Studies in Ancient Monarchies

Edited by
ULRICH GOTTER (Konstanz), MATTHIAS HAAKE (Bonn),
NINO LURAGHI (Oxford) and KAI TRAMPEDACH (Heidelberg)

Volume 11

www.steiner-verlag.de/brand/Studies-in-Ancient-Monarchies

The Same, but Different?

*Monarchical Rule and Representation
in the Hellenistic World*

Edited by
Christoph Michels
with Hans Beck and Achim Lichtenberger

Franz Steiner Verlag

Bibliographic information published by the German National Library:
The German National Library lists this publication in the Deutsche Nationalbibliografie;
detailed bibliographic information is available at
dnb.d-nb.de.

www.steiner-verlag.de
Layout and production by Franz Steiner Verlag
Print: Beltz Grafische Betriebe, Bad Langensalza
Printed on acid-free and age-resistant paper.
Printed in Germany.
ISBN 978-3-515-13636-5 (Print)
ISBN 978-3-515-13642-6 (E-Book)
DOI 10.25162/9783515136426

Preface

This volume has its origins in an international conference of the same name, held at the University of Münster in March of 2022. The conference, in turn, was inspired by the complementary research interests of its organizers on cultural interactions in the Hellenistic world on the one hand and the study of ancient monarchies and their ideological expressions on the other. More immediately, the gathering was part of Christoph Michels' wider research agenda on the Hellenistic period, carried out as Heisenberg fellow of the Deutsche Forschungsgemeinschaft (DFG) at the University of Münster. We fondly remember the lively discussions between the participants, who joined in both via zoom and in person, despite the restrictions imposed by the pandemic at the time. Most of the presentations given at this conference are published here. Following the practice at the conference, we have decided to leave it up to each contributor to decide whether to publish in English or German.

We owe many debts of gratitude. First and foremost, we thank the DFG for funding the conference and the publication of its proceedings via the research funds of Christoph Michels' Heisenberg project. We would also like to express our thanks to the editors of Studies in Ancient Monarchies for welcoming this volume into their wonderful series and the peer reviewers for their valuable comments and suggestions. Eylihan Ayhan provided crucial support for the organization and realization of the conference. We would like to thank the student assistants, Daniel Hagen, Ann-Kathrin Hönerloh and Daniel Schlageter, and especially Lukas Duisen for their help both during the conference and with the work on the conference proceedings. Once again, we also thank all contributors for their efforts and patience and Johannes Wienand for agreeing to offer concluding remarks to this volume. Finally, Katharina Stüdemann of Steiner Verlag supported this project with great enthusiasm and professionalism.

Christoph Michels, Hans Beck, and Achim Lichtenberger   Münster, May 2024

Table of Contents

Part 2:
The Second and First Centuries

Comparing Themes and Structures of Representation and Communication / Themen und Strukturen der Repräsentation und Kommunikation im Vergleich

The Image of the Ruler between Tradition and Innovation / Das Herrscherbild zwischen Tradition und Innovation

Concluding Remarks / Schlussbetrachtungen

Abbreviations

What follows is a list of abbreviations for standard works and lexica, as well as for epigraphical, numismatic, and papyrological corpora. Abbreviations for ancient authors and their works generally follow the rules of DNP.

Agora XVI	Woodhead, A. Geoffrey, The Athenian Agora. Results of Excavations conducted by the American School of Classical Studies at Athens, XVI. The Decrees, Princeton 1997
ANET³	Pritchard, James B. (ed.), Ancient Near Eastern Texts Relating to the Old Testament, Princeton ³1969
ANRW	Temporini, Hildgard – Haase, Wolfgang (eds.), Aufstieg und Niedergang der römischen Welt: Geschichte und Kultur Roms im Spiegel der neueren Forschung, Berlin 1972–
Austin ²2006	Austin, Michel, The Hellenistic World from Alexander to the Roman Conquest. A Selection of Ancient Sources in Translation, Cambridge ²2006
BCHP	Babylonian Chronographic Texts from the Hellenistic Period, ed. I. L. Finkel, R. J. van der Spek, R. Pirngruber, https://www.livius.org/sources/content/mesopotamian-chronicles-content/ (last access 20.5.2024)
BE	Bulletin épigraphique, in: Revue des études grecques, Paris 1888–
BGU	Ägyptische (Griechische) Urkunden aus den Kaiserlichen (from vol. 6 Staatlichen) Museen zu Berlin, 13 vol.s., Berlin 1895–1976
BMC Galatia	Wroth, Warwick, Catalogue of the Greek Coins of Galatia, Cappadocia, and Syria, A Catalogue of the Greek Coins in the British Museum 20, London 1889
BMC Phoenicia	Hill, George F., Catalogue of Greek Coins of Phoenicia, A Catalogue of Greek Coins in the British Museum 26, London 1910
BNJ	Worthington, Ian (ed.), Brill's New Jacoby, Leiden, 2012– (online: https://scholarlyeditions.brill.com/bnjo/) last access: 20.5.2024

Bop.	Bopearachchi, Osmund, Monnaies gréco-bactriennes et indo-grecques, Paris 1991
CAH²	Cambridge Ancient History, Cambridge ²1961–
CID	Corpus des Inscriptions de Delphes, Paris 1977–
CIG	Corpus Inscriptionum Graecarum, 4 vols., Berlin 1828–77
CII	Corpus Inscriptionum Iranicarum, Wiesbaden et al. 1972–
CIIP	Corpus Inscriptionum Iudaeae/Palaestinae: A Multi-Lingual Corpus of the Inscriptions from Alexander to Muhammad, ed. H. Cotton – L. Di Segni – W. Eck – B. Isaac – E. Lupu – M. Heimbach – A. Kushnir-Stein – N. Schneider, Berlin, 2010
CIL	Corpus Inscriptionum Latinarum, Berlin 1863–
CIS	Corpus Inscriptionum Semiticarum, Paris 1881–1962
C.Jud.Syr.Eg.	van't Dack, Edmond – Clarysse, Willy – Cohen, Getzel M. – Quaegebeur, Jan – Winicki, Jan K., The Judean-Syrian-Egyptian Conflict of 103–101 B.C. A Multilingual Dossier Concerning a "War of Sceptres", Brussels 1989
CPE	Lorber, Catharine, Coins of the Ptolemaic Empire, 5 vol.s, New York 2018–2024
CPI	Bowman, Alan et al. (eds.), Corpus of Ptolemaic Inscriptions, Oxford 2021
CT	Cuneiform Texts from Babylonian Tablets in the British Museum, London, 1896–
DNP	Der Neue Pauly, Leiden 1996–
FD	Fouilles de Delphes, Paris 1902–
FGrH	Jacoby, Felix, Die Fragmente der griechischen Historiker, Berlin – Leiden 1923
HGIÜ	Brodersen, Kai – Günther, Wolfgang – Schmitt, Hatto H. (eds.), Historische griechische Inschriften in Übersetzung, Darmstadt 2011
I.Amyzon	Robert, Jeanne and Louis, Fouilles d'Amyzon en Carie I: Exploration, histoire, monnaies et inscriptions, Paris 1983
I.Beroia	Hatzopoulos, Miltiades B. – Gounaropoulou, Loukretia (eds.), Inscriptiones Macedoniae Inferioris, Fasc. 1: Inscriptiones Beroeae, Athens 1998
I.Cret.	Guarducci, Margherita, Inscriptiones Creticae, Rome 1935–1950
IDélos	Durrbach, François et al., Inscriptions de Délos, Paris 1926–1972
I. Didyma	Rehm, Albert – Harder, Richard, Didyma II. Die Inschriften, Berlin 1958
I.Estremo Oriente	Canali de Rossi, Filippo, Iscrizioni dello estremo oriente Greco, IK 65, Bonn 2004

I.Fay.	Bernand, Étienne, Recueil des inscriptions grecques du Fayoum, 3 vols., Leiden et al. 1975–1981
IG	Inscriptiones Graecae, Berlin 1873–
IGCyr	Dobias-Lalou, Catherine, Inscriptions of Greek Cyrenaica, Bologna 2017
IGLS	Jalabert, Louis et al., Inscriptions grecques et latines de la Syrie, Paris 1929
IGR	Cagnat, René et al., Inscriptiones Graecae ad Res Romanas Pertinentes. Paris 1901–1927
IGUR	Moretti, Luigi, Inscriptiones Graecae urbis Romae, 4 vols., Rom 1968–1990
I.gr.Eg.Nub.Louvre	Bernand, Étienne, Inscriptions grecques d'Egypte et de Nubie au Musee du Louvre, Paris 1992
I.Herm.Magn.	Bernand, Étienne, Inscriptions grecques d'Hermoupolis Magna et de sa nécropole, Cairo 1999
I.Iasos	Blümel, Wolfgang, Die Inschriften von Iasos, IK 28, Bonn 1985
I.Ilion	Frisch, Peter, Die Inschriften von Ilion, IK 3, Bonn 1975
IK	Inschriften griechischer Städte aus Kleinasien, Bonn 1972–
I.Kaunos	Marek, Christian, Die Inschriften von Kaunos, Munich 2006
I.Labraunda	Crampa, Jonas, Labraunda. Swedish Excavations and Researches III. Greek Inscriptions. 2 vols., Lund 1969 and Stockholm 1972
I.Magnesia	Kern, Otto, Die Inschriften von Magnesia am Maeander, Berlin 1900
I.Milet	Die Inschriften von Milet, Berlin 1914–
I.Mylasa	Blümel, Wolfgang, Die Inschriften von Mylasa, IK 34–35, Bonn 1987–1988
IvP	Die Inschriften von Pergamon, Berlin 1890-
I.Priene B – M	Blümel, Wolfgang – Merkelbach, Reinhold, Die Inschriften von Priene, IK 69.1-2, Bonn 2014
I.Prose	Bernand, André, La prose sur pierre dans l'Égypte hellénistique et romaine, 2 vols., Paris 1992
I.Prusa	Corsten, Thomas, Die Inschriften von Prusa ad Olympum, IK 39–40, Bonn 1991–1993
I.Teos	McCabe, Donald F., Teos Inscriptions. Texts and List, Princeton 1985
IThSy	Bernand, André, De Thèbes à Syène, Paris 1989
I.Varsovie	Lajtar, Adam – Twardecki, Alfred, Catalogue des inscriptions grecques du Musée National de Varsovie, Warsaw 2003
KAI	Donner, Herbert – Röllig, Wolfgang, Kanaanäische und Aramäische Inschriften, Wiesbaden [5]2002

LexAM	Heckel, Waldemar – Heinrichs, Johannes – Müller, Sabine – Pownall, Francis (eds.), Lexicon of Argead Makedonia, Berlin 2020
LexHell	Schmitt, Hatto H. – Vogt, Ernst (eds.), Lexikon des Hellenismus, Wiesbaden 2005
LIMC	Lexicon Iconographicum Mythologiae Classicae, Zurich – Munich 1981–2009
Mamroth, Philippos	Mamroth, Alfred, Die Silbermünzen des Königs Philippos V. von Makedonien, Zeitschrift für Numismatik 40, 1930, 277–303
OGIS	Dittenberger, Wilhelm, Orientis Graeci Inscriptiones Selectae, 2 vols., Leipzig 1903–1905
P.Berol.	Schubart, Wilhelm, Papyrae graecae Berolinenses, Bonn 1911
P.Carlsberg	The Carlsberg papyri, Copenhagen 1991–
P.Eleph.	Ägyptische Urkunden aus den Königlichen Museen in Berlin: Griechische Urkunden, Sonderheft. Elephantine-Papyri, ed. O. Rubensohn, Berlin 1907
P.Hib.	The Hibeh Papyri. London. vol. 1, ed. B. P. Grenfell – A. S. Hunt, 1906; vol. 2, ed. E. G. Turner – M.-Th. Lenger 1955
P.Köln	Kölner Papyri, Opladen 1976–
P.Lille	Papyrus grecs (Institut Papyrologique de l'Université de Lille), ed. P. Jouguet – P. Collart – J. Lesquier – M. Xoual, Paris 1907–1928
P.Lond.	Greek Papyri in the British Museum, London 1893–
P.Mich.	Michigan Papyri, Ann Arbor 1931–
P.Oxy.	The Oxyrhynchus Papyri. London 1898–
P.Polit.Iud.	Cowey, James M. S. – Maresch, Klaus, Urkunden des Politeuma der Juden von Herakleopolis: (144/3–133/2 v. Chr.) (P. Polit. Iud.). Papyri aus den Sammlungen von Heidelberg, Köln, München und Wien, Wiesbaden 2001
P.Tebt.	Grenfell, Bernard P. et al. (eds.), The Tebtunis Papyri, London 1902–1976
P.Tor.Choach.	Pestman, Pieter W., Il Processo di Hermeias e altri documenti dell'archivio dei choachiti, papiri greci e demotici conservati a Torino e in altre collezioni d'Italia, Turin 1992
RC	Welles, Charles B., Royal Correspondence in the Hellenistic Period. A Study in Greek Epigraphy, New Haven 1934
RE	Paulys Realencyclopädie der classischen Altertumswissenschaft, Stuttgart 1893–1980
RPC	Burnett, Andrew – Amandry, Michel – Ripollès, Pere Pau (eds.), Roman Provincial Coinage, London 1992– (cf. https://rpc.ashmus.ox.ac.uk/ (last access: 20.5.2024)

Sachs – Hunger I	Sachs, Abraham – Hunger, Hermann (eds.), Astronomical Diaries and Related Texts from Babylon, I, Diaries from 625 B. C. to 262 B. C., Wien 1988
SB	Sammelbuch griechischer Urkunden aus Ägypten (Inschriften und Papyri), vols. 1–2: F. Preisigke (ed.), 1913–22; vols. 3–5: F. Bilabel (ed.), 1926–1934
SC	Houghton, Arthur – Lorber, Catharine, Seleucid Coins. A Comprehensive Catalogue I: Seleucus I through Antiochus III, Lancaster et al. 2002 and Houghton, Arthur – Lorber, Catharine – Hoover, Oliver, Seleucid Coins. A Comprehensive Catalogue II: Seleucus IV through Antiochos XIII, Lancaster et al. 2008
SEG	Supplementum Epigraphicum Graecum, ed. A. Chaniotis – R. S. Stroud – J. H. M. Strubbe (et al.), Amsterdam, 1955–
SH	Lloyd-Jones, Hugh et al. (eds.), Supplementum Hellenisticum, Berlin – Boston 1983
SNG	Sylloge Nummorum Graecorum
StV	Die Staatsverträge des Altertums vol. 3: H. H. Schmitt (ed.), Die Verträge der griechisch-römischen Welt 338 bis 200 v. Chr., Munich 1969
Svor.	Svoronos, Ioannes N., Ta Nomismata tou Kratous ton Ptolemaion. Die Münzen der Ptolemäer, Athen 1904–1908
Syll.³	Dittenberger, Wilhelm, Sylloge Inscriptionum Graecarum, Leipzig ³1915–1924
TAM	Tituli Asiae Minoris, Vienna 1901–
UPZ	Wilcken, Ulrich, Urkunden der Ptolemäerzeit (ältere Funde). vol. 1: Papyri aus Unterägypten; vol. 2: Papyri aus Oberägypten, Berlin – Leipzig 1922–27 / 1957

Introduction

CHRISTOPH MICHELS

1. Hellenistic kingdoms and kingship

Just as interest in the Hellenistic world with its complex cultural interactions and inter-connected economies has intensified in recent decades, the dominant political struc-tures of this time, the Hellenistic kingdoms, have also increasingly come into focus of scholarship – albeit from quite different perspectives. Two distinct approaches can be characterised as follows:[1] One line of scholarship, which is particularly influential in the Anglo- and Francophone world, focuses on the institutional foundations of the great realms. In this context, it has proved quite fruitful to examine the Macedonian monarchies in terms of their organisational structures by conceptualizing them as "em-pires".[2] This is especially convincing in the case of the Seleukid realm. With its different cultural zones, it comes close to modern concepts of empire and its categorisation as such helps to analyse its multifaceted character.[3] In a recent volume, this is also argued for the Ptolemaic kingdom, and both realms have been – despite their apparent dif-ferences in territorial extension and morphology – conceived as multi-ethnic empires and accordingly compared.[4]

A comparative approach is in many ways also important for the conference which formed the basis for this volume. However, its theme follows the second identifiable approach in scholarship on the Hellenistic kingdoms, namely the study of the ideologi-cal staging of the persona of the king and his dynasty, that is on 'symbolic aspects of the Hellenistic monarchies.'[5] This is a field of research that has admittedly been influenced

---

1   Wiemer 2017, 332–338.
2   Ma 2013. Cf. Schäfer 2014, who – based on the criteria developed by Herfried Münkler – also counts the Antigonids as an empire, with some qualifications. Cf. also Kaye 2022, 2 who sees the Attalid kingdom after 188 as an 'overnight empire'. Reflections on the notion of empire and its uses in Sinopoli 1994; Gehler – Rollinger 2022.
3   Cf., e. g., Strootman 2013.
4   Fischer-Bovet – von Reden 2021b. If one agrees with Strootman 2019, who characterises the Ptole-maic realm of the 3rd century as a maritime empire, this is all the more the case.
5   Bilde – Engberg-Pedersen – Hannestad – Zahle 1996, 12.

to no small extent by recent empire studies.[6] To give only some examples: The role of imperial ideology in motivating action is stressed. Empires are understood not only as a set of centralised and autonomous institutions but as networks of communication. It is recognised that the evocation of an "imagined empire" in texts (e. g. through the mention of interlocutors participating in the respective communication or alluding to the extension of the realm) emanating from the centre or mirrored in civic texts is also part of royal representation.[7] The studies by Paul Kosmin on the construction of space and time in the Seleukid empire are only one example of this trend in scholarship.[8]

Particularly in German-language research, increased attention has been paid in the past decades to the symbolic and ritual communication of the Hellenistic monarchies, after the earlier, primarily constitutional approach to kingship in this era had proved to be insufficient.[9] This is in line with a general trend in scholarship on ancient monarchic systems, which is increasingly focusing on ritual and symbolic communication and the underlying "ideologies" as one of the foundations of the monarch's acceptance.[10] This approach has shown to be very fruitful for Alexander the Great,[11] but it is also a useful starting point for the study of the Hellenistic kingdoms following Alexander's world empire, since these were dominions which (especially in the case of the multicultural and multi-ethnic Seleukid empire) had no basis for a common citizenship but had their only centre in the person of the monarch.[12] This is already evident linguistically when kings describe their domination as their "affairs" (*pragmata*) or their "royal rule" (*basileia*) in the sources. In fact, it was not possible to describe a kingdom without reference to the person of the Hellenistic monarch. When a Samian decree from ca. 201–197 BC refers to a time when the polis had been won back by the Ptolemies, this is naturally described as 'when the city was restored to the *pragmata* of King Ptolemaios (V)' (ἔν τε τῆι ἀποκαταστάσει τῆς πόλεως εἰς τὰ τοῦ βα[σιλέ]ως Πτολεμαίου πράγματα).[13]

In this field of research, a particularly influential approach has been to draw on Max Weber's "Herrschaftssoziologie" and his models of legitimate rule, wherein rulership or domination is the probability that a command will be obeyed by a certain group of persons and legitimacy is to be understood as the acceptance by the ruled both of authority and of the need to obey its commands.[14] In an influential contribution, Hans-

---

6   Cf., e. g., Degen 2022, 40–51.
7   Cf. Sinopoli 1994; Fischer-Bovet – von Reden 2021a, 4; Ma 2003, 185.
8   Kosmin 2014 and 2019.
9   Wiemer 2017, 308–309.
10   Cf. the overview in Rebenich – Wienand 2017. This is especially apparent in the case of the Roman principate; cf., e. g., Zimmermann 2011.
11   Among recent works on the topic, which has long been a subject of debate among scholars, see Trampedach – Meeus 2020b.
12   Chamoux 2003, 249–250.
13   IG XII.6.1 12 ll. 26–28 (=Austin ²2006, no. 145; cf. 162 n. 3 with further examples).
14   Weber 1978. Cf. Trampedach – Meeus 2020a, 9–10: 'Two findings of Max Weber are fundamental in this regard: first, the distinction between power ("Macht") and domination ("Herrschaft"),

Joachim Gehrke has used Weber's ideal type of the charismatic ruler to emphasize the military victoriousness of the Hellenistic king as the very basis of his acceptance by his subjects.[15] This has, of course, been differentiated in recent decades.[16] Warfare was most certainly a 'defining element of the Hellenistic world'.[17] The "charismatic" facet of Hellenistic monarchy was, however, not limited to the military dimension. Rather, the charismatic authority of the kings derived from an ostentatious performance that went beyond the possibilities of a "normal" human being in various areas: in the display of splendor (*tryphe*), for example, at the table at court, but also in the context of large festive processions and in his impressive benefactions.[18] Also, the display of the public image of kings and their families in portraits and coin imagery cultivated nuanced ideas of monarchic rule and kingship. While the identification of such "charismatic" facets is certainly conducive to making this form of monarchical rule more comprehensible – especially in comparison with other monarchic system – the question arises as to whether there actually was a uniform phenomenon of monarchical rule in the Hellenistic age.

2. Hellenistic kingship – the same, but different?

Whether there was "a" Hellenistic kingship at all is still a matter of controversy, but especially when compared with other systems like the Roman principate or its predecessor, Argead kingship, sufficient similarities between the Macedonian dynasties that emerged in the succession wars after Alexander's untimely death can be identified to

which invite us to analyse how (military) power developed into (political) domination. Which means did Alexander apply in order to transform the many countries which he victoriously crossed with his army into areas of domination?'.

15 Gehrke 2013. Weber 1978, 241 defines charisma as: 'a certain quality of an individual personality by virtue of which he is considered extraordinary and treated as endowed with supernatural, superhuman, or at least specifically exceptional powers or qualities. These are such as are not accessible to the ordinary person, but are regarded as of divine origin or as exemplary, and on the basis of them the individual concerned is treated as a "leader"'. cf. Gotter 2008; Luraghi 2013b, 20–22. On Weber's conception of charisma and its foundations, see Joosse 2014.

16 Cf. Wiemer 2017. An overview of the development of scholarship building on Weber concerning different fields of the Ancient world is provided by Näf 2015. While Koehn 2007, 77–88 created an unnecessary division by insisting that the wars of the Diadochi are to be explained 'machtpolitisch' and not 'machtsoziologisch', Lendon 2015 has argued forcefully against the use of any of Weber's legitimacy concepts and against the notion of "strategies of legitimation" mainly by the Roman emperors. Roisman 2020, 58–60 remains sceptical about what is gained by characterising the kings as "charismatic".

17 Serrati 2007, 461.

18 See, e. g., Theokr. 17. On *tryphe* see Heinen 1983. For royal banquets see Vössing 2004 and for *pompai* Köhler 1996. Following Gehrke 2013, Gotter 2013 reduces this rather one sided to victory.

constitute a 'specific political category of monarchy'.[19] When during the so-called "Year of the Kings" 306/305 BC, the Diadochi proclaimed themselves *basileus* and took the diadem as visual expression of their new status in a kind of chain reaction, this title had neither territorial nor national restrictions, but rather referred to nothing other than the superior status of the person of the king.[20]

That the in some respects excessive, "charismatic" image of these new kings was in fact perceived by contemporaries as distinct and novel is particularly evident in that it instantly became a point of reference for other rulers who oriented themselves on this model as *the* expression of monarchical power and rule of the time. Examples for this phenomenon can be found in the West, where immediately in 304 BC the Syracusan tyrant Agathokles proclaimed himself king (fig. 1) and married a stepdaughter of Ptolemaios I,[21] and in the East as well, where non-Greek rulers deemed it necessary to stress their parity with the Macedonian monarchs by joining the club of the kings. The rulers of Bithynia may serve as an example here, as the dynast Zipoites probably used a military victory against generals of Lysimachos to declare himself *basileus* in 297/296 BC.[22] Others, like the Attalid Philetairos, did not dare to take this step. Zipoites' son and successor Nikomedes (note also the now Greek name which, however, changes again to Thracian under his successors) then started to mint coins (fig. 2) following primarily the Seleukid example.[23]

Fig. 1 Agathokles. Bronze coin. Obv.: Bust of Artemis Soteira right, with quiver over shoulder. ΣΩΤΕΙΡΑ. Rev.: Winged thunderbolt; ΑΓΑΘΟΚΛΕΟΣ || ΒΑΣΙΛΕΟΣ.

19 Quote after Eckstein 2009, 385 who argues mainly on the basis of Walbank 1984. On the successors see Bosworth 2002; on the Argeads cf. now Müller 2016. Wallace-Hadrill 1982 is still important for the difference between Hellenistic monarchy and the Roman principate.

20 Gruen 1985. On the diadem, its significance(s) and its possible origins see Lichtenberger et al. 2012.

21 De Lisle 2021, 139–177.

22 Paganoni 2019, 37–44.

23 Michels 2009, 158–162.

Fig. 2 Nikomedes I. Tetradrachm. Obv.: Diademed portrait of Nikomedes right. Rev.: Bendis sitting to left, holding two spears; in front shield. ΒΑΣΙΛΕΩ[Σ] || ΝΙΚΟΜΗΔΟ[Υ].

At first glance, this uniformity seems to fit well with the interconnection of the different Afro-Eurasian spheres that constituted the Hellenistic world and might be seen as an expression of the "globalisation" of this time.[24] Recent studies have nonetheless illustrated and stressed the diversity of monarchical rule in the Hellenistic world. In a way, this also becomes tangible in the specific coin images just referred to. The coins of Agathokles lack a royal portrait, which has often been taken as the most important innovation of Hellenistic royal coins, while Nikomedes did choose to depict his portrait with a diadem on the obverse, but he also associated himself with the specifically Thracian goddess Bendis shown on the reverse.[25]

The main reason for these profound differences lies of course in the diverse framework conditions and traditions under which the different monarchies emerged. The contrast, for example, between the Antigonids ruling in the Macedonian heartland on the one hand and the Seleukids and Ptolemies – 'exiles from their ethnic homeland' –[26] ruling over a diverse body of subjects on the other hand is especially stark, yet not great enough to see them as completely different entities.[27]

However, the issue here is not only that there were different specifics in the various kingdoms. There is also no uniform picture within the great empires. This is to a large extent the result of the constellation of foreign rule of the Macedonian monarchs over diverse populations. As a foreign ruler, the Macedonian king assumed a variety of roles that were based on locally coded models.[28] This xenocratic constellation applies to the

24   Cf. Versluys – Riedel 2021, 17–18. Chaniotis 2018, 6: 'Because of the interconnection of vast areas in Europe, Asia and North Africa, the Hellenistic world and the Roman Empire have justly been considered as early examples of Globalisation.'
25   Michels 2009, 159–160.
26   Shipley 2000, 295.
27   Walbank 1984, 65.
28   Stressed, e. g., by Ma 2003, 186.

cultures of the Near and Middle East with their oftentimes longstanding monarchic traditions as well as to the old and new Greek cities. To recognize the key expectations emanating from the political culture(s) of the subjects was crucial for the successful exercise of power –[29] Alexander in Egypt whom we meet here as Horus 'the ruler of the rulers of the entire land' or 'the strong-armed' being probably the most-quoted example.[30] How consciously the Ptolemies then – in conversation with the powerful priestly elite – specifically addressed traditions of the indigenous population is apparent, e. g., in the Rosetta stone when it is decreed that the planned statues of Ptolemaios V are to be placed beside accompanying statues of the main deity of the respective sanctuary which gives Ptolemaios the weapon of victory made 'in the Egyptian fashion.'[31] Also, the choice of Pharaonic iconography and local stones in some Ptolemaic royal portraits underline this specific target group orientation towards local audiences.[32]

Other "rules" had to be recognized by the kings when dealing with the Greek city states both of their realm, and also of the wider Aegean, which formed, so to speak, the core of the Hellenistic world of states: When Lykortas, the father of Polybios, wanted to induce the Achaian League to give military aid to the Ptolemaic side against Antiochos IV in 169/168 BC, he read out a register contrasting the past benefactions of the Ptolemies to the league with those of the Seleukids.[33] Of course, kings showed their munificence also towards their other subjects as is strikingly illustrated by the Kanopos Decree from 238 BC which praises Ptolemaios III for having given grain not only to the residents of the temple but to all the inhabitants of Egypt which suffered from a drought at the time.[34] Nevertheless, the euergetic exchange between kings and *poleis* (and *koina*) brought forth culturally specific rituals with their own language.[35]

When considering monarchical representation (rather than propaganda[36]) – to be understood as visual and textual expressions of rulership as well as all actions connected with or referring to the king – special attention must therefore be paid to the respective communication partner and context.[37] The various roles to be assumed by the ruler, his virtues, norms of behaviour, and his canon of duties and responsibilities

29   But see Chamoux 2003, 251: 'No other state model was ever less eager for pretence, less keen on any attempt to justify the power it held.'
30   Bosch-Puche 2013, 134.
31   OGIS 90 (= Austin ²2006, no. 283), ll. 39–40: κατεσκευασμέν[α τὸν τῶν Αἰγυπτίων] | τρόπον. The reconstruction is based on the Hieroglyphic text.
32   Kyrieleis 1975.
33   Pol. 29.24.11–16.
34   Kanopos Decree (= Austin ²2006, no. 271), ll. 14–19.
35   Bringmann 2000; Ma ²2002.
36   Whether the term "propaganda" is at all applicable for the ancient world is still debated today. Oftentimes, cf. Baynham 2021, the problem of anachronism is rather brushed aside. Especially the discussions on the Roman empire and "propaganda" (see, e. g., Weber – Zimmermann 2003a; Meister 2021) have shown that the term should rather be avoided and replaced with representation.
37   Cf. Eich 2003; Gotter 2008.

were not prescribed by the ruler alone, but rather resulted from interaction with different communication partners.[38]

Many instances of monarchical interaction in the Hellenistic world may be described
as having a decidedly "glocal" character, which means that they comprised both imperial or global elements that can be classified with the cultural containers "Graeco-Macedonian" and "Achaimenid" as well as aspects endowed with meaning on a local, respectively meso-regional level.[39] Whether it is possible to clearly differentiate between 'local
roleplaying and unitary ideology' or if the impulses and guidelines provided at the level
of local interaction also had consequences for the general ruler-image of the respective
realms is certainly a complex question complicated by the scarcity of sources.[40]

Fig. 3 Ptolemaios VI Philometor, seal, diademed and bearded portrait bust left.

Fig. 4 Ptolemaios VI Philometor, seal, bearded portrait bust left,
with pschent and diadem, pectoral.

38   Cf. also Lichtenberger 2015.
39   Cf. Lichtenberger 2021.
40   Ma 2003, 186.

Staying with the "Janus-like" Ptolemaic kingship,[41] the famous example of two seals now in the Louvre (figs. 3–4) which probably both show Ptolemaios VI on the one hand as a Hellenistic king and on the other hand as an Egyptian pharaoh seem to prove the point. Integrated into the Egyptian crown there is a diadem perhaps pointing to the overarching quality of Graeco-Macedonian Hellenistic kingship.[42]

However, the communication processes seem to have been multi-layered. While court culture in Alexandreia was essentially Graeco-Macedonian, scholars have pointed out how elements of Egyptian traditions of kingship were adapted in court poetry (e. g., in Kallimachos' *Hymn to Delos*).[43] The differences between the dynasties resulting from this constellation could be consciously shaped, but they also shifted or were levelled out by innovations in the staging of power.

3. The scope of this volume

The focus of this volume can be described as twofold. First, it concentrates on the emergence and cross-fertilisation of concepts of power and ideologies between the Macedonian and "indigenous" Hellenistic dynasties among themselves and in conversation with local traditions of rule. A study of the "ideology" of Hellenistic monarchy is therefore necessarily also a cultural history of Hellenistic kingship, as called for by John Ma.[44] As already mentioned, the reasons for the obedience of the ruled and the interests of the local elites are to be considered – that is the origins of monarchic legitimacy.[45] This is a field that has also received important impulses directly and indirectly from postcolonial studies.[46] Even if the 'binary model of colonial relations is simplistic too' and has also shown itself insufficient to grasp the complex cultural processes,[47] the approach of moving away from simple top-down models, taking into account the polyphony of the various actors, and considering the repercussions of adaptation strategies on the centre has in many cases enabled important differentiations. To concentrate exclusively on these disparate (and often temporally isolated) individual acts of

---

41   Koenen 1993, 25.
42   Koenen 1993, 25–27
43   Koenen 1983.
44   Ma 2003, 191–194.
45   On the role and the agency of local elites see Dreyer – Mittag 2011; cf. also the respective chapters in Fischer-Bovet – von Reden 2021b.
46   The use and usability of post-colonial concepts is rightly hotly debated. Already advocated by Will 1985, Bagnall 1997 has pointed out the problem of transferring modern colonialism which is virtually defined by the existence of a metropolitan centre outside the colonized land on the Seleukids and Ptolemies. On past views and perspectives for future research cf. Hoo 2018.
47   Strootman 2021, 84.

communication, however, carries the danger of obscuring commonalities among the dynasties.[48]

Another, quite different factor, also seems important for our topic: the competition of the kings before a primarily Greek world public was a central framework condition of the multipolar Hellenistic world of states. This 'superpower competition'[49] often played out as war, but not exclusively so. As "peers", the kings fought for influence and status, and this produced a monarchical habitus and "royal style"[50] that was only secondarily the result of actual communication between ruler and ruled.[51] The example set by Ptolemaios II with the foundation of a dynastic sacrificial festival was imitated not only by the other major dynasties, especially by the Antigonids, the great rivals of the Ptolemies in the Aegean. Even before Antigonos Gonatas established the *Antigoneia* and *Stratonikeia*, Philetairos, the founder of the Attalid dynasty, had followed the Ptolemaic model and donated a capital of 4,000 drachmas for the newly founded sacrificial festival of the *Philetaireia*.[52]

For an analysis of the development of monarchical representation, one important dimension seems to be which communication channels can be identified and what "agents" can be discerned for the transfer of ideologies. Likely candidates are, for example: members of the various courts which constituted social spheres where power was concentrated and redistributed but which also were intellectual centres,[53] royal women who moved between dynasties because of marital connections,[54] and non-human "actors" such as coins. Of central interest are also the historical constellations and events that were responsible for the adoption or (conscious?) rejection of "new" ideologies.

This brings us to the second focus of this volume – a diachronic view on Hellenistic kingship and its evolution. Much changed in the approximately three centuries commonly counted as the Hellenistic Age.[55] One of the most profound changes certainly was the "coming of Rome". That the Roman Republic emerged as the hegemonic power in the East in the second century BC had repercussions on the basic mechanisms

---

48   As advocated by Gotter 2008, 186: 'Auf die oben genannten konkreten historischen Fallbeispiele angewandt, hieße das, die Differenzen zwischen hellenistischer Monarchie und römischem Prinzipat am ehesten über die verschiedene normative Ausrichtung der jeweils disparaten Untertanenverbände zu beschreiben, nicht über das Formenspektrum der Herrscher und ihren unterschiedlichen Reinheitsgrad in puncto Charisma.'

49   Ma 2013, 352.

50   On Early Hellenistic royal style cf., e. g., Wallace 2014; peers: Ma 2003, 188.

51   Cf. Veyne 1990, 23: 'Le roi se doit d'exprimer sa grandeur parce qu'il est le roi: il ne se rend pas roi en exprimant sa grandeur.'

52   Bringmann 2000, 87.

53   Erskine – Llewellyn-Jones – Wallace 2014.

54   Cf. among many recent publications Coşkun – McAuley 2016.

55   What counts as the Hellenistic Age has of course been debated since the inception of the term; on the inconsistencies already present in Droysen's work cf. Bichler 1983. Recently, Chaniotis 2018 had the Hellenistic Age end with the emperor Hadrian.

of the Hellenistic state system. It is debatable whether, and if yes to what extent, this also had fundamental implications for the persona of the Hellenistic king, for example regarding his victoriousness as Ulrich Gotter has forcefully argued with regard to the "Day of Eleusis" of 168 BC.[56] Prusias II's servile appearance in the senate in 167 certainly points in this direction.[57] Antiochos IV, however – although or rather because the public humiliation by the Roman ambassador Laenas at Eleusis 'undermined not merely the foundation of his power but that of the monarchy as a whole'[58] – presented his might in an ostentatious display of his economic and military resources during the procession of Daphne shortly thereafter.[59] Eumenes II, on the other hand, had already freely admitted in his correspondence with the inhabitants of the Phrygian town Toriaion in the 180s that he had the power to grant privileges in this area 'having received it from the Romans who have prevailed in war and through treaties'.[60]

4. Contents: themes, concepts, and communication

The subject matter is undoubtedly complex, and this volume attempts to approach it through a thematic structure devoted to different thematic fields and media of communication. In order to factor in the considerable change in the general conditions from the late 4th to the 1st century BC, it is divided into two sections: the first encompasses the time from the Wars of the Diadochi until the end of the 3rd century BC and the second focuses on the 2nd and 1st centuries BC. Therefore, one dimension of the chapters is to explore whether such a division makes sense in every field or whether some developments are either actually more gradual or less chronological in nature but rather geographical respectively specific to individual dynasties.

The contributions by Sabine Müller, Jordan Christopher, and Ralf von den Hoff open with three very different views on the time of the Diadochi, a period of upheaval and change that fundamentally influenced the character of the monarchies that arose from the decades of conflict. Müller concentrates on the main themes of Argead representation developed in her view mainly by Alexander I "Philhellen" and Philipp II: the representation of the Argeads as a clan, the spaces of action of royal women, and the major iconographic features of coinage in the sense of dynastic iconography. Her chapter shows how the Argead strategies of representation served in a way as a blue-

---

56   Gotter 2013, 207: 'Much more than Augustus' victory over Cleopatra, the day of Eleusis marked the end of Hellenistic monarchy as it had existed from the time of Alexander the Great.'
57   Pol. 30.18.
58   Gotter 2013, 208.
59   Mittag 2015.
60   Austin ²2006, no. 236 l. 20–21: (…) διὰ τὸ παρὰ τῶν κρατησάντων καὶ πολέμωι καὶ σ[υν]|θήκαις εἰληφέναι Ῥωμαίων.

print for the members of Hellenistic dynasties. Argead representation was, however, not slavishly imitated. We rather see different dynasties selectively borrowing from it.

Christopher parallelizes the time of the Diadochi Wars with the Eighteen Kingdoms Period of Early China (209–202 BC), the *tertium comparationis* being that both saw intracultural interstate chaos in the wake of major imperial collapses. By drawing comparisons between several key individuals, especially between Antigonos I Monophthalmos and Xiang Yu of Chu, and by exploring different fields like the formation of coalitions and the recognition of the status of others in the peer group of rivalling warlords he reveals key dynamics. The common characterisation of Argead collapse as "internal" and Qin collapse as "external" is questioned and the Diadochi are shown to be influenced by a larger conception of "Macedon" than just that represented by Argead rule.

Ralf von den Hoff treats the distinctive royal portraiture that developed in the time between Alexander's death and the late 3rd century BC with a special focus on similarities and differences between royal and civic portraiture of the early Hellenistic period. Despite all differences he stresses the homogeneity of the royal "portrait concept" of this time and its similarities to civic portrait concepts. A change can be observed from the dynamic, "live like" presentation of the Diadochi to a calmer and more distanced portrait concept of their successors. That the diversity of royal portraits later grew in the course of the third century is perhaps to be explained by an increased need for competitive distinction of the royal dynasties.

The complex connection of the king and the divine is certainly a central dimension of the study of Hellenistic monarchy and the focus of the chapters by Gregor Weber, Stefan Pfeiffer, and Sonja Richter. Gregor Weber deals with a phenomenon that is attested already in Homer but which has not yet been studied systematically concerning Hellenistic kings: protective deities. Being well attested for the different dynasties, it seems obvious to ask for the reasons of the preferences of kings and dynasties, possible target groups, and the media of implementation. Closer studies show the need to differentiate, however: between relationships to indigenous deities, equations of members of the royal dynasties with gods, and the situational claim to protective deities in military contexts (e. g., Demetrios and Poseidon – Antigonos Gonatas and Pan). The chapter aims at outlining the phenomenon and illustrates the possibilities of further research on this topic.

Hellenistic ruler cult – 'not the root' of Hellenistic monarchy but 'rather the leaves on its branches'[61] – is the topic of the two contributions by Stefan Pfeiffer and Sonja Richter, and it also plays a role in several other chapters. Pfeiffer throws a light on one aspect closely connected to dynastic ruler cult in Ptolemaic kingship, the invention of tradition and genealogy as well as the construction of a dynastic past, present and fu-

---

61   Adcock 1953: 'It was not the root of Hellenistic monarchy: it was rather the leaves on its branches.'

ture. He argues that the dynasty is to be understood as a "community of memory" and considers both the Graeco-Macedonian and Egyptian representation. In both spheres homonymy, *similitudo*, endogamy, divinity and divine descent are central elements. As the material makes clear, however, a distinction is necessary between self-representation of the Ptolemies on the one hand and representation of the royal couple by subjects on the other hand. Richter focuses on the problematic evidence for a Seleukid state-sponsored dynastic cult which remains uncertain. If one considers the specific respective context of the diverse evidence, it rather points to local or regional phenomena. In the vast and culturally heterogeneous Seleukid empire, coins were a central medium of communication that propagated Apollon as mythical dynastic founder. While for some elements of Seleukid representation – like the concept of sibling marriage – Ptolemaic parallels and potential examples have to be considered, especially coins show that there was also a unique "Seleukid" dimension of representation.

Three chapters explore themes and communication channels of Hellenistic monarchical representation focussing on the 3rd century. Shane Wallace uses contested epithets, especially the epithet *megas* and the title *basileus megas*, as a case study to explore inter-dynastic court rivalry in the early Hellenistic period. Focusing mainly on the Seleukid and Ptolemaic dynasties, he also includes both earlier and later uses of these elements in the Antigonid and Euthydemid dynasties. While claims to supremacy over other monarchic peers and the ideology of oikoumenic rule were universal features of all dynasties, local influences and regional variation can be detected in the use of both the epithet and the title from mainland Greece to Baktria. As one of the main observations of the chapter, however, Wallace argues that beyond the court it was apparently local communities and royal officials that played an important role in the development of the royal titulature.

Starting from the much-discussed Borsippa cylinder, Christoph Michels examines the significance of the use of the ethnikon "Makedon" in this indigenous context, which has been interpreted very differently with regard to the character of the Seleukid realm. The chapter explores the context within which this element should be embedded, and discusses which concepts were attached to (royal) Macedonian ethnicity. Apart from the notion of conquest, proximity to the Greek world and – resulting from this – the patronage of Greek cultural elements at court also seem to have been associated with Macedonicity. The latter activities were one aspect of transdynastic competition. They should not, however, be subsumed under the label of cultural policy as this presupposes a separate social sphere of "culture" in antiquity.

Although the victoriousness of the Hellenistic king undoubtedly played an important role in his representation, Charalampos Chrysafis opens up another perspective on the king's persona by stressing the importance of his role as an agent of *eirene* and *homonoia* for his legitimacy. Starting from the observation that peace and internal concord were concepts which were not only valued in the Greek sources but also frequently appeared in non-Greek contexts, the chapter discusses evidence for the role of the king as peacemaker and peacekeeper as a legitimizing factor. Likewise, the centrality of "peace" (an abstract term filled with specific concepts in different cultures) as an object of the subjects' expectations is discussed.

In a world shaped by transimperial and supralocal connections and interactions it is not surprising that we find similarities between the different dynasties but at the same time very different expressions of kingship in the various regions reacting to local traditions and specific communicative frameworks. Moving from the Greek mainland to the extreme east and then to the far west, the chapters by Hans Beck, Milinda Hoo, and Linda-Marie Günther explore the specific settings of monarchic rule and representation.

Hans Beck focuses on the third century rivalry between the Ptolemies and the Antigonids over influence in mainland and Aegean Greece – in a way a form of xenocracy, considering on the one hand the general Hellenic distaste of monarchic rule and on the other hand the traditional reservations against Macedonians. The scenario resulted in the curious constellation that for the actors in the diverse poleis the Ptolemies appeared as somewhat dubious but remote and therefore less dangerous agents, whereas the Antigonids may have been regarded as a more immediate threat. The remoteness of the Ptolemaic imperial centre in relation to Greece called not only for special strategic planning and careful conduct on the ground, but also influenced how the notion of their Macedonian otherness played out in the arena of politics.

Milinda Hoo analyses royal representation in Hellenistic Baktria. She sees royal practices as neither distinctly Macedonian nor globally uniform, but as translocally networked practices of sameness and differentiation. In Baktria, although the position as legitimate king depended on local acceptance by soldiers, administrators, elites, and to an extent the broader populace, the kings showed conscious efforts to participate in broader networks of power and prestige, engaging with visual languages of legitimacy and distinction that resonated both globally and locally. The charismatic royal persona derived from the presentation of military success, prestigious material display, and an increasing "heroisation" – situated in a highly competitive milieu of rival kings and adversaries.

Moving to the west, Linda-Marie Günther stresses the strong recourses of the kings of Syracuse to Sicilian history and tradition. Hieron II, on whom the chapter focuses, claimed descent from the Deinomenid tyrants. There existed manifold contacts with the eastern Adriatic zone, yet the Syracusan kings apparently did not adopt any specific Macedonian or Epirotic forms of representation. Hieron's coinage reflects elements of the traditional iconography, while the diademed portraits documented his royal status. A similar intent has often been ascribed to his lavish donations to Rhodos in 228/227, but they are rather to be interpreted against the background of the Deinomenid's descent from Gela, archaic colony of Rhodos.

While these studies illustrate the range and differences of monarchical rule and analyse communication embedded in different contexts, the following four chapters –

moving to the time frame of the second century BC – follow a comparative approach and explore the interrelation of common, or at least similar, themes and structures.

Peter Mittag discusses the interrelations (metrology, iconography, design) between Ptolemaic and Seleukid coinage and studies several cases of potential echoes and borrowings which, as he argues upon closer inspection, are quite rare, though. While coins produced under Antiochos IV in Antiocheia during the Sixth Syrian War may have symbolised the king's dual rule over the Seleukid and Ptolemaic empires, Phoinikian coins minted under Antiochos V and Demetrios I that take up Ptolemaic elements might be explained with the intention to meet local expectations. The most complex picture emerges from the coinage connected to the marriage between the Ptolemaic Kleopatra Thea and Alexander Balas and the ensuing events, as it combines elements of both empires in its different stages.

Galatian victories probably counted among the most prestigious for the Hellenistic kings, as it was possible to frame these as altruistic efforts for the Greeks. Giovanna Pasquariello compares aspects of the role of the "Galatersieger" in both a diachronic and synchronic analysis. She analyses the "Graeco-centrism" that is characteristic of this type of royal representation (and linked to practices such as royal philhellenism and euergetism) in a "multidimensional" model. This means that she employs a "vertical" perspective (diachronic depth of Greek tropes of barbarians and the fight of chaos and order) while "horizontally" looking at contemporaneous Greek attitudes towards the Galatian migration and their repercussions on royal representation, as well as royal competition in front of a mainly Graeco-Macedonian audience.

Alex McAuley situates the two attested instances of brother-sister marriage among the Mithradatids of Pontos (Mithradates IV with his sister Laodike, and Mithradates VI's first marriage to his sister Laodike) in the cultural and political context of the kingdom to determine how this phenomenon relates to the unique Anatolian/Iranian/Greek environment of Pontos. While these marriages have been viewed as an imitation of either Ptolemaic or Achaimenid practice and therefore as an indication of the dynasty's cultural alignment, the chapter argues against this exclusivity. Rather, an alignment with the emerging power of the Arsakids of Parthia should be taken into account. The phenomenon may thus be seen as part of a wider effort to draw on common Iranian heritage and may be an instance of the Zoroastrian practice of xwēdōdah.

Benedikt Eckhardt offers a comparative study of organised groups of loyalists with regard to their origin and function. Much has to remain uncertain, of course, due to the lack of sources, but it can be shown, e. g., how the Ptolemaic *basilistai* were connected with the military and the gymnasion or, in the case of the Attalistai, to agonistic networks. In the Seleukid empire, evidence for similar groups is lacking, but maybe gymnasia and groups like "the Antiochians in Ptolemais" played a comparable role. Royal regulations of civic gymnasia by the Antigonids maybe aimed to curb associationalism and ensure loyalty. It is a heterogeneous picture, but precisely because of the great differences it is capable of shedding light on the constellations that were responsible for the diverse manifestations of the phenomenon.

The final five chapters are explicitly concerned with possible consequences of the coming of Rome for monarchic power politics and the development of Hellenistic kingship since roughly 200 BC that presumably accompanied this fundamental change.

Noah Kaye proposes that the use of Weber's concept of "charismatic kingship" discussed above actually obscures a fundamental change in the representation and practice of kingship following ca. 200 BC that evolved around ideals of cosmic order and ethical discipline. To grasp this change, it is necessary in his view to use a new schema, one based on anthropologist Alan Strathern's recent comparative study of sacred kingship in world history. In response to Roman dominance, the later Hellenistic kings more actively cultivated traditional authorities such as cities, temples, and villages. Other phenomena may be linked to this change: the disappearance of the royal portrait from coinage such as on the Attalid kistophoroi and the so-called autonomous coinages of the Antigonids and the fact that rulers of this period begin to appear as parties to civic oaths.

Katharina Martin treats similar phenomena in her numismatic study on monarchical representation concerning the interaction between kings and cities (and their elites), and focuses on the Seleukid Empire. She compares the so-called quasi-municipal coinage in the Seleukid Empire since Antiochos IV with the so-called pseudo-autonomous coins of Mithradates VI in Pontos and Paphlagonia. Martin explores the silver coinage of the late Seleukids from Mallos, Tarsos and Damaskos, and analyses how references to indigenous cults integrated civic traditions into monarchical representation. As an outlook, she also touches upon the Attic-weight wreathed coinages circulating in the Seleukid Empire which in her view illustrate the increasing opportunities of presenting civic structures within the framework of monarchical systems.

Patrick Sänger asks for possible changes in the representation of the later Ptolemies (2nd and 1st century) due to the loss of power at an international level. His focus lies on the possible instrumentalization of ethnic groups and concepts in the administrative and social realm and takes the institution of the *politeuma* (probably introduced by Ptolemaios VI) as object of analysis. This specific form of association with ethnic designations may have been intended to keep Egypt attractive for immigrants from foreign cities or regions. In a way, it possibly was a compensatory strategy that evoked patterns which had been formative for the dynasty's self-image and asserted its former status as a maritime power on an ideological level.

Taking another perspective, Martin Kovacs, in examining the Seleukid portraits of the late 3rd and 2nd centuries BC, comes to a rather different conclusion concerning the "charisma" of the kings. Apart from visual references to the forefathers, another "transgressive" phenomenon can be identified, namely allusions to the imagery of Alexander the Great. This can be shown for Antiochos IV and even more so for the usurper Diodotos Tryphon. The *imitatio Alexandri* seems to have aimed at creating the ruler's own (not dynastic) legitimacy. In his view, the allusions – not to be found in the generation of the Diadochi and their successors – function as a promise to repeat and match Alexander's achievements as conqueror. Thus, they might be an attempt to style the respective rulers in a decidedly charismatic way – a dimension surely different from the phenomena described in the preceding chapters.

Finally, Achim Lichtenberger treats one of the most important "royal activities", the (re)foundation of cities (or settlements) with dynastic names – powerful markers of the claim to rule. This phenomenon can also be observed in the late Hellenistic period, but with a new twist. In this time, we also encounter cities named after members of the Roman imperial family. To name cities after "foreign" ruling dynasties seems to be specific not only to this time frame but also to the relationship to Rome, because in situations that were not dissimilar to this constellation with kingdoms dependent on Parthia this apparently did not happen. This may in fact suggest that Rome's client kings did not develop this gesture of loyalty themselves but reacted to expectations of the Roman imperial centre.

5. Outlook

The picture of Hellenistic monarchical representation presented here is inevitably incomplete, yet it clearly illustrates the dynamics and the heterogeneity of monarchical rule, and the multiple roles associated with the ruler. The chapters concentrating on regional peculiarities or the comparison of fields of representation found in several dynasties illustrate how problematic the label "Hellenistic" is when used as an all-encompassing descriptor. Equally, concepts like "globalisation" tend to rather obscure the specifics of the different dynasties if the local/regional dimension of political communication is left out of the picture. Of course, it is not enough to state the dissimilarities. Rather, the value of pointing these out is that it makes it possible to ask about, and ideally identify, the respective reasons for adoption or demarcation.

Nevertheless, the use of the term "Hellenistic kingship" goes beyond a mere chronological definition of monarchic rule and has explanatory value. As many chapters show, the norms, roles and practices attributed as defining characteristics of this monarchical system are conducive to explaining the behaviour of individual rulers beyond personal preferences as well as character strengths and weaknesses.

Asking for the agency and cultural baggage of the diverse (local) actors helps to explain the development of ideologies – and illustrates why notions of one-sided, concerted royal propaganda are problematic. The constraints and traditions that came into play for the kings when interacting with local elites, but also impulses of honouring the kings emanating from this level, could have an impact on the imperial centre. At the same time, it is evident that on another level, inter-dynastic competition – beyond concrete ruler-subject relationships – could also play a significant role, as could the courts as communication platforms. While notions of empire certainly played a role in different chapters, it is not necessarily an explanatory model that replaces other perspectives on the monarch and his rule.

Those chapters that are explicitly concerned with the consequences of the coming of Rome clearly illustrate its profound impact on the Hellenistic world of states but also on the image of the ruler. Easily identifiable trends in the development of Hellenistic kingship, however, turn out to be more complex and, depending on the perspective, quite contradictory upon closer examination. Dates (200 BC?, 168 BC?) associated with radical changes prove to be of heuristic value in some regard, but seem not to have had any significant influence on other aspects of the persona of the king.

Thus, the studies collected in this volume – sometimes explicitly so – call for further studies on Hellenistic kingship that embrace the multifaceted nature of this monarchic system without overstating the idiosyncrasies of the rivalling dynasties: the same, but different.

Bibliography

Adcock 1953: Adcock, Frank E., Greek and Macedonian Kingship, Proceedings of the British Academy 39, 1953, 163–180

Bagnall 1997: Bagnall, Roger S., Decolonizing Ptolemaic Egypt, in: P. Cartledge – P. Garnsey – E. Gruen (eds.), Hellenistic Constructs: Essays in Culture, History, and Historiography, Berkeley, Los Angeles et al. 1997, 225–241

Baynham 2021: Baynham, Elizabeth, "Selling Alexander": the Concept and Use of "Propaganda" in the Age of Alexander, in: J. Walsh – E. Baynham (eds.), Alexander the Great and propaganda. New York et al. 2021, 1–13

Bichler 1983: Bichler, Reinhold, "Hellenismus". Geschichte und Problematik eines Epochenbegriffs, Darmstadt 1983

Bilde – Engberg-Pedersen – Hannestad – Zahle 1996: Bilde, Per – Engberg-Pedersen, Troels – Hannestad, Lise – Zahle, Jan, Introduction, in: P. Bilde et al. (eds.), Aspects of Hellenistic Kingship, Aarhus 1996, 9–14

Bosch-Puche 2013: Bosch-Puche, Francisco, The Egyptian Royal Titulary of Alexander the Great I: Horus, Two Ladies, Golden Horus, and Throne Names, Journal of Egyptian Archaeology 99, 2013, 131–154

Bosworth 2002: Bosworth, Albert B., The Legacy of Alexander. Politics, Warfare, and Propaganda under the Successors, Oxford et al. 2002

Bringmann 2000: Bringmann, Klaus, Geben und Nehmen. Monarchische Wohltätigkeit und Selbstdarstellung im Zeitalter des Hellenismus, Berlin 2000

Bringmann – von Steuben 1995: Bringmann, Klaus – von Steuben, Hans (eds.), Schenkungen hellenistischer Herrscher an griechische Städte und Heiligtümer, Berlin 1995

Chamoux 2002: Chamoux, Francois, Hellenistic Civilization, tr. M. Roussel, Chichester 2002

Chaniotis 2018: Chaniotis, Angelos, Age of Conquests The Greek World from Alexander to Hadrian 336 BC–AD 138, London 2018

Coşkun – McAuley 2016: Coşkun Altay – McAuley, Alex (eds.), Seleukid Royal Women. Creation, Representation and Distortion of Hellenistic Queenship in the Seleukid Empire, Stuttgart 2016

Dreyer – Mittag 2011: Dreyer, Boris – Mittag, Peter F. (eds.), Lokale Eliten und hellenistische Könige. Zwischen Kooperation und Konfrontation, Berlin 2011

Eich 2003: Eich, Armin, Die Idealtypen "Propaganda" und "Repräsentation" als heuristische Mittel bei der Bestimmung gesellschaftlicher Konvergenzen und Divergenzen von Moderne und römischer Kaiserzeit, in: Weber – Zimmermann 2003b, 41–84

Eckstein 2009: Eckstein, Arthur M., Hellenistic Monarchy in Theory and Practice, in: R. K. Balot (ed.), A Companion to Greek and Roman Political Thought, Oxford et al. 2009, 247–265

Erskine – Llewellyn-Jones – Wallace 2014: Erskine, Andrew – Llewellyn-Jones, Lloyd –Wallace, Shane (eds.), The Hellenistic Court. Monarchic Power and Elite Society from Alexander to Cleopatra, Swansea 2017

Fischer-Bovet – von Reden 2021a: Fischer-Bovet, Christelle – von Reden, Sitta, Introduction, in: Fischer-Bovet – von Reden 2021b, 1–14

Fischer-Bovet – von Reden 2021b: Fischer-Bovet, Christelle, von Reden, Sitta (eds.), Comparing the Ptolemaic and Seleucid Empires. Integration, Communication, and Resistance, Cambridge 2021b

Gehler – Rollinger 2022: Gehler, Michael – Rollinger, Robert, Imperial Turn. Challenges, Problems and Questions of Empire History, in: M. Gehler – R. Rollinger (eds.), Empires to be Remembered. Ancient Worlds through Modern Times, New York 2022, 3–39

Gehrke 2013: Gehrke, Hans-Joachim, The Victorious King. Reflections on the Hellenistic Monarchy, in: N. Luraghi (ed.), The Splendors and Miseries of Ruling Alone. Encounters with Monarchy from Archaic Greece to the Hellenistic Mediterranean, Stuttgart 2013, 73–98 (engl. tr. of Gehrke, Hans-Joachim, Der siegreiche König. Überlegungen zur hellenistischen Monarchie, Archiv für Kulturgeschichte 64, 1982, 247–277)

Gotter 2008: Gotter, Ulrich, Die Nemesis des Allgemein-Gültigen: Max Webers Charisma-Konzept und die antiken Monarchien, in: P. Rychterová – S. Seit – R. Veit (eds.), Das Charisma – Funktionen und symbolische Repräsentationen. Historische, philosophische, islamwissenschaftliche, soziologische und theologische Perspektiven, Berlin 2008, 173–186

Gotter 2013: Gotter, Ulrich, The Castrated King, or: The Everyday Monstrosity of Late Hellenistic Kingship, in: Luraghi 2013b, 207–230

Gruen 1985: Gruen, Erich, The Coronation of the Diadochi, Karanos 1, 2018, 109–119 (rep. id., The Coronation of the Diadochi, in: J. Eadie – J. Ober (eds.), The Craft of the Ancient Historian, Maryland 1985, 253–272)

Heinen 1983: Heinen, Heinz, Die Tryphè des Ptolemaios VIII. Euergetes II. Beobachtungen zum ptolemäischen Herrscherideal und zu einer römischen Gesandtschaft in Ägypten (140/39 v. Chr.), in: id. (ed.), Althistorische Studien: FS Hermann Bengtson, Wiesbaden 1983, 116–128

Hoo 2018: Hoo, Milinda, Ai Khanum in the Face of Eurasian Globalisation: A Translocal Approach to a Contested Site in Hellenistic Bactria, 2018, 161–186

Joose 2014: Joosse, Paul, Becoming a God. Max Weber and the Social Construction of Charisma, in: Journal of Classical Sociology 14, 2014, 266–283

Kaye 2022: Kaye, Noah, The Attalids of Pergamon and Anatolia. Money, Culture, and State Power, Cambridge 2022

Köhler 1996: Köhler, Jens, Pompai. Untersuchungen zur hellenistischen Festkultur, Frankfurt a. M. et al. 1996

Koenen 1983: Koenen, Ludwig, Die Adaption ägyptischer Königsideologie am Ptolemäerhof, in: E. van't Dack – P. van Dessel – W. van Gucht (eds.), Egypt and the Hellenistic World, Leuven 1983, 143–190

Koehn 2007: Koehn, Clemens, Krieg – Diplomatie – Ideologie. Zur Außenpolitik hellenistischer Mittelstaaten, Historia ES 195, Stuttgart 2007

Koenen 1993: Koenen, Ludwig, The Ptolemaic King as a Religious Figure, in: Bulloch, Anthony et al. (eds.), Images and Ideologies. Self-Definition in the Hellenistic World, Berkeley 1993, 25–38

Kosmin 2014: Kosmin, Paul J., The Land of the Elephant Kings: Space, Territory, and Ideology in the Seleucid Empire, Cambridge 2014

Kosmin 2019: Kosmin, Paul J., Time and Its Adversaries in the Seleucid Empire, Cambridge 2019

Kyrieleis 1975: Kyrieleis, Helmut, Bildnisse der Ptolemäer, Berlin 1975

Lendon 2006: Lendon, Jon E., The Legitimacy of the Roman Emperor: Against Weberian Legitimacy and Imperial "Strategies of Legitimation", in: A. Kolb (ed.), Herrschaftsstrukturen und Herrschaftspraxis. Konzepte, Prinzipien und Strategien der Administration im römischen Kaiserreich, Berlin 2006, 53–63

Lichtenberger 2015: Lichtenberger, Achim, Herod, Zoilos, Philopappos. Multiple Identities in the Graeco-Roman World, Eretz-Israel 31, 2015 (Ehud Netzer Volume), 110*–122*

Lichtenberger 2021: Lichtenberger, Achim, Hellenistic Commagene in Context. Is 'Global' the Answer and Do We Have to Overcome Cultural 'Containers'?, in: M. Blömer et al. (eds.) Common Dwelling Place of all the Gods. Commagene in its Local, Regional and Global Hellenistic Context, Stuttgart 2021, 579–587

Lichtenberger et al. 2012: Lichtenberger, Achim et al. (eds.), Das Diadem der hellenistischen Herrscher. Übernahme, Transformation oder Neuschöpfung eines Herrschaftszeichens, Bonn 2012

Luraghi 2013a: Luraghi, Nino, Ruling Alone: Monarchy in Greek Politics and Thought, in: Luraghi 2013b, 11–24

Luraghi 2013b: Luraghi, Nino (ed.), The Splendors and Miseries of Ruling Alone, Encounters with Monarchy from Archaic Greece to the Hellenistic Mediterranean, Stuttgart 2013b

Ma 2002: Ma, John, Antiochos III and the Cities of Western Asia Minor, ²Oxford 2002

Ma 2003: Ma, John, Kings, in: A. Erskine (ed.), A Companion to the Hellenistic World, Oxford et al. 2003, 177–195

Ma 2013: Ma, John, Hellenistic Empires, in: P. F. Bang – W. Scheidel (eds.), The Oxford Handbook of the State in the Ancient Near East and Mediterranean, Oxford 2013, 324–360

Meister 2021: Meister, Jan B., Antike und moderne Propaganda, Historische Zeitschrift 312.3, 2021, 587–613

Michels 2009: Michels, Christoph, Kulturtransfer und monarchischer "Philhellenismus" Bithynien, Pontos und Kappadokien in hellenistischer Zeit, Göttingen 2009

Mittag 2015: Mittag, Peter F., Der potente König. Königliche Umzüge in hellenistischen Hauptstädten, in: D. Boschung – K.-J. Hölkeskamp – C. Sode (eds.), Raum und Performanz. Rituale in Residenzen von der Antike bis 1815, Stuttgart 2015, 75–98

Müller 2016: Müller, Sabine, Die Argeaden. Geschichte Makedoniens bis zum Zeitalter Alexanders des Großen, Paderborn 2016

Näf 2015: Näf, Beat, Das Charisma des Herrschers. Antike und Zeitgeschichte in der ersten Hälfte des 20. Jahrhunderts, in: D. Boschung – J. Hammerstaedt (eds.), Das Charisma des Herrschers, Paderborn 2015, 11–50

Paganoni 2019: Paganoni, Eloisa, Forging the Crown: a History of the Kingdom of Bithynia from its Origin to Prusias I, Rome 2019

Pownall – Asirvatham –Müller 2021: Pownall, Frances – Asirvatham, Sulochana R. – Müller, Sabine (eds.), The Courts of Philip II and Alexander the Great. Monarchy and Power in Ancient Macedonia, Berlin et al. 2021

Rebenich 2017: Rebenich, Stefan (ed.), Monarchische Herrschaft im Altertum, Berlin 2017

Rebenich – Wienand 2017: Rebenich, Stefan – Wienand, Johannes, Monarchische Herrschaft im Altertum. Zugänge und Perspektiven, in: Rebenich 2017, 1–41

Roisman 2020: Roisman, Joseph, Charismatic Leaders in Ancient Greece, in: J.P. Zúquete (ed.), Routledge International Handbook of Charisma, Abingdon 2020, 53–64

Schäfer 2014: Schäfer, Christoph, Die Diadochenstaaten: "Imperien" oder doch konkurrierende Territorialstaaten?, in: M. Gehler – R. Rollinger (eds.), Imperien und Reiche in der Weltgeschichte 1, Wiesbaden 2014, 387–400

Serrati 2007: Serrati, John, Warfare and the State, in: P. Sabin – H. van Wees – L.M. Whitby (eds.), The Cambridge History of Greek and Roman Warfare. Cambridge 2007, 461–497

Shipley 2000: Shipley, Graham, The Greek World after Alexander. 323–30 BC, London et al. 2000

Sinopoli 1994: Sinopoli, Carla M., The Archaeology of Empires, Annual Review of Anthropology 23, 1994, 159–180

Strootman 2013: Strootman, Rolf, Babylonian, Macedonian, King of the World: The Antiochos Cylinder from Borsippa and Seleukid Imperial Integration, in: E. Stavrianopoulou (ed.), Shifting Social Imaginaries in the Hellenistic Period. Narrations, Practices, and Images, Leiden 2013, 67–97

Strootman 2019: Strootman, Rolf, The Ptolemaic Sea Empire, in: R. Strootman – F. van den Eijnde – R. van Wijk (eds.), Empires of the Sea: Maritime Power Networks in World History, Leiden et al. 2019, 113–152

Strootman 2021: Strootman, Rolf, The Introduction of Hellenic Cults in Seleukid Syria. Colonial Appropriation and Transcultural Exchange in the Creation of an Imperial Landscape, in: H. Bru – A. Dumitru – N. Sekunda (eds.), Colonial Geopolitics and Local Cultures in the Hellenistic and Roman East (3rd Century B.C.–3rd century A.D.), Oxford 2021, 73–91

Trampedach – Meeus 2020a: Trampedach, Kai – Meeus, Alexander, Introduction: Understanding Alexander's Relations with His Subjects, in: Trampedach – Meeus 2020b, 9–18

Trampedach – Meeus 2020b: Trampedach, Kai – Meeus, Alexander (eds.), The Legitimation of Conquest. Monarchical Representation and the Art of Government in the Empire of Alexander the Great, Stuttgart 2020

Versluys – Riedel 2021: Versluys, Miguel J. – Riedel, Stefan, Beyond East & West. Hellenistic Commagene between Particularism and Universalism, in: M. Blömer et al. (eds.), Common Dwelling Place of all the Gods. Commagene in its Local, Regional and Global Hellenistic Context, Stuttgart 2021, 11–30

Veyne 1990: Veyne, Paul, Propagande expression roi, image idole oracle, L'Homme 114, 1990, 7–26

Vössing 2004: Vössing, Konrad, Mensa Regia. Das Bankett beim hellenistischen König und beim römischen Kaiser, Munich et al. 2004

Walbank 1984: Walbank, Frank W., Monarchies and Monarchic Ideas, CAH² 7.1, Cambridge [u.a.] 1984, 62–100

Wallace 2014: Wallace, Shane, Court, Kingship, and Royal Style in the Early Hellenistic Period, in: Erskine – Llewellyn-Jones – Wallace 2014, 1–30

Wallace-Hadrill 1982: Wallace-Hadrill, Andrew, Civilis Princeps: Between Citizen and King, The Journal of Roman Studies 72, 1982, 32–48

Weber 1978: Weber, Max, Economy and Society. An Outline of Interpretive Sociology, 2 vols., ed. by G. Rothand – C. Wittich, Berkeley et al. 1978

Weber – Zimmermann 2003a: Weber, Gregor – Zimmermann, Martin, Propaganda, Selbstdarstellung und Repräsentation. Die Leitbegriffe des Kolloquiums in der Forschung zur frühen Kaiserzeit, in: Weber – Zimmermann 2003b, 11–40

Weber – Zimmermann 2003b: Weber, Gregor – Zimmermann, Martin (eds.), Propaganda, Selbstdarstellung, Repräsentation im römischen Kaiserreich des 1. Jhs. n. Chr., Wiesbaden 2003

Wiemer 2017: Wiemer, Hans-Ulrich, Siegen oder untergehen? Die hellenistische Monarchie in der neueren Forschung, in: Rebenich 2017, 305–339

Will 1985: Will, Édouard, Pour une "anthropologie coloniale" du monde hellénistique, in: W. J. Eadie – J. Ober (eds.), The Craft of the Ancient Historian: Essays in Honor of Chester G. Starr, Lanham 1985, 273–301

Zimmermann 2011: Zimmermann, Martin, Die Repräsentation des kaiserlichen Ranges, in: A. Winterling (ed.), Zwischen Strukturgeschichte und Biographie. Probleme und Perspektiven einer neuen römischen Kaisergeschichte zur Zeit von Augustus bis Commodus, Munich 2011, 181–205

Figures

Fig. 1: Münzsammlung der Universität Münster, M 3961, Photo by Robert Dylka.

Fig. 2: Münzkabinett, Kunsthistorisches Museum, ID103163. Photo by Margit Redl.

Fig. 3: Musée du Louvre, Département des Antiquités grecques, étrusques et romaines; NIII 1472; Bj 1093.

Fig. 4: Musée du Louvre, Département des Antiquités grecques, étrusques et romaines; NIII 1471; Bj 1092.

Christoph Michels has been a Heisenberg Fellow at the University of Münster since 2020. He studied History, Classical Archaeology and Art History at the University of Bochum. In 2008, he received his doctorate in a co-tutelle programme at the Universities of Innsbruck/Frankfurt with a thesis on the kingdoms of Bithynia, Pontos, and Kappadokia (published 2009). In 2016, he completed his habilitation at Aachen University with a thesis on the representation of the Roman princeps using Antoninus Pius as example (published 2018). Michels is co-editor of *Athen und/oder Alexandreia?* (2014), *Jenseits des Narrativs. Antoninus Pius in den nicht-literarischen Quellen* (2017), *Erinnerung. Studien zu Konstruktionen, Persistenzen und gesellschaftlichem Wandel* (2018). He has held substitute professorships in Bayreuth, Düsseldorf, Münster, and Tübingen. From 2014–2017, he was member of the Junges Kolleg of the AWK NRW. His research focuses on cultural history and the history of monarchy as well as on political communication in antiquity.

Part 1:
The Diadochi and the Third Century

The Formation Phase / Die Formationsphase

Argead Representation and Its Impact[*]

SABINE MÜLLER

Abstract: Argead representation as a kind of success story that had proven its ideological worth had much to offer to the Successors and their heirs. This paper explores the major features of the Argead dynastic image, essentially designed and developed by Alexander I in the fifth century BC and by Philip II in the fourth century BC. To the end of offering some answers to the question of what political actors after the Argeads might have learned from them concerning their political self-fashioning, the following aspects are examined: the representation of the Argeads as a clan, the spaces of action of Argead royal women, and the major iconographic features of Argead coinage as dynastic iconography. Thereby it will be shown that the dynastic image of the Argeads and their strategies of representation could serve in multiple ways as a blueprint for the members of Hellenistic dynasties and triggered selective borrowings.

1. Introduction

Argead representation can be regarded as effective. As one of the means to justify and safeguard the leading position of the Argeads and to keep the Macedonians – particularly the influential families – loyal to Argead rule, the representation of the Argeads served to spread and keep alive the belief that their family was the only house fit for rule.[1]

In all likelihood, Alexander I was the "mastermind" who created the essentials of the dynastic public image preserved by his successors and designed the strategies of its

---

[*] I am grateful to Christoph Michels, Hans Beck and Achim Lichtenberger for their kind invitation to their conference.

[1] On the Argeads see Wirth 1985, 9–25; Borza 1990; Ogden 1999, 3–40; Roisman 2010; Mari 2011; Psoma 2014; Psoma 2015; Müller 2016; Hatzopoulos 2017; King 2018; Hatzopoulos 2020; Heckel – Heinrichs – Müller – Pownall 2020. For recent definitions of the nature of the Argead monarchy see Landucci Gattinoni 2003a; Hatzopoulos 2020, 103–116; Kholod 2020; Mari 2020. On some elements of Argead representation used by the Successors see Meeus 2020.

representation.[2] There were multiple ways to propagate the values and advantages of
Argead power, such as an own foundation myth that was occasionally revised, coin images, public appearances (at festivals, games, performances of cultic duties, weddings,
or burials), dedications, benefactions, dynastic names, or the patronage of artists, writers, or scientists. As for Argead cultural patronage, it was particularly Archelaos who
assembled Greek artists and intellectuals at his court and gained the reputation of being a generous patron.[3] For example, he was the patron of the Athenian tragic poets
Agathon and Euripides, the painter Zeuxis, the epic poet Choirilos of Samos and the
dithyrambic poet Timotheos of Miletos.[4] Archelaos was also responsible for a "refreshment" including new images of the Argead coin iconography.[5] Besides Alexander I and
Archelaos, Philip II played a major role in developing the representation of his house.[6]
His military and political successes opened up new spaces, also concerning the politics
of representation, for example paving the way f increased visibility of individual royal
women.

As for the aforementioned effectiveness, the Argeads were able to preserve the
majority consensus within the population of their realm that rule rested exclusively
with them as long as there was a male successor. Thus, while Alexander IV ruled only
formally, doomed to be a puppet and a prisoner, his murder was a watershed in Macedonian history. The teenager's elimination freed the Successors from the problem of
dealing with his legitimate claim while trying to justify their own power.

On a literary level, Greek historiographers such as Herodotos and Thukydides
bought the Argeads' propagandistic claim to Greek Temenid descent, ostentatiously
confirmed by the participation of Alexander I at the Olympic Games: only free Greeks
could take part in the Games.[7]

In the transitional times after the death of Alexander III, there emerged new ways to
represent Macedonian power and ruling qualities. Since the Successors had grown up
with Argead rulership, it was the obvious example to turn to. Argead strategies of representation influenced the political self-fashioning and public images of the Successors
and their heirs.[8]

2   On Alexander I see Heinrichs – Müller 2008; Heinrichs 2017; Müller 2017, 76–83; Heinrichs 2020a;
     Heinrichs 2020d.
3   See Pownall 2020a, 97–98; Pownall 2020b, 228–220; Pownall 2020c, 383–384.
4   Agathon: Plut. mor. 177a-b; Ail. var. 2.21; 13.4; Euripides: Aristot. pol. 1311b; Plut. mor. 177a; 531d-e;
     Ail. var. 2.21; 13.4; Zeuxis: Ail. var. 14.17; cf. Plin. nat. 35.63; Choirilos: Istros, BNJ 334 F 61; Suda s. v.
     Χοιρίλος; Timotheos: Plut. mor. 177b-c; 334b; Steph. Byz. s. v. Μίλητος.
5   Cf. Heinrichs 2020c, 172.
6   On Philip II see Wirth 1985; Anson 2008; Beck – Buckler 2008, 233–276; Worthington 2008; Müller
     2016, 236–276; Müller 2019, 43–47; Wirth 2020; Hatzopoulos 2020, 128–169.
7   Hdt. 8.137–139; Thuk. 2.99. Cf. Vasilev 2011. On Alexander I at Olympia: Hdt. 5.22.2; Iust. 7.2.14.
8   Some examples are provided by Landucci Gattinoni 2003a, 93; Landucci Gattinoni 2010.

Against this background, this paper explores the messages spread by the Argeads about the Macedonian *basileia*. It will examine how they possibly wanted to be perceived, primarily by the Macedonians, and how they tried to convince the population of their realm, particularly the leading circles, that they were the only family fit to rule.

To the end of providing some examples of what the Successors might have learned from the Argeads regarding their political self-fashioning, this paper will focus on (1) Argead clan nature, (2) the spaces of action of Argead royal women, and (3) the major iconographic features of Argead coinage as a possible source of inspiration.

2. The representation of the Argead clan

The clan nature of the Argead *basileia* was of particular importance to Argead representation.[9] The earliest attested version of the Argead foundation myth already tells the story of a family: three brothers, standing together. Perdikkas I, the founder of the Argead realm, overcame dangers and toils together with his two elder brothers and supporters Gauanes and Aëropos.[10] Since Argead family life – or family business – was essentially political, all of its members could or had to represent their house and help to propagate its image and ideology as its agents.

For example, although Arrhidaios, the son of Philip II and his Thessalian wife Philinna, was mentally disabled and in constant need of a guardian, he was expected to support the dynasty in accordance with his – however limited – possibilities.[11] It is likely that he was present at public events such as festivals, celebrations of his father's military victories, and marriages or burials of Argeads. Apparently, it seemed to be sufficient regarding his role as an Argead representative that Arrhidaios was able to perform basic public duties when being guided.[12] Philip tried to integrate Arrhidaios in his marriage politics.[13] Alexander let him participate in his cultic duties.

---

9   Cf. Carney 2003, 251; Carney 2016, 7–8; Carney 2019a, 8. See also Ogden 1999, 3–41.
10   Hdt. 8.137–138. Cf. Müller 2016, 85–91.
11   On Arrhidaios' intellectual disability: Diod. 18.2.2; Heidel. Epit. F 1.2; Iust. 13.2.8; 13.11.2; Plut. Alexander 77.5; Plut. Phokion 33.5–6; Plut. mor. 337d-e; Curt. 10.7.13; 10.8.2. Cf. Hamilton 1969, 217; Bosworth 1988, 28, 174; Carney 2001, 78–82; Bosworth 2002, 30, n. 9; Carney 2006, 92, 149, 155; Atkinson 2009, 188–189; Müller 2020; Heckel ²2021, 383–384. The descriptions by our sources are too imprecise to know about its nature.
12   Curt. 10.7.7–8.20; 10.9.16–19.
13   Plut. Alexander 10.1. Preparing his Persian campaign, Philip tried to connect with Pixodaros, the satrap of Karia via a marital bond between Arrhidaios and Pixodaros' daughter (to the end of establishing Argead control over the important port of Halikarnassos). The plan came to naught, however apparently not because of Arrhidaios' disability but because of the intervention of the Persian king who took efforts to keep the Macedonians away from the Karian coast (Strab. 14.2.17). Cf. Wirth 1989, 124–125; Briant 2010, 156–160; Olbrycht 2010, 347; Ruzicka 2010, 6–7; Müller 2019, 59–61; Heckel 2020, 17.

Thus, in Asia, apparently guided by Alexander, Arrhidaios appeared as his half-brother's 'associate in sacrifices and ceremonies (*sacrorum caerimoniarumque consors*).'[14] It was a specific dual representation of Argead cultic responsibility, displayed by a pair of brothers. Unfortunately, it is unknown if Arrhidaios was staged as a kind of Alexander's "brother-loving" dynastic support. In this case, their appearance would have foreshadowed the theme of the brother-loving part of the Ptolemaic couple. This famous type of the dual representation of the Ptolemies served to stress the strength of the dynasty through unity and harmony.[15] However, the scarce information on Arrhidaios' public appearances in association with Alexander does not allow for certain conclusions.

In any case, the Argead imagery of the rule of a clan, bonded by solidarity and unity, offered the Successors and their heirs some politically useful lessons to learn and examples to follow. In Hellenistic times, the emphasis on the clan nature of the Macedonian *basileia* did not cease to be of ideological importance.[16] To return to the Ptolemaic example, the public staging of harmony, unity, and mutual love in the royal family was a key aspect of the legitimization of the early Ptolemies. Ptolemaios II initiated and developed the theme in order to stress the ruling qualities of his specific family branch as a token of his legitimacy.[17] Newly created images of mutual love between the members of this branch mirrored this ideology in its emphasis on dynastic harmony and unity.

The most prominent example of this theme formed part of the carefully arranged public image of the inseparable loving royal couple, Ptolemaios II and his sister-wife Arsinoë II, both during Arsinoë's lifetime and posthumously. She was represented as a Ptolemaic goddess; after her death, the illusion was kept alive that she carried on taking care for her husband (who did not remarry), his realm, and its population.[18] Poets at the Ptolemaic court stressed that Ptolemaios II and Arsinoë II were completely devoted to each other. They also emphasized that the first and third Ptolemaic couple – Ptolemaios I and Berenike I, Ptolemaios III and Berenike II (his cousin, formally styled as his sister) – were happily in love. In addition, they praised Ptolemaios II's

---

14   Curt. 10.7.2. Cf. Atkinson 2009, 186. On Alexander's pious practice in general see von den Hoff
      2020. On knowledge of Alexander's deeds in the Greek world in general see Wallace 2020.
15   Cf. Müller 2009, 136–138; Ager 2021, 346–347; Pfeiffer 2021, 96. 100–101.
16   Cf. Landucci Gattinoni 2003a, 87–93; Landucci Gattinoni 2010, 121.
17   Cf. Ogden 1999, 78–79; Müller 2009, 136–138; Lianou 2020, 130–132; Carney 2013, 37; Ager 2021,
      346–347; Müller 2021b, 44–45. As for the background, Ptolemaios II had innerdynastic problems
      with his accession. Although his father, Ptolemaios I, had taken efforts to secure Ptolemaios II's
      succession and made him his co-regent in 285 BC, when he died in 282/281 BC, Ptolemaios II's rule
      was contested by his half-brothers. Thus, Ptolemaios II chose to promote his family branch as the
      one predestined to rule.
18   Cf. Ogden 1999, 78–79; Müller 2009, 134–155, 262–266 (*theoi adelphoi*), 280–300 (*Thea Philadel-
      phos*); Carney 2013, 83–128; Pfeiffer 2021, 96–98. On the coins visualizing these images see Le Rid-
      er – Callataÿ 2006, 51–52. On the impact of this image regarding the third Ptolemaic couple see
      McAuley 2020, 182–183. On this topic in general see the chapter of Stefan Pfeiffer in this volume.

cultic acts in honor of his beloved parents and attested to the great pride he took in the panhellenic victories of his close relatives.[19]

Another way to express this theme of dynastic love was the adoption of an *epitheton* expressing the loving attitude (e. g. Philadelphos or Philopator).[20] The dynastic harmony theme transported the message that the ruling house stood solid as a rock guaranteeing a stable rule, untroubled by inner-dynastic strife. Furthermore, the image of the happy royal couple in love served to emphasize that the offspring was legitimate.

As for an Antigonid example, while anecdotal in character and often reminiscent of gossip, some of the stories told by Plutarch about the mutual love between Antigonos Monophthalmos and Demetrios Poliorketes may reflect their genuine propagandistic effort to create a public image of particular closeness between father and son.[21] Thus, Plutarch characterizes Demetrios as *philopator* and stresses that a faithful Antigonos even let his son sit down by his side while Demetrios, arriving from a hunt, was carrying his weapons. This ostentatious demonstration of faith and harmony was effectively staged at the public event of an audience.[22] Granted that there is some authenticity to this story, this public display of harmony between father and son served to emphasize their political strength and inseparable bond in order to attract potential allies searching for strong and reliable partners and intimidate their enemies (or at least be a warning addressed to their opponents).

3. The visibility of Argead royal women

The clan nature of Argead rule also shaped the spaces of action of Argead royal women.[23] As defined by Elizabeth Carney, female Argeads were 'participants in an interlocking web of relationships that dominated the public life of Macedonia.'[24] Some of them became visible beyond marriage policy and reproduction in the fields of politics, diplomacy, war, succession advocacy, euergetism, and patronage. While in Argead times there is no evidence for the use of female titles for royal women, Elizabeth Carney sug-

---

19   Theokr. 17.38–42, 128–130; Catull. 66.11–25; Kall. fr. 110 Pf.; Poseidipp. ep. 78 AB. On Ptolemaios III
     and Berenike II as ideological siblings: OGIS 54, ll. 1–2; OGIS 55, ll. 2–3; OGIS 56, l.1; Kall. Ait. 3.58
     Asper (*SH* 254 + 383 Pf.); Poseidipp. ep. 82 AB. Cf. McAuley 2020, 179–181; Pfeiffer 2021, 98–99. On
     the political meaning of maternity in Kallimachos see Manakidou 2020.
20   On the meaning of royal Hellenistic epithets see Muccioli 2013, 203–255.
21   Plut. Demetrios 18.1. On the biased nature of Demetrios' literary portraits see Pownall 2016.
22   Plut. Demetrios. 3.1–3. On the career of Demetrios see Wheatley – Dunn 2020.
23   Cf. Carney 2003, 251; Carney 2016, 7–8, 11; Carney 2019a, 8; Müller 2021a, 294.
24   Carney 2010a, 409.

gests that in some individual cases, the personal names of female Argeads had special dynastic implications and carried a kind of royal 'trademark quality'.[25]

Argead women's spaces of action and public visibility expanded in accordance with their dynasty's rise. In consequence, the reign of Philip II under whom Argead Macedonia became a major power in the Mediterranean world and Greece's new hegemon, was a watershed also regarding the public space of female Argeads. Philip's own elevation of rank in relation to his leading circles, that is, the first steps of distancing the ruler from the traditional position of the *primus inter pares* (further developed by Alexander III), also increased the visibility of female Argeads in the monarchical presentation.[26]

However, the first female Argead with a public profile had entered the political scene some years before, when Philip was still a minor: Eurydike, his mother, the wife of Amyntas III.[27] In 368/367 BC, when the future of her two minor sons Perdikkas and Philip was threatened by the invasion of the impostor Pausanias, likely a member of another Argead branch, Eurydike hired the Athenian general Iphikrates and his *mistophoroi*. Iphikrates happened to be in the North on an Athenian mission, trying to re-establish Athenian control over Amphipolis. While he failed in this matter, he successfully expelled Pausanias.[28] Embedded in the web of personal connections associated with the Argead house, Eurydike made use of the *philia* networks of her dead husband. Amyntas had cultivated close connections to Iphikrates.[29] The ancient authors prefer to depict Eurydike as a pleading mother in despair and not as a political actor on a diplomatic mission. Thus, they fail to mention the payment for Iphikrates and his troops. However, this must have been a central part of the negotiations. It is suggested that Eurydike had an own income at her disposal, a kind of apanage she could use.[30]

During the reign of her youngest son Philip, Eurydike was still a visible figure, acting as a representative of her house. For example, dated to the 350s BC, she made two dedications at the sanctuary of Eukleia in Aigai to the goddess Eukleia of which two inscribed statue bases and a *peplos* figure survive.[31] Eurydike is mentioned with her pat-

---

25   Carney 2010b, 44. See also Carney 1991. Thus, occasionally, Argeads used their daughters' names to commemorate their political and military accomplishments. Philip II named his daughters Thessalonike, "victory over the Thessalians" (perhaps at the Krokos Field in 352 BC) and Europe (born after Chaironeia). Alexander III's sister Kleopatra honored her brother's defeat of the Thebans in 335 (that had begun by attacking the Macedonian garrison on the Kadmeia: Diod. 17.13.3–4; Iust. 11.3.8–4.9) by calling her baby daughter Kadmeia: Plut. Pyrrhos 5.5. The word *basilissa* for a Macedonian royal woman is earliest attested for Demetrios Poliorketes' wife Phila after 306 BC: Syll.³ 333.8–9. Cf. Carney 1991, 161.

26   Cf. Carney 2019b on Olympias and Philip as a couple.

27   On Eurydike see Carney 2019a.

28   Aischin. 2.27–29; Nep. 11.3.2; Suda s. v. Karanos (κ 356 Adler). Cf. Carney 2019a, 38–40, 64–67.

29   Aischin. 2.28. Cf. Carney 2000, 43; Roisman 2010, 160, 162.

30   Cf. Macurdy 1927, 212. On the spaces of action of Argead widows see Carney 2019c; Müller 2021a, 301.

31   Cf. Carney 2019a, 82–92.

ronymic as dedicant: 'Eurydike, daughter of Sirras'.[32] The statue's identity (Eukleia, a priestess, or Eurydike herself) is debated. A damaged inscription from near Palatitsia, a village about two kilometers away from Aigai, also mentions Eurydike and her patronymic. It is suggested that it points at a lost portrait statue of her.[33] Further, Plutarch refers to a dedication made by Eurydike in association with the Muses, celebrating her acquisition of education comparatively late in life.[34]

A statue of her was also included in the dynastic group made by the sculptor Leochares of gilded marble which Philip commissioned for the so-called Philippeion after his victory at Chaironeia in 338 BC.[35] The group showed his dynastic past and present: his father and mother, Philip himself, his wife Olympias, and their son Alexander III.

According to a plausible suggestion, Eurydike's statue also hints at her past role of safeguarding the succession for Philip.[36] Apparently, the memory of her as the savior of the royal future of her minor sons was preserved at Philip's court: probably, Aischines had every reason to recall the event when he gave a speech to Philip at Pella in 346 BC.[37] As one of the ten Athenian ambassadors sent to negotiate the Peace of Philokrates, Aischines was expected to improve the Athenian position without displeasing Philip. The subject of Eurydike's dealings with Iphikrates gave Aischines the chance to point out that Philip owed a lot to Athens while simultaneously honoring the memory of his mother. Probably, Aischines knew that her commitment was still remembered favorably at Pella. Thus, Philip could be expected to be pleased. As for another argument in favor of this suggestion, Aischines recalled the content of his speech when being charged with misconduct on the second embassy to Philip. Prosecuted by Demosthenes in 343 BC, Aischines had to convince the Athenian jury that he had done his very best in the interests of Athens and could not be blamed for the outcome, namely the unpopular treaty that favored Philip.[38]

In any case, the family group of the Philippeion may have been a source of inspiration regarding the theme of a mother-loving ruler and for family group monuments

32   SEG 36.556. Cf. Kottaridi 2004; Carney 2019a, 76–95; Müller 2021a, 294–295.
33   Cf. Carney 2019a, 92–95. It is considered to have been a portrait statue that formed part of a double of the family group in the Philippeion.
34   Plut. mor. 14b.
35   Paus. 5.17.4; 5.20.10. Cf. Worthington 2008, 164–166; Carney 2010a, 417; Carney 2019a, 108–112; Carney 2020. According to archaeological results, there was no change in the original statue program and contrary to Pausanias' claim, the statues were not made of ivory and gold. On the visibility of Eurydike in Philip's reign in general see Carney 2000, 44; Carney 2010b, 43; Carney 2019a, 44–52, 76–117.
36   Cf. Carney 2020, 421.
37   Aischin. 2.27–29.
38   Demosthenes accused Aischines of having sold the *polis* and its interests to Philip: Demosth. 19.110–111, 118–120, 178, 201. On the evocation of emotions as a stylistic device of the Attic orators see Michels 2022, 234–235.

symbolizing dynastic unity. Both elements are known from the Ptolemaic dynastic representation.[39]

The public visibility of individual Argead royal women did not cease to exist after the accession of Philip's successor Alexander. His mother Olympias and full sister Kleopatra were particularly prominent public figures. During Alexander's absence in Asia, the influential general Antipatros was in charge of the European affairs.[40] While he could be expected to defend the interests of Macedonia and its leading circles, these could differ from Argead interests. Hence, Alexander was in need of trustworthy agents of his own house working for him. His obvious choice were Olympias and Kleopatra.

He sent them plunder which they used for distribution policy, dedications, and other benefactions for the sake of the Argead dynasty.[41] For example, after the establishment of Macedonian control over the Kyrenaika, a granary, in 331/330 BC, Olympias and Kleopatra were able to sell Kyrenaian grain during a time of shortage in Greece, likely cheaper than the expensive famine price.[42] Olympias made dedications at Athens to the goddess Hygieia and ordered a dedication of crowns to Delphic Apollon to be paid with Persian *dareikoi*.[43] After the death of Kleopatra's uncle-husband Alexander I of Molossia in 331 BC, she seems to have functioned as guardian and regent for her minor son Neoptolemos. Thus, she received religious ambassadors, and sponsored the tomb of a Greek flute-player, probably her court musician and, as Elizabeth Carney has recently suggested, her agent and diplomat.[44]

Thus, individual female Argeads such as Eurydike, Olympias, and Kleopatra played a major role in defining the spaces of action and public images of Macedonian royal women. Their careers mirror a wide range of activity besides succession advocacy, and marriage politics, namely dedications, benefactions, diplomacy, piety, politics, cultural policy, and patronage. As for the impact of these royal female appearances in Hellenistic representation, because of the ubiquitous character of war in Argead and Hellenistic times, a particularly interesting example is the legacy of warlike appearances of Argead royal women. Again, the reign of Philip II is crucial to the association of Argead women with war. His Illyrian wife Audata and their daughter Kynnane are said to have received a military education and Kynnane is reported to have joined her father on an

39   For example, Ptolemaios VI bore the epithet Philometor. Family groups: Athen. 5.205e-f; IG IX 1².
      1.56. For the illusion of a family group created by poetry: Theokr. 17.121–128; Poseidipp. ep. 78 AB.
      Cf. Kosmetatou 2002, 103–111; Kosmetatou 2004.
40   Arr. an. 1.11.3; Curt. 4.1.39; Diod. 18.12.1.
41   Plut. Alexander 16.8; 25.4; 39.7; Hyp. 4.19; Syll.³ 252. Cf. Carney 2006, 50–51, 96; Müller 2013, 35.
42   SEG 9.2; Lykurg. 26. Cf. Carney 1995, 386; Carney, 2006, 49–51. On the establishment of control
      over the Kyrenaika see Curt. 4.7.9–10; Diod. 17.49.2–3.
43   Syll.³ 252.
44   Iust. 12.2.3–4; Aischin. 3.242; SEG 23.189, l. 11. Cf. Carney 2000, 89; Carney 2010b, 52; Meyer 2013,
      122. On the court musician as Kleopatra's agent: Elizabeth D. Carney, Complicating the "Agency"
      of Royal Women, Paper at the Conference: Power, Royal Agency, and Elite Women in the Hellen-
      istic and Roman World, Waterloo Institute for Hellenistic Studies, 22.10.2021.

Illyrian campaign.[45] Kynnane's daughter Adea, twice an Argead since her father was Philip's nephew Amyntas, son of Perdikkas III, gave speeches to the troops in Asia and appeared in the – perhaps symbolic – role of a military leader at the battlefield of Euia against Olympias in 317 BC.[46]

As for the reception of this warlike aspect of female Argeads emerging in the literary sources, there seems to be an echo from Ptolemaic Egypt. Since the legend of the Macedonian *Mimallones*, connecting proto-historical Macedonian women with war and the cult of Dionysos, is first mentioned by Kallimachos, it is suggested that it may have emerged in a Ptolemaic context.[47] This would also explain the pre-eminence of Dionysos, the mythical progenitor of the Ptolemies.[48]

According to the tale, the proto-historical Argead ruler Argaios tricked the invading Illyrians into believing that his small force was a huge one. He ordered Macedonian girls, female devotees of Dionysos, to show themselves atop a mountain carrying *thyrsoi* instead of spears and having their faces covered with wreaths. The Illyrian ruler mistook them for men and retreated. A grateful Argaios built a temple to Dionysos Pseudanor ("sham man") and called the priestesses *Mimallones* ("imitators of men").[49]

Francesca Angiò suggests that the military aspect of the public role of some individual Argead women – at least in the sense of symbolic leadership – inspired the tradition of the Macedonian *Mimallones*. For example, Olympias was associated with an appearance on the battlefield of Euia and also with Dionysiac rites.[50] In addition, according to Angiò, the legend associated those Argead women who were said to have gone into combat with some Ptolemaic royal women to whom a military aspect was ascribed (f. i., Arsinoë II, Berenike II, or Arsinoë III).[51] For example, one of the epigrams

---

45   Polyain. 8.60. Cf. Carney 1993; Carney 2000, 69; Carney 2004, 185.
46   Diod. 19.11.2; 19.11.9; Athen. 13.560f; Arr. succ. BNJ 156 F1.23. Cf. Carney 1987.
47   Kall. fr. 503 Pf. Cf. Angiò 2020, 344.
48   OGIS 54, l. 1–6; Satyros BNJ 631 F1; P.Oxy. 27.2465.
49   Kall. fr. 503 Pf.; Polyain. 4.1. Argaios is mentioned in the Argead genealogy preserved by Hdt. 8.139. Cf. Borza 1990, 81. Argaios may be fictitious. Next to nothing is known about him. The legend of the *Mimallones* is also thought to reflect a transition rite for Macedonian adolescent girls that included cultic female travesty: Hatzopoulos 1994, 73–85. Polyainos emphasizes the association of the *Mimallones* with Dionysos. In the first book of his *Stratagems*, Polyainos ascribes a similar ruse to Dionysos himself: conquering India, the god ordered his army to hide their weapons under thyrsi and ivy in order to trick the inhabitants of the cities to let them in. In addition, when he waged war against the Baktrians, Dionysos was supported by the Amazons and his female bacchants who tricked the Baktrians into leaving their safe camp (Polyain. 1.1).
50   Reportedly, she raised pet-snakes, appeared on the battlefield of Euia surrounded by snakes, and conceived Alexander by a huge snake (*drakon*), either Zeus(-Ammon) in disguise, or, according to variants of the *Alexander Romance*, the Egyptian magician Nektanebos II: Plut. Alexander 2.5–7; Athen. 13.560f; Ps.-Kall. 1.3–7.7. Cf. Carney 2006, 96–101, 120–123; Carney 2010b, 46.
51   Angiò 2018; Angiò 2020, 344–345. On Arsinoë II and war: Poseidipp. ep. 36 AB. On Berenike II as a warlike royal woman: Catull. 66.25–28; Hyg. astron. 2.24.11–18. On Arsinoë III (addressing the troops before the battle of Raphia in 217 BC): Pol. 5.83.3; 5.84.1; 5.87.6; 3 Makk 1.4. Carney 2004, 184 divides their warlike appearances into three categories: battlefield command, symbolic leader-

of the Milan papyrus, as a whole ascribed to the Macedonian poet Poseidippos of Pella by the majority of scholars, has the Macedonian girl Hegeso remember a dream about Arsinoë II as Kypris Zephyritis who apparently returns from the toils of a battlefield like a warrior, sweating and carrying a spear and shield.[52] Thus, the female Argeads may have been treated as archetypes and the Ptolemaic royal women were modelled on them in literature.

4. The iconography of Argead coins

The iconography of Argead coins specifically mirrors Argead symbols, messages, and images, probably in accordance, at least to some extent, with expectations and demands of the Macedonians when it came to their ruling house.[53] It has been suggested that Philip II and Alexander III were instrumental in selecting the designs to be placed on their coins.[54] Probably, other Argead rulers also played a role in deciding about the images of their emissions.

Stressing the Argeads' mission as the only family divinely chosen to rule, the iconography of their coins particularly refers to their claim to Heraklid lineage. Frequent images are the head of Herakles (and his symbols) as their mythical progenitor or Zeus as the dynasty's protector and his eagle.[55] Other symbolic animals on Argead coins are goats referring to their capital Aigai, and the Argive wolf-dog borrowed from the coins of Argos, the hometown of their proclaimed ancestor Temenos.[56]

Likely mirroring practical requirements of rule in mostly hard-pressed Macedonia, war and warrior skills were central to the iconography of Argead coins. The earliest Argead coin image known is the so-called Macedonian rider on coins minted by Alexander I who initiated Argead coinage in the 480s BC.[57] Perhaps showing how to visualize

ship, and administrative leadership. On Ptolemaic women as "power brokers" see Strootman 2021, 338–340.

52 Poseidipp. ep. 36 AB. Cf. Gutzwiller 2007, 196; Müller 2009, 216–221; Müller 2015, 149–151.

53 On Argead coins see Gaebler 1935, 148–177, with pl. 28–32; Raymond 1958; Kraay 1976, 144–147; Le Rider 1977; Westermark 1989; Price 1991; Greenwalt 1994; Price ²1997; Troxell 1997; Psoma 1999; Le Rider 2003; Nicolet-Pierre 2002, 188–211; Tsangari 2008; Heinrichs 2012; Heinrichs 2017; Alonso Troncoso 2018; Heinrichs 2020b; Heimrichs 2020c; Heinrichs 2020d.

54 Cf. Price ²1997, 171, 174.

55 Herakles: Raymond 1953, 59–60; Price 1991, 31; Nicolet-Pierre 2002, 190; Alonso Troncoso 2018, 143; Heinrichs 2020c, 172. Zeus: Raymond 1953, 59–60; Price 1991, 31; Nicolet-Pierre 2002, 190; Alonso Troncoso 2018, 143–144; Heinrichs 2020c, 172.

56 Aigai: Raymond 1953, 46–47, 49–52, 59; Nicolet-Pierre 2002, 190; Heinrichs 2020c, 171. Argos: Heinrichs 2011; Alonso Troncoso 2018, 145; Heinrichs 2020c, 172.

57 Cf. Gaebler 1935, 148; Raymond 1953, 43, 57; Nicolet-Pierre 2002, 189; Liampi 2020, 168; Heinrichs 2020c, 171–172; Heinrichs 2020d, 458. On Alexander I's coinage in general: Gaebler 1935, 149–153, with pl. 28; Raymond 1953, 100–107; Nicolet-Pierre 2002, 188–189; SNG ANS 8 Macedonia II, pl. 1–2, 1–36; SNG Greece 2,1 Alpha Bank Macedonia I, pl. I–IV, 1–81.

the qualities of Argead rule, the rider, an armed cavalryman, may hint at the Argead ruler as conqueror and protector of his realm.[58]

Alexander I's successor Perdikkas II minted two series that both preserved his father's iconography, probably as a legitimizing device. One series of Perdikkas' silver tetrobols shows the armed Macedonian rider and the lion, the other a horse and a helmet.[59] Besides the loyalty to his father and thus the duty to preserve his political legacy, the iconography may have stressed Perdikkas' military skills that were so desperately needed in his troubled reign that witnessed his struggles to keep his realm autonomous during the Peloponnesian War.

After having preserved the traditional Argead iconography, late in his reign, about 400 BC, Perdikkas' son and successor Archelaos introduced new images in a dynastic silver series.[60] Likely in accordance with the refreshment of the Argead foundation myth put on the stage by Euripides, Archelaos displayed on his coins major elements such as the Argeads' mythical ancestor Herakles, the Nemean lion, the eagle of the Argead patron Zeus, and the Argive wolf-dog.[61] Forming part of this revision of the dynastic legitimization that explained the Argead right to rule by recalling the legendary deeds of the family's founder, the newly introduced obverse image of the male youth wearing a *tainia* was to be the new Argead founder figure.[62] Under Archelaos, this founder bore his own name, Archelaos; later on, during the fourth century BC, and after another revision of the myth, the founder came to be Karanos.[63]

In the time of Amyntas III, his Thessalian allies from Larissa adopted the Argead eagle standing with a reverted head as a coin symbol.[64] This iconographical borrowing may have visualized their alliance since the Thessalians had helped to restore Amyntas to his kingdom when he had been expelled by the Illyrians in 393/392 BC.[65]

---

58   Cf. Gaebler 1935, 148–149; Raymond 1953, 53–57; Heinrichs – Müller 2008, 295; Olbrycht 2010, 344–345; Alonso Troncoso 2018, 138–139; Heinrichs 2020c, 172; Heinrichs 2020d, 458–459.

59   Cf. Gaebler 1935, 153–155, with pl. 28–29; Raymond 1953, 18–19, 136–166; Kraay 1976, 144; Psoma 1999; Nicolet-Pierre 2002, 190; Heinrichs 2012, 129, 132; Müller 2017a, 43–45; Alonso Troncoso 2018, 141–142; Heinrichs 2020c, 172.

60   Cf. Gaebler 1935, 155–156 with pl. 29; Greenwalt 2003; Westermark 1989, 302–304; Borza 1999, 10; Heinrichs 2020c, 172, with 534, pl. 2.

61   Euripides' *Archelaos*: Hyg. fab. 219. Cf. Müller 2016, 97–100; Pownall 2020b, 228. On the new iconography of Archelaos' coins see Kraay 1976, 145; Westermark 1989, 303–304; Borza 1990, 173; Heinrichs 2020b.

62   Cf. Kraay 1976, 144; Le Rider 1977, 368; Borza 1990, 173; Price 1991, 32; Müller 2016, 94–95; Alonso Troncoso 2018, 149; Heinrichs 2020b, 99; Heinrichs 2020c, 172, with 534, pl. 2, 6. The male youth does not wear a distinguishing laurel wreath, indicative for Apollon. *Pace* Westermark 1989, 304; Nicolet-Pierre 2002, 190 (however, hesitating).

63   Theop. BNJ 115 F 393; Diod. 7 F 15, F 17; Iust. 7.1.7–12; Liv. 45.9.3; Vell. Pat. 1.6.5; Plut. Alexander 2.1.

64   SNG Cop. 505; SNG Alpha Bank 153. Cf. Lorber 2008, 120; Müller 2016, 22, 314, fig. 10; Heinrichs 2020c, 171. On the Aleuads and Larissa see Beck 1997, 119–134.

65   Diod. 14.92.3. On the traditionally close connections between Aleuads and Argeads see Beck 1997, 123.

Philip II combined continuity and innovation – preservation and variation of traditional Argead symbols and introduction of new ones. He gave his coinage a special "Hellenic" touch addressing also the Greek world.[66] Sometime after the conquest of the Chalkidike and the destruction of Olynthos (in 348 BC), Philip adopted the youthful laureate head of Apollon from the obverse of its coins. Simultaneously, Apollon hinted at Philip's role in the Third Sacred War as the god's avenger fighting the Phokians.[67] Philip also introduced the laureate head of Olympian Zeus as an obverse type and commemorated his Olympian victory in 356 BC by showing a mounted jockey.[68] Achim Lichtenberger has suggested that the laureate, bearded Zeus was a well-known image in the region of the Olympos and that Philip's Zeus on his coins was thus a reference to the Zeus Olympios of the Macedonian-Thessalian Olympos.[69] While the younger tetradrachm type depicts the jockey in heroic nudity crowned with an olive wreath and holding a palm of victory, the elder version is a variant of the Macedonian rider, wearing a beard and the Macedonian hat.[70] This horseman is often interpreted as an image of Philip himself.[71] In any case, the Macedonian jockey shows Philip skilfully playing with the Argead tradition.

Alexander III's early bronze and silver eagle series are inspired by the coin iconography of his grandfather Amyntas III and uncle Perdikkas III.[72] As for new designs, after the conquest of Tarsos in 333/332 BC and apparently inspired by the Tarsian coin image of Baal, Alexander introduced an enthroned Zeus holding an eagle as a reverse type, but paired him with the traditional image of the youthful Herakles on the obverse.[73] In the name of Alexander's successors Philip III and Alexander IV, the types of him and his father Philip continued as a means to visualize the claim to political continuity.[74]

---

66   Cf. Kraay 1976, 147; Price 1991, 28; Price ²1997, 171; Alonso Troncoso 2018, 148; Heinrichs 2020c, 172.
67   Iust. 8.2.3–6; Diod. 16.35.6. Cf. Kraay 1976, 146; Ritter 2002, 139; Nicolet-Pierre 2002, 192; Le Rider 2003, 31; Müller 2016, 252–254, 317, fig. 19; Heinrichs 2020c, 173; Wirth 2020, 417–418. On Philip's involvement in the Third Sacred War see Pownall 2020d.
68   Plut. Alexander 3.5.
69   Lichtenberger 2021, 116.
70   Cf. Kraay 1976, 146–147; Heinrichs 2020c, 173, with 533, pl. 1, 4. On the rider see also Heinrichs 2020d, 459.
71   Cf. Kraay 1976, 146; Price ²1997, 171; Nicolet-Pierre 2002, 192; Heinrichs 2020c, 173. In addition, the rider recalls some well-known staters from Thessalian Pharsalos, an ally of Philip.
72   Cf. Gaebler 1935, 168–169, with pl. 31; Le Rider 1977, 393–394; Westermark 1989, 308; Price 1991, 28, 30–32; Mørkholm 1991, 42; Le Rider 1996, 91–94; Troxell 1997, 31–37; Price ²1997, 172; Le Rider 1999, 521–522; Liampi 1998, 247–248, 252, with pl. 54–55; Nicolet-Pierre 2002, 192–193; Heinrichs 2012, 119–121. See also Price 1991, 28: "His first issues reflect the continuation of Philip's policies, with no break in the minting arrangements."
73   Cf. de Callataÿ 1982; Troxell 1997, 86–89; Le Rider 1999, 519; Nicolet-Pierre 2002, 193; Heinrichs 2020c, 173. It was not meant to be a (disguised) portrait of Alexander, cf. Price 1991, 33; Price ²1997, 171; Nicolet-Pierre 2002, 189.
74   Cf. Gaebler 1935, 170–172, with pl. 31–32; Price 1991, 25–28; Troxell 1997, 50–64, 95–97; Price ²1997, 174; Nicolet-Pierre 2002, 208–210; Heinrichs 2020c, 174; Wheatley – Dunn 2021, 163.

As for the impact of the lessons regarding representation that the Successors and their heirs could have learnt from the iconography of Argead coinage, there are certain examples of an iconographic borrowing. Thus, the display of divine patrons or progenitors and of elements of the dynastic founding myth can also be found on coins in Hellenistic times. The portrait of the founder of the royal house was shown on Ptolemaic (Ptolemaios I) and Attalid (Philetairos) coins as an obverse type; the Seleukids chose their mythical progenitor (Apollon) as one standard reverse image.[75] Ptolemaios I adopted the Argead eagle of Zeus with the thunderbolt that became the standard reverse type in Ptolemaic Egypt.[76]

As for the use of re-issues to the end of claiming the preservation of a political tradition, Kassandros, for example, tried to create an artificial continuum to Argead times in Macedonia before Alexander III by re-issuing Philip's coin types. In addition, he used Perdikkas III's coin images of the lion breaking the javelin.[77] During the First Mithradatic War against Rome, the mints of Mithradates VI of Pontos in Messembria and Odessos struck imitations of Alexander's tetradrachms while in Byzantion, imitations of Lysimachos' tetradrachms with Alexander's portrait adorned with a diadem and the ram's horn were minted.[78] The imitation of famous coins that had circulated for a long time in this area and were regarded as precious and worthy, triggered associations of financial security and welfare.

Regarding the adoption of coin types or iconographic symbols as a sign of an alliance, Lysimachos hinted at the alliance with Kassandros by minting the same reverse type (lion and spearhead).[79] After his marriage to Ptolemaios' daughter Arsinoë (about 300 BC), Lysimachos mirrored this alliance by introducing the horn of Ammon's ram to the head of Alexander on the obverse of his tetradrachms.[80] As for the commemoration of certain successful events (such as Philip II's Olympic success), Demetrios Poliorketes, for example, hinted at his naval victory at Salamis in 306 BC

75 Ptolemies (Ptolemaios I as the standard obverse type of the tetradrachms until the end of the Ptolemaic Empire): Nicolet-Pierre 2002, 214–220; Le Rider – de Callataÿ 2006, 50–54; CPE. Attalids (Philetairos as an obverse type from Attalos I to sometime in the reign of Eumenes II): Westermark 1961; Michels 2011, 119; Nicolet-Pierre 2002, 222–225; Seleukids (Apollon as the standard reverse type starting with the coins of Antiochos I): Nicolet-Pierre 2002, 220–222; SC I–II; Le Rider – de Callataÿ 2006, 45–48. On the Seleukid representation in general see the chapter of Sonja Richter in this volume.

76 Cf. Le Rider – de Callataÿ 2006, 50; CPE, 25–26.

77 Cf. Gaebler 1935, 173, with pl. 32; Miller 1991, 49–55; Mørkholm 1991, 58–60; Landucci Gattinoni 2003a, 136, 144.

78 Cf. Bohm 1989, 173; de Callataÿ 1997, 111; Højte 2009, 149; Michels 2009, 205–206, 208–209. On other parallels between the Mithratids and Hellenistic dynasties see the chapter of Alex McAuley in this volume.

79 Cf. Müller 2017b, 125. On their alliance see Diod. 20.106.2–3; Iust. 15.21.2. Cf. Thompson 1968, 164; Landucci Gattinoni 2003a, 64.

80 Cf. Müller 2017b, 125–127. On Ptolemaios' obverse type showing the deified Alexander with the horn of Ammon and the elephant headdress see CPE, 25.

by showing Poseidon and the ship's prora on his coins.[81] Apparently, many elements of Argead coinage responded to the political needs of Hellenistic rulers.

5. Conclusions

Selectively borrowing from the treasury of Argead representation could connect the present with the past as a legitimizing strategy, conceal the interruption of political continuity, and appease the Macedonian recipients by the use of traditional, well-known images.

Argead representation provided political actors of Hellenistic times with a number of ideologically useful elements that had served their purpose in the past. For example, there was a dynastic foundation myth including the claims to divine descent, protection, election, and predestination to rule. There were images of dynastic strength and unity, names with a dynastic significance, and coins with a special iconography propagating the dynastic image. Furthermore, Argead representation provided the first Macedonian family group (in the Philippeion), a son honoring his mother who had taken efforts to secure his future, the performance of cultic rites by a pair of brothers, cultural patronage, and individual royal women as public figures, becoming visible as agents of their house. Serving as blueprints, such elements of Argead representation could be made compatible with the needs and requirements of Macedonian political actors after Argead rule had ended.

Bibliography

Ager 2021: Ager, Sheila, Royal Brother-Sister Marriage, Ptolemaic and Otherwise, in: Carney – Müller 2021, 346–358

Alonso Troncoso 2018: Alonso Troncoso, Victor, The Animal Types on the Argead Coinage, Wilderness and Macedonia, in: T. Howe – F. Pownall (eds.), Ancient Macedonians in the Greek and Roman Sources, Swansea 2018, 137–162

Angiò 2018: Angiò, Francesca, Callimaco Fr. 503 Pf., Posidippo e le *Mimallones*, Papyrologia Lupiensia 27, 2018, 7–16

Angiò 2020: Angiò, Francesca, s. v. Mimallones, in: LexAM, 344–345

Anson 2008: Anson, Edward M., Philip II and the Transformation of Macedonia: A Reappraisal, in: T. Howe – J. Reames (eds.), Macedonian Legacies, Claremont 2008, 17–30

Atkinson 2009: Atkinson, John E., A Commentary on Q. Curtius Rufus' *Historiae Alexandri Magni*. Book 10, Oxford 2009

Beck 1997: Beck, Hans, Polis und Koinon, Stuttgart 1997

---

81   Cf. Gaebler 1935, 180–181, with pl. 33; Nicolet-Pierre 2002, 212. On Antigonos Gonatas' refreshed use of Poseidon see Panagopoulou 2020, 337.

Beck – Buckler 2008: Beck, Hans – Buckler, John, Central Greece and the Politics of Power in the 4th c. BC, Cambridge 2008

Bohm 1989: Bohm, Claudia, Imitatio Alexandri im Hellenismus, Munich 1989

Borza 1990: Borza, Eugene N., In the Shadow of Olympus. The Emergence of Macedon, New Jersey 1990

Bosworth 1988: Bosworth, Albert B., Conquest and Empire. The Reign of Alexander the Great, Cambridge 1988

Bosworth 2002: Bosworth, Albert B., The Legacy of Alexander the Great. Politics, Warfare and Propaganda under the Successors, Oxford 2002

Briant 2010: Briant, Pierre, Alexander the Great and his Empire, Princeton 2010

de Callataÿ 1997: de Callataÿ, François, L'histoire des guerres Mithridatiques vue par les monnaies, Louvain-la-Neuve 1997

Carney 1987: Carney, Elizabeth D., The Career of Adea-Eurydike, Historia 36, 1987, 496–502

Carney 1993: Carney, Elizabeth D., Foreign Influence and the Changing Role of Macedonian Royal Women, Ancient Macedonia 5, 1993, 313–323

Carney 1995: Carney, Elizabeth D., Women and *basileia*. Legitimacy and Female Political Action in Macedonia, Classical Journal 90, 1995, 367–391

Carney 2000: Carney, Elizabeth D., Women and Monarchy in Macedonia, Norman 2000

Carney 2001: Carney, Elizabeth D., The Trouble with Philip Arrhidaeus, The Ancient History Bulletin 15, 2001, 63–89

Carney 2003: Carney, Elizabeth D., Women in Alexander's Court, in: J. Roisman (ed.), Brill's Companion to Alexander the Great, Leiden et al. 2003, 227–252

Carney 2006: Carney, Elizabeth D., Olympias, Mother of Alexander the Great, London et al. 2006

Carney 2010a: Carney, Elizabeth D., Macedonian Women, in: Roisman – Worthington 2010, 409–427

Carney 2010b: Carney, Elizabeth D., Putting Women in their Place: Women in Public under Philip II and Alexander III and the Last Argeads, in: Carney – Ogden 2010, 43–54

Carney 2013: Carney, Elizabeth D., Arsinoë of Egypt and Macedon. A Royal Life, Oxford 2013

Carney 2016: Carney, Elizabeth D., King and Court in Ancient Macedonia: Rivalry, Treason, and Conspiracy, London et al. 2016

Carney 2019a: Carney, Elizabeth D., Eurydice and the Birth of Macedonian Power, Oxford 2019

Carney 2019b: Carney, Elizabeth D., An Exceptional Argead Couple: Philip II and Olympias, in: A. Bielman Sánchez (ed.), Power Couples in Antiquity: Transversal Perspectives, London et al. 2019, 16–31

Carney 2019c: Carney, Elizabeth D., Royal Macedonian Widows: Merry and not, Greek, Roman, and Byzantine Studies 59, 2019, 368–396

Carney 2020: Carney, Elizabeth D., Philippeion, in: LexAM, 420–421

Carney – Müller 2021: Carney, Elizabeth D. – Müller, Sabine (eds.), The Routledge Companion to Women and Monarchy in the Ancient Mediterranean World, New York et al. 2021

Carney – Ogden 2010: Carney, Elizabeth D. – Ogden, Daniel (eds.), Philip II and Alexander the Great: Father and Son, Lives and Afterlives, Oxford 2010

Cusset – Belenfant – Nardone 2020: Cusset, Christophe – Belenfant, Pierre – Nardone, Claire-Emmanuelle (eds.), Féminités hellénistiques: Voix, genre, representations, Leuven 2020

Gaebler 1935: Gaebler, Hugo, Die antiken Münzen von Makedonia und Paionia II, Berlin 1935

Greenwalt 1994: Greenwalt, William S., The Production of Coinage from Archelaus to Perdikkas III and the Evolution of Argead Macedonia, in: I. Worthington (ed.), Ventures into Greek History, Oxford 1994, 105–134

Greenwalt 2003: Greenwalt, William S., Archelaus the Philhellene, The Ancient World 34, 2003, 131–153

Gutzwiller 2007: Gutzwiller, Kathryn J., A Guide to Hellenistic Literature, London 2007

Hamilton 1969: Hamilton, James R., Plutarch, *Alexander*. A Commentary, Oxford 1969

Hatzopoulos 1994: Hatzopoulos, Miltiades B., Cultes et rites de passage en Macédoine, Athens 1994

Hatzopoulos 2015: Hatzopoulos, Miltiades B., Federal Makedonia, in: H. Beck – P. Funke (eds.), Federalism in Greek Antiquity, Cambridge 2015, 319–340

Hatzopoulos 2020: Hatzopoulos, Miltiades B., Ancient Macedonia, Berlin et al. 2020

Heckel 2020: Heckel, Waldemar, In the Path of Conquest. Military and Political Resistance to Alexander the Great, Oxford 2020

Heckel ²2021: Heckel, Waldemar, Who's Who in the Empire of Alexander the Great, Oxford ²2021

Heinrichs 2011: Heinrichs, Johannes, Athen und Argos in der Mitte des 5. Jhs., Zeitschrift für Papyrologie und Epigraphik 177, 2011, 23–25

Heinrichs 2012: Heinrichs, Johannes, Münzen als Krisensymptome? Zur makedonischen Silberprägung unter Amyntas III. und Perdikkas III. (ca. 393–359), Zeitschrift für Papyrologie und Epigraphik 181, 2012, 117–139

Heinrichs 2017: Heinrichs, Johannes, Coins and Constructions. The Origins of Argead Coinage under Alexander I, in: S. Müller et al. (eds.), A History of the Argeads – New Perspectives, Wiesbaden 2017, 79–98

Heinrichs 2020a: Heinrichs, Johannes, Alexander I, in: LexAM, 55–60

Heinrichs 2020b: Heinrichs, Johannes, Archelaos, Founder Hero, in: LexAM, 99

Heinrichs 2020c: Heinrichs, Johannes, Coinage, Argead, in: LexAM, 171–176

Heinrichs 2020d: Heinrichs, Johannes, Rider, Makedonian, on Coins, in: LexAM, 458–459

Heinrichs – Müller 2008: Heinrichs, Johannes – Müller, Sabine, Ein persisches Statussymbol auf Münzen Alexanders I. von Makedonien, Zeitschrift für Papyrologie und Epigraphik 167, 2008, 283–309

Højte 2009: Højte, Jakob M., Portraits and Statues of Mithridates VI., in: J. M. Højte (ed.), Mithridates VI and the Pontic Kingdom, Aarhus 2009, 145–161

Hoover 2016: Hoover, Oliver D., Handbook of Coins of Macedon and its Neighbors I, Lancaster et al. 2016

Kholod 2020: Kholod, Maxim M., On the Titulature of Alexander the Great: The Title *basileus*, in: Trampedach – Meeus 2020, 219–242

King 2018: King, Carol J., Ancient Macedonia, London et al. 2018

Kosmetatou 2002: Kosmetatou, Elizabeth, Remarks on a Delphic Dynastic Group Monument, Tyche 17, 2002, 103–111

Kosmetatou 2004: Kosmetatou, Elizabeth, Constructing Legitimacy: the Ptolemaic *Familiengruppe* as a Means for Self-Definition in Posidippus' *Hippika*, in: B. Acosta-Hughes – E. Kosmetatou – M. Baumbach (eds.), Labored in Papyrus Leaves. Perspectives on an Epigram Collection attributed to Posidippus (P. Mil. Vogl. VIII 309), Cambridge 2004, 225–246

Kottaridi 2004: Kottaridi, Angeliki, The Lady of Aigai, in: D. Pandermalis (ed.), Alexander the Great: Treasures from an Epic Era of Hellenism, New York 2004, 139–148

Kraay 1976: Kraay, Colin M., Archaic and Classical Greek Coins, London 1976

Landucci Gattinoni 2003a: Landucci Gattinoni, Franca, L'arte del potere. Vita e opere di Cassandro di Macedonia, Stuttgart 2003

Landucci Gattinoni 2003b: Landucci Gattinoni, Franca, Tra monarchia nazionale e monarchia militare: il caso della Macedonia, in: C. Bearzot – F. Landucci Gattinoni – G. Zecchini (eds.), Gli stati territoriali nel mondo antico, Milan 2003, 199–224

Landucci Gattinoni 2010: Landucci Gattinoni, Franca, Cassander and the Legacy of Philip II and Alexander III in Diodorus, in: Carney – Ogden 2010, 113–122

Le Rider 1977: Le Rider, Georges, Le monnayage d'argent et d'or de Philippe II frappé en Macédoine de 359 à 294, Paris 1977

Le Rider 1996: Le Rider, Georges, Le monnayage et finances de Philippe II. Un état de la question, Athens 1996

Le Rider 1999: Le Rider, Georges, Les tétradrachmes macédoniens d'Alexandre: réflexions sur leur classement, le nombre d'ateliers et les lieux de frappe, in: E. Papaefthymiou – F. de Callataÿ – F. Queyrel (eds.), Études d'histoire et financière du monde grec. Écrits 1958–1998, II, Athens 1999, 519–528

Le Rider 2003: Le Rider, Georges, Alexandre le Grand. Monnaie, finances et politique, Paris 2003

Le Rider – de Callataÿ 2006: Le Rider, Georges – de Callataÿ, Francois, Les Séleucides et les Ptolémées: L'héritage monétaire et financier d' Alexandre le Grand, Paris 2006

Liampi 1998: Liampi, Katerini, A Hoard of Bronze Coins from Alexander the Great, in: R. Ashton – S. Hurter (eds.), Studies in Greek Numismatics in Memory of M. J. Price, London 1998, 247–253

Lianou 2010: Lianou, Margarita, The Role of the Argeadai in the Legitimation of the Ptolemaic Dynasty: Rhetoric and Practice, in: Carney – Ogden 2010, 123–134

Lichtenberger 2021: Lichtenberger, Achim, Der Olymp: Sitz der Götter zwischen Himmel und Erde, Stuttgart 2021

Lorber 2008: Lorber, Catharine C., Thessalian Hoards and the Coinage of Larissa, American Journal of Numismatics 20, 2008, 119–142

Macurdy 1927: Macurdy, Grace H., Queen Eurydice and the Evidence for Woman-Power in Early Macedonia, American Journal of Philology 48, 1927, 201–214

Manakidou 2020: Manakidou, Flora P., Maternity in Callimachus' Hymns 1 and 4: Interweaving poetics and politics, in: Cusset – Belenfant – Nardone 2020, 195–222

Mari 2011: Mari, Manuela, Archaic and Classical Macedonia, in: R. Lane Fox (ed.), Brill's Companion to Ancient Macedon, Leiden 2011, 79–92

Mari 2020: Mari, Manuela, Alexander, the King of the Macedonians, in: Trampedach – Meeus 2020, 197–218

McAuley 2020: McAuley, Alex, Between Hera and Heroine: The Virginity, Marriages, and Queenship of Berenike II, in: Cusset – Belenfant – Nardone 2020, 177–194

Meeus 2020: Meeus, Alexander, The Strategies of Legitimation of Alexander and the Diadochoi: Continuities and Discontinuities, in Trampedach – Meeus 2020, 291–318

Meyer 2013: Meyer, Elizabeth A., The Inscriptions of Dodona and a New History of Molossia, Stuttgart 2013

Michels 2009: Michels, Christoph, Kulturtransfer und monarchischer 'Philhellenismus'. Bithynien, Pontos und Kappadokien in hellenistischer Zeit, Göttingen 2009

Michels 2011: Michels, Christoph, Dionysos Kathegemon und der attalidische Herrscherkult. Überlegungen zur Herrschaftsrepräsentation der Könige von Pergamon, in: L.-M. Günther – S. Plischke (eds.), Studien zum vorhellenistischen und hellenistischen Herrscherkult, Berlin 2011, 114–140

Michels 2022: Michels, Christoph, Erinnerung und Emotion in Reden vor der Volksversammlung, in: V. Räuchle – S. Page – V. Goldbeck (eds.), Pathos und Polis, Tübingen 2022, 231–252

Miller 1991: Miller, M. C. J., The Regal Coinage of Cassander, The Ancient World 22, 1991, 49–55

Mørkholm 1991: Mørkholm, Otto, Early Hellenistic Coinage from the Accession of Alexander to the Peace of Apamea (336–188 B. C.), Cambridge 1991

Muccioli 2013: Muccioli, Federicomaria, Gli epiteti ufficiali dei re ellenistici, Stuttgart 2013

Müller 2009: Müller, Sabine, Das hellenistische Herrscherpaar in der medialen Repräsentation. Ptolemaios II. und Arsinoë II., Berlin 2009

Müller 2015: Müller, Sabine, Poseidippos of Pella and the Memory of Alexander's Campaigns at the Ptolemaic Court, in: W. Heckel – S. Müller – G. Wrightson (eds.), The Many Faces of War in the Ancient World, Cambridge 2015, 135–165

Müller 2016: Müller, Sabine, Die Argeaden. Geschichte Makedoniens bis zum Zeitalter Alexanders des Großen, Paderborn 2016

Müller 2017a: Müller, Sabine, Perdikkas II. – Retter Makedoniens, Berlin 2017

Müller 2017b: Müller, Sabine, Visualizing Political Friendship, Family Ties, and Links to the Argead Past in the Time of the Successors, in: F. Landucci Gattinoni – C. Bearzot (eds.), Alexander's Legacy. Texts, Documents, Fortune, Rome 2017, 121–140

Müller 2019: Müller, Sabine, Alexander der Große. Eroberung – Politik – Rezeption, Stuttgart 2019

Müller 2020: Müller, Sabine, Arrhidaios, in: LexAM, 114–115

Müller 2021a: Müller, Sabine, Argead Women, in: Carney – Müller 2021, 294–306

Müller 2021b: Müller, Sabine, Political Marriages in Antiquity, in: F. Jacobs – J. A. Mohammed (eds.), Marriage Discourses in Early Modern and Modern Times, Berlin 2021, 25–49

Nicolet-Pierre 2002: Nicolet-Pierre, Hélène, Numismatique grecque, Paris 2002

Ogden 1999: Ogden, Daniel, Polygamy, Prostitutes and Death. The Hellenistic Dynasties, Swansea 1999

Olbrycht 2010: Olbrycht, Marek J., Macedonia and Persia, in: Roisman –Worthington 2010, 342–369

Panagopoulou 2020: Panagopoulou, Katerina, The Early Antigonids. Coinage, Money, and Economy, New York 2020

Pfeiffer 2021: Pfeiffer, Stefan, Royal Women and Ptolemaic Cults, in: Carney – Müller 2021, 96–107

Pownall 2016: Pownall, Frances, Folly and Violence in Athens under the Successors, in: T. Howe – S. Müller (eds.), Folly and Violence in the Court of Alexander the Great and the Successors? Greco-Roman Perspectives, Bochum et al. 2016, 47–58

Pownall 2020a: Pownall, Frances, Archelaos, in: LexAM, 94–99

Pownall 2020b: Pownall, Frances, Euripides, in: LexAM, 228–229

Pownall 2020c: Pownall, Frances, Patronage, royal, in: LexAM, 382–387

Pownall 2020d: Pownall, Frances, Third Sacred War, in: LexAM, 495–498

Price 1991: Price, Martin J., The Coinage in the Name of Alexander the Great and Philip Arrhidaeus I–II, London et al. 1991

Price ²1997: Price, Martin J., Alexander's Policy on Coinage, in: J. Carlsen – B. Due – O. S. Due – B. Poulsen (eds.), Alexander the Great. Reality and Myth, Rome ²1997, 171–176

Psoma 1999: Psoma, Selene, Monnaies de poids réduit d'Alexandre I et Perdiccas II de Macédoine, Zeitschrift für Papyrologie und Epigraphik 128, 1999, 273–282

Psoma 2014: Psoma, Selene, Athens and the Macedonian Kingdom from Perdikkas II to Philip II, Revue des Études Anciennes 116, 2014, 133–144

Psoma 2015: Psoma, Selene, Naming the Argeads, Ktèma 40, 2015, 15–26

Raymond 1953: Raymond, Doris, The Macedonian Regal Coinage to 413 B. C., New York 1953

Roisman 2010: Roisman, Joseph, Classical Macedonia to Perdiccas III, in: Roisman – Worthington 2010, 145–165

Roisman – Worthington 2010: Roisman, Joseph – Worthington, Ian, (eds.), A Companion to Ancient Macedonia, Oxford et al. 2010

Ruzicka 2010: Ruzicka, Stephen, The 'Pixodarus Affair' Reconsidered again, in: Carney – Ogden 2010, 3–11

Ritter 2002: Ritter, Stefan, Bildkontakte. Götter und Heroen in der Bildsprache griechischer Münzen des 4. Jahrhunderts v. Chr., Berlin 2002

Strootman 2021: Strootman, Rolf, Women and Dynasty at the Hellenistic Imperial Courts, in: Carney – Müller 2021, 333–344

Thompson 1968: Thompson, Margaret, The Mints of Lysimachus, in C. M. Kraay – G. K. Jenkins (eds.), Essays in Greek Coinage, Oxford 1968, 163–182

Trampedach – Meeus 2020: Trampedach, Kai – Meeus, Alexander (eds.), The Legitimation of Conquest, Monarchical Representation and the Art of Government in the Empire of Alexander the Great, Stuttgart 2020

Troxell 1997: Troxell, Hyla A., Studies in the Macedonian Coinage of Alexander the Great, New York 1997

Tsangari 2008: Tsangari, Dimitria, Coins of Macedonia in the Alpha Bank Collection, Athens 2008

Vasilev 2011: Vasilev, Miroslav I., Thucydides II,99 and the Early Expansion of the Argeadai, Eirene 47, 2011, 93–105

von den Hoff 2020: von den Hoff, Ralf, Alexander's Dedication to the Gods: Sacred Space, Pious Practice and Public Legitimation, in: Trampedach – Meeus 2020, 99–122

Wallace 2020: Wallace, Shane, Communication and Legitimation: Knowledge of Alexander's Asian Conquests in the Greek World, in: Trampedach – Meeus 2020, 123–144

Westermark 1961: Westermark, Ulla, Das Bildnis des Philetairos von Pergamon: Corpus der Münzprägung, Stockholm 1961

Westermark 1989: Westermark, Ulla, Remarks on the Regal Macedonian Coinage, ca. 413–359 B. C., in: G. Le Rider et al. (eds.), Essays Kraay – Mørkholm, Leuven 1989, 301–315

Wheatley – Dunn 2020: Wheatley, Pat – Dunn, Charlotte, Demetrius the Besieger, Oxford 2020

Wheatley – Dunn 2021: Wheatley, Pat – Dunn, Charlotte, Coinage and Propaganda: Alexander and his Successors, in: J. Walsh – E. Baynham (eds.), Alexander the Great and Propaganda, London et al. 2021, 162–198

Wirth 1989: Wirth, Gerhard, Der Kampfverband des Proteas. Spekulationen zu den Begleitumständen der Laufbahn Alexanders, Amsterdam 1989

Wirth 2020: Wirth, Gerhard, Philip II, in: LexAM, 415–420

Worthington 2008: Worthington, Ian, Philip II of Macedon, Oxford 2008

Sabine Müller is Professor of Ancient History at Marburg University. She studied Medieval and Modern History, Art History and Ancient History. Her research focuses on the Persian Empire, Argead Macedonia, the Hellenistic Empires, Macedonian royal women, Lucian, and reception studies. Her publications include monographs on Alexander the Great, Ptolemaios II and Arsinoë II, and Perdikkas II. She is co-editor of the *Lexicon of Argead Makedonia* (2020) and *The Routledge Companion to Women and Monarchy in the Ancient Mediterranean World* (2021).

Diadochi of the Qin
Early Hellenistic and Chu-Han Ruler Dynamics Compared

JORDAN THOMAS CHRISTOPHER

Abstract: The Early Hellenistic Period (323–301) is parallel in several ways with the Qin-Han interregnum of Early China (209–202) as eras of intracultural interstate chaos in the wake of major imperial collapses (the fall of Alexander's Empire and the fall of the Qin Dynasty), with further parallels between several key individuals, especially between Antigonos I Monophthalmos and Xiang Yu of Chu. Comparison of the two periods reveals key dynamics highlighting how elite Macedonians rejected Alexander's imperial autocratic framework (and indeed, the rule of the Argead house) over them. The common characterization of Argead collapse as "internal" and Qin collapse as "external" is problematized through comparing the two cases. Key differences in warlord behavior between Macedonian and Early Chinese cases are identified: Macedonians form military coalitions easier and without the insistence on hierarchical structures found in Early Chinese equivalent groupings. Macedonian rulers recognize each other's equivalent stature and rank outside of mutual subservience to a third figure, unlike the Early Chinese examples. Explanations for these differences can be found ultimately in earlier Macedonian traditions of multiple Macedonian basileis beyond just those of the Argead clan. The Diadochi, therefore, are shown to be influenced by a larger conception of "Macedon" than just that represented by Argead rule. Accordingly, the destruction of the Argead clan is arguably not to be conflated with the understanding of a persistent greater Macedonian empire that outlives their clan. Separately, comparison with Macedonian cases suggests an understanding of Qin governance in conquered lands as ineffective, while Macedonian governance was shallow, and that furthermore, Qin mass population deportations seemingly had little effect on breaking down local identities or severing connections between local elites and mass groups.

1. Introduction

In the 4th century BC,[1] the kingdom of Argead Macedon and the state of Qin 秦, a semi-feudal polity in the fragmented Eastern Zhou Dynasty (771–221), rapidly rose in military and political significance. The cultural places of Argead Macedon and Qin were uniquely similar; both were culturally semi-outsiders, with no firm contemporary consensus on their belonging among the greater Greek/Zhou cultural worlds. Both existed at the geographic periphery of their larger cultural worlds, before then unifying their cultural spheres, dominating them for a few decades, and then collapsing as quickly as they had arisen. The military-political unifications brought about by these states cast them as culture brokers, if not culture unifiers, permanently changing the trajectory of Greek and Zhou history. On the rises of these two polities in a comparative perspective, I have written extensively elsewhere.[2] Instead, this paper will seek to highlight dynamics of the chaotic periods following the collapses of these two polities. Specifically, I aim to compare rulership dynamics of the early Hellenistic period, and more specifically the first generation of successors (corresponding roughly to a 20-year span from Alexander's death in 323 to Antigonos I Monophthalmos's death in 301), to equivalent cases from Early China during the period of Qin's collapse and the following interregnum, known as the "Eighteen Kingdoms" 十八國 and its seminal conflict, the Chu-Han Contention 楚漢相爭 (209–202).[3]

Before going any further, however, it is appropriate to briefly explain the nature and benefits of comparative historiography, especially in light of this volume which seeks to engage in comparative analysis. Fundamentally, historical comparison works by allowing insight into a given case to be compared by virtue of highlighting *what that case is not*. This approach has its limitations, like any other, especially when applied improperly. A scholar cannot produce a history of a state by writing only what that state was not. Comparison is best applied when there is uncertainty or question as to the nature of any specific aspect of a case. It works by finding similarities and differences with other cases that appear similar, and it aids one in understanding the distinctions and particularities of the case under study. This study uses comparative approaches to identify peculiarities of the dynamics of the Early Hellenistic and Eighteen Kingdoms eras. By examination of one case and its sources, one is often led to ask new questions of another case and its own body of evidence. By this method, bodies of historical evidence as thoroughly mined by centuries of academics as the historiographies of

---

1   All dates in this study are BC unless otherwise noted.
2   Christopher 2022.
3   The choice of dates to boundary this study does not imply that the period right after Antigonos' death entails a fundamental shift in how leadership dynamics worked – just that they are the years in which Antigonus and Xiang Yu's lives can be fully explored in comparison, while not leaving an (admittedly subjectively decided) overlarge gap in timespans for their use as comparanda.

ancient Greece (and in the case of this article, early China as well) can be made to yield
new and fresh insights. In sum, in the asking of such questions as comparison inspires,
what is old is made new.

In the case of this paper, historical comparison allows for insight into how those
individuals caught up in the collapses of Argead and Qin authority saw themselves
and each other, how they understood themselves in relation to their founders of world
empire, Alexander III and Ying Zheng (the First Emperor of Qin), how they formed
coalitions to join forces, and how these dynamics all come together to reframe the
early Hellenistic period as a revolt, of sorts, against the Argead domination of a Macedonian empire that lasted much longer than is often thought. To do this, I will first go
over the basic facts of the Chinese point of comparison and those following the death
of Alexander III. I will highlight the lives of two similar figures, Antigonos I Monophthalmos (~382–301) and Xiang Yu 項羽 of Chu 楚 (232–202), upon which I will begin
comparative analyses to gain further insight into their similar experiences and their
time periods. With the two cases clearly established and comparisons drawn, I will
examine the dynamics of collective action in each and will examine distinct features of
the Macedonian case.

2. The comparability of the Early Hellenistic Period and the Eighteen Kingdoms

The periods set for comparison share more in common than just a rough chronological
synchronicity.[4] Beyond the numerous parallels in the rises of Macedon and Qin, they
both collapse into comparable periods as well. In each case, what had been a singular
imperial unity under a single family line (the Argead and Ying 嬴 clans) was fractured.
The former imperial family lines would ultimately be destroyed. Personnel who had
formerly been associated with the imperial project in some capacity turned against
it, and no clear successor was found to carry on the imperial frameworks as they had
existed before. The results were two separate, yet similar periods of interstate anarchy
wherein numerous competing authority figures variously fought against or aligned
with each other in various efforts to recreate a unified hegemonic dominion. Of course,
these periods were not exact parallels – the Hellenistic period in total lasted centuries, and none of the successor "states" of Alexander's empire succeeded in recreating
it (though Antigonos and Seleukos got close). The Eighteen Kingdoms period was

---

4   Chronological synchronicity is, in the personal experience of this author, often erroneously held
     up as being a major factor of whether a comparison is "valid" or not. This is not a view this author
     shares – a comparison of Athenian democracy and American democracy is a valid comparison –
     the vastly different historical periods and technologies available would simply be factors needing
     to be accounted for in laying out a comparison.

fleeting by contrast. From the outbreak of the revolt that destroyed Qin in 209 to the establishment of the Han Dynasty in 202 boundaries a period lasting less than a decade. However, parallel dynamics of interstate anarchy and interpersonal tension and confusion were clearly in operation in both cases, and individuals in both cases faced at times strikingly similar circumstances and challenges: Both periods were times of constant warfare between members of a discernible singular cultural in-group (that is, on the one hand, between Macedonians, and on the other, between individuals belonging to the larger post-Zhou cultural sphere). Both periods saw tensions over handouts of the land of the former empire, questionable loyalty to nominal authorities, intensely personal dynamics of "state" behavior and diplomacy, challenges of conquering groups and native populations, and much more.

As I see it, that the two periods resulted in very different outcomes, far from indicating an invalid comparison, inspires a major research question which this article can only offer the beginnings of an answer to: Given the many similarities between the rise and fall of Macedon and Qin, why did Alexander's empire collapse never to be restored, while the Qin dynasty collapsed, only to see the Han Dynasty succeed at reconstructing something that resembled it within a decade?

3. Summary case: The death of Alexander, the fall of the Argead clan, and the Wars of the Diadochi

It may seem unnecessary to readers versed in the classical tradition to provide an extremely brief summary of the Early Hellenistic period here. However, in the interest of making my work accessible to both Classicists *and* Sinologists, I include one nevertheless. Specialists in the field may skip to the equivalent brief summary on the fall of Qin and the Eighteen Kingdoms.

After a decade-long reign spent almost exclusively on campaigns to conquer the entirety of the Achaimenid Empire and then some, Alexander III died in Babylon in 323.[5] He left no legitimate heirs, save for an unborn child within his Sogdian wife Roxana.[6] Disputes over the future of his empire began immediately. In the event, the Macedonian infantry clashed with the more aristocratic elements of the army over the succession.[7] The infantry held that Arrhidaios (359–317), a semi-invalid brother of Alexander who had been passed over for succession due to an unclear malady, should be named

---

5   Plut. Alexander 75–77; Arr. an. 7.26; Diod. 17.117; Curt. 10.5; Iust. 12.15–16.
6   Plut. Alexander 77.4; Iust. 12.15.9; Green 1991, 467 n. 75. There is also the contentious matter of his supposed illegitimate son by Barsine, Herakles. Whatever one concludes, whether with Tarn 1921 that he was not a son of Alexander or with Errington 1970 that he was, he clearly was not favored for succession.
7   See the full discussion of various perspectives, interests, and factions in Billows 1990, 49–58.

basileus.[8] The cavalry favored waiting until the birth of Roxana's child, and if male, naming it as basileus. The compromise reached determined that Arrhidaios be named basileus (and re-named Philippos) and that Alexander's unborn child, if a male, was to be made basileus as well.[9] The general Perdikkas was named as regent, and set about allotting satrapies to his supporters and the other powerful Macedonian generals.[10] Support for his position was shaky, and when he tried to marry Alexander III's sister Kleopatra, order among the satraps broke down, and a revolt against his authority was initiated.[11] Seeking to subdue this revolt, Perdikkas campaigned against Ptolemaios in Egypt, Perdikkas ended up murdered by his own soldiers in a mutiny around 320 possibly instigated by Ptolemaios.[12] With the regency vacant, Ptolemaios named Arrhidaios (not Alexander's brother) and Peithon as co-regents, but these immediately ceded the position to Antipatros, who had ruled over Macedon since Alexander III's departure.[13] Antipatros's death in 319 and choice of successor sparked further revolts, supported by several satraps including Antigonos and Ptolemaios.[14] By 317, Kassandros had seized Macedonia, and by 310 he had executed Alexander III's mother Olympias, Roxana, and Alexander's young son Alexander IV, bringing an end to the Argead dynasty.[15] Separately, the satrap Antigonos had accumulated a significant amount of power in Asia, and was potentially on the cusp of being powerful enough to subdue the other Macedonian dynasts.[16] A major coalition of Seleukos, Lysimachos, Kassandros, and Ptolemaios formed to defeat Antigonos, meeting him and his son Demetrios I "Poliorketes (City-Besieger)" at the Battle of Ipsos in 301, killing Antigonos, and with him, the best chance of any full restoration of Alexander's dominion.[17]

4. Summary case: The Fall of Qin, The Eighteen Kingdoms, and the Chu-Han Contention

The best account of the period under study remains the *Shiji* 史記 of Sima Qian (145– c. 86), itself reliant on the now-lost *Chu-Han Chunqiu* 楚汉春秋 of Lu Jia 陸賈 (mid-2nd

---

8   Curt. 10.6.20–10.8.10; Diod. 18.2.3.

9   Iust. 13.4.3; Arr. succ. BNJ 156 F1.1; Diodoros omits discussion of this arrangement, but begins referring to the rulers in plural from 18.6 onwards. For much more on this dynamic and evidence for it, see Habicht 1973 and Funke 2005.

10   Curt. 10.10.1–8; Iust. 13.4; Diod. 18.3–4.

11   Diod. 18.23; Arr. succ. BNJ 156 F1.3–4.

12   Diod. 18.36; Arr. succ. BNJ 156 F9.28.

13   Diod. 18.36.6–7 and 18.39.2; Arr. succ. BNJ 156 F9.30–32.

14   See the segment on Antigonos below.

15   Diod. 19.105.2.

16   See the segment on Antigonos below.

17   Plut. Demetrios 29.3–5; Diod. 21.1. The next-closest chance would have been Seleukos at Kouroupedion, though even had he not been assassinated shortly after, he had not yet conquered Egypt.

century) for its account of events.[18] As with sources for Alexander, literary embellish-
ment clouds the historical account and makes discerning history from narrative fancy
during this short and chaotic period quite difficult.[19] Still, the following can be said with
certainty: After Qin's 4th century reforms, its power grew tremendously, and in the 3rd
century Qin ended 500 years of political disunity in China under the reign of its *wang*
王 (conventionally translated as king), Ying Zheng 嬴政.[20] Ying Zheng oversaw the conquest of the other early Chinese territorial states and their *wangs* and in 221 brought the
whole of the proto-Chinese cultural domain under his authority. Given that his own
power exceeded all prior *wangs*, he invented a new title for himself: *huangdi* (emperor)
皇帝.[21] When Ying Zheng died in 210, his youngest son Huhai 胡亥 (231–207)[22] took the
throne and became Qin Er Shi 秦二世 (Qin's Second Emperor). We are told by Sima
Qian, however, that there were significant irregularities with Huhai's accession, and
that he was incompetent and over trusting of his self-interested officials.[23] Regardless of
the truth of these assertions, Qin authority began to precipitously collapse a year into
his rule.[24] Newly conquered areas rebelled, sectors of Qin's own expansive governing
body joined the rebels and recreated several of the fallen Warring States polities, and
some figures broke away entirely. I must stress this point: this was not just a revolt of
the conquered; Qin personnel are themselves clearly depicted as having an active hand
in turning against the authority of Qin.[25] These rebels quickly formed themselves into

18   Cao and Liu 2020. I have opted to provide references to translations of the *Shiji* (where available;
      the major translation effort of William H. Nienhauser Jr. is not yet completed). This is in order to
      better allow readers without a sinology background (that is to say, most Classicists) to follow my
      research and argumentation.

19   For example, see the discussions in Shibata 2013, 3–4 and Nienhauser 2002, 98 about the literary
      nature of Sima Qian's depiction of nearly parallel encounters where both Xiang Yu and Liu Bang
      separately watch Ying Zheng touring his domain (in *Shiji*, 7:296 (Nienhauser 1994, 180) and 8:344
      (Nienhauser 2002, 9–10)), with their separate reactions being intended as indicative of their per-
      sonalities.

20   Sima Qian, *Shiji*, 6:234–236 (Nienhauser 1994, 134–135). There is a certain tension with using the
      word "king" for both *wang* and basileus in a comparative piece, so I have opted to try to avoid
      translating the terms to more clearly highlight the difference in the titles. On this, see Christopher
      2022, 91–92.

21   Sima Qian, *Shiji*, 6:236 (Nienhauser 1994, 135–136).

22   Loewe 2000, 652–653 notes that Huhai's age at accession is contradictory in the *Shiji* and that he
      may have been a child at the time of becoming ruler, born around 222. I side with Kinney 2004, 10
      n. 9's reasoning that the younger age possibility is the less likely.

23   Sima Qian, *Shiji*, 6:264–269 (Nienhauser 1994, 154–158), 87:2548–2552 (Nienhauser 2021, 643–
      649), and 88:2567–2568 (Nienhauser 2021, 675–678).

24   Sima Qian, *Shiji*, 6:269–270 (Nienhauser 1994, 158–159) and 87:2553 (Nienhauser 2021, 649–651)
      recount the situation from the Qin perspective, and 48:1950–1955 specifically recounts the initial
      rebellions and claims to kingship of Chen She 陳涉 and Wu Chen 武臣.

25   Sima Qian, *Shiji*, 6:273 (Nienhauser 1994, 160–161) and 7:308–309 (Nienhauser 1994, 188–189) and
      Ban Gu, *Hanshu*, 1A:20 sees the Qin general Zhang Han 章邯, who was tasked with resisting the
      rebellion, defect to Xiang Yu and take his entire army with him along with the Qin high officials
      Sima Xin 司馬欣 and Dong Yi 董翳. Zhang Han was then enfeoffed by Xiang Yu as a leader of

new iterations of the lands that Qin had conquered, and were loosely unified only in their common goal, the destruction of Qin rule. This did not mean, however, that they answered to each other or arose in collaboration. Eventually, many warlords, "kings," and others coalesced into a loose coalition under Xiang Yu of Chu by 207.[26] That year, Xiang Yu seized the Qin capital, burned it to the ground, and killed the Qin ruler and the entire ruling clan of Qin.[27] He divided up Qin's remaining lands and formalized the division of the Qin Dynasty into 18 Kingdoms, and aimed to set himself up as a kind of hegemon under a puppet emperor that all kingdoms would nominally be subordinate to.[28] However, ambitions among rulers and Xiang Yu's own overbearing behavior to these newly restored kingdoms quickly became intolerable and the kingdoms ended up again in conflict very soon.[29] One prominent quasi-vassal of Xiang Yu, the peasant leader turned noble Liu Bang 劉邦 (256–195), seized on the building discontent towards Xiang Yu's attempts at hegemony. Building his own coalition of kingdoms, Liu Bang warred against Xiang Yu for five years, eventually defeating him at Gaixia 垓下 in 202, and claiming the title of emperor for himself and establishing the Han Dynasty.[30] Renaming himself Han Gaozu 漢高祖, his early reign saw some rebellions of individ-

---

one of the eighteen kingdoms. The Qin army itself under Zhang Han fared more poorly, as the men were so worried about Qin reprisals on their families that they appeared potentially disloyal to Xiang Yu's faction and were executed en masse. Note, however, the explicit wording in Sima Qian, *Shiji*, 7:310 (Nienhauser 1994, 189) that "[if Xiang Yu and his coalition] now are able to enter the pass and defeat Qin, that will be good; if they can't, the nobles will take us east as prisoners, [and therefore] Qin will certainly exterminate our parents, wives, and children (今能入關破秦，大善；即不能，諸侯虜吾屬而東，秦必盡誅吾父母妻子)." Clearly, the soldiers are not depicted as being particularly concerned with the fate of the state as much as the fates of their own families, worrying less about the vengeance of the rebels than about the vengeance of Qin, and cannot be seen to have been particularly loyal to Qin. *Shiji*, 7:297 (Nienhauser 1994, 180) sees Yin Tong 殷通, governor of Kuaiji 會稽, prepared to revolt; *Shiji*, 8:349 (Nienhauser 2002, 18–20) depicts the prefect of Pei 沛 specified as a Qin official wishing to revolt; *Shiji*, 89:2574 (Nienhauser 2008, 8–10) depicts the previously loyal magistrate of Fanyang as eager to surrender when the revolt occurred; *Shiji*, 96:2675 (Nienhauser 2008, 205–206) notes that Zhang Cang 張蒼 was a Qin imperial secretary, was punished, and joined up Liu Bang when he took over the area; *Shiji*, 113:2967 sees Qin commander Zhao Tuo 趙佗 and Qin official Ren Xiao 任囂, willingly revolting against their own government.

26 Sima Qian, *Shiji*, 7:307 (Nienhauser 1994, 187–188) and 8:365–366. The list of individuals invested as *wangs* by Xiang Yu in the aftermath of the destruction of the Qin capital can be taken to be a loose list of who Xiang Yu believed to be the major players in the anti-Qin cause.

27 Sima Qian, *Shiji*, 6:275 (Nienhauser 1994, 163), 7:315 (Nienhauser 1994, 194), and 8:365 (Nienhauser 2002, 41).

28 Sima Qian, *Shiji*, 7:316–317 (Nienhauser 1994, 194–196) and 8:365 (Nienhauser 2002, 41–43). It is unnecessary to list the full 18 kingdoms here, but note that *all* former feudal states before Qin's unification were restored under kings, though most were broken up into several sovereign kingdoms rather than restored whole, likely to ensure Chu's ability to dominate them. Note also that Shibata 2013, 10 suggests that the extent to which this figure was a puppet of Xiang Yu might be exaggerated for dramatic effect.

29 Sima Qian, *Shiji*, 7:320–321 (Nienhauser 1994, 196–197).

30 Sima Qian, *Shiji*, 8:378–380 (Nienhauser 2002, 63–66).

ual vassals, each successfully put down, and the Han Dynasty would rule (with a brief interruption in 9 CE – 23 CE) until the 3rd century CE.

5. Comparing eras by comparing lives: Antigonos I and Xiang Yu

With the periods under study sufficiently outlined, one can go further to establish parallels. In pursuing a biographical comparison of Xiang Yu and Antigonos I, one finds common experiences and concerns, similar outcomes, but drastically different policies and behaviors. Both figures came close to establishing their own hegemonic authority over the fragmented empire of their era, before failing at a very late stage. Xiang Yu's failure, however, led to the establishment of the Han Dynasty – Antigonos' entrenched the political divisions of the Hellenistic period for generations to come.

5.1 Antigonos I Monophthalmos

The early life of Antigonos son of Philippos, later known as Antigonos I "Monophthalmos" (The One-Eyed) is poorly attested. He was born around 382.[31] Little is known of his parents, though Richard Billows, in his thorough biography of the man, concluded that a background of anything other than Macedonian aristocracy makes little sense.[32] Of his youth nothing can be known. He would presumably have been raised to appreciate 'Greek culture and … the martial pursuits of a warrior aristocracy,' the latter of which was no doubt aided by his tall stature.[33] As a young adult he witnessed the accession to power of Philippos II, father of Alexander, whose reign saw Macedon go from a point of near-collapse to indisputable hegemon over the Greek world. Antigonos' activities in the reign of Philippos are unclear, but there is enough evidence to suggest that he must have gained some prominence in activities under Philippos, likely during which time he lost an eye in battle.[34]

Under Alexander, Antigonos was a competent though not extremely prominent high officer. He was initially placed in command of the Allied Greek infantry and likely participated at the Granikos.[35] Antigonos was soon made satrap of Phrygia in 333, where he acted to secure Alexander's rear and entrenched his authority over the area.[36]

---

31   Billows 1990, 16.
32   Billows 1990, 16–18 and n. 3. I have largely followed Billows in the major outlines of the life of Antigonos.
33   Plut. Demetrios 2.2.
34   Billows 1990, 24 and 27–29 makes the case for Perinthos being the site of Antigonos losing his eye.
35   Arr. an. 1.29.3. For his participation at the Granikos, see the arguments of Billows 1990, 36–38.
36   Arr. an. 1.29.3; Curt. 3.1.8; Iust. 13.4.14; Billows 1990, 36–39. Anson 1988 examines his function in this role in detail.

Ernst Badian noted that Antigonos stayed on as satrap through the duration of Alexander's rule (unlike most others picked for that title), and was not impacted by Alexander's mass purge of governors upon his return from India.[37] By Alexander's death in 323 (which Antigonos was not present in Babylon for, nor for the politicking that came after), Antigonos was about 59; a generation older than many of the successors who would also become prominent in this chaotic period, and in command of an independent force of Macedonians, as well as 'the key Macedonian commander in Asia Minor, at the head of a huge satrapy, much of which he had himself conquered'.[38]

Perdikkas, the chosen regent for the empire, ordered Antigonos to conquer a new satrapy to be handed over to Eumenes, which Billows has suggested was an order designed to force Antigonos to create a political and military counterweight to himself.[39] Antigonos did not act, and Perdikkas eventually had to conquer the area himself, following this up by demanding Antigonos arrive to stand trial for, as Diodorus Siculus describes the charges, 'fraudulent lies and unjust accusations.'[40] Antigonos fled to Europe and aligned himself with Antipatros and Krateros, before moving back into Anatolia and stabilizing his position there.[41] With the death of Perdikkas in Egypt, Antigonos became one of the primary contenders for power at the conference at Triparadeisos, and saw his former dominions in Asia Minor restored.[42] Antigonos was appointed as general of the war in Asia against the remainder of Perdikkas' faction, in which Antigonos proved victorious, though Antipatros's death in 319 destabilized the power framework Antigonos had been operating in.[43]

Kassandros and Antipatros refused to recognize the authority of Polyperchon as successor regent to Antipatros, and further conflicts were waged by Antigonos to maintain his position.[44] To trace the campaigns and shifting political constellations of the ensuing years in detail while remaining intelligible would be beyond the scope of this short paper.[45] Suffice to say, Antigonos led further campaigns against Eumenes, killing him in 316 and expanding his own domain into Mesopotamia, where he made an enemy of

---

37 Badian 1961.
38 Billows 1990, 48 and 56. Billows notes that only Antigonos and Antipatros had conducted major successful campaigns independent of Alexander's activities.
39 Plut. Eumenes 3.2; Billows 1997, 56–58.
40 Plut. Eumenes 3.3; Arr. succ. BNJ 156 F9.20; Diod. 18.23.4 provides the description of the charges, quoted above, as διαβολὰς ψευδεῖς καὶ κατηγορίας ἀδίκους.
41 Diod. 18.23.4–25.2; Arr. succ. BNJ 156 F9.24–26.
42 Arr. succ. BNJ 156 F9.37; Diod. 18.39.
43 Diod. 18.40.1, 18.47.4; Billows 1990, 74–80.
44 Diod. 18.49.1–50.2.
45 Even in such a large study as Billows 1990, the biographer notes on page 81 that there is no way to discern the legitimacy or legal basis (if any) of Antigonos' position between 319 and 311. Antigonos seems to have considered himself continuing on officially as *strategos* (general), as attested in Diod. 19.61.3. On this treaty, see also Meeus 2013, 129.

Seleukos.[46] The other Macedonian rulers demanded Antigonos cede significant lands to them to rebalance power among them away from Antigonos.[47] Antigonos refused and in the ensuing Third War of the Diadochi, he eventually fought his adversaries into a compromise peace.[48] Crucially, the peace agreement reached in 311 maintained the legal stance, at least, that all signatories (which notably excluded Seleukos), including Antigonos, were still subordinate to Alexander's young son, Alexander IV.[49] Kassandros then had Alexander IV and his mother murdered, and hostilities erupted again not long after the peace was signed.[50] While Seleukos caused considerable setbacks for Antigonos' position in the east, a major victory of Antigonos' fleet at Salamis in 306 provided the opportunity for Antigonos to take for himself and his son Demetrios the titles of basileis.[51] The ensuing years saw further campaigns, culminating ultimately in a coalition of all other major Macedonian dynasts to form against him, leading into the battle of Ipsos in 301, which saw Antigonos defeated and killed (though he was given a royal burial by his enemies), and his lands divided between the victors.[52]

5.2 Xiang Yu of Chu

As with the larger period of the Eighteen Kingdoms in which he is a prominent figure, the best source for Xiang Yu is Sima Qian's biography of the man. Sima Qian gave a prominence of place to Xiang Yu's biography, between the account of Ying Zheng and that of Liu Bang, that has often proven disturbing to later scholars.[53] That there are authorial stylings (whether those of Sima Qian himself or his sources) which seem to present Xiang Yu and Liu Bang as polar opposites has been suggested, though given that Liu Bang's biography is filled with supernatural elements, it seems likelier that Liu Bang has been "built up" moreso than Xiang Yu, whose biography is comparatively

---

46   Diod. 19.43.8–19.44.3; Plut. Eumenes 17.1–19.1 for Eumenes and Diod. 19.55; App. Syr. 53 for the schism between Antigonos and Seleukos.
47   Diod. 19.57.1–2; Iust. 15.1; App. Syr. 53. On the justifiability of the demands made of Antigonos, see Billows 1990, 109–110.
48   For an account of the events of that war, see Billows 1990, 109–134.
49   Diod. 19.105.
50   Diod. 19.105.2 and 20.19.3.
51   On the campaign against Seleukos: Billows 1990, 146. On the taking of the title "basileus", see the discussion in Gruen 2018, and the list of sources he provides in n. 2.
52   Plut. Demetrios 29.3–5; Diod. 21.1. Billows 1990 suggests that the burial was the work of Seleukos due to his magnanimity, which is possible but unknowable. See Meeus 2013, 131, discussing the major events of the Early Hellenistic period after Ipsos, unfortunately beyond the scope of this short paper to address.
53   On this issue, see Shibata 2013, 2–3. Note that there are discrepancies between some details of campaigns and events for the period, which Nienhauser 1994, 209 suggests is the result of Sima Qian being reliant on further, unknown sources which are providing contradictory information.

more grounded.[54] What follows is, therefore, a summarized account of Sima Qian's biography of Xiang Yu.

Xiang Yu was born in ~232 and raised in what is now Jiangsu.[55] Exceptionally for the *Shiji*, his parents are not named.[56] The Xiang clan, however, had been a well known as a powerful family of the Chu state which had been destroyed by Qin in 223, and he was related to a famous Chu general of the late Warring States, Xiang Yan 項燕 (d. 223).[57] Raised by his uncle Xiang Liang 項梁, son of Xiang Yan, Sima Qian attests that the boy was disinterested in scholastic pursuits or swordsmanship, but was passionate about studying generalship, and unusually tall and physical strong.[58] At the behest of his uncle, he joined the revolt against Qin around 208 in an incident involving a murderous overthrow of the local Qin governor, after which the provincial administration fell under his uncle's sway.[59] Xiang Yu set about pacifying outlying areas, and in a few instances demonstrated a tendency towards anger and brutality which persists throughout his depiction in the *Shiji*.[60] When Chen Sheng 陳涉 (the first of the anti-Qin rebels) was killed, Xiang Liang convened a meeting of various Chu-aligned anti-Qin rebel leaders, (which at that time included Liu Bang). On the advice of his strategist Fan Zeng 范增 (c. 277–207), Liang emplaced a commoner descendant of Chu Huai *Wang* (r. 328–399) as Chu Huai 懷 *Wang* II (later titled Chu Yi 義 *Di*, r. 208–206) as a figurehead who could unite several of the Chu-aligned rebel armies into one cohesive group.[61] After several further victories against Qin and a brief intervention in Qi 齊, Xiang Liang was himself killed at Dingtao 定陶.[62] Chu Huai *Wang* II emplaced Song Yi 宋義 over Chu's combined forces, and when the latter delayed rather than engage enemy forces, Xiang Yu murdered him in his tent and claimed (falsely) to have acted on the orders of Chu Huai *Wang* II. The army fell completely under his sway and Huai *Wang* was forced to accept the matter as a fait accompli.[63] Xiang Yu won a major victory against Qin at Julu

---

54 Shibata 2013, 5. On the question of Sima Qian being author or transmitter/editor of these attitudes towards Xiang Yu, see Cao and Liu 2020.

55 Sima Qian, *Shiji*, 7:295 (Nienhauser 1994, 179).

56 Shibata 2013, 5.

57 Sima Qian, *Shiji*, 7:295 (Nienhauser 1994, 179). Shibata 2013, 7 n. 23 points out how often this is played up to create another distinction between Xiang Yu and the commoner Liu Bang. Shibata, however, emphasizes that the family appears to have been subsumed into commoner status under Qin systems, with little to suggest any Qin recognition of their prior standing or fame.

58 Sima Qian, *Shiji*, 7:295–296 (Nienhauser 1994, 179–180).

59 Sima Qian, *Shiji*, 7:297 (Nienhauser 1994, 180–181).

60 Sima Qian, *Shiji*, 7:297 (Nienhauser 1994, 181). Xiang Yu's anger might be slightly played into a literary trope to distinguish him from Liu Bang, on this see Shibata 2013. There are certainly other cases of Xiang Yu being brutally impetuous (at least in the eyes of this author) to be found, including *Shiji*, 7:306, 7:307, 7:310–311, 7:315, 7:320, 7:326, and 7:328 (Nienhauser 1994, 187, 189–190, 194, 197, 200, and 202), to provide a few examples.

61 Sima Qian, *Shiji*, 7:300 (Nienhauser 1994, 183).

62 Sima Qian, *Shiji*, 7:303 (Nienhauser 1994, 185).

63 Sima Qian, *Shiji*, 7:304–307 (Nienhauser 1994, 186–187)

鉅鹿 in 207, after which he captured the entirety of Qin's field army there and eventually had them executed en masse.[64] After the battle, the variant rebel forces outside of Chu control submitted to his nominal authority as a kind of coalition field leader.[65]

Political machinations of Chu Huai *Wang* II delayed Xiang Yu from advancing on Qin's capital at Xianyang 咸陽, causing Liu Bang, at this time also nominally under the authority of Chu Huai *Wang* II, to be first to take it, whereupon he treated the population and Qin rulership gently.[66] Infuriated, Xiang Yu's advisors suggested assassinating Liu Bang, but we are told Xiang Yu did not approve it, and attempts to go through with it regardless and without his approval failed.[67] Liu Bang's treatment of the city and surrendered Qin royals contrasted greatly with Xiang Yu's handling of both once he arrived – he razed the capital city and executed the Qin royal clan entirely.[68] Following the destruction of Qin, Xiang Yu divided out enfeoffments to nobles of the former Warring States and his own supporters in 206. Attempting to move Liu Bang, already perceived as a threat, far enough away that he would cease to be a threat, Xiang Yu granted him the lands of what is now Sichuan. The territorial divisions Xiang Yu had set up began to fall apart immediately, partially because of his own meddling to remove those that Sima Qian suggests he did not respect.[69] Liu Bang and his army moved into the former Qin heartland and seized it, and diverted Xiang Yu's attention from the matter by drawing him into conflict with the states of Qi and Zhao 趙.[70] After handling this, Xiang Yu won a major victory at Pengcheng 彭城 against Liu Bang, and was in the ascendancy until a rift opened between Xiang Yu and his primary advisor Fan Zeng, which Sima Qian attributes to trickery on the part of Liu Bang.[71] The two sides came to a gradual stalemate, while Chu faced serious challenges arising from internal rebellions, and a peace treaty between the two adversaries was signed around 203.[72] This peace was immediately broken by Liu Bang who pursued Xiang Yu and his army, defeating him at Gaixia in 202.[73] Sima Qian attests that Xiang Yu himself, pursued by Liu Bang's forces and eventually cornered, killed hundreds of men before eventually slitting his own throat.[74] His body was dismembered by individuals eager to claim the

---

64   Sima Qian, *Shiji*, 7:307–310 (Nienhauser 1994, 187–189).
65   Sima Qian, *Shiji*, 7:307 (Nienhauser 1994, 187–188).
66   Sima Qian, *Shiji*, 8:362–365 (Nienhauser 2002, 37–41).
67   Sima Qian, *Shiji*, 7:311–314 (Nienhauser 1994, 190–193); 8:364 (Nienhauser 2002, 39–40); See Liu 2000, 3 for the corresponding fragment from the *Chu-Han Chunqiu*.
68   Sima Qian, *Shiji*, 7:313–315 (Nienhauser 1994, 192–193); 8:362–365 (Nienhauser 2002, 37–41).
69   Sima Qian, *Shiji*, 7:315–320 (Nienhauser 1994, 194–197).
70   Sima Qian, *Shiji*, 7:321 (Nienhauser 1994, 198).
71   Sima Qian, *Shiji*, 7:321–325 (Nienhauser 1994, 197–200). On the role of Fan Zeng in Xiang Yu's campaigns, see Xue and Zhu 2021.
72   Sima Qian, *Shiji*, 7:327–331 (Nienhauser 1994, 201–204).
73   Sima Qian, *Shiji*, 7:331–334 (Nienhauser 1994, 204–206).
74   Sima Qian, *Shiji*, 7:334–336 (Nienhauser 1994, 206–207).

land Liu Bang had promised for it – which Liu Bang divided into five pieces to match the divided condition of the body.[75]

6. A revolt vs A collapse?

There are obviously many striking differences and similarities between the lives of these two figures. Xiang Yu's youth at his time of death (dying around the age of 30) highlights Antigonos' advanced age at death (about 80). Their interactions with coalition diplomacy stand out as key similarities. However, before engaging in any of those analysis, one key factor must be addressed: the major apparent dissimilarity between the larger trajectories of the eras of the two men. It appears on the surface that the fall of the Argead empire was a case of internal collapse – Antigonos, like other Diadochi, had been a competent and loyal servant of Alexander III (and of Philippos II before him). Xiang Yu and his uncle Xiang Liang held no comparable role in the Qin administration. Glancing at figures like Xiang Yu, Chen Sheng, and others, one might walk away with the following (and quite standard) impression: the fall of Qin occurred through an external revolt, and the fall of Argead control over Macedon was an internal collapse.[76] However, comparing these collapses more closely, the matter isn't quite as clear-cut as this. There are elements of collapse that precede the revolts against Qin authority, and there are elements of revolt in the "collapse" of Argead authority. It has been pointed out that Qin administrators and generals do not appear to have resisted particularly firmly, and some elements of the Qin state simply broke away from it, as occurred in the south, when the Qin official-general Zhao Tuo formed his own kingdom with Qin military and civilian personnel in what is now modern Guangdong, claiming himself to be *huangdi* in defiance of Liu Bang's claim to that title. I'd also point out that the successors of Alexander, while eager in some ways to follow Alexander's example, were not necessarily any more loyal to the *Argead dynasty*'s state institutions than many Qin officials were to Qin. To be sure, some figures are noted for persisting

75   Sima Qian, *Shiji*, 7:336 (Nienhauser 1994, 207).
76   For a few examples of this depiction of the fall of Qin as a revolt, see Dull 1980, Yoshinami 1978, and He 1955. Sanft 2018, 156 identifies, however, that prior to the wave of revolts, Qin underwent an intense purge of qualified personnel for political reasons which severely weakened it, collapsing its ability to firmly handle resistance. For depictions of post-Alexander Macedonian history as an internal collapse, see Adams 2006, 28–30; Bosworth 2002, 1, and note that essentially all depictions of the period immediately after the death of Alexander (rightfully) do not note the conquered peoples of Alexander's empire as major factors in this immediate collapse. However, as I aim to show below, revolt can be internal as well. By "revolt" and "collapse," I mean that the one is typically understood as an expression of dissent against governing systems or figures, and the other is typically understood as a kind of internal systemic failure even when participants might be otherwise satisfied with the extant sociopolitical structures in operation. The two are not mutually exclusive, though in the cases of these two examples, are rarely discussed together.

in serving the Argead dynasty with something like loyalty including Polyperchon, and Eumenes, but the more successful figures of this era were those who went their own way to break from Argead authority.[77] It can be pointed out that there were clear elements of mass revolt under Qin that do not appear to have occurred following Alexander's death. After all, while the Greeks were violently resistant (discussed more below), the Persians, Egyptians, Sogdians, and countless other peoples of the Macedonian empire did not explode into revolt following Alexander's death, whereas the depiction of Qin rebellion usually appears to be bottom-up.[78] This is a key difference but can be explained clearly. Qin governance penetrated vastly deeper into society at all levels than Macedonian governance did.[79] It practiced a large-scale bureaucratic mode of administration internally and seems to have attempted to enforce this system on newly conquered lands.[80] Contrastingly, Alexander's conquest of Asia seems to have had a limited immediate impact on most of the peoples he had conquered.[81] Aside from the gradual incorporation of Persian nobility and personnel which in 323 was still

77 Perdikkas might be included in this list, and he was made regent over the joint basileis in 323 and died during a mutiny of soldiers in 320 which was brought about through military setback. Meeus 2013, 122–123, Coblentz 2019, 87–88, and Boiy 2017, 42 suggest, however, that Perdikkas may have wanted to become basileus himself, and was seen as threat and potential claimant to Macedonian throne, so his activities as regent in the name of the Argead house should not be taken too literally as proof of his loyalty as his activities may well have been self-serving. Polyperchon became regent at the death of Antipatros in 319. He ultimately fared poorly in this role, but seems to have genuinely tried to rally Argead authority in Macedonia, Epeiros, and the Greek mainland (Heckel ²2016, 206–216). Eumenes' loyalist stance is unquestionable, but belies the fact that his own ambitions as a Greek were best served by tying himself to the Argead house than in making a bid for power under his own name and alienating the core of his forces (Macedonians) in the process. On this, see Anson 2004, 9 n. 55, and 28.

78 On the characterization of the revolt against Qin, see Dull 1983. I am not making the claim that it was a mass peasant revolt, but that it is usually depicted as a revolt of non-Qin actors.

79 For a brief discussion of some examples of the thorough complexity of Qin bureaucratic ordinances, see Christopher 2022, 147–148. On the notion of administrative penetration in a comparative sense, see Beck 2021, esp. 193–195.

80 On this, see the major study of Qin administrative practices in southern China in Korolkov 2021, 90–147.

81 See Cohen 2013, 46–52 for the ongoing dispute as to how many foundations of cities Alexander undertook in his campaign. However, even if one goes with the extreme high number of around 70 proposed by Plut. mor. 328–329a and accepted by Hammond 1998, this does not in itself prove a massive impact: it seems likely that Macedonian control of conquered regions was essentially a matter of fortified outposts and cities, and that control of the hinterlands of the Asian acquisitions was limited (Tarn – Griffith ³1952, 162; also see Cohen 2013, 43). Moreover, the extreme difficulty of archaeologically locating a number of these settlements suggests that even if one goes with a higher number of foundations, that many dissolved relatively quickly (Fraser 1996, 201). Further still, Bosworth 2006, 18–19 points out how even communities of Greeks in established urban areas like Babylon do not appear to have mixed with locals significantly in this early period, such that the actual impact of Hellenic rulership and immigrants appears to be extremely minimal. Nor does there seem to have been any Macedonian (or, for that matter, any Greek) structure capable of imposing central control on areas far from urban centers akin to the vast bureaucratic structures of China, such that in the absence of well-established Macedonian powerbases, one struggles to see

a burgeoning factor rather than an a well-established one, Alexander's personnel were Graeco-Macedonians.[82] In the facts of Greek rebellion at the deaths of Philippos *and* Alexander, one *does* see mass rebellion against Macedonian rule comparable to that of Qin.[83] I would suggest that where Macedonian rule *had* penetrated deeper, where it was most felt, (that is to say, among the Greeks and Macedonians elites), there was an equivalent depth of revolt upon Alexander's death.[84] Therefore, one must not be misled into thinking that the collapse of Qin is qualitatively different from the collapse of Argead dominion because the former has popular elements to it: each state structure was destabilized proportional to the depth of its administrative penetration and no further. Lastly, note that the Qin dynasty was built on the backs of its bureaucratic apparatus, and the collapse of the Qin was characterized by the breakdown of control over these bureaucrats as they themselves revolt. Comparatively, the Argead dominion of Philippos and Alexander was built on the backs of its aristocracy, and it is among this aristocracy that we most clearly see behavior that can be characterized as breakdown and revolt, but this is a matter I will return to later.

7. Coalition and collective

A major part of the chaotic period following the deaths of Alexander and Ying Zheng were wars involving free agent warlords and nominally sovereign polities with forces which could normally or potentially have been mutually hostile gathering together to oppose a mutually agreed upon adversary, after which the coalition. Antigonos and Xiang Yu were caught up as both participants in and victims of such coalitions, and

---

how Macedonian rulership could have penetrated deeply into the lives of those who did not live near to these bases.

82   On this, see Bosworth 1980. Cf. also the chapter by Christoph Michels in this volume.

83   On the revolts that followed the death of Philippos II, see Iust. 11.1.5–6; Diod. 17.3; Green 1991, 113–114; Cartledge 2004, 56–57. On the breakout of the Lamian War (323–322) following the death of Alexander, see Diod. 18.8; Arr. succ. BNJ 156 F1 9, 12; Plut. Demosthenes 27 and Phokion 23–26; Hyp. 6.10–20; Iust. 13.5; Paus. 1.25.3–5. There is even direct parallel to be made with the Greek mercenary revolt in the far east of Alexander's empire being comparable as having elements of mass revolt not dissimilar to many of the rebels against Qin, on the former see Iliakis 2013.

84   Understanding the revolt of the Greeks after Alexander III's death as being a rejection of further submission to Argead despotism is not a new idea, for this see Badian 1982, 43. Note as well that Greece would also have "felt" Macedonian hegemony more keenly than other "conquered" peoples in the east because it had no real tradition of submission to royalty – indeed, ever since the Persian Wars particularly, it had developed an ideological opposition to it. The mass of Persian subjects were likely not immediately impacted to a great degree by the shift in regime. The Greeks were still in living memory of sovereignty without kings at all. That said, it is also important to acknowledge that, just as Pol. 18.14 indicates, the rise of Philip in Greece probably came with benefits for several Greek regions, though it is beyond the scope of this paper to examine each region's reasons for supporting or opposing Macedonian rule in the wake of Alexander's death.

they were far from the only ones – such coalitions formed and disbanded frequently in the periods under study. To illustrate this with only a few examples:[85] the alliance of Antipatros, Krateros, and Antigonos against Perdikkas, the alliance of Kassandros, Antigonos, and Ptolemaios against Polyperchon and Eumenes, and most famously, the coalition of Kassandros, Lysimachos, Ptolemaios, and Seleukos, which was raised to oppose Antigonos I Monopthalmos, who met his end opposing this coalition at Ipsos in 301.[86] The Chu-Han contention saw the same dynamic: the initial rebellion of Chen Sheng can be argued to have resulted in an unstable anti-Qin coalition which collapsed with the death of Chen Sheng.[87] Another loose anti-Qin coalition was formed against the second Qin emperor led by Xiang Yu, though nominally under the auspices of Chu Huai *Wang*. Following the defeat of Qin, Xiang Yu's behavior resulted in a loose coalition formed against him led by Liu Bang.[88] The ultimate victor of that conflict was Liu Bang, leaving him in a position to claim the title of *huangdi* for himself, and his reign saw the destruction of his former allies and vassals piecemeal, entrenching the powerbase of his nascent Han dynasty. In this area of comparison, one finds the real substantive differences in how Macedonians and early Chinese elites behaved, which in turn resulted in marked differences in how their histories play out.

First, we note a key similarity: Macedonian and early Chinese coalitions are fundamentally interpersonal affairs. In China, this is unremarkable as all interstate diplomacy was conducted between rulers and rulers or between rulers and their vassals in this period as with earlier stages in Chinese history.[89] The Macedonian case, however, stands in stark distinction from Greek precedents. Whereas Classical Greek leagues listed poleis as sovereign communities, the Macedonian tradition of personal rule carried through into the Hellenistic period. This was such that, outside of Greece and a few other cities, interstate diplomacy following the death of Alexander was interpersonal diplomacy.[90] However, there are marked differences between the coalitions of

---

85   For a fuller list, see Meeus 2018, 131–136.

86   For the coalition of Antipatros, Krateros, and Antigonos, see Diod. 18.23–25; for the coalition of Kassandros, Antigonos, and Ptolemaios, Diod. 18.54–55; for the coalition of Kassandros, Lysimachos, Ptolemaios, and Seleukos, Diod. 20.113; Plut. Demetrios 29.

87   This earliest phase saw rebelling warlords display some hostility to each other which was blunted only by their mutual fear of Qin. For example, see Zhao's betrayal of Chen Sheng in Sima Qian, *Shiji*, 48:1955 (Watson 1993, 5); see also the dispute between Song Yi and Xiang Yu regarding whether letting Qin destroy Zhao would weary or strengthen them (with the subtext that if it was the latter, that Zhao must be rescued before Qin defeated them) in *Shiji*, 7:305 (Nienhauser 1994, 186–187).

88   Sima Qian, *Shiji*, 7:321 (Nienhauser 1994, 198), but note also the separate coordinated efforts of Zhao and Qi against Xiang Yu in a kind of separate front entirely in *Shiji*, 7:320–321 (Nienhauser 1994, 197–198).

89   For a general overview, see Selbitschka 2015.

90   On this dynamic in context see Grainger 2017, 1–4. Note when Macedon is involved in Greek interstate treaties in the Classical period, Macedonian personal rulership is clear through identifying individuals rather than communities as signatories. Consider how IG II² 236 (= Rhodes and Os-

persons in the Chu-Han period and those in the early Hellenistic period. Early Chinese coalitions are based around the existence of a figure who is the acknowledged superior of all members. There is *no* concept of a first among equals relationship in early China. I would go as far as to say that such a conception was not only alien but even unethical in the cultural calculus of that world. What of Macedon, then? To say that there are no particularly prominent figures in Macedonian coalitions is perhaps an overstatement, the idea of alliance has to come from *someone* after all. However, the cooperation of Kassandros, Lysimachos, Seleukos, and Ptolemaios is at no point specified as a relationship of mastery of any given one of these figures over the others, and generally the legal fiction was maintained (till the death of Alexander IV) that these figures were all subordinates of the Argead house.[91] These major Diadochi were able to see where their interests aligned and entreat each other as equals in this capacity. These coalitions were never particularly stable in either case, but that the Macedonians could repeatedly recognize common interest without a master forcing them into it while the early contention-era warlords could not is a key difference.[92]

8. Temporary supremacy of the Qin?

There is a further dynamic that is apparent concerning the legitimacy of emplaced rulers in this period. It is held by scholars such as Anthony Barbieri-Low and Chun-Shu Chang that Qin's population redistribution activities were massively disruptive to local traditions and local identities, and may have helped create a strong pan-Chinese

borne 2003, 373–375), the oath of the League of Corinth, specifies that communities owe loyalty to Philippos rather than Macedon. Also, consider how in a 5th century inscription between Athens and Perdikkas II (Bengtson 1975, no. 186, lines 16–28, 47–52, and 61), Macedonians are treated by names as individuals while Athens is treated as an incorporated entity. See also Polyperchon's decree to the Greeks in Diod. 18.55–56.

91   Diod. 21.2 phrases it most bluntly: τι Πτολεμαῖος καὶ Σέλευκος καὶ Λυσίμαχος συνέδραμον ἐπ' Ἀντίγονον τὸν βασιλέα· οὐχ οὕτως ὑπὸ τῆς πρὸς ἀλλήλους εὐνοίας προκληθέντες, ὡς ὑπὸ τοῦ καθ' ἑαυτοὺς φόβου συναναγκασθέντες ὥρμησαν ἑτοίμως πρὸς τὴν τῶν ὅλων κοινοπραγίαν. ('Ptolemaios, Seleukos, and Lysimachos gathered against King Antigonos. Inspired less by good feelings towards each other than coerced by fear for themselves, they readily undertook all aspects of joint action together'). The nominal authority, at least, of the Argead house is suggested through the activities of Perdikkas as regent, and Ptolemaios' efforts to undermine that (for which, see Adams 2010, 210–212). No Macedonian successor claimed the title of basileus until *after* the death of Alexander IV, further suggesting a sense of not wishing to be too audacious in their power-grabs until the framework of Argead hegemony was truly gone. On how flimsy these alliances and coalitions were, see Meeus 2018.

92   This is particularly significant in light of Meeus 2013 pointing out that more likely than not, all diadochi were likely to harbor ambitions over the whole, or at least, more of Alexander's realm and were not, in fact, "separatists." This is not to say that these coalitions were at all stable or led to anything more than fleeting cooperation, but even this fleeting cooperation appears to occur more often than in the Chinese case.

identity that existed oppositionally to Qin.[93] However, a comparison with the behaviors of emplaced rulers in the early Hellenistic period challenges this idea. Figures like Ptolemaios, Seleukos, and Peukestas entrenched their standing over their holdings only through their activities while in control of their respective territories.[94] However, as Macedonian invaders in these lands, none of them claimed any authority that derived from something before Alexander's conquests. In fact, their own individual and personal activities seem to build up their hold on their areas from nothing, save for their initial allotment of territories as satraps. In direct contrast to this, the Chu-Han contention saw a clear dynamic where certain individuals claimed an ancestral, area-specific legitimacy to rule an area that predated the Qin dynasty.[95] Moreover, there is a direct equivalent in the Chu-Han contention to the scenes of satrapal distribution one finds in Diodoros.[96] Xiang Yu emplaces a number of *wangs* based in places that they are explicitly noted or presumed to have had powerbases and familiarity with the local area/population.[97] Given that satraps having too strong a grip over their domains appears to have been something undesirable for the Macedonians, one might suggest that Xiang Yu did not intend to attain mastery over these areas, and instead genuinely sought to break up Qin's empire. However, his near immediate about-face and interventions into these kingdoms contradict such an interpretation.[98] Indeed, the Xiang clan also emplaced a rather unimpressive figure (literally grabbing a shepherd from the fields) as emperor over all nobility in early China including themselves as a means to facilitate cooperation between the nobility.[99] This and the further practice of recognizing descendants of former warring states as latter day rulers was seen as necessary for the anti-Qin maneuvers, but not desirable in itself, and when Qin had been destroyed, these figures had served their purpose. Emperor Yi was murdered by Xiang Yu, and rul-

---

93   Barbieri-Low 2021 and Chang 2007, 1:56–60.
94   Ptolemaios secures firm command over Egypt through kindness in rule (Diod. 18.14.1; Iust. 13.6) and the alliance of other Macedonian elites through kind treatment of them (Diod. 19.55–56). Gorre 2009, 487, 624; and Gorre 2013, 101–105 note that it is likely only with Ptolemaios II that a very active interest is taken by the dynasty in securing Egyptian cooperation, but the so-called "Satrap Stela" (published in Brugsch 1871, 1–13, see the discussion in Ladynin 2007) suggests already in the reign of Ptolemaios I cooperative relations between Ptolemaios and Egyptian natives were strengthening his rule there. See also the discussion of the importance of possessing the body of Alexander already in Erskine 2002; Seleukos: Grainger 1990, esp. 95–113; Peukestas: Diod. 19.14.4–5, 19.22, and 19.48.5.
95   Beyond the Xiang clan's emplacement of King Huai II (discussed below), there is also the matter of the Qin commanders emplaced in former Qin lands (Sima Qian, *Shiji*, 7:316–319 (Nienhauser 1994, 194–196)), but also rulers of Wei, Zhao, Yan, and Qi were recognized for seemingly no reason other than their ancestral legitimacy, but with their powers curtailed by being forced to divide their territory with vassals Xiang Yu believed to be worthy.
96   Specifically, compare Diod. 18.3 to Sima Qian, *Shiji*, 7:316–317 (Nienhauser 1994, 194–197).
97   Sima Qian, *Shiji*, 7:316–317 (Nienhauser 1994, 194–197).
98   Sima Qian, *Shiji*, 7:320–321 (Nienhauser 1994, 196–197).
99   Sima Qian, *Shiji*, 7:300 and 315–316 (Nienhauser 1994, 183 and 194).

ers who did not serve as contributing commanders to aid Xiang Yu in the anti-Qin war had much of their lands partitioned and handed out to generals who had served Xiang Yu.[100] Whereas the diadoch-basileis attained their positions through personal glories, and cemented their power through engagement with local legitimacy traditions, many Chu-Han leaders of kingdoms were emplaced by others for ancestral lines having little to do with their own personal merit, and it is observed that Xiang Yu bestowed the imperial title of Yi *Di* 義帝 ("Righteous Emperor", but with a second meaning of artificial, i.e. "Fake Emperor") on Chu Huai *Wang* II, likely as an ironic joke, given his total lack of personal participation in events.[101] There is a demonstrable concern in the Chu-Han period for a warlord to seek political power through *the act of* recognizing the (only semi-symbolic) political authority of individuals who have ancestral ties to those lands as rightful owners of those lands.[102] Such a concern is not apparent in the Macedonian case. Peukestas dressed like a Persian to appeal to the Persians, Ptolemaios proclaims himself Pharaoh, and Seleukos becomes king of Babylon, but in each case these are foreign lords appropriating local traditions to be deployed in interest of Macedonian concerns.[103] It's a fascinating difference, then, that the Macedonians even believe they are themselves capable of performing these local functions and not needing local inhabitants to fill these roles (no doubt inspired by prior kingship traditions of the Achaimenids and of Alexander alike), despite their own complete lack of ties to these areas.[104] For Chu-Han rulership, it was seen to be unwise or immoral to try to

---

100   Sima Qian, *Shiji*, 7:315–317 (Nienhauser 1994, 194–197).

101   Sima Qian, *Shiji*, 7:315–316 (Nienhauser 1994, 194 and n. 139). Note also the famous definition in the *Suda*, s.v. *basileia*.

102   See Sima Qian, *Shiji*, 7:316–317 (Nienhauser 1994, 194–197) for a number of cases of this occurring.

103   Peukestas: Diod. 19.14.4–5, 19.22, and 19.48.5; Ptolemaios: Hölbl 2013, 21; Seleukos: Grainger 1990, esp. 95–113, see also Sachs – Wiseman 1954, 205. All of this also points to the importance placed on gaining the support of local elites for Macedonians seeking to build their authority in any given area. Cf. on this the chapters by Stefan Pfeiffer, Sonja Richter, and Christoph Michels in this volume. The recognition of local priests and cults by Macedonians is a similar dynamic, but differentiated by the scale of the authority being recognized by Chinese warlords. It is beyond the scope of this paper to probe the consequences of the absence of Mediterranean cult practices in China and how that might force recognition of ancestral ties to be political rather than "purely" religious.

104   This may perhaps derive or be in some way related to their understanding of their lands as being legitimately held through being "spear-won" (δορίκτητον). However, this would itself be likely an instance of the successors imitating Alexander rather than some earlier Macedonian tradition. Going with Mehl 1980, Alexander's famous declaration, in Diod. 17.17.2, that Asia was δορίκτητον ("spear-won") has a Homeric precedent, but not one tied to territoriality. Alexander's use of the term is obviously expansionistic in nature, but the term itself appears in Homeric use relating to the taking of captives or plunder (as in Hom. Il. 9.344), and is further used in that sense in cases like that of Eur. Andr. 155. The use of the term in Lykophron, Alexandra, applies to both captives and land (l. 934 for herds, l. 1116 for a captured woman, and l. 1361 for lands in Italy), but the attribution of *Alexandra* to Lykophron is disputed due to its depiction of Roman dominance which is fitting only as early as the 2nd century. Even if the attribution is correct, however, it is sufficiently late that its use of the term to describe lands may well be inspired by Alexander's usage rather than indicating a common understanding of the term as applicable to lands in use well before Alexan-

emplace a foreign ruler over these areas, given that the only cause that unified them was their opposition to foreign (Qin) rule. The Qin systems of bureaucracy and deep intrusion of state life into government and mass deportations of hundreds of thousands of people, by all accounts a much larger imposition into the lived experiences of individuals in conquered areas, seems in this comparison, to have utterly failed to break local resistances and may even have strengthened local identities. By contrast, the conquests of Alexander, which are taken to have been far more surface-level administrative changes rather than top-to-bottom revolutions in lived experience for conquered peoples, appear to have in this case allowed Macedonians to insert themselves into local traditions without much immediate backlash. Either the accounts of Qin's population redistribution activities are massively overblown in Sima Qian's history, or, just as likely, large population transfers failed to significantly impact the realities on the ground in conquered areas – claimants to local nobility still existed in these areas, and their claims were considered strong enough that they were to be recognized even in the absence of other redeeming features of these individuals.

A fascinating early Chinese counterpoint exists, however. Far in the south of the Qin realm, the Qin general Zhao Tuo took a Qin army, along with a number of Qin settlers, broke off from Qin control during the collapse of Qin, and established his own state.[105] The Zhao dynasty of Nanyue established itself as a Huaxia-Yue hybrid kingdom and lasted a century as a counter-claimant to the title of *huangdi* against the Han Dynasty.[106] Zhao Tuo's overlordship of the area seems to have been well received by Yue locals, and may have much resembled that of Seleukos and Ptolemaios in "Asia" and Egypt. The exact dynamics that underlay his successful arrival as a foreign overlord in this culturally distinct area are unclear. One might speculate that rather than this having to do with Yue particularities, that there may have been systems that bound noble Huaxia lineages to their land and perhaps even the local inhabitants there, that were not in operation among a clearly foreign cultural group such as the Yue, but this is speculation beyond the scope of this article to pursue. Instead, I would point out a clear difference between Zhao Tuo's relationship with the Han dynasty and the early Hellenistic basileis' relationship with each other. In the Chu-Han period, the *wangs*

der's reign. On the dating of the *Alexandra*, see Fraser 2000 and West 2006. On the afterlife of the term "Spear-won" in the Hellenistic period, see Barbantani 2007. Note lastly the minority position of Zahrnt 1996, Lehmann 2015, and Degen 2018 that Alexander's use of the term and the throwing of the spear are entirely literary constructs and ahistorical. Degen's point that there are literary tropes to the scene of spear-throwing is well-taken, but the fact that the term seems to suddenly shift in meaning away from precedent of captured booty and persons and towards conquered lands suggests nevertheless that Alexander may well have said something to the effect of the speech attributed to him by Diodoros, whether or not the dramatic arrival and spear-throwing scene is historical.

105   Sima Qian, *Shiji*, 113:2967–2968 (Nienhauser 2020, 1–4).
106   On this, see the discussion in Brindley 2010–2011.

were effectively warlord-kings who, while acknowledging each other as nominally co-equals, could not effectively cooperate outside of the framework of single figures who could dominate others.[107] Whereas the Zhao clan's claim to being the *huangdi* was taken extremely negatively by the Han, equivalent title claims were less the case among Macedonians.[108] Alexander never took a title to supercede basileus, and even his lordship of Asia was phrased as βασιλεὺς τῆς Ἀσίας.[109] Critically, this was not a title that was taken up by the Diadochi.

Famously, the successors of Alexander modeled themselves in several ways on Alexander. While the infantry and some of the officer corps may have had greater affection for Philippos II, it is Alexander who is the model for such Hellenistic dynamics as the absorption of non-Hellenic power traditions, and the founding of cities.[110] The situation in Qin, however, is harder to pin down. In popular imagination, the First Emperor was a tyrant king whose rule through fear inspired a colossal revolt.[111] And yet, there is evidence to argue that he provided a model for those who followed no less than Alexander. Sima Qian seems fairly clear that it is not Ying Zheng but his successor Hu Hai who seems to have brought on a collapse through trying to consolidate a questionably legitimate reign.[112] The very title of "Emperor," *huangdi*, was according to Sima Qian, the personal invention of Zheng.[113] It was quite quickly taken up by opponents of Qin, first by Xiang Yu and Yi Di, and then by Liu Bang who declared himself to be *huangdi* of the Han.[114] Critically, no figure claimed the title of *huangdi until* Ying Zheng's death, with the revolt against Qin rule exploding right afterwards. Thus, despite having

107   This is most obviously on display in the account of how various lords, despite having an interest in relieving the kingdom of Zhao from Qin assault, ultimately left the matter in the hands of Xiang Yu, whose victory at Julu led to his recognition as a kind of superior force. On this, see Sima Qian, *Shiji*, 7:307 (Nienhauser 1994, 187). Note also the wording, conveyed by Sima Qian, *Shiji*, 8:379 (Nienhauser 2002, 66), of the vassals who desired to elevate Liu Bang to the emperorship. They claimed that, "… 大王不尊號，皆疑不信. [… if you do not elevate your title, all titles will be suspect and unreliable. (trans. Nienhauser)]."

108   Sima Qian, *Shiji*, 113:2969–2971 (Nienhauser 2020, 5–9).

109   Attested in Plut. Alexander 34.1. Whatever foreign titles Alexander, Ptolemaios, Seleukos, and the rest may have taken unto themselves seem to have been targeted at non-Graeco-Macedonian audiences, and it does not seem likely that the successors were much troubled by their assumption, as they sought to simultaneously appeal to non-Greek subjects while maintaining their Hellenistic veneer to each other and the larger Greek world. On this, see the discussion in Plischke 2017, esp. 164–165 and n. 3 and 6.

110   Bosworth 2002, 1–5. Note Hadley 1974, struggling to discern if a Seleukid coin depicted Seleukos or Alexander. On the coin portraits of the Diadochi see the chapter by Ralf von den Hoff in this volume.

111   Zheng is often depicted as a megalomaniacal autocrat: Lewis 2007, 164; Andrew 2018, 49; Caldwell 2018, 2. This view derives ultimately from the essay of Jia Yi included in the *Shiji*, in Sima Qian, *Shiji*, 6:276–284 (Nienhauser 1994, 163–169).

112   Sanft 2018, 156.

113   Sima Qian, *Shiji*, 6:236 (Nienhauser 1994, 133–134).

114   Sima Qian, *Shiji*, 8:379 (Nienhauser 2002, 65–66).

a complicated relationship with his subjects that can certainly not be called universal adoration, the First Emperor was a model for imitation regardless. One notes that
there were clear tensions between Alexander and his Macedonians discernible at every
level and every stage of his career. To provide only a short list here, one need only recall
the questioning of his legitimacy as heir, suspicions of his involvement in Philippos'
death, the torture and execution of Philotas, the drunken murder of Kleitos, and the
entire package of his so-called "Orientalizing".[115] After his death, his will was either virtually ignored or one was forged entirely, and the murder of his son Alexander IV did
not seem to elicit a vast outcry.[116] I suggest, then, a minor but important point: One
doesn't need to love the king to want to imitate the king, at least in some respects, and
whatever emotions a Diadoch held towards Alexander as a man, the best way to make
sense of their behavior is to understand them as completely self-interested.[117]

9. The durable Macedonian Empire

If one concedes the standard lines about competition between basileis and the need
for victory to legitimate one's kingship and all the rest for the Macedonian basileis,
then I would ask why *don't* they deny each other's legitimacy as basileis?[118] Traditionally, it is argued that the successors acknowledged each other's kingship because they
were satisfied with their own realms and do not see themselves as rulers over a greater
Macedonian empire. By this view, the Diadochi took the title of basileus as a way to
stake their claims on their limited domains, with the exception of Antigonos Monophthalmos, who, it is held, had ambitions to reunify the whole of Alexander's domain
and thus genuinely become a successor to the Argeads.[119] Erich Gruen in 1985 showed
that the traditional answer to this question is invalid.[120] Against this vision of a self-con-
ceived partition of the realm, Gruen pointed out the following: First of all, Antigonos'
claim to the title of basileus did not, as often supposed, result in the immediate dec-

---

115   On his legitimacy: Plut. Alexander 9.4–6; On the death of Philippos: Plut. Alexander 10.4; Iust.
       9.7.1–6; on the execution of Philotas: Heckel 1977, 10–17; on the death of Kleitos, see Plut. Alex-
       ander 50–52.1; Arr. an. 4.8–9; Curt. 8.1.22–55; on Alexander's so-called "Orientalizing," see Plut.
       Alexander 45.1–3; Diod. 17.77.5; Eratosthenes BNJ² 241 F30 for just a few examples.
116   On the will being ignored: Diod. 18.4.2–6 (on whether it was even genuine, see Heckel 1988, 85–
       87). On the death of Alexander IV: Diod. 19.105.1; Iust. 9.2.5; Paus. 9.7.2.
117   On this, see also their behavior towards each other as analyzed by Meeus 2018 and the discussion
       of Alexander's image among the successors in Meeus 2009.
118   On the importance of victory to Hellenistic Kingship, see Gehrke 2013. That the Diadochi greeted
       each other *as* basileis: Plut. Demetrios 18.2.
119   Gruen 2018, 109 n. 1 lists major works that take this view up to 1985.
120   Gruen 2018, expanded by Billows 1990, 155–160 and 351–352, and accepted by Bosworth 2002, 246–
       247 and n. 3, though Bosworth notes that the position remains under contention. Anson 2014, 157
       takes a similar stance.

larations of similar status by the other successors.[121] They surely were influenced by Antigonos, but there is at least two years duration between Antigonos' seizure of the title and the accession of Seleukos and Ptolemaios to that title, spurred on by separate victories which would legitimate their claims to such a stature.[122] None of Alexander's successors, save for Kassandros, who in epigraphic texts is represented as βασιλεὺς Μακεδόνων [King of the Macedonians], are attested in any coins, epigraphy, or other known contemporary documents as depicting themselves as basileis *of* Egypt, Thrace, Syria, or otherwise.[123] Gruen further noted that Kassandros, in the unique position of controlling Macedon itself, identified himself as King of the Macedonians, and can be understood to have been claiming kingship over Macedonians *everywhere*, and not just those within the confines of Macedon.[124] Critically, however, the office of basileus of Macedon was not at this time institutionalized in the way of Greek magistracies, and had never been so under the several centuries of Argead rule. Its very flexibility and fluidity amounted to there being no firm regulations restricting it to being one man. This very culturally specific sense of kingship meant that the successors and army were free to make the power-compromise of naming Arrhidaios basileus with (at that time, possibly) another basileus-to-be in Alexander IV, and later for Antigonos to declare himself joint king with Demetrios.[125] It must be remembered that in Macedonia at the time of Philippos II's accession, there had been a notable tradition of several individuals claiming to be basileis over Macedonians.[126] Philippos II's domination of these other Macedonian kings did *not* come with any title change. For the Successors old enough to remember conditions under Philippos, including Antigonos and Antipatros, multiple basileis in Macedon was the norm from time immemorial. For those who were too young to have lived through Philippos' rise, such as Ptolemaios and Kassandros, these matters would at least have been common knowledge, with a reminder coming in the form of Alexander of Lynkestis accused of plotting to murder Alexander in 334.[127] Con-

---

121   Gruen 2018, 113–115.
122   Gruen 2018, 114.
123   Gruen 2018, 115. In fact, their generation that follows them also does not take up titles denoting specific limited areas of authority, either.
124   Gruen 2018, 115 and 117. On this matter of "Hellenistic Universalism," see also Strootman 2014, Meeus 2013, which illustrate the principle further that no diadoch was likely "satisfied" with their limited territorial holdings, and all likely had ambitions on more or all of the remainder of Alexander's realm.
125   On the former case, Iust. 13.4.5. Diod. 18.2 omits reference to the situation, but shifts to mentioning more than one king already by 18.23. On the joint kingship of Antigonos and Demetrios, see Diod. 20.53.2; Plut. Demetrios 18.1. See also the later joint kingship of the sons of Kassandros discussed in Anson 2014, 177.
126   Thuk. 2.99.2–6 notes that there were several basileis outside of the rule of the Argeads; Bengtson 1975, no. 186 is a 5th century inscription that strongly suggests a reading indicating the presence of several basileis within the factions of an Argead and a Lynkestian basileus.
127   Arr. an. 1.25.3. This conspiracy is usually phrased as Alexander wishing to usurp the throne of Alexander III. Whether it was a true conspiracy or fiction designed to destroy Alexander of Lynkestis,

sidering the Macedonian traditions of multiple basileis, one sees that Argead absolute authority over all Macedon and Macedonians was, in perspective, a very brief period of Macedonian history lasting only for a few decades, from the 340s to 323.[128]

Whereas there is no reason to posit hard territorial delineations for the Diadochi, the same cannot be said of Early Chinese ruler titles. Rulership in Early China was tied inextricably to territory. Early Chinese states, emerging out of the Western Zhou dynasty (1045–771) developed from semi-feudal enfeoffments of royal clan members and worthy vassals.[129] The very status of being a ruler in the Zhou cultural sphere was tied therefore to the legitimacy of the Zhou *wang*, whose authority "validated" territorial control. When Ying Zheng declared himself Emperor, there was a strong desire among some in his court to repeat this process of infeudations in the vein of remembered/ imagined Western Zhou practice.[130] Ying Zheng ultimately refused, preferring to emplace his own bureaucratic structures over conquered areas, but this is clearly not the approach taken by Xiang Yu or Liu Bang, who both distributed out lands similarly to the earlier Zhou practice.[131] The ties of Chinese rulers to their lands can be further illustrated through a brief look at Chinese ruler nomenclature: in the period under study, a Chinese ruler is identified by three components in a given title: First, the name of their territorial kingdom, second, their posthumous regnal name, and third, their rank. Jin Wen *Gong* 晋文公 (r. 636–628) is therefore the *Gong* of Jin whose posthumous regnal name was Wen. Qin Shi *Huangdi* did away with regnal names, but his name still bears out the significance of the territorial name: He was the *Huangdi* of Qin, with "First" in place of a regnal name. The state names were ancient, deriving from an earlier era over 500 years before the fall of Qin. The name of the territorial state was a clear signifier known to everyone and tied into the name of the ruler in a way not seen in Macedon. While very early Chinese infeudations could completely change territories, this was arguably no different than early poleis, where a few in specific circumstances could "move", but were otherwise rooted in place.[132]

Hellenistic kingdoms were fundamentally personal rather than institutional, even in the terms used to label them – *basileia* (rulership) and *pragmata* (affairs [of the ruler]).[133] Beyond these fundamentally personal terms for the dominions of rulers which

the nobility of Lynkos had once had their own kings and contended against the Argeads in prior eras.

128   Though later kings like the Antigonids would rule alone in Macedon later, they never had control of the larger Macedonian empire and its own segments of Macedonians abroad, making the situation distinct.

129   For a comparative study of Greek and early Chinese traditions of kingship, which examines how early Chinese rulership was tied to recognition by the figure of the *wang* who distributed land to worthy vassals in the Western Zhou period, see Christopher 2022, 89–146.

130   Sima Qian, *Shiji*, 6:237–239 and 6:254–255.

131   Sima Qian, *Shiji*, 7:315–317; 8:365–366; 8:380.

132   On moving poleis and *bang*, see Christopher 2022, 170–173.

133   On this matter, see Capdetrey 2010 and Strootman 2013, 41 n. 6.

demarcated the boundaries of one from another, Edson and Plischke noted that later historians did *not* demarcate Macedonian states by name (i. e., how moderns refer to "The Seleucid Empire"), calling the entire lot of the post-Diadoch states as the lands or dominion of the *Macedonians*.[134] There was not, it would seem, much particular recognition of the partition of territory in the naming of administrations by particular basileis, save for the case of Egypt.[135]

10. Conclusion

This paper has touched on only a few of the comparative analyses one could pursue with these two periods, but even this limited look into the topic yields interesting results. As the volume this article is included in is oriented towards classical rather than sinological issues, I will only briefly summarize my sinological conclusions here: A study of the Chu-Han contention in light of the early Hellenistic period raises serious questions as to the efficacy of Qin bureaucratic structure in the new territories conquered by the First Emperor. It raises questions about the structures of Warring States governance outside of Qin; Qin bureaucratic structure did not bind bureaucrats to local areas and populations in the way that local rebelling nobility during the Chu-Han contention were bound to their ancestral claims. It also raises questions about the utility of Chinese historical periodization through the politically motivated understanding of Chinese history as a succession of dynasties. Lastly, it suggests *why* the rebirth of the Warring States period in the wake of Qin's conquests was so short-lived – it is yet another consequence of the early Chinese refusal to engage in collectivist activities which even the hyper-agonal Macedonian elites were able to engage in.

And what of Macedon and the Hellenistic Period? We have noted how Hellenistic sources conceive of the Macedonian dominion being taken as a singular large cultural whole. We have noted the Macedonian ideas and practices of kingship in the form of the basileus that has a tradition of multiple titleholders co-existing. The group of elites who survived the brief period of Argead ascendancy, were, in my view, eager to ensure that, with the Argead house gone, nobody (if not, of course, themselves as individuals) would take their place. The weakness of the Argead house combined with resentment at the autocratic direction of the institution of kingship that the Argeads had taken led to an opportunistic revolt of older Macedonian practices. Macedonian elites competed with each other by whatever means they could for influence, power, and authority, presumably just as the pre-Philippian Argeads had done previously, just on a vastly larger stage. The early Hellenistic period was thus a revolt of an older Macedonian

---

134 Edson 1958. See also Plischke 2017, 164–165.
135 Edson 1958, 164–165. And on the matter of Ptolemaios and his supposedly distinct 'separatism', see Meeus 2013.

mentality re-asserting itself: it was in full swing through 301, and the death of Antigonos at Ipsos confirmed, then, that, Argead masters notwithstanding, the Macedonian
Empire was alive and well.

It has been unfortunately beyond the scope of this short paper to handle topics of
comparing sources, examining the loaded conceptions of "culture" in each case, and
other matters that would no doubt add great depth to pursuit of a comparative study of
these eras and dynamics. Scholarly comparisons of the Hellenistic and Early Imperial
Chinese historical experiences are exceedingly rare, and this short contribution should
be seen as beginning a discussion rather than exhaustively resolving one.

Bibliography

Adams 2006: Adams, Winthrop L., The Hellenistic Kingdoms, in: G. Bugh (ed.), The Cambridge
    Companion to the Hellenistic World, Cambridge 2006, 28–51
Adams 2010: Adams, Winthrop L., Alexander's Successors to 221 BC, in: J. Roisman – I. Worthing-
    ton (eds.), A Companion to Ancient Macedonia, Malden 2010, 208–224
Anson 1988: Anson, Edward, Antigonos, the Satrap of Phrygia, Historia 37, 1988, 471–477
Anson 2004: Anson, Edward, Eumenes of Cardia. A Greek among Macedonians, Leiden 2004
Badian 1961: Badian, Ernst, Harpalus, The Journal of Hellenic Studies 81, 1961, 16–43
Barbantani 2007: Barbantani, Silvia, The Glory of the Spear. A Powerful Symbol in Hellenistic
    Poetry and Art. The Case of Neoptolemus 'of Tlos' (And Other Ptolemaic Epigrams), Studi
    Classici e Orientali 53, 2007, 67–138
Barbieri-Low 2021: Barbieri-Low, Anthony, Coerced Migration and Resettlement in the Qin Im-
    perial Expansion, Journal of Chinese History 5.2, 2021, 181–202 (doi:10.1017/jch.2019.1) last ac-
    cess: 20.5.2024
Beck 2021: Beck, Hans, Registers of 'the People' in Greece, Rome, and China, in: H. Beck –
    G. Vankeerberghen (eds.), Rulers and Ruled in Ancient Greece, Rome, and China, Cambridge
    2021, 193–224
Bengtson 1975: Bengtson, Hermann, Die Staatsverträge des Altertums. vol. 2: Die Verträge der
    griechisch-römischen Welt von 700 bis 338 v. Chr., Munich 1975
Billows 1990: Billows, Richard, Antigonos the One-Eyed and the Creation of the Hellenistic State,
    Los Angeles 1990
Boiy 2007: Boiy, Tom, Between High and Low. A Chronology of the Early Hellenistic Period,
    Frankfurt 2007
Bosworth 1980: Bosworth, Albert B., Alexander and the Iranians, The Journal of Hellenic Studies
    100, 1980, 1–21
Bosworth 1988: Bosworth, Albert B., Conquest and Empire. The Reign of Alexander the Great,
    Cambridge 1988
Bosworth 2002: Bosworth, Albert B., The Legacy of Alexander: Politics, Warfare, and Propaganda
    under the Successors, Oxford 2002
Bosworth 2006: Bosworth, Albert B., Alexander the Great, in: G. Bugh (ed.), The Cambridge
    Companion to the Hellenistic World, Cambridge 2006, 9–27
Brindley 2010/2011: Brindley, Erica, Representations and Uses of Yue Identity along the Southern
    Frontier of the Han, ca. 200–111 B. C. E., Early China 33, 2010/2011, 1–35

Brugsch 1871: Brugsch, Heinrich, Ein Dekret Ptolemaios' des Sohnes Lagi, des Satrapen, Zeitschrift für ägyptische Sprache und Altertumskunde 19, 1871, 1–13

Capdetrey 2010: Capdetrey, Laurent, Espace, territoires, et souveraineté dans le monde hellénistique. L'exemple du royaume séleucide, in: I. Savalli-Lestrade – I. Cogitore (eds.), Des rois au Prince: Pratiques du pouvoir monarchique dans l'Orient hellénistique et romain (IVᵉ siècle avant J.-C. – IIᵉ siècle après J.-C.), Grenoble 2010, 17–36

Cao – Liu 2020: Cao, Yang 曹阳 – Liu, Yanqing 刘彦青, Jiyan yu 'Xiang Yu Benji' de Wenxuexing renshi: Jianlun yuanshi sucai dui Shiji wenben fengge yingxiang 记言与《项羽本纪》的文学性认识. 兼论原始素材对《史记》文本风格的影响 [Recorded Dialogue and the 'Basic Annal of Xiang Yu': On the Influence of Original Materials on the Textual Style of the Records of History], Journal of Weinan Normal University 35, 2020, 25–33

Coblentz 2019: Coblentz, David K., Macedonian Succession. A Game of Diadems, Diss. Washington 2019

Cohen 2013: Cohen, Getzel M., The Hellenistic Settlements in the East from Armenia and Mesopotamia to Bactria and India, Los Angeles 2013

Chang 2007: Chang, Chun-shu, The Rise of the Chinese Empire I: Nation, State, and Imperialism in Early China, ca. 1600 B. C.–A. D. 8, Ann Arbor 2007

Christopher 2022: Christopher, Jordan T., Periphery Triumphant. The Pioneer Kingdoms of Macedon and Qin, Diss. Münster 2022

Degen 2018: Degen, Julian, Alexander III., Dareios I. und das speererworbene Land (Diod. 17, 17, 2), Journal of Ancient Near Eastern History 6, 2018, 53–95

Dull 1983: Dull, Jack, Anti-Qin Rebels. No Peasant Leaders Here, Modern China 9, 1983, 285–318

Edson 1958: Edson, Charles, Imperium Macedonicum. The Seleucid Empire and the Literary Evidence, Classical Philology 53, 1958, 153–170

Errington 1970: Errington, Robert M., From Babylon to Triparadeisos. 323–320 B. C., The Journal of Hellenic Studies 90, 1970, 49–77

Erskine 2002: Erskine, Andrew, Life after Death. Alexandria and the Body of Alexander, Greece and Rome 49, 2002, 163–179

Fraser 1996: Fraser, Peter M., Cities of Alexander the Great, Oxford 1996

Fraser 2000: Fraser, Peter M., Lycophron, in: S. Hornblower – T. Spawforth (eds.), Who's Who in the Classical World, Oxford 2000, 895–897

Funke 2005: Funke, Peter, Philippos III. Arrhidaios und Alexandros IV. 'von Amun auserwählt', Gerión Anejos 9, 2005, 45–56

Gehrke 2013: Gehrke, Hans-Joachim, The Victorious King. Reflections on the Hellenistic Monarchy, in: N. Luraghi (ed.), The Splendors and Miseries of Ruling Alone. Encounters with Monarchy from Archaic Greece to the Hellenistic Mediterranean, Stuttgart 2013, 73–98

Gorre 2009: Gorre, Gilles, Les relations du clergé égyptien et des Lagides d'après les sources privées, Leuven 2009

Gorre 2013: Gorre, Gilles, Self-Representation and Identity of the Egyptian Priests, in: E. Stavrianopoulou (ed.), Shifting Social Imaginaries in the Hellenistic Period, Leiden 2013, 99–114

Grainger 1990: Grainger, John D., Seleukos Nikator. Constructing a Hellenistic Kingdom, London 1990

Grainger 2017: Grainger, John D., Great Power Diplomacy in the Hellenistic World, London 2017

Green 1991: Green, Peter, Alexander of Macedon, 356–323 BC. A Historical Biography, Berkeley 1991

Gruen 2018: Gruen, Erich, The Coronation of the Diadochi, Karanos 1, 2018, 109–119 [Updated Republishing of Gruen, Erich, The Coronation of the Diadochi, in: J. Eadie – J. Ober (eds.), The Craft of the Ancient Historian, Maryland 1985, 253–272]

Habicht 1973: Habicht, Christian, Literarische und epigraphische Überlieferung zur Geschichte Alexanders und seiner ersten Nachfolger, in: Akten des VI. Internationalen Kongresses für Griechische und Lateinische Epigraphik, München 1972, Munich 1973, 367–377

Hadley 1974: Hadley, Robert A., Seleukos, Dionysus, or Alexander?, The Numismatic Chronicle, 7. Ser. 14, 1974, 9–13

Hammond 1998: Hammond, Nicholas G. L., Alexander's Newly Founded Cities, Greek, Roman, and Byzantine Studies 39, 1998, 243–269

He 1955: He, Ciquan 何兹全, Qin-Han shilüe秦漢史略 [A Brief History of the Qin and Han Periods], Shanghai 1955

Heckel 1988: Heckel, Waldemar, The Last Days & Testament of Alexander the Great. A Prosopographic Study, Stuttgart 1988

Heckel ²2016: Heckel, Waldemar, Alexander's Marshals. A Study of the Makedonian Aristocracy and the Politics of Military Leadership, London ²2016

Hölbl 2013: Hölbl, Gunther, A History of the Ptolemaic Empire, London 2013

Iliakis 2013: Iliakis, Michael, Greek Mercenary Revolts in Bactria. A Re-Appraisal, Historia 62, 2013, 182–195

Kinney 2004: Kinney, Anne B., Representations of Childhood and Youth in Early China, Stanford 2004

Ladynin 2007: Ladynin, Ivan A., Two Instances of the Satrap Stela. Tokens of the Graeco-Egyptian Linguistic and Cultural Interrelation at the Start of Hellenism?, in: P. Kousoulis – K. Magliveras (eds.), Moving across Borders: Foreign Relations, Religion, and Cultural Interactions in the Ancient Mediterranean, Leuven 2007, 337–354

Lehmann 2015: Lehmann, Gustav A., Alexander der Große und die "Freiheit der Hellenen". Studien zu der antiken historiographischen Überlieferung und den Inschriften der Alexander-Ära, Berlin 2015

Liu 2000: Liu, Xiaodong 劉曉東 (ed.), Ershiwu Bieshi 二十五別史 [Twenty-Five Other Histories], Jinan 2000

Loewe 2000: Loewe, Michael, A Biographical Dictionary of the Qin, Former Han, and Xin Periods (221 BC-AD 24), Leiden 2000

Meeus 2009: Meeus, Alexander, Alexander's Image in the Age of the Successors, in: W. Heckel – L. Tritle (eds.), Alexander the Great. A New History, Malden 2009, 235–250

Meeus 2013: Meeus, Alexander, Confusing Aim and Result? Hindsight and the Disintegration of Alexander the Great's Empire, in: A. Powell (ed.), Hindsight in Greek and Roman History, Swansea 2013, 113–147

Meeus 2018: Meeus, Alexander, Friendship and Betrayal: The Alliances Among the Diadochoi, in: T. Howe – F. Pownall (eds.), Ancient Macedonians in the Greek and Roman Sources: From History to Historiography, Swansea 2018, 103–136

Mehl 1980: Mehl, Andreas, Doriktetos Chora. Kritische Bemerkungen zum 'Speererwerb' in Politik und Völkerrecht der hellenistischen Epoche, Ancient Society 11, 1980, 173–212

Nienhauser 1994–2020 (Ongoing): Nienhauser Jr., William H. (ed.), The Grand Scribe's Records, Bloomington 1994–2020 (Ongoing)

Plischke 2017: Plischke, Sonja, Persianism under the early Seleukid Kings? The Royal Title 'Great King', in: M. J. Versluys – R. Strootman (eds.), Persianism in Antiquity, Stuttgart 2017, 163–176

Sachs – Wiseman 1954: Sachs, A. J. – Wiseman, D. J., A Babylonian King List of the Hellenistic Period, Iraq 16, 1954, 202–212

Sanft 2018: Sanft, Charles Theodore, The Qin Dynasty, in: P. Goldin (ed.), The Routledge Handbook of Early China, London 2018, 146–159

Selbitschka 2015: Selbitschka, Armin, Early Chinese Diplomacy. 'Realpolitik' versus the So-called Tributary System, Asia Major Third Series 28, 2015, 61–114

Shibata 2013: Shibata, Noboru柴田昇, Shiki kou-u hongi kou '史記' 項羽本紀考 [A Study on Shiji Xiang Yu Benji], Aichikonantanki University Minutes 42, 2013, 1–12

Strootman 2013: Strootman, Rolf, Dynastic Courts of the Hellenistic Empires, in: H. Beck (ed.), A Companion to Greek Government, Hoboken 2013, 38–53

Strootman 2014: Strootman, Rolf, Hellenistic Imperialism and the Ideal of World Unity, in C. Rapp – H. A. Drake (eds.), The City in the Classical and Post-Classical World: Changing Contexts of Power and Identity, Cambridge 2014, 38–61

Tarn 1921: Tarn, William W., Heracles, Son of Barsine, The Journal of Hellenic Studies 41, 1921, 18–28

Tarn – Griffith ³1952: Tarn, William W. – Griffith, Guy T., Hellenistic Civilization, New York ³1952

Watson 1993: Watson, Burton, Sima Qian. The Records of the Grand Historian. Han Dynasty I, Revised Edition, New York 1993

West 2006: West, Stephanie, Lycophron, in: N. G. Wilson (ed.), Encyclopedia of Ancient Greece, London 2006, 433–435

Xue – Zhu 2021: Xue, Congjun 薛从军 – Zhu, Zhaoyuan 祝兆源, Lun Fan Zeng Zhengzhi Celüe 论范增政治策略 [On Fan Zeng's Political Stratagems], Journal of Weinan Normal University 36, 2021, 38–44

Yoshinami 1978: Yoshinami, Takashi, Shin-Kan taikokushi kenkyui 秦漢帝国史研究 [Historical Research on the Qin and Han Empires], Tokyo 1978

Zahrnt 1996: Zahrnt, Michael, Alexanders Übergang über den Hellespont, Chiron 26, 1996, 129–147

Jordan T. Christopher is a Lecturer in the Department of Classics and Archaeology at Loyola Marymount University. He completed his PhD in 2022 at the University of Münster (formerly WWU), in the Seminar für Alte Geschichte, under Hans Beck and Armin Selbitschka. His work focuses on comparative approaches to the study of Ancient Greece and Rome and Early China. More specifically, he analyzes the intersections between cultural beliefs and political practices in these cultures. His dissertation, *Periphery Triumphant: The Pioneer Kingdoms of Macedon and Qin*, traced the rise of Argead Macedon and Qin as political entities facing parallel challenges in vastly different cultural environments. The revised manuscript has just been contracted with Cambridge University press to be published as part of their new series: *Antiquity in Global Context*.

Early Hellenistic Royal Portrait Concepts
"Zeitgesicht", Differences and Civic Portraiture

RALF VON DEN HOFF

Abstract: Between Alexander's death and the late 3rd century BC, a distinctive royal portraiture came into being in the Mediterranean world. While the identification and the messages of many royal portraits in various visual media of this period have been extensively studied, comparative approaches that focus upon broader differences and similarities between the royal dynasties and regions and that also include civic portraiture are rare. It is the aim of this paper to lay further ground for such an approach by comparing 'portrait concepts' of the royal and civic portraiture of the early Hellenistic period and by studying interpictorial relations of the different design of the portraits' faces and hairstyles.

As a result, besides local, traditional portrait concepts such as in Egypt, in the early Hellenistic period, male royal portraiture appears rather homogeneous as far as the diademed portraits' hairstyles and beardless appearance as well as the basic distance to the portraits of Alexander the Great are concerned. Homogeneity was even more obvious in female portraiture. Similarities to civic portrait concepts are undeniable. A change can be observed from the dynamic, 'live like' presentation of the Diadochi to a calmer and more distanced portrait concept of their successors, which almost resulted in a royal "period face" ("Zeitgesicht"). However, already since Demetrios Poliorketes, motifs of wealth and luxury (*tryphe*) appeared. Furthermore, single motifs of assimilation to the portraiture of Alexander were applied ("Bildnisangleichung"). In the course of the 3rd century, the diversity and the distinctive charging of royal portraits were growing, which resulted in an increasing individuality and in different forms of un-bearded and bearded portraits. This was possibly a sign of growing needs for a competitive legitimation and distinction of the royal dynasties after the middle of the 3rd century BC.

1. Introduction

If one asks for the contribution of visual testimonia to the understanding of differences and sameness in early Hellenistic kingdoms, three answers immediately come to mind: First, since the "year of the kings" (306/305 BC), the diadem was the new and only visually explicit royal sign of the new Hellenistic rulers.[1] Related to the old Greek custom of giving fillets to winners in agonistic competitions, the fillet-like diadem visualized the idea of the victorious king who had conquered his "spear-won land" (*doryktetos chora*).[2] As recent studies have underlined, visually projecting the diadem back to Alexander (even though he did possibly wear it in particular situations, yet never in portraits created during his lifetime) symbolically intertwined victory, the present king, and the tradition of Alexander.[3] Second, the portraits of the diademed kings became one of the most visible and widespread features of royal presence and dominated the visual representation in almost every early Hellenistic kingdom.[4] This relates well to the fact that Hellenistic monarchy was a personal rule with strong charismatic elements.[5] Finally, the design and choice of royal portraits in different dynasties and regions was heterogeneous.[6] To mention only some examples, on coins, Lysimachos relied on the retrospective image of Alexander. The Ptolemies, however, preferred the portrait of the founder of their dynasty besides rare portraits of actual kings and queens, even though images of contemporary Ptolemies were widespread in sculpture, while, for the Seleukids, the image of the ruling king on coins was of higher importance than portraying kings in retrospect.

Hence, comparing royal portraiture in different kingdoms and dynasties allows conclusions regarding the notions of rule, competitiveness, tradition, and presence in royal representation. It is the objective of this paper to lay further ground for such a comparative approach during the first three generations of early Hellenistic kings until around 220/210 BC. I will argue that, besides the separate comparison of particular visual records, the comparison of "portrait concepts" allows bridging differences in media and embedding royal portraiture in the visual culture of early Hellenistic portraiture as a whole.

1   Smith 1988, 34–38; Lichtenberger et al. 2012; Haake 2014.
2   Lehmann 2012; Lichtenberger 2012; Mileta 2012. – However, the distinction of diadems and victory fillets in Hellenistic portraiture needs reevaluation due to possibly 'diademed' portraits of athletes: Kazakidi 201, particularly 282 no. 40.E1/Γ7 pl. 7.
3   Dahmen 2012; Haake 2012.
4   Smith 1988; Ma 2010.
5   Gehrke 1982; cf. Wiemer 2017.
6   Smith 1988 is still the comprehensive reference work for Hellenistic royal portraiture; see now also Pangerl 2021 (restricted to portrait coins). – For single dynasties and regions: Fleischer 1991; von den Hoff 2021 (Seleukids); Kyrieleis 1975; Ashton 2001; Stanwick 2002; Lorber 2014; Queyrel 2019; von den Hoff 2021 (Ptolemies); Queyrel 2003; Gans 2006; von den Hoff 2011; Andreae 2015 (Attalids); Michels 2009; de Callataÿ 2009 (Kappadokia, Bithynia, Pontos); Dumke 2012; Mittag 2013 (Baktria); Caccamo Caltabiano et al. 1997 (Syracuse).

2. Early Hellenistic royal portraits: conditions

The visual image of a Hellenistic king consists of his visual representations – those are his portraits – in different media.[7] Speaking of royal portraiture, this includes portraits of the king's wife, children, and relatives. Royal portraits were neither necessarily "true likenesses", nor the product of pure propaganda, nor regularly products of the "king's will". Rather, they were media of a reciprocal communication related to how the king should be and was visible in public.[8] This is due to the typical conditions of the production and use of media of royal portraits in the Hellenistic world.[9]

A political community, a group or an individual could set up a statue of a king in order to honor him, to dedicate his image to the gods, or to participate in a royal cult. This happened locally and without central organization; the royal family itself rarely initiated (let alone controlled) royal statues. Small-scale portrait statuettes, used in houses or sanctuaries, or portraits on finger rings – even portraits decorating metal or clay vessels – could evoke an ideal nearness or allegiance to a king, but they did not rely on official commissions, even though they sometimes followed identical models.[10]

The most widespread royal portraits were those on coins.[11] In the late 4th century, this was a revolution. Ancient Greece had not been familiar with numismatic portraits of human beings. Rather, on Greek coins, divine images had been the rule. After Alexander, the king's portrait head replaced them on the coins' obverses.[12] Through it, royal portraits fulfilled a new need for guaranteeing currency value.[13] In addition to portraits in other media, this resulted in a high visibility and symbolic elevation of the king to a figure similar to the gods.

Coins could be issued by poleis, but the most valuable ones were issued under royal supervision.[14] However, in contrast to what we know from Roman emperors since Augustus, Hellenistic kings did not regularly enforce the spread of official portrait models, which, even far away from the court, were copied on coins and in the round alike.[15] Hence, coin portraits of a king or queen could differ in different mints, on globally spread silver issues, on more locally or regionally used bronze coins and on special gold emissions. These differences concern, for example, physiognomic details, motifs of the hairstyle, attributes, or inscriptions. However, we can observe simultaneous changes of

---

7   Ma 2010, 149–154.
8   Ma 2010, 158.
9   For the following: Ma 2010, 154–161.
10 Statuettes: Thomas 2002; von den Hoff – Azoulay 2017, 189–190; cf. Svenson 1995. – Finger rings and other small-scale portraits: Schreiber 2014/2015; Galbois 2018. – Cf. also seals: Kyrieleis 2015.
11 Cf. Ma 2010, 151–152, 161; Lorber 2014.
12 Kroll 2007; cf. Lorber 2014, 115–117; in a wider perspective: Papaefthymiou 2021.
13 Cf. Lorber 2014, 118.
14 Ma 2010, 161 ('sans besoin d'initiative d'autres acteurs que le roi'), is possibly too strict.
15 Smith 1988, 30–31; Ma 2010, 161–163.

the visual appearance of a royal portrait across different mints.[16] This is pointing to procedures that were officially framed, even though not necessarily centrally organized. Furthermore, the series of typologically identical coin portraits of Ptolemaios I from 304 to the late Hellenistic period in many regions of the Ptolemaic empire testifies to a high degree of acceptance of an almost uniform royal image.[17] Apart from this, already in the 3rd century, we observe punctual typological relations between royal portraits on coins, in reliefs and in the round. Clear replicas of Ptolemaic portraits in the round appear during the 2nd century BC.[18] This requires the existence of exemplary models, available for different workshops, by whatever means they were disseminated. Hence, we do not know how exactly the similarities and the differences of the portraits of a specific king or queen came into being, but both existed. Admittedly, it is rather unclear how exactly differences in portrait design were related to different messages, let alone how a message precisely reached a viewer using a coin. However, coin portraits – as well as other portraits – were public images. They were both, carefully designed and elaborately worked out, no matter how intensively they were looked at. Together with the observations mentioned above, this leads to the conclusion that neither random design, nor a complete independency of different workshops were the leading factor of the production of royal portraits. On the other hand, a completely consistent and centralized organization of royal portrait representation in the early Hellenistic period is also unlikely.

3. Portrait concepts: methodology

In order to cope with these conditions of an officially framed freedom of choice, one has to look at those features of the royal portraits of *one* king or queen that were similar in different media. This will allow identifying the crucial elements of his/her representation, and it could result in constructing something like his/her ideal image. This image might have existed physically as a kind of "Urbild". However, as mentioned above, this was rather unlikely in the late 4th and 3rd century BC. Instead, the ideal image has to be conceived as a heuristic concept in order to virtually imagine what was typical for the visual imagination of a specific royal person in different portrait media. As already described in a recent article,[19] I will call this ideal portrait a "portrait concept". The "portrait concept" stands for the 'components of the visual design tying together

---

16   Fleischer 1991, 31–34; von den Hoff 2021, 175–176 (Antiochos III); Fleischer 1991, 44–52; Kovacs 2022, 406–411 (Antiochos IV).

17   Lorber 2014, 118; von den Hoff – Azoulay 2017, 191–192.

18   Stanwick 2002, 57; von den Hoff – Azoulay 2017, 171–174, 192–193; Queyrel 2019, 213–217; von den Hoff 2021, 174–175.

19   von den Hoff 2021, 165–166.

portraits of a single king' or of another member of the dynasty including typological, iconographical, physiognomic, and mimic features, traditions and conventions.[20]
It must be made clear here that a portrait concept, even though it is an imagination,
can only be perceived in particularly representative portraits on coins or in the round
today, and that a portrait concept could change over time.

In order to understand fundamental relations and differences of portraits of *different* royal personnel in different periods, regions or dynasties, the approach has to be
comparative. Portrait studies already provide a terminology, a methodology and some
semiotic schemata. As we know, for example, from the Roman imperial period, two or
more portraits that are identical in a high number of motifs are called replicas. They
were copied from the same, physically existing model ("Urbild"), which was accessible by plaster casts. Portraits of such a degree of typological identity depict the same
person and constitute a "portrait type".[21] However, as mentioned above, in this strict
sense, copying and portrait types did not exist before the 2nd century BC. Hence, one
has to be careful in applying the concept of "portrait types" to earlier periods. In the
3rd century BC, media as well as political preconditions of ruler portraits were different
from the Roman imperial world.

However, we know of interpictorial relations between portraits of different persons.[22]
The portraits of Augustus' intended and real successors stand out due to clear motif relations to the portraits of the first princeps. This phenomenon is called "Bildnisangleichung" (portrait assimilation);[23] it did not illustrate biological kinship, but was aimed
at the symbolic legitimation of succession by creating a visual "community" of those
belonging to the *domus Augusta*. "Bildnisangleichung" as a claim of succession also
appeared in the Hellenistic period. Examples are the imitation of Alexander's portraits
or the portraits of members of the same philosophical "school".[24]

On the other hand, in Roman imperial portraiture, also simple citizens adopted the
hairstyles of imperial portraits. Usually, we call this "Modefrisur" (fashion hairstyle),
and the fashion is usually set by the imperial family.[25] Even the physiognomies of por-

20   von den Hoff 2021, 165. This concept is borrowed from Landwehr 1998, who used it in order to
      describe visual traditions in Roman ideal sculpture.
21   Boschung 1993; Fittschen 1999, 10–12; Fittschen 2010, 226; Fittschen 2015.
22   For recent methodological reflections on interpictoriality/intericonicity see Dorka Moreno 2019,
      32–42; Hijmans 2022. These studies open up necessary discussions concerning the meaning of
      similarities of images as such.
23   Massner 1982; Boschung 1993; Fittschen 2010, 236–239; Fittschen 2011; Fittschen 2015, 65; Fittschen
      2017, 20 n. 136; Boschung 2021, 201–204.
24   Smith 1991, 35; von den Hoff 1994 (philosophers); Fleischer 2002, 67–71; Kovacs 2022 (Alexan-
      der imitations). As for the *imitatio Alexandri*, Hijmans 2022 now would allow questioning direct
      assimilation; in reference to Dorka Moreno 2019, he rather suggests a 'common ground' of similar
      signs, which "anchor" the images' meaning. For the *imitatio Alexandri* in coin portraits see Martin
      Kovacs in this volume.
25   Cf. Franken 1994; Schröder 2012, 502–510; Schröder 2020.

traits of the *domus Augusta* were imitated, which we call "Zeitgesicht" (period face).[26] These two phenomena are chronological indicators describing 'prevailing types of appearance' typical of the time.[27] Clearly, they were not meant as claims of imperial succession or of belonging to the imperial court. Rather they were visual statements of the civic acceptance of the principate, of being part of this political system and of nearness to the social establishment.[28] It should be emphasized that what portraits present in terms of "Zeitgesicht" and "Modefrisur", is formally almost indistinguishable from "Bildnisangleichung". For sure, the multiplication of "Bildnisangleichung" could lead to "Zeitgesicht". However, why were "Bildnisangleichung" and "Zeitgesicht/Modefrisur" similar as interpictorial phenomena, but different in meaning?[29] How could we distinguish comparable formal relations in Hellenistic royal and civic portraits?[30]

Other Greek examples add to the complexity of these interpictorial phenomena. The civic portrait head of one of the almost 2000 preserved late Classical Attic grave reliefs, today in Copenhagen,[31] resembles the portrait head of Demosthenes[32] in many details of the hairstyle, beard and physiognomy – even though both heads are no replicas. Demosthenes honorific statue was set up in Athens in 280/279 BC, around 30 years after the end of the Attic grave relief production. There was no kinship relation between a random Attic citizen and the honored politician Demosthenes. The formal relations cannot be a sign of an intentional direct assimilation ("Bildnisangleichung"), since no one cared for a portrait on a random grave relief in Athens, when designing Demosthenes' portrait. Another case of portrait similarity is the portrait of Metrodoros, a student of Epikuros, who around 280/270 BC received a statue in the *kepos* of the Epikureans.[33] Metrodoros' portrait resembles conventional heads on Attic grave reliefs from around 320/10,[34] even though different from those related to the portrait of

26   Zanker 1982; Fittschen 2010, 237–238; Schröder 2012, 502–510; Boschung 2021, 227–235.

27   Fittschen 2010, 237.

28   Zanker 1982.

29   Fittschen 2015, 65, now suggests to no longer use the term 'period face' because of its 'imprecision', cf. Fittschen 2017, 20 n. 136. This does not solve the problem described here. If the more precise term "Bildnisangleichung" is always 'based on a conscious individual decision' (Fittschen 2015, 65) – while Bosching 2021, 227 speaks of an 'eher unbeabsichtigte Wirkung' –, does this mean that every similarity between two portraits is meant as a direct assimilation of one to the other? What is the difference between the similarities of a portrait of C. Caesar and of a private portrait to those of Augustus? Cf. Dorka Moreno 2019, 32–42.

30   For the Attalid portraiture, Queyrel 2009 applied the concept of 'family resemblance', which is not without problems, in order to identify a Hellenistic royal portrait; cf. Fleischer 2005. – For the possible imitation of Hellenistic royal portraits in civic portraits cf. Schreiber 2014/2015, 265–267, and below n. 119 (Kypros).

31   Ny Carlsberg Glyptotek Inv. 1816: von den Hoff 1994, 55 with n. 21 fig. 16; Moltesen 1995, 111 no. 52; Bergemann 1997, 170 Naiskos no. 482.

32   Richter 1965, 215–223; Fittschen 1988, pl. 109–115; cf. von den Hoff 2009b; Raeck 2021.

33   Richter 1965, 200–203; von den Hoff 1994, 63–69.

34   Cf. Berlin, Staatliche Museen – Antikensammlung Inv. 1972.15: Scholl et al. 2012, 118 no. 63; Bergemann 1997, 175 Naiskos no. 630 pl. 75,3–4.

Demosthenes: long-bearded, with full hair and almost no motion of the calm face. In the Epikurean case, the idea behind this similarity seems obvious. Metrodoros was no Attic citizen, nor should he appear as a man of the time around 320/310, when he was still a child ("Zeitgesicht"). Rather, his portrait aimed at presenting him as a beautiful, conventional, middle-aged civic person lacking all emotional tension – like men living in Athens had been depicted for decades. This relates well to the emotional balance (*eudaimonia*) and the negation of references to political controversies, which were part of the Epikurean life model.[35] In contrast to this, Demosthenes' appearance related to engagement and physical tension appropriate for politically active citizens as they also appeared in Attic grave reliefs. Different portrait concepts were related to different meanings.

However, the use of an identical portrait concept could also result in an explicit reference: Around 260/250 BC, the hairstyle of the portrait of another Epicurean philosopher, Hermarchos, was explicitly related to the appearance of the portrait of Epikuros, his predecessor and highly worshipped founder of the school, which proves the existence of "Bildnisangleichung" in early Hellenistic portraiture.[36]

What can we conclude methodologically from these observations for a comparative approach to early Hellenistic royal portraits? Formal, interpictorial similarities and differences between portraits of different individuals or groups relate to and evoke an ideal nearness or distance between the depicted human beings. However, the semantics of these relations are not self-evident. Before talking about (intentional) "Bildnisangleichung" or (period-related, fashionable) "Zeitgesicht" as phenomena with a definite meaning, the formal relations need a clear description. Hence, identifying and comparing "portrait concepts" and links to these concepts, as defined above, is a valid basis for detecting similarities and differences between royal portraits of different dynasties and contemporaneous other portraits, as will be presented in the following parts of this paper. This will lay ground for understanding the visual system in which royal portraits were designed and have to be explained. In order to understand Hellenistic royal portrait representation as a visual system,[37] many recent studies have analyzed the portraits as a whole, including body types, attributes, inscriptions and, on coins, the combination of images on obverse and reverse.[38] In contrast to this, in the following, only the portrait heads itself will be studied including their physiognomies, pathognomies (mimic motion)[39] and hairstyles. This will allow additional and com-

---

35   von den Hoff 1994, 82–83; Zanker 1995, 118.

36   Richter 1965, 203–206; von den Hoff 1994, 78–82.

37   Basic insights were already expressed by Smith 1988; Fleischer 1996 and Fleischer 2002; cf. von den Hoff 2009a; von den Hoff 2021.

38   For portraits on coins, Lorber 2014 is exemplary in this sense; for some body types see Masséglia 2013, 19–47.

39   For this terminology: Giuliani 1986.

plementary results regarding the imagination of the royal figures in relation to other, particularly civic portraits of the early Hellenistic period.

4. Seleukid portrait concepts

The Seleukid portrait representation started with Seleukos I's posthumous coin portraits and a lifetime sculptural portrait known by an early Augustan copy from the "Villa dei Papiri" in Herculaneum (fig. 1).[40] The diadem defines Seleukos' portrait concept together with the clean-shaven face and the individual, lifelike, and energetic appearance of a man aged about 50 or more, testified by deep lines in the face and a reclining hairline. The hair leaves the ears uncovered.

The portraits of his successor, Antiochos I (fig. 5), followed a slightly different concept.[41] Still clean-shaven, with short hair and wearing a diadem, the hairline above the forehead is now full and regular. Individual features of a man aged of about 40 are visible. However, Antiochos' portrait was rather that of a quiet, less energetic and more distanced man.

His successors Antiochos II (fig. 16) and Seleukos II as well as Antiochos Hierax followed up on this line, as far as the hairstyle and the quiet appearance are concerned, even though they were depicted as younger men. Mimic tensions disappeared completely. The early portraits of Antiochos III do not reveal any fundamental changes, while the later portraits of Antiochos III turn to gaunt cheeks and a deliberately individual, naturalistic outfit.[42] Apart from bearded portraits, which are discussed below, coins struck under Antiochos Hierax and representing himself or Antiochos I are another interesting phenomenon of Seleukid portraits of the 3rd century.[43] Above the portrait's forehead, an Alexander-like *anastole* was inserted in order to underline a visual relation to the Macedon king. Later assimilations of Seleukid male royal portraits to the images of their predecessors and relatives ("Bildnisangleichung") have already been observed.[44]

---

40 Smith 1988, 73–74; Fleischer 1990; Fleischer 1991; cf. von den Hoff 2021, 166–169. – For the coinage: SC I; cf. now Pangerl 2020, 57–59 no. 107–109, 107, 110, 90 no. 185–186 (Seleukos I); 90–92 no. 187–191 (Antiochos I); 92–93 no. 193–194 (Antiochos II); 93–94 no. 196–199 (Seleukos II).

41 von den Hoff 2021, 170–171, also for the following remarks. – The diademed portrait head in Florence, Galleria degli Uffizi Inv. 1914.54, could well be a Roman imperial copy of a portrait of a 3rd century Seleukid king: Smith 1988, 83, 161 no. 32 pl. 26,1–3, *pace* Fleischer 1991, 196. – It still remains open if the remnants of a royal bronze statue from Kal-e Chendar, today in Tehran, National Museum of Iran Inv. 2477, depict a 3rd century Seleukid: Smith 1988, 173 no. 95 pl. 57,1; Lindström 2021.

42 von den Hoff 2021, 175–176; cf. Martin Kovacs in this volume.

43 Mørkholm 1991, 124 no. 397 pl. 26; Fleischer 1991, 21–22 pl. 12c; Salzmann 2012, 359, 378 fig. 74; Pangerl 2020, 95–96 no. 199–200; Kovacs 2022, 396–400 fig. 106; cf. Sonja Richter and Martin Kovacs in this volume.

44 Fleischer 1991, 128–129; Fleischer 2002; cf. von den Hoff 1994, 51.

5. Ptolemaic portrait concepts

The knowledge of Ptolemaios I's portrait concept is based on coin portraits (fig. 2), some already on emissions from the late 4th century, and on sculpted portraits.[45] It resembles Seleukos I. Ptolemaios Soter, wearing the diadem and short hair, appears with a clean-shaven, wrinkled face. The reclining hairline testifies to his age, and signs of energy and individuality are clearly visible. His portraits in the round, created not before the 3rd century, rejuvenated his outer appearance.[46] On the other hand, his coin portraits remained the "back bone" of Ptolemaic coin portraiture until the late Hellenistic period; possibly some of these coin portraits of Ptolemaios I adopted features of the reigning kings and vice versa, which would be a sign of "Bildnisangleichung".[47]

Energy, age and individuality receded in the portraits of Soter's successors, Ptolemaios II Philadelphos (fig. 6) and Ptolemaios III Euergetes (fig. 7), as witnessed by coin portraits and portraits in the round.[48] This could have been due to their young age when they took over the reign, but it remained unchanged until they died aged over 60. Hence, after 285/0 BC, the early Ptolemaic diademed portrait concept was rejuvenated. Like in the case of Antiochos II and Seleukos II, the almost regular hairline above the forehead and the lack of signs of energy and mimic motion contribute to a calm and distanced appearance. On the other hand, the rather fleshy, more rounded faces of Ptolemaios II and III add the specific notion of *tryphe* to the Ptolemaic portraits of the 3rd century.[49]

An alternative Ptolemaic portrait concept in Egypt was the statue in the dress of an Egyptian pharaoh. In the late 4th and most of the 3rd century BC, such portraits were clearly distinct from those with Greek hairstyles and physiognomies as described above.[50] To date, no clear evidence exists for early "hybrid" portraits combining Greek-style hair above the forehead with a typically Egyptian headdress, like the Nemes, as known from later statues since Ptolemaios VI.[51] Apparently, in the first generations of Macedonian rule in Egypt, pharaonic traditions were presented as rather independent

45   Kyrieleis 1975, 4–16; Smith 1988, 90; von den Hoff 2021, 166–169. – For the coinage: Lorber 2014, 114–118; CPE; Pangerl 2020, 171–174 no. 440–443, 448–449.
46   von den Hoff 2021, 166 n. 14.
47   Fleischer 2002, 65–67; Lorber 2014, 120–132; CPE, 120, 171.
48   Kyrieleis 1975, 17–42; Smith 1988, 91; Queyrel 2002; Queyrel 2009; Lorber 2014, 120–127, 140–147; Pangerl 2020, 174–175 no. 446–447, 450, 177–178 no. 452–454, 456; von den Hoff 2021, 169–174.
49   Cf. Lorber 2014, 122; von den Hoff 2021, 173 n. 47 with further bibliography. For the concept of "tryphe": Heinen 1983.
50   Ashton 2001; Stanwick 2002; Stanwick 2005; Albersmeier 2002.
51   Stanwick 2002, 50, 56–57, 61–62. It remains dubious if the "hybrid" portrait head of the Ptolemaic royal statue in Frankfurt, Liebieghaus, with Egyptian dress, Nemes and Greek-style hair, is indeed an image of Alexander. It rather does not belong to the early Hellenistic period, see Kovacs 2022, 151. – Cf. Kovacs 2022, 152–158 pl. 37,1, 3, for a possibly early Hellenistic Egyptian style statue with a Greek style portrait head.

Fig. 1 Seleukos I. Roman copy of the head
of a portrait statue (ca 305/4 BC). Naples,
Museo Archeologico Nazionale Inv. 5590.

Fig. 2 Ptolemaios I. Tetradrachm
(ca 290/80 BC). Berlin, Staatliche Museen
Münzkabinett – SMPK Object No. 18258950.

Fig. 3 Menandros. Roman copy of the head
of a portrait statue (ca 291/0 BC).
Venice, Seminario Patriarcale (plaster cast
Göttingen).

Fig. 4 Nikomedes I. Tetradrachm
(278–255 BC). Wien, Kunsthistorisches
Museum Münzkabinett Inv. GR 15918.

Fig. 5 Antiochos I. Tetradrachm (281 –261 BC). Wien,
Kunsthistorisches Museum Münzkabinett Inv. GR 20304.

from notions of Greekness. Towards an Egyptian audience, they were used particularly
in old Egyptian sanctuaries and in Upper Egypt in order to underline the locally based,
traditional legitimacy of the Pharaoh king.[52]

6. Antigonid portrait concept

Portraits of Antigonid rulers are less numerous than those of the Seleukid and Ptolemaic kings.[53] Shortly after 301 BC, or around 292/1 at the latest, Demetrios Poliorketes
was the first Antigonid king appearing on coins, at a time when he was slightly older
than 40 (fig. 12).[54] A Roman copy of his portrait in the round (fig. 15) and rare further
portraits attributed to him add to our knowledge of his portrait concept.[55] Demetrios
was regularly depicted diademed and beardless. His hair is short and leaves the ears
uncovered. Clear signs of aging are missing. Rather, his full cheeks are signs of his
youth; no mimic tension is perceivable. As such, in contrast to the contemporaneous,
early, energetic portraits of the Diadochi, Demetrios rather resembles the Seleukids

52   Stanwick 2002.
53   For Antigonid portrait representation: Wagner 2017, 157–171.
54   Newell 1927; Mørkholm 1991, 76–81 no. 169; 172–175 pl. 10; Pangerl 2020, 22–26 no. 22, 23–26;
      Wheatley – Dunn 2020, 15–21; cf. also Gregor Weber in this volume.
55   Naples, Museo Archeologico Nazionale Inv. 6149: Smith 1988, 64, 156 no. 4 pl. 4–5; von den Hoff
      2007a, 37–38 fig. 47; von den Hoff 2007b, 55 fig. 42. – A further possible portrait of Demetrios is
      in Rome, Musei Vaticani Inv. 10312: Smith 1988, 157 no. 9 pl. 10,1–2; Vorster 2004b, 121–123 no. 66
      pl. 85; cf. Smith 1988, 65–66; Wheatley – Dunn 2020, 15–16, 21–25.

and Ptolemies of the second generation. This was not only due to his real age. Plutarch later testifies to earlier records about his beauty in relation to his portraits and his royal qualities:

> Demetrios had features of rare and astonishing beauty, so that no painter or sculptor ever achieved a likeness of him. They had at once grace (*charis*) and strength (*baros*), fright (*phobos*) and beauty (*hōra*), and there was blended with their youthful eagerness a certain heroic (*heroike*) look and a kingly majesty (*basilike semnotes*) that were hard to imitate.[56]

Diodoros speaks of Demetrios' heroic appearance as a sign of his royal superiority.[57] Apparently, Demetrios' portraits were related to these attributions. However, his portrait concept could be modified significantly. On some coins minted after 290, his physiognomy was more pronounced and even fleshy (fig. 13) – adding something like a *tryphe* formula to his image before the Ptolemies did so.[58] Finally, for the first time in the history of Hellenistic royal portraiture, Alexander's typical *anastole*, the fountain-like hair raising above his forehead, was added to some of Demetrios' coin portraits (fig. 14)[59] in order to signify an explicit legitimation as a real successor of the comparably young and beautiful Macedonian king.[60]

In how far Antigonos II Gonatas, Demetrios' son and the Antigonid king since 277/6 BC, followed a particular portrait concept is hard to decide. His rare coin portraits were blended with iconographic features of the god Pan when a head with Pan's physiognomy wearing the royal diadem appeared on Gonatas' coins.[61] However, there is no reason to doubt that the short hair and the beardless face, common to all portraits of the successors of the Diadochi, were also typical for Antigonos Gonatas' representation.

---

56   Plut. Demetrios 2.2.
57   Diod. 20.92.3.
58   Newell 1927, no. 89, 144; Salzmann 2012, 356, 377 fig. 68a. – Demetrios and *tryphe*: Plut. Demetrios 41–42.
59   Newell 1927 no. 120, 156, 159. – Kovacs 2022, 196–197, mentions other features adopted from Alexander.
60   It still remains unclear if (or in how far) a Roman late Republican bronze statuette from Herculaneum, now in Naples, Museo Archeologico Nazionale Inv. 5026, reproduces a portrait statue(tte) of Demetrios Poliorketes: Smith 1988, 154 no. 10 pl. 70,5; Laubscher 1985, 336–337 pl. 68,1, 69,1; Marquardt 1995, 311–313 pl. 31,3. The head of the statuette resembles the short haired early Hellenistic royal portrait concept. However, the motion of the hair above the forehead is different from Demetrios' portraits and a feature of the god Pan, like the horns growing out of the hair.
61   Laubscher 1985, 341–346 pl. 71, 1–4; Panagopoulou 2020, 107–109; Kovacs 2022, 205–206 fig. 39; cf. Gregor Weber in this volume. – As for the 'Demetrios' statuette in Naples (see note before), it remains unclear, how the iconographies of Pan and of Antigonos Gonatas (?) are related in an early Hellenistic bronze statuette now in Berlin, Antikensammlung Inv. Fr. 2233: Smith 1988, 154 no. 19 pl. 71,7–8; Laubscher 1985, 333–345 pl. 66–67; Marquardt 1995, 320–321. Here, Pan's horns are fixed on the fillet. The individual physiognomy of the statuette's head could well be related to Pan. The human form of the legs indicates the representation of a human being, which then must be a king.

Fig. 6 Ptolemaios II. Head of a portrait statue (3rd century BC). Paris, Musée du Louvre Inv. Ma 4709.

Fig. 7 Ptolemaios III. Stater (246–222 BC). New York, American Nusmismatic Society Inv. 1944.100.77199.

Fig. 8 Philetairos. Tetradrachm (262–241 BC). Berlin, Staatliche Museen: Münzkabinett – SMPK Object No. 18269737.

Fig. 9 Philetairos. Roman copy of the head of a portrait statue (ca 270–240 BC). Naples, Museo Archeologico Nazionale Inv. 6148 (plaster cast Göttingen).

Fig. 10 Poseidippos. Roman copy of the head of a portrait statue (ca 260/50 BC). Geneva, Musée d'Art et d'Histoire Inv. MF 1330 6148. (plaster cast Bonn).

Fig. 11 Hieron II. (269–216 BC). Berlin, Staatliche Museen: Münzkabinett – SMPK Object No. 18203196.

7. Lysimachos' portrait concept?

Until recently, no portraits of Lysimachos, king of Thrace and Macedonia until 281 BC, had been convincingly identified. In 2008, Achim Lichtenberger, Helge Nieswandt and Dieter Salzmann argued that the longhaired, diademed, beardless portraits on local bronze coins from Lysimacheia should be identified as Lysimachos, who founded this city in 309/308.[62] The emission date of the coins is unclear, but good arguments exist in favor of an early date shortly after the foundation of the city and not after 300.[63] Before 2008, the Lysimacheia coin portraits had mostly been identified as Alexander the Great. The three authors argue that there was no clear relation between Lysimacheia and Alexander, and thus no reason to depict him on local coins. Rather Lysimachos was the city's *ktistes*, and portraits of *ktistai* were common on local coins. Furthermore, they underline the differences between the bronze coin portraits and the slightly later Alexander portraits on Lysimachos' silver coins. Indeed, images of *ktistai* appear on local coins, but also other images could appear, like portraits of kings not directly related to a city, or images of gods and heroes worshiped in this city. Furthermore, it is true that the horn of Zeus Ammon, essential for Alexander on Lysimachos' silver emissions, is missing in Lysimachaia. However, this attribute was not 'constitutive' for Alexander's portraits, let alone before 300/290, as Alexander images on early Ptolemaic coins prove.[64] Finally, as Martin Kovacs already observed, the design of the bronze coin portraits' hair is almost identical to Alexander's portraits on the later silver coins, Thus, typologically these are their immediate successors.[65] It was Lysimachos who put new portraits of Alexander on his silver coins since the early 3rd century BC, and these portraits were the most widespread icons of the Macedonian king. As such, they were also minted in Lysimacheia. Thus, there is no clear argument in favor of the idea that Lysimacheia put Lysimachos' portrait on its coins shortly after 308 BC and later, since 300/290 BC, changed this to a portrait of Alexander: Why shouldn't he have gone along with his own portraits? Rather, it seems convincing to place the Lysimacheia portraits within the general line of experimenting with coin portraits of Alexander before around 300, which can also be observed on Ptolemaic and "anti-Ptolemaic" Seleukid coins.[66] The bronze coins minted in Lysimacheia in the late 4th century testify to Lysimachos taking part in this competitive 'search for Alexander' in the city related to his own name and kingship.[67] Later, he remained the only Diadoch relying on Alexander's portrait on coins as a conceptual sign of legitimacy, rather than on his own portraits.

62   Lichtenberger – Nieswandt – Salzmann 2008.
63   For the chronology of Lysimachos' coins from Lysimacheia: Riedel 2016.
64   Dahmen 2012, 286–287; Lorber 2014, 112–114.
65   Kovacs 2022, 187 n. 323.
66   Dahmen 2012, 288; Lorber 2014, 112–114.
67   Cf. for Lysimachos' strategies of legitimation: Plischke 2011.

8. Bithynian portrait concept

Shortly after 280 BC, portraits of Bithynian kings appeared for the first time, when Nikomedes I put his image on coins (fig. 4).[68] His portrait concept was not a new one: a diademed, middle-aged man with short hair, leaving the ears uncovered. The profile line of his face and the bulging forehead demonstrate his energy. The wrinkles between his nose and chin add to his physical presence. This follows the portraits of the early Diadochi Seleukos I and Ptolemaios I, as Christoph Michels has pointed out.[69] However, it remains unclear why Nikomedes adopted this concept, which was already outdated when he came to rule. This was rather a demonstration of a concept of rule and royal "presence", similar to the Diadochi, than of claiming a clear relation to Seleukos I, who died before Nikomedes I became king.

9. Baktrian portrait concept

During the middle of the 3rd century BC, conflicts with Antiochos II lead to the independency of Diodotos I's Baktrian kingdom. His coin portraits are preserved.[70] His portrait concept comes as no surprise: a diademed head, beardless and with short hair leaving his ears uncovered. The regular line of the hair above the forehead, the lack of clear signs of age and the quiet appearance of the face do not relate to the Diadochi's portraits. Rather the similarities to Antiochos I's images are obvious. This points to the idea that Diodotos I aimed at imitating a contemporaneous Seleukid portrait concept. On the other hand, multiple coin portraits add a small *anastole* above his forehead. Such a motive could not appear more than once by accident. It has been argued that this was meant to relate Diodotos' portraits to Alexander's images in order to legitimate his claims of being an independent ruler in Macedonian tradition.[71] Similar visual strategies of "Bildnisangleichung" have been observed in coin portraits of Demetrios Poliorketes and of Antiochos Hierax.[72]

---

68   Mørkholm 1991, 130 no. 414–416 pl. 28; Michels 2009, 158–162; Pangerl 2020, 48–49 no. 86–88.
69   Michels 2009, 159.
70   Mørkholm 1991, 120–12 no. 374 pl. 24; Dumke 2012; von den Hoff 2013, 87; Pangerl 2020, 146 no. 358–360; Kovacs 2022, 434–438; cf. Alram 2009.
71   von den Hoff 2013.
72   See above n. 43 and 59.

10. Attalid portrait concepts

In Pergamon,[73] Philetairos, son of Attalos, had been the local representative of Lysimachos, later of Seleukos I, before he reinforced his independence since around 270 BC.
After his death in 263, Eumenes I, his adopted son, followed him, without taking the
diadem. Pergamon formally became a kingdom under Attalos I around 230 BC. The
first portraits of Attalids were posthumous images of Philetairos disseminated on Pergamene coins under Eumenes I (fig. 8).[74] Furthermore, a portrait of Philetairos, which
is typologically identical to the coin portraits, was copied in marble and was set up in
the late republican "Villa dei Papiri" in Herculaneum (fig. 9).[75] It cannot be decided
if the model of this copy was already created before Philetairos died (and where this
happened) or if it was a retrospective creation of his successor. However, according to
what we know about the portraiture of the 3rd century BC, a date around the middle of
the century, between ca. 270 and 240, is stylistically undeniable. Philetairos is beardless. He is wearing short hair that leaves his ears uncovered, like all other royal portraits
of this period. However, the hair above his forehead is in a very dynamic motion. This
is why one of the curls of hair was attached separately in the Roman copy. In contrast
to the more definite *anastole* in Baktrian portraits, Philetairos' hairdo is not enough to
suggest explicit relations to Alexander the Great.[76] Rather, it testifies to the imagination of a dynamic king. This is supported by the energetic turn of his head and by his
facial expression: He is pulling his eyebrows together, which was a conventional sign
of emotional activity and motion. Two further characteristics of Philetairos' portraits
are remarkable. He was more than 70 years old before his portrait was designed. Even
though his appearance is not unrealistically youthful, compared to the early Diadochi's
portraits, clear signs of his real age are avoided, while his mimic motion relates to the
Diadochi. Furthermore, Philetairos' rather fleshy, rounded face and neck adopted the
notion of wealthy *tryphe*, which characterized some earlier portraits of Demetrios Poliorketes on coins (figs. 13) and Ptolemaic (even though younger) portraits (figs. 6–7)
just in the period of the creation of the Attalid portrait head.[77]

---

73   For Attalid royal portraits: Queyrel 2003; Gans 2006; von den Hoff 2011; Andreae 2015.
74   Westermark 1961; Mørkholm 1991, 128–130 no. 409–410 pl. 27; Salzmann 2012, 377 fig. 70, 379
      fig. 76; Pangerl 2020, 59–62 no. 112–114.
75   Naples, Museo Archeologico Nazionale Inv. 6148: Smith 1988, 74–75, 159 no. 22 pl. 17; Queyrel
      2003, 74–78; von den Hoff 2011, 126; Grüßinger et al. 2011, 498–499 no. 5.7. (M. R. Hofter).
76   However, the arrangement of Philetairos' hair above the forehead is not too far from Pompeius'
      portrait of the 1st century BC (Junker 2007; Trunk 2008; Kovacs 2015, 53–57; Kovacs 2022, 54–55;
      Boschung 2021, 175–183), where a direct (even though not typologically correct) imitation of Alex-
      ander the Great's *anastole* is clear due to literary records (Plut. Pompeius 2.1).
77   Michels 2011, 135–136; von den Hoff 2011, 126; von den Hoff 2021, 174.

11. Further male royal portraits and iconographies

Royal portraits from other regions of the early Hellenistic world existed, of which only a selection can be discussed here.[78]

A bronze portrait head of Seuthes III, ruler of the Odrysians in Thrace, was found in 2004 in his tomb not far from Kasanlak in Bulgaria.[79] The portrait can be dated to the last decade of the 4th or the early 3rd century BC. Seuthes is not wearing a diadem, even though Diodoros later calls him a king.[80] He appears as a rather old man with long hair covering his ears and with a full beard.

Only by coins from Karystos on Euboia do we know of the portrait of a "nameless dynast"[81] of the middle of the 3rd century BC. In different emissions, the heads differ in detail, while the portrait concept is always the same as in the case of Antiochos I and II.[82] However, the *anastole* above the forehead was added in order to relate the portrait to Alexander the Great.

In Sparta, royal portraits did not appear on coins before Kleomenes III (fig. 17).[83] His portrait follows the diademed, short haired, beardless concept of a young king.

In Syracuse, multiple early Hellenistic royal portraits appeared on coins under Hieron II.[84] Beardless faces with a short and rather calm hairdo, which relate to the portrait concepts used in the Ptolemaic and Seleukid realm, were the male standard.[85] Hieron II (fig. 11) adopted the fleshy version of this portrait concept that we already know from the Ptolemies and from Philetairos. His son Gelon and his grandson Hieronymos followed up on this path appearing as young kings[86] like Kleomenes III, the 3rd century Seleukids and Ptolemies.

Early Hellenistic portraits of the kings of Kappadokia are preserved on coins.[87] As far as the attributes are concerned, the early images adopted local, Iranian concepts, which is comparable to the local pharaonic Ptolemaic portraits in Egypt. Greek por-

---

78   The portraiture of Pyrrhos of Epeiros, who does not appear on coins, still remains a problem in terms of identification and dates, cf. Smith 1988, 64–65, 156–157 no. 5–6 pl. 6–7; Winkes 1992; Brown 1995; Fleischer 1999, 555; von den Hoff 2007a, 39 fig. 50; Katsikoudes 2009.

79   Sofia, National Archaeological Museum: Saladino – Formigli 2012/2013; Lehmann 2022.

80   Diod. 18.4.2; 19.73.8.

81   Mørkholm 1991 157–158 no. 564 pl. 37; Salzmann 358 (no diadem). 378 fig. 71; Pangerl 2020, 38 no. 59; cf. now Kovacs 2022, 400–403.

82   Hence, Kovacs 2022, 402, identifies Antiochos I.

83   Grunauer-von Hoerschelmann 1978; Walthall 2013. – Kleomenes III: Mørkholm 1991, 149–150 no. 505 pl. 34; Palagia 2006, 209–210; Salzmann 2012, 349, 370 fig. 39. – Nabis: see below n. 94.

84   Caccamo Caltabiano et al. 1997; Lehmler 2005, 84–95; Günther 2011, 103–104; Salzmann 2012, 349 fig. 40–43, 366 fig. 20, 371 fig. 42–43, 370 fig. 40–41; Pangerl 2020, 17–20 no. 8–13, 15. On Hieron II as "Hellenistic king" cf. the chapter by Linda-Marie Günther in this volume.

85   Lehmler 2005, 90.

86   Cf. Salzmann 2012, 366 fig. 20, 371 fig. 42–43.

87   Simonetta 1977; Mørkholm 1991, 131–132; Michels 2009, 220–235; Pangerl 2020, 72–73 no. 144–146, 73 no. 147–148 (Ariarathes IV in Iranian and in Greek style).

Fig. 12 Demetrios Poliorketes. Drachm
(301–295 BC). New York, American
Nusmismatic Society Inv. 1944.100.13712.

Fig. 13 Demetrios Poliorketes. Tetradrachm
(289/88 BC). New York, American
Numismatic Society Inv. 1944.100.13767.

Fig. 14 Demetrios Poliorketes. Tetradrachm
(289/88 BC). New York, American
Numismatic Society Inv. 1944.100.13786.

Fig. 15 Demetrios Poliorketes. Roman copy
of the head of a portrait statue (305/300 BC).
Naples, Museo Archeologico Nazionale
Inv. 6149.

Fig. 16 Antiochos II. Tetradrachm (256–246 BC). Wien, Kunsthistorisches Museum: Münzkabinett Inv. GR 20364.

Fig. 17 Kleomenes III. Tetradrachm (227–217 BC). Berlin, Staatliche Museen Münzkabinett – SMPK Object No. 18200217.

Fig. 18 Meleagros. Head of the Roman copy of a statue made by Skopas of Paros (4th century BC). Rome, Musei Vaticani, Museo Pio Clementino Inv. 490.

Fig. 19 "Praying Boy". Statue of a boy (ca. 300 BC). Berlin, Staatliche Museen: Antikensammlung (bronze cast Berlin).

trait concepts did not appear before Ariarathes IV in the latest 3rd century, but details of identification are disputed.

In Pontos, royal portraits are not known before Mithradates III in the latest 3rd century.[88] Even though his portraits – and even more so those of his son and successor Pharnakes I – adopted the concept of short haired kings, they stand out for their beards and for their high physiognomic individualization. This was clearly a distinguishing feature, even though individualization as such was an important factor also for other kings of the latest 3rd century, like for Antiochos III in the Seleukid realm.

Finally, the bearded faces of the Pontic kings lead us to another feature of early Hellenistic male royal portraits. Despite the clear change from bearded to beardless portraits after Alexander, images of bearded kings did not disappear completely. This phenomenon has not been sufficiently explained, and a consistent explanation does not seem to exist.[89] Local traditions of bearded portraits remained in use for example in the portraiture of the Iranian Frataraka rulers.[90] For the first time in Seleukid portraiture, portraits of Seleukos II show a beard growing in time.[91] Simultaneously, Antiochos Hierax is wearing a long, later a short beard; Achaios is wearing a beard as an usurper.[92] Seleukid bearded portraits have been explained in relation to military activities.[93] In Macedonia, since 221, Philip V was consistently depicted with a beard, as were Nabis in Sparta and Prusias I in Bithynia.[94] What seems to be clear is that, after around 230/220, the beard became more familiar as a distinguishing iconographic feature and that the original 4th century meaning of a bearded portrait as a representation of a mature man was diversified since the late 3rd century. Different forms of beards now were related to more specific political and cultural conditions.

---

88   Mørkholm 1991 131 no. 420 pl. 28; de Callataÿ 2009; Michels 2009, 190–193; Pangerl 2020, 40 no. 69, 44 no. 70.
89   Lorber – Iossif 2009; Günther 2011, 99–100, 105–109; Pangerl 2020, 144 no. 350–351; Wünsch 2020; cf. already Smith 1988, 46 with n. 2; Queyrel 2004, 205. – Dieter Salzmann's study on varying forms of beards in Hellenistic royal portraiture, which he already presented in lectures since 2013/4, has not been published yet.
90   Mørkholm 1991 74 no. 146–147 pl. 8; Müseler 2018; Wünsch 2020, 278 fig. 4.
91   Mørkholm 1991, 124 no. 396 pl. 26; Lorber – Iossif 2009, 95–96.
92   Antiochos Hierax: Lorber – Iossif 2009, 96. – Achaios: Mørkholm 1991, 126 no. 403 pl. 27; Lorber – Iossif 2009, 104–105; Pangerl 2020, 100 no. 212; Wünsch 281 fig. 9.
93   Lorber – Iossif 2009.
94   Philip V: Mørkholm 1991, 135 no. 438 pl. 29. – For the portraiture of Philip V see lately Palagia 2017. – Nabis: Mørkholm 1991, 150 no. 511 pl. 35; Salzmann 2012, 357, 377 fig. 69; Pangerl 2020, 38 no. 61; Walthall 2013. – Prusias I: Mørkholm 1991, 130 no. 417 pl. 28; Michels 2009, 164–175; Pangerl 2020, 49–51 no. 88–94.

12. Female portrait concepts

Female royal portraits were not rare in the early Hellenistic period, as epigraphic evidence suggests.[95] However, only some early Hellenistic queens appear on coins and/or can be identified in preserved portraits in the round. This is true for the Ptolemaic queens.[96] We know portraits of Berenike I, wife of Ptolemaios I, of Arsinoë II, sister and wife of Ptolemaios II Philadelphos, and of Berenike II, wife of Ptolemaios III. The attributes differ (horn of Zeus Ammon, veil, *stephane*), and Berenike II has a fuller *tryphe* face than the others. Nevertheless, the female portrait concept was almost identical. Ptolemaic queens appear rather "ideal" with ageless faces, a melon coiffure and/or the hair parted at the center above the forehead. This was a convention for many female heads – human and divine alike – since the 4th century BC.[97] The ideal, anti-individualistic character of female Greek portraiture has often been observed,[98] and this holds true for the Ptolemaic queens as well. As 'ideal beauties'[99] they appear almost indistinguishable from each other and from civic portraits. Coin portraits of Arsinoë, Lysimachos' wife, from Ephesos and of Philistis from Syracuse confirm the homogeneity of the female portrait concept in the early Hellenistic period also in other regions of the Hellenistic world.[100] Even later Seleukid and possibly Attalid female royal portraits did not differ fundamentally.[101]

13. Comparative synthesis

To sum up the observations presented so far, it appears that the 4th century tradition of depicting rulers and kings as bearded men was still alive in the latest 4th century,[102] as attested by Seuthes III's portrait in Thrace. Different from other Greek royal portraits after Alexander, Seuthes III's portrait concept had been conventionally used during the 4th century in order to depict kings, military leaders, and citizens, like king Archidamos III from Sparta.[103]

---

95 Müller 2013; Martin 2011; Ager – Hardiman 2016; Carney 2021; Ager 2021.
96 Kyrieleis 1975, 78–102; Smith 1988, 89–92; Stanwick 2002, 55; Lorber 2014, 139–148; CPE *passim*; Pangerl 2020, 177–183 no. 451, 457–468; cf. also Albersmeier 2002.
97 Vorster 2004a, 423–428; Dillon 2010, 103–134.
98 Dillon 2007; Dillon 2010, 103–134; Masséglia 2013, 47; cf. Vlachogianni 2018.
99 Dillon 2007, 77.
100 Arsinoë: Mørkholm 1991, 93 no. 257–258 pl. 15. – Philistis: Caccamo Caltabiano et al. 1997, 65–82 pl. 3–23; Lehmler 2005, 90–95 fig. 34–35; Pangerl 2020, 20 no. 13, 205. Cf. also the chapter by Linda-Marie Günther in this volume.
101 For later, Seleukid queens: Meyer 1992/1993; Meyer 2020. – Identifications of Attalid queens are still hypothetical: Queyrel 2003, 263–275.
102 von den Hoff 2017.
103 Archidamos III: Richter 1965, 160; Fittschen 1988, 101–105 pl. 72; von den Hoff 2017, 284–286 fig. 13.

However, from the death of Alexander onwards, early Hellenistic royal portraits in Greece, Asia Minor, Egypt and later in Baktria and on Sicily adopted a different portrait concept: the beardless face with rather short hair, which leaves the ears uncovered (figs. 1–2; 5–9; 11–17). This also relied on a 4th century portrait concept, originally used for young men, heroes and gods (figs. 18–19).[104] Simultaneously, by adopting this portrait concept, the new kings took up the beardless fashion of Alexander's portraits, which after his reign became conventional also for portraits of mature citizens.[105] However, they avoided any explicit relation to Alexander's long hair and – except for singular cases – his typical *anastole*.[106] Hence, despite all political boundaries, rather than differences, similarity seems to be typical for early Hellenistic portraits of kings – and even more so of queens. This is even more striking, if one compares completely different civic portrait concepts of the early Hellenistic period, like the long-bearded philosophers or the short-bearded Attic orator-politicians like Demosthenes or Olympiodoros.[107]

On the other hand, differences in iconographic details on the chronological and on the regional level can be observed. After Alexander, the new Diadochi's anti-Alexander portrait concept of high aged and energetic "real live" kings with mimic tension made the beginning. Ptolemaios I and Seleukos I were its representatives (figs. 1–2).[108] Even though, immediately after Alexander's death, they experimented with portraits of the Macedon king on their coins, they then abandoned this strategy in favor of presenting their own, individual portraits. This was an additional measure to make Alexander become a distant and unreachable ideal figure. Disregarding Alexander's iconography in their own portraits was an explicit decision of the kings, as is confirmed by the fact that Alexander's portraits were both well-known everywhere and thus available for imitation and use – as Lysimachos' Alexander coins document –, and a possible choice for non-royal portraits. More precisely than in any king's portrait, Alexander motives were adopted in civic portraits of the late 4th and early 3rd century.[109]

In a broader perspective, the Diadochi's portrait concept perfectly fits into what we know about civic portraits of the time around and shortly after 300 BC, of which the portrait of the comic poet Menandros (fig. 3) is a good example. His statue was set up in Athens around 291/290, when he died at the age of over 50 years.[110] The rather wrinkled, beardless face, the slightly sunken cheeks and the bulging forehead vividly reflect

104   Smith 1988, 68.
105   Lorber – Iossif 2009, 87–89; cf. Schmidt 2007.
106   Smith 1988, 68: 'distinct or separate from Alexander's images'; 'avoid the anastole'; cf. von den Hoff 2009a, 51; cf. Martin Kovacs in this volume.
107   Philosophers: von den Hoff 1994; Zanker 1995. – Demosthenes: Richter 1965, 215–223; von den Hoff 2009b; Raeck 2021. – Olympiodoros: Richter 1965, 162.
108   Fleischer 2002, 61; cf. von den Hoff 2007b, 55; von den Hoff 2009a, 51; von den Hoff 2017, 295.
109   von den Hoff 1994, 51; von den Hoff 2013, 84, 89–93.
110   Fittschen 1991; Palagia 2005

his real age and are similar to the royal images. Thus, the Diadochi's portrait concept was also innovative insofar as its civic connotation is concerned.

Demetrios Poliorketes did not follow that line. In his portraits (figs. 12–15), his well-known youthful beauty was adopted, which created a clear contrast to the energetic and aged other kings. However, Demetrios' portrait concept was nothing new. The short, curly hair and the face without any wrinkles resembled portraits of athletes and images of mythical heroes of the 4th century BC (figs. 18–19).[111] In addition, Apollon appeared in the same manner already on Philip II's 4th century coinage.[112] Plutarch and Diodoros later called Demetrios' appearance heroic and dignified.[113] Further royal portraits of the period around 300 and shortly after, which cannot be identified with certainty, took up the same tradition.[114] On the other hand and in contrast to the Diadochi's concept, Demetrios youthful portraits could be loaded with an explicit reference to Alexander (*anastole*) and with signs of *tryphe* (figs. 13–14). Thus, the new (anti-Alexander) civic portrait concept of "mature men of action" stood in contrast to other, more athletic and heroic portraits of younger kings, who, however, only rarely tried to establish a more explicit relation to Alexander.

The period around 280 meant a break from this system. Old age features almost completely disappeared. This was due to the young age of some of the Diadochi's successors (figs. 6–7; 16–17). However, together with the youthful appearance, the new royal portraits lost their mimic tension and dynamic appearance like Demetrios' portrait had already done. They became calm, static and dignified, letting the kings appear serene and more distant to the real world.[115] This cannot be related exclusively to their young age. Ptolemies, Seleukids, early Baktrian kings and the kings of Syracuse as well as local rulers, like in Karystos, adopted this portrait concept. Apparently, this did not seem suitable for an older ruler like Philetairos in Pergamon. After 280, for him and for Nikomedes I in Bithynia (fig. 4) the Diadochi's concept of an energetic, more aged appearance was reactivated. However, this old concept could then be loaded with new references to luxury and wealth (*tryphe*) in Pergamon (figs. 8–9), as was the new calm and serene royal portrait concept in Egypt and Sicily (figs. 6–7; 11). As can be seen

---

111 Portraits of athletes, like Lysippos' Apoxyomenos (Maderna 2004, 351–353 fig. 319g-h) and the statue of Agias in Delphi (Spahlinger 2020, fig. 10–12; Geominy 2007, 69 fig. 71), or the slightly later "Berlin Athlete", the "Getty Athlete" and the "Praying Boy" (fig. 19; von den Hoff 2007a, 28–30 fig. 32–34). – Meleagros (fig. 18): Maderna 2004, 340 fig. 310–311. – Herakles: Kansteiner 2000. – Cf. Smith 1988, 66 ('a combination of fourth–century athletic and heroic models, with a slight admixture of individuality', 'Meleager type').

112 Le Rider 1977; Mørkholm 1991, 57 no. 55–56 pl. 4, 145 no. 545 pl. 36, 157 no. 563 pl. 37; Pangerl 2020 no. 20.

113 See above n. 56–57.

114 Smith 1988, 66, 157 no. 9–12 pl. 10–11, 158 no. 17 pl. 10–11, no. 19 pl. 27, 1–2, 162 no. 35 pl. 27,1–2; cf. Vorster 2004b, 122, and above n. 55 with a similar further portrait of Demetrios.

115 von den Hoff, 2021, 170–175; 188.

from this, since the second quarter of the 3rd century BC, the variation of portrait concepts became more flexible.

This tendency is confirmed by other variations of the young royal portrait concept.
After 280, Alexander's *anastole* was used more often as an additional royal sign, as
demonstrated by the portraits on coins of Antiochos Hierax, the portraits of Diodotos I in Baktria and of an unknown ruler in Karystos. Here, we observe "Bildnisangleichung". Philetairos' portrait (figs. 8–9) – initiated by him or by his successor – did not
imitate Alexander's hairstyle, but only its dynamic motion. Possibly, increasing struggles about succession and separation of kingdoms gave rise to such additional features
of distinction and thus to a visual legitimation. Nevertheless, this strategy remained
restricted to single motifs of Alexander's portraits.

The relation of royal portraiture to civic portraiture remained unchanged after 280,
as attested by some conventionally young, short haired and beardless male civic portraits (cf. fig. 19).[116] However, we know other versions of this civic portrait concept. The
statue of Poseidippos from Kassandreia (fig. 10), a comic poet of the early to the middle 3rd century,[117] testifies that the regular hairline above the forehead and the fleshy face
related to *tryphe* must also have been common features in non-royal portraiture of the
3rd century. The *tryphe* physiognomy relates well to single coin portraits of Lysimachos
(fig. 13) and to the Ptolemies (figs. 6–7) as well as to the royal portraits from Syracuse
(fig. 11) and from Pergamon (figs. 8–9). Private portraits from Kypros demonstrate that
the *tryphe* concept was familiar in different regions of the Hellenistic world.[118] While
the Kypriot portraits could possibly have been imitation of Ptolemaic *tryphe* portraits,[119] this is rather unlikely for Poseidippos' portrait. Hence, the use of this concept
was not "Bildnisangleichung", but a form of "Zeitgesicht" that kings also embraced.

Finally, the beard, which reappeared in late 3rd-century royal portraits, had been out
of fashion in royal portraits since the beginning of the century. Its use in civic portraiture was mostly restricted to portraits of philosophers and poets and of some orators
and politicians who thus were related to the glorious past of the 4th century, like Demosthenes and Olympiodoros.[120] However, during the 3rd century, other bearded civic
portraits reappear.[121] When beards were applied to royal portraits in the later 3rd century,

116   Olympia, Museum Inv. L 99: Geominy 2007, 71–72 fig. 92; Lehmann 2008; Spahlinger 2020, 20
       with n. 47 fig. 18–19. – London, British Museum Inv. 1600 ('Head Aberdeen'): Stewart 1977, 104–
       105 pl. 46c–d; Vorster 2004b, 122 with n. 10 (king?); Geominy 2007, 72 fig. 89. – Cf. the slightly
       earlier 'Praying Boy', Berlin, Staatliche Museen: Antikensammlung Sk 2 (fig. 19; see above n. 111). –
       For Hellenistic statues of athletes cf. Spahlinger 2020.
117   Fittschen 1992; Zanker 1995 134–139; La Rocca – Bucchino 2011, 152 no. 2.47 (R. di Cesare); cf. von
       den Hoff 2021, 174.
118   Connelly 1988, 57 no. 17 fig. 72–73, 57–58 no. 18 fig. 74–77, 90 no. 34 fig. 121–122, 102–103 no. 56–57
       fig. 171–172.
119   Senff 1993, 43.
120   See above n. 32 and 107.
121   Cf. Connelly 1988, 88 no. 31 fig. 116; Schmidt 2007.

the meaning had changed. Different beards were rather new signs of distinction than a motif purely related to age.

To sum up this comparative approach: Male royal portraits of the early Hellenistic period until around 220/210 BC were far more similar than different. Only a restricted number of variations of the beardless, shorthaired royal portrait concept – distinct in multiple facets from Alexander's portraiture – was in use. There were clear relations to civic portraits, which demonstrates that early Hellenistic royal portraiture was visually nothing particular but rather "civic" – except for distinctive attributes like the diadem and a particularly honorific vocabulary of divine attributes, not discussed here.

However, the similarities of early Hellenistic royal portraits did not result in uniformity. The Diadochi's concept underlined the real live presence of the dynamic kings, while after around 280, a calmer and more distant concept of the king's image seems to have been familiar. This concept appears like a royal "Zeitgesicht" of the 3rd century in different dynasties. In Pergamon and Bithynia the Diadochi's concept was reapplied after ca 280, when it ended for reigning kings in the Ptolemaic and Seleukid realm. As time went by, variations became more numerous. The application of Alexander motives ("Bildnisangleichung") was growing in number.[122] The use of *tryphe* motives in some dynasties as in civic portraiture testifies to regionally particular, but also broadly used applications related to luxury and wealth that were, however, not in use in Seleukid portraiture. Furthermore, differently bearded portraits appeared more often since the second half of the 3rd century. Finally, while in Egypt local traditions of old pharaonic iconographies remained familiar, elsewhere, like in Kappadokia, local traditions were newly complemented by Greek iconographies during the 3rd century.

Hence, what we may observe over the course of the 3rd century is a certain trend towards diversity and distinctive charging of the royal "period face". This is possibly a sign of growing needs for a competitive legitimation that no longer aimed at homogeneity. It could also be a sign of an interest in distinction in times of crisis like in Baktria or for Antiochos Hierax.

Royal portraits of the latest 3rd and 2nd century have not been discussed here. However, even without a detailed analysis, three final points can be made for these portraits. First, the concept of the calm, dignified beardless royal portrait remained alive locally. Second, as an additional sign of diversity, the individuality of male royal portraits – as well as differently bearded portraits – received more attention, as the late portraits of Antiochos III, royal portraits in Pontos and Ptolemaic portraiture since Ptolemaios VI bear witness to.[123] Finally, from the 2nd century onward, Alexander's portrait concept – rather than just individual Alexander motives – were a more important

---

122   Kovacs 2022; see also Martin Kovacs in this volume.
123   von den Hoff 2021, 175–187.

choice.[124] As a clearly retrospective portrait concept, this had been unfamiliar during the 3rd century. Hence, royal portraits of the late 3rd and 2nd century overcame the relative sameness of "Zeitgesicht" of the early Hellenistic period. They enhanced differences, while consequently sameness in terms of "Bildnisangleichung" became an even more visible visual strategy.

Bibliography

Ager 2021: Ager, Sheila, Dynastic Images in the Early Hellenistic Age: Queen's Power or King's Will?, The Ancient History Bulletin 35, 2021, 36–55

Ager – Hardiman 2016: Ager, Sheila – Hardiman, Craig, Female Seleukid Portraits. Where are they?, in: A. Coşkun – A. McAuley (eds.), Seleucid Royal Women: Creation, Representation and Distortion of Hellenistic Queenship in the Seleukid Empire, Stuttgart 2016, 143–172

Albersmeier 2002: Albersmeier, Susanne, Untersuchungen zu den Frauenstatuen des ptolemäischen Ägypten, Mainz 2002

Alram 2009: Alram, Michael, Münzprägung in Baktrien und Sogdien. Von den graeco-baktrischen Königen bis zu den Kuschan, in: S. Hansen – A. Wieczorek – M. Tellenbach (eds.), Alexander der Große und die Öffnung der Welt, Regensburg 2009, 183–191

Andreae 2015: Andreae, Bernhard, Attaliden-Bildnisse. Eine Apologie, in: R. Grüßinger et al. (eds.), Pergamon als Zentrum der hellenistischen Kunst. Bedeutung, Eigenheiten und Ausstrahlung, Berlin 2015, 30–37

Ashton 2001: Ashton, Sally-Ann, Ptolemaic Royal Sculpture from Egypt. The Interaction between Greek and Egyptian Traditions, Oxford 2001

Bergemann 1997: Bergemann, Johannes, Demos und Thanatos. Untersuchungen zum Wertsystem der Polis im Spiegel der attischen Grabreliefs des 4. Jahrhunderts v. Chr. und zur Funktion der gleichzeitigen Grabbauten, Munich 1997

Boschung 1993: Boschung, Dietrich, Die Bildnistypen der iulisch-claudischen Kaiserfamilie. Ein kritischer Forschungsbericht, Journal of Roman Archaeology 6, 1993, 39–79

Boschung 2021: Boschung, Dietrich, Effigies. Antikes Porträt als Figuration des Besonderen, Paderborn 2021

Brown 1995: Brown, Blanche R., Royal Portraits in Sculpture and Coins. Pyrrhos and the Successors of Alexander the Great, New York 1995

Caccamo Caltabiano et al. 1997: Caccamo Caltabiano, Maria et al., Siracusa ellenistica. Le monete 'regali' di Ierone II, della sua famiglia e dei Siracusani, Messina 1997

Carney 2021: Carney, Elisabeth D., Women in Antigonid Monarchy, in: E. D. Carney – S. Müller (eds.), The Routledge Companion to Women and Monarchy in the Ancient Mediterranean World, London 2021, 307–318

Connelly 1988: Connelly, John B., Votive Sculpture of Hellenistic Cyprus, New York 1988

Dahmen 2012: Dahmen, Karsten, Alexander und das Diadem. Die archäologische und numismatische Perspektive, in: Lichtenberger et al. 2012, 281–292

124 Kovacs 2022; cf. Fleischer 2002, 67–71.

de Callataÿ 2009: de Callataÿ, François, The First Royal Coinages of Pontos (from Mithridates III to Mithridates V), in: J. M. Højte (ed.), Mithridates VI and the Pontic Kingdom, Aarhus 2009, 63–94

Dillon 2007: Dillon, Sheila, Portraits of Women in the Early Hellenistic Period, in: von den Hoff – Schultz 2007, 49–62

Dillon 2010: Dillon, Sheila, The Female Portrait Statue in the Greek World, Cambridge 2010

Dorka Moreno 2019: Dorka Moreno, Martin, Imitatio Alexandri? Ähnlichkeitsrelationen zwischen Götter- sowie Heroenbildern und Porträts Alexanders des Großen in der griechisch-römischen Antike, Rahden 2019

Dumke 2012: Dumke, Gunnar R., Diadem = Königsherrschaft?: der Fall des Diodotos I. von Baktrien, in: Lichtenberger et al. 2012, 385–393

Fittschen 1988: Fittschen, Klaus, Griechische Porträts, Darmstadt 1988

Fittschen 1991: Fittschen, Klaus, Zur Rekonstruktion griechischer Dichterstatuen I: Die Statue des Menander, Mitteilungen des Deutschen Archäologischen Instituts. Athenische Abteilung 106, 1991, 243–279

Fittschen 1992: Fittschen, Klaus, Zur Rekonstruktion griechischer Dichterstatuen II: Die Statuen des Poseidippos und des Pseudo-Menander, Mitteilungen des Deutschen Archäologischen Instituts. Athenische Abteilung 107, 1992, 229–271

Fittschen 1999: Fittschen, Klaus, Prinzenbildnisse antoninischer Zeit, Mainz 1999

Fittschen 2010: Fittschen, Klaus, The Portraits of Roman Emperors and their Families. Controversial Positions and Unsolved Problems, in: B. C. Ewald – C. F. Noreña (eds.), The Emperor and Rome. Space, Representation and Ritual, Cambridge 2010, 221–246

Fittschen 2011: Fittschen, Klaus, Il fenomeno dell'assimilazione delle immagini nella ritrattistica romana di età imperiale, in: La Rocca – Bucchino 2011, 246–252

Fittschen 2015: Fittschen, Klaus, Methodological Approaches to the Dating and Identification of Roman Portraits, in: B. Borg (ed.), A Companion to Roman Art, Chichester 2015, 52–70

Fittschen 2017: Fittschen, Klaus, Halbierte Köpfe?, Trierer Winckelmannsprogramme 28, Mainz 2017

Fleischer 1991: Fleischer, Robert, Studien zur seleukidischen Kunst I: Herrscherbildnisse, Mainz 1991

Fleischer 1996: Fleischer, Robert, Hellenistic Royal Iconography on Coins, in: P. Bilde et al. (eds.), Aspects of Hellenistic Kingship, Aarhus 1996, 28–40

Fleischer 1999: Fleischer, Robert, Rev. of: Brown 1995, Gnomon 71, 1999, 555–558

Fleischer 2002: Fleischer, Robert, True and False Ancestors in Hellenistic Rulers' Portraiture, in: J. M. Højte (ed.), Images of Ancestors, Aarhus 2002, 59–74

Fleischer 2005: Fleischer, Robert, Rev. of: Queyrel 2003, Gnomon 77, 2005, 616–628

Franken 1994: Franken, Norbert, Modefrisuren als Grundlage zur Datierung römischer Büstengewichte, in: J. Ronke (ed.), Akten der 10. Internationalen Tagung über Antike Bronzen, Stuttgart 1994, 147–153

Galbois 2018: Galbois, Estelle: Images du pouvoir et pouvoir de l'image. Les 'médaillons-portraits' miniatures des Lagides, Bordeaux 2018

Gans 2006: Gans, Ulrich-Walter, Attalidische Herrscherbildnisse. Studien zur hellenistischen Porträtplastik Pergamons, Wiesbaden 2006

Gehrke 1982: Gehrke, Hans-Joachim: Der siegreiche König. Überlegungen zur hellenistischen Monarchie, Archiv für Kulturgeschichte 64, 1982, 247–277

Geominy 2007: Geominy, Wilfred, Die allmähliche Verfertigung hellenistischer Stilformen (280–240 v. Chr.), in: P. C. Bol (ed.), Geschichte der antiken Bildhauerkunst III: Hellenistische Plastik, Mainz 2007, 43–101

Giuliani 1996: Giuliani, Luca, Bildnis und Botschaft, Frankfurt a. M. 1996

Grunauer-von Hoerschelmann 1978: Grunauer-von Hoerschelmann, Susanne, Die Münzprägung der Lakedaimonier, Berlin 1978

Grüßinger et al. 2011: Grüßinger, Ralf et al. (eds.), Pergamon – Panorama der antiken Metropole, Petersberg 2011

Günther 2011: Günther, Linda-Marie, Herrscher als Götter – Götter als Herrscher? Zur Ambivalenz hellenistischer Münzbilder, in: Günther – Plischke 2011, 98–113

Günther – Plischke 2011: Günther, Linda-Marie – S. Plischke (eds.), Studien zum vorhellenistischen und hellenistischen Herrscherkult, Mainz 2011

Haake 2012: Haake, Matthias, Diadem und basileus. Überlegungen zu einer Insignie und einem Titel in hellenistischer Zeit, in: Lichtenberger et al. 2012, 393–313

Haake 2014: Haake, Matthias, Das Diadem, königliches Symbol in hellenistischer Zeit, in: K. Ehling – G. Weber (eds.), Hellenistische Königreiche, Darmstadt 2014, 24–28

Heinen 1983: Heinen, Heinz, Die 'Tryphe' des Ptolemaios VIII. Euergetes II. Beobachtungen zum ptolemäischen Herrscherideal und zu einer römischen Gesandtschaft in Ägypten (140/39 v. Chr.), in: id. (ed.), Althistorische Studien. Hermann Bengtson zum 70. Geburtstag, Wiesbaden 1983, 116–130

Hijmans 2022: Hijmans, Steven E., Alexander or not? The Problem of Alexander-like Portraits in Roman Art, in: F. Pownall – S. R. Asirvatham – S. Müller (eds.), The Courts of Philip II and Alexander the Great, Berlin 2022, 275–298

Junker 2007: Junker, Klaus, Die Porträts des Pompeius Magnus und die mimetische Option, Mitteilungen des Deutschen Archäologischen Instituts. Römische Abteilung 113, 2007, 69–93

Kansteiner 2000: Kansteiner, Sascha, Herakles. Die Darstellungen in der Großplastik der Antike, Cologne 2000

Katsikoudes 2009: Katsikoudes, Nikolaos, Πύρρος βασιλεύς ηγήτωρ, Archaiologike Ephemeris 148, 2009, 97–120

Kazakidi 2015: Kazakidi, Natalia, Εἰκόνες ἐν γυμνασίῳ. Ἔργα γλυπτικῆς στο ελληνιστικό γυμνάσιο, Thessaloniki 2015

Kovacs 2015: Kovacs, Martin, Imitatio Alexandri – zu Aneignungs- und Angleichungsphänomenen im römischen Porträt, in: R. von den Hoff et al. (eds.), Imitatio heroica. Heldenangleichung im Bildnis, Würzburg 2015, 47–84

Kovacs 2022: Kovacs, Martin, Vom Herrscher zum Heros. Die Bildnisse Alexanders des Großen und die Imitatio Alexandri, Rahden 2022

Kroll 2007: Kroll, John, The Emergence of Ruler Portraiture on Early Hellenistic Coins. The Importance of Being Divine, in: R. von den Hoff – P. Schultz (eds.), Early Hellenistic Portraiture. Image, Style, Context, Cambridge 2007, 113–122

Kyrieleis 1975: Kyrieleis, Helmuth, Bildnisse der Ptolemäer, Berlin 1975

Kyrieleis 2015: Kyrieleis, Helmuth, Hellenistische Herrscherporträts auf Siegelabdrücken aus Paphos, Wiesbaden 2015

La Rocca – Bucchino 2011: La Rocca, Eugenio – Bucchino, Laura (eds.), Ritratti. Le tante facce del potere, Roma 2011

Landwehr 1998: Landwehr, Christa, Konzeptfiguren. Ein neuer Zugang zur römischen Idealplastik, Jahrbuch des Deutschen Archäologischen Instituts 113, 1998, 139–194

Laubscher 1985: Laubscher, Hans-Peter, Hellenistische Herrscher und Pan, Mitteilungen des Deutschen Archäologischen Instituts, Athenische Abteilung 100, 1985, 333–353

Le Rider 1977: Le Rider, Georges, Le monnayage d'argent et d'or de Philippe II frappé en Macédoine de 359 à 294, Paris 1977

Lehmann 2008: Lehmann, Stephan, Der Kopf einer hellenistischen Athletenstatue in Olympia, in: C. Franek et al. (eds.), Thiasos. Festschrift für Erwin Pochmarski, Vienna 2008, 579–590

Lehmann 2012: Lehman, Stephan, Sieger-Binden im agonistischen und monarchischen Kontext, in: Lichtenberger et al. 2012, 181–208

Lehmann 2022: Lehmann, Stefan, Seuthes III. und Lysimachos. Ihre Gräber, Bildnisse und Stadtgründungen als historische Zeugnisse frühhellenistischer Herrscher im Diadochenreich Thrakien, Antike Welt 2022. Heft 1, 55–63

Lehmler 2005: Lehmler, Caroline, Syrakus unter Agathokles und Hieron II. Die Verbindung von Kultur und Macht in einer hellenistischen Metropole, Frankfurt a. M. 2005

Lichtenberger 2012: Lichtenberger, Achim, Gibt es eine vorhellenistische makedonische Tradition für das Diadem?, in: Lichtenberger et al. 2012, 163–179

Lichtenberger et al. 2012: Lichtenberger, Achim et al. (eds.), Das Diadem der hellenistischen Herrscher. Übernahme, Transformation oder Neuschöpfung eines Herrschaftszeichens, Bonn 2012

Lichtenberger – Nieswandt – Salzmann 2008: Lichtenberger, Achim – Nieswandt, H.-Helge – Salzmann, Dieter, Ein Porträt des Lysimachos? Anmerkungen zu einem anonymen Herrscherbild auf den Münzen von Lysimacheia, in: E. Winter et al. (eds.), Vom Euphrat bis zum Bosporus. Kleinasien in der Antike. Festschrift für Elmar Schwertheim zum 65. Geburtstag, Bonn 2008, 391–407

Lindström 2021: Lindström, Gunvor, The Portrait of a Hellenistic Ruler and other Bronze Sculptures from Kal-e Chendar/Shami. Results of the 2015 and 2016 Studies in the National Museum of Iran, The Journal of Iran National Museum 2, 2021, 177–196

Lorber 2014: Lorber, Catharine C., The Poyal Portrait on Ptolemaic Coinage, in: A. Lichtenberger et al. (eds.), BildWert. Nominalspezifische Kommunikationsstrategien in der Münzprägung hellenistischer Herrscher, Bonn 2014, 111–181

Lorber – Iossif 2009: Lorber, Catharine – Iossif, Panagiotis P., Seleucid Campaign Beards, L'Antiquité Classique 78, 2009, 87–115

Ma 2010: Ma, John, Le roi en ses images. Essai sur les représentations du pouvoir monarchique dans le monde hellénistique, in: I. Savalli-Lestrade – I. Cogitore (eds.), Des rois au prince. Pratiques du pouvoir monarchique dans l'Orient hellénistique et romain, Grenoble 2010, 147–164

Maderna 2004: Maderna, Caterina, Die letzten Jahrzehnte der spätklassischen Plastik, in: P. C. Bol (ed.), Geschichte der antiken Bildhauerkunst II: Klassische Plastik, Mainz 2004, 303–382

Marquardt 1995: Marquardt, Nathalie, Pan in der hellenistischen und kaiserzeitlichen Plastik, Bonn 1995

Martin 2011: Martin, Katharina, Göttliche Herrscherin – herrschende Göttin? Frauenbildnisse auf hellenistischen Münzen, in: N. Holmes (ed.), Proceedings of the XIVth International Numismatic Congress Glasgow 2009, London 2011, 285–292

Masséglia 2013: Masséglia, Jane, Body Language in Hellenistic Art and Society, Oxford 2013

Massner 1982: Massner, Anne-Kathrein, Bildnisangleichung. Untersuchung zur Entstehungs- und Wirkungsgeschichte des Augustusporträts (43 v. Chr.–68 n. Chr.), Berlin 1982

Meyer 1992/1993: Meyer, Marion, Mutter, Ehefrau und Herrscherin. Darstellungen der Königin auf seleukidischen Münzen, Hephaistos 11–12, 1992/1993, 107–132

Meyer 2020: Meyer, Marion, Frauen für Krisen. Die raren Münzbildnisse der Seleukiden, in: Pangerl 2020, 263–275

Michels 2009: Michels, Christoph, Kulturtransfer und monarchischer 'Philhellenismus'. Bithynien, Pontos und Kappadokien in hellenistischer Zeit, Göttingen 2009

Michels 2011: Michels, Christoph, Dionysos Kathegemon und der attalidische Herrscherkult. Überlegungen zur Herrschaftsrepräsentation der Könige von Pergamon, in: Günther – Plischke 2011, 114–140

Mileta 2012: Mileta, Christian, Ein Agon um Macht und Ehre. Beobachtungen zu den agonalen Aspekten der Königserhebungen im 'Jahr der Könige', in: Lichtenberger et al. 2012, 315–334

Mittag 2013: Mittag, Peter F., Geschichte und Münzprägung Baktriens von den Seleukiden bis zum Ende der graeco-baktrischen Herrschaft, in: G. Lindström et al. (eds.), Zwischen Ost und West. Neue Forschungen zum antiken Zentralasien, Darmstadt 2013, 115–124

Moltesen 1995: Moltesen, Mette, Catalogue 'Greece in the Classical Period'. Ny Carlsberg Glyptotek, Copenhagen 1995

Mørkholm 1991: Mørkholm, Otto, Early Hellenistic Coinage from the Accession of Alexander to the Peace of Apameia (336–188 B.C.), Cambridge 1991

Müller 2013: Müller, Sabine, The Female Element of the Political Self-fashioning of the Diadochi: Ptolemy, Seleucus, Lysimachus, and their Iranian Wives, in: V. Alonso Troncoso – E. M. Anson (eds.), After Alexander: The Time of the Diadochi (323–281 BC), Oxford 2013, 199–214

Müseler 2018: Müseler, Wilhelm, The Dating and the Sequence of the Persid Frataraka Revisited, Koinon. The International Journal of Classical Numismatic Studies 1, 2018, 84–106

Newell 1927: Newell, Edward T., The Coinages of Demetrius Poliorcetes, Oxford 1927

Palagia 2005: Palagia, Olga, A New Interpretation of Menander's Image by Kephisodotos II and Timarchos, Annuario della scuola archeologica di Atene e delle missioni italiane in Oriente 83, 2005, 287–296

Palagia 2017: Palagia, Olga, A Royal Macedonian Portrait Head from the Sea off Kalymnos, in: J. M. Daehner – K. Lapatin – A. Spinelli (eds.), Artistry in Bronze. The Greeks and their Legacy. XIXth International Congress on Ancient Bronzes, Los Angeles 2017, 40–45 = https://www.getty.edu/publications/artistryinbronze/large-scale-bronzes/4-palagia (last access: 20.5.2024)

Pangerl 2020: Pangerl, Andreas (ed.), Portraits. 400 Years of Hellenistic Portraits, Munich 2020

Papaefthymiou 2021: Papaefthymiou, Eleni, Le portrait monétaire grec dans l'Antiquité, in: D. Boschung – F. Queyrel (eds.), Formate und Funktionen des Porträts / Formats et fonctions du portrait, Paderborn 2021, 69–114

Plischke 2011: Plischke, Sonja, Herrschaftslegitimation und Städtekult im Reich des Lysimachos, in: Günther – Plischke 2011, 55–76

Panagopoulou 2010: Panagopoulou, Katerina, The Early Antigonids: Coinage, Money, and the Economy, New York 2020

Queyrel 2002: Queyrel, François, Les portraits de Ptolemée III Évergète et la problématique de l'iconographie lagide de style grec, Journal des Savants 2002, 3–73

Queyrel 2003: Queyrel, François, Les portraits des Attalides. Fonction et représentation, Athens 2003

Queyrel 2009: Queyrel, François, Iconographie de Ptolémée II, in: J.-Y. Empereur (ed.), Alexandrina III, Le Caire 2009, 7–61

Queyrel 2019: Queyrel, François, The Portraits of the Ptolemies, in: O. Palagia (ed.), Handbook of Greek Sculpture, Berlin et al. 2019, 194–224

Raeck 2021: Raeck, Wulf, Demosthenes, der Ratgeber. Überlegungen zum Politikerporträt in der athenischen Demokratie, in: J. Lang – C. Marcks-Jakobs (eds.), Arbeit am Bildnis. Porträts als Zugang zu antiken Gesellschaften. Festschrift für Dietrich Boschung, Regensburg 2021, 195–207

Rebenich 2017: Rebenich, Stefan (ed.), Monarchische Herrschaft im Altertum, Berlin 2017

Richter 1965: Richter, Gisela M. A., The Portraits of the Greeks, London 1965

Riedel 2016: Riedel, Stefan, ΘΕΟΙ ΤΟΥ ΒΑΣΙΛΕΩΣ ΚΑΙ ΤΗΣ ΠΟΛΕΩΣ. Die Götterwelt(en) des Lysimachos und seiner Residenzstadt Lysimacheia im Spiegel der Münzen, in: H. Schwarzer – H.-Helge Nieswandt (eds.), "Man kann es sich nicht prächtig genug vorstellen". Festschrift für Dieter Salzmann zum 65. Geburtstag, Marsberg 2016, 171–182

Saladino – Formigli 2012/2013: Saladino, Vincenzo (appendice de Formigli, Edilberto), Il ritratto di Seuthes III., Jahrbuch des Deutschen Archäologischen Instituts 127–128, 2012/2013, 125–206

Salzmann 2012: Salzmann, Dieter, Anmerkungen zur Typologie des hellenistischen Königsdiadems und zu anderen herrscherlichen Kopfbinden, in: Lichtenberger et al. 2012, 337–383

Schmidt 2007: Schmidt, Stefan, Fashion and Meaning. Beardless Portraits of Artists and Literati in the Early Hellenistic Period, in: von den Hoff – Schultz 2007, 99–112

Scholl et al. 2012: Scholl, Andreas et al. (eds.), Staatliche Museen zu Berlin. Die Antikensammlung, Mainz ⁴2012

Schreiber 2014/2015: Schreiber, Torben, Herrscher ohne Diadem oder ptolemäisches 'Zeitgesicht'? Zu den sogenannten Ptolemäerringen im Archäologischen Museum der Westfälischen Wilhelms-Universität Münster, Boreas 37–38, 2014/2015, 227–283

Schröder 2012: Schröder, Thoralf, Im Angesichte Roms. Überlegungen zu kaiserzeitlichen männlichen Porträts aus Athen, Thessaloniki und Korinth, in: T. Stephanidou-Tiveriou – P. Karanastasis – D. Damaskos (eds.), Κλασική παράδοση και νεωτερικά στοιχεία στην πλαστική της ρωμαϊκής Ελλάδας, Thessaloniki 2012, 497–512

Schröder 2020: Schröder, Thoralf, Grüppchenbildung oder homogene Selbstdarstellung? Zu den Porträts der städtischen Eliten im römischen Griechenland, in: D. Boschung – F. Queyrel (eds.), Porträt und soziale Distinktion / Portrait et distinction sociale, Paderborn 2020, 307–331

Senff 1994: Senff, Reinhard, Das Apollonheiligtum von Idalion. Architektur und Statuenausstattung eines zyprischen Heiligtums, Jonsered 1994

Simonetta 1977: Simonetta, Bono, The Coins of the Cappadocian Kings, Fribourg 1977

Smith 1988: Smith, Roland R. R., Hellenistic Royal Portraits, Oxford 1988

Smith 1991: Smith, Roland R. R., Hellenistic Sculpture. A Handbook, London 1991

Spahlinger 2020: Spahlinger, Florian, "Die aus dem Gymnasion". Studien zu Ikonologie und Funktion von Athletenstandbildern in Hellenismus und Römischer Kaiserzeit, Regensburg 2020

Stanwick 2002: Stanwick, Paul E., Portraits of the Ptolemies. Greek Kings as Egyptian Pharaohs, Austin 2002

Stanwick 2005: Stanwick, Paul E., Ägyptische Statuen der Ptolemäer, in: H. Beck – P. C. Bol – M. Bückling (eds.), Ägypten, Griechenland, Rom. Abwehr und Berührung, Tübingen 2005, 244–251

Stewart 1977: Stewart, Andrew, Skopas of Paros, London 1977

Svenson 1995: Svenson, Dominique, Darstellungen hellenistischer Könige mit Götterattributen, Frankfurt a. M. 1995

Thomas 2002: Thomas, Renate, Eine postume Statuette Ptolemaios' IV. und ihr historischer Kontext. Zur Götterangleichung hellenistischer Herrscher, Mainz 2002

Trunk 2008: Trunk, Markus, Studien zur Ikonographie des Pompeius Magnus. Die numismatischen und glyptischen Quellen, Jahrbuch des Deutschen Archäologischen Instituts 123, 2008, 101–168

Vlachogianni 2018: Vlachogianni, Elena, The Art of Hairstyling: Hairstyles in the Greco-Roman
    World and their Semiology, in: M. Lagogianni-Georgakarakos (ed.), The Countless Aspects of
    Beauty in Ancient Art, Athens 2018, 303–316
von den Hoff 1994: von den Hoff, Ralf, Philosophenporträts des Früh- und Hochhellenismus,
    Munich 1994
von den Hoff 2007a: von den Hoff, Ralf, Die Plastik der Diadochenzeit, in: P. C. Bol (ed.),
    Geschichte der antiken Bildhauerkunst III: Hellenistische Plastik, Mainz 2007, 1–40
von den Hoff 2007b: von den Hoff, Ralf, Naturalism and Classicism. Style and Perception of Early
    Hellenistic portraits, in: von den Hoff – Schultz 2007, 49–62
von den Hoff 2009a: von den Hoff, Ralf, Alexanderporträts und Bildnisse frühhellenistischer
    Herrscher, in: S. Hansen – A. Wieczorek – M. Tellenbach (eds.), Alexander der Große und die
    Öffnung der Welt, Regensburg 2009, 47–53
von den Hoff 2009b: von den Hoff, Ralf, Die Bildnisstatue des Demosthenes als öffentliche
    Ehrung eines Bürgers in Athen, in: M. Haake – C. Mann – R. von den Hoff (eds.), Rollen-
    bilder in der athenischen Demokratie. Medien, Gruppen, Räume im politischen und sozialen
    System, Wiesbaden 2009, 193–220
von den Hoff 2013: von den Hoff, Ralf, Alexanderbildnisse und Imitatio Alexandri in Baktrien, in:
    G. Lindström et al. (eds.), Zwischen Ost und West. Neue Forschungen zum antiken Zentral-
    asien, Darmstadt 2013, 83–98
von den Hoff 2017: von den Hoff, Ralf, König, Tyrann, Bürger, Heros, Gott: Bilder von Monar-
    chen in der visuellen Kultur des antiken Griechenland, in: Rebenich 2017, 263–304
von den Hoff 2021: von den Hoff, Ralf, The Visual Representation of Ptolemaic and Seleucid
    Kings. A Comparative Approach to Portrait Concepts, in: S. von Reden – C. Fischer-Bovet
    (eds.), Comparing the Ptolemaic and Seleucid Empires. Integration, Communication, and Re-
    sistance, Cambridge 2021, 164–190
von den Hoff – Azoulay 2017: von den Hoff, Ralf – Azoulay, Vincent, Dissémination: statues-por-
    traits multiples et diffusion sur d'autres médias, in: F. Queyrel – R. von den Hoff (eds.),
    Eikones. La vie des portraits grecs. Ve–Ier siècles av. J.-C., Paris 2017, 151–194
von den Hoff – Schultz 2007: von den Hoff, Ralf – Schultz, Peter (eds.), Early Hellenistic Portrai-
    ture. Image, Style, Context, Cambridge 2007
Vorster 2004a: Vorster, Christiane, Die Porträts des 4. Jahrhunderts v. Chr., in: P. C. Bol (ed.),
    Geschichte der antiken Bildhauerkunst II: Klassische Plastik, Mainz 2004, 383–428
Vorster 2004b: Vorster, Christiane, Römische Skulpturen des späten Hellenismus und der Kai-
    serzeit. Vatikanische Museen, Museo Gregoriano Profano Ex Lateranense: Katalog der Skulp-
    turen 2.2, Wiesbaden 2004
Wagner 2017: Wagner, Stefan E. A., Herrscherrepräsentation im frühen Hellenismus. Studien zu
    Entstehung und Funktion königlicher Selbstdarstellung in der Diadochenzeit, Diss. Erlangen
    2017
Walthall 2013: Walthall, D. Alexander, Becoming Kings. Spartan Basileia in the Hellenistic Period,
    in: N. Luraghi (ed.), The Splendors and Miseries of Ruling Alone. Encounters with Monarchy
    from Archaic Greece to the Hellenistic Mediterranean, Stuttgart 2013, 129–163
Westermark 1961: Westermark, Ulla, Das Bildnis des Philetairos von Pergamon. Corpus der Münz-
    prägung, Stockholm 1961
Wheatley – Dunn 2020: Wheatley, Pat – Dunn, Charlotte, Demetrius the Besieger, Oxford 2020
Wiemer 2017: Wiemer, Hans Ulrich, Siegen oder untergehen? Die hellenistische Monarchie in
    der neueren Forschung, in: Rebenich 2017, 305–339

Winkes 1992: Winkes, Rolf, The Pyrrhus Portrait, in: T. Hackens (ed.), The Age of Pyrrhus. Papers Delivered at the International Conference at Brown University, Leuven 1992, 175–188

Wünsch 2020: Wünsch, Julian, Bärtige Seleukiden, in: Pangerl 2020, 277–291

Zanker 1982: Zanker, Paul, Herrscherbild und Zeitgesicht, in: Wissenschaftliche Zeitschrift der Humboldt-Universität zu Berlin. Reihe Gesellschaftswissenschaften 31, 1982, 307–312

Zanker 1995: Zanker, Paul, Die Maske des Sokrates. Das Bild des Intellektuellen in der antiken Kunst, Munich 1995

Figures

Fig. 1: Naples, Museo Archeologico Nazionale Inv. 5590. Photo after: B. Andreae, Skulptur des Hellenismus, München: Hirmer 2001, pl. 6.

Fig. 2: Berlin, Münzkabinett, Staatliche Museen zu Berlin 18258950. Photo by Lutz-Jürgen Lübke (Lübke und Wiedeman). Public Domain 1.0 / CC BY-SA 4.0.

Fig. 3: Venice, Seminario Patriarcale (plaster cast Göttingen, Universität: Abgussammlung des Archäologischen Instituts Inv. A 1536). © Archäologisches Institut der Universität Göttingen, Foto Stephan Eckardt.

Fig. 4: Wien, Kunsthistorisches Museum: Münzkabinett Inv. GR 15918. © Kunsthistorisches Museum Wien / KHM-Museumverband.

Fig. 5: Wien, Kunsthistorisches Museum: Münzkabinett Inv. GR 20304. © Kunsthistorisches Museum Wien / KHM-Museumverband.

Fig. 6: Paris, Musée du Louvre Inv. Ma 4709. © Réunion des Musées Nationaux – Grand Palais (Musée du Louvre), Photo by Hervé Lewandowski: https://collections.louvre.fr/ark:/53355/cl010278258; last access: 20.5.2024.

Fig. 7: New York, American Nusmismatic Society Inv. 1944.100.77199. Courtesy of the American Numismatic Society.

Fig. 8: Berlin, Münzkabinett, Staatliche Museen zu Berlin 18269737. Photo by Bernhard Weisser.

Fig. 9: Naples, Museo Archeologico Nazionale Inv. 6148 (plaster cast Göttingen, Universität: Abgussammlung des Archäologischen Institits Inv. A 1547). © Archäologisches Institut der Universität Göttingen, Photo Stephan Eckardt.

Fig. 10: Geneva, Musée d'Art et d'Histoire Inv. MF 1330 6148 (plaster cast Bonn, Akademisches Kunstmuseum Inv. 2352). © Forschungsarchiv für Antike Plastik, Photo by Gisela Geng.

Fig. 11: Berlin, Münzkabinett, Staatliche Museen zu Berlin 18203196. Photo by Reinhard Saczewski.

Fig. 12: New York, American Nusmismatic Society Inv. 1944.100.13712. Courtesy of the American Numismatic Society.

Fig. 13: New York, American Numismatic Society Inv. 1944.100.13767. Courtesy of the American Numismatic Society.

Fig. 14: New York, American Numismatic Society Inv. 1944.100.13786. Courtesy of the American Numismatic Society.

Fig. 15: Naples, Museo Archeologico Nazionale Inv. 6149. Photo: Deutsches Archäologisches Institut Rom, D-DAI-ROM-59.759.

Fig. 16: Wien, Kunsthistorisches Museum: Münzkabinett Inv. GR 20364. © Kunsthistorisches Museum Wien / KHM-Museumverband.

Fig. 17:   Münzkabinett, Staatliche Museen zu Berlin 18200217. Photo by Lutz-Jürgen Lübke (Lüb-
           ke und Wiedeman).
Fig. 18:   Rome, Musei Vaticani, Museo Pio Clementino Inv. 490. Photo: Deutsches Archäologi-
           sches Institut Rom, D-DAI-ROM-94Vat.89 / Klaus Anger.
Fig. 19:   Berlin, Staatliche Museen: Antikensammlung – SMPK Sk 2 (bronze cast Berlin, Abguss-
           Sammlung antiker Plastik der Freien Universität Inv. VII 850–07/8). Photo: Freie Uni-
           versität Berlin, Abguss-Sammlung antiker Plastik 3304784_01_AAPN3_461.

Ralf von den Hoff is professor of Classical Archaeology at the University of Freiburg i. Br., where he
is the executive director of the Freiburg Institute for Advanced Studies (FRIAS). Since 2012, he has
been directing the Collaborative Research Center 948 "Heroes – Herozations – Heroisms. Transformations and Conjunctures from Antiquity to the Modern Day". His research foci are Greek sculpture, ancient portraits and the representation of rulers as well as on the iconology and visual culture
of the ancient Greek and Roman world. Among his publications is *Handlungsporträt und Herrscherbild. Die Heroisierung der Tat in Bildnissen Alexanders des Großen* (Göttingen 2020); together with
F. Queyrel he co-edited *La vie des portraits grecs. Statues-portraits du Ve au Ier siècle av. J.-C. – Usages
et re-contextualisations* (Paris 2017; German edition 2019), together with P. Schultz *Early Hellenistic
Portraiture: Image, Style and Context* (Cambridge 2007).

The Royal Family and the Divine /
Die Königsfamilie und das Göttliche

————————

Königliche Schutzgottheiten im frühen Hellenismus
*‚Konzepte' und Umsetzungen**

GREGOR WEBER

Abstract: Already the Homeric heroes were ascribed protective deities who sometimes actively intervened in the events of the Trojan War, and in the world of the Greek poleis there were also corresponding preferences that were implemented cultically. If we look at the Hellenistic Era, the use of Zeus, Apollon, Dionysos or Athena as patron deities of the great dynasties is obvious, sometimes also connected with genealogically oriented legends. This manifests itself in the minting of coins, in cult buildings and festivals, and in the implementation of the dynasty founders in mythological contexts; the claim to Zeus by the Ptolemies exemplifies this. Therefore, questions about the reasons for the specific selection, the target groups and the media of implementation virtually force themselves upon us, as do questions about the general developments and the preferences of a king.

On closer inspection, however, the phenomenon proves to be much more complex, especially since there is also a lack of uniform ancient terminology and conceptual focus: Some Hellenistic kings stood in a special relationship to indigenous deities, such as Ahura Mazda, Marduk or Amun-Re, which generated target groups and communication contexts of their own kind. Then a new level was reached with equations, e. g., of Arsinoë II with Isis and Aphrodite, especially since the queen herself then performed a protective function.

Finally, there are cases, especially in a political-military context, in which the claiming of protective deities was implemented situationally and probably linked to concrete occasions: Poseidon by Demetrios Poliorketes and Pan by Antigonos Gonatas, which can be seen above all – but by no means exclusively – in the coinage. For these two historical constellations, the contexts are

*   Den Herausgebern danke ich für die Einladung, an der Tagung in Münster teilnehmen zu dürfen, außerdem etlichen Teilnehmerinnen und Teilnehmern für ihre kritischen und weiterführenden Fragen. Charalampos Chrysafis, Kay Ehling, Jürgen Malitz und Stefan Pfeiffer haben wichtige Hinweise zum Thema des Beitrags gegeben, ebenso der anonyme Reviewer des Bandes. Für die Überlassung der Abbildungen aus der Staatlichen Münzsammlung München, die Nicolai Kästner und Sergio Castelli angefertigt haben, bin ich Kay Ehling zu großem Dank verpflichtet, ebenso Thomas Seidler. Der Duktus des Vortrags wurde beibehalten und um einige Literaturhinweise ergänzt (vgl. dazu Anm. 6).

examined and possible intentions discussed. In both cases, complex networks of references are revealed – right up to a specific perception in Athenian inscriptions and a coin series of portraits of Pan with a royal diadem. From these findings, some perspectives for further research will be developed.

1. Einführung

Vor einigen Jahren wurde ich gebeten, für einen Supplementband zum Neuen Pauly über „Religion in Context" einen Beitrag über Religion an den Königs- und Kaiserhöfen beizusteuern.[1] Gerade für den Hellenismus entwickelte sich dieses Unterfangen zu einer Spurensuche, waren doch explizite Aussagen bei antiken Autoren selten bzw. anekdotisch überformt. Bei den archäologischen Zeugnissen stieß man auf die Schwierigkeit, dass generell Kultstätten in den Ausgrabungsbefunden der Palastareale nicht ohne weiteres nachweisbar sind, was ebenso für spezifisches Fundmaterial gilt. Dennoch ließen sich Eckdaten plausibel machen, zumal die Höfe *jenseits* einer kultischen Praxis auch als Schalt- und Kommunikationszentralen fungierten, in denen auf Initiativen innerhalb der Königreiche (und außerhalb) reagiert und reichsweit umzusetzende Planungen im Rahmen königlicher Selbstdarstellung konzipiert wurden – auch im Bereich der Religion. Für die hellenistische Zeit habe ich diese Thematik mit Blick auf „Herrscherkulte, Dynastiekulte und Schutzgottheiten" nochmals intensiver untersucht und im Rahmen einer Tagung zur Diskussion gestellt.[2]

Dabei kam die Frage auf, was eine Schutzgottheit eigentlich sei und was sie ausmache:[3] Sie schien mir zunächst nicht wirklich weiterführend zu sein, denn der Begriff ‚Schutzgottheit' kam bislang zur Anwendung, wenn zum Ausdruck gebracht wurde, dass eine Gottheit einen König konkret oder dauerhaft unterstützte, bzw. beiden ein entsprechendes Verhältnis zugeschrieben wurde. Bei näherem Nachdenken erwies sich die Antwort auf die Frage aber als deutlich komplexer, weil hierbei nämlich Phänomene zusammenkamen, die es auseinanderzuhalten gilt, weil sie nicht zwingend zusammengehören müssen bzw. im gleichen Kontext entstanden sind. Denn es macht Sinn, unterschiedliche Stränge legitimatorischen Handelns zu unterscheiden und zu gewichten.[4] Darüber hinaus hat man bei aller heuristisch gerechtfertigten und angebrachten Feindifferenzierung aber stets danach zu schauen, ob und wie ein Konzept in der Antike im Allgemeinen und in einem bestimmten regionalen oder epochenspezifischen Kontext überhaupt verankert ist.

---

1   Weber 2024a.
2   Vgl. Weber 2024b.
3   Für diese Anregung danke ich Gunnar Dumke (Winterthur).
4   In den differenzierten Ausführungen von Edelmann 2007 zur Herrschaftslegitimation der hellenistischen Könige (bes. 212–327) wird das Konzept der Schutzgottheiten nicht eigens behandelt.

Im Folgenden möchte ich zunächst die angesprochenen Ansätze ausdifferenzieren, in einem zweiten Abschnitt mögliche Vorläufer und Vorbilder benennen und in einem dritten drei Beispiele betrachten und terminologische Implikationen zu berücksichtigen versuchen. In den Blick zu nehmen sind die zugrundeliegenden Mechanismen, die beteiligten Akteure und ein mögliches Experimentierpotential seitens der Könige und ihrer Umgebung, von dem durchaus auszugehen ist.[5] Außerdem hat man nach den Gründen für die Auswahl, den Zielgruppen und den Medien der Umsetzung zu fragen. Im letzten Abschnitt sollen die Ergebnisse auf einige Leitfragen dieses Bandes hin ausgewertet werden.[6]

2. Die Phänomene

Das Quellenspektrum für die hellenistischen Könige lässt fünf hier relevante Phänomene erkennen, zu denen verwandte Bereiche hinzukommen, die ebenfalls kurz anzuschneiden sind:[7]

(a) Die Inanspruchnahme von Zeus, Apollon oder Dionysos, auf die sich ein König und seine Dynastie genealogisch zurückführten: Dies konnte sich – etwa bei Argeaden, Ptolemaiern oder Seleukiden – in Gründungs- bzw. Abstammungslegenden manifestieren,[8] was aber nicht ausschließt, dass die Schutzfunktion betont wurde. Das besondere Verhältnis zeigte sich auch in Orakeln oder Träumen, die

---

5 Dazu bereits exemplarisch Weber 2011.

6 Hervorzuheben ist, dass zum Thema insgesamt kein Forschungsstand vorliegt, nur zu einzelnen Aspekten, worauf dann an der jeweiligen Stelle verwiesen wird. Die Literatur zu einzelnen Protagonisten und Aspekten geht inzwischen ins Uferlose; auch wenn die Bibliographie insgesamt umfangreich geraten ist, können die verarbeiteten Titel nur ansatzweise einen Eindruck von bestimmten Problemlagen vermitteln und erheben keinen Anspruch auf Vollständigkeit für den jeweiligen Sachverhalt.

7 Wichtige Differenzierungen finden sich bei Schmitt 2005, außerdem bereits Taeger 1957, 29, der mehrere Aspekte zusammenbringt: "Im allgemeinen nahm man ein ganz besonders inniges Verhältnis zwischen der Könige und den Göttern an, sei es, daß es als ein Schutzverhältnis im weitesten Sinne, das auch die älteren Vorstellungen gern in sich aufnahm, betrachtet wurde, sei es, daß es, eine gleichfalls sehr weit verbreitete, auf älteste, oft wohl totemistische Vorstellungen zurückgehende Idee, als Verwandtschaft angesehen wurde. Man konnte aber auch die Grenze zwischen den Göttern und dem Menschen ganz aufheben und den sterblichen König als die irdische Erscheinung eines Gottes oder als Gott sui generis verehren, ohne daß dadurch der Schutzgedanke im Raume der Königsideologie aufgehoben worden wäre."

8 Schmitt 2005 unterscheidet die Herleitung einer Dynastie von einem göttlichen oder heroischen Ahnherrn und die Zeugung durch einen göttlichen Vater. Zu den Argeaden: Müller 2016, 85–99, und 2017, 184–192; zu den Ptolemaiern: Lianou 2010; zu den Seleukiden: Ogden 2017, der deutlich macht, wie sich die Alexander- und die Seleukos-Legende parallel entwickelt haben und letztere unter Antiochos III. nochmals einen ‚Schub' erhielt; bes. Nawotka 2019, demzufolge der Apollon-Bezug erst nach 301 v. Chr. in Form der Abstammungslegende hergestellt wurde und in die Münzprägung Einzug hielt, während das Anker-Symbol früher aufgekommen war und damit zunächst nichts zu tun hatte: Während Seleukos anfangs Zeus zuneigte, sei im Kontext der Beziehungen zu Milet/Didyma die Erwählung und Abstammung von Apollon verkündet worden, so dass dann

als Vermittlungsinstanz fungierten, auf die man sich wiederum beziehen konnte.[9] Sichtbar wurde der Zusammenhang in Münzprägung, Kultbauten und Festen, ebenso in der höfischen Literatur. Die Beziehung zu einer bestimmten Gottheit musste keineswegs exklusiv sein, sondern *mehrere* Könige konnten sich parallel auf die genannten Götter berufen. Eine Konkurrenz darum dürfte es ebenso wenig gegeben haben, wie bekanntlich Gottheiten an *verschiedenen* Orten – bisweilen mit einem zusätzlichen Epitheton bzw. einer spezifischen Epiklese versehen – verehrt wurden.[10]

(b) Die Rückführung auf Herakles als Ahnherrn und über ihn wiederum auf Zeus.[11] Hier gilt das zuvor Gesagte, nur dass Herakles eine Doppelrolle als Gott *und* Heros zukam. Vergöttlichte Könige konnten mit ihm auf eine Ebene gerückt werden, was eine Art Gleichrangigkeit suggerierte. Die genannten Konstellationen definieren aber dennoch einen Unterschied zwischen König bzw. Dynastie und schützender Gottheit.

(c) Die besondere Beziehung zu Göttern, zu denen König oder Königin *nicht* in einem genealogischen Zusammenhang standen, was aufgrund bestimmter Charakteristika – z. B. bei Athena die Jungfräulichkeit – nicht möglich war; deshalb konnten spezifische Eigenheiten wie Klugheit oder Wehrhaftigkeit, für die die Göttin stand, zum Tragen kommen.[12]

(d) Die Bezugnahme auf eine Gottheit, die in einer bestimmten, nicht selten historischen Situation konkret-individuellen Schutz geboten hatte, etwa Poseidon im Falle von Demetrios Poliorketes oder Pan bei Antigonos Gonatas.[13]

(e) Das spezielle Verhältnis eines Königs zu einer indigenen Gottheit, zum Beispiel zu Ahura Mazda, Marduk oder Amun-Re. Diese Beziehung generierte Zielgruppen und Kommunikationskontexte eigener Art, lässt aber auch Rückwirkungen auf Elite und Bevölkerung des jeweiligen Königreichs vermuten.[14]

Davon sind Phänomene wie die Herrscher- und Dynastiekulte abzugrenzen, mit denen die Könige in eine andere Sphäre gelangten. Hierher gehört die kultische Praxis

---

von einem ἀρχηγέτης bzw. ἀρχηγὸς τοῦ γένους gesprochen werden konnte (OGIS 212 und 219, dazu Nawotka 2019, 265–266).

9 Dazu Schmitt 2005, 252–253; außerdem bereits Weber 1999. Siehe auch unten Anm. 75.

10 Vgl. dazu Chaniotis 1997, 1119–1120; aufschlussreich für die Behandlung signifikanter Beispiele sind die Beiträge in Riboldi 2016.

11 Dazu grundlegend Huttner 1997, 253–270.

12 Vgl. zu den Göttern bei den Attaliden, etwa Athena und Dionysos Kathegemon, Taeger 1957, 338–352, sowie vor allem Michels 2011.

13 Dazu siehe unter 4.

14 Hierzu sind wir im Falle Ägyptens und der ägyptischen Priester vergleichsweise gut informiert; zu diesem komplexen Verhältnis Pfeiffer 2017, 44–50, außerdem die hilfreiche Systematisierung der verschiedenen Ebenen und Aktionsradien bei Huß 1994. Vgl. zu dem Komplex auch die Beiträge von Sonja Richter und Christoph Michels in diesem Band.

der Verehrung als σύνναος θεός, insofern ein verstorbener König oder eine Königin aufgrund der Hinzufügung einer eigenen Kultstatue in einem bestehenden Heiligtum als ‚tempelteilende Gottheit' verehrt wurde – ein offenkundig nicht so seltenes Phänomen, zu dem es aber bislang noch an systematischer Forschung mangelt.[15] Außerdem haben Könige, etwa Ptolemaios XII., Epitheta wie ‚Neos Dionysos' und damit eine neue Qualität für sich beansprucht, während Gleichsetzungen, etwa von Arsinoë II. mit Isis sowie mit Aphrodite Zephyritis und Euploia, für eine neue Stufe standen; in diesem Fall nämlich nahm die Königin eine göttliche Schutzfunktion für andere wahr.[16]

Zwischen den beschriebenen Phänomenen gab es Überschneidungen, und die kultische Verehrung eines lebenden oder verstorbenen Königs stand nicht im Widerspruch zu dessen Inanspruchnahme oder Zuerkennung von Schutzgottheiten – auch wenn dies implizierte, dass der König des göttlichen Schutzes tatsächlich bedurfte und er hierarchisch *unter* der Gottheit stand. In den mythologisch unterfütterten Abstammungslegenden wurde ein anderer Akzent gesetzt, da der König den Status als Abkömmling eines Gottes erhielt: Im Gefüge antiker religiöser Vorstellungen und kultischer Praxis war dies freilich unproblematisch, mehr noch: Mit den Konzepten von Heros oder Halbgott standen bereits aus der Vergangenheit Zwischenstufen zur Verfügung, die entsprechend eingesetzt oder modifiziert werden konnten. Die Inanspruchnahme eines Schutzes wurde jedenfalls keineswegs als ‚Minuspunkt' angesehen, sonst hätten sich keine Belege dafür gefunden – und sei es nur als ‚Versuchsballon' oder Zwischenschritt.[17]

3. Vorbilder

Mit den hellenistischen Königen als Referenzpunkt wird man davon ausgehen dürfen, dass sie sich – wie so oft – mit Vorbildern auseinandersetzen: in makedonischer Tradition, in der griechischen Poliswelt und in indigenen Kontexten. Der Umgang damit konnte affirmativ sein, in Abgrenzung münden oder auch eklektisch nur Aspekte aufnehmen. Insbesondere Philipp II. und Alexander der Große stellten solche Referenzpunkte dar, die für entgegengesetzte Pole standen: der Vater für eine Profilierung des Makedonischen, die seit König Archelaos (413–399 v. Chr.) *auch* in klarer Orientierung an griechischer Kultur erfolgte;[18] der Sohn wiederum für eine Monarchie *sui ge-*

---

15   Dazu bislang Nock 1930, Schmidt-Dounas 1993, Queyrel 2015 und Newman 2020.

16   Konkret Arsinoë II. von ihrem Heiligtum am Kap Zephyrion aus für Seefahrer, dazu Barbantani 2005, Kleibl 2009, 113–114 und Acosta-Hughes 2021.

17   Eine weitere Fragestellung, der hier nicht nachgegangen werden kann, wäre die nach der Relevanz des Genderaspektes für die Schutzgottheiten, d. h. wie es mit dem Schutz der Könige durch weibliche Gottheiten aussah und ob Königinnen nur weibliche Schutzgottheiten oder auch männliche besaßen.

18   Dazu Hecht 2017 und Pownall 2017; zuvor bereits ausführlich Weber 1992, 64–67.

neris, die *auch* achaimenidischem Erbe verpflichtet war. Dies lässt sich daran ersehen, dass nach Alexanders Tod die späteren Könige, die fast alle seinem engsten Umfeld entstammten, verschiedentlich von seinem Herrschaftshabitus abrückten, um gleichzeitig, wo immer opportun, – etwa durch Heiratsavancen gegenüber seiner Schwester Kleopatra, im Umgang mit seinem Leichnam oder in der Münzprägung – an ihn ‚anzudocken'.[19] Für unseren Zusammenhang ist hier die Frage relevant, wie Alexander selbst es mit dem göttlichen Schutz hielt und wie sich Diadochen und Epigonen auf sein Vorbild im Umgang mit Schutzgöttern beziehen konnten.

Betrachten wir zunächst die Alexander vertraute homerische Welt: Dort wurden den Helden individuelle Schutzgottheiten zugeschrieben, etwa Athena für Diomedes und Odysseus.[20] Sie griffen – auch im Sinne einer Familientradition – aktiv in das Geschehen des Trojanischen Krieges ein und konnten mittels Gebet aktiviert werden. Der Erfolg musste nicht nur militärischer Art sein, sondern konnte auch über eine ‚Wesensverwandtschaft' wie Klugheit wirken.[21] Als Gegenleistung wurde eine Reverenz erwartet, die der Held dem Gott entgegenbrachte. Anders als bei Thetis' Unterstützung für ihren Sohn Achilleus spielte bei Athena die Abstammung keine Rolle.

Auch jenseits des individuellen Schutzes, in der Welt der griechischen Poleis, gab es entsprechende Präferenzen, die – sichtbar etwa in der Münzprägung – kultisch umgesetzt wurden: Athena schützte Athen, Apollon Milet usw., wobei ein doppelter oder mehrfacher göttlicher Schutz nicht unüblich war.[22] Parallel dazu kam es zu einer Übertragung auf Alleinherrscher in vorhellenistischer Zeit: Peisistratos stand bei seinem zweiten Einzug in Athen unter dem Schutz der Athena-Phye, und Pindar zufolge besaß Hieron von Syrakus einen θεὸς ἐπίτροπος,[23] zumal nach der Epinikienliteratur in den Wettkämpfen immer wieder Gottheiten ihre adligen Schützlinge unterstützten.[24]

19 Dazu etwa Lianou 2010 und Wallace 2018. Zu den Argeaden als Bezugspunkt siehe auch den Beitrag von Sabine Müller in diesem Band.
20 Dazu Hirschberger 2011, bes. 281–282, außerdem Deacy 2008, 59–73.
21 Huttner 1997, 253–257: „Durch Paränese, Verleihung von Mut, Kraft und Einsicht und nicht zuletzt durch persönlichen Beistand verhilft also die Göttin dem Helden zu seinem Erfolg" (255); außerdem bereits Taeger 1957, 56.
22 Brackertz 1976, die das Phänomen für die Poleis untersucht und dabei auch Fragen der praktischen Umsetzung behandelt hat (6–7), verweist auf die Unterscheidung zwischen dem Schutz einer Stadt durch *alle* Götter und dem durch eine einzelne, dann exponierte Gottheit. Ein wichtiges Ergebnis besteht in der Erkenntnis, dass als Schutzgottheiten *alle* aus dem griechischen Pantheon infrage gekommen seien; außerdem Huttner 1997, 253–253.
23 Pind. O. 1.106–112: θεὸς ἐπίτροπος ἐὼν τεαῖσι μήδεται | ἔχων τοῦτο κᾶδος, Ἱέρων, | μερίμναισιν· εἰ δὲ μὴ ταχὺ λίποι, | ἔτι γλυκυτέραν κεν ἔλπομαι | σὺν ἅρματι θοῷ κλεΐ|ξειν ἐπίκουρον εὑρὼν ὁδὸν λόγων | παρ' εὐδείελον ἐλθὼν Κρόνιον („Gott ist dein Fürsprecher, Hieron, er waltet – dies ist seine Sorge – über deinem Bestreben. Wenn er dich nicht plötzlich verlässt, hoffe ich von einem noch beglückenderen Sieg mit dem schnellen Wagen künden und die willkommen dienende Weise des Gesangs finden zu können beim weithin sichtbaren Kronoshügel", Übersetzung: E. Dönt). Dazu Taeger 1957, 83 und 89–90.
24 Huttner 1997, 257–258.

Kurz noch zu Makedonien, obwohl sich viel dazu sagen ließe (und in der Forschung bereits gesagt wurde): Zeus und Herakles als Ahnherren und Gründern der Argeadendynastie kam eine herausragende Bedeutung zu,[25] u. a. ersichtlich an der offenkundigen Relevanz des Zeus-Heiligtums in Dion am Olymp.[26] Philipp II. legte um die Mitte des 4. Jh.s einen Schwerpunkt auf Zeus-Münzen, wobei Porträts des jugendlichen Herakles schon seit Archelaos geprägt wurden.[27] Alexander selbst bewegte sich in einer Sphäre, die von mythologischen Gestalten durchdrungen war: Sie lebte – so suggerieren die verschiedenen Ausgestaltungen in der Alexander-Literatur – einerseits von göttlichem Eingreifen, andererseits von Alexanders Bestreben, Vorbilder aus dem Mythos noch zu übertreffen:[28] Vielfach wird auf die Zeussohnschaft, die Verwandtschaft mit Achilleus und Herakles sowie auf dionysische Implikationen verwiesen, um die wichtigsten Bezüge zu nennen.[29] In der Münzprägung fand eine Entwicklung von traditionellen Herakles-Prägungen hin zu einer Angleichung an den König statt,[30] dazu Darstellungen des thronenden Zeus mit Adler und Szepter, der Athena und der Nike, d. h. eine Mischung von Abstammungs- und Schutzelementen.[31] Gleichzeitig hat Alexander – auch im Rahmen seiner Legitimationsbestrebungen und mit großem kommunikativem Talent – viel dafür investiert, sich, wie Ralf von den Hoff aufgezeigt hat, als „a pious, but autonomous devotee in Greek sanctuaries, tied to historical, mythological and local traditions" zu erweisen.[32]

4. Beispiele

Für die in Abschnitt 2 genannten Phänomene seien drei besonders signifikante Beispiele herausgegriffen, wobei bestimmte Könige bzw. Dynastien, etwa die Seleukiden, nicht berücksichtigt sind. Sie können aber eine Vorstellung sowohl vom Potential, das dem Thema innewohnt, als auch den damit verbundenen Problemen vermitteln.

25   Hatzopoulos 2020, 82.
26   Kreutz 2007, 197–198; Christesen – Murray 2010, 430–431, bes. Hatzopoulos 2013, 165–167, Lichtenberger 2021, 104–111. Makedonischer Tradition zufolge hat man seitens der Argeadendynastie und auch seitens der Lokalbarone offenkundig keine *großen* Tempelbauten errichtet bzw. es ist nur ein diesbezüglicher Plan Alexanders des Großen bekannt, der aber nicht mehr realisiert werden konnte. Dion mit seinem Zeus-Heiligtum stellt folglich eine signifikante Ausnahme dar.
27   Kreutz 2007, 200; Lianou 2010, 129–130; Müller 2016, 90 mit Anm. 348, dort auch zu den Adler-Münzen seit Amyntas III., sowie 95–96. Dazu siehe auch den Beitrag von Sabine Müller in diesem Band.
28   Antela-Bernárdez 2016, 240–246; zur Religiosität Alexanders vgl. Orth 2014, 560–561; zuletzt systematisch: Hölscher 2020.
29   Dazu Taeger 1957, 187; Huttner 1997, 266–268; Kreutz 2007, 201–205; Antela-Bernárdez 2016, 246–251; Müller 2017, 194.
30   Dazu Schulze 2013; Dahmen 2013, 157–158, außerdem Kissel 2005, 46 mit Abb. 2.
31   Dazu Dahmen 2007, passim; bes. Dahmen 2013; zu Athena und Nike: Ehling 2013.
32   So von den Hoff 2020, 121.

4.1 Zeus bei den frühen Ptolemaiern

Bereits unter dem Dynastiegründer Ptolemaios I. wurde der Zeus-Bezug stark gemacht: Hierzu trug die Abstammungslegende von Ptolemaios als Bruder Alexanders und ebenso die notorische Wiederholung des Adlers als Dynastieemblem auf den Münzen bei (Abb. 1).[33] Außerdem fand *insgesamt* ein starker Rückbezug auf die Argeaden statt, zumal Ptolemaios als erster Alexanders Porträt auf seine Münzen setzte und es auch als erster durch sein eigenes ersetzte (Abb. 2 und 3).[34] Dass die höfische Dichtung solche Assoziationen aufgriff, verwundert nicht, etwa Theokrit im 17. Eidyllion, dem Enkomion auf Ptolemaios II.: In ihm werden Kernelemente der Königsideologie angesprochen, u. a. die Nahbeziehung des Dynastiegründers zu Alexander und Herakles.[35] Einige Verse erwähnen dessen Frau Berenike und des Sohnes Geburt auf Kos.[36] Dieser Teil des Enkomions ist von zwei aufschlussreichen Aussagen gerahmt. Am Ende heißt es: „Und dreimal kreischte von oben her aus den Wolken ein mächtiger Adler, der Vogel des Glückes. Dies war ein Zeichen von Zeus wohl; denn Zeus, der Kronide, behütet ehrwürdige Könige stets, doch besonders den, der ihm lieb ist gleich von Geburt an."[37] Es fällt der mehrfach explizit hergestellte Bezug zu Zeus auf, zumal es im letzten Vers des Enkomions heißt: „Vollendung (ἀρετή) aber erbitte Dir von Zeus",[38] außerdem die Formulierung der Beziehung, konstruiert unpersönlich mit μέλει, etwa: „Die Könige liegen Zeus am Herzen" oder „Zeus kümmert sich um die Könige". Zuvor wird auf Berenike Bezug genommen: „Herrin du, Aphrodite, der Göttinnen erste an Schönheit, ja, du nahmst Berenike dich an …".[39] Mit σοὶ … μεμέλητο wird – kaum zufällig – dasselbe Wort verwendet. Beide Formulierungen suggerieren,

---

33   Abb. 1: Tetradrachme, Alexandreia, ca. 295–285 v. Chr. (CPE 137 (p. 278–279) mit Taf. X); Lianou 2010, 128–129.

34   Abb. 2: Tetradrachme, Alexandreia, ca. 306–300 v. Chr. (CPE 70 (p. 265) mit Taf. V); Abb. 3: wie Abb. 1. Dazu Lianou 2010, 125 und 133, dort auch der Verweis auf Poseidipp. ep. 31 AB, in dem ausdrücklich Adler und Blitz als Siegeszeichen genannt und mit Alexander zusammengebracht werden; mit der expliziten Bezugnahme auf die Argeadenkönige im Epigramm dürften die Ptolemaier gemeint sein. Iossif 2018, 274, geht von „sometime around the 290s" aus.

35   Theokr. 17.13–33. Der Text beginnt mit der Vergöttlichung von Ptolemaios I. und Berenike I., also des ersten Ptolemaierpaares, reicht über die Wohltaten, die der König dem Land und seinen Bewohnern zukommen ließ, bis hin zu einer Beschreibung des ptolemaiischen Herrschaftsgebietes. Dazu Weber 1993, 220–221 und passim; außerdem Hunter 2003. In OGIS 54, der Adulis-Inschrift, wird die ptolemaiische Abstammung von Dionysos und Herakles, die beide auf Zeus zurückgehen, formuliert. Vgl. dazu den Beitrag von Stefan Pfeiffer in diesem Band.

36   Theokr. 17.53–71.

37   Theokr. 17.71–75: ὁ δ᾽ ὑψόθεν ἔκλαγε φωνᾷ / ἐς τρὶς ἀπὸ νεφέων μέγας αἰετὸς αἴσιος ὄρνις. / Ζηνός που τόδε σᾶμα. Διὶ Κρονίωνι μέλοντι / αἰδοῖοι βασιλῆες· ὁ δ᾽ ἔξοχος, ὅν κε φιλήσῃ / γεινόμενον τὰ πρῶτα. Dazu Hunter 2003, 151–155.

38   Theokr. 17.137: ἀρετήν γε μὲν ἐκ Διὸς αἰτεῦ. Hunter 2003, 197–199, verweist mit Recht darauf, dass nur Zeus ἀρετή verleihen konnte.

39   Theokr. 17.45–46: κάλλει ἀριστεύουσα θεᾶν πότν᾽ Ἀφροδίτα, / σοὶ τήνα μεμέλητο. Dazu Hunter 2003, 134 (mit weiteren Belegen): „μέλειν is commonly used of a divinity's special interest in a par-

dass König und Königin unter dem Schutz spezifischer, auf die konkrete Situation zugeschnittener Götter stehen. Andernorts, etwa im kallimacheischen Zeus-Hymnos, wird von der Auswahl eines Königs durch Zeus gesprochen.[40]

Abb. 1 Adler nach links mit geschlossenen Schwingen auf einem Blitzbündel.

Abb. 2 Alexanderkopf nach rechts mit Elefantenskalp.

Abb. 3 Kopf von Ptolemaios I. mit Diadem nach rechts mit Aigis um den Hals.

Zeus fungiert hier als Schutzgottheit, und nimmt man die Münzrückseiten und weitere Zeugnisse hinzu, erscheint die Intention eindeutig: Könige und Dynastie proklamierten den Schutz und versuchten, durch die Nähe zur göttlichen Sphäre einen Prozess der Legitimation anzustoßen.[41]

---

ticular human or institution." Die explizite Verbindung zu einem Schutzgott-Konzept wird freilich nicht hergestellt; siehe dazu unten unter 5.

40 Kall. h. Zeus 79–90, bes. 80–81. Dazu Brumbaugh 2019, 183–186. Der kallimacheische Apollonhymnos, in dem auch auf Ptolemaios II. Bezug genommen wird, handelt von göttlichem Schutz, ohne dass sich dies im expliziten Agieren des Königs selbst widerspiegelt.

41 Zu Hinweisen auf weitere Götter, auf die ptolemaiische Münzen anspielen, vgl. dezidiert Iossif 2018, 275 mit Anm. 29.

4.2 Poseidon bei Demetrios Poliorketes

Dass Demetrios gemeinhin als eine der auffälligsten Gestalten der Diadochenzeit gilt, dürfte eine zutreffende Einschätzung sein, auch wenn sich Überlieferung und Forschung, wie Sabine Müller herausgearbeitet hat, oftmals auf diskreditierende Aspekte konzentriert haben.[42] Indem er den Tod seines Vaters in der Schlacht von Ipsos 301 v. Chr. überlebte und danach seine Herrschaft zu etablieren vermochte, hatte sich Demetrios zäher gezeigt, als die Konkurrenten wohl anfangs dachten.

Abb. 4/5 Auf dem Avers Nike mit Trompete und Signalmast auf dem Schiffsbug. Revers: kämpfender Poseidon mit Dreizack nach links einschließlich der Umschrift Δημητρίου βασιλέως.

Abb. 6/7 Auf dem Avers Porträt von Demetrios Poliorketes mit Diadem und Hörnern nach rechts. Revers: Poseidon nach links, sitzend auf einem Felsen, mit Dreizack und einer Schiffszier, Umschrift Δημητρίου βασιλέως.

---

42   Dazu Müller 2010. Zu den deplorablen, aber auch spektakulären Umständen seines Todes: Wheatley – Dunn 2020, bes. 427–436.

Seine Münzprägung erweist sich allerdings in der Datierung als ausgesprochen schwierig, zumal in den Befunden für einzelne Münzstätten. Nach der üblichen Interpretation begann Demetrios bereits um 300 v. Chr. – sein Territorium beschränkte sich auf einige Hafenorte, vor allem Ephesos und Salamis auf Zypern – qualitativ hochwertige Tetradrachmen in mehreren Münzstätten zu prägen, was auch nach der Etablierung in Makedonien fortgeführt wurde: Der Avers zeigt Nike mit Trompete und Signalmast auf dem Schiffsbug, der Revers einen kämpfenden Poseidon mit Dreizack einschließlich der Umschrift Δημητρίου βασιλέως (Abb. 4 und 5).[43] Damit wurde vermutlich die Erinnerung an den Seesieg beim zyprischen Salamis von 306 bemüht und – statt eines Rückgriffs auf die Motivik der Alexander-Statere – der Schutz durch den Meeresgott Poseidon sowie die aktuelle Seeherrschaft des Demetrios betont.[44] Mit Blick auf die griechischen Städte und Söldner als Zielgruppe bzw. als Zahlungsmittel für diese Gruppe macht das Sinn, wenngleich auch eine Frühdatierung zwischen 306 und 304 v. Chr. nicht auszuschließen ist.[45] Einige Jahre später, ca. 292/291, wurden Münzen mit einem Demetrios-Porträt mit Diadem und Hörnern samt einem modifizierten Poseidon auf dem Revers geprägt (Abb. 6 und 7).[46] Dies zielte gängiger Interpretation zufolge auf die Göttlichkeit des Königs, ganz unabhängig davon, welche Gottheit man mit den Hörnern verbindet.[47] Hierzu passt die Passage im athenischen Ithyphallikos von 291/290 v. Chr., Demetrios stamme von Poseidon und Aphrodite ab:[48] Während Poseidon als Vater auf derselben Ebene wie Zeus und Alexander bzw. Apollon und Seleukos liegt, irritiert Aphrodites Mutterschaft, denn üblicherweise besaßen hellenistische Könige keine göttlichen Mütter, und auch eine Verbindung von Aphrodite und Poseidon scheint kaum zu passen. Angelos Chaniotis hat deshalb plausibel eine metaphorische

---

43 Abb. 4/5: Tetradrachme, Salamis, 300 v. Chr. oder früher (SNG München 1038, Taf. 44 = Newell 1927, Nr. 23, Taf. III, Nr. 1 [dieses Stück]); dazu Mørkholm 1991, 77–81 mit Nr. 162; Wheatley – Dunn 2020, 267–268 mit Abb. 14.

44 So auch Mittag 2023. Weitere Poseidon-Darstellungen stehen in Kombination mit einem Demetrios-Porträt, das Alexander-Anklänge aufweist, dazu Wheatley – Dunn 2021, 180–181.

45 Mitteilung von Kay Ehling am 2. März 2022; die konventionelle Datierung dieses Münztyps für Salamis (ca. 300–295 v. Chr.) und Ephesos (ca. 301–294 v. Chr.) bei Newell 1927, 24 und 64, akzeptiert etwa von Bernhardt 2014, 59–67.

46 Abb. 6/7: Tetradrachme, Amphipolis, 292/91 v. Chr. (SNG München 1048, Taf. 45 = Newell 1927, Nr. 107, Taf. X, Nr. 1 [dieses Stück]), dazu Mørkholm 1991, 79–80 mit Nr. 172; außerdem Ehling 2000; Wheatley – Dunn 2021, 182; Iossif 2018, 275. Wheatley – Dunn 2020, passim favorisieren hingegen eine Datierung gleichzeitig mit den Nike-Prägungen.

47 In Demetrios kamen weitere Facetten zusammen: Demetrios als σύνναος der Athena Parthenos und des Apollon von Delos, die Angleichung an Dionysos (dazu Müller 2010, 562–565; Orth 2014, 562–564) und in der Annäherung an Demeter – und eben die besondere Beziehung zu Poseidon, so explizit Ehling 2000, 158–159, gegen Taeger 1957, 271–273, demzufolge die göttlichen Implikationen im Hymnos bunt zusammengewürfelt gewesen seien. Zu den Tierhörnern auf den Münzen der hellenistischen Könige generell: Lücke 2020, 299–302.

48 Hermokles (?) von Kyzikos (Athen. 6.253d-f = CA S. 173–175,13–14.): ὦ τοῦ κρατίστου παῖ Ποσειδῶνος θεοῦ, / χαῖρε, κἀφροδίτης. („O du, des stärksten Gottes Poseidon Sohn und der Aphrodite, sei gegrüßt!").

Deutung zum Verständnis der Wesenszüge des Königs vorgeschlagen; möglicherweise intendierte Beziehungen zu Aphrodite sind von den Zeitgenossen aber offenkundig auch missverstanden worden.[49]

Vorbehaltlich der umstrittenen Datierung der Münzen liegt eine signifikante Entwicklung vor: Verband sich die Sieghaftigkeit des Königs, an die in prekärer Situation erinnert wurde, mit dem Schutz des Königs durch Poseidon, hat sich später – basierend auf entsprechender Abstammung – das Paradigma von der Göttlichkeit des Königs selbst ausgebildet. Die Nike-Poseidon-Prägung stellt jedenfalls eine Abkehr von allem Bisherigen dar und dürfte mit einem konkreten Sieg des Königs verbunden gewesen sein.[50]

4.3 Pan bei Antigonos Gonatas

Eine besondere Konstellation ergab sich für Antigonos II. Gonatas im Kontext seines Sieges über die Kelten bei Lysimacheia im Jahre 277 v. Chr.; damit war ihm der Weg auf den makedonischen Thron geebnet.[51] Auch wenn er bald darauf von Pyrrhos von Epeiros zeitweilig vertrieben wurde, behauptete er sich seit 272 dauerhaft.[52] Dieser Keltensieg wurde seit Usener 1874 mit einem neuen Münztyp, nämlich Pan-Prägungen, zusammengebracht: Bekannt sind Tetradrachmenserien mit einem – jüngeren oder auch älteren – Pan-Kopf als zentralem Emblem eines makedonischen Schildes,[53] umgeben von sieben eingefassten Sternen mit einer unterschiedlichen Anzahl an Strahlen, auf dem Avers und Athena mit einem Blitzbündel auf dem Revers (Abb. 8 und 9);[54] außerdem eine Bron-

---

49   „He had been victorious in the element of Poseidon – the sea – near the island of Aphrodite – Cyprus", so Chaniotis 2011, 184–185, dort auch zu weiteren Implikationen aus athenischer Sicht; außerdem Wheatley – Dunn 2020, 349–351; Müller 2010, 566–570, hat weitere Bezüge, zumal in athenischem Kontext, herausgearbeitet und verweist darauf, dass Demetrios' Bezüge zu Aphrodite schnell konterkariert wurden. In jedem Fall musste die Ausgestaltung aus athenischer Perspektive so gewählt worden sein, dass sie von Demetrios in der konkreten Situation zumindest nicht als anstößig empfunden werden und kontraproduktiv wirken konnte.

50   Wheatley – Dunn 2021, 181. Ehling 2000, 159, sieht in der Darstellung des Poseidon in drei verschiedenen Positionen quasi einen Beleg für die Darstellungsabsicht des Demetrios als Gottessohn. Dies ist keineswegs ausgeschlossen, wobei die Entwicklungen in den verschiedenen Prägeorten sich z. T. auch überlagern; für die spätere Phase Wheatley – Dunn 2020, 368–375.

51   Für den historischen Kontext immer noch instruktiv: Will ²1979, 107–110 („Antigonos Gonatas, roi de Macédoine"). Überliefert findet sich die Begebenheit bei Iust. 25,1,2–2,7. Zu den Keltensiegen als legitimatorischem Instrument vgl. den Beitrag von Giovanna Pasquariello in diesem Band.

52   Dazu Panagopoulou 2020, 224–229, mit weiterer Literatur.

53   Makedonische Schilde auf dem Avers wurden bereits unter Demetrios Poliorketes geprägt, und zwar auf Bronzenominalen von der Münzstätte Pella aus der Zeit zwischen 294 und 288 v. Chr., allerdings ohne ein Porträt im Zentrum, dazu Newell 1927, 118–120 mit Nr. 125–133.

54   Abb. 8/9: Tetradrachme, Amphipolis (Gaebler 1935, 186, Antigonos Gonatas Nr. 3, Taf. XXXIV, Nr. 3). Umstritten ist, um welches Athena-Statuen-Vorbild es sich handelt – Alkidemos (aus Pella) oder Promachos (aus Athen) –, wobei wichtig ist, dass im vorliegenden Fall Athena nicht den Speer, sondern ein Blitzbündel schwingt (zum Blitzbündel Lücke 2020, 293–295): Für entsprechende Alex-

zeprägung mit einem Athena-Kopf und einer Panfigur in mehreren Varianten, die ein Tropaion errichtet, das wiederum aus keltischen Waffen bestand (Abb. 10 und 11).[55] Man zog den Schluss, dass durch die auch nach Antigonos' Tod fortgeführten Prägeserien die Erinnerung daran wach gehalten werden sollte, Antigonos habe mit ‚panischer Hilfe' die Kelten besiegt; damit hätte er sich als Retter der griechischen Welt vor den gefürchteten Barbaren präsentieren können.[56] Allerdings – darauf wurde vermehrt hingewiesen – verbinden die Quellen nirgends explizit diesen Keltensieg mit einem πανικὸς φόβος.[57] Panagopoulou kam bei ihrer Analyse des Münzmaterials zum Ergebnis, dass sich der Einführungszeitraum des neuen Typs auf 268/267 bis 265/264 v. Chr. eingrenzen lässt, womit man sich vom bislang favorisierten Datum 271/270 v. Chr. entfernt und in den Kontext der Anfangsphase des Chremonideischen Krieges (267–261 v. Chr.) gelangt.[58] Nach der neuen Deutung hat Antigonos mit der Münzprägung ein komplexes Interpretationsgeflecht mit Reminiszenzen an die Perser- und Keltenabwehr bemüht, womit er und Makedonien zu ‚den Guten' gehörten[59] – dass der Pan-Kopf Bestandteil eines makedonischen Schildes samt Sternen ist, unterstreicht den *legitimatorischen* Konnex,

---

ander-Prägungen will Bernhardt 2014, 62–63 mit Anm. 56 die Frage des Athena-Bezugs offenlassen; Voutiras 1998 zeigt – unter Verweis auf eine Fehlinterpretation des Livius – den Kontext der makedonischen Poleis für Athena Alkidemos auf, ebenso den Bezug zu den Königen. Nichts zu Athena und ihrer Verbindung zu den hellenistischen Königen bei Deacy 2008. Charalampos Chrysafis wies mich noch auf den Panzer aus dem Königsgrab in Vergina hin, der auf der rechten Seite eine Applikation mit einer schreitenden Athena trägt und damit auch eine Art Schutzfunktion übernehmen sollte. Eine eigene Untersuchung wäre auch die Frage Wert, ob es einen direkten Zusammenhang zwischen einer konkreten Schutzgottheit und getragenen Amuletten gegeben hat; das Problem dabei besteht freilich darin, dass sich der dafür notwendige Kontext bei den Trägern der Amulette kaum wird hinreichend ausleuchten lassen, zumal die Zeitstellung der Amulette in magischem Kontext zumindest im erhaltenen Material erst mit dem 2./1. Jh. v.Chr, beginnt, dazu Kotansky 1994, xvii–xix.

55   Abb. 10/11: geprägte Kleinbronze, Pella oder Amphipolis, 271/270–239 v. Chr. (SNG München 1096, Taf. 47; Gaebler 1935, 187 Antigonos Gonatas Nr. 6, Taf. XXXIV, Nr. 4), Mørkholm 1991, Nr. 430 und 432; Weber 1995, 313 mit Anm. 157; vor allem die ausführlichen Analysen von Panagopoulou 2020, passim (bes. 228–229 zum Athena-Kult in Makedonien) und 356–358 (mit Taf. 61/13) zu den Bronzeprägungen. Eine spezifische Kelten-Symbolik findet sich nicht, sondern der eindeutig zu identifizierende Pan-Kopf ist stets von sieben makedonischen Schilden umgeben, in deren Mitte sich ein Stern befindet. Zu klären wäre, ob der Zahl sieben hier eine besondere Bedeutung zugemessen wurde (siehe unten Anm. 58). Mit den sieben *somatophylakes* Alexanders des Großen dürften die Schilde nichts zu tun haben, zumal mögliche historische Umstände, wie es zu dieser Personenanzahl gekommen war, unbekant sind. vgl. aber die Ausdeutungen bei Panagopoulou 2020, 226–228.

56   So auch Waterfield 2021, 123–124.

57   Dazu Nachtergael 1977, 177–180; außerdem Weber 1995, 306 mit Anm. 112; ausführlich Voutiras 2018, 404–405.

58   Panagopoulou 2020, 291–303 und passim (die Indizes in diesem Werk verweisen vielfach auf falsche Seiten); außerdem Weber 1995, 313, Anm. 157. Zur Darstellung siehe auch den Beitrag von Ralf von den Hoff in diesem Band.

59   Bezug genommen wird auch auf eine Revolte keltischer Söldner in Megara, die Antigonos niederzuschlagen vermochte (dazu Voutiras 2018, 405 mit Anm. 66; Panagopoulou 2020, 14, 298, 300–301 und 303); Iustin berichtet darüber im Proömium zu Buch 26 und in 26.2, während sich die andere, mehrfach zitierte Passage in Paus. 3.6 nicht darauf bezieht.

wie denn auch die Errichtung des Tropaion durch Pan auf den Bronzeprägungen die *militärische* Aussageintention verstärkt.[60] Auch wenn kein *konkreter* Sieg angezielt sein sollte, handelt es sich um eine militärische bzw. siegessymbolische Konnotation, die – und dieser Hintergrund wiegt stark – bei Prägungen aus dem frühen Hellenismus nur sehr punktuell anzutreffen ist. Dies entspricht bemerkenswerterweise genau der Praxis der Poleis, Münzen in aller Regel gerade *nicht* mit einem konkreten Siegesbezug auszuprägen und damit eine konkrete Kommemorationskultur herzustellen. Die Abweichung, die auch für Demetrios zu vermuten ist, erscheint deshalb umso signifikanter.

Abb. 8/9 Avers: Makedonischer Schild mit sieben Sternen, im Episema der gehörnte Kopf des unbärtigen Pan nach links mit einem Ziegenfell um den Hals, dahinter ein Wurfholz (lagobolon). Revers: Athena mit Helm, Schild und Blitzbündel nach links schreitend, unten links ein Helm, Umschrift βασιλέως Ἀντιγόνου.

Abb. 10/11 Bronzeprägung mit Athena-Kopf mit korinthischem Helm nach rechts auf dem Avers, eine Panfigur im Ausfallschritt, die ein Tropaion errichtet, auf dem Revers.

---

60 Grundlegende Varianten im Material scheint es nicht zu geben, nur variiert die Zahl der Strahlen der Sterne zwischen sechs und acht (vgl. dazu den Katalog von Panagopoulou 2020). Waterfield 2021, 124, sieht einen Bezug zum ‚Keltensieg' von Ptolemaios II. (dazu Hölbl 1994, 36; Pfeiffer 2017, 68), der ebenfalls kommemoriert wurde, nicht zuletzt durch die Abbildung von *Kelten*schilden. Mittag 2023 verbindet nur die Bronzeprägungen mit dem Tropaion direkt mit dem Keltensieg bei Lysimacheia, während die Tetradrachmen, zumal mit der wehhaften Athena auf dem Revers, auf die „allgemeine Wehrfähigkeit des Königs" anspielen würden, wobei der Pan-Kopf wohl doch eine Reminiszenz an Lysimacheia darstelle.

Warum aber Pan, zumal die Gottheit eng mit Arkadien verbunden und durch ihre theriomorphe Gestalt mehr als ungewöhnlich ist? Denn zur Ausrichtung großer Opfer oder zur Errichtung eines großen Pan-Heiligtums in Makedonien kam es offenkundig ebenso wenig wie zur Ausbildung einer Abstammungslegende des Antigonos oder (wie im Falle des athenischen Hymnos für Demetrios) seiner Vorfahren, was mit Pan vielleicht auch schwierig gewesen wäre, bzw. überhaupt zu einer Geschichte mit Pan – außer eben in dem aufgezeigten militärischen Kontext. Dabei liegen Belege für Pan-Darstellungen in Makedonien seit dem Ende des 5. Jh.s v. Chr. durchaus vor;[61] aber es stellt sich die Frage, ob damit eine exklusive Beziehung zwischen König und Gott intendiert war und das Schutzgott-Konzept greift. Immerhin, nach den antigonidischen Seesiegen gegen die Ptolemaier bei Andros und Kos wurden Soteria und Paneia auf Delos eingerichtet,[62] und zumindest mit Aratos von Soloi hat sich ein mit dem Hof des Antigonos verbundener Dichter auf Pan bezogen. Ihm schreibt der Suda-Artikel neben einem Enkomion auf Antigonos selbst und einem Gedicht auf seine Frau Phila (εἰς Φίλαν) einen Hymnos εἰς Πᾶνα zu; von ihm hat sich jedoch nur der Titel erhalten, so dass sich nichts über Inhalt und mögliche Bezugspunkte zum König sagen lässt.[63] Einen weiteren Pan-Hymnos hat Arats Landsmann Kastorion verfasst: Von ihm sind zwar fünf Verse überliefert, doch sind die Indizien für eine konkrete Verbindung nicht stark genug.[64]

---

61 Dazu Voutiras 2018, 399–404, mit Belegen und Abbildungen; bereits Borgeaud 1979, 169–170 mit Anm. 135; Weber 1995, 313, Anm. 158. Zur grundsätzlichen Bedeutung von Pan als Gottheit der Liminalität und Transgression vgl. Cardete del Olmo 2016. – Makedonische Münzen verschiedener Nominale trugen bereits vom Ende des 6. Jh.s v. Chr. an das Bild einer Ziege bzw. eines Ziegenbocks: Die Ziege spielte im Kontext der argeadischen Gründungsmythen um König Karanos eine wichtige Rolle (dazu Müller 2016, 93–104); außerdem findet sich das Motiv vor allem auf Münzen aus Aigai, was wiederum mit – problematischen – etymologischen Herleitungen erklärt wurde (dazu Fischer-Bossert 2007). Eine dezidierte Verbindung zu Pan liegt aber nicht vor, sieht man von dem Von auf den Porträtmünzen getragenen Ziegenfell einmal ab.

62 Weber 1995, 313, Anm. 158; Voutiras 2018, 405–406; mit Belegen; Panagopoulou 2020, 224.

63 SH 99, 115 und 116. Dazu Weber 1995, 308–309, dort auch zu weiteren Zuweisungen, die sich aber inzwischen nicht als plausibel erwiesen haben. Evident ist außerdem, dass in mehreren Gedichten auf Galaterkämpfe und auf Meder Bezug genommen wurde – wer auch immer dann damit gemeint sein sollte; außerdem Voutiras 2018, 404–405 mit Anm. 54; Waterfield 2021, 123: „in the hymn he seems to have raised the god Pan to the status of a major deity, whereas previously he had scarcely figured in Macedonian worship, and before long (beginning probably in 271), Antigonus began to strike coins, silver tetradrachms (four-drachma pieces), which prominently featured the head of the god".

64 SH 310 (Athen. 10.454f–455a): Σὲ τὸν βολαῖς νιφοκτύποις δυσχείμερον / ναίονθ' ἕδραν, θηρονόμε Πάν, χθόν' Ἀρκάδων, / κλήσω γραφῇ τῇδ' ἐν σοφῇ πάγκλειτ' ἔπη / συνθείς, ἄναξ, δύσγνωστα μὴ σοφῷ κλύειν, / (5) μωσοπόλε θήρ, κηρόχυτον ὃς μείλιγμ' ἱεῖς („Dich, Tierherr Pan, der Du bewohnst den winterlich / von Schneestürmen bedrängten Ort, Arkaderland, / will preisen ich in dieser Schrift mit Ruhmeswort, / das ich verfasst, mein Herr, das nur der Kluge hört, / (5) du Musentier, das Töne lockt aus der Schalmei"). Dazu Weber 1995, 308, Anm. 120; außerdem Bing 1995 und Magnelli 2015. Meyer 2014, 181, betont vor allem die literarische Gestaltung der Zeilen, die damit ganz im Trend der Zeit liegt.

Anders verhält es sich mit einer 1997 publizierten Inschrift auf einer Statuenbasis aus Beroia:[65] Es handelt sich um eine Weihung für Pan, in der der Stifter Hippokles einem Antigonos für die Erneuerung der Atelie dankt. Der verwendete Begriff πνεῦμα … σύμμαχον, also ein Atemzug oder Wind, mit dem Pan Makedonien half, impliziert einen militärischen Zusammenhang, der zu Antigonos Gonatas passen könnte; die Datierung der Inschrift scheint mit der Zeit dieses Königs vereinbar zu sein.

Abb. 12 Poseidon-Kopf nach rechts auf dem Avers.

Von Gonatas liegen, wenn ich es richtig sehe, keine Münzen mit eigenem Porträt vor, sondern diese variieren auf beiden Seiten – neben anfangs Alexander, Herakles und sitzendem Zeus – Abbildungen von Athena auf den Reversen und gegen Ende der Regierungszeit noch Poseidon auf den Aversen (Abb. 12),[66] und eben statt des Königs-porträts:[67] Pan. Diese scheinen so eng mit Antigonos verbunden gewesen zu sein, dass damit genau die in den Inschriften vom athenischen Asklepieion seit 256/255 v. Chr.

---

65   Ἐπιγραφές Κάτω Μακεδονίας (EKM) A. Beroia 37 = SEG 47.893: Πᾶν καὶ ἐν Ἀρκαδίαι μέγα τίμιος, ἀλλὰ | πόθος 'με' πνεῦμα Μακηδονίαι σύμμαχον ἠγάγετο, | Ἱπποκλέους δὲ ἀρετά με τεθαλότα καὶ νέον ὧδε | θῆκέ γέ τε ἐκ προγόνων κισσὸν ἀναψάμενος. |⁵ ἀθάνατος βασίλει<ο>ς ἐπεὶ χάρις ἅδε Φιλίππου | καὶ τέκνων τέκνοις ἀϊδίως ἐδόθη | καὶ κτεάνων ἀτελῆς δόμος ἅτε ἐπίσημος, | Ἀντιγόνου φάμα τόνδε ἐφύλαξε νόμον. Dazu Voutiras 2018, 407–409, mit einer französischen Übersetzung und weiterer Literatur; Panagopoulou 2020, 224. Unzutreffend Waterfield 2021, 124, der von einer „recently discovered base" spricht.

66   Das Stück von Abb. 12 stammt aus der Zeit von Antigonos Doson, der die Prägung fortsetzte, und lässt sich aufgrund eines Hortfundes recht genau datieren: Tetradrachme, Amphipolis (?), 227–225 v. Chr. (SNG München 1121, Taf. 48). Die Prägungen mit dem Poseidonkopf auf dem Avers und Apollon auf einem Schiffsbug sitzend auf dem Revers (Panagopoulou 2020, 304–309) dürften mit dem Seesieg bei Andros (246/245 v. Chr.) zusammenhängen (so auch Mittag 2023). Ob der Poseidon-Bezug etwas mit Demetrios Poliorketes zu tun hat (s. o.), bedarf noch einer genaueren Untersuchung. Drachmenprägungen liegen noch mit einem Zeuskopf und einer kämpfenden Athena vor, dazu Mørkholm 1991, 134 und Nr. 431.

67   Die Zusammenstellung nach Panagopoulou 2020, 7–10.

erwähnten τετρᾱχμα Ἀντιγόνεια gemeint gewesen sein dürften.[68] Dies impliziert rein ikonographisch eine Abkehr von der inzwischen entwickelten Porträttradition für die hellenistischen Könige, sondern knüpft eigentlich eher wieder an den Poliskontext mit einem Emblem oder Porträt der städtischen Schutzgottheit(en) an. Spekulativ bleiben müssen frühere Überlegungen, die in bestimmten Pan-Porträts den König sehen wollten.[69] Hervorzuheben ist aber, dass in der von Panagopoulou konstituierten Periode III, die von 246/245 bis 229 v. Chr. reichte, der Pan-Kopf mit einem Diadem geschmückt war:[70] Durch die generelle Angabe βασιλέως Ἀντιγόνου auf dem Revers wird aber der Schutz von König und – so wird man ergänzen dürfen – Land auch *ohne* dezidierten Siegeskontext herausgestellt, zumal für eine griechische Zielgruppe. Es lässt sich vermuten, dass die im diademierten Pan zum Ausdruck gebrachte nochmals engere Verbindung zwischen Gott und König eine über Griechenland hinausgehende Zielrichtung haben sollte, da sowohl bei den Ptolemaiern als auch bei den Seleukiden 246/245 v. Chr. einschneidende Herrscherwechsel stattgefunden hatten. Antigonos könnte hiermit die so wichtigen Übergänge – zwischen dem König als Mensch, der des göttlichen Schutzes bedurfte, und dem König, der sich quasi mit dem Gott verbindet bzw. von letzterem aus angeglichen wurde – für sich genutzt haben.

Insgesamt hebt sich Antigonos durch zwei Besonderheiten von seinen ‚Königskollegen' ab, deren Schutzgottreservoir Porträts bzw. Attribute von Zeus, Apollon und Herakles aufwies.[71] Insbesondere die Verbreitung der Bronzeprägungen von Athena und Pan mit Tropaion in Griechenland verstärken dieses Bild nochmals erheblich.[72] Während Pan in einem ‚Götter-Rating' keinesfalls die Prominenz von Zeus erreichen kann, besticht seine Inanspruchnahme in antigonidischem Kontext durch Exzeptio-

68 Z. B. IG II/III³ 1, 1010 (248/247 v. Chr.), Z. 72, 122, 157, 163, 170, dazu Panagopoulou 2020, 220–221, 291 mit Anm. 292, 295.

69 Voutiras 2018, 406f mit Abb. 9, verweist auf Teile der Prägungen, bei denen Pan „un bandeau semblable à un diadème royal" trägt, was „peut-être l'assimilation du dieu à un souverain hellénistique" suggeriert, wobei sich die Assimilation auch bei Statuen ausmachen lässt; Panagopoulou 2020, 147 mit Anm. 26.

70 SNG München 1080, Taf. 46. Vgl. die Gruppen 27–31 unter III 127–136 bei Panagopoulou 2020, die freilich dem Diadem keine besondere Bedeutung zumisst; auch bei Lichtenberger et al. 2012 findet diese Gruppe keine Berücksichtigung.

71 Kreutz 2007, 207, betont, dass „in der antigonidischen Kultpolitik Zeus nicht an erster Stelle stand", was vor der Folie der Argeaden umso signifikanter erscheint. Insbesondere „das angebliche Vater-Sohn-Verhältnis, das Alexander in bislang einzigartiger Weise mit dem höchsten Gott verbunden hatte", habe dazu geführt, dass „die antigonidischen Herrscher andere Gottheiten zu ihren besonderen Schutzmächten" wählten.

72 Athena kam insofern vielleicht eine noch größere Bedeutung zu als gedacht, da mit dem makedonischen Ort Kyrrhos, der als Sammelpunkt des makedonischen Heeres gelten darf, ein bedeutendes, wohl überregional wirkendes Heiligtum der Athena Kyrrhestis verbunden war, das Diod. 18.4.5 zufolge Alexander der Große zu monumentalisieren gedacht hatte, dazu Voutiras 1998, 124–125 und Daubner 2012, 159–160.

nalität und Situationsbezogenheit[73] – die Wahrnehmung in den athenischen Inschriften im Asklepieion zeigt jedenfalls, dass die Münzen und damit auch der Pan-Bezug in eindeutiger Verbindung mit Antigonos wahrgenommen wurden. Zumindest die frühen Antigoniden haben sich genealogisch gerade *nicht* an die Argeaden angebunden, sondern entsprechende Aussagen finden sich erst unter Philipp V. und Perseus.[74]

5. Zusammenfassung

Die behandelten Beispiele zeigen Strategien von Königen mit verschiedenen Versuchen, ihre Position individuell und punktuell, aber auch auf Dauer angelegt zu festigen, zum Teil mit beträchtlichem ideologischem und vor allem auch finanziellem Aufwand, zum Teil aber auch in der Zuschreibung durch andere, von denen Initiativen aufgegriffen wurden. Allerdings stellt das Schutzgott-Konzept oftmals einen Baustein in einem größeren Ensemble dar, durchaus auch mit Überschneidungen. Ausgehend von bestimmten Stereotypisierungen werden Abweichung und ,Experimente' umso deutlicher, ebenso wie Kontinuitäten und Brüche. Der Bezug auf Alexander als Schutzgott, etwa auf derselben Ebene wie Herakles, wurde hingegen nicht stark forciert, nicht einmal von den Ptolemaiern, denn dabei handelte es sich nicht zuletzt aufgrund der Exzeptionalität des großen Makedonen um eine äußerst ,heikle Materie'[75] – deren In-

---

73   Möglicherweise ist auch eine Reminiszenz an die Schlacht von Marathon intendiert, bei der nach Hdt. 6.105–106 Pan auch eine Rolle spielte (dazu Mastrapas 2013); indem die Galater mit den Persern gleichgesetzt wurden (Cardete del Olmo 2016, 228), kommt dem Sieger das Prädikat des Befreiers von Griechenland zu, dazu Panagopoulou 2020, 301–302.

74   Die Belege bei Schmitt 2005, 252.

75   Es ist vielleicht kein Zufall, dass eine prominente Inanspruchnahme in die frühe Diadochenzeit fällt, und zwar von einem Protagonisten, dem der Aufbau einer Dynastie gerade nicht gelang – dem Griechen Eumenes von Kardia, von dem Plutarch in seiner entsprechenden Biographie gleich zwei Träume überliefert. Im einen (Plut. Eumenes 12.4–6) fungiert Alexander selbst als Traumfigur – er habe Eumenes ein königliches Zelt gezeigt, darin einen Thron, auf dem er selbst virtuell anwesend sei und alle in seinem Namen geführten Unternehmungen unterstützen würde; auch wenn der Text dies als Inszenierung ausgibt, wird die Wirkmächtigkeit deutlich (dazu Weber 1999, 16 f. mit Anm. 53, zur Parallelüberlieferung). Im anderen Traum sah Eumenes zwei Alexander gegeneinander kämpfen, die von Athena und – letztendlich siegreich – Demeter unterstützt wurden (Plut. Eumenes 6.8–12, dazu Weber 1999, 15–18). Der Träumende fungierte selbst als Deuter, gab als Konsequenz die Losung ,Demeter und Alexander' aus und ließ die Soldaten ihre Waffen mit Ähren schmücken, behielt aber den Traum für sich. Der Text suggeriert, dass die Verbreitung der Begebenheit erst nach dem Erfolg umgesetzt wurde. Ob man sich hier die Erscheinung Alexanders als Gott vorstellen muss, ist nicht eindeutig zu klären, aber auch nicht auszuschließen. In jedem Fall konnte auf diese Weise den bekannten Rekursen auf Alexander eine weitere Variante hinzugesetzt werden.

anspruchnahme war mit einem erheblichen Risiko des Scheiterns verbunden, wenn die damit verbundenen Ansprüche nicht adäquat eingelöst werden konnten.[76]

Die Beispiele machen aber auch deutlich, wie persistent manche Motive und Bezüge gewesen sein können, und zwar jenseits konkreter Anlässe: Im Falle der Pan-Porträts von Antigonos Gonatas lässt sich beobachten, dass die Münzen auch nach dem Tod des Königs weitergeprägt wurden, etwa in Periode IV (nach Panagopoulou) unter Antigonos Doson,[77] somit also Kontinuität hergestellt wurde. Die Poseidon-Prägungen des Demetrios hingegen erfuhren nach dem Tod des Prägeherrn keine Fortführung, sondern wurden – dann aber in modifizierter Form als Porträt – erst wieder nach 250 v. Chr. gezeigt. Der Zeus-Bezug bei den Ptolemäern, den der Adler als Wappentier repräsentiert, wurde bis zum Ende der Dynastie fortgeführt.

Insgesamt verwundert es nicht, dass für die beschriebenen Phänomene keine übergeordnete antike Terminologie besteht, mehr noch: Es scheint auch kein einheitliches Konzept von Schutzgottheit(en) im Sinne einer definitorischen Klarheit vorzuliegen. Dennoch gehörten die oben genannten Phänomene zur Lebensrealität der antiken Zeitgenossen, wie sie sich in der alltäglichen Praxis und in den Brechungen durch verschiedene literarische Gattungen zeigen. Weitere Untersuchungen verdienen die terminologischen Implikationen aber dennoch, denn es gilt zu prüfen, wie das Verhalten der schützenden Gottheiten bzw. deren Anspruch und Aktionsfeld formuliert wurden. In der historiographischen Literatur, die zudem oftmals deutlich nach solchen Ereignissen Beschreibungen und Analysen vornimmt, wird man entsprechende Aussagen nicht erwarten, am ehesten noch in Hymnen oder Epigrammen, jedenfalls in Literatur in einem höfischen oder städtischen Kontext, der eine Rückbindung an die Könige aufweist. Eine Richtung könnten die kallimacheischen Hymnen aufzeigen, in denen das Wortfeld μέλει μοι … für den göttlichen Schutz und die Sorge der Gottheit um den jeweiligen König verwendet wird; Inschriften setzen hingegen voraus, dass ein König im Rahmen seiner eigenen Repräsentationsbestrebungen von sich aus die Thematik anspricht oder es sich um Zuschreibungen anderer handelt.[78] Bei Bildzeugnissen hingegen, etwa den behandelten Münzen, besteht immer die Gefahr, ikonographische

---

76 Alexander konnte zu einem späteren Zeitpunkt im Rahmen der Herleitung einer Dynastie von einem bedeutenden Herrscher(geschlecht) aus früherer Zeit durchaus relevant werden; Schmitt 2005, 452, verweist auf Mithradates VI. von Pontos und Antiochos I. von Kommagene.

77 Panagopoulou 2020, 192–205. Eine bemerkenswerte Weiterentwicklung stellt eine Münze Philipps V. dar, auf der das Pan-Porträt ersetzt ist durch eine Darstellung des Heros Perseus, der möglicherweise Züge des Königs trägt; dazu und zu den Zuweisungen Lücke 2020, 298–299.

78 Einschlägig ist SEG 39.1334, worauf Christoph Michels mich freundlicherweise aufmerksam gemacht hat: Παῖς ὁ Δεινοκράτους με σοί, Θυώνης | κοῦρε, καὶ βασιλῆι τὸν φίλοινον | Ἀττάλωι Διονυσόδωρος εἶσεν | Σκίρτον οὐξικύωνος – ἁ δὲ τέχνα | Θοινίου, τὸ δὲ λῆμμα πρατίνειον – | μέλοι δ᾽ ἀμφοτέροισιν ὁ ἀναθεὶς [με] („Der Sohn des Deinokrates, Dionysodoros aus Sikyon, hat mich, den weinliebenden Skirtos, zu deinen Ehren, Sohn der Thyone, und zu Ehren von König Attalos aufgestellt [das Werk stammt von Thoinias, das Sujet aber ist von Pratinas angeregt]. Möge beiden lieb sein der, der mich geweiht hat").

Details nicht zu verstehen oder falsch zu deuten bzw. komplexe Aussageebenen oder offene Rezeptionsangebote nicht wahrzunehmen;[79] dennoch sind es gerade Münzen, die aufgrund ihrer immensen Stückzahlen, die z. B. für die Panbronzen anzunehmen sind, und ihrer weiten Verbreitung probate Medien für den Transfer von Herrschaftsideologie abgaben. Die behandelten Beispiele lassen aber auch erkennen, dass sich zumindest für uns das Phänomen ‚Schutzgottheit' erst aus der Kombination *mehrerer* Quellen(arten) richtig erschließen lässt.

Perspektivisch ergeben sich daraus weitere Ansatzpunkte für eine künftige Beschäftigung mit der Thematik, wobei man aufgrund des Quellenmaterials nicht immer zu zufriedenstellenden Lösungen gelangen wird: (1) Wie haben sich die für den Beginn der Epoche beschriebenen Phänomene weiterentwickelt, auch mit Blick auf die numismatische Kommemorierung von Einzelereignissen?[80] Solche blieben, zumal im militärischen Bereich, ja keineswegs aus, was ebenso für die Berücksichtigung des religiösen Bereichs durch die Herrscher zutrifft.[81] (2) Finden sich bestimmte Formulierungen im Sinne von Standards, mit denen ein König selbst sein Verhältnis zu einer Gottheit beschrieben hat? Hier ergibt sich die Schwierigkeit, dass etwa die mit Münzdarstellungen verbundenen Intentionen seitens der Könige nicht schriftlich niedergelegt wurden. (3) Gab es besondere Formen königlicher Ehrerbietung den Schutzgöttern gegenüber? Denn Demetrios und Antigonos haben – wie bereits formuliert – zumindest nach unserem Kenntnisstand *keine* Heiligtümer für Poseidon und Pan errichten lassen. Vielleicht war ihnen auch die Zeit dafür nicht vergönnt – oder die makedonische Tradition stand dem entgegen.[82]

79   Vgl. dazu auch Lücke 2020, 303: „Vielmehr entsteht der Eindruck, dass die Herrscher es ganz bewusst vermieden haben, eindeutige Aussagen auf diesem Wege (sc. den Münzporträts mit Götterattributen) zu kommunizieren. Heute wie damals schwebt über diesen Darstellungen ein Assoziationsgefüge, das im Wesentlichen auf dynastische Abstammungslegenden oder herausragende Fähigkeiten oder Leistungen der Dargestellten anspielt."

80   Den Beginn machte wohl – zumindest nachweisbar – Alexander mit seinen Poros-Prägungen.

81   Hier könnte man den ptolemaiischen Adler anführen, insofern Ralf von den Hoff nach der Bedeutung des Doppeladlers unter Ptolemaios VI. und VIII. gefragt hat. Wenn der Adler (auch) für den göttlichen Schutz steht, ließe sich argumentieren, dass – angezeigt durch die Verdoppelung des Adlers – beide Könige geschützt würden, was aber vielleicht nicht intendiert gewesen sein dürfte. Plausibler erscheint eine Entwicklung, derzufolge sich der Adler von einem Symbol für den Schutz zu einem Herrschaftssymbol verselbständigt hat.

82   Zu fragen wäre außerdem noch, inwieweit man mit dem römischen *tutela*-Konzept weiterkommt (dazu Bolder-Boos 2014) bzw. ob Vorstellungen, wie sie mit dem Daimonion des Sokrates verbunden sind, hier rezipiert wurden.

Literaturverzeichnis

Acosta-Hughes 2021: Acosta-Hughes, Benjamin, That I be your Plaything. The Cult of Arsinoe-Aphrodite in Image and Text, in: M. A. Harder et al. (eds.), Women and Power in Hellenistic Poetry, Leuven et al. 2021, 13–34

Antela-Bernárdez 2016: Antela-Bernárdez, Borja, Like Gods among Men. The Use of Religion and Mythical Issues during Alexander's Campaign, in: K. Ulanowski (ed.), The Religious Aspects of War in the Ancient Near East, Greece and Rome, Leiden et al. 2016, 235–255

Barbantani 2005: Barbantani, Silvia, Goddess of Love and Mistress of the Sea. Notes on a Hellenistic Hymn to Arsinoe-Aphrodite (P. Lit. Goodsp. 2, I–IV), Ancient Society 35, 2005, 135–165

Bernhardt 2012: Bernhardt, Johannes Chr., Das Nikemonument von Samothrake und der Kampf der Bilder, Stuttgart 2012

Bing 1985: Bing, Peter, Kastorion of Soloi's Hymn to Pan (Supplementum Hellenisticum 310), American Journal of Philology 106, 1985, 502–509

Bolder-Boos 2014: Bolder-Boos, Marion, Tutelary Deities in Roman Citizen Colonies, in: T. D. Stek – J. Pelgrom (eds.), Roman Republican Colonization. New Perspectives from Archaeology and Ancient History, Rom 2014, 279–294

Borgeaud 1979: Borgeaud, Philippe, Recherches sur le dieu Pan, Genf 1979

Brackertz 1975: Brackertz, Ursula, Zum Problem der Schutzgottheiten griechischer Städte, Diss. Berlin 1975 [1976]

Brumbaugh 2019: Brumbaugh, Michael, The New Politics of Olympos. Kingship in Kallimachos' *Hymns*, Oxford 2019

Cardete del Olmo 2016: Cardete del Olmo, María C., El dios Pan y los paisajes pánicos. De la figura divina al paisaje religioso, Sevilla 2016

Chaniotis 1997: Chaniotis, Angelos, Epiklese, DNP 3, 1997, 1118–1121

Chaniotis 2011: Chaniotis, Angelos, The Ithyphallic Hymn for Demetrios Poliorketes and Hellenistic Religious Mentality, in: P. P. Iossif – A. S. Chankowski – C. C. Lorber (eds.), More than Men, Less than Gods. Studies on Royal Cult and Imperial Worship, Leuven et al. 2011, 157–195

Christesen – Murray 2010: Christesen, Paul – Murray, Sarah C., Macedonian Religion, in: J. Roisman – I. Worthington (eds.), A Companion to Ancient Macedonia, Malden 2010, 428–445

Dahmen 2011: Dahmen, Karsten, The Legend of Alexander the Great on Greek and Roman Coins, London et al. 2011

Dahmen 2013: Dahmen, Karsten, König, Vorbild, Held, Legende. Darstellungen Alexanders des Großen im antiken Münzbild, in: Gebhard – Rehm – Schulze 2013, 157–163

Daubner 2012: Daubner, Frank, Götter der Makedonen außerhalb Makedoniens, in: G. A. Lehmann – D. Engster – A. Nuss (eds.), Von der bronzezeitlichen Geschichte zur modernen Antikenrezeption, Göttingen 2012, 157–162

Deacy 2008: Deacy, Susan, Athena, London et al. 2008

Edelmann 2007: Edelmann, Babett, Religiöse Herrschaftslegitimation in der Antike. Die religiöse Legitimation orientalisch-ägyptischer und griechisch-hellenistischer Herrscher im Vergleich, St. Katharinen 2007

Ehling 2000: Ehling, Kay, Stierdionysos oder Sohn des Poseidon. Zu den Hörnern des Demetrios Poliorketes, Göttinger Forum für Altertumswissenschaften 3, 2000, 153–160

Ehling 2013: Ehling, Kay, Alexander Thalassokrator. Der Makedonenkönig als Herrscher der Meere, in: Gebhard – Rehm – Schulze 2013, 170–173

Fischer-Bossert 2007: Fischer-Bossert, Wolfgang, Die Ziegen von Aigai, Schweizerische numismatische Rundschau 86, 2007, 23–29

Gaebler 1935: Gaebler, Hugo, Die antiken Münzen Nord-Griechenlands III: Die antiken Münzen von Makedonia und Paionia. Zweite Abteilung, Berlin 1935

Gebhard – Rehm – Schulze 2013: Gebhard, Rupert – Rehm, Ellen – Schulze, Harald (eds.), Alexander der Große – Herrscher der Welt, Darmstadt et al. 2013

Günther – Plischke 2011: Günther, Linda-Marie – Plischke, Sonja (eds.), Studien zum vorhellenistischen und hellenistischen Herrscherkult, Berlin 2011

Hatzopoulos 2013: Hatzopoulos, Miltiades B., Was Dion Macedonia's Religious Centre?, in: P. Funke – M. Haake (eds.), Greek Federal States and Their Sanctuaries, Stuttgart 2013, 163–172

Hatzopoulos 2020: Hatzopoulos, Miltiades B., Ancient Macedonia, Berlin et al. 2020

Hecht 2017: Hecht, Christine, Zwischen Athen und Alexandria. Dichter und Künstler beim makedonischen König Archelaos, Wiesbaden 2017

Hirschberger 2011: Hirschberger, Martina, Götter, in: A. Rengakos – B. Zimmermann (eds.), Homer-Handbuch. Leben – Werk – Wirkung, Stuttgart 2011, 278–292

Hölbl 1994: Hölbl, Günther, Geschichte des Ptolemäerreiches. Politik, Ideologie und religiöse Kultur von Alexander dem Großen bis zur römischen Eroberung, Darmstadt 1994

Hölscher 2020: Hölscher, Tonio, From Early On To Become A Hero (‚Held‘). Mythical Models of Alexander's Image and Biography, in: Trampedach – Meeus 2020, 21–44

Hunter 2003: Hunter, Richard, Encomium in Ptolemy Philadelphus, Berkeley 2003

Huß 1994: Huß, Werner, Der makedonische König und die ägyptischen Priester. Studien zur Geschichte des ptolemaiischen Ägypten, Stuttgart 1994

Huttner 1997: Huttner, Ulrich, Die politische Rolle der Heraklesgestalt im griechischen Herrschertum, Stuttgart 1997

Iossif 2018: Iossif, Panagiotis P., Divine Attributes on Hellenistic Coinages. From Noble to Humble and Back, in: P. P. Iossif – Fr. De Callataÿ – R. Veymiers (eds.), ΤΥΠΟΙ. Greek and Roman Coins seen through their Images. *Noble* Issuers, *Humble* Users?, Liège 2018, 269–296

Kissel 2005: Kissel, Theodor, Lockruf des Mythos. Im Wettstreit mit den homerischen Helden eroberte Alexander die Welt, Antike Welt 36.3, 2005, 45–52

Kleibl 2009: Kleibl, Kathrin, Bündnis und Verschmelzung zweier Göttinnen. Isis und Aphrodite in hellenistischer und römischer Zeit, in: M. Seifert (ed.), Aphrodite. Herrin des Krieges, Göttin der Liebe, Mainz 2009, 111–125

Kotansky 1994: Kotansky, Roy, Greek Magical Amulets. The inscribed Gold, Silver, Copper and Bronze *Lamellae*. I: Published Texts of Known Provenance, Köln 1994

Kreutz 2007: Kreutz, Natascha, Zeus und die griechischen Poleis. Topographische und religionsgeschichtliche Untersuchungen von archaischer bis in hellenistische Zeit, Rahden 2007

Liampi 2001: Liampi, Katerini, Sylloge Nummorum Graecorum (SNG) Deutschland. Staatliche Münzsammlung München, 10./11. Heft: Makedonien, Könige, Nr. 1–1228, München 2001

Lianou 2010: Lianou, Maria, The Role of the Argeadai in the Legitimation of the Ptolemaic Dynasty: Rhetoric and Practice, in: E. D. Carney – D. Ogden (eds.), Philip II and Alexander the Great: Father and Son, Lives and Afterlifes, Oxford 2010, 123–133

Lichtenberger 2021: Lichtenberger, Achim, Der Olymp. Sitz der Götter zwischen Himmel und Erde, Stuttgart 2021

Lichtenberger et al. 2012: Lichtenberger, Achim et al. (eds.), Das Diadem der hellenistischen Herrscher. Übernahme, Transformation oder Neuschöpfung eines Herrschaftszeichens?, Bonn 2012

Lücke 2020: Lücke, Stephan, Darstellungen hellenistischer Herrscher mit Götterattributen im Münzbild, in: A. Pangerl (ed.), Portraits. 400 Years of Hellenistic Portraits. 400 Jahre hellenistische Portraits, München 2020, 293–312

Magnelli 2015: Magnelli, Enrico, A Note on Castorion's Hymn to Pan (SH 310): Metre and Syntax, Reading and Listening, Greece & Rome 62.1, 2015, 87–91

Mastrapas 2013: Mastrapas, Antonis, The Battle of Marathon and the Introduction of Pan's Worship to Athens. The Political Dimension of a Legend Through Written Evidence and Archaeological Find, in: Chr. Carey – M. Edwards (eds.), Marathon – 2,500 Years: Proceedings of The Marathon Conference 2010, London 2013, 111–122

Meyer 2014: Meyer, Doris, Hymnen und Kultdichtung, in: B. Zimmermann – A. Rengakos (eds.), Handbuch der griechischen Literatur der Antike II: Die Literatur der klassischen und hellenistischen Zeit, München 2014, 179–190

Michels 2011: Michels, Christoph, Dionysos Kathegemon und der attalidische Herrscherkult. Überlegungen zur Herrschaftsrepräsentation der Könige von Pergamon, in: Günther – Plischke 2011, 114–140

Mittag 2023: Mittag, Peter F., Sieghaftigkeit und Frieden auf hellenistischen Münzen, in: Ch. Chrysafis et al. (eds.), Basileus eirenophylax. Friedenskultur(en) und monarchische Repräsentation in der alten Welt, Stuttgart 2023, 161–180

Mørkholm 1991: Mørkholm, Otto, Early Hellenistic Coinage. From the Accession of Alexander to the Peace of Apamea (336–188 B. C.), Cambridge 1991

Müller 2010: Müller, Sabine, Demetrios Poliorketes, Aphrodite und Athen, Gymnasium 117, 2010, 559–573

Müller 2016: Müller, Sabine, Die Argeaden. Geschichte Makedoniens bis zum Zeitalter Alexanders des Großen, Paderborn 2016

Müller 2017: Müller, Sabine, The Symbolic Capital of the Argeads, in: S. Müller et al. (eds.), The History of the Argeads. New Perspectives, Classica et Orientalia 19, Wiesbaden 2017, 183–198

Müller 2020: Müller, Sabine, Foundation Myth, in: LexAM, 236–240

Nachtergael 1977: Nachtergael, Georges, Les Galates en Grèce et les Sotèria de Delphes, Brüssel 1977

Nawotka 2019: Nawotka, Krzysztof, Apollo, the Tutelary God of the Seleucids, and Demodamas of Miletus, in: Z. Archibald – J. Haywood (eds.), The Power of Individual and Community in Ancient Athens and Beyond, Swansea 2019, 261–284

Newell 1927: Newell, Edward T., The Coinages of Demetrius Poliorcetes, London 1927 (ND Chicago 1978)

Newman 2020: Newman, Alana N., Arsinoë II as Synnaos Thea, in: C. Cusset – P. Belenfant – C.-E. Nardone (eds.), Féminités hellénistiques. Voix, genre, représentations, Leuven et al. 2020, 157–176

Nock 1930: Nock, Arthur D., Synnaos theos, Harvard Studies in Classical Philology 41, 1930, 1–62 (= id., Essays on Religion and the Ancient World, ed. Z. Stewart, Oxford 1972, 202–251)

Ogden 2017: Ogden, Daniel, The Legend of Seleucus. Kingship Narratives and Mythmaking in the Ancient World, Cambridge 2017

Orth 2014: Orth, Wolfgang, Der fromme Diadoche. Zur Situation der großen griechischen Heiligtümer um 300 v. Chr., in: H. Hauben – A. Meeus (eds.), The Age of the Successors and the Creation of the Hellenistic Kingdoms (323–276 BC), Leuven et al. 2014, 559–575

Panagopoulou 2020: Panagopoulou, Katerina, The Early Antigonids. Coinage, Money, and the Economy, New York 2020

Pfeiffer 2017: Pfeiffer, Stefan, Die Ptolemäer. Im Reich der Kleopatra, Stuttgart 2017

Pownall 2017: Pownall, Frances, The Role of Greek Literature at the Argead Court, in: S. Müller et al. (eds.), The History of the Argeads. New Perspectives, Wiesbaden 2017, 215–229

Queyrel 2015: Queyrel, François, Synnaoi theoi. Die sakrale Inszenierung der Königsstatuen, in: D. Boschung – J. Hammerstaedt (eds.), Das Charisma des Herrschers, Paderborn 2015, 213–234

Riboldi 2016: Riboldi, Chiara (ed.), Epitheta deorum, Mailand 2016

Schmidt-Dounas 1993: Schmidt-Dounas, Barbara, Statuen hellenistischer Könige als synnaoi theoi, Egnatia 4, 1993, 71–132

Schmitt 2005: Schmitt, Hatto H., Herrscherlegenden, in: LexHell, 452–453

Schulze 2013: Schulze, Harald, Alexander und Herakles, in: Gebhard – Rehm – Schulze 2013, 188–193

Taeger 1957: Taeger, Fritz, Charisma, Stuttgart 1957

Trampedach – Meeus 2020: Trampedach, Kai – Meeus, Alexander (eds.), The Legitimation of Conquest. Monarchical Representation and the Art of Government in the Empire of Alexander the Great, Stuttgart 2020

von den Hoff 2020: von den Hoff, Ralf, Alexander's Dedications to the Gods. Sacred Space, Pious Practice and Public Legitimation, in: Trampedach – Meeus 2020, 99–122

Voutiras 1998: Voutiras, Emmanuel, Athèna dans les cités de Macédoine, Kernos 11, 1998, 111–129

Voutiras 2018: Voutiras, Emmanuel, Pan en Macédoine, in: M. Kalaitzi et al. (eds.), Βορειοελλαδικά. Tales from the Lands of the Ethne. Essays in Honour of Miltiades B. Hatzopoulos, Athen 2018, 397–412

Wallace 2018: Wallace, Shane, Metalexandron. Receptions of Alexander in the Hellenistic and Roman Worlds, in: K. R. Moore (ed.), Brill's Companion to the Reception of Alexander the Great, Leiden et al. 2018, 162–196

Waterfield 2021: Waterfield, Robin, The Making of a King. Antigonus Gonatas of Macedon and the Greeks, Chicago 2021

Weber 1992: Weber, Gregor, Poesie und Poeten an den Höfen vorhellenistischer Monarchen, Klio 74, 1992, 25–77

Weber 1993: Weber, Gregor, Dichtung und höfische Gesellschaft. Die Rezeption von Zeitgeschichte am Hof der ersten drei Ptolemäer, Stuttgart 1993

Weber 1995: Weber, Gregor, Herrscher, Hof und Dichter. Aspekte der Legitimierung und Repräsentation hellenistischer Könige am Beispiel der ersten drei Antigoniden, Historia 44.3, 1995, 283–316

Weber 1999: Weber, Gregor, Herrscher und Traum in hellenistischer Zeit, Archiv für Kulturgeschichte 81.1, 1999, 1–33

Weber 2011: Weber, Gregor, Der ptolemäische Herrscher- und Dynastiekult – ein Experimentierfeld für Makedonen, Griechen und Ägypter, in: Günther – Plischke 2012, 77–97

Weber 2024a: Weber, Gregor, Religion an Herrscherhöfen? Eine Spurensuche in der griechischen und römischen Welt, in: J. N. Bremmer – G. Petridou – J. Rüpke (eds.), Religion in Context, Stuttgart 2024 (im Druck)

Weber 2024b: Weber, Gregor, Religion an den Höfen der hellenistischen Könige: Herrscherkulte, Dynastiekulte und Schutzgottheiten – eine Spurensuche, erscheint in: S. Blaschek – G. Dumke (eds.), Macht – Sprache – Herrscher. Herrscherrepräsentation und Herrscherkult in den außerägyptischen Besitzungen und Einflussgebieten der Ptolemäer (323 bis 30 v. Chr.), Leuven 2024 (im Druck)

Wheatley – Dunn 2020: Wheatley, Pat – Dunn, Charlotte, Demetrius the Besieger, Oxford 2020

Wheatley – Dunn 2021: Wheatley, Pat – Dunn, Charlotte, Coinage as Propaganda. Alexander and his Successors, in: J. P. Walsh – E. Baynham (eds.), Alexander the Great and Propaganda, London et al. 2021, 162–198

Will ²1979/1982: Will, Edouard, Histoire politique du monde hellénistique (323–30 av. J.-C.) 2 vols., Nancy ²1979/1982

Abbildungsverzeichnis

Alle Abbildungen © Staatliche Münzsammlung München (Abb. 1–11: Nicolai Kästner, Abb. 12: Sergio Castelli).

Gregor Weber is a full Professor of Ancient History at the University of Augsburg. He has been researching various aspects of kingship in Hellenism for many years, especially in the combination of philological and historical questions. His project on the "Basileus eirenophylax" in this era has resulted in the anthology *Friedenskultur(en) und monarchische Repräsentation* (2023); his monograph *Studien zur hellenistischen Monarchie* was published in spring 2024 (C. H. Beck). Other foci of his research relate to ancient and modern democracy as well as dreams, visions and dream interpretation books from Greco-Roman antiquity and their reception into modern times; he also edits the bibliographic database "Dreams of Antiquity 2.0" (https://dreamsofantiquity.ku.de) and serves as co-editor of the "Gnomon Bibliographic Database" (www.gbd.digital). He is currently working on a cultural history of mushrooms in antiquity.

Eine prospektive Erinnerungsgemeinschaft
Dynastie und Genealogie in der Repräsentation der Ptolemaier

STEFAN PFEIFFER

Abstract: In Ptolemaic kingship, the invention of tradition and genealogy as well as the construction of dynastic past, present and future played a decisive role. This paper argues that for this reason the understanding of dynasty in Ptolemaic kingship went far beyond the concept of "family" – the dynasty was a prospective "community of memory". The present study traces the interconnection of the three time levels past, present and future with a view to the representation of dynasty and family in word and image. In this context, the "double face" of the monarchy, i.e., its Graeco-Macedonian and its Egyptian representation, is also considered. To this end, a distinction is made between self-representation on the one hand and representation of the royal couple by (groups of) subjects on the other.

Homonymy, similitudo, endogamy, divinity and divine descent are elaborated as central elements of the dynastic representation of the Ptolemies, both in the Greek and the Egyptian context.

1. Herkunft und Wirkmacht

Jan Assmann konstatiert in seinem epochalen Werk zum *Kulturellen Gedächtnis* zutreffend: „Herrschaft braucht Herkunft".[1] Doch es gibt keine Regel ohne Ausnahme: Im Hellenismus kann bekanntlich Charisma Herkunft als Herrschaftsvoraussetzung ersetzen, denn Herrschaft beruht auf Gefolgschaft, die auch durch persönliche Wirkmacht erzielt werden kann, wie es Gehrke auf Basis von Max Weber vor nunmehr 40 Jahren in seinem programmatischen Aufsatz zum siegreichen König ausgeführt hat.[2]

---

1   Assmann ⁸2018, 71.
2   Gehrke 1982, 247–277.

Ptolemaios, der Sohn des Lagos und Begründer der nach ihm benannten Dynastie, ist im Grunde genommen ein idealtypischer Vertreter dieser charismatischen Form von Herrschaft: Er kam aus einer derart unbekannten Familie, dass er, wie es eine Hofanekdote zu berichten weiß, noch nicht einmal den Namen seines Großvaters väterlicherseits benennen konnte.[3] Ob die Anekdote nun historisch ist oder nicht, ob Ptolemaios dies vorgab, weil es ebenfalls das Gerücht gab, er sei ein illegitimer Sohn Philipps II.,[4] oder ob er wirklich nicht wusste, wer seine väterlichen Ahnen waren, ist unerheblich. Die Anekdote, die möglicherweise als Angriff auf seine Legitimität verstanden werden kann, charakterisiert den Lagiden andererseits als Repräsentant einer Sorte von Monarchen, die nach der vielzitierten und vielbemühten Definition der Suda die Nachfolger Alexanders des Großen ausmachten: Nicht ihre Herkunft – die *phýsis* –, sondern ihre Fähigkeit, ein Heer zu führen und die politischen Angelegenheiten kompetent zu handhaben, also die persönliche Wirkmacht war es, die sie zum Königtum bestimmte.[5]

Nun hatte aber Ptolemaios eine Dynastie begründet, in der gerade die Herkunft aus der regierenden Familie zweifelsfrei Voraussetzung war, den Thron zu besteigen. Seit der zweiten Generation gilt also tatsächlich das, was Jan Assmann so treffend formuliert hat, dass Herrschaft Herkunft braucht. Der erste Lagide selbst hatte das dynastische Ideal in dem Moment vorgegeben, als er seinen Sohn zum Mitherrscher erklärte. Bereits mit dem zweiten Ptolemaier war damit klar, dass die Nachfolge ausschließlich von einem Sohn des Königs übernommen werden kann, die „Herkunft" bzw. mit den Worten der Suda die *phýsis* war mithin wichtiger als das persönliche Charisma. In den folgenden zwölf Generationen kam es deshalb zwar zu blutigen Konflikten in den stets prekären Phasen eines Thronwechsels, aber fast nie stand es zur Debatte, dass ein Knabe, der nicht dem königlichen Blute entsprungen war, die Nachfolge antreten könnte.

Wie sehr *phýsis* seit Ptolemaios II. ausreichte, um Gefolgschaft zu erhalten, zeigte sich drei Generationen später: Im Jahr 217 v. Chr. standen sich bei Raphia Ptolemaios IV. und Antiochos III. an der Spitze zweier großer Heere gegenüber. Vor der Schlacht hielt jeder König eine Rede an seine Truppen, deren Inhalt Polybios kurz

---

3   Plut. De cohib. ira 9 = mor. 457c–458c: Πτολεμαῖος δὲ γραμματικὸν εἰς ἀμαθίαν ἐπισκώπτων ἠρώτησε τίς ὁ τοῦ Πηλέως πατὴρ ἦν· κἀκεῖνος Ἂν σὺ πρότερον εἴπῃς ἔφη τίς ὁ τοῦ Λάγου· Τὸ δὲ σκῶμμα τῆς δυσγενείας ἥπτετο τοῦ βασιλέως, καὶ πάντες ἠγανάκτησαν ὡς οὐκ ἐπιτήδειον ὂν καὶ ἄκαιρον· ὁ δὲ Πτολεμαῖος Εἰ μὴ τὸ φέρειν ἔφη σκαπτόμενον, οὐδὲ τὸ σκάπτειν βασιλικόν ἐστιν; „Ptolemaios fragte einst einen Grammatiker, um ihn wegen seiner Unwissenheit zu verspotten, wer Peleus' Vater gewesen sei. ‚Sag du mir erst', versetzte der Grammatiker, ‚wer des Lagos Vater gewesen ist'. Dieser Spott warf dem König seine niedrige Herkunft vor, und alle waren darüber aufgebracht, rieten ihm auch, dass er dies nicht ungeahndet lassen sollte. Aber Ptolemaios antwortete: ‚Wenn ein König keinen Spott annehmen soll, so darf er auch keinen ausgeben.'" (Übersetzung: Apelt 1926/1927).

4   Paus. 1.6.2; Curt. 9.8.22.

5   Suda, s. v. *basileia* no. 147: Οὔτε φύσις οὔτε τὸ δίκαιον ἀποδιδοῦσι τοῖς ἀνθρώποις τὰς βασιλείας, ἀλλὰ τοῖς δυναμένοις ἡγεῖσθαι στρατοπέδου καὶ χειρίζειν πράγματα νουνεχῶς. οἷος ἦν Φίλιππος καὶ οἱ διάδοχοι Ἀλεξάνδρου.

zusammenfasst.[6] Auch wenn unklar bleibt, inwiefern Polybios hier Autor oder tatsächlich Referent des Inhalts der Reden ist, so bietet seine Zusammenfassung doch trotzdem einen Einblick in das Denken seiner Zeit über die Grundlagen von soldatischer Gefolgschaft im hellenistischen Königtum, wie es sich in den auf die Diadochenzeit folgenden Jahren entwickelt hatte. Beide Könige hätten, so Polybios, erst vor kurzem den Thron bestiegen, weshalb keiner von beiden auf „ein eigenes sichtbares und würdiges Werk verweisen" (ἴδιον μὲν γὰρ ἔργον ἐπιφανὲς καὶ κατηξιωμένον) könne. Ptolemaios IV. hatte in der Tat ein Problem: Obzwar bereits seit drei Jahren König und mit 27 Lebensjahren in einem Alter, in dem Alexander der Große schon die Welt erobert hatte, war es dem Ptolemaier bisher nicht gelungen, das zwei Jahre zuvor von Antiochos geraubte Koilesyrien zurückzuerobern. So musste der Lagide in der Tat den „Geist und Mut" (φρόνημα καὶ θάρσος) der Soldaten auf andere Art und Weise stärken. Hierzu wiederum verwies er, wie Antiochos auch, auf den Ruhm, die *dóxa*, und die Taten der Vorfahren (τῆς δὲ τῶν προγόνων δόξης καὶ τῶν ἐκείνοις πεπραγμένων), die mithin als dynastische Qualitäten auf ihn übertragen wurden.

Für meine folgenden Überlegungen ist entscheidend, dass am Vorabend der Schlacht von Raphia auf ptolemaiischer Seite ein König das Heer führte, der zunächst ausschließlich aus traditionalen Gründen König war. Trotz der bisher nicht erwiesenen Leistungsfähigkeit war der vierte Ptolemaier unbestritten König, denn er konnte seine bisher mangelnde militärische Erfahrung mit dem Verweis auf seine Herkunft wettmachen: Er nahm also die Leistungen der Ahnen, deren Charisma, oder in der Sprache der Quellen, ihre *dóxa*, für seine eigene Leitungsfunktion in Anspruch: Sie waren integraler Bestandteil seiner eigenen *phýsis*. In diesem Sinne inkarnierte sich in der Tat nach ptolemaiischer Selbstdarstellung die Qualität des Vaters und die Sakralität der Vorfahren im amtierenden Sohn: Die Ptolemaier sind als Könige aufgrund ihrer Heiligkeit anerkannt, die sich aus der dynastischen Tradition begründete.[7] Dass die Übertragung von progonaler Wirkmächtigkeit bereits in der zweiten Generation wichtiger Bestandteil königlicher Repräsentation war, legt ein Gedicht des Theokrit auf Ptolemaios II. nahe, wo es heißt, dass Berenike I. dem Krieger Ptolemaios den Krieger Ptolemaios gebar.[8]

Da der ptolemaiische König seit dieser Zeit zudem nicht ohne seine Gemahlin, die gleichzeitig seine Schwester war, zu denken ist, betraf die Übertragung progonaler *dóxa* zudem auch seine Gemahlin, die gleichen Blutes war. Dies bringt ein Epigramm

---

6   Pol. 5.83.3–6 (Übersetzung: Ziegler 1961/1963).

7   Um die hellenistische Herrschaft trotzdem weiterhin als charismatisch zu charakterisieren, bedient man sich deshalb des Hilfskonstrukts eines Erbcharismas: Gehrke 1982, 256–257; 270; vgl. Weber ⁵1976, 140–148; vgl. die Kritik am Erbcharisma-Konzept für die Zeit nach den Diadochen bei Wiemer 2017, 334–336.

8   Theokr. 17.56–57: αἰχμητά Πτολεμαῖε, αἰχμητᾷ Πτολεμαίῳ ἀρίζηλος Βερενίκα: „und dich, Lanzenkämpfer Ptolemaios, gebar dem Lanzenkämpfer Ptolemaios die glorreiche Berenike" (Übersetzung: Effe ²2013).

des Poseidippos auf Berenike II.[9] zum Ausdruck, die er nach einem Wagensieg in Olympia sagen lässt, dass ihr „Ruhm", ihre δόξα [παλαιόγονος], bis auf den Großvater zurückgehe – die Ergänzung von παλαιόγονος ist zumindest plausibel –, der ebenfalls mit dem Wagen in Olympia gewonnen habe.[10]

Aufgrund der enormen Bedeutung der Ahnen für die Selbstdarstellung der ptole-maiischen Herrschaft werde ich im Folgenden genauer auf die kultische Repräsenta-tion der Dynastie eingehen. Einerseits möchte ich hierbei die Selbstdarstellung vor-stellen und andererseits auf die Repräsentation des Königshauses durch verschiedene Untertanengruppen eingehen, um zu zeigen, wie unterschiedlich verschiedene Unter-tanengruppen aufgrund ihres jeweiligen kulturell-religiösen Hintergrundes mit der von oben gesetzten dynastischen Konzeption umgehen konnten.

2. Das dynastische Konzept der Ptolemaier

Als Idee geht das dynastische Konzept, wie gesagt, bereits auf Ptolemaios I. zurück, der seinen Sohn als Nachfolger betrachtete, ihn, um dessen Nachfolge zu sichern, bereits zu Lebzeiten zum Mitkönig erklärt und durch die Namensvergabe an den Sohn das Prinzip der Homonymie von Vater und Sohn zu einem entscheidenden Kennzeichen der Pto-lemaier gemacht hatte. So drücken es auch die Epigramme des Poseidippos aus, wenn er zu Ptolemaios II. schreibt: „der König, der von seinem Vater, der auch König war, den Namen erhielt".[11] Ptolemaios II. wiederum ließ Vater und Mutter als Rettergötter vergöttlichen. Nach der Hochzeit mit der Schwester vergöttlichte er sich mit Arsinoë II. ebenfalls. Goldmünzen mit Doppelporträts seines Vaters und seiner Mutter sowie mit dem seiner selbst und der Schwestergemahlin erhielten die Umschrift „(Münze) der Geschwistergötter"[12] und markierten das zentrale Element dynastischer Herrschaft: Vorgänger- und Herrscherpaar bilden eine Medaille mit zwei Seiten. Die verstorbe-nen göttlichen Vorgänger erhalten im lebenden göttlichen Herrscherpaar eine irdische Manifestation.[13] Bis zum Ende der Dynastie erschien zudem das Porträt Ptolemaios' I. auf den Bronze- und Silberprägungen der Ptolemaier, was zeigt, wie wichtig gerade er

9   Schwerlich ist Berenike, die Tochter Ptolemaios' II. und Arsinoës I., gemeint (so Thompson 2005, 274–278); zumindest gibt es keinen Hinweis darauf, da das gesamte Epigramm gut in die Reprä-sentation der Dynastie als Herrscherfamilie passt.
10 Poseidipp. fr. 78 (Austin/Bastianini).
11 Poseidipp. fr. 78,6–7 (Austin/Bastianini): ἐκ βασιλέως βασιλεὺς | πατρὸς ἔχων ὄνομα (Übersetzung Hose 2015).
12 Olivier – Lorber 2013, 50–78; zur Herrschaftsideologie und Sukzession der Zeit zwischen erstem und zweitem Ptolemaier vgl. Caneva 2016; zur Interpretation von den Hoff 2021, 171–173.
13 Es ist die Liebe zwischen den Eltern, die diese Ähnlichkeit weitergibt: Theokr. 17.38–44; nach Kall. h. 4.170, zeigt Ptolemaios II. „das Wesen des Vaters" (ἤθεα πατρός).

für die Identifikation der Dynastie bis zu ihrem Ende war.[14] In späterer Zeit kam es sicherlich auch wegen der Bedeutung der dynastischen Herkunft in der Kunst zu einer Bildnisangleichung zwischen regierendem Sohn und verstorbenem Vater.[15] Damit zeigt sich, dass die dynastische Konzeption der Ptolemaier auf vier Kernelementen beruhte: Homonymie, Endogamie, *similitudo* und Göttlichkeit.

2.1 Der Dynastiekult

Der deutlichste Ausdruck der dynastischen Selbstdarstellung ptolemaiischer Herrschaft ist sicherlich in dem, was wir modern als den „alexandrinischen Dynastiekult" bezeichnen, zu sehen. Es handelt sich um eine Form des Kultes und der Vergöttlichung, die vollumfänglich auf die Initiative des Königshauses selbst zurückgehen dürfte.[16] Gleichzeitig wirft dieser Dynastiekult aber auch Fragen auf, denn er bricht mit der eben herausgestellten dynastischen Tradition, weil er erstens an Alexander den Großen gebunden ist, und weil zweitens zunächst Ptolemaios I. nicht in den Kult integriert war – letzterer kam erst unter Ptolemaios IV. hinzu.[17]

Es ist deshalb wichtig herauszustellen, dass die Bezeichnung dieses Kultes als Dynastiekult eine moderne ist,[18] denn in seiner Ausgestaltung verbindet der Kult das Prinzip der Anknüpfung an die Ahnen mit der Nachfolge Alexanders. Seinen Ursprung hat der Kult unter Ptolemaios II., der sich – erstmals belegt 272/271 v. Chr. – mit seiner Schwestergemahlin Arsinoë II. und unter dem bereits erwähnten Kulttitel „Geschwistergötter" an den unter Ptolemaios I. wohl 290/289 v. Chr. eingerichteten Reichskult Alexanders des Großen[19] anschließen ließ.[20] Neben das Geschwisterpaar der Dioskuren, die bisher die beiden „Retter" waren, traten nun also zwei neue göttliche Geschwister, die eine ähnliche Funktion erhielten.

Zwar hatte der König seinen Vater und seine Mutter als Rettergötter deifiziert, wie er auch in seiner Selbstdarstellung einen engen Bezug zu Vater und Mutter suchte, doch seine eigene Vergöttlichung betrieb er in Anschluss an den Kult Alexanders des Großen. Reichsweite Verbreitung fand der Kult Alexanders und der Ptolemaier

14   Galbois 2012, 280.
15   Von den Hoff 2021, 189.
16   Fraser 1972, I, 213–246; Koenen 1993, 50–57.
17   Minas 2000, 112–114.
18   Ob man deshalb freilich erst ab dieser Zeit von einem Dynastiekult reden darf (etwa Caneva 2016, 163: „this definition is not appropriate for the Alexandrian eponymous priesthood before the reform of Ptolemy IV."), ist eine Frage der Definition des Begriffes selbst, den die antiken Menschen nicht kannten.
19   Zur Einrichtung des Alexanderkultes: Minas 2000, 87–89.
20   P.Hib. II 199,17; Caneva 2016, 163–173. Unklar muss bleiben, weshalb Ptolemaios II. nicht seinen Vater als Ankerpunkt des Kultes wählte. Zur Einrichtung des Arsinoëkultes: Collombert 2008, 83–101.

im Institut eines jährlich wechselnden Priesters, der in jeder Urkunde nach der Nennung des Regierungsjahres eines Königs mit anzuführen war. Existiert hat der eponyme Alexanderkult bis mindestens unter die Herrschaft Ptolemaios' X. Alexander I. (84/83 v. Chr.).[21]

Da stets die Königsgemahlin Teilhaberin des Kultes war, ist es offensichtlich, dass ptolemaiischer Herrscherkult im Grunde genommen immer ein Herrscher*paar*kult war. Der Gemahlin kam in der kultischen Repräsentation der Dynastie sogar eine wichtigere Rolle zu als dem König selbst, weil die Ptolemaierinnen zunächst postum eigene eponyme Priesterinnen erhielten, die in den Urkunden nach dem Alexanderpriester angeführt wurden. Anders als der König konnten Gemahlinnen auch über eigene Tempel verfügen.[22]

Diese offensive Einbindung der Königsgemahlin in den Kult könnte ihre Wurzeln bei den Argeaden haben, denn schon das Philippeion in Olympia integrierte die Königsgemahlinnen Olympias und Eurydike[23] als weibliche Ahnen Alexanders. So macht dieses Gebäude gleichzeitig auch die dynastische Konzeption von Herrschaft im makedonischen Bereich deutlich, da nicht nur Alexander und Philipp, sondern auch Amyntas, der Vater Philipps, als Statuen aufgestellt waren.[24] Falls das Philippeion also eine Stiftung von Philipp II. selbst sein sollte, so war er es, der nach der Schlacht von Chaironeia seine militärische Sieghaftigkeit erstmals an die Ahnen rückband,[25] wobei er über die Nähe des Baus zum Pelopion gleichzeitig einen Bezug zum Gründer der Argeadendynastie Herakles herstellte, der den Kult des Pelops in Olympia begründet hatte.[26]

Sicherlich aufgrund der Nähe zum Philippeion weihte der Flottengeneral Kallikrates von Samos dem Zeus an der gegenüberliebenden Seite der Altis später dann auch das Ptolemaieranathem mit den Statuen Ptolemaios' II. und Arsinoës II.[27]

Mit Blick auf den Dynastiekult bleibt erstens festzuhalten, dass, obwohl die Dynastie gemeinsam mit Alexander verehrt wurde, die Ptolemaier Alexander *nicht* in ihre Genealogie eingebunden haben – sie waren allerhöchstens fiktiv mit ihm verwandt –, und dass zweitens, auch wenn Ptolemaios I. zunächst *nicht* Bestandteil des Dynastiekultes war, er dennoch, wie es die oben angeführten Beispiele der frühen Ptolemaierzeit zeigen, für alle Ptolemaier als wichtiger Ahn, als Begründer des Königshauses galt.

Sicherlich wollten deshalb Ptolemaios II. und seine Nachfolger den Gründervater des Geschlechts nicht ,zurückstellen', als sie ihn nicht in den Alexanderkult aufnah-

---

21   Clarysse – van Derveken 1983, Nr. 207.
22   Vgl. für Arsinoë II. etwa den Tempel im Hafen von Alexandreia und den am Kap Zephyrion; Quellen zum Tempel zusammengestellt bei: Scherf 2002, 767.
23   Paus. 5.17.4; 20.9–10.
24   Zuletzt von den Hoff 2020, 100–106, der es, m. E. nicht überzeugend, keinesfalls für einen Tempel, sondern ein Schatzhaus hält („treasury with sacral charakter").
25   Paus. 5.20.9–10.
26   Von den Hoff 2020, 106–107.
27   Hoepfner 1971, 11–54; zuletzt Caneva 2016, 152–153.

men. Möglicherweise ist es eher so, dass Ptolemaios I. zunächst die gleiche Position hatte wie Alexander, weshalb er nicht an den Dynastiekult angeschlossen werden musste. Eine solche Gleichwertigkeit der beiden Zeitgenossen Ptolemaios und Alexander postuliert auch Theokrit. In seinem 17. Idyll sitzen Alexander und Ptolemaios nebeneinander auf goldenen Thronen im Saal des Zeus und beiden gegenüber sitzt Herakles, „denn beide haben sie den gewaltigen Herakliden zum Ahnen / beide leiten sich bis von Herakles her."[28] Ptolemaios I. und Berenike hatten deshalb auch einen eigenen Tempel.[29]

2.2 Die Kultnamen der Ptolemaier

Es sind insbesondere die kultischen Beinamen der Ptolemaier, die die enge familiäre Bindung, die sich auch im Institut der Geschwisterheirat nach dem Vorbild von Ptolemaios II. und Arsinoë II. für die nachfolgenden Herrscherpaare ausdrückte, deutlich zu erkennen geben: Auf einen Kultnamen, der mit der Qualität des Königspaares mit Blick auf die Untertanen in Zusammenhang steht – Rettung, Wohltat und Erscheinung –, folgt in den ersten knapp 200 Jahren immer in der nächsten Generation ein Kultname, der die Liebe innerhalb der Familie betont – die Geschwister-, Vater- und Mutterliebe.[30]

Tab. 1 Die epitheta der ptolemaiischen Herrscherpaare (grün = Geschwisterbezug; blau = Mutterbezug; rot = Vaterbezug)

Ptolemaios I.	theoi soteres	
Ptolemaios II.		theoi adelphoi
Ptolemaios III.	theoi euergetai	
Ptolemaios IV.		theoi philopatores
Ptolemaios V.	theoi epiphaneis	
Ptolemaios VI.		theoi philometores
Ptolemaios VIII.	theoi euergetai	
Ptolemaios IX. Soter II.	theoi philometores soteres	
Ptolemaios X. Alex. I.	theos philometor (soter) + thea philadelphos	
Ptolemaios XI. Alex. II.	--	

28   Theokr. 17.26–27 (Übersetzung: Staiger 1970); hierzu Huttner 1997, 140–144.
29   Theokr. 17.123.
30   Vgl. zu den Kultnamen umfassend die entsprechenden Abschnitte bei Muccioli 2013. Zur Geschwisterheirat bei den pontischen Königen vgl. den Beitrag von Alex McAuley in diesem Band.

Ptolemaios XII.	theos neos Dionysos philopator philadelphos	
Ptolemaios XIII.		theoi philopatores
Ptolemaios XIV.		theoi philopatores philadelphoi
Kleopatra VII.		thea Neotera philopator philopatris
Ptolemaios XV.		theos philopator philometor

Des Weiteren fällt auf, dass nach dem anfänglichen Wechsel zwischen göttlicher Wirk-macht und Familienliebe, die der Kultname ausdrückt, seit dem 1. Jh. v. Chr. die Kö-nige und Königinnen in ihrem Kultnamen auf göttliche Eigenschaften, die die Unter-tanen berücksichtigen, verzichten, und ausschließlich die familiäre Abkunft betonen, wobei deutlich das patrilineare Element im Vordergrund steht. Das geschieht, obwohl es gerade in der späten Ptolemaierzeit die Königinnen waren, die teils sogar eigenstän-dig die Regierungsgeschäfte führten.

Schon die antiken Autoren wussten freilich, dass es mit der Familienliebe in einer Dynastie, in der ständig das eine Mitglied das andere ums Leben brachte, nicht weit her war. So schreibt Pausanias etwa über Ptolemaios IX.: „Philometor, der achte Nach-komme des Ptolemaios, des Sohnes des Lagos, bekam seinen Beinamen zum Spott, denn keiner von den Königen wurde unseres Wissens so sehr von seiner Mutter ge-hasst."[31]

2.3 Die Reaktion der griechischen Welt: Retrospektive und prospektive Loyalität

Der Spott des Dichters Sotades über die Geschwisterehe des zweiten Ptolemaiers ist ein seltener Hinweis darauf, dass eine Herrschaft, die auf dem Prinzip Endogamie basierte, bei den Untertanen nicht unstrittig war.[32] Im städtischen Lob der Ptolemaier hingegen ist die dynastische Konzeption von Homonymie, *similitudo*, Endogamie und Göttlichkeit präsent, so präsent, dass selbst freie Städte, wie etwa Athen, die ,interge-nerationale' Anbindung des lebenden Königs an die Ahnen aufgriffen. Nach dem Tod der königlichen Schwestergemahlin Arsinoë II. heißt es im Chremonides-Dekret der

---

31   Paus. 1.9.1: ὁ δὲ Φιλομήτωρ καλούμενος ὄγδοος μέν ἐστιν ἀπόγονος Πτολεμαίου τοῦ Λάγου, τὴν δὲ ἐπίκλησιν ἔσχεν ἐπὶ χλευασμῷ. οὐ γάρ τινα τῶν βασιλέων μισηθέντα ἴσμεν ἐς τοσόνδε ὑπὸ μητρός (Übersetzung: Eckstein 1986).
32   Athen. 14.621; Plut. mor. 11a.

Athener, dass „König Ptolemaios, in Übereinstimmung mit der Haltung seiner Vorfahren und seiner Schwester, um die gemeinsame Freiheit der Hellenen" bemüht sei.[33]

Die Nesioten wiederum reagierten positiv auf die Bitte Ptolemaios' II., die von ihm zu Ehren seines Vaters eingerichteten Festspiele der Ptolemaia als isolympische anzuerkennen, wobei sie nicht nur die Leistungen des ersten Ptolemaiers betonten, sondern auch die *eúnoia*, die „gute Gesinnung" Ptolemaios' II. gegenüber den Ahnen.[34] Eine ähnliche Rückbindung des lebenden Königs an seine Dynastie zeigen auch die Opfer, die die Nesioten auf Delos darbrachten: Sie waren gerichtet „an die Götter und den Soter Ptolemaios und den König Ptolemaios."[35]

Wenn nun ein Ptolemaier einen Herrscherkult erhielt, ohne dass er zuvor große Leistungen vollbracht hatte bzw. die Einrichtung des Herrscherkultes ohne Verweis auf die persönliche Leistungsfähigkeit erfolgte, so zeigt sich, dass sich mit der *dóxa* der Ahnen auch deren Göttlichkeit auf den Sohn übertragen hatte. Das illustriert ein Beispiel aus der Stadt Itanos auf Kreta, die den Kult für das dritte Ptolemaierpaar schlicht wie folgt begründete:

> Da König Ptolemaios, als er die Stadt der Itaner und die Bürger von seinem Vater, dem König Ptolemaios, und *von seinen Vorfahren übernahm*, (…) und mit Wohlwollen die Gesetze, die er bei der Regierung übernahm, bewahrte.[36]

Für Milet wiederum spielte ebenfalls die Anknüpfung von Ptolemaios II. an seinen Vater eine entscheidende Rolle für die Einrichtung des Herrscherkultes, doch verwiesen die Milesier noch auf einen weiteren Punkt: Ihnen war es nach eigener Auskunft wichtig, dass die Herrschaft des Königs prospektiv in der Familie bleiben möge. Auch Ptolemaios II. hatte schließlich nach dem Vorbild des Vaters den Sohn in die Herrschaft integriert.[37] So sollte, genauso wie es der König in einem Brief erwünscht hatte – „auch bitten wir euch, in Zukunft dieselbe Haltung uns gegenüber einzunehmen"[38] –, nach dem Ehrenbeschluss die zukünftige Generation der Stadt selbst dem Königshaus loyal bleiben:

---

33   Syll.³ 434/5,16–18: ὅ τε βασιλεὺς Πτολεμαῖος ἀκολούθως τεῖ τῶν προγόνων καὶ τεῖ τῆς ἀδελφῆς προ[α]ιρέσει φανερός ἐστιν σπουδάζων ὑπὲρ τῆς κοινῆς τ[ῶν] Ἑλλήνων ἐλευθερίας.

34   Syll.³ 390,23–24: καὶ τὴμ πρὸς τοὺς π[ρογόνου]ς εὔνοιαν διατηρῶν; vgl. Pfeiffer ²2020, Nr. 6.

35   IG XI 4, 1038,23–26 = OGIS 67: ὅπως δὲ καὶ τῶν ἱερῶν ὧν θύουσιν οἱ νησιῶται ἐν Δήλωι τοῖς τε ἄλλοις θεοῖς καὶ Σωτῆρι Πτολεμαίωι καὶ βασιλεῖ Πτολεμαίωι ἀποστέλληται.

36   Syll.³ 463,1–6 = http://s.phrc.it/phrc011: ἀγαθᾶι τύχαι· ἐπειδὴ βασιλεὺς Πτολεμαῖος παραλαβὼν τὰν τῶν Ἰτανίων πόλιν καὶ πολίτας παρὰ τῷ πατρὸς βασιλέως Πτολεμαίω καὶ τῶν προγόνων, (…) διαφυλάσσων μετ' εὐνοίας ἐν οἷς παρέλαβε πολιτευομένος τοῖς αὐτῶν νόμοις.

37   Zu Ptolemaios, dem Sohn, zuletzt Criscuolo 2017, 1–15.

38   I.Milet I 139,12–13: παρακαλοῦμεν δὲ καὶ εἰς τὸν λοιπὸν χρόνον τὴν αὐτὴν ἔχειν αἵρεσιν πρὸς ἡμᾶς. (Übersetzung: Bringmann – von Steuben 1995, KNr. 275 [E 2]).

Damit sich aber das Volk auch *künftig* dem Sohn und ihm bereitwillig zeigt, sollen alle Bürger aufgerufen und eidlich verpflichtet werden, dass sie die für die Stadt bestehende Freundschaft und Bundesgenossenschaft mit dem König Ptolemaios und seinen Nachkommen *für alle Zeit* bewahren werden: Es sollen aber auch die jeweils heranwachsenden Epheben (…) schwören, den vom Volk getroffenen Entscheidungen treu zu bleiben und die Freundschaft und Symmachie mit König Ptolemaios *und seinen Nachkommen* durchgängig zu bewahren.[39]

Zwar fehlen bei der Weihung einer Statuengruppe der Ptolemaier in Thermon die Ahnen des Königs, doch wird hier umso mehr die Zukunft der Dynastie durch das Vorhandensein der männlichen und weiblichen Nachkommen betont.[40]

Die Einbindung der Nachfahren in die Ehrungen entspricht dabei durchaus dem Usus der Ehrendekrete für verdiente Bürger, was unterstreicht, dass die Städte herrscherliche Selbstdarstellung in traditionelle Formeln einbanden.[41] Wie sehr die Städte mit ihren Beschlüssen zu Ehren der Dynastie als Ganzes aber gleichzeitig auch die Erwartungen und damit die Repräsentation des Königs spiegeln, zeigt ein Brief Ptolemaios' III. an die Stadt Xanthos:

Wir loben nun euch, dass ihr immer dieselbe Gesinnung hegt, und dass ihr euch dankbar *an meine, meines Vaters und meines Großvaters Wohltaten* erinnert, und fordern euch auf, auch zukünftig dieselbe Gesinnung zu bewahren.[42]

So wie also die Könige *eúnoia* gegenüber den Ahnen zeigen, sich an deren *exempla* halten, so erwarten sie ebenfalls eine loyale Gesinnung von den beherrschten Städten. Wir sehen damit, dass die griechischen Städte die amtierenden Könige vor allem als Mitglieder ihrer Dynastie verstanden, und das nicht nur retrospektiv, sondern auch prospektiv.

---

39 I.Milet I 139,42–51: ἵνα] δὲ κ[αὶ εἰς τ]ὸ λοιπὸν ὁ δῆμος φαίνηται πρόθυμον αὐτὸμ παρεχόμενος τῶι τ[ε υἱῶι κ]αὶ αὐτῶι, παρακεκλῆσθαι μὲν τοὺς πολίτας ἅπαντας καὶ ἔνορκον αὐ[τ]οῖς εἶναι διαφυλάξειν τὴμ φιλίαν καὶ τὴν συμμαχίαν τὴν ὑπάρχουσαν [τ]ῆι πόλει πρὸς τὸμ βασιλέα Πτολεμαῖον καὶ τοὺς ἐκγόνους αὐτοῦ τὸν ἀεὶ χρόνον· ὀμνύειν δὲ καὶ τοὺς ἐφήβους τοὺς ἀεὶ γινομένους, (…) ἐμμενεῖν τοῖς ὑπὸ τοῦ δήμου κυρωθεῖσιν καὶ διατηρήσειν τὴμ φιλία[ν κ]αὶ τὴν συμμαχίαν τὴμ πρὸς τὸμ βασιλέα Πτολεμαῖον καὶ τοὺς ἐκγόν[ους α]ὐτοῦ. (Übersetzung: Rebecca Kreßner, unpubl. Masterarbeit Halle).

40 IG IX 1², 56; vgl. hierzu den Beitrag von Hans Beck im vorliegenden Band.

41 Vgl. Veligianni-Terzi 1997, 263. Ich danke Matthias Haake für diesen Hinweis.

42 SEG 36.1218, Z. 2–28: Ἐπαινοῦμεν οὖν ὑμᾶς τὴν αὐτὴν αἵρεσιν διὰ παντὸς ἔχοντας καὶ μεμνημένους εὐχαρίστως ὧν εὐεργετήθητε καὶ ὑπ᾽ ἐμοῦ καὶ ὑπὸ τοῦ πατρὸς καὶ τοῦ πάππου, καὶ παρακαλοῦμεν καὶ εἰς τὸ λοιπὸν ἐν τῆι αὐτῆι διαθέσει μένειν (Übersetzung: Kotsidu 2000, Nr. 293 [E]).

2.4 Die Reaktion der Ägypter.
Die Modifikation des pharaonischen Ahnenkultes

Ein Pharao der klassisch-pharaonischen Epochen verstand sich als Bestandteil einer über Generationen hinwegreichenden Linie. Das zeigen Darstellungen, die ihn beim Ritualvollzug vor all diesen Vorgängern präsentieren. So ist in einer Szene in der soge- nannten Festhalle Thutmosis' III. im Tempel von Karnak besagter König beim Opfer vor ursprünglich 61 sitzenden Königen zu sehen.[43] Im Tempel von Abydos wiederum opfert Sethos I. in Begleitung seines Sohnes, des zukünftigen Ramses' II., vor den in Kartuschen präsenten Namen seiner 76 Vorgänger bis zur mythischen Anfangszeit, dem König Menes der 1. Dynastie und letztlich vor Ptah-Sokar.[44] Hier ist gleichzeitig auch schon der Nachfolger einbezogen, womit auf den prospektiven Aspekt des ägyp- tischen Ahnenkultes verwiesen ist.[45]

Der königliche Kult für die Amtsvorgänger war, wie es schon die Anbringung der Szene Sethos' I. im Osiristempel von Abydos zeigt, unmittelbar mit dem ägyptischen Totenkult verbunden, weshalb auch königliche Beamte den Kult für die verstorbenen Pharaonen in ihren thebanischen Privatgräbern thematisierten.[46] So zeigt eine Dar- stellung aus dem Grab des Imiseba in Theben-West das sogenannte Talfest, bei dem eine Barke des Amun von Karnak die Westseite besucht. Während dieser Prozession begleiten den Gott Amun die Statuen sowohl der verstorbenen Könige als auch hoher verstorbener Würdenträger, die sich damit an den königlichen Kult anbinden. Folgen- der Auszug beschreibt die Riten, die dabei stattfinden:

> Opfer niederlegen vor den Statuen der Pharaonen, der Götter im Gefolge des Horus, der Priester, Gottesväter-Priester und Wabpriester (...). Zu rezitieren durch die obersten Vor- lesepriester: (...) Oh Kollegium des Horusgefolges, ihr Pharaonen, ihr Königinnen und Königsmütter, ihr Priester, Gottesväter-Priester (...). Ihr Thebaner und Thebenpilger: Möge euer Ba, möge euer Ka empfangen Opfergaben und Speisen, Brot und Bier, Wasser aus der Schöpfstelle, wovon die Götter leben. Wein, Milch und Libation.[47]

Ganz ähnlich findet sich auch im Grab des Inherchau (TT 359; Zeit Ramses' III./IV.) die Darstellung eines Räucheropfers, das der Grabinhaber in Begleitung seiner Ge- mahlin vor den Pharaonen, ihren Gemahlinnen und Königssöhnen vollzieht.[48] Zwar fehlen also in den offiziellen königlichen Listen die Königsgemahlinnen und -mütter, doch zeigen beide Privatdarstellungen, dass diese sehr wohl im Kult mitbedacht wur-

---

43   Wildung 1974, 41–48; Redford 1986, 29–34.
44   Redford 1986, 18–20.
45   Minas 2000, 76.
46   Liste bei Redford 1986, 45–55.
47   Übersetzung: Assmann 2011, 139.
48   Cherpion – Corteggiani 2010. Zu den Darstellungen von solchen Königsreihen in ramessidischen Gräbern: Bickel – Münch 2014, 188–191.

den/werden konnten. Die Gemahlinnen waren es schließlich, die nach ägyptischer Vorstellung durch die Vereinigung mit Amun, der die Gestalt ihres Gatten angenommen hatte, den zukünftigen König zur Welt brachten.[49]

Wie man sich das Ausführen der Königsstatuen im Zusammenhang mit dem Totenkult vorstellen kann, zeigt wiederum eine Darstellung des Min-Festes im Ramesseum, dem Totentempel Ramses' II., auf der thebanischen Westseite.[50] Die Könige sind hier nicht in Schreinen, sondern als Statuen präsentiert und entscheidend für die Verbindung von Toten- und Königskult ist, dass auch eine Statue des amtierenden Königs Ramses II. an erster Stelle von den Priestern ausgeführt wird.

Als die ägyptischen Priester nun daran gingen, die griechischen Vorstellungen des Dynastiekultes in die Tempel einzufügen, griffen sie auf den alten pharaonischen Ahnenkult zurück, wählten aber einen anderen Weg der dynastischen Repräsentation, weil sie das ägyptische an das griechische Konzept anpassen mussten. Aus diesem Grund schlossen sie einerseits die nicht-ptolemaiischen Pharaonen aus der Ahnenverehrung aus, führten die Ahnenverehrung aber gleichzeitig insofern weiter, als dass sie seit der Zeit Ptolemaios' III. den lebenden Pharao und teils seine Gemahlin bei einem Rauchopfer vor den eigenen genetisch-dynastischen Ahnen, sowohl den Männern als auch den Frauen, zeigen.[51]

Solche Szenen der Ahnenverehrung sind, wie es der Tradition entspricht, ebenfalls im Kontext des Totenkultes zu verorten, schließlich geht es um die *verstorbenen* Vorgänger. Hieraus erklärt sich, dass die Szenen des ptolemaiischen Ahnenkultes auch mit Szenen des Opfers vor dem lebenden und dem toten Herrn der Unterwelt, Osiris, vergesellschaftet sind.[52] Auf diese Weise ist der König gleichzeitig, wie es die Priesterdekrete verschriftlichen, deutlich als Horus auf Erden gekennzeichnet.[53]

Die Szenen des ptolemaiischen Ahnenkultes stehen aber in einem Ritualzusammenhang, der über den schlichten Totenkult hinausgeht und der klar auf die göttliche Legitimation des regierenden Königs verweist, denn sie sind mit zwei Szenentypen gekoppelt, die die Qualität des regierenden Königs und seiner Gemahlin betreffen. Einerseits sind das Darstellungen, in denen das amtierende Königspaar die ewige Dauer seiner Regierungsjahre von den Göttern in Jahresrispen eingetragen bekommt.[54]

---

49   Zum Geburtsmythos: Brunner ²1986; Assmann 1982, 13–61.
50   Maher-Taha – Loyrette 1979, Taf. 5; Redford 1986, 34–36.
51   Zu den Szenen der Ahnenverehrung: Winter 1978, 147–158; Quaegebeur 1989, 93–116; Minas 2000, 61–64; Preys 2022, 172, 174–177.
52   Preys 2015a, 203–209.
53   Preys 2015a, 164–165.
54   Zu den Entwicklungslinien zwischen der Zeit Ptolemaios' III. und Ptolemaios' XII.: Quaegebeur 1989, 96; Minas-Nerpel 2020, 168–172; Preys 2015b, 157–160; Preys 2016, 389–418. In diesen Szenen wiederum steht das regierende Königspaar auf der göttlichen Seite und jeder von beiden hält zudem das Götterzepter in der Hand. Deutlich sind Ptolemaios und seine Gemahlin damit als Götter zu erkennen, die aber durch die Sandalen und den sogenannten makedonischen Mantel, einem

Abb. 1 Das Giebelfeld der Stele von Nobaireh, die eine Kopie des bekannten Rosetta-Dekrets von 196 v. Chr. enthält. Ptolemaios V. speert den besiegten Feind und erhält vom Gott Schu das Siegesschwert. Begleitet ist der Gott von Tefnut und den Ahnen des Königs.

Andererseits sind das seit der Zeit Ptolemaios' IV. Darstellungen, die das Überreichen des Siegesschwertes durch einen Gott an den König zeigen.[55] Das bringt wiederum zum Ausdruck, dass stabile Herrschaft, Verehrung des Osiris und der Ahnen auf das engste miteinander verbunden sind.

Einen Spiegel finden die Ritualdarstellungen der Tempel in den Texten und Darstellungen der bereits erwähnten ägyptischen Priesterdekrete zu Ehren der Ptolemaier.[56] In den erhaltenen Giebelfeldern der Stelen sehen wir häufig den mit dem Dekret bedachten Ptolemaier beim Erschlagen oder Erstechen eines vor ihm knienden Feindes. Er vollzieht diesen Ritus in Gegenwart einer Gottheit, die ihm im Gegenzug dafür das Schwert des Sieges reicht. Besonders eindrücklich ist dabei die Verbindung von göttlicher und menschlicher Genealogie in der Nobaireh-Stele, die eine Version des Rosetta-Dekretes zum Inhalt hatte, zum Ausdruck gebracht: Der König ersticht in Be-

---

neuen Element der Königsdarstellung, ikonographisch auch gleichzeitig von den Göttern abgesetzt sind, vgl. hierzu Preys 2015b, 150–154.

55 Preys 2015b, 160: „Couronnement, culte des ancêtres, rédaction des annales et remise de l'épée sont donc des sujets connexes."

56 Vgl. Hoffmann – Pfeiffer 2021, 125–126.

gleitung seiner Gemahlin den Feind. Es ist hier Schu, der Sohn des Re, der ihm im
Gegenzug das Siegesschwert reicht, womit ein Rückbezug auf Re und Schu und damit
auf den Ursprung der göttlichen Genealogie selbst gegeben ist. Begleitet ist Schu von
seiner Gemahlin Tefnut und es folgen die Ptolemaierpaare.[57]

Auf anderen Stelen sieht man das Motiv des ‚Einschreibens der Regierungsjahre'.
Komplett erhalten ist eine solche Darstellung noch auf der Tanis-Stele des Dekretes
von Kanopos. Ptolemaios III. und seine Gemahlin stehen hier den Göttern des Gaus
von Kom el-Hisn gegenüber. Hinter dem Königspaar befinden sich Thot und Seschat,
die dem Herrscherpaar die Regierungs- und Lebensjahre in Palmrispen einschreiben. Den beiden Göttern folgen die Ahnen.[58] Eine ähnliche Szene wird sich auf dem
nicht mehr vollständig ausgeführten Bildfeld der Stele mit dem Priesterdekret von
243 v. Chr. befunden haben.[59] So präsentieren also die Giebelfelder der ptolemaiischen
Priesterdekrete die beiden Szenen – ‚Einschreiben der Regierungsjahre' und ‚Überreichen des Siegesschwertes' –, die sich monumental dargestellt auch in den Reliefs
ägyptischer Tempel finden: Entweder werden Herrschaftsjahre garantiert oder aber
Feinde vernichtet und beides wird mit Elementen der Ahnenverehrung verbunden.

Mit Blick auf Ptolemaios I. weist aber der ptolemaiische Ahnenkult im Tempel eine
Besonderheit auf, die genauso schwer zu erklären ist wie dessen anfängliches Fehlen
im alexandrinischen Dynastiekult. In den Ritualszenen wird nämlich das erste Ptolemaierpaar niemals angeführt: Die Reihe der Vorfahren endet immer mit Ptolemaios II. und Arsinoë II. Das geschieht, obwohl Ptolemaios I. und Berenike häufig in den
Synodaldekreten in einer Klausel über die Erweiterung der kultischen Ehren für die
Dynastie Erwähnung finden. Mittels dieser Dekrete banden nämlich die Priester das
hellenistische Konzept von der Göttlichkeit des lebenden Königs und seiner Gemahlin in die ägyptische Tempelreligion ein,[60] was dazu führte, dass in ptolemaiischer Zeit
erstmals überhaupt der *lebende* König und seine Gemahlin auch am Kult im Tempel als
sýnnaoi theoí partizipierten. Eingeführt haben die Priester diesen Kult erst unter dem
zweiten Ptolemaier, denn Ptolemaios II. und Arsinoë II. sind das erste Herrscherpaar,
das als *sýnnaoi theoí* Erwähnung findet. Möglicherweise ist es dann genau diesem Umstand geschuldet, dass also der ägyptische Herrscherkult erst unter Ptolemaios II. und

---

57 Hoffmann – Pfeiffer 2021, 27–31.
58 Vgl. die Beschreibung bei Pfeiffer 2004, 28–38.
59 Vgl. Abb. in Pfeiffer ²2020, 88.
60 Dass es jetzt einen Personenkult für die Herrscherpaare in den Tempeln gab, ist eine theologische
    Neuerung, schließlich war der Pharao, auch wenn man es des Öfteren liest, und wie es teils schon
    Griechen falsch verstanden haben (vgl. Diod. 1.90.2–3 = FGrH 265 F 25,1488–1497; vgl. im leichten
    Widerspruch dazu Diod. 1.95.5), kein Gott in den ägyptischen Tempeln: Es gab keinen Kult für
    ihn. Vgl. hierzu etwa Hornung 2005, 147–148. Baines 1995, 39 verweist darauf, dass Fälle, in denen
    der Pharao als Gott angesprochen wird, metaphorisch seien und in einem „role-playing context"
    zu verorten seien.

Arsinoë II. eingeführt wurde, dass auch die Ahnenreihen in den Ritualszenen erst mit diesen beginnen.

Wie neu die Ptolemäergötter im Tempel waren, sieht man auch daran, dass die ägyptischen Priester nun auch jeweils dem Kulttitel, den sie für ihren jeweiligen Hauptgott führten, die neuen Götter anfügten. Vergleichbares ist aus pharaonischer Zeit unbekannt. Da jeder Priester offiziell nun nicht mehr nur ein Priester etwa des Amun war, sondern auch des regierenden Königspaares und der Ahnen, verlängerte sich gleichzeitig auch die Priestertitulatur mit jeder Generation.[61] Die Priester des Chnum von Elephantine etwa waren unter dem sechsten Ptolemäer

> Priester des Chnum, Herr von Elephantine, und der Geschwistergötter, Wohltätergötter, Vaterliebenden Götter, Erschienenen Götter, des Gottes Eupator und der Mutterliebenden Götter.[62]

Hieran zeigt sich, dass die Ptolemaier einen Dynastiekult im Tempel erhielten, in dem nur eben Ptolemaios I. fehlte. Vergleichbar zum griechischen Dynastiekult ist die Tatsache, dass es sich nicht ausschließlich um einen Kult für die Dynastie handelte, sondern dass dieser Kult immer an den Kult der jeweiligen Hauptgottheit eines Tempels angebunden war, so wie eben auch der griechische Dynastiekult mit dem Kult Alexanders verbunden war. Wir sehen hier also eine deutliche Parallele zum griechischen Dynastiekult, nur dass Alexander durch die jeweiligen lokalen Gaugötter Ägyptens ersetzt ist.

Die zum Alexanderkult vergleichbare Position der Ptolemaier kommt ebenfalls in den sogenannten Ahnenreihen seit der Zeit Ptolemaios' III. zum Ausdruck,[63] die sich in Tempelinschriften, auf Gründungstäfelchen von Tempeln, Stelen, Obelisken und Sokar-Osirismumien finden.[64] Hier heißt es stets, dass der regierende König nicht nur von dem betreffenden Gott des Tempels erwählt (wörtlich: geliebt) ist,[65] sondern auch von dessen eigenen Ahnen, abgesehen vom ersten Ptolemaierpaar, das allem Anschein nach nicht zu den *sýnnaoi theoí* gehörte.

---

61   Dass nur die Ptolemaier und nicht die übrigen tempelteilenden Götter genannt sind, mag daran liegen, dass die Ahnen „an der Spitze der Mitgötter" standen: Winter 1978, 152, mit Anm. 5.

62   OGIS 111,20–24.

63   Minas 2000, 181–187. Minas-Nerpel 2006, 36–42 zeigt, dass dies schon unter Ptolemaios III. begann.

64   Zu letzterem Minas-Nerpel 2006.

65   Zur Erwählung: Simpson 1977, 493–498; Minas 2000, 55–59. Ebenso können die Ahnen aber auch gemeinsam mit dem König als Geliebte der Gottheit erscheinen.

3. Die göttliche Genealogie der Ptolemaier in der griechischen Welt

Was wir bisher noch nicht thematisiert haben, ist die Frage der göttlichen Abkunft der ptolemaiischen Könige, denn eine solche gehörte im Grunde genommen zur ,Standardausstattung' hellenistischen Königtums. Mit Blick auf die Kultnamen zeigt sich das bei den Ptolemaiern aber erst ganz am Ende der Dynastie, bei Ptolemaios XII., der sich nicht nur als *philopátor* und *philádelphos*, sondern auch als „junger Dionysos" bezeichnet. Es geht ihm hiermit darum, sich als lebende Inkarnation des Dionysos auf Erden zu qualifizieren. Gleichzeitig betont er auf diese Weise umso deutlicher seine dynastische Herkunft, denn die Ptolemaier führten ihre Familie auf ebenjenen Gott zurück. Nicht von ungefähr befand sich etwa in der Thalamegos Ptolemaios' IV. im Raum des Dionysos eine Statuengalerie der Familie des Königs.[66]

Über Dionysos und zudem über Herakles[67] schrieben die Ptolemaier ihre Genealogie dann bis auf Zeus zurück. Das zeigt etwa die mir einzige bekannte Siegesinschrift der hellenistischen Welt. Sie ist uns durch eine Abschrift eines Mönches erhalten, der sie im 6. Jh. an der Küste des Roten Meeres, in der ptolemaiischen Elefantenjagdstation Adulis, kopiert hatte. Der Text, der uns Ptolemaios als ,siegreichen König' vorstellt, beginnt mit der Bedeutung dynastischer Herkunft:

> Großkönig Ptolemaios,
> Sohn des Königs Ptolemaios und der Königin Arsinoë, der Geschwistergötter,
> den Kindern von König Ptolemaios und Königin Berenike, den Rettergöttern,
> von Vaterseite Nachkomme des Herakles, des Sohnes des Zeus,
> von Mutterseite des Dionysos, des Sohnes des Zeus.[68]

Ist die Annahme des Titels ,Großkönig' noch eine Besonderheit der Inschrift – der Titel wird von den Ptolemaiern nur äußerst selten verwendet[69] –, so ist die Betonung der Abkunft nicht nur von den göttlichen Eltern und Großeltern, sondern über diese auch von Herakles, Dionysos und damit von Zeus wichtig für eine Gleichstellung der eigenen Abkunft mit derjenigen anderer Dynastien und griechischer Eliten. Ein weiterer Punkt ist, dass sie gerade über die Abkunft von Herakles Blutsgemeinschaft

---

66 Athen. 5.205e–f: προάγοντι δὲ ἐπὶ τὴν πρῷραν οἶκος ὑπέκειτο Βακχικὸς τρισκαιδεκάκλινος περίπτερος, ἐπίχρυσον ἔχων τὸ γεῖσον ἕως τοῦ περιτρέχοντος ἐπιστυλίου· στέγη δὲ τῆς τοῦ θεοῦ διαθέσεως οἰκεία. ἐν δὲ τούτῳ κατὰ μὲν τὴν δεξιὰν πλευρὰν ἄντρον κατεσκεύαστο, οὗ χρῶμα μὲν ἦν ἔχον τὴν πετροποιίαν ἐκ λίθων ἀληθινῶν καὶ χρυσοῦ δεδημιουργημένον· ἵδρυτο δ᾽ ἐν αὐτῷ τῆς τῶν βασιλέων συγγενείας ἀγάλματα εἰκονικὰ λίθου λυχνέως.

67 Vgl. Theokr. 17.20–27.

68 OGIS 56,1–5 = Pfeiffer ²2020, Nr. 11: βασιλεὺς μέγας Πτολεμαῖος, υἱὸς βασιλέως Πτολεμαίου καὶ βασιλίσσης Ἀρσινόης θεῶν Ἀδελφῶν, τῶν βασιλέω<ς> Πτολεμαίου καὶ βασιλίσσης Βερενίκης θεῶν Σωτήρων ἀπόγονος, τὰ μὲν ἀπὸ πατρὸς Ἡρακλέος τοῦ Διός, τὰ δὲ ἀπὸ μητρὸς Διονύσου τοῦ Διός.

69 Vgl. hierzu Pfeiffer 2022, 313–330. Zu diesem Titel vergleiche auch die Beiträge von Sonja Richter und Shane Wallace in diesem Band.

mit den Dorern und den Argeaden aufweisen konnten. Entsprechendes findet sich in einem Brief der Dorer von Kytenion, den ein Ehrendekret der Stadt Xanthos zitiert, herausgestellt.[70]

Wie kommt es aber, dass sich Ptolemaios III. bis auf Zeus zurückführen konnte, wo doch Ptolemaios I. angeblich nicht wusste, wer sein Großvater väterlicherseits war? Dieses Problem lässt sich mit einer ptolemaiischen Genealogie klären, die uns der antiochenische Bischof Theophilos im 2. Jh. n. Chr. für Ptolemaios IV. überliefert. Zwar gibt es die Ansicht, dass dieser Stammbaum nicht helfe, die von Ptolemaios III. in der Adulitana angegebene Genealogie zu erklären,[71] doch bei genauerem Hinsehen ist es vielleicht doch möglich.

Der Bischof paraphrasiert den Dichter Satyros aus Kallatis und dessen Beschreibung der Demen von Alexandreia aus der Wende vom 3. zum 2. Jh. v. Chr.[72] Unter Nennung der jeweiligen Vatersnamen und teils auch der Mutternamen führt Satyros die Herkunft des vierten Ptolemaiers mütterlicherseits – Ankerpunkt ist Arsinoë, die *Gemahlin* des Lagos – über 24 Generationen auf Dionysos zurück.[73] Wenn also explizit die Genealogie ausschließlich auf die Frau des Lagos, Arsinoë, und nicht auf den Vater Lagos selbst zurückgeht, so ist hier die Fiktion, dass Ptolemaios I. seine Ahnen nicht kennt, als eine dynastische Tatsache gegeben. Die eingangs erwähnte Anekdote spiegelt mithin tatsächlich die Selbstdarstellung des Königs. Wie kann es aber sein, dass sich Ptolemaios III. trotzdem nach Auskunft der Adulitana väterlicherseits auf Herakles zurückführt?

Auch hierfür könnte die mütterliche Genealogie der Lagiden eine Lösung bieten: Da Satyros explizit erwähnt, dass die Tochter des Dionysos Deianeira mit Herakles den Ahnen Hyllos zeugte, ist die Urahnin der Dynastie eine Tochter des Dionysos, der Urahn ein Sohn des Herakles und so ist zwar Herakles ebenfalls ein Urahn der Arsinoë, doch ließe er sich als Erzeuger des Hyllos auch als patrilinearer Ahn der Dynastie vereinnahmen.[74] Über Herakles wiederum hatten die Ptolemaier und Alexander zudem

---

70 SEG 32.1476, Z. 40–42 (206/205 v. Chr.): καὶ μάλιστα τῶι βασιλεῖ Πτ[ο]λεμαίωι ὄντι συγγενεῖ Δωριέων κατὰ τοὺς βασιλεῖς. τοὺς ἀφ' Ἡρακλέους Ἀργεάδας.

71 Huttner 1997, 125: Die Rekonstruktion „hilft (…) nicht weiter, die Zweiteilung im Stammbaum des Ptolemaios III. zu erklären."

72 Fr. F* 29 (Schorn) = FGrH 631 F 1. Zur Datierung und zum Ort: Schorn 2004, 5–10.

73 Der teils erhebliche Eingriff des Theophilos in die Genealogie zeigt sich daran, dass er die Ptolemaier selbst nicht mit ihren vollständigen Kulttiteln versieht. Statt also von den Rettergöttern zu sprechen, spricht er von Ptolemaios Soter, Ptolemaios Philadelphos, Ptolemaios Euergetes und Ptolemaios Philopator. Hier folgt er der hellenistischen historiographischen Tradition, denn schon Polybios spricht von ihnen auf diese Weise. Der Bischof betont des Weiteren eigens, dass Berenike II. die Tochter des Magas ist, mithin nicht die Schwester von Ptolemaios III., was ebenfalls der dynastischen Tradition widerspricht.

74 Möglich ist auch, dass Ptolemaios als unehelicher Sohn Philipps II. betrachtet wurde, was ihn zu einem illegitimen Argeaden gemacht hätte; vgl. Paus. 1.6.2.

die gleiche Abstammung, oder, um es mit Theokrit zu formulieren: „Und von Herakles leiten sie beide am Ende den Stamm ab."[75]

Die Genealogie der Ptolemaier nach dem Demenfragment des Satyros

Dionysos + Aletheia

Deianeira + Herakles

Hyllos

Kelodaios

18 weitere Namen

Meleagros

Arsinoë + Lagos

Ptolemaios Soter

Ptolemaios Philadelphos

Ptolemaios Euergetes

Ptolemaios Philopator

(grün = Herkunftslinie der Arsinoë;
rot = Herkunftslinie des Lagos)

Da wiederum Zeus mit seiner Schwester Hera Kinder hervorgebracht hatte, erklärt es sich, dass die Dichtung am Ptolemaierhof die Ehe von Ptolemaios II. und Arsinoë II. genau mit dieser Hierogamie verglich,[76] wohingegen Pausanias in seiner Invektive gegen den König auf die fehlende makedonische Präzedenz der Geschwisterheirat hinweist und eine ägyptische Sitte als Vorbild geltend macht.[77]

4. Die göttliche Genealogie der Ptolemaier in der ägyptischen Welt

Durch die Anknüpfung an Dionysos und Herakles stehen die Lagiden gleichberechtigt an der Seite von griechischen Aristokraten klassischer Zeit, schließlich gehörte es in diesen Kreisen seit Homer zum guten Ton, eine lange Reihe von Ahnen aufzählen zu können.[78] Das verdeutlicht ein bekanntes Beispiel aus den Historien des Herodot, der berichtet, dass der Gelehrte Hekataios von Milet den dortigen Priestern stolz berichtet habe, er könne sich über 16 Generationen hinweg auf einen Gott zurückführen. Rechnen wir die 200 Jahre zwischen Hekataios und den Ptolemaiern hinzu, so entspricht die Länge seines Stammbaums proportional also dem der Ptolemaier. Das griechische Zeitkontinuum zwischen historischer und göttlicher Zeit war folglich konsistent; die Griechen wussten sehr genau, wann noch Götter auf Erden gewandelt waren und Kinder gezeugt hatten.

---

75 Theokr. 17.27.
76 Theokr. 7.131–132; Kall. Ait. 3.58.2 Asper = P.Lille 82.
77 Paus. 1.7.1.
78 Vgl. Plut. Alkibiades 1 (bis auf Zeus).

Doch gerade das Beispiel des Hekataios zeigt, dass die göttliche Abstammung und Genealogie der Ptolemaier für ägyptische Untertanen Probleme mit sich bringen konnten, denn der Priester, dem Hekataios so stolz von seiner Genealogie berichtete, nahm ihn einfach bei der Hand und führte ihn in den Tempel. Hier zeigte der Priester die Statuen seiner eigenen Vorgänger, von denen jeder eine Statue im Tempel hatte. Das wiederum seien 354 Statuen gewesen und jeder Vorgänger stelle einen, wie es bei Herodot unübersetzt heißt, *piromis* dar, einen Menschen, der von einem Menschen geboren sei.[79] In der Zeit also, in der die Götter in Griechenland auf Erden weilten, hätten in Ägypten bereits seit 300 Generationen ausschließlich Menschen gelebt, nur davor hätten Götter mit Menschen auf Erden geweilt.[80]

Es gibt keine erhaltene Priesterahnenreihe, die tatsächlich die von Herodot beschriebene Fülle von Vorfahren aufweist, doch kam es in Ägypten durchaus vor, dass Priester sich ihrer Vorfahren besannen, diese notierten und ehrten,[81] denn es stellte ein gesellschaftliches Ideal dar, dass der Sohn dem Vater im Amte folgte.[82] So meint ein memphitischer Priester, seine Ahnenreihe über 60 Generationen, umgerechnet 1300 Jahre, von der Zeit Scheschonks V. (22. Dynastie, 767–730 v. Chr.) bis zur Zeit Mentuhoteps I. (2061–2010 v. Chr.), zurückverfolgen zu können.[83]

So sehr also Herodots Bericht über Hekataios von einer Erzählintention geprägt ist,[84] so ist doch eines nicht von der Hand zu weisen: Die Vorstellung von zeitlicher Tiefe, der nicht nur die Griechen klassischer Zeit, sondern auch die Ptolemaier in Ägypten begegneten, übertraf die Vorstellungen griechischer Chronologie bei weitem. So klingen für die Griechen die 24 Generationen, die ein Ptolemaios IV. als Ahnen aufweisen kann, vielleicht nach einer langen Zeit, doch in ägyptischen Augen ist das nur ein Wimpernschlag der Vergangenheit. Selbst Priester konnten schließlich über Ahnenreihen verfügen, die die ptolemaiische um ein Vielfaches übertrafen.

Zwar ist es schwer vorstellbar, dass ägyptische Priester mit einem ptolemaiischen König ähnlich umgegangen wären wie mit Hekataios: Die Hand, die einen füttert, beißt man schließlich nicht. Sollten die Ptolemaier Herodot gelesen haben, so hätten sie gewusst, dass schon zur Zeit des Herodot die ägyptische Geschichte auf eine Chronologie von 331 Königen zurückblickte.[85] Sollten sie Herodot nicht konsultiert haben,

---

79   Hdt. 2.143–144. Zu Herodot und Hekataios: West 1991, 144–160.

80   Hdt. 2.144.1.

81   Perdu 2014, 107–139. In ptolemaiischer Zeit war das freilich nicht mehr der Fall: Jansen-Winkeln 2005, 137.

82   Vgl. auch zu den Problemen, wenn keine genealogische Sukzession möglich war: von Lieven 2017, 85–112. Zudem Bickel – Münch 2014, 177–202.

83   Redford 1986, 62–64; Borchardt 1932, 618–622; Bickel – Münch 2014, 191–193.

84   Für vorliegende Fragestellung ist es unerheblich, ob sich das von Herodot Berichtete wirklich ereignete, oder ob Herodot die Geschichte erfunden hat und sie dazu dient, sich von Hekataios abzusetzen und zudem das enorme Alter der ägyptischen Kultur und Religion zu verdeutlichen, vgl. zu letzterem etwa Moyer 2011, 63–68.

85   Hdt. 2.99–100.

hätten sie dies auch durch das Werk des Manetho erfahren,[86] und gewusst, dass die ägyptische Chronologie um viele Jahrhunderte älter war als die griechische, dass also in der Zeit, in der der ptolemaiische Ahnherr Dionysos auf Erden weilte, die ägyptischen Pharaonen bereits seit Jahrhunderten auf dem Thron saßen, vor denen 20.000 Jahre lang erst die Götter und danach Halbgötter geherrscht hatten.[87]

Ein ptolemaiischer König muss sich also im Klaren darüber gewesen sein, dass seine Genealogie für einen Ägypter entweder nicht wirklich beeindruckend oder sogar unglaubhaft war. Da aber das dynastische Prinzip und damit das Vorhandensein einer Genealogie, die ihren Ursprung bei den Göttern hatte, zu den entscheidenden Kriterien des ptolemaiischen Herrscherkultes, sowohl in seiner griechischen als auch in seiner ägyptischen Ausprägung, zählte, mussten die Ptolemaier bzw. die ägyptischen Priester andere Formen der göttlichen Anbindung und dynastischen Repräsentation schaffen, um auf diese Weise den griechischen Dynastiekult in die ägyptische Welt einzubinden. Aus diesem Grund stellten die Priester die Ptolemaier mit Blick auf deren göttliche Herkunft in die Tradition ägyptischen Pharaonentums.

Wir begegnen einem illustrativen Beispiel für die ägyptische Konzeption göttlicher Herkunft der Ptolemaier in der gleichen historischen Situation, in der Polybios das eingangs angesprochene griechische Verständnis progonaler *dóxa* formuliert hatte: im Kontext der Schlacht von Raphia. Anlässlich des Sieges hatten die ägyptischen Priesterschaften das bekannte Dekret von Raphia für Ptolemaios IV., den „jugendlichen Horus", „den sein Vater hat erscheinen lassen", verfasst. Nach Auskunft der Priester sind es wiederum „alle Götter und Göttinnen Ägyptens", die dem König im Traum offenbart hatten, dass er den Feind besiegen werde. Und so überwand Ptolemaios die Feinde „wie Horus, der Sohn der Isis, ehedem seine Feinde massakriert hatte."[88] Die Konzeption des regierenden Königs als eines Horus *redivivus* findet sich ebenfalls im Dekret von Rosetta für Ptolemaios V.: „Er bemächtigte sich der Feinde, die in ihr waren. Er metzelte sie entsprechend dem, was Schu, Sohn des Re, zusammen mit Horus, Sohn der Isis, vordem(?) an diesem Ort denen angetan hatten, die sich gegen sie aufgelehnt hatten."[89]

Hier ist es also nicht der Ruhm der Vorfahren, der sich im König inkarniert, sondern es sind die Götter Ägyptens, die ihn zur Sieghaftigkeit befähigen und nach deren Präzedenz sein Handeln gedeutet ist. Als Wiedergänger des Horus tritt der Pharao gleichzeitig als Schützer und Rächer seines Vaters auf. Das verdeutlicht besonders der Titel der Statue von Ptolemaios IV., die auf Veranlassung der Priester in jedem Tempel aufgestellt wird: „Horus, Rächer seines Vaters, dessen Sieg schön ist."[90] So wie im

86   Hierzu etwa Moyer 2011, 84–141.
87   Diod. 1.43–45; Manetho, fr. 1 (Waddell) = Eus. Chronicon I.
88   Vittman o. D.
89   Hieroglyphischer Text; Übersetzung: Hoffmann – Pfeiffer 2021, 70.
90   Thissen 1966, 24: καλέσαι δὲ αὐτὴν βασιλέα Πτολεμαῖον Ὧρον τὸν ἐπαμύνοντα τῶι πατρὶ καλλίνικον.

Mythos Horus das Unrecht an seinem Vater Osiris gerächt hatte, so tat dies nun der Horus-Ptolemaios für seinen Vater Osiris-Ptolemaios.

Für die ägyptischen Vorstellungen vom Pharao war es entscheidend, dass er sich auch genealogisch legitimieren konnte, und die Erwähnung der ägyptischen Götter und des Horus zeigt, dass natürlich auch der ptolemaiische Pharao ein „Sohn des Re" war und gleichzeitig als Inkarnation des Horus auf Erden dessen Funktion übernahm. Als solcher war er zudem Sohn des Osiris und stand damit, wie alle seine Vorgänger bis zurück in die Vorzeit, mit diesem Gott in Verbindung. Osiris selbst wiederum ist aus einer Göttergenealogie hervorgegangen, die sich auf den Schöpfergott Atum-Re zurückführt,[91] was sich im gerade erwähnten Königstitel „Sohn des Re" ausdrückte.[92] Deshalb ist es kein Widerspruch, wenn der Pharao sowohl Sohn des Re als auch Sohn des Osiris ist.

Wie jeder Pharao, so kann der ptolemaiische König damit auf die göttliche Genealogie Atum-Re, Schu, Geb, Osiris und Horus verweisen, was vor allem deshalb gut zu ptolemaiischen Vorstellungen passte, weil auch die Nachfolger des Atum alle ihre jeweiligen Schwestern geehelicht hatten.

5. Ergebnisse

Wie eingangs erwähnt, sind die vier zentralen Elemente der dynastischen Repräsentation der Ptolemaier Homonymie, *similitudo*, Endogamie und Göttlichkeit. Die Göttlichkeit bezeugt sich nicht nur in der eigenen Wirkmacht und der Göttlichkeit der Vorgänger, sondern auch in der göttlichen Genealogie, also der Abkunft von den Unsterblichen, die als fünftes Element hinzutritt. Durch die Rückschreibung der Genealogie in die mythische Vorzeit Griechenlands und die Verknüpfung des lebenden Herrscherpaares mit Dionysos und Herakles ist es zudem das Ziel, die aus unbekannten makedonischen Gefilden stammende Familie nicht nur an Alexander den Großen, sondern auch an die großen griechischen Familien in den verschiedenen Poleis anzubinden, um sich auf diese Weise auch in das gesamtgriechische mythohistorische Gedächtnis einzuschreiben.

Es ist wohl nicht zu bezweifeln, dass die Ptolemaier ihre auf Dionysos und Herakles und darüber hinaus auf Zeus zurückgehende Genealogie mit Blick auf ihre Herrschaftsrepräsentation für ihre griechischen Untertanen ebenso wie die dynastischen Konkurrenten der hellenistischen Welt propagierten. Für die ägyptischen Untertanen hingegen schufen die Priester eine Genealogie, die die Ptolemaier, unter Auslassung der indigenen Pharaonen, unmittelbar an Horus und dessen göttliche Herkunft an-

---

91 Etwa Assmann 2011, 138.
92 Vgl. die Übergabe des Königtums über die Göttergenerationen von Re bis Horus in Edfu: Kurth 1994, Nr. 46.

band. Da nun die vielen hundert Generationen an Trägern des Horusamtes verschwiegen wurden, fiel auf diese Weise die chronologische Differenz zwischen griechischer und ägyptischer Chronologie nicht mehr ins Gewicht. Gleichzeitig konnte das Ideal der Geschwisterheirat, das meines Erachtens seine maßgebliche Legitimation in der Heirat von Zeus und Hera hatte, unproblematisch auch aus der ägyptischen Göttergenealogie erklärt werden, wo Schu und Tefnut, Geb und Nut sowie Osiris und Isis ebenfalls Geschwister waren.

Eins wird aber in beiden Konstruktionen von dynastisch-göttlicher Genealogie deutlich: Das Verständnis von Dynastie meint weit mehr als Familie. Sie ist eine bereits durch Ptolemaios II. konstruierte und nachhaltig bis zum Ende der Dynastie wirkmächtig geglaubte und propagierte „Erinnerungsgemeinschaft",[93] die Vergangenheit, Gegenwart und vor allem auch Zukunft im Herrscherpaar miteinander verband. Im griechischen Verständnis diente diese Gemeinschaft dazu, die von den Ahnen erwiesene *dóxa* auf die gegenwärtige und zukünftige Generation zu übertragen. Denn auch das Vorhandensein des Erben ist von Bedeutung für die Selbstdarstellung und Wahrnehmung der Dynastie.[94] So verlangte der König von seinen Untertanen, dass die Kulte nicht nur für ihn, sondern *auch* für seine Kinder vollzogen werden.[95] Dass dem Wunsch von Untertanenseite noch unter den späten Ptolemaiern nachgekommen wurde, zeigt eine Inschrift aus Kyrene, wo es für Ptolemaios IX. Soter II. heißt:

> Die Damiurgen und Hierathyten sollen das Prytaneion und die Stoen schmücken und Opfer vollziehen lassen für das Heil der Stadt beim König Ptolemaios und der Königin Kleopatra, der Schwester, den Rettergöttern, *und ihrem Sohn Ptolemaios* und ihren Eltern und Großeltern und allen anderen Göttern.[96]

Die derart konstruierte, klar griechisch ausgerichtete Erinnerungsgemeinschaft erstreckt sich damit über vier Zeitstufen: Die mythische Vergangenheit bis zu Arsinoë, der Gemahlin des Lagos, die innerdynastische Vergangenheit bis zum jeweiligen Elternpaar, die Gegenwart des Königspaars und die Zukunft in der gesicherten Thronfolge. Ein wichtiges Ziel scheint es nämlich gewesen zu sein, dass die eigene Herrschaft in Zukunft überdauert.

Im Ägyptischen wiederum spielen die Ahnen Ptolemaios' II. keine Rolle. Sogar sein Vater findet selten Erwähnung. Das liegt wohl daran, dass erst Ptolemaios II. und Arsinoë II. zur Ehre der Altäre in den Tempeln erhoben wurden. Erst mit diesen beginnt deshalb auch eine göttliche dynastische Erinnerungsgemeinschaft, die sich unmittel-

---

93   Assmann [8]2018, 202–203.
94   Vgl. I.Fay. III 152; vgl. Heinen 2009, 248–249.
95   P.Tebt. I 6,47–49.
96   IGCyro11100,28–35: Οἱ δὲ δαμιεργοὶ καὶ ἱαροθύται [τ]ὸ πρυτανεῖον καὶ τὰς στωιὰς κοσμησάντων καὶ θυσάντων ὑπὲρ τᾶς πόλιος βασιλεῖ [Π]τολεμαίωι καὶ βασιλίσσαι Κλευπάτραι [τ]ᾶι ἀδελφᾶι, θεοῖς Σωτῆρσι, καὶ τῶι υἱῶι [α]ὐτῶν Πτολεμαίωι καὶ τοῖς γονεῦσι [κ]αὶ τοῖς προγόνοις αὐτῶν καὶ τοῖς ἄλλοις [θεο]ῖς παῖσιν.

bar an die ägyptische Götterwelt anschließt. Es sind die Götter, die gleichzeitig den König mit seinen Qualitäten dauerhafter Herrschaft und militärischer Sieghaftigkeit versehen: Seine Leistung beruht auf seiner Funktion als Inkarnation des Horus auf Erden. Hier unterscheiden sich die priesterlichen Darstellungen also von der königlichen Selbstdarstellung, wie wir sie in der Adulitana kennenlernen.

Auch im ägyptischen dynastischen Konzept spielt nicht nur die mythische Vergangenheit – Ptolemaios siegte wie Horus über die Feinde des Vaters –, sondern auch die Zukunft eine Rolle. Das zeigt die Traumoffenbarung der Isis für Hor über den Abzug des Antiochos IV. aus Ägypten:

> Alexandria ist gesichert gegen die Zerstörung. Der König registriert Dinge darin mit seinen Geschwistern. Der älteste Sohn des Königs ist angekündigt. Sein Sohn ist nach ihm angekündigt. Der Sohn dieses Sohnes ist angekündigt nach ihm. Der Sohn des Sohnes des Sohnes dieses Sohnes ist angekündigt nach ihm für eine lange Zeit, die sehr umfangreich ist. Der Beweis dafür: Die Königin gebiert ein männliches Kind.[97]

Eine gesicherte Nachfolge gehörte zum pharaonischen ebenso wie zum griechischen dynastischen Ideal.

Eine vollkommen neue dynastische Konzeption brachte dann die letzte Vertreterin der Dynastie, Kleopatra VII., ins Spiel, eine Konzeption, die aufgrund ihres Scheiterns überaus ephemer war, die aber durchaus im offiziellen Namen ihres Sohnes Ptolemaios Kaisar und in dessen Kultnamen Philopator Philometor angelegt ist.

Ein Zeugnis für die neue dynastische Konzeption bietet eine Stele aus dem Faijum. Ihre Weihinschrift hat die Königin sicherlich nie zu Gesicht bekommen: Es handelt sich um ein rein privates Dokument eines Untertanen, das sicherlich auch nicht von Kleopatra autorisiert wurde. Und trotzdem denke ich, dass die Inschrift die Zukunft spiegelt, wie sie sich die Königin vorstellte. Der Stiftungstext lautet:

> Zugunsten der Königin Kleopatra, der Vaterliebenden Göttin und des Königs Ptolemaios, der auch Kaisar heißt, des Vaterliebenden und Mutterliebenden Gottes, und ihrer Ahnen, dem Suchos, dem zweimalgroßen, dem Vatersvater (geweiht).[98]

Wir sehen also, dass Kleopatra für ihren Sohn das Prinzip der Ptolemaierepitheta übernommen hat. Wenn aber Ptolemaios Kaisar, der allein schon aufgrund seines Namens von der Königin deutlich als Sohn Caesars deklariert ist, hier nicht nur die „Mutterliebe", sondern auch die „Vaterliebe" als Beinamen erhält, dann zeigt sich, dass wir am Beginn einer neuen dynastischen Konzeption stehen, die nun die ptolemaiisch-makedonische Linie mit der römischen des Caesar, die auf Venus zurückgeht, verbinden sollte; schließlich ist die Stele den Ahnen – und damit kann ja nur die ptole-

---

97   O.Hor 1.14–17. Übersetzung: Quack 2008, 378.
98   SB I 1570; vgl. hierzu die Interpretation von Heinen 2009.

maiische und die julische Linie gemeint sein – geweiht.[99] Nicht von ungefähr begann Kleopatra (wahrscheinlich) auch mit der Errichtung eines Tempels des Caesar in Alexandreia.[100]

Das lokale Objekt zeigt wiederum, wie Ägypter versuchten, diese neue Form in ihre Vorstellungen zu integrieren. Im Giebelfeld sieht man einen Pharao – es sollte dann wohl Ptolemaios Kaisar sein – bei einer Ritualhandlung vor zwei Erscheinungsformen des Sobek mit dem Beinamen Vatersvater.

Literaturverzeichnis

Apelt 1926/1927: Apelt, Otto, Plutarch. Moralische Schriften, Leipzig 1926/1927

Assmann 1982: Assmann, Jan, Die Zeugung des Sohnes. Bild, Spiel, Erzählung und das Problem des ägyptischen Mythos, in: J. Assmann – W. Burkert – F. Stolz (eds.), Funktionen und Leistungen des Mythos. Drei altorientalische Beispiele, Fribourg et al. 1982, 13–61

Assmann 2011: Assmann, Jan, Steinzeit und Sternzeit. Altägyptische Zeitkonzepte, München 2011

Assmann ⁸2018: Assmann, Jan, Das kulturelle Gedächtnis. Schrift, Erinnerung und politische Identität in frühen Hochkulturen, München ⁸2018

Baines 1995: Baines, John, Kingship, Definition of Culture, and Legitimation, in: D. B. O'Connor – D. P. Silverman (eds.), Ancient Egyptian Kingship, London et al. 1995, 3–48

Bickel – Münch 2014: Bickel, Susanne – Münch, Hans-Hubertus, Götter – Herrscher – Amtsinhaber. Beispiele zu Genealogie als Denkform im Alten Ägypten, in: A.-B. Renger – I. Toral-Niehoff (eds.), Genealogie und Migrationsmythen im antiken Mittelmeerraum und auf der arabischen Halbinsel, Berlin 2014, 177–202

Borchardt 1932: Borchardt, Ludwig, Stammbaum memphitischer Priester, SPAW 24, 1932, 618–622

Bringmann – von Steuben 1995: Bringmann, Klaus – von Steuben, Hans, Schenkungen hellenistischer Herrscher an griechische Städte und Heiligtümer, Berlin 1995

Brunner ²1986: Brunner, Hellmut, Die Geburt des Gottkönigs. Studien zur Überlieferung eines altägyptischen Mythos, Wiesbaden ²1986

Caneva 2016: Caneva, Stefano G., From Alexander to the Theoi Adelphoi. Foundation and Legitimation of a Dynasty, Leuven 2016

Cherpion – Corteggiani 2010: Cherpion, Nadine – Corteggiani, Jean-Pierre, La tombe d'Inherkhâouy (TT 359) à Deir el-Medina, Cairo 2010

Clarysse – van Derveken 1983: Clarysse, Willy – van Derveken, Griet, The Eponymous Priests of Ptolemaic Egypt. Chronological Lists of the Priests of Alexandria and Ptolemais with a Study of the Demotic Transcriptions of their Names, Leiden 1983

Collombert 2008: Collombert, Philippe, La „stèle de Saïs" et l'instauration du culte d'Arsinoé II dans la Chôra, Ancient Society 38, 2008, 83–101

Criscuolo 2017: Criscuolo, Lucia, Ptolemy the Son. A Pretended Co-Regency?, Ancient Society 47, 2017, 1–15

99 Heinen 2009, 250.
100 Vgl. Cass. Dio 51.15; Diskussion etwa bei Fraser 1972 II, 68, Anm. 156.

Eckstein 1986: Eckstein, Felix, Pausanias. Reisen in Griechenland I: Athen, Zürich 1986

Effe 2013: Effe, Bernd (ed.) Theokrit, Gedichte, Berlin ²2013

Fraser 1972: Fraser, Peter M., Ptolemaic Alexandria, 3 vols., Oxford 1972

Galbois 2012: Galbois, Estelle, Les portraits miniatures des Ptolémées. Fonction et modes de représentation, in: P. Ballet (ed.), Grecs et Romains en Égypte. Territoires, espaces de la vie et de la mort, objets de prestige et du quotidien, Paris 2012, 271–284

Gehrke 1982: Gehrke, Hans-Joachim, Der siegreiche König. Überlegungen zur hellenistischen Monarchie, Archiv für Kulturgeschichte 64, 1982, 247–277

Heinen 2009: Heinen, Heinz, Eine Darstellung des vergöttlichten Iulius Caesar auf einer ägyptischen Stele? Beobachtungen zu einem mißverstandenen Denkmal (SB I 1570 = IG Fay. I 14), in: id., Kleopatra-Studien. Gesammelte Schriften zur ausgehenden Ptolemäerzeit, Konstanz 2009, 244–257

Hoepfner 1971: Hoepfner, Wolfram, Zwei Ptolemaierbauten. Das Ptolemaierweihgeschenk in Olympia und ein Bauvorhaben in Alexandria, Berlin 1971

Hoffmann – Pfeiffer 2021: Hoffmann, Friedhelm – Pfeiffer, Stefan, Der Stein von Rosetta, Stuttgart 2021

Hornung 2005: Hornung, Erik, Der Eine und die Vielen. Altägyptische Götterwelt, Darmstadt 2005

Huttner 1997: Huttner, Ulrich, Die politische Rolle der Heraklesgestalt im griechischen Herrschertum, Stuttgart 1997

Jansen-Winkeln 2005: Jansen-Winkeln, Karl, Die Entwicklung der genealogischen Informationen nach dem Neuen Reich, in: M. Fitzenreiter (ed.), Genealogie. Realität und Fiktion von Identität, London 2005, 137–145

Koenen 1993: Koenen, Ludwig, The Ptolemaic King as a Religious Figure, in: A. Bulloch et al. (eds.), Images and Ideologies. Self-Definition in the Hellenistic World, Berkeley et al. 1993, 25–115

Kotsidu 2000: Kotsidu, Haritini, ΤΙΜΗ ΚΑΙ ΔΟΞΑ. Ehrungen für hellenistische Herrscher im griechischen Mutterland und in Kleinasien unter besonderer Berücksichtigung archäologischer Denkmäler, Berlin 2000

Kurth 1994: Kurth, Dieter, Treffpunkt der Götter. Inschriften aus dem Tempel des Horus von Edfu, Zürich 1994

von Lieven 2017: von Lieven, Alexandra, „Er war mit keinem einzigen von ihnen zufrieden, außer als ich ihm deinen Namen sagte." Religiöse Sukzession im Alten Ägypten, in: A.-B. Renger – M. Witte (eds.), Sukzession in Religionen. Autorisierung, Legitimierung, Wissenstransfer, Berlin et al. 2017, 85–112

Maher-Taha 1979: Maher-Taha, Mahmoud – Loyrette, Anne-Marie, Le Ramesseum XI: Les fêtes du dieu Min, Cairo 1979

Minas 2000: Minas, Martina, Die hieroglyphischen Ahnenreihen der ptolemäischen Könige. Ein Vergleich mit den Titeln der eponymen Priester in den griechischen und demotischen Papyri, Mainz 2000

Minas-Nerpel 2006: Minas-Nerpel, Martina, Die ptolemäischen Sokar-Osiris-Mumien. Neue Erkenntnisse zum ägyptischen Dynastiekult der Ptolemäer, Mitteilungen des Deutschen Archäologischen Instituts Kairo 62, 2006, 36–42

Minas-Nerpel 2020: Minas-Nerpel, Martina, Ptolemaic Queens as Ritualists and Recipients of Cults. The Cases of Arsinoe II and Berenike II, Ancient Society 49, 2020, 168–172

Moyer 2011: Moyer, Ian S., Egypt and the Limits of Hellenism, Cambridge 2011

Muccioli 2013: Muccioli, Federicomaria, Gli epiteti ufficiali dei re ellenistici, Stuttgart 2013

Olivier – Lorber 2013: Olivier, Julien – Lorber, Catharine C., Three Gold Coinages of Third-Century Ptolemaic Egypt, Revue belge de numismatique et de sigillographie 159, 2013, 49–150

Perdu 2014: Perdu, Olivier, Une statue stéléphore très particulière, Revue d'Égyptologie 65, 2014, 107–139

Pfeiffer 2004: Pfeiffer, Stefan, Das Dekret von Kanopos. Kommentar und historische Auswertung eines dreisprachigen Synodaldekretes der ägyptischen Priester zu Ehren Ptolemaios' III. und seiner Familie, München et. al. 2004

Pfeiffer ²2020: Pfeiffer, Stefan, Griechische und lateinische Inschriften zum Ptolemäerreich und zur römischen Provinz Aegyptus, Berlin ²2020

Pfeiffer 2022: Pfeiffer, Stefan, Great King Ptolemy III and Great King Antiochos III. Remarks on the Significance of a „Persian" Title in their Representation, in: id. – E. Anagnostou-Laoutides (eds.), Culture and Ideology under the Seleukids. Unframing a Dynasty, Berlin et al. 2022, 313–330

Preys 2015a: Preys, René, La royauté lagide et le culte d'Osiris d'après les portes monumentales de Karnak, in: Chr. Thiers (ed.), Documents de Théologies Thébaines Tardives 3 (D3T 3), Montpellier 2015a, 159–215

Preys 2015b: Preys, René, Roi vivant et roi ancêtre. Iconographie et idéologie royale sous les Ptolémées, in: Chr. Zivie-Coche (ed.), Offrandes, rites et rituels dans les temples d'époques ptolémaïque et romaine, Montpellier 2015b, 149–184

Preys 2016: Preys, René, Les scènes du culte royal à Edfou. Pour une étude diachronique des scènes rituelles des temples de l'époque gréco-romaine, in: S. Baumann – H. Kockelmann (eds.), Der ägyptische Tempel als ritueller Raum. Akten der internationalen Tagung Haus der Heidelberger Akademie der Wissenschaften, 9.–12. Juni 2015, Wiesbaden 2016, 389–418

Preys 2022: Preys, René, Le culte des Ptolémées dans les temples égyptiens. Les décrets royaux et la décoration des temples, in: G. Lenzo – Chr. Nihan – M. Pellet (eds.), Les cultes aux rois et aux héros à l'époque hellénistique. Continuités et changements, Tübingen 2022, 171–195

Quack 2008: Quack, Joachim F., Demotische magische und divinatorische Texte, in: B. Janowski – G. Wilhelm (eds.), Texte aus der Umwelt des Alten Testaments. Neue Folge, IV: Omina, Orakel, Rituale und Beschwörungen, Gütersloh 2008, 331–385

Quaegebeur 1989: Quaegebeur, Jan, The Egyptian Clergy and the Cult of the Ptolemaic Dynasty, Ancient Society 20, 1989, 93–116

Redford 1986: Redford, Donald B., Pharaonic King-Lists, Annals and Day-Books. A Contribution to the Study of the Egyptian Sense of History, Mississauga 1986

Scherf 2002: Scherf, Johannes, Zephyritis, DNP 12/2, 2002, 767

Schorn 2004: Schorn, Stefan, Satyros aus Kallatis. Sammlung der Fragmente mit Kommentar, Basel 2004

Simpson 1977: Simpson, William K., Amor Dei. nṯr mrr rmt m tꜣ wꜣ (Sh. Sai. 147–148) and the Embrace, in: J. Assmann – E. Feucht – R. Grieshammer (eds.), Fragen an die altägyptische Literatur. Studien zum Gedenken an Eberhard Otto, Wiesbaden 1977, 493–498

Staiger 1970: Staiger, Emil, Theokrit. Die echten Gedichte, Zürich et al. 1970

Thissen 1966: Thissen, Heinz-Joseph, Studien zum Raphiadekret, Meisenheim am Glan 1966

Thompson 2005: Thompson, Dorothy J., Posidippus. Poet of the Ptolemies, in: K. Gutzwiller (ed.), The New Posidippus. A Hellenistic Poetry Book, Oxford 2005, 269–283

Veligianni-Terzi 1997: Veligianni-Terzi, Chryssoula, Wertbegriffe in den attischen Ehrendekreten der klassischen Zeit, Stuttgart 1997

Vittman o. D.: Vittman, Günther, Raphia-Dekret, in: Thesaurus Linguae Aegyptiae (online: http://aaew.bbaw.de/tla) last access: 20.5.2024 von den Hoff 2020: von den Hoff, Ralf, Alexander's Dedications to the Gods. Sacred Space, Pious Practice and Public Legitimation, in: K. Trampedach – A. Meeus (eds.), The Legitimation of Conquest. Monarchical Representation and the Art of Government in the Empire of Alexander the Great, Stuttgart 2020, 99–121

von den Hoff 2021: von den Hoff, Ralf, The Visual Representation of Ptolemaic and Seleucid Kings. A Comparative Approach to Portrait Conepts, in: Chr. Fischer-Bovet – S. von Reden (eds.), Comparing the Ptolemaic and Seleucid Empires. Integration, Communication and Resistance, Cambridge 2021, 164–190

Weber ⁵1976: Weber, Max, Wirtschaft und Gesellschaft. Studienausgabe, Tübingen ⁵1976

West 1991: West, Stefanie, Herodotus' Portrait of Hecataeus, The Journal of Hellenic Studies 111, 1991, 144–160

Wiemer 2017: Wiemer, Hans-Ulrich, Siegen oder untergehen? Die hellenistische Monarchie in der neueren Forschung, in: S. Rebenich (ed.), Monarchische Herrschaft im Altertum, München 2017, 305–339

Wildung 1974: Wildung, Dietrich, Aufbau und Zweckbestimmung der Königsliste von Karnak, Göttinger Miszellen 9, 1974, 41–48

Winter 1978: Winter, Erich, Herrscherkult in den ägyptischen Ptolemäertempeln, in: H. Maehler – V. M. Strocka (eds.), Das ptolemäische Ägypten, Berlin 1978, 147–158

Ziegler 1961/1963: Ziegler, Konrad, Polybios. Geschichte, Zürich 1961/1963

Abbildungsverzeichnis

Abb. 1: © Patrick Brose, München.

Stefan Pfeiffer is Full Professor in Ancient History at Martin-Luther-Universität Halle-Wittenberg (since 2013), before this he was Professor for "Ancient World and Europe" at Technische Universität Chemnitz (2010–2013). His areas of specialization are the history of Graeco-Roman Egypt, ruler cult in antiquity and Judaism in Alexandria. He has among other aspects worked on multilingual texts from Egypt (the Decree of Canopus, which was his PhD-thesis, and the victory stela of C. Cornelius Gallus) and has published a book on emperor cult in Egypt (2010). He furthermore has written a study-book on Greek and Latin epigraphical records from Egypt (2015, second augmented edition 2020) and has published a general overview on the Ptolemaic Empire (2017). In 2021 he has published a commentary on 3 Makkabees and together with Friedhelm Hoffmann a small book on the decree of Rosetta.

Zwischen West und Ost
Zur Konzeption von Herrschaft, Dynastie und Kult im Seleukidenreich[*]

SONJA RICHTER

Abstract: This contribution focuses on our evidence for a Seleukid dynastic cult and its context. Given the vast expanse of the empire, the problematic nature of sources and inevitable comparisons with other dynasties (especially the Ptolemies) in modern scholarship, it offers a reassessment of the ancient material. In a careful reading of the available written sources, both literary and epigraphical, it becomes clear that a state-sponsored, top-down cult is far from certain. Rather, all evidence in these media points to local or regional contexts in which the material is best understood. As the paper shows, the main medium for Seleukid self- and dynastic representation were numismatics; coins being an attractive and flexible medium which could cater to the vastly different parts of the Seleukid empire. A main feature of dynastic representation can be found in the image of Apollon, whose role as mythical dynastic founder makes him the ideal standard-bearer. All Seleukid self-representation must be viewed alongside their Ptolemaic counterparts, but while it is clear that some elements (like the adoption of the title of basileus megas or the representation of sibling marriage) are to be understood in this context, other media, especially in numismatics, show a unique Seleukid way of representation – same, but different.

1. Einleitung und Fragestellung

Die Seleukiden nehmen unter den hellenistischen Herrscherhäusern aus verschiedenen Gründen eine Sonderstellung ein: Kein anderes hellenistisches Reich umfasste in

[*]   Ich danke den Organisatoren der Münsteraner Tagung, PD Dr. Christoph Michels, Prof. Dr. Hans Beck und Prof. Dr. Achim Lichtenberger, für die Möglichkeit, mich noch einmal vertieft mit den Seleukiden beschäftigen zu können und meine wissenschaftlichen Überlegungen zur Bedeutung des Dynastiekultes einbringen und zur Diskussion stellen zu dürfen. Des Weiteren bedanke ich mich bei meinen Essener Kollegen, insbesondere Prof. Dr. Justus Cobet, Dr. Carsten Binder und Dr. Isidor Brodersen, die diesen Beitrag in seinen unterschiedlichen Entstehungsphasen begleiteten und mir immer wieder zu neuen Denkanstößen verhalfen.

seiner maximalen Ausdehnung einen solch immensen Raum, und keine andere Dynastie herrschte über eine solch heterogene Bevölkerung mit einer Vielzahl an unterschiedlichen Sprachen, an kulturellen wie religiösen Traditionen und an soziopolitischen und gesellschaftlichen Systemen. In der antiken Literatur wie auch in Teilen der modernen Forschung haftete den seleukidischen Herrschern von Beginn an das Bild einer ,Fremdherrschaft' an, wenn mit Trogus-Iustin gesprochen Seleukos als *rex Macedonus*[1] in einem *Imperium Macedonium*[2] wahrgenommen wird oder die Seleukiden, wie etwa bei Strabon, grundsätzlich als Makedonen verstanden werden.[3] In dieser Beobachtung sah sich die Forschung zunächst durch die krisenhaften Entwicklungen ab der Mitte des 3. Jhs. v. Chr. bestätigt, als besonders in den östlichen Gebieten jenseits des Zagros lokale Satrapen versuchten, sich von der seleukidischen Herrschaft zu lösen und unabhängige Reiche zu etablieren.[4] Die Schwierigkeiten einer herrschaftlichen Durchdringung des Raumes wurden durch die Dichotomie des Gebietes grob in West und Ost noch deutlich verstärkt, wobei das mesopotamische Kernland eine weitere Sonderrolle einnahm. Eine in allen Regionen tragende Akzeptanz griechisch-makedonischer Traditionen als Grundlage der Legitimation der Herrschaft war nicht gegeben. Vielmehr mussten zur Sicherung der Herrschaft die jeweiligen lokalen Traditionen und Voraussetzungen berücksichtigt werden. Die Seleukiden hatten daher kaum die Möglichkeit, eine einheitliche Herrschaftsstrategie zu entwickeln. Ebenso wenig konnten überall die gleichen Kommunikationskanäle und -medien zur Sicherung der dynastischen Herrschaft zum Erfolg führen. Aus dieser Konstellation resultierte ein an Praktikabilität orientierter seleukidischer Sonderweg.

Diese Bedingungen erklären zudem, weshalb sich die Seleukiden nur bedingt am kompetitiven Ringen um Herrschaftsanspruch und monarchische Repräsentation im östlichen Mittelmeerraum beteiligten bzw. beteiligen konnten. Vor dem Hintergrund der diesen Beitrag kontextualisierenden Frage nach „Gleich, nur anders?" möchte ich meine Überlegungen im Folgenden auf die beiden miteinander verbundenen Aspekte

---

1   Iust. 36.1.10.
2   Edson 1958. So bezeichnet etwa Brüggemann 2010, 52 das Seleukidenreich als „eine formal unbestreitbar makedonische Monarchie". Strootman 2011, 89 wies der indigenen Kultur am seleukidischen Königshof lediglich ein Schattendasein zu, da die Herrschaftsideologie griechisch geblieben sei. Jüngst erklärte Brüggemann 2022 die Außenwahrnehmung des Seleukidenreiches als „Makedonisches Reich" damit, dass die Heterogenität des Reiches für außenstehende Zeitgenossen und die Nachwelt in gleicher Weise das Seleukidenreich nicht greifbar gemacht hätte, weshalb man sich in der Bezeichnung auf die einzige Konstante, das makedonische Element im Herrschaftsgefüge, konzentriert hätte. Vgl. dazu auch den Beitrag von Christoph Michels in diesem Band.
3   Strab. 11.11.6/7.2/9.1; 15.3.3/24.
4   Ungeachtet dessen ist jedoch zu betonen, dass bereits ab der zweiten Generation die seleukidische Dynastie in größerem Maße iranisch geprägt war und eben jener Antiochos I. Soter, der selbst nie griechischen bzw. makedonischen Boden betreten hatte, mit der aus dem Hause der Antigoniden stammenden Stratonike eine Frau zur Gattin nahm, die die seleukidische Herrschaft vor allem im westlichen Teil sichern und für die Bevölkerung ,akzeptabel' machen sollte. Vgl. etwa Plischke 2016.

Kult und Herrschaft bzw. Kult als herrschaftsstabilisierende Komponente im Seleukidenreich richten, um ihre dynastische Bedeutung, ihre mediale Repräsentation und ihre herrschaftliche Kontextualisierung aufzuzeigen.

Die Frage nach der Bedeutung des Dynastiekultes im Seleukidenreich hat in den letzten Jahren und Jahrzehnten bereits großes Interesse erfahren. Während sich die Forschung dahingehend einig ist, dass unter Antiochos III. ein seleukidischer Herrscherkult existierte, divergieren die Ansichten hinsichtlich der Einführung eines solchen Kultes. So geht ein Teil[5] der Forschung von der Existenz eines vom Herrscherhaus bereits unter Antiochos I. eingeführten Dynastiekultes aus. Ein anderer Teil[6] hingegen vertritt die Meinung, dass erst Antiochos III. für die Einrichtung des seleukidischen Herrscherkultes verantwortlich gewesen sei, wobei verschiedene Zeitpunkte einer möglichen Einführung diskutiert werden.

Hinter dieser zunächst chronologischen Unterscheidung verbirgt sich jedoch auf zweiter Ebene eine differierende Wahrnehmung der seleukidischen Herrschaft. Als Eckpunkte einer durchaus facettenreichen Bandbreite lassen sich in etwa folgende Ansichten benennen: So hätten die Seleukiden entweder ihre Herrschaft nach iranischem Vorbild ausgeübt, wodurch mögliche Anknüpfungspunkte an die Achaimeniden in den Fokus gerieten,[7] oder sie seien – als Nachfolger Alexanders III.? – griechisch-makedonischen Traditionen gefolgt, wodurch ihnen wie bereits angedeutet mitunter das Label einer Fremdherrschaft anhaftete.[8] Bereits 1958 wies Charles Edson darauf hin, dass das gleichzeitig entstandene Ptolemaierreich in Ägypten im Gegensatz zum Seleukidenreich nie als ‚makedonisch' bezeichnet oder angesehen worden sei. Daraus folgerte er, dass das Seleukidenreich im Ganzen – auch im seleukidischen Selbstverständnis – ‚makedonisch' geprägt gewesen sei, die Seleukiden es jedoch nicht so hätten bezeichnen können, da in Makedonien und den griechischen Kerngebieten bis 168 v. Chr. ein von den Antigoniden beherrschtes, ‚makedonisches Reich' existiert habe.[9] Im ptolemaiischen Raum findet sich hingegen durchaus die Wahrnehmung und Propagierung des Seleukidenkönigs als Nachfolger der Achaimeniden, bspw. in der Bezeichnung „König Perserfreund",[10] deren Genese jedoch als Abwertung eines konkurrierenden Feindbildes verstanden werden muss.[11] Mögliche Konsequenzen, die

---

5   So etwa Gruen 1999; Sartre 2006; Erickson 2018a, jedoch jeweils mit unterschiedlichen Begründungen.
6   Bikerman 1938; Sherwin-White – Kuhrt 1993; Van Nuffelen 2004; Iossif 2014; Plischke 2014.
7   Eine strukturelle Kontinuität von den Achaimeniden bis zu den Seleukiden betont besonders Engels 2017.
8   Eine Wahrnehmung der Seleukiden als Makedonen findet sich in jüngerer Zeit etwa bei Capdetrey 2008; Tuplin 2008. Hiervon zu unterscheiden ist die Sichtweise bei Briant 1979, 330, der die
     seleukidische Herrschaft zwar als makedonisch geprägt, nicht jedoch in der Nachfolge Alexanders
     versteht, da Philipps Sohn vielmehr „le dernier des Achéménides" gewesen sei.
9   Edson 1958, 154–165.
10   Funck 1996, 201. Tuplin 2008, 113–114 lehnt diese Ansicht jedoch ab.
11   Müller 2011, 4.

sich aus der zweiten Position ergeben können, schlagen sich dann etwa in der Formulierung von Erich S. Gruen nieder, der die zeitliche Verortung des Herrscherkults mit dem augenscheinlich nicht kausal verbundenen Spannungsfeld zu anderen hellenistischen Dynastien und dem kompetitiven Ringen um Machtdemonstration verknüpft: „There is no reason to believe that this (*scil.* Ruler) cult first saw the light of day in the time of Antiochus III. It seems unlikely that the Seleucids would have lacked a centrally organized cult when the Ptolemies had long had one."[12]

Ausgehend von der dieser Ansicht zugrunde liegenden Annahme, dass es nicht nachvollziehbar sei, warum die Seleukiden nicht den gleichen – erfolgreichen – Weg beschritten hätten wie insbesondere die Ptolemaier, zu denen die Seleukiden in direktester und schärfster Konkurrenz standen, nachdem sich die Etablierung eines Herrscherkults – retrospektiv – als legitimatorisch funktionierendes und zielführendes Mittel der Herrschaftsetablierung, -sicherung und -festigung erwiesen hatte und pauschalisiert alle hellenistischen Dynastien sich eines solchen bedienten hätten, möchte ich im Folgenden die beiden Punkte zur zeitlichen Verortung und zu möglichen hellenistischen Vorbildern aufgreifen, sie jedoch in anderer Weise miteinander verknüpfen. Zwei Fragen werden diesbezüglich im Fokus stehen: Welche Einflussnahme kann dem auf westlicher Tradition beruhenden Dynastiekult im Spannungsgefüge der hellenistischen Monarchien zugeschrieben werden? Und: Lassen sich im Sinne eines ‚seleukidischen Sonderwegs' andere Kommunikationswege und -medien ausmachen, mittels derer sich die Seleukiden im Konkurrenzkampf um Kult und Herrschaft positionierten und ihre Dynastie legitimierten? Hierfür erfolgt zunächst eine Untersuchung der schriftlichen Quellen, vornehmlich der epigraphischen Überlieferung, um ihren Quellenwert für die Beantwortung der Frage, welche Bedeutung dem Dynastiekult bzw. der kultischen Repräsentation im Seleukidenreich zugrunde lag, zu bestimmen. In einem zweiten Schritt stehen die nichtschriftlichen Quellen im Fokus, um aufzuzeigen, welche Funktion insbesondere den Münzen im Sinne eines herrschaftlichen Sonderwegs zur kultisch-religiösen Selbstdarstellung unter den Seleukiden zukam. Den Abschluss bildet die Antwort auf die Frage, in welcher Hinsicht das Ptolemaierreich im Sinne von Angleichung und Abgrenzung eine besondere Rolle für das Seleukidenreich spielte, deren kompetitive Resonanzbeziehung vor allem in der Herrschaftszeit Antiochos' III. zu fassen ist.

Wenn im Folgenden die Genese, Existenz und Ausprägung des Dynastiekultes unter den Seleukiden untersucht wird, sind ausschließlich Formen der kultischen Verehrung gemeint, die vom Herrscher selbst initiiert und propagiert wurden und imperialen, das (gesamte) Reich betreffenden Charakter hatten. Gemeint ist also ein ‚Staatskult', der von oben nach unten das Reich durchdringen sollte. Hiervon ist der Städtekult abzugrenzen, dem ein vornehmlich lokaler Charakter zukommt und dessen Initiatoren

---

12 Gruen 1999, 33. Erickson 2018a, 99 zielt bei seiner Neubewertung des seleukidischen Dynastiekultes auf Basis der Münzprägung darauf ab, „to support Gruen's questioning of the traditional view of Seleucid ruler cult".

einzelne Personen oder *poleis* sind, die von sich aus mit einer Ehrbekundung an die Dynastie herantraten, um ihre Dankbarkeit für Zuwendungen auszudrücken oder umgekehrt Zuwendungen zu erbitten. In gleicher Weise zu verstehen sind Zuwendungen der Herrscher bzw. der Dynastie, die diese einzelnen *poleis* zukommen ließen, um ihrerseits das Verhältnis zu stärken.[13] Diese Form der kultischen Verehrung ist auch aus Teilen des Seleukidenreiches bereits seit dem frühen 3. Jh. v. Chr. bekannt und lokal verbreitet.

2. Vorbemerkungen zur Quellensituation

Fragen sowie unterschiedliche Ansätze und Blickwinkel auf das Seleukidenreich haben in der Vergangenheit immer wieder zu umfangreichen Diskussionen hinsichtlich der Herrschaftsprägung geführt, wobei die den Diskussions- und Interpretationsrahmen bedingenden Quellen in ihrer Aussagekraft weder über- noch unterschätzt werden sollten. So ist neben der Heterogenität des Reiches an sich eben auch in besonderem Maße die Unterschiedlichkeit in der Quellenlage zu berücksichtigen, also einerseits quantitativ die Anzahl der überlieferten Quellen, andererseits die Inhomogenität der Quellenarten für das gesamte Herrschaftsgebiet. Hierbei gilt grundsätzlich, dass die Quellenlage als recht dürftig zu bezeichnen ist. Ein Grund hierfür ist sicherlich, dass sich die herrschaftlichen Bestrebungen in den Hauptphasen der politischen und militärischen Tätigkeit in östlichen Gebieten bewegten bzw. der Mittelpunkt des Reiches in von der Ägäis aus gesehen weit östlichen Territorien lag. Somit standen die Seleukiden nur in geringem Maße im Blickfeld griechisch-römischer Autoren, die sich auf den Mittelmeerraum konzentrierten. In den literarischen Werken einiger Autoren wie Polybios, Diodor, Appian oder Plutarch lassen sich natürlich einige wenige Hinweise und Informationen zur seleukidischen Herrschaft finden, doch waren sie alle keine Zeitgenossen der Ereignisse und besaßen erst recht keine tieferen Kenntnisse über iranische und andere indigene Traditionen. Darüber hinaus operierten die Seleukiden zumindest im Osten in einem Gebiet, das nicht die aus der griechisch-römischen Kultur bekannten Tendenzen zur literarischen Textualisierung und Reflexion besaß, so dass aus den iranischen Gebieten kein Äquivalent zu den uns bekannten literarischen Quellen auf uns gekommen ist. Als weitere Gattung schriftlicher Quellen spielen natürlich die epigraphischen Quellen eine wichtige Rolle, doch lässt sich auch hier eine geographische bzw. kulturelle Diskrepanz in Quantität und Qualität feststellen. Wäh-

---

13 Die Trennung zwischen dem lokalen Städtekult und dem dynastischen Herrscherkult wurde durch die Arbeiten von Bikerman 1938 und Habicht ²1970 in der Forschung etabliert. „This picture of the relations between city and ruler as diplomacy and cordial reciprocity is of course exactly the image which the rituals and the documents of the cities sought to publicize in permanent form. This is not a reliable source to evaluate the place of the cities within the Seleukid empire and their relation with the kings"; Ma 1999, 38. Grundsätzlich zu diesem Aspekt auch Chaniotis 2003; Debord 2003.

rend aus den griechischen *poleis* im Westen zahlreiche Inschriften bzw. Verwaltungsdo-
kumente und Briefe bekannt sind, die Einblicke in lokale Strukturen von Herrschaft,
Dynastie und Kult und in das Verhältnis zwischen Herrscher und Stadt bzw. Bevölkerung ermöglichen, ist auch hier der Befund jenseits des mesopotamischen Kernlandes
im Verhältnis zum Westen und erst recht im Verhältnis zu westlichen hellenistischen
Reichen recht mager, so dass Fragen nach einheitlichen Herrschaftspraktiken, die im
gesamten Seleukidenreich eingeführt wurden oder Anwendung fanden, auf Grund
der Quellenbasis kaum beantwortet werden können. Dieser Umstand bestimmt jede
Untersuchung zum Seleukidenreich und muss zwangsläufig zu unterschiedlichen, vor
allem unterschiedlich belastbaren Ergebnissen aus West und Ost führen.

3. Der seleukidische Herrscherkult in den epigraphischen Quellen

Eine Vorstufe des Dynastiekultes, der die Verehrung des lebenden Herrschers ein-
schließt, bildet die Einrichtung eines Ahnenkultes zur Verehrung der verstorbenen
progonoi. So ließ Ptolemaios II. Philadelphos nach deren Tod seine Eltern Ptolemaios I.
Soter und Berenike I. kultisch als *theoi soteres* verehren.[14] Einen Kult für sich und seine
Gattin Arsinoë II. ließ er noch zu Lebzeiten etwa 272/271 v. Chr. einrichten, in dem das
Herrscherpaar als *theoi adelphoi*[15] verehrt wurde.

Ungeachtet der im weiteren Verlauf diskutierten Frage nach der Einsetzung des seleukidischen Dynastiekultes finden sich mit den frühen ptolemaiischen Entwicklungen vergleichbare Tendenzen. So ließ Antiochos I. nach dem Tod seines Vaters den
Dynastiegründer im Rahmen eines Ahnenkultes verehren. Greifbar ist dieser Akt im
sogenannten Nikatoreion,[16] einem Tempel mit *temenos*, in dem er Seleukos in Seleukeia
Piereia[17] bestatten ließ. Einen epigraphischen Beleg für den Kult des verstorbenen Herr-

---

14   P. Eleph. 2. Dieser Kult war getrennt von dem etwa 285 v. Chr. durch Ptolemaios I. eingerichteten
      Kult zur göttlichen Verehrung Alexanders III.; vgl. Herklotz 2005, 155–156. Vgl. zu diesem Komplex
      den Beitrag von Stefan Pfeiffer in diesem Band.

15   Erstmalig belegt in P.Hib. II,199. Eine Zusammenführung aller Kulte in einen Dynastiekult er-
      folgte erst unter Ptolemaios IV. Philopater (erstmalig belegt in BGU 6, 1276 aus dem Frühjahr
      214 v. Chr.).

16   Nur zwei kultische Gebäude zur Verehrung seleukidischer Herrscher sind bekannt: der Naos in
      Lemnos (Phylarch. BNJ 81 F 29) und das Nikatoreion in Seleukeia Piereia (App. Syr. 63).

17   Die Stadt wurde laut Strabon (16.1.5) um 300 v. Chr. von Seleukos an der östlichen Mittelmeer-
      küste als Hafenstadt Antiocheias am Orontes gegründet und war Teil der Tetrapolis Antiocheia
      am Orontes, Apameia am Orontes, Laodikeia und Seleukeia Piereia. Im 3. Syrischen Krieg fiel
      die Stadt unter die Herrschaft Ptolemaios' III. Erst Antiochos III. gelang es, Seleukeia Piereia
      219 v. Chr. im Rahmen des 4. Syrischen Krieges zurückzuerobern. Neben der wirtschaftlichen und
      politischen Bedeutung für das Seleukidenreich spielte die Stadt auch kultisch bzw. dynastisch eine
      besondere Rolle, die sich etwa in Polybios' Bericht (5.58.4) über den Kriegsrat zeigt, wenn im Kon-
      text der Überlegungen hinsichtlich eines Einmarsches nach Koile-Syrien vor dem 4. Syrischen

schers[18] liefert eine jährliche Priesterliste aus der Zeit Seleukos' IV., die einen Priester für alle verstorbenen Seleukidenherrscher nennt sowie einen weiteren Priester für den Kult des lebenden Herrschers. Zu betonen ist ebenfalls, dass die *progonoi* mit ihren jeweiligen Kultepitheta bezeichnet werden und Seleukos und Antiochos darüber hinaus eine göttliche Zuordnung erhalten:

> [...] Priester des Jahres Hundertund[...] (Priester) des Zeus Olympios und des Zeus Koryphaios, Nikeratos, Sohn des Nikeratos; (Priester) des Apolls von Daphne, Kallikles, Sohn des Diogenes; (Priester) des Apolls, Zenobios, Sohn des Zenon; (Priester) des Seleukos [I.] Zeus Nikator und des Antiochos [I.] Apollon Soter und des Antiochos [II.] Theos und Seleukos [II.] Kallinikos und des Seleukos [III.] Soter und des Antiochos und des Antiochos [III.] des Großen, [...]genes, Sohn des Artemon; (Priester) des [Köni]gs Seleukos (IV.), [...].[19]

Die Priesterliste belegt somit eindeutig, dass in der ersten Hälfte des 2. Jhs. v. Chr. ein Dynastiekult im Seleukidenreich etabliert war, und gibt insoweit Einblicke in die Kultpraxis, als die Priestereinsetzung und die Kultepitheta der Herrscher deutlich werden. Unklar bleibt jedoch, wann der seleukidische Herrscherkult tatsächlich eingerichtet wurde und inwieweit er aus dem ursprünglich von Antiochos I. gegründeten Ahnenkult[20] hervorgegangen sein kann.[21]

Krieg der Bewohner Seleukeias Apollophanes die Stadt als „Wiege des Reiches" bzw. „heiligen Herd" bezeichnet.

18 Die Gründe, weshalb es sich bei der Kulteinrichtung in Seleukeia Piereia nicht um einen Kult für den Stadtgründer, sondern um einen dynastischen Ahnenkult handelt, wurden bereits von Iossif 2014, 141 Anm. 67 ausführlich diskutiert, der einerseits die dynastische Komponente durch Antiochos I. im Gründungsakt betont und andererseits in der Rede des Apollophanes einen weiteren Beleg dafür sieht, da dieser Seleukeia Piereia nicht als Ort beschreibt, in dem der Stadtgründer bestattet ist, sondern der Gründer der Dynastie. Zudem blieb der Ahnenkult für den verstorbenen Herrscher nicht auf Seleukeia Piereia beschränkt, sondern weitete sich auf weitere Städte Ioniens aus.

19 OGIS 245 (187–175 v. Chr.). Zur Übersetzung vgl. bes. Stroud 1985, 32–37. Vgl. auch Dumke 2022, 51–52. Eine weitere Priesterliste ist aus Teos bekannt; OGIS 246 (150–100 v. Chr.).

20 Ladynin 2020, 46–58 hat daher jüngst geschlussfolgert, dass auch das Begräbnis des Dynastiegründers im Spiegel ptolemaiischer Handlungen verstanden werden sollte. So weise einerseits die geographische Lage der jeweiligen Begräbnisstätten in Seleukeia Piereia und Alexandreia große Parallelen auf, andererseits zeigten sich durch die Berichterstattung (Diod. 18.28.3–4; Ioh. Mal. 8.12–19; Curt. 1.30–33) über die Begräbnisse große Übereinstimmungen in der Wahrnehmung, so dass Antiochos I. die Absicht unterstellt werden könne, durch die Bezugnahme auf Alexander und im Kontext eines Konkurrenzverhältnisses mit den Ptolemaiern Seleukos als Dynastiegründer und einendes Element im Reich zu überhöhen. Auch von Reden – Strootman 2021, 36 sehen in der Frühzeit eindeutige Parallelen zwischen Seleukeia Piereia und Alexandreia.

21 Sartre 2006 versteht den von Antiochos begründeten Ahnenkult bereits als Dynastiekult. Nach Iossif 2014, 134–136 muss jedoch nicht zwingend von einer Entwicklung von einer städtischen hin zu einer dynastischen Kultverehrung ausgegangen werden, da die Inschriften zum Teil lediglich auf den Umgang mit den Ahnen verweisen, diese jedoch nicht in einen kultischen Kontext gestellt werden. Vgl. hierzu auch seine Bewertung zur Aussagekraft von P. Berol. 21286.

In der Forschung lassen sich zwei Strömungen hinsichtlich der zeitlichen Begründung des seleukidischen Dynastiekultes ausmachen: eine Frühdatierung in die Herrschaftszeit Antiochos' I. und eine Spätdatierung in die Herrschaftszeit Antiochos' III.
Drei epigraphische Zeugnisse bilden den Ausgangspunkt für die sogenannte Frühdatierung: ein Dekret der ionischen Städte aus Klazomenai anlässlich des Geburtstags
Antiochos' I.,[22] ein Brief Antiochos' I. an Erythrai, in dem er auf seine Ahnen und deren Städtepolitik in Erythrai Bezug nimmt,[23] und ein Dekret aus Ilion für einen König
Antiochos, dessen Datierung insofern unsicher ist, als es offen bleibt, ob es sich auf
Antiochos I. oder Antiochos III. bezieht.[24] Unabhängig davon, dass die Quantität der
überlieferten Quellen kaum davon überzeugen kann, dass bereits unter Antiochos I.
ein flächendeckender Dynastiekult im Seleukidenreich eingerichtet wurde, sind diese
Zeugnisse in den Bereich des lokalen Städtekults zu verorten, der vor allem in den
poleis im westlichen Kleinasien eine besondere Rolle spielte.[25] Weitere Beispiele für die
Stiftung städtischer Kulte für die Seleukiden sind etwa aus Milet, Priene oder Aigai in
der Aiolis[26] bekannt.

Die Quellenlage für die sogenannte Spätdatierung weist im Gegensatz dazu große Unterschiede auf, bleibt aber ähnlich problematisch. Hinsichtlich der Existenz des
Dynastiekultes unter Antiochos III. auf Basis der Inschriften herrscht zunächst grundsätzlich Einigkeit. Drei identische inschriftliche Zeugnisse geben Auskunft darüber,
dass Antiochos 193 v. Chr. die Einrichtung eines Kultes für seine Gattin Laodike ver-
anlasste. Gefunden wurden sie bei Eriza[27] an der Grenze Kariens und Phrygiens, in Laodikeia[28] in Medien und in der Nähe von Kirmānšāh.[29]

(...) und jetzt haben wir entschieden, dass – so wie für uns ernannt werden (ἀποδείκνυνται)
im Königreich Oberpriester – auch für sie eingesetzt werden (καθίστασθαι) in denselben
Bezirken Oberpriesterinnen, die tragen sollen goldene Kränze mit einem Bild von ihr, und
die ferner genannt werden sollen in den Kontrakten nach den Oberpriestern für unse-
re Vorfahren und für uns. Da nun ernannt ist für die unter deiner Verwaltung stehenden
Gebiete Laodike (die Tochter), ist alles auszuführen den oben gemachten Anordnungen
zufolge, und die Abschriften der Briefe sind auf Stelen aufzuzeichnen und aufzustellen an

---

22   OGIS 222; Habicht ²1970, 91–93; Orth 1977, 97–100.
23   OGIS 223. Bikerman 1938, 136 datiert den Brief in die Zeit Antiochos' II. Vgl. auch Habicht ²1970,
      96–99; Orth, 1977, 87–97; Capdetrey 2007, 211.
24   OGIS 219. Antiochos I.: etwa Ma 1999, 254–259; Antiochos III.: etwa Iossif 2011, 244–246.
25   Auf Grund der spärlichen Überlieferung verneint Iossif 2014, 135–137 auch die Annahme eines
      „evolutionist' model" (135), nach dem der Dynastiekult aus dem Städtekult hervorgegangen sei,
      da die Vorfahren hier lediglich hinsichtlich ihrer Verdienste erwähnt, nicht jedoch in einen kulti-
      schen Kontext gesetzt werden.
26   Vgl. hierzu bes. Hasan – Ricl 2009. Neu dazu Habicht 2020.
27   OGIS 224; Merkelbach – Stauber 2005, Nr. 302.
28   Merkelbach – Stauber 2005, Nr. 301.
29   Merkelbach – Stauber 2005, Nr. 303.

den am besten sichtbaren Stellen, damit jetzt und in Zukunft allen die Einstellung deutlich werde, die wir hierin gegenüber unserer Schwester hegen. (…).[30]

Dieses *prostagma* an den Funktionär Menedemos ist zunächst ein Zeugnis dafür, dass der Laodike-Kult eingerichtet und mit demjenigen für den Herrscher gleichgestellt werden soll. Dies setzt voraus, dass der Herrscherkult zum Zeitpunkt der Einsetzung des Laodike-Kultes bereits existieren musste, woraus die Diskussion darüber entstand, wann der Kult zur Verehrung des lebenden Herrschers eingerichtet wurde. Die spätestmögliche Einsetzung wäre somit 193 v. Chr., die Susan Sherwin-White und Amélie Kuhrt präferieren, da sie ἀποδείκνυνται als gleichzeitige Handlung zu καθίστασθαι verstehen.[31] Frühere Datierungsvorschläge ergeben sich aus inschriftlichen Belegen der Jahre 205 v. Chr. bzw. 209 v. Chr., in denen bereits Priester für die Verehrung der seleukidischen Herrscher genannt werden. So datieren die Bewohner Antiocheias in der Persis im Rahmen eines Briefwechsels ihr Schreiben im Jahre 205 v. Chr. an Magnesia am Maiander hinsichtlich der dortigen Festspiele nach einem gewissen „Herakleitos, Sohn des Zoes, der Priester des Seleukos Nikator und des Antiochos Soter und des Antiochos Theos und des Seleukos Kallinikos und des Königs Seleukos und des Königs Antiochos und dessen Sohnes des Königs Antiochos" war.[32] Ein Briefwechsel aus dem Jahre 209 v. Chr. zwischen Philotas, Zeuxis und Antiochos III. gibt Aufschluss darüber, dass der seleukidische König den Leiter der königlichen Finanzkanzlei Nikanor zum Oberpriester aller kultischen Angelegenheiten jenseits des Tauros ernannt hat.[33] Panagiotis Iossif konnte zuletzt jedoch überzeugend aufzeigen, dass beide inschriftlich dokumentierten Ereignisse dem Städtekult bzw. lokalen Kultpraktiken zuzuordnen sind und keinen Nachweis für einen bereits etablierten seleukidischen Dynastiekult darstellen.[34] Zu berücksichtigen ist an dieser Stelle die besondere geographische Situation, die sich durch die bereits seit Jahrhunderten etablierte griechische Polisstruktur und die damit einhergehende Inschriftentradition in Kleinasien ergibt. Nikanor scheint an dieser Stelle durchaus die kultischen Pflichten über einen mehrere Städte bzw. Regionen umfassenden Raum übernommen zu haben; Priester im seleukidischen Dynastiekult war er jedoch nicht, was durch seine Nennung als Oberpriester im Städtekult in Amyzon in den Jahren 202 bzw. 201 v. Chr. deutlich wird.[35] Ähnliches gilt für die Situation in Antiocheia

---

30 Übersetzung nach HGIÜ 462.

31 Sherwin-White 1993, 209–210.

32 OGIS 233; Merkelbach – Stauber 2005, Nr. 306. Zur Auslassung des *epitheton* für Seleukos III. und seiner grundsätzlichen *epitheta* vgl. Muccioli 2013, bes. 104; Iossif 2014, 139.

33 SEG 37.1010; BE 89.276.

34 Iossif 2014, 136–140.

35 Ma 1999, Nr. 9; 10. Überzeugend hierzu Iossif 2014, 136–138, der Nikanors Nennung vor der Erwähnung des städtischen Priesters über die Anweisung Antiochos' III. erklärt, Nikanor solle in allen Verträgen und anderen Dokumenten, in denen es üblich sei, genannt werden (SEG 37.1010). Nikanor habe somit in hierarchischem Sinne an der Spitze eines Kollegiums gestanden.

in der Persis. Die Stadt wurde durch Antiochos I. (wieder-)gegründet, indem er Bürger der Polis Magnesia am Maiander dorthin übersiedeln ließ. Somit war Antiocheia trotz seiner geographischen Verortung in Westiran eng mit griechischen Traditionen und Praktiken verknüpft, was seine Bürger in ihrem Brief an Magnesia betonen.[36] Die weiteren Briefe im Rahmen dieser Korrespondenz, die Schreiben Antiochos' III.[37] und Antiochos' des Jüngeren[38] an Magnesia am Maiander, weisen jedoch keinerlei vergleichbare Formulierung auf, was darauf hindeutet, dass die Datierungsformel einer lokal in Antiocheia in der Persis[39] zugehörigen Kultpraxis entspringt. Zudem weist die in dieser Inschrift verwendete Formulierung hinsichtlich des Priesteramtsumfangs einen deutlichen Unterschied zu den Befugnissen der Priester im seleukidischen Dynastiekult aus späterer Zeit auf: Herakleitos war Priester sowohl im Kult für die Ahnen als auch im Kult für den lebenden Herrscher und für dessen designierten Nachfolger. Die angesprochene Priesterliste aus der Zeit Seleukos' IV. aus Seleukeia Piereia benennt hingegen zwei Priester, einen für den Kult der Ahnen und einen für den lebenden Herrscher. Zudem weist die Priesterliste, wie bereits gezeigt, Seleukos und Antiochos ihre mit Göttern assoziierten Beinamen zu, wenn der Dynastiebegründer als Seleukos Zeus Nikator und sein Sohn als Antiochos Apollon Soter bezeichnet werden.[40]

Des Weiteren belegt das *prostagma*, dass für den Laodike-Kult eine Oberpriesterin ernannt wird, die goldene Kränze/Kronen[41] mit Bildnissen der Königin tragen soll. In Laodikeia und Kirmānšāh handelt es sich hierbei um die Tochter Laodike, der diese Aufgabe im Kult ihrer Mutter übertragen wird. In Eriza wird der Abschrift nach Berenike, Tochter des Ptolemaios, der ein Sohn des semi-unabhängigen Herrschers Lysimachos in Telmessos war, als Oberpriesterin eingesetzt. Zudem sollen öffentlich Abschriften ausgestellt werden an den „am besten sichtbaren Stellen". Es fehlt somit jeglicher Hinweis auf ein kultisches Gebäude, also die Errichtung eines Tempels oder ähnliches, oder die eigentliche Kultpraxis bzw. den -ritus. Daher folgert Iossif, dass der Kult für die Königin durch ihre die Bildnisse tragende Oberpriesterin vergegenwärtigt sei und ausgeübt werde:

> the recipient of the cult [the queen] was supposed to be present through her likeness when her cult was performed, in the same way gods were present in their rituals through their statues. This can only mean that the queen/goddess could receive a cult virtually every-

---

36   OGIS 233.
37   OGIS 231; Merkelbach – Stauber 2005, Nr. 304.
38   OGIS 232; Merkelbach – Stauber 2005, Nr. 305.
39   Vgl. hierzu auch Capdetrey 2007, 216.
40   OGIS 245. Gleiches gilt für die Priesterliste aus Teos (OGIS 246). Vgl. auch Iossif 2014, 139–140.
41   Iossif 2014, 144 geht von einem griechisch-makedonischen bzw. hellenisierten Publikum aus, das durch die goldenen Kränze/Kronen angesprochen wurde, da er den Ursprung der Krone ebenfalls im makedonischen Raum verortet.

where in the satrapy, where her high-priestess, the mediator par excellence, would bring her image.

Die Ernennung einer das Bildnis der Königin tragenden Oberpriesterin ohne Zuordnung zu einem spezifischen Heiligtum findet zudem keine Parallelen in den Kultpraktiken anderer hellenistischer Dynastien, sondern unterstreicht die spezifisch seleukidische Ausrichtung in der Einrichtung des Laodikekultes.

Zuletzt sei ein Aspekt erwähnt, der sich augenscheinlich nicht auf den Dynastie- bzw. den Laodikekult bezieht, meiner Ansicht nach jedoch einen verstärkten Einblick in das dynastische Selbstverständnis der Seleukiden im ausgehenden 3. Jh. v. Chr. gibt: Antiochos nennt sich selbst ‚König Antiochos'; die Königin Laodike, die als Tochter Mithradates' II. von Pontos eine Cousine des Seleukiden war, bezeichnet er durchgehend als „Schwester".[42]

Aus der Analyse der inschriftlichen Überlieferung ergibt sich, dass die gemeinhin als seleukidischer Dynastiekult bezeichnete Herrscherverehrung unter Antiochos III. eindeutig zu greifen ist und vermutlich auch erst in seiner Herrschaftszeit eingerichtet wurde. Die wenigen erhaltenen Zeugnisse reduzieren jedoch die Aussagekraft der *prostagmata* deutlich. Zwei Sichtweisen sind grundsätzlich möglich: Wenn die drei erhaltenen Abschriften als Beleg für eine reichsweite und flächendeckende Einführung des seleukidischen Dynastiekults verstanden werden, wofür etwa die Pluralform ἀρχιερεῖς ins Feld geführt werden kann, muss davon ausgegangen werden, dass der Großteil der diesbezüglichen Inschriften verloren gegangen ist und daher keine weiteren Aussagen etwa hinsichtlich einer nachhaltigen oder herrschaftsstabilisierenden Wirkung getroffen werden können, zumal sich Antiochos' Anordnung lediglich auf die Kulteinrichtung als solche konzentriert, die praktische Ausübung jedoch keine Rolle zu spielen scheint bzw. nicht thematisiert wird. Werden die drei erhaltenen Zeugnisse hingegen als bewusst in ihren jeweiligen Lokalisationen eingesetzte Selbstzeugnisse des Herrschers verstanden, verlieren sie ihren möglichen Wert für die Annahme eines etablierten Dynastiekultes im Seleukidenreich. In diesem Fall geben die *prostagmata* jedoch einen tieferen Einblick in das politisch-dynastische Geflecht im ausgehenden 3. Jh. v. Chr. So lassen sich zwei Inschriften in der Region verorten, die sich nur wenige Jahrzehnte zuvor im Rahmen der Revolte unter Molon vom Seleukidenreich loszusagen versuchte. Dieser Umstand kann als hinreichende Erklärung dafür verstanden werden, warum sich Antiochos dieser Region besonders annahm und sie einerseits durch eine intensivierte Kontrolle, andererseits durch die Vergabe von Sonderrollen stärker in das herrschaftspolitische Geflecht einzubinden versuchte. Ähnliches lässt sich für die Lokalisation der dritten Abschrift vermuten, die aus einer Region stammt,

42 Die hierdurch ausgedrückte Selbstwahrnehmung bzw. das dahinter liegende Dynastieverständnis werden in Kapitel 5 noch einmal aufgegriffen. Zu den Mithradatiden und den mit Mithradates IV. einsetzenden Inzestehen siehe den Beitrag von Alex McAuley in diesem Band.

die den Usurpator Achaios während seines Aufstands unterstützt hatte. Indem Berenike zur Oberpriesterin im Kult der Königin ernannt wurde, stärkte der seleukidische
Herrscher die Beziehung zur Herrscherfamilie des Lysimachos in Telmessos. Nach
diesem Verständnis handelt es sich bei der Einsetzung des Laodike-Kultes und insbesondere seiner regionalen Verbreitung um ein politisches Mittel zur Stärkung der dynastischen Akzeptanz, das losgelöst vom spärlichen Quellenbefund auch in weiteren
Reichsteilen zum Einsatz gekommen sein kann.[43]

Weiteren Einblick in das seleukidische Selbstverständnis und die dynastische Außendarstellung gibt ein keilschriftlicher Zylinder aus der Zeit Antiochos' I., benannt
nach der nahe Babylon gelegenen Stadt Borsippa. Der Text beschreibt, dass Antiochos – persönlich als Bauherr – den Ezida-Tempel wieder habe aufbauen lassen und
um göttliche Unterstützung gebeten habe.[44] Der Zeitpunkt der Aufstellung des Zylinders im Monat Nisanu impliziert seine inhaltliche Kontextualisierung mit dem babylonischen Neujahrsfest, dem *akītu*-Fest.[45] Der Text nennt zunächst die Titel, die Antiochos führt: großer König (*šarru rabû*), König der Welt (*šar kiššati*), König von Babylon
(*šar Bābili*), König der Länder (*šar mātāti*). Dieser Teil erinnert an die textliche Gestaltung früherer Zylinder. Einen deutlichen Bruch mit dieser Tradition bildet jedoch
die Zeile 5, in der Antiochos seinen Vater Seleukos explizit als Makedonen bezeichnet.[46] Im Anschluss beschreibt Antiochos seine Aktivitäten bei der Wiedererrichtung
der Heiligtümer Esagil in Babylon und Ezida in Borsippa.[47] Im dritten Abschnitt richtet
Antiochos ein Gebet an den babylonischen Gott Nabû, in dem der König Nabû bittet,
ihn beim Sieg über Feinde zu unterstützen, ihm und seiner Dynastie ein langes Leben
zu gewähren, seiner Herrschaft Stabilität zu verschaffen und weitere Eroberungen zu
begünstigen. Im Gegenzug verspricht Antiochos, seine Erfolge dazu zu nutzen, dass
der Esagil und der Ezida fortdauernd kultisch gepflegt werden. Den Schluss bildet Antiochos' Bitte um göttlichen Beistand für sich, seinen Sohn und Thronfolger Seleukos
sowie seine Ehefrau und Mitregentin Stratonike.[48]

Eine Analyse des Textes zeigt, dass die inhaltliche Ausgestaltung auf den ersten
Blick besonders im ersten Abschnitt stark mesopotamischen Traditionen folgt. Die
Selbstvorstellung des Sprechers und Erschaffers des Zylinders durch die Nennung

43   Iossif – Lorber 2007, 64 betonen bereits die strategische Bedeutung der Oberpriesterinnen im
     Laodike-Kult. Vgl. auch Iossif 2014, 145–146, der die Einsetzung des Laodike-Kultes als strategi-
     sches Mittel in einer schwierigen Herrschaftsperiode versteht, das bereits nach kurzer Zeit wieder
     scheiterte, da sich keine nachhaltige Wirkung erkennen lässt.
44   BM 36277.
45   Das *akitu*-Fest wurde sowohl unter achaimenidischer wie auch seleukidischer Herrschaft zele-
     briert; Sherwin-White 1983, 156–159; Bidmead 2004, 143–145; Erickson 2011, 59–62; Plischke 2014,
     164–165.
46   Col. 1.1–6. Vgl. dazu auch den Beitrag von Christoph Michels in diesem Band.
47   Col. 1.6–16.
48   Col. 1.16; Col. 2.29.

bzw. geradezu Zurschaustellung der Titel findet sich in sehr ähnlicher Weise auf den Zylindern Nabonids[49] und des Kyros,[50] und auch die Selbstpräsentation Dareios' I. in der Bisutun-Inschrift[51] weist Parallelen auf. Daraus folgt, dass der Titel „großer König", den Antiochos laut Zeile 1 führt, als Rückgriff auf eine Vorstellung nach neubabylonischer bzw. mesopotamischer Tradition verstanden werden sollte.[52] Zudem findet sich kein weiteres schriftliches Zeugnis, das für Antiochos I. den Titel „Großer König" – weder als Fremd- noch als Selbstzeichnung – belegt.

Besondere Berücksichtigung gilt daher dem Bruch, den Zeile 5 markiert. Während die Nennung des Vaters, hier Seleukos, noch traditionell begründet ist, stellt die Herkunftsbezeichnung „der Makedone" eine deutliche Abkehr von den bisherigen Vorläufern dar und muss als spezifisch seleukidisches Element verstanden werden. Auf den ersten Blick scheint die Betonung der makedonischen Herkunft einen Widerspruch zu Antiochos' Ambitionen auszudrücken, sich in den östlichen Gebieten im Sinne der jeweiligen lokalen Tradition zu präsentieren. Doch stellt vielleicht genau diese Mischung aus West und Ost, aus (griechisch-)makedonischen und indigenen Traditionen, die die Herrschaft der Seleukiden bereits seit der ersten Generation auszeichnete,[53] eine Besonderheit dar, die Antiochos tatsächlich zu betonen suchte – denn sein Vater ist der Makedone, nicht Antiochos selbst.[54] Die jüngere Forschung hat daher zurecht vermehrt den interkulturellen Charakter des Zylinders betont und ihn als Ausdruck eines seleukidischen Selbstverständnisses aufgefasst. Deutlich greifbar sind die seleukidischen Einflüsse ebenfalls in der Nennung, der Bezeichnung und der prominenten Stellung, die Stratonike als „Mitregentin und Königin"[55] erhält.[56] Die für die Entstehung

49 Eḫulḫul-Zylinder: „(1) Ich bin Nabû-na'id, der große König, der mächtige König, (2) der König der Welt, der König von Bābil, der König der vier Weltgegenden, (3) der Versorger von Esangil und Ezida, (4f) als dessen Schicksal Sîn und Nîngal im Leibe seiner Mutter das Königtum bestimmten, (6) der Sohn des Nabû-balāssu-iqbi, der weise Fürst, der die großen Götter fürchtet, bin ich"; Schaudig 2001, 2.12 I 1–6.

50 „(20) Ich bin Kyros, König der Welt, Großer König, Mächtiger König, König von Babylonien, König von Sumer und Akkad, König in allen vier Himmelsrichtungen, (21) Sohn von Kambyses, Großer König, König von Anschan, Enkel von Kyros, Großer König, König von Anschan, Urenkel von Teispes, Großer König, König von Anschan [...]"; BM 90920.

51 „(1.1) Ich (bin) Dareios, der große König, König der Könige, (1.2) König in Persien, König der Länder, (1.3) des Hystapes Sohn, des Arsames Enkel, ein Achaimenide"; DB § 1.1–3.

52 Vgl. Stevens 2014, 69–72. Worthington 2012, 146–156 nennt diese Methode „„cut and paste'-reduction". Mehl 2022, bes. 197–198 betont an dieser Stelle ebenfalls, dass die bloße Nennung durch Dritte kein hinreichender Beweis dafür ist, dass Antiochos I. – und gleiches gilt für das singuläre Zeugnis bezüglich Antiochos' II. – diesen Titel tatsächlich geführt hat.

53 Vgl. hierzu die Funktion der seleukidischen Königin als Bindeglied zwischen West und Ost an den Beispielen Apames und Stratonikes; Plischke 2016.

54 Anders Michels in diesem Band.

55 BM 36277, II 27.

56 Widmer 2019, 264–279 versteht die herausragende Bedeutung der seleukidischen Königin als für babylonische Traditionen fremdes und somit spezifisch seleukidisches Element. Vor diesem Hintergrund bewertet sie den Zylinder als „result of the dialogical functioning of Seleucid Power"

des Textes verantwortlichen Funktionäre müssen somit eng mit dem seleukidischen Herrscherhaus verbunden gewesen sein, so dass die Textgestaltung als Ausdruck der interkulturellen Verständigung zwischen dem seleukidischen Herrscherhaus und der lokalen Elite in Borsippa verstanden werden sollte.[57] Eine solche Wahrnehmung erhöht natürlich den Wert dieser Inschrift für das Verständnis von Interaktion zwischen dem Herrscherhaus und lokalen Eliten, beweist jedoch ebenso seine grundsätzliche Bedeutung für den geographischen Einzelfall und ordnet den Zylinder, wie wir es aus den griechischen *poleis* im Westen kennen, in eine Tradition lokaler[58] Verehrung und Gunstbezeugungen ein, die keinen Aufschluss über oder kein Indiz für einen vom Herrscher vorgegebenen Staats- oder Dynastiekult gibt.[59]

Eine kultisch-dynastische Bedeutung des Zylinders ergibt sich jedoch an anderer Stelle. So ist durch das abschließende Gebet an Nabû eine Fokussierung auf den babylonischen Gott erkennbar, den Antiochos hier explizit anspricht, zum Schutzpatron seiner Herrschaft und seiner Familie macht und in besonderer Weise verehren lässt. Ein tatsächlicher Synkretismus in der Verehrung des griechischen Apollon und des babylonischen Nabû, der sich etwa im Apollon-Nabû-Tempel aus Palmyra zeigt, ist ab der zweiten Hälfte des 2. Jhs. v. Chr. sicher belegt.[60] Da Apollon jedoch seit der Zeit Antiochos' I. im Seleukidenreich eine besondere Bedeutung zukommt,[61] wurde jüngst vermehrt die These vertreten, dass die Gleichsetzung Apollons mit Nabû schon früher anzusetzen und im Gebet an Nabû im Borsippa-Zylinder bereits eine Huldigung Apollons zu erkennen sei.[62]

Mit der oben diskutierten Einrichtung des Ahnenkultes liegt uns somit ein singuläres Zeugnis für eine kultische Verehrung vor, die in ihrem Gründungsakt tatsächlich zunächst ortsgebunden war und durchaus als parallele Entwicklung etwa zu den Ptolemaiern zu verstehen ist. Die Anordnung Antiochos' III. zur Einsetzung des Laodike-Kults belegt einerseits die Existenz des seleukidischen Dynastiekultes, gibt andererseits jedoch nur wenig Einblick in die tatsächliche Zielsetzung des Dynastiekultes und seiner Kultausübung.[63] Der Borsippa-Zylinder wiederum ist ebenfalls als singuläres

(279). McAuley 2022, 27–29 versteht das seleukidische Herrschaftskonzept als eine Triade aus dem Herrscher und Vater, der Königin und Mutter und dem Nachfolger bzw. Erben und Sohn. Einen deutlichen Beleg für diese Herrschaftsauffassung sieht er im Borsippa-Zylinder gegeben, der mit dieser Triadennennung schließt.

57   Vgl. etwa Strootman 2013, 67–97; Kosmin 2014, 173–198; Stevens 2014, 66–88.
58   Ausführlich und überzeugend erarbeitet bei Stevens 2014, 66–88.
59   Ähnlich Shayegan 2011, 45–59 für Babylonien in parthischer Zeit: Mithradates II. als ‚König der Könige'. Vgl. auch Plischke 2017.
60   Aus postseleukidischer Zeit sind vielfache Belege für eine Apollon-Nabû-Symbiose erhalten. Vgl. etwa Doura-Europos, Palmyra, Edessa und Hierapolis.
61   Vgl. Kap. 4.
62   Erickson 2011, 57–59; Beaulieu 2014; Erickson 2019, 81–90. Zur Verbindung von Apollon-Nabû vgl. auch Ambos 2003, 232–233.
63   Iossif 2014, 146 sieht hier eine Verbindung von „traditional elements from the available ‚tool kit' of traditional religion (sacrifices, relation to the divine, eponymy etc.) and innovative features (dia-

Zeugnis zu verstehen, das einerseits einen Einblick in das gesellschaftliche Verhältnis zwischen der Dynastie und einer lokalen Elite ermöglicht – erneut in einer Region, die hinsichtlich der Dichte der Quellen und deren Aussagewert eine Sonderrolle einnimmt –, andererseits überregional herrschaftspolitische bzw. dynastische Aspekte beinhaltet, sofern die Verehrung Nabûs auf Apollon übertragen wird. Ebenso deutlich wird aber auch, dass über inschriftliche Quellen die Frage nach einem herrschaftlichen und kultischen Dynastieverständnis im Seleukidenreich kaum beantwortet werden kann, da die äußerst dürftige Überlieferungslage diesbezüglich keine Aussagen zulässt oder aber – und diesem Ansatz möchte ich im Folgenden nachgehen – die Gattung der textlichen Quellen nicht das Medium ist, das die Seleukiden als geeignet für die Verbreitung eines dynastischen Konzepts ansahen.

4. Der seleukidische Herrscherkult in den materiellen Quellen

Münzen als Quellen zeichnen sich allgemein durch folgende Aspekte aus: Auf Grund ihrer geringen Größe spielt die textliche Gestaltung kaum eine Rolle, sondern der Fokus liegt auf der ikonographischen Gestaltung. Sie sind gesellschaftsübergreifend als Wertmittel anerkannt, so dass ihre Verbreitung und geographische Durchdringung als sehr hoch eingeschätzt werden können. Durch die Verwendung unterschiedlicher Metalle können unterschiedliche Adressaten angesprochen werden. Das Bildprogramm ist veränderlich. Es können mehrere parallel ausgegebene Bildprogramme vorhanden sein, Bildprogramme können speziell auf verschiedene Zielgruppen zugeschnitten sein und die Entwicklung neuer Bildprogramme muss nur kaum bestimmten Vorgaben entsprechen. Der Kreativität und der Neuschöpfung bzw. der Schaffung neuer Motive, in denen traditionell verankerte, aber unterschiedlich begründete Aspekte neu zusammengefügt werden, sind kaum Grenzen gesetzt. All diese Voraussetzungen weisen die Münzen als ideales Medium aus, in einer solch diversen Herrschaftsstruktur, wie sie im Seleukidenreich vorzufinden ist, eine gewisse Form von Einheitlichkeit durch Uneinheitlichkeit zu etablieren. Gleichzeitig beinhalten sie einen immensen Interpretationsspielraum. Daher soll im Folgenden untersucht werden, inwieweit die seleukidische Münzprägung Auskunft über das dynastische und kultische Herrschafts–verständnis geben kann.[64]

Den Anfang der Betrachtung bilden zwei Prägungen aus der Zeit Seleukos' I., die in ihrer Aussage umstritten sind. Es handelt sich jeweils um Silberprägungen im Nominal der Tetradrachme mit der Legende ΒΑΣΙΛΕΩΣ ΣΕΛΕΥΚΟΥ. Der Avers der Prägung

---

dem bearing the image of the queen/goddess, priestess in the head of a hierarchy not attached to a specific sanctuary etc.)".

64 Iossif 2014, 147 ist der Ansicht, dass die Seleukiden sich in äußerst diskreter Weise auf den Münzen mit göttlichen Symbolen assoziierten, und spricht in diesem Zusammenhang den Bronzeprägungen mit ihrem lokal begrenzten Wirkungsgrad eine hohe Bedeutung zu.

aus Susa (Abb. 1), deren Ausgabe etwa in die Zeit zwischen 305/304–295 v. Chr. fällt,
zeigt einen behelmten Portraitkopf, auf dem ein Pantherfell drapiert ist; seitlich sind
Stierohren und Stierhörner zu erkennen.[65] Auf dem unproblematischeren Revers ist
die Göttin Nike zu sehen, die ein *tropaion* bekränzt, so dass dieses Münzbild ganz im
Kontext eines militärischen Erfolges zu verstehen ist und die kriegerische Überlegenheit des seleukidischen Heeres und seines Königs symbolisiert. Bei der etwa 295 v. Chr.
in Ekbatana ausgegebenen Prägung (Abb. 2) stellt hingegen weniger der dem Beispiel
Alexanders III. folgende Avers ein Problem dar, auf dem ein Portrait des jungen Herakles mit Löwenfell als Kopfschmuck zu sehen ist; problematisch ist vielmehr die
Deutung des Revers, der einen mit einem Pantherfell geschmückten Reiter auf einem
Pferd zeigt.[66] Die Köpfe beider Figuren sind mit Stierhörnern und der Kopf des Reiters
ebenfalls mit Stierohren versehen. Nach Ansicht von Arthur Houghton und Andrew
Stewart trägt der Reiter zudem persische Tracht.[67]

Abb. 1 Seleukos I. Av.: Helmtragender Portraitkopf (Seleukos' I.?); Rev.: ein tropaion
bekränzende Nike, ΒΑΣΙΛΕΩΣ ΣΕΛΕΥΚΟΥ.

Abb. 2 Seleukos I. Av.: Kopf des jungen Herakles mit Löwenfell; Rev.: mit einem Pantherfell
geschmückter Reiter auf gehörntem Pferd, ΒΑΣΙΛΕΩΣ ΣΕΛΕΥΚΟΥ.

65   SC 173.
66   SC 203.
67   Vgl. Houghton – Stewart 1999.

Der Portraitkopf und der Reiter, deren Identifikation Arthur Houghton und Catharine Lorber lediglich als „Head of Hero (assimilating Seleucus, Alexander, and Dionysus)" umschreiben,[68] werden in der Forschung als dieselbe Person verstanden und auf Grund ihrer dionysischen Attribute seit dem richtungsweisenden Beitrag von Robert A. Hadley mit Alexander identifiziert.[69] Für eine Darstellung Alexanders – und die gleiche Argumentation gilt für eine Identifikation mit Dionysos – weist das Portrait jedoch zu wenig Ähnlichkeit mit den bekannten Alexanderportraits[70] auf. Ein Alexander in persischen Hosen wird von der modernen Forschung zudem auf der Basis Diodors ausgeschlossen, der uns berichtet, dass sich Alexander das persische Diadem um das Haupt gelegt und sich mit dem weißen Gewand, dem persischen Gürtel sowie all dem sonstigen Ornat bekleidet habe, aber niemals persische Hosen getragen habe.[71] Zudem werden Alexander, dem ansonsten keine weitere Bedeutung in der dynastischen Legitimation der Seleukiden zukommt,[72] auf Grund der Zeus-Ammon-Verehrung Widderhörner zugeschrieben, keine Stierhörner. Oliver D. Hoover hat sich daher dafür ausgesprochen, wieder der im ausgehenden 19. Jh. und beginnenden 20. Jh. vorherrschenden Ansicht, die Person als Seleukos zu identifizieren, den Vorzug zu geben,[73] und wurde in jüngerer Zeit von Kyle Erickson in dieser Wahrnehmung unterstützt.[74] Ein Beleg hierfür sei durch die spätere literarische Überlieferung gegeben, die für Se-

---

68   SC 173.
69   Hadley 1974, 9–13.
70   Zur Assimilierung des Herakleskopfes und des Alexanderportraits vgl. besonders Huttner 1997, 119: „Freilich muß man sich dessen bewußt bleiben, daß sicher nicht jeder, der die Silbernominale Alexanders in der Hand hielt, in dem Herakleskopf den Herrscher erkannte. Alexander hatte ja keinen Befehl erteilt, ihn auf den Münzen gezielt als Herakles darzustellen [...] Man darf natürlich auch nicht voraussetzen, daß das Alexanderporträt überall dort bekannt war, wo die Münzen umliefen." Vgl. hierzu auch den Beitrag von Ralf von den Hoff in diesem Band.
71   Diod. 17.77.5.
72   Deutlich wird der Umstand, dass Alexander in der seleukidischen Herrschaftsbegründung und -ausprägung keine Rolle spielte, neben dem Gründungsmythos und der Form der Bestattung in Seleukeia Piereia auch durch die Einführung der seleukidischen Zeitrechnung 312/311 v. Chr. nach der Einnahme Babylons. Vgl. auch Kosmin – Moyer 2021. Vgl. hierzu jüngst auch Kovacs 2022, 228–231.
73   Hoover 2002, 51–60. Vgl. auch Hoover 2011.
74   Dies macht er vorrangig daran fest, dass die persische Tracht des Reiters nicht der Alexandertradition entspräche (Diod. 17.77.5). Zudem habe Seleukos seine eigene Herrschaftsetablierung nicht in die Tradition Alexanders gestellt, sondern vielmehr mit Alexander verbundene Motive genutzt, um sie seleukidisch umzuformen. Zudem sieht er in der (späteren) literarischen Überlieferung (App. Syr. 56; Curt. 2.28; Lib. or. 11.92; vgl. auch Erickson 2019, 40–42) mehrere Parallelen, die rechtfertigen, Seleukos mit Stierhörnern zu identifizieren – jedoch (noch?) nicht zu deifizieren. So seien die Hörner „a common iconographic trope in Persian, Babylonian and Greek cultures" und „recognisable as a symbol of either of divinity or of heroised kingship"; Erickson 2012, 123. Problematisch ist in dieser Hinsicht jedoch der vorausgesetzte Bedeutungswandel innerhalb weniger Jahrzehnte, sowohl auf Seiten des Münzauftraggebers als auch des Rezipienten, wenn Erickson 2018a, 101 Hörner und Flügel eindeutig als „divine iconography" versteht und diese Symbole auf Münzen zur Mitte des 3. Jhs. v. Chr. als eindeutigen Versuch versteht, einen seleukidischen Dynastiekult zu etablieren.

leukos einen deutlichen Stierbezug kennt. So berichtet Appian, dass Seleukos im Rahmen eines göttlichen Ritus unter Alexander, als der Opferstier sich losreißen konnte, das Tier bei den Hörnern gepackt und mit seinen bloßen Händen eingefangen habe.[75] Auf Grund dieser Ereignisse seien Seleukosstatuen zur eindeutigen Identifikation mit Stierhörnern versehen worden, wie sie Libanios[76] im 4. Jh. n. Chr. in Antiocheia noch sehen konnte. Darüber hinaus lassen sich auf den Münzen, die unter Seleukos ausgegeben wurden, weitere Beispiele finden, auf denen Tiere, vornehmlich Pferde und Elefanten, mit Stierhörnern versehen wurden. Das Horn ist hier als *pars pro toto* sowohl als Rückgriff auf die Stiersymbolik zu verstehen als auch besonders im indigenen Verständnis als Ausdruck von Göttlichkeit. Vor diesem Hintergrund erhält die Annahme, in beiden Münzenabbildungen Seleukos zu erkennen, deutlich mehr Gewicht. Ausgehend davon, dass im achaimenidisch geprägten Osten die Herrschervergöttlichung keine Vorläufer kennt,[77] bedeutete eine solche Interpretation, dass sich Seleukos, anders als bisher vermutet, dem Konkurrenzkampf mit den anderen Diadochen um das Münzportrait, Demetrios Poliorketes[78] und Ptolemaios[79] im Besonderen, offensiv stellte, indem er nicht nur das eigene Portrait auf den Avers prägen ließ, sondern diesem bereits ein göttliches Antlitz verlieh. Unklar bleibt natürlich, inwieweit die Botschaft, die ein Münzherr durch die Ausgabe eines Bildprogramms mitteilen wollte, auch von den Adressaten als solche verstanden wurde. Deutlicher fassbar ist der militärische Kontext und die seleukidische Sieghaftigkeit, die beide Prägungen ausdrücken, weshalb Gunnar Dumke sie jüngst als „Visitenkarte Seleukos' für seine östlichen Soldaten" bezeichnete, die in gleicher Weise die östliche Bevölkerung adressierten.[80]

Sollte diese Deutung korrekt sein, muss das ganze Projekt dennoch als Versuchsballon[81] bezeichnet werden, der keine flächendeckende Nachhaltigkeit entwickelte. Die Nike-Tropaion-Prägung wurde vornehmlich in Susa emittiert, hier aber zumindest in jeglichen Silbernominalen von der Tetradrachme bis zur Obole;[82] zwei Exemplare die-

---

75   App. Syr. 56.

76   Lib. or. 11.92.

77   Vgl. hierzu Rollinger 2009.

78   Newell 1927, Nr. 112; 153. Eine detaillierte Analyse zur Bedeutung der Stierhörner auf den Portraits des Demetrios Poliorketes findet sich bei Ehling 2000.

79   Einen Vergleich der Portraitentwicklung bei den Seleukiden und den Ptolemaiern findet sich bei von den Hoff 2021.

80   Dumke 2022, 47.

81   Marest-Caffey 2016 hat sich jüngst noch einmal mit Seleukos' Siegesprägung auseinandergesetzt. Ihrer Ansicht nach sollte der ikonographische und somit auch interpretatorische Schwerpunkt nicht auf dem Portrait bzw. auf der Frage nach der dargestellten Person liegen; sie betont vielmehr die Attribute des Portraits, die Stierhörner und das Pantherfell, deren Wahl sie darin begründet sieht, dass Seleukos eine Siegesprägung – ihrer Ansicht nach in Erinnerung an die Schlacht bei Ipsos 301 v. Chr. – ausgab, mit der sich alle Gesellschaften des Seleukidenreiches identifizieren konnten.

82   SC 173–176.

ses Typs mit aramäischer Legende werden einer Prägestätte in der Persis zugewiesen.[83] Aus der Drangiane sind ebenfalls wenige Exemplare bekannt, die den gleichen Avers zeigen, auf Grund der Legende ΒΑΣΙΛΕΩΣ ΑΝΤΙΟΧΟΥ jedoch zumindest der Phase der Koregentschaft ab 294 v. Chr. oder sogar der Herrschaftszeit Antiochos' I. zuzuschreiben sind.[84] Das Bildprogramm des mit Hörnern versehenen Reiters, das sich an die Emission aus Susa zeitlich anschloss, ist nur aus Ekbatana bekannt.[85]

Der Befund zur Münzprägung unter Antiochos I. ist im Gegensatz dazu eindeutiger. Zunächst spielt die bereits erwähnte Einrichtung des Ahnenkultes für den verstorbenen Dynastiebegründer eine wichtige Rolle, da hiermit drei Edelmetallprägungen aus der Zeit der direkten Herrschaftsübernahme korrelieren, die vermutlich in oder in der Nähe von Ai Khanum geprägt wurden: Auf dem Avers ist ein mit Stierhörnern verziertes Portrait des verstorbenen Dynastiebegründers Seleukos zu sehen.[86] Einige Jahre später, ab etwa 276 v. Chr., ließ Antiochos in Sardeis,[87] wo er sich im Kontext des 1. Syrischen Krieges aufhielt, AR-Tetradrachmen mit dem gleichen hornverzierten Seleukosportrait auf dem Avers prägen; auf dem Revers ist neben der Legende ΒΑΣΙΛΕΩΣ ΑΝΤΙΟΧΟΥ entweder wie auch in Baktrien ein gehörnter Pferdekopf[88] oder der auf dem Omphalos[89] sitzende Apollon[90] zu sehen (Abb. 3). In Verbindung mit der Priesterliste aus Seleukeia Piereia geben die Münzen somit Rückschluss auf ein zweites Motiv, das Antiochos' Herrschaft in besonderer Weise prägte: die Fokussierung auf Apollon als göttlichen Stammvater. Nachdem bereits Seleukos die direkte Bezugnahme auf Apollon begründet hatte, wie sie etwa in der Fürsorge und Pflege des didymeischen Apollon in Milet oder auch in einigen Münzbildern[91] zu erkennen ist, erhielt Apollon unter Antiochos eine

---

83 SC 195–197.

84 SC 198–199.

85 Kovacs 2022, 233 hat sich jüngst noch einmal deutlich dafür ausgesprochen, im gehörnten Reiter Seleukos zu sehen, der sich in dieser Weise stilisiert, um sowohl als erfolgreicher Makedone wahrgenommen zu werden als auch „orientalische Konventionen" aufzunehmen und „die Gunst der persischen Aristokratie zu gewinnen".

86 SC 469; 471; 472. Auch wenn zwei Münzen die Legende ΒΑΣΙΛΕΩΣ ΣΕΛΕΥΚΟΥ tragen, können sie auf Grund ihrer ikonographischen Ausgestaltung in die Herrschaftszeit Antiochos' I. verortet werden; SC I, p. 161. Vgl. ebenfalls Kovacs 2022, 232–233.

87 Wenn Iossif 2011, 268–272 mit seiner Annahme Recht hat, dass der Ursprung dieser Serie in Seleukeia am Tigris zu verorten ist, kam das vergöttlichte Seleukosportrait vor Antiochos' Ankunft in Sardeis in Umlauf.

88 SC 322.

89 Die Bedeutung des Omphalos innerhalb des Münzbildes über seine Wahrnehmung als Nabel der Welt hinaus kann nicht abschließend geklärt werden. Dass grundsätzlich die Darstellung des Gottes im Vordergrund stand, zeigen spätere Prägungen Seleukos' II., der den stehenden Apollon auf Münzen prägen ließ; der Omphalos wurde nicht mehr abgebildet. Auch praktische Gründe mögen die Wahl des Omphalos begünstigt haben, da eine sitzende Person einfacher auf einer Münze abzubilden ist, wie es schon vorherige Zeus-, Herakles- und Nike-Prägungen belegen. Zu parthischen Übernahmen seleukidischer Münzbilder vgl. Günther 2012.

90 SC 323.

91 Vgl. etwa SC 145; 256; 267; 289 (Anker) und SC 148 (Apollon).

allumfassende und reichseinende Aufgabe. Hierfür sind zwei Kennzeichen besonders wichtig: zuerst die seleukidische Abkunftlegende. Einzig überliefert ist diese Legende, nach der Seleukos' Mutter geträumt habe, von Apollon ein Kind zu empfangen und zur Bestätigung einen Ring mit einem eingraviertem Anker erhielt, bei Trogus-Iustin[92], doch reiht sie sich ein in eine Tendenz, die in allen Diadochenreichen zu greifen ist: den Versuch, die eigene Herrschaft durch eine göttliche Abkunft zu legitimieren.[93] Die besondere Bedeutung Didymas für Seleukos begründet Pausanias damit, dass Seleukos die im Zuge der persischen Zerstörung des Didymeions 479 v. Chr. geraubte Statue Apollons, den er als Schutzgottheit der seleukidischen Dynastie ausgemacht habe, nach Didyma zurückgeführt habe.[94] Diodor hingegen berichtet bereits im Kontext des Jahres 311 v. Chr., dass Seleukos, als er mit einer kleinen Streitmacht auf dem Weg nach Babylonien gewesen sei, um die Satrapie zurückzuerobern, seine Gefährten, die die Übermacht der gegnerischen Truppen fürchteten, beruhigt habe, indem er ihnen erzählte, dass die Gottheit, als er das Orakel von Didyma befragt habe, ihn mit König Seleukos angesprochen habe, wodurch sein zukünftiger Erfolg bestätigt worden sei.[95]

Eine tatsächliche Verbreitung dieser Abkunftlegende und der damit verbundenen göttlichen Schutzfunktion setzte jedoch erst unter Antiochos I. ein, was sich in dem zweiten Kennzeichen niederschlägt: die Fokussierung auf Apollondarstellungen[96] auf seleukidischen Münzen. Nachdem Seleukos vornehmlich Zeusdarstellungen[97] hatte prägen lassen, ersetzte Antiochos diesen durch Apollon, der ab diesem Zeitpunkt den Revers seleukidischer Münzen im gesamten Reich zierte (Abb. 4); der Avers blieb nun dem Herrscherportrait vorbehalten.[98] Dies unterstreicht die verbindende Funktion, die Antiochos Apollon zuwies, wodurch die Lesart, bereits im Borsippa-Zylinder eine

---

92   Iust. 15.4.1–6.

93   In diesem Kontext kommt auch dem Bezug zu Alexander III. und Didyma eine besondere Bedeutung zu. So sei nach Strabon (17.1.43) das Orakel in Didyma nach der Zerstörung während der Perserkriege wieder aufgesprudelt, als sich Alexander 331 v. Chr. in Ägypten aufhielt; es habe ihn als Sohn des Zeus bezeichnet und ihm den Sieg bei Gaugamela prophezeit. Vgl. zur Präsenz dieses Aspekts bereits bei den Argeaden den Beitrag von Sabine Müller in diesem Band. Vgl. zur Konzeption der Abkunftlegende auch Kovacs 2022, 234–236.

94   Paus. 1.16.3; 8.46.3. Zu Seleukos und Milet vgl. Habicht ²1970, 103; Orth 1977, 17–32/153–158; Funck 1996, 210–213.

95   Diod. 19.90.1–4.

96   Iossif 2011 betont zurecht die Darstellung Apollons als Bogenschütze, ausgedrückt durch die Attribute Pfeil und Bogen, wodurch eine Verbindung griechischer (Apollon als Teil des griechischen Pantheons) und mesopotamisch-iranischer („topos of the ‚king as the perfect archer'", hier 274) Elemente geschaffen wurde.

97   Laut Wright 2018 spiegelt sich Seleukos' Präferenz des Göttervaters Zeus ebenfalls in der Wahl und Gründung Seleukeias Piereias wider, die Antiochos in der Errichtung des Nikatoreion weiter betont habe. Vgl. hierzu auch Ogden 2011, der Zeus' Rolle im mythologischen Gründungskontext herausgearbeitet hat. Auch von Reden – Strootman 2021, 38–39 betonen die Bedeutung des Göttervaters im Gründungsmythos.

98   Diese Zuordnung spiegelt sich auch in der Priesterliste aus Seleukeia Piereia wider, in der ein Priester für Antiochos Apollon Soter und einer für Seleukos Zeus Nikator benannt wird; OGIS 245.

Apollon-Nabû-Symbiose[99] zu erkennen, weitere Unterstützung erhält. In den folgenden Jahren und Jahrzehnten setzten die Seleukidenherrscher die Fokussierung auf Apollon fort.

Abb. 3 Antiochos I. Av.: Antiochos I. mit Königsbinde; Rv.: auf dem Omphalos sitzender Apollon mit Pfeil und Bogen, ΒΑΣΙΛΕΩΣ ΑΝΤΙΟΧΟΥ.

Abb. 4 Antiochos I. Av.: Seleukos I. mit Königsbinde und Stierhörnern; Rv.: auf dem Omphalos sitzender Apollon mit Bogen, ΒΑΣΙΛΕΩΣ ΑΝΤΙΟΧΟΥ.

Die Herrschaft Antiochos' I. und auch die ersten Jahre unter seinem Nachfolger Antiochos II.[100] waren zunächst von Stabilität geprägt. Aus den dynastischen Heiratsallianzen, die Antiochos II. durch die Ehen mit seiner Cousine Laodike und Berenike der Jüngeren, einer Tochter Ptolemaios' II., einging, resultierten jedoch innerdynastische Krisen, die zur Mitte des 3. Jhs. v. Chr. im Osten zahlreiche Abfallbewegungen und Separationstendenzen auslösten und das Seleukidenreich bis zum Ende dieses Jahrhunderts beschäftigen sollten. Die Zeit nach dem Tode Antiochos' II. 246 v. Chr. war

Zur Etablierung Apollons als wichtigste Gottheit, speziell auf Münzen, seit der Zeit der Koregentschaft 294 v. Chr. vgl. auch Erickson 2011, 51–53; Erickson 2019, 62–115.

99   Aus postseleukidischer Zeit sind vielfache Belege für eine Apollon-Nabû-Symbiose erhalten, etwa in Doura-Europos, Palmyra, Edessa und Hierapolis. Hierzu bereits Kap. 3.

100   Antiochos II. übernahm auf dem Revers die von Antiochos I. geprägte Darstellung Apollons auf dem Omphalos. Den Avers zitierte zunächst das Portrait Antiochos' I., das als bewusster Ausdruck einer dynastischen Kontinuität verstanden werden kann, und später dann das eigene Herrscherportrait, das sowohl Kontinuität als auch Stabilität implizieren sollte; vgl. auch Erickson 2019, 117–122.

daher zunächst von innerseleukidischen Thronwirren geprägt, da die beiden mündigen Söhne, der ältere Seleukos II. und der jüngere Antiochos Hierax, im sogenannten Bruderkrieg um die Herrschaftsnachfolge rangen.[101]

Die unterschiedlichen Strategien, sich als legitimer und potenter Nachfolger zu präsentieren, spiegeln sich in den nun ausgegebenen Bildprogrammen wider, die jüngst neu in den Blickpunkt geraten sind. Kyle Erickson hat unlängst den Ansatz verfolgt, die göttlichen Symbole auf seleukidischen Münzen als Ausdruck eines „royal cult" zu verstehen, dessen Anfänge spätestens unter Seleukos II. und Antiochos Hierax zu fassen seien. So habe Seleukos auf Bronzeprägungen aus Susa (Abb. 5)[102] und Seleukeia am Tigris[103] sein mit Hörnern versehenes Portrait prägen lassen.[104] Als Antwort darauf habe Hierax in Ilion[105] in Silber Portraits Antiochos' I. ausgeben lassen, die eine hornähnliche Haarlocke über der Königsbinde zeigen. Da noch Seleukos IV. Münzen dieses Typs prägen ließ, schließt Erickson auf eine frühere Vergöttlichung Antiochos' I. sowie auf eine sich etablierende Tradition hinsichtlich dieses Münzbildnisses.[106] Zudem habe Hierax ein weiteres Motiv mit göttlicher Funktion aufgegriffen, indem er das ursprünglich von Antiochos II. lokal in Alexandreia Troas[107] ausgegebene Portrait mit kleinen Flügeln an der Königsbinde in Lampsakos und zwei weiteren Städten der Troas[108] prägen ließ. Diesen Befund deutet Erickson als Hinweis auf einen mehrere Städte umfassenden „local cult", der dann Einfluss auf die herrscherliche Darstellung am Königshof genommen habe und sich in der Existenz eines „royal cult" zeige.[109]

Dieser Rückschluss ist meiner Ansicht nach jedoch eine Überinterpretation des Quellenbefundes. Einerseits handelt es sich erneut um lokal begrenzte Emissionen, denen daher keine reichsweite Funktion oder Einflussnahme zugeschrieben werden kann. Andererseits verstehe ich die facettenreichen Bildprogramme der Seleukiden nicht wie Erickson als numismatischen Beleg für die Existenz eines hellenistischen Herrscherkults, sondern zunächst als Ausdruck einer herrschaftlichen Legitimationsstrategie und als Medium zur Verbreitung einer göttlichen Herrscherwahrnehmung. So kann ich in diesen Münzbildern auch kein Konzept zur dynastischen Vergöttlichung

---

101 Diese Phase der Instabilität nutzte Ptolemaios III. dann zu seinem Vorstoß, um offiziell die Ermordung seiner Schwester Berenike zu rächen, tatsächlich aber um eigene territoriale Ambitionen nach dem Ende des 2. Syrischen Krieges zu bedienen. Vgl. auch Coşkun 2018, der eine umfassende Neubewertung der Ereignisse um den 3. Syrischen Krieg und den Bruderkrieg zwischen Seleukos II. und Antiochos Hierax vorgelegt hat.

102 SC 800–801.

103 SC 767–768.

104 Erickson 2018a, 104–105.

105 SC 866–867.

106 Erickson 2018a, 105–107.

107 SC 491.

108 Lampsakos: SC 850; Ilion: SC 871–872; Alexandreia Troas: 874–886.

109 Vgl. Erickson 2018a, 107–111, der hier Parallelen zu den Entwicklungen unter den Ptolemaiern erkennen möchte.

Abb. 5 Seleukos II. Av.: gehörntes Portrait Seleukos' II. in der ¾-Ansicht; Rev.: Elefant.

Abb. 6 Antiochos Hierax. Av.: Antiochos (I.?) mit Königsbinde und kleinen Flügeln am Kopf;
Rev.: auf dem Omphalos sitzender Apollon mit Pfeil und Bogen, ΒΑΣΙΛΕΩΣ ΑΝΤΙΟΧΟΥ.

Abb. 7 Seleukos II. Av.: Seleukos II. mit Königsbinde; Rev.: an ein Dreibein gelehnter,
stehender Apollon mit Pfeil, ΒΑΣΙΛΕΩΣ ΣΕΛΕΥΚΟΥ.

erkennen. Der Fokus liegt vielmehr auf dem Konkurrenzkampf zweier Thronanwärter.
Während Seleukos II. sich auf Grund seines Status als ältester Sohn problemlos in die
Tradition des verstorbenen Herrschers hätte stellen können, indem er das Münzpro-
gramm seines Vaters übernommen hätte – was er jedoch nicht tat –, musste der jüngere Hierax[110] einen kreativeren Weg gehen. Daher wählte er mit dem mit kleinen Flü-

---

110   Zu Antiochos Hierax' (Selbst-)Darstellung als legitimer Seleukidenherrscher vgl. Chrubasik 2016,
      72–81. Zum Verhältnis der Münzbilder unter Antiochos I. und Antiochos Hierax jüngst auch Ko-
      vacs 2022, 396–400.

gelchen verzierten Portrait (Abb. 6) ein lokal begrenztes Motiv seines Vaters, das ihn durch das Portrait Antiochos' I. jedoch gleichzeitig in dynastischer Weise legitimieren sollte. Seleukos[111] hingegen entwickelte die Münzbildnisse seiner Vorfahren weiter, indem er neue Apollondarstellungen schuf.[112] Charakteristisch war nun der stehende Apollon mit Pfeil[113] in der Hand, entweder an einen Bogen (Abb. 7)[114] oder ein Dreibein[115] gelehnt. Dieses Münzbild wurde in nahezu allen seleukidischen Prägestätten und in allen Edelmetallnominalen fortan ausgegeben. Die Elefantendarstellung[116] auf dem Revers der Prägung, deren Vorderseite das gehörnte Portrait[117] Seleukos' II. zeigt, ordnet die Prägung zudem eindeutig einem kriegerischen Kontext zu. Die im Avers identische Prägung[118] aus Seleukeia am Tigris, auf deren Revers ein Reiter zu sehen ist, deuten Houghton und Lorber als „Siegesprägung", die die zeitweisen seleukidischen Erfolge im 3. Syrischen Krieg gegen Ptolemaios III. verdeutlichen soll.[119] In Analogie dazu verstehe ich die Bronzeprägungen aus Susa im Kontext der kriegerischen Bemühungen im Osten gegen die Parther, in deren Zusammenhang auch Prägungen[120] entstanden, die den Herrscher im Portrait Bart tragen ließen.

Die bisherigen numismatischen Befunde deuten meines Erachtens darauf hin, dass spätestens seit der Zeit Antiochos' I. durchaus eine dynastische Tendenz zu fassen ist, die seleukidische Herrschaft in religiöser Hinsicht zu legitimieren, indem Antiochos die Ahnenverehrung initiierte und zeitgleich die göttliche Abkunft der Seleukiden von

111   Eine Inschrift (OGIS 227) aus dem Jahr 246 v. Chr. belegt, dass Seleukos die Politik seiner Vorfahren hinsichtlich Milets und Apollons fortsetzte. Zeitlich ist die Inschrift in den Konflikt mit Ptolemaios III. zu verorten, so dass Seleukos die Position der Stadt vor diesem Hintergrund stärkte.

112   Aus Gründen der Chronologie sieht Erickson 2019, 123 Seleukos' stehenden Apollon nicht als Reaktion auf Hierax' Revolte; vielmehr habe das neue Apollon-Münzbild Hierax die Möglichkeit eröffnet, seinen eigenen Herrschaftsanspruch durch den Rückgriff auf traditionelle Apollondarstellungen zu legitimieren. Wenige Münzstätten, am prominentesten diejenige in Ekbatana, prägten auch weiterhin das Münzbild Apollons auf dem Omphalos.

113   Erickson 2019, 124 sieht in dem charakteristischen Pfeil in der Hand Apollons eine Symbolisierung des für Nabû typischen *stylos*.

114   Vgl. etwa SC 643–655; 664; 668–669; 672; 674; 676–681.

115   Vgl. etwa SC 656; 671; 682–684.

116   SC 800.

117   Dodd 2009, 131–132 betont bereits zurecht die vielfältige Breite, die die Portraits Seleukos' II. aufweisen. Lorber – Iossif 2020 haben zudem den göttlichen Charakter des Avers betont, da Seleukos II. hier erstmals als Büste in der ¾-Ansicht zu sehen ist, eine Darstellung, die zuvor lediglich Göttern bzw. Heroen vorbehalten war. Dies sollte Seleukos' Fähigkeiten als potenter, erfolgreicher und legitimer Nachfolger im Seleukidenreich stärken.

118   SC 767–768. Dodd 2009, 141–142 versteht das gehörnte Portrait Seleukos' II. als Machtdemonstration im Konflikt mit Ptolemaios III.

119   SC I, p. 274.

120   SC 685; 749–750; 788. Dodd 2009, 134–140 stellt die Sinnhaftigkeit, den König Bart tragen zu lassen, um einem Erfolg in Parthien Ausdruck zu verleihen, im Sinne einer (un-)möglichen Abgrenzung in Frage. Ihrer Ansicht nach können die bärtigen Portraits eher dazu gedient haben, sich ihm Bruderkrieg von Antiochos Hierax bildhaft abzugrenzen.

Apollon[121] propagiert wurde. Die ikonographische Neuausrichtung der Münzen zeugt zumindest von einer deutlich fassbaren Tendenz der Vereinheitlichung. Das von Ralf von den Hoff unlängst als „a concept of a quiet king, distant from the world"[122] bezeichnete Bildprogramm der Seleukiden – besonders im Vergleich zu den Ptolemaiern – verweist ebenfalls darauf, dass Antiochos in der ikonographischen Portraitdarstellung einen Weg wählte, der einer kultisch-göttlichen Verehrung im Seleukidenreich auf der Basis einer Seleukos-Zeus- und Antiochos-Apollon-Symbiose den Boden ebnen sollte. Das mit Hörnern versehene Portrait des verstorbenen Herrschers unterstreicht ebenfalls eindeutig die Absicht, Seleukos' Vergöttlichung zu propagieren.[123] Die inschriftliche Überlieferung flankiert diese Tendenzen und scheint zumindest in Borsippa das Apollon-Motiv aufzugreifen. Die nachfolgenden Herrscher setzten die Apollontradition fort, doch schuf sich Seleukos II. mit seiner reichsweiten Verbreitung des stehenden Apollons ein neues Alleinstellungs- bzw. Identifikationsmerkmal. Göttliche Symbole wie Stierhörner und Flügel tauchen immer wieder auf Münzen auf, vermehrt jedoch in Verbindung mit Elefanten oder Pferden. Die wenigen gehörnten Herrscherportraits lassen sich zumeist konkreten und lokal begrenzten Ereignissen zuschreiben und können nicht als flächendeckendes göttliches Attribut des Herrscherportraits verstanden werden.

5. Antiochos III. – Die herrschaftliche Neuausrichtung im seleukidisch-ptolemaiischen Spannungsfeld

Nach der nur drei Jahre andauernden Herrschaft Seleukos' III., die keinen nachhaltigen Einfluss auf die Entwicklung der Dynastie nehmen konnte,[124] folgte mit Antiochos III., auch bekannt als der Große, ein Seleukidenherrscher, dem in der Rückschau eine dem

---

121 Der früheste Beleg für eine Bezugnahme auf Apollon als Ahnherr der Seleukiden findet sich in Ilion (OGIS 212) nach dem Zusammenbruch des Herrschaftsgebietes des Lysimachos, also nach 281 v. Chr. Dieser Befund korreliert mit der kleinasiatischen Wahrnehmung, Seleukos als ‚Befreier' vom Joch des Lysimachos zu sehen. Zudem wurde Antiochos I. 280/297 v. Chr. zum *stephanephoros* ernannt; I.Milet I 123 Z. 37; Habicht ²1970, 82–83. Zeitgleich begann die Apollon-Omphalos-Prägung im Seleukidenreich.

122 Von den Hoff 2021, 170. Vgl. auch Dodd 2009.

123 Aus der späten Herrschaftszeit Antiochos' I. ist der gleiche Typ in Bronze aus Doura-Europos bekannt; SC 363; 364. Die Bronzeprägungen deuten jedoch eher auf einen lokalen Städtekult hin, der für den Städtegründer Seleukos eingerichtet worden ist; vgl. auch Dodd 2009, 181.

124 In der Münzprägung kehrte Seleukos III. zum ursprünglichen Bild des auf dem Omphalos sitzenden Apollon zurück, worin vermutlich sein proklamierter Herrschaftsanspruch auf den seleukidischen Thron losgelöst von den vorangegangenen innerdynastischen Zwistigkeiten zum Ausdruck kommen sollte. Erickson 2019, 124–125 erkennt auf Herrscherportraits Seleukos' III. „increasingly hornlike locks of hair" bzw. „quasi-horned representation" (SC 925; SC I, p. 335 noch vorsichtiger in ihrer Deutung; einzig SC 942 aus UM 52 (zu Seleukeia am Tigris zugehörig?) scheint einen Typus eines mit Hörnern versehene Portraits geprägt zu haben), die dessen Herrschaftsanspruch unterstützen sollten.

eigentlichen Dynastiegründer nahezu ebenbürtige Rolle beigemessen wird. Diese Wahrnehmung resultiert u. a. daraus, dass ihm, wie bereits gesehen, die Einrichtung des seleukidischen Dynastiekultes zugeschrieben wird. Im Folgenden soll daher die Herrschaftszeit Antiochos' III. noch einmal in den Fokus gerückt werden, um die Absichten und Ziele seiner herrschaftlichen und dynastischen Handlungen aufzuzeigen. Den Ausgangspunkt bilden erneut die *prostagmata* zur Einrichtung des Laodike-Kultes, deren Aussagekraft und Absicht um eine neue bzw. andere Lesart erweitert werden sollen. Im Vordergrund steht die Beobachtung, dass Antiochos in diesen Selbstzeugnissen Laodike, eigentlich seine Cousine, durchgehend als „Schwester-gemahlin" bezeichnet.[125] Aus Iasos[126] in Karien liegen aus dem Kontext des lokalen Städtekultes um 196 v. Chr. Texte vor, in denen ähnliche Formulierungen verwendet werden.

Neben der Inszenierung als Geschwister, auf die unten eingegangen wird, fällt vor allem auf, dass die Iasier in ihrem Antwortschreiben auf Laodikes Brief[127] an die Stadt Antiochos konsequent als βασιλεὺς μέγας bezeichnen.[128] Dieser Befund leitet über zu der Frage nach der Bedeutung und der Funktion der Bezeichnung als μέγας. Der literarische Kontext findet sich bei Appian,[129] nach dem die Übertragung der Bezeichnung als μέγας eng mit Antiochos' Erfolgen in den östlichen Gebieten verknüpft ist. Diese Wahrnehmung spiegelt sich zudem in Inschriften wider, die in die Zeit kurz nach Antiochos' Rückkehr von seiner *anabasis* 205/204 v. Chr. zu datieren sind. John Ma konnte auf Basis der unterschiedlichen Wortstellung bereits überzeugend die Entwicklung zweier Phasen aufzeigen, wonach das μέγας in der frühen Formulierung βασιλεὺς Ἀντίοχος Μέγας[130] als *epitheton* zu verstehen ist, das dem Umfeld des Königshofes entsprungen zu sein scheint und ausschließlich in kultischen Belangen genutzt wurde.[131] Die seit etwa 199/198 v. Chr. aufkommende Bezeichnung als βασιλεὺς μέγας Ἀντίοχος,[132] die auch in den Dekreten aus Iasos, nicht aber in den *prostagmata* zur Einsetzung des Laodike-Kultes Verwendung fand, unterscheidet sich dahingehend, dass

---

125   Merkelbach – Stauber 2005, Nr. 301–303.
126   Ma 1999, Nr. 26–28.
127   Ma 1999, Nr. 26 A.
128   Ma 1999, Nr. 26 B; Nr. 27; Nr. 28.
129   App. Syr. 1.1.
130   Ma 1999, Nr. 9–10; 18. Dekrete aus Amyzon und Teos; Frühdatierung (203 v. Chr.); zur Spätdatierung (197/196 v. Chr.) vgl. Ma 1999, 260–265.
131   Ma 1999, 273. Zu „royal nicknames" vgl Bickerman, 1938, 236–242. Zur Entwicklung dieses Elements im Kontext der höfischen Gesellschaft(en) siehe den Beitrag von Shane Wallace in diesem Band.
132   Inschrift aus Antiocheia am Orontes aus 198/197 v. Chr., die einen Seleukiden für sein Wohlwollen ehrt (BE 65.436); Weihung aus Soloi aus 197 v. Chr. an Leto, Artemis und Apollon; Korrespondenz aus Iasos von 196 v. Chr.; Ma 1999, Nr. 26b; 27; 28; Weihung einer Statue an den „Großen König" Antiochos durch den seleukidischen Botschafter Menippos auf Delos (OGIS 239); Weihung einer Statue an den Sohn Antiochos auf Klaros vor 193 v. Chr.; Ma 1999, Nr. 42; Weihinschrift der Athener auf Delos für zwei Statuen an Antiochos IV., den Sohn des „Großen Königs" Antiochos (OGIS 249; 250). Vgl. auch Ma 1999, 273–276.

sie zwar auch in kultischen Kontexten in Erscheinung tritt, geographisch jedoch vornehmlich in den Regionen zu finden ist, die im Zuge des 5. Syrischen Krieges unter seleukidischen Einfluss gerieten. Zudem handelt es sich an keiner Stelle um eine Selbstbezeichnung, wofür die *prostagmata* zur Einsetzung des Laodike-Kultes, in denen eine solche Erwähnung gänzlich fehlt, ein deutlicher Beleg sind. Urheber einiger der frühesten Zeugnisse ist hingegen ein gewisser Ptolemaios,[133] Sohn des Thraseas, der ursprünglich als *strategos* der Provinzen Syrien und Phoinikien im Dienst der Ptolemaier stand,[134] unter der Herrschaft Ptolemaios' V. jedoch zusammen mit den von ihm verwalteten Satrapien auf die Seite der Seleukiden wechselte. Daraus ergibt sich, dass sich „Großer König" als Fremdbezeichnung direkt auf die Inschrift von Adulis bezieht. Nachdem Ptolemaios III. im Kontext des 3. Syrischen Krieges im Seleukidenreich eingefallen war, um Rache für die Ermordung seiner Schwester Berenike zu nehmen, hatte er sich in seinem sogenannten Tatenbericht als ‚Großer König' betiteln lassen.[135] Das Aufkommen der Bezeichnung auf seleukidischer Seite korreliert somit eindeutig mit der Konfliktsituation zwischen den Ptolemaiern und den Seleukiden bzw. der Eroberung Koilesyriens und den weiteren Erfolgen im 5. Syrischen Krieg. Die Genese der Bezeichnung als μέγας und/oder deren Verwendung können somit in keiner Weise mit einer gezielten oder vom Herrscher gesteuerten Verehrung im Rahmen des Dynastiekultes verbunden werden, auch wenn das *epitheton* als kultischer Beiname fungierte, wie es die Priesterliste[136] aus Seleukeia Pieria belegt. Die Bezeichnung „Großer König" ist ausschließlich als Replik mit seleukidischem[137] Inhalt auf das Verhalten der Ptolemaier zu verstehen. Stefan Pfeiffer hat sich zur ptolemaiischen Nutzung des Titels jüngst folgendermaßen geäußert: „The title became attractive again to praise oneself as a great conqueror, who has defeated a Seleukid enemy, who was imagined as a Persian foe."[138] Was läge daher näher für einen seleukidischen Herrscher, der durch seine Erfolge im Westen in Kleinasien und seine Rückeroberungen im Osten ein „great conqueror" war und das ptolemaiische Heer besiegt hatte, als seinen Erfolg mit genau dem Titel zu zelebrieren, der zuvor gegen die Seleukiden Verwendung gefunden hatte?

---

133   Bittstellung des Ptolemaios, Sohn des Thraseas, Statthalter und Hohepriester von Koile-Syrien; SEG 29.1613. Weihung wieder des Ptolemaios, Sohn des Thraseas, in Soloi an Hermes, Herakles und βασιλεῖ μεγάλωι Ἀντιόχωι aus dem Jahr 197 v. Chr.; OGIS 230.

134   Pol. 5.63–87. Dreyer – Gerardin 2021, 277–279 betonen daher, dass Antiochos den 5. Syrischen Krieg sowohl diplomatisch wie auch militärisch gewann, da es ihm gelang, die Unterstützung der lokalen Eliten zu gewinnen, die zuvor auf ptolemaiischer Seite gestanden hatten: „Local power was Antiochus III's strongest weapon" (279).

135   OGIS 54; HGIÜ 403. In diesem Kontext war es Ptolemaios III. ebenfalls gelungen, Seleukeia Piereia unter ptolemaiische Herrschaft zu bringen.

136   OGIS 245.

137   Bereits Plischke 2017, 75: „The former title ‚Great King', for the first time used in Greek, was connected to Seleukid modes of ruling at that time." und Strootman 2020, 126–127: „It was a contemporaneous Seleukid title and not a reference to the Achaemenid past."

138   Pfeiffer 2022, 323. Anders Tuplin 2008; Barbantani 2014.

Als zweites fällt auf, dass Laodike in ihrem Brief an die Bewohner von Iasos, der deren Dekreten vorangegangen ist, Antiochos durchgehend als „Bruder" bezeichnet.[139] Der Text ist also ein weiterer Beleg dafür, dass sich das Herrscherpaar in der Selbstbezeichnung mittels des Bildes einer Geschwisterehe präsentiert.[140] Auch dieser Aspekt muss vor dem Hintergrund des seleukidisch-ptolemaiischen Spannungsverhältnisses verstanden werden, das in der Selbst- bzw. Außendarstellung der Dynastie deutlich fassbar wird. So beschreiben der Laodike-Brief und die *prostagmata* zur Einrichtung des Laodike-Kults das Bild einer angeblichen Geschwisterehe, die in der Form in der Seleukidendynastie bisher nicht von Bedeutung war. Antiochos und Laodike legten aber anscheinend besonderen Wert darauf, die Dynastie in noch stärkerem Maße als Einheit[141] zu präsentieren. Dies zeigt sich auch darin, dass Antiochos seine Tochter Laodike – nach ptolemaiischem Vorbild[142] – nicht nur zur Oberpriesterin im Kult für die Mutter einsetzte, sondern sie 196 v. Chr. mit ihrem ältesten Bruder und designiertem Thronfolger Antiochos verheiratete.[143] Damit wurde die erste echte Geschwisterehe in der Seleukidendynastie geschlossen. Auch diese dynastische Neuausrichtung kann als Reaktion auf das ptolemaiische Handeln verstanden werden.

Zudem stärkte Antiochos die bildliche Darstellung der seleukidischen Königin,[144] die nun eine neue Form der Sichtbarkeit erhielt. Seit der Dynastiebegründung hatten die Gattinnen der Herrscher oder designierten Nachfolger eine herrschaftsstabilisierende Funktion inne.[145] Ikonographisch sichtbar – wie im Falle der Ptolemaier durch Münzportraits[146] seit Arsinoë II. – wurden die seleukidischen Königinnen jedoch erst Anfang des 2. Jhs. v. Chr., als Laodikes Bildnis von der Oberpriesterin an goldenen Kränzen getragen wurde.

---

139   Ma 1999, Nr. 26 A.
140   In einem in der Datierung umstrittenen Dekret aus Teos (um 203 v. Chr. oder um 197 v. Chr.) für Antiochos III. und Laodike III. wird ebenfalls durch die Bezeichnung als Schwester das Bild einer Geschwisterehe durch die Teianer erzeugt; SEG 41.1003 = Ma 1999, Nr. 17/18. Vgl. ebenfalls Ma 1999, 260–265; Chaniotis 2007.
141   Im Kontext der Analyse des Berichts bei Polybios zur Eheschließung zwischen Antiochos III. und Laodike III. betont auch D'Agostini 2021, 203 die „pan-Seleukid" Außenwirkung für das „reunited Seleukid Empire", die das Herrscherpaar verkörpert sehen wollte.
142   Besonders das Beispiel um Berenike II. und ihre Tante und (Schwieger-)Mutter Arsinoë II. zeigt die direkte Einbindung und Verflechtung der lebenden Königin in die kultische Verehrung der Vorgängerinnen; vgl. etwa auch Cole 2023, 54–68. Zur medialen Herrscherrepräsentation der Ptolemaier vgl. auch Müller 2009.
143   App. Syr. 4.
144   Laodike III. und ihre Tochter Laodike IV. sind bereits auf Tonsiegel im ausgehenden 3. Jh. v. Chr. abgebildet; vgl. auch Iossif – Lorber 2007, 65.
145   So fungierten besonders Apame als Gattin des Dynastiebegründers und Stratonike als Gattin seines Nachfolgers als Bindeglied zwischen West und Ost; vgl. hierzu Plischke 2016.
146   Müller 2009, 452, Abb. 8.

In der Edelmetallprägung blieb Antiochos hingegen seleukidisch beständig, indem er wie bereits sein Bruder auf das unter Antiochos I. etablierte Apollonbildnis[147] auf dem Omphalos zurückgriff, das er reichsweit und seine gesamte Herrschaft hindurch prägen ließ. Die Darstellungen unterscheiden sich regional nur in wenigen Einzelheiten, wie etwa in der Gestaltung der Diademenden des Herrscherportraits[148] oder des Apollon (nackt auf dem Omphalos sitzend oder mit einem Mantel um die Hüften).[149] Zudem finden sich Prägungen,[150] auf denen das Herrscherportrait anscheinend mit einem Horn über dem Ohr versehen ist. Die Hörner als göttliches Symbol bleiben jedoch weiterhin vornehmlich den Elefanten- und Pferdedarstellungen vorbehalten. In den Bronzeemissionen findet sich jedoch eine Prägung, die es noch einmal näher zu betrachten gilt. So hatte Antiochos bereits Ende des 3. Jhs. v. Chr. in Susa Bronzemünzen prägen lassen, auf deren Avers anscheinend ein weibliches Portrait mit Elefantenkopfschmuck zu sehen ist; den Revers ziert neben der Legende ΒΑΣΙΛΕΩΣ ΑΝΤΙΟΧΟΥ Artemis als Jägerin mit Fackel und Bogen.[151] Während die Elefantendarstellung an die militärischen Erfolge im Osten erinnern soll, ein Motiv, das eine Prägestätte in Koile-Syrien nach dem Erfolg im 5. Syrischen Krieg aufnahm,[152] handelt es sich, sofern die Deutung korrekt ist, um das erste Portrait einer weiblichen Person auf seleukidischen Münzen. Artemis[153] als Schwester des göttlichen Dynastieahnen Apollon kann vor diesem Hintergrund als göttliche Mutter der weiblichen Angehörigen der Seleukidendynastie verstanden werden, weshalb Sara Cole jüngst eine Identifizierung mit Laodike in Erwägung gezogen hat.[154] Spätestens unter Seleukos IV. finden sich dann auch weibliche Dynastiemitglieder auf Münzen, wenn seine Gattin Laodike IV. auf Bronzeprägungen aus Antiocheia am Orontes und Ptolemaïs zu sehen ist.[155]

---

147 SC 961–1295. Erickson 2019, 126 hat zurecht herausgestellt, dass das Bild des sitzenden Apollon deutlich besser dazu geeignet war, den seleukidischen Herrschaftsanspruch auszudrücken, da es die eigenen Ambitionen mit Antiochos I. verknüpfte und zudem an die Erfolge Antiochos' II. in Kleinasien erinnerte, die für Antiochos III. ebenfalls von Bedeutung waren.

148 Vgl. etwa SC 961 und 962.

149 Vgl. etwa SC 1141.

150 Vgl. etwa SC 1170.

151 SC 1224–1225.

152 SC 1084–1090.

153 Eine auf nach 204 v. Chr. datierte, seltene Bronzeprägung aus Seleukeia am Tigris zeigt auf dem Avers das Doppelportrait von Artemis und Apollon (Apollon in der ¾-Ansicht, Artemis im Hintergrund); den Revers ziert ein Dreibein; SC 1189.

154 Cole 2023, 73–74.

155 SC 1318; 1332; Hoover 2002, 81–87. Ager – Hardiman 2016 haben die Münzen, die Laodike IV. zeigen (können – eine entsprechende Legende fehlt gänzlich), ausführlich besprochen. Zudem betonen sie die numismatische Unsichtbarkeit der seleukidischen Königin vor Laodike IV., heben aber zurecht die epigraphische Sichtbarkeit von Stratonike und Laodike III. oder die literarische Sichtbarkeit Laodikes I. hervor. In gleicher Weise betonen sie die Unterschiede im Vergleich mit den Ptolemaiern, die durch die besonderen Bedingungen in Ägypten zu erklären seien: „It seems likely that the need to reinforce strong family connections, dynastic successions, and the legitimacy of incestuous marriage, coupled with the millennia-old tradition of public images of Pharaonic

Die literarische Überlieferung verweist zudem auf eine weitere Analogie, die Antiochos bei der Eheschließung mit Laodike verfolgte. Während bereits in der Vergangenheit mehrere eheliche Verbindungen mit Mitgliedern der pontischen Dynastie
geschlossen wurden, betont Polybios in seinem Bericht zu Laodike die Abkunft Mithradates' II. von einem der sieben Perser, die mit Dareios den Mager getötet hätten.[156]
Die Ehe zwischen Antiochos und Laodike symbolisiere damit eine Verbindung der
Seleukiden mit einer iranischstämmigen Dynastie, was an die Ehe zwischen Seleukos
und Apame erinnere.[157] Eine solche Wahrnehmung wird vorrangig daraus resultieren,
dass sich Antiochos in seinem Herrschaftsverständnis grundsätzlich an demjenigen
des Dynastiebegründers orientierte. In Erinnerung an Seleukos stellte Antiochos seinen Zug nach Osten und die Stilisierung seiner Erfolge deutlich in die Tradition von
dessen *anabasis*. Aus diesem Verständnis heraus erklären sich auch die Wichtigkeit,
Seleukeia Piereia zurückzuerobern,[158] Antiochos' Anspruch auf und der Kampf um
Koilesyrien sowie das besondere Spannungsfeld von Konkurrenz und Vorbild, dem
es nachzueifern und das es zu übertrumpfen galt. In der späteren Verheiratung Kleopatras I. mit Ptolemaios V. ist zudem der Versuch zu erkennen, nach den Erfolgen im
5. Syrischen Krieg das Ptolemaierreich über dynastische Allianzen zu kontrollieren.[159]
Diese Stränge, in denen Antiochos bis zum Beginn des 2. Jhs. vornehmlich Erfolge ver-
zeichnen konnte, führten in Summe dazu, dass das Seleukidenreich im ausgehenden
3. Jh. eine Position inne hatte, in der Neuerungen und eigene machtpolitische Akzente
nach den Wirren der zweiten Hälfte des 3. Jhs. v. Chr. das erste Mal bewusst umgesetzt
werden konnten.

queens throughout Upper and Lower Egypt, would have presented a unique set of cultural circumstances that would make the distribution of royal queen portraits throughout Ptolemaic Egypt
thoroughly desirable and acceptable. There was no such need or tradition in the Seleukid East."
(168).

156   Pol. 5.43.1–4.

157   Vgl. auch D'Agostini 2021, 202–203. Kosmin 2020, 76–77 sieht die Bezugnahme auf Seleukos und
       Apame auch in der geographischen Lage, da Antiochos Laodike in Seleukeia am Zeugma bzw. am
       Euphrat geheiratet habe, das gegenüber seiner Gründung Apameia am Euphrat lag; beide Städte
       sollen zudem mit einer Brücke über den Euphrat verbunden gewesen sein. Vgl. auch Sherwin-
       White – Kuhrt 1993, 15.

158   Ptolemaios III. hatte die Stadt im Zuge seines Einmarsches im Seleukidenreich 246 v. Chr. erobern
       können.

159   Vgl. hierzu ausführlich Ager 2020, die überzeugend aufzeigen kann, wie durch die persönlichen
       Ambitionen königlicher Frauen, hier am Beispiel Kleopatras I., eigene Einflussnahmen möglich
       waren, so dass die Ehe zwischen Ptolemaios V. und Kleopatra I. vielmehr der ptolemäischen Sta-
       bilisierung diente und der Königin eigene Spielräume für die Herrschaftsausübung schuf.

6. Fazit

Aus den vorangegangenen Überlegungen ergibt sich, dass der aus dem Reich der Ptolemaier bekannte, inschriftlich fassbare Dynastiekult als Herrschaftsinstrument mit imperialem Charakter im Seleukidenreich anscheinend nur wenig Bedeutung hatte. Möchte man die drei erhaltenen *prostagmata* zum Laodike-Kult als Zeichen für einen reichsweit etablierten Dynastiekult werten, lassen sich auf Grund der dann äußerst spärlichen Überlieferung kaum belastbare Schlüsse hinsichtlich der Ausrichtung und der Bedeutung des Kultes ziehen oder Aussagen über dessen Nachhaltigkeit treffen. Interpretiert man die drei Zeugnisse hingegen nicht als Zufallsfunde, sondern misst den Fundorten eine größere Bedeutung bei, können die *prostagmata* als Kommunikationsmedium dahingehend verstanden werden, dass Antiochos III. in diesen Regionen im beginnenden 2. Jh. v. Chr. besonderen Wert auf eine Stabilisierung der Herrschaft legte. Eine solche Wahrnehmung wiese den Texten jedoch eine vornehmlich lokale Funktion zu.

Abb. 8 Antiochos IV. Av.: Antiochos IV. mit Königsbinde; Rv.: thronender Zeus mit Nike auf der Rechten, ΒΑΣΙΛΕΩΣ ΑΝΤΙΟΧΟΥ ΘΕΟΥ ΕΠΙΦΑΝΟΥΣ ΝΙΚΕΦΟΡΟΥ.

Für die Verbreitung der göttlichen Dynastiewahrnehmung nutzten die Herrscher vielmehr das Medium der Münzen mit seinen Bildern,[160] da es im Sinne des seleukidischen Sonderwegs unter dem Motto „Gleich, nur anders" deutlich besser geeignet war, individuell alle Teile des Reiches zu adressieren und weniger die Gefahr barg, im Sinne einer ‚Fremdherrschaft' wahrgenommen zu werden. Dieses Selbstverständnis spiegelt sich bereits in der ikonographischen Reform unter Antiochos I. wider. Die vereinzelten und kontextgebundenen göttlichen Symbole, die unter seinen Nachfolgern auf Münzen zu fassen sind, zeigen die bewusste Strategie der Dynastie für eine

---

160   Vgl. Dodd 2009, 164. Das Beispiel Susas zeigt auch die Bedeutung lokaler Emissionen. So ließ Antiochos III. nach seiner Rückeroberung Susas nach der Molonrevolte 220 v. Chr. Bronzemünzen prägen, auf deren Avers sein eigenes, mit Hörnern verziertes Portrait zu sehen ist. Es handelt sich hierbei jedoch um lokale Kultbestrebungen, die in Susa bereits unter Seleukos II. ähnlich zu beobachten waren.

göttliche Legitimation auf. Im Gegensatz zu den Ptolemaiern, die auch in den späteren Generationen das Portrait Ptolemaios' I. als Traditionsmerkmal prägen ließen, zeichnete sich das seleukidische Herrschaftsverständnis jedoch dadurch aus, dass nicht das Herrscherportrait Kontinuität vermitteln sollte, sondern Apollon als wichtigste Gottheit im Dynastiekonzept diese Funktion übernahm.[161] Antiochos III. war dann in der Lage, diese eher implizite Symbolik westlich des Zagros auszuweiten und deutlich flächendeckender im Reich zu etablieren. Explizit[162] lässt sich die herrscherliche Vergöttlichung[163] dann erst auf Münzen Antiochos' IV.[164] fassen, der sich auch textlich als ΘΕΟΣ ΕΠΙΦΑΝΗΣ ΝΙΚΕΦΟΡΟΣ (Abb. 8)[165] bezeichnete und dessen Herrschaft daher in vielerlei Hinsicht eine einschneidende Zäsur darstellt.

---

161   Von den Hoff 2021, 189 sieht bei den Seleukiden im Vergleich zu den Ptolemaiern ein weniger zentralisiertes Herrschaftskonzept, was sich darin niederschlägt, dass der Fokus bei den Seleukiden auf der Darstellung des aktuellen Herrscherportraits lag und Seleukos I., im Gegensatz zu Ptolemaios I. im Ptolemaierreich, von seinen Nachfolgern nicht zur strategischen Legitimation auf späteren Münzen abgebildet wurde. Auch Dumke 2022, 52: „Zu dem immer gleichen Porträt Ptolemaios' I. auf den ptolemaiischen Münzen gesellten sich im Laufe der Zeit eine ganze Reihe seleukidischer Herrscher."

162   Deutlich pessimistischer Iossif 2014, 147: „The aborted attempts of Antiochos III to establish an empire-wide cult or those of Antiochos IV to present himself with numerous divine attributes indicate that either the kings were reluctant in using those artifices for strengthening their power, or their subjects weren't willing to follow."

163   Vgl. hierzu besonders Iossif – Lorber 2009, die zurecht sowohl das Problem im Verständnis griechischer *epitheta* auf Münzen im iranischen Raum als auch die ikonographische Bedeutung himmlischer bzw. göttlicher Symbole betonen, die eben ohne Sprach- bzw. Textkenntnisse eine dynastische bzw. herrschaftliche Intention vermitteln können.

164   Vgl. hierzu auch die Nikephoros-Prägungen Antiochos' IV.; Iossif – Lorber 2009. Zu Antiochos IV. grundsätzlich vgl. Mittag 2006.

165   Etwa SC 1400. Aus dem 3. Jh. v. Chr. ist ebenfalls die Antiochos Soter-Münzserie bekannt, die erstmals das göttliche *epitheton* eines Herrschers benennt. Auf dem Avers ist ein Portrait Antiochos' I. zu sehen, den Revers ziert der sitzende Apollon. Weder Prägestätte noch Münzherr der in drei Nominalen vorliegenden Emission sind jedoch bekannt. Erickson 2019, 128–131 verortet sie in die Herrschaftszeit Antiochos' II. Einerseits ist diese Serie zwar ein singulärer Versuch zum Ausdruck der seleukidischen Dynastieausprägung, andererseits belegt das Münzbild jedoch eindeutig die Bedeutung Apollons als (Schutz-)Gott der Dynastie. Zudem erinnert der Avers an die von den Ptolemaiern bekannte herrschaftliche Legitimationsstrategie, nicht das eigene Münzportrait abzubilden, sondern das der Vorfahren, um dadurch die dynastische Tradition stärker zu betonen. Eine solche Wahrnehmung betonte aber die Bedeutung Antiochos' I. im Gegensatz zum eigentlichen Dynastiebegründer Seleukos I. Vgl. auch Erickson 2018b, 253–273.

Literaturverzeichnis

Ager 2020: Ager, Sheila, „He Shall Give Him the Daughter of Women …“: Ptolemaic Queens in the Seleukid House, in: Oetjen 2020, 183–201

Ager – Hardiman 2016: Ager, Sheila – Hardiman, Craig, Female Seleukid Portraits: Where Are They?, in: A. Coşkun – A. McAuley (eds.), Seleukid Royal Women. Creation, Representation and Distortion of Hellenistic Queenship in the Seleukid Empire, Stuttgart 2016, 143–172

Ambos 2003: Ambos, Claus, Nanaja – eine ikonographische Studie zur Darstellung einer altorientalischen Göttin in hellenistisch-parthischer Zeit, Zeitschrift für Assyriologie 93, 2003, 231–272

Anagnostou-Laoutides – Pfeiffer 2022: Anagnostou-Laoutides, Eva – Pfeiffer, Stefan (eds.), Culture and Ideology under the Seleukids. Unframing a Dynasty, Berlin et al. 2022

Barbantani 2014: Barbantani, Silvia, „Attica in Syria“: Persian War Reenactments and Reassessments of the Greek-Asian Relationship: A Literary Point of View, Erga-Logoi, 2, 2014, 21–91

Beaulieu 2014: Beaulieu, Paul-Alain, Nabû and Apollo: The Two Faces of Seleukid Religious Policy, in: F. Hoffmann – K. S. Schmidt (eds.), Orient und Okzident in hellenistischer Zeit, Vaterstetten 2014, 13–30

Bidmead 2004: Bidmead, Julye, The Akitu Festival. Religious Continuity and Royal Legitimation in Mesopotamia, Piscataway 2004

Bikerman 1938: Bikerman, Elias, Institutions des Séleucides, Paris 1938

Briant 1979: Briant, Pierre, Des Achéménides aux rois hellénistiques: continuités et ruptures. Bilan et propositions (1979), in: P. Briant (ed.), Rois, tributs et paysans. Etudes sur les formations tributaires au Moyen-Orient ancien, Paris 1982, 291–330

Brüggemann 2010: Brüggemann, Thomas, Vom Machtanspruch zur Herrschaft. Prolegomena zu einer Studie über die Organisation königlicher Herrschaft im Seleukidenreich, in: T. Brüggemann (ed.), Studia Hellenistica et Historiographica. Festschrift für Andreas Mehl, Gutenberg 2010, 19–57

Brüggemann 2022: Brüggemann, Thomas, Mehr als Schall und Rauch? Das Seleukidenreich und seine antiken Namen, in: Anagnostou-Laoutides – Pfeiffer 2022, 331–350

Capdetrey 2007: Capdetrey, Laurent, Le pouvoir séleucide. Territoire, administration, finances d'un royaume hellénistique (312–129 avant J.-C.), Rennes 2007

Capdetrey 2008: Capedetrey, Laurent, Le royaume séleucide: un empire impossible, in: F. Hurlet (ed.), Les Empires. Antiquité et Moyen Âge, Rennes 2008, 57–80

Chaniotis 2003: Chaniotis, Angelos, The Divinity of Hellenistic Rulers, in: A. Erskine (ed.), A Companion to the Hellenistic World, Oxford 2003, 431–445

Chaniotis 2007: Chaniotis, Angelos, La divinité mortelle d'Antiochos III à Téos, Kernos 20, 2007, 153–171

Chrubasik 2016: Chrubasik, Boris, Kings and Usurpers in the Seleukid Empire. The Men Who Would Be King, Oxford 2016

Cole 2023: Cole, Sara E., Seleukid and Ptolemaic Imperial Iconography in the Syrian Wars (274–168 BC): The Role of Dynastic Women, in: T. Daryaee – R. Rollinger – M. Canepa (eds.), Iran and the Transformation of Ancient Near Eastern History: the Seleucids (ca. 312–150 BCE), Wiesbaden 2023, 49–85

Coşkun 2018: Coşkun, Altay, The War of Brothers, the Third Syrian War, and the Battle of Ankyra (246–241 BC): a Re-appraisal, in: K. Erickson (ed.), The Seleukid Empire, 281–222 BC. War Within the Family, Swansea 2018, 197–252

D'Agostini 2021: D'Agostini, Monica, Seleukid Marriage Alliances, in: E. D. Carney – S. Müller (eds.), The Routledge Companion to Women and Monarchy in the Ancient Mediterranean World, Abingdon et al. 2021, 198–209

Debord 2003: Debord, Pierre, Le culte royal chez les Séleucides, in: F. Prost (ed.), L'Orient méditerranéen de la mort d'Alexandre aux campagnes de Pompée, Toulouse 2003, 281–308

Dodd 2009: Dodd, Rebecca, Coinage and Conflict. The Manipulation of Seleucid Political Imagery, Glasgow 2009

Dreyer – Gerardin 2021: Dreyer, Boris – Gerardin, François, Antiochus III, Ptolemy IV, and Local Elites. Deal-Making Politics at Its Peak, in: Fischer-Bovet – von Reden 2021, 262–300

Dumke 2022: Dumke, Gunnar, Alexander vs. Soter vs. Nikator. Die Rolle Alexanders, Ptolemaios' I. und Seleukos' I. in der politischen Legitimation ihrer Nachfolger, in: Anagnostou-Laoutides – Pfeiffer 2022, 41–56

Edson 1958: Edson, Charles, Imperium Macedonicum: The Seleucid Empire and the Literary Evidence, Classical Philology 53, 1958, 153–170

Ehling 2000: Ehling, Kay, Stierdionysos oder Sohn des Poseidon. Zu den Hörnern des Demetrios Poliorketes, Göttinger Forum für Altertumswissenschaft 3, 2000, 153–160

Engels 2017: Engels, David, Benefactors, Kings, Rulers. Studies on the Seleucid Empire between East and West, Leuven et al. 2017

Erickson 2011: Erickson, Kyle, Apollo-Nabû: the Babylonian Policy of Antiochus I, in: K. Erickson – G. Ramsey (eds.), The Seleucid Dissolution. The Sinking of the Anchor, Wiesbaden 2011, 51–65

Erickson 2012: Erickson, Kyle, Seleucus I, Zeus and Alexander, in: L. Mitchell – C. Melville (eds.), Every Inch a King. Comparative Studies in Kings and Kingship in the Ancient and Medieval Worlds, Leiden 2012, 109–128

Erickson 2018a: Erickson, Kyle, Another Century of Gods? A Re-evaluation of Seleucid Ruler Cult, Classical Quarterly 68, 2018a, 97–111

Erickson 2018b: Erickson, Kyle, Antiochos Soter and the Third Syrian War, in: K. Erickson (ed.), The Seleukid Empire, 281–222 BC. War within the Family, Swansea 2018b, 253–273

Erickson 2019: Erickson, Kyle, The Early Seleukids, their Gods and their Coins, Abingdon et al. 2019

Fischer-Bovet – von Reden 2021: Fischer-Bovet, Christelle – von Reden, Sitta (eds.), Comparing the Ptolemaic and Seleucid Empires. Integration, Communication, and Resistance, Cambridge et al. 2021

Funck 1996: Funck, Bernd, „König Perserfreund". Die Seleukiden in der Sicht ihrer Nachbarn. Beobachtungen zu einigen ptolemäischen Zeugnissen des 4. und 3. Jhs. v. Chr., in: B. Funck (ed.), Hellenismus. Beiträge zur Erforschung von Akkulturation und politischer Ordnung in den Staaten des hellenistischen Zeitalters, Tübingen 1996, 195–215

Gruen 1999: Gruen, Erich S., Seleucid royal ideology, Society of Biblical Literature Seminar Papers 38, 1999, 24–53

Günther 2012: Günther, Linda-Marie, Seleukidische Vorbilder der parthischen Münzikonographie, in: P. Wick – M. Zehnder (eds.), Das Partherreich und seine Religionen – Studien zu Dynamiken religiöser Pluralität, Frankfurt 2012, 53–66

Habicht 2020: Habicht, Christian, Aigai in der Aiolis im frühen Hellenismus, in: Oetjen 2020, 623–631

Habicht ²1970: Habicht, Christian, Gottmenschentum und griechische Städte, München ²1970

Hadley 1974: Hadley, Robert A., Seleucus, Dionysus, or Alexander?, Numismatic Chronicle 14, 1974, 9–13

Hasan – Ricl 2009: Hasan, Malay – Ricl, Marijana, Two New Hellenistic Decrees from Aigai in Aiolis, Epigraphica Anatolica 42, 2009, 39–60

Herklotz 2005: Herklotz, Friederike, Der Ahnenkult der Ptolemäer, in: M. Fitzenreiter (ed.), Genealogie – Fiktion und Realität sozialer Identität, London 2005, 155–164

Hoover 2002: Hoover, Oliver D., The Identity of the Helmeted Head on the „Victory" Coinage of Susa, Schweizerische numismatische Rundschau 81, 2002, 51–60

Hoover 2011: Hoover, Oliver D., Never Mind the Bullocks: Taurine Imagery as a Multicultural Expression of Royal and Divine Power under Seleukos I Nikator, in: P. Iossif – A. Chankowski – C. Lorber (eds.), More than Men, less than Gods. Studies on Royal Cult and Imperial Worship, Leuven et al. 2011, 197–228

Houghton – Stewart 1999: Houghton, Arthur – Stewart, Andrew, The Equestrian Portrait of Alexander the Great on a New Tetradrachm of Seleucus I, Schweizerische numismatische Rundschau 78, 1999, 27–35

Huttner 1997: Huttner, Ulrich, Die politische Rolle der Heraklesgestalt im griechischen Herrschertum, Stuttgart 1997

Iossif 2011: Iossif, Panagiotis, Apollo Toxotes and the Seleukids: Comme un air de famille, in: P. Iossif – A. Chankowski – C. Lorber (eds.), More than Men, less than Gods. Studies on Royal Cult and Imperial Worship, Leuven et al. 2011, 229–291

Iossif 2014: Iossif, Panagiotis, The Apotheosis of the Seleucid King and the Question of Highpriest/priestess: A Reconsideration of the Evidence, in: T. Gnoli – F. Muccioli (eds.), Divinizzazione, culto del sovrano e apoteosi. Tra Antichità e Medioevo, Bologna 2014, 129–148

Iossif – Lorber 2007: Iossif, Panagiotis – Lorber, Catharine, Laodikai and the Goddess Nikephoros, L'Antiquité Classique 76, 2007, 63–88

Iossif – Lorber 2009: Iossif, Panagiotis – Lorber, Catharine, Celestial Imagery on the Eastern Coinage of Antiochus IV, Mesopotamia 44, 2009, 129–146

Kosmin 2014: Kosmin, Paul, Seeing Double in Seleucid Babylonia: Rereading the Borsippa Cylinder of Antiochus I, in: A. Moreno – R. Thomas (eds.), Patterns of the Past: Epitēdeumata in the Greek Tradition, Oxford 2014, 173–198

Kosmin 2020: Kosmin, Paul, No Island is a Man. The Marriage of Antiochus III to ‚Euboea', in: Oetjen 2020, 71–79

Kosmin – Moyer 2021: Kosmin, Paul – Moyer, Ian, Imperial and Indigenous Temporalities in the Ptolemaic and Seleucid Dynasties. A Comparison of Times, in: Fischer-Bovet – von Reden 2021, 129–163

Kovacs 2022: Kovacs, Martin, Vom Herrscher zum Heros. Die Bildnisse Alexanders des Großen und die *Imitatio Alexandri*, Rahden/Westf. 2022

Ladynin 2020: Ladynin, Ivan, The Burial of Seleucus I Nicator in Appian (Syr. 63): A Replica of the Ptolemaic Eponymous Cult?, in: Oetjen 2020, 46–58

Lorber – Iossif 2020: Lorber, Catharine – Iossif, Panagiotis, Draped Royal Busts on the Coinage of the Early Seleucids, in: Oetjen 2020, 158–180

Ma 1999: Ma, John, Antiochos III and the Cities of Western Asia Minor, New York 1999

Marest-Caffey 2016: Marest-Caffey, Laure, Seleukos I's Victory Coinage of Susa Revisited: A Die Study and Commentary, American Journal of Numismatics 28, 2016, 1–64

McAuley 2022: McAuley, Alex, The Seleukid Royal Family as a Reigning Triad, in: Anagnostou-Laoutides – Pfeiffer 2022, 23–40

Mehl 2022: Mehl, Andreas, How to Understand Seleukids as Babylonian „Great Kings", in: Anagnostou-Laoutides – Pfeiffer 2022, 187–202

Merkelbach – Stauber 2005: Merkelbach, Reinhold – Stauber, Josef, Jenseits des Euphrat. Griechische Inschriften. Ein epigraphisches Lesebuch, Leipzig 2005

Mittag 2006: Mittag, Peter Franz, Antiochos IV. Epiphanes. Eine politische Biographie, Berlin 2006

Muccioli 2013: Muccioli, Federicomaria, Gli epiteti ufficiali dei re ellenistici, Stuttgart 2013

Müller 2009: Müller, Sabine, Das hellenistische Königspaar in der medialen Repräsentation. Ptolemaios II. und Arsinoë II., Berlin et al. 2009

Müller 2011: Müller, Sabine, Die frühen Perserkönige im kulturellen Gedächtnis der Makedonen und in der Propaganda Alexanders d. Gr., Gymnasium 118, 2011, 1–29

Newell 1927: Newell, Edward T., The Coinage of Demetrios Poliorcetes, London 1927

Ogden 2011: Ogden, Daniel, Seleucid Dynastic Foundation Myths: Antioch and Seleuceia-in-Pieria, in: K. Erickson – G. Ramsey (eds.), The Seleucid Dissolution. The Sinking of the Anchor, Wiesbaden 2011, 149–160

Oetjen 2020: Oetjen, Roland (ed.), New Perspectives in Seleucid History, Archaeology and Numismatics. Studies in Honor of Getzel M. Cohen, Berlin et al. 2020

Orth 1977: Orth, Wolfgang, Königlicher Machtanspruch und städtische Freiheit. Untersuchungen zu den politischen Beziehungen zwischen den ersten Seleukidenherrschern (Seleukos I., Antiochos I., Antiochos II.) und den Städten des westlichen Kleinasiens, München 1977

Pfeiffer 2022: Pfeiffer, Stefan, Great King Ptolemy III and Great King Antiochos III: Remarks on the Significance of a „Persian" Title in their Representation, in: Anagnostou-Laoutides – Pfeiffer 2022, 313–329

Plischke 2014: Plischke, Sonja, Die Seleukiden und Iran. Die seleukidische Herrschaftspolitik in den östlichen Satrapien, Wiesbaden 2014

Plischke 2016: Plischke, Sonja, Apame und Stratonike – Die seleukidische Königin als Bindeglied zwischen West und Ost, in: C. Binder – H. Börm – A. Luther (eds.), Diwan. Untersuchungen zu Geschichte und Kultur des Nahen Ostens und des östlichen Mittelmeerraumes im Altertum. Festschrift für Josef Wiesehöfer zum 65. Geburtstag, Duisburg 2016, 325–345

Plischke 2017: Plischke, Sonja, Persianism under the Early Seleukid Kings? The Royal Title ‚Great King', in: M. J. Versluys – R. Strootman (eds.): Persianism in Antiquity, Stuttgart 2017, 163–176

Sartre 2006: Sartre, Maurice: Religion und Herrschaft: Das Seleukidenreich, Saeculum 57, 2006, 163–190

Schaudig 2011: Schaudig, Hanspeter, Die Inschriften Nabonids von Babylon und Kyros' des Großen, Münster 2011

Shayegan 2011: Shayegan, M. Rahim, Arsacids and Sasanians. Political Ideology in Post-Hellenistic and Late Antique Persia, Cambridge 2011

Sherwin-White 1983: Sherwin-White, Susan, Ritual for a Seleucid King at Babylon?, Journal of Hellenic Studies 103, 1983, 156–159

Sherwin-White – Kuhrt 1993: Sherwin-White, Susan – Kuhrt, Amélie, From Samarkhand to Sardis. A New Approach to the Seleucid Empire, London 1993

Stevens 2014: Stevens, Kathryn, The Antiochus Cylinder. Babylonian Scholarship and Seleucid Imperial Ideology, Journal of Hellenic Studies 134, 2014, 66–88

Strootman 2011: Strootman, Rolf, Hellenistic Court Society. The Seleukid Imperial Court Under Antiochos The Great, 223–187 BCE, in: J. Duindam – T. Artan – M. Kunt (eds.), Royal Courts in Dynastic States and Empires. A Global Perspective, Leiden et al. 2011, 63–89

Strootman 2013: Strootman, Rolf, Babylonian, Macedonian, King of the World: The Antiochos Cylinder from Borsippa and Seleukid imperial integration, in: E. Stavrianopoulou (ed.), Shifting Social Imaginaries in the Hellenistic Period: Narrations, Practices, and Images, Leiden et al. 2013, 67–97

Strootman 2020: Strootman, Rolf, The Great Kings of Asia. Imperial Titulature in the Seleukid and Post-Seleukid Middle East, in: Oetjen 2020, 123–157

Tuplin 2008: Tuplin, Christopher J., The Seleucids and Their Achaemenid Predecessors: A Persian Inheritance, in: S. M. Darbandi – A. Zournatzi (eds.), Ancient Greece and Ancient Iran. Cross-Cultural Encounters, Athens 2008, 109–136

Van Nuffelen 2004: Van Nuffelen, Peter, Le culte royal de l'empire des Séleucides: une réinterprétation, Historia 53, 2004, 278–301

von den Hoff 2021: von den Hoff, Ralf, The Visual Representation of Ptolemaic and Seleucid Kings: A Comparative Approach to Portrait Concepts, in: Fischer-Bovet – von Reden 2021, 164–190

von Reden – Strootman 2021: von Reden, Sitta – Strootman, Rolf, Imperial metropoleis and Foundation Myths. Ptolemaic and Seleucid Capitals Compared, in: Fischer-Bovet – von Reden 2021, 17–47

Widmer 2019: Widmer, Marie, Translating the Seleucid ΒΑΣΙΛΙΣΣΑ: Notes on the Titulature of Stratonice in the Borsippa Cylinder, Greece & Rome 66, 2019, 264–279

Worthington 2012: Worthington, Martin, Principles of Akkadian Textual Criticism, Boston et al. 2012

Wright 2018: Wright, Nicholas L., Seleukos, Zeus and the Dynastic cult at Seleukeia in Pieria, in: K. Erickson (ed.), The Seleukid Empire, 281–222 BC. War within the Family, Swansea 2018, 83–99

Abbildungsverzeichnis

Abb. 1: Roma Numismatics Ltd, Auction XXV, Lot 499, 22.09.2022.

Abb. 2: Nomos AG, Auction 1, Lot 119, 06.05.2009.

Abb. 3: Leu Numismatik AG, Web Auction 23, Lot 3400, 22.08.2022.

Abb. 4: CNG Triton XXIV, Lot 752, 09.01.2021.

Abb. 5: http://catalogue.bnf.fr/ark:/12148/cb41762640f.

Abb. 6: GM Auction 207, Lot 409, 15.10.2012.

Abb. 7: Leu Numismatik AG, Web Auction 20, Lot 1525, 16.07.2022.

Abb. 8: GM Auction 280, Lot 361, 11.10.2021.

Sonja Richter is administrative coordinator of the Departement of History at the University Duisburg-Essen. She studied History and Classical Philology at the Ruhr-Universität Bochum. Afterwards, she received her PhD in Ancient History from the Christian-Albrechts-Universität zu Kiel in 2012 and published her dissertation with Harrassowitz Verlag in 2014 under the title *Die Seleukiden und Iran. Die seleukidische Herrschaftspolitik in den östlichen Satrapien*. From 2014 to 2022, she was Lecturer in Ancient History at the University Duisburg-Essen. She is co-editor of the volume *Studien zum vorhellenistischen und hellenistischen Herrscherkult* (2011). She works primarily on the Hellenistic period with a focus on the Seleucid Empire.

Themes and Contexts of Monarchic Representation /
Themen und Felder monarchischer Repräsentation

———————

Contesting Greatness
The Epithet Megas *in the Hellenistic Courts*

SHANE WALLACE

Abstract: This chapter seeks to explore similarities and differences across the Hellenistic courts through the prism of contested epithets, specifically the epithet megas and the title basileus megas. Focusing on the Antigonid, Ptolemaic, Seleukid, and Euthydemid dynasties between the late 300s and the 190s, I examine the degree to which the epithet megas and the title basileus megas function as markers of inter-dynastic court rivalry. While the main focus lies on the Seleukid and Ptolemaic dynasties and the well-documented contested uses of the title basileus megas between Ptolemaios III, Ptolemaios IV, and Antiochos III, I examine both earlier and later uses of the epithet megas and the title basileus megas in the Antigonid and Euthydemid dynasties. Claims to personal greatness, supremacy over one's royal opponents, and the ideology of oikoumenic rule were universal features of all dynasties in the early Hellenistic period, from Antigonid Athens to Euthydemid Baktria. While local influences and regional variation can be detected, the ideology of oikoumenic rule marks similarity across time and space. What is striking, however, is the important role played by local communities and royal officials in developing royal epithets/titles and contesting them beyond the court, across the Hellenistic dynasties.

1. Introduction

An epithet is, according to the *Oxford English Dictionary*, 'an adjective indicating some quality or attribute which the speaker or writer regards as characteristic of the person or thing described'.[1] In the Hellenistic world, official epithets were used to present the ruler in different guises, of which Federicomaria Muccioli has identified five: political (*Soter, Euergetes*), familial (*Philadelphos, Philopator*), familiar (*Philhellen, Philopatris*),

---

1 https://www.oed.com (last access: 20.5.24). All dates, unless noted, are BC. I am indebted to the numerous helpful comments of the editors and the external reader. I would particularly like to thank the conference organisers for their generous invitation to present and their kind hospitality in Münster.

divine (*Theos, Eusebes*), and military (*Nikator, Kallinikos*).[2] Unofficially, epithets could describe a ruler by emphasising some distinctive physical feature (*Monophthalmos, Gonatas, Physkon, Monodontos*) or punning on an official epithet (*Epiphanes* 'the Manifest' becomes *Epimanes* 'the Mad'[3]). Literary historians also used popular, unofficial epithets to differentiate rulers (*Auletes, Grypos*).[4] In the Ptolemaic dynasty, which numbered at least fifteen distinct Pharaohs each named Ptolemaios, epithets were frequently used to distinguish between rulers.[5] Some epithets were assumed by the ruler and used thereafter by subjects. Others were developed and used by courtiers or subject groups, and occasionally repeated in literary sources, in order to convey a particular feature of the king or ruler, often something that describes their character or unites both ruler and subject.[6] Frequently, a ruler had multiple epithets defining different aspects of their character or actions to different audiences. Demetrios I of Macedon was commonly known as *Poliorketes* in literary sources,[7] but was known as both *Soter*[8] ('Saviour') and *Katabates*[9] ('the Descender') as a recipient of cult in Athens. He may also have been known, or perhaps presented by the Antigonids, as *Philopator*[10] in his youth and as *Euergetes*[11] by the Athenians. Notably, he appears in a dedication by Athenian soldiers in 303/302 as *Megas* 'the Great'.[12]

In antiquity, *megas* could be used as a descriptive adjective to denote stature, as in body size, or maturity, as in age,[13] though it was also used abstractly to describe an indi-

2   Muccioli 2013.
3   Pol. 26.1.
4   Van Nuffelen 2009, focusing in particular on the late third century when the phenomenon of epithets became increasingly common and important.
5   The phenomenon became more noticeable as the third century wore on. For an early epigraphic example, see the Siphnian honours for Ptolemaios II Philadelphos, c. 246 (SEG 62.597, ll. 12–14: πρ[ό]τερομ βασιλεὺς Πτ[ολε]|[μαῖος – – – – – – – βασιλέ]ως Πτολεμαίου Σωτῆρ[ος..]|[– – – – – – – – – βασιλίσσ]ης Ἀρσινόης Φιλαδέλ[φου …]).
6   By way of a modern example, Queen Elizabeth II has been called both 'the Diamond Queen' (Marr 2012, tellingly subtitled *Elizabeth II and Her People*) and 'the Steadfast' (Hurd 2015), epithets emphasising longevity and stability.
7   Plut. Demetrios 42.11.
8   Diod. 20.46.2; Plut. Demetrios 10.3, 13.2; Agora XVI 114, ll. 16–17; SEG 25.149, l. 17.
9   Plut. Demetrios 10.5.
10   Plut. Demetrios 3.1.
11   Plut. Demetrios 9.1.
12   SEG 25.149, l. 1.
13   *Stature*: Hom. Il. 16.776: ὁ δ᾽ ἐν στροφάλιγγι κονίης κεῖτο μέγας μεγαλωστί; Hom. Od. 9.508: ἀνὴρ ἠΰς τε μέγας τε, 9.513: φῶτα μέγαν καὶ καλόν, 15.418: καλή τε μεγάλη τε, 18.4: εἶδος δὲ μάλα μέγας ἦν ὁράασθαι; Soph. Oid. T. 740–742: {ΟΙΔ} φύσιν | τίν᾽ εἶχε φράζε, τίνα δ᾽ ἀκμὴν ἥβης ἔχων. | {ΙΟ} μέγας; Hdt. 3.1: κάρτα μεγάλη τε καὶ εὐειδής. *Maturity*: Hom. Od. 2.314: νῦν δ᾽ ὅτε δὴ μέγας εἰμί; Aischyl. Ag. 358: μήτε μέγαν μήτ᾽ οὖν νεαρῶν τινα; Paul Hebr. 11.24: Μωϋσῆς μέγας γενόμενος; Septuagint Ex. 2.11: μέγας γενόμενος Μωυσῆς; Zonar. 3.146: ὁ Ὠδέναθος μέγας γενόμενος καὶ Ῥωμαίοις πιστός.

vidual's moral greatness.[14] Aristophanes, unsurprisingly, sometimes used it to describe a comically large penis.[15] As a personal epithet, *megas* (or ὁ μέγας) was also employed as a religious title[16] – famously so for Antiochos III in the late third century – and was applied as a personal epithet to Hellenistic kings from at least the late fourth century onwards. The most famous historical figure to whom this epithet was applied is Alexander who is first called 'the Great' in Plautus' *Mostellaria* of ca. 193.[17] He is not called 'the Great' in surviving Greek sources until at least the first century AD. The situation is anomalous, particularly since the earliest reference to a Greek or Macedonian being called *megas* in Greek sources is Demetrios Poliorketes in Athens, ca. 303/2. Connected with *megas*, but conceptually distinct from it, is the Achaimenid royal title 'Great King', rendered in Greek as βασιλεύς μέγας. 'Great King' was part of the standard titulature of the Persian king, though its antecedents stretch back to the third millennium. It appears on the cylinder of Kyros the Great, ca. 539–530, and was used thereafter by his successors, such as Dareios I in the Behistun inscription of ca. 522–486. Among the early Hellenistic kings, it was used in Akkadian by Antiochos I on the Borsippa cylinder and was in Greek used by or applied to Antiochos III, Ptolemaios II, III, IV, and V, and in a modified form by Euthydemos I of Baktria.

In this chapter, I focus on the epithet *megas* and the associated title *basileus megas*, which appear in the Antigonid, Ptolemaic, Seleukid, and Euthydemid dynasties between the late 300s and the 190s. Stefan Pfeiffer has recently examined the title *basileus megas* and its contested use between the Ptolemaic and Seleukid empires from the reign of Ptolemaios III to that of Antiochos III. He argues, following Strootman, that the Hellenistic use of this title was not connected directly with Achaimenid precedents – indeed, Antiochos III was a 'Great King' from Asia claiming to liberate the Greeks, not enslave them like the Persian 'Great Kings' Dareios and Xerxes – but rather served a similar function to the associated title 'King of Kings' in that it expressed the king's claims to oikoumenic victory and subordination of all other kings to his rule.[18] Pfeiffer also argues that we should disassociate the epithet *megas* from the title *basileus megas* since some kings, such as Ptolemaios III, used the title without using the epithet; in another instance the epithet *megas* was used in Antiochos' ruler cult, while 'Great King' was an unofficial title and not apparent in his cultic honours. These are fair points, and the distinction drawn by Pfeiffer holds, but nonetheless both epithet and title are conceptually associated and can be fruitfully analysed in tandem. As we shall

---

14 Mette 1961. On the use of the adjective μέγας generally in Greek literature, see Bissinger 1966. On the epithet 'the Great' throughout history, see Schieder 1984.
15 Stone 1978.
16 Kazarow 1931; B. Müller 1913; Spranger 1958, 23–24; Bissinger 1966, 64–74; Versnel 1998, 194–196, 237–241; Chaniotis 2010.
17 Plaut. Most. 3.2.775.
18 Strootman 2020; Pfeiffer 2022. On the title King of Kings, see Schäfer 1974, esp. 1–49; Wiesehöfer 1996.

see, the context for Demetrios Poliorketes' acclamation as *megas*, like Antiochos III's, shares many features with uses of the title *basileus megas*, such as oikoumenic rule and victory over and subordination of other kings. Further, while Ptolemaios III may not have used both epithet and title, Antiochos III did and while he switched from the form Antiochos 'the Great' (c. 204–200) to the form 'Great King' Antiochos (post-200), his Greek audience would perhaps have seen similarity more than difference in both usages. Indeed, despite his longer use of the official title *basileus megas*, Antiochos remained commonly known as *megas*, as the literary sources amply attest.

Building on Pfeiffer's work and broadening the focus by including the personal epithet *megas* and bringing in material beyond the Ptolemaic and Seleukid empires, I examine the degree to which the epithet *megas* and the title *basileus megas* function as markers of inter-dynastic and inter-court rivalry. Royal epithets and titles could signify similarity or difference between courts. In the Ptolemaic dynasty, for instance, epithets were particularly important for differentiating between homonymous rulers. Some epithets, such as Soter, were used in almost all dynasties and reveals that the king's wish to be seen as a saviour or protector was a universal aspect of Hellenistic monarchic ideology. Other epithets, however, seem to have been favoured within specific dynasties, such as variations on *philo-* within the Ptolemaic dynasty (Philadelphos, Philopator, Philometor), and mark some degree of difference, or at least localised emphasise, between the Hellenistic courts.[19]

In what follows, I stress the following four points. First, claims to personal greatness, supremacy over one's royal opponents, and the ideology of oikoumenic rule were universal in the early Hellenistic period, from Antigonid Athens to Euthydemid Baktria (though to my knowledge no Attalid was described as 'the Great' or 'Great King'). Second, and following Pfeiffer, the title 'Great King' was contested between courts, specifically the Ptolemaic, Seleukid, and Euthydemid. Third, the epithet 'the Great' and the title 'Great King' were connected in each court with claims to universal or oikoumenic rule, in which form they reflected the common claims to global dominion voiced across the Hellenistic empires. Fourth, the Hellenistic use of the *megas* form arose from deep roots whereby almost every major ruler of an Afro-Asian land empire since the third millennium used claims to greatness as part of generic universalistic pretension: claiming to be 'great' might be taken to reflect a king's personal exemplarity, but assuming the title 'Great King' or, though it is outside the scope of this paper, 'King of Kings' (again a title with a millennia-old history of use) marked a competitive claim to royal superiority over other kings, often as a result of victory over another king, as we shall see with victories by or against Antiochos III, or claims to oikoumenic rule, as was the case with Demetrios Poliorketes or Ptolemaios III. So, while the

---

19   On the epithet Philopatris, see Muccioli 2006. On Philadelphos cf. the chapter by Alex McAuley in this volume.

use of *megas* within the Hellenistic courts marks a degree of universality in use and understanding at the level of the Graeco-Macedonian courts, local uses within Athens, Phoinikia, Egypt, and Babylonia suggest a degree of regional variation arising from the deep history of engagement by local populations with a myriad of earlier Near Eastern empires. *Megas* and *basileus megas*, therefore, provide a fruitful case study for examining the development of royal representation in the early Hellenistic period, conflict between dynasties and courts, as well as tracing similarity and difference in use across the Hellenistic courts at a macro (court) and micro (local) level.

2. Antigonids: Demetrios 'the Great'

Greek historical figures of the fifth and fourth centuries were sometimes called 'Great' or 'the Great', but only it would appear by later sources: the first century philosopher Amphikrates of Athens referred to Themistokles as either 'Great' or 'the Great' in his work *On Distinguished Men*[20] while Plutarch called Agesilaos 'the Great' in the late first or early second century AD.[21] The first contemporary description of a Greek historical individual as 'Great' or 'the Great' in Graeco-Roman antiquity comes from an Athenian inscription of ca. 303/2 that was dedicated by a private group of volunteer troops serving with Demetrios Poliorketes. The inscription records the erection of a bronze equestrian statue of the king next to the statue of *Demokratia* in the Athenian agora in thanks for his liberation of Greece and expulsion of the opponents of democracy.[22]

[ἔδοξε]ν τοῖς ἐθελονταῖς ἐπ[ιλέκτοις· ἐπειδὴ πρότερον μὲν Δημήτριος] | ὁ μέγας ἀφικόμενος
εἰς τὴν [Ἀττικὴν μετὰ ναυτικῆς καὶ πεζικῆς δυνά]|μεως τοὺς ὑπεναντίους τῆι δ[ημοκρατίαι
ἐξέβαλε καὶ ἠλευθέρωσε τὴν] | χώραν τὴν Ἀθηναίων καὶ τῶν ἄλ[λων πλείστων Ἑλλήνων,
νῦν δ' Ἀθηναίοις πα]|⁵ραγέγονεν βοηθήσων μετὰ δυν[άμεως καὶ μείζονος καὶ τῶν ἐχθρῶν
περι]|γενόμενος πολλὰς μὲν ἤδη πόλ[εις ὑπέταξεν τῆι τοῦ πατρὸς Ἀντιγόνου] | βασιλείαι,
κίνδυνον καὶ πόν[ον αὐτὸς μὲν πάντα ὑπομένων, τοὺς δὲ μετ' αὐ]|τοῦ τιμῶν καὶ περὶ πλεῖστο[υ

---

20   FGE 1158–1159; Athen. 13.37 [576c]: ὡς Ἀμφικράτης ἱστορεῖ ἐν τῷ Περὶ Ἐνδόξων Ἀνδρῶν συγγράμματι·
      Ἀβρότονον Θρήισσα γυνὴ γένος· ἀλλὰ τεκέσθαι | τὸν μέγαν Ἕλλησιν φασὶ Θεμιστοκλέα, though
      the text of Plut. Themistokles 1.1 and Anth. Graec. 7.306 is to be preferred with the use of the
      first-person singular verb φημί in the second clause of this (funerary?) epigram. See Duff 2008,
      159–160, 165–167, where he argues that the couplet 'serves a very literary function ... μέγας and its
      compounds will recur frequently ... [it] introduces and foreshadows the theme of the greatness of
      Themistokles'.
21   Plut. mor. 208b: Ἀγησίλαος ὁ μέγας παρὰ πότον ποτὲ λαχὼν συμποσίαρχος, ἐρωτηθεὶς ὑπὸ τοῦ
      οἰνοχόου πόσον ἑκάστῳ προσφέροι, 'εἰ μὲν πολὺς οἶνός ἐστιν' ἔφη 'παρεσκευασμένος, ὅσον ἕκαστος
      αἰτεῖ· εἰ δ' ὀλίγος, ἐξ ἴσου δίδου πᾶσι.' He is described elsewhere as becoming of great importance
      (213b: ὡς τοῦ πολέμου τὸν Ἀγησίλαον αὔξοντος καὶ ποιοῦντος ἐνδοξότατον καὶ μέγιστον). Plutarch
      also has Agesilaos contrast himself with the Persia 'Great King' (mor. 213c): Περσῶν βασιλέα μέγαν
      προσαγορεύειν, 'τί δαὶ ἐκεῖνος ἐμοῦ μείζων' ἔφη, 'εἰ μὴ καὶ δικαιότερος καὶ σωφρονέστερος.'
22   SEG 25.149. Trans. Mikalson 1998, 84–85 (adapted). On the date, see Muccioli 2013, 77 with n. 226.

ποιούμενος τὴν σωτηρίαν αὐτῶν, τούτων δὲ] | καὶ δεηθέντων ἡγεῖσθαι τῆ[ς ἐλευθερίας καὶ
συναντιλαμβάνεσθαι τῶν] |¹⁰ κατὰ Πελοπόννησον πράξεων πο[ρευθεὶς εὐθὺς σὺν τοῖς |
ἐθελονταῖς ἐπιλέ]|κτοις ἐξέβαλεν ἐκ τῆς χώρας τοὺ[ς ὑπεναντίους, ν τύχηι οὖν ἀγαθῆι
δεδό]|[χ]θαι τοῖς ἐθελονταῖς ἐπιλέκτοι[ς ἐπαινέσαι ἀρετῆς ἕνεκα καὶ εὐνοίας] | [Δ]ημήτριον
Ἀντιγόνου βασιλέα β[ασιλέως υἱὸν καὶ στῆσαι αὐτοῦ εἰκόνα] | [ἐ]φ' ἵππου ἐν ἀγορᾶι παρὰ
τὴν Δημο[κρατίαν· παρακαλέσαι δὲ Ἀθηναίους καὶ] |¹⁵ [τ]οὺς ἄλλους Ἕλληνας ἱδρύσασθαι
Δ[ημητρίωι βωμοὺς καὶ τεμένη· τοὺς δὲ κα]|θιισταμένους εἰς τὰς θυσίας τὰς [συντελουμένας
ὑπὲρ Ἀντιγόνου καὶ Δημητ]|ρίου καὶ Δημητρίωι Σωτῆρι θύειν [θύματα παριστάνοντας εἰς
τὴν θυσία]ν ὡς σεμνότατα καὶ κάλλιστα καὶ[ι ἀνειπεῖν τὰς τιμὰς τὰς ὑπὸ τῶν ἐθελον]|τῶν
ἐπιλέκτων τῶι βασιλεῖ δεδ[ομένας, ὅπως ἄν, καθάπερ αὐτοὶ ἐκ τῶν ἰδί]|²⁰ων τετιμήκασιν τοὺς
εὐεργέτ[ας, καὶ ἄλλοι αὐτοὺς ἐπιφανεστάταις τι]|μαῖς τιμῶσιν ἐπ[α]κο[λουθο]ῦντ[ες – – – –
– – – – – – – – – – – – – | –]

The select volunteers voted: [whereas, Demetrios] *megas* [previously] came into [Atti-
ca with a naval and infantry] force and [threw out] the opponents of [democracy and
set free] the land of the Athenians and [most other Greeks, and now] has stood by [the
Athenians] to help with an [even greater] force, and, having overcome [his enemies, has
already aligned] many cities under the kingship [of his father Antigonos, himself enduring
every] danger and labour, and he honours [those with him] and is very concerned [with
their safety,] and he leads those in need of [freedom and helpfully takes part with us] in
the affairs in the Peloponnese, and he [immediately went there with select volunteers]
and threw out the [enemy] from the land, [with good fortune] it was voted by the select
volunteers [to praise because of his virtue and goodwill] Demetrios, son of Antigonos,
a king, [son of a king, and to erect] an equestrian [statue of him] in the Agora next to
Demokratia, and [to encourage Athenians and] the other Greeks to set up [for Demetrios
altars and sanctuaries], and for those participating in the sacrifices [performed on behalf
of Antigonos and Demetrios] to sacrifice also to Demetrios *Soter*, [presenting] the most
sacred and beautiful [victims for sacrifice,] and to [proclaim the honours] given to the
king by the select volunteers [so that, just as they themselves] have honoured their benefactors [at their own expense, so also others] may follow and honour [them with the most
illustrious] honours.

The private dedication of the 'Select Volunteers' was erected in ca. 303/2 and must be
understood in the context of Demetrios' return to Athens and Greece in summer 304,
his first arrival on Greek shores since his father's declaration of kingship in spring 306.
Plutarch is clear that within a few years Ptolemaios, Seleukos, Lysimachos, Kassandros, and Agathokles followed suit and took the royal title.[23] Quickly, the title that had

23   Plut. Demetrios 18.1–4, 25.7; Diod. 20.53.2–54.1. The Antigonid declaration of kingship took place
     in spring 306, after the victory at Salamis (Wheatley – Dunn 2020, 159–163), that of Seleukos be-
     tween March 305 and April 304 (Boiy 2011), though contrary to Plut. Demetrios 18.2, Seleukos
     did not assume the royal title prior to the declaration of kingship in 305/4 (Boiy 2002, 251–254);

marked Antigonos' and Demetrios' superiority over their opponents was now claimed by all. As Rolf Strootman has argued, Antigonos' assumption of the royal title and diadem meant that he was laying claim to the entirety of Alexander's empire, so when Ptolemaios, Lysimachos, Seleukos, Kassandros, and Agathokles in turn assumed the royal title they too made the same claim; they could do no less.[24] The ideology of Hellenistic monarchy at this time was essentially universal and opportunistic in expansion – rapacity without borders – with each successor claiming to be heir to Alexander and legitimate ruler of his empire. Each subsequent declaration of kingship was a direct challenge to Antigonid legitimacy, but the interaction of the new Macedonian monarchies with Greek *poleis* and other subject communities stimulated new directions in monarchic ideology. Contrary to Plutarch's claim,[25] the Athenians did not declare the Antigonids to be kings. Cities did not make kings, but their recognition of the royal title was an important legitimising element in Hellenistic monarchy and, having recognised the royal title, cities or civic groups could do interesting things with it, thus emphasising their agency as influential allies of the new monarchs.[26] In Demetrios' case, a group of volunteer troops acclaimed him *megas*.

The dedication of the select volunteers opens by calling Demetrios *megas* (ll. 1–2: [Δημήτριος] | ὁ μέγας) and describes his whirlwind campaigns against Kassandros in Attica and the Peloponnese[27] and his victories on behalf of freedom and democracy. *Megas* was probably a spontaneous acclamation by Demetrios' troops reflecting his victories that brought freedom and democracy to the city-states of mainland Greece[28] and may, as Adolf Wilhelm argued, owe something to Demetrios' impressive stature, which is frequently described as *megas* or *megethos* in ancient sources.[29] Demetrios

---

that of Ptolemaios perhaps between November 305 and July 304 (Samuel 1962, 4–11; Gruen 1985, 257–258; Worthington 2016, 160–162), that of Lysimachos and Kassandros around the same time as Ptolemaios in spring 304 (Lund 1992, 156–158; Landucci Gattinoni 1992, 129–134; 2003, 124–127), and that of Agathokles in 304 (Consolo Langher 2000, 203; de Lisle 2021, 140–147). See, in general, Gruen 1985.

24 Strootman 2014a, 317–320; 2014b; 2020. Only Kassandros and Agathokles took the title but not the diadem (O. Müller 1973, 122–124; Hauben 1974, 106; de Lisle 2021, 140–142). On the universal pretensions of early Hellenistic monarchy, see also Gruen 1985 (cautious); Lund 1992, 51–52; Bosworth 2002, 246–247; Paschidis 2013.

25 Plut. Demetrios 10.3.

26 Paschidis 2013, emphasising Athens' and Rhodos' roles in perpetuating the Antigonid and Ptolemaic declarations of kingship, respectively.

27 SEG 25.149; Diod. 20.100.5–6, 102–103.

28 Spranger 1958, 26–28; Moretti 1967, 15; Muccioli 2013, 77–78. J. & L. Robert BÉ 1948 num.47, like Moretti, date the text to 303/2, but 295/4 cannot be excluded (Moretti 1967, 14–15).

29 Wilhelm 1943, 161 n. 25, a point rejected by Muccioli 2013, 77 n. 227. Martin 1998, 31 concludes that 'it is impossible to make a definitive conclusion'. For the ancient evidence, which must go back to contemporary descriptions, see Plut. Demetrios 2.2: (Δημήτριος δὲ μεγέθει μὲν ἦν τοῦ πατρὸς ἐλάττων, καίπερ ὢν μέγας); 10.2 (οὕτως λαμπρὸν ἐν ταῖς εὐεργεσίαις καὶ μέγαν φανέντα τὸν Δημήτριον); Diod. 19.81.4 (ἦν δὲ καὶ τῷ κάλλει καὶ τῷ μεγέθει διάφορος); 20.92.3 (ἦν δὲ καὶ κατὰ τὸ μέγεθος τοῦ σώματος καὶ κατὰ τὸ κάλλος ἡρωικὸν ἀποφαίνων ἀξίωμα).

also appears as *Soter* (l. 17), an official cult-name in Athens, where he and his father Antigonos were worshipped as the *theoi soteres*, and references a religious dimension to his rule as saviour of the Greeks.[30] When he is referred to with the royal title it is as an inherited position received as a result of his biological relationship with Antigonos (l. 13: [Δ]ημήτριον Ἀντιγόνου βασιλέα β[ασιλέως υἱὸν]).[31] By 303/2, however, Lysimachos, Ptolemaios, Seleukos, Agathokles, and Kassandros had also declared themselves kings, so Demetrios' troops emphasise that which marks him out as superior to his royal opponents: hereditary kingship, personal greatness, his victories on behalf of Greek freedom and democracy, and his role as *soter*. Notably, Kassandros is neither named nor titled within the dedication, he is only referred to periphrastically as one of 'the enemies of democracy' (l. 3: τοὺς ὑπεναντίους τῆι δ[ημοκρατίαι]). Demetrios was *soter* to the Greeks because of his liberation of Greece from Kassandros and his defence of freedom and democracy, but he was *megas* to his troops because of his military victories. The epithet emphasises the troops' bond with the king and showcases their agency in fashioning the ideology of Hellenistic kingship; that it appears programmatically at the opening of the text is important and must have been striking to the reader, particularly when the dedication was set against the gilded equestrian statue that it describes.[32]

As we shall see below with Ptolemaios II and Ptolemaios III, Demetrios' acclamation as *megas* can be connected with contemporary claims to universal rule. Plutarch and Diodoros claim repeatedly that the Antigonids coveted the *oikoumene*.[33] In Demetrios' Athens, the honorary decree for Lykourgos of 307/6 described Alexander as having conquered 'all of Asia and the other parts of the *oikoumene*',[34] perhaps echoing Antigonid oikoumenic ambitions. An Athenian private dedication of statues of the Antigonid *soteres* refers to the kings, if Adolf Wilhelm's restoration is correct, as '[*he*

30 Diod. 20.46.2; Plut. Demetrios 10.3, 13.2; Agora XVI 114, ll. 16–17.
31 Note the similar construction in Poseidipp. ep. 78 AB, ll. 25–26: νίκην εἷλε πατὴρ ἐ<κ> βασιλέω[ς] βασ[ι]λεὺς | πατρὸς ἔχων ὄνομα.
32 The remains of a gilded equestrian statue of early Hellenistic date were found in a well in the north-western corner of the agora in 1971 (Shear 1973, 165–168 with pl. 36; Houser 1982). These remains (left leg, sword, two sections of drapery, and a Pegasos from the helmet) are currently on display in the Agora Museum (B 1382–5).
33 Plut. Demetrios 8.3: οὐ προσέσχεν ὁ Ἀντίγονος, ἀλλ' ἐπιβάθραν μὲν ἔφη καλὴν καὶ ἀσάλευτον εἶναι τὴν εὔνοιαν, τὰς δ' Ἀθήνας, ὥσπερ σκοπὴν τῆς οἰκουμένης, ταχὺ τῇ δόξῃ διαπυρσεύσειν εἰς ἅπαντας ἀνθρώπους τὰς πράξεις; Diod. 18.50.1: περιβαλλόμενος (Ἀντίγονος) δὲ ταῖς ἐλπίσι τὴν τῶν ὅλων ἡγεμονίαν ἔγνω μὴ προσέχειν μήτε τοῖς βασιλεῦσι μήτε τοῖς ἐπιμεληταῖς αὐτῶν; 19.56.2: πᾶσαν τὴν Μακεδόνων βασιλείαν.
34 IG II² 457, ll. 10–12: Ἀλε|[ξάνδρωι Θηβῶν ἐπικρατήσα]ντι καὶ πᾶσαν τὴν Ἀσίαν κ|[αὶ τὰ ἄλλα τῆς οἰκουμένης? μ]έρη καταστρεψαμένωι; Plut. mor. 852c: Ἀλεξάνδρου τε τοῦ βασιλέως ἅπασαν μὲν τὴν Ἀσίαν κατεστραμμένου. Note also Aischines' description (or. 3.165) in early 331 of Alexander as having 'withdrawn to the uttermost regions of the north, almost beyond the borders of the *oikoumene*' (he was in Mesopotamia at the time); in 323, Deinarchos too placed Alexander in India at the time of Agis' revolt (1.34).

gemones of Greece and kings of] Asia, rich in gold'.[35] Duris of Samos describes a marvellous robe that Demetrios wore with the heavens embroidered on it and records that in the 290s Demetrios was depicted on the *skene* during the Athenian Dionysia festival 'riding atop the *oikoumene*'.[36] P.Köln VI 247 claims, in a negative context, that Antigonos aspired to conquest of the *oikoumene*, a sentiment perhaps similarly shared by the famous *Suda* entry on kingship.[37] By claiming the *oikoumene*, Demetrios laid symbolic claim to his peers' territories and, implicitly, their titles as kings.

We can also connect Demetrios' acclamation as *megas* with contested claims to sole kingship. In the dedication of the select volunteers, *megas* is a personal epithet that enforces Demetrios' greatness as a true king. Other contemporary sources show how both Demetrios and the Athenians denied the royal title to his opponents. An Athenian honorary decree for the Antigonid courtier Eupolis (304/3) refers to Demetrios, without mentioning his name, as 'the King', intrinsically associating him and him alone with legitimate kingship.[38] The phrasing may owe something to Greek literary descriptions of the Persian king. Another Athenian honorary decree for the Antigonid commander [---]otimos (post-306/5) describes 'Kings Antigonos and Demetrios' fighting for freedom but 'Kassandros' fighting for slavery, again using the royal title to emphasise legitimacy and status.[39] These are civic documents that emphasise the city's concern with legitimising Demetrios' rule, but a royal toast of c.302 reveals Antigonid claims to sole kingship and shows how the new royal title was employed and contested at court. Plutarch records that:

ἐκεῖνος δὲ χλευάζων καὶ γελῶν τοὺς ἄλλον τινὰ πλὴν τοῦ πατρὸς καὶ αὐτοῦ βασιλέα προσαγορεύοντας, ἡδέως ἤκουε τῶν παρὰ πότον ἐπιχύσεις λαμβανόντων Δημητρίου βασιλέως, Σελεύκου δ' ἐλεφαντάρχου, Πτολεμαίου δὲ ναυάρχου, Λυσιμάχου δὲ γαζοφύλακος, Ἀγαθοκλέους δὲ τοῦ Σικελιώτου νησιάρχου.

---

35   IG II² 3424, l. 16: [Ἑλλάδος ἡγεμόνες βασιλεῖς τ'] Ἀσίας πολυχρύσου, following the restorations of Wilhelm 1937. Interestingly, the dedication is described on l. 17 as [παρ]άδειγμα μέγιστον.

36   Plut. Demetrios 41.6–7. Duris of Samos BNJ 76 F14: ἐπὶ τῆς οἰκουμένης ὀχούμενος. On the astral symbolism of Demetrios' cosmic regalia, see Michels 2017.

37   P.Köln VI 247, col. 1, ll. 21–25: πεπεισμένος | [τοὺς μ]ὲν ἐν τοῖς ἀξιώμα|[σιν πάν]τας ἀρεῖσθαι ῥαι|[δίως, αὐ]τὸς δ' ἡγήσεσθαι | [τῆς οἰκο]υμένης ἁπάσης; Suda β147 s. v. Βασιλεία: τοὺς δὲ μηδὲν προσήκοντας βασιλεῖς γενέσθαι σχεδὸν ἁπάσης τῆς οἰκουμένης.

38   IG II² 486, ll. 11–12 (Prytany XII, 304/3): [περὶ οὗ ὁ βασιλ]|εὺς ἐπέστειλεν τεῖ [βουλεῖ καὶ τῶι δήμωι]. Numerous Athenian decrees refer to the Antigonids as *basileis* without their personal names: IG II² 492 (303/2), 558 (Prytany VIII, 304/3), 560 (307–301).

39   IG II² 469, ll. 4–10: ἐκείνου ἀπέδωκε Χα[λκιδεῦσιν τ]|[ὸν Ε]ὔριπον κα[ὶ] α[ἴ]τιος ἐγένετο [τοῦ τὴν πόλ|ιν] αὐτῶν ἐλευθέραν γενέσθαι κα[τὰ τὴν προ|α]ίρεσιν τῶν βασιλέων Ἀντιγόνο[υ καὶ Δημη|τρ]ίου καὶ νῦν ἐπιστρατεύσαντ[ος ἐπὶ τὸν δ|ῆμ]ον τὸν Ἀθηναίων Κασσάνδρ[ου ἐπὶ δουλεί||α τ]ῆς πόλεως. After his defeat at the battle of Ipsos, Demetrios was pointedly denied the royal title by the Athenians, though it was granted to others (IG II³.1 877, ll. 16–18 [Prytany III, 283/2]: καὶ νικήσαντος Λυ|σιμάχου τοῦ βασιλέως [τὴ]ν μάχην τὴν Ἰψῶι γενομέν|ην πρὸς Ἀντίγον[ον κα]ὶ Δημήτριον).

Demetrios used to rail and mock all those who gave the title of King to anyone except his father and himself, and was well pleased to hear his revellers toast Demetrios as King, but Seleukos as *Elephantarch*, Ptolemaios as *Nauarch*, Lysimachos as *Gazophylax*, and Agathokles of Sicily as *Nesiarch*.[40]

Plutarch also unfavourably compares Demetrios with Alexander, who never claimed the title King of Kings and was content to acknowledge other kings.[41] As Hans Hauben has pointed out, the toast delegitimised Antigonos' and Demetrios' opponents by making the Antigonids alone real and true kings, espousing a rhetoric of royal authority and legitimacy by claiming that other kings were no more than Demetrios' subordinate officials.

Demetrios' acclamation as *megas*, his claims to universal rule, and his denial of the royal title to his opponents all show the important role played by the interaction of court and subject communities in fashioning Hellenistic kingship. Plutarch is clear that the toast of 302 took place at court and that it was Demetrios' courtiers, his *philoi*, who toasted him as king and delegitimised his opponents by denying them the royal title, just as it was Antigonos' *philoi* who crowned him king in spring 306;[42] the Athenian state furthered this process by referring to Demetrios as 'King' but Kassandros by his personal name alone.[43] Similarly, the dedication of the select volunteers shows that Demetrios was acclaimed *megas* by his troops. Paschalis Paschidis has recently emphasised the role played by subject states, particularly Athens and Rhodos, in legitimising the declaration of kingship in 306.[44] In these three instances, we can see how court, city, and subjects interacted and played with royal terminology, promoting Demetrios as the only legitimate king, furthering his claims to oikoumenic rule, and developing new forms of acclamation by called him *megas*.

---

40   Trans. Loeb Classical Library, adapted. The toast is preserved in numerous sources, with slight variations: Plut. *Demetrios* 25.6–7 (Phylarch. BNJ 81 F31); mor. 823d; Athen. 6.261b. On the date and context, see Hauben 1974. Gruen 1985, 259–260 argues for a date after 297 due to the absence of Kassandros. The toast is generally interpreted as indicative of Antigonid global ambitions: Ritter 1965, 87; O. Müller 1973, 88–89; Hauben 1974, 107; Lehmann 1988, 2; Waterfield 2011, 143; Strootman 2014, 316–319; though Gruen 1985, 260 is cautious. On Agathokles' presence, see de Lisle 2021, 145; cf. also the chapter by Linda-Marie Günther in this volume.

41   Plut. *Demetrios* 25.7.

42   Plut. *Demetrios* 18.1. Ptolemaios too was crowned by his *philoi*, see P.Köln VI 247, col. II, ll. 28–31; Plut. *Demetrios* 18.1.

43   Note also the toast to the kings in Alexis' *Apothecary* or *Krateias*, Athen. 6.64 (254a-b): <ἕν'> Ἀντιγόνου τοῦ βασιλέως νίκης καλῶς | καὶ τοῦ νεανίσκου κύαθον Δημητρίου with Arnott 1996, 308–315, 324–9. Demetrios also appears without his royal title in the honorary decree for Medeios of Larissa of prytany XII, 303/2, IG II² 498, ll. 15–17: ὅτε ὁ βασιλ|εὺς Ἀντίγονος ἀπέστελλεν τὸν ὑὸν α|ὑτοῦ Δημήτριον, on which see the insightful comments of Paschidis 2008, 110–112.

44   Paschidis 2013.

3. Ptolemies: Ptolemaios II and Ptolemaios III

Demetrios' epithet 'the Great' (*megas*) was unofficial and was given to him by his troops, it was not a formally-assumed epithet and it is not the same as the official title 'Great King,' which had a long history in the east, from third millennium Sumeria through the Egyptian, Hittite, Babylonian, Mitanni, Assyrian, Persian, Seleukid, and Ptolemaic empires.[45] Greek knowledge of the titles 'Great King' and 'King of Kings' would have filtered through usage in the Persian empire where Kyros II appears as 'King of the World … Great King … Mighty King … King of Babylon … King of Sumer and Akkad' in the Kyros Cylinder of ca. 539–530, in which his ancestors Cambyses, Kyros I, and Teispes are also all called 'Great King'.[46] Kyros is called 'the Great' by Greek sources.[47] On the Behistûn inscription of ca. 522–486 Dareios I is termed 'Great King … King of Kings … King of Persia … King of the lands'.[48] He, too, is called 'King of Kings' in Greek sources.[49] 'Great King' was part of the traditional Achaimenid royal titulature and is attested for all Persian Kings up to Artaxerxes III.[50] For the Greeks, from Herodotos to Appian, the Persian king was frequently described as the 'Great King'.[51] As Rolf Strootman has recently shown: ' "Great King" does not designate a specific, well-defined "office" but is the most popular of several generic expressions of the universalistic pretension characteristic of virtually all pre-modern land empires in Afro-Eurasian history'.[52]

There is some scattered evidence for Ptolemaic use of the title 'Great King' in the mid-third century, but the evidence is late, regional, or otherwise somewhat difficult to interpret. Ptolemaios II Philadelphos is called 'Great King' in the *Letter of Aristeas*, but the work is probably of mid-second century date and most likely reflects traditions of its own time.[53] A private Phoinikian dedication from Kypros of ca. 255, in Semitic, is

---

45 Schäfer 1974; Artzi – Malamat 1993. The near eastern precedents of the epithet have recently been examined by Engels 2014, 334–336; Plischke 2017, 165–166; Strootman 2020, 128–131. See also Kelder – Waal 2019 on the titles *lugal gal* and *wanax* in the late Bronze Age, especially Waal 2019, 11–14.

46 BM 90920, ll. 20–22a.

47 Agathokles of Kyzikos BNJ 472 F6: Κῦρος … ὁ μέγας; App. civ. 4.80: Κύρῳ τῷ μεγάλῳ.

48 King – Thompson 1907, 1, col. I §I.

49 See n. 51.

50 Plischke 2017, 166.

51 Aischyl. Pers. 24: βασιλῆς βασιλέως ὕποχοι μεγάλου; Hdt. 1.188: βασιλεὺς ὁ μέγας; 192: βασιλεύς τε μέγας; 5.49.7: βασιλεύς τε μέγας; 8.140: βασιλεύς γε ὁ μέγας; Aristoph. Plut. 170: μέγας δὲ βασιλεύς; Xen. an. 1.4.11: πρὸς βασιλέα μέγαν εἰς Βαβυλῶνα; Plut. mor. 213c: Περσῶν βασιλέα μέγαν προσαγορεύειν. Note also Aischyl. Pers. 666: δέσποτα δεσποτᾶν; I.Magnesia 115, ll. 1–4: Βασιλεὺς [βα]σιλέ|ων Δαρεῖος ὁ Ὑσ|τάσπεω Γαδάται | δούλοι τάδε λέγε[ι] with Wiesehöfer 1987; Briant 2003; Tuplin 2009.

52 Strootman 2020, 127, 148–150.

53 [Ps.-]Aristeas § 29: βασιλεῖ μεγάλῳ; 261: μέγιστε βασιλεῦ; 280: μέγιστε βασιλεῦ; 290: βασιλεὺς μέγας; on the date, see Hunter 2011; Wright 2015, 21–30.

translated as referring to Ptolemaios Philadelphos as *dominus regum* (*'dn mlkm*).[54] In a fragmentary and undated letter from the Zenon archive, Ptolemaios' *dioiketes* Apollonios describes (most likely) Ptolemaios Philadelphos as 'Great King'.[55] So, while there is contemporary evidence for Ptolemaios Philadelphos being described as "Great King", we are not able to say under what circumstances exactly this title originated.

The earliest dateable evidence for the assumption of the title "Great King" by a Hellenistic ruler can be seen in the Third Syrian War of 246–241. Interestingly, use of the title appears to have been stimulated primarily by control over Koile Syria, whose liminal space on the borders between the Ptolemaic and Seleukid empires, between Libya and Asia, is significant. In the sixth century AD the traveller Kosmas Indikopleustes copied what is now known as the Adulis inscription, a royal decree from Adulis in Eritrea and dating from ca. 245–243. The inscription describes Ptolemaic victories in the Third Syrian War stretching from Thrace in the west to Baktria and India in the east:[56]

βασιλεὺς μέγας Πτολεμαῖος, υἱὸς βασιλέως Πτολεμαίου | καὶ βασιλίσσης Ἀρσινόης θεῶν ἀδελφῶν, τῶν βασιλέω<ς> | Πτολεμαίου καὶ βασιλίσσης Βερενίκης θεῶν Σωτήρων, | ἀπόγονος τὰ μὲν ἀπὸ πατρὸς Ἡρακλέους τοῦ Διὸς, τὰ δὲ ἀπὸ μη|⁵τρὸς Διονύσου τοῦ Διός, παραλαβὼν παρὰ τοῦ πατρὸς | τὴν βασιλείαν Αἰγύπτου καὶ Λιβύης καὶ Συρίας | καὶ Φοινίκης καὶ Κύπρου καὶ Λυκίας καὶ Καρίας καὶ τῶν | Κυκλάδων νήσων, ἐξεστράτευσεν εἰς τὴν Ἀσίαν μετὰ | δυνάμεων πεζικῶν καὶ ἱππικῶν καὶ ναυτικοῦ στόλου |¹⁰καὶ ἐλεφάντων Τρωγλοδυτικῶν καὶ Αἰθιοπικῶν, οὓς ὅ τε πατὴρ | αὐτοῦ καὶ αὐτὸς πρῶτο<ι> ἐκ τῶν χωρῶν τούτων ἐθήρευσαν | καὶ καταγαγόντες εἰς Αἴγυπτον κατεσκεύασαν <πρὸς τὴν> | πολεμικὴν χρείαν. κυριεύσας δὲ τῆς τε ἐντὸς Εὐφράτου | χώρας πάσης καὶ Κιλικίας καὶ Παμφυλίας καὶ Ἰωνίας καὶ τοῦ Ἑλ|¹⁵λησπόντου καὶ Θράικης καὶ τῶν δυνάμεων τῶν ἐν ταῖς χώραις | ταύταις πασῶν καὶ ἐλεφάντων Ἰνδικῶν, καὶ τοὺς μονάρχους τοὺς ἐν | τοῖς τόποις πάντας ὑπηκόους καταστήσας, διέβη τὸν Εὐφράτην | ποταμὸν καὶ τὴν Μεσοποταμίαν καὶ Βαβυλωνίαν καὶ Σουσι|ανὴν καὶ Περσίδα καὶ Μηδίαν καὶ τὴν λοιπὴν πᾶσαν ἕως |²⁰ Βακτριανῆς ὑφ᾽ ἑαυτοῦ ποιησάμενος καὶ ἀναζητήσας ὅσα | ὑπὸ τῶν Περσῶν ἱερὰ ἐξ Αἰγύπτου ἐξήχθη καὶ ἀνακο|μίσας μετὰ τῆς ἄλλης γάζης τῆς ἀπὸ τῶν τόπων εἰς Αἴ|γυπτον δυνάμεις ἀπέστειλεν διὰ τῶν ὀρυχθέντων πο|ταμῶν [...]

The Great King Ptolemaios (III), son of King Ptolemaios (II) and Queen Arsinoë, the Brother–Sister Gods (*theoi adelphoi*), children of King Ptolemaios (I) and Queen Berenike the Saviour Gods (*theoi soteres*), descended on his father's side from Heracles son of Zeus and on his mother's side from Dionysus son of Zeus, having taken over from his father the kingdom of Egypt, Libya, Syria, Phoinikia, Kypros, Lykia, Karia and the Kyklades islands, marched out into Asia with a force of infantry and cavalry, a fleet and elephants

---

54   KAI, no. 40 = CIS 93, l. 1: *anno XXXI domini regum Ptolem[aei]* with Huß 1977. Engels 2014, 352 n.101 argues for mistranslation of royal titles between Egyptian, Greek, and Phoinikian.

55   P.Mich. 76: [Ἀ]πολλώνιος Ζήνωνι χα[ίρειν c ? | εὐ]γενεστάτων κοπρισα[c ? | κα]ταφυτεύετε ὡς πλειστα.[c ? | τῶι] βασιλεῖ μεγάλαι τῶι μ[εγέθει c ? || c ?] Χοίαχ 7. Ζήνωνι.

56   I.Estremo Oriente 451 (= OGIS 54). Trans. Austin ²2006, no. 268.

from the Troglodytes and Ethiopia, which his father and he himself were the first to hunt from these places, and (which) they brought to Egypt and equipped for use in war. Having secured control of all the territory within (i. e. to the west of) the Euphrates and of Cilicia, Pamphylia, Ionia, the Hellespont, Thrace, and of all the forces in those places and of the Indian elephants, and having reduced to his obedience all the rulers (*monarchoi*) in the provinces (*topoi*), he crossed the river Euphrates, and having subdued Mesopotamia, Babylonia, Susiana, Persis, Media and all the remaining territory as far as Baktria, and having sought out all the sacred objects that were removed from Egypt by the Persians and having brought them back to Egypt together with the rest of the treasure from the provinces (*topoi*), he sent his forces across the dug-out rivers (i. e. canals) [...]

The Third Syrian War was a rollicking success that saw Ptolemaios III advance as far as Susa, at least, but it was not the *oikoumenic* multi-continental campaign that the decree claims. Nonetheless, the Adulis inscription is not alone in making such claims for Ptolemaios III.[57] Polyainos claims that Ptolemaios III conquered from the Taurus mountains to India,[58] while Catullus states that he added Asia to Egypt.[59] Other sources claim that Ptolemaios would have advanced past Babylonia were it not for a native revolt in Egypt.[60] A hieroglyphic inscription from the temple of Khnum, Nebtu, and Heqa at Esna, built during the reign of Ptolemaios III, appears to record conquests in Macedon, Thrace, Persia, Elam, and Susiana.[61] The recently discovered Alexandreia Edict of December 243 records victories in Syria, Phoinikia, Kilikia, Bablyonia/Persis, and Susiana.[62] Imperial ideology need not always be based in reality, but the fanciful claim that Ptolemaios III conquered all of Asia appears to have been widespread and likely developed from the Ptolemaic court where victory over the Seleukids could be globalised to claim suzerainty over the entirety of their empire as spear-won land. We should perhaps connect the Adulis inscription with a mid-third century petition from one Aigyptos which opens by addressing an unidentified Ptolemaic king as 'Great King Ptolemaios' and closes by referring to him as 'king of the entire *oikoumene*'.[63] The

---

57 Beyer-Rotthoff 1993, 42–67; Fauvelle-Aymar 2009; and especially Strootman 2014b.
58 Polyain. 8.50.
59 Catull. 66.36.
60 Iust. 27.1.9; P.Haun. 6 = FGrH 1127, ll. 14–17.
61 Sauneron 1952, 31–34; Abdel-Rahmen Ali 2009, 2–5; Burstein 2016, 82.
62 Altenmüller 2010; El-Masry – Altenmüller – Thissen 2012, 22–25, 100–102, see also the useful discussion of the Third Syrian War on pages 151–167; Burstein 2016, 83.
63 PSI V 541: [β]ασιλεῖ μ[εγ]άλωι Πτολεμαίωι | χαίρειν Αἴγυπτος. διὰ σὲ σωθε[ὶς] | καὶ νῦν δέομαί σου, εἴ σοι δοκεῖ, | πρόσταξον κατατάξαι με οὗ σοι || φαίνεται, ἵνα εὐσχημονῶν καὶ | ἀνέγκλητός σοι ὢν τὸν βίον ἔχω, | σοῦ τῆς οἰκουμένης πάσης | βασιλεύοντος. | εὐτύχει; Gerardin 2017, 98–99. Pfeiffer 2022, 318 connects this letter with Ptolemaios II. For the Ptolemies' oikoumenic pretensions, once may also note P.Berol. 13045, ll. 28–29 (first century): αἱ μὲν γὰρ ἄλλαι πόλε[ις] τῆς ὑποκειμέ[νης χώ]ρας πόλεις εἰσίν, | Ἀλεξανδρείας δὲ κῶμαι· τῆς γὰρ οἰκουμένης Ἀλ[ε]ξάνδρεια πόλις ἐστίν with Amendola 2022, 230–231, 304–309.

connection between the title "Great King" and universal rule is strikingly similar to that seen in the Adulis inscription and reinforces the suggestion that we should read the Ptolemaic assumption of the title as stimulated by victory over the Seleukids in the Third Syrian War which lead to claims of universal, *oikoumenic* rule and the subordination of other kings, such as the Seleukids, to Ptolemaios III as "Great King".[64] The title "Great King" was most likely applied to or used by Ptolemaios III quite widely.[65]

As Stefan Pfeiffer has shown, Ptolemaios III is not following Achaimenid precedent when describing himself as *basileus megas*.[66] Rather, there is a deep history of Ptolemaic claims to universal rule that may have stimulated Ptolemaios III's oikoumenic claims. Two strikingly innovative coins of Ptolemaios I emphasise his claims to rulership on Alexander's model.

Fig. 1 Alexander in elephant scalp. Tetradrachm of Ptolemaios I, Alexandreia, Egypt, ca. 315–305 BC.

Fig. 2 Alexander driving an elephant quadriga. Gold stater of Ptolemaios I, Alexandreia, Egypt, ca. 300 BC.

---

64   Pfeiffer 2022, 317. Strootman 2020, 136 compares the situation with Ptolemaios VI's invasion of the Seleukid empire in 145 (1 Makk 11.13).

65   Gerardin 2017, 99. Like Ptolemaios II before him, Ptolemaios III also appears as 'Lord of Kings' in a Phoinikian dedication of 222 (KAI, no. 19).

66   Pfeiffer 2022, 316; contra Gerardin 2017, 97. See also Strootman 2020 for the Seleukid, rather than Achaimenid, context for Antiochos III's use of the title Great King.

First, a series of Ptolemaic tetradrachms minted ca. 319 or shortly thereafter depict Alexander on the obverse with an elephant scalp and horns of Ammon (fig. 1).[67] The elephant scalp symbolises Dionysos' and Alexander's conquests in India and claims to global victory; an early marker of Hellenistic kingship, the elephant headdress was to Ptolemaios 'a symbol of unassailable universal hegemony ... the invulnerable instrument and symbol par excellence of the invincible word conqueror.'[68] Second, a Ptolemaic gold stater of ca. 304 depicts a diademed Ptolemaios Soter on the obverse and Alexander the Great holding a thunderbolt and driving an elephant quadriga on the reverse (fig. 2).[69] Like the grandiose claims of Ptolemaios III in the Adulis inscription, these coins are not based on real Ptolemaic victories in India, rather they present the king as legitimate successor to Alexander and heir to his empire. The Ptolemies may elsewhere have attributed universal empire to Alexander. The recently discovered Egyptian titulature of Alexander from the Bahariya oasis, which is unique and which Ivan Ladynin has argued was created under the early Ptolemies, appeals to global conquest and refers to Alexander as 'The Horus: ruler of rulers of the entire land'.[70]

Claims to universal rule were a perennial feature of the reign of Ptolemaios II and provide a plausible context for the attribution to him of the title 'Great King.' In his *Encomium to Ptolemaios Philadelphos*, dating to the late 270s, Theokritos describes the geographical scope of his rule: Phoinikia, Arabia, Syria, Libya, Ethiopia, the Pamphylians, the Kilikians, Lykians, Karians, and the Kyklades; 'the entire land and sea and all the roaring rivers are ruled by Ptolemaios'.[71] Kallimachos' *Hymn to Delos*, which also dates from the mid- to late 270s, describes Ptolemaios Philadelphos ruling 'both continents and the lands which are set in the sea, far as where the end of the earth is and again whence his swift horses carry the sun'.[72] Kallixeinos of Rhodos' description of the grand procession of Ptolemaios Philadelphos, which probably took place in the

---

67   Kuschel 1961; Zervos 1967; Mørkholm 1991, 63–66, 92–93; Stewart 1993, 233–237. On the date of c.319, see Lorber 2005, esp. 62. On the elephant medallions of Alexander the Great, see Holt 2003. On elephant scalps, Svenson 1995, 106–115 remains useful.

68   Stewart 1993, 236. On the elephant headdress, see Smith 1988, 41. Agathokles of Syracuse imitated these issues and may have represented his Karthaginian campaign of c. 310–307 as the western continuation of Alexander's victory over Persia, if we see his gold commemorative staters depicting Alexander in an elephant headdress as *imitatio Alexandri*, see Coarelli 1982, 549; Stewart 1993, 266–269, 432–433; Portale 2011; de Lisle 2021, 128–130.

69   Matz 1952, 29; Toynbee 1973, 39; Scullard 1974, 254 and pl. XVc; Stewart 1993, 231–243; van Oppen de Ruiter 2019.

70   SEG 59.1764; Ladynin 2014a-b; 2016. Both Bosch-Puche (2008) and Naiden (2020) argue that the inscription is contemporary with Alexander.

71   Theokr. 17.77–94, esp. ll. 91–92: θάλασσα δὲ πᾶσα καὶ αἶα | καὶ ποταμοὶ κελάδοντες ἀνάσσονται Πτολεμαίῳ; Hunter 2003, 3–7, on the date.

72   Kall. h. 4.166–170: ᾧ ὑπὸ μίτρην | ἵξεται οὐκ ἀέκουσα Μακηδόνι κοιρανέεσθαι | ἀμφοτέρη μεσόγεια καὶ αἳ πελάγεσσι κάθηνται | μέχρις ὅπου περάτη τε καὶ ὁππόθεν ὠκέες ἵπποι || Ἠέλιον φορέουσιν. Mineur 1984, 10–18 suggests that it was first delivered on the occasion of Ptolemaios Philadelphos' birthday on 7th March 274. For a date c. 275/4–270, see also Meincke 1965, 116–124; Weber 1993, 213 n. 3.

early 270s in connection with one of the Great Ptolemaia festivals, displayed the global reach and projection of Ptolemaic kingship.[73] Indians and Ethiopians appeared in the procession, along with Indian, Hyrkanian, and Molossian dogs, Ethiopian birds and sheep, Arabian, Euboian, and Indian cows, a white bear, leopards, panthers, lynxes, a giraffe, and a rhinoceros – an oikoumenic zoology of kingship. Kallixeinos also describes an astonishing twenty-four elephant quadriga, a golden statue of Alexander drawn in an ivory chariot, and a statue of Dionysos carried atop an elephant, all of which made the association between Dionysos, Alexander, and India explicit.[74] Finally, a number of Poseidippos' poems, though fragmentary, reference the Nabataeans and Arabia,[75] the Hydaspes,[76] and India,[77] which may reflect Ptolemaios II's claims to global conquest on his father's model, following Alexander the Great.

Ptolemaios IV may also have used the title 'Great King,' but the reference in a papyrus recording his imperial titulature is restored.[78] The title is certainly applied to him after his victory over Antiochos III in the Fourth Syrian War at the Battle of Raphia in June 217, which ensured Ptolemaic control of Koile Syria. A statue-base dedication made at Joppa that same year by Anaxikles, the priest Ptolemaios IV, addressed the king as 'Great King Ptolemaios'.[79] Once again, it seems that victory over the Seleukids in Koile Syria stimulated use of the title. Ptolemaios V also appears as 'Great King of Upper and Lower Egypt' on the Rosetta Stone in 196, a Greek translation of traditional Pharaonic titulature to be sure but one that chooses to emphasise in a striking way the king as 'Great.'[80] Thereafter, only scattered references to later Ptolemaic use of the title survive: Ptolemies VI and VIII are addressed as 'Great King,'[81] Ptolemaios XII was

---

73 BNJ 627 F2 apud Athen. 5.197d–203b. Still the standard treatment of the procession, Rice (1983, 182–187) dates it to 280–275. Keyser (2016) has recently argued for a date of 279/8.

74 Kallixeinos of Rhodos BNJ 627 F2 § 31–32, 34 apud Athen. 5.200d–f, 202a–b; Rice 1983, 83–86, 90–92. An early third century bronze statuette depicts Ptolemaios Philadelphos with elephant scalp and club of Herakles (British Museum, EA38442). For the connection between animals and Ptolemaic kingship, see now Miziur-Mozdzioch 2024.

75 Ep. 10 AB, col. 2.7–16.

76 Ep. 1 A-B, col. 2.2–5.

77 Ep. 2 A-B, col. 1.6–9.

78 P.Münch. 3.45, ll. 7–9: [κύριος] τριακοντετη[ρίδων καθάπερ ὁ | Ἥφαιστος] ὁ μέγας, βασιλεὺς καθάπερ [ὁ Ἥλιος, μέγας βασιλεὺς τῶν τε ἄ]νω καὶ τῶν κάτω χωρ[ῶν], though see the comments of Hagedorn – Hagedorn – Hübner – Shelton 1986, 6. The restoration is apparently based on the description of Ptolemaios V in the Rosetta Stone of 196 (see below n. 80). Ptolemaios III is described earlier in the text as κύριος βασιλ[ειῶν] (l. 2).

79 CIIP 2172 (=SEG 20.467, 53.1846): Βασιλέα μέγαν Πτολεμαῖον | θεὸν φιλοπάτορα τὸν ἐγ βασιλέως | Πτολεμαίου κα<ὶ> βασιλίσσης | Βερενίκης θεῶν εὐεργετῶν || καὶ Πτο[λε]μα[ίο]υ βασιλέως | [φιλ] αδ[έλ]φ[ου ἔκγο]νον, Ἀναξικλῆς | [-- ἱ]ερεὺς τοῦ βασι[λέως]. For date, commentary, and discussion see Pfeiffer 2015, 118–21; Gerardin 2017.

80 OGIS 90, l. 3: μέγας βασιλεὺς τῶν τε ἄνω καὶ τῶν κάτω χωρῶν. Placing μέγας before βασιλεὺς is anomalous, but see Aristoph. Plut. 170: μέγας δὲ βασιλεὺς οὐχὶ διὰ τοῦτον κομᾷ.

81 UPZ 1 10, ll. 20–21; UPZ 1 41, l. 4; Stud. Pal. IV 54; col. I ll. 5–7; P.Lond. III 879, ll. 10–12.

called 'Great King,'[82] while his daughter Kleopatra VII was acclaimed 'Queen of Kings' and Kaisarion 'King of Kings' at the Donations of Alexandreia in autumn 34.[83] The 'golden age' of the Ptolemies as 'great kings' occurred in the mid- to late third century, was connected with claims to oikoumenic rule, and arose from conflict with the Seleukids over Koile Syria.

4. Seleukids: Antiochos III

In the Seleukid empire, the Borsippa Cylinder, an archaic ceremonial Babylonian cuneiform text dating from 268, calls Antiochos I 'Great King (*šarru rabû*) (…) Mighty King (…) King of the World (…) King of Babylon (…) and King of the Lands.'[84] As with Ptolemaios II, Antiochos' description as 'Great King' is connected with claims to universal rule, only here the title *šarru rabû* echoes earlier uses by Assurbanipal, Nabonidos, and Kyros II, each of whom was adapting an Assyrian model.[85] Recent scholarship has emphasised both the local dynamics of the Borsippa cylinder as a Babylonian document and the many ways in which it communicates Seleukid imperial ideology.[86] We cannot be sure of how widely the text of the cylinder circulated or whether its Babylonian and Achaimenid royal titulature influenced Seleukid practice in the Greek world, but we should expect that versions of the text were known at court and perhaps beyond it, furthering the interaction of Babylonian and Seleukid traditions of kingship. Kathryn Stevens argues that the cylinder melds imperial ideology with local Babylonian and Borsippan traditions, suggesting a nuanced blend of cultural traditions and openness to such at the court. Paul Kosmin has recently emphasised how texts such as this would have been translated and circulated at court; Irving Finkel has shown that versions of the text of the Kyros Cylinder circulated in Babylonia.[87]

---

82   SEG 39.1705, ll. 1–2: βασιλέα μέγαν Πτο|λεμαῖον θεὸν (Tebtynis, c.55); Delta I 416 (5), l. 1: βασιλέα μέγαν Πτολεμαῖον θεὸν (Schedia, 59); IG XII.4.2 983, ll. 1–2: βασιλέα μέγαν Πτολεμαῖον τὸ[ν] | Φιλοπάτορα καὶ Φιλάδελφον (Kos, 80–51); cf. Junker – Daum 1958, 214, l. 5.

83   Cass. Dio 49.40.2–41.3: ἐκείνην τε βασιλίδα βασιλέων καὶ τὸν Πτολεμαῖον, ὃν Καισαρίωνα ἐπωνόμαζον, βασιλέα βασιλέων καλεῖσθαι ἐκέλευσε; see Strootman 2010; 2014b, 45–47; Gerardin 2017, 101–102.

84   Translations after Stevens 2014, who examines Antiochos' royal titulature on pages 73–77. Kosmin 2014, 189 describes it as 'a bricolage of Neo-Assyrian, Neo-Babylonian, and Achaimenid royal titles'. The text of the Borsippa cylinder can be most easily accessed in English as Austin ²2006, no. 166.

85   Stevens 2014, 73–74; see also Haratta 1971; Kuhrt 1983; Schaudig 2001, 550–556.

86   Sherwin-White 1991; Strootman 2013; Kosmin 2014; Stevens 2014; Plischke 2017, 168–171. Stevens 2014, 85 describes it as 'a product of collaboration between the Borsippan elite and the Seleucid authorities.' Cf. also the contributions by Sonja Richter and Christoph Michels in this volume.

87   Stevens 2014; Kosmin 2014, 193–194. Fragments of a tablet copy of the Kyros cylinder have been found at the small site of Dailem near Babylon. They show that versions of the text circulated and that the cylinder text developed from the tablet text (Finkel 2013, 15–26).

Antiochos' characterisation as 'Great King' in the Babylonian tradition may, therefore, have been well-known at the Seleukid court and perhaps beyond it. Achaimenid and local Babylonian traditions again influence the descriptions of Antiochos I Soter and Antiochos II Theos as 'Great King' in a later Babylonian king list of the mid-second century.[88]

Evidence for the Greek use of the epithet *megas* and the title *basileus megas* comes primarily from the reign of Antiochos III, the first Seleukid to use the Greek form of the title or have it attributed to him in official documents.[89] After the siege of Baktra in 206, the culmination of his eastern *anabasis*, Antiochos III recognised Euthydemos I of Baktria's claim to kingship and married his daughter to Euthydemos' son.[90] Upon his return to the Seleukid heartland, Antiochos assumed the epithet *megas ca.* 204/3.[91] According to Rolf Strootman, the epithet *megas* referred to Antiochos III himself, was linked with the extent of his empire, and reflected Seleukid claims to universalist victories and eastern conquests, on the model of Herakles, Dionysos, Kyros, Alexander, Seleukos I, and perhaps others.[92] Concerning its origins, Spranger suggested that it developed from court usage, John Ma claims that it 'belongs to the category of "royal nicknames"', and Stefan Pfeiffer argues that it was Antiochos' cultic name.[93] Strootman argues that the regional and chronological breadth and scope of its use suggests that it was an official title and that it was not connected with Achaimenid precedent.[94] The issue is complicated somewhat by the fact that each of the four known contemporary epigraphic attestations of Antiochos as *megas* occur in civic texts, not in documents of the Seleukid royal chancellery.[95] We do not know the origins of the epithet – court

---

88   Sachs – Wiseman 1954; Boiy 2002, 249; Austin ²2006, no. 158, obv. ll. 10–13. Simonides of Magnesia (BNJ 163 T1) describes a victory by 'Antiochos the Great' over the Galatians, though the identification of this Antiochos is debated, see Coşkun 2012; Engels 2014, 336–338. Cf. also the discussion by Giovanna Pasquariello in this volume.

89   In the later Seleukid empire, Antiochos VII Sidetes also appears to have called himself "the Great", again in the context of victories in the eastern portion of the Seleukid realm (Iust. 38.10.6; SC II, no. 2134).

90   Pol. 11.34.

91   App. Syr. 1. Spranger 1958, 29–33; Engels 2014, 338–340; Strootman 2020, 145–148. Walbank (1957, 451; 1967, 638) suggests that the title *megas* was adopted by 205 (on Pol. 4.2.7; 6.2.7). Virgilio 2011, 124 prefers to place it during the conquest of Koile Syria from the Ptolemies, ca. 200. For Antiochos' use of *megas* and *basileus megas*, see usefully Ma 1999, 271–276; see also Richter in this volume.

92   Strootman 2020, 135–148.

93   Spranger 1958, 30; Ma 1999, 273; Pfeiffer 2022, 315.

94   Strootman 2020.

95   Teos, c. 203 (Ma 1999 no. 18 = SEG 41.1003, l. 11: β[ασιλέως] Ἀντιόχου Μεγάλου, l. 30: βασιλεῖ Ἀντιόχωι Μεγάλωι); Amyzon, Oct.–Nov. 202 (Ma 1999 no. 9, l. 1: Βασιλευόντων Ἀντιόχου Μεγάλου); Amyzon, Nov.–Dec. 201 (Ma 1999 no. 10, l. 1: [Βασιλε]υόντων Ἀντιόχου Μεγάλου); Nysa, c. 203–200 (RC 64: [Ἀντι]όχου δὲ τοῦ μεγάλου). See also Seleukeia-in-Pieria, mid-2ⁿᵈ century (OGIS 245 = IGLS 3 (2) 1184, ll. 18 and 40: Ἀντιόχου μεγάλου); Teos, mid-2ⁿᵈ century (OGIS 246 = SEG 35.1521, ll. 2 and 7: Ἀντιόχου μεγάλου).

usage, army acclamation,[96] cult epithet – but whatever the case, it was assumed after Antiochos' conquests in the Upper Satrapies and was not used for long.

By ca. 201, upon his conquest of Koile Syria in the Fifth Syrian War of 202–195, Antiochos dropped the epithet *megas* in favour of the title *basileus megas*, a formal and well-attested title for which at least seventeen examples are known from ca. 200–160.[97] Interestingly, the title 'Great King Antiochos' does not appear in any extant royal letter, rather surviving examples, which cluster tightly in the years 200–195, are private dedications, communications from royal officials, or civic documents. Official statements, of course, but not court documents. Of the very earliest examples, we can count private dedications by Proteas[98] and Themison[99], civic documents from Xanthos[100] and Iasos[101], a letter of the royal official Zeuxis[102], and, most conspicuously, two documents from the turncoat governor of Koile Syria, Ptolemaios[103] son of Thraseas, whose defection was instrumental in bringing Koile Syria to the Seleukid fold and ensuring victory in the Fifth Syrian War.

Again, an oikoumenic context may inform Antiochos III's adoption of the epithet *megas* and, later, the title *basileus megas*. As is well-established, Antiochos III claimed that his victories were aimed at least in part to restore the Seleukid empire to the extent controlled by Seleukos I, which at the moment of his death covered in name at

---

96 Cf. Lukian, Zeuxis 11.

97 Pergamon, c. 201–187 (IvP I 182 = OGIS 240: βασιλέα [μέγαν Ἀντίοχ]ον | βασιλέως Σ[ελεύκου Καλλ]ινίκου | [Πρ]ωτᾶς Μεν[ίππου νο]μοφύλαξ); Koile Syria, 199/8 (SEG 29.1613, ll. 21: [βασ]ιλεῖ μεγάλω[ι] Ἀντιόχωι); Antiocheia on the Orontes, 198/7 (BÉ 65: 436: εἰς βασιλέα μέγαν Ἀντίοχον); Aigeai, 197 (Ma 1999, no. 20: ὑπὲρ βασιλέως μεγάλου | Ἀντιόχου καὶ Ἀντιόχου | τοῦ υἱοῦ καὶ βασιλίσσης | Λαοδίκης καὶ τῶν παιδίων || Θεμίσων ὁ ἀδελφιδοῦς | τοῦ βασιλέως | Διὶ Κασίωι); Iasos, 197 (Ma 1999, no. 26b, ll. 41–42: βασιλέως μεγάλου Ἀντιό|[χο]υ; l. 67: βασιλέα μέγαν Ἀντίο[χον]; ll. 72–73: βασ[ιλέως μεγάλου Ἀντιό]|χου); Kildara, c. 197 (I.Mylasa 962 = Ma 1999, no. 25, ll. 4–5: ὑπὸ τοῦ βασιλέως | [μεγάλου] [Ἀ]ν[τι]ό[χ]ου); Soloi, 197 (OGIS 230 = Ma 1999, no. 21: Πτολεμαῖος Θρασέα | στρατηγὸς καὶ ἀρχιερεὺς | Συρίας Κοίλας καὶ Φοίνικας | Ἑρμᾶι vac. καὶ vac. Ἡρακλεῖ vac. καὶ | βασιλεῖ μεγάλωι Ἀντιόχωι); Xanthos, 197 (Ma 1999, no. 22: βασιλεὺς μέγας Ἀντίοχος | ἀφιέρωσεν τὴν πόλιν | τῆι Λητῶι καὶ τῶι Ἀπόλλωνι | καὶ τῆι Ἀρτέμιδι διὰ τὴν || πρὸς αὐτοὺς συνάπτουσαν | συνγένειαν); Euromos, post-197 (Ma 1999, no. 30, ll. 7–8: τῆς συμμαχίας τῆς συντεθειμένης | πρὸς βασιλέα μέγαν Ἀντίοχον διὰ Ζεύξιδος); Iasos, c. 196 (Ma 1999, no. 27, l. 3: βασιλεῖ τε μεγάλωι Ἀ[ντιόχωι]); Iasos, c. 196 (Ma 1999, no. 28, l. 11: βασιλέως μεγάλου Ἀντιόχου); Delos, 193/2 (IG XI.4 1111: [β]ασιλέα [μέγαν] | Ἀντίοχο[ν] | βασιλέως Σελεύκ[ου] | Κ]αλλινίκου || Μακεδόνα | τὸν α[ὐ] το[ῦ] σωτῆρ[α | κ]αὶ ε[ὐ]εργέτ[ην] | Μένιππος Φανίου | ἀνέ[θηκεν]); Klaros, c. 197–193 (Ma 1999, no. 42: Βασιλέα Ἀντίοχον | βασιλέως μεγάλου Ἀντιόχου | Διοσκουρίδης Χάρητος); Iasos, c. 195–190 (I.Iasos 4, l. 67: βασιλέα μέγαν Ἀντίο[χον –]); Amyzon, post-188 (I.Amyzon, no. 23, l. 15: [β]ασιλεῖ μεγάλωι); Delos, c. 166–163 (IDélos 1540 (= OGIS 249), ll. 1–2: β[ασιλέα] Ἀν[τίοχον Ἐπιφανῆ] | βα[σιλέ]ως Μεγ[άλου Ἀντιόχου]); Delos, c. 166–163 (IDélos 1541, ll. 1–2: [βασιλέα Ἀντίοχον] Ἐπιφανῆ | [βασιλέως μεγ]άλου Ἀντιόχου).

98 IvP I 182 = OGIS 240.

99 Ma 1999, no. 20.

100 TAM II 266 = Ma 1999, no. 22.

101 I.Iasos 4 = Ma 1999, no. 26b.

102 I.Mylasa 962 = Ma 1999, no. 25.

103 SEG 29.1613; OGIS 230 = Ma 1999, no. 21; see also Richter in this volume.

least, through the principle of spear-won land, the entirety of Alexander's empire from India to Macedon, excluding Egypt. Antiochos' victories in the east, the Levant, Asia Minor, and Europe were routinely presented as reconquering lost Seleukid territory and restoring the empire to its size under Seleukos I Nikator.[104] In a description strikingly similar to that of the Adulis inscription, Appian describes Seleukos' victories as including 'Mesopotamia, Armenia, the so-called Seleukid Kappadokia, the Persians, Parthians, Baktrians, Arabs, Tapyri, Sogdiani, Arachotes, Hyrkanians, and all the other adjacent peoples that had been subdued by Alexander, as far as the river Indus'.[105] While we cannot know whether the title "Great King" was assumed first by Antiochos III himself or applied to him by courtiers and subjects, the prominence of the satrap of Koile Syria in our evidence suggests two things. First, the importance of royal officials and the court in the development and promulgation of new royal titles, arising out of contexts of inter-court rivalry. Second, Seleukid control of Koile Syria and victory over the Ptolemies as a key element in Antiochos' standing as "Great King", a neat parallel to Ptolemaios III's and Ptolemaios IV's victories over the Seleukids and control of Koile Syria before their attestation as "Great King" in the 240s and 210s respectively. In this regard, Antiochos' use of the title likely echoes Ptolemaios III's in that, in the aftermath of his victories in the Upper Satrapies, Antiochos III as *basileus megas* staked a claim to universal victory and pre-eminence over other subordinate kings, whom he had defeated, came into agreements with, or to whom he had married his daughters, such as Ariarathes IV of Kappadokia, Xerxes of Armenia, Euthydemos I in Baktria, Arsakes II in Parthia, Sophagasenos of India.[106] The conquest of Koile Syria during the Fifth Syrian War and the marriage of Antiochos' daughter Kleopatra I to Ptolemaios V was the most dramatic statement of a process which Strootman has termed 'vassalisation' whereby the Ptolemies became, in a manner of speaking, vassals of the Seleukids and local kings of Egypt, under the suzerainty of the newly-termed "Great King" Antiochos.[107]

---

104   Pol. 18.50.4–52.5; Liv. 33.39.3–41.4; Diod. 28.12; App. Syr. 2–3. In a general sense, Antiochos was also operating in the spirit of Ptolemaios III, Alexander, Kyros, and other Afro-Eurasian rulers who made claims to universal empire, see Ma 1999, 273–276; Grainger 2002, 90–97; Muccioli 2013, 399; Plischke 2017, 173–174; Strootman 2017; 2020.

105   App. Syr. 9.55.

106   Ariarathes IV of Kappadokia (Diod. 31.19.7; App. Syr. 5.18.8); Xerxes of Armenia (Pol. 8.23.1–5); Euthydemos I in Baktria (Pol. 11.34); Arsakes II in Parthia (Iust. 41.5); Sophagasenos of India (Pol. 10.28–31). Note also Polybios' account of Antiochos' proposed marriage alliance with Eumenes II (Pol. 21.19.1–21.11; App. Syr. 5.18.9).

107   Engels 2014 (employing the term feudalisation); Plischke 2014, 269–270; 2017, 173–174; Strootman 2014b, 54; 2017, 193; 2020, 140–145; Pfeiffer 2022, 319–321.

5. Euthydemids

Similar contexts of inter-court rivalry and contestation over royal titles can be detected in the modified use of the epithet "Great" by Antiochos III and Euthydemos I in the late third and early second centuries. A recently published inscription from Tajikistan records religious dedications made in the mid-190s by one Heliodotos, a member of Euthydemos' court:

Τόνδε σοι βωμὸν θυώδη, πρέσβα κυδίστη θεῶν | Ἑστία, Διὸς κ(α)τ᾽ ἄλσος καλλίδενδρον
ἔκτισεν | καὶ κλυταῖς ἤσκησε λοιβαῖς ἐμπύροις Ἡλιόδοτος | ὄφρα τὸμ πάντων μέγιστον
Εὐθύδημον βασιλέων |⁵ τοῦ τε παῖδα καλλίνικον ἐκπρεπῆ Δημήτριον | πρευμενὴς σώιζηις
ἐκηδεῖ(ς) σὺν τύχαι θεόφρον[ι].

> This fragrant altar to you, august Hestia, most honoured among the gods, Heliodotos established in the grove of Zeus with its fair trees, furnishing it with splendid libations and burnt-offerings, so that you may graciously preserve free from care, together with divine good fortune, Euthydemos, greatest of all kings, and his outstanding son Demetrios, renowned for fine victories.[108]

It is striking that in the dedication Euthydemos is called 'greatest of all kings' (τὸμ πάντων μέγιστον Εὐθύδημον βασιλέων). This cannot but be a biting reference to Antiochos' assumption of the personal epithet "the Great" or, perhaps more likely, the official title "Great King" a few years after his recent compact with Euthydemos. In a context of inter-court rivalry, Euthydemos was not to be outdone or demeaned by Antiochos; Antiochos may have declared himself *megas* after his campaigns in Baktria, but Euthydemos responded by being acclaimed as *megistos*.[109] The Heliodotos dedication is important evidence for the spread of monarchic ideology between the Hellenistic courts and it is worth noting that, as with Demetrios, Ptolemaios II and IV, and Antiochos III, the surviving evidence documents a royal official, not the king or the royal chancellery, first using new titles. There is no evidence for claims to oikoumenic rule or victory by Euthydemos I, but his compact with Antiochos III must have been presented by him as a great victory, as it was presented by Antiochos, and here too, like Antiochos, we see Euthydemos presented by his courtiers as a king greater than all others, just as Demetrios Poliorketes had been at the famous toast of 302.[110] Notably, however, after Euthydemos a number of Graeco-Baktrian and Indo-Greek rulers begin

---

108 SEG 54.1569. Trans. from Hollis 2011, adapted.
109 Other examples of contested epithets exist. Federicomaria Muccioli (2013, 285–286) has argued that the epithet Epiphanes was created by Aristomenes of Akarnania, tutor of Ptolemaios V, in the 190s in order to reinforce his authority after the deaths of Ptolemaios IV and Arsinoë III.
110 This example prefigures the somewhat similar description of Ptolemaios VI as 'greatest king', see UPZ 1.10, ll. 20–21: μέγιστε βασιλεῦ καὶ | βασίλισσα; UPZ 1.41, l. 4: μέγιστε βασιλεῦ.

using the title *basileus megas*, most famously Eukratides I, as exemplified on a truly colossal 169.2 g gold 20-stater coin of 58 mm diameter named the Eukratidion (fig. 3).

Fig. 3 The "Eukratideion". Eukratides I, 20-stater gold coin, unknown mint, Baktriane.

6. Conclusion

The earliest evidence for a Graeco-Macedonian ruler being given the epithet *Megas* or the title *Basileus Megas*, likely influenced by earlier description of Persian rulers, comes from a spontaneous acclamation given to Demetrios Poliorketes by Athenian troops in 303/2. Thereafter, neither epithet nor title reappears in the Greek tradition until the reign of Ptolemaios Philadelphos who is called 'Great King' in a letter of his *dioikistes* Apollonios[111] and, in a separate tradition, '*dominus regum*' by a Phoinikian subject.[112] In the Seleukid kingdom, Antiochos I was called 'Great King,' 'King of the World,' and 'King of the Lands' in the Borsippa Cylinder following long-established Babylonian tradition. In each of these early cases, we can identify distinct local variations at play – Babylonian, Phoinikian, Greek – as well as common features, such as universal rule, royal primacy, and the importance of court officials and subject communities in shaping royal titulature and forms of address. Ptolemaios III lays claim to the title 'Great King' in the aftermath of his spectacular victories over the Seleukids in the Third Syrian War;[113] once again a connection is made with universal rule while the idea of Ptolemaic royal superiority over the Seleukids is implied. *Megas basileus* thereafter becomes a regular feature of the Ptolemaic and Seleukid empires in the late third and early second centuries and is used by Ptolemaios IV, Ptolemaios V, and Antiochos III (as well as the personal epithet *megas*), again in the context of Ptolemaic-Seleukid conflict over Koile Syria, the "ground zero" for claims to the title.[114] Use of the title Great

---

111   P.Mich. 76.
112   KAI, no. 40 (= CIS 93), l. 1: '*dn mlkm*.
113   I.Estremo Oriente 451; PSI V 541.
114   Gerardin 2017; Pfeiffer 2022, both emphasising the importance of Koile Syria.

King expands hereafter and we find it being used in the Euthydemid, Parthian, Pontic, and Armenian kingdoms.[115]

The origins of the epithet *megas* and the title *basileus megas* are difficult to decipher, but we can detect a number of important influences. Demetrios' acclamation as *megas* by Greek troops shows no direct influence from Achaimenid or near eastern traditions, though the epithet had of course been applied to Persian rulers in the Greek literary tradition, so its origin can probably be detected in a perfect storm of the declaration of kingship in 306, Antigonid claims to sole rule of the *oikoumene* as heirs to Alexander, court praise of the new monarch, and Athenian self-fashioning as a privileged ally of the Antigonids. This early example is an outlier, but the influences at play are diagnostic and see reflection is later uses of the title *basileus megas*.

Universal rule, along with claims to monarchic primacy, can be detected behind the examples of Demetrios, Ptolemaios II, Ptolemaios III, and perhaps Antiochos III. While there are local precedents of universal rule and use of the title King of Kings in both Babylonian and Achaimenid tradition, there does not appear to have been the same tradition in Pharaonic monarchic ideology. In the case of Ptolemaios II,[116] therefore, the origins of his acclamation as Great King must lie in the long history of Ptolemaic claims of oikoumenic rule stretching back to Ptolemaios Soter and Alexander, or attributed to Alexander by the early Ptolemies. In this regard, the Adulis inscription of Ptolemaios III reflects the confluence, whether direct or not, of numerous different traditions: Ptolemaic/Alexandrian claims of oikoumenic rule (seen already with the Antigonids) and, for the first time, victory over the Seleukids in the east, which grounded Ptolemaic claims to oikoumenic rule in tangible achievements.

The local traditions of subject communities were important yet often overlooked influences on the development of royal titles. In literary sources, Diodoros records that upon his arrival in Persis in 316 Antigonos was given royal honours and called "Lord of Asia", possibly an early example of the importance of local communities in acclaiming rulers and influencing the development of royal titles.[117] Antigonos is termed [lú]RAB UQU (the Akkadian rendering of *strategos*) in Babylonian cuneiform documents from late 316 to 312, which notably do not mention king Alexander IV; indeed, one

---

115 See, for example, Sciandra 2008; Engels 2014, 342–354; Plischke 2017, 175–176; Strootman 2017; 2020, 151–156; Ballesteros Pastor 2017.

116 P.Mich. 76.

117 Diod. 19.48.1: τιμῆς μὲν ὑπὸ τῶν ἐγχωρίων ἠξιώθη βασιλικῆς ὡς ἂν κύριος ὢν ὁμολογουμένως τῆς Ἀσίας. The description may reflect Antigonos' appointment as στρατηγός τῆς Ἀσίας at Triparadeisos in 320 (Diod. 18.40.1) or even owe something to Alexander's characterisation as 'Lord of Asia', on which see Arr. an. 2.14.7–9, 7.1.2–3; Plut. Alexander 14.1, 34; Curt. 4.1–14; cf. Iust. 11.14.6; BNJ 532 F1, § 38: κύριος γενόμενος τᾶς Ἀσίας; Strootman 2020, 131–137. Memnon of Herakleia describes Antigonos as Ἀντιγόνῳ δὲ τὴν Ἀσίαν κατέχοντι (BNJ 434 F1 4.6) in a line of rulers in Asia that extends from Alexander the Great (§ 4.1: Ἀλέξανδρον περιφανῶς ἤδη τῆς Ἀσίας κρατοῦντα) down to the Seleukids (§ 8.1: Σέλευκος … τὴν δὲ Ἀσίαν Ἀντιόχῳ παραθέσθαι τῷ παιδί).

text describes Antigonos as ^{lú}GAL ERIN₂ KUR.KUR ("Strategos of the Lands"), which parallels the Achaimenid royal title LUGAL KUR.KUR ("King of the Lands") as used by Alexander the Great.[118] In Greece, Athenian troops called Demetrios *Megas* in 303/2, the earliest example from the Hellenistic world. At Borsippa, local Babylonian traditions lead to Antiochos being called "Great King". Ptolemaios II's Phoinikian subjects acclaimed him *dominus regum*, perhaps translating court terminology.[119] While this of course suggests different local nuance and emphasis, it also implies the importance of the Persian empire as a shared precedent which consolidated and then globalised the ideology of universal rule and claims to greatness. Broad similarity, yet local difference.

Courts appear to have been, perhaps, the most important centre for the development and dissemination of royal titulature. It is noticeable that from Demetrios Poliorketes to Antiochos III, *megas* and *basileus megas* are rarely used by kings themselves or appear in official documents surviving from the royal chancellery. Rather, the evidence shows that the titles were used first and most frequently by local communities or royal officials close to the courts. This is strikingly similar across the early Hellenistic empires. Plutarch records that it was at a royal toast that Demetrios' courtiers acclaimed him king and denied the title to his peers; in Egypt our evidence for Ptolemaios II being called "Great King" consists of a letter of his *dioikistes* Apollonios, a high ranking royal official; after the battle of Raphia Ptolemaios V is described as "Great King" on a statue-base dedication made by the king's priest Anaxikles; for Antiochos III, our earliest evidence of his use of the title "Great King" consist of a private dedication by the Seleukid commander Themison, a letter of Zeuxis, and two documents from Ptolemaios son of Thraseas, the duplicitous former Ptolemaic governor of Koile Syria who handed the province to Antiochos during the Fifth Syrian War; at the Euthydemid court in Baktria a royal official named Heliodotos described Euthydemos as "the greatest of all kings" in a pointed gesture to Antiochos' use of similar titles. While the use of the epithet/title across different dynasties in closely-connected contexts suggests similarity of use and conception, differentiation is also found. Beyond a single unofficial use under Demetrios Poliorketes, the Antigonids do not use *megas*, which might have been unsuitable for Macedonian or Greek subjects on the mainland, though it is strange then to find the first ever use of the epithet appearing in an Athenian inscription. Conflict between the Seleukids and Ptolemies turns *megas/basileus megas* into a spoil of war and an epithetic manifestation of competing claims to oikoumenic rule, from which, thereafter, the epithet and title become globalised and their use spreads throughout the Hellenistic world. The Hellenistic courts were centres of information exchange and inter-dynastic competition, and epithets were a part of that. Courtiers and royal officials were themselves the sinews of communication and, as we have seen,

---

118   CT 49, 34, l.24; Boiy 2002: 247–248, 254–256. It may translate Antigonos' position as στρατηγός τῆς Ἀσίας, see Del Monte 1997, 17–18, 215–219.
119   Engels 2014, 352 n. 101.

instrumental in developing, disseminating, and competing royal titles throughout the Hellenistic world.

Bibliography

Abdel-Rahman Ali 2009: Abdel-Rahman Ali, Mohamed, The Lost Temples of Esna, Bulletin de l'Institut français d'archéologie orientale 109, 2009, 1–8

Altenmüller 2010: Altenmüller, Hartwig, Bemerkungen zum Ostfeldzug Ptolemaios' III. nach Babylon und in die Susiana im Jahre 246/245, in: J. C. Fincke (ed.), Festschrift für Gernot Wilhelm anlässlich seines 65. Geburtstages am 28. Januar 2010, Dresden 2010, 27–44

Amendola 2022: Amendola, Davide, The Demades Papyrus (P.Berol. inv. 13045). A New Text with Commentary, Berlin 2022

Artzi – Malamat 1993: Artzi, Pinhas – Malamat, Abraham, The Great King – A Royal Title in Cuneiform Sources and in the Bible, in: M. E. Cohen (ed.), The Tablet and The Scroll, Bethesda, MD 1993, 28–38

Ballesteros Pastor 2017: Ballesteros Pastor, Luis, Pharnaces II and his Title 'King of Kings', Ancient West and East 16, 2017, 297–303

Beyer-Rotthoff 1993: Beyer-Rotthoff, Brigitte, Untersuchungen zur Außenpolitik Ptolemaios' III, Bonn 1993, 42–67

Bissinger 1966: Bissinger, Margaret, Das Adjektiv ΜΕΓΑΣ in der griechischen Dichtung, Munich 1966

Boiy 2002: Boiy, Tom, Royal Titulature in Hellenistic Babylonia, Zeitschrift für Assyriologie und Vorderasiatische Archäologie 92, 2002, 241–257

Boiy 2007: Boiy, Tom, Between High and Low: A Chronology of the Early Hellenistic Period, Frankfurt 2007

Boiy 2011: Boiy, Tom, The Reigns of the Seleucid Kings According to the Babylon King List, Journal of Near Eastern Studies 70, 2011, 1–12

Bosch-Puche 2008: Bosch-Puche, Francisco, L''autel' du temple d'Alexandre le Grand à Bahariya retrouvé, Bulletin de l'Institut français d'archéologie orientale 108, 2008, 29–44

Bosworth 2002: Bosworth, Albert B., The Legacy of Alexander. Politics, Warfare, and Propaganda under the Successors, Oxford 2002

Briant 2003: Briant, Pierre, Histoire et archéologie d'un texte: la lettre de Darius à Gadatas entre Perses, Grecs et Romains, in: M. Giorgieri et al. (eds.), Licia e Lidia prima dell'ellenizzazione, Rome 2003, 107–144

Burstein 2016: Burstein, Stanley M., Ptolemy III and the Dream of Reuniting Alexander's Empire, The Ancient History Bulletin 30, 2016, 77–86

Chaniotis 2010: Chaniotis, Angelos, Megatheism. The Search for the Almighty God and the Competition between Cults, in: S. Mitchell – P. van Nuffelen (eds.), One God: Pagan Monotheism in the Roman Empire, Cambridge 2010, 112–140

Coarelli 1982: Coarelli, Filippo, La pugna equestris di Agatocle nell'Athenaion di Siracusa, in: L. Beschi et al., (eds.) ΑΠΑΡΧΑΙ. Nuove ricerche e studi sulla Magna Grecia e la Sicilia antica in onore di Paolo Enrico Arias, Pisa 1982, 547–557

Consolo Langher 2000: Consolo Langher, Sebastiana N., Agatocle: da capoparte a monarca fondatore di un regno tra Cartagine e i Diadochi, Messina 2000

Coşkun 2012: Coşkun, Altay, Deconstructing a Myth of Seleucid History: the So-Called "Elephant Victory" Revisited, Phoenix 66, 2012, 57–73

Del Monte 1997: Del Monte, Giuseppe, Testi dalla Babilonia Ellenistica. Volume I: Testi Cronografici. Pisa-Roma 1997

Duff 2008: Duff, Timothy, The Opening of Plutarch's Life of Themistokles, Greek, Roman, and Byzantine Studies 48, 2008, 159–179

El-Masry – Altenmüller – Thissen 2012: El-Masry, Yahia – Altenmüller, Hartwig – Thissen, Heinz-Josef, Das Synodaldekret von Alexandria aus dem Jahre 243 v. Chr., Hamburg 2012

Engels 2014: Engels, David, "Je veux être calife à la place du calife"? Überlegungen zur Funktion der Titel "Großkönig" und "König der Könige" vom 3. zum 1. Jh. v. Chr., in: V. Cojocaru – A. Coşkun – M. Dana (eds.), Interconnectivity in the Mediterranean and Pontic World during the Hellenistic and Roman Periods, Cluj-Napoca 2014, 333–362

Fauvelle-Aymar 2009: Fauvelle-Aymar, François-Xavier, Les inscriptions d'Adoulis (Érythrée). Fragments d'un royaume d'influence hellénistique et gréco-romaine sur la côte africaine de la mer Rouge, Le Bulletin de l'Institut français d'archéologie orientale 109, 2009, 135–160

Finkel 2013: Finkel, Irving, The Cyrus Cylinder: the Babylonian Perspective, in: id. (ed.), The Cyrus Cylinder. The King of Persia's Proclamation from Ancient Babylon, London 2013, 4–34

Gerardin 2017: Gerardin, François, D'un grand roi à l'autre: la Syrie-Coélé entre rivalités idéologiques et transition impériale de Ptolémée IV à Antiochos IV, in: C. Feyel – L. Graslin-Thomé (eds.), Antiochos III et l'Orient. Actes du Colloque organisé à Nancy, 6–8 juin 2016, Nancy 2017, 81–106

Grainger 2002: Grainger, John D., The Roman War of Antiochos the Great, Leiden 2002

Gruen 1985: Gruen, Erich. S., The Coronation of the Diadochoi, in: J. Eddie – J. Ober (eds.), The Craft of the Ancient Historian: Essays in Honour of C. G. Starr, Lanham 1985, 253–271

Hagedorn – Hagedorn – Hübner – Shelton 1986: Hagedorn, Ursula – Hagedorn, Dieter – Hübner, Robert – Shelton, John C. (eds.), Die Papyri der Bayerischen Staatsbibliothek München III.1: Griechische Papyri (Nr. 45–154): Griechische Urkundenpapyri, Stuttgart 1986

Harmatta 1971: Harmatta, János, The Literary Patterns of the Babylonian Edict of Cyrus, Acta Antiqua Academiae Scientiarum Hungaricae 19, 1971, 217–231

Hauben 1974: Hauben, Hans, A Royal Toast in 302 B. C., Ancient Society 5, 1974, 105–106

Hollis 2011: Hollis, Adrian S., Greek Letters in Hellenistic Bactria, in: D. Obbink – R. Rutherford (eds.), Culture in Pieces. Essays on Ancient Texts in Honour of Peter Parsons, Oxford 2011, 104–118

Holt 2003: Holt, Frank, Alexander the Great and the Mystery of the Elephant Medallions, Berkeley 2003

Houser 1982: Houser, Caroline, Alexander's Influence on Greek Sculpture as Seen in a Portrait in Athens, in B. Barr-Sharrar – E. N. Borza (eds.), Macedonia and Greece in Late Classical and Early Hellenistic Times, Washington, D. C. 1982, 229–240

Hunter 2003: Hunter, Richard, Encomium of Ptolemy Philadelphus, Berkeley 2003

Hunter 2011: Hunter, Richard, The Letter of Aristeas, in: A. Erskine – L. Llewellyn-Jones (eds.), Creating a Hellenistic World, Swansea 2011, 47–60

Hurd 2015: Hurd, Douglas, Elizabeth II: The Steadfast, London 2015

Huß 1977: Huß, Werner, Der "König der Könige" und der "Herr der Könige", Zeitschrift des Deutschen Palästina-Vereins 93, 1977, 131–140

Junker – Daum 1958: Junker, Hermann – Daum, Otto, Der große Pylon des Tempels der Isis in Phila, Vienna 1958

Kazarow 1931: Kazarow, Gavril, Megas, in: RE 15/1, 1931, 221–230

Kelder – Waal 2019: Kelder, Jorritt – Waal, Willemijn (eds.), From 'Lugal.Gal' to 'Wanax'. Kingship and Political Organisation in the Late Bronze Age Aegean, Leiden 2019

Keyser 2016: Keyser, Paul T., Venus and Mercury in the Grand Procession of Ptolemy II, Historia 65, 2016, 31–52

King – Thompson 1907: King, Leonard W. – Thompson, Reginald C., The Sculptures and Inscription of Darius the Great on the Rock of Behistûn in Persia, London 1907

Kosmin 2014: Kosmin, Paul, Seeing Double in Seleucid Babylonia: Rereading the Borsippa Cylinder of Antiochus I, in: A. Moreno – R. Thomas (eds.), Patterns of the Past: Epitēdeumata in the Greek Tradition, Oxford 2014, 173–198

Kuhrt 1983: Kuhrt, Amélie, The Cyrus Cylinder and Achaemenid Imperial Policy, Journal for the Study of the Old Testament 25, 1983, 83–97

Kuschel 1961: Kuschel, Brigitte, Die neuen Münzbilder des Ptolemaios Soter, Jahrbuch für Numismatik und Geldgeschichte 11, 1961, 9–18

Ladynin 2014a: Ladynin, Ivan, The Altar from the Temple of Amun at the Bahariya Oasis with the Egyptian Royal Names of Alexander the Great I: Inscriptions of the Monument, Vestnik drevnei istorii 289, 2014a, 3–12

Ladynin 2014b: Ladynin, Ivan, The Altar from the Temple of Amun at the Bahariya Oasis with the Egyptian Royal Names of Alexander the Great II: Interpretation and Dating, Vestnik drevnei istorii 290, 2014b, 3–20

Ladynin 2016:Ladynin, Ivan, Defense and Offence in the Egyptian Royal Titles of Alexander the Great, in: K. Ulanowski (ed.), The Religious Aspects of War in the Ancient Near East, Greece and Rome, Leiden 2016, 256–271

Landucci Gattinoni 1992: Landucci Gattinoni, Franca, Lisimaco di Tracia: un sovrano nella prospettiva del primo ellenismo, Milan 1992

Landucci Gattinoni 2003: Landucci Gattinoni, Franca, L'arte del potere: vita e opere di Cassandro di Macedonia, Stuttgart 2003

Lehmann 1988: Lehmann, Gustav Adolf, Das neue Kölner Historiker-Fragment u. d. χρονικὴ σύνταξις des Zenon von Rhodos, Zeitschrift für Papyrologie und Epigraphik 72, 1988, 1–17

de Lisle 2021: de Lisle, Christopher, Agathokles of Syracuse: Sicilian Tyrant and Hellenistic King, Oxford 2021

Lorber 2012: Lorber, Catharine, Dating the Portrait Coinage of Ptolemy I, American Journal of Numismatics 24, 2012, 33–44

Lund 1992: Lund, Helen S., Lysimachus. A Study in Early Hellenistic Kingship, London 1992

Ma 1999: Ma, John, Antiochos III and the Cities of Western Asia Minor, Oxford 1999

Marr 2012: Marr, Andrew, The Diamond Queen: Elizabeth the Second and her People, London 2012

Martin 1998: Martin, Devon, Did Pompey Engage in imitatio Alexandri?, in: C. Deroux (ed.), Studies in Latin History and Literature 9, Brussels 1998, 23–51

Matz 1952: Matz, Friedrich, Der Gott auf dem Elefantenwagen, Wiesbaden 1952

Meincke 1966: Meincke, Werner, Untersuchungen zu den enkomiastischen Gedichten Theokrits. Ein Beitrag zum Verständnis hellenistischer Dichtung und des antiken Herrscherenkomions, Kiel 1966

Mette 1961: Mette, Hans-Joachim, Der 'große Mensch', Hermes 89, 1961, 332–344

Michels 2017: Michels, Christoph, Überlegungen zum 'kosmischen' Herrscherornat des Demetrios I. Poliorketes, in H. Beck et al. (eds.), Von Magna Graecia nach Asia Minor. Festschrift für L.-M. Günther, Wiesbaden 2017, 211–224

Mikalson 1998: Mikalson, John, Religion in Hellenistic Athens, Berkeley 1998

Miziur-Mozdzioch 2024: Miziur-Mozdzioch, Maya, 'Ptolemy's Zoo'. Exotic Animals in Third-Century BC Egypt, Leuven 2024

Moretti 1967: Moretti, Luigi, Iscrizioni storiche ellenistiche I: Attica, Peloponneso, Beozia, Florence 1967

Mørkholm 1991: Mørkholm, Otto, Early Hellenistic Coinage from the Accession of Alexander to the Peace of Apamea (336–186 BC), Cambridge 1991

Muccioli 2006: Muccioli, Federicomaria, Philopatris e il concetto di patria in età ellenistica, Studi Ellenistici 19, 2006, 365–398

Muccioli 2013: Muccioli, Federicomaria, Gli epiteti ufficiali dei re ellenistici, Stuttgart 2013

B. Müller 1913: Müller, Bruno, Μέγας Θεός, Diss.: Halle 1913

O. Müller 1973: Müller, Olaf, Antigonos Monophthalmos und 'Das Jahr der Könige', Bonn 1973

Naiden 2020: Naiden, Fred, The Self-Definition of Alexander the Great, in: E. Mackil – N. Papazarkadas (eds.), Greek Epigraphy and Religion. Papers in Memory of Sara B. Aleshire from the Second North American Congress of Greek and Latin Epigraphy, Leiden 2020, 295–309

van Nuffelen 2009: van Nuffelen, Peter, The Name Game: Hellenistic Historians and Royal Epithets, in: id. (ed.), Faces of Hellenism. Studies in the History of the Eastern Mediterranean (4th Century B.C.–5th Century A.D.), Leuven 2009, 93–112

Paschidis 2008: Paschides, Paschalis, Between City and King: Prosopographical Studies on the Intermediaries between the Cities of the Greek Mainland and the Aegean and the Royal Courts in the Hellenistic Period (322–190 BC), Athen 2008

Paschidis 2013: Paschidis, Paschalis, Agora XVI 107 and the Royal Title of Demetrius Poliorcetes, in: V.A. Troncoso – E.M. Anson (eds.), After Alexander: The Time of the Diadochi (323–281 BC), Oxford 2013, 121–141

Pfeiffer 2015: Pfeiffer, Stefan, Griechische und lateinische Inschriften zum Ptolemäerreich und zur römischen Provinz Aegyptus, Berlin 2015

Pfeiffer 2022: Pfeiffer, Stefan, Great King Ptolemy III and Great King Antiochos III: Remarks on the Significance of a "Persian" Title in their Representation, in: id. – E. Anagnostou-Laoutides (eds.), Culture and Ideology under the Seleukids: Unframing a Dynasty, Berlin 2022, 313–329

Plischke 2014: Plischke, Sonja, Die Seleukiden und Iran. Die seleukidische Herrschaftspolitik in den östlichen Satrapien, Wiesbaden 2014

Plischke 2017: Plischke, Sonja, Persianism under the Early Seleukid kings? The Royal Title of 'Great King', in: R. Strootman – M.J. Versluys (eds.), Persianism in Antiquity, Stuttgart 2017, 163–176

Portale 2011: Portale, Elisa C., L'immagine di Agatocle e l'arte dell'età di Agatocle, Archivio Storico Siracusano 46, 2011, 269–232

Rice 1983: Rice, Ellen E. The Grand Procession of Ptolemy Philadelphus, Oxford 1983

Ritter 1965: Ritter, Hans-Werner, Diadem und Königsherrschaft. Untersuchungen zu Zeremonien und Rechtsgrundlagen des Herrschaftsantritts bei den Persern, bei Alexander dem Großen und im Hellenismus, Munich 1965

Sachs – Wiseman 1954: Sachs, Abraham – Wiseman, Donald J., A Babylonian King List of the Hellenistic Period, Iraq 16, 1954, 202–211

Samuel 1962: Samuel, Alan E., Ptolemaic Chronology, Munich 1962

Sauneron 1952: Sauneron, Serge, Le Dégagement du Temple d'Esné: Mur Nord, Annales du Service des Antiquités de l'Égypte 52, 1952, 29–39

Schäfer 1974: Schäfer, Gerd, König der Könige – Lied der Lieder. Studien zum Paronomastischen Intensitätsgenitiv, Heidelberg 1974

Schaudig 2001: Schaudig, Hanspeter, Die Inschriften Nabonids von Babylon und Kyros' des Großen, Münster 2001

Schieder 1984: Schieder, Theodor, Über den Beinamen "der Große". Reflexionen über historische Größe, Opladen 1984

Sciandra 2008: Sciandra, Roberto, Il 'Re dei Re' e il 'Satrapo dei Satrapi': note sulla succession tra Mitradate II e Gotarze I a Babilonia (ca. 94–80 a. e. v.), Studi Ellenistici 20, Pisa 2008, 471–488

Scullard 1974: Scullard, Howard H., The Elephant in the Greek and Roman World, London 1974

Shear 1973: Shear, Theodore L. Jnr., The Athenian Agora: Excavations of 1971, Hesperia 42, 1973, 121–179

Sherwin-White 1991: Sherwin-White, Susan, Aspects of Seleucid Royal Ideology: The Cylinder of Antiochus I from Borsippa, Journal of Hellenic Studies 111, 1991, 71–86

Smith 1988: Smith, Roland R. R., Hellenistic Royal Portraits, Oxford 1988

Spranger 1958: Spranger, Peter P., Der Große: Untersuchungen zur Entstehung des historischen Beinamens in der Antike, Saeculum 9, 1958, 22–58

Stevens 2014: Stevens, Kathryn, The Antiochus Cylinder, Babylonian Scholarship and Seleucid Imperial Ideology, Journal of Hellenic Studies 134, 2014, 66–88

Stewart 1993: Stewart, Andrew, Faces of Power: Alexander's Image and Hellenistic Politics, Berkeley 1993

Stone 1978: Stone, Laura M., The Obscene Use of ΜΕΓΑΣ in Aristophanes, American Journal of Philology 99, 1978, 427–432

Strootman 2010: Strootman, Rolf, Queen of Kings: Cleopatra VII and the Donations of Alexandria, in: M. Facella – T. Kaizer (eds.), Kingdoms and Principalities in the Roman Near East, Stuttgart 2010, 140–157

Strootman 2013: Strootman, Rolf, Babylonian, Macedonian, King of the World: The Antiochos Cylinder from Borsippa and Seleukid Imperial Integration, in: E. Stavrianopoulou (ed.), Shifting Social Imaginaries in the Hellenistic Period: Narrations, Practices, and Images, Leiden 2013, 67–97

Strootman 2014a: Strootman, Rolf, 'Men to Whose Rapacity Neither Sea nor Mountains Set a Limit': The Aims of the Diadochs, in: H. Hauben – A. Meeus (eds.), The Age of the Successors and the Creation of the Hellenistic Kingdoms (323–276 B. C.), Leuven 2014a, 307–322

Strootman 2014b: Strootman, Rolf, Hellenistic Imperialism and the Idea of World Unity, in: C. Rapp – H. A. Drake (eds.), The City in the Classical and Post-Classical World: Changing Contexts of Power and Identity, Cambridge 2014b, 38–61

Strootman 2017: Strootman, Rolf, Imperial Persianism: Seleukids, Arsakids and Fratarakā, in: id. – M. J. Versluys (eds.), Persianism in Antiquity, Stuttgart 2017, 177–200

Strootman 2020: Strootman, Rolf, The Great Kings of Asia: Universalistic Titulature in the Seleukid and post-Seleukid East, in: R. Oetjen – F. X. Ryan (eds.), Seleukeia: Studies in Seleucid History. Archaeology and Numismatics in Honor of Getzel M. Cohen, Berlin 2020, 123–157

Svenson 1995: Svenson, Dominique, Darstellungen hellenistischer Könige mit Götterattributen, Bern 1995

Toynbee 1973: Toynbee, Jocelyn, Animals in Roman Life and Art, London 1973

Tuplin 2009: Tuplin, Christopher, The Gadatas Letter, in: L. Mitchell – L. Rubinstein (eds.), Greek History and Epigraphy: Essays in Honour of P. J. Rhodes, Swansea 2009, 155–184

van Oppen de Ruiter 2019: van Oppen de Ruiter, Branko, Monsters of Military Might: Elephants in Hellenistic History and Art, Arts 8/4, 2019, article no. 160, 1–37

Versnel 1998: Versnel, Henk, Inconsistencies in Greek and Roman Religion I: Ter Unus. Isis, Dionysos, Hermes. Three Studies in Henotheism, Leiden 1998

Virgilio 2011: Virgilio, Biagio, Le Roi Écrit. Le Correspondance du Souverain hellénistique, suivie de Deux Lettres d'Antiochos III à Partir de Louis Robert et d'Adolf Wilhelm, Pisa 2011

Waal 2019: Waal, Willemijn, 'My Brother, a Great King, my Peer'. Evidence for a Mycenaean Kingdom from Hittite Texts, in: Kelder – Waal 2019, 9–29

Walbank 1957/1967: Walbank, Frank, A Historical Commentary on Polybius I–II, Oxford 1957/1967

Wallace 2017: Wallace, Shane, Court, Kingship, and Royal Style in the Early Hellenistic Period, in: id. – A. Erskine – L. Llewellyn-Jones (eds.), The Hellenistic Court. Monarchic Power and Elite Society from Alexander to Cleopatra, Swansea 2017, 1–30

Weber 1993: Weber, Gregor, Dichtung und höfische Gesellschaft. Die Rezeption von Zeitgeschichte am Hof der ersten drei Ptolemäer, Stuttgart 1993

Wheatley – Dunn 2020: Wheatley, Pat – Dunn, Charlotte, Demetrius the Besieger, Oxford 2020

Wiesehöfer 1987: Wiesehöfer, Josef, Zur Frage der Echtheit des Dareios-Briefes an Gadatas, Rheinisches Museum 130, 1987, 396–398

Wiesehöfer 1996: Wiesehöfer, Josef, 'King of Kings' and 'Philhellen': Kingship in Arsacid Iran, in: P. Bilde et al. (eds.), Aspects of Hellenistic Kingship, Aarhus 1996, 55–66

Wilhelm 1937: Wilhelm, Adolf, Ein Gedicht zu Ehren der Könige Antigonos und Demetrios (IG II/III 3424), Ἀρχαιολογικὴ Ἐφημερίς 1937, 203–207

Wilhelm 1943: Wilhelm, Adolf, Beschluss zu Ehren des Demetrios ὁ μέγας, Jahreshefte des österreichischen archäologischen Instituts in Wien 35, 1943, 157–63

Worthington 2016: Worthington, Ian, Ptolemy I. King and Pharaoh of Egypt, Oxford 2016

Wright 2015: Wright III, Benjamin. G., The Letter of Aristeas. 'Aristeas to Philocrates' or 'On the Translation of the Law of the Jews', Berlin 2015

Zervos 1967: Zervos, Orestes H., The Early Tetradrachms of Ptolemy I, American Numismatic Society Museum Notes 13, 1967, 1–16

Figures

Fig. 1: Classical Numismatic Group, Electronic Auction 314, 6.11. 2013, Nr. 184 (27mm).

Fig. 2: Classical Numismatic Group, Mail Bid Sale 84, 5.5.2010, Nr. 751 (17mm).

Fig. 3: Cabinet des Médailles, Paris (http://ark.bnf.fr/ark:/12148/cb41759042z) last access: 20.5.2024.

Shane Wallace is Walsh Family Assistant Professor in Classics and Ancient History at Trinity College Dublin. He has edited the books *The Hellenistic Court* (2017) and the forthcoming volume *The Antigonid Empire in Greece*, to be published in 2024.

It's All Greek to Me
*Ethnicity, Culture, and Hellenistic Kingship**

CHRISTOPH MICHELS

Abstract: This chapter has its starting point in the unique testimony of the so-called Borsippa Cylinder. At first glance, it documents how the Seleukid Antiochos I inscribed himself into a local, Babylonian tradition through his patronage of a local temple. Even though long-established elements dominate the text, scholars have, however, recently emphasised the innovative way in which the imperial power dealt with these traditions. Remarkably, Antiochos also describes himself as the son of the Macedonian Seleukos. This explicit reference to the ethnic background of the ruler's family disrupts the local context of communication and points to the centre of the empire. The following reflections concentrate on the interpretation of the ethnikon in this text and on what can and what should not be derived from it concerning the character of the Seleukid realm and the view of its rulers on their old homeland. Furthermore, it explores the context in which this element should be embedded (Achaimenid tradition or "Hellenistic" practices?). The Seleukid emphasises his Macedonian, not Greek, roots and yet the promotion of Greek cultural elements has often been seen as the very core of the Macedonian empires with their Graeco-Macedonian elites. The paper explores possible concepts associated with Macedonian ethnicity like the conquest of Asia but also proximity to the Greek world and the patronage of art, science, literature, and poetry at their court. Like other royal activities, the promotion of Greek cultural elements can be seen as a forum for competition with other dynasties. Monarchic patronage and the development of a common elite culture have frequently been combined with distinctly different phenomena of representation such as euergetism and dedications in sanctuaries and have been subsumed under the label of cultural policy. However, since this presupposes a separate social sphere of "culture" in antiquity, it is advisable to disentangle these rather distinct aspects of monarchic representation.

*   I am grateful to Achim Lichtenberger and Hans Beck for reading the manuscript and discussing with me various important aspects; I also thank the anonymous peer reviewer for valuable remarks.

1. Introduction

Scholars have rightly emphasised the universalistic pretensions of the Hellenistic kings and the personal nature of their rule.[1] Their claim to power, however, had to be enforced and legitimised on the ground under the most diverse conditions – be it in conversation with the priesthoods of Egypt and Babylonia or with the Greek poleis.[2] Especially in the case of the Seleukids as masters of a multi-ethnic empire, one might summarize with Anagnostou-Laoutides that, 'in terms of their practices' they 'were primarily "kings" and secondarily "Macedonians".'[3] A prime example of the need to accommodate the local expectations seemed to be the so-called Antiochos or Borsippa Cylinder from the eponymous city, located about seventeen kilometres southwest of Babylon.[4] The cuneiform inscription of the clay cylinder is a foundation text dating to 27 March 268 BC which records Antiochos I's reconstruction of the temple of Nabû, the main deity at Borsippa. The text was discovered in the ruins of this temple called Ezida. Being the sole surviving example of a Seleukid royal inscription in cuneiform the text gives us a unique snapshot of the Seleukid patronage in Babylonia and – on a more general level – of the local interaction between king and non-Greek city.[5]

> [i] Antiochos, the great king, | the mighty king, king of the world, king of Babylon, king of (all) countries, | caretaker of Esagila and Ezida, | foremost son of Seleukos, the king, |[5] the Macedonian, king of Babylon, | am I. When I desired to build | Esagila and Ezida, | the (first) bricks | of Esagila and Ezida |[10] in the land of Hatti with my pure hand(s) | I moulded with fine quality oil and | for the laying of the foundation of Esagila | and Ezida I transported them. In the month of Addaru, on the 20th day, | of year 43, I laid the foundation of Ezida, |[15] the true temple, the temple of Nabû, which is in Borsippa. | O Nabû, lofty son, | the wise one of the gods, the proud one, | who is eminently worthy of praise, | firstborn son |[20] of Marduk, offspring of Erûa | the queen, who creates offspring, | regard

---

1   Bickerman 1938, 11: 'Le royauté des Séleucides n'est ni nationale ni territoriale. Conformément aux conceptions grecques, elle est personnelle'; cf. Mehl 1986, 37; Virgilio ²2003, 131–132; Wiemer 2017, 329; but cf. Kosmin 2014b.

2   Mehl 1999, 32–37, 40; Ma 2003. On the comparison between Babylonia and Egypt see now Pfeiffer – Klinkott 2021. Concerning Alexander, the theme of legitimation is now treated in Trampedach – Meeus 2020.

3   Anagnostou-Laoutides 2017, 174.

4   Weissbach 1911, 132–135; BM 36277; ANET³ 317; Austin ²2006, no. 166; van der Spek – Stol 2020; Stevens 2014. On this interpretation of the cylinder cf., e. g., Virgilio ²2003, 184.

5   Visscher 2020, 88. Because the cylinder was deposited as a foundation document in the ziggurat and was therefore withdrawn from the public, it has been questioned whether we can at all interpret it as a source for monarchical representation; cf. Mehl 2022, 194–195. But since the inscription of the cylinder was probably read aloud (Visscher 2020, 83) when it was deposited (but see Mehl 2022, 195) and because it apparently was part of a ritual, the Borsippa Cylinder can be compared to royal letters in Greek in its significance as 'performative utterance' of the king; on differences between the two text forms cf. Kosmin 2014a, 193.

me joyfully and, | at your lofty command | which is unchanging, |[25] may the overthrow of the country of my enemy, | the achievement of my triumphs, | the predominance over the enemy through victory, | kingship of justice, a reign | of prosperity, years of happiness, |[30] (and) the full enjoyment of very old age be the gift | [ii] for the kingship of Antiochos | and king Seleukos, his son, | forever. O Son of the Prince (Marduk), | Nabû, son of Esagila, |[ii.5] first-born son of Marduk, | offspring of queen Erûa: | at your entry into Ezida, the true house, | the house of your Anu-ship, the dwelling of your heart's desire, | with rejoicing and jubilation, |[ii.10] may – at your true command, | which cannot be annulled – my days be long, | my years many, | may my throne be secure, my reign long-lasting, | on your sublime writing board |[ii.15] which sets the boundary of heaven and earth. | May my good (fate) constantly be established in your pure mouth, | may my hands conquer the countries from sunrise | to sunset | that I might inventory their tribute |[ii.20] and bring it to make perfect Esagila | and Ezida. O Nabû, | foremost son, when you enter Ezida, | the true house, | may good (fate) for Antiochos, king of (all) countries, |[ii.25] king Seleukos, his son, | (and) Stratonike, | his consort, the queen, | may their good (fate), | be established by your command (lit.: in/by your mouth).

The document illustrates how Antiochos I inscribed himself into a local tradition by styling himself a pious ruler of Babylonia, and insofar presents us Antiochos' 'Babylonian voice'.[6] Unlike the bilingual stelae of the Ptolemaic/Egyptian priests, the text is exclusively written in an archaizing Akkadian script.[7] Antiochos calls himself caretaker of Esagila, the temple of Marduk, centre of the Babylonian state cult, and of the temple Ezida.[8] Long established elements are prominent. That the king moulds the bricks for the building of the temple with his own ritually purified hands is certainly a powerful image.[9] Recent studies have, however, emphasised the innovative way in which the imperial power dealt with the indigenous traditions.[10] These unusual features include among others the prominent role of Queen Stratonike, the non-Babylonian setting for the brick-making ritual in Hatti (that is Northern Syria), and the fact that Antiochos does not present his actions as based on the wish of the gods, but attributes them to his own will thus reflecting the language of Hellenistic euergetism.[11]

---

6   Ma 2003, 180.
7   Stevens 2014, 71–72; Haubold 2013, 9, 141.
8   Cf. Pfeiffer – Klinkott 2021, 249–250. Haubold 2013, 139.
9   Pfeiffer – Klinkott 2021, 251. This conservatism manifests itself not least in the traditional medium of the inscription, cf. Plischke 2014, 203–204.
10   Strootman 2013, 68 pointed out the 'entanglement of the global and the local in an imperial context'. Stevens 2014, 86: 'The combination, with all its tensions and disjunctions, is Hellenistic.' Admittedly, 'Hellenistic' does not describe anything concrete. Kuhrt – Sherwin-White 1991, 83 had stressed that despite some non-Babylonian features the 'royal ideology expressed in the text is a totally Babylonian one'.
11   Haubold 2013, 139; Strootman 2013; Stevens 2014; Kosmin 2014b, 192–193; Beaulieu 2014, 25–27; Widmer 2019; Visscher 2020, 87–90. McAuley 2022 stresses the fact that not the whole family of

In the following, however, I will focus on another remarkable element that can be found in the introduction of the text. In his titulary, Antiochos combines Akkadian epithets used by Persian, Assyrian and Babylonian rulers.[12] He is 'Antiochos, the great king, the mighty king, king of the world, king of Babylon, king of (all) countries'. But he also describes himself as 'foremost son of Seleukos, the king, the Macedonian, king of Babylon'. The ethnic label Makkadunāya, 'Macedonian', probably does not refer to Antiochos himself but to his father Seleukos.[13] Nevertheless, this explicit reference to the ethnic background of the ruler's family, an element with no Babylonian tradition, in a way disrupts the local context of communication, and points outwards – to the centre of the empire. Its interpretation will serve as a starting point and anchor for the following reflections on the significance of Macedonian ethnicity as element of monarchical representation and its connection to the promotion of elements of Greek culture, often subsumed under the heading "cultural policy". I aim to contextualize these phenomena through a comparison with the other dynasties and to point out similarities and differences which are inclined to shed light on the underlying mechanisms.

This is all the more necessary since the appearance of the ethnic label Macedonian in the Borsippa Cylinder has been interpreted very differently over the past decades with regard to its meaning as well as its relevance considering that it is only mentioned once in the singular text.[14] Amélie Kuhrt and Susan Sherwin-White saw the gentilic, in fact, not as an innovative element at all but rather in line with the 'genealogical self-definitions used by the Persian emperors in their royal inscriptions'.[15] To give only one example of what is meant: in an inscription from Susa, Dareios refers to himself as 'great king, king of kings, king of countries, king on this great earth far and wide, son of Hystaspes, an Achaemenid, a Persian, son of a Persian, an Aryan, of Aryan lineage'.[16] Pierre Briant has, however, rightly pointed out the profound differences in concepts of empire and 'ethno-classe dominante' that are typical for the Achaimenid inscriptions which refer to 'la place de la Perse (et des Perses) dans l'Empire, et, d'autre part et en même temps, à la conception des liens qui les unissaient au berceau du pouvoir perse

---

the king but only Antiochos, his son Seleukos, and his wife Stratonike, the 'ruling triad', are mentioned in the text – which should also be seen as a reflection of "official" ideology.

12   Boiy 2002, 248; Stevens 2014, 75; cf. also Mehl 2022 who sees these elements not as titles but as attributtions.

13   Weissbach 1911, 133; Kosmin 2014. Cf. Kuhrt – Sherwin-White 1991, 83; Briant, 1994, 459–460, and Ma 2003, 189 who linked it to Antiochos I. Ultimately, one cannot rule out the possibility that something got mixed up here by the non-Greek scribe. In Greek inscriptions, the ethnikon also appears after the filiation (cf., e.g., IG XI.4 1111: [β]ασιλέα [Μέγαν] Ἀντίοχο[ν] βασιλέως Σελεύκ[ου] [Κ]αλλινίκου Μακεδόνα). The concluding 'king of Babylon', however, obviously refers to Seleukos, since Antiochos has already been identified as such.

14   Cf., e.g., Erickson 2011, 56 who stresses that the single reference rather shows the receptiveness towards local traditions.

15   Sherwin-White – Kuhrt 1991, 83; followed inter alia by Barbantani 2014, 35; Visscher 2020, 85.

16   Kuhrt 2007, 11.12 (Kent DSe).

et achéménide (le Fars)'.[17] Briant rather stressed the contemporary use of the ethnikon Μακεδών by the Diadochi and their dynasties.

This has been well studied with regard to the Ptolemies and among them especially for Ptolemaios I.[18] Pausanias underlines in two passages that Ptolemaios – at a time when he had not yet assumed the title king – explicitly referred to himself as a Macedonian.[19] The first case is a dedication in Olympia, probably dating to around 308 BC, the second case concerns a victory in a chariot race during the 69th Pythian Games in Delphi dated 314/310 BC.[20] On one level, this can be explained by the context and the participation in Panhellenic Games from which non-Greeks were excluded.[21] Beyond that, however, Ptolemaios seems to have set himself up as the "true" successor to Alexander.[22] On his way to continental Greece, he visited Delos in 308 BC. In the Artemision, he offered a therikleios kylix and an ivy crown to Aphrodite dedicating it as 'Ptolemaios, son of Lagos, Macedonian'.[23] Even if his efforts eventually came to nothing, Ptolemaios apparently used the dedications and his Macedonian ethnicity at these important religious centres as part of his bid for Alexander's empire.

Somewhat in line with Pausanias, who stresses that the Ptolemies respectively 'the kings of Egypt liked to be called Macedonians' (ἔχαιρον γὰρ δὴ Μακεδόνες οἱ ἐν Αἰγύπτῳ καλούμενοι βασιλεῖς),[24] modern scholars have used the ethnic to evaluate how

---

17   Briant 1994, 461. The differences were already stressed by Bickerman 1966, 97. On the ethno-linguistic marking of rulership which is specific for the Achaimenids cf. also Rollinger 2017, 201–202.

18   Bearzot 1992 who also discusses possible references to Ptolemaios' Macedonicity in his history of Alexander.

19   Paus. 6.3.1: Δαμίσκου δὲ ἐγγύτατα ἕστηκεν ἀνὴρ ὅστις δή, τὸ γὰρ ὄνομα οὐ λέγουσιν ἐπ' αὐτῷ, Πτολεμαίου δὲ ἀνάθημά ἐστι τοῦ Λάγου· Μακεδόνα δὲ αὐτὸν ὁ Πτολεμαῖος ἐν τῷ ἐπιγράμματι ἐκάλεσε, βασιλεύων ὅμως Αἰγύπτου. Paus. 10.7.8: διαλιπόντες δὲ ἀπὸ ταύτης μίαν κέλητι ἔθεσαν δρόμον πώλῳ, ἐνάτῃ δὲ ἐπὶ ταῖς ἑξήκοντα συνωρίδι πωλικῇ, καὶ ἐπὶ μὲν τῷ πώλῳ τῷ κέλητι Λυκόρμας ἀνηγορεύθη Λαρισαῖος, Πτολεμαῖος δὲ ἐπὶ τῇ συνωρίδι Μακεδών· ἔχαιρον γὰρ δὴ Μακεδόνες οἱ ἐν Αἰγύπτῳ καλούμενοι βασιλεῖς, καθάπερ γε ἦσαν. Bearzot 1992, 39 erroneously speaks of two dedications. This is not unimportant as contrary to the dedication in Olympia (where Pausanias mentions the inscription), in the Delphian case, it is actually not clear (although not unlikely) that Ptolemaios identified himself as Macedonian on that occasion or whether Pausanias (or his source) adds this information on his own account.

20   Bringmann – von Steuben 1995, KNr. 57 [L]. The dedication is often seen in context of Ptolemaios' Peloponnesian activities, but if we take Paus. 6.3.1 who mentions Ptolemaios being king verbatim, the dedication would date after 306 BC. Contrary to Howe 2018, 174 n. 116 it was not a dedication by the Eleans but by Ptolemaios himself. Van Bremen 2007, 363 stresses that the statue which Pausanias mentions did not depict Ptolemaios himself, and that the periegetes does not mention a victory at the Olympic games. A chariot victory of Ptolemaios I at Olympia is however documented by Poseidipp. ep. 78 and 88. Lagos, a son of Ptolemaios I, won at the Lykaia in 308/7 BC (Syll.³ no. 314V).

21   Fantuzzi 2005, 251–252.

22   Hauben 2014, 259; Howe 2018, 174–175.

23   Tréheux 1992, 15, s. v. Πτολεμαῖος Λάγου Μακεδών, for later activities as king see s. v. Πτολεμαῖος βασιλεὺς Σωτήρ. Cf. also a dedication of Ptolemaios, son of Lagos, Macedonian (from 334?) in Miletos; Bringmann – von Steuben 1995, KNr. 273.

24   Paus. 10.7.8.

these kings perceived themselves.[25] However, since we cannot gain insight into their minds, it seems more fruitful to ask how they presented themselves.[26] Of course, due to the lack of sources, we do not have a complete picture, and it is therefore difficult to judge whether one dynasty laid more emphasis on this element than another house in the same way as it is possible to say that the Ptolemies apparently valued agonistic victories much more than the Seleukids.[27] It is rather the question to what extent similarities but also differences in the use of ethnicity can be identified. That there were differences is illustrated by two observations. Firstly, from Ptolemaic Egypt where a foreign rule which has been oftentimes explicitly compared to the situation that existed in Babylonia, no reference to the Macedonian descent of the Ptolemies in a similar communicative context (king – indigenous elites) has survived as far as I know.[28] At most, and apart from the Greek inscriptions of the bilingual stelae, there are indications of the ruler's foreignness in the iconography – for example, in the relief on the trilingual stele of the Raphia Decree which depicts Ptolemaios IV as a Macedonian cavalryman with a spear on horseback, alien to pharaonic art.[29] Secondly, the Macedonian ethnikon was apparently given as an honorary title in the Ptolemaic Empire, whereas this is not attested for the Seleukids.[30] The "character" of the large Hellenistic empires and the question of their "herrschende Gesellschaft" cannot be separated from these questions, but I will only touch upon them.[31]

Of fundamental importance in this context is the relationship between Macedonicity and Hellenicity respectively between the Macedonian kings and the Greeks. In his treatment of the Borsippa Cylinder, Rolf Strootman notes in passing that 'with his Macedonian identity Antiochos distances himself from the Greeks as well'.[32] This interpretation seems not to be supported by the available evidence.[33] On the contrary, rather

---

25   Cf., e.g., Hannestad 2020a, 110 who takes the Borsippa Cylinder as testimony that Seleukos saw himself as a Macedonian. Cf. also generally Brüggemann 2022, 337.
26   Although the comments on the Macedonicity of the kings in Mari 2020, 213–215 are not very fruitful overall, she is certainly right that the use of the ethnikon should be seen as an element of self-representation or, in her words, should be interpreted "ideologically".
27   Cf. Fantuzzi 2005, 251. On the agones cf. Kainz 2016; Mann 2018.
28   Pfeiffer 2018, 4.
29   Laubscher 1991, 226–227. The comparison is also made by Ma 2003, 189 who sees a 'rupture of ethnically determined visual discourse'. On depictions of the victorious Ptolemaic king in pharaonic tradition and on the way the Egyptian priests constructed divine descent for the Ptolemies see the paper by Stefan Pfeiffer in this volume. Too little is known of the context of depictions of the Ptolemaic ruler with kausia in seal impressions as well as in kameos, cf. Janssen 2007, 51–54, to say more on the target audience. A portrait head from the Faijum shows a king with a kausia entwined by a diadem. Attached to this is a uraeus snake above the forehead. This again illustrates the Janus-headed nature of Ptolemaic rule.
30   Brüggemann 2022, 388.
31   Habicht 1958; cf. Mehl 2003 with a critique of the concept.
32   Strootman 2013, 88 n. 67.
33   Anson ²2015, 241–261, e.g., argues against the common notion that Eumenes of Kardia eventually failed because of ethnic prejudices of the Macedonian Diadochi.

the opposite seems to have been the case and it is therefore a potential level of meaning of the ethnic in this text.[34]

The relationship between Macedonians and Greeks is notoriously disputed and a topic too vast to cover in more detail in this context.[35] Suffice it to say then that from a modern perspective it is already problematic to ask whether the Macedonians really were Greeks in antiquity, because the definitional basis of Greekness shifted profoundly over time.[36] Concerning the perspective of the ancient Greek sources, the development from Classical to Imperial times is palpable. While differences certainly were perceived and could be stressed in times of conflict (Demosthenes being the prime example), the latent Macedonian and Greek antagonism was eventually (increasingly so since the second century BC) overshadowed by a sense of cultural unity of Macedonia and the Greek world.[37] It is, however, clearly an etic perspective when primarily Jewish authors speaking of the Seleukid empire call it the 'Kingdom of the Greeks',[38] and to equate 'Greek' and 'Macedonian' rule is at least problematic.[39]

It is one thing, however, how the Greeks perceived their relationship to the Macedonians. An entirely different question is how the Macedonian kings used their ethnicity when interacting with the Greek world. In the documented instances in which kings of the Antigonid, Seleukid and Ptolemaic dynasties explicitly used their ethnika in Greek inscriptions, it is not to alienate the Greeks but rather to stress or rather construct common ground often in competition with similar claims of other dynasties. Correspondingly, it is of course also of interest when Greek poleis, leagues or single individuals saw it fit to mention the ethnikon of the kings when honouring them. For the Greeks, such wording had in a way already a tradition as is illustrated by a proxeny decree for Antigonos Monophthalmos from 334 (that is long before he became king), in which he is identified as Antigonos, son of Philip, Macedonian.[40] But is the Makkadunāya of the cylinder even meant in an ethnic sense?

---

34   Rather too strong in this regard is Ma 2003, 191, however, who sees here an 'openly asserted Greekness of the kings'.
35   Cf. the overview by Hatzopoulos 2020, 49–124. For the spectrum of opinion concerning the question whether the Macedonians were "Greeks" see only on the one hand Badian 1982; Borza 1996; Engels 2010 and on the other hand Hatzopoulos 2011; cf. Anson ²2015, 213–240. Mari 2020, 198 unconvincingly argues that the main reason for Greek authors to doubt Macedonian Hellenicity was the institution of monarchy.
36   Hall 2001; cf. Hatzopoulos 2020, 123–124.
37   Adams 1995.
38   Cf. 1 Makk 1.1; 1.10; 6.2; 8.18; Edson 1958, 165.
39   Cf., e. g., Sherwin-White 1987 who equals Seleukid rule with 'Greek rule' in Babylonia while Hammond 1993 insists on the 'Macedonian imprint' of the large kingdoms on the Hellenistic world.
40   I.Priene B – M 15, l. 5. (= HGIÜ 261). It is therefore problematic when Tracy – Habicht 1991, 221 state: 'The Ptolemaic kings, as well as the Seleucids and the Antigonids, were accustomed to add the ethnic their names as a means of pointing to their glorious origin. They were followed in this practice by their subordinates.' Cf. Mari 2020, 213–215 on evidence for the importance of Macedonicity for the Macedonian kings prior to Alexander.

2. Seleukos, Macedonian king?

It is important to underline that we are dealing with Antiochos' Macedonian origin
on an ethnic level, because Kathryn Stevens has argued some years ago (similar to the
argumentation of Kuhrt and Sherwin-White) that the text does not actually refer to
Seleukos' ethnicity, but that 'Macedonian' rather qualifies the preceding word 'king'
and is supposed to convey that Seleukos had 'royal status beyond the Babylonian context'.[41] However, this hardly seems plausible. Apart from the linguistic problems of this
interpretation,[42] king of the Macedonians, βασιλεὺς Μακεδόνων, was probably not a
title that Seleukos I ever took. To rule over the Macedonian heartland had, of course,
been his ambition after the triumph over Lysimachos in 281 BC. But these plans had
found a sudden end when Seleukos was murdered on his way to Macedonia by Ptolemaios Keraunos. I do not see how this failed attempt at conquest could have been
transformed into a positive characteristic of Seleukos in the Borsippa Cylinder roughly
a decade later. The view of some modern scholars that Seleukos had already been proclaimed king of Macedonia by his soldiers directly after the victory is not supported
by the extant sources.[43] When the local historian Memnon of Herakleia applies the
highly unsusual title 'ruler of Asia and the Macedonians' (τῆς Ἀσίας βασιλεύοντος καὶ
τοῦ Μακεδόνων) to Seleukos – in a passage concerned with the politics and victories
of the Bithynian king Zipoites – this rather reflects the later perception of this author
and not the actual self-description of the first Seleukid.[44]

---

41   Stevens 2014, 76–77; 2022, 119; Hannestad 2021b, 257. Cf. also Boiy 2002, 248.
42   Stevens 2014, 76. I am grateful to Kristin Kleber for pointing out to me that traditionally gentilizia
      after 'king' are extremely rare and that rather place/country names come after 'king'.
43   Lehmann 1905 believed that Seleukos was acclaimed king of Macedonia by his soldiers after his
      victory over Lysimachos, and he took the Borsippa Cylinder as evidence for this title; against this
      see however already Reuss 1907, 595–600 but again Lehmann-Haupt 1907 and 1909 and on this
      Reuss 1909. Cf. Stähelin 1921, 1226. Again considered by Musti 1966, 90; but see Heinen 1972, 46–
      50. Segre 1930, 500 thought the text showed that Antiochos 'riconosceva diritti sulla Macedonia a
      suo padre, non a sè stesso'. Why should he do that in an inscription directed at his own subjects
      and just after having called himself 'king of the world'? Pol. 18.51.4 stresses that Seleukos had a
      claim to Lysimachos' kingdom by right of conquest. Stevens 2014, 76 n. 52 believes that there is
      'no reason why a Babylonian redactor could not have coined such an expression independently'.
      If we assumed such freedom of formulation, then the value of the cylinder's information for the
      representation of the Seleukids would be very limited indeed.
44   Memnon BNJ 434 F 1 12.5: οὐ παῖς τῆς ἀρχῆς διάδοχος Ζιποίτης, λαμπρὸς ἐν πολέμοις γεγονώς,
      καὶ τοὺς Λυσιμάχου στρατηγοὺς τὸν μὲν ἀνελών, τὸν δὲ ἐπὶ μήκιστον τῆς οἰκείας ἀπελάσας ἀρχῆς,
      ἀλλὰ καὶ αὐτοῦ Λυσιμάχου, εἶτα καὶ Ἀντιόχου τοῦ παιδὸς Σελεύκου ἐπικρατέστερος γεγονώς, τοῦ
      τε τῆς Ἀσίας βασιλεύοντος καὶ τοῦ Μακεδόνων, κτίζει πόλιν ὑπὸ τῶι Λυπερῶι (?) ὄρει τῆι αὐτοῦ
      κλήσει ἐπώνυμον. ('His son and successor in the rule, Zipoites, became illustrious in war and of the
      generals of Lysimachos killed one and drove the other as far as possible from his own realm. But
      after he had also gained the upper hand over Lysimachos himself and then over Antiochos, son of
      Seleukos, ruler of Asia and the Macedonians, he founded a city named after himself at the foot of
      Mount Luperos.'); Brüggemann 2022, 340; Keaveney – Madden 2011 ad loc. do not comment on
      this title given to Seleukos (or Antiochos?; cf. Heinemann 2010, 227 who thinks that the conflict

Among the Diadochi, the appellation 'king of the Macedonians' was only used by Kassandros.[45] After him, it is attested exclusively for the Antigonids (or, more specifically, for Philip V) who actually ruled over the traditional land Macedonia.[46] But even they never put this title on coins. The title 'king of the Macedonians/of Macedon' therefore did not signify royal status as such in a way that could be compared to a title like 'the mighty king' or 'king of the world' or be an equivalent to the Achaimenid 'king of Anshan', titles used by Kyros II in the "Cyrus cylinder".[47] In the case of Seleukos and Antiochos, it could not, therefore, 'confer extra legitimacy upon him and his son'.[48] 'Macedonian' is thus not part of Seleukos' 'royal title' in a strict sense.[49]

3. Macedonicity and conquest

Why then was Seleukos' "Macedonicity" mentioned? André Aymard believed that Antiochos intended to underline that his father had been one of the companions of Alexander.[50] This goes in a direction that was already advocated by William Tarn not regarding the Borsippa Cylinder but the cases of qualifications of kings as Macedonians in Greek inscriptions. Tarn thought that the kings adopted the title Μακεδών as 'a mark of distinction by those kings who reigned over Orientals; and the desire to distinguish himself from the Asiatic must be the reason of its so frequent use by the private Macedonian'.[51] This is certainly too sweeping a statement. In view of the pride of individual Macedonians as well as Macedonian colonies of their heritage on the one hand and the ethnic conflicts that are attested in the sources on the other hand, it would, however, also be rash to brush it aside, and I will come back to this point.[52]

---

therefore can be dated in the time between 281 and 279, when Antigonos Gonatas became king). In Diod. 19.55.3 (reporting the events 315/314), Seleukos questions the authority of Antigonos over him by pointing out that he has received his position by the Macedonians for his achievements under Alexander (I thank the anonymous peer reviewer for the reference), but even if this claim were authentic, it does not follow that the (later) title is correct. On the interpretation of this passage see Meeus 2022 ad loc.

45   Aymard 1950, 119–120; Errington 1974, 23, who, however, stresses that it was used 'purely for internal political reasons and was clearly intended for purely internal consumption' but see Bringmann – von Steuben 1995, KNr. 113. Gruen 1985, 259 is wrong in stating that the title "king of the Macedonians" also appears on Kassander's bronze coins.

46   Cf. Aymard 1950 and Errington 1974.

47   Kuhrt 2007, 3.21, ll. 20–21.

48   Cited after Stevens 2014, 77.

49   Pace Hannestad 2020b, 257 and already Tarn 1909, 269. As ethnicity is never mentioned on coins, Muccioli 2013 rightly does not treat it in the context of his comprehensive study on the epithets of the Hellenistic kings.

50   Aymard 1950, 104. A connection to Alexander as legitimation is implied for example in Diod. 19.55.3.

51   Tarn 1909, 269.

52   Billows 1995, 28–29, 172. Cf. below p. 269–275.

That Macedonian ethnicity or Macedonia as such could in fact be linked to the notion of conquest and more specifically could serve as symbol for the conquest of 'Asia' may perhaps be drawn from an entirely different kind of source, a scene (fig. 1) of a wall painting from the villa of P. Fannius Synistor in Boscoreale.[53] The famous scene belongs to a picture frieze that is probably a copy of a 3rd century original from a royal court.[54] It most likely shows the personification of Makedonia sitting on a rock, identified by the kausia she wears and a Macedonian shield next to her, and Asia, wearing an oriental headdress seated below Makedonia, on opposite sides of the Hellespont.[55] Makedonia's spear is stretched across the water and planted in the territory of Asia. As Smith has argued, this is a vivid depiction of the concept of spear-won land.[56] In my opinion, it also shows the association of Macedonia as such and conquest possibly also manifested in the frequent use of the Macedonian shield on the coins of Seleukid colonies.[57] In the fresco, the conquest acquires another level through the philosopher who watches the scene from the panel to the left of Makedonia – apparently approvingly. His presence probably refers to Greek sentiments of Hellenic and (to a somewhat lesser degree)[58] Macedonian superiority over the barbarians prevalent in Isokrates and Aristoteles.[59] Even in conquest there are thus hints at the cultural dimension of Macedonian ethnicity linking it to the Greeks.

While the connotation with conquest may thus indeed have been an aspect of Seleukos' Macedonicity, it was probably not the purpose of the ethnic to convey that Antiochos belonged to a Macedonian 'Herrenvolk' and thus to deliberately antagonize the Babylonians.[60] Although recent scholarship has warned not to paint an all too rosy picture of the situation of Babylonia under the Seleukids, in the concrete text

---

53   Cf. Fittschen 1975; Smith 1994 with bibliography.
54   Smith 1994, 125; Fittschen 1975, 99 opts for late 3rd/early 2nd century. Smith 1994, 125 (among others) argues for an Antigonid setting for the following reason: 'Seleukos Nikator claimed all Asia, but he ruled in Syria where the emphasis on Macedonia as a country would be less appropriate. The early Antigonid kings of Macedonia are perhaps the strongest candidates'. That this is not a sufficient argument will hopefully become clear in the course of this article. The royal couple depicted with other figures in panels 3–5 has been variously identified. Smith 1994, 125–126 concludes that the ruler must be an Antigonid, cf. Billows 1995, 51–53, but see Zanker 2019, 197.
55   Both figures are clearly female; cf. Billows 1995, 47. The interpretation of Palagia 2014, 213–214, who identifies the figure with kausia as Alexander the Great, therefore lacks any basis. The left figure, however, does not signify Europe, as Kosmin 2014b, 124 claims, or the 'Graeco-Macedonian mainland', as Kaye 2022, 317 thinks, but specifically Makedonia.
56   Smith 1994; cf. also Billows 1995, 45–55.
57   Billows 1995, 179–182; Liampi 1998.
58   Isokr. or. 5.154.
59   Smith 1994, 112; Muccioli 2004, 122.
60   As Adcock 1953, 177 thought: 'Here and there, there is a trace of the belief that they belonged to a *Herrenvolk*, in the curt addition to their title of the single word *Makedon*, a Macedonian.' In the Achaimenid royal inscriptions, this sentiment is much more evident; cf. Briant 1994, 461. But see Ma 2003, 189: 'Even as they interacted in locally defined spaces and gestures, both foreign king and local priest knew that the former belonged to a *Herrenvolk* of external conquerors'.

Fig. 1 Wall painting from the Villa of P. Fannius Synistor in Boscoreale. Panels 1 and 2.

of the Borsippa Cylinder this would fly in the face of Antiochos' efforts to stress his commitment to local religion and traditions of kingship.[61] That a certain amount of cooperation with the members of the Babylonian elite was in fact a prerequisite for this integration is illustrated in a Babylonian Chronicle.[62] It reports for the time when Antiochos I was still co-regent of his father that, he, 'the crown prince at the instruction of a certain Bab[ylonian performed] regular [offerings] for Sîn of Egišnugal and Sîn of Enit[enna]'.[63] The passage documents that Antiochos acted on advice of a Babylonian expert when performing sacrifices for the Mesopotamian moon god Sîn. Concerning the perspective and expectations of the Babylonians keeping the chronicle, it is significant that the local expert is mentioned explicitly in the text.[64]

Another chronicle entry illustrates, however, that the Seleukids also deviated from local practice. During a visit of the crown prince to the 'ruins' of the temple Esagila and while Antiochos was conducting what must have been a Babylonian ritual, apparently an accident happened.[65] Antiochos slipped on the debris of the unrestored temple. The crown-prince then made sacrifices 'in the Greek fashion' respectively 'in the manner

61   Dirven 2014.
62   Cf. Dillery 2015, xviii.
63   BCHP 5 (Antiochus I and Sin Temple Chronicle) ll. 8–9.
64   Haubold 2013, 142.
65   BCHP 6 (Ruin of Esagila Chronicle), obv. ll. 4–8.

of the land of Yauna', which probably means that he made offerings that were followed by a communal meal.[66] The text does not say so but the fall probably was taken as a bad omen and Antiochos switched to his own rites to be sure to propitiate the gods.[67] The chronicle gives no explicit judgement on the events, but they at least seem ambivalent, for shortly after a lightning strike in a building is mentioned.[68] In the Borsippa Cylinder, Antiochos likewise appears both as an insider and an outsider.[69] That Babylonia is, after all, only part of a larger empire is expressed quite clearly by the unusual elements mentioned above, and it manifests in the Macedonian ethnic.[70]

4. Seleukos' ethnikon as an indicator of a turning away from Macedonia?

Seleukos' final campaign to Macedonia is mentioned in another Babylonian chronicle that narrates the final two years of Seleukos' reign. It notes that '[Seleukos mustered] his [troops] from the land of Sard[is]. He and his army crossed the sea to Macedonia', which is called 'his own land' or 'homeland'.[71] The passage in the chronicle again shows that the first Seleukid is perceived as a foreign ruler in Babylonia.[72] Furthermore, scholars have linked the passage to the literary texts on this campaign, notably Nymphis/ Memnon, who stresses that Seleukos after his victory against Lysimachos 'was eager to cross over to Macedonia, with a longing for his fatherland (πόθον ἔχων τῆς πατρίδος) from which he had set out on campaign with Alexander, and being old by this time, he intended to finish the remainder of his life there and to entrust Asia to his son Antiochos'.[73] It is debatable whether the phrasing of the chronicle and Memnon's narrative echo Seleukos' representation at the time concerning the nature of his expedition as

---

66   Van der Spek 2006, 274; see Dirven 2014, 210 with n. 41; Haubold 2013, 133–134.
67   Erickson 2011, 54–55; Haubold 2013, 133; van der Spek – Stol 2020 ad loc.
68   I thank Kristin Kleber for pointing this out to me. It seems to me doubtful, therefore, whether the chronicle actually 'celebrates the empire's ability to harness competing cultural idioms' as Haubold 2013, 133 thinks.
69   Strootman 2013, 88; Kosmin 2014a, 192.
70   Cf. Kosmin 2014a, 193: 'The Cylinder, therefore, encodes the dynasty's Macedonian origins, Syrian heartland, and restless mobility. The ultimate effect is to provincialize Babylonia.'
71   BCHP 9 (End of Seleucus I Chronicle), rev. 1–4 (trans. van der Spek – Stol).
72   Briant 1994, 466. Barbantani 2014, 35 stresses that there is a difference between the Macedonicity of the Seleukid king and the cultural identity of his troops called Haneans in the Babylonian sources, i. e., a term applied to hostile foreigners in earlier times. But the meaning of the Land Ḫanî seems to be complex, and it is the homeland of Alexander the Great in Sachs – Hunger I, 191; Briant 1994, 463–464; Haubold 2013, 134–135; Kosmin 2014b, 91–92; Heller 2015.
73   BNJ 434 F1 8.1; cf. Paus. 1.16.2. Briant 1994, 463–466. On the account of Nymphis/Memnon/Photios cf. Mehl 1986, 316–320; Primo 2009, 109–117; Heinemann 2010; Ogden 2017, 247–252.

Paul Kosmin argues.[74] It is important to note, however, that in my opinion (and contrary to Kosmin) a contrast between Seleukos and Antiochos cannot be derived from the observation that Antiochos apparently does not carry the ethnikon 'Macedonian' himself in the Borsippa-Cylinder. This could be significant and has been linked to the fact that Antiochos was descended from an Iranian woman, the Baktrian princess Apame, and actually never saw Macedonia himself.[75] Thus, Kosmin (among others) has interpreted the 'dramatic absence' of the Macedonian ethnic in the case of Antiochos as an indicator that Macedonia was no longer of decisive importance as a point of reference during his reign – in stark contrast to the 'Homeward Bound campaign' of his father only twelve years earlier.[76] As it was by no means necessary to mention the ethnic at all, its presence is deliberate. I find it hardly plausible, however, that a contrast between father and son should be the intended message of the text because this would entail that 1) Antiochos wished to distance himself from his predecessor in this aspect and that 2) Macedonicity was something negative from which the king had to distance himself.[77] Both points seem unlikely. Rather, the ethnicity of the father also extended to the son even if no direct connection is made in the text.[78] This seems all the more likely since the Iranian ancestry of Antiochos on his mother's side is nowhere mentioned in the text. Antiochos would thus simply lack an ethnic affiliation.[79]

---

74   Kosmin 2014b, 82–85. I do not think, though, that it has been 'proven' as Nawotka 2017, 38 states. Critical is Ogden 2017, 252 n. 15. Heller 2015 stresses that the phrase 'his own land' is not so uncommon as Kosmin thinks. Briant 1994, 466 ponders that the passage in the chronicle might indeed be understood as critical of the foreign ruler. A problem might be that Kosmin seems to assume that Seleukos took up (and inverted) a sense of *pothos* that had developed under Alexander. But it is not sure if this is contemporaneous; cf. Strootman 2022 who thinks it is a product from later Hellenistic imperial cosmography. Hannestad 2021b, 255 seems to have misunderstood Kosmin's argument.

75   Briant 1994, 467; Stevens 2014, 77: 'Antiochus himself is not described as "Macedonian", which we might have expected if there was a deliberate stress on his own ethnicity or that of the dynasty as a whole'.

76   Kosmin 2014b, 87, 114.

77   This, however, is the intention according to Musti 1966, 105: 'egli confessa certo così l'origine macedone, ma non sembra volersi fregiare dell'etnico, almeno di fronte agli Orientali.' Wiesehöfer 1996, 33 assumes that Antiochos deliberately 'verzichtet' on mentioning his ethnic. On this question cf. also the chapter by Sonja Richter in this volume.

78   Strootman 2013, 88.

79   Pace Kosmin 2014b, 114 who thinks that the missing ethnic for Antiochos 'acknowledges more than Antiochus' half-Iranian ethnicity and Asian upbringing'. Likewise, it is problematic when Barbantani 2014, 35 states: 'The fact that Antiochus I was half-Iranian was certainly put in good use in his relationship with the local philoi and population' as I don't know any evidence which would suggest that a stress of an Iranian descent would have benefited acceptance of Seleukid rule in Babylonia. Cf. on the other hand Ma 2003, 187: 'identity was defined by a Macedonian father, and hence could survive marriage with non-Macedonian women (Antiochos I, the son of Seleukos I and the Iranian Apame, was nonetheless a Macedonian)'.

Therefore, I cannot follow Kosmin in his interpretation that the cylinder 'encodes the abandonment of Macedonia from Seleucid space'.[80] This point is part of a larger argument that I can only touch upon, but which to me certainly seems sophisticated but nevertheless flawed for several reasons. As some of these reasons concern how the sources for the interaction between the Macedonian kings and the Greek poleis are to be interpreted, it is necessary to comment on them. In his discussion of the development of the perception of the space over which the Seleukids ruled, Kosmin analyses what he calls the 'metamorphosis of the dynasty's westward gaze',[81] in short, he traces how – from Seleukos I to Antiochos IV – Macedonia and the Seleukids' Macedonicity lost their importance for the dynasty.

Apart from the Borsippa Cylinder, there is just one other inscription in which a Seleukid king is given the label 'Macedonian'. The inscription belonged to a statue of Antiochos III which was dedicated on Delos probably in 192 by Menippos, a high-ranking general of Antiochos and an ambassador to Rome. It is thus the only text from the Graeco-Macedonian world in which a Seleukid king is given this ethnikon.[82]

[β]ασιλέα [Μέγαν] | Ἀντίοχο[ν] | βασιλέως Σελεύκ[ου] | [Κ]αλλινίκου |⁵ Μακεδόνα | τὸν
α[ὐ]το[ῦ] σωτῆρ[α] | [κ]αὶ ε[ὐεργέτ]ην | Μένιππος Φανίου | ἀνέ[θηκεν].[83]

Menippos, son of Phanias, has erected (the statue of) the Great King Antiochos, son of king Seleukos Kallinikos, Macedonian, his saviour and benefactor.

Although it is a "private" dedication, the fact that Menippos was a courtier undoubtedly allows to see the ethnic as part of the "official" image of Antiochos.[84] The ethnic is probably meant to convey at a Panhellenic place that Antiochos is a plausible champion for the Greeks against the Romans – and perhaps even more so than the Antigonid Philip V.[85] Antiochos' statue competed with several Antigonid dedications. Probably Gonatas (Doson, however, cannot be excluded) had been a very active benefactor to the Delian sanctuary of Apollon after the victory over the Ptolemaic fleet near Kos around 255 BC. Among the dedications erected to illustrate his new dominance over the Aegean, especially the progonoi monument stressed his Macedonian

---

80 Kosmin 2014b, 114.
81 Kosmin 2014b, 115.
82 Mistakenly identified as Antiochos I by Bearzot 1992, 39 n. 1 and 3.
83 IG XI.4 1111; Durrbach, Choix 75 f. Nr. 59.
84 Brüggemann 2022, 340; it is 'private' for Ma ²2002, 207 n. 10. On this aspect cf. the contribution of Shane Wallace in this volume.
85 Pfeiffer 2022, 322; similar Kosmin 2014b, 115–116. The deliberate intent is also illustrated by the fact that a roughly contemporaneous dedication (OGIS 240) in Pergamon (also by a Seleukid courtier?) does not give the ethnic; on this dedication cf. Chrubasik 2013, 101.

identity.[86] Toward the end of the 3rd century, Philip V added another stoa.[87] A likely parallel to the Seleukid dedication that strengthens this reading may be seen in the dedication of a family group for Ptolemaios III Euergetes and his wife and children by the Aitolian League in Thermon (and a possible twin monument set up in Delphi by a private individual).[88] The king and all the other male and female members of the royal house are explicitly identified as Macedonians. The exedra probably dates to the time of the Kleomenian War, that is 224–221 BC.[89] In both cases, the power politics of the various actors on the Greek mainland and the Ptolemaic-Antigonid struggle for control of this sphere form the background of the dedications.[90] Ptolemaios is not only honoured because of his benefactions for the league (ἀρετᾶς ἕνεκεν καὶ εὐεργεσίας τᾶς εἰς τὸ ἔθν[ος]) but also for all the other Hellenes (καὶ τοὺς ἄλλους Ἕλλανας). While the latter could be interpreted as reacting to the Hellenic league of Antigonos Doson and the associated claim to represent all Greeks,[91] the prominent Macedonicity maybe also stressed competition with regard to the Antigonids as kings of Macedon.

For Kosmin, the honours for Antiochos III are an 'important echo of Seleucus I's post-Corupedium proclamation of homesickness' but the conflict as a whole, in his view, rather illustrates a fundamental difference between the two kings insofar as Macedonia itself is not Antiochos' target, nor are his Macedonian roots basis of his legitimation during the conflict. Rather, the 'southern Balkan peninsula had been reduced to a proxy pawn of Great Power competition.'[92] Without going into detail, I find it, however, hardly surprising that in the conflict with Rome, in which Antiochos styled him-

---

86 IG XI.4 1096. See Bringmann – von Steuben 1995, 190–192; Aymard 1950, 107–108; Buraselis 1982, 161–162; H. Thompson 1982, 177; Ma 2013, 226. When the Epidaurians wanted to honour Doson and later Philip V, they also added the ethnikon to the king's name. IG IV²,1 589 and 590 (ἁ πόλις τῶν Ἐ[πιδαυρίων βασιλέα] | Ἀντίγονον Δ[ημητρίου Μακε]δόνα; [ἁ πόλις τῶν Ἐπιδαυρί]ων ἀνέθη[κε βασιλέα] | [Φίλιππον βασιλέως] Δημητρ[ίου Μακεδόνα]); cf. Aymard 1950, 107–108.

87 H. Thompson 1982, 176–177.

88 IG IX,1² 1,56: βασιλέα Πτολεμαῖον | βασιλέως Πτολεμαίου | Μακεδόνα. | Πτολεμαῖον βασιλέως | Πτολεμαίου Μακεδόνα. | βασίλισσαν Β[ερ]εν[ίκαν] | βασιλέως Μάγα | Μακέταν. | βα[σί]λισσα[ν Ἀρσ]ινόαν | βασιλέως Πτ[ολ]εμαίου | Μακέ[τ]αν. | βασίλισσαν [Βε]ρενίκαν | βασιλέως Πτολεμαίου | Μακέταν. | . . . c. 10 . . . βασιλέως | [Πτολεμαίου] Μακεδόνα. | Ἀλέ[ξαν]δρον βασιλέως | Πτολεμαίου Μακεδόνα. | Μάγαν βασιλέως | Πτολεμαίου Μακεδόνα. | Αἰτωλῶν τὸ κοινὸν ἀρετᾶς ἕνεκεν καὶ εὐεργεσίας τᾶς εἰς τὸ ἔθν[ος] καὶ τοὺς ἄλλους Ἕλλανας; Huss 1975; Kotsidu 2004; KNr. 104; on the Delphic monument see Kosmetatou 2003. On the Ptolemaic connections to the Aitolians as well as other leagues of Aegean Greece see the chapter by Hans Beck in this volume.

89 Habicht 1982, 111 n. 148 argued for the Kleomenian war. But cf. Bennett 2002 who places it in the time of the Demetrian war.

90 For the aims of Ptolemaios III in mainland Greece cf. Scherberich 2009.

91 Habicht 1982, 113 n. 148. It does not have to be connected to the league, however, as is illustrated by an inscription from Teos (I.Teos 30 l. 6–8) from 204/3 BC in which it is said about Antiochos III that he decided to be the 'common [benefactor] both of the other Greek [cit|ies and] of our city' (κοινὸς [εὐ]|[ἐργέτης πρ]οείρηται γίνεσθαι τῶν τε ἄλλων Ἑλληνίδωμ [πό]|[λεων καὶ τ]ῆς πόλεως τῆς ἡμετέρας). Cf. also IG XII.4 1 ll. 11–17.

92 Kosmin 2014b, 116. Cf. Briant 1994, 467.

self liberator of the Greeks and guarantor of freedom for the autonomous Greek cities in Asia Minor, Macedonia, in which the Antigonids had reigned for nearly a century, was not the prime focus. Insofar, I do not see this conflict as comparable to Seleukos' campaign and thus not as evidence for a development of the Seleukids' Macedonicity.

Kosmin, however, sees the way in which Antiochos III acted during the conflict as one step further on the way to the situation under Antiochos IV which he links to the euergetism of the latter and characterises as follows:

> Father and son, Antiochus III and IV, manifest the transformation of the dynasty's offi-
> cial attitude to the Graeco-Macedonian mainland over the course of the third century: a
> waning of affective, homeland ties; a southward trajectory from Macedonia to central and
> southern Greece, from Macedonicity to Hellenicity; the preference for political sponsor-
> ship and euergetical performance over territorial possession; and the untroubled recogni-
> tion of this region's existence outside the kingdom's territory.[93]

The territorial aspirations of the Seleukids are too large a subject to deal with here. What is important to our topic, however, is that Kosmin perceives a stark contrast between the gifts made by Seleukos I and Antiochos IV to Greek cities. He explicitly compares the gift of probably a pair of tigers by Seleukos I to Athens with the donations of Antiochos IV as in his view only these two kings 'directed ideologically charged and meaningful acts of beneficence toward the poleis of central and southern Greece'.[94]

For Antiochos IV, who spend huge sums promoting the cultural and urban attrac-tiveness of Greek cities, Kosmin rightly sees the sponsoring of 'Old World classical Greek identity' as an important factor.[95] However, the way in which Kosmin frames this is problematic. While the 'flamboyant exoticism' of the tigers in his view documents Seleukos' confidence in his Graeco-Macedonian identity, Antiochos' 'stereotypical Hellenism betrays the exaggerated compensation of a colonial Mimic Man'.[96] One should probably not assume that we have a complete picture of Seleukid euergetism.[97] My criticism is, however, another. In my opinion, Kosmin is comparing things that do not belong together. That Seleukos also gave the island of Lemnos to Athens is mentioned by Kosmin but because 'nesiotic assignments were a recurrent feature of the early Hellenistic period's geopolitics' he sees them as 'of limited significance here'.[98] In my view, however, the gift of Lemnos would have been precisely that what can be compared to the architectural donations of Antiochos IV while the tigers might best

---

93   Kosmin 2014b, 118.
94   Kosmin 2014b, 117; on the tigers see Bringmann – von Steuben 1995, KNr. 20 [L].
95   Kosmin 2014b, 118.
96   Kosmin 2014b, 118.
97   E. g., benefactions by Antiochos III for Athens, that are nowhere documented, are probably to be
      inferred from IG XI 1056 (= OGIS 771 = Bringmann – von Steuben 1995, KNr. 35); cf. Ma 2002, 92
      n. 146.
98   Kosmin 2014b, 117.

be compared to the 'woollen curtain, adorned with Assyrian weaving and Phoenician purple' which Antiochos IV (or III?) dedicated at Olympia.[99]

So, why is this differentiation significant? For the question of the supposed development, it is important to consider the framework of royal euergetism to a greater extent than Kosmin does.[100] The fact that the ritualised exchange of giving and taking in the discourse between city and ruler could be instrumentalised in this sense can only be explained by a specifically Greek morality of reciprocity, which demanded strict reciprocation in both the positive and the negative. The moral obligations established through royal benefactions on the one hand and appropriate honours by the cities on the other hand were designed to last and aimed at mutual political good will. As recent scholarship has shown, both in the time of Seleukos I and of Antiochos IV, i. e., in the early 3rd century and in the 2nd century, kings generally responded to urban initiatives. Lemnos, for example, was returned to Athens by Seleukos on the initiative of an Athenian delegation under the hipparch Komeas.[101] Because the international conditions had changed in the 2nd century primarily due to the coming of Rome, the cities now no longer requested help in the case of war and catastrophe or in the pursuit of concrete power politics but concerning objects of representation. These not only served the cities' need for prestige, but also promoted their economic interests.[102] The kings likewise were concerned with prestige. The elaborate commemoration of royal generosity in the cities constituted considerable symbolic capital for which the kings competed in front of a Graeco-Macedonian world audience. In an honorary decree of the Ionian League for Eumenes II, the king is praised for having helped the cities to build many things that contribute to their external splendour and glory, and he is called upon to continue to do so in the future, so that he may receive from the cities everything that is conducive to his honour and glory.[103] The continued euergetical exchange thus could become a 'self-perpetuating spiral'.[104]

Civic *eunoia* in reaction to royal generosity could result in concrete political decisions. This is clearly illustrated by an episode reported by Polybios. In 169 BC, the Achaian statesman Lykortas demanded military support for Alexandreia against Antiochos IV on the grounds that the Ptolemies had done much more for the Achaian League than their rivals in the past. He did so by enumerating in his speech the benefits they had received both from the Ptolemies and the Seleukids.

99 Bringmann – von Steuben 1995, KNr. 23 [L].

100 Cf. Bringmann 1993; 2000; Bringmann– von Steuben 1995; Ma ²2002.

101 Mehl 1986, 306–307.

102 Bringmann 2000, 151–156, 156: 'Die Schwerpunktverlagerung des monarchischen Euergetismus im zweiten Jahrhundert v. Chr. scheint von den Städten initiiert worden zu sein.'

103 OGIS 763 l. 36–37: οὕτω γὰρ καὶ μετὰ ταῦτά με πάντων τεύξεσθαι τ]ῶν εἰς τιμὴν καὶ δόξαν ἀνηκόντων (= Bringmann – von Steuben 1995, KNr. 285 [E] = Austin ²2006, no. 239).

104 Ma ²2002, 185.

For there was a great difference between the two kingdoms in comparison, since only rare instances could be found in which there had been any close relations between that of Antiochos and Greece, in former times at least – for the present king had acted with conspicuous generosity toward the Greeks – but the favours which the Achaians had received from the kingdom of Ptolemaios in former times had been so great and frequent, that no one could have expected more. Lykortas, by arguing thus, made a great impression, as the comparison showed the difference to be complete. For while it was not easy to enumerate the benefits conferred by the kings in Alexandreia, there was not a single act of kindness of any practical value to be found which the Achaians had met with from the kingdom of Antiochos.[105]

Even if Lykortas' request eventually was not accepted but rather that of his rival Kallikrates, and the Achaians thus decided to send a mediating legation to both courts, the possibility of the political instrumentalization of benefactions becomes clear. The fact that Antiochos committed himself in such a way in mainland Greece was probably because he tried to compensate for the deficits of his forefathers.[106] Two of the cities that profited from Antiochos' munificence were Tegea and Megalopolis – small poleis but both members of the Achaian League.[107] The discrepancy between Seleukos I and Antiochos IV noted by Kosmin thus does not result from a change in cultural self-perception of the Seleukids ('from Macedonicity to Hellenicity') but it is rather a reflection of royal competition in drastically different international political landscapes. The passage in Polybios also clearly illustrates that the Seleukids had not been as active in the Western Aegean as the Ptolemies and Antigonids in the 3rd century.[108]

This leads to the other equally important aspect. Kosmin at this point of his argument exclusively focuses on the Seleukid activities in the 'Graeco-Macedonian mainland'.[109] He establishes this geographical category in another context as counterpart to the Greek term Asia as a designation for the Seleukid kingdom. However, this is hardly plausible since a unified geographical concept of Macedonia plus mainland Greece is

---

105 Pol. 29.24.12–16: αἵ τε γὰρ βασιλεῖαι συγκρινόμεναι μεγάλην εἶχον διαφοράν· ὑπὸ μὲν γὰρ τῆς Ἀντιόχου σπάνιον ἦν εὑρεῖν οἰκεῖόν τι γεγονὸς καθόλου πρὸς τοὺς Ἕλληνας ἔν γε τοῖς ἀνώτερον χρόνοις· καὶ γὰρ ἡ τοῦ τότε βασιλεύοντος μεγαλοψυχία <διά>δηλος ἐγένετο τοῖς Ἕλλησιν· ὑπὸ δὲ τῆς Πτολεμαίου τοσαῦτα καὶ τηλικαῦτα τοῖς Ἀχαιοῖς ἐγεγόνει φιλάνθρωπα κατὰ τοὺς ἀνώτερον χρόνους ὥστ' ἂν μηδένα πλεῖον ἀξιοῦν. ἃ διατιθέμενος ὁ Λυκόρτας μεγάλην ἐποιεῖτο φαντασίαν, ἅτε τῆς παραθέσεως ὁλοσχερῆ τὴν διαφορὰν ἐχούσης· καθ' ὅσον γὰρ οὐκ ἐξαριθμήσασθαι ῥᾴδιον ἦν τὰς τῶν ἐν Ἀλεξανδρείᾳ βασιλέων εὐεργεσίας, κατὰ τοσοῦτον ἁπλῶς οὐδὲν ἦν εὑρεῖν φιλάνθρωπον ἐκ τῆς Ἀντιόχου βασιλείας ἀπηντημένον εἰς πραγμάτων λόγον τοῖς Ἀχαιοῖς. (trans. Loeb, modified).
106 Bringmann 1993, 19. On Antiochos' IV. euergetism cf. Mittag 2006, 103–118.
107 Bringmann – von Steuben 1995, KNr. 55 [L], 56 [L].
108 Ma ²2002, 92 identifies the limited control over the Western coast of Asia minor as a reason for this.
109 Kosmin 2014b, 124–125.

to my knowledge nowhere to be found in the sources.[110] It becomes especially problematic when used in the context of euergetism. Are the Seleukids' benefactions for Miletos (and Didyma) or Rhodos not evidence of their interaction with "Greece"? Concerning the regional focus of royal euergetism there are several differences between the large and the diverse smaller dynasties.[111] That the Panhellenic sanctuary of Delos was seen as a place fit for advertising Antiochos' III Macedonicity in preparation for his plans for the Greek mainland, again illustrates the unity of the Aegean (and the Greek world beyond).[112] All in all, then, the context for the interpretation of the Macedonian ethnic proposed by Kosmin is rather unplausible.

5. The Macedonian kings and Greek "culture"

The dedications discussed above and comparable monuments in Panhellenic sanctuaries are examples of culturally encoded political communication with the Greek world – similar in a way to the foundation of Hellenic leagues by the Macedonian kings. Yet, Pausanias in his description of Ptolemaios I's activities in Olympia and Delphi perhaps points to another reason for the wish of Ptolemaios and his descendants to be referred to as Macedonians. As I already mentioned, in 10.7.8, the perieget widens the scope insofar as he does not only refer to the first king of the dynasty but to all Ptolemies in stating that 'the kings of Egypt liked to be called Macedonians, as in fact they were'.[113] While Pausanias acknowledges the Macedonicity of the Ptolemies here, he just calls them 'Egyptians' in other passages.[114] In 6.3.1, Pausanias explicitly constructs a contradiction between Ptolemaios I being both Macedonian and king of Egypt: ἐν τῷ ἐπιγράμματι ἐκάλεσε, βασιλεύων ὅμως Αἰγύπτου.[115] The latter title (which Pausanias also uses on other occasions) was of course never used as a self-description by the Ptolemies but – similar to the Seleukids in Babylonia – they went to great

---

110   It is also not mentioned by Muccioli 2004; 2006 whom Kosmin follows in his discussion of the term Asia. Cf. Erskine 2013, 353 who stresses concerning Polybios' perspective: 'It is noticeable that while he freely talks of Greeks and Greek affairs when his focus is on the Greek mainland *and the Aegean* (my emphasis) he does not do so nearly as readily when his subject is Asia or Egypt.'

111   Bringmann 2000, 313–319.

112   H. Thompson 1982, 177 and similarly Erskine 2013, 356 connect the importance of Delos to a shift of the centre of the Greek world to the east.

113   Similarly, Ptolemaios X Alexandros I Theos Philometor is called 'king of the Egyptians' in Paus. 1.9.3 (ὃν αὐτὴ βασιλεύειν ἔπραξεν Αἰγυπτίων).

114   Paus. 1.9.4: Αἰγυπτίους; Paus. 1.5.5: Πτολεμαίου τοῦ Αἰγυπτίου; Paus. 1.36.5: Πτολεμαῖον τὸν Αἰγύπτιον and 10.10.2: Πτολεμαῖον τὸν Αἰγύπτιον.

115   I am not sure whether we should think with Kainz 2016, 345 that in the later passage 10.7.8 near the end of his work 'Pausanias has made up his mind and understands why a Ptolemaic king should have called himself a Macedonian rather than an Egyptian'. The two passages rather seem to me to illustrate the ambivalent picture of the Ptolemies.

lengths to be good pharaohs in communication with their Egyptian subjects and to a certain extent also adapted Egyptian ideology of kingship at court.[116] Although Pausanias does not present a contemporary picture, he probably transmits a reflection of the "old world's" reserved view on this kingdom in Hellenistic times. This view can also be found in Polybios, most prominently in the episode of the Theban pankratiast Kleitomachos and the "Egyptian" boxer Aristonikos promoted by Ptolemaios IV at the Olympic games.[117]

A radically different setting is evoked in court poetry. This is a milieu in which the Macedonian ethnicity could be explicitly used to underline the difference to the "barbarians". In Kallimachos' *Hymn to Delos* – clearly aimed at the court society –[118] Apollon prophesises that all the lands facing the sea, from the East to the West, 'do not refuse to have a Macedonian king'.[119] This dichotomy is especially prevalent in the epigrams of Poseidippos of Pella. At no point of his victory poems are we made aware of the Egyptian dimension of the Ptolemaic kingdom.[120] The ethnic chauvinism of Poseidippos, who was apparently proud of his Macedonian origin and saw Macedonians as his primary audience, is not necessarily to be found to the same extent in all authors of the Ptolemaic court, and the existence of cultural translators like Berossos and Manetho probably point to a wider phenomenon.[121] Nevertheless, court culture was essentially Graeco-Macedonian.[122] Royal patronage concentrated on the promotion of Greek cultural elements that constituted an elite culture which has often been seen as

116 Aymard 1948, 240. 'Egyptian king' also Paus. 1.8.6 and 3.6.8 for the Ptolemies as pharaohs cf. only Pfeiffer 2018, 9–18.
117 Erskine 2013, 353–354; Freitag – Fündling – Michels 2014, 11–12; Kainz 2016, 346–348; Mann 2018, 456–457.
118 Weber 1993, 307–309.
119 Kall. h. 4.166–170: ᾧ ὑπὸ μίτρην ἵξεται οὐκ ἀέκουσα Μακηδόνι κοιρανέεσθαι ἀμφοτέρη μεσόγεια καὶ αἳ πελάγεσσι κάθηνται, μέχρις ὅπου περάτη τε καὶ ὁππόθεν ὠκέες ἵπποι Ἤελιον φορέουσιν· (trans. Stephens 2015, 175). Koenen 1993, 81–84 stresses the incorporation of 'Egyptian ideology' in the hymn. In the following line, Ptolemaios II is styled as a protector of the Ἕλληνες against the Galatians, the 'later born Titans'; cf. on this theme the paper by Pasquariello in this volume.
120 Stephens 2005, 234. Bingen 2002, 48 describes Poseidippos as "le prophète d'une idéologie de prestige, la divinisation des souverains doublée de la pureté de leur hellénisme et (…) de la 'Macédonité' de la dynastie". It was without the knowledge of Poseidippos whose epigrams had not yet been rediscovered that Edson 1958, 164–165 could claim that it is 'indeed striking that Alexandrian poetry all but entirely disregards the Ptolemies' Macedonian connection'.
121 Fantuzzi 2005, 252; D. Thompson 2005, 269–270. Poseidippos expresses his hope in ep. 118.13–16 'that the Macedonians – those on [the islands] and those / along the coast of Asia, end to end / may honour me' (ὦ ἄνα, καὶ κατ' ἐμοῦ, / ὄφρα με τιμήσωσι Μακηδόνες, οἵ τ' ἐπὶ ν[ήςων / οἵ τ' Ἀςίης πάσης γείτονες ἠϊόνος). D. Thompson 2005, 270 stresses: 'Only twice in the full corpus do we find instead a mention of the wider category of Greeks'. On non-Greek scholars who however integrated themselves into the Greek intellectual milieu see Dillery 2015; Gruen 2017.
122 Often cited in this context is Plut. Antonius 27.3–4 who reports that only the last member of the dynasty, Kleopatra VII, learned the Egyptian language.

the very core of the Macedonian empires and which helped define who belonged to the imperial elite.[123]

Numerous studies have treated the promotion of Greek arts, science, literature, and poetry at the Hellenistic courts and showed that this was no selfless commitment to Greek paideia but rather a further aspect of the competition between the kings.[124] However, it is problematic to classify this commitment under the umbrella term of cultural policy.[125] The problem already arises from the fact that scholars tend to have very different understandings of what constitutes culture in this case. For Michel Austin, for example, culture includes literature and philology, medicine, military technology, and philosophy.[126] Caroline Lehmler, in her study on the cultural policy of Agathokles and of Hieron II of Syracuse, also includes the promotion of religion, dedications and euergetism, buildings, monuments, festivals, and the instrumentalization of cultural means such as coins and portraits.[127] Defined in this way, the activities documented in the Borsippa Cylinder would fall just as much under cultural policy as the Seleukid city foundations. An even more fundamental problem, however, is to presuppose a separate social sub-system of "culture" for ancient societies (arts, music, literature) to which a specific policy could be dedicated. When the term is used in this chapter, I rather follow a holistic, ethnological concept of culture, and it is thus to be understood as 'the conscious reification of ideas, beliefs, values, attitudes and practices, selectively extracted from the totality of social existence and endowed with a particular symbolic signification for the purposes of creating exclusionary distinctiveness' by different groups within a society.[128] Therefore, it seems more practical to disentangle the above mentioned, rather distinct aspects of monarchical representation that were all aimed at increasing the prestige of the ruler but followed distinct rules.

Patronage of "art and literature" at court obviously played a central role for the Ptolemies and later for the Attalids, and the kings were prepared to invest considerable resources for the prestige gained in this field – following the example of earlier Greek and then Macedonian rulers.[129] For the Ptolemies, as well as later for the Attalids as late-comers in the club of kings, the special motivation for this commitment evidently

---

123 Weber 1993; Müller 2009, 206–210; Strootman 2010. Although Habicht 1958 lacked sufficient evidence for his view of a Graeco-Macedonian ruling elite in the Hellenistic kingdoms, Strootman 2017, 132–133 stresses that looking back on research done since his article, Habicht was basically right and that the royal philoi were mainly Greeks and Macedonians. For Ma 2003, 187 the question of the ethnicity of the Hellenistic king is identical to the question of his 'Greekness'.
124 Erskine 1995; Weber 1997, 61–64; 2007, 104–111.
125 Cf., e. g., Schalles 1985; Gruen 2000; Kainz 2016, 349 n. 74; Mann 2018, 459; Montana 2020; Visscher 2020, 169.
126 Austin 2001, 95.
127 Lehmler 2005 following Schalles 1985; similar Barbantani 2014, 37–38 who, however, 67–68 (mis)-understands the phrase "cultural policy" as a policy of Hellenization (and rightly rejects this).
128 Hall 2004, 45–46; Kohl ³2012, 131–133.
129 Erskine 1995, 46.

arose from the need to emphasise their affiliation with the Greek world. Thus, in a way this lies on the same level as the reference to the Macedonian ethnicity which, as argued above, plays an important role in court literature. It also was, as recent studies have shown, closely linked to the agonistic activities of the Ptolemies.[130]

This again becomes most apparent in the epigrams of Poseidippos, namely in the ἱππικά (AB 71–88) composed on the occasion of equestrian victories of Ptolemaic kings and queens.[131] In one epigram, Poseidippos singles out Berenike I's chariot victory with foals. The speaking young horses (or their monument?)[132] stress Berenike's Macedonicity and compare her success to that of Kyniska, daughter of the Spartan king Archidamos II.[133]

> When we were still foals we won the Olympic crown,
> for Macedonian Berenike, O people of Pisa,
> which has a much praised reputation; with it we eclipsed
> the ancient kudos of Kyniska in Sparta.[134]

In epigram 88, Philadelphos himself speaks. He boasts of his victories as well as of those of his ancestors (especially his mother's) and of his Macedonian heritage, which is made more specific by the reference to the dynasty's origin in the Upper Macedonian canton Eordaia (Ἐορδαία γέννα):

> We are the first and only trio of kings to win
> the chariot race at Olympia, my parents and I.
> I, named after Ptolemaios and born the son of Berenike,
> of Eordaean descent, am one, my parents the other two:
> and of my father's glory I boast not, but that my mother,
> a woman, won in her chariot – that is great![135]

At the end of epigram 78, which belongs to a series of epigrams that celebrate Philadelphos' daughter Berenike, the "target audience" of the victory poetry is clearly identified: 'Sing, Macedonian women, of queen Berenice's crown, / for her four-horse

---

130   Cf. Fantuzzi 2005; Kainz 2016; Mann 2018.

131   Fantuzzi 2005; van Bremen 2007; Barbantani 2012; Kainz 2016.

132   Hose ad loc. in: Seidensticker – Stähli – Wessels 2015, 315.

133   On this comparison see Fantuzzi 2005, 253–264.

134   Poseidipp. ep. 87 AB: π[ῶλοι] ἔθ' ἁμὲς ἐοῦσαι Ὀλυμ[πια]κὸν Βερενίκας, / Π[ι]cᾶ[τ]αι Μακέτας ἀγάγομ[ε]ς / cτέφανον, / ὃc τὸ [πο]λυθρύλατον ἔχει κλέος, ὧι τὸ Κυνίcκας / ἐν Cπά[ρ]ται χρόνιον κῦδος ἀφειλόμεθα. (trans. Stephens).

135   Poseidipp. ep. 88 AB: πρῶτο[ι] τρεῖς βαcιλῆες Ὀλύμπια καὶ μόνοι ἁμὲς / ἅρμαcι νικῶμες καὶ γονέες καὶ ἐγώ· / εἷc μὲν ἐγὼ [Π]τολεμαίου ὁμώνυμος, ἐκ Βερενίκας / υἱ[όc], Ἐορδαία γέννα, δύω δὲ γονεῖc· / †πρου μέγα πατρὸς εμου† τίθεμαι κλέος, ἀλλ' ὅτι μάτηρ / εἷλε γυνὰ νίκαν ἅρματι, τοῦτο μέγα. (trans. Nisetich).

chariot'.[136] When the Ptolemies of the 3rd century promoted athletics, participated in international agones and founded isolympic games in Alexandreia this likewise aimed at a Graeco-Macedonian public both in their realm (where Macedonicity was taken as a mark of distinction) and in the Aegean.[137] Fantuzzi suspected that concrete Realpolitik stood behind their activities primarily in the hippic disciplines and that it was directed against the dominance of the Antigonids over the Greek mainland.[138] We might, however, rather see it – like euergetism and literary patronage – as part of a policy of prestige that was equally aimed primarily at the Graeco-Macedonian world.

But can these elements also be found in the case of the Seleukids? That is to say, can the Seleukids be shown to have engaged in court culture on a scale comparable to the Ptolemies? At first glance, the evidence is as meagre as it is late, and it is only in the time of Antiochos III that a library is attested in Antiocheia.[139] In a recent study, Kathryn Stevens accordingly concluded that Seleukid patronage of Greek scholars was only sporadic and restricted to a few individual kings. This finding has been explained in quite different ways. According to Stevens, we are dealing with a deliberate difference in royal style.[140] The Antigonids, for whom the tradition is similarly scarce, did not consider it necessary, in her view, to emphasise their affiliation to the Greek world in this way because for them, it was more important not to appear authoritarian.[141]

This might be comparable, at first glance, to the agonistic activities of the Hellenistic dynasties as the Antigonids and the Seleukids apparently did not engage in agonistics to the same degree as is attested for the Ptolemies.[142] The underlying reasons for this are still being debated. It was certainly not a necessary element to show oneself in the tradition to Alexander, as the great Macedonian had (in contrast to his father) neither participated in agones nor founded any himself.[143] Perhaps the Ptolemies stood under particular pressure to show their Graeco-Macedonian affiliation in this way because with the Egyptian royal tradition there was a powerful – and consistent – counter-

---

136 Poseidipp. ep. 78 AB: τεθρίππου δὲ τελείου ἀείδετε τὸν Βερ[ε]νίκη[ς / τῆς βασιλευούςης, ὦ Μακέτα[ι], ςτέφανον. (trans. Stephens with changes). D. Thompson 2005, 270 with n. 5 probably is right that ὦ Μακέτα[ι] refers to females; but cf. Hose ad loc. in: Seidensticker – Stähli – Wessels 2015, 302. In IG IX,1² 1,56 the differentiation is clear. Kosmetatou 2004.

137 Remijsen 2010; Müller 2009, 212; Kainz 2016; Mann 2018, 455–456. On the importance of their ethnicity for the Macedonians in Egypt cf. Kosmetatou 2004, 25–29. That the Ptolemies actually had to prove that they were Greek in order to participate in the Panhellenic games as Kainz 2016, 243–249 assumes starting from the famous episode of Alexander I Philhellen reported by Herodotos, seems to me unlikely.

138 Fantuzzi 2005, 251–252; but cf. van Bremen 2007, 373; Mann 2018, 454–455.

139 Austin 2001, 95–102; Stevens 2019, 250.

140 Stevens 2019, 246.

141 Stevens 2019, 244.

142 Mann 2018, 451. Seleukid courtiers and princes are, however, listed as participants in Panhellenic agones; cf. van Bremen 2007, 362–363; Barbantani 2012, 52–54; 2014, 37.

143 Mann 2018, 457–458.

image which led to a Janus-faced monarchy.[144] This did not exist in the case of the Seleukids who certainly integrated themselves into local and regional monarchic traditions but who never strove to emulate the Achaimenids to a degree which would be comparable to the Pharaonic persona of the Ptolemies.[145] This does not mean that the Seleukid realm was not perceived as foreign and therefore ambivalent by the Greeks of the "old world" as the Ptolemaic empire was,[146] but it seems that since the non-Greek elements of the Seleukids remained much more obscure, their Asian empire could be conceptualized as an *imperium Macedonicum* much more easily in later sources.[147] Thus, they perhaps did not perceive the same need to promote athletics as a mark of their Graeco-Macedonian identity on an "international" level.[148] On a local level within their realm, the Seleukids certainly did promote Greek cultural institutions (without ever following a concerted policy of Hellenization).[149] This is illustrated, e. g., by the Greek settlement (apparently not a polis) on the small island Ikaros, modern Failaka, near the head of the Persian Gulf lying off Kuwait where a gymnastic agon was established by a Seleukid functionary around 241–237 BC.[150] A decidedly Macedonian note was given to the Seleukid realm when the early Seleukids not only founded new cities and remarkably often gave them names from cities from Macedonia or Greece, but also named rivers and some regions after rivers and landscapes in the old home of the settlers.[151] Likewise, it seems that specifically Macedonian gods were promoted.[152]

Concerning the promotion of Greek scholarship at the Seleukid court, the difference to the picture of the Ptolemaic court (that Stevens emphasizes) possibly rather results from the coincidence of extant tradition and the fact that the Seleukids (and the Antigonids) did not create a capital like Alexandreia but had several residences.[153] One factor which should also be taken into account is the promotion of intellectuals not at court but in the Greek cities of the Seleukid realm.[154] Silvia Barbantani and recently Marijn Visscher have therefore painted a much brighter picture of Seleukid patronage

144 Kainz 2016, 335; cf. Koenen 1993, 25 on the 'Janus head' of Ptolemaic kingship.
145 Rightly remarked by Kainz 2016, 335. Tuplin 2009. Barbantani 2014, 31 argues that the fact that the Seleukids were apparently not stylised by the Ptolemies as an archenemy in Persian tradition possibly also speaks against a close emulation of the Achaimenids.
146 Erskine 2013, 353.
147 Edson 1958; cf. Musti 1966; Hammond 1993; Billows 1995.
148 Ultimately not convincing is Mann 2018 who points at the ambivalences of agonistic victories as possible reasons. The ambivalence certainly did not stop the Greek tyrants, Philip II or the Ptolemies.
149 Austin 2001, 94.
150 Roueché – Sherwin-White 1985, 32–34; Sherwin-White 1987, 30; Cohen 2013, 140–154.
151 Brodersen 2001; Kosmin 2014b, 108–109; Scharrer 2006; Brüggemann 2022, 344–346.
152 Daubner 2017.
153 The scantiness of the sources is stressed by Austin 2001, 94; Ehling 2002; contra Stevens 2019, 246. On the Antigonid residences cf. Weber 2007, 105.
154 Ehling 2002, 52. I thank Gregor Weber for pointing this out during our conference.

of Greek literature and scholarship.[155] The connotation of the Macedonian ethnicity of the king with his role as a promoter of Greek intellectual life can thus probably also be claimed for the Seleukids.[156]

6. Conclusion

The analysis of the instrumentalization of ethnicity by the Hellenistic kings is significantly influenced by the underlying preconceptions of modern scholars concerning the topic and its context, and it pays to reflect on both of them. Given the uniqueness of the Borsippa Cylinder and the few sources on the use of the Macedonian ethnikon, its precise meaning in the cylinder's text remains in a way enigmatic.[157] As there is no other source from the Seleukid (or another Hellenistic) realm with which it could be paralleled regarding its context and purpose, it is rather more possible to say what the Macedonicity of the Seleukid kings likely was not intended to convey.

It is most likely that the term is meant in an ethnic sense and not related to the nature of Seleukos' kingship. In the Borsippa Cylinder, it therefore does qualify the monarch as an outsider, and in a way, this stands in contrast to his efforts to integrate his rule into the Babylonian tradition. Whether its use in an indigenous context was also prompted by earlier, Achaimenid practice cannot be ruled out, contrary to the Persians it, however, never became a standard element of the royal titulature and the contemporary parallels rather point to a separate context in the Graeco-Macedonian world.[158] On an ethnic level, one probably should not ask for a precise meaning due to the wide range of the ethnic's meaning and associations. In Greek inscriptions, that is on an "international level" in the contexts of honours for kings by Greek cities, leagues, and individuals, the cases discussed point to a use of the ethnicity in competition with the Antigonids. In the case of Ptolemaios I's emphasis on his Macedonicity, a reference to Alexander has been claimed, but it probably was less in the person of the latter than in the Macedonian heartland. Conquest does indeed seem to have been an aspect that was linked to the concepts of Macedonia and Macedonicity, and it reminds of the Achaimenids' usage of their ethnicity. A decidedly different aspect is the link of the kings' Macedonicity with Greek culture made most clearly in the court poetry of the Ptolemies, but which can to a certain degree also be claimed for the Seleukids.

---

155   Barbantani 2014, 46–59; Visscher 2020; cf. Primo 2009.
156   Barbantani 2014.
157   It is not as simple as Ma 2003, 187 implies: 'The king was Macedonian, identified as such in public documents both Greek and non-Greek'.
158   Kuhrt 2002, 25: 'And in this purely Babylonian setting, too, Antiochus employs the epithet, thus reminding all that, while he may be a Babylonian king, he is simultaneously a Macedonian, member of the conquering group which now wields power. The emphasis on the ruler's ethnicity echoes the Achaemenid stress on the Persian identity and nature of their rule.' But see Briant 1994, 461.

Although it is problematic to subsume all the activities under one unified concept of "cultural policy", euergetism, the promotion of elements of Greek culture and the engagement in typical Greek activities apparently were an important aspect of the royal image and explicitly linked to their ethnicity. The target audience of these activities was (at least culturally) Graeco-Macedonian.

An entirely different communicative context must be assumed in the case of the Borsippa Cylinder. That Seleukos' (and therefore also Antiochos') Macedonicity was mentioned here, points to the importance the early Seleukids attached to their Macedonian roots in their representation very much akin to that of the Ptolemies at their court. If one wanted to claim the Borsippa Cylinder as evidence of a general approach to communication, they may therefore have chosen a different path than the Ptolemies who did not explicitly stress their Macedonicity in communication with their Egyptian subjects. The ethnikon does not, however, need to be explained in a monocausal way, rather, this mosaic piece again illustrates the multifaceted nature of the Hellenistic king's persona. This has recently been emphasised for the Ptolemies,[159] and it must in any case be stressed just as much, and probably to a greater extent, for the Seleukids.

Bibliography

Adams 1995: Adams, Winthrop L., Historical Perceptions of Greco-Macedonian Ethnicity in the Hellenistic Age, Balkan Studies 36, 1995, 205–222

Adcock 1953: Adcock, Frank E., Greek and Macedonian Kingship, Proceedings of the British Academy 39, 1953, 163–180

Anagnostou-Laoutides 2017: Anagnostou-Laoutides, Eva, In the Garden of the Gods: Models of Kingship from the Sumerians to the Seleucids, London 2017

Anagnostou-Laoutides – Pfeiffer 2022: Anagnostou-Laoutides, Eva – Pfeiffer, Stefan (eds.), Culture and Ideology under the Seleukids. Unframing a Dynasty, Berlin et al. 2022

Anson ²2015: Anson, Edward, Eumenes of Cardia. A Greek among Macedonians, Leiden et al. ²2015

Austin 2001: Austin, Michel, War and Culture in the Seleucid Empire, in: T. Bekker-Nielsen – L. Hannestad (eds.), War as a Cultural and Social Force. Essays on Warfare in Antiquity, Copenhagen 2001, 90–109 (German in Brodersen 1999)

Aymard 1948: Aymard, André, Le protocol royal grec et son évolution, Revue des Études Anciennes 50, 1948, 232–263

Aymard 1950: Aymard, André, Βασιλεὺς Μακεδόνων, Revue internationale des droits de l'antiquite 4, 1950, 61–97 (repr. in: id., Études d'Histoire ancienne, Paris 1967, 100–122)

Badian 1982: Badian, Ernst, Greeks and Macedonians, in: Barr-Sharrar – Borza 1982, 33–51

Barbantani 2011: Barbantani, Silvia, Callimachus on Kings and Kingship, in: B. Acosta-Hughes – L. Lehnus – S. Stephens (eds.), Brill's Companion to Callimachus, Leiden 2011, 178–200

159   Pfeiffer 2018, 18.

Barbantani 2012: Barbantani, Silvia, Hellenistic Epinician, in: P. Agócs – Chr. Carey – R. Rawles (eds.), Receiving the Komos. Ancient & Modern Receptions of the Victory Ode, London 2012, 37–55

Barbantani 2014: Barbantani, Silvia, "Attica in Syria": Persian War Reenactments and Reassessments of the Greek-Asian Relationship: A Literary Point of View, Erga-Logoi 2, 2014, 21–91 (https://doi.org/10.7358/erga-2014-001-barb) last access: 20.5.2024

Barr-Sharrar – Borza 1982: Barr-Sharrar, Beryl – Borza, Eugene (eds.), Macedonia and Greece in Late Classical and Early Hellenistic Times, Washington, D. C. 1982

Bearzot 1992: Bearzot, Cinzia S., Πτολεμαῖος Μακεδών. Sentimento nazionale macedone e contrapposizioni etniche all'inizio del regno tolemaico, in: M. Sordi (ed.), Autocoscienza e rappresentazione dei popoli nell'antichità, Milan 1992, 39–53

Beaulieu 2014: Beaulieu, Paul-Alain, Nabû and Apollo: the Two Faces of Seleucid Religious Policy, in: F. Hoffmann (ed.), Orient und Okzident in hellenistischer Zeit, Vaterstetten 2014, 13–30

Bennett 2002: Bennett, Chris, The Children of Ptolemy III and the Date of the Exedra of Thermos, Zeitschrift für Papyrologie und Epigraphik 138, 2002, 141–145

Bickerman 1938: Bickerman, Elias, Institutions de Séleucides, Paris 1938

Bickerman 1966: Bickerman, Elias, The Seleucids and the Achaemenids, in: Accademia Nazionale dei Lincei (ed.), La Persia e il mondo greco-romano, Rom 1966, 87–117

Billows 1995: Billows, Richard A., Kings and Colonists: Aspects of Macedonian Imperialism, Leiden 1995

Bingen 2002: Bingen, Jean, Posidippe: Le poète et les princes, in: G. Bastianini (ed.), Un poeta ritrovato. Posidippo di Pella, Milan 2002, 47–59

Boiy 2002: Boiy, Tom, Royal Titulature in Hellenistic Babylonia, Zeitschrift für Assyriologie und Vorderasiatische Archäologie 92, 2002, 241–257

Borza 1996: Borza, Eugene N., Greeks and Macedonians in the Age of Alexander: The Source Traditions, in: R. W. Wallace – E. M. Harris (eds.), Transitions to Empire. Essays in Greco-Roman History; 360–146 B. C., in Honor of E. Badian, Norman 1996, 122–139

Briant 1994: Briant, Pierre, De Samarkand a Sardes et de la ville de Suse au pays des Haneens, Topoi 4, 1994, 455–467

Bringmann 1993: Bringmann, Klaus, The King as Benefactor: Some Remarks on Ideal Kingship in the Age of Hellenism, in: Bulloch et al. 1993, 7–24

Bringmann 2000: Bringmann, Klaus, Geben und Nehmen. Monarchische Wohltätigkeit und Selbstdarstellung im Zeitalter des Hellenismus, Berlin 2000

Bringmann – von Steuben 1995: Bringmann, Klaus – von Steuben, Hans (eds.), Schenkungen hellenistischer Herrscher an griechische Städte und Heiligtümer, Berlin 1995

Brodersen 1999: Brodersen, Kai (ed.), Zwischen West und Ost. Studien zur Geschichte und Gesellschaft des Seleukidenreiches, Hamburg 1999

Brodersen 2001: Brodersen, Kai, "In den städtischen Gründungen ist die rechte Basis des Hellenisierens". Zur Funktion seleukidischer Städtegründungen, in: S. Schraut – B. Stier (eds.) Stadt und Land. Bilder, Inszenierungen und Visionen in Geschichte und Gegenwart. Wolfgang von Hippel zum 65. Geburtstag, Stuttgart 2001, 355–371

Brüggemann 2022: Brüggemann, Thomas, Mehr als Schall und Rauch? Das Seleukidenreich und seine antiken Namen, in: Anagnostou-Laoutidis – Pfeiffer 2022, 331–350

Bulloch et al. 1993: Bulloch, Anthony et al. (eds.), Images and Ideologies. Self-Definition in the Hellenistic World, Berkeley 1993

Buraselis 1982: Buraselis, Kostas, Das hellenistische Makedonien und die Ägäis. Forschungen zur Politik des Kassandros und der drei ersten Antigoniden (Antigonos Monophthalmos, Demetrios Poliorketes und Antigonos Gonatas) im Ägäischen Meer und in Westkleinasien, Munich 1982

Chrubasik 2013: Chrubasik, Boris, The Attalids and the Seleukid Kings, 281–175 BC, in: P. Thonemann (ed.), Attalid Asia Minor: Money, International Relations, and the State, Oxford 2013, 83–119

Cohen 2013: Cohen, Getzel M., The Hellenistic Settlements in the East from Armenia and Mesopotamia to Bactria and India, London 2013

Daubner 2017: Daubner, Frank, Makedonische Götter in Syrien und Kleinasien: Erwägungen zur Identität der Siedler in hellenistischen Stadtgründungen, in: R. Raja (ed.), Contextualizing the Sacred in the Hellenistic and Roman Near East Religious Identities in Local, Regional, and Imperial Settings, Turnhout 2017, 49–61

Dillery 2015: Dillery, John D., Clio's Other Sons. Berossus and Manetho with an Afterword on Demetrius, Ann Arbor 2015

Dirven 2014: Dirven, Lucinda, Religious Continuity and Change in Parthian Mesopotamia: A Note on the Survival of Babylonian Traditions, Journal of Ancient Near Eastern History 1.2, 2014, 201–229

Edson 1958: Edson, Charles, Imperium Macedonicum: The Seleucid Empire and the Literary Evidence, Classical Philology 53, 1958, 153–170

Ehling 2002: Ehling, Kay, Gelehrte Freunde der Seleukidenkönige, in: A. Goltz – A. Luther – H. Schlange-Schöningen (eds.), Gelehrte in der Antike. Alexander Demandt zum 65. Geburtstag, Cologne 2002, 41–58

Engels 2010: Engels, Johannes, Macedonians and Greeks, in: J. Roisman – I. Worthington (eds.), Blackwell's Companion to Ancient Macedonia, Oxford et al. 2010, 81–98

Erickson 2011: Erickson, Kyle, Apollo-Nabû: the Babylonian Policy of Antiochus I, in: id. – G. Ramsey (eds.), Seleucid Dissolution. The Sinking of the Anchor, Wiesbaden 2011, 51–66

Errington 1974: Errington, Robert M., Macedonian 'Royal Style' and Its Historical Significance, The Journal of Hellenic Studies 94, 1974, 20–37

Erskine 1995: Erskine, Andrew, Culture and Power in Ptolemaic Egypt: The Museum and Library of Alexandria, Greece & Rome 42, 1995, 38–48

Erskine 2013: Erskine, Andrew, The View from the Old World. Contemporary Perspectives on Hellenistic Culture, in: Stavrianopoulou 2013, 339–363

Erskine – Llewellyn-Jones – Wallace 2017: Erskine, Andrew – Llewellyn-Jones, Lloyd – Wallace, Shane (eds.), The Hellenistic Court. Monarchic Power and Elite Society from Alexander to Cleopatra, Swansea 2017

Fantuzzi 2005: Fantuzzi, Marco, Posidippus at Court: The Contribution of the Hippika of P. Mil. Vogl. VIII 309 to the Ideology of Ptolemaic Kingship, in: Gutzwiller 2005, 249–268

Fischer-Bovet – von Reden 2021: Fischer-Bovet, Christelle – von Reden, Sitta (eds.), Comparing the Ptolemaic and Seleucid empires. Integration, Communication, and Resistance, Cambridge 2021

Fittschen 1975: Fittschen, Klaus, Zum Figurenfries der Villa von Boscoreale, in: B. Andreae – H. Kyrieleis (eds.), Neue Forschungen in Pompeji und den anderen vom Vesuvausbruch 79 n. Chr. verschütteten Städten, Recklinghausen 1975, 93–100

Freitag – Fündling – Michels 2014: Freitag, Klaus – Fündling, Jörg – Michels, Christoph, Hellenicity ohne Hellenen? Eine Einleitung in die Thematik, in: K. Freitag – C. Michels (eds.), Athen oder Alexandria? Aspekte von Identität und Ethnizität im hellenistischen Griechenland, Cologne 2014, 7–18

Gruen 1985: Gruen, Erich S., The Coronation of the Diadochi, in: J. W. Eadie – J. Ober (eds.), The Craft of the Ancient Historian. Essays in Honor of Chester G. Starr, New York 1985, 253–271

Gruen 2000: Gruen, Erich S., Culture as Policy: The Attalids of Pergamon, in: N. de Grummond – B. Ridgway (eds.), From Pergamon to Sperlonga: Sculpture and Context, Berkeley 2000, 17–31

Gruen 2017: Gruen, Erich S., Hellenistic Patronage and the Non-Greek World, in: Erskine – Llewellyn-Jones – Wallace 2017, 295–318

Gutzwiller 2005: Gutzwiller, Kathryn (ed.), The New Posidippus. A Hellenistic Poetry Book, New York 2005

Habicht 1958: Habicht, Christian, Die herrschende Gesellschaft in den hellenistischen Monarchien, Vierteljahrschrift für Sozial- und Wirtschaftsgeschichte 48.1, 1958, 1–16

Habicht 1982: Habicht, Christian, Studien zur Geschichte Athens in hellenistischer Zeit, Göttingen 1982

Hall 2001: Hall, Jonathan M., Contested Ethnicities: Perceptions of Macedonia within Evolving Definitions of Greek Identity, in: I. Malkin (ed.), Ancient Perceptions of Greek Ethnicity, Washington, D. C. 2001, 159–186

Hall 2004: Hall, Johnathan M., Culture, Cultures and Acculturation, in: R. Rollinger – C. Ulf (eds.), Griechische Archaik. Interne Entwicklungen – Externe Impulse, Berlin 2004, 35–50

Hammond 1993: Hammond, Nigel G. L., The Macedonian Imprint on the Hellenistic World, in: P. Green (ed.), Hellenistic History and Culture, Berkeley 1993, 12–23

Hannestad 2020a: Hannestad, Lise, Nicator. Seleukus I and his Empire, Aarhus 2020a

Hannestad 2020b: Hannestad, Lise, The Macedonian: Seleukos I – the Foreign King, in: I. B. Maehle – P. B. Ravnå – E. H. Seland (eds.), Methods and Models in Ancient History. Essays in Honor of Jørgen Christian Meyer, Athens 2020b, 253–260

Hatzopoulos 2011: Hatzopoulos, Miltiades B., Macedonians and other Greeks, in: R. Lane Fox (ed.), Brill's Companion to Ancient Macedon. Studies in the Archaeology and History of Macedon, 650 BC-300 AD, Leiden et al. 2011, 51–78

Hatzopoulos 2020: Hatzopoulos, Miltiades B., Ancient Macedonia, Berlin 2020

Hauben 2014: Hauben, Hans, Ptolemy's Grand Tour, in: Hauben – Meeus 2014, 235–261

Hauben – Meeus 2014: Hauben, Hans – Meeus, Alexander (eds.), The Age of the Successors and the Creation of the Hellenistic Kingdoms (323–276 B. C.), Leuven 2014

Haubold 2013: Haubold, Johannes, Greece and Mesopotamia. Dialogues in Literature, Cambridge 2013

Heinemann 2010: Heinemann, Uwe, Stadtgeschichte im Hellenismus: die lokalhistoriographischen Vorgänger und Vorlagen Memnons von Herakleia, Munich 2010

Heinen 1972: Heinen, Heinz, Untersuchungen zur hellenistischen Geschichte des 3. Jahrhunderts v. Chr. Zur Geschichte der Zeit des Ptolemaios Keraunos und zum chremonideischen Krieg, Wiesbaden 1972

Heller 2015: Heller, André, Rev. of Kosmin 2014b, H-Soz-Kult, 09.02.2015, (www.hsozkult.de/publicationreview/id/reb-21919) last access: 20.5.2024

Howe 2018: Howe, Timothy, Kings Don't Lie: Truthtelling, Historiography and Ptolemy I Soter, in: id. (ed.), Ptolemy I Soter. A Self-Made Man, Oxford 2018, 155–184

Huss 1975: Huss, Werner, Die zu Ehren Ptolemaios' III und seiner Familie errichtete Statuengruppe von Thermos (IG IX 1,1², 56), Chronique d'Egypte 50, 1975, 312–320

Janssen 2007: Janssen, Eric, Die Kausia. Symbolik und Funktion der makedonischen Kleidung, Diss. Göttingen 2007

Kainz 2016: Kainz, Lukas, 'We are the Best, We are One, and We are Greeks!' Reflections on the Ptolemies' Participation in the Agones, in: Mann – Remijsen – Scharff 2016, 331–353

Kaye 2022: Kaye, Noah, The Attalids of Pergamon and Anatolia: Money, Culture, and State Power, Cambridge 2022

Keaveney – Madden 2011: Keaveney, Arthur – Madden, John A., Memnon (434), in: I. Worthington (ed.), Jacoby Online. Brill's New Jacoby III, Leiden 2011 (http://dx.doi.org/10.1163/1873-5363_bnj_a434) last access: 20.5.2024

Koenen 1993: Koenen, Ludwig, The Ptolemaic King as a Religious Figure, in: Bulloch et al. 1993, 25–38

Kohl ³2012: Kohl, Karl-Heinz, Ethnologie – die Wissenschaft vom kulturell Fremden. Eine Einführung, München ³2012

Kosmetatou 2003: Kosmetatou, Elizabeth, Remarks on a Delphic Ptolemaic Dynastic Group Monument, Tyche 18, 2003, 103–111

Kosmetatou 2004: Kosmetatou, Elizabeth, Bilistiche and the Quasi-Institutional Status of Ptolemaic Royal Mistress, Archiv für Papyrusforschung und verwandte Gebiete 50.1, 2004, 18–36

Kosmin 2014a: Kosmin, Paul J., Seeing Double in Seleucid Babylonia: Rereading the Borsippa Cylinder of Antiochus, in: A. Moreno – R. Thomas (ed.), Patterns of the Past. Epitēdeumata in the Greek Tradition, Oxford 2014, 173–198

Kosmin 2014b: Kosmin, Paul J., The Land of the Elephant Kings. Space, Territory, and Ideology in the Seleucid Empire, Cambridge 2014

Kuhrt 2002: Kuhrt, Amélie, 'Greeks' and 'Greece' in Mesopotamian and Persian Perspectives, Oxford 2002

Kuhrt 2007: Kuhrt, Amélie, The Persian Empire: A Corpus of Sources from the Achaemenid Period, New York 2007

Kuhrt – Sherwin-White 1991: Kuhrt, Amélie – Sherwin-White, Susan M., Aspects of Seleucid Royal Ideology: The Cylinder of Antiochus I from Borsippa, The Journal of Hellenic Studies 111, 1991, 71–86

Laubscher 1991: Laubscher, Hans P., Ptolemäische Reiterbilder, Mitteilungen des Deutschen Archäologischen Instituts. Athenische Abteilung 106, 1991, 223–238

Lehmann 1905: Lehmann, Carl F., Hellenistische Forschungen, 2. Seleukos, König der Makedonen, Klio 5, 1905, 244–254

Lehmann-Haupt 1907: Lehmann-Haupt, Carl F., Seleukos Nikators makedonisches Königtum, Klio 7, 1907, 449–453

Lehmann-Haupt 1909: Lehmann-Haupt, Carl F., Nochmals Seleukos Nikators makedonisches Königstum, Klio 9, 1909, 248–251

Lehmler 2005: Lehmler, Caroline, Syrakus unter Agathokles und Hieron II. Die Verbindung von Kultur und Macht in einer hellenistischen Metropole, Frankfurt a. M. 2005

Liampi 1998: Liampi, Katerini, Der makedonische Schild, Bonn 1998

Ma ²2002: Ma, John, Antiochos III and the Cities of Western Asia Minor, Oxford ²2002

Ma 2003: Ma, John, Kings, in: A. Erskine (ed.), A Companion to the Hellenistic World, Oxford et al. 2003, 177–195

Ma 2013: Ma, John, Statues and Cities. Honorific Portraits and Civic Identity in the Hellenistic World, Oxford 2013

Mann 2018: Mann, Christian, Könige, Poleis und Athleten in hellenistischer Zeit, Klio 100.2, 2018, 447–479

Mann – Remijsen – Scharff 2016: Mann, Christian – Remijsen, Sofie – Scharff, Sebastian (eds.), Athletics in the Hellenistic World, Stuttgart 2016

Mari 2020: Mari, Manuela, Alexander, King of the Macedonians, in: Trampedach – Meeus 2020, 197–217

McAuley 2022: McAuley, Alex, The Seleukid Royal Family as a Reigning Triad, in: Anagnostou-Laoutides – Pfeiffer 2022, 23–40

Meeus 2022: Meeus, Alexander, The History of the Diadochoi in Book XIX of Diodoros' 'Bibliotheke'. A Historical and Historiographical Commentary, Berlin 2022

Mehl 1986: Mehl, Andreas, Seleukos Nikator und sein Reich. Teil 1: von Triparadeisos bis Pydna, Leuven 1986

Mehl 1999: Mehl, Andreas, Zwischen West und Ost / Jenseits von West und Ost. Das Reich der Seleukiden, in: Brodersen 1999, 10–43

Mehl 2003: Mehl, Andreas, Gedanken zur "herrschenden Gesellschaft" und zu den Untertanen im Seleukidenreich, Historia 52, 2003, 147–160

Mehl 2022: Mehl, Andreas, How to Understand Seleukids as Babylonian "Great Kings", in: Anagnostou-Laoutides – Pfeiffer 2022, 187–202

Mittag 2006: Mittag, Peter F., Antiochos IV. Epiphanes. Eine politische Biographie, Berlin 2006

Montana 2020: Montana, Fausto, Hellenistic Scholarship, in: F. Montanari (ed.), History of Ancient Greek Scholarship from the Beginnings to the End of the Byzantine Age, Leiden 2020, 132–259

Muccioli 2004: Muccioli, Federicomaria, 'Il re dell' Asia': Ideologia e propaganda da Alessandro Magno a Mitridate VI, Simblos 4, 2004, 105–158

Muccioli 2006: Muccioli, Federicomaria, Antioco IV 'salvatore dell'Asia' (OGIS 253) e la campagna orientale del 165–164 a. C., in: A. Panaino – A. Piras (eds.), Proceedings of the 5th Conference of the Societas Iranologica Europaea Held in Ravenna, 6–11 October 2003, Milan 2006, 619–634

Muccioli 2013: Muccioli, Federicomaria, Gli epiteti ufficiali dei re ellenistici, Stuttgart 2013

Müller 2009: Müller, Sabine, Das hellenistische Königspaar in der medialen Repräsentation: Ptolemaios II. und Arsinoe II., Berlin et al. 2009

Musti 1966: Musti, Domenico, Lo stato dei Seleucidi. Dinastie popoli città da Seleuco I ad Antioco III, Studi Classici e Orientali 15, 1966, 61–197

Nawotka 2017: Nawotka, Krzysztof, Seleukos I and the Origin of the Seleukid Dynastic Ideology, Scripta Classica Israelica 36, 2017, 31–43

Ogden 2017: Ogden, Daniel, The Legend of Seleucus: Kingship, Narrative and Mythmaking in the Ancient World, Cambridge 2017

Palagia 2014: Palagia, Olga, The Frescoes from the Villa of P. Fannius Synistor in Boscoreale as Reflections of Macedonian Funerary Paintings of the Early Hellenistic Period, in: Hauben – Meeus 2014, 207–231

Pfeiffer 2018: Pfeiffer, Stefan, The Ptolemies: Hellenistic Kingship in Egypt, in: http://www.oxfordhandbooks.com (https://doi.org/10.1093/oxfordhb/9780199935390.013.23) last access: 20.5.2024

Pfeiffer 2022: Pfeiffer, Stefan, Great King Ptolemy III and Great King Antiochos III: Remarks on the Significance of a "Persian" Title in their Representation, in: Anagnostou-Laoutides – Pfeiffer 2022, 313–329

Pfeiffer – Klinkott 2021: Pfeiffer, Stefan – Klinkott, Hilmar, Legitimizing the Foreign King in the Ptolemaic and Seleucid Empires: The Role of Local Elites and Priests, in: Fischer-Bovet – von Reden 2021, 233–261

Plischke 2014: Plischke, Sonja, Die Seleukiden und Iran. Die seleukidische Herrschaftspolitik in den östlichen Satrapien, Wiesbaden 2014

Primo 2009: Primo, Andrea, La storiografia sui Seleucidi da Megastene a Eusebio di Cesarea, Pisa 2009

Rebenich 2017: Rebenich, Stefan (ed.), Monarchische Herrschaft im Altertum, Berlin et al. 2017

Reuss 1907: Reuss, Friedrich, Hellenistische Beiträge, Rheinisches Museum für Philologie. N. F. 62, 1907, 591–600

Reuss 1909: Reuss, Friedrich, Das makedonische Königtum des Seleukos Nikator, Klio 9, 1909, 76–79

Rollinger 2017: Rollinger, Robert, Monarchische Herrschaft am Beispiel des teispidisch-achaimenidischen Großreichs, in: Rebenich 2017, 189–215

Rouché – Sherwin-White 1985: Rouché, Charlotte M. – Sherwin-White, Susan M., Some Aspects of the Seleucid Empire: the Greek Inscriptions from Failaka, in the Arabian Gulf, Chiron 15, 1985, 1–39

Schalles 1985: Schalles, Hans-Joachim, Untersuchungen zur Kulturpolitik der pergamenischen Herrscher im 3. Jahrhundert vor Christus, Tübingen 1985

Scharrer 2006: Scharrer, Ulf, Die Einwanderung griechischer und makedonischer Bevölkerungsgruppen in den hellenistischen Osten, in: E. Olshausen – H. Sonnabend (eds.), "Troianer sind wir gewesen". Migrationen in der antiken Welt, Stuttgart 2006, 337–363

Scherberich 2009: Scherberich, Klaus, Zur Griechenlandpolitik Ptolemaios' III., in: J.-F. Eckholdt – M. Sigismund – S. Sigismund (eds.), Geschehen und Gedächtnis: die hellenistische Welt und ihre Wirkung; Festschrift für Wolfgang Orth zum 65. Geburtstag, Berlin 2009, 25–44

Seidensticker – Stähli – Wessels 2015: Seidensticker, Bernd – Stähli, Adrian – Wessels, Antje (eds.), Der Neue Poseidipp. Text – Übersetzung – Kommentar, Darmstadt 2015

Sherwin-White 1987: Sherwin-White, Susan M., Seleucid Babylonia: a Case Study for the Installation and Development of Greek Rule, in: A. Kuhrt – S. M. Sherwin-White (eds.), Hellenism in the East. The Interaction of Greek and Non-Greek Civilizations from Syria to Central Asia After Alexander, Berkeley 1987, 1–31

Sherwin-White – Kuhrt 1993: Sherwin-White, Susan M. – Kuhrt, A., From Samarkhand to Sardis: A New Approach to the Seleucid Empire, London 1993

Smith 1994: Smith, Roland R. R., Spear-Won Land at Boscoreale: On the Royal Paintings of a Roman Villa, The Journal of Roman Archaeology 7, 1994, 100–128

Stähelin 1921: Stähelin, Friedrich, Seleukos (2.) (I.), RE 2, A 1, 1921, 1208–1234

Stavrianopoulou 2013: Stavrianopoulou, Eftychia (ed.), Shifting Social Imaginaries in the Hellenistic Period. Narrations, Practices, and Images, Leiden 2013

Stephens 2005: Stephens, Susan A., Battle of the Books, in: Gutzwiller 2005, 229–248

Stephens 2015: Stephens, Susan A., Callimachus. The Hymns, Oxford 2015

Stephens 2018: Stephens, Susan A., The poets of Alexandria, London 2018

Stevens 2014: Stevens, Kathryn, The Antiochus Cylinder, Babylonian Scholarship and Seleucid Imperial ideology, The Journal of Hellenic Studies 134, 2014, 66–88

Stevens 2019: Stevens, Kathryn, Between Greece and Babylonia. Hellenistic Intellectual History in Cross-Cultural Perspective, Cambridge 2019

Stevens 2022: Stevens, Kathryn, "After Him a King Will Arise": Framing Resistance in Seleucid Babylonia, in: P. J. Kosmin – I. Moyer (eds.), Cultures of Resistance in the Hellenistic East, Oxford 2022, 95–124

Strootman 2010: Strootman, Rolf, Literature and the Kings, in: J. Clauss – M. Cuijpers (eds.), A Companion to Hellenistic Literature, Malden 2010, 30–45

Strootman 2013: Strootman, Rolf, Babylonian, Macedonian, King of the World: The Antiochos Cylinder from Borsippa and Seleukid Imperial Integration, in: Stavrianopoulou 2013, 67–97

Strootman 2014: Strootman, Rolf, Courts and Elites in the Hellenistic Empires, Edinburgh 2014

Strootman 2017: Strootman, Rolf, Eunuchs, Renegades and Concubines: The 'Paradox of Power' and the Promotion of Favorites in the Hellenistic Empires, in: Erskine – Llewellyn-Jones – Wallace 2017, 121–142

Strootman 2022: Strootman, Rolf, Pothos or Propaganda? Alexander's Longing to Reach the Ocean and Argead Imperial Ideology, in: F. Pownall – S. R. Asirvatham – S. Müller (eds.), The Courts of Philip II and Alexander the Great. Monarchy and Power in Ancient Macedonia, Berlin et al. 2022, 189–207

Tarn 1909: Tarn, William W., The Battles of Andros and Cos, The Journal of Hellenic Studies 29, 1909, 264–285

D. Thompson 2005: Thompson, Dorothy J., Posidippus, Poet of the Ptolemies, in: Gutzwiller 2005, 269–283

H. Thompson 1982: Thompson, Homer A., Architecture as a Medium of Public Relations Among the Successors of Alexander, in: Barr-Sharrar – Borza 1982, 173–189

Tracy – Habicht 1991: Tracy, Stephen V. – Habicht, Christian, New and Old Panathenaic Victor Lists, Hesperia 60, 1991, 187–236

Trampedach – Meeus 2020: Trampedach, Kai – Meeus, Alexander (eds.), The Legitimation of Conquest: Monarchical, Representation and the Art of Government in the Empire of Alexander the Great, Stuttgart 2020

Tréheux 1992: Tréheux, Jacques, Inscriptions de Délos. Index 1: Les étrangers, à l'exclusion des Athéniens de la clérouchie et des romains, Paris 1992

Tuplin 2009: Tuplin, Christopher J., The Seleucids and their Achaemenid Predecessors. A Persian inheritance, in: S. M. R. Darbandi, – A. Zournatzi (eds.), Ancient Greece and Ancient Iran: Cross-Cultural Encounters, Athens 2009, 109–136

van Bremen 2007: van Bremen, Riet, The Entire House is Full of Crowns. Hellenistic Agones and the Commemoration of Victory, in: S. Hornblower – C. Morgan (eds.), Pindar's Poetry, Patrons, and Festivals. From Archaic Greece to the Roman Empire, Oxford 2007, 345–375

van der Spek 2006: van der Spek, Robartus J., The Size and Significance of the Babylonian Temples und the Successors, in: P. Briant – F. Joannès (eds.), La transition entre l'empire achéménide et les royaumes hellénistiques (vers 350–300 av. J.-C.), Paris 2006, 261–307

van der Spek – Stol 2020: van der Spek, Robartus J. – Stol, Marten, 'Antiochus Cylinder' (https://www.livius.org/sources/content/mesopotamian-chronicles-content/antiochus-cylinder/) last access: 20.5.2024

Virgilio ²2003: Virgilio, Biagio, Lancia, diadema e porpora. Il re e la regalità ellenistica, Studi Ellenistici 14, Pisa et al. ²2003

Visscher 2020: Visscher, Marijn S., Beyond Alexandria. Literature and Empire in the Seleucid World, New York 2020

Weber 1993: Weber, Gregor, Dichtung und höfische Gesellschaft: die Rezeption von Zeitgeschichte am Hof der ersten drei Ptolemäer, Stuttgart 1993

Weber 1995: Weber, Gregor, Herrscher, Hof und Dichter. Aspekte der Legitimierung und Repräsentation hellenistischer Könige am Beispiel der ersten drei Antigoniden, Historia 44.3, 1995, 283–316

Weber 1997: Weber, Gregor, Interaktion, Repräsentation und Herrschaft. Der Königshof im Hellenismus, in: A. Winterling (ed.), Zwischen "Haus" und "Staat": Antike Höfe im Vergleich, Munich 1997, 27–71

Weber 2007: Weber, Gregor, Die neuen Zentralen. Hauptstädte, Residenzen, Paläste und Höfe, in: id. (ed.), Kulturgeschichte des Hellenismus, Stuttgart 2007, 99–117

Weissbach 1911: Weissbach, Franz H., Die Keilinschriften der Achämeniden, Leipzig 1911

Widmer 2019: Widmer, Marie, Translating the Seleucid ΒΑΣΙΛΙΣΣΑ: Notes on the Titulature of
Stratonice in the Borsippa Cylinder, Greece & Rome 66.2, 2019, 264–279

Wiemer 2017: Wiemer, Hans-Ulrich, Siegen oder untergehen? Die hellenistische Monarchie in
der neueren Forschung, in: Rebenich 2017, 305–339

Wiesehöfer 1996: Wiesehöfer, Josef, Discordia et Defectio. Dynamis kai Pithanourgia. Die frühen
Seleukiden und Iran, in: B. Funck (ed.), Hellenismus, Tübingen 1996, 29–56

Zanker 2019: Zanker, Paul, The Frescoes from the Villa of Publius Fannius Synistor at Boscoreale
in The Metropolitan Museum of Art, in: S. Hemingway – K. Karoglou (eds.), Art of the Hellenistic Kingdoms from Pergamon to Rome, New Haven et al. 2019, 190–204

Figures

Fig. 1: https://upload.wikimedia.org/wikipedia/commons/8/80/Wall_painting_-_
unexplained_figure_scene_-_Boscoreale_%28Villa_of_P_Fannius_Synistor_
oecus_H%29_-_Napoli_MAN_-_01.jpg (last access: 20.5.2024) © ArchaiOptix

Christoph Michels has been a Heisenberg Fellow at the University of Münster since 2020. He studied History, Classical Archaeology and Art History at the University of Bochum. In 2008, he received
his doctorate in a co-tutelle programme at the Universities of Innsbruck/Frankfurt with a thesis on
the kingdoms of Bithynia, Pontos, and Kappadokia (published 2009). In 2016, he completed his
habilitation at Aachen University with a thesis on the representation of the Roman princeps using
Antoninus Pius as example (published 2018). Michels is co-editor of *Athen und/oder Alexandreia?*
(2014), *Jenseits des Narrativs. Antoninus Pius in den nicht-literarischen Quellen* (2017), *Erinnerung.
Studien zu Konstruktionen, Persistenzen und gesellschaftlichem Wandel* (2018). He has held substitute
professorships in Bayreuth, Düsseldorf, Münster, and Tübingen. From 2014–2017 he was member
of the Junges Kolleg of the AWK NRW. His research focuses on cultural history and the history of
monarchy as well as on political communication in antiquity.

Der hellenistische König als Friedenswächter
Untersuchungen der Bedeutung des Friedens
in der hellenistischen monarchischen Ideologie
aus transdynastischer Perspektive[*]

CHARALAMPOS I. CHRYSAFIS

Abstract: The conceptions of the king as a warrior, victor or as a wealthy benefactor and city founder are the most common representational strategies that have been explored. There is a tendency in research to emphasize the warlike qualities of the Hellenistic king and to create the impression that he could establish its legitimacy exclusively through victorious military actions. Here the question arises whether the aspect of the king as an agent of peace and ὁμόνοια was less relevant to Hellenistic royal ideology. But an exclusively warlike and militaristic message would contradict the importance that ancient societies attached to these values. Peace and internal concord were widespread demands in the Hellenistic era, which were not limited to the Greek world, but could also be found in other traditions, such as Egypt and Mesopotamia. The aim of the paper is therefore to show where the concept of peace can be found in different areas of royal activity and self-representation in a transdynastic perspective and that the various, already consolidated approaches to the Hellenistic king as victor and benefactor partly or completely carry the image of the king as peacekeeper. Moreover, the influence of Philippos II's and Alexandros III's (self-) representation, through which they sought to legitimize their newly created hegemony over the Greek poleis, on the incorporation of peace into Hellenistic royal ideology is examined. Peace played an essential role as a goal of fundamental ideological constructs of the ancient Greek world, such as the promotion of the polis, federalism and panhellenism. Using examples of royal action in the aforementioned areas, an attempt is made to highlight the importance of the king's role as a peacekeeper and peacemaker as a legitimizing factor, but also the centrality of peace

[*]   Ich danke Christoph Michels, Hans Beck und Achim Lichtenberger für ihre freundliche Einladung zu ihrer Konferenz, sowie für wertvolle Kommentare zum Entwurf dieses Beitrags. Des Weiteren bedanke ich mich bei meinen Augsburger Kollegen Gregor Weber und Andreas Hartmann für ihre kritischen und weiterführenden Fragen, die diesen Beitrag in seinen unterschiedlichen Entstehungsphasen begleiteten und mir immer wieder zu neuen Denkanstößen verhalfen. Eventuelle Fehler und Irrtümer bleiben natürlich meine eigenen.

as an object of the subjects' expectations. Since the concept of peace is an abstract term, whose definition depends largely on how a culture perceives it, it can be concluded that its transdynastic manifestation in the royal self-representation of the Hellenistic dynasties exhibited a sufficient degree of homogeneity when addressed to a consistent audience.

1. Einführung

Die Konzeptionen des Königs als Krieger, Sieger oder wohlhabender Wohltäter und Stadtgründer sind die häufigsten Darstellungsstrategien, die in der Forschung über die hellenistische Monarchie untersucht worden sind. Es besteht zuweilen die Tendenz, die kriegerischen Eigenschaften des hellenistischen Königs zu betonen und den Eindruck zu erwecken, dass die hellenistische Monarchie ihre Legitimität ausschließlich durch siegreiche militärische Aktionen begründen konnte.[1] Wir hören in der Forschung vergleichsweise wenig über den hellenistischen König als Agenten des Friedens und der inneren Ordnung. Der griechische Begriff εἰρήνη wird dabei mit dem Konzept des äußeren Friedens in Verbindung gebracht und oft im Gegensatz zum Krieg als einer der beiden Zustände, in denen sich eine Stadt befinden kann, ausgedrückt, wie etwa in den Proxenie-Ehrenbeschlüssen. Ab dem 4. Jh. wird der Begriff auch im Sinne von zwischenstaatlichen Verträgen verwendet. Mit dem inneren Frieden einer Stadt oder Gesellschaft werden andere Begriffe wie ὁμόνοια, d. h. Eintracht, Zusammenarbeit und Einigkeit zwischen allen Mitgliedern der sozialen Organisation gleichgesetzt. Andere Begriffe, die einen friedlichen Zustand beschreiben, sind ἀσφάλεια (Schutz vor äußeren Feinden) und ἡσυχία (Ruhe, Fehlen von Unruhen).[2] Hierbei stellt sich die Frage, ob dieser Aspekt für die hellenistische königliche Ideologie weniger relevant war.

Auf einer ersten Ebene mag eine solche Lesart gerechtfertigt sein, insbesondere auf der praktischen Ebene des königlichen Verhaltens, wie es sich in Plutarchs bekanntermaßen negativer Beurteilung der hellenistischen Könige widerspiegelt, „deren Raubgier weder Meer noch Gebirge noch die unbewohnbare Wüste eine Grenze setzen", dass sie zudem nicht mit dem, was sie haben, zufrieden sein können, und sie ständig einander Unrecht tun. Wenn wir insgesamt die Geschichte der hellenistischen Reiche betrachten, stellen wir tatsächlich fest, dass sich die hellenistischen Könige fast durchgehend im Krieg befanden und, wenn wir zurück zu Plutarch blicken, „sie die beiden

---

[1]   Die Problematik der Forschung zu diesem Thema wird in der Einleitung zu dem in Kürze erscheinenden Band mit dem Titel „Basileus Eirenophylax: Friedenskulturen und monarchische Repräsentation in der hellenistischen Staatenwelt" (herausgegeben von Ch. Chrysafis, A. Hartmann, Chr. Schliephake und G. Weber) ausführlich erörtert.

[2]   Vgl. Graeber 1992, 116–162; Bolmarcich 2020.

Worte Krieg und Frieden wie gängige Münzen behandeln, indem sie ohne Rücksicht auf die Gerechtigkeit das benutzen, was ihnen gerade zum Vorteil gereicht".[3]

Der Topos der königlichen πλεονεξία (Raubgier) ist oft in der Forschung nur als eine negative Übertragung der königlichen Selbstdarstellung als triumphierende Eroberer interpretiert worden.[4] Es ist jedoch nicht zu übersehen, dass der Krieg und die ständige Beschäftigung der Könige damit in den Quellen negativ behandelt werden. Ein gutes Beispiel für die positive und negative Übertragung dieser königlichen Darstellung ist Antiochos III. Gehrke zeigte beispielsweise anhand von Polybios' Beschreibung (11.34.15) der militärischen Erfolge Antiochos' III. im Osten die „importance of reputation and recognition, prestige and victory, for Hellenistic kingship".[5] Ähnliche Eroberungsaktionen wie die in Koilesyrien und Thrakien werden jedoch von den Römern bei Appian benutzt, um den Seleukidenkönig zu beschuldigen, aus Habgier einen ungerechten Krieg zu führen.[6]

Insbesondere auf der Ebene der antiken politischen Theorie wird die Habgier systematisch als ein Element verurteilt, das mit Tyrannei, d. h. mit illegitimen Herrschaftstypen verbunden ist. Der Symposionteil des Aristeasbriefes (§ 222–223) zum Beispiel, der eine Zusammenfassung der Laienwahrnehmung der politischen Philosophie jener Zeit enthält, beschreibt als guten König denjenigen, der sich selbst beherrschen kann und nicht den Begierden nachgibt, ohne Maß nach Land zu streben.[7] Darüber hinaus

---

3   Plut. Pyrrhos 12.3–5: οἷς γὰρ οὐ πέλαγος, οὐκ ὄρος, οὐκ ἀοίκητος ἐρημία πέρας ἐστὶ πλεονεξίας, οὐδ' οἱ διαιροῦντες Εὐρώπην καὶ Ἀσίαν τέρμονες ὁρίζουσι τὰς ἐπιθυμίας, πῶς ἂν ἁπτόμενοι καὶ ψαύοντες ἀλλήλων ἀτρεμοῖεν, ἐν τοῖς παροῦσι μὴ ἀδικοῦντες, οὐκ ἔστιν εἰπεῖν· (4) ἀλλὰ πολεμοῦσι μὲν ἀεί, τὸ ἐπιβουλεύειν καὶ φθονεῖν ἔμφυτον ἔχοντες, δυεῖν δ' ὀνομάτων ὥσπερ νομισμάτων, πολέμου καὶ εἰρήνης, τῷ παρατυχόντι χρῶνται πρὸς τὸ συμφέρον, οὐ πρὸς τὸ δίκαιον· (5) ἐπεὶ βελτίους γε πολεμεῖν ὁμολογοῦντές εἰσιν, ἢ τῆς ἀδικίας τὸ ἀργοῦν καὶ σχολάζον δικαιοσύνην καὶ φιλίαν ὀνομάζοντες. Die betreffende Passage von Plutarch ähnelt stark der These von der grundsätzlichen Nichtexistenz des Friedens, wie ein kretischer Redner in Platons Gesetzen behauptet, die weitgehend aus der Beobachtung der Instabilität der griechischen Welt durch die häufigen Kriege des 5. und 4. Jh.s abgeleitet wurde; Plat. leg. 626A: ἣν γὰρ καλοῦσιν οἱ πλεῖστοι τῶν ἀνθρώπων εἰρήνην, τοῦτ' εἶναι μόνον ὄνομα, τῷ δ' ἔργῳ πάσαις πρὸς πάσας τὰς πόλεις ἀεὶ πόλεμον ἀκήρυκτον κατὰ φύσιν εἶναι. Diese Position wird von Platon in seinem Werk ausgebaut, nur um wenig später von dem athenischen Gesprächspartner des Dialogs dekonstruiert zu werden, Plat. leg. 628c: τό γε μὴν ἄριστον οὔτε ὁ πόλεμος οὔτε ἡ στάσις, ἀπευκτὸν δὲ τὸ δεηθῆναι τούτων, εἰρήνη δὲ πρὸς ἀλλήλους ἅμα καὶ φιλοφροσύνη. Die Bedeutung des Friedens für das antike griechische Denken, insbesondere im 5. und 4. Jh., wird von Raaflaub (2009, 225–250; 2016, 122–157), und den verschiedenen Beiträgen des Münsteraner Katalogs über den Frieden in der Antike (Lichtenberger – Nieswandt –Salzmann 2018) sowie des Bandes von Ager 2020 für die Kulturgeschichte des Friedens in der Antike mit vielen Verweisen auf ältere Literatur hervorgehoben.

4   Strootman 2014, 308.

5   Gehrke 2013, 77–78.

6   App. Syr. 38.194–196. Pol. 15.20.1–8 übt eine ähnlich starke Kritik an der Habgier von Antiochos III. und Philippos V. im Zusammenhang mit dem so genannten „Raubvertrag", den sie schlossen, um die äußeren Besitztümer des minderjährigen Ptolemaios V. zu teilen, vgl. Diod. 28.3.

7   Siehe Wright 2015, 43–58, 327–335, 424–429 mit Verweisen auf ältere Literatur für den Symposionteil des Aristeasbriefes als eine leichter verständliche Wiedergabe der hellenistischen politischen

wurde in der Forschung bereits hervorgehoben, dass in der hellenistischen Epoche die Suche und der Wunsch nach Frieden trotz der zentralen Bedeutung des Krieges in dieser Epoche nicht aufhörten.[8] Es ist daher nicht verwunderlich, dass diese Thematik bei der königlichen (Selbst-)Darstellung in der Tat aufgenommen und nicht zurückgewiesen wird. Der Hauptgrund dafür ist, dass die Friedensbotschaft tatsächlich den Erwartungen der damaligen Rezipienten (entweder der Untertanen oder der griechischen Städte) entsprach, wie weiter unten in der Analyse von Beispielen aus dieser Zeit gezeigt wird, und auf diese Weise das Prestige der Monarchie und ihre Legitimation als akzeptables Regime besonders gestärkt wurden.

Deshalb wird z. B. im Aristeasbrief (§ 291) auf die allerletzte Frage des Symposiums nach der wichtigsten Aufgabe einer Königsherrschaft geantwortet, dass die Untertanen immer in Frieden leben und schnellen Rechtsentscheid erlangen müssen. Zusammengefasst unterscheidet sich die hellenistische politische Theorie nicht sehr von den Schlussfolgerungen der modernen Herrschaftssoziologie, da sie die ordnungskonstituierenden und -stabilisierenden Effekte des Königtums positiv bewertet und diese als Kern der Legitimation für die Herrschaft der hellenistischen Könige untermauert.[9] Ziel dieses Beitrages ist es daher, aufzuzeigen, wo sich der Friedensbegriff in verschiedenen Bereichen königlicher Tätigkeit und Selbstdarstellung in einer trans-

---

Theorie, die hauptsächlich aus den weitgehend verlorenen hellenistischen Abhandlungen über das Königtum stammt. Ein anderes Beispiel der theoretischen Debatte über die πλεονεξία als negatives Merkmal befindet sich in der sehr späten Quelle von Pollux (1.42). Einige der Vorwürfe, die man nach ihm verwenden könnte, um einen Tyrannen zu tadeln, sind die Begrifflichkeiten πλεονέκτης (gierig) und πολεμοποιός (kriegerisch). Diese negative Stimmung der Griechen gegenüber dem königlichen Landerwerb ist auch in der antiken Geschichtsschreibung nachzuweisen, z. B. in der pro-ptolemaiischen und anti-antigonidischen Erzählung des P.Köln VI 247 über die Ereignisse des „Jahres der Könige", in der die universalistischen Ansprüche des Antigonos als eine Bedrohung empfunden wurden; z. B. col. I Z. 18–27: [Ἀντί|γονος] ὁ Φιλίππου προσ|[²⁰ηγόρε]υσεν ἑαυτὸν βασι|[λέα πρ]ῶτος πεπεισμένος | [τοὺς μ]ὲν ἐν τοῖς ἀξιώμα|[σιν πάν]τας ἀρεῖσθαι ῥαι|[δίως, αὐ]τὸς δ' ἡγήσεσθαι | [τῆς οἰκο]υμένης ἁπάσης | [καὶ καθ]ά[[περ]] Ἀλέξανδρος π[α|ρα]λήψεσ]θαι τὰ πράγματα, G. A. Lehmann 1988; Billows 1990, 351–352. Ptolemaios hingegen scheint aus Sicht der Rhodier der bessere König zu sein, da er einerseits ein Gegengewicht zu Antigonos bilden würde und andererseits keine Ambitionen hat, dem Vorbild Alexanders als Weltkönig zu folgen, P.Köln VI 247 col. II Z. 28–38.

8   Siehe die entsprechende Analyse von Chaniotis 2005, 71–72, 184–186, 252–253, der auch die sehr interessante Inschrift IG IV 12.687 zitiert, in welcher der (uns sonst unbekannte) Historiker Philippos von Pergamon (BNJ 95) hofft, die Griechen durch seine Beschreibung des Übels von Kriegen und Unruhen zu lehren, wie sie ihre Lebensweise verbessern können, vgl. Jones 2020, 120–127. Ein ähnliches Problem wurde für die klassische Periode der griechischen Antike identifiziert, wo zwar auf den ersten Blick der Eindruck einer an kriegerischen und heroischen Vorbildern orientierten Gesellschaft entsteht, in der aber gleichzeitig die Bedeutung des Friedens als Wert und erstrebenswerter Zustand der Menschheit nicht unterschätzt werden sollte, wie von Raaflaub 2009; 2010; 2016, 1–11, 12–42, 122–157 sehr deutlich herausgestellt wird; vgl. Wilker 2012a; Moloney – Williams 2017; Ager 2020.

9   Die moderne Herrschaftssoziologie ist erst von Max Weber in der Tiefe definiert und untersucht worden, Weber 1922, 1–12; 1980, 122–176. Ein prominentes Beispiel für seine Rezeption in der althistorischen Forschung stellt Gehrke 1982 (2013) dar, der versucht, die hellenistische Monarchie

dynastischen Perspektive wiederfindet und dass die verschiedenen, bereits gefestigten Ansätze zum hellenistischen König als Sieger und Wohltäter teilweise oder vollständig das Bild des Königs als Friedenswächter in sich tragen.

2. Der erste „eirenophylax": Zur historischen Konstellation der Aufnahme der Rolle des Friedenswächters in die (Selbst-)Darstellung hellenistischer Könige

Die Darstellung des Königs als Beschützer des Friedens und folglich des Wohlstands seines Reiches und seiner Untertanen ist ein fast überzeitliches, wenn nicht sogar universelles Phänomen, das natürlich variierend in vielen Kulturen und historischen Epochen wiederzufinden ist.[10] Die hellenistische Monarchie ist in der Tat eine komplexe Institution, in der sich Einflüsse aus vielen verschiedenen Traditionen wie dem pharaonischen Ägypten (hauptsächlich für die Ptolemaier) und Mesopotamien (für die Seleukiden) nachweisen lassen. Obwohl die Bedeutung des Friedens in den beiden oben genannten Traditionen und deren Einfluss auf die hellenistische königliche Selbstdarstellung auf lokaler Ebene diskutiert werden kann, wurde die gesamte hellenistische Monarchie eher von der griechischen/makedonischen Tradition, aus der sie hervorging, und von der persischen Tradition, die sie ersetzte, beeinflusst. Die sogenannte ‚pax Achaemenidica', die in der Forschung als Ideologem vorgestellt ist, kann zwar als ein Modell erkannt werden, an dem sich die hellenistische Monarchie hätte orientieren können.[11] Aber das erste bewusste und intensive Bemühen, den hellenisti-

---

im Sinne der Weberschen Herrschaftstypologie (und hier unter Zugrundelegung des Typs der charismatischen Herrschaft) zu analysieren.

10   Zu den Gemeinsamkeiten und Unterschieden der verschiedenen antiken Traditionen in der Herangehensweise an Theorien und Konzepte des Friedens siehe die Hinweise in Raaflaub 2016.

11   Die persische königliche Darstellung betonte besonders die Funktion der göttlichen Unterstützung des Königs, die ihn leitet, gerecht zu handeln und sieghaft zu sein. Der persische König ist daher durch seine militärische Stärke und Kompetenz ein Bewahrer des Friedens. Von besonderer Bedeutung ist aber auch die Darstellung des Königs, der seinem Hofstaat, seiner Armee und seinen Untertanen eine Audienz gewährt, indem er sich um Ruhe, Frieden und religiös-politische Ordnung bemüht; Brosius 2014; Wiesehöfer 2023; vgl. Tuplin 2017, 31–54. Inwieweit diese persische Ideologie die Herausbildung der entsprechenden hellenistischen Ideologie beeinflusst hat, ist sicherlich eine legitime Frage, und die Feststellung des Ausmaßes ihres Einflusses ist vor allem wegen des Umfangs der griechisch geprägten Quellen im Verhältnis zu anderen schwieriger zu ermitteln. Problematisch ist auch, dass die antike griechische Wahrnehmung des persischen Reiches nicht mit der Selbstdarstellung der Perser übereinstimmt und viele Elemente eines kulturellen Missverständnisses in sich trägt; vgl. Tuplin 2017. Bewusste Versuche, hellenistische Monarchien mit der persischen Tradition zu verbinden, finden sich vor allem in einer Reihe von Königreichen mit ausgeprägteren iranischen Elementen, die an der Peripherie des seleukidischen Reiches entstanden, Michels 2017, 41–56; 2021, 471–496; Canepa 2021, 71–101. Für die Seleukiden selbst, auf deren Territorium sich der größte Teil des persischen Reiches befand und für die wir theoretisch die meisten Belege für eine Kontinuität haben sollten, ist die Beweislage so dürftig, dass Tuplin 2008,

schen Monarchen in enger Verbindung mit der Durchsetzung des Friedens insbesondere in der griechischen Welt darzustellen, kam als Folge der anhaltenden Kriege des
5. und 4. Jh.s und einer intensiven ideologischen Ausarbeitung im Geiste der panhellenischen Idee.

Vor allem die problematischen Erfahrungen dieser beiden Jahrhunderte in der
griechischen Welt führten dazu, dass die Intellektuellen der Zeit versuchten, das Übel
des Krieges durch seinen ‚Export' zu beseitigen. Das bedeutet, dass eine Trennung
zwischen den Griechen und den ‚Barbaren' vorgenommen wurde. So wurde versucht,
Kriege zwischen den Erstgenannten abzuschaffen oder zu verurteilen, während die
letzteren, nämlich primär Persien, als die größte Macht unter den Barbaren, die Rolle
eines gemeinsamen Feindes annehmen und so die griechische Welt einen sollten.[12] Im
Allgemeinen wurden die Barbaren im griechischen Denken als eine Antithese zum
Griechentum und als von Natur aus dazu prädestiniert konzipiert, in Konflikt mit den
Griechen zu geraten und von diesen rechtmäßig beherrscht zu werden.[13]

Hier ist die antike Unterscheidung von gerechten und ungerechten Kriegen besonders hervorzuheben, da sie für das Verständnis des Krieges als ein grundsätzlich negativer Aspekt des menschlichen Lebens von besonderer Bedeutung ist. Ein Übergang
vom Frieden zum Krieg musste dementsprechend angemessen gerechtfertigt werden,
und sehr oft wurde der negative Ausgang eines kriegerischen Konflikts mit dem Unrecht seiner Auslösung als göttliche Strafe in Verbindung gebracht. Kriege sollten also
immer gerechtfertigt werden, und die hellenistischen Könige waren in diesem Bereich

109–136 der Ansicht ist, dass wir besonders skeptisch sein sollten, was die Sicherheit einer Verbindung oder eines Bruchs zwischen diesen beiden königlichen Traditionen angeht. Ein Beweis für
die Übernahme älterer königlicher Traditionen durch die Seleukiden ist der „Antiochos-Zylinder"
von Borsippa, obwohl dieser eher in die Fußstapfen der noch älteren mesopotamischen Monarchien tritt, und es zudem zweifelhaft ist, ob das Vokabular des Textes eine bewusste Entscheidung
der seleukidischen Monarchie widerspiegelt oder einfach das Ergebnis der üblichen Formulierung
babylonischer Schreiber in offiziellen Dokumenten ist; Plischke 2017, 168–171; vgl. zudem die Beiträge von Sonja Richter; Shane Wallace und Christoph Michels in diesem Band.

12   Die Notwendigkeit der Einheit der Griechen und der Beendigung der innerhellenischen Kriege
      wird nicht zufällig bereits von Herodot (z. B. Hdt. 7.9) formuliert, welcher durch die Idealisierung
      der Heldentaten der Perserkriege ein Eckpfeiler dieser ideologischen Bewegung ist. Wenn zudem
      die Angaben Plutarchs zutreffen, scheint die Auffassung von der Notwendigkeit der Einheit der
      Griechen zum Zwecke der Kriegsführung gegen die Perser bereits in der Mitte des 5. Jh.s in den
      führenden Kreisen Athens verbreitet gewesen zu sein, Plut. Perikles 4–6, 17.2. Viel stärker mani-
      festierte sich diese Bewegung nach dem Ende des katastrophalen Peloponnesischen Krieges mit
      Gorgias und seinem Schüler Isokrates als ihren Hauptvertretern; siehe Chrysafis 2023 mit Verwei-
      sen auf ältere Literatur.

13   Clavadetscher-Thürlemann 1985, 30–45. Diese Auffassung wurde von den Diadochen geteilt, wie
      die Aussage von Demetrios Poliorketes in seinen fruchtlosen Verhandlungen mit Seleukos kurz
      vor seiner Niederlage und anschließenden Gefangennahme sehr deutlich zeigt. Er verdiene es, zu-
      mindest die Gelegenheit zu erhalten, ein kleines Königreich unter einigen Barbaren zu erwerben,
      die noch nicht erobert sind, Plut. Demetrios 47.4.

keine Ausnahme.[14] Noch wichtiger für diesen Beitrag ist der philosophische Versuch der Einordnung des Kriegs als Mittel, um Frieden zu schaffen.[15] Ein gerechter und legitimer Krieg sollte also nach außen hin der Sicherung des Friedens dienen. Dieser Versuch zeigt einerseits, dass ein pazifistischer Ansatz in der Antike nicht haltbar war – realistischerweise gab es für eine antike Gemeinschaft keine Möglichkeit, den Krieg für immer zu vermeiden –, und andererseits, dass der Wert des Friedens konsequent über dem Wert des Krieges eingestuft wurde, auch wenn der letztgenannte aufgrund seiner Notwendigkeit ideologisch überhöht wurde und im Mittelpunkt der Aufmerksamkeit stand.[16]

Um auf die Entwicklungen des 4. Jh.s v. Chr. und die Suche nach Frieden in der griechischen Welt zurückzukommen, sei Folgendes angemerkt: auf praktischer Ebene wurde schnell klar, dass ein solches Vorhaben aufgrund der widersprüchlichen Interessen der griechischen Stadtstaaten ohne die Präsenz einer fähigen Hegemonialmacht als durchsetzende Instanz kaum zu verwirklichen war. Andererseits wurde einer solchen Macht durch diese Rolle die Möglichkeit gegeben, die positive Botschaft des Friedens zu manipulieren, um auf zynische Weise eigene Interessen durchzusetzen und zu legitimieren.[17] Die Suche nach dieser hegemonialen Macht lässt sich vor allem

---

14 Clavadetscher-Thürlemann 1985, 53–83. Ein gutes Beispiel dafür bietet die Erklärung und Argumentation des Philippos V. und seiner Verbündeten zur Rechtfertigung des Bundesgenossenkrieges gegen die Aitoler als δίκαιος πόλεμος im Jahre 220 v. Chr.; Pol. 4.25–26.

15 Plat. leg. 628c–e, 803d: τὰ γὰρ περὶ τὸν πόλεμον ἡγοῦνται σπουδαῖα ὄντα τῆς εἰρήνης ἕνεκα δεῖν εὖ τίθεσθαι; Aristot. pol. 1333a35: πόλεμον μὲν εἰρήνης χάριν, 1334a10; eth. Nic. 1177b4–12: δοκεῖ τε ἡ εὐδαιμονία ἐν τῇ σχολῇ εἶναι· ἀσχολούμεθα γὰρ ἵνα σχολάζωμεν, καὶ πολεμοῦμεν ἵν' εἰρήνην ἄγωμεν. τῶν μὲν οὖν πρακτικῶν ἀρετῶν ἐν τοῖς πολιτικοῖς ἢ ἐν τοῖς πολεμικοῖς ἡ ἐνέργεια, αἱ δὲ περὶ ταῦτα πράξεις δοκοῦσιν ἄσχολοι εἶναι, αἱ μὲν πολεμικαὶ καὶ παντελῶς (οὐδεὶς γὰρ αἱρεῖται τὸ πολεμεῖν τοῦ πολεμεῖν ἕνεκα, οὐδὲ παρασκευάζει πόλεμον· δόξαι γὰρ ἂν παντελῶς μιαιφόνος τις εἶναι, εἰ τοὺς φίλους πολεμίους ποιοῖτο, ἵνα μάχαι καὶ φόνοι γίνοιντο, vgl. Dinkler 1972, 444–445. Das Konzept des gerechten Krieges bei den Griechen ist ausführlich von Clavadetscher-Thürlemann 1985, 17–126 untersucht worden.

16 Gleichzeitig finden wir aber im antiken griechischen Denken die Existenz des Grundsatzes, dass die gewaltsame Eroberung fremden Landes einen rechtmäßigen Besitz begründet, Chaniotis 2004, 194–199. Die meisten Beispiele für die Legitimierung von Landbesitz durch Eroberung stammen aus der Zeit der Diadochen (Diod. 18.39.5, 43.1, 85.3, 19.105.5, 20.76.7), über deren Vorgehen wir die meisten Informationen haben. Später wird diese Position von Antiochos III. und Antiochos IV. in aller Deutlichkeit vertreten, als sie ihre laufenden Annektierungen mit der Vererbung des durch siegreichen Kampf ihres Vorfahrens gewonnenen Eigentums rechtfertigten (Pol. 18.51.3–6, 28.1.4, 28.20.6–9). Das Quellenmaterial zum Argument des „speererworbenen" Landes als Rechtfertigung des territorialen Eigentums ist von Mehl 1980 gesammelt worden, vgl. Degen 2018, 67–77. Die sorgfältige Analyse der Quellen zeigte jedoch, dass die absolute Gültigkeit des Speererwerbs nicht in die Struktur des hellenistischen Großmachtsystems passt und die Legitimität der Landbesetzung durch einen Sieg auch direkt von den gerechten Gründen abhängt, aus denen der Krieg begonnen wurde, wie zum Beispiel Rachekrieg oder Darstellung des Kriegsausbruches als Schuld der Besiegten, vgl. Bickerman – Sykoutris 1928, 26–29; Chaniotis 2004, 197–199.

17 Die erste relativ erfolgreiche institutionelle Durchsetzung des Friedens in großem Maßstab in der gesamten griechischen Welt war die koine eirene von 387/386 v. Chr., die ironischerweise vom persischen König Artaxerxes diktiert worden war, Jehne 1994, 7–29; Wilker 2012b, 95–117. Dabei

in den Schriften des athenischen Publizisten und Hauptvertreters dieser Ideen, Isokrates, nachvollziehen. Schließlich, nach vielen misslungenen Versuchen, identifizierte er 346 v. Chr. Philippos II. von Makedonien als den einzigen, der diese Vision verwirklichen konnte.[18]

Betrachtet man die charakteristischen Vorbilder und Begründer der hellenistischen Monarchien, Philippos II. und Alexandros III., so stellt sich das Ende der ewigen innergriechischen Kriege und die Durchsetzung des Friedens als eine grundlegende Errungenschaft ihrer informellen Oberherrschaft über Griechenland dar. Philippos II. übernahm Entwicklungen und Ideen der griechischen Welt, um seiner Macht über die griechischen Städte nicht nur Legitimität, sondern auch Stabilität zu verleihen. Der Höhepunkt von Philippos' Handeln war die Gründung des Korinthischen Bundes (338/337 v. Chr.) mit ihm als Friedensgaranten, der seine militärisch errungene Hegemonialstellung auf eine legale Basis stellte und festigte.[19] Die Details dieses Machtsystems sind entscheidend. Der Vertrag der griechischen Poleis mit Philippos II. erwähnt eine Nichtangriffsbestimmung und den Schutz der Verfassungen der Mitglieder.[20] Innerhalb des Bündnisses mussten Streitigkeiten durch die Institution der Schiedsverfahren beigelegt werden, wie zum Beispiel die Beilegung des Streits zwischen Melos und Kimolos über einige Inseln durch die Vermittlung von Argos, welches gemäß dem Beschluss des συνέδριον der Bündner darüber geurteilt hat.[21] Gleichzeitig ist der Bund jedoch schon im Gründungsgedanken auf einen Rachekrieg gegen Persien ausgerichtet. Dieser Krieg gegen die Barbaren fungiert als das verbindende Schlüsselelement des Bündnisses und verweist nochmal auf das grundlegende Element des Friedenskonzepts im antiken griechischen Denken, das durch die Übertragung des Krieges und seiner zerstörerischen Folgen auf die Gebiete des Feindes gestärkt oder geschützt wird. Nach den Bestrebungen des Philippos II. in diese Richtung versuchte auch Alexander III., sich als Vorkämpfer und Rächer der Griechen zu präsentieren.[22]

Die teilweise positive Rezeption des Philippos als guter Herrscher in der antiken Literatur beruhte zudem weitgehend auf der Art und Weise, wie er die makedonische Hegemonie nach seinem Sieg bei Chaironeia durch das griechische Bündnis von Korinth aufbaute. Vor allem die makedonischen Könige (Argeaden und Antigoniden) versuchten, ausgehend von diesen ‚Errungenschaften' der Herrschaft des Philippos

---

spielten Sparta und Persien die Rolle des Garanten des Friedens, Sparta als προστάτης τῆς εἰρήνης, Xen. Hell. 5.1.36; Artaxerxes II. als φύλαξ τῆς εἰρήνης, Isokr. 4.175.

18   Isokr. 5.14–16. Es scheint auch, dass Philippos II. selbst seitdem begonnen hatte, sich diese Slogans anzueignen und zu versuchen, sie in seine Kommunikation mit der griechischen Welt einzubeziehen, Diod. 16.60.3–5.

19   Zahrnt 2009, 21–25.

20   IG II³ 1.318, Z. 5–15. Der Vertrag ist durch Alexandros III. 336 v. Chr. erneuert worden, Demosth. 18.2–30.

21   Ager 1996, Nr. 3, vgl. Ager 2015, 484–486; Smarczyk 2015, 453–458.

22   Wallace 2011, 148–157; 2020, 125–135, 143–144; Trampedach 2020, 53–54.

eine positive Darstellung ihrer Macht über die Griechen aufzubauen. Eines der frühesten Beispiele ist die Anordnung des Philippos-Arrhidaios III. bezüglich der Freiheit der Griechen. Durch diese Anordnung versuchte Arrhidaios, sich als ein echter Nachfolger von Philippos II. und Alexander III. darzustellen. Der erste Satz des Edikts verweist unmittelbar auf die Verdienste der Vorfahren des Arrhidaios zu Gunsten der Griechen und seine Absicht, ihr Werk fortzusetzen.[23] Die Herstellung des Friedens wird unmittelbar danach ausdrücklich als ein Verdienst des Philippos II. bezeichnet, womit das Bündnis von Korinth und dessen Statuten gemeint sind. Anschließend werden in diesem Diagramma die kritischen Ereignisse der Jahre 323–319 v. Chr. so dargestellt, wie die makedonische Monarchie sie offiziell darstellen möchte, wobei die Kriege und Katastrophen auf die Entscheidungen einiger fehlgeleiteter Griechen und unglückliche Initiativen makedonischer στρατηγοί zurückgeführt werden. Das Ziel des Arrhidaios ist es jedoch, zur vorherigen (idealisierten) Situation zurückzukehren und, explizit gesagt, den Frieden wiederherzustellen (ἡμεῖς δὲ τιμῶντες τὴν ἐξ ἀρχῆς προαίρεσιν κατασκευάζομεν ὑμῖν εἰρήνην).[24]

---

23 Diod. 18.56.1: ἐπειδὴ συμβέβηκε τοῖς προγόνοις ἡμῶν πολλὰ τοὺς Ἕλληνας εὐεργετηκέναι, βουλόμεθα διαφυλάττειν τὴν ἐκείνων προαίρεσιν καὶ πᾶσι φανερὰν ποιῆσαι τὴν ἡμετέραν εὔνοιαν ἣν ἔχοντες διατελοῦμεν πρὸς τοὺς Ἕλληνας. Dieser besondere Ausdruck, der in mehrfacher Hinsicht die dynamische Kontinuität zeigt und die Stabilität der Leistungen im Laufe der Zeit unterstreicht, erweist sich als eine Konstante der hellenistischen königlichen Kommunikation mit der griechischen Welt, z. B. I.Milet I 139 (Brief des Ptolemaios II. an Milet), Z. 2–5: πρότερον τὴμ πᾶσαν ἐποιούμην σπουδὴν ὑπὲρ τῆς πόλεως ὑμῶν (…) διὰ τὸ καὶ τὸμ πατέρα τὸν ἡμέτερον ὁρᾶν οἰκείως τὰ πρὸς τὴμ πόλιν διακείμενον καὶ πολλῶν ἀγαθῶν παραίτιον ὑμῖν γενόμενον. Für die Attaliden, Liv. 33.2.1; Für die Seleukiden I. Didyma 493 (Brief des Seleukos II. an Milet) Z. 2–3: τῶμ προγόνων ἡμῶν καὶ τοῦ πατρὸς πολλὰς καὶ μεγάλας εὐεργεσίας κατατεθειμένων εἰς τὴν ὑμετέραμ πόλιν. Auf diese Weise wird die Legitimität des Herrschers gestärkt, nicht nur als „charismatischer" König, durch sein individuelles Handeln zum Wohle des Ganzen, sondern auch als Erbe eines ebenso „charismatischen" Vorfahren. Die griechischen Städte wiederum übernehmen diese Darstellung in ihr Vokabular zur Ehrung des Herrschers und verschaffen ihm damit eine äußere Anerkennung seiner Kommunikationsziele, siehe z. B. für die Ptolemaier IG XII.7 506 (Nikouria-Dekret) Z. 10–20: ἐπειδὴ ὁ βασιλεὺς καὶ σωτὴρ Πτολεμαῖος πολλῶν καὶ μεγάλων ἀγαθῶν α αἴτιος ἐγένετο τοῖς Ἕλλησι (…) Καὶ νῦν ὁ βασιλεὺς Πτολεμαῖος, διαδεξάμενος τὴμ βασιλείαν παρ[ὰ] τοῦ πατρός, τὴν αὐτὴν εὔνοιαν καὶ ἐπιμέλειαν [π]αρεχόμενος διατελεῖ εἰς τε τοὺς νησιώτας κα[ὶ] τοὺς ἄλλους Ἕλληνας; I.Milet I 139. Z. 23–32; Für die Seleukiden: IK 28.4 (Iasos) Z. 41–43: ἐπειδὴ βασιλέως μεγάλου Ἀντιό[χο]υ προγονικὴν αἵρεσιν διατηροῦντος εἰς πάντας [το]ὺς Ἕλληνας καὶ τοῖς μὲν τὴν εἰρήνην παρέχοντος; Für die Attaliden I.Milet I 307 Z. 2–5: ἐπειδὴ βασιλεὺς Εὐμένης συγγενὴς κ[αὶ φί]λος καὶ εὔνους καὶ εὐεργέτης ὑπάρχων τῆς πόλεως διὰ προγόνων καὶ πρὸς ἅπαντας μὲν τοὺς Ἕλληνας φιλοδόξως ἀπὸ τῆς ἀρχῆς διακείμενος.

24 Diod. 18.56.2–3: ἡγούμενοι δεῖν ἐπαναγαγεῖν πάντας ἐπὶ τὴν εἰρήνην καὶ τὰς πολιτείας ἃς Φίλιππος ὁ ἡμέτερος πατὴρ κατέστησεν, ἐπεστείλαμεν εἰς ἁπάσας τὰς πόλεις περὶ τούτων. [3] ἐπεὶ δὲ συνέβη, μακρὰν ἀπόντων ἡμῶν, τῶν Ἑλλήνων τινὰς μὴ ὀρθῶς γινώσκοντας πόλεμον ἐξενεγκεῖν πρὸς Μακεδόνας καὶ κρατηθῆναι ὑπὸ τῶν ἡμετέρων στρατηγῶν καὶ πολλὰ καὶ δυσχερῆ ταῖς πόλεσι συμβῆναι, τούτων μὲν τοὺς στρατηγοὺς αἰτίους ὑπολάβετε γεγενῆσθαι, ἡμεῖς δὲ τιμῶντες τὴν ἐξ ἀρχῆς προαίρεσιν κατασκευάζομεν ὑμῖν εἰρήνην, πολιτείας δὲ τὰς ἐπὶ Φιλίππου καὶ Ἀλεξάνδρου καὶ τἆλλα πράττειν κατὰ τὰ διαγράμματα τὰ πρότερον ὑπ᾿ ἐκείνων γραφέντα.

Obwohl diese königliche Anordnung in ihren praktischen, objektiven Zielen scheiterte, da Philippos-Arrhidaios III. und sein Aufseher (ἐπιμελητής) Polyperchon militärisch und politisch ihre Macht nicht halten konnten, hatte sie doch ideologisch äußerst wichtigen Einfluss.[25] Der einschlägige Slogan von der Freiheit und dem Frieden der Griechen wurde in der ersten Phase von Antigonos Monophthalmos und Ptolemaios I. in Zusammenhang mit ihren Bestrebungen in Griechenland übernommen.[26] Auch die von ihnen gegründeten Dynastien (Antigoniden und Ptolemaier) hielten an der spezifischen Argumentation fest und versuchten jeweils mehr oder weniger, sie zu ihrem Vorteil zu nutzen.[27] Es ist kein Zufall, dass die Antigoniden, in deren Wirkungskreis Makedonien selbst und die griechischen Poleis, einst Großmächte und Akteure des klassischen Zeitalters, lagen, 302 und 224 v. Chr. zweimal versuchten, den griechischen Bund wiederherzustellen.[28] In den Bestimmungen des Bundes von 302 v. Chr. finden sich unter den verbotenen Handlungen zudem wieder Angriffe gegen den territorialen Bestand der anderen Mitgliedsstaaten und gegen die antigonidische Monarchie.[29]

Vor allem die Antigoniden versuchten durch eine konstruierte Nachkommenschaft von Philippos II. gerade dessen positive Wahrnehmung als Friedenswächter zu kultivieren und auszunutzen. Ein Beispiel für diese späte pro-makedonische Rhetorik findet sich bei Polybios, wo Philippos II. als Wohltäter Griechenlands beschrieben und außerdem dafür gelobt wird, dass er das Schiedsverfahren als einzige Möglichkeit zur

---

25   Poddighe 2013, 225–240.
26   Antigonos Monophthalmos war einer der ersten, der erkannte, wie nützlich es war, die Griechen durch solche Slogans zu mobilisieren, um seine Konkurrenten bei der Aufteilung von Alexanders Reich zu besiegen. Bereits 315 v. Chr. machte er in Tyros mit Alexandros, dem Sohn des Polyperchon, eine ähnliche Proklamation, um damit symbolisch an die frühere Proklamation des Philippos III. Arrhidaios von 318 v. Chr. anzuknüpfen, Diod. 19.61.1–5, Dmitriev 2011, 115–18. Die Wiederherstellung des Friedens wird in der von Diodor gegebenen Zusammenfassung des Inhalts nicht erwähnt, aber es ist nicht ausgeschlossen, dass sie schon damals von Monophthalmos als Argument verwendet wurde. Kurz darauf, 311 v. Chr., stellt sich Antigonos in einem Brief (OGIS 5) als Hauptverteidiger der Rechte der griechischen Poleis dar und macht sogar schmerzhafte Zugeständnisse um des Friedens willen. Relevant sind hier insbesondere Antigonos' Bemerkungen in den Z. 1–2, 12–26, 32–37, 43–46, 51–69. Natürlich darf man nicht übersehen, dass der Friedensschluss vor allem das Ergebnis der militärischen Misserfolge des Antigonos und der Bestätigung des *status quo* mit den anderen Diadochen war, aber es ist dennoch wichtig, dass er versuchte, den Frieden und seine positive Botschaft auf diplomatischem Gebiet zu nutzen, um sein Image als wohlwollender Herrscher zu stärken. Ebenfalls sehr schnell folgte Ptolemaios I. dem Beispiel des Antigonos, indem er ein ähnliches Dekret erließ, um die Griechen wissen zu lassen, dass er nicht weniger an ihrer Autonomie interessiert sei als Antigonos; Diod. 19.62.1. Später scheint Ptolemaios I. im Rahmen des Feldzugs von 308 v. Chr., der sich symbolisch auch auf die Einnahme von Korinth konzentrierte, weiter nachdrücklich den Slogan der Freiheit der Griechen zu verwenden. Er wurde jedoch wenig später von der mangelnden materiellen Unterstützung der griechischen Poleis enttäuscht; Diod. 20.37.1–2.
27   Dmitriev 2011, 112–144; Meeus 2020, 314.
28   Griechischer Bund von 302 v. Chr., Plut. Demetrios 25.3; IG IV 1², 68; Wallace 2013, 147–151. Griechischer Bund von 224 v. Chr. Pol. 4.9.3–4, 24.4–5; Scherberich 2009.
29   IG IV² 1.68 Z. I 13–15.

Beilegung von Streitigkeiten zwischen den Mitgliedern des Korinthischen Bündnisses eingeführt hat.[30] Dasselbe politische Vokabular der griechischen Freiheit und panhellenischen Einheit wird jedoch auch von den Ptolemaiern ausgiebig gegen die Antigoniden verwendet. Obwohl diese nicht beim Namen genannt werden, rekurriert das Chremonides-Dekret beispielsweise auf die Perserkriege, um dem von Ptolemaios II. geschützten Bündnis zwischen Athen und Sparta im Krieg gegen Antigonos Gonatas für die Freiheit der Griechen Ansehen zu verleihen.[31]

Mit anderen Worten kann man argumentieren, dass viele Elemente der hellenistischen monarchischen Ideologie, insbesondere im Hinblick auf die propagandistische und politische Rolle des Friedens bei der königlichen (Selbst-)Darstellung, vor allem in der griechischen Poliswelt, Resultate von Entwicklungen der klassischen Zeit und ein Erbe der Griechenlandpolitik Philippos' II. sind.

3. Frieden in der hellenistischen Herrschaftsdarstellung

Die Diadochen und nach dem ‚Jahr der Könige' (307/306 v. Chr.) die hellenistischen Monarchien übernahmen wie gesehen in ihrer Selbstdarstellung eine bereits verfeinerte Ideologie, die den Frieden als Instrument der Machtstiftung und -legitimation konzipierte. Die wichtigsten Mittel waren der Aufbau hegemonialer Allianzen, ihre Beteiligung an der Institution der Schiedsgerichtsbarkeit und ihre Teilnahme im Kampf gegen die Barbaren. Diese Strategien dienten als Maßnahme der Friedenserzwingung (auch wenn sie gerade so manipuliert wurden, dass sie mehr der Erhaltung der Macht und Autorität des Königs als den Interessen der jeweils beteiligten Mitglieder dienten) und damit der Bildung einer positiven Selbstdarstellung der hellenistischen Monarchien.

---

30   Z. B. Pol. 9.33.6–7, 11–12: ἐν οἷς καιροῖς Φίλιππος ἐθελοντὴν αὑτὸν ἐπιδοὺς ἐπανείλετο μὲν τοὺς τυράννους, ἠσφαλίσατο δὲ τὰ κατὰ τὸ ἱερόν, αἴτιος δ᾽ ἐγένετο τοῖς Ἕλλησι τῆς ἐλευθερίας, ὡς αὐτὰ τὰ πράγματα μεμαρτύρηκε καὶ τοῖς ἐπιγενομένοις. [7] οὐ γὰρ ὡς ἠδικηκότα Φίλιππον Θετταλούς, καθάπερ οὗτος ἐτόλμα λέγειν, ἀλλ᾽ ὡς εὐεργέτην ὄντα τῆς Ἑλλάδος, καὶ κατὰ γῆν αὐτὸν ἡγεμόνα καὶ κατὰ θάλατταν εἵλοντο πάντες (…) [11] (…) καταπληξάμενος δὲ κἀκείνους καὶ τούτους ἐπὶ τῷ κοινῇ συμφέροντι διὰ λόγου τὴν ἐξαγωγὴν ἀμφοτέρους ἠνάγκασε ποιήσασθαι περὶ τῶν ἀμφισβητουμένων, [12] οὐχ αὑτὸν ἀποδείξας κριτὴν ὑπὲρ τῶν ἀντιλεγομένων, ἀλλὰ κοινὸν ἐκ πάντων τῶν Ἑλλήνων καθίσας κριτήριον. Es handelt sich um die Interpretation einer Rede eines Lykiskos, eines akarnanischen Gesandten in Sparta aus dem Jahr 211 v. Chr. (Pol. 9.32–39), die zusammen mit der antimakedonischen Position eines aitolischen Gesandten (Pol. 9.28–31) literarisch als eine Darstellung des rhetorischen Argumentationskrieges für oder gegen die makedonische Hegemonie von Polybios verwendet wird, vgl. Dmitriev 2011, 340–341, 354–362.
31   IG II³ 912, Heinen 1972, 117–142; Wallace 2011, 160–164.

3.1 Frieden, Könige und die föderalen Makrostrukturen
(Hegemoniale Bündnisse und föderale Verbände)

Das erste Instrument, das hier vorgestellt werden soll, ist die Tätigkeit des Königs bei der Schaffung hegemonialer Bündnisse nach dem Vorbild der panhellenischen Allianz des Philippos II. und die damit verbundene wohltätige königliche Aktivität gegenüber den verschiedenen Bündnissen und Föderationen der hellenistischen Welt.[32] In all diesen föderalen Organisationsformen, ob es sich nun um hegemoniale Verbände oder um gleichberechtigte Föderationen handelt, werden intensive Anstrengungen unternommen, um den Schutz vor äußeren Feinden und inneren Frieden zu bewahren. Dies zeigt sich zum einen in Kriegserklärungen an dritte Parteien, die die territoriale Integrität und das Eigentum der Mitglieder der Organisation bedrohten, und zum anderen in der friedlichen Beilegung von Streitigkeiten zwischen den Mitgliedern der Organisation selbst.[33] Auf diese Weise sollte durch direkte königliche Initiativen oder indirekt durch die Bundesorgane der äußere Frieden zwischen den Bundesmitgliedern gewährleistet werden.

Es sei darauf hingewiesen, dass der durch solche hegemonialen Bündnissysteme erzwungene Frieden für die dominierende Macht ein wesentliches Instrument zur Durchsetzung der eigenen Vormachtstellung durch die Aufrechterhaltung eines positiven *Status quo* ist. Die dominante Macht konnte dadurch die Außenpolitik des Bündnisses und der Mitglieder, die seinen Einflussbereich bildeten, so weit bestimmen, dass sie auch das innenpolitische Leben der Stadt, deren Freiheit und Autonomie theoretisch geschützt war, beeinflusste.[34] Dennoch hatte diese besondere politische Option in der griechischen Welt eine positive Resonanz, da sie sowohl die Illusion von Autono-

---

32   Zur Bedeutung hegemonialer Bündnisse im Rahmen des griechischen Föderalismus siehe Raaflaub 2015, 434–451; Smarczyk 2015, 452–470.
33   Als weitere Beispiele für die Sicherung des Friedens durch die Instrumente eines hegemonialen Bündnisses sind die Erklärung des hellenischen Bündnisses des Philippos V. im Jahr 220 v. Chr., in der die programmatischen Ziele des Bundesgenossenkrieges gegen die Aitoler genannt werden, und der königliche Brief mit dem Ultimatum an die Aitoler zu nennen; Pol. 4.25, 26.3–4. Die räuberischen Überfälle der Aitoler und die dadurch verursachten Katastrophen werden ausführlich erwähnt, um die Notwendigkeit einer Kriegserklärung zu dokumentieren, den Schutz der Verbündeten zu erreichen und indirekt die Möglichkeit, ohne Angst vor Invasionen zu leben, zu schaffen. Zur fehlenden Überlieferung für eine Verpflichtung zur friedlichen Beilegung von Streitigkeiten zwischen den Mitgliedern der griechischen Allianz von 224 v. Chr. siehe Scherberich 2009, 188–89. Das Fehlen eines solchen Hinweises schließt jedoch keineswegs aus, dass es für die Mitglieder dieses Bündnisses keine solchen Verpflichtungen gab, insbesondere wenn sie Feindseligkeiten und Kriegserklärungen gegen Nichtmitglieder rechtfertigen mussten, wie 220 v. Chr. gegen die Aitoler und 201 v. Chr. die Akarnanen gegen Athen; Liv. 31.14.6–9.
34   Smarczyk 2015, 464–470.

mie als auch eine größere Bewegungsfreiheit im Vergleich zur alternativen Option der Besetzung einer Stadt durch königliche Garnisonen ermöglichte.[35]

Außerdem konnten die hellenistischen Könige die neue Entwicklung der griechischen Verfassungsinstitutionen bezüglich des Föderalismus verfolgen, die sie wegen des Erfolgs der Einrichtung und ihrer allgemeinen Akzeptanz in der griechischen Welt nicht ignorieren konnten. Die Föderationen verliehen den griechischen Poleis eine neue Dynamik, da sich teilweise der Schwerpunkt der Entscheidungen und Entwicklungen in der hellenistischen Ära in Gebiete wie Westgriechenland (Aitolien, Arkadien, Achaia) verlagerte, die zuvor als Randgebiete galten. Ptolemaier-, Antigoniden-, Attaliden- und Seleukidenkönige versuchten also, durch Wohltaten, Stiftungen oder sogar durch die Förderung des Föderalismus (mitunter gar durch die Gründung von *koina*), die neuen Verbände in ihre Einflusssphären einzubinden und gegen ihre Rivalen einzusetzen.[36] So nahmen beispielsweise Ptolemaios III., Antigonos Doson und Philippos V. den Achaiischen Bund unter ihren Schutz, förderten ihn und setzten ihn gegen ihre Feinde ein.[37] Das hegemoniale griechische Bündnis von 224 v. Chr. wurde selbst als ein Bündnis von Föderationen und nicht, wie die früheren Versuche des 4. Jh. v. Chr., von autonomen Städten charakterisiert.[38]

Ein Unterschied zwischen den Antigoniden und den anderen hellenistischen Monarchien besteht darin, dass die griechischen Bünde, die unter ihrem Einfluss standen, im Allgemeinen eine geringere Unabhängigkeit und Flexibilität in ihrem Handeln besaßen. Könige, deren Machtzentrum sich außerhalb der griechischen Halbinsel befand, ermöglichten den Föderationen eher, mit ihnen gleichrangige Verträge zu schließen. Andererseits versuchten die Antigoniden, deren unmittelbarer Aktionsraum die Wirkungsbereiche des Aitolischen und Achaiischen Bundes umfasste, eine engere und dauerhaftere Kontrolle auszuüben.[39]

---

35   Ein Beispiel für diese Perspektive ist der Ratschlag des Aratos an Philippos V., dass er über seine Verbündeten durch τὴν πίστην, d. h. das gegenseitige Vertrauen herrschen solle und nicht durch die Garnisonen; Pol. 7.12.

36   Buraselis 2003a, 39–50; 2021, 95–101. Andererseits ist festzustellen, dass die Aktivitäten der Attaliden und Seleukiden in Bezug auf die Entwicklung ihrer Beziehungen zu den verschiedenen *koina* des griechischen Kernlandes ihren Höhepunkt in der Zeit nach der Niederlage der Makedonen im Zweiten Makedonischen Krieg erreichten. Unter den Seleukiden sticht auch der Fall von Antiochos III. hervor, dem 192 der Titel eines στρατηγὸς αὐτοκράτωρ des Aitolischen Bundes angeboten wurde, App. Syr. 12.46–47; Liv. 35.45.9. Die Attaliden wurden auch besonders aktiv bei der Unterstützung von föderalen Bündnissen durch Wohltaten oder den Abschluss von Sondervereinbarungen, wie zum Beispiel die finanzielle Unterstützung von Eumenes II. für das achaiische *koinon* im Jahr 185 v. Chr. (Pol. 22.7.3) und der Vertrag desselben Königs mit dem kretischen *koinon* im Jahr 183 v. Chr. (I. Cret. iv 179).

37   Ptolemaios III., Plut. Aratos 24.4; Paus. 2.8.5. Antigonos III. Doson, Pol. 2.52.3–7, 54.1–4, 54.13; Plut. Aratos 42, 45.1–3. Philippos V. Pol. 1.3.1, 2.37.1, 4.9.1–4, 22.2, 25, 26.8, 5.1.6–12; Plut. Aratos 47.6. Ptolemaios V. Pol. 22.9.

38   Scherberich 2009, 193–194; Smarczyk 2015, 462–464.

39   Buraselis 2021, 97.

Wichtige Belege für den königlichen Einfluss liefern auch die *koina* der Nesioten und der Kreter. Der Nesiotenbund wurde von Antigonos Monophthalmos oder Ptolemaios I. gegründet, um den größten Teil der Ägäis unter einem Dach zu vereinen, und war weitgehend eine vom König abhängige Föderation.[40] Der Nesiarchos während der ptolemaiischen Phase des *koinon* war fast immer ein hochrangiger ptolemaiischer Beamter, der nicht von einer ägäischen Insel stammte.[41] Seine Beschlüsse zielten auch darauf ab, das positive Bild der Ptolemaier als Wohltäter und Retter hervorzuheben.[42]

Der kretische Bund war ein äußerst eigenartiger Verband, dessen Struktur instabil und locker war.[43] Das *koinon* wurde wahrscheinlich erstmals auf Initiative von Ptolemaios II. oder Sparta im ersten Viertel des 3. Jh. v. Chr. gegründet.[44] Darüber hinaus fungierte dieser Verband während eines Großteils seines Bestehens im Wesentlichen als Mittel hellenistischer Monarchen, um Kreta unter Kontrolle zu bringen. Sein Schutz wurde von verschiedenen Königen wie Philippos V. und Ptolemaios VI. übernommen.[45] Besonders die Ptolemaier bemühten sich im Hinblick auf ihre eigenen Interessen um eine Befriedung der Region Kreta. Ein auf Delos aufgestelltes kretisches Dekret ehrt sogar Ptolemaios VI., weil ὑπάρχων ὁ βασιλεὺς [καὶ] ὅσιος καὶ εὐσεβὴς καὶ πάντων ἀνθρώ[πων] ἡμερώτατος ἐποήσατο τήν τε φιλία[ν καὶ] τὴν εἰρήνην.[46]

3.2 Frieden, der König und die griechische Polis

Abgesehen von multilateralen Bündnissen investierten die hellenistischen Könige viel Zeit in direkte Kontakte mit einzelnen Städten. Diese Kommunikation, die hauptsächlich durch königliche Briefe erfolgte, weist auf die Freundschaft (φιλία) und das Bünd-

---

40   Buraselis 2015, 358–376 mit Verweisen auf ältere Literatur.

41   Buraselis 1982, 81–83, 184–186.

42   Aus der ptolemaiischen Phase des *koinon* sind siebzehn Dekrete erhalten, mit denen der Nesiotenbund seinen ptolemaiischen Gönnern und deren Beamten dankt und diese ehrt; Buraselis 1982, 180–183.

43   Chaniotis 2015, 377–385 mit Verweisen auf ältere Literatur.

44   Das Hauptargument für diese Position ist, dass die früheste Erwähnung der *Kretaieis* (d. h. der Bürger der Poleis, die sich an dieser Föderation beteiligten) aus dem Chremonides-Dekret (IG II³ 912) stammt, Chaniotis 2015, 379–380.

45   Philippos V. Plut. Aratos 48.3; Pol. 7.11.8–9. Ptolemaios VI. Strab. 10.4.11; IDélos 1517, 1518; I.Cret. III iv.9. Z. 107–108.

46   IDélos 1518, Z. 5–8. Die Charakterisierung von Ptolemaios VI. als „Friedensstifter" mag paradox erscheinen, da aus dem Inhalt des restlichen Beschlusses hervorgeht, dass der König Soldaten aus Kreta im Krieg gegen seinen Bruder Ptolemaios VIII. auf Zypern anführte. Der Frieden bezieht sich also auf den positiven Ausgang des Krieges (den Sieg, der den Krieg beendete) oder, was wahrscheinlicher ist, auf Philometors Aktivitäten zur Schaffung eines Friedens in Kreta. Im letzteren Fall befürworteten die Kreter zudem den Krieg außerhalb der Insel, durch den sie Lohn und Beute erhalten konnten. Siehe Buraselis 2011, 151–160 mit Verweisen auf die Belege für eine solche Friedenstätigkeit der Ptolemaier in Kreta.

nis (συμμαχία) zwischen den beiden Akteuren hin und propagiert das schon in der Forschung intensiv untersuchte Bild des Königs als Wohltäter, der zum Vorteil seiner Untertanen und Verbündeten handelt. Die Poleis als unmittelbare Nutznießer betonen durch ihre Ehrenbeschlüsse sogar besonders diesen Parameter in ihrer Kommunikation mit den Königen, die aus Prestigegründen, aber auch zur Aufrechterhaltung ihrer Legitimität, ein unmittelbares Interesse daran hatten, dieses Bild zu fördern.[47] Die Fähigkeit eines Königs, Verbündete zu schützen, insbesondere ihre territoriale Integrität, und sie vor der Plünderung durch Feinde zu bewahren, ist ein starker Ausdruck seiner Macht und Legitimität.[48] Alles andere würde die Akzeptanz des Königs bei den Untertanen und den Verbündeten erheblich beeinträchtigen.[49] In diesem Zusammenhang finden wir als Teil der königlichen Aktivitäten den Schutz des Friedens in der Stadt, der auf verschiedene Weise zum Ausdruck kam.

An erster Stelle ist die Tätigkeit des Königs zu nennen, verbündete Städte und ihr Umland vor Feinden zu schützen. Außerdem wird aus den Begründungen der Poleis für die Ehrendekrete die besondere Bedeutung des königlichen Beitrags zum Schutz einer problemlosen Ernte hervorgehoben.[50] Die Polis Itanos auf Kreta ist ein sehr gutes Beispiel für diese Beziehung, da sie uns eine Reihe von Ehrendekreten und anderen Dokumenten liefert, in denen besonders die Dienste der Ptolemaier und der von ihnen zum Schutz der Stadt und deren Territorium (χώρα) eingesetzten Offiziere

---

47   Bringmann 1993, 7–24; Bringmann – von Steuben 1995; Bringmann 2000; Hofmann 2015, 139–152; Wiemer 2017, 316–318; Kotsidu 2000; Schmidt-Dounas 2000.

48   Pol. 6.7.4.

49   Die Plünderung des Gebietes von Argos durch den spartanischen König Kleomenes III. war z. B. eine persönliche Herausforderung für den in der Stadt anwesenden Antigonos Doson, da die verärgerten Bürger so weit gingen, vor dem Haus, in dem er wohnte, zu demonstrieren, während sogar gefordert wurde, ihn durch einen anderen, fähigeren Herrscher zu ersetzen; Plut. Kleomenes 25.4–5. Auch der Ton des Briefes von Ptolemaios II. an Milet und der dazugehörige Volksbeschluss zeigen, dass die Schwierigkeiten des Krieges, in den die Stadt wegen dem König involviert war, zu Unzufriedenheit unter den Bürgern geführt und die Unterstützung für die Ptolemaier verringert haben könnte; I.Milet I 139, Z. 32–34. Ptolemaios bat im Wesentlichen um eine Bestätigung der Loyalität der Stadt, indem er die Vergünstigungen aufzählte, die er und sein Vater Milet gewährt hatten und deren Fortbestand von der Fortführung der pro-ptolemaiischen Ausrichtung der Außenpolitik dieser Polis abhing; I.Milet I 239, Z. 2–14. Milet kommt der Bitte des Ptolemaios sofort nach und beschließt, dass die gegenwärtigen und zukünftigen Bürger (zudem im Rahmen der Institution der Epheben) schwören, die Freundschaft und das Bündnis mit dem König zu wahren. Was die Stadt aber wirklich möchte, geht aus den Z. 30–34 hervor, wo neben den bereits erwähnten kriegsbedingten Schwierigkeiten aufgeführt wird, dass Ptolemaios für τὴν εἰρήνην παρασκευάζων τῶι δήμωι gelobt wird.

50   Z. B. ein Dekret der Polis Teos für Antiochos III., SEG 41.1003 II Z. 50–53: ἐπειδὴ οὐ μόνον εἰρήνην ἡμῖν ὁ βασιλεὺς παρέσχεν, ἀλλὰ καὶ (…) λυσιτελεῖς τὰς ἐν τῇ χώραι μετ' ἀσφαλεί[ας π]εποίηκεν ἐργασίας καὶ τὰς καρπείας. Außerdem versuchten Könige in Krisenzeiten, die Plünderung des Hinterlandes oder die Unzugänglichkeit desselben durch die Entsendung von Getreide und anderen Vorräten in die Stadt auszugleichen. Eine Sammlung von dieser Kategorie der Schenkungen hellenistischer Herrscher findet sich bei Bringmann – von Steuben 1995, passim.

und Soldaten erwähnt werden.[51] In einem Urteil, das Magnesia in der Funktion eines Schlichters im Konflikt zwischen Itanos und Hierapytna fällte, wird auf die Leistungen Ptolemaios' VI. Philometor für die kollektive Sicherheit auf Kreta hingewiesen und gleichzeitig indirekt die Gleichgültigkeit seines Nachfolgers Ptolemaios VIII. Physkon kritisiert. Der Abzug der ptolemaiischen Truppen wird im Text explizit mit dem Ausbruch des Krieges in Zusammenhang gebracht.[52]

Antiochos III. legte besonderen Wert auf die Förderung seiner Rolle als Verfechter bzw. Stifter des Friedens und des Wohlstands. Dies zeigte sich speziell, als sich seine Ambitionen zur Wiederherstellung der Autorität und des Territoriums der Seleukiden im westlichen Kleinasien, in Thrakien und den dortigen griechischen Poleis herauskristallisierten. Eine solche Darstellungsstrategie diente der Festigung seines Einflusses in der Region im Hinblick auf seine Expansionsbestrebungen auf dem griechischen Festland vor dem Frieden von Apameia.[53]

In diese Kategorie von Aktivitäten können wir auch die königliche Beteiligung an dem Phänomen der antiken Asylie einbeziehen, das im äußerst instabilen Kontext der internationalen Beziehungen in der hellenistischen Welt große Bedeutung gewann; nicht nur, wenn die Könige dieses Recht bereitwillig anerkannten, wenn Städte mit wichtigen Heiligtümern, wie Kos und Magnesia, darum baten, sondern auch, wenn sie aktiv solche Privilegien einführten und intensiv durch Gesandte und Briefe unterstützten.[54] Der praktische Nutzen, den ein König aus der Förderung und Anerkennung einer Asylie einer verbündeten Stadt zog, bestand darin, dass ein Sicherheitsnetz für diese Stadt geschaffen werden konnte, insbesondere wenn er aus verschiedenen Gründen nicht mehr persönlich in dem Gebiet agierte.[55] Die Tätigkeit von Königen zugunsten

---

51 Siehe außerdem ein Ehrendekret von Itanos für Patroklos, der „im Sinne des Willens des Königs" für die Sicherheit (ἀσφάλεια) in der Stadt und den Vororten sorgte; I.Cret. II iv.2. Ein ähnliches Beispiel aus Samothrake für Hippomedon; IG XII.8 156.

52 I.Cret. III iv.9 Z. 40–46.

53 Dmitriev 2011, 138–139, 215–217, 361–362. FD III 4.162–163 (= OGIS 234) Z. 19–22: περὶ βασιλέος Ἀντιόχου τοῦ εὐεργέτα Ἀντιοχέων (in Chrysaoreia) εὐλόγηκε εὐχαριστῶν αὐτῶι διότι τὰν δαμοκρατίαν καὶ τὰν εἰράναν ἐν τοῖς Ἀντιοχεῦσιν διαφυλάσσει κα[τ] τὰν τῶν προγόνων ὑφάγησιν. SEG 41.1003 (Teos) Z. 50: ἐπειδὴ οὐ μόνον εἰρήνην ἡμῖν ὁ βασιλεὺς παρέσχεν; IK 28.4 (Iasos) Z. 41–43: ἐπειδὴ βασιλέως μεγάλου Ἀντιό[χο]υ προγονικὴν αἵρεσιν διατηροῦντος εἰς πάντας [το]ὺς Ἕλληνας καὶ τοῖς μὲν τὴν εἰρήνην παρέχοντος. Vgl. Ma 1999, 194–206, 212–219, 305–308, 311–317, 329–335. Es bleibt umstritten, welcher Antiochos in Ilion für die Wiederherstellung des Friedens geehrt wurde; IK 3 Ilion 32 (= OGIS 219) Z. 4–6, 11–15. Obwohl es sehr wahrscheinlich bleibt, dass es sich wiederum um Antiochos III. handelt, insbesondere wegen der sprachlichen Parallelen und der möglichen Korrelation der in der Inschrift erwähnten Probleme seiner frühen Regierungszeit (so Piejko 1991, 9–50), tendiert die Forschung dazu, den Seleukidenkönig mit Antiochos I. zu identifizieren, vgl. Ma 1999, 254–259.

54 Eine Untersuchung der Belege und Verweise auf die ältere Literatur bietet Knäpper 2018, 75–248.

55 In der Anerkennung der Unverletzlichkeit Smyrnas durch Delphi (OGIS 229; 245–240 v. Chr.) wird beispielsweise erwähnt, dass der Petition der Smyrnaier ein Empfehlungsschreiben von Seleukos II. beigefügt war, das die Anerkennung bereits vollzogen hatte. Für Buraselis 2003b, 145–146 steht das Ereignis im Zusammenhang mit den Katastrophen, die die Region Smyrna im Zweiten

der Anerkennung einer Unverletzlichkeit findet sich oft in Poleis aus neugewonnenen oder umstrittenen Einflussgebieten und kann daher als politisch motivierte Handlung interpretiert werden, die u. a. der Etablierung der königlichen Macht diente.[56]

Noch interessanter ist die Tatsache, dass Könige oft Asylrechte für Städte anerkannten, die zum Einflussbereich anderer Herrscher gehörten, wie im Fall von Kos, das von nahezu allen Königen der hellenistischen Welt als ἱερός und ἄσυλος erklärt wurde.[57] Dies sollte als Teil der Konkurrenzlogik zwischen den Königen in Bezug auf ihre Leistungen gesehen werden. Aus diesem Grund tritt häufig das Phänomen auf, dass Könige beim Wechsel einer Polis von einem Einflussbereich zu einem anderen die Privilegien anderer Könige bestätigten, während sie gleichzeitig verkündeten, andere hinzuzufügen.[58]

Im Allgemeinen ist es kaum möglich, Unterschiede in diesem Teil der königlichen Tätigkeit festzustellen. Die geringere Aktivität der Ptolemaier in diesem Bereich im Vergleich zu anderen Königen wurde hauptsächlich durch die Probleme ihrer Außenpolitik auf dem Höhepunkt des hellenistischen Asyliephänomens erklärt.[59] Andererseits neigten Könige in der Peripherie der hellenistischen Welt oder mit geringerem Bezug zur griechischen Tradition dazu, ihre Positionierung hinsichtlich der Asylieanfragen ausführlicher darzulegen, vermutlich um explizit ihre kulturelle Identifikation mit dem Griechentum hervorzuheben.[60]

Die Aufrechterhaltung des inneren Friedens in einer Stadt ist ein weiterer thematischer Bereich, in dem die hellenistischen Könige sehr aktiv waren. Es handelte sich um die Gewährleistung der ὁμόνοια, die die innere Einheit des Staatswesens einer Polis oder eines Reiches gewährleistet und deren Antithese die στάσις (innerer Zwist) darstellt.[61] Symbolisch und rhetorisch wurde die ὁμόνοια in einer Polis vor allem durch die

Syrischen Krieg erlitten hatte, und war eine Möglichkeit für Seleukos, eine befreundete Polis zu stärken und zu sichern, während er und seine Armee in Kleinasien abwesend waren; vgl. Knäpper 2018, 84–87. Andere Beispiele einer Asylieempfehlung bietet Knäpper 2018, 225–27.

56   Charakteristische Fälle sind neben der bereits erwähnten Unterstützung Smyrnas durch Seleukos II. die jeweiligen Anerkennungen und diplomatischen Aktivitäten zugunsten der Asylie von Kyzikos durch Philippos V. und Teos durch Antiochos III.; siehe Knäpper 2018, 84–87, 137–144, 161–163.

57   IG XII.4 208–213. Neufunde sind jüngst von Bosnakis – Hallof 2020 publiziert worden. Die Bemerkungen von Buraselis 2004, 15–20 zum Interesse der Könige an der Anerkennung der Unverletzlichkeit von Städten und Heiligtümern in Bezug auf ihren internationalen Hintergrund sind immer noch aktuell. Ähnlicher Weise wurde die internationale Anerkennung der Asylie von Teos durch diplomatische Interventionen sowohl von Antiochos III. als auch von Philippos V. unterstützt; Knäpper 2018, 141–44. Noch ein Beispiel in dieser Richtung bietet Magnesia am Maiander, z. B. I.Magnesia 16 Z. 30–33 ἀποδεξαμένων τῶμ βασιλέων [κ]αὶ τῶν ἄλλ[ων ἀπάν]τωμ, πρὸς οὓς ἐπρέσβευσαν, κατὰ ἔθνη καὶ πό[λεις ψηφισαμ]ένων, τιμᾶν Ἄρτεμιν [Λε]υκοφρυηνήν· κα[ὶ ἄσυλον εἶναι τ]ὴμ Μαγνήτωμ πόλιν καὶ χώραν.

58   Hofmann 2015, 149–150.

59   Knäpper 2018, 221–222.

60   Knäpper 2018, 223–224.

61   Thraede 1994, 176–199.

Wiederherstellung der πάτριοι νόμοι, der sogenannten „Gesetze der Väter", oder der πάτριος πολιτεία, der „Verfassung der Väter", erreicht. Dieser rhetorische Slogan entspricht mehr oder weniger der Etablierung einer gemischten Verfassung, einer Art begrenzten Demokratie, die seit dem 5. Jh. als Lösung für soziale und politische Konflikte innerhalb einer Stadt angesehen wurde.[62] Die Könige haben nicht nur versucht, symbolisch in ihren Briefen an die Poleis als Garant und Wiederhersteller der väterlichen Verfassung zu fungieren,[63] sondern waren außerdem in praktischer Form besonders aktiv durch Gesetzgebung[64] oder die Entsendung von Richtern, um die Probleme der Rechtsprechung in den Städten zu lösen und die Eintracht innerhalb der Bürgerschaft wiederherzustellen.[65]

Der König fungierte zudem als Agent der Gerechtigkeit innerhalb seines Königreiches. Deren Bedeutung für die hellenistische politische Theorie der Monarchie ist in der Forschung bereits hervorgehoben und als „Kern aller Herrschertugend" beschrieben worden.[66] Der Philosoph Diotogenes, der eine Abhandlung über das Königtum verfasste, beschreibt den König als νόμος ἔμψυχος, die Verkörperung der Rechtsprechung in seinem Staat.[67] Durch Gerechtigkeit erlangt ein Staat die εὐνομία (die gute Gesetzgebung und das ordnungsgemäße und gerechte Funktionieren einer Verfassung), was wiederum den inneren sozialen Frieden sichert und die Legitimität eines Regimes begründet. An dieser Stelle kann erneut die Aussage des Aristeas (§ 291–2) zitiert wer-

---

62 Raaflaub 2009, 229–230.
63 Dieses politische Vokabular ist auch eine Übernahme der früheren politischen Entwicklungen des klassischen Zeitalters. Das Bündnis von Korinth unter Philippos II. und die Anordnung von Philippos III. Arrhidaios (Diod. 18.56.2–4) gehören zu den ersten Beispielen für die Einbeziehung dieses Slogans in die positive Projektion der Monarchie gegenüber den Städten. Andere spätere Beispiele: für Antiochos III: IK 28.4 (Iasos) Z. 9–10; für Antigonos Doson und Tegea (Pol. 2.70.4–5) und Sparta (Pol. 9.36.4–5). Die Poleis ehrten die Könige auch für die Wiederherstellung der väterlichen Gesetze: Ptolemaios II. und Ägäische Inseln; IG XII.7 506, Z. 10–16; Ptolemaios III.: I.Cret. III iv.4 (Itanos) Z. 1–6; Antiochos III, FD III 4.162–163 Z. 19–22: περὶ βασιλέος Ἀντιόχου τοῦ εὐεργέτα Ἀντιοχέων (In Chrysaoreia) εὐλόγηκε εὐχαριστῶν αὐτῶι διότι τὰν δαμοκρατίαν καὶ τὰν εἰράναν ἐν τοῖς Ἀντιοχεῦσιν διαφυλάσσει κα[τ] τὰν τῶν προγόνων ὑφάγησιν; Antiochos II.: IK 2.504 Z. 14–18: [παρακαλείτω]σαν δὲ οἱ πρέσβεις τόμ βασι[λέα Ἀντίοχον πᾶσαν ἐπιμ]έλειαν ποιεῖσθαι τῶμ πόλε [ων τῶν Ἰάδων ὅπως καὶ τὸ λοιπὸ]ν ἐλεύθεραι οὖσαι καὶ δημο[κρατούμεναι μεθ' ὁμονοίας πολι] τεύωνται κατὰ τοὺς πατρί[ους] νόμους; Antigonos Gonatas oder Doson IG XII Suppl. 168 (Ios), Z. 2–4. Eumenes II. SEG 2.663 (wahrscheinlich Apollonia am Rhyndakos), Z. 8–10.
64 Als Beispiel kann man den Fall der Gesetzgebung in Megalopolis durch Vermittlung des Antigonos Doson anführen; Pol. 5.93.8. Es gibt jedoch auch den Fall von Kyrene, bei dem Ptolemaios I. eingreift und eine gemischte Verfassung ausarbeitet, um den internen politischen Konflikt zu lösen: SEG 9.1; Buraselis 2018, 257–258.
65 Die Tätigkeit der ptolemaiischen (z. B. I.Labraunda 43) oder antigonidischen Richter (z. B. IG XII.5 1065) ist mehrmals inschriftlich überliefert, wie auch das Lob der Poleis für die entsprechenden Könige, die diese Beamten oder Gesandten beauftragt haben. Ausführlichere Beispiele dieser Tätigkeit listet Buraselis 2018, 253–264 auf.
66 Schubart 1937, 6–8; vgl. Onasch 1976, 242.
67 Diotog., Fr. 1, p. 71 Z. 20–23, 72 Z. 19–23. Scrofani 2020, 71–89; Roskam 2020, 133–134 mit Verweisen auf ältere Literatur.

den, nach der die schnelle und gerechte Rechtsprechung neben dem Frieden die wichtigste Aufgabe des Königtums ist. Des Weiteren wurde nach Aristeas (§ 267) der hellenistische König auch dazu angehalten, die Gerechtigkeit als seine politische Richtlinie zu benutzen, um sich den Bedürfnissen der vielfältigen Menschenmengen anzupassen.

Diese Position ist nicht nur für die theoretische Konstruktion der idealen Monarchie von Bedeutung, sondern hatte auch praktische Auswirkungen auf die tatsächliche Machtausübung. Häufiger als die Niederlage werden als Ursachen für die Delegitimierung eines hellenistischen Herrschers die Entfremdung von seinen Untertanen durch die Vernachlässigung seiner Pflichten als Richter oder sogar der Missbrauch seiner absoluten Macht durch die ungerechte Aneignung von Besitz und Eigentum angeführt. Probleme mit den Petitionen, die in einem Fall zum Unterstützungsverlust und in einem anderen zu offenen Konflikten führten, werden zum Beispiel bezüglich des Demetrios Poliorketes in Makedonien[68] und des Seleukiden Demetrios I. in Syrien[69] erwähnt.

Ein weiteres Handlungsfeld der Könige im Sinne des Friedens beinhaltet mit dem wirtschaftlichen Aufschwung verbundene Aktivitäten wie die Gewährung oder Verleihung von Privilegien, z. B. Steuererleichterungen oder Schenkungen, inkl. Landesschenkungen.[70] So steht im Mittelpunkt dieser Selbstdarstellung die Verknüpfung der königlichen Macht mit dem Wohlstand der Polis. Die Affinität von Reichtum und Wohlstand mit Frieden hatte bereits in der Klassik auch visuellen Ausdruck gefunden, was sich im Hellenismus – unter monarchischen Vorzeichen – weiterentwickelte.[71]

---

68 Plut. Demetrios 41.4–42.

69 Ios. ant. Iud. 3.35–37; Diod. 31.32a.

70 Ein Dekret der Stadt Teos über Antiochos III. (ca. 203–190 v. Chr.) erwähnt die Befreiung der Polis von Tribut und Steuern, die sie an die früheren Attaliden-Herrscher zahlen musste; SEG 41.1003 II Z. 50–53. Ein kleinerer Fürst aus der erweiterten Familie der Ptolemaier in Telmessos beispielsweise unterstützte die Polis, nachdem sie ihm geschenkt worden war, dabei, sich von ihren finanziellen Problemen zu erholen, die zum Teil durch die Kriege des Ptolemaios Euergetes hervorgerufen worden waren; TAM II 1.1 Z. 7–21. Diese Art des finanziellen königlichen Euergetismus umfasst zudem Fördermittel für den Wiederaufbau von Städten. Bezeichnend ist auch hier die Tendenz des Bieterwettbewerbs der hellenistischen Könige, wie sie in den Fällen von Theben (IG VII² 4; Buraselis 2014, 159–170; Kalliontzis – Papazarkadas 2019, 293–315) und Rhodos (Pol. 5.88–90) zu beobachten ist.

71 Papini 2018, 63–73; Meyer 2018; 2019. Die Zurschaustellung von Reichtum durch die hellenistischen Könige war ein wichtiges Merkmal ihrer Repräsentation, mit der sie ihre Fähigkeit demonstrieren wollten, den Wohlstand ihrer Untertanen und Verbündeten zu erhalten und zu mehren. Solche Motive des Reichtums, des Überflusses und der Freigiebigkeit, die im Luxus der Hofhaltung und der Paläste, in der Förderung der Künste und Wissenschaften, in der Stiftung von Tempeln und öffentlichen Bauten oder in prunkvollen Festen und Prozessionen ersichtlich werden, können mit einer Botschaft des Friedens in Bezug gebracht werden. Dieser Standpunkt kommt am ehesten in den höfischen Gedichten zum Ausdruck, z. B. Herondas 1,26–34; Kall. h. 1.70–96. Die Verbindung des Friedens mit der Ideologie der großen Prozessionen Ptolemaios' II. und Antiochos' IV. wurde von Strootman 2023 behandelt.

Selbstverständlich konnte eine Polis königliche Schenkungen und Förderungen nur in einem friedlichen Zustand genießen.[72] Die Bereitstellung von Geldspenden durch Könige konnte auch direkt den inneren Frieden einer Stadt aufrechterhalten, insbesondere wenn sie zur Rehabilitierung von Verbannten oder zur Lösung kritischer Probleme eingesetzt wurden, um die Bürger nicht zu belasten, wie es Aratos mit den Spenden des Ptolemaios III. an Sikyon tat.[73]

Ein weiterer Punkt für die Bedeutung des Friedens in der königlichen Darstellung besteht darin, dass der ultimative Grund für die Ehrenverleihung, auch göttlicher Ehren, an Könige ihre wohltätige Wirkung in der realen Welt war.[74] In dieser Hinsicht ist es äußerst bezeichnend, dass in vielen Fällen in der Begründung dieser kultischen Ehren der Frieden erwähnt wird. Die Friedensvereinbarungen zwischen den Diadochen aus dem Jahr 311 v. Chr. gaben z. B. den Anlass zu einer solchen Reihe von Ehrungen, wie sie in dem Dekret von Skepsis erwähnt werden, in welchem dem Antigonos Monophthalmos ein Temenos, ein Altar und ein Kultbild gewidmet wurden.[75] Der ithyphallische Hymnos, der eben diese Überlegenheit von Demetrios Poliorketes über die anderen Götter beschreibt, da sein Handeln durch seine Präsenz in der Welt unmittelbare praktische Ergebnisse brachte, erwähnt ebenfalls den Frieden als zentrale Errungenschaft des Königs.[76] Der Frieden, den Demetrios wiederherstellen muss, steht in engem Zusammenhang mit seinen erhofften kriegerischen Aktivitäten gegen die Aitoler. Dieses Element zeigt eine Unterordnung des Krieges als Instrument zur Erreichung eines Friedens in einer Situation, die so gestaltet sein wird, dass sie den politischen und wirtschaftlichen Wünschen des Königs, seiner Verbündeten und seiner Untertanen entspricht. Dieses Thema führt uns zum nächsten Abschnitt über den Krieg als Instrument zur Durchsetzung und zum Schutz von Frieden und Wohlstand.

---

72 Eine solche Verbindung ist ausdrücklich von Kall. h. 6.134–138 genannt worden.

73 Plut. Aratos 12.1, 13.6–14.4, Bringmann – von Steuben 1995, 119–122. In ähnlicher Weise löste Antiochos IV. den internen Zwist in Megalopolis über die Größe der Stadtmauer, indem er sie finanzierte, Pol. 5.93.1–8.

74 Bringmann – von Steuben 2000, 166–183; Kotsidu 2000, 559–578; Chaniotis 2003, 173–189 mit Verweisen auf ältere Literatur.

75 OGIS 6 Z. 11–23, Kotsidu 2000, 309–312. OGIS 6 Z. 11–13: ἐπειδὴ Ἀντίγονος τῆι τε [π]όλει καὶ τοῖς ἄλλοις Ἕλλησιν μεγάλων ἀγαθῶν αἴτιος γεγένηται. Als ein Element des Guten, dessen Urheber Antigonos war, ist auch ausdrücklich der Frieden erwähnt worden: Z. 15–18, συνησθῆναι δὲ τὴν πόλιν καὶ τοῖς Ἕλλησιν ὅτι ἐλευθερ[ρ]οι καὶ αὐτόνομοι ὄντες ἐν εἰρήνηι [εἰς] τὸ λοιπὸν διάξουσιν.

76 Duris BNJ² 76 F13 (= Athen. 6, 253d-f). In Vers 21 dieses Paians, den die Athener gesungen haben, um sich bei Demetrios für die Wiederherstellung der demokratischen Verfassung (295 oder 294 v. Chr.) und seine anderen Schenkungen zu bedanken, wird erwähnt, dass der liebste Demetrios als erstes den Frieden bringen soll (πρῶτον μὲν εἰρήνην ποίησον, φίλτατε). Siehe Chaniotis 2011 mit Verweisen auf ältere Literatur.

3.3 Der König als Krieger und Sieger um des Friedens willen

So wirkungsmächtig das Bild des Königs als siegreicher Krieger war, schwingt bei dieser Rolle doch auch der Faktor der Friedensstiftung mit. Diese Darstellung wird noch deutlicher, wenn der Gegner, zumeist ‚barbarische Stämme', mit dem Chaos und der König mit der Wiederherstellung der göttlichen Ordnung identifiziert wurden.[77] Das bekannteste Beispiel dieser königlichen Selbstdarstellung sind ohne Zweifel die attalidischen Monumente, die sich auf die Siege über die Galater beziehen. Die kämpferischen Werte des Königs werden in dieser Erzählung als Mittel zur Herstellung des Friedens und zum Schutz der Untertanen und Verbündeten eingesetzt.[78] Diese Selbstdarstellung kommt auch in einem Brief Eumenes' II. an das Ionische Koinon (167 v. Chr.) zum Ausdruck, in dem festgehalten ist, dass Eumenes sich „als Wohltäter der Griechen erwiesen" hat, indem er „viele und große Kämpfe gegen die Barbaren unternommen und allen Eifer und alle Voraussicht darauf verwandt (hat), dass die Bewohner der griechischen Poleis immer in Frieden und in bester Verfassung leben könnten".[79]

---

77 Vgl. dazu auch den Beitrag von Giovanna Pasquariello in diesem Band. Dazu trug insbesondere die Tatsache bei, dass ein Krieg gegen die Barbaren immer als gerechter Krieg wahrgenommen wurde; Clavadetscher-Thürlemann 1985, 35–45. Darüber hinaus wurde in der Forschung die königliche Jagd, eine der beliebteren königlichen Aktivitäten Alexanders des Großen und der frühen Diadochen, nach dem mesopotamischen Modell als religiöses Symbol für die Bändigung des Chaos und für die Wiederherstellung der Ordnung interpretiert. Diese Perspektive könnte auch als eine Kontinuität der hellenistischen Herrschaftslegitimation mit den mesopotamischen und persischen monarchischen Traditionen verstanden werden. Für die mesopotamischen Herrschaftskonzepte und die Bedeutung der Jagd, Selz 2001, 14, vgl. Wagner-Durand 2019, 235–272. Eine ausführliche Analyse bezüglich der Verbindung der königlichen Jagd mit Herrschaftsansprüchen und mit der Legitimation der Herrschaft bei den Persern und Makedonen bietet Seyer 2007. Greenwalt 2019, 11–17 argumentiert zudem, dass die königliche Jagd schon vor Alexander III. ein wichtiges Legitimationsritual für die Argeadenkönige war und die Bändigung des Chaos, die Wiederherstellung der Sicherheit und den Beginn des Wohlstandes symbolisierte. Palagia 2000, 167–206 zeigte jedoch, dass diese Art der Darstellungen in der hellenistischen Kunst nur kurzlebig war und das Konzept die erste Generation der Diadochen nicht zu überleben scheint. Sie argumentiert daher, dass die Ikonographie der Löwenjagd durch die Eroberung Alexanders aus dem Osten übernommen wurde, um die Nähe der Teilnehmer zum König zu betonen, und dass sie in erster Linie im Propagandakrieg der Nachfolger verwendet wurde, um deren Anspruch auf die Herrschaft über das Reich durch die Nachahmung Alexanders zu legitimieren.

78 Walbank ²1984, 81–82 betont zudem, dass die hellenistische Theorie des Königtums mehr Gewicht auf die Tatsache des Sieges als auf den blutigen Prozess seiner Erringung legt, und ebenso auf die Fähigkeit des Königs, seine eigenen Bürger zu retten und zu schützen, anstatt, wie in einigen nahöstlichen Kulturen, eine große Zahl von Feinden zu erschlagen. Die Brutalität der attalidischen Monumente bildet einen interessanten Gegensatz zu dieser Äußerung. Teil dieser monarchischen Repräsentation ist zudem die Ikonographie des pergamenischen Zeus-Altars (erbaut wohl unter Eumenes II.) mit der Gigantomachie. Diese Ikonographie symbolisierte die Überwindung der Unordnung und der Chaos bringenden Giganten, die die Galater widerspiegelten, und somit letztlich auch die Schaffung der Ordnung und des Friedens; vgl. dazu Pasquariello in diesem Band.

79 SEG 4.443 Z. 7–13: καὶ κοινὸν ἀναδείξας ἐμαυτὸν εὐεργέτην τῶν Ἑλλήνων πολλοὺς μὲν καὶ μεγάλους ἀγῶνας ὑπέστην πρὸς τοὺ[ς] βαρβάρους, ἅπασαν σπουδὴν καὶ πρόνοιαν ποιού[με]νος ὅπως οἱ τὰς Ἑλληνίδας κατοικοῦντες πόλε[ις] διὰ παντὸς ἐν εἰρήνηι καὶ τῆι βελτίστηι καταστάσ[ει] ὑπάρχωσιν.

Dieses Element ist nicht nur bei den Attaliden, sondern auch bei anderen Dynastien zu finden. Das antigonidische Makedonien wird zum Beispiel in den ihm freundlich gesinnten Quellen oft als Schutzschild Griechenlands vor Barbareneinfällen aus dem Norden dargestellt.[80] Darüber hinaus versuchte die pro-makedonische Propaganda, bei den Griechen Sympathien zu wecken, indem sie das Vorhandensein der Römer als Feinde und die panhellenischen Einheit, die unter makedonischer Hegemonie in Frieden lebte, als starke Verteidigungsinstanz betonte.[81] Bei Pausanias ist die Beschreibung eines Denkmals in Olympia erhalten,[82] auf dem die Personifikation von Hellas Antigonos Doson und Philippos V. bekrönt. Nach Thomas Kruse steht diese Darstellung in einem symbolischen Zusammenhang mit einer anderen Statuengruppe vom selben Ort, in welcher die personifizierte Ἐκεχειρία (der heilige Friede) Iphitos, den mythischen Gründer der Olympischen Spiele, krönt. Möglicherweise handelt es sich um einen bewussten Versuch der Antigoniden, sich als Garanten des panhellenischen Friedens und als Stifter der Spiele zu präsentieren.[83]

Ein weiteres ähnliches Beispiel dieser Darstellung des siegreichen Herrschers aus einer anderen Dynastie besteht in einer Gruppe von Bronzestatuetten ptolemaiischer Herrscher, die einen Gegner beim Ringen besiegen. Das Thema der so genannte Ringergruppen stieß im griechisch-römischen Ägypten auf großes Interesse, wobei sich die ptolemaiische Gruppe auf den König selbst konzentrierte, der über einen Barbaren triumphiert.[84]

Außerdem finden wir ähnliche Elemente dieser Botschaft in der Kommunikation der Ptolemaier mit ihren einheimischen Untertanen, indem sie Darstellungsstrategien aus der pharaonischen Monarchie übernahmen: die Aufteilung zwischen Ägypten, dessen Schutz und Wohlstand die höchsten Prioritäten eines Herrschers waren, und

Die Darstellung von Eumenes II. und seiner Dynastie als Wohltäter und Beschützer aller Griechen findet sich auch in den Beschlüssen der Aitoler und der Amphiktyonen zur Annahme der Asylie der Athena Nikephoros wieder, FD III.240 Z. 1–6; 261 Z. 1–10.

80   Pol. 9.35.3; 18.37.9; 31.29.3–5.

81   Elemente dieser politischen Rhetorik sind bei Polybios in einer Reihe von (wahrscheinlich fiktiven) Reden erhalten, die er in sein Werk aufgenommen hat; Pol. 5.104, 9.32–39, 11.4–6. Siehe Dmitriev 2011, 147–151 mit Verweisen auf ältere Literatur.

82   Paus. 6.16.3.

83   Kruse 1992, 273–293; Wallace 2014, 235–246.

84   Die Unterlegenen sind in der Forschung durch Haartracht und Physiognomie mit verschiedenen Feinden der Ptolemaier (Galater, Afrikaner oder Seleukiden) in Verbindung gebracht worden. Die siegreichen Ringer sind dagegen als verschiedene Könige von Ptolemaios II. bis zum VI. identifiziert worden; Kyrieleis 1975, 170, 173; St. Lehmann 1988, 296; Rabe 2010, 53–54. Die bronzenen Ringergruppen gingen vermutlich einer großplastischen Statuengruppe voraus, die als politisches Monument für die Symbolisierung des Triumphes eines Ptolemaiers über den barbarischen Feind hergestellt wurde. Thomas 2002, 39 geht sogar noch weiter, indem sie annimmt, „dass hinter dieser Gruppenkomposition ein Ehrenmonument steht, welches Alexander den Großen im Kampf gegen Barbaren darstellte". Ferner, wie St. Lehmann 1988, 297 betont, führen die Darstellungen mit diesem agonalen Thema zudem allegorisch die Überlegenheit des Griechentums vor.

dem Rest der Welt, der als die Ordnung bedrohendes Chaos verstanden wurde.[85] Besonders augenscheinlich wird dies in den Synodaldekreten der ägyptischen Priester, die an traditionell ägyptische Vorstellungen anknüpfen und an die ägyptischen Tempel und die Bevölkerung gerichtet waren, auch wenn die Botschaft als Dekret gemäß typisch griechischer Kommunikation zwischen König und Untertan übermittelt wurde.[86] Das Kanopos-Synodaldekret erwähnt beispielsweise, dass Ptolemaios Euergetes „ferner das Land in Frieden bewahrte, indem er für es gegen viele Völkerschaften und die bei ihnen Herrschenden Krieg führte".[87] Auch hier steht die siegreiche Führung des Krieges im Ausland als Mittel zur Sicherung des Friedens und des Wohlstands des Königreichs im Vordergrund.

4. Schlussfolgerungen

Zusammenfassend lässt sich sagen, dass Frieden ein recht vages und vielseitiges Konzept ist, das nicht einfach als Abwesenheit von Krieg definiert werden kann. Die Suche nach Frieden in der königlichen Selbstdarstellung ist vielmehr ein komplexer Prozess, der uns zu einer Reihe von Handlungsfeldern der hellenistischen Monarchie führt. Der Frieden im antiken griechischen Denken ist in Dichtung, Kunst und Philosophie mit vielen Schlüsselbegriffen der antiken politischen Theorie und Kultur verknüpft und kombiniert worden, wie z. B. mit Gerechtigkeit, guter Gesetzgebung und innerer Ordnung, Reichtum, gottgegebenem Recht, Frömmigkeit und Wohlstand. In der Tat ist die Darstellung des inneren und äußeren Friedens als positives und höchstes Gut für die Menschheit in der antiken Philosophie und Geschichtsschreibung weit verbreitet.[88] Darüber hinaus wurde der Frieden als der ideale Zustand angesehen, durch den Wohlstand erreicht wird.[89] Die Legitimität eines Regimes hängt also zu einem großen Teil davon ab, wie es ihm gelingt, den Frieden zu erhalten oder durchzusetzen,

---

85 Herz 1996, 32–33.
86 Von Recklinghausen 2018, 182–189; Gorre – Veisse 2020, 113–139.
87 Pfeiffer 2015, Nr. 14, Z. 12–13: τήν τε χώραν ἐν εἰρήνηι διατετήρηκεν προπολεμῶν ὑπὲρ αὐτῆ[ς π]ρὸς πολλὰ ἔθνη καὶ τοὺς ἐν αὐτοῖς δυναστεύοντας. In ähnlicher Weise lobten auch andere Synodaldekrete den König als Garant und Stifter des Friedens und der Sicherheit in Ägypten, Pfeiffer 2015, Nr. 13 Z. 116; Nr. 22 Z. 21. Die ägyptische Wahrnehmung der königlichen Herrschaft ist in der hieroglyphischen und demotischen Version des Dekretes deutlicher erkennbar; Pfeiffer 2004, 89–93. Die Feinde des Pharaos werden nach ägyptischer Praxis mit dem Chaos gleichgesetzt; Assmann 2017, 43–60. Sie bildeten also eine Analogie mit den „Barbaren" der griechischen Welt.
88 Plat. rep. 465b; leg. 863d–e; Pol. 12.26.6.
89 Besonders in der Dichtung: Herondas 1,26–28: κεῖ δ' ἐστὶν οἶκος τῆς θεοῦ· τὰ γὰρ πάντα, / ὅσσ' ἔστι κου καὶ γίνετ', ἔστ' ἐν Αἰγύπτωι· / πλοῦτος, παλαίστρη, δύναμι[ς], εὐδίη, δόξα; Theokr. 17.95–105; Kall. h. 6.134–137: χαῖρε, θεά, καὶ τάνδε σάω πόλιν ἔν θ' ὁμονοίᾳ / (135) ἔν τ' εὐηπελίᾳ, φέρε δ' ἀγρόθι νόστιμα πάντα· / φέρβε βόας, φέρε μᾶλα, φέρε στάχυν, οἶσε θερισμόν, / φέρβε καὶ εἰράναν, ἵν' ὃς ἄροσε τῆνος ἀμάσῃ; IG IV 1² 128, Z. 21–23: καὶ ἐπεύχεσθαι πολιάταις / πᾶσιν ἀεὶ διδόμεν τέκνοις τ' ἐρατὰν ὑγίειαν, / εὐνομίαν τε καὶ εἰράναν καὶ πλοῦτον ἀμεμφῆ, vgl. Weber 2023.

sei es als innere Harmonie oder als Schutz vor äußeren Bedrohungen. Das ist so, weil eine legitime Herrschaft, d. h. eine Herrschaft, die von den Beherrschten als legitim anerkannt wird, auch als ein Mechanismus der Konfliktregelung fungiert, der in der Lage ist, Verteilungskonflikte beizulegen und das höchste kollektive Gemeinwohl zu schaffen. Dieses Denken ist in den Debatten über die Legitimität demokratischer Verfassungen herausgearbeitet worden, während es in entsprechenden Diskursen über die Monarchie teilweise unterschätzt wird.

In diesem Beitrag wurde das entsprechende Handeln des hellenistischen Königs in diesen Bereichen und sein Versuch, sich als Akteur des Friedens zu präsentieren, herausgestellt. Da es sich um einen abstrakten Begriff handelt, dessen Definition weitgehend davon abhängt, wie eine Kultur ihn wahrnimmt, ist es nicht verwunderlich, dass seine transdynastische Manifestation in der königlichen Selbstdarstellung der hellenistischen Dynastien ein ausreichendes Maß an Homogenität aufwies, wenn es sich an ein gleichbleibendes Publikum, nämlich die griechischen Städte, richtete. Bei den hellenistischen Königen ging es vor allem darum, sich im Wettbewerb durchzusetzen und zu zeigen, wer den besten Lebensstandard ohne Entbehrungen und den größten Wohlstand bieten konnte. Dies drückte der König auf verschiedene Weise durch königliche Briefe, Anordnungen, Monumente und Feste aus, während Poleis und Bünde aus eigenem Interesse diese Projektion der Herrschaftsideologie durch Volksbeschlüsse und verliehene (kultische) Ehren beförderten.

Auf der praktischen Ebene können wir natürlich bezweifeln, ob der hellenistische König wirklich an diese Botschaft glaubte, und den Ansatz formulieren, dass sein Handeln eher dem Zweck diente, seine autoritäre Macht positiv zu verkleiden und ihr damit eine Akzeptanz zu verleihen.[90] Die hellenistische Monarchie verfügte zwar über eine dem einzelnen Stadtstaat weit überlegene Durchsetzungsgewalt, widersprach aber den entschieden antimonarchischen Überzeugungen der griechischen Poliswelt, die, kulturell bereits fest verankert, in dieser Epoche dominant blieben. Die Vorherrschaft der hellenistischen Monarchien in Folge von Philippos II. und Alexandros III. zwang die antiken griechischen Intellektuellen, ihre antimonarchische Haltung bis zu einem gewissen Grad aufzugeben, um die neuen Realitäten mit den etablierten politischen und sozialen Werten der griechischen Polis in Einklang zu bringen.[91]

---

90   Dies hängt weitgehend vom Charakter des jeweiligen Königs ab; vgl. Pol. 32.4.2. Die Ansicht, dass die Ermahnungen der antiken Philosophen und die antike politische Theorie im praktischen Bereich der Formulierung königlicher Politik und Macht keinen großen Einfluss hatten, abgesehen von der Art und Weise, wie sie den Untertanen positiv dargelegt werden musste, wird insbesondere von Chaniotis 2005, 71–72 und Eckstein 2009, 255–259 vertreten.

91   Bis zu einem gewissen Grad lässt sich eine freundliche Haltung gegenüber der Monarchie schon vor der makedonischen Herrschaft in der zweiten Hälfte des 4. Jh. v. Chr. nachweisen. Positive Ansichten über die Monarchie als wirksame Regierungsform werden von Isokrates in seinen Reden über die zypriotischen Könige Euagoras und Nikokles (um 375 v. Chr.) und von Xenophon in seinen Biografien über Agesilaos und Kyros II. (um 370 v. Chr.) vertreten, Barceló 1993, 248–58. Auch

So ist ein Bild des hellenistischen Idealherrschers entstanden, das kurz als eine Umkehrung des klassischen Stereotyps des Tyrannen beschrieben werden kann. Diese Darstellung ist besonders in den hellenistischen Abhandlungen „Über das Königtum" ausgedrückt worden.[92] Die guten Könige sollten also durch ihre Kriegskunst, Gesetzgebung und Frömmigkeit die Ordnung, den Schutz nach außen und den Wohlstand ihrer Untertanen gewährleisten. Sie sollten außerdem eine Art effektiven und wohlwollenden Herrscher verkörpern, der sowohl die Ordnung schützt und seinen Untertanen Vorteile verschafft als auch Selbstbeherrschung und alle typischen Tugenden zeigt. Die hellenistische Monarchie folgte also den Regeln, die die kulturelle Hegemonie der griechischen Poleis aufgestellt hatte, um sich als Partner und nicht als Eroberer zu präsentieren und Legitimität herzustellen. Der Kampf gegen die Feinde (insbesondere die Barbaren) und die Nutzung des griechischen Föderalismus zum eigenen Vorteil waren zwei Instrumente, die die hellenistischen Könige ausgiebig einsetzten und bei denen der durch die königlichen Handlungen geschützte Frieden eine grundlegende Rolle in ihrer Repräsentation spielte.

Darüber hinaus scheint die Bedeutung und der Einsatz des Friedens in der königlichen Selbstdarstellung nicht stark differenziert zu sein, selbst wenn hellenistische Könige versuchten, sich an ein nicht-griechisches Publikum zu wenden, wie es die Ptolemaier in Ägypten taten. Auch wenn das Phänomen in diesem Beitrag nicht so detailliert untersucht wurde wie die Kommunikation zwischen Königen und griechischen Städten, gibt es in der antiken Welt generell starke Ähnlichkeiten zwischen den verschiedenen Traditionen, was die Wahrnehmung des Friedens als einen mit dem Krieg kompatiblen Zustand angeht, wenn er siegreich geführt wird, um die Sicherheit und Ordnung des Reiches zu schützen und das Wohlergehen der Untertanen zu steigern. Im Gegensatz zur Welt der Poleis gab es zudem für die kosmologische Sichtweise der orientalischen Untertanen kein Problem, die monarchische Institution als Verwaltungssystem zu legitimieren, und ihre Einwände richteten sich weitgehend ausschließlich gegen die Person oder die Dynastie, und die gewählte Lösung bestand darin, sie durch einen anderen König oder eine andere Dynastie zu ersetzen, der bzw. die die Rolle eines Garanten der Ordnung und des Wohlergehens besser zu spielen verstand.[93]

Andererseits muss betont werden, dass die hellenistische Monarchie nie die Intensität und das Ausmaß der charakteristischen Ikonographie und der Verwendung des Schlagworts ‚pax Romana' in der römischen Kaiserzeit erreichte. Der Frieden als Begriff und Personifikation wird beispielsweise auf hellenistischen königlichen Münzen nicht thematisiert, anders als auf den römischen Prägungen.[94] Auch gibt es von Seiten

---

Platon (polit. 291e) und Aristoteles (pol. 1284a, 1287a–1288a) verstanden die legitime Monarchie (βασιλεία) als eine gute Staatsform.

92   Haake 2003; 2013.
93   Herz 1996, 27–40.
94   Lichtenberger – Martin – Nieswandt – Salzmann 2018; Mittag 2023; Noreña 2023.

der hellenistischen Könige keine Bauprogramme und Staatsmonumente wie unter Augustus, um die programmatische Rolle des Friedens im neuen goldenen Zeitalter des neuen Römischen Reiches zu unterstreichen.[95]

Was jedoch den normativen Aspekt für die hellenistische Epoche betrifft, so dürfen wir die Bedeutung des Friedenskonzepts und der darunterfallenden Aktivitäten nicht unterschätzen, insbesondere wenn es um die Legitimität der königlichen Macht und um ihre Akzeptanz durch die Untertanen geht. Der Pythagoreer Diotogenes erklärt beispielsweise, dass der König die Rolle eines Generals, Richters und Priesters innehatte.[96] Oftmals konzentriert sich die Forschung nicht zu Unrecht auf seine Rolle als Feldherr, durch dessen Macht ein König überleben und sich gegenüber seinen Gegnern durchsetzen konnte. In der antiken politischen Theorie dient diese Rolle jedoch keineswegs ihrem Selbstzweck und beinhaltet nur einen Teil der königlichen Pflichten eines Idealherrschers. So haben die militärische Tüchtigkeit, die Rechtsprechung und die Frömmigkeit eines Königs die Funktion, diesen idealen Zustand der Menschheit, der mit dem vagen Begriff des Friedens beschrieben wird, in ihrem Staat zu schützen und durchzusetzen. In Pollux' Katalog des Herrscherlobes können nur sehr wenige Begrifflichkeiten mit direktem militärischem Bezug gefunden werden. Dagegen betonte er ausdrücklich die Wichtigkeit der Funktion des Königs als Friedenswächter – εἰρηνοφύλαξ.[97]

Literaturverzeichnis

Ager 1996: Ager, Sheila L., Interstate Arbitrations in the Greek World, 337–90 B. C., Berkeley 1996

Ager 2015: Ager, Sheila L., Peaceful Conflict Resolution in the World of the Federal States, in: Beck – Funke 2015, 471–486

Ager 2020: Ager, Sheila L. (ed.), A Cultural History of Peace in Antiquity, London et al. 2020

Alonso Troncoso – Anson 2013: Alonso Troncoso, Victor –Anson, Edward M. (eds.), After Alexander. The Time of the Diadochi (323–281 BC), Oxford 2013

Assmann 2017: Assmann, Jan, Schöpfung und Herrschaft: Die altägyptische Sakralmonarchie, in: S. Rebenich (ed.), Monarchische Herrschaft im Altertum, Berlin et al. 2017, 43–60

Barceló 1993: Barceló, Pedro, Basileia, Monarchia, Tyrannis: Untersuchungen zu Entwicklung und Beurteilung von Alleinherrschaft im vorhellenistischen Griechenland, Stuttgart 1993

Beck – Funke 2015: Beck, Hans – Funke, Peter (eds.), Federalism in Greek Antiquity, Cambridge 2015

Bickerman – Sykoutris 1928: Bickerman, Elias – Sykoutris, Ioannis, Speusipps Brief an König Philipp: Text, Übersetzung, Untersuchungen, Leipzig 1928

Billows 1990: Billows, Richard A., Antigonos the One-eyed and the Creation of the Hellenistic State, Berkeley 1990

---

95   Faust 2018; id. 2023.
96   Diotog., fr. 1, p. 71 Z. 23–72, Z. 20.
97   Poll. 1.41: φιλοστρατιώτης, πολεμικὸς μὲν οὐ φιλοπόλεμος δέ, εἰρηνικός, εἰρηνοποιός, εἰρηνοφύλαξ.

Blömer et al. 2021: Blömer, Michael et al. (eds.), Common Dwelling Place of all the Gods: Commagene in its Local, Regional and Global Hellenistic Context, Oriens et occidens 34, Stuttgart 2021

Bolmarcich 2020: Bolmarcich, Silvia, Definitions of Peace, in: Ager 2020, 19–36

Bosnakis – Hallof 2020: Bosnakis, Dimitris – Hallof, Klaus, Alte und Neue Inschriften aus Kos VI, Chiron 50, 2020, 287–326

Bringmann 1993: Bringmann, Klaus, The King as Benefactor: Some Remarks on Ideal Kingship in the Age of Hellenism, in: A. Bulloch – E. S. Gruen – A. A. Long – A. Stewart (eds.), Images and Ideologies: Self Definition in the Hellenistic World, Berkeley 1993, 7–24

Bringmann – von Steuben 1995: Bringmann, Klaus – von Steuben, Hans (eds.), Schenkungen hellenistischer Herrscher an griechische Städte und Heiligtümer, Berlin 1995

Bringmann 2000: Bringmann, Klaus, Geben und Nehmen: monarchische Wohltätigkeit und Selbstdarstellung im Zeitalter des Hellenismus, Berlin 2000

Brosius 2014: Brosius, Maria, Pax persica: Königliche Ideologie und Kriegführung im Achämenidenreich, in: B. Meißner – O. Schmitt – M. Sommer (eds.), Krieg – Gesellschaft – Institutionen: Beiträge zu einer vergleichenden Kriegsgeschichte, Berlin 2014, 135–162

Buraselis 1982: Buraselis, Kostas, Das hellenistische Makedonien und die Ägäis: Forschungen zur Politik des Kassandros und der drei ersten Antigoniden (Antigonos Monophtalmos, Demetrios Poliorketes und Antigonos Gonatas) im Ägäischen Meer und in Westkleinasien, München 1982

Buraselis 2003a: Buraselis, Kostas, Considerations on Symmachia and Sympoliteia in the Hellenistic Period, in: K. Buraselis – K. Zoumboulakis (eds.), The Idea of European Community in History: Conference Proceedings II: Aspects of connecting Poleis and Ethne in Ancient Greece, Athen 2003a, 39–50

Buraselis 2003b: Buraselis, Kostas, Zur Asylie als außenpolitischem Instrument in der hellenistischen Welt, in: M. Dreher (ed.), Das antike Asyl: kultische Grundlagen, rechtliche Ausgestaltung und politische Funktion, Köln et al. 2003b, 143–158

Buraselis 2004: Buraselis, Kostas, Some Remarks of the Koan Asylia (242 B. C.) against its International Background, in: K. Höghammar (ed.), The Hellenistic Polis of Kos: State, Economy and Culture, Uppsala 2004, 15–20

Buraselis 2011: Buraselis, Kostas, A Lively ,Indian Summer': Remarks on the Ptolemaic Role in the Aegean under Philometor, in: A. Jördens – J. F. Quack (eds.), Ägypten zwischen innerem Zwist und äußerem Druck: die Zeit Ptolemaios' VI. bis VIII., Wiesbaden 2011, 151–160

Buraselis 2015: Buraselis, Kostas, Federalism and the Sea. The Koina of the Aegean Islands, in: Beck – Funke 2015, 358–376

Buraselis 2018: Buraselis, Kostas, A Royal Peace. The Hellenistic King and His Officials as Mediators / Arbitrators and Social Guarantors, in: M. Kalaitzi – P. Paschidis – Cl. Antonetti – A.-M. Guimier-Sorbets (eds.), Βορειοελλαδικά: tales from the lands of the ethne: essays in honour of Miltiades B. Hatzopoulos, Μελετήματα 78, Athen 2018, 253–264

Buraselis 2021: Buraselis, Kostas, Symbiosis of „Koinon" and King: Remarks on the Interconnections between Greek „Koina" and Hellenistic Monarchs, in: C. Grandjean (ed.), The „Koina" of Southern Greece: Historical and Numismatic Studies in Ancient Greek Federalism, Bordeaux 2021, 95–101

Canepa 2021: Canepa, Matthew P., Commagene before and beyond Antiochos I: Dynastic Identity, Topographies of Power and Persian Spectacular Religion, in: Blömer et al. 2021, 71–101

Chaniotis 2003: Chaniotis, Angelos, The Divinity of Hellenistic Rulers, in: A. Erskine (ed.), A Companion to the Hellenistic World, Malden 2003, 431–445

Chaniotis 2004: Chaniotis, Angelos, Justifying Territorial Claims in Classical and Hellenistic Greece: the Beginnings of International Law, in: E.M. Harris – L. Rubinstein (eds.), The law and the courts in ancient Greece, London 2004, 185–213

Chaniotis 2005: Chaniotis, Angelos, War in the Hellenistic World: A Social and Cultural History, Oxford 2005

Chaniotis 2011: Chaniotis, Angelos, The Ithyphallic Hymn for Demetrios Poliorcetes and Hellenistic Religious Mentality, in: P. Iossif – A.S. Chankowski – C.C. Lorber (eds.), More than Men, Less than Gods. Studies in Royal Cult and Imperial Worship, Leuven 2011, 157–195

Chaniotis 2015: Chaniotis, Angelos, Federalism on Crete: The Cretan Koinon and the Koinon of the Oreioi, in: Beck – Funke 2015, 377–385

Chrysafis 2023: Chrysafis, Charalampos I., Griechische Voraussetzungen und Kontexte: Die Suche nach Frieden in der griechischen Poliswelt und die Entstehung des Basileus Eirenophylax-Konzeptes, in: Chrysafis – Hartmann – Schliephake – Weber 2023, 99–125

Chrysafis – Hartmann – Schliephake – Weber 2023: Chrysafis, Charalampos I. – Hartmann, Andreas – Schliephake, Christopher – Weber, Greger (eds.), Basileus Eirenophylax: Friedenskultur(en) und monarchische Repräsentation in der alten Welt, Stuttgart 2023

Clavadetscher-Thürlemann 1985: Clavadetscher-Thürlemann, Silvia, ΠΟΛΕΜΟΣ ΔΙΚΑΙΟΣ und Bellum Justum: Versuch einer Ideengeschichte, Zürich 1985

Degen 2018: Degen, Julian, Alexander III., Dareios I. und das speererworbene Land (Diod. 17, 17, 2), Journal of Ancient Near Eastern History 6, 2018, 53–95

Dinkler 1972: Dinkler, Erich, Friede, Reallexikon für Antike und Christentum 8, 1972, 435–505

Dmitriev 2011: Dmitriev, Sviatoslav V., The Greek Slogan of Freedom and Early Roman Politics in Greece, Oxford et al. 2011

Eckstein 2009: Eckstein, Arthur M., Hellenistic Monarchy in Theory and Practice, in: R.K. Balot (ed.), A Companion to Greek and Roman Political Thought, Oxford et al. 2009, 247–265

Faust 2018: Faust, Stephan, Altar des Friedens: Friedensideologie unter Kaiser Augustus, in: Lichtenberger – Nieswandt – Salzmann 2018, 131–147

Faust 2023: Faust, Stephan, Das Templum Pacis. Bedeutungsebenen des Friedens im kaiserzeitlichen Rom, in: Chrysafis – Hartmann – Schliephake – Weber 2023, 349–376

Gehrke 2013: Gehrke, Hans-Joachim, The Victorious King. Reflections on the Hellenistic Monarchy, in: N. Luraghi (ed.), The Splendors and Miseries of Ruling Alone. Encounters with Monarchy from Archaic Greece to the Hellenistic Mediterranean, Stuttgart 2013, 73–98 (engl. tr. of Gehrke, Hans-Joachim, Der siegreiche König. Überlegungen zur hellenistischen Monarchie, Archiv für Kulturgeschichte 64, 1982, 247–277)

Gorre – Veisse 2020: Gorre, Gilles, – Veisse, Anne, Birth and Disappearance of the Priestly Synods in the Time of the Ptolemies, in: G. Gorre – S. Wackenier (eds.), Quand la fortune du royaume ne dépend pas de la vertu du prince: Un renforcement de la monarchie lagide de Ptolémée VI à Ptolémee X (169–88 av. J.-C.), Leuven et al. 2020, 113–139

Graeber 1992: Graeber, Andreas, Friedensvorstellung und Friedensbegriff bei den Griechen bis zum Peloponnesischen Krieg, Zeitschrift der Savigny-Stiftung für Rechtsgeschichte. Romanistische Abteilung 109.1, 116–162

Greenwalt 2019: Greenwalt, William, The assassination of Archelaus and the significance of the Macedonian royal hunt, Karanos 2, 2019, 11–17

Haake 2003: Haake, Matthias, Warum und zu welchem Ende schreibt man Peri Basileias? Überlegungen zum Historischen Kontext einer Literarischen Gattung im Hellenismus, in: K. Piepenbrink (ed.), Philosophie und Lebenswelt in der Antike, Darmstadt 2003, 84–138

Haake 2013: Haake, Matthias, Writing Down the King: The Communicative Function of the Treatises On Kingship in the Hellenistic Period, in: N. Luraghi (ed.), The Splendors and Miseries of Ruling Alone. Encounters with Monarchy from Archaic Greece to the Hellenistic Mediterranean, Stuttgart 2013, 165–206

Heinen 1972: Heinen, Heinz, Untersuchungen zur hellenistischen Geschichte des 3. Jahrhunderts v. Chr. Zur Geschichte der Zeit des Ptolemaios Keraunos und zum Chremonideischen Krieg, Wiesbaden 1972

Herz 1996: Herz, Peter, Hellenistische Könige: zwischen griechischen Vorstellungen vom Königtum und Vorstellungen ihrer einheimischen Untertanen, in: A. M. Small (ed.), Subject and Ruler. The Cult of the Ruling Power in Classical Antiquity, Ann Arbor 1996, 27–40

Hofmann 2015: Hofmann, Vera, Communications between City and King in the Hellenistic East, in: L. Reinfandt – S. Tost – S. Procházka (eds.), Official Epistolography and the Language(s) of Power, Wien 2015, 139–152

Jehne 1994: Jehne, Martin, Koine eirene: Untersuchungen zu den Befriedungs- und Stabilisierungsbemühungen in der griechischen Poliswelt des 4. Jahrhunderts v. Chr, Stuttgart 1994

Jones 2020: Jones, Christopher P., The Historian Philip of Pergamon, The Journal of Hellenic Studies 140, 2020, 120–127

Knäpper 2018: Knäpper, Katharina, Hieros kai asylos: territoriale Asylie im Hellenismus in ihrem historischen Kontext, Stuttgart 2018

Kotsidu 2000: Kotsidu, Hariteni, TIMH KAI ΔΟΞΑ: Ehrungen für hellenistische Herrscher im griechischen Mutterland und in Kleinasien unter besonderer Berücksichtigung der archäologischen Denkmäler, Berlin 2000

Kruse 1992: Kruse, Thomas, Zwei Denkmäler der Antigoniden in Olympia: eine Untersuchung zu Pausanias 6,16,3, Mitteilungen des Deutschen Archäologischen Instituts. Athenische Abteilung 107, 1992, 273–293

Kyrieleis 1975: Kyrieleis, Helmut, Bildnisse der Ptolemäer, Berlin 1975

G. A. Lehmann 1988: Lehmann, Gustav A., Das neue Kölner Historiker-Fragment (P. Köln Nr. 247) und die χρονικὴ σύνταξις des Zenon von Rhodos (FGrHist 523), Zeitschrift für Papyrologie und Epigraphik 72, 1988, 1–17

St. Lehmann 1988: Lehmann, Stephan, Ptolemaios III. Euergetes-Hermes Enagonios als Pentathlos und Pankratiast: zur Bedeutung zweier alexandrinischer Bronzestatuetten in Stuttgart, in: K. Gschwantler – A. Bernhard-Walcher (eds.), Griechische und römische Statuetten und Grossbronzen. Akten der 9. Internationalen Tagung über antike Bronzen, Wien 1988, 290–301

Lichtenberger – Nieswandt – Salzmann 2018: Lichtenberger, Achim – Nieswandt, Helge – Salzmann, Dieter (eds.), Eirene / Pax: Frieden in der Antike, Münster 2018

Lichtenberger – Martin – Nieswandt – Salzmann 2018: Lichtenberger, Achim – Martin, Katharina – Nieswandt, Helge-H. – Salzmann, Dieter, Ausgeprägter Friede? Eirene/Pax in der antiken Münzprägung, in: Lichtenberger – Nieswandt –Salzmann 2018, 115–129

Ma 1999: Ma, John, Antiochos III and the Cities of Western Asia Minor, Oxford et al. 1999

Meeus 2020: Meeus, Alexander, The Strategies of Legitimation of Alexander and the Diadochoi: Continuities and Discontinuities, in: Meeus – Trampedach 2020, 291–317

Meeus – Trampedach 2020: Meeus, Alexander – Trampedach, Kai (eds.), The Legitimation of Conquest: Monarchical Representation and the Art of Government in the Empire of Alexander the Great, Stuttgart 2020

Mehl 1980: Mehl, Andreas, Δορίκτητος χώρα. Kritische Bemerkungen zum „Speererwerb" in Politik und Völkerrecht der hellenistischen Epoche, Ancient Society 11–12, 1980, 173–212

Meyer 2018: Meyer, Marion, Abstraktion und dionysischer Rausch: Eirene in der griechischen Bilderwelt, in: Lichtenberger – Nieswandt –Salzmann 2018, 49–57

Meyer 2019: Meyer, Marion, Frieden in der Bilderwelt der Griechen, in: G. Althoff et al. (eds.), Frieden: Theorien, Bilder, Strategien von der Antike bis zur Gegenwart, Dresden 2019, 58–85

Michels 2017: Michels, Christoph, The Persian Impact on Bithynia, Commagene, Pontus and Cappadocia, in: S. Müller et al., The History of Argeads. New Perspectives, Wiesbaden 2017, 41–56

Michels 2021: Michels, Christoph, ‚Achaemenid‘ and ‚Hellenistic‘ Strands of Representation in the Minor Kingdoms of Asia Minor, in: Blömer et al. 2021, 476–496

Mittag 2023: Mittag, Peter F., Sieghaftigkeit und Frieden auf hellenistischen Münzen, in; Chrysafis – Hartmann – Schliephake – Weber 2023, 161–180

Moloney 2017: Moloney, Eoghan P. – Williams, Michael S. (eds.), Peace and Reconciliation in the Classical World, London et al. 2017

Noreña 2023: Noreña, Carlos, Coinage in the Early and High Roman Empire: Pax, Victory and Monarchic Ideology, in: Chrysafis – Hartmann – Schliephake – Weber 2023, 303–317

Onasch 1976: Onasch, C., Zur Königsideologie der Ptolemäer in den Dekreten von Kanopus und Memphis (Rosettana), Archiv für Papyrusforschung und Verwandte Gebiete 24–25, 1976, 237–254

Palagia 2000: Palagia, Olga, Hephaestion's Pyre and the Royal Hunt of Alexander, in: A. B. Bosworth – E. J. Baynham (eds.), Alexander the Great in fact and fiction, Oxford 2000, 167–206

Papini 2018: Papini, Massimiliano, Frieden bringt Reichtum: Die Eirene des Kephisodot, in: A. Lichtenberger – H. Nieswandt – D. Salzmann (eds.), Eirene/Pax: Frieden in der Antike, Münster 2018, 63–73

Pfeiffer 2004: Pfeiffer, Stefan, Das Dekret von Kanopos (238 v. Chr.): Kommentar und historische Auswertung eines dreisprachigen Synodaldekretes der ägyptischen Priester zu Ehren Ptolemaios' III. und seiner Familie, München 2004

Pfeiffer 2015: Pfeiffer, Stefan, Griechische und lateinische Inschriften zum Ptolemäerreich und zur römischen Provinz Aegyptus, Münster 2015

Piejko 1991: Piejko, Francis, Antiochus III and Ilium, Archiv für Papyrusforschung und verwandte Gebiete 37, 1991, 9–50

Plischke 2017: Plischke, Sonja, Persianism under the early Seleukid kings? The royal title ‚Great King‘, in: R. Strootman – M. J. Versluys (eds.), Persianism in Antiquity, Stuttgart 2017, 163–176

Poddighe 2013: Poddighe, Elisabetta, Propaganda Strategies and Political Documents: Philip III's „Diagramma" and the Greeks in 319 BC, in: Alonso Troncoso – Anson 2013, 225–240

Raaflaub 2009: Raaflaub, Kurt A., Conceptualizing and Theorizing Peace in Ancient Greece, Transactions of the American Philological Association 139, 2009, 225–250

Raaflaub 2010: Raaflaub, Kurt A., Friedenskonzepte und Friedenstheorien im griechischen Altertum, Historische Zeitschrift 290, 2010, 593–619

Raaflaub 2015: Raaflaub, Kurt A., Forerunners of Federal States: Collaboration and Integration Through Alliance in Archaic and Classical Greece, in: Beck – Funke 2015, 434–451

Raaflaub 2016: Raaflaub, Kurt A. (ed.), Peace in the Ancient World: Concepts and Theories, Chichester et al. 2016

Rabe 2010: Rabe, Brigitte, Zu Herstellung und Bedeutung der Ptolemäischen Ringergruppe, Antike Kunst 53, 2010, 49–61

Roskam 2020: Roskam, Geert, How to Date the Timeless? The Difficult Problem of the Pseudo-Pythagorean Treatises on Kingship, Ktèma 20, 2020, 125–141

Scherberich 2009: Scherberich, Klaus, „Koinè symmachía": Untersuchungen zum Hellenenbund Antigonos' III. Doson und Philipps V. (224–197 v. Chr.), Stuttgart 2009

Schmidt-Dounas 2000: Schmidt-Dounas, Barbara, Geschenke erhalten die Freundschaft: Politik und Selbstdarstellung im Spiegel der Monumente: Historische und archäologische Auswertung, Berlin 2000

Schubart 1937: Schubart, Walter, Das hellenistische Königsideal nach Inschriften und Papyri, Archiv für Papyrusforschung und verwandte Gebiete 12, 1937, 1–26

Scrofani 2020: Scrofani, Francesca, Royauté et loi: de Platon aux Traités sur la royauté, Ktèma 45, 2020, 71–89

Selz 2001: Selz, Gebhard J., Guter Hirte, Weiser Fürst – Zur Vorstellung von Macht und zur Macht der Vorstellung im altmesopotamischen Herrschaftsparadigma, Altorientalische Forschungen 28, 2001, 8–39

Seyer 2007: Seyer, Martin, Der Herrscher als Jäger: Untersuchungen zur königlichen Jagd im persischen und makedonischen Reich vom 6.–4. Jh. v. Chr. sowie unter den Diadochen Alexanders des Großen, Wien 2007

Smarczyk 2015: Smarczyk, Bernhard, The Hellenic Leagues of Late Classical and Hellenistic Times and their Place in the History of Greek Federalism, in: Beck – Funke 2015, 452–470

Strootman 2014: Strootman, Rolf, „Men to Whose Rapacity Neither Sea nor Mountain sets a Limit": the Aims of the Diadochs, in: H. Hauben – A. Meeus (eds.), The Age of the Successors and the Creation of the Hellenistic Kingdoms (323–276 BC), Leuven 2014, 307–322

Strootman 2023: Strootman, Rolf, Die große Prozession von Ptolemaios II. Philadelphos: wie das Ptolemäische Reich als Zeitalter von ewigem, weltweitem Frieden präsentiert wird, in: Chrysafis – Hartmann – Schliephake – Weber 2023, 207–229

Thomas 2002: Thomas, Renate, Eine postume Statuette Ptolemaios' IV. und ihr historischer Kontext: zur Götterangleichung hellenistischer Herrscher, Mainz 2002

Thraede 1994: Thraede, Klaus, Homonoia (Eintracht), Reallexikon für Antike und Christentum 16, 1994, 176–289

Trampedach 2020: Trampedach, Kai, Staging Charisma: Alexander and Divination, in: Meeus – Trampedach 2020, 45–60

Tuplin 2008: Tuplin, Christopher J., The Seleucids and their Achaemenid predecessors: a Persian inheritance, in: S. M. Darbandi – A. Zournatzi, Ancient Greece and Ancient Iran. Cross-cultural encounters, Athen 2008, 109–136

Tuplin 2017: Tuplin, Christopher J., War and Peace in Achaemenid Imperial Ideology, Electrum 24, 2017, 31–54

von Reckinghausen 2018: von Recklinghausen, Daniel, Die Philensis-Dekrete: Untersuchungen über zwei Synodaldekrete aus der Zeit Ptolemaios' V. und ihre geschichtliche und religiöse Bedeutung, Wiesbaden 2018

Wagner-Durand 2019: Wagner-Durand, Elisabeth, Narration. Description. Reality: The Royal Lion Hunt in Assyria, in: E. Wagner-Durand – B. Fath – A. Heinemann (eds.), Image – Narration – Context: Visual Narration in Cultures and Societies of the Old World, Heidelberg 2019, 235–272

Walbank ²1984: Walbank, Frank W., Monarchies and Monarchic Ideas, in: CAH² 7.1, Cambridge et al. 1984, 62–100

Wallace 2011: Wallace, Shane, The Significance of Plataia for Greek ἐλευθερία in the Early Hellenistic Period, in: A. Erskine – Ll. Llewellyn-Jones (eds.), Creating a Hellenistic World, Swansea 2011, 147–176

Wallace 2013: Wallace, Shane, Adeimantus of Lampsacus and the Development of the early Hellenistic „Philos", in: Alonso Troncoso – Anson 2013, 142–157

Wallace 2014: Wallace, Shane, Defending the Freedom of the Greeks: Antigonos, Telesphoros, and the Olympic Games of 312 B.C., Phoenix 68.3–4, 2014, 235–246

Wallace 2020: Wallace, Shane, Communication and Legitimation: Knowledge of Alexander's Asian Conquests in the Greek World, in: Meeus – Trampedach 2020, 123–144

Weber 1922: Weber, Max, Die drei reinen Typen der legitimen Herrschaft, Preußische Jahrbücher, 1922, 1–12

Weber 1980: Weber, Max, Wirtschaft und Gesellschaft. Grundriss einer verstehenden Soziologie, Tübingen 1980

Wiemer 2017: Wiemer, Hans-Ulrich, Siegen oder untergehen? Die hellenistische Monarchie in der neueren Forschung, in: S. Rebenich (ed.), Monarchische Herrschaft im Altertum, Berlin et al. 2017, 305–339

Wiesehöfer 2023: Wiesehöfer, J., Frieden und Friedensvorstellungen im achaimenidischen Iran, in: Chrysafis – Hartmann – Schliephake – Weber 2023, 41–51

Wilker 2012a: Wilker, Julia (ed.), Maintaining Peace and Interstate Stability in Archaic und Classical Greece, Mainz 2012a

Wilker 2012b: Wilker, Julia, War and Peace at the Beginning of the Fourth Century. The Emergence of Koine Eirene, in: Wilker 2012a, Mainz, 92–117

Wright 2015: Wright, Benjamin G., The Letter of Aristeas. Commentaries on early Jewish literature, Berlin 2015

Zahrnt 2009: Zahrnt, Michael, The Macedonian Background, in: W. Heckel – L.A. Tritle (eds.), Alexander the Great. A New History, Oxford 2009, 7–25

Charalampos I. Chrysafis is a Research Associate in Ancient History at the University of Augsburg. He earned his Ph.D. in Ancient History from the National Kapodistrian University of Athens with a thesis focused on the Antigonid garrisons in Greek poleis. Since 2019, he has been actively involved in research projects on Hellenistic monarchy at the University of Augsburg, with a primary emphasis on the central role of peace in the context of monarchical ideology. Moreover, his current research delves into the intricate dynamics of the ideological tension surrounding representations of Hellenistic kings, whether they are seen as universal rulers or deeply rooted in localist/regionalist identities.

Impact and Foreign Domination /
Ausstrahlung und Fremdherrschaft

———————

King and Koinon
*Ptolemaic Interactions with Greek Federalism**

HANS BECK

Abstract: The Hellenistic Age is often labelled the era of federalism in Greek history. Organizations such as the Achaian and Aitolian Leagues are seen as innovative instruments of resilience against Macedonian rule: (trans-)regional cooperation made them a force to be reckoned with, while at the same time they safeguarded time-honored principles of local self-governance. This contribution examines how one of the major Hellenistic monarchies dealt with the koina of Greece. From the outset, overlapping strategies among Ptolemies and Antigonids (and others, for that matter) might be expected. Emanating from different locations of power, the spatial dynamics in the implementation of those strategies put the Ptolemies, however, on a distinct trajectory. The article discusses Ptolemaic interactions with the Nesiotic League, the Boiotian League, the (somewhat unexpected case of the) Amphictyony of Kalaureia, and the Aitolian as well as Achaian Leagues. It is argued that federalism provided the Ptolemies with an ideal toolkit to pursue their strategic goals in a political arena far remote from their court in Alexandreia. Both in practical terms and in the ways they fashioned themselves before Hellenic audiences, support of federalism was intuitive to their agency. In conclusion, such an assessment of Ptolemaic policies complicates the more general verdict that federalism was geared toward the purpose of resistance against the Hellenistic monarchies.

1. Introduction

The rule of the Hellenistic monarchies drew on different methods and means to wield power over a diverse body of subjects. Understood not merely as the exercise of military force and the pervasive organization of state power, their reign was characterized by the close interplay between rulers and ruled, sensitive to the need of culture-specific interactions. Due recognition of the key expectations emanating from the political

*   Thanks to Christoph Michels and Alex McAuley for helpful comments on an earlier version.

culture of their subjects was crucial for the successful exercise of power. For instance, in Egypt Ptolemaic rule was notoriously built on the recognition of time-honored legacies and traditions in place, a circumstance that was acknowledged also by Ptolemaios I's acclamation to the title of Pharaoh in 305 BC.

In the Aegean and in mainland Greece, which had never come under their direct military sway, the Ptolemies devised other strategies which were again developed in careful consideration of the circumstances on the ground. The starting condition was altogether different from Egypt. On the one hand, interventions of a Macedonian dynasty were prone to potential push-back against foreign influence and the reactions this provoked in discourses of self-governance and freedom; no matter how their foreignness was conceived, it put Ptolemaic agents on a potentially xenocratic footing. On the other hand, rivalry with the Antigonid dynasty, while adding another layer of complexity to interstate relations, created a constellation where the Ptolemies operated as agents from afar, whereas the Antigonids could be regarded a more direct threat. Ptolemaic possessions throughout the Aegean and Saronic regions, including strongholds in Attica and on the Peloponnese among others, no doubt complicated this picture as these possessions gave the Ptolemies an immediate presence in Greece and the Aegean. Yet their center of power was remote from Greece, and the avenues of communication and control were maritime. As pointed out by Rolf Strootman, Ptolemaic imperialism in the third century was seaborne, following the dynamics of a Sea Empire: its imperial policy aimed first of all 'at securing sea routes through the control of harbors'.[1] In the convoluted political environment of Aegean Greece, this called for special strategic planning and careful conduct in accordance with the prevailing traditions and expectations. Remoteness might have been an advantage over the Antigonids, but it also represented a structural challenge, if not a risk.

From the 3rd century BC, the federal states of central and southern Greece were among the main Ptolemaic (and Antigonid) interlocutors in conversations of power. Kostas Buraselis has recently surveyed the relations between what he labels 'symbiotic creatures' – kings and koina – in the period prior to the arrival of Rome. His study reveals the utilitarian undertone in their exchanges. The Macedonian dynasties found the various federal states of the mainland and the Aegean too powerful to ignore them; hence, they attempted to win them over and integrate them into their designs of power. The federal leagues, geared toward advanced models of statecraft, were of course unable to ignore the Macedonians either. Their interests intersected and found a common denominator with the great dynasties in the flow of cash and manpower. The favors worked both ways: while federal organization served the needs of kings, because they presented themselves as effective, region-wide partners, assailing compartmen-

---

1   Strootman 2020, citation 117.

talized agencies of a plethora of cities, the ruling dynasties of Macedon and Egypt were promising allies with staggering financial funds and other resources at their disposal.[2]

In light of complementary interests, it will be worthwhile to explore how the Ptolemies made efforts to enlarge the potential of collaboration: that is, to examine if and how they made use of the mechanics of federalism, and how this policy left its marks on federal affairs in Greece. The Hellenistic Age has often been declared the era of federalism. Most eminently, Frank Walbank observed that federalism 'exemplif[ied] the continuing ability of the Greeks to respond to a new political challenge with new solutions. (…) Federalism offered the possibility of transcending the limitations of size and relative weakness of the separate city-state'.[3] The implicit motive behind this verdict is that federalism safeguarded an ever-shrinking degree of freedom and independence from foreign domination. While this assertion is certainly true, complementary interests between king and koinon could also contribute to the spread of federal policies. For instance, the League of Corinth from 338/337 BC amply witnessed the desire of Philip II to make the most of the federal principle in his designs of power: organized as an alliance along federal structures, the members of the league were themselves mostly federal states that were instrumental in extending Philip's rule across central and southern Greece.[4] Over a century later, Antigonos Doson in 224 BC applied a similar blend of measures to the renewal of a Hellenic League that consisted for the most part of federal states. Based on loose contractual relationships yet with a firm Macedonian grip on the decision-making process, Doson's league both safeguarded his own position of power in Greece and endorsed the lived tradition of federal arrangements.[5] Between these instances, the following sections tease out Ptolemaic dealings with federalism, carried out from their particular place of power and enacted with the goal of gaining ground in mainland Greece and the Aegean.

2. The League of Islanders: federalism from the scratch

The most eminent and also earliest example of Ptolemaic experiments with federalism was the κοινὸν τῶν νησιωτῶν, or League of Islanders. Seated on the island of Delos and comprising members from the Kyklades as well as a few islands beyond the "circle" (κύκλος), the league was subject to a unique maritime dynamic. A full catalogue of its membership seems to be out of reach, but the koinon certainly included the islands of Delos, Mykonos, Naxos, Paros, Andros, Amorgos, and presumably Samos.[6] Other

---

2   Buraselis 2021, citation 101.
3   Walbank 1981, 157–158.
4   Buckler 2008b; Jehne 1994, 139–197.
5   See only Scherberich 2009a; Smarczyk 2015.
6   For a discussion, see Buraselis 1982, 78; Meadows 2013, 35.

powers had pushed into the core region of the Aegean before, most notably the Athenians, seeking to integrate the scattered island world into the design of naval empire. As an organization in its own right, however, the Nesiotic League had no forerunner in the Aegean. Its foundation was a novelty, unprecedented and built from the scratch. From its inception, then, the κοινὸν τῶν νησιωτῶν attests to the desire to explore new paths of federal cooperation. If Philip's League of Korinth appeared innovative for its mix of federal union and military alliance, the makers of the Nesiotic League deserve credit for bringing federalism to the sea.[7]

Just who they were and when the foundation happened exactly is a bone of contention in scholarship. According to the previous orthodoxy that dated its beginnings between ca. 314 and 288 BC, the league was considered an Antigonid creation, established under the leadership of Antigonos Monophthalmos and Demetrios Poliorketes. Since this rendering is based on the mention of the festivals of Antigoneia und Demetrieia in but one inscription from Delos,[8] an Antigonid phase has been challenged. For instance, appreciating that the full swing of league inscriptions runs under Ptolemaic aegis, the reign of Ptolemaios II Philadelphos (284–246) in particular, Andrew Meadows has argued that the league was a Ptolemaic construct altogether. As such, it would have been a critical piece in the puzzle of political, religious, and commercial designs for the Aegean world envisioned by Ptolemaios II.[9] There is no need to revisit the lively epigraphic debate behind these positions here; it goes back to the days of Félix Dürrbach.[10] Beyond Antigonids and Ptolemies, Christy Constantakopoulou has drawn attention to the fact that the earliest beginnings of the league most likely did not reflect its character as a royal tool of power in a highly contested space of the Mediterranean but a 'positive act of affirmation of identity in the southern Aegean' .[11] As such, the koinon of Islanders was, at the moment of its inception, an expression of and contribution to a strong sense of belonging among multiple islands. While this observation is certainly correct, the inscriptions evidence a steep trajectory in league activities throughout the first half of the 3rd century BC, with a sizable number of documents attributed to the Ptolemaic period.[12] The distribution is too striking to be dismissed as an accident of survival. If the league had an Antigonid phase, and a launch-period before that, driven by self-assertion and senses of togetherness, it is difficult to judge how lively this start might have been. The koinon spread its wings only under the suzerainty of Ptolemaios Philadelphos.

---

7   Cf. Billows 1990, 220–225; Constantakopoulou 2012; Buraselis 2015.
8   IG XI.4, 1036.
9   Meadows 2013, also suggesting a lower date for IG XI.4, 1036 (reign of Ptolemaios II).
10   See Dürrbach 1907; subsequent scholarship is covered by Meadows 2013.
11   Constantakopoulou 2012, 53.
12   17 documents survive; cf. the compilation by Buraselis 1982, 180–183.

The inscriptions reveal the basic outline of the league. Its main bodies included a synedrion (συνέδριον), or koinon synedrion, that met on Delos. The council was staffed with representatives, σύνεδροι, from the member-states; delegates were sent on basis of equal representation.[13] Reporting to the synedrion, an ἐπιμελητής oversaw financial contributions and federal spendings, including costs for the inscription of the league's decrees.[14] At the head of the organization stood the νησίαρχος, the "archon of the islands", who appears to have been an 'imported governor'.[15] None of the attested individuals hailed from Nesiotic origins: Bakchon came from Boiotia, Hermias, most likely from Halikarnassos, and a certain Apollodoros from Kyzikos.[16] In similar fashion, incumbents of the office of "οἰκονόμος of the islands" were seemingly appointed by royal order. The arrangement required a creative collaboration between the *epimelētēs* of the synedrion and the *oikonomos* dispatched by the king.[17]

The basic outline suggests a light organization – no traces of a federal law court or common coinage survive, although the absence of the latter might have had to do with the seabound nature of the koinon. Light mechanics did not imply loose agency. The surviving epigraphic material says nothing about participation in military expeditions alongside their Ptolemaic masters, nor is there any mention of contributions to a common war chest, *vel sim*. Instead, the inscriptions attest to a flurry of honorary decrees for the first two Ptolemies and the royal officials of the koinon. In some cases, the rights of *asylia* and *proxenia* were granted, which recipients carried happily across the islands; the image is one of lively exchanges that brought, among other benefits, also economic assets with them. Although there was no joint federal citizenship, the koinon awarded its benefactors with the full bundle of citizenships of each of its member-states. Effectively, this might have implied – the issue is debated – that the citizens of the league themselves were united by mutual bonds of *isopoliteia*. Either way, the personal character of these federal relationships with the Ptolemies and their agents is certainly noteworthy.[18]

The koinon undertook major efforts to coordinate the sending of *theoroi*, festival delegations. In the famous decree from Nikouria (c. 281/280 BC) on the southeastern perimeter of the Kylades, regulations are made for the dispatch of official representatives to the Ptolemaieia in Alexandreia, newly established feasts and games of Ptolemaios II in honor of his father.[19] Whereas the celebrations for Ptolemaios directed the

13   On the synedrion, Buraselis 1982, 78–87; Constantakopoulou 2012, 58–59.
14   IG XI.4, 1040 and 1041.
15   Buraselis 2015, 362.
16   On nesiarchs, cf. Bagnall 1976, 138; Buraselis 1982, 81–83, 184–186; Constantakopoulou 2012. For Bakchon, see also Hennig 1989, 177–180; Meadows 2013, 32. The Delian temple accounts record two golden phialai dedicated by him.
17   IG XII Suppl. 169; Constantakopoulou 2012, 57.
18   Cf. Billows 1990, 220–221; Buraselis 2015, 362–363.
19   IG XII.7 506 = Syll.³ 390; Constantakopoulou 2012, 55–57.

focus of the league toward the ruling dynasty and the splendour of its new capital, the language of the decree assured members that the league's cause, although a new foundation, remained committed to motivations of old. In lines 13 to 15, Ptolemaios I is honored because he 'freed the cities and gave them back their laws and reestablished their "ancestral constitution"' (τὴμ πάτριομ πολιτείαμ).[20] Another decree of the Nesiotic League from Delos, roughly contemporary with the Nikouria decree, documents the inauguration of the festival of Ptolemaieia there, too. Issued as an honorary decree for a man named Sostratos from Knidos who had played a vital role in the communications between certain league VIPs and the Ptolemaic court, the inscription highlights the attempt to cultivate relations through facilitating personal access to the king.[21]

Dating to the earliest years of Philadelphos' reign, the establishment of the Ptolemaieia as federal games on Delos and the koinon's official participation in the festival celebrated in the royal capital Alexandreia show a gripping interplay between league affairs and cultic agencies, in the Aegean and in Egypt. Whatever the military arm of the Nesiotic League was and no matter how strong its firepower, in its core the koinon served the purpose of structuring the communication between Ptolemaios II (and maybe his father) on the one hand and the island world of Aegean Greece on the other. Its political body allowed the king to address a plethora of island states at once; in return, exchanges between members and the king in Alexandreia could be funneled through the federal synedrion. Rather than steering communications through league institutions and officials alone, however, the κοινὸν τῶν νησιωτῶν fostered an extensive, carefully conceived cultic agenda that occupied much of its activities. In the lived history of federalism in the two centuries leading up to the League of Islanders, federal games had absorbed a key role in the process of regional integration. For instance, in Boiotia, home of Bakchon the nesiarch, translocal sanctuaries and federal festivals were indispensable features of the region's federal togetherness (below). With the Ptolemaieia, the tradition of federal cults and festivals was both continued and given a new direction: the festival invited the members of the league to celebrate their union, and it provided a platform for them to honor and venerate their patron. In the decades of Ptolemaic leadership, then, the Nesiotic League offered almost an object lesson of the creative interplay between king and koinon.

3. Boiotia: immersion in regional exchange

On the mainland, the Thebans had launched a notorious revolt against Macedon in 335 BC, with detrimental consequences for their city. Aided by several Boiotians and

---

20   IG XII.7 506, ll. 13–15.
21   IG XI.4 1038, cf. Constantakopoulou 2012, 58. Sostratos was probably the donor of the Pharos of Alexandreia. On the phenomenon cf. also the chapter by Benedikt Eckhardt in this volume.

ordered by the council of the League of Korinth, Alexander destroyed Thebes, enslaved the greatest part of the surviving population, and parceled out its chora to other
poleis in eastern Boiotia. Maybe Alexander ordered the dissolution of any remaining
federal league, but the political landscape of Boiotia remains largely unknown at the
time.[22] In 316/315 Kassandros ordered the rebuilding of Thebes and the city resurfaced
as a player in regional affairs. But only by 288 did the Thebans regain the status of political self-governance within the league. Fifty years after the battle of Chaironeia and
after a troubled period of defeat, turmoil, and destruction Thebes had consolidated
its stance as a genuine citizen community, however, with a decimated population and
a much-reduced territory. The future of the Boiotian League, an organization deeply
intertwined with hegemonic ambitions of Thebes, was yet to be determined.[23]

Along the road to Theban recovery, an inscription from before 281 honored Ptolemaios' daughter Arsinoë II, at the time wife of Thracian king Lysimachos, for her
καλοκαγαθία. The text survives on two fragments of a statue base kept in the museum
in Thebes; their provenance in the city is unknown:

[Πτ]ολεμαῖ[ο]ς Λυσιμάχου
[ὑπ]ὲρ βασιλέως [Λ]υσιμάχο[υ]
[Ἀρ]σινόην τὴν αὐτοῦ
[γυν]αῖκα καλοκ[α]γαθίας ἕνεκ[α]

The inscription explains that the dedication was commissioned by Ptolemaios Epigonos, first-born son of Lysimachos with Arsinoë, on his father's behalf. While Arsinoë is
the recipient of honors – the dedication is motivated by her *kalokagathia* –, the inscription says it was made for the king in honor of Arsinoë his wife. The family constellation
is accentuated by reference to Lysimachos as father and king, and Arsinoë as the king's
wife. Arsinoë most likely distinguished herself through financial contributions to the
recovery of Thebes in one way or another and her engagement was subsequently remembered by Ptolemaios Epigonos (died 240).[24]

The famous catalogue inscription from Thebes that lists donations made in response
to Lysimachos' call to rebuild the city (IG VII 2419 = Syll.³ 337) dates a little earlier
than the honorific decree for Arsinoë. Maurice Holleaux offered a masterful study of
the text in 1895 which laid the groundwork for all subsequent research. Recently, in
2019, Yannis Kalliontzis and Nikolaos Papazarkadas provided a profound reexamina-
tion, as part of the ongoing work on their Theban fascicle of the new Boiotian corpus (IG VII² 4). Their reassessment of the stone also benefits from the discovery of
a second, previously unknown fragment identified and masterfully edited by Kostas

22   Cf. Beck – Ganter 2015, 150–152; Gullath 1982, 86–113.
23   Gullath 1982, 107–113 (Thebes sending delegates to the sanctuary of Apollon Ptoios in Akraiphia:
      IG VII 2723, 2724, 2724a, 2724b); Knoepfler 1999 and 2001.
24   SEG 25.516, with Robert 1933, 485–491; Gullath 1982, 206, note 4 (between 284 and 281).

Buraselis in 2014. The second fragment, now figuring as (a), joins the older text (b) at the top of the stone. It adds another 20 lines to two columns of donors. The assembled fragments are on display in the Hellenistic section of the museum in Thebes.[25]

The catalogue inscription makes no mention of Arsinoë. Holleaux has suggested, however, to see Arsinoë's husband king Lysimachos among the donors, who maybe appears as Βασιλ[εὺς Λυσίμαχος] in the lower part of the stone (line II 41). The issue is complicated by the fact that lines II 32–42 in the royal section of donors are extremely poorly preserved. At least four different kings are mentioned (lines II 32, 37, 39, 41). Scholars have made various attempts to fill these lacunae; among others, with Kassandros, Lysimachos, Ptolemaios I, Pyrrhos, and Damaratos. For line II 40, Kalliontzis and Papazarkadas now suggest [δραχμὰς Λουσιμα]|χίας, which lends further support to earlier suggestions that Lysimachos was one of the kings in lines II 39–41.[26] Both Lysimachos and his then wife Arsinoë were thus involved in the rebuilding of Thebes in one way or another; Arsinoë in particular was singled out from the circle of benefactors on the catalogue inscription through the award of individual honors; presumably she had distinguished herself through financial support of a specific project, for instance, the restoration of one of the sanctuaries in the city or countryside. A few years later she is reported to have made a similar financial contribution on Samothrake. Arsinoë came to the island during her flight from Kassandreia to Egypt in ca. 280. Her brother Ptolemaios II Philadelphos had commissioned there a monumental gatehouse that led visitors into the sanctuary of the Kabiroi; the impressive building marked the transition into the sacred space of the temenos.[27] Arsinoë made a similar contribution. She financed the erection of an imposing tholos complex of 17 m in diameter, the Rotunda of Arsinoë.[28] Upon her visit to the sanctuary, she was also initiated into the Mysteries of the Kabiroi, a ritual charged with a special meaning to Macedonian royal families: Philip had famously met his fourth wife Olympias at a celebration of the Mysteries on Samothrake.[29] The Mystery lead was picked up before by Arsinoë's father, Ptolemaios I. When refashioning the worship of Serapis in Alexandreia to marry it with his ruler cult, he incorporated significant elements of the Greek Mysteries into the corresponding rituals. In doing so, Ptolemaios was said to have been inspired by a priest of the Eleusinian Mysteries, with which, effectively, he had proclaimed privileged relations.[30]

---

25   Holleaux 1895/1938; Buraselis 2014; Kalliontzis – Papazarkadas 2019.

26   Kalliontzis – Papazarkadas 2019, 305, adding that Lysimachos first struck royal tetradrachms in 297 BC. See Holleaux 1895/1938, 38; Gullath 1982, 89–97, esp. 96; Knoepfler 2001b (one of the kings in lines II 39–41 Lysimachos).

27   See Frazer 1990, 231–3; Carney 2013, 94. The dedicatory inscription suggests a later date than the rotunda of Arsinoë, see IG XII.8 228 = Samothrace 11.

28   IG XII.8 227 = Samothrace 10; Blakely 2011, 81; Carney 2013, 37–39.

29   Plut. Alexander 2.2; Greenwalt 2008; Landucci 2015.

30   The details are discussed by Pfeiffer 2008.

While Arisinoë made lavish spendings on Samothrake and in Thebes, the people of Samothrake might also have aided the rebuilding of Thebes. In line I 33 of the donor catalogue, Holleaux found the restauration of Σαμοθρ]ακες 'tout à fait vraisemblable', although the case is rather tentative.[31] If correct, the image is one of triangular relations between Thebes, Samothrake, and Arsinoë, along with a conspicuous interest of the leading figures of the Ptolemaic dynasty in the celebration of Mystery cults.

Thebes had its own Mysteries in the Sanctuary of the Kabiroi, although the beginnings of the Mystery cult on site are debated. In the literary sources, corresponding cult practices are only attested to by Pausanias, whose account contains no reliable information on when the veneration of the Kabiroi was first fused with rituals revolving around a Mystery cult.[32] The Kabirion was located ca. 5 km to the west of the Kadmeia in the Theban plain. Excavations at the sanctuary have brought to light a deep transformation of the site in the late 4th and early 3rd centuries BC. The overhaul was massive. An extensive oval terrace was placed into the center of the site, measuring ca. 40 m long and 20 m wide and surrounded by a low wall. In addition, an impressive entry complex and a well were built; the latter carried water via an underground pipe into the central area. On the terrace, a rectangular podium and a round structure were placed on the eastern and western part respectively. Both stood in plain sight of the natural *cavea* that was now banked up and extended. In addition, a large stoa was built to the south of the temenos.[33]

Coinciding with this building program, the first stone inscriptions from the Kabirion document the full-fledged organization of the cult of the Kabiroi, including a college of ἱαρειαδδοί. They are superseded by an ἄρχων who was assisted by two καβιριαρχαί as well as a secretary, γραμματίδδος.[34] In another text, the καβιριαρχαί are followed by twelve παραγωγεῖες. Their function is difficult to assert. It has been argued that they discharged the role of *mystagogoi* elsewhere, hence they were "leaders of initiands", which implies that they related to the administration of a Mystery cult. If correct, this is the first firm attestation of a Mystery cult on site.[35] It is best, therefore, to see the rise of the Mystery cult in causal connection with the changes to the monumental architecture of the Kabirion in the first two decades of the 3rd century.

So, the transformation of the site and changes to the ritual practice will have gone hand in hand. Who inspired this change, and who picked up the bills? With the destruction of Thebes and the parceling out of its countryside, the economic basis of the local elites that had carried the sanctuary for the past two centuries had vanished if the

---

31   Holleaux 1895/1938, 40; cf. Gullath 1982, 91–92. Kalliontzis – Papazarkadas 2019, 298 have reservations against Holleaux's supplement.
32   Paus. 9.25–26.
33   Schachter 2003/2016, 318–325; Beck 2024.
34   IG VII 2420; Wolters and Bruns 1940, 27.4; also IG VII 2428. Cf. Roesch 1965, 202–203.
35   IG VII 2428; Paus. 9.25.5–10; cf. Bremmer 2014, 44–45; Schachter 2003/2016, 323.

families weren't killed altogether. By the 300s and 290s, signs of recovery suggest that some Theban money was available, but these funds were hardly sufficient. Note that the metamorphosis of the sanctuary also assigned a new role to the Kabirion in regional conversations in Boiotia. Formerly an extraurban sanctuary of the city of Thebes, the Kabirion now extended its catchment area into the surrounding region, attracting local elites from elsewhere. The evidence of theophoric personal names (Kabiros, Kabirichos, Kabirinos, and others) betrays a dissemination of these names across various Boiotian cities, including Thespiai, Tanagra, Thisbe, and Oropos. With the exception of the earliest of these (a Theban archon from the 370s), all of the surviving cases date from the early Hellenistic period. The name choice signals the eminence of the cult in regional conversations.[36] Hailing from different corners of the region, it suggests that the local elites of Boiotia saw the new Kabirion as a place where participation in ritual and the celebration of elite distinction were two sides of the same coin.

The Ptolemies must have realized this potential. Engagement in the Kabirion allowed Arsinoë and her dynasty to branch out, that is, to communicate with elites beyond the local horizon. Conversations promised to be practical and symbolic – and they went both ways, as they allowed elite circles in Boiotia in turn to foster ties with powerful partners. Pointing the Kabirion cult into a new direction was, therefore, instrumental to these mutual goals. Support of the Kabirion complemented the agenda of Arsinoë's father and brother, as it aligned with their aid of Mysteries elsewhere. When she came forth in Thebes, her actions were carried out ostentatiously before the backdrop of family: the aforementioned dedication of her honorary statue by Ptolemaios Epigonos praised the ideal scenario of husband, wife, and son. In the Theban Kabirion, such family engagement was part and parcel in the performance of the cult since the late 6th century. Prior to 335 BC, the Kabirion was a site famed for ritual celebrations of families – husbands and wives who typically accompanied their sons at the moment of initiation into adult life.[37] It is unlikely that this rootedness of family in cult went unnoticed to the queen. In Thebes, it seems, Arsinoë acted in recognition of precisely this tradition. At the same time, her support allowed not only to rebuild but also to advance the site, that is, to steer the Kabirion into the new direction of a Mystery cult.

It is difficult although maybe not impossible to relate these actions seamlessly to the scattered history of the Boiotian League at the time. After 308, the koinon witnessed a phase of formidable consolidation through the integration of Eretria and Chalkis; in or around 287 BC Oropos was added, which broadened the basis of league operations. In the two decades between, Thebes solidified its role within the league. By 292, the city

---

36   The surviving theophoric names have been compiled by Schachter 2003/2016, 317, note 4.
37   The so-called Kabirion ware provides ample evidence for this type of ritual agency, see only the Kabiros and Pais kotyle from ca. 410 (Athens, National Museum 10426; Wolters and Bruns 1940, 96.K1 and tables 5 and 44.1); cf. Schachter 2003/2016, 323–35, with exemplary discussion.

was considered one of the leaders in an attempted revolt against Antigonid control.[38] In light of muddled terrains, subject to swiftly changing alliances and volatile constellations on the ground, engagement in a sanctuary appeared a convenient way to forge ties with the local elites. In the case of the Kabirion, such involvement was all the more persuasive because the site was surrounded by tales about recognition and respect. Pausanias tells the story that the Macedonians were particularly fearful of the Theban Kabiroi. During the sack of Thebes some Macedonian soldiers – out of ignorance – had violated the sanctuary; they were killed by thunder and lightning from heaven in return.[39] The anecdote added a nice piece to the puzzle of local traditions about the site, Macedonian intervention, and the prestige of the sanctuary.

4. Kalaureia: tampering with tradition

Two decades or so after the reception of honors on Samothrake and in Thebes, Arsinoë, now queen and wife of her brother Ptolemaios II Philadelphos, appeared again as critical agent in cultic conversations between king and koinon. In the Chremonidean War (267–261 BC), a coalition of cities and leagues challenged the power of the Antigonids in Greece. Both sides resorted to programmatic slogans: while the Hellenic symmachy fully immersed itself in the language of freedom and independence from domination, the Antigonids, claiming to contain local rivalries of old, styled themselves as deliverers of both.[40] The anti-Antigonid coalition received major support from Egypt. Although allied with Athens at the time, the Ptolemies had no access to the Peiraieus because the harbor was held by Antigonos Gonatas' party. The Ptolemies established a series of naval bases stitched into the perimeter of the Saronic region. Their presence is traceable at Koroni near Porto Raphti on the Aegean coast of Attica, at Rhamnous, on Keos, and the small islet named Patroklos Island, opposite Cape Sounion (Sounion itself was under the control of the Antigonids).[41] The central base of operations was placed on the Methana peninsula of the Peloponnese, in the city of Methana. Ptolemaic influence there was so impactful that Methana at the time changed its name to Arsinoë. The city continued to bear the name for roughly a century.[42]

In 2007–2008, ongoing excavations in the Sanctuary of Kalaureia on Poros, a few kilometers south of Methana, brought to light an inscribed statue base comprising four blocks made from greyish limestone. These were retrieved from a rubble area in the

---

38 For a comprehensive narrative, see Gullath 1982, 169–206.
39 Paus. 9.25.10.
40 See Dreyer 1999, 331–376; O'Neil 2008.
41 The standard account is still Bagnall 1976, 117–158; cf. also Huss 2001, 275–280; Hölbl 2001, 40–43.
42 See Gill 2007, 60–61. Ptolemaic influence also imprinted through religious activities, encouraging the worship of Serapis and Isis, see Wallensten – Pakkanen 2009, 164.

southeastern section outside the peribolos wall of the temple. The inscription, written in well-cut regular letters, runs across three blocks of the base. It survives in full and can be easily read:[43]

Βασιλῆ Πτολεμαῖον καὶ Ἀρσινόαν Φιλάδελφον ἁ πόλις | ἁ τῶν Ἀρσυνοέων ἀπὸ Πελοποννάσου Ποδειδᾶνι

The polis of Arsinoë for King Ptolemaios and Arsinoë Philadelphos to Poseidon of the Peloponnese.

In other words, the people of Methana/Arsinoë, home to the Ptolemaic fleet in the Saronic, offered statues of Ptolemaios II and his sister-wife to be set up on an impressive base (c. 2 m wide). With the dedication, Methana/Arsinoë not only proclaimed its allegiance and honored its benefactors, but the city presented its new outlook before a high volume of visitors to the sanctuary, in a prominent spot. Contents and context of the inscribed dedication allow for a dating after death of Arsinoë (the moment of her assuming the name Philadelphos) and in the lifetime of Ptolemaios II, ca. 270 to 246 BC.[44]

From the Sanctuary of Poseidon derives another well-known inscription.

[– – –]ωνος vacat(?) | [ʽΗγ]ελόχου {[Μεν]ελόχου?} | [–]ι τὰν νᾶσον | [Πο]σειδᾶνος |⁵ [ὑπ] ἐρ δὲ τῶν |[–]ας, καθὼς καὶ τοῖς | [ἱα]ρομναμόνων | [–]α ἐκ τὰς νάσου |¹⁰ κὴν Ἀμφικτ[ύοσι].[45]

Chiselled into white marble and retrieved from the peribolos wall of the temple during first excavations in 1894, the fragmented inscription speaks of Kalaureia as 'the island of Poseidon' (ll. 3–4). The text refers to a board of sacred officials who represented the amphictyony of the sanctuary (ll. 7–9). The date established by the excavators is the 3rd century BC, which overlaps broadly with Methana's dedication for Ptolemaios II and Arsinoë but places the document otherwise at an uncertain moment in a crowded timeline. Since the Lamian War of 323–322 BC, the Saronic was in Antigonid possession. Despite challenges to their supremacy in the Chremonidean War, Antigonos Gonatas was able to defended his interests in the northern sector of the Saronic. The city of Athens received an Antigonid garrison that remained in the city until 255, in the Piraeus even until 229; when Antigonos visited Eleusis (prior to 243?), the pro-Macedonian parties had arranged for a splendid reception.[46] The incorporation of Korinth, Megara, Troizen, and Epidauros into the Achaian League in 243/242 posed however a serious threat to the Macedonian presence. The situation was aggravated when Ptolemaios III in the same year became nominal leader and military commander of the

43 Wallensten – Pakkanen 2009.
44 Wallensten – Pakkanen 2009, 163.
45 IG IV 842.
46 Palagia – Tracy 2003. Eleusis: SEG 65.106.

Achaian League. The league annexed the Peloponnesian shores of the Saronic, which left no doubts about the firepower of the Achaian-Ptolemaic alliance as well as the sympathies it enjoyed across the Peloponnese.[47]

Kalaureia was on a volatile trajectory amidst these troubles. From the early days of Antigonid interventions in the Saronic, the settlement for the first time proclaimed for itself the status of a polis with an associated body of citizens, the πόλις τῶν Καλαυρεατᾶν.[48] If articulated in conjunction with the amphictyony of IG IV 842, the new status might have been a claim to fame, heralding transregional importance. Usage of the label ἀμφικτυονία, with its strong sense of primordial neighborhood ties, would have supplemented this; by the 3rd century BC, the term clearly had an archaizing ring. Among the few epigraphic pieces that attest to the polis of Kalaureia is a collective grant of *ateleia*, immunity and/or exemption from duties, to the island of Siphnos, gateway through the open perimeter of the Saronic into the Aegean. It is perfectly conceivable that the city and amphictyony, building off the notion of connectedness in the Saronic, resorted to the theme of immunity, which would have bolstered its reputation both as a tax haven and asylum.[49]

The age of the Amphictyony of Kalaureia is notoriously debated. A high number of contributions to the discussion concentrates on footprints that might indicate early beginnings. Indeed, there is a fascination with potentially late-Iron Age or Archaic roots, a chronology that would put the amphictyony on the same timeline as the (Anthelian-)Delphic amphictyony.[50] While the issues at stake are of obvious attraction, it seems that the intensity of the debate is disproportionate to the available body of evidence, which is next to nothing (below). Only occasionally is the organization discussed in the time context for which there are sources available, that is, from the 3rd century BC. Whenever founded initially, a fresh start in the 3rd century BC is undeniable. In light of the Saronic's factual – and inspirational – connectedness in quotidian affairs, Kalaureia's majestic location and prestigious sanctuary made it a prime, if not compelling hub were amphictyonic ideas might have converged. Accelerated conditions in the course of the 3rd century added to the sense of vibrant exchanges clustering at Kalaureia. No matter how substantiated claims to a heritage of old were, the Hellenistic amphictyony surely will have found it convenient to promote itself as an organisation with time-honored roots.[51]

Beyond the inscription from the 3rd century, only one single piece of evidence survives that sheds light on the enigmatic amphictyony. It derives from Strabon, who says that 'there was some amphictyony relating to the sanctuary (of Poseidon) of seven

---

47   Cf. below.
48   IG IV 839 (Syll.³ 359; late 4th century); IG IV 841 and 848 (2nd century). See Robertson 1982, 11.
49   IG IV 839 = Syll.³ 359.
50   Cf. Tausend 1992, 12–19, 57–61; Funke 2013, 460–462; Constantakopoulou 2007, 29–38.
51   Beck 2023, 51–60.

cities who shared in the sacrifices'.[52] The member-list is spelled out as follows: 'Hermione, Epidauros, Aigina, Athens, Prasiai, Nauplion, and Minyan Orchomenos.' Strabon explains that the participating city behind Nauplion was Argos, whereas the Spartans contributed on behalf of Prasiai.

It is unclear from where Strabon drew his archaizing catalogue. Several possibilities arise. If from Ephoros, who is referenced in the surrounding sections of Strabon's text, it is intriguing to note that Ephoros would have written about the Kalaurian amphictyony roughly at a time when quarrels over the Amphictyony of Delphi had thrown the Greek world into the turmoil of the Third Sacred War (356–346 BC), events that were critical and indeed instrumental to the rise of Philip II's power in Greece. Reference to Orchomenos rather than Thebes as mainland outpost in the north might suggest that the list derived from a time when Alexander had erased Thebes from the topography of power politics, after 335 (above).[53] But there were more Macedonian connections. Strabon reports that Poseidon's sanctuary was famous for its inviolability. Indeed, its function as an asylum was so much respected that a Macedonian detachment, although in possession of the temple at the time, did not dare to extract the Athenian Demosthenes from the sanctuary in 322, who had sought refuge there. Intimidated by Poseidon's force – note how the motive resembles that of respect for the Theban Kabiroi –, the Macedonians let Demosthenes commit suicide in the sanctuary rather than violating the sacred *asylia*.[54]

Curiously enough, all these stories bear a Macedonian signature. Given the chronological uncertainties, it is not possible to determine with certainty whether the amphictyony rose to prominence under Antigonid (specifically Demetrios Poliorketes?) or Ptolemaic control of the Saronic; maybe both were involved in the project at different moments in time. However, Ptolemaios and Arsinoë's presence in the sanctuary, along with the stability this lent to the central and southern Saronic region, highlights the influence the Ptolemies wielded over Kalaureia from the time of the Chremonidean War. Under the circumstances prevailing, it is altogether difficult to conceive of the amphictyony as something that was unwanted or untolerated by them.

While Ptolemaic impact is obvious, it should be noted how deeply the royal intervention engaged with conditions on the ground. Poseidon's temple at Kalaureia was a center in cultic conversations across the Saronic since the Archaic Period; its foundations date from the second half of the 6th century BC, although they mark only one, relatively late development in the site's history.[55] Much like in the Kabirion at Thebes, Ptolemaic involvement in Kalaureia thus occurred in dialogue with the time-honored

---

52   Strab. 8.6.14: ἦν δὲ καὶ Ἀμφικτυονία τις περὶ τὸ ἱερὸν τοῦτο ἑπτὰ πόλεων αἳ μετεῖχον τῆς θυσίας.
53   The presence of Orchomenos has triggered a lively discussion, see only Tausend 1992, 12–16.
54   Paus. 2.33.3–5, whose depiction of Kalaureia, regrettably brief, is almost entirely concerned with Demosthenes' fate there.
55   See Penttinen et al. 2009; Mylona 2015; Beck 2023, 49.

traditions on site. A priori, Ptolemaios II and Arsinoë were determined to act in accordance with and advance these traditions. The proclamation of a (new) Saronic
amphictyony, seated in and supplementing the region's prime sanctuary, suggests this
much. In practical terms, the amphictyony structured royal communications with its
participating members and provided them with a joint, quasi-federal frame of reference (the actual workings of this "league" are of course unknown). The organization
not only streamlined exchanges with multiple stake holders but, effectively, safeguarded Ptolemaic movements through the Saronic. Vice versa, and not dissimilar to the
Nesiotic League one generation earlier (above), resorting to the idea of integration
provided members with a joint platform for interactions with the royal court. Most
eminently, and no matter if initially formed under Ptolemaios' aegis or brought under
his wings along the way, the amphictyony was a loud-voiced commitment to an ancestral way of organizing politics. Through Kalaureia, Ptolemaic policies were presented
with the opportunity but also put before the challenge to creatively refashion these
traditions and adapt them to their designs of power in and over the Greek world.

5. Aitolia and Achaia: power politics and symbolic communication

After their victory over the Celts in 279 BC, the Aitolians and their koinon were on
a stark rising trajectory. In the course of the next two generations, the league spread
across most regions of Central Greece, drawing not only key cities but entire federal
states into its orbit: the exchange of *isopoliteia* with the Akarnanian League in the late
260s, known from a bronze stele discovered in the excavations at Thermon, marked
but one prominent case of hegemonic expansion by the means of federalism.[56] In
the later 240s, the Aitolians pushed into the Peloponnese, exercising some degree of
control over its western regions while raiding others: a massive invasion of Lakonia
and the looting of Poseidon's temple at Cape Tainaron in ca. 240 followed suit. These
movements were complemented in the Aegean war theater, where Aitolians gradually grew to become a contender. From the late 260s and 250s, when the League of
Islanders dropped from the Ptolemaic fold, individual Aitolians and their syndicates
were among those who filled the vacuum. In the absence of a regular Aitolian navy, the
league's naval policy was governed by the steady growth of collective treaty agreements
with Aegean states – Chios, Tenos, Delos, Smyrna, among others – that variably granted *asphaleia*, *asylia*, and/or exchanges of *isopoliteia*.[57]

These developments were closely monitored in Egypt. Due to the scattered nature
of the sources, however, Ptolemaic responses are not fully understood, especially in the

---

56 IG IX I² I 3A (from Thermon); Klaffenbach 1955; Scholten 2000, 253–256; Freitag 2015, 76. On the
     impact of the Celtic victory cf. also the chapter by Giovanna Pasquariello in this volume.
57 See only Scholten 2000, 96–130; Funke 2008.

early days of Aitolian expansion. Soon after the Aitolian defeat of the Celts, the temple at Delphi, under the protection of the Aitolians since 290, granted Ptolemaios II the right of *promanteia*. A few years later, the ampictyonic council voted to recognize the festival of Ptolemaieia in Alexandreia, which boosted its prestige in the Greek world.[58] While both measures had an anti-Antigonid sting, their wider implications for the bilateral relations between Aitolia and Alexandreia are shrouded in silence.

Affairs with another federal state, the Achaian koinon, provide some insight. With the death of Ptolemaios II in 246, his first-born son Ptolemaios III Euergetes rose to the throne, who for the time being continued his father's ties of friendship with the Achaian League. Amicable relations between both went back to Aratos of Sikyon's famous journey to the court in Alexandreia some time between 250 and 246/245 that, in addition to establishing personal ties with the king, filled the Achaian treasury with 150 talents of silver. The funds were critical to the league's subsequent expansion.[59] When the koinon extended its membership to Korinth, Megara, Troizen, and Epidauros in 243/242, the sweep also prompted the conferral of the honorary title of "hegemon in war on land and sea" to Ptolemaios III (ἡγεμονῶν πολέμου καὶ κατὰ γῆν καὶ θάλατταν). Plutarch says that the move was one of Aratos' master strokes, but interests on both sides were more complex.[60] Adoption of the title was conspicuous enough: Ptolemaios' father and grandfather had refrained from taking up official league titles which appeared counterintuitive to the understanding of king and pharaoh. Ptolemaios Euergetes signaled a different approach. This was the first time since the days of Philip II and his hegemonia of the League of Korinth that a dynast of Macedonian descent adopted the nominal leadership of a federal alliance. Ptolemaios never commanded an Achaian army or fleet so his leadership was of symbolic weight. The message was, however, clear: highlighting the importance that was given to the renewed alliance between Egypt and Achaia, the title of hegemon triggered sentiments of Philip looming on the horizon. The overall atmosphere after the Achaians' most recent gains in the Peloponnese was euphoric enough to invoke aspirations of something great.

More immediately, the declaration of Ptolemaios' Achaian hegemonia put the Aitolians under *Zugzwang*. In light of increasing alienation from its oldest ally and immediate neighbor to the northwest, the Epeirote kingdom, the koinon couldn't ignore the need to secure its position on the mainland.[61] Rapport with Achaia appeared both appealing and advisable. In 239 or 238, both concluded a treaty that established piece and an alliance.[62] At the same time, the Aitolians sought the support of Ptolemaios III.

58   Syll.³ 404 (c. 278 BC); Scholten 2000, 137.
59   Plut. Aratos 12–13; Buraselis 2015, 95. On the date, Paschidis 2008, 523–532, who argues for the winter of 246/5, hence, a date after the death of Ptolemaios II.
60   Plut. Aratos 21–22 with Shipley 2018, 171–192; Grabowksi 2012, 86–87; for the title, Plut. Aratos 24.4. Korinth, Megara, Troizen, Epidauros: IG IV² 1 70 and 71.
61   Scholten 2000, 132–136.
62   Pol. 2.44; Plut. Aratos 33.

In the literary record, their alliance transpires only for the year 229, but the course of the Demetrian War (239 to 229 BC) suggests that Aitolians, Achaians, and Ptolemaios acted shoulder to shoulder.[63] For Ptolemaios, an alliance with the Aitolian League was valuable not only because of its anti-Antigonid thrust: in Greece, it forged a powerful triangle that appeared virtually impeccable, while in the Aegean, friendly relations with the Aitolians eased the pressure on the few strongholds of Ptolemaic influence there were after the defeat by an Antigonid fleet in the battles of Kos and Andros, ca. 246 BC.[64]

From this period dates the famous exedra of statues in the Sanctuary of Apollon at Thermon, erected by the Aitolian koinon in honor of Ptolemaios Euergetes and his family. It comprised seven marble blocks of ca. 6 m width m in total, arranged in a rectangular ⊓ shape and surmounted with the bronze statues of eight members of Ptolemaios' house. None of the statues survive, three stones are also missing. The remaining blocks are kept in the museum in Thermon today. The joining pieces bear the inscribed names of the people on display, so the overall arrangement is clear. On the left wing of the exedra stood Ptolemaios, who was accompanied by his family lined up along the horizontal bar of the ⊓. Only on the right wing, opposite Ptolemaios and like him moved to the foreground, the figure on display is unknown (the block with the corresponding inscription is among those missing).[65] The monument has typically been dated to the final years of the Demetrian War, or later. In-depth study of its prosopography by Chris Bennett has made it not unlikely however that it derives from the earliest phase of the war, maybe from the first year and in causal connection with the forging of triangular relations between Aitolia, Achaia, and the Ptolemies.[66]

The monument from Thermon had a twin in the Sanctuary of Apollon at Delphi, of which five non-joining fragments survive. Its surviving inscription (IG IX I² I 202) identifies the offering as dedication [ἀ]ρετ[ᾶ]ς [ἕνεκεν καὶ εὐεργεσίας τᾶς εἰς αὐτὸν καὶ κοινὸν τῶν Α]ἰτωλῶν [Ἀπόλ]λωνι [Πυθίωι]. Nothing is known about the original setup but the preserved sections, along with surviving names of three members of Ptolemaios III's family, makes it clear that it was a dynastic group monument. The restoration by Robert Flacelière suggests an oblong base of 8 to 9 m, which left ample room for the representation of the figures from Thermon. Most likely, the dedication comprised the entire royal family.[67] Unlike its twin, the monument had an individual

---

63   For discussion, see Scholten 2000, 138.
64   Literature on these events and the subsequent lessening of Ptolemaic influence in the Aegean is enormous, see only Reger 1994; Dreyer 1999 (416–419 on the Battle of Kos); Grabowski 2012.
65   IG IX I² I 56 with reconstruction of the monument by G. Klaffenbach; cf. Huss 1975; Kotsidu 2000, 168–169, KNr. 104; Scherberich 2009b. Cf. also the chapter by Christoph Michels in this volume p. 265.
66   Bennett 2002, pointing to the presence of Berenike (E), daughter of Ptolemaios III, who is known from the Kanopus Decree to have died in 238 BC.
67   Kosmetatou 2002; Grzesik 2018; cf. R. Flacelière's restoration in FD III.4.2 ad no. 233.

sponsor, a man named Λαμι[(Lamios?) who would have been a high ranking official of the Aitolian koinon. The date of the dedication is debated and cannot be established with certainty. It is obvious enough that there was a thematic connection with the Thermon group. Honoring the Ptolemies in Egypt for services to the league (and its elusive dedicant?), the monument heralded the friendship of the Aitolian koinon with Alexandreia, vocally so, before visitors to Delphi from near and far.[68]

The inscription from Thermon documents the message the parties wished to convey with their dedications (IG IX I² I 56). Ptolemaios III is followed by his son Ptolemaios (B) and wife Berenike (C). Five further children follow of which three are otherwise attested (D, E, H). One name is unreadable (F), while no Alexander (G) has been known as son of Ptolemaios so far.[69]

A   βασιλέα Πτολεμαῖον | βασιλέως Πτολεμαῖου | Μακεδόνα

B   Πτολεμαῖον βασιλέως | Πτολεμαίου Μακεδόνα

C   βασίλισσαν Β[ερ]εν[ίκαν] | βασιλέως Μάγα | Μακέταν

D   βα[σί]λισσα[ν Ἀρσ]ινόαν | βασιλέως Πτ[ολ]εμαίου | Μακέ[τ]αν

E   βασίλισσαν [Βε]ρενίκαν | βασιλέως Πτολεμαίου | Μακέταν

F   [.. c.10 ..] βασιλέως | [Πτολεμαίου] Μακεδόνα

G   Ἀλέ[ξαν]δρον βασιλέως | Πτολεμαίου Μακεδόνα

H   Μάγαν βασιλέως | Πτολεμαίου Μακεδόνα

Across the lower section of the horizontal ⊓ base runs the dedication formula:

Αἰτωλῶν τὸ κοινὸν ἀρετᾶς ἕνεκεν καὶ εὐεργεσίας τᾶς εἰς τὸ ἔθν[ος] καὶ τοὺς ἄλλους Ἕλλανας

The koinon of the Aitolians for the virtue and benefaction bestowed up the ethnos and the other Greeks.

The names of the honored individuals appear in purposeful order and fashion. Each member of Ptolemaios' family is addressed with their name, regal title if applicable, and family relations, i. e., their relation to Ptolemaios. Each entry concludes proclaiming the ethnic identity of every single person as "Macedonian": Μακεδόνα for the male, Μακέταν for the female members of the family. What appears as a somewhat repetitive fashion could also be read as a loud statement. Previous monumental dedications, made by the Ptolemies themselves or set up in their honor, made no explicit reference to the dynasty's Macedonian origins. To begin with, then, the inscription from Thermon attests to a relaxed attitude towards animosities of old. Whether the Macedonians were conceived of (and stigmatized) as foreign or not was a question

68   On the date, see Kosmetatou 2002, 110–111; Lamios: Paschidis 2008, 333.
69   This is not the place for discussion about the identity of F and G, cf. Bennett 2002. The surviving blocks from Delphi attest to the presence of Arsinoë III, the young Ptolemaios IV, and Berenike III (E in Thermon).

that left the dedicants unmoved. Maybe Thermon, meeting place in the heartland of the Aitolian League, was a place that was particularly immune to quarrels such as these. Being looked down upon by polis-Greeks ever since the 5th century as μειξοβάρβαροι, "semi-barbarians",[70] the Aitolians most likely had turned a deaf ear to such conversations. Note, however, that the dedication in Delphi refrained from mentioning the Macedonian label. Whether the difference was deliberate or circumstantial is difficult to assert. Emphasis on ethnic origins in northern Greece was also a firm statement that recalled the Macedonian rootedness of the family.[71] In turn, this blanketed the Egyptian home base of their power; the frequent repetition of Μακεδόνα and Μακέταν in the Aitolian variant of the monument virtually marginalized this background.

Although the dedication in Delphi chose a different wording, it also fostered the sentiment of the Macedonicity of its honorees. Already before Ptolemaios III, his grandfather Ptolemaios Soter and father Ptolemaios Philadelphos had resorted the motive of family representation – that is, the deliberate inclusion not only of heirs but of women and other children – to proclaim dynastic ties to Philip. Under Ptolemaios II, respective offerings focused on associating the king with his sister-wife Arsinoë.[72] Yet none of these dedications were set up in a major transregional sanctuary. The first and thus far unfollowed dedication was the one commissioned by Philip in Olympia, the Philippeion, a magnificent tholos that contained the statues of himself and his family: his wife Olympias, Alexander, and his parents Amyntas and Eurydike.[73] Honors for Ptolemaios Euergetes and his family could, therefore, be understood as a symbolic reverence for, and return to, the early days. Similar to Ptolemaios' role as hegemon of the Achaian League, family honors in Thermon and Delphi in particular inevitably evoked images of Philip and the dawn of Macedon's leadership in Greece.

The dedication formula from Thermon picked up on this, and it amplified the message. It explains that the monument brought three distinct groups in conversation with one another, each one with a different public outlook and body within: the ethnos of the Aitolians, singled out as lead actor, and all other Greeks, two collectives; and a royal dynasty, also a collective, yet comprising a number of individuals and a shared ethnic identity complementary with but different from that of Aitolians and Hellenes:

---

70 Eur. Phoen. 138; cf. Thuk. 1.5.2–3.

71 For a similar case of highlighting royal Macedonian ethnicity, cf. the dedication of the courtier Menippos for Antiochos III on Delos (IG XI.4 1111; cf. the discussion in the chapter of Michels in this volume).

72 Paus. 1.6.2 reports the curious case Ptolemaios' descendancy from Philip. Dedications by Ptolemaios II and Arsione, e. g., during the Alexandreian Ptolemaieia: Thompson 2000. On the significance of dynastic representation cf. the chapter by Stefan Pfeiffer in this volume.

73 Paus. 5.20.9–10, which is the only literary reference to complement the material evidence. Kosmetatou 2002, 109–110 points to other Ptolemaic Familiengruppen, but none of the cited examples is as strident in its monumental representation of dynastic continuity as the installations in Thermon and Delphi.

Macedonians. Once again, the monument displayed the juxtaposition of these parties with ease. From a more programmatic point of view, the dedication visualized an ideal scenario of concerted action, assigning each party their designated place: the Aitolians, foremost of the Hellenes; all other Greeks, casually subsumed under the collective plural; and the Macedonians, whose leadership was both quintessential and also beneficial to all, for as long as they acted as "good" Macedonians, that is, in Philip's spirit. This was, most likely, the exedra's anti-Antigonid punchline. Accentuating the Macedonicity of Ptolemaios' family, the Aitolians endorsed the image of a role-model dynasty that showed itself as benefactors to the Greeks – contrary, the implicit argument will have went, to the 'bad' dynasty of the Antigonids. The tandems of Aitolians/Greeks on the one hand and Ptolemies/Macedonians on the other thus were a clear shout out to what united both: their joint efforts to safeguard the interests of all of Greece.

6. Conclusion

Assessing the interactions between Ptolemaios III and the Achaian League, Angelos Chaniotis recently observed

> a recurring pattern: a group of Greek cities, united to face an enemy of their independence, accepted as their leader a monarch whose policy seemed at the moment to favour their plan; and a monarch accepted the leadership, not out of love of freedom, but rather to gain prominence on a Panhellenic stage.[74]

The verdict of opportunistic relations, bleak in its perspicuity, resonates with scholarly assessments that see the relations between Hellenistic kings and the koina of Greece governed by the volatile nature of power politics. If common interests suggested closer ties, closer ties surfaced; when the common ground faded, so did the collaboration. Friends became enemies at the blink of an eye – in the name of freedom and independence.

It is certainly correct to see federal-dynastic relations from the vantage point of Hellenistic interstate anarchy that set the pace for the exchanges between state actors of all sizes and shapes. At the same time, the study of king and koinon-affairs reveals a curious cross-fertilization that complicates the picture of power. On a more general level, the cases discussed above suggest that Ptolemaic interventions in Aegean Greece effected a traceable invigorating of federalism both in scope and depth. Therefore, if federalism was a means to preserve room for polis concerns and strengthen its survival in a world dominated by forces that transcended the capacities of the city-state, it is

74   Chaniotis 2018, 80.

puzzling to observe that the intervention of the Hellenistic dynasties also lent resilience to the polis and its federal engagements.

The interplay was not a Ptolemaic doing, fostered by the court in Alexandreia exclusively. There is always the danger to oversimplify the differences between the Hellenistic royal houses by deducing them from the vastly different cultures zones they occupied and interacted with in the quotidian exercise of power. With regards to Greece and the Aegean, royal agencies were enveloped by their common Macedonian background. Antigonos Doson, great-grandson of Ptolemaios I through his grandmother Ptolemais, the sister of Ptolemaios Philadelphos II and third wife of Demetrios Poliorketes, found this background as formative to his actions as members of the Seleukid or Ptolemaic dynasties did. Not surprisingly then, Antigonid dealings with federalism resemble those of their counterparts from Alexandreia. If the League of Islanders had an Antigonid phase to it, it too witnessed the establishment of celebrations in honor of its patrons on Delos, the federal Antigoneia (above). After the troubled 250s, Antigonid presence on the island was voiced also by a two-aisled stoa at the north boundary of the Sanctuary of Apollon; the donation was not dissimilar to Ptolemaic building activity on Samothrake and, presumably, near Thebes. Aegean involvement was in any case supplemented by the new launch of a federal league on the island of Euboia under the aegis of the Antigonids.[75] In 225, the Achaian League was won over by Antigonos in a similar personal accord with Aratos as before in the 240s by the Ptolemies.[76] And after 223 BC, Mantineia was effectively renamed Antigoneia, a measure that recalled the Ptolemaic renaming of Methana a few decades earlier.[77] Their appears to have been even a back ripple to the political organization of Macedon itself which, from the rule of Philip and again under the Antigonids, took on the outlook of a quasi-federal state, different from the federal states of central and southern Greece, but akin to federal leagues of Epeiros and Thessaly.[78]

Since the time of Philip, Macedonian courts were keen to present their actions in accordance with the tenets of Greek political culture. In the arena of federalism, too, Philip had set the pace. Witnessing the rise of the Boiotian League in the 360s during his stay in Thebes with his own eyes, the king was intimately familiar with the workings of a koinon. In 352, he became life-time archon of the Thessalian League, six years later a regular council member and nominal leader of the amphictyony in Delphi.[79] In 338/337, all these previous experiences paved the way for the foundation of the League of Korinth, an ingenious political creation that amalgamated Macedonian leadership

75 See Knoepfler 2015, 168 for the circumstances.
76 Plut. Aratos 36–44.
77 Plut. Aratos 45.6; Paus. 8.8.11; cf. IG V 2, 299.
78 Cf. Scholten 2003, 156; Hatzopoulos 2015.
79 There is no need here to elaborate on the details. Stay in Thebes, cf. Buckler 2008a; Thessalian League, Bouchon – Helly 2015; Delphi, Buckler 1989, 111–142.

and Panhellenic affairs in purposeful fashion. The innovative potential of the arrangement is often overlooked, especially when reduced to its goal to cement Macedon's
position in and wield power over Greece. Integrating the various cities and leagues
of Greece into a common body that was based on effective governance (something
various voices in Athens and elsewhere had advocated for decades) and principles of
proportional representation, the treaty of Korinth from 338/7 opened a promising new
chapter in Hellenic interstate affairs. Relations with the ruling Macedonian dynasties
remained volatile over the next generations, and they played out differently in different
corners of the Greek world. Advocacy of federal concerns, articulated in the support
of leagues and symbolically showcased through exchanges of friendship and other distinctions, was however a sure expression of adherence to the precedent set by Philip.
Rather than targeting or dismantling leagues as potential loci of power (something the
Spartans had done in the decades before the rise of Philip), patronage was the more
promising strategy.

The true point of difference in the dealings with federalism was the location of power from where this strategy was pursued, and the means of communication and control
with which it was endorsed. If the Ptolemies appear as particularly eager supporters of
federalism, this had to do with their geopolitical position. Anchored in the Aegean and
mainland Greece through various naval bases and other depots, the bases of supplies
in this quadrant of their naval empire were removed from the central command in
Egypt. Sure enough, dealings with the Achaian and Nesiotic Leagues and backing of
the amphictyony in the temple of Poseidon at Kalaureia were motivated by questions
of power politics. But there was an implicit undertone of return to Philip's policies
to this, something the Ptolemies will have felt particularly important to their perception in Greece. Support of federalism, practically and symbolically, was a gesture that
brought stability and buttressed the standing of a dynasty engaging from afar in swiftly
changing circumstances in Greece.

This observation aligns prima facie with royal respect for the concerns of polis governance. But there was also a quantitative difference. One of the key traits of federal
leagues was that they baled a multitude of local voices, streamlining exchanges of their
members with others. The koinon was a relay station of political communication. For
Hellenistic dynasties this trait of leagues made them principally promising partners
in the attempt to secure existing spheres of interest and to win over new ones. The
Ptolemies will have found this quality particularly beneficial, again because of their remoteness from Greece. For instance, their involvement in the Kabirion in Thebes was
not simply a religious affair but allowed them to branch out and network with elites
throughout Boiotia. In similar vein, federal alliances with the Achaian, Aitolian, and
Nesiotic Leagues helped to unlock wider regional arenas of influence, the Peloponnese, Central Greece, and the Aegean.

The impact was magnified again by the place of interaction. Sanctuary sites on Delos
and near Thebes, in Thermon or Kalaureia were locations with a supreme prestige, foci

of traditions of belonging and religious conduct, places where the presence of the divine was evoked in prayer, sacrifice, and song. As such they provided not only an obvious space for dedications that celebrated allegiance but actually elevated ties. Surrounding them with a sacred aura, federal sanctuaries provided again a specific twist of sanction and authority – and imparted them with meaning. For dedications for the Ptolemies in Thermon and the sanctuary of Poseidon in Kalaureia that placed the members of the dynasty in the inner core of the temenos heightened both the perception of the honoured and, most eminently, the authority of the site, extending the relevance and purpose of federal traditions from the past into the present day, rich in subtlety and nuance. Beyond power politics, kings and koina were truly "symbiotic creatures".

Bibliography

Bagnall 1976: Bagnall, Roger S., The Administration of the Ptolemaic Possessions outside Egypt, Leiden 1976

Beck 2023: Beck, Hans, Refitting the Local Horizon of Ancient Greek Religion (Including some Remarks on the Sanctuary of Poseidon on Kalaureia), in: id. – J. Kindt (eds.), The Local Horizon of Ancient Greek Religion, Cambridge 2023, 28–66

Beck (in press): Beck, Hans, The Long Road to a Mystery Cult: Thebes and the Kabirion, in: H. Bowden – A. Iliana Rassia (eds.), The Oxford Handbook of Ancient Mystery Cults (in press)

Beck – Funke 2015: Beck, Hans – Funke, Peter (eds.), Federalism in Greek Antiquity, Cambridge 2015

Beck – Ganter 2015: Beck, Hans – Ganter, Angela, Boiotia and the Boiotian League, in: Beck – Funke 2015, 132–157

Bennett 2002: Bennett, Chris, The Children of Ptolemy III and the Date of the Exedra of Thermos, Zeitschrift für Papyrologie und Epigraphik 138, 2002, 141–145

Billows 1990: Billows, Richard A., Antigonos the One-Eyed and the Creation of the Hellenistic State, Berkeley et al. 1990

Blakely 2011: Blakely, Sandra, Kadmos, Jason, and the Great Gods of Samothrace: Initiation as Mediation in a Northern Aegean Context, Electronic Antiquity 11, 2011, 67–95

Bouchon – Helly 2015: Bouchon, Richard – Helly, Bruno, The Thessalian League, in: Beck – Funke 2015, 231–249

Bremmer 2014: Bremmer, Jan N., Initiation into the Mysteries of the Ancient World, Berlin et al. 2014

Buckler 2008a: Buckler, John, Pammenes, the Persians, and the Sacred War, in: J. Buckler – H. Beck (eds.), Central Greece and the Politics of Power in the Fourth Century BC, Cambridge 2008, 224–232 (revised version in English of id., Pammenes, die Perser und der heilige Krieg, in H. Beister – J. Buckler (eds.), Boiotika, Munich 1989, 155–162)

Buckler 2008b: Buckler, John, Philip's Designs on Greece, in: J. Buckler – H. Beck, Central Greece and the Politics of Power in the Fourth Century BC, Cambridge 2008, 259–276 (orig. id., Philip's Designs on Greece, in: R. W. Wallace – E. M. Harris (eds.), Transitions to Empire: Essays in Greco-Roman History, 360–146 B. C., in Honor of E. Badian. Norman 1996, 77–97)

Buckler 1989: Buckler, John, Philip II and the Sacred War, Leiden 1989

Buraselis 1982: Buraselis, Kostas, Das hellenistische Makedonien und die Ägäis: Forschungen zur
Politik des Kassandros und der drei ersten Antigoniden im Ägäischen Meer und in Westkleinasien, Munich 1982

Buraselis 2014: Buraselis, Kostas, Contributions to Rebuilding Thebes: the Old and a New Fragment of IG VII 2419 = Sylloge3 337, ZPE 188, 2014, 159–170

Buraselis 2015: Buraselis, Kostas, Federalism and the sea. The koina of the Aegean islands, in:
Beck – Funke 2015, 358–376

Carney 2013: Carney, Elizabeth D., Arsinoe of Egypt and Macedon: A Royal Life, Oxford 2013

Chaniotis 2018: Chaniotis, Angelos, Age of Conquests. The Greek World from Alexander to Hadrian (336 BC–AD 138), London 2018

Constantakopoulou 2007: Constantakopoulou, Christie, The Dance of the Islands. Insularity,
Networks, the Athenian Empire, and the Aegean World, Oxford 2007

Constantakopoulou 2012: Constantakopoulou, Christie, Identity and Resistance: The Islanders'
League, the Aegean Islands and the Hellenistic Kings, Mediterranean Historical Review 27,
2012, 51–72

Dillon 2010: Dillon, Sheila, Marble Votive Statuettes of Women from the Sanctuary of the Great
Gods on Samothrace, in: O. Palagia – B. D. Wescoat (eds.), Samothracian Connections. Essays
in honor of James R. McCredie, Oxford 2010, 165–172

Dreyer 1999: Dreyer, Boris, Untersuchungen zur Geschichte des spätklassischen Athen (322–
ca. 230 v. Chr.), Stuttgart 1999

Dürrbach 1907: Dürrbach, Félix, ΑΝΤΙΓΟΝΕΙΑ – ΔΗΜΗΤΡΙΕΙΑ. Les origines de la Confédération des insulaires, Bulletin de Correspondance Hellénique 31, 1907, 208–227

Frazer 1990: Frazer, Alfred, Samothrace. Excavations conducted by the Institute of Fine Arts of
New York University X: the Propylon of Ptolemy II., Princeton 1990

Freitag 2015: Freitag, Klaus, Akarnania and the Akarnanian League, in: Beck – Funke 2015, 66–85

Funke 2008: Funke, Peter, Die Aitoler in der Ägäis. Untersuchungen zur sogenannten Seepolitik
der Aitoler im 3. Jh. v. Chr., in: E. Winter (ed.), Vom Euphrat bis zum Bosporus. Kleinasien in
der Antike, Bonn 2008, 253–267

Funke 2013: Funke, Peter, Greek Amphiktyonies. An Experiment in Transregional Governance,
in: H. Beck (ed.), A Companion to Ancient Greek Government, Malden 2013, 451–465

Gill 2007: Gill, David W., Arsinoe in the Peloponnese: the Ptolemaic Base on the Methana Peninsula, in: T. Schneider – K. Szpakowska (eds.), Egyptian Stories: a British Egyptological Tribute to Alan B. Lloyd, Münster 2007, 87–110

Grabowski 2012: Grabowski, Tomasz, The Ptolemies versus the Achaean and Aetolian Leagues in
the 250s–220s BC, Electrum 19, 2012, 83–97

Greenwalt 2008: Greenwalt, William, Philip II and Olympias on Samothrace: A Clue to Macedonian Politics during the 360s, in: T. Howe – J. Reames (eds.), Macedonian Legacies. Studies
in Ancient Macedonian History and Culture in Honor of Eugene M. Borza, Claremont 2008,
79–106

Grzesik 2018: Grzesik, Dominika, The Power of Space and Memory: The Honorific Statuescape
of Delphi, Antichthon 52, 2018, 23–42

Gullath 1982: Gullath, Brigitte, Untersuchungen zur Geschichte Boiotiens in der Zeit Alexanders
und der Diadochen, Frankfurt 1982

Hatzopoulos 2015: Hatzopoulos, Miltiades B., Federal Makedonia, in: Beck – Funke 2015, 319–340

Hennig 1989: Hennig, Dieter, Böoter im ptolemäischen Ägypten, in: H. Beister – J. Buckler (eds.),
Boiotika. Vorträge vom 5. Internationalen Böotien-Kolloquium zu Ehren von Professor Dr.
Siegfried Lauffer, Munich 1989, 169–182

Hölbl 2001: Hölbl, Günther, A History of the Ptolemaic Empire, London 2001

Holleaux 1895: Holleaux, Maurice, Sur une inscription de Thèbes, Revue des Études Grecques 8.29,1895, 7–48

Huss 1975: Huss, Werner, Die zu Ehren Ptolemaios' III. und seiner Familie errichtete Statuengruppe von Thermos (IG IX I² I 56), Chronique d'Égypte 50, 1975, 312–320

Huss 2001: Huss, Werner, Ägypten in hellenistischer Zeit 332–30 v. Chr., Munich 2001

Jehne 1994: Jehne, Martin, Koine Eirene: Untersuchungen zu den Befriedungs- und Stabilisierungsbemühungen in der griechischen Poliswelt des 4. Jahrhunderts v. Chr., Stuttgart 1994

Kalliontzis – Papazarkadas 2019: Kalliontzis, Yannis – Papazarkadas, Nikolaos, The Contributions to the Refoundation of Thebes, Annual of the British School at Athens 114, 2019, 293–315

Klaffenbach 1955: Klaffenbach, Günther, Die Zeit des ätolisch-akarnanischen Bündnisvertrages. Δεύτεραι φροντίδες, Historia 4.1, 1955, 46–51

Kosmetatou 2002: Kosmetatou, Elizabeth, Remarks on a Delphic Ptolemaic Dynastic Group Monument, Tyche 17, 2002, 103–111

Kotsidu 2000: Kotsidu, Haritini, TIMH KAI ΔΟΞΑ. Ehrungen für hellenistische Herrscher im griechischen Mutterland und in Kleinasien unter besonderer Berücksichtigung der archäologischen Denkmäler, Berlin 2000

Knoepfler 1999: Knoepfler, Denis, L'épigraphie de la Grèce centro-méridionale (Eubée, Béotie, Phocide et pays voisins, Delphes). Publications récentes, documents inédits, travaux en cours, in: XI Congresso Internazionale di Epigrafia Greca e Latina, Rome 1999, 229–255

Knoepfler 2001: Knoepfler, Denis, La réintégration de Thèbes dans le Koinon béotien après son relèvement par Cassandre, ou les surprises de la chronologie épigraphique, in: R. Frei-Stolba – K. Gex (eds.), Recherches récentes sur le monde hellénistique, Vienna 2001, 11–26

Knoepfler 2015: Knoepfler, Denis, The Euboian League – an 'Irregular' Koinon?, in: Beck – Funke 2015, 158–178

Landucci 2015: Landucci, Franca, The Sanctuary of the Great Gods at Samothrace and the Rulers of the Early Hellenism, Aevum 89.1, 2015, 67–82

McKechnie – Guillaume 2008: McKechnie, Paul – Guillaume, Philippe (eds.), Ptolemy II Philadelphus and his World, Leiden et al. 2008

Meadows 2013: Meadows, Andrew, The Ptolemaic League of Islanders, in: K. Buraselis et al. (eds.), The Ptolemies, the Sea and the Nile, Cambridge 2013, 19–38

Merker 1970: Merker, Irwin L., The Ptolemaic Officials and the League of the Islanders, Historia 19, 1970, 141–160

Mylona 2015: Mylona, Dimitra, From Fish Bones to Fishermen: Views from the Sanctuary of Poseidon at Kalaureia, in: D. C. Haggis – C. M. Antonaccio (eds.), Classical Archaeology in Context. Theory and Practice in Excavation in the Greek World, Berlin et al. 2015, 385–418

O'Neil 2008: O'Neil, James L., A Re-Examination of the Chremonidean War, in: McKechnie – Guillaume 2008, 65–90

Palagia – Tracy 2003: Palagia, Olga – Tracy, Stephen V. (eds.), The Macedonians in Athens, 322–229 B.C., Oxford 2003

Paschidis 2008: Paschidis, Paschalis, Between City and King. Prosopographical studies on the intermediaries between the cities of the Greek mainland and the Aegean and the royal courts in the Hellenistic period (322–190 BC), Athens 2008

Penttinen et al. 2009: Penttinen, Arto et al., Report on the Excavations in the years 2007 and 2008 southeast of the temple of Poseidon at Kalaureia, Opuscula. Annual of the Swedish Institutes at Athens and Rome 2, 2009, 89–141

Pfeiffer 2008: Pfeiffer, Stefan, The God Serapis, his Cult and the Beginnings of the Ruler Cult in
    Ptolemaic Egypt, in: McKechnie – Guillaume 2008, 387–408
Reger 1994: Reger, Gary, The Political History of the Kyklades 260–200 B.C., Historia 43, 1994,
    32–69
Robertson 1982: Robertson, Noel, The Decree of Themistocles in its Contemporary Setting,
    Phoenix 36, 1982, 1–44
Roesch 1965: Roesch, Paul, Thespies et la confédération Béotienne, Paris 1965
Schachter 2016: Schachter, Albert, Evolutions of a Mystery Cult: the Theban Kabiroi, in: id. (ed.),
    Boiotia in Antiquity: Selected Papers, Cambridge 2016, 315–343 (orig. M.B. Cosmopoulos
    (ed.), Greek Mysteries: the Archaeology and Ritual of Ancient Greek Secret Cults, London
    et al. 2003, 112–142)
Scherberich 2009a: Scherberich, Klaus, Koine Symmachia. Untersuchungen zum Hellenenbund
    Antigonos' III. Doson und Philipps V., Stuttgart 2009a
Scherberich 2009b: Scherberich, Klaus, Zur Griechenlandpolitik Ptolemaios' III., in: J.-F. Eck-
    holdt – M. Sigismund – S. Sigismund (eds.), Geschehen und Gedächtnis: die hellenistische
    Welt und ihre Wirkung; Festschrift für Wolfgang Orth zum 65. Geburtstag, Berlin 2009b,
    25–44
Scholten 2000: Scholten, Joseph B., The Politics of Plunder. Aitolians and their Koinon in the
    Early Hellenistic Era, 279–217 B.C., Berkeley 2000
Scholten 2003: Scholten, Joseph B., Macedon and the Mainland, 280–221 BC, in: A. Erskine (ed.),
    A Companion to the Hellenistic World, Malden 2003, 134–158
Shipley 2018: Shipley, D. Graham J., The Early Hellenistic Peloponnese. Politics, Economics, and
    Networks 338–197 BC, Cambridge 2018
Smarczyk 2015: Smarczyk, Bernhard, The Hellenic leagues of late Classical and Hellenistic times
    and their place in the history of Greek federalism, in: Beck – Funke 2015, 452–470
Strootman 2020: Strootman, Rolf, The Ptolemaic Sea Empire, in: id. et al. (eds.), Empires of the
    Sea. Maritime Power Networks in World History, Leiden 2020, 113–152
Tausend 1992: Tausend, Klaus, Amphiktyonie und Symmachie. Formen zwischenstaatlicher Be-
    ziehungen im archaischen Griechenland, Stuttgart 1992
Thompson 2000: Thompson, Dorothy J., Philadelphus' Procession. Dynastic Power in a Mediter-
    ranean Context, in: L. Mooren (ed.), Politics, Administration, and Society in the Hellenistic
    and Roman World, Leuven 2000, 365–388
Walbank 1981: Walbank, Frank W., The Hellenistic World, Cambridge 1981
Wallensten – Pakkanen 2009: Wallensten, Jenny – Pakkanen, Jari, A New Inscribed Statue Base
    from the Sanctuary of Poseidon at Kalaureia, Opuscula. Annual of the Swedish Institutes at
    Athens and Rome 2, 2009, 155–165
Wolters – Bruns 1940: Wolters, Paul H.A. – Bruns, Gerda, Das Kabirenheiligtum bei Theben I,
    Berlin 1940

Hans Beck is Professor and Chair of Greek History at Münster University and Adjunct Professor
in the Faculty of Arts at McGill University Montreal. Previous appointments include the Universities of Cologne and Frankfurt, and the Center for Hellenic Studies in Washington, DC. He has
published widely on the history and culture of ancient Greece, including *The Local Horizon of Ancient Greek Religion* (jointly edited with J. Kindt, Cambridge UP 2023), *Localism and the Ancient*

Greek City-State (University of Chicago Press 2020), *Federalism in Greek Antiquity* (jointly edited with P. Funke, Cambridge UP 2015). He is the co-editor of *Hermes* and *Hermes Einzelschriften*, of *Teiresias Journal* and *Supplements Online* (TJO, TSO) and of the series *Antiquity in Global Context* (Cambridge UP). Among other distinctions, Hans Beck is the recipient of the German Humboldt Foundation's Anneliese Maier Research Prize, an elected Fellow of the Royal Society of Canada, and a corresponding member of the German Archaeological Institute.

Hieron II. und das ‚hellenistische Königtum'
im syrakusanisch-ostadriatischen Spannungsfeld

LINDA-MARIE GÜNTHER

Abstract: In discussing the representation of monarchical power with regard to the Sicilian kings, I aim to emphasize the role of their strong recourses to Sicilian history and self-reliance. This disposition differs from the mainstream of preponderant Italian publications on the topic.

The main focus of the following reflections will lie on Hieron II (270–215 BC): Claiming descent from the Deinomenid tyrants (5th cent.), he was surely a member of the local aristocracy as well as his wife Philistis, whose descent from the family of Dionysios I and his courtier Philistos seems highly plausible. When the couple's son Gelon married a young princess from Epeiros (230?), the Syracusan court renewed the dynastic networks with the Molossian house, which had begun with Agathokles' daughter Lanassa as second wife of Pyrrhos (294?). At any rate, manifold contacts of Syracuse with the eastern Adriatic zone, where the colonisatory impact of Korinth, Syracuse's mother city, was still significant, existed at least since Dionysios I's expansionistic interests in that region. But there is no hint of Sicilian assimilation of specific Macedonian or Epirotic forms in Agathokles' or Hieron's monarchical representation.

The latter's coinage reflects the traditional iconography of the Syracusans, while shaping of the royal portraits shows the spirit of the times, for example the diademed and veiled head of Philistis. Nevertheless, there were similar female heads on bronze coins of Pyrrhos in Syracuse – and earlier ones form Thessaly and Kos – which could have served as models for the queen's coins. Lastly, I prefer to interpret the donations of Hieron to Rhodos in 228/227, especially the frequently discussed statues of the Syracusan demos crowning the Rhodian, on the background of the Deinomenid's descent from Gela, archaic colony of Rhodos.

1. Einleitung

„Gleich, nur anders?" Für die hellenistische Monarchie in Syrakus lautet meine Antwort:

Nur bedingt gleich, unter zentralen Aspekten anders. Diese Perspektive mag insofern plausibel erscheinen, als in der Forschung zur hellenistischen Zeit der Westen der

griechischen Welt ein weniger behandeltes Thema ist, nicht zuletzt, weil hier die auf-
steigende Großmacht Rom und ihre Rivalin Karthago in den Blick kommen – und es
waren auch Agathokles und Hieron II., die als die hellenistischen Monarchen Siziliens
gelten dürfen, in militärische Konflikte mit Karthago bzw. in den Ersten Punischen
Krieg involviert.

Allerdings fällt in der überwiegend italienischen Literatur zu den beiden Machthabern auf, dass hier das forschungsleitende Interesse auf die Gleichartigkeit mit der
hellenistischen Welt im östlichen Mittelmeerraum fokussiert ist: Sizilien wird als re-
levanter Akteur gesehen, der auch im späten 4. und im 3. Jh. v. Chr. in die Politik und
Kultur des Hellenentums integriert ist; dabei finden die Eigenheiten der politischen
Kultur der Insel seltener die gebührende Aufmerksamkeit.[1] Im Mittelpunkt soll hier
mit Hieron II. (270–215) ein Machthaber stehen, der fast das ganze 3. Jh. v. Chr. mit-
erlebt und die neue Dominanz Roms im westlichen Mittelmeerraum mitgestaltet hat.

Als Hieron, Sohn des Hierokles, im Jahr 306 in Syrakus geboren wurde, herrschte in
Sizilien Agathokles (317–289),[2] der in jenem Jahr seinen Krieg mit Karthago siegreich
beendete, während im Osten die Kämpfe um das Alexanderreich mit der Seeschlacht
beim zyprischen Salamis in eine neue Phase traten. Zuerst nahmen die Sieger Demetrios und sein Vater Antigonos, dann auch ihre Gegner den Titel ‚Basileus‘ an – zwei
Jahre später ebenso der sizilische Tyrann. Dass dieser von den neuen Machthabern
im werdenden hellenistischen Osten eher mild belächelt und kaum auf Augenhöhe
wahrgenommen wurde, lässt sich den spöttischen Trinksprüchen im Freundeskreis
des Demetrios entnehmen:[3]

> Auf Seleukos den Elefantenfürsten!
> Auf Ptolemaios den Admiral!
> Auf Lysimachos den Schatzwächter!
> Auf Agathokles den Inselfürsten von Sizilien!“

Dabei mag es retrospektiv eine Rolle gespielt haben, dass es dem Syrakusaner nicht
gelungen war, mit einer Dynastiegründung die Herrschaft über seinen Tod hinaus zu
stabilisieren. Es ist aber zu betonen, dass Syrakus im letzten Jahrzehnt des 3. Jh.s ein
geostrategischer Baustein im Netzwerk Ptolemaios' I. geworden war[4] und seine Be-

---

1   Vgl. Prag – Crawley Quinn 2013; eine Ausnahme stellt Vacanti 2012 dar, der den Ersten Punischen
     Krieg als einen primär ‚sizilischen‘ Konflikt behandelt.
2   Zu Agathokles ist auf folgende Literatur zu verweisen: Berve 1967, 441–457: Lehmler 2005, 36–48;
     de Lisle 2021.
3   Plut. Demetrios 25,4–5: Σελεύκου δὲ ἐλεφαντάρχου, Πτολεμαίου δὲ ναυάρχου, Λυσιμάχου δὲ
     γαζοφύλακος, Ἀγαθοκλέους δὲ τοῦ Σικελιώτου νησιάρχου.
4   Kontakte zu dem Diadochen in Ägypten scheint Agathokles schon um 310 gehabt zu haben, denn
     sie sind vorauszusetzen für seine konfliktreiche Kooperation mit dem ptolemaiischen Statthalter
     in Kyrene bei seinem Afrika-Feldzug gegen Karthago, nämlich Ophellas, den Agathokles eigen-
     händig getötet haben soll. Dessen Nachfolger in Kyrene wurde Magas, Stiefsohn Ptolemaios' I.;

deutung auch nach dem Tod des Agathokles nicht verloren hatte. Inwieweit dabei das expansive Rom eine Rolle gespielt hat, soll hier aber nicht thematisiert werden.

Eine Generation später, als Hieron sich anlässlich eines militärischen Sieges in Ostsizilien zum König ausrufen ließ (269), waren die Rahmenbedingungen freilich andere: Alle Diadochen waren tot, ihre nachfolgenden Söhne arrangierten sich mit den jeweiligen Gegebenheiten ihres Herrschaftsgebiets – und mit der Tatsache, dass es im zentralen Mittelmeerraum mit Sizilien einen starken Machtfaktor gab.

2. Traditionslinien sizilischer Herrschaftsrepräsentation

Indessen waren für Hierons II. Herrschaft ältere und jüngere lokale Traditionen von entscheidender Bedeutung. Daher seien zwei relevante historische Referenzpunkte seines Selbstverständnisses und seiner davon beeinflussten Politik aufgezeigt, die in die Zeit der sizilischen Tyrannen im 5. und 4. Jh. v. Chr. zurückreichen, nämlich sein Bezug auf die Deinomeniden und auf die seit Dionysios I. intensivierten Kontakte mit den Molossern.

2.1 Deinomeniden

Im 5. Jahrhundert hatte die Herrscherfamilie der Deinomeniden aus Gela Syrakus von 485 bis 466 autokratisch regiert; Gelon und Hieron hatten Ruhm als Sieger über Karthager und Etrusker gewonnen.[5] Hieron II., der sich als deren Nachfahren sah, seinen Sohn Gelon und eine Tochter Damarete nannte, orientierte sich in seiner Münzprägung an den seit Jahrhunderten üblichen Bildtypen,[6] insbesondere an der Verwendung von Vier- und Zweigespannen (Abb. 1) auf den Reversen.

---

ihn hatte Berenike, die zweite Gattin des Königs, in ihrer ersten Ehe geboren, ebenso wie ihre beiden Töchter, die – neben Magas – für das Netzwerk im zentralen Mittelmeerraum entscheidend wurden: Theoxena heiratete – vermutlich um 300 – den ‚Inselfürsten', ihre Schwester Antigone wurde Gattin des Molossers Pyrrhos, der seit 301 am Hof in Alexandreia als Geisel für Demetrios lebte. Ihn führte sein Gönner Ptolemaios im Jahr 298/297 mit Waffengewalt auf den väterlichen Thron in Epeiros zurück. Nach dem Tod der Antigone heiratete Pyrrhos Lanassa, eine Tochter des Agathokles. Da deren Sohn Alexander (II.) später seine Halbschwester Olympias, das Kind der Antigone, ehelichte, zählten alle weiteren molossischen Könige sowohl Ptolemaios I. als auch Agathokles zu ihren Ahnherren. Vgl. Consolo Langher 1996, 151–190; Huß 2000, 202–203 mit Anm.108; Günther 2011, 89–109.

5   Vgl. Mann 2013.

6   Charakteristisch ist seit dem späten 6. Jh. in der Münzprägung sikeliotischer Städte das – oft durch Hinzufügung einer Nike mit Kranz – siegreiche Vier- oder Zweigespann auf den Vorderseiten: vgl. e. g. Franke – Hirmer 1964 Tafel 12–15; 17; 21–22. Dionysios I. führte diese Bildmotive ebenso fort wie im späten 4. Jh. Agathokles und dann Hierons unmittelbarer Vorgänger Hiketas: vgl. e. g. Franke – Hirmer 1964 Tafeln 43–46 mit Text S. 52–54 (Dionysios I), Tafel 48 mit Text S. 55 (Aga-

Abb. 1 Hieron II. (269–216 v. Chr.), Bronzemünze, Syrakus. Rev.: Von Nike gelenkte Biga n. r.

Abb. 2 Hieron II. (269–216 v. Chr.), 16-Litren-Silbermünze für Philistis.

Abb. 3 Gelon, Sohn und Mitregent Hierons II. Didrachme (8 Litrae).

Er verwendete das Vier- bzw. Zweigespann vornehmlich für seine Gold- und Silbermünzen sowie für die im Namen seiner Gattin Philistis (Abb. 2) und seines Sohnes Gelon (Abb. 3) geprägten Silbernominale.[7] Allerdings werden diese Prägeserien von

thokles) und Tafel 49 mit Text S. 56 (Golddrachme des Hiketas). Lehmler 2005, 93 begründet die Übernahme von Biga und Quadriga auf den Münzrückseiten als Motive „des frühen 4. Jhs. v. Chr." mit einer Suggestion des Fortlebens lokaler Traditionen, wie es „auch Agathokles schon versucht" hatte.

7 Vgl. Franke – Hirmer 1964 Tafel 49 (Golddrachme), Tafel 50 (32-Litren), Tafel 51 (8-Litren für Gelon) und Tafel 49 (16-Litren für Philistis, nur die Vorderseiten mit dem Kopf der Königin abgebildet); Texte dazu S. 55–56 – Abbildungen der Quadriga auf den Rückseiten dieser Silbermünzen e. g. Lehmler 2005, 92 Abb. 34.

der neueren numismatischen Forschung für relativ spät gehalten und in die Zeit nach der Erhebung des Sohnes zum Mitregenten (um 230) bzw. in die Jahre 218–215 datiert.[8] Zuvor emittierte Hieron nur Bronzemünzen, die auf der Vorderseite den Kopf des Prägeherrn mit Diadem zeigen, während die Legende auf der Rückseite auf den Basileus-Titel verzichtet.[9]

Abb. 4 Hieron II. Bronzemünze. Rev.: Reiter im Galopp n. r.; in der rechten Hand Lanze.

Mit dem im Rahmen der beherrschenden Münzikonographie des 4. Jh.s neuartigen Bildmotiv der Rückseite, einem gepanzerten Reiter mit Speer (Abb. 4),[10] adaptierte er freilich ein geloisches Avers-Motiv (Abb. 5) des 5. Jh.s[11] und demonstrierte in diesem Medium die alte Dignität seiner Abstammung.

Abb. 5 Gelon I. Didrachme, Gela. Av.: Nackter, bärtiger Reiter mit phrygischem Helm und Speer.

---

8   Vgl. Lehmler 2005, 85 mit Anm. 86 unter Verweis auf die Forschungen von M. Caccamo Caltabiano.

9   Die sog. königliche Bronzeprägeserie, die auf der Rückseite das Viergespann darstellt, verzichtete indessen nicht auf den Basileus-Titel: vgl. e. g. Lehmler 2005, 92 Abb. 31.

10   Vgl. Lehmler 2005, 88 Abb. 28–29.

11   Vgl. e. g. Franke – Hirmer 1964, Tafel 55–56, Text S. 58 f.

2.2 Molosser

Wenn auch in der – insgesamt wesentlich variantenreicheren – Münzprägung des
Agathokles die motivische Reproduktion älterer Emissionen vorherrschte,[12] begegnet
auf seinen Gold- und Bronze-Emissionen, die auf der Vorderseite Athena oder Artemis zeigen, als neuartiges Rückseitenmotiv ein waagerechter geflügelter Blitz, über-
und unterhalb dessen die Legende – ΣΥΡΑΚ-ΟΣΙΩΝ bzw. nach 304 ΒΑΣΙΛΕΩΣ
ΑΓΑΘΟΚΛΕΟΣ – angebracht ist.[13]

Abb. 6 Agathokles. Bronzemünze, Syrakus. Rev.: Geflügeltes Blitzbündel,
ΑΓΑΘΟΚΛΕΟΣ ‖ ΒΑΣΙΛΕΩΣ.

Abb. 7 Pyrrhos. Bronzemünze, Syrakus. Rev.: Blitzbündel. ΒΑΣΙΛΕΩΣ ‖ ΠΥΡΡΟΥ.

12   Zu nennen sind die Wiederaufnahme der Quadriga sowie die Fortführung der seit Timoleon auf
      den als Stateren geprägten Münzen übernommenen korinthischen Ikonographie mit Pegasos und
      behelmten Frauenkopf; in allen diesen Emissionen lautet die Legende ΣΥΡΑΚΟΣΙΩΝ, es wird
      aber mit dem Beizeichen der Triskelis dann bald auf den Prägeherrn Agathokles verwiesen; vgl.
      e. g. Franke – Hirmer 1964 Tafel 47 mit Text S. 54; vgl. Lehmler 2005, 62–65.
13   Vgl. Lehmler 2005, 81–83 mit Abb. 25; betont wird (mit Anm. 77), dass die Goldstater-Emission
      mit dem Athenakopf auf der Vorderseite eine Imitation einer Prägung Alexanders III. aus dessen
      frühen Jahren (336–333) sei. Übersehen wird dabei, dass bereits Alexander I. von Epeiros – Onkel
      mütterlicherseits von Alexander III. von Makedonien – den Blitz (und auf der Münzvorderseite
      den Zeuskopf) bei seinen Prägungen verwendet hat, was für eine Adaption durch den Neffen Ale-
      xander III. spricht.

Abb. 8 Hieronymos. 5-Litren-Silbermünze. Rev.: Geflügeltes Blitzbündel,
ΒΑΣΙΛΕΟΣ ΙΕΡΩΝΥΜΟΥ.

Das gleiche Zeus-Symbol prägte um 278 Pyrrhos auf einer in Syrakus emittierten Bronzemünze mit der Legende ΒΑΣΙΛΕΩΣ ΠΥΡΡΟΥ (Abb. 7).[14] Dasselbe Bildmotiv nahm Hierons II. Enkel und Nachfolger Hieronymos auf seinen Silbermünzen wieder auf (Abb. 8), vor allem wohl wegen seiner Abstammung mütterlicherseits von Nereïs, einer Urenkelin Pyrrhos' I.[15] Obgleich der langjährige Herrscher Hieron, der in der syrakusanischen Entourage des Molosserkönigs seine militärische Karriere begonnen und damit den Grund für seinen wenige Jahre späteren politischen Erfolg gelegt hatte,[16] verzichtete er in seiner gesamten Münzprägung auf den Zeus-Blitz. Möglicherweise nahm er in der Wahl seines Bildprogramms der Bronzeprägung – die ja stattdessen auf die geloischen Ahnen verweist (s. o.) – Rücksicht auf die Römer wegen der mit dem Blitz verbundenen Assoziation mit Pyrrhos: Ihn hatten seine neuen Verbündeten schließlich besiegt und ihnen verdankte er den Erhalt seiner Herrschaft.[17]

Wesentlich älter als Pyrrhos' Feldzug in Sizilien waren indessen die Beziehungen zwischen Syrakus und Epeiros, nämlich basierend auf der geographischen Lage diesseits und jenseits der Adria.[18] Darauf rekurrierte bereits Dionysios I., der für seine expansiven Interessen im adriatischen Raum teils mit den Epiroten, teils mit illyrischen Stämmen kooperierte; so fand der Molosser Alketas nach seiner Vertreibung aus Epeiros gastliche Aufnahme in der Tyrannenfamilie, schloss enge Freundschaft mit Leptines, dem Bruder des Tyrannen, und kehrte mit deren tatkräftiger Unterstützung 385 auf

14 Vgl. Lehmler 2005, 88 Abb. 26. – Zu dem gänzlich neuen Vorderseitenbild, einem Frauenkopf mit Hinterkopfschleier, s. u. S. 356–357.

15 Zwar wurde wenige Jahre nach der Heirat der Molosserin mit Gelon ihre Herrscherfamilie in Epeiros gestürzt, doch visualisierte Hieronymos mit dem Münzbild seinen Anspruch auf Epeiros, *notabene* aufgrund seiner Rivalität mit Philipp V. von Makedonien, einem Sohn von Nereïs' Tante Phthia.

16 Zu den Anfängen Hierons: Berve 1967, 462–465; Lehmler 2005, 50–53.

17 Pol. 1,16,3–10; Diod. 23,4,1; Schmitt 1969, 137–140 (Nr. 479); vgl. Lehmler 2005, 53–54.

18 Bedeutsam waren seit dem 8. Jh. v. Chr. in diesem Raum die vornehmlich kommerziellen Interessen Korinths, das die Apoikien Korkyra und Syrakus, aber später auch weitere Pflanzstädte entlang der ostadriatischen Küste bis hinauf nach Epidamnos/Dyrrhachium (Durrës) gründete; vgl. Stickler 2010, 72–75.

den Molosserthron zurück.[19] Diese Politik, zu der die syrakusanische Besiedlung der dalmatinischen Insel Pharos gehört hatte,[20] revitalisierte Agathokles, wofür wiederum numismatische Argumente sprechen, insofern in den nun massenhaft geprägten Pegasi eine Art Gemeinschaftswährung für eine kontinuierliche und dichte Kommunikation zwischen Sizilien und dem nordwestgriechischen Raum gesehen werden kann.[21]

Die verdichtete ,Vernetzung' der Sizilier im Adriaraum unter Agathokles, wo gleichzeitig die Epiroten unter den mit Makedonien teils verbündeten, teils verfeindeten Molosserkönigen ihren Einfluss erweiterten, bezeugen weitere syrakusanische Tochtergründungen von Pharos und Lissos/Lissa/Issa aus in den ersten Jahrzehnten des 3. Jh., die – wie die Besiedlung von Korkyra Melaina – unter Beteiligung auch illyrischer Stämme stattfanden.[22] Als Kronzeuge für die expansiven Ambitionen des vom Tyrannen zum Basileus gewandelten Syrakusaners darf nicht zuletzt seine militärische Eroberung der geostrategisch wichtigen Insel Korkyra (301) gewertet werden, durch die Agathokles in Rivalität zum makedonischen Diadochen Kassander geraten war.[23]

Dass ein hochrangiger Feldherr des Agathokles den Namen Leptines trug und auch der Schwiegervater Hierons ebenso hieß,[24] lässt in der onomastischen Kontinuität familiäre Beziehungen zum Bruder Dionysios' I. (s. o.) erkennen, nämlich durch den Namen der Gattin Hierons, Philistis, der auf Philistos, den engen Vertrauten (und Geschichtsschreiber) Dionysios' I. verweist: Als dieser wie Leptines um 386/385 verbannt wurde, begaben sich beide Männer ins Exil, zunächst nach Thurioi, dann zu Alketas, wo sich Philistos bis zum Tod des Machthabers aufhielt, während dessen Bruder schon bald nach Syrakus zurückkehren durfte.[25]

Anlass für die Verbannung soll die dem Dionysios unerwünschte Heirat des Philistos mit einer Tochter des Leptines gewesen sein. Es ist daher sehr wahrscheinlich, dass sich in jenen Jahren des Exils auch die junge Gattin des Philistos und anzuneh-

---

19 Stroheker 1958, 119–27; ein epigraphisches Zeugnis legt die Vermutung nahe, dass ein Sohn des Leptines nach dem molossischen Freund benannt worden ist: Stroheker 1958, 121 mit 224 Anm. 79.

20 Stroheker 1958, 122–124, 224–226 Anm. 85–109.

21 Bis ins 3. Jh. reichte die quantitativ erstaunliche Prägung syrakusanischer ,Pferdchen' nach Vorbild Korinths, in deren ostadriatischen Apoikien seit der Mitte des 4. Jh., zweifellos im Gefolge des Timoleon-Unternehmens, eine erstaunliche Ausweitung der Prägestätten und der Emissionen zu beobachten ist: Vgl. Calciati 1990 II; Günther 2016, 450–452.

22 Consolo Langher 1996, 188–190.

23 Diod. 21,2,1: Agathokles beendete mit der Zerstörung der makedonischen Flotte die Belagerung der Insel. – Nach Diod. 21,2,2 trieb den – ebenso wie Kassander – maßlos ehrgeizigen Agathokles die Ruhmsucht zu seinem Angriff auf Korkyra. Diese Einlassung ist nicht geeignet zu klären, ob etwa der Syrakusaner aufgrund seiner Beziehungen zu Epeiros gegen Kassander agierte.

24 Meister 1999, 75 vermutet, dass der Militär der Großvater der Philistis war.

25 Philistos, die versierteste Machtstütze Dionysios' II., starb als syrakusanischer Nauarch 356; nach Meister 2000, 818–819, soll er von Dionysios II. mit dem Aufbau eines ,adriatischen Kolonialreiches' betraut worden sein, doch ist die zugrundeliegende Notiz nicht belastbar, zumal ihre Interpretation wegen der Unsicherheiten über die Chronologie der weiteren syrakusanischen Gründungen in jener Region problematisch ist.

mende gemeinsame Kinder bei Alketas aufhielten und dass Hierons Gattin Philistis in vierter Generation von jenem Paar abstammen dürfte. Dass bei den Nachkommen der beiden Männer aus dem engeren Umkreis des Tyrannen Dionysios, die der syrakusanischen Führungselite zuzurechnen sind,[26] die früheren Beziehungen der Familie zu Epeiros noch lebendig waren, ist daher mehr als eine vage Vermutung. In jedem Fall belebten zum einen die Heirat der Lanassa mit Pyrrhos, zum anderen der Aufenthalt des Molossers in Sizilien als Feldherr/Condottiere der Syrakusaner in ihrem Krieg mit Karthago die früheren Beziehungen. Darauf gründete sich dann nicht zuletzt das persönliche Interesse Hierons an Kontakten mit dem Herrscherhaus von Epeiros, das in der Verheiratung seines Sohnes mit Nereïs kulminierte.[27]

Kurz: Die starke Orientierung an den historischen Leistungen der Syrakusaner und der Wille zur Bewahrung der lokalen Traditionen heben Hieron II. deutlich von den anderen hellenistischen Monarchen seiner Zeit ab.

3. Hierons II. Kontakte mit dem östlichen Mittelmeerraum

3.1 Ptolemaier

Neben den neuerlich vertieften Beziehungen zu Epeiros gehörten zum ‚Erbe' von Agathokles und Pyrrhos, das Hieron II. übernahm, höchstwahrscheinlich auch enge Kontakte zum Hof in Alexandreia. Unter Ptolemaios II. (285–246) und Ptolemaios III. (246–222) erlangte das hellenistische Ägypten sowohl Stabilität als auch Dominanz im hellenistischen Machtgefüge.[28] Für Hierons II. Beziehungen zu den Ptolemaiern ist das bekannteste Zeugnis das monumentale Schiff ‚Syrakosia', das angeblich nur im Hafen von Alexandreia ankern konnte und daher als Geschenk an Ptolemaios III. gesandt wurde.[29]

---

26   Vgl. Berve 1967, 467: Hieron habe sich von allen früheren Tyrannen unterschieden durch seine dezidierte Begünstigung der ‚Oligarchen' seiner Heimatstadt.

27   Vgl. o. S. 352–353.

28   Zu den Beziehungen zu Rom, deren Verbesserung Ptolemaios II. nach dem Pyrrhos-Krieg mit einer Gesandtschaft an den Tiber initiierte und die in eine *amicitia* mündeten, vgl. Huß 2000, 294–297, 367–368.

29   Athen. 5.206d–209e. – Berve 1959, 70–75; Huß 2000, 368 sieht in dem Geschenk an – vermutlich – Ptolemaios III. ein Zeichen der Ergebenheit Hierons II., betont aber gleichzeitig: „Die ptolemäische Regierung hatte offensichtlich daran Interesse, das zwischen Alexandreia und Syrakosai bestehende gute Verhältnis zu pflegen"; ausführlich Lehmler 2005, 210–232; das Riesenschiff nebst seiner Getreideladung diente nach Lehmler als „Repräsentationsmittel" (228) und „Prestigeobjekt" Hierons II. (232).

Abb. 9 Münzporträt der Arsinoë II.

Abb. 10 Münzporträt der Berenike II.

Ebenso gilt als Beleg die Übernahme der Münzporträts von Arsinoë II. und Berenike II.[30] in den syrakusanischen Prägereihen der 16-Litren-Silbermünzen für Philistis (Abb. 2). Die Ähnlichkeiten mit der sizilischen Basilissa sind im Hinterkopf-Schleier und dem darunter verborgenen Haarknoten nicht zu verkennen; es handelt sich aber beim Bildnis der Philistis keineswegs um eine ‚Imitation' der Ptolemaierinnen, wie oft behauptet worden ist:[31] Bereits auf syrakusanischen Münzen des Pyrrhos, geprägt 278/286, begegnet ein entsprechend gestalteter Frauenkopf (Abb. 7), der mit der Beischrift ΦΘΙΑΣ auf eine Personifikation der Landschaft Phthias in Thessalien, der Heimat des molossischen Ahnherrn Achilleus, oder auf Phthia, die Mutter des Molossers,

30   Die Abbildungen der Arsinoë II. auf Gold-Oktodrachmen sowie Silber-Deka- und Tetradrachmen
      datieren in die Zeit nach 270, diejenigen Berenikes II., Tochter des Magas, in die Zeit der Herrschaft Ptolemaios' III., der nun auch Kyrene direkt vereinnahmte; vgl. e. g. Franke – Hirmer 1964
      Tafel 219 u. XX mit Text S. 163–165; vgl. Lehmler 2005, 94 Abb. 36–37; vgl. 91 mit Anm. 111 zu den
      Ähnlichkeiten und zur Annahme, „daß nur das Porträt der Berenike Vorbild für das der Philistis
      gewesen sein kann".
31   Vgl. Lehmler 2005, 89–90; Günther 2012, 39–40 betont zwar auch die Orientierung am ptolemaiischen Vorbild Berenikes II., lehnt aber die Kategorisierung als Herrscherinnenporträt ab.

verweisen mag.[32] Entscheidend ist m. E., dass es in Syrakus selbst ein älteres Vorbild für das Münzbildnis der Philistis gab, das offenbar mit kleinen ptolemaiischen Retuschen verwendet wurde.[33] Ungeachtet dieser Frage ist die Bildaussage des Philistis-Kopfes evident, da in der auf Hieronymos' Herrschaft folgenden so genannten republikanischen Phase in Syrakus, die mit der römischen Eroberung der Stadt 211 endete, Silbermünzen mit einem sehr ähnlichen Götterkopf geprägt wurden, der zweifellos Demeter darstellt.[34]

3.2 Rhodos

Nachdem im Jahr 228/227 ein schweres Erdbeben Rhodos verheert hatte, trafen von allen Seiten Hilfsgüter auf der Insel ein, wie Polybios ausführlich berichtet – darunter auch Lieferungen vom syrakusanischen Monarchen und seinem Sohn und Mitregenten Gelon:[35]

> Hieron und Gelon gaben nicht nur 75 Silbertalente für den Wiederaufbau der Mauern und eine ausreichende Summe für den Ölbedarf im Gymnasion, teils sofort, teils mit ganz kurzer Frist, sondern sie weihten auch silberne Becken und die Untersätze für sie, dazu einige silberne Wasserkrüge, ferner 10 Talente für die Opfer und weitere zehn für die

32 Auf diese Münze verweist auch Lehmler 2005, 91 (und Abb. 26), erkennt aber wegen des fehlenden königlichen Status in der Dargestellten, hier für die Mutter des Pyrrhos gehalten, keine Parallele bzw. kein Vorbild für die Darstellung der Philistis. – Phthia ist ein bei den Aiakiden mehrfach bezeugter Frauenname, beginnend im 5. Jh., mit der Gattin des Admetos (Plut. Themistokles 24). Da Pyrrhos' Mutter aus dem thessalischen Pharsalos stammte, könnte sie den ‚molossischen' Namen erst bei ihrer Heirat erhalten haben; das gleiche wäre freilich gleichermaßen für eine Gattin des Pyrrhos zu vermuten, etwa die Syrakusanerin Lanassa! – Vgl. Günther 2012, 42–44 (und 53 Abb. 13). Zu ähnlichen Frauenköpfen mit Hinterkopfschleier und lockigem Stirnhaar auf Silbermünzen von Kos um 350/40 Günther 2012, 44–46 (und 53 Abb. 16). Auch die thessalische Polis Pelinna verwendete im 3. Jh. auf Bronzemünzen einen vergleichbaren Frauenkopf: Vgl. Gießener Münzhandlung GmbH, Auktionskatalog 102, 24.5.2000, Nr. 188.
33 Vgl. den Beitrag von Ralf von den Hoff in diesem Band, S. 111.
34 Günther 2012, 40–41; 52 Abb. 8.
35 Pol. 5.88: Ἱέρων γὰρ καὶ Γέλων οὐ μόνον ἔδωκαν ἑβδομήκοντα καὶ πέντ' ἀργυρίου τάλαντα πρὸς τὴν εἰς τὸ ἔλαιον τοῖς ἐν τῷ γυμνασίῳ χορηγίαν, τὰ μὲν παραχρῆμα, τὰ δ᾽ ἐν χρόνῳ βραχεῖ παντελῶς, ἀλλὰ καὶ λέβητας ἀργυροῦς καὶ βάσεις τούτων καί τινας ὑδρίας ἀνέθεσαν, πρὸς δὲ τούτοις εἰς τὰς θυσίας δέκα τάλαντα καὶ τὴν ἐπαύξησιν τῶν πολιτῶν ἄλλα δέκα, χάριν τοῦ τὴν πᾶσαν εἰς ἑκατὸν τάλαντα γενέσθαι δωρεάν. καὶ μὴν ἀτέλειαν τοῖς πρὸς αὐτοὺς πλοϊζομένοις ἔδοσαν καὶ πεντήκοντα καταπέλτας τριπήχεις. καὶ τελευταῖον τοσαῦτα δόντες, ὡς προσοφείλοντες χάριν, ἔστησαν ἀνδριάντας ἐν τῷ τῶν Ῥοδίων δείγματι, στεφανούμενον τὸν δῆμον τῶν Ῥοδίων ὑπὸ τοῦ δήμου τοῦ Συρακοσίων. Die Geschenke anderer Könige und Helfer referiert Pol. 5.89–90: genannt sind Ptolemaios III., Antigonos III. Doson und dessen Gattin, Seleukos II.; als weitere Schenkende Prusias II. und Mithradates II., die kleinasiatischen Dynasten Lysanias, Olympichos und Limnaios sowie – ohne Spezifizierung – viele Poleis; vgl. Bringmann – von Steuben 1995, KNr. 199–200; 205; 207; 215 und 216–220 sowie Kobes 1996.

Unterstützung der Bürger, damit bei der Schenkung eine Gesamtsumme von 100 Talenten herauskäme. Sodann gewährten sie den rhodischen Kaufleuten Zollfreiheit in ihren Häfen, überwiesen der Stadt fünfzig drei Ellen große Katapulte, und schließlich, als wären sie ihnen noch Dank schuldig, stellten sie zu all diesen Geschenken noch zwei Standbilder auf dem Markt der Rhodier auf, das Volk der Rhodier von dem der Syrakusaner bekränzt.

In der Forschung ist unbestritten, dass die syrakusanischen Machthaber bei den Schenkungen für Rhodos einerseits im Sinne des hellenistischen Euergetismus in Konkurrenz zu den anderen beteiligten Monarchen traten, andererseits mit der gestifteten Statuengruppe die Rolle des Demos betonten.[36] Die Ansicht des Polybios, mit der visualisierten Ehrung des rhodischen Demos durch den syrakusanischen hätten die sizilischen Könige einen schuldigen Dank dafür ausdrücken wollen, hat kaum Widerspruch hervorgerufen; allenfalls wird darauf verwiesen, dass mit dem kränzenden Demos der Syrakusaner die Bürgerschaft in der Rolle der Hilfeleistenden zu sehen sei.[37] Dieser Gedanke führt indessen m. E. auf eine andere Interpretation als die einer typisch hellenistischen internationalen Repräsentation von Hieron II. und Gelon: So oft auch auf die ökonomische Bedeutung des sizilischen Handels mit Rhodos verwiesen wird, fehlt der Bezug auf die Beziehungen beider Poleis in archaischer Zeit: Rhodos war die Mutterstadt von Gela, der Heimatstadt der Deinomeniden (s. o.), die von dort aus einst Syrakus groß und historisch bedeutsam gemacht hatten. Insofern dürften im Hintergrund der Bekränzung des rhodischen Demos durch den syrakusanischen (der zugleich für Sizilien stellvertretend erscheinen konnte) die zeitlosen (und gegenseitigen) Verpflichtungen zwischen Mutter- und Tochterstadt stehen. Mit ihrer Ehrung betonten Hieron II. und Gelon nicht nur ihre konkurrenzlos altehrwürdige Beziehung zu Rhodos, sondern vermittels dieser historischen Dimension auch eine spezifische Würde ihrer – wenn auch im Vergleich mit Ptolemaiern, Seleukiden und Antigoniden recht kleinen – Herrschaft. Ein Aspekt dieser Würde ist die wiederum einzigartige Genese ihrer Macht auf der Basis einer Polis. Somit erwies sich Hieron II. in der Zugabe der Statuengruppe zu den Hilfsleistungen für die Metropolis gerade nicht als typisch hellenistischer Monarch, der mit den anderen Königen in jeder Beziehung mitzuhalten suchte.

---

36   Ausführlich zur Erdbebenhilfe für Rhodos: Lehmler 2005, 203–205, wo die Demonstration von Reichtum, kulturellem Potenzial und hohem technischen Entwicklungsstand im Reich von Hieron II. und Gelon herausgestellt wird.

37   Lehmler 2005, 204 spitzt Polybios' Bemerkung noch zu: als Dank „dafür, dass sie sich an der Spendenaktion beteiligen durften." – Im Übrigen bleibt zu konstatieren, dass es keinen einzigen Beleg dafür gibt, dass ein hellenistischer König oder Potentat einer Polis in der Weise dankte, dass er sie mit einem Kranz ehrte.

4. Resümee

Für den hellenistischen König Hieron II., dessen Reich auf Syrakus und Teile Ostsiziliens beschränkt war, hatten lokale Traditionen und historische Bezugspunkte bei der Außendarstellung seiner Herrschaft, zumal in der Münzprägung, einen viel größeren Einfluss als Vorbilder der hellenistischen Monarchen der ostmediterranen Welt. Dabei spielten Bezüge auf die Deinomeniden und auf die Ambitionen früherer Machthaber im östlichen Adriaraum einschließlich der Kontakte mit den epirotischen Molossern eine wesentliche Rolle. Hieron II. verhielt sich somit – ungeachtet der gewandelten Rahmenbedingungen im Verlauf des 3. Jh. – ähnlich wie schon Agathokles, der eigentliche ‚Innovator' monarchischer Herrschaft in Sizilien, betonte aber konsequenter die ins 5. Jh. hinaufreichenden Reminiszenzen.

Literaturverzeichnis

Berve 1959: Berve, Helmut, König Hieron II., München 1959

Berve 1967: Berve, Helmut, Die Tyrannis bei den Griechen, 2 vols., München 1967

Bringmann – von Steuben 1995: Bringmann, Klaus – von Steuben, Hans (eds.), Schenkungen hellenistischer Herrscher an griechische Städte und Heiligtümer. Teil I Zeugnisse und Kommentare, Berlin 1995

Calciati 1990: Calciati, Romolo, Pegasi, 2 vols., Mortara 1990

Consolo Langher 1996: Consolo Langher, Sebastiana N., Siracusa e la Sicilia greca tra età arcaica ed alto elenismo, Messina 1996

de Lisle 2021: de Lisle, Christopher, Agathocles of Syracuse. Sicilian Tyrant and Hellenistic King, Oxford 2021

De Sensi Sestito 1977: De Sensi Sestito, Giovanna, Gerone II. Un monarca elenistico in Sicilia, Palermo 1977

Franke – Hirmer 1964: Franke, Peter R. – Hirmer, Max, Die griechische Münze, München 1964

Günther 2011: Günther, Linda-Marie, Syrakus unter Agathokles und die ptolemäische Expansion, Archivio Storico Siracusano 46, 2011, 89–109

Günther 2012: Günther, Linda-Marie, Polis und Königin: Zur Interpretation von Frauenköpfen auf hellenistischen Münzen, Jahrbuch für Numismatik und Geldgeschichte 62, 2012, 35–53

Günther 2016: Günther, Linda-Marie, Münze und Macht. Eine Währungsunion bei den ‚alten Griechen'? Numismatisches Nachrichtenblatt 65, 2016, 450–452

Huß 2000: Huß, Werner, Ägypten in hellenistischer Zeit (332–30 v. Chr.), München 2000

Kobes 1996: Kobes, Jörn, Rhodos und das Erdbeben von 227 v. Chr., Münstersche Beiträge zur antiken Handelsgeschichte 12.1, 1993, 1–26

Lehmler 2005: Lehmler, Caroline, Syrakus unter Agathokles und Hieron II. Die Verbindung von Kultur und Macht in einer hellenistischen Metropole, Frankfurt 2005

Mann 2013: Mann, Christan, The Victorious Tyrant: Hieron of Syracuse in the Epinicia of Pindar and Bacchylides in: N. Luraghi (ed.), The Splendors and Miseries of Ruling Alone. Encounters with Monarchy from Archaic Greece to the Hellenistic Mediterranean, Stuttgart 2013, 25–48

Meister 1999: Meister, Klaus, Leptines Nr. 4–5, DNP 7, 1999, 75

Meister 2000: Meister, Klaus, Philistos, DNP 9, 2000, 818–819

Prag – Crawley Quinn 2013: Prag, Jonathan R. W. – Crawley Quinn, Josephine (eds.), The Helle-nistic West: Rethinking the Ancient Mediterranean, Cambridge 2013

Schmitt 1969: Schmitt, Hatto H., Die Staatsverträge des Altertums III, München 1969

Stickler 2010: Stickler, Timo, Korinth und seine Kolonien. Die Stadt am Isthmus im Machtgefüge des klassischen Griechenland, Berlin 2010

Stroheker 1958: Stroheker, Karl F., Dionysios I. Gestalt und Geschichte des Tyrannen von Syra-kus, Wiesbaden 1958

Vacanti 2012: Vacanti, Claudio, Guerra per la Sicilia e guerra della Sicilia. Il ruolo delle città sicilia-ne nel primo conflitto romano-punico, Neapel 2012

Abbildungsverzeichnis

Abb. 1: © Archäologisches Museum der Universität Münster, ID 804.

Abb. 2: © Archäologisches Museum der Universität Münster, M 6360.

Abb. 3: © Archäologisches Museum der Universität Münster, ID 805.

Abb. 4: © Archäologisches Museum der Universität Münster, ID 799.

Abb. 5: Gorny & Mosch Giessener Münzhandlung, Auction 240 (10.10.2016), Lot number 26.

Abb. 6: © Archäologisches Museum der Universität Münster, M 3961.

Abb. 7: © Archäologisches Museum der Universität Münster, ID 792.

Abb. 8: © Archäologisches Museum der Universität Münster, ID 813.

Abb. 9: Classical Numismatic Group, Triton XXVI (10.01.2023), Lot number 433.

Abb. 10: Classical Numismatic Group, Triton XIII (5.12010), Lot number 238.

Linda-Marie Günther was Professor of Ancient Greek History at the Ruhr-Universität Bochum from 1999 to 2018. Her research interests included all epochs of Classical Antiquity from Archaic Greece to the Late Roman Empire. Special interest concerned Hellenistic History, giving priority to epigraphic and numismatic material besides well-known literary sources. She has published mono-graphs, among others on Sicily and Carthage (1993), Herod the Great (2005), and Milesian Women (2014) as well as a study-book on Greek history (utb 2008, ²2011). She has written numerous articles in journals and edited several proceedings of workshops and congresses.

The Power to Impress and Impressing to Power
*Translocal Developments in Baktrian Kingship and Royal Representation in the Third and Second Centuries BC**

MILINDA HOO

Abstract: In Hellenistic Eurasia, kingship and royal power were dependent on dynamic networks of power, ideological interplay, and cultural exchange in a world shaped by transimperial and supralocal connections and interactions. Hellenistic kingship practices were, however, neither distinctly Macedonian nor globally uniform, but should be seen as translocally networked practices of sameness and differentiation. In Baktria, the historical context within which such practices took place hint at conscious efforts to participate in broader networks of power and prestige, engaging with visual languages of legitimacy and distinction that resonated both globally and locally. As in other Hellenistic empires and post-satrapal kingdoms, legitimate kingship in Baktria seemed to have been charismatic in nature which matured in a dynamic world of strife and war. Kingship was neither natural nor absolute but was contingent upon claims to royal power based on (impressions of) grand military success, prestigious material display, and increasing heroization of a strong victorious leader in a highly competitive milieu of rival kings and adversaries. Although the position as legitimate king depended on local acceptance by soldiers, administrators, elites, and to an extent the broader populace, Baktrian rulers advocated an ideology of kingship that deeply engaged with and developed from translocally networked practices of power and differentiation across Hellenistic Eurasia.

*   I warmly thank Christoph Michels, Hans Beck, and Achim Lichtenberger for inviting me to a most inspiring conference in Münster, as well as providing valuable comments on the draft of this paper. Faults and errors remain, of course, my own.

1. Introduction

In 1938, William W. Tarn proclaimed in his book *The Greeks in Bactria and India* that the elusive dynasties of the Graeco-Baktrian kingdoms in Central Asia were a lost chapter of Hellenistic history. Their untold story, he argued, was a Hellenistic one that ought to be considered on the same level of grandeur and achievement as the Antigonid, Ptolemaic, and Seleukid kings.[1] 85 years of research, excavations, new discoveries, and timely paradigm shifts have unfolded unprecedented layers of Baktria's history which, though sometimes corrective of Tarn's often-fantastical historical reconstructions, substantiated his central thesis with firm evidentiary ground: the kings of Baktria were not distant and isolated from the Hellenistic world but their stories were deeply entangled with the histories and practices across the wider Afro-Eurasian landmass.

Indeed, consideration of the Graeco-Baktrian kingdoms (modern Afghanistan and parts of southern Tajikistan and Uzbekistan) as an integral part of the Hellenistic world has become imperative in recent historiography of Greek antiquity. Few scholars today would approach this world of kingdoms and empires as a mosaic of isolated and unitary political entities with sharply defined domains of influence and stable control over distinct territories. Rather, kingship and royal power across Afro-Eurasia were dependent on dynamic networks of power, ideological interplay, and cultural exchange in a world shaped by transimperial and supralocal connections and interactions.[2] Hellenistic kingship practices were, however, not distinctly Greek, Macedonian, or globally uniform but should be seen as translocally networked practices of sameness and differentiation. In Baktria, the historical contexts within which such practices took place hint at conscious efforts to participate in broader networks of power and prestige, engaging with visual languages of legitimacy and distinction that resonated both globally and locally. This paper accordingly argues that developments of kingship and royal representation in Baktria during the third and second centuries BC should be considered as *translocal* (glocal) phenomena of the entangled, globalized world of Hellenistic Afro-Eurasia.[3]

To analyse the perimeters of Baktrian kingship, this paper builds on Hans-Joachim Gehrke's influential theory of charismatic kingship as a typical form of legitimate gov-

---

1   Tarn 1938, xix.
2   Von Reden 2020b; see also Bang 2012; Strootman 2014; Versluys 2017.
3   For a translocal approach, see Hoo 2022, 229–270. Afro-Eurasia refers here to the broad arena of the continental landmass of Europe and Asia (Anatolia to China) whose geographies and histories are interconnected and entangled with those of the wider Mediterranean including North Africa and the Near East. For Afro-Eurasia as a suitable term for world history, see Bentley 1998; Chase-Dunn – Hall 1997, 149–186; and recent usages in relation to global history in e. g. von Reden 2020a/2021; Versluys forthcoming.

ernment in the Hellenistic period.[4] His analytical observations invites to consider that kingship in Baktria, too, was neither natural nor absolute but tied to the charismatic persona of individual kings – and possibly their families. Legitimate royal power was not automatically hereditary but contingent on (impressions of) military success, prestigious material display, and the heroization of a strong victorious leader in a highly competitive milieu of rival kings and adversaries. Assessing the spaces, forms, and strategies of Baktrian kings to differentiate themselves from delegitimate others, this paper surveys the clues to kingship in the evidence at hand, focusing on three interrelated articulations of royal representation: charismatic achievements, prestigious display, and the ruler's relationship with the divine. It will become clear that Baktrian rulers not only depended on local acceptance by soldiers, administrators, elites, and to an assumed extent the broader populace but also advocated an ideology of kingship that deeply engaged with and developed from translocally networked practices of differentiation that resonated both within Central Asia and across Afro-Eurasia.

2. Historical background

2.1 Pre-Hellenistic traditions of kingship

Central Asia was not alien to concepts of kingship before the coming of Alexander the Great, and it is necessary to first embed kingship practices in Hellenistic Baktria in the context of deeper and dynamic traditions of kingship in Afro-Eurasian history. According to Diodoros, sourcing from Ktesias, Central Asia had been subject to imperial desire by Neo-Assyrian kings who made arduous efforts to incorporate Baktria into their empire, known as a wealthy land of numerous cities of which Baktra was most famed for the palace of the king – one named by Diodoros as Oxyartes.[5] Although the Assyrian campaigns to Baktria by the mythical king Ninos and his (future) wife Semiramis probably form a literary trope of conquest of the world's farthest edges to evoke Assyria's royal prestige, concepts of kingship were not unfamiliar to Central Asia before the Hellenistic period.[6] Nevertheless, whether or not Assyrian rule actually reached

---

4   Gehrke 2013 departing from Max Weber's sociology of legitimate rule. On the applicability of this ideal type see also the chapter by Noah Kaye in this volume.

5   Diod. 2.6.1–8. Oxyartes is a local Baktrian name after the most important Central Asian waterway: the Oxos river. It is quite possible that Diodoros (con)fused the name of this king presumably ruling over Baktria in Neo-Assyrian times with the later Baktrian-Sogdian warlord and father of Roxane (whom Alexander the Great would marry in 327 BC), who also bore the name Oxyartes. That Baktria was known for its numerous cities – a proverbial "thousand cities" – is reflected by Strab. 15.1.3; Iust. 41.1, 41.4, and Sima Qian, *Shiji* 123 (tr. Watson 1961, 235).

6   Diod. 2.5.3–2.7.1; cf. OGIS 54. Diodoros' narrative of Assyrian campaigns to Bactria probably served a teleological narrative of the succession of empires, culminating in the Roman empire; cf.

Baktria and whether or not Baktria was ruled by a local king who came in contact with Near Eastern kings in the late ninth or early eighth century BC, any transdynastic transfer of knowledge of Assyrian royal ideology in Central Asia, such as artificial paradisal gardens, must have been mediated through Achaimenid developments of Iranian kingship.[7]

From the mid-sixth century onward, Baktria's experience with concepts of kingship certainly became (more) immediate when Kyros II the Great (r. 559–530 BC) conquered Baktria-Margiana and incorporated the region as a far eastern satrapy of the Achaimenid Empire in the 540s or 530s BC.[8] From Herodotos' *Histories*, we know that Baktria was one of the satrapies paying significant tribute of 360 talents to the Achaimenid treasury.[9] The trilingual rock inscription of Dareios I (r. 522–486 BC) at Bisutun in north-western Iran affirms the integration of Baktria-Margiana in the Achaimenid empire, presenting these regions as formerly rebellious lands that were reconquered by Dareios.[10] In this text and other royal inscriptions, Dareios proclaimed himself as a just, fearless, and divinely sanctioned warrior-king, blessed by Ahura Mazda with the skills of the spear and the bow, excelling both on horseback and on foot.[11] As the Bisutun inscription makes clear, such self-presentation not only served to legitimize his own rise to power – considering that Dareios was not a dynastic heir – but particularly to *delegitimize* other kings, who were stigmatized as rebellious evildoing kings 'who followed the Lie'.[12] In doing so, Dareios could ideologically frame his own military campaigns across the empire as 'acts of righteousness' befitting a truthful king while overruling other (indigenous) claims to kingship.[13]

Entangled in imperial and social networks of the Achaimenid empire, it may be assumed that Baktrians and other Central Asian populations became well aware of Iranian discourses of power and kingship. Baktrians are represented bearing gifts on the reliefs of the eastern staircase of the Apadana at Persepolis, while objects from the

     Vell. Pat. 1.1.6. Possible but unsubstantial material traces of Assyrians in Central Asia are discussed in Ball et al. 2019, 268.

7   For Assyrian royal gardens, see esp. Carroll 2003; Farrar 2016. For Achaimenid royal gardens (*pairidaiza/pairidaida*, Gr. *paradeisoi*), see Stronach 1989; Tuplin 1996; Canepa 2018, 345–352.

8   The chronology of Kyros' eastern campaigns and the question whether they were undertaken before or after the conquest of Babylon in 539 BC, is impossible to reconstruct from the available evidence; see discussion in Briant 1984, 69–71; 2002, 38–40, 752–754. Briant 1984 remains essential for Baktria under Achaimenid rule, with further recent discussion in Briant 2020; Wu 2020; Rapin 2021.

9   Hdt. 3.93.1; 3; see also Xen. Kyr. 1.1.4.

10   DB § 6, § 38–39 (trans. Lecoq 1997, as for all further references to Achaimenid inscriptions).

11   Esp. DB § 9, § 51–70; DNb § 9–10.

12   DB § 10, 52, 54–55. Foremost among them, Gaumata: the Magos who had killed Kambyses' brother and legitimate heir Bardiya (Gr. Smerdis) and assumed the throne, pretending to be him (DB § 12–13).

13   DB § 63. The rebellious kings received cruel punishment by mutilation and subsequent public display (DB § 32–33); further discussion in Lincoln 2007; Rollinger 2010; Muller 2016.

Oxos Treasure discovered in southern Tajikistan reflect local (elite) familiarity with Persian ideology of the warrior-king: gold Daric coins depicting a king with a bow and spear and a cylinder seal with battle scenes in which a royal figure prevails over his enemies.[14] Dated around 500 BC, the Persepolis Fortification Archive moreover sheds light on regular royally authorized travel between Persis, eastern Iran, and Central Asia during the reign of Dareios I. This archive provides record not only of Central Asians among frequent travellers on official mission to trade and (re)distribute goods, but also of Baktrians and Sogdians working as specialist workers in Persepolis – the quintessential city of kingship in the imperial heartland.[15] Baktria further held exceptional significance for the Achaimenid dynasty, as sons and brothers of the king – close kinsmen but also potential threats to the throne – would be appointed satrap of Baktria and so kept at bay while ensuring continued imperial control over strategic routes and passes of the northern Hindu Kush region.[16] More specific information on later Baktrian interaction with Achaimenid kingship after Dareios I, however, remains unclear. Aramaic documentary inscriptions from an archive of the satrap of Baktria of the fourth century BC do record considerable administrative continuity in the transition from Achaimenid to Alexandrian rule, including the use of Official Aramaic and local functionaries, though they tell us little about performative and representational practices of kingship.[17]

It is with the conquest of the Achaimenid empire by Alexander the Great in the fourth century BC that kingship and royal representation in Baktria come into clearer historiographical purview. Alexander's presence and reign in Central Asia was short (329–327 BC) yet received ample attention in lively literary narratives by the Alexander historians, dated mostly to the first or second centuries AD, and thus written with distinct Roman interests.[18] Although Plutarch famously praised Alexander for bringing civilization to the Far East by founding Greek cities, it was in Central Asia that Alexander began to 'Persianize' as he took up Iranian traditions of royal ceremony, regal attire,

---

14   Resp. BM 124080; BM 124015. The Oxos Treasure was discovered on the south banks of the Amu Darya in the region of Takht-i Kuvad near Takht-i Sangin – the site of the Oxos Temple. For Persian coins in the treasure, see Bellinger 1962, 53–54, 56–57; and discussion in Pichikyan 1992, 69–82. On the cylinder seal: Wu 2010, 548–549, 558.

15   Henkelman 2018; cf. DSf § 10. For the Persepolis Fortification Archive, see Hallock 1969; Garrison – Root 2001. Further discussion on the dense connectivity and communication across the Achaimenid empire in Briant 2012; and esp. Colburn 2013; 2016.

16   Hdt. 9.113.1–2; Diod. 11.69.2; further discussion in Briant 1984, 75–76; Garcia Sanchez 2014. Revolts in Baktria against the Achaimenid throne, sometimes initiated by the satrap of Baktria, i. e. a close relative of the Great King, did occur; see esp. Hdt. 9.113.1–2 and further Briant 1984, 76–77; Wu 2010; 2017.

17   Naveh – Shaked 2012, esp. 198–212 which record a year 7 of Alexander; see further Gzella 2021.

18   With the exception of Diodoros of Sicily, who flourished from the 20s BC until the AD 20s, and Justin, whose work is conventionally considered to date to the second or third centuries AD (Yardley – Develin 1994, 4), though some scholars attribute the work to the late fourth century AD (Schmidt 1999).

and other Persian customs, and demanded his men to do the same.[19] Alexander not only presented himself as an Iranian king, but also married into noble and royal Iranian families, and recruited Baktrian horsemen.[20] Baktrian warriors seemed to have enjoyed a good reputation, as they had also been mobilized by Xerxes I for his invasion of Greece (480 BC) and played a significant role in the royal army of Dareios III against Alexander (333 and 331 BC).[21] This consideration is relevant, as Baktrians – whether as soldiers or elites – were important among the targeted audiences for royal ideology propagated by kings ruling over Central Asia. Soon after Alexander left the region for India, his new settlers joined hands with local populations and rebelled against his rule, leaving Central Asia in an interregnum by the time of Alexander's death in 323 BC.[22]

2.2 Kings in Hellenistic Baktria

Although his reign in Central Asia was brief and turbulent, Alexander's transformation of kingship into a charismatic institution of rule and leadership – a power network formed around the king's exceptional persona – remained influential under his successors in Asia.[23] In 308 BC, Seleukos I marched to the Far East to reclaim and incorporate Baktria as part of the Upper Satrapies and crossed into India to renew diplomatic relations with the Mauryan king Chandragupta. Seleukid eastern campaigns served both military and ideological purposes of legitimizing claims to imperial territory; immediately after his anabasis, which gained him a supposed number of 500 elephants, Seleukos I adopted the title of King (*Basileus*) in 305 BC.[24] He appointed his son and dynas-

---

19   Diod. 17.77.4–7, Curt. 6.1–8; Iust. 12.3.8–12. Alexander's adoption of Persian ways caused controversy, tension, and even mutiny among his men; see recent discussion in Heckel 2020, 201–220. This episode only exists in the 'Vulgate' version based on the lost work of Kleitarchos, but is absent in Arrian's narrative. Arrian does mention that Alexander, upon entering Central Asia, gave Iranian nobleman honourable positions while punishing Greeks who had fought in the Achaimenid army (Arr. an. 3.23.7); further discussion in Olbrycht 2014.

20   For Alexander civilizing the East, see Plut. mor. Alex. 328f–329a. In 327 BC, Alexander married Roxane, the daughter of the Baktrian-Sogdian nobleman Oxyartes (Curt. 8.4.23–26; Plut. Alexander 47.4) and additionally took Parysatis and Stateira, daughters of resp. Artaxerxes III and Dareios III, as his wives during the mass weddings at Susa in 324 BC (Curt. 3.13.12; Arr. an. 7.4.4–5). Stateira is sometimes confused as Barsine (Arr. an. 7.4.4), the daughter of Artabazanos whom Alexander appointed satrap of Baktria.

21   For Baktrians in the Achaimenid royal army, see e.g. Hdt. 8.113.2; Curt. 4.6.2–3, 4.15.18. For Baktrians in Alexander's army, see e.g. Curt. 8.5.1; more specifically Arr. an. 7.6.3. Central Asia was known for its 'heavenly horses' bred in Ferghana (Dayuan), north of Baktria, a legacy that reached the report of Sima Qian in the second century BC (*Shiji* 123, tr. Watson 1961, 233, 245).

22   Diod. 17.99.5–6; Curt. 9.7.1–2; further discussion in Holt 1989, 70–99; 2005, 105–120; Iliakis 2013.

23   See fruitful discussion, among others, in Luraghi 2013; Plischke 2014, 22–172; Trampedach – Meeus 2020; Von den Hoff 2021; Degen 2022.

24   For Seleukos I's eastern campaigns in light of legitimizing strategies, see Kosmin 2014, 32–78; Plischke 2014, 22–172.

tic successor Antiochos I as coregent in the Upper Satrapies, who cultivated Seleukid rule in Central Asia from 294 until 281 BC. The Central Asian lands held special meaning to Antiochos, since he was half Baktrian or Sogdian through his mother Apame, whom Seleukos I had married during the mass weddings at Susa in 324 BC. During his coregency, Antiochos founded the city of Ai Khanum in Baktria and opened a royal eastern mint.[25] He upheld Seleukid rule in Central Asia until the death of Seleukos I in 281 BC forced him to return to turbulent affairs in western Asia. Antiochos' dynastic successors remained preoccupied with conflicts in Syria and Asia Minor, providing opportunity for Central Asian satraps to assert more influence.

The political history of post-Seleukid Baktria is notoriously sketchy, as only few literary passages by later Greek and Latin authors have survived traditions of textual transmission, most notably Polybios, Strabon, and Pompeius Trogus (via Justin's epitome), who were primarily interested in the rise of Baktria's neighbours, the Arsakids, on the imperial stage east of the Roman Mediterranean.[26] These authors provide secure record of the names of eight kings of post-Seleukid Baktria, a stark contrast to the roughly forty additional rulers known from coins alone.[27] Justin mentions that Diodotos, the Seleukid satrap of Baktria, revolted against Macedonian domination which possibly took place around 250 BC, a date which conventionally marks the beginnings of the Graeco-Baktrian kingdom.[28] Although the extent and gradation of "state independence" is a point of scholarly debate – considering that coins with the portrait of Diodotos I still bore the name of Antiochos II in the legend – the coins of his son Diodotos II make a definite claim to royal authority, propagating Diodotos' own name and portrait with the title of king (fig. 1).[29]

---

25 Martinez-Sève 2015; Kritt 2016; Glenn 2020.

26 For an overview of textual sources on Hellenistic Baktria, see Holt 1999, 174–184. For an overview of evidence focused on Central Asia's economic history, see Morris 2020a.

27 Hoo – Wiesehöfer 2022, 273–274 with further methodological implications. Kings mentioned in literary sources are: Diodotos I, Diodotos II, Euthydemos I, Demetrios I, Apollodotos, Eukratides I, and Menander I. The eighth king is Demetrios 'rex Indorum' whose identity remains obscure (see fn. 39). Epigraphical sources further record the names of Eumenes and Antimachos II (CII 2.1, no. 92) and Antialkidas in India (Salomon 1998, 265–267). Bopearachchi 1991 remains essential for coins of the Baktrian kings. For a recent reconstruction of the chronological order of kings, see Morris 2020b, 65.

28 Iust. 41.4.5; see also Strab. 11.9.3, 11.11.1. Justin provides three temporal anchors for the Baktrian revolt: 1. 'at the same time' of the revolt by Andragoras, the Seleukid satrap of Parthia (Iust. 41.4.4: eodem tempore, but cf. Strab. 11.9.3); 2. when Lucius Manlius Vulso and Marcus Atilius Regulus were consuls (256 BC, Iust. 41.4.3, though this could be an error by Justin); 3. made possible by the Seleukid focus on the intradynastic "War of the Brothers" between Seleukos II and Antiochos Hierax (239–236 BC, Iust. 41.4.4). Reconstruction of the chronology of events is puzzling; see esp. relevant discussion in Lerner 1999, 13–32; Wolski 1999; Coloru 2009, 157–193; Overtoom 2020.

29 Iust. 41.4.9 mentions that Diodotos had a son with the same name. Diodotos II's coins have been considered an outright declaration of independence, but recent scholarship proposed a common practice of indirect rule under Seleukid suzerainty; see discussion in Chrubasik 2016, 48–52; En-

Fig. 1 Coin of Diodotos II, inscribed in his own name.

Around 230 or the early 220s BC, Euthydemos seized power from the Diodotids. Polybios tells us that Euthydemos was a settler from Magnesia in Asia Minor who, in a fictive
speech, justifies his claim to kingship by expressly distancing himself from Diodotos
and his lineage, portraying them as rebel kings: 'He himself (Euthydemos) had never revolted against the king, but after others (the Diodotids) had revolted he had possessed
himself of the throne of Baktria by destroying their descendants.'[30] The context of this
defensive passage is another Seleukid eastern anabasis, this time by Antiochos III (212–
205 BC) who besieged Baktra for two years.[31] Euthydemos, by then already ruling Baktria for over two decades, appealed to the Seleukid king with a common cause to protect
civilization from "great hordes of nomads" on the north-eastern frontier, and a treaty
was formed that formally acknowledged Euthydemos as king of Baktria, supposedly
sealed with a marriage between his son Demetrios and an unnamed daughter of Antiochos.[32] The treaty allowed Euthydemos to maintain and further consolidate his realm together with Demetrios, who succeeded him around 190 BC and expanded the kingdom
southwards into the Paropamisadai, Arachosia, and Gandhara in the 180s BC.[33]

The thriving success of these Euthydemids finds echo in Strabon and the Kulob
inscription (discussed further below) but literary sources are silent about royal succes-

gels 2017, 318–322. For comparison, it should be mentioned that the Diadochi (e. g. Lysimachos)
initially continued to mint coins in the name of Alexander.

30   Pol. 11.34.1–2 (trans. Paton – Walbank – Habicht 2011): γεγονέναι γὰρ οὐκ αὐτὸς ἀποστάτης τοῦ
βασιλέως, ἀλλ᾽ ἑτέρων ἀποστάντων ἐπανελόμενος τοὺς ἐκείνων ἐκγόνους, οὕτως κρατῆσαι τῆς
Βακτριανῶν ἀρχῆς. In the context of the narrative, we may assume that βασιλεύς refers to the Seleukid dynastic monarchy, although we can also entertain the possibility that it refers to a more general concept of *legitimately obtained* kingship. For relevant discussion on Seleukid rule in relation to
local rulers, see Chrubasik 2016, 48–52; Engels 2017, 318–322.

31   For discussion on Antiochos' anabasis in Baktria-Sogdiana, see Martinez-Sève 2017.

32   Pol. 11.34.3–6: πλήθη οὐκ ὀλίγα τῶν Νομάδων.

33   It might be that conquests across the Hindu Kush by Demetrios I took place earlier than 190 BC,
possibly during a coregency between Euthydemos I and Demetrios I, considering that Euthydemos I already held possession over war elephants which he had to concede to Antiochos III as a
condition to the treaty of 205 BC (Pol. 11.34.10–11). Additionally, copper coins of Euthydemos have
been found south of the Hindu Kush (MacDowall 2005, 198–199).

sions after Demetrios I, save for an uninformative mention in the *Periplus Maris Erythraei* of coins in Barygaza (western India) of Apollodotos and Menander, 'rulers who came after Alexander'.[34] We do know from coins that several short-reigning kings ruled north and south of the Hindu Kush after Demetrios I in the 170s BC: an Euthydemos II (possibly Demetrios I's son), followed by Pantaleon and Agathokles (presumably close relatives), three co-reigning kings Antimachos I, Eumenes, and Antimachos II (the latter two probably sons of the former, also documented in a leather tax receipt), and lastly Apollodotos.[35] Although it has been suggested that the majority if not all of these rulers were kinsmen of Euthydemos, acting as sub-kings or satraps under Euthydemid suzerainty, the precise relations between them remain unclear.[36] Coins of a second Demetrios also shortly circulated in Baktria around this time, but his identity and kinship to the Euthydemids or Antimachos remain similarly unknown.[37]

Around 171 BC, Eukratides asserted power in Baktria and ruled until around 145 BC, his reign contemporaneous to Mithradates I of Parthia (r. 171–139/138 BC). He was the last Graeco-Baktrian king known from literary sources which immortalized him as a great and formidable king.[38] Eukratides, too, marched across the Hindu Kush into north-west India, where he clashed with a mysterious Demetrios 'king of the Indians' and with Menander, an Indo-Greek king ruling around 165 BC whose rivalling greatness is documented in both Greek and Indic sources.[39] Eukratides' son and coregent, Eukratides II, reigned in Baktria while his father campaigned in the southeast. According to Justin, this son turned against him, brutally killed Eukratides upon his return, and publicly drove a chariot through his blood, parading his deed.[40] After Eukratides' death

34 For the success of Demetrios, see Strab. 11.11.1, and perhaps alluded to in 15.1.27; CII 2.1, no. 255. For Apollodotos and Menander, see Peripl. m. Eryth. 47: [δραχμαὶ, γράμμασιν Ἑλληνικοῖς ἐγκεχαραγμέναι ἐπίσημα] τῶν μετ᾽ Ἀλέξανδρον βεβασιλευκότων Ἀπολλοδότου καὶ Μενάνδρου (trans. Casson 1989). Apollodotos may have been named in CII 2.1, no. 92 as proposed by Jakobsson – Glenn 2018.

35 Coins of Pantaleon and Agathokles (Bopearachchi 1991, pl. 7–9) are extremely similar and it is often presumed that they were brothers (but cf. Glenn 2020, 127). For the leather tax receipt, see CII 2.1, no. 92; and CII 2.1, no. 93; further discussion below and fn. 57–58.

36 Tarn 1938, 90–91. Further discussion in Rapin 2010, 242–243.

37 Bopearachchi 1991, pl. 14 (cf. pl. 5). Coins of Demetrios II did not feature the elephant-helmet, while a standing Athena was chosen as deity on the reverse. This makes it unlikely that Demetrios II was related to Demetrios I, whose coins included the king wearing the elephant helmet on the obverse combined with Herakles on the reverse.

38 Strab. 11.11.2; Iust. 41.6.1.

39 Justin describes an epic battle between Eukratides and Demetrios 'rex Indorum', king of the Indians (Iust. 41.6.4). Though Bopearachchi 1991, 65–66 suggests that this king was Demetrios II, the coins of Demetrios II do not reflect any Indian imagery (see fn. 33). Who Demetrios 'rex Indorum' was, remains unclear (see discussion in Coloru 2009, 109–113, 225–227; Rapin 2010, 240–241). On the rivalry between Menander and Eukratides, see Bopearachchi 1991, 76–88; Bordeaux 2018, 37–46 (on dynastic relations), 112–117. For Menander in Greek sources: Strab. 11.11.1, possibly referred to in 15.1.27; Plut. mor. 821e. For Menander in Indic sources: *Milindapañhā* (Questions of King Milinda), *passim*, but cf. Kubica 2020.

40 Iust. 41.6.5.

in 145 BC, Baktria was plagued by internal political conflicts, local strife, and encroach-
ment by expansionist Arsakid kings from the west and migrating nomadic pastoralists
from the north, which drove kings with Greek names to move their attention south of
the Hindu Kush, where the Indo-Greek kingdom continued to exist until ca. AD 10.

3. The warrior-king in image and name

Although literary and documentary sources allow for a rough historical outline of kings
of Hellenistic Baktria, much remains unclear. Compared to other parts of Hellenistic
Afro-Eurasia, there is a significant lack (or absence) of evidence on royal matters: no
civic decrees, no letters between kings and cities, no written thanksgivings for royal
benefactions, no victory lists of athletic or artistic competitions, and no extensive literary accounts that inform us about how kings represented themselves in interaction
with their subjects.[41] Nevertheless, valuable insights into the workings of Baktrian
kingship and royal representation can be gleaned from coinage, epigraphy, and archaeological remains.

Coinage of the Graeco-Baktrian kings north of the Hindu Kush engaged with familiar coin traditions across Hellenistic Afro-Eurasia: they were locally minted according
to an Attic weight standard and had designs that were artistically and linguistically
similar to numismatic practices in western Asia and Asia Minor.[42] Coin obverses featured a personalized, beardless portrait of the living king wearing the diadem, while
the reverse displayed their patron deity with a Greek legend in the genitive, proclaiming the king's name with the title of *Basileus* ('[coin of] King'). Aligned with Seleukid
coinage, yet unlike coins of the Ptolemies and the Arsakids, the Baktrian kings did not
seem to celebrate a single dynastic founder, propagated through a recurring dynastic
name and deity on their coins.[43] While they kept to similar designs for reasons of recognition and commensurability – coins and their value needed to be acknowledged
in order to be used as payment in local economies – new kings consciously promoted
their own name with a different deity on their reverse types, disassociating themselves
from previous kings. Diodotos elected thundering Zeus (fig. 1) instead of the Seleukid
Apollon, coins of Euthydemos and his son Demetrios featured Herakles (fig. 2), while
Eukratides favoured the Dioskouroi twins on horseback (fig. 6). Menander, ruling
south of the Hindu Kush, likewise disassociated himself from Eukratides, assuming

41   See now Mairs 2020 on various aspects of the Graeco-Baktrian and Indo-Greek world and Morris
      2020ab; 2021ab for valuable reconstructions of the economic history of the 'imperial space' of Cen-
      tral Asia.
42   Cribb 2007, 336–339.
43   The Diodotids, both propagating thundering Zeus on their coin reverses, may form an exception
      and perhaps an example of a failed attempt to start a dynasty.

the patronage of thundering Athena (fig. 7). Where much remains unknown about the identities of the short-reigning kings between Demetrios and Eukratides and those following Menander in India, we may assume that Diodotos, Euthydemos, Eukratides, and Menander represented different royal houses, as literary sources specifically mention them as rebels, usurpers, or rivals to previous or contemporaneous royal power-holders across Central Asia.

That Baktrian kingship developed in distinctly regional contexts of royal strife and competition becomes clear in coin innovations of the first half of the second century BC. In the early 180s BC, with the push into northwest India, headdresses that allude to military victory start to appear on royal coin portraits. Demetrios I is the first of the Baktrian kings to present himself wearing a helmet in the shape of an elephant scalp on coins (fig. 2), an attribute referring to the conquest of India, known in slightly different form from early Ptolemaic coin types depicting Alexander the Great.[44]

Fig. 2 Coin of Demetrios I wearing the elephant scalp helmet.

Demetrios' extensive campaigns in India are confirmed by literary sources, as his achievements were lauded by Strabon and likely referred to by Isidoros of Charax who includes the name-city Demetrias in Arachosia in his periegetic work *Parthian Stations*, written in the first century BC.[45] The depiction of headdresses as a visual tool of military acumen and distinction remained a common feature on coins of the 170s BC. Coin obverses of Antimachos I portrayed him diademed and wearing the *kausia*, a flat Macedonian army cap which symbolized a claim to power and military leadership, evoking connections with Alexander and Macedonian (Hellenistic) kingship, possibly combined with associations with eastwards (Indian) campaigns (fig. 5).[46] Coins

44 For discussion, see Glenn 2020, 35–36. Alexander wearing the elephant scalp likely referred to his Indian campaign and victory over king Poros in the Battle of the Hydaspes in 326 BC but cf. Lorber 2012. Alexander never minted coins in Baktria, but it is likely that his coins did circulate in Central Asia – perhaps posthumously via the Seleukids – as they occur in several Baktrian hoards (Glenn 2020, 26).

45 Strab. 11.11.1; Isid. Char. Parthian Stations 19.

46 Cribb 2007, 340; Janssen 2007, 60–66; Kingsley 1981; cf. Glenn 2020, 37–39. The diadem was tied around the *kausia*.

of Eukratides too featured the king with a military headdress, this time in the form of a crested cavalry helmet – the so-called Boiotian helmet, decorated with a bull's horn and ear (fig. 6).[47]

Other timely innovations in royal representation can be attributed to the decades of the 180s and 170s BC, particularly on coins of Pantaleon and Agathokles and swiftly followed by those of Antimachos. Under Pantaleon but to a greater extent under Agathokles, royal coinage started to include new types in copper and bronze that were square in form and lighter in weight, deviating from the Attic weight standard in adherence to a regional (North-Indian) one.[48] Circulating on both sides of the Hindu Kush, these coins adopted Indic bilingual and biscriptural legends and imagery that appealed to various audiences, an innovation most probably connected to the geopolitical and economic expansion of Baktrian royal influence into northwest India.[49] In Greek language and script on the reverse and Pali language in Brahmi or Kharoshthi script on the obverse, Agathokles proclaimed himself not only as *Basileus* but also as *Raja*. Instead of the royal portrait, these coins graced the depiction of deities of Indian pantheons whose support were invoked, sometimes on both sides but more often with a panther on the reverse (fig. 3). The issuing of bilingual square coins remained a common practice of kings ruling south of the Hindu Kush until the end of the Indo-Greek kingdoms.

Fig. 3 Bilingual coin of Agathokles with an Indian deity, inscribed with Rajane Agathuklayasa (in Brahmi) and ΒΑΣΙΛΕΩ[Σ] – ΑΓΑΘΟΚΛΕΟ[ΥΣ].

Another novelty that seems to have started with the reign of Agathokles is the inclusion of a royal epithet for the living king on coins, a feature unprecedented on Baktri-

---

47   For horns as a marker of divinity on Central Asian coins, see Shenkar 2017, 58–60.
48   Audouin – Bernard 1974; Bopearachchi 1991, pl. 7–8, séries 9–11; and recent discussion in Glenn 2020, 131–148; see also Morris 2021, 455–465 in relation to fiscal regimes and monetization. The output of Pantaleon was much lower, and only included bronze square coins of various weights.
49   On Indic horizons of meaning (*Sinnhorizonte*), see excellent discussion in Dumke 2014. Glenn 2020, 148 is rather cautious in connecting this innovation to political expansion and considers the possibility of the coins facilitating commercial relations with various groups. For economic activities, see Morris 2021.

an – or other Hellenistic (west Asian) – coins before.[50] On his standard monolingual round tetradrachms, characterized by Greek imagery, Agathokles adopted the epithet 'the Just' (*Dikaios*) along his king title on the obverse, while the reverse depicted a standing Zeus holding a tiny figure of Hekate. A local context is the probable reason why Agathokles singled out *Dikaios* out of a repertoire of possible epithets, as this epithet allowed to culturally align himself with Indian ethical views on the righteous conqueror (*dharmavijaya*).[51] Royal epithets are also included in another innovative coin series, the so-called 'pedigree issues'. On these coins, Agathokles advertised a constructed lineage to illustrious kings of the past by presenting their respective coin types with their portrait, name, epithet, and patron deity, combined with his own king title and epithet on the reverse (fig. 4).

Fig. 4 Coin of Agathokles Dikaios, pedigree series with Alexander as Herakles wearing the lion scalp and Zeus enthroned.

In reconstructed order, Agathokles' proclaimed a royal pedigree that reached back to Alexander, son of Philip (*Philippou*), Diodotos the Saviour (*Soter*), Diodotos the God (*Theos*), Antiochos the Victorious (*Nikator*, possibly a Diodotid king), Euthydemos the God (*Theos*), Demetrios the Unconquered (*Aniketos*), and lastly Pantaleon the Saviour (*Soter*).[52] Whether these epithets had been used by the earlier kings them-

---

50   Until the second quarter of the second century BC, royal epithets on coins only occurred on Ptolemaic coins and were reserved for deceased kings only (de Callataÿ – Lorber 2011, 422–423), with the exception of early Arsakid coinage. See extensive discussion on Hellenistic epithets in Muccioli 2013, esp. 281–309, cf. below.

51   *Kauṭiliya Arthaśāstra* 12.1.10–11 (trans. Olivelle 2013). For concepts of kingship in early historic India, see Dwivedi 2020, 108–111.

52   Bopearachichi 1991, 60–61, 177–180, pl. 8, séries 12–19. It has long been assumed that the Antiochos in Agathokles' declared pedigree was the Seleukid king Antiochos II (known as *Theos*; App. Syr. 11.65), whose epithet presumably got mixed up with the epithet of Seleukos I *Nikator*. It has recently been argued that Antiochos *Nikator* was a Baktrian king, rather than a Seleukid overlord (Jakobsson 2010; Glenn 2020, 139–140). NB: Alexander III never adopted the epithet "the Great" (*Megas*) during his reign; this familiar epithet was posthumously ascribed to him – the earliest attestation is by Plautus (Mostell. 3.2.775), a comic playwright of the Roman Republic whose works date to shortly after Baktria's 'independence' in the mid-third century BC.

selves, is difficult to ascertain, if not unlikely. A dedicatory inscription to Hestia, found at Kulob in southern Tajikistan, does provide us with a case of nicknames – sobriquets rather than epithets – given unofficially to the kings. In this text, the dedicator Heliodotos speaks of offerings made to Hestia to bestow good fortune on Euthydemos and his son Demetrios, named respectively as 'the Greatest' (*Megistos*) and '[Winner] of Noble Victory' (*Kallinikos*).[53] Both nicknames notably deviate from the royal epithets in Agathokles' pedigree and were possibly venerable cult titles, considering the nature of the text. The Kulob inscription bespeaks the reception and recognition of the achievements of the Euthydemids by their subjects, though it remains unclear to what extent these nicknames interacted with official epithets with which the kings represented themselves.

Lauranne Martinez-Sève suggested that Heliodotos probably did not invent these epithets on his own and that they were popularized by Euthydemos and Demetrios, whose epithet *Kallinikos* would serve to align himself to (and possibly assimilate with) Herakles and his heroic exploits in the Far East.[54] It is a compelling interpretation which, however, complicates the use of different epithets in Agathokles' pedigree: if Euthydemos and Demetrios initiated the use of the epithets mentioned in the Kulob inscription, why did Agathokles not use the same ones? He was likely not uninformed: *Aniketos* evokes a similar warrior-like quality as *Kallinikos* but with significantly grander implications. Considering the unruly times of the 180s BC, it is most plausible that Agathokles posthumously conferred and manipulated royal epithets in the pedigree series to suit his timely self-stylization, which allowed him to adapt and appropriate numerous exceptional, and indeed, divine qualities through this professed lineage on coins. Antimachos I, ruling after Agathokles, also issued "pedigree coins" with types and epithets of Diodotos *Soter* and Euthydemos *Theos*, although a recent die study suggests that they seem to have been intended for limited circulation.[55]

The practice of including glorifying epithets for living kings in coin legends appears to have had more consistent ideological appeal than the pedigree tradition – which reoccurred only once in a later series issued by Laodike and Heliokles.[56] The tradition of epithets progressed further under Antimachos I. His standard silver coinage portrayed

---

53   The Kulob inscription: CII 2.1, no. 151, published by Bernard et al. 2004; see also Hollis 2011.

54   Martinez-Sève 2010a, 14. The epithet *Kallinikos* was also used by Seleukos II but Demetrios' adoption of the title, if this was the case, probably signified a more general connection to Herakles rather than a specifically Seleukid connection. On the usage of *Kallinikos*, see discussion in Muccioli 2013, 342–345.

55   Glenn 2020, 152–153, 157–158. Only a small number of pedigree coins and only with obverse portraits of Diodotos Soter and Euthydemos Theos are known to have been issued by Antimachos. These were minted with reused obverse dies from Agathokles' pedigree series and produced only shortly at the beginning of Antimachos I's reign – Glenn suggests a pragmatic motive for this: to uphold the coin production to pay soldiers in the face of the power transition.

56   See fn. 67.

him wearing the *kausia* and, for the first time, with the epithet God (*Theos*) which proclaimed the king as divine (fig. 5).

Fig. 5 Coin of Antimachos I Theos wearing the *kausia*.

The accepted use of the divine title is confirmed by the Asangorna parchment, a formal tax receipt on leather which used the following dating formula: 'in the reign of God Antimachos and Eumenes and Antimachos … year 4, month of Olöus … in Asangorna'.[57] The absence of epithets for Eumenes and Antimachos, presumably sons of Antimachos I, stands in stark contrast with the lofty appellation for Antimachos I.[58] This lack may indicate their subordinance as sub-kings of different areas of an expanding kingdom. It is notable that the epithet *Theos* was not invoked immediately when Antimachos came to power, but seemed to have been adopted later in his reign. An older inscription of a similar tax receipt from a place called Amphipolis used a dating formula *without* the divine epithet while logging according to an different calendar: 'in the reign of Antimachos in year 30 in Amphipolis …'.[59] The difference in administrative time-keeping in the Amphipolis inscription and in the Asangorna inscription not only indicates a significant ideological change in Antimachos I's royal status, but also provides a glimpse of the actual consequences involved. The shift from 'year 30' to 'year 4' indicates recent abandonment of an old calendar and instalment of a new one to regulate administrative affairs, its beginnings marked by the coregency between An-

57 CII 2.1, no. 92: [βασιλευό]ντων θεοῦ Ἀντιμάχου καὶ Εὐμένους καὶ Ἀντιμάχο[υ] τ[ῶν υἱῶν αὐτ]οῦ, ἔτους δ', μηνὸς Ὀλώιου, ἐν Ἀσαγγώρνοις … Published by Bernard – Rapin 1994; Rea – Senior – Hollis 1994; Rapin 1996; further discussion in Rapin 2010; and recently Jakobsson – Glenn 2018. Olöus or Loios was a Macedonian month name, its usage common in calendars of the Seleukid, Ptolemaic, and Antigonid kings.

58 On Eumenes and Antimachos as sons, see Rea – Senior – Hollis 1994, 275–176.

59 CII 2.1, no. 93: Βασιλεύοντος Ἀντιμάχου ἔτους τριακοστοῦ [μηνὸς – –] ἐν Ἀμφιπόλει … Published by Clarysse – Thompson 2007, 275–277. Amphipolis is assumed to have been in Baktria. Both the Amphipolis inscription and the Asangorna inscription originated from the northern Hindu Kush regions.

timachos I, Eumenes, and the younger Antimachos II.[60] Such a power move – the introduction of a new dating system and the proclamation of an explicitly divine epithet while still alive – was likely prompted by a revolutionary historical event that merited the heralding of a new age. An appealing explanation, Claude Rapin argued that the occasion must have been a grand geopolitical unity of both sides of the Hindu Kush, presumably achieved through an allied victory by Antimachos (in the north) and Apollodotos (in the south) – their coins shared the same monogram and depiction of the king wearing the *kausia* – over a common rival, Agathokles.[61] Recent infrared analysis of the Asangorna parchment even raises the possibility that Apollodotos was included in the royal dating formula as fourth joint-king of Baktria under Antimachos I.[62] Rapin proposed to date this grand achievement to the year 175 BC, identifying Antimachos' inaugural age as the Yona era ('Greek' era), known from an inscription on a Buddhist reliquary, and aligning it with the reign of Antiochos IV (175–164 BC), who adopted the same divine epithet on his lifetime coinage for the first time as he declared himself God Manifest (*Theos Epiphanes*).[63]

The innovations of royal representation in the dynamic years of the 180s and 170s carried momentum into the following decades, with the reign of Eukratides (171–145 BC). His coins portrayed him wearing a military headdress (the Boiotian helmet) and later glorified him with the epithet 'the Great': *Basileos Megalou Eukratidou* ([coin of the] great king Eukratides).[64] Eukratides' grandiose title was probably connected to geopolitical victories in India, although the precise circumstances of this feat remain unclear. With the inclusion of the epithet in the legend, the position of the inscription changed to a circular line along the contours of the coin, combined with a horizontal line below (fig. 6). Eukratides not only (visually and ideologically) extended the royal title but also expanded the imagery on the reverse of his coins. Instead of a single standing deity, he evoked divine patronage of the Dioskouroi in an elaborate military scene of the twin gods holding spears, palms, or both, striding or galloping on horseback. According to Greek myth, as Diodoros informs us, the divine twins Polydeukes

60   This new dating system of 'year 4' most likely reflected the introduction of a new era rather than a regnal period of a single king; for references see fn. 57. For discussion on the beginning of the preceding era, that of 'year 30', see Clarysse – Thompson 2007, 275–277; Rapin 2010.

61   Rapin 2010, 242–245; but cf. Martinez-Sève 2015, 38 fn. 120. See also Rea – Senior – Hollis 1994, 275; Widemann 2007, 11–12; Coloru 2009, 198–202.

62   Jakobsson – Glenn 2018, 65.

63   Rea – Senior – Hollis 1994, 277; Coloru 2009, 198 (176 BC); Rapin 2010, 242. On the date of 175/174 BC for the beginning of the 'Yona era' (Yavana era i. e. [Indo-]Greek era), see Cribb 2005, 214, corroborated by Falk 2007, 135–136; Falk – Bennett 2009; Rapin 2010; cf. Mittag 2006, 32–33. Further discussion in Coloru 2009, 187–199. It should be noted that coins of Ptolemaios V *Epiphanes* (r. 204–180 BC) already included a royal epithet, but this referred to the deified status of his father Ptolemaios IV *Philopator*, not to his own divinity (de Callataÿ – Lorber 2011, 423–424).

64   ΒΑΣΙΛΕΩΣ ΜΕΓΑΛΟΥ ΕΥΚΡΑΤΙΔΟΥ; Bopearachchi 1991, pl. 16–22, séries 4–8, 11–12, 17–24. On the title great king cf. also the chapter by Shane Wallace in this volume.

and Kastor were known for their exceptional valour, manly spirit and military skill –
heroic qualities that were visibly asserted on Eukratides' coin imagery.[65] A particular
obverse type showcased a notable part of Eukratides' nude bust rather than a head
portrait, which allowed him to boast his muscular shoulder and arm while throwing
a spear (fig. 6) – a most explicit visualization of the king's military prowess which not
only alluded to the Hellenistic justification of 'spear-won-land' (*doriktetos chora*) but
also echoed thundering Zeus on Diodotid coins.[66] This image was innovative in another aspect as well, as the king faced to the left rather than to the right as in all other
Graeco-Baktrian coins.

The effective appeal of Eukratides' royal representation is demonstrated by a later
"pedigree series" issued by Laodike and Heliokles – joint rulers whose identities remain unknown – which visually and textually invoked the authority of a helmeted or
spear-throwing Eukratides on their reverse.[67] South of the Hindu Kush, Menander I
also interacted with the innovative royal imagery of Eukratides, his rival in India.
Emphasizing royal and god-like qualities of heroic courage and military prowess,
Menander's coins similarly brandished the king's spear-throwing skills with a bust
facing to the right (fig. 7), sometimes depicted with the Boiotian helmet. Different
than Eukratides' nude bust, however, a shield covered Menander's left shoulder on
his early obverse types which visually mirrored the reverse image of his patron deity,
thundering Athena holding her aegis over her arm.[68] This obverse type is commonly
referred to Athena *Alkidemos* (Defender of the People), known from Antigonid coin
types, but it is highly questionable whether this 'Macedonian' Athena, associated with
her worship at Pella, retained its specific meaning under Menander and his intended audience in India.[69] From the start of his reign, Menander's coins, including types
featuring thundering Athena, were issued with bilingual and biscriptural legends that
proclaimed him as 'Saviour' in Greek on the obverse and Kharoshthi on the reverse:
Basileos Soteros Menandrou and *Maharajasa Tratarasa Menamdrasa*, respectively. Rather than propagating a Macedonian connection, Menander's coinage with a patron deity in the iconography of Athena likely articulated the king's warlike persona as a heroic
saviour, a message designed to be legible in cultural realms on both sides of the Hindu

65   Diod. 6.6.
66   Bopearachchi 1991, pl. 19, série 8.
67   Bopearachchi 1991, pl. 19–20, séries 13–16. It was long thought that these "pedigree coins" were
      issued by Eukratides who advertised his lineage to his parents Laodike and Heliokles with their
      jugate busts on the obverse. However, a die study by Glenn 2014 convincingly demonstrated that
      it were Laodike and Heliokles (possibly sub-kings or later kings) who asserted (royal?) power
      through Eukratides, rather than the other way around.
68   Bopearachchi 1991, pl. 26–27, séries 3–8.
69   Brett 1950, esp. 64–65. Tarn 1938, 261 interpreted the presence of Athena on Menander's coins as a
      move to signify Menander's Greekness. Athena *Alkidemos* also appeared on coins of Ptolemaios I,
      depicted to right rather than to left – a type quickly substituted for Zeus enthroned.

Kush, shaped by Menander's rivalry with Eukratides whom he outruled in India.[70] The warlike figure of Athena may further have been interpreted by some audiences as Nana who later became an important royal patron deity under the Kushan kings.[71] It is notable that the Kharoshthi legend presented Menander as 'Great King' (*Maharaja*), possibly echoing the grandiose epithet of Eukratides, whereas the Greek version only used the standard royal title. This may suggest a greater importance attached to presenting himself as such to Indian-speaking contingents of Menander's intended audience in light of his defeat of Eukratides, possibly aimed towards other, more eastern political rivalries in the Punjab.

Fig. 6 Coin of Eukratides I throwing the spear.

Fig. 7 Bilingual coin of Menander I throwing the spear, inscribed with ΒΑΣΙΛΕΩΣ ΣΩΤΗΡΟΣ | ΜΕΝΑΝΔΡΟΥ and *Maharajasa tratarasa Menamdrasa* (in Kharoshthi).

Royal representations on coins of the first half of the second century BC testify to an accepted notion of kingship that was intimately tied to Achaimenid and Hellenistic ideas of the warrior king, yet different in its operationalization. Rulers of Baktria, whether they were each other's kinsmen, allies, or opponents, all integrated and innovated visual and textual statements on coins that differentiated and elevated the king

---

70   Kubica 2020, 435–438; also relevant is Dumke 2014.
71   On Nana in Central Asia, see Shenkar 2014, 119–127, cf. fig. 95.

through his personalized heroic (and increasingly divine) qualities, portraying them as exceptionally brave, noble, personally engaged in battle, and above all, great in victory.

4. Material display of wealth and prestige

But coins were not the only tools of royal representation. Apart from the dissemination of the king's exceptional qualities and achievements via coins, kings in Baktria made extensive efforts to advertise their glory and power through material displays of wealth and prestige.[72] A unique site in its monumentality and the massive extent of excavations it received by the *Délégation archéologique française en Afghanistan* (1964–1978), the city of Ai Khanum in eastern Baktria illuminates essential contexts of kingship beyond the numismatic material.[73] Founded by Seleukos I or Antiochos I at the strategic intersection of the Oxos and the Pandj rivers, the town was planned to be a site of power and royalty, forming a central node of control in a network of garrisons and strongholds across the Upper Satrapies.[74] Yet, nothing is known about Ai Khanum – a modern Uzbek name – from ancient literary sources. Although the site and its mixed material culture entered modern historiography as a splendid example of an "outpost of Hellenism in the East", Ai Khanum only gradually gained its urban appearance in several phases which can be linked to distinct ambitions of royal representation of the Graeco-Baktrian kings (fig. 8).[75]

4.1 Builder-kings and monumentalizing efforts

The first buildings at Ai Khanum date to the years of the coregency of Antiochos I (291–281 BC) with continuing works undertaken by the first Graeco-Baktrian kings, a period which saw the construction of defensive ramparts, a main street, and at least two religious structures: a central shrine set in a wider sanctuary and an intramural mausoleum (sometimes termed a *heroon*).[76] It is well possible that the temple outside the city walls, a second mausoleum (the 'stone-vault mausoleum'), and the cultic platform on the acropolis also saw their construction in the first half of the third century BC. Substantial investment in religious structures was ingrained in Seleukid royal ideology which developed in distinct interaction with and emulation of Near East-

---

72   Gehrke 2013, 81.
73   See now Mairs 2022. For the excavation history of Ai Khanum by the DAFA, see Bernard 2001; Martinez-Sève 2020, 218–225.
74   Martinez-Sève 2014.
75   For a discussion on Ai Khanum in relation to Hellenism, see Hoo 2018; 2022, 73–108, 244–251; for Ai Khanum's material culture reflecting a distinct Graeco-Baktrian *koine*, see Mairs 2014b, 57–101.
76   Martinez-Sève 2014; 2015. This phase stretches across Ceramic Periods I–III: Lyonnet 2012; 2013.

ern (particularly Babylonian) traditions of kingship: a good king was a builder king.[77] Indeed, the earliest version of the town under Antiochos I was defined by religious structures; these were square and symmetrical in ground plan and all raised on a high podium oriented to the east which spatially and visually evoked an aura of eminence and authority. Recipients of cults remain hypothetical; the only securely known recipient is Kineas, presumably the founding hero of Ai Khanum who was buried in the mausoleum and named in a dedicatory inscription in Greek, alongside five verses of

Fig. 8a Plan of Ai Khanum, ca. 150 BC. The palatial district, including the palace complex, the gymnasium, the mausolea, and the main sanctuary, is located on the west side of the main street.

77   On the development of a distinctly Seleukid vocabulary of power, see Canepa 2015a; 2015b; 2020.

the Delphic maxims that were engraved on a stele in the shrine's antechamber.[78] These early religious structures at Ai Khanum coincided with the construction of the monumental Oxos Temple at Takht-i Sangin and the cultic terrace at Torbulok (both in southern Tajikistan) which similarly saw their beginnings in the third century BC.[79]

Baktrian kingship practices, in turn, engaged with and developed from established ways of Hellenistic rule. Apart from adapting Seleukid royal coinage, the first Graeco-Baktrian rulers also carried out similar reconstructions of religious structures at Ai Khanum in the second half of the third century BC, befitting the notion of a great builder king. Under Diodotos I or Diodotos II, after assuming the royal title, the main temple at Ai Khanum was completely levelled and built anew while preserv-

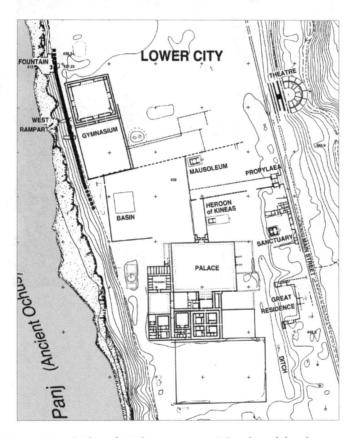

Fig. 8b Plan of Ai Khanum, ca. 150 BC, enlarged detail.

78 CII 2.1, no. 97a, 97b; published in Robert 1973, 211, 213. Further discussion in Mairs 2014a; 2022, 306–309.
79 For Takht-i Sangin, see Litvinsky – Pichikyan 2002, 19, 37. For Torbulok, see Lindström 2014; 2017; 2021.

ing its squared form: distinctive indented niches were added to the outer walls, a new staircase was cut into the platform to form a monumental entrance, while the interior space was renovated to house a broad antechamber, a main vestibule, and two smaller L-shaped side rooms, possibly to house a divine triad – a layout that was retained until the destruction of the city (fig. 9).[80]

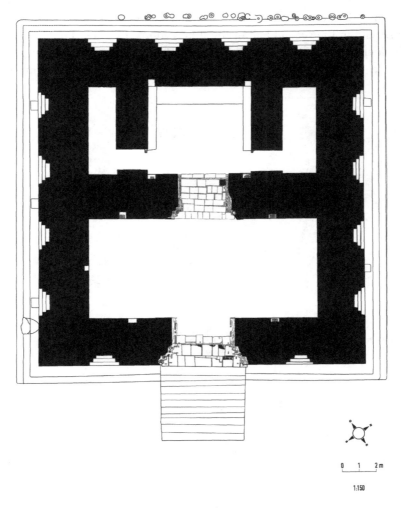

Fig. 9 Plan of the main temple at Ai Khanum (phase III: le temple à niches indentées), beginning of the second century BC.

80   Martinez-Sève 2010b, 202–203; further discussion on the temple in relation to ethnic and civic identity in Mairs 2013. Coins of Diodotos, issued with his name in the royal legend, were found in this layer.

At the beginning of the second century BC, Ai Khanum entered a new phase of demographic growth and increasing monumentalization that transformed its urban landscape, probably on initiative of Euthydemos I after his treaty with Antiochos III in 205 BC.[81] Coins of Euthydemos are most heavily represented in the coin record of Ai Khanum.[82] Standing his ground against the Seleukid incursion, Euthydemos capitalized on the ideological weight of the treaty – a significant moment of royal endorsement that called for a matching reflection in the built environment. He commissioned an extensive building programme which resulted in the development of Ai Khanum into a proper town with different buildings. A grand gateway was constructed on the main street which spatially marked the beginnings of a new royal district that represented the might of the Graeco-Baktrian king. Euthydemos likely began the construction of the palace concurrently with the *propylaia*, although the precise chronology of this complex remains obscure. The early second century BC also saw the building of private mansions in the southern part of the lower city, innovations in ceramic forms that testify to new trends in drinking and eating, and major renovations of the main sanctuary and the mausoleum of Kineas.[83] This building programme may have been financed by riches gained from military victories in India: Strabon mentions Euthydemos as a mighty king who gained mastery over the fertile lands of Ariana and India, while Demetrios' coin portraits donned him with the elephant helmet; especially Demetrios, as discussed above, was hailed as a noble victor in the Kulob inscription.[84]

The drive to aggrandize the city carried momentum into the second quarter of the second century BC. Possibly on commission of Antimachos I, notable building activities took place north of the palace, which included the construction of a sizable bathing complex.[85] But it was in the final decades before its destruction around 145 BC, that Ai Khanum reached its peak. Eukratides commissioned another grand building programme that brought the urban landscape of Ai Khanum to new heights, with the construction of a gymnasion in place of the structures north of the palace, a massive theatre on the slopes of the acropolis, and further city-wide renovations.[86] Although the gymnasion and the theatre made the city famous in modern historiography as an

---

81 Martinez-Sève 2015, 35–38; this phase aligns with Ceramic Period IV (Lyonnet 2012; 2013); see further Holt 1999, 126–133; Coloru 2009, 175–193.

82 Petitot-Biehler – Bernard 1975; numismatic discussion in Kritt 2001, 70–127.

83 Renovations of the main sanctuary received recent publication in Martinez-Sève 2021. For the ceramic forms, see Lyonnet 2013; further recent discussion in Junker 2021.

84 Strab. 11.1.1; CII 2.1, no. 151.

85 Veuve 1987, 52–56. Much remains unknown about these buildings.

86 This peak is attributed to Eukratides rather than to Antimachos, as his greatness was remembered in narratives of literary sources (Iust. 41.6.1–5; Strab. 11.11.2) while the construction of the theatre and the gymnasium during this building phase outdate the reign of Antimachos. Coins of Eukratides are moreover heavier represented in Ai Khanum's numismatic record, although it can be assumed that Antimachos held the city for a short period (Cribb 2005, 210–212; Ball et al. 2019, 338–339).

outpost of Hellenism in the East, signifying the ethnic Greek belonging of its settlers, their construction should be seen as inherent part of a royal agenda of monumentalization to display the building accomplishments of the king.[87]

4.2 The palatial district at Ai Khanum

Not much is known about the palace before Eukratides, but it was in the last grand building programme during his reign in the second quarter of the second century BC that this structure became an opulent mega complex, set in a public royal district which came to occupy almost a third of the lower city (fig. 8) – comparable to the *basileia* in Ptolemaic Alexandreia.[88] The beginnings of this prominent district had already been undertaken under Euthydemos after 205 BC, as he had commissioned the construction of the monumental *propylaia* on the main street which routed movement to the palatial complex.[89] Strabon's mention of the royal name-city Eukratideia – if we assume that it referred to Ai Khanum as renovated under Eukratides – as well as the overall monumentality suggests that this enormous complex was royal rather than satrapal in nature.[90] The presence of residential sections donned with pebbled-mosaic floored bathrooms indicates that this complex was not only a ceremonial centre for official audiences at the court but also fulfilled the function of a residence for the king (and his family) and possibly his coregent.[91] Its colossal ground plan has been compared to palatial architecture in Achaimenid Babylonia and Susiana, particularly the palace of Dareios I at Susa.[92] It had several large courtyards and a markedly symmetrical and modular structure of space, regulated by long and narrow peripheral corridors around and between distinct yet connected units of the complex. These peripheral corridors regulating movement and spatial access were typical for Ai Khanum as well as for regional Baktrian architecture.[93]

Visitors would have to cross a grandiose peristyle courtyard in order to enter the inner palace through an impressive 'forest of columns' of a hypostyle hall. This entrance hall created an atmosphere of verticality perhaps similar to the *apadana* in Susa and

---

87   For critical discussion, see Hoo 2018; 2022.

88   Strab. 17.1.8: τὰ βασίλεια. Fraser 1972 remains relevant for Alexandreia; see now also Riedel 2020. Bernard 2009, 41 states that from the onset, this area was intended for the development of a palace; see further discussion in Martinez-Sève 2014.

89   On zoning strategies in Ai Khanum, see Mairs 2014b, 65–66 (in relation to the palace district). Mairs 2014b 77–78 argues for a much earlier date of a palatial district, presuming an earlier Achaimenid palace that was replaced by a Hellenistic one.

90   Strab. 11.11.2; Bernard 2009, 42.

91   Bernard 2009, 42; Mairs 2014b, 69–72. For the residential sections, see Lecuyot 2013, 194–197; further discussion on the mosaics of Ai Khanum in Giesser 2017.

92   Bernard 1976, 253–254.

93   Mairs 2014b, 79–82 analyses these as part of a Graeco-Baktrian architectural koine.

Persepolis, though on a much smaller scale.[94] The walking distance from the *propylaia* to this hall (around 100 meters) would provide visitors ample time for awe and admiration. The enormous dimensions and monumentality of the palatial complex, especially its impressive peristyle courtyards and hypostyle hall, decorated with Corinthian and Doric columns, clearly reflect power practices to express royal rule through the built environment, as was done by previous and contemporaneous imperial power holders. Additionally, the empty spaces adjacent to the north and the west of the palace, or on the enormous southern courtyard within its enclosure may have functioned as garden and hunting areas (*paradeisoi*), similar to Mesopotamian and Iranian palaces, boasting of the kingdom's wealth, extent, and diversity through its flora and fauna.[95] This would certainly suit the ideological programme behind the aggrandizement of the palatial district of Ai Khanum: the palace was not only intended to receive visitors but also to visually remind observers of the king and his power, to be an impressive royal monument that provided his might with material permanence, also in absentia – when he was away on military campaign.

Under the reign of Eukratides, a royal treasury was added in the west wing of the palace, though its construction never saw its completion when Ai Khanum came to its end.[96] Here, inscriptions record the storage of olive oil and incense which allude to convivial and ritual ceremonies that took place elsewhere in the palace.[97] The treasury also hints at royal patronage of the arts, though it should be noted that these sections could only be accessed from the residential quarters of the palace. In one storage room, likely a royal library, the imprints of two decomposed manuscripts written in Greek were unearthed: a dramaturgical text in iambic trimeter and a philosophical dialogue outlining the Platonic theory of ideas.[98] Paleographically dated between the mid-third and early second century BC, Rapin proposed these texts to have originated from the Mediterranean before they were brought to Ai Khanum, where their storage in the palace library – adjacent to a peristyle courtyard that accommodated reflective strolls by learned visitors – would fit the role of the king and his court as learned patrons of culture.[99]

That patronage of scholarship, literature, and the arts and attendant investment in appropriate infrastructure for the cultured elites formed part of kingship practices by the time of Eukratides can also be seen elsewhere in the royal precinct. A construction

94 For the palace of Ai Khanum being modelled after Achaemenid and Neo-Babylonian examples, see Bernard 1976, 253–257. For columned halls, see Gopnik 2010.
95 Nielsen 1994, 127–128; Farrar 2016, 112–113. Cf. Canepa 2018, 353, postulates a *paradeisos* situated within the space of the southernmost courtyard of the palace of Ai Khanum.
96 Rapin 1987, 49.
97 CII 2.1, no. 99–120, published by Rapin 1992, 95–114. In relation to economic history, Morris 2020a, 408–410.
98 CII 2.1, no. 131–132, published by Rapin – Hadot – Cavallo 1987; Rapin 1992, 115–123.
99 Rapin 1987, 50. Cf. the chapter of Christoph Michels in this volume on this aspect of Hellenistic kingship.

that similarly remained unfinished when Ai Khanum was destroyed around 145 BC
was the grand gymnasion north of the palace, which provided a more public venue
for academic and athletic activities than the royal library in the inner palace. Here,
the French archaeologists excavated small finds such as limestone sundials and strigil
fragments to scrape off sweat and oil from the skin, while a pool enclosure to the south
and a fountain to the north possibly provided washing facilities.[100] A statue of a bearded herm bore a dedicatory inscription to Hermes and Herakles, patron deities of the
gymnasion, which reflected cultural understandings that were shared across the Hellenistic world.[101] The gymnasion, probably constructed upon royal commission, provided an arena not only for cultural activities but also for competition among wealthy
civic and regional elites that frequented these quarters.[102] One early example of such an
elite member is Klearchos, the notable dedicator of the inscribed stele with Delphic
maxims which was set up in the mausoleum of Kineas, situated on the promenade
leading to the palace and thus part of the royal precinct. The mausoleum inscription
not only named Kineas as the chief occupant of the tomb-shrine but especially boasted
of Klearchos' travels and intellectual acquaintance with a prominent site in the wider
world, appropriate to the self-representation of a *pepaideumenos*: 'There [at the Apollon temple at Delphi], Klearchos copied them [the maxims] conscientiously and set
them up here in the sanctuary of Kineas, blazing from afar.'[103] His descendants may
well have been among those that frequented another arena that facilitated culture and
competition: the grand theatre on the slope of the acropolis across the palatial district,
constructed in mud brick around the same time as the gymnasium, in the last decades
of the city under Eukratides.

4.3 Kingship and the divine

Baktrian kings were mostly away to war, not only to expand their influence and control
over networks and resources but above all to uphold and increase their charismatic
persona as victorious warrior-kings to ensure the loyalty of their army and subjects.

---

100   Veuve 1987, 33.
101   CII 2.1, no. 98, published by Robert 1968; Bernard 1973, 208–211. On the cultural understandings
       connected to the gymnasion in Hellenistic times, see Bringmann 2004.
102   The location of the gymnasion, within the palatial quarter, suggests that it was built upon royal
       commission. It was, moreover, built after the demolition of an older monumental structure, pos-
       sibly a pool complex (Bernard 1978, 429; Veuve 1987, 43–58, 107–108; Lecuyot 2013, 198). The im-
       mense efforts of deconstructing this building to replace it with a gymnasium, prominently located
       across the palace proper, suggests that this was done upon royal commission, although involve-
       ment of intellectual elites should not be excluded.
103   CII 2.1, no. 97a: (…) Πυθοῖ ἐν ἠγαθέαι ἔνθεν ταῦτ[α] Κλέαρχος ἐπιφραδέως ἀναγράψας εἴσατο
       τηλαυγῆ Κινέου ἐν τεμένει. Published by Robert 1968, see esp. 443–454 on Klearchos; further dis-
       cussion in Mairs 2014a.

That the persona of the king increasingly gained divine associations is not only suggested by developments in the iconography and inscriptions on royal coins, but also
in the transformation of Ai Khanum's urban landscape in the first half of the second
century BC. The monumental building programmes of Euthydemos and later Eukratides saw the construction of the *propylaia* and the development of a grand royal district
which was deliberately built around the early structures of the main sanctuary and the
mausoleum of Kineas (fig. 8). This new urban zone therefore spatially and ideologically incorporated important older religious buildings, integrating them in the sphere of
the palace to signify close proximity between the royal and the divine. We may entertain the thought that the promenade that connected the palace to the main street may
have facilitated ceremonial or religious processions that paraded the greatness of the
king. It can only be imagined that such processions journeyed from outside, routing
from the plain of Ai Khanum along the extramural temple via the northern ramparts
into the city, and via the main road to the palatial district. Spectators and participants
of such processions from across the kingdom would flock to Ai Khanum, although the
limited evidence leaves us with mere speculations. The grand dimensions of both the
gymnasion and the theatre do suggest that these buildings accommodated more people than actually inhabited the city.[104] Thus, *if* royal processions took place, they may
well have been organized (or envisioned to take place) in combination with athletic
and theatrical games – theories which can only be entertained for the second quarter
of the second century BC, when the theatre and the gymnasion were built.

There are, however, more archaeological indications of an exceptional relationship
to the gods that was proclaimed by Baktrian kings. Ai Khanum's main temple and its
wider temenos were not only seamlessly integrated in the palace district, but were also
the focus of regular royal building efforts, receiving continuous architectural renova-
tion and maintenance throughout its existence (fig. 9). Furthermore, fragments of anthropomorphic statues were found in the main temple. The sandaled foot of the cult
statue, decorated with a thunderbolt, is most famous among these, which led to the
hypothesis that Zeus – possibly syncretized with an Iranian deity – was worshipped
here.[105] But this was not the only statue in the sanctuary: clay and plaster diademed
heads of once life-sized naturalistic statues, one female and one male, were unearthed
in the pronaos of the temple; they were originally placed on mud brick pedestals on
either side of the doorway to the main chamber.[106] Elsewhere in the wider temenos, in
a chapel on the north side of the courtyard, a sculpted finger of another cult statue was
found, one likewise raised on a mud brick pedestal. Martinez-Sève suggested that the
statue in the chapel and the statues in the temple's pronaos represented royal figures

---

104 The theatre is estimated to facilitate over 6,000 visitors (Bernard 1978, 432–433).
105 See e. g. Bernard 1969, 340–341; Francfort 1984, 35–37, 125–125; Grenet 1991; Martinez-Sève 2010a,
     13; Francfort 2012.
106 Bernard 1969, 344; Martinez-Sève 2010b, 203.

(the king and members of the royal family), possibly as recipients of a ruler cult.[107] Rachel Mairs agrees while also reminding of the possibility that these statues could have presented these royals in a mere civic capacity, as patrons of royal cult.[108] The identities of the figures and the precise circumstances of related ritual activities remain unclear, but the fact that these representations were placed in the interior of the temple and the chapel, within the main temenos in close proximity to the palace, does hint at certain ideological connections to royal personae.

Other sculpted ruler portraits have been discovered in the grand Oxos Temple at Takht-i Sangin, a monumental Baktrian sanctuary dedicated to the Central Asian river Oxos (Vakhsh) and probably built on royal initiative in the third century BC. Among its votive collections were two beardless diademed portraits of an older man (fig. 10) and a younger man, which stylistically echoed images of other Hellenistic rulers, while a third portrait represented a bearded man wearing the *kyrbasia* – an Iranian satrapal headdress.[109] The diademed heads crowned once half-life-sized statues, while the third portrait was part of a smaller statue that was roughly a third in life-size. If the diademed portraits represented kings and the bearded man a satrap, governor, or client-king, it would indicate that various rulers – kings and representative governors – could have their statue placed in a temple and receive honours if not some form of cultic worship.[110] Significantly so, no remains of a cult statue of the Oxos god were found. The diademed portraits were found deposited in the long corridors in the rear part of the Oxos Temple, which functioned as storage galleries for votive gifts. Gunvor Lindström argued that the stored objects were likely moved there after having initially been more accessible or visible elsewhere, either in the columned hall of the temple or on the courtyard of the sanctuary.[111] It might well have been the case that the statues were originally presented in the front part of the Oxos Temple, in similar fashion as the statues in the pronaos of the niched temple at Ai Khanum. In the same corridor as one of the diademed portraits, the broken statues of two draped half-life-sized female figures and two other unidentifiable statues were unearthed, indicating, perhaps, that cultic honours were extended to royal family members who received effigies within sacred premises.[112]

---

107   Martinez-Sève 2018, 383–384 suggests Eukratides as possible recipient; see also 2010a, 18; 2010b, 203.
108   Mairs 2022, 302.
109   Hansen – Wieczorek – Tellenbach 2009, 351–352, nos. 232, 233, 234. Another example of a royal portrait is the faience diademed head which presumably originated from Ai Khanum, but without secure archaeological context; see discussion in Bopearachchi 1998.
110   See recent discussion in Mairs 2022, 300–302. It should be noted that the *kyrbasia* could also signify conquest (as discussed further below).
111   Lindström 2013a, 302–303; 2013b, 103.
112   Hansen – Wieczorek – Tellenbach 2009, 351–352, no. 237; Lindström 2013b, 103–104.

Fig. 10 Diademed portrait unearthed in corridor 2, Oxus Temple, Takht-i Sangin.

The female statues were already broken before they were deposited, since the upper and lower bodies were unearthed some meters away from each other.[113] Anjelina Drujinina and Lindström therefore argued that the movement of the sculptures to storage must have happened shortly after the sanctuary experienced a destruction wave, which they associate with either an Arsakid invasion under Mithradates I (between 163–150 BC) or a nomadic invasion under the Yuezhi (between 140–130 BC).[114] But if the female statues originally were part of a royal group, together with the statues with the diademed portraits, we may entertain a different possibility here, connecting the question of why and when the statues were moved to storage with the elusive identity of those they represented. While Boris Litvinsky, the main excavator of the Oxos temple, suggested that the diademed portraits were likely local governors with royal authority, Kazim Abdullaev more compellingly argued that they may have represented the kings Euthydemos and Demetrios.[115] Abdullaev pointed out that this father-son

113   Lindström 2016, 295.
114   I. e. before 'Fußboden 2' was laid on top of the votive collection; Drujinina – Lindström 2013, 184 consider this layer as an act of restoration after the invasion and therefore evidence for the cultic continuity of the temple. On possible dates for the Parthian invasion of Mithradates I, see Olbrycht 2010, 237; Lerner 2015, 46.
115   Litvinsky 2003, 55; (but cf. Litvinsky – Pichikyan 1994, 61); Abdullaev 2017, 227–229.

pair not only makes sense because of the stylistic similarity and the different ages of the portraits but also, particularly, in light of their glorifying mention in the Kulob inscription. The inscription states that sacrifices were made to Hestia for the fortune of Euthydemos and Demetrios and, as discussed above, praises their honourable qualities that merited divine fortune. Even if the text does not explicitly state that the rulers themselves were recipients of cultic worship, it does place them in a context of worship. Martinez-Seve suggested on the basis of numismatic finds that the Oxos Temple may have been completely rebuilt during Euthydemos' reign at the beginning of the second century BC, replacing an older temple.[116] The decision to place and display royal statues of himself and his son in the Temple of the Oxos would be a bold move that would fit Euthydemos' contemporaneous grand building programme at Ai Khanum which saw the beginnings of the palatial district in proximity of the divine. If the identification of the diademed portraits with Euthydemos and Demetrios is correct, it may well be possible that the removal of their royal effigies from visible places to storage in the rear end of the temple was a delegitimizing act by those ruling after them, in the context of the highly competitive royal milieu during the first half of the second century BC.

Are these royal statues then to be considered as evidence for a Baktrian ruler cult? Recent discussion by Mairs cautions for over-interpretation: we ultimately do not know who dedicated these sculptures, who precisely they represented, and whether they were actually objects of worship. What these sculptures do affirm, according to Mairs, is royal patronage of local religious institutions, indicating 'efforts by Graeco-Bactrian kings to cement their legitimacy by association with powerful temples', rather than testifying to their cultic incorporation as recipients of worship.[117] But whether or not the diademed portraits were votive or honorary in nature – i.e. commissioned by kings to associate themselves with the temples, or gifted by the civic community to honour the kings for their benefactions – the presence of ruler sculptures in the inner space of important sanctuaries at Ai Khanum and at Takht-i Sangin must have elicited distinct impact. Their visual placement and presence in houses of the gods, combined with royal investments in religious buildings and royal coinage that increasingly alluded to god-like qualities of the kings, starting with Demetrios, thus likely reflect developments towards kingship concepts of a heroic if not divine king, foreshadowing later developments of deified kingship in Baktria under the Kushan kings.[118]

---

116   Martinez-Sève 2010a, 11. This would be contemporaneous to Euthydemos' grand building programme at Ai Khanum.
117   Mairs 2022, 302.
118   As most explicitly testified by the Rabatak inscription (Sims-Williams 2004). Further discussion on divine kinship under the Kushans, interacting with Graeco-Baktrian precedents, by Shenkar 2017; Canepa 2020, 71–74.

5. Same, but different: Translocal contexts for Baktrian kingship

As elsewhere in Hellenistic Afro-Eurasia, royal representations in Baktria worked to assert and endorse charismatic achievements of the kings in such manner that they increasingly invited interpretations of the king as a heroic, if not a godly ruler. The previous sections accordingly showed that the notion of the warrior king circulated in image and name on Baktrian coins, that royal prestige and wealth were expressed through material display in the form of monumental building projects as well as patronage of cultural infrastructure and activities, and that the royal persona began to appropriate divine associations. These power practices, however, should not be considered as a sheer continuation of Hellenic or Macedonian ways of conduct that diffused from West to East in an acculturative process of Greek 'sameness' – of Hellenization under Alexander and the Seleukid kings. Practices that communicated legitimate rule were not homogenous nor territorialized (tied to particular geographical origins) but constituted a set of behaviours that gained transregional network power in broader dynamics of increasing interactions, interconnectedness, and interdependence of localities across the Afro-Eurasian world in the third and second centuries BC.[119] Such universalized practices with network power could guarantee recognition of power and authority on various geographical scales, even when it was precarious. The king's dependence on charismatic conduct and recognition thereof meant that the foundations of kingship were extremely volatile. Claims to kingship were contingent on projections of success and stability which paradoxically, were most imperative in unstable times of agonistic strife and war. This context made the performance of power crucial: to render their actions not only as legitimate but also as most authoritative, rulers interacted with a transregional repertoire of effective practices, routines, and symbols of kingship that could communicate and signify royal power and authority both within the locality as well as to those who threatened it from beyond. The insights we gain from the evidence of Hellenistic-period Baktria, therefore, not only provide impressions of power but also the power to impress various translocal audiences.

The third century BC saw Antiochos I as coregent over the Upper Satrapies (280s), the Baktrian assertion of autonomous power by Diodotos II (240s), the emergence of Arsakes I in Parthia (240s), and Antiochos III's eastern anabasis which affirmed Graeco-Baktrian hegemony over Central Asia under Euthydemos and Demetrios (205) – these respective royals all formed translocal actors that engaged in the power play for influence in Central Asia, each interacting with royal statements of others. Cultural power practices manifested themselves particularly in royal coinage and large building projects with a notable focus on constructing and renovating local sanctuaries: both

---

119 On network power, see Grewal 2009; Hoo 2021, 21–22; Versluys forthcoming. Globalization in relation to Hellenism and Hellenization are extensively discussed in Hoo 2022, esp. 65–70, 229–231 with further bibliography. For globalization and Baktrian historiography, see Hoo 2020.

the Oxos temple and the main temple at Ai Khanum saw their beginnings under the Seleukids in the early third century BC and continued to thrive under the Baktrian kings. While co-opting the Attic weight system and Greek coin imagery as used by Alexander, the Diadoch kings developed new monetary designs with personalized portraits and new patron deities. In turn, Diodotos II and the Euthydemids build on the network power of such coin practices and skilfully adapted their coins to distinguish their royal persona from the Seleukids as well as from other rivals in Central Asia. Significantly so, Euthydemos' city-wide building programme at Ai Khanum, initiated after his treaty with Antiochos III, spatially incorporated existing religious structures built under the Seleukids and renovated under the Diodotids within a grand new palatial district, with which Euthydemos not only surpassed his predecessors but also signified an increasing divine significance of the king and his family. Such performances of kingship had distinct local impact as the palatial district cultivated wealth, prestige, loyalty, industry, and trade, yet they simultaneously reflect engagement with translocally networked models of royal representation across Afro-Eurasia. By the time that Ai Khanum started to monumentalize under Euthydemos, the Ptolemaic kings at Alexandreia and the Seleukid kings at Babylon, Dura Europos, Seleukeia-Tigris, and Jebel Khalid had manifested their royal presence and power through the built environment, endowing major constructions of public buildings and royal architecture.[120]

Practices to bolster the king's charisma intensified and diversified in the first half of the second century BC, especially from the 180s into the 150s BC. The political context for this period was shaped by the push into India under Demetrios (180s), the intense dynastic wars and conflicts in Baktria (170s), the rise of Eukratides and the simultaneous rise of and competition with Menander in India and Mithradates I in Parthia (150s). It is during these warring times in Central Asia that we see the crystallization of Baktrian concepts of charismatic kingship. This is most visible on the innovative developments on coinage of Demetrios, Agathokles, Antimachos, and Eukratides (the military headdresses, royal epithets, bicultural issues, and pedigree coins) which proliferated royal representation on coins in image and name and progressively alluded to divine associations of the reigning king. The elaboration of coin imagery and legends in the 170s BC clearly reacted to royal representations of competing kings in Baktria, yet was done so in distinct interaction with developments across the Hellenistic world. By the time that Demetrios adopted the elephant-helmet in his royal portrait on coins, the elephant headdress had been circulating on Ptolemaic coins, albeit in a different form (as a scalp, rather than a helmet). While Ptolemaic coins could be ambiguously interpreted by various audiences to refer to Alexander's Indian victories as well as the Syrian elephant hunt by the pharaoh Thutmose III in a distant past, both signifying the

120   On Seleukid palatial districts, see Canepa 2018, 308–314; discussion of Hellenistic Babylon and Seleukeia in Hoo 2022, 155–167, 176–196 with further bibliography. Excavations at Seleukeia by the Turin mission (CRAST) have resumed in autumn 2022.

conquest of Asia, Demetrios' elephant helmet likely referred to his own victories south of the Hindu Kush – a glorious feat remembered by Strabon and likely praised in the Kulob inscription.[121]

Although Demetrios seemed aware of the powerful symbolism of the elephant on coins, engaging with Greek geographical ideas of India as the eastern edge of the *oikoumene*, the adoption of military headgear to proclaim a victorious king need not be a direct Ptolemaic influence from the far west. Closer to home, the Baktrian kings were in constant interaction and competition with their Central Asian neighbours in Parthia, as accounted by classical sources.[122] Arsakid coins since Arsakes I (r. 247–217 BC) bore portraits of the king wearing the *kyrbasia* tied with a diadem. According to Marek-Jan Olbrycht, this headgear emulated the Achaimenid satrapal headdress but was used to signify military conquest.[123] It has been argued that innovative coins of Phriapatios (r. 191–176 BC), father of Mithradates I, combined the image of the king wearing a headdress signifying victory with the Greek title *Basileus* and the epithet *Theos*; coins of Mithradates I followed suit with the title *Theopatros* (son of god).[124] Although Arsakes I had already included the titles *Autokratos* and *krny* (*karny*, Lord in Aramaic) in his bilingual coin legends, a pioneering move that combined a Greek title with the Old Persian title *kara-na* to signify supreme local authority, it was only in the 170s BC that epithets for living kings became widely popular on royal coinage across the Hellenistic East.[125]

In Baktria, Agathokles seemed to have been the first to adopt an additional epithet alongside his royal title on coins (as well as appropriating posthumous epithets of kings in his proclaimed pedigree); his innovations were quickly trailed by Antimachos. The moment that Antimachos explicitly proclaimed himself *Theos*, combined with a coin portrait of the king wearing the *kausia*, may thus have interacted with earlier claims to divinity under the Arsakids – if the attribution of the *Theos* coin-types to Phriapatios is correct. This strategy to impress to power was further enhanced by Antimachos' grand move to install a new calendar, asserting dominance over time in the form of a new

---

121   On the Egyptian interpretation of the elephant scalp on Alexander portraits, see Lorber 2012. Seleukos I also depicted an elephant on his coin reverses, though in standing or walking pose, not in the form of headdress.

122   Strab. 11.11.2; Iust. 41.4.8–9, 41.6.1–3. Relevant discussion in Olbrycht 2010; Lerner 2015; Overtoom 2016.

123   Olbrycht 2021, 246.

124   Assar 2004, 82, 88; Olbrycht 2021, 247–248 thus attribute the elusive issues of Sellwood 1980, type 10.15 to Phriapatios rather than Mithradates I. NB epithets evoking divinity occurred earlier on Ptolemaic coins of Ptolemaios II and Arsinoë II (*Theoi Adelphoi*, 'Sibling Gods, from 273 BC; see de Callataÿ – Lorber 2011, 423 and the chapter by Stefan Pfeiffer in this volume), though regional competition with the neighbouring Arsakids provides a more likely context for Baktrian adoption of the epithet *Theos*.

125   The title *krny*, however, did not last on later coins after Arsakes I. See instructive discussion in Olbrycht 2013; 2021, 249–254.

imperial presence, in similar fashion as the Seleukids had done earlier.[126] The divine epithet and the declaration of a new epoch served Antimachos' royal charisma to out-perform other contenders to power north and south of the Hindu Kush. Further west, the epithet *Theos Epiphanes* also appeared on contemporaneous coins of Antiochos IV in western Asia around 175 BC. While Antiochos IV is often considered to have been the source of inspiration for Antimachos' claim to divinity, it is more likely that the divine epithet had gained transregional network power across Hellenistic Asia as a uni-versalized (standardized) practice which kings increasingly adopted to be recognized as legitimate and to partake in global tendencies towards divine kinship in the second quarter of the second century BC. These tendencies matured in a particularly warring period, both in Central Asia as in West Asia, which shaped the translocal agonistic contexts for kings across Hellenistic Eurasia to assert (immortal) titles of grandeur for various translocal audiences.

The selection of forms of royal representation by Eukratides reflect similar inno-vative participation in and negotiation of translocal power practices of prominence and distinction. Eukratides adopted the title Great King on coins after his victories in northern India, following previous and contemporaneous kings in Hellenistic Asia. Seleukos I had assumed the royal title *Basileus* after the Treaty of the Indus with Chan-dragupta Maurya, while Antiochos III took on the epithet *Megas* upon his return from his eastern anabasis a century later. In Baktria, Antimachos not only proclaimed him-self *Theos* but also introduced a new dating system, presumably after his allied victory over Agathokles which gained him rule over both sides of the Hindu Kush – if Rapin's theory is correct. Similarly, Mithradates I of Parthia, Eukratides' contemporary and rival who transformed the Arsakid kingdom into an empire, adopted the epithet *Megas* only after his grand conquest of Seleukid Babylonia in 141 BC. The coin designs of Eu-kratides further interacted with distinct regional peers: his coin portrait that boasted his muscular upper body while throwing the javelin (fig. 6) innovatively emulated the depiction of thundering Zeus on Diododit coins (fig. 1), combining it with an elabo-rate martial scene of the horse-riding Dioskouroi. Menander's coins, in turn, innovated those of his rival Eukratides with thundering Athena on the reverse; his obverse por-trait mirrors Athena's thundering stance on the reverse, which could be read to assert close proximity, if not assimilation with the martial goddess (fig. 7).

Translocal trails can also be discerned in material culture beyond coins. Eukrati-des' vast building programme at Ai Khanum, which invested distinctly in the palatial district and infrastructure for elite activities in the arts, science, and culture, is dated to the final decades before 145 BC. This coincided with, or shortly predated the grand building project at (Old) Nisa under Mithradates I. As at Ai Khanum, this enormous

---

126   For the Seleukid strategies of domination over time, see now Kosmin 2018. Significantly so, Anti-
        machos' new calendar adopted a Macedonian month-name used in the Seleukid calendar as well.

royally-commissioned undertaking transformed Nisa from a fortress into a grand ceremonial centre dedicated to the celebration of the Arsakid dynasty.[127] In Justin's *Epitome*, Eukratides receives mention in the same breath as Mithradates, described as 'both great men' – a quality not only proclaimed on coins but also echoed in the monumentalization and material culture of Ai Khanum and Nisa.[128] In the Round Hall at Nisa, larger-than-life-sized statues of unbaked clay were unearthed, sculpted in Greek style. The Round Hall was a monumental structure with white-washed plastered walls somewhat secluded from the public courtyard; the Italian archaeologists of the Turin mission (CRAST) tentatively interpreted the building as a dynastic mausoleum, a celebratory space dedicated to the memory of one of the early Arsakid kings or their ancestors, implemented under Mithradates I.[129] Amongst the statues was a portrait head of a bearded male with the facial features of Mithradates I according to his coin portraits. Some scholars, Edward Dąbrowa most actively, have suggested that the Round Hall was the nucleus for a ruler cult of Mithradates I, perhaps combined with the celebration of other (ancestral) members of his lineage such as Arsakes I who, according to Ammianus Marcellinus, would have received divine posthumous honours.[130] Such an interpretation is not implausible in light of the diademed portraits and the fragmented statues found in the Baktrian temples at Takht-i Sangin and Ai Khanum, which hint at increasing translocal claims to divinity across Central Asia in the second century BC. Embedding kingship practices in trans-scalar (local, regional, and transregional) contexts of the second century BC thus provides valuable insights in the networked ways in which Baktrian kings innovated distinct ideologemes and behaviours with the power to impress both locally and globally.

6. Conclusion

Baktria was not an isolated part of the ancient *oikoumene* but was deeply connected and enmeshed in imperial networks of power and political practices across Afro-Eurasia. Clues to performative practices of kingship in the available evidence suggest that royal power in Baktria, like elsewhere in the Hellenistic period, depended on the king's success on the battlefield to acquire resources, prestige, and legitimacy to rule. While we can assume that Baktria was well familiar with imperial representations of the warrior king since the sixth century BC, it were the competitive times of the third and second century BC that mobilized the notion of the victorious king as most imperative for charismatic kingship practices. It is in contexts of military prowess, expansion, and in-

---

127 Pilipko 2008, 47–50; Lippolis 2019, 225–226.
128 Iust. 41.6.1.
129 Invernizzi 2001a, 141–147; 2001b, 308–310; Bollati 2008, 191–192.
130 Amm. 23.6.4; Dąbrowa 2009; 2011.

terstate war that we hear about the Baktrian kings in the few literary sources at hand. In ancient narratives, Diodotos, Euthydemos, and Eukratides are all remembered as ambitious and aggressive rulers that usurped power and raised to greatness by conquering and subjugating far foreign lands. This matched the realities of Hellenistic Afro-Eurasia, a violent world of war which cultivated a culture of agonistic imperialism that became codified in royal ideologies. As their Antigonid, Ptolemaic, Seleukid, Indian, Arsakid, and other Central Asian peers, the Baktrian kings spent most of their time warring for influence. They displayed military strength and leadership on the physical battlefield and made extensive efforts to communicate their exceptional persona as formidable warriors through coinage, visual representations, and the built environment. Boasting ever-greater glory and prestige, the royal representations of the Baktrian kings progressively diversified in the first half of the second century BC, appropriating increasingly divine features that brought their personas into the folds of immortal glory. Such bold moves were not isolated developments but were particularly driven by the timely conditions of the volatile political environment of eastern Baktria where royal power was difficult to last. Yet, while the investment to present themselves as victor, builder, and heroic individuals had immediate local impacts, such charismatic practices also actively engaged with and contributed to broader networked idioms of authority circulating in competitive spheres of influence across Afro-Eurasia, making Baktrian charismatic conduct inherently *translocal* in nature. In the warring times of the second century BC, the kings of Baktria were increasingly bound with the power to impress as with impressing oneself to power in the face of competitors for influence within and beyond the locality.

Bibliography

Abdullaev 2017: Abdullaev, Kazim, The Royal Portrait in Hellenistic Bactria, in: D. Boschung – F. Queyrel (eds.), Bilder der Macht. Das griechische Porträt und seine Verwendung in der antiken Welt, Leiden et al. 2017, 213–253

Assar 2004: Assar, G. R. Farhad, Genealogy and coinage of the early Parthian rulers I, Parthica 6, 2004, 69–93

Audouin – Bernard 1974: Audouin, Rémy – Bernard, Paul, Trésor de monnaies indiennes et indo-grecques d'Aï Khanoum, Afghanistan. II. Les monnaies indo-grecques, Revue numismatique Ser. 6, 16, 1974, 6–41

Ball et al. 2019: Ball, Warwick – Glenn, Simon – Lyonnet, Bertille – MacDowall, David – Taddei, Maurizio, The Iron Age, Achaemenid and Hellenistic Periods, in: R. Allchin – N. Hammond – W. Ball (eds.), The Archaeology of Afghanistan from the Earliest Times to the Timurid Period, Edinburgh 2019, 260–343

Bang 2012: Bang, Peter F., 'Elephant of India': Universal Empire through Time and Across Cultures, in: P. F. Bang – D. Kolodziejczyk (eds.), Universal Empire. A Comparative Approach to Imperial Culture and Representation in Eurasian History, Cambridge 2012, 1–40

Bellinger 1962: Bellinger, Alfred R., The Coins from the Treasure of the Oxus, American Numismatic Society Museum Notes 19, 1962, 51–67

Bentley 1998: Bentley, Jerry H., Hemispheric Integration, 500–1500 C. E., Journal of World History 9/2, 1998, 237–254

Bernard 1969: Bernard, Paul, Quatrième campagne de fouilles à Aï Khanoum (Bactriane), Comptes rendus des séances de l'Académie des Inscriptions et Belles-Lettres 113.3, 1969, 313–355

Bernard 1973: Bernard, Paul (ed.), Fouilles d'Aï Khanoum I (campagnes 1965, 1966, 1967, 1968). Rapport préliminaire, Paris 1973

Bernard 1976: Bernard, Paul, Les traditions orientales dans l'architecture gréco-bactriennes, Journal Asiatique 264, 1976, 245–275

Bernard 1978: Bernard, Paul, Campagne de fouilles 1976–1977 à Aï Khanoum (Afghanistan), Comptes rendus séances de l'Académie des Inscriptions et Belles-Lettres 122.2, 1978, 421–463

Bernard 2001: Bernard, Paul, Aï Khanoum en Afghanistan hier (1964–1978) et aujourd'hui (2001): un site en péril. Perspectives d'avenir, Comptes rendus séances de l'Académie des Inscriptions et Belles-Lettres 145.2, 2001, 971–1029

Bernard 2009: Bernard, Paul, La découverte et la fouille du site hellenistique d'Ai Khanoum en Afghanistan: comment elles se sont faites, Parthica 11, 2009, 33–56

Bernard – Pinault – Rougemont 2004: Bernard, Paul – Pinault, Georges-Jean – Rougemont, Georges, Deux nouvelles inscriptions grecques de l'Asie centrale, Journal des Savants, 2004, 227–356

Bernard – Rapin 1994: Bernard, Paul – Rapin, Claude, Un parchemin gréco-bactrien d'une collection privée, Comptes rendus séances de l'Académie des Inscriptions et Belles-Lettres 138.1, 1994, 261–294

Bollati 2008: Bollati, Ariela, Le sculture in argilla cruda dipinta, in: A. Invernizzi – C. Lippolis (eds.), Nisa Partica. Ricerche nel complesso monumentale arsacide 1990–2006, Florence 2008, 167–195

Bopearachchi 1991: Bopearachchi, Osmund, Monnaies gréco-bactriennes et indo-grecques. Catalogue raisonné, Paris 1991

Bopearachchi 1998: Bopearachchi, Osmund, A faience head of a Graeco-Bactrian king from Bulletin of the Asia Institute N. S. 12, 1998, 23–30

Bordeaux 2018: Bordeaux, Olivier, Les Grecs en Inde. Politiques et pratiques monétaires (IIIe s. a. C. – Ier s. p. C.), Bordeaux 2018

Brett 1950: Brett, Agnes B., ATHENA ΑΛΚΙΔΗΜΟΣ of Pella, American Numismatic Society Museum Notes 4, 1950, 55–72

Briant 1984: Briant, Pierre, L'Asie centrale et les royaumes proche-orientaux du premier millénaire avant notre ère (c. VIIIe-Ve siècle avant notre ère), Paris 1984

Briant 2002: Briant, Pierre, From Cyrus to Alexander. A history of the Persian empire, trans. by P. T. Daniels, Winona Lake 2002

Briant 2012: Briant, Pierre, From the Indus to the Mediterranean Sea: The Administrative Organization and Logistics of the Great Roads of the Achaemenid Empire, in: S. E. Alcock – J. Bodel – J. A. Talbert (eds.), Highways, Byways and Road Systems in the Pre-Modern World, Oxford et al. 2012, 141–170

Bringmann 2004: Bringmann, Klaus, Gymnasion und Griechische Bildung im Nahen Osten, in: P. Scholz – D. Kah (eds.), Das Hellenistische Gymnasion, Berlin 2004, 323–334

Canepa 2015a: Canepa, Matthew P., Seleukid Sacred Architecture: Royal Cult and the Transformation of Iranian Culture in the Middle Iranian Period, Iranian Studies 48.1, 2015, 71–97

Canepa 2015b: Canepa, Matthew P., Dynastic Sanctuaries and the Transformation of Iranian Kingship between Alexander and Islam, in: S. Babaei – T. Grigor (eds.), Of Architecture and Kingship. Strategies of Power in Iran from the Achaemenids to the Pahlavis, London et al. 2015, 65–117

Canepa 2017: Canepa, Matthew P., Rival Images of Iranian Kingship and Persian Identity in post-Achaemenid Western Asia, in: R. Strootman – M. J. Versluys (eds.), Persianism in Antiquity, Stuttgart 2017, 201–222

Canepa 2018: Canepa, Matthew P., The Iranian Expanse. Transforming Royal Identity through Architecture, Landscape, and the built Environment, 550 BCE-642 CE, Oakland 2018

Canepa 2020: Canepa, Matthew P., "Afghanistan" as a Cradle and Pivot of Empires: Reshaping Eastern Iran's Topography of Power under the Achaemenids, Seleucids, Greco-Bactrians and Kushans, in: R. E. Payne – R. King (eds.), The Limits of Empire in Ancient Afghanistan. Rule and Resistance in the Hindu Kush, circa 600 BCE-600 CE, Wiesbaden 2020, 45–79

Carroll 2003: Carroll, Maureen, Earthly Paradises. Ancient Gardens in History and Archaeology, Los Angeles 2003

Casson 1989: Casson, Lionel, The Periplus Maris Erythraei. Text with Introduction, Translation, and Commentary, Princeton 1989

Chase-Dunn – Hall 1997: Chase-Dunn, Christopher – Thomas D. Hall, Rise and Demise. Comparing World-Systems, Boulder 1997

Chrubasik 2016: Chrubasik, Boris, Kings and Usurpers in the Seleukid Empire. The Men Who Would be King, Oxford 2016

Clarysse – Thompson 2007: Clarysse, Willy – Thompson, Dorothy J., Two Greek Texts on Skin from Hellenistic Bactria, Zeitschrift für Papyrologie und Epigraphik 159, 2007, 273–279

Colburn 2013: Colburn, Henry P., Connectivity and Communication in the Achaemenid Empire, Journal of the Economic and Social History of the Orient 56, 2013, 29–52

Colburn 2016: Colburn, Henry P., Globalization and the Study of the Achaemenid Persian Empire, in: T. Hodos (ed.), The Routledge Handbook of Archaeology and Globalization, London et al. 2016, 871–884

Coloru 2009: Coloru, Omar, Da Alessandro a Menandro. Il regno greco di Battriana, Pisa et al. 2009

Cribb 2005: Cribb, Joe, The Greek Kingdom of Bactria, its Coinage and its Collapse, in: O. Bopearachchi – M.-F. Boussac (eds.), Afghanistan. Ancien carrefour entre l'Est et l'Ouest. Actes du colloque international de Lattes (5–7 mai 2003), Turnhout 2005, 207–225

Cribb 2007: Cribb, Joe, Money as Marker of Cultural Continuity and Change in Central Asia, in: J. Cribb – G. Herrmann (eds.), After Alexander. Central Asia before Islam, Oxford 2007, 333–376

Curtis 2005: Curtis, John, The Oxus Treasure in the British Museum, Ancient Civilizations from Scythia to Siberia 10, 2005, 293–338

Curtis – Simpson 2010: Curtis, John – Simpson, St. John (eds.), The World of Achaemenid Persia. History, Art and Society in Iran and the Ancient Near East, London et al. 2010

Dąbrowa 2009: Dąbrowa, Edward, Mithradates I and the Beginning of the Ruler-Cult in Parthia, Electrum 15, 2009, 41–51

Dąbrowa 2011: Dąbrowa, Edward, ΑΡΣΑΚΗΣ ΘΕΟΣ: Observations on the Nature of the Parthian Ruler-cult, in: C. Lippolis – S. de Martino (eds.), Un impaziente desideriodi scorrere il mondo. Studi in onore di Antonio Invernizzi per il suo settantesimo compleanno, Florence 2011, 247–253

de Callataÿ – Lorber 2011: de Callataÿ, François – Lorber, Catharine C., The Pattern of Royal Epithets on Hellenistic Coinages, in: P. P. Iossif – A. S. Chankowski – C. C. Lorber (eds.), More than Men, Less than Gods. Studies on Royal Cult and Imperial Worship, Leuven 2011, 417–455

Degen 2022: Degen, Julian, Alexander III. zwischen Ost und West, Stuttgart 2022

Drujinina – Lindström 2013: Drujinina, Anjelina – Lindström, Gunvor, Kultgefäße im Oxos-Tempel: Zur Frage der Kultkontinuität im unruhigen 2. Jh. v. Chr., in: G. Lindström et al. (eds.), Zwischen Ost und West. Neue Forschungen zum antiken Zentralasien, Darmstadt 2013, 171–186

Dumke 2014: Dumke, Gunnar, Nicht nur im Auge des Betrachters: Zu visuellen und haptischen Unterschieden baktrischer Münzen als Ausdruck unterschiedlicher Kommunikationsstrategien, in: A. Lichtenberger et al. (eds.), Bildwert. Nominalspezifische Kommunikationsstrategien in der Münzprägung hellenistischer Herrscher, Bonn 2014, 79–106

Dwivedi 2020: Dwivedi, Mamta, Evidence for Early South Asia, in: von Reden 2020a, 423–267

Engels 2017: Engels, David, Benefactors, Kings, Rulers. Studies on the Seleukid Empire between East and West, Leuven 2017

Falk 2007: Falk, Harry, Ancient Indian Eras: An Overview, Bulletin of the Asia Institute 21, 2007, 131–145

Falk – Bennett 2009: Falk, Harry – Bennett, Chris, Macedonian Intercalary Months and the Era of Azes, Acta Oiientalia 70, 2009, 197–216

Farrar 2016: Farrar, Linda, Gardens and Gardeners of the Ancient World. History, Myth & Archaeology, Oxford 2016

Francfort 1984: Francfort, Henri-Paul, Fouilles d'Aï Khanoum III. Le sanctuaire du temple à redans. Les trouvailles, Paris 1984

Francfort 2012: Francfort, Henri-Paul, Ai Khanoum "Temple with Indented Niches" and Takht-i Sangin "Oxus Temple" in historical cultural perspective: outline of a hypothesis about the cults, Parthica 14, 2012, 109–136

Fraser 1972: Fraser, Peter M., Ptolemaic Alexandria, 2 vols., Oxford 1972

García Sánchez 2014: García Sánchez, Manel, The Second after the King and Achaemenid Bactria in Classical Sources, in: B. Antela-Bernárdez – J. Vidal (eds.), Central Asia in Antiquity. Interdisciplinary Approaches, Oxford 2014, 55–63

Garrison – Root 2001: Garrison, Mark – Root, Margaret C., Seals on the Persepolis Fortification Tablets 1: Images of heroic encounter, Chicago 2001

Gehrke 2013: Gehrke, Hans-Joachim, The Victorious King. Reflections on the Hellenistic Monarchy, in: N. Luraghi (ed.), The Splendors and Miseries of Ruling Alone. Encounters with Monarchy from Archaic Greece to the Hellenistic Mediterranean, Stuttgart 2013, 73–98 (engl. tr. of Gehrke, Hans-Joachim, Der siegreiche König. Überlegungen zur hellenistischen Monarchie, Archiv für Kulturgeschichte 64, 1982, 247–277)

Giesser 2017: Giesser, Valentine, Les mosaïques de galets d'Ai Khanoum (Afghanistan, IIe siècle avant J.-C). Survivance d'une technique à l'extrême périphérie d'un "Empire", in: N. Bock – I. Foletti – M. Tomasi (eds.), Survivals, revivals, rinascenze. Studi in onore di Serena Romano, Rome 2017, 97–110

Glenn 2014: Glenn, Simon, Heliocles and Laodice of Bactria: A Reconsideration, The Numismatic Chronicle 174, 2014, 45–59

Glenn 2020: Glenn, Simon, Money and Power in Hellenistic Bactria, New York 2020

Gopnik 2010: Gopnik, Hilary, Why Columned Halls?, in: Curtis – Simpson 2010, 195–207

Grenet 1991: Grenet, Frantz, Mithra au temple principal d'Aï Khanoum?, in: P. Bernard – F. Grenet (eds.), Histoire et cultes de l'Asie centrale préislamique. Sources écrites et documents archéologiques. Actes du colloque international du CNRS, Paris 22–28 novembre 1988, Paris 1991, 147–151

Grewal 2009: Grewal, David S., Network Power. The Social Dynamics of Globalization, New Haven et al. 2009

Gzella 2021: Gzella, Holger, Bactria, in: B. Jacobs – R. Rollinger (eds.), A Companion to the Achaemenid Empire II, Hoboken 2021, 951–964

Hallock 1969: Hallock, Richard T., The Persepolis Fortification Tablets, Chicago 1969

Hansen – Wieczorek – Tellenbach 2009: Hansen, Svend – Wieczorek, Alfried – M. Tellenbach, Michael (eds.), Alexander der Große und die Öffnung der Welt. Asiens Kulturen im Wandel, Mannheim 2009

Heckel 2020: Heckel, Waldemar, In the Path of Conquest, Oxford 2020

Henkelman 2018: Henkelman, Wouter, Bactrians in Persepolis – Persians in Bactria, in: A Millennium of History. The Iron Age in Southern Central Asia (2nd and 1st millennia BC), Berlin 2018, 223–255

Hollis 2011: Hollis, Adrian S., Greek letters in Hellenistic Bactria, in: D. Obbink – R. Rutherford (eds.), Culture in Pieces. Essays on Ancient Texts in Honour of Peter Parsons, Oxford 2011, 104–118

Holt 1989: Holt, Frank L., Alexander the Great and Bactria. The Formation of a Greek Frontier in Central Asia, Leiden 1989

Holt 1999: Holt, Frank L., Thundering Zeus. The making of Hellenistic Bactria, Berkeley 1999

Holt 2005: Holt, Frank L., Into the Land of Bones. Alexander the Great in Afghanistan, Berkeley 2005

Hoo 2018: Hoo, Milinda, Ai Khanum in the Face of Eurasian Globalisation: A Translocal Approach to a Contested Site in Hellenistic Bactria, 2018, 161–186

Hoo 2020: Hoo, Milinda, Globalization and Interpreting Visual Culture, in: Mairs 2020, 553–569

Hoo 2021: Hoo, Milinda, Globalization beyond the Silk Road: Writing Global History of Ancient Economies, in: von Reden 2021, 7–28

Hoo 2022: Hoo, Milinda, Eurasian Localisms. Towards a Translocal Approach to Hellenism and Inbetweenness in Central Eurasia, Third to First Centuries BCE, Stuttgart 2022

Hoo – Wiesehöfer 2022: Hoo, Milinda – Wiesehöfer, Josef, An Empire of Graeco-Bactrians and Indo-Greeks?, in: M. Gehler – R. Rollinger (eds.), Empires to be Remembered. Universal- und kulturhistorische Studien, Wiesbaden 2022, 273–297

Iliakis 2013: Iliakis, Michael, Greek Mercenary Revolts in Bactria: A Reappraisal, Historia 62.2, 2013, 182–195

Invernizzi 2001a: Invernizzi, Antonio, Arsacid Dynastic Art, Parthica 3, 2001, 133–157

Invernizzi 2001b: Invernizzi, Antonio, Arsacid Palaces, in: I. Nielsen (ed.), The Royal Palace Institution in the First Millennium BC, Aarhus 2001, 295–312

Jakobsson 2010: Jakobsson, Jens, Antiochus Nicator, the Third King of Bactria?, The Numismatic Chronicle 170, 2010, 17–33

Jakobsson – Glenn 2018: Jakobsson, Jens – Glenn, Simon, New Research on the Bactrian Tax-Receipt, Ancient History Bulletin 32.1–2, 2018, 61–71

Janssen 2007: Janssen, Erik, Die Kausia. Symbolik und Funktion der makedonischen Kleidung, Diss. Göttingen 2007

Junker 2021: Junker, Kristina, Deconstructing the 'Greekness' of Bactrian pottery: On the Greek-Mediterranean influences on the local pottery production in Bactria during the Hellenistic period, Studia Hercynia 25.2, 2021, 42–63

Kingsley 1981: Kingsley, Bonnie M., The Cap that Survived Alexander, American Journal of Archaeology 85.1, 1981, 39–46

Kosmin 2014: Kosmin, Paul J., The Land of the Elephant Kings. Space, Territory, and Ideology in the Seleucid Empire, Cambridge et al. 2014

Kosmin 2018: Kosmin, Paul J., Time and its Adversaries in the Seleucid Empire, Cambridge et al. 2018

Kritt 2001: Kritt, Brian, Dynastic Transitions in the Coinage of Bactria. Antiochus-Diodotus-Euthydemus, Lancaster 2001

Kritt 2016: Kritt, Brian, The Seleucid Mint of Aï Khanoum, Lancaster 2016

Kubica 2020: Kubica, Olga, Reading the Milindapañha: Indian Historical Sources and the Greeks in Bactria, in: Mairs 2020, 430–445

Lecoq 1997: Lecoq, Pierre, Les inscriptions de la Perse achéménide, Paris 1997

Lecuyot 2013: Lecuyot, Guy (ed.), Fouilles d'Ai Khanoum IV. L'habitat, Mémoires de la Délégation archéologique française en Aghanistan 34, Paris 2013

Lerner 1999: Lerner, Jeffrey D., The Impact of Seleucid Decline on the Eastern Iranian Plateau. The Foundations of Arsacid Parthia and Graeco-Bactria, Stuttgart 1999

Lerner 2015: Lerner, Jeffrey D., Mithridates I's Conquest of Western Greek-Baktria, Проблемы Истории Филологии Культуры = Journal of History, Philology and Cultural Studies 47.1, 2015, 45–55

Lhuillier 2021: Lhuillier, Johanna (ed.), Archaeology of Central Asia during the 1st Millennium BC, from the Beginning of the Iron Age to the Hellenistic Period, Vienna 2021

Lincoln 2007: Lincoln, Bruce, Religion, Empire, and Torture. The Case of Achaemenian Persia, with a Postscript on Abu Ghraib, Chicago 2007

Lindström 2013a: Lindström, Gunvor, Baktrien – Votive und Votivpraxis in den hellenistischen und kuschanzeitlichen Heiligtümern (3. Jh. v. Chr. – 3. Jh. n. Chr.), in: I. Gerlach – D. Raue (eds.), Sanktuar und Ritual. Heilige Plätze im archäologischen Befund, Rahden 2013, 299–306

Lindström 2013b: Lindström, Gunvor, Votivdeponierungen im Oxos-Tempel (Baktrien) – Tradierung griechischer Kultpraxis?, in: A. Schäfer – M. Witteyer (eds.), Rituelle Deponierungen in Heiligtümern der hellenistisch-römischen Welt, Mainz 2013, 97–114

Lindström 2014: Lindström, Gunvor, Torbulok: Tadschikistan. Ein neuentdecktes Heiligtum im hellenistischen Osten, e-Forschungsberichte des DAI 2014-1, 120–124

Lindström 2016: Lindström, Gunvor, Der Oxos-Tempel: Räumliche Aspekte und Kultkontinuität im Spiegel der Votivpraxis, in: S. Hansen – D. Neumann – T. Vachta (eds.), Raum, Gabe und Erinnerung. Weihgaben und Heiligtümer in prähistorischen und antiken Gesellschaften, Berlin 2016, 281–310

Lindström 2017: Lindström, Gunvor, Torbulok, Tadschikistan: Die Arbeiten der Jahre 2014 bis 2016, e-Forschungsberichte des DAI 2017-1, 174–183

Lindström 2021: Lindström, Gunvor, The Hellenistic sanctuary at Torbulok, Tajikistan, in: Lhuillier 2021, 89–104

Lippolis 2014: Lippolis, Carlo, Parthian Nisa: Art and Architecture in the Homeland of the Arsacids, in: P. Leriche (ed.), Art et civilisation de l'Orient hellénisé. Rencontres et échanges culturels d'Alexandre aux Sassanides. Hommage à Daniel Schlumberger, Paris 2014, 223–230

Litvinsky 2003: Litvinsky, Boris A., Hellenistic Clay Portraits from the Temple of the Oxus, Parthica 5, 2003, 37–62

Litvinsky – Pichikyan 1994: Litvinsky, Boris A. – Pichikyan, Igor R., The Hellenistic Architecture and Art of the Temple of the Oxus, Bulletin of the Asia Institute 8, 1994, 47–66

Litvinsky – Pichikyan 2002: Litvinsky, Boris A. –Pichikyan, Igor R., Taxt-i Sangīn. Der Oxus Tempel. Grabungsbefund, Stratigraphie und Architektur, Mainz 2002

Lorber 2012: Lorber, Catherine C., An Egyptian Interpretation of Alexander's Elephant Headdress, American Journal of Numismatics 24, 2012, 21–31

Luraghi 2013: Luraghi, Nino (ed.), The Splendors and Miseries of Ruling Alone. Encounters with Monarchy from Archaic Greece to the Hellenistic Mediterranean, Stuttgart 2013

Lyonnet 2012: Lyonnet, Bertille, Questions on the date of the Hellenistic pottery from Central Asia (Ai Khanoum, Marakanda and Koktepe), Ancient Civilizations from Scythia to Siberia 18.1, 2012, 143–173

Lyonnet 2013: Lyonnet, Bertille, La céramique de la maison du quartier sud-ouest d'Aï Khanoum, in: G. Lecuyot (ed.), Fouilles d'Ai Khanoum IV. L'habitat, Paris 2013

MacDowall 2005: MacDowall, David W., The Role of Demetrius in Arachosia and the Kabul Valley, in: O. Bopearachchi – M.-F. Boussac (eds.), Afghanistan. Ancien carrefour entre l'Est et l'Ouest, Turnhout 2005, 197–206

Mairs 2013: Mairs, Rachel, The "Temple with Indented Niches" at Ai Khanoum: Ethnic and Civic Identity in Hellenistic Bactria, in: R. Alston – O.M. van Nijf – C. Williamson (eds.), Cults, Creeds and Identities in the Greek City after the Classical Age, Leuven 2013, 85–111

Mairs 2014a: Mairs, Rachel, The Founder's Shrine and the Foundation of Ai Khanoum, in: N. Mac Sweeney (ed.), Foundation myths in ancient societies. Dialogues and discourses, Philadelphia 2014, 103–128

Mairs 2014b: Mairs, Rachel, The Hellenistic Far East. Archaeology, language, and identity in Greek Central Asia, Berkeley 2014

Mairs 2020: Mairs, Rachel (ed.), The Graeco-Bactrian and Indo-Greek worlds, London et al. 2020

Mairs 2022: Mairs, Rachel, Kingship and Ruler Cult in Hellenistic Bactria: Beyond the Numismatic Sources, in: E. Anagnostou-Laoutides – S. Pfeiffer (eds.), Culture and ideology under the Seleukids, Berlin 2022, 297–312

Martinez-Sève 2010a: Martinez-Sève, Laurianne, Pouvoir et religion dans la Bactriane hellénistique. Recherches sur la politique religieuse des rois séleucides et gréco-bactriens, Chiron 40, 2010, 1–27

Martinez-Sève 2010b: Martinez-Sève, Laurianne, À propos du temple aux niches indentées d'Aï Khanoum: quelques observations, in: P. Carlier – C. Lerouge-Cohen (eds.), Paysage et religion en Grèce antique, Paris 2010, 195–207

Martinez-Sève 2014: Martinez-Sève, Laurianne, The Spatial Organization of Ai Khanoum, a Greek City in Afghanistan, American Journal of Archaeology 118.2, 2014, 267–283

Martinez-Sève 2015: Martinez-Sève 2015: Martinez-Sève, Laurianne, Ai Khanoum and Greek domination in Central Asia, Electrum 22, 2015, 17–46

Martinez-Sève 2017: Martinez-Sève, Laurianne, Les opérations d'Antiochos III en Bactriane-Sogdiane: L'apport de la documentation archéologique, in: C. Feyel – L. Graslin-Thomé (eds.), Antiochos III et l'Orient, Paris 2017, 271–302

Martinez-Sève 2018: Martinez-Sève, Laurianne, Ai Khanoum after 145 BC: The post-palatial occupation, Ancient Civilizations from Scythia to Siberia 24, 2018, 354–419

Martinez-Sève 2020: Martinez-Sève, Laurianne, Afghan Bactria, in: Mairs 2020, 217–248

Martinez-Sève 2021: Martinez-Sève, Laurianne, The Chapels of the Main Sanctuary at Ai Khanoum, in: Lhuillier 2021, 105–127

Mittag 2006: Mittag, Peter F., Methodologische Überlegungen zur Geschichte Baktriens: Könige und Münzen, Schweizerische Numismatische Rundschau 85, 2006, 27–46

Morris 2020a: Morris, Lauren, Evidence for Central Asia, in: von Reden 2020a, 381–421

Morris 2020b: Morris, Lauren, Central Asian empires, in: von Reden 2020a, 53–93

Morris 2021a: Morris, Lauren, Tools of Economic Activity from the Greek Kingdoms of Central Asia to the Kushan Empire, in: von Reden 2021, 449–490

Morris 2021b: Morris, Lauren, Economic Actors under the Greek Kingdoms of Central Asia to the Kushan Empire, in: von Reden 2021, 159–207

Muccioli 2013: Muccioli, Federicomaria, Gli epiteti ufficiali dei re ellenistici, Stuttgart 2013

Muller 2016: Muller, Yannick, Religion, Empire and Mutilation: A Cross-Religious Perspective on Achaemenid Mutilation Practices, in: D. V. Edelman – A. Fitzpatrick-McKinley – P. Guillaume (eds.), Religion in the Achaemenid Persian Empire. Emerging Judaisms and trends, Tübingen 2016, 197–227

Naveh – Shaked 2012: Naveh, Joseph – Shaked, Shaul, Aramaic Documents from Ancient Bactria (Fourth Century B. C. E.). From the Khalili Collections, London 2012

Nielsen 1994: Nielsen, Inge, Hellenistic Palaces. History and Renewal, Aarhus 1994

Olbrycht 2010: Olbrycht, Marek J., Mithradates I of Parthia and his Conquests up to 141 BC, in: E. Dąbrowa et al. (eds.), Hortus Historiae. Studies in honour of professor Józef Wolski on the 100th anniversary of his birthday, Kraków 2010, 229–245

Olbrycht 2013: Olbrycht, Marek-Jan, The Titulature of Arsaces I, King of Parthia, Parthica 15, 2013, 63–74

Olbrycht 2014: Olbrycht, Marek J., An Admirer of Persian ways: Alexander the Great's Reforms in Parthia-Hyrcania and the Iranian Heritage, in: T. Daryaee – K. Rezakhani (eds.), Excavating an Empire. Achaemenid Persia in longue durée, Costa Mesa 2014, 37–62

Olbrycht 2021: Olbrycht, Marek J., Early Arsakid Parthia (ca. 250–165 B. C.). At the Crossroads of Iranian, Hellenistic, and Central Asian History, Leiden et al. 2021

Olivelle 2013: Olivelle, Patrick, King, Governance, and Law in Ancient India. Kauṭilya's Artha-śāstra, Oxford 2013

Overtoom 2016: Overtoom, Nikolaus L., The Power-Transition Crisis of the 240s BCE and the Creation of the Parthian State, The International History Review 38.5, 2016, 984–1013

Overtoom 2020: Overtoom, Nikolaus L., Reign of Arrows. The Rise of the Parthian Empire in the Hellenistic Middle East, Oxford 2020

Paton – Walbank – Habicht 2011: Polybius, The Histories, Books 9–15. trans. by W. R. Paton, revised by Frank W. Walbank and Christian Habicht, Cambridge et al. 2011

Petitot-Biehler – Bernard 1975: Petitot-Biehler, Claire-Yvonne – Bernard, Paul, Trésor de monnaies grecques et gréco-bactriennes trouvé à Aï Khanoum (Afghanistan), Revue Numismatique 6, 17, 1975, 23–69

Pichikyan 1992: Pichikyan, Igor R., Oxos-Schatz und Oxos-Tempel. Achämenidische Kunst in Mittelasien, Berlin 1992

Pilipko 2008: Pilipko, Viktor N., The Central Ensemble of the Fortress Mihrdatkirt: Layout and chronology, Parthica 10, 2008, 33–51

Plischke 2014: Plischke, Sonja, Die Seleukiden und Iran. Die seleukidische Herrschaftspolitik in den östliche Satrapien, Wiesbaden 2014

Rapin 1987: Rapin, Claude, La trésorerie hellénistique d'Aï Khanoum, Rev. Archéologique 1, 1987, 41–70

Rapin 1992: Rapin, Claude, Fouilles d'Aï Khanoum VIII. La trésorerie du palais hellénistuqe d'Aï Khanoum. L'apogée et la chute du royaume grec de Bactriane, Paris 1992

Rapin 1996: Rapin, Claude, I. Nouvelles observations sur le parchemin gréco-bactrien d'Asangôrna, Topoi Orient-Occident 6, 2, 1996, 458–469

Rapin 2010: Rapin, Claude, L'ère Yavana d'après les parchemins gréco-bactriens d'Asangorna et d'Amphipolis, in: K. Abdullaev (ed.), The traditions of East and West in the antique cultures of Central Asia. Papers in honour of Paul Bernard, Tashkent 2010, 234–252

Rapin 2021: Rapin, Claude, The Empire's Northeast, in: B. Jacobs – R. Rollinger (eds.), A Companion to the Achaemenid Empire, Hoboken 2021, 311–323

Rapin – Hadot – Cavallo 1987: Rapin, Claude – Hadot, Pierre – Cavallo, Guglielmo, Les textes littéraires grecs de la trésorerie d'Aï Khanoum, Bulletin de Correspondance Hellénique 111.1, 1987, 225–266

Rea – Senior – Hollis 1994: Rea, John R. – Senior, Robert C. – Hollis, Adrian S., A Tax Receipt from Hellenistic Bactria, Zeitschrift für Papyrologie und Epigraphik 104, 1994, 261–280

Riedel 2020: Riedel, Stefan, Die Basileia von Alexandria. Topographisch-urbanistische Untersuchungen zum ptolemäischen Königsviertel, Turnhout 2020

Robert 1968: Robert, Louis, De Delphes à l'Oxus, inscriptions grecques nouvelles de la Bactriane, Comptes rendus des séances de l'Académie des Inscriptions et Belles-Lettres 112, 3, 1968, 416–457

Rollinger 2010: Rollinger, Robert, Extreme Gewalt und Strafgericht: Ktesias und Herodot als Zeugnisse für den Achaimenidenhof, in: B. Jacobs – R. Rollinger (eds.), Der Achämenidenhof / The Achaemenid Court, Wiesbaden 2010, 559–666

Rougemont 2012: Rougemont, Georges, Inscriptions grecques d'Iran et d'Asie centrale. Corpus inscriptionum Iranicarum II: Inscriptions of the Seleucid and Parthian periods of eastern Iran and central Asia. I: Inscriptions in non-Iranian languages 1, London 2012

Salomon 1998: Salomon, Richard, Indian Epigraphy. A Guide to the Study of Inscriptions in Sanskrit Prakrit and other Indo-Aryan Languages, New York et al. 1998

Schmidt 1999: Schmidt, Peter L., s. v. M. Iunian(i)us Iustinus, in: DNP 6, 1999, 106.

Sellwood 1980: Sellwood, David, An Introduction to the Coinage of Parthia, London 1980

Shenkar 2014: Shenkar, Michael, Intangible Spirits and Graven Images. The Iconography of Deities in the Pre-Islamic Iranian World, Leiden 2014

Shenkar 2017: Shenkar, Michael, Royal Regalia and the "Divine Kinship" in the pre-Islamic Central Asia, Parthica 19, 2017, 55–74

Sims-Williams 2004: Sims-Williams, Nicholas, The Bactrian Inscription of Rabatak: A New Reading, Bulletin of the Asia Institute 18, 2004, 53–68

Stronach 1989: Stronach, David, The Royal Garden at Pasargadae: Evolution and Legacy, in: L. De Meyer – E. Haerinck – H. Haerinck (eds.), Archaeologia Iranica et Orientalis. Miscellanea in Honorem Louis Vanden Berghe I, Ghent 1989, 475–502

Strootman 2014: Strootman, Rolf, Courts and Elites in the Hellenistic Empires. The Near East after the Achaemenids, c. 330 to 30 BCE, Edinburgh 2014

Tarn 1938: Tarn, William W., The Greeks in Bactria and India, Cambridge 1938

Thierry 2005: Thierry, François, Yuezhi et Kouchans: Pièges et dangers des sources chinoises, in: O. Bopearachchi – M.-F. Boussac (eds.), Afghanistan. Ancien carrefour entre l'Est et l'Ouest, Turnhout 2005, 421–539

Trampedach – Meeus 2020: Trampedach, Kai – Meeus, Alexander (eds.), The Legitimation of Conquest. Monarchical Representation and the Art of Government in the Empire of Alexander the Great, Stuttgart 2020

Tuplin 1996: Tuplin, Christopher, The Parks and Gardens of the Achaemenid Empire, in: Achaemenid Studies, Stuttgart 1996, 80–131

Versluys 2017: Versluys, Miguel J., Visual Style and Constructing Identity in the Hellenistic World. Nemrud Dağ and Commagene under Antiochos I, Cambridge 2017

Versluys forthcoming: Versluys, Miguel John (ed.), A Global Revolution? Objects and Change in Afro-Eurasia in the Final Centuries BCE, Cambridge (forthcoming)

Veuve 1987: Veuve, Serge, Fouilles d'Aï Khanoum VI. Le gymnase. Architecture, céramique, sculpture, Paris 1987

von den Hoff 2021: von den Hoff, Ralf, The Visual Representation of Ptolemaic and Seleucid Kings: A Comparative Approach to Portrait Concepts, in: C. Fischer-Bovet – S. von Reden (eds.), Comparing the Ptolemaic and Seleucid Empires. Integration, Communication, and Resistance, Cambridge 2021, 164–190

von Reden 2020a/2021: von Reden, Sitta (ed.), Handbook of Ancient Afro-Eurasian Economies, 2 vols., Berlin 2020/2021

von Reden 2020b: von Reden, Sitta, The Hellenistic Empires, in: von Reden 2020a, 15–52

Watson 1961: Watson, Burton, Records of the Grand Historian by Sima Qian. Han Dynasty II, Hong Kong et al. 1961

Widemann 2007: Widemann, François, Civil Wars and Alliances in Bactria and North-Western India after the Usurpation of King Eucratides, East and West 57.1/4, 2007, 9–28

Wolski 1999: Wolski, Józef, The Seleucids. The Decline and Fall of their Empire, Kraków 1999

Wu 2010: Wu, Xin, Enemies of Empire: A Historical Reconstruction of Political Conflicts between Central Asia and the Persian Empire, in: Curtis – Simpson 2010, 454–606

Wu 2017: Wu, Xin, Ruling the Unrule-able: Bactria in the Achaemenid Empire, in: K. O. Weber et al. (eds.), Fitful Histories and Unruly Publics. Rethinking Temporality and Community in Eurasian Archaeology, Leiden et al. 2017, 258–287

Wu 2020: Wu, Xin, Central Asia in the Achaemenid Period, in: Mairs 2020, 595–618

Yardley – Develin 1994: Yardley, John C. – Develin, Robert, Justin. Epitome of the Philippic History of Pompeius Trogus, Atlanta 1994

Figures

Fig. 1:   ANS 1995.51.44, courtesy of the American Numismatic Society.

Fig. 2:   ANS 1944.100.64188, courtesy of the American Numismatic Society.

Fig. 3:   Staatliche Museen zu Berlin, Münzkabinett, 18234578, Lutz-Jürgen Lübke (Lübke und Wiedemann).

Fig. 4:   Bibliothèque nationale de France, département Monnaies, médailles et antiques, Y 6432 ark:/12148/btv1b10317199b.

Fig. 5:   ANS 1944.100.74409, courtesy of the American Numismatic Society.

Fig. 6:   ANS 1995.51.78, courtesy of the American Numismatic Society.

Fig. 7:   Staatliche Museen zu Berlin, Münzkabinett, 18200225, Reinhard Saczewski.

Fig. 8:   © DAFA: J.-C. Liger, C. Rapin, courtesy of Laurianne Martinez-Sève.

Fig. 9:   © DAFA: J.-C. Liger, A.-B. Pimpaud, courtesy of Laurianne Martinez-Sève.

Fig. 10:   © DAI-Eurasien-Abteilung: Gunvor Lindström.

Milinda Hoo is Assistant Professor of Ancient History and Identity Formation at Utrecht University. Her research examines the impact of globalization on cultural interaction, geographical imagination, and identity construction in the history and archaeology of central Eurasia, with a particular focus on eastern Iran, Central Asia, and the Eurasian steppes. She earned her PhD from Kiel University in 2018 and published her dissertation with Franz Steiner Verlag in 2022 under the title *Eurasian Localisms: Towards a Translocal Approach to Hellenism and Inbetweenness in Central Eurasia, Third to First Centuries BCE*. From 2018 to 2023, she was employed as Assistant Professor of Ancient History at the University of Freiburg, and was active as associate member of the ERC Project 'Beyond the Silk Road: Economic Development, Frontier Zones, and Inter-Imperiality in the Afro-Eurasian World Region, 300 BCE to 300 CE'. She currently works on a second monograph on the mnemohistory and spatiocultural imagination of 'the North-East'.

Part 2:
The Second and First Centuries

Comparing Themes and Structures of Representation
and Communication /
Themen und Strukturen der Repräsentation
und Kommunikation im Vergleich

Gleichungen mit vielen Unbekannten
Ptolemaiisches auf seleukidischen Münzen[*]

PETER FRANZ MITTAG

Abstract: Reliable echoes of or borrowings from Ptolemaic coinage are comparatively rare among the Seleukids. Metrological aspects and the adoption of Ptolemaic design are often very closely connected. Apart from these cases, the other adoptions ultimately go back to the marriage between the Ptolemaic Kleopatra Thea and Alexander Balas and their further actions in the Seleukid Empire.

The earliest secure example is the coin series of Antiochos IV, which was probably produced in Antiocheia during the Sixth Syrian War. It was possibly an attempt to reform the Seleukid coinage system by copying the sophisticated Ptolemaic bronze coinage in order to save silver. The design of the coin's obverse and reverse could thus symbolise the king's dual rule over the Seleukid and Ptolemaic empires. Towards the end of his reign, his son Antiochos V resumed the minting of tetradrachms of reduced weight in Ptolemaïs-Ake, which in weight and appearance were reminiscent of the tetradrachms minted here in Ptolemaic times. Many successors also had coins minted in various Phoenician cities to a reduced weight standard and 'Ptolemaic' design. A gold coinage of Demetrios I, which exceptionally does not show the portrait of the ruler on the obverse but Tyche, bears a legend on the obverse following the round of the coin and the 'Ptolemaic' double cornucopia. Whether this is more a coincidental product of not very skilled die cutters or a deliberate imitation of the coinage of the Ptolemies, with whom Demetrios I was at war at the time, cannot be decided. The fourth case are rare gold staters of Kleopatra Thea, which were produced according to Seleukid weight standards and with Seleukid style but Ptolemaic design, perhaps in the context of her marriage to Alexander Balas. The tetradrachms minted on this occasion tend to follow Seleukid traditions also, with the attributes of Kleopatra Thea alone potentially pointing to Egypt. The tetradrachms from the sole reign of Kleopatra Thea were struck according to Seleukid weight standards. Only the queen's hairstyle and the double horn of plenty copy Ptolemaic models.

---

[*] Alle Münzen werden in Originalgröße abgebildet, die Durchmesser finden sich zudem im Abbildungsverzeichnis.

1. Einleitung

Sowohl die Ptolemaier als auch die Seleukiden schöpften bei der Gestaltung ihrer Münzen aus demselben Setzkasten der numismatischen Traditionen und ikonographischen Konventionen. Parallelen sind daher grundsätzlich naheliegend; dennoch entwickelten sich die Münzen der beiden Dynastien bereits unter den ersten Königen in unterschiedliche Richtungen. Das lag u. a. daran, dass einzelne Gottheiten und Mythen für die Ptolemaier und die Seleukiden eine jeweils ganz besondere Bedeutung besaßen. Die Seleukiden führten ihr Geschlecht auf Apollon zurück,[1] weshalb sich Darstellungen von Apollon und seiner Schwester Artemis phasenweise sehr prominent auf seleukidischen Münzen finden. Die Ptolemaier ihrerseits hielten Zeus und Dionysos für ihre Urahnen väterlicher- bzw. mütterlicherseits,[2] und der mit Zeus auf das Engste verbundene Adler ist das typische Reversbild auf ptolemaiischen Münzen. Darüber hinaus gibt es eine Reihe von Gestaltungselementen und technischen Details, die sich entweder allein bei den Ptolemaiern finden oder doch so prominent auf ihren Münzen sind, dass sie hier als ptolemaiisch erachtet werden sollen. Einige dieser spezifisch ptolemaiischen Merkmale wurden von den Seleukiden gelegentlich übernommen und könnten gezielt eingesetzt worden sein, um spezifische Botschaften zu vermitteln. Diese Münzen sollen im Zentrum der folgenden Überlegungen stehen. In einem ersten Schritt sollen zunächst die typisch ptolemaiischen Gestaltungsmerkmale zusammengestellt werden, um auf dieser Grundlage in einem zweiten Schritt diejenigen seleukidischen Münzen genauer in den Blick zu nehmen, die einige dieser Merkmale aufweisen.

Abb. 1 Ptolemaios I., Tetradrachme, Alexandreia, ca. 294–285 v. Chr., CPE 137.

1　　Iust. 15.4.3–6.
2　　Siehe besonders prominent den Stammbaum, den Ptolemaios III. in der Adulisinschrift (OGIS 54) nennt. Siehe auch die Beiträge von Gregor Weber (insbesondere S. 134–135) und Stefan Pfeiffer (S. 168–170) in diesem Band.

Abb. 2 Ptolemaios II., Drachme, Alexandreia, ca. 230–222 v. Chr., CPE B395.

2. Typische ptolemaiische Charakteristika

Ptolemaios I. und Seleukos I. prägten zunächst die von Alexander dem Großen verwendeten Münztypen weiter. Während die Seleukiden auch in den folgenden Generationen an einigen wesentlichen Merkmalen dieser Münzprägung festhielten, indem sie beispielsweise das attische Gewichtssystem übernahmen und die Legende in senkrechten Linien auf dem Revers platzierten (um die beiden wichtigsten Übernahmen zu nennen), beschritt bereits Ptolemaios I. in verschiedenen Etappen abweichende Wege. Zum einen reduzierte er in mehreren Stufen das Gewicht der Edelmetallmünzen (ptolemaiischer Standard), und die Reverslegende wurde in der letzten Serie dem Münzrund folgend angebracht.[3] Der Avers dieser Münzen zeigt das Bildnis Ptolemaios' I., der Revers einen mit angelegten Flügeln auf einem Blitzbündel nach links stehenden Adler (Abb. 1). Die meisten der bis zum Ende der Ptolemaierherrschaft in Alexandreia geprägten Tetradrachmen folgen diesen Gestaltungsprinzipien, und der Adler ist auch das gängige Reversmotiv der ptolemaiischen Bronzemünzen (Abb. 2). Sowohl diese Bildmotivik als auch die runde Legendenanordnung sind sicher die typischsten Erkennungszeichen ptolemaiischer Münzen.

Darüber hinaus finden sich einige Motive zunächst auf den ptolemaiischen Münzen und könnten als Vorbild für andere Könige gedient haben. Hierzu zählen etwa die zwischen 282 und 272 v. Chr. erstmals ausgeprägten gestaffelten Doppelbüsten von Königen und Königinnen[4] und seit 270 v. Chr. Bildnisse von Königinnen allein auf dem Avers[5]. Die Reverse der letztgenannten Münzen zeigen in der Regel ein Füllhorn oder ein Doppelfüllhorn und nennen den Namen der Königin. Neben dem stehenden

---

3   Die verschiedenen Schritte lassen sich gut nachvollziehen anhand der Darstellung bei Noeske 2000, 22–23.
4   CPE 307–319.
5   CPE 320–330.

Adler sind auch diese Füllhörner ein typisch ptolemaiisches Reversmotiv, da sie erst
mit großem zeitlichen Abstand auch auf den Münzen anderer Dynastien erscheinen.
Zudem finden sich Epitheta und Strahlendiademe zuerst auf ptolemaiischen Münzen.
Auch diese beiden Elemente könnten eine Vorbildfunktion entfaltet haben. Unter
technischen Gesichtspunkten ist neben dem reduzierten Gewicht der Edelmetallmünzen zudem insbesondere das sogenannte Zentrierloch auf Bronzemünzen auffällig (Abb. 2), das die seleukidischen Münzen nicht aufweisen.[6] Folgende Tabelle, in der
neben den genannten Aspekten der ptolemaiischen Münzprägung auch die seleukidischen Pendants aufgeführt werden, soll den Überblick erleichtern.

Tab. 1: Ikonographische und technische Spezifika ptolemaiischer und seleukidischer Münzen

	Ptolemaier	Seleukiden
Avers	Silber: i. d. R. Ptolemaios I.	Gold/Silber: ab Antiochos I. i. d. R. regierender König
	ab 282/272: Doppelporträts	
	ab ca. 270: auch Königinnen	
Revers	sehr häufig: Adler auf Blitzbündel n. l. ; bei Prägungen für Königinnen: Füllhorn	280 bis 175: Silber i. d. R. Apollon
	dem Münzrund folgende Legende	parallele Legenden
Randgestaltung	Perlkreis	Perlkreis, Perlstab oder Wollbinde
Technik	Gold/Silber: ptolemaiischer Gewichtsstandard	attischer Gewichtsstandard
	Zentrierloch	

Abgesehen davon, dass es natürlich keinen Patentschutz auf die erstmalige Verwendung bestimmter ikonographischer Details gab, konnten viele der genannten Charakteristika auch unabhängig von den Ptolemaiern andernorts entstehen. Selbst wenn
sich manche der typischen ptolemaiischen Charakteristika auf seleukidischen Münzen finden, muss daher keine direkte Nachahmung vorliegen. Das wird im Folgenden
an einer Reihe von Beispielen deutlich.

---

6   Das Zentrierloch rührt wahrscheinlich daher, dass der Schrötling vor dem Prägevorgang geglättet
    wurde. Zu verschiedenen Deutungsansätzen siehe etwa Wagner 1999 (Glättung der Münzoberflä-
    che durch fräserartigen Bohrer – nicht auf einer Drehbank, da die Bohrlöcher häufig nicht gegen-
    überliegen), Butcher 1988, 67 (Glättung des Münzrandes), Guey – Picon 1968a und Guey – Picon
    1968b (allgemein zum Phänomen), Hall 1926 (Glättung der Münzoberfläche durch fräserartigen
    Bohrer).

2. Ptolemaiisches auf seleukidischen Münzen

2.1 Kollaboration mit den Ptolemaiern: Achaios

Die früheste potentielle Übernahme eines der typischen ptolemaiischen Merkmale findet sich auf den Bronzemünzen des Achaios, dem nach dem Tod Seleukos' III. als engem Verwandten vom Militär die Herrschaft angetragen wurde. Achaios schlug zwar zunächst aus, usurpierte 220 v. Chr. aber gegen Antiochos III. Während er sich bei der Gestaltung der Gold- und Silbermünzen eher an Philipp V. von Makedonien anlehnte (Abb. 3–4),[7] zeigen seine Bronzemünzen auf dem Revers einen stehenden Adler, der die durch Polybios[8] belegte enge Zusammenarbeit mit Ptolemaios III. symbolisieren könnte. Allerdings steht der Adler nicht nach links, sondern nach rechts, es fehlt das Blitzbündel und der Adler hält mit seinem linken Flügel einen Palmzweig (Abb. 5). Diese drei Abweichungen sind so auffällig, dass es sich trotz der Zusammenarbeit mit den Ptolemaiern nicht um eine Übernahme eines ptolemaiischen Motivs zu handeln scheint. Gerade der Palmzweig deutet auf einen konkreten Sieg hin, und Achaios, der vor seiner Usurpation sehr erfolgreich in Kleinasien operierte, dürfte damit auf seine eigene Sieghaftigkeit angespielt haben. Der Adler ist ein viel zu weit verbreitetes Reversbild in der griechischen Numismatik,[9] als dass ein antiker Betrachter von dem ikonographisch deutlich vom ptolemaiischen Adler abweichenden Adler auf den Münzen des Achaios eine direkte Beziehung zu den Ptolemaiern gezogen haben müsste. Grundsätzlich könnte der Adler auf die Unterstützung durch den obersten griechischen Gott verweisen.[10]

Abb. 3 Philippos V., Tetradrachme, Pella oder Amphipolis, Mamroth, Philippos 1.

---

7   SC 952–953, siehe auch den Kommentar bei SC I, p. 348.
8   Pol. 4.51.1–6.
9   Siehe etwa Icard 1979, Nr. 1486–1621.
10   So auch SC I, p. 348.

Abb. 4 Achaios, Goldstater, Sardeis, 220–213 v. Chr., SC 952.

Abb. 5 Achaios, Bronzemünze, Sardeis, 220–213 v. Chr., SC 955a.

Abb. 6 Seleukos IV., Bronzemünze, Antiocheia, 187–173 v. Chr., SC 1318.1d.

2.2 Die erste Königin: Laodike IV.

Etwa eine Generation später findet sich erstmals das Bildnis einer Königin auf seleukidischen Münzen. Bronzemünzen aus Antiocheia am Orontes, die von der Herrschaftszeit Seleukos' IV. (187–175 v. Chr.) bis etwa 173 v. Chr. geprägt wurden, zeigen auf dem Avers Laodike IV. (Abb. 6).[11] Seleukos IV. hatte seine Schwester geheiratet – was in gewisser Weise als Anlehnung an die bei den Ptolemaiern gängige Heiratspraxis angesehen werden könnte –, doch hätte er auch unabhängig davon ein Bildnis seiner Gattin auf die Münzen prägen lassen können. Eine direkte Beeinflussung von ptolemaiischen Vorbildern ist nicht nachweisbar, auch wenn die Darstellung demselben Schema folgt wie bei den Ptolemaiern: eine verschleierte Büste mit Haarknoten am Hinterkopf und *stephanē*. Abgesehen davon, dass ältere Darstellungen von Seleukidinnen fehlen, entspricht dieses Schema den späteren Darstellungen von Olympias.[12] Sollten die Olympias-Darstellungen auf zeitgenössische Vorbilder zurückgehen, wäre

11   SC 1318 und 1371; Hoover 2002.
12   Besonders prominent ist die Darstellung auf den Abukir-Medaillons aus dem frühen 3. Jh. n. Chr.;
     siehe bereits Dressel 1906, 31–40, der auf S. 34 vermutete, dass es ein zeitgenössisches Vorbild für
     die späteren Olympiasdarstellungen gegeben habe.

das Darstellungsschema bereits vor den 270er Jahren entwickelt worden. Sowohl die Ptolemaier als auch die Seleukiden hätten sich damit eines älteren Vorbildes bedient, Seleukos IV. brauchte sich also nicht an den ptolemaiischen Vorbildern orientieren. Dafür spricht auch, dass im Gegensatz zu den ptolemaiischen Münzen die Bronzemünzen Seleukos' IV. auf dem Revers nicht den Namen der Königin, sondern den des Königs nennen (ΒΑΣΙΛΕΩΣ ΣΕΛΕΥΚΟΥ).

Abb. 7 Laodike IV. und Antiochos, Gold-Oktadrachme, Antiocheia, 175 v. Chr., SC 1368.

Ebenso scheinen auch die im Herbst 175 in Antiocheia am Orontes geprägten Gold-Oktadrachmen, die auf dem Avers die gestaffelten Büsten von Laodike IV. und ihrem Sohn Antiochos zeigen (Abb. 7),[13] keine bewusste Anlehnung an ptolemaiische Vorbilder darzustellen. Dort zeigen Doppelbüsten stets Ehepartner oder Geschwister, hier sind es Mutter und Sohn. Darüber hinaus nehmen die Legenden bei den ptolemaiischen Beispielen Bezug auf beide Personen, während die Legende hier lediglich auf Antiochos verweist. Es geht also im vorliegenden Fall nicht darum, die Eintracht innerhalb einer Doppelherrschaft zu symbolisieren, sondern die Gold-Oktadrachmen zeigen eher die prekäre Lage, in der sich das Königshaus befand. Nach der Ermordung von Seleukos IV. durch dessen Kanzler Heliodoros war die seleukidische Herrschaft geschwächt und die ungewöhnlich großen Goldmünzen dürften als Geschenke gedient haben, um die Unterstützung für die Witwe und ihren Sohn zu sichern.[14] Die Mutter war ein Symbol für die Stabilität der Herrschaft des noch unmündigen Sohnes.

Abb. 8 Antiochos IV. und Laodike IV., Bronzemünze, Tripolis, 166/165 v. Chr., SC 1441.

13   SC 1368.
14   So auch SC II, p. 37.

2.3 Doppelporträts

Während bei Laodike IV. und ihrem Sohn die Legende und die konkreten historischen Umstände eine bewusste Kopie ptolemaiischer Vorbilder nicht sehr wahrscheinlich machen, ist es beim zeitlich nächsten seleukidischen Doppelporträt der Prägeort, der die Münzen nicht zum Beleg für die Übernahme ptolemaiischer Vorbilder durch die Seleukiden machen kann (Abb. 8). Für die Gestaltung der in Tripolis im Jahr 166/165 v. Chr. entstandenen Bronzemünzen war in erster Linie die Stadt zuständig. Der König dürfte keinen Einfluss auf die Münzgestaltung genommen haben. Warum man sich dort dazu entschied, ein Doppelporträt auf den Avers zu setzen, und nicht wie alle anderen damals Bronzemünzen prägenden seleukidischen Städte ein Porträt Antiochos' IV., lässt sich allenfalls erraten. Eine mögliche Deutung ergibt sich aus dem Reversbild, das die nach rechts reitenden Dioskuren zeigt. Die Dioskuren scheinen für Tripolis eine besonders Bedeutung besessen zu haben, denn sie erscheinen nicht nur auf dem Revers der Bronzemünze, sondern auch auf Tetradrachmen der Stadt aus dem Jahr 110/109, die auf dem Avers ein gestaffeltes Doppelporträt der beiden Geschwister zeigen.[15] Vielleicht entschied man sich wegen dieser besonderen Nähe zu den Dioskuren für ein Doppelporträt auf den Bronzemünzen des Jahres 166/165.

Abb. 9 Demetrios I. und Laodike V., Tetradrachme, Seleukeia am Tigris,
162–150 v. Chr., SC 1687.

Ein gestaffeltes Doppelporträt erscheint noch ein drittes Mal auf seleukidischen Münzen (Abb. 9). Aber auch in diesem Fall ist ein ptolemaiisches Vorbild eher unwahrscheinlich, denn die Tetradrachmen, die Demetrios I. und Laodike V. zeigen,[16] wurden in Seleukeia am Tigris geprägt, wo kaum jemand von den ptolemaiischen Pendants Kenntnis besessen haben dürfte.

15　　BMC Phoenicia, Tripolis 2–7; de Callataÿ 1993, 123 kurz zur Bedeutung der Dioskuren, die auch
　　　davor und danach auf den Münzen aus Tripolis zu finden sind; siehe auch Cohen 2011, 715.
16　　SC 1686–1689.

All diese Beispiele zeigen, dass einige der genannten Charakteristika ptolemaiischer Münzen sich auch unabhängig von diesen andernorts herausbilden konnten.

2.4 Göttliche Attribute und Epitheta zu Lebzeiten: Antiochos IV.

Es gibt aber auch Beispiele, bei denen eine Beeinflussung seleukidischer Münzen durch ptolemaiische Vorbilder sicher ist. Die frühesten Beispiele finden sich unter Antiochos IV., der nach zehnjähriger Geiselhaft in Italien und anschließendem Aufenthalt in Athen mit der Unterstützung Eumenes' II. auf den seleukidischen Thron gelangte. Antiochos IV. adoptierte den amtierenden seleukidischen König, den Sohn seines von Heliodor ermordeten Bruders, als dessen Rächer er sich zunächst stilisierte.[17] Trotz dieser Versuche, sich als legitimen Nachfolger Seleukos' IV. zu etablieren, dürfte der Herrschaftsbeginn nicht einfach gewesen sein. Antiochos IV. sah sich sowohl den Anhängern von Heliodor als auch den *philoi* seines Bruders gegenüber, die in erster Linie den Sohn des ermordeten Königs unterstützt haben dürften. Antiochos IV. reagierte darauf, indem er sich bei seiner Selbstdarstellung ganz bewusst von seinem ermordeten Bruder absetzte und sich einerseits an den Dynastiegründer Seleukos I. anlehnte sowie andererseits eine starke Anbindung an die göttliche Sphäre suchte. Er war nicht der von außen kommende Usurpator, sondern der an den Dynastiegründer anknüpfende göttliche, rechtmäßige König. Zwar existierte spätestens seit seinem Vater Antiochos III. ein reichsweiter Dynastie- und Herrscherkult, bisher hatten es die Seleukiden aber weitgehend vermieden, sich zu Lebzeiten auf den Münzen mit göttlichen Attributen zu präsentieren oder entsprechende Epitheta zu tragen.

Abb. 10 Antiochos IV., Tetradrachme, Antiocheia am Orontes, 173–168 v. Chr., SC 1396.

Abb. 11 Antiochos IV., Hemidrachme, Antiocheia am Orontes, 169 v. Chr., SC 1405.

17 Bunge 1974, 60 und Mittag 2006, 46.

Abb. 12 Ptolemaios V., Tetradrachme, unbekannte Münzstätte in Phoinikien, Svor. 1263.

Mit dieser Tradition brach Antiochos IV., als er spätestens 173 v. Chr. ein neuartiges Diadem einführte, an dessen Enden sich jeweils ein Stern befindet (Abb. 10);[18] zuweilen trug er auch ein Strahlendiadem (Abb. 11)[19] und nutzte ab diesem Zeitpunkt das Epitheton θεὸς ἐπιφανής.[20] Für alle drei Aspekte existierten Vorbilder in der ptolemaiischen Münzprägung. Ptolemaios V. (204–180 v. Chr.), der Schwager Antiochos' IV., hatte bereits eine (allerdings mit Kornähren) verzierte Königsbinde getragen,[21] eine Strahlenkrone trug Ptolemaios III. auf posthumen Prägungen,[22] und die ersten kultischen Epitheta nutzte bereits Ptolemaios II.[23] Inwiefern sich Antiochos IV. von diesen Vorbildern inspirieren ließ, lässt sich aber kaum abschätzen. Manches konnte sich wie die bereits behandelten Doppelbüsten unabhängig herausbilden. Bereits frühere Seleukiden hatten Epitheta erhalten,[24] und es war letztlich nur eine Frage der Zeit, bis solche Epitheta auch auf Münzen verwendet wurden. Hierbei mussten keineswegs die Ptolemaier das Vorbild geliefert haben, denn auch der baktrische König Agathokles, der im frühen 2. Jh. regierte, wurde auf seinen Münzen zuweilen mit seinem vollständigen Namen tituliert (ΒΑΣΙΛΕΩΣ ΔΙΚΑΙΟΥ ΑΓΑΘΟΚΛΕΟΥΣ).[25] Das Strahlendiadem als Anlehnung an die Kopfbedeckung des Sonnengottes Helios[26] war

---

18   SC 1396–1397. Zur Typologie des hellenistischen Herrscherdiadems siehe grundsätzlich Salzmann 2012.

19   Z. B. SC 1405.

20   Siehe auch die Beiträge von Sonja Richter und Martin Kovacs (S. 602–607) in diesem Band.

21   Kyrieleis 1973, 244–246 und Mørkholm 1979 deuten die ungewöhnliche Königsbinde als Hinweis auf eine besondere Verbindung oder gar Identifikation zu bzw. mit Triptolemos oder Harpokrates, die für landwirtschaftlichen Überfluss sorgten.

22   Goldmnaeia, die zwischen 221 und 204 v. Chr. in Alexandreia geprägt wurden: CPE 887–890.

23   Es handelt sich um Golddidrachmen, die auf der einen Seite die gestaffelten Büsten von Ptolemaios I. und Berenike I. sowie die Legende ΘΕΩΝ, auf der anderen Seite die gestaffelten Büsten von Ptolemaios II. und Arsinoë II. sowie die Legende ΑΔΕΛΦΩΝ tragen und zwischen 282 und 272 v. Chr. in Alexandreia geprägt wurden: CPE 307–319.

24   Zu Seleukos I. siehe beispielsweise Muccioli 2013, 94–107.

25   In Baktrien scheinen sie zunächst nur posthum genutzt worden zu sein; siehe zu Diodotos I. und II. Bop. Sér. 16. Erst Agathokles propagierte das Epitheton Dikaios bereits zu Lebzeichen (Bop. Sér. 3–4).

26   Zur Verbindung des hellenistischen Strahlendiadems mit dem Sonnengott s. Bergmann 1998, 40–57.

grundsätzlich nicht ungewöhnlicher als die ebenfalls auf einzelne Götter verweisenden Stierhörner oder Flügel, die einige frühere Seleukiden als Kopfschmuck trugen.[27] Auch für das Strahlendiadem bedurfte es somit nicht unbedingt des ptolemaiischen Vorbildes. Letztlich sind auch die Sternenden des Diadems wohl kaum vom Ährendiadem Ptolemaios' V. direkt inspiriert worden. Insofern können alle drei außergewöhnlichen Merkmale der Münzen Antiochos' IV. durchaus unabhängig von ptolemaiischen Vorlagen erklärt werden.

Das gilt aber nicht für eine Reihe von Münzen, die wahrscheinlich 169/168 v. Chr. in Antiocheia am Orontes entstanden. Sie sind sowohl ikonographisch als auch technisch zu deutlich an ptolemaiische Prägungen angelehnt. Die Rückseite zeigt stets einen mit angelegten Flügeln nach rechts auf einem Blitzbündel stehenden Adler, die Bronzemünzen weisen das typisch ptolemaiische Zentrierloch auf und zwei Bronzenominale zeigen auf den Aversen die ägyptischen Götter Serapis bzw. Isis (Abb. 13–17).

Abb. 13 Antiochos IV., Drachme, Antiocheia am Orontes, 169 v. Chr., SC 1404.

Abb. 14 Antiochos IV., Bronzemünze (Avers: Zeus), Antiocheia am Orontes, 169 v. Chr., SC 1412.

27 Nach Lib. or. 11.92 befand sich beispielsweise in Antiocheia eine Statue Seleukos' I. mit Stierhörnern. Zur Aneignung von Götterattributen durch hellenistische Könige s. Bergmann 1998, 16–38; dort 23–25 zu den Stierhörnern des Demetrios Poliorketes.

Abb. 15 Antiochos IV., Bronzemünze (Avers: Serapis), Antiocheia am Orontes,
169 v. Chr., SC 1413.

Abb. 16 Antiochos IV., Bronzemünze (Avers: Isis), Antiocheia am Orontes, 169 v. Chr., SC 1414.

Abb. 17 Antiochos IV., Bronzemünze (Avers: Antiochos IV.), Antiocheia am Orontes,
169 v. Chr., SC 1415.

Diese ungewöhnliche Serie hat früh die Aufmerksamkeit der Forschung erregt. Während Ioannes Svoronos 1908 noch annahm, die Münzen seien während des für Antiochos IV. militärisch erfolgreichen Sechsten Syrischen Krieges in Ägypten geprägt worden, wird seit den Arbeiten von Edward Newell von den meisten Bearbeitern angenommen, die Münzen seien in Antiocheia am Orontes hergestellt worden.[28] Nach wie vor umstritten ist jedoch der Zweck dieser ausgewöhnlichen Serie. Deutete Svoronos sie als Münzen für den Gebrauch in Ägypten, sah Newell in ihnen nachträglich geprägte Erinnerungsmünzen. Otto Mørkholm betonte dagegen die propagandistische Wirkung

---

28 Svor. 1415–1419, Newell 1918, 25–27, Mørkholm 1963, 22–23; anders: Weiser 1995, 94–97, der annimmt, die Münzen seien in Ägypten gefertigt worden und ihnen läge der 600-Rechen-Bronzedrachmen-Standard zugrunde.

während des Krieges für die Bewohner des seleukidischen Kerngebietes und unterstrich die Funktion als Münzen. Die Bronzemünzen hätten dazu gedient, den Bedarf an Silbermünzen zu reduzieren.[29] Das wäre insofern eine Imitation des ptolemaiischen Vorbildes, als im silberarmen Ägypten bereits seit längerer Zeit Bronzemünzen Silbergeld ersetzten.[30] Georges Le Rider hob folgerichtig das Gesamtkonzept der Münzprägung in Antiocheia hervor; die neuen Bronzemünzen hätten die gleichzeitig geprägten Drachmen, Hemidrachmen und Obolen ergänzt, die auf ihren Reversen ebenfalls einen stehenden Adler zeigen (Abb. 13).[31] Die von Le Rider angenommenen Wertrelationen wurden jedoch von Arthur Houghton, Catharine Lorber und Oliver Hoover in Zweifel gezogen,[32] so dass die Frage nach dem Zweck der Serie wieder offen ist.

Die übliche Datierung in die Jahre 169/168 v. Chr. basiert auf verschiedenen Überlegungen. Spätestens nach dem erzwungenen Rückzug aus Ägypten nahm Antiochos IV. den Beinamen Nikephoros an, der auch auf Münzen verwendet wurde.[33] Da die hier interessierende Serie dieses Epitheton noch nicht aufweist, scheint sie bis spätestens 168 v. Chr. geprägt worden zu sein. Als frühester Zeitpunkt kommt das Jahr 173/172 v. Chr. in Frage, da erst ab diesem Jahr die auf den Münzen zu findenden Epitheta Theos und Epiphanes Verwendung fanden.[34] Die genauere zeitliche Eingrenzung auf die Jahre 169/168 v. Chr. ergibt sich über die Gestaltung. Die Avers- und Reversdarstellungen stellen keineswegs eine exakte Kopie der ptolemaiischen Münzen dar, sondern wurden ganz bewusst abgewandelt. Das gilt insbesondere für die Entscheidung, die Averse von zwei der vier Nominale mit Serapis und Isis zu schmücken. Zwar wurden Serapis und Isis auch in seleukidischen Städten verehrt,[35] beide Gottheiten waren aber auf das Engste mit den Ptolemaiern verbunden, und bisher hatten diese Götter nicht zum Repertoire der seleukidischen Münzprägung gehört. Sozusagen gerahmt wurden

---

29 Mørkholm 1982, 303–305.

30 Maresch 1996, 7–11. Allerdings ließ bereits Antiochos III. deutlich größere Bronzemünzen prägen als die bisher bei den Seleukiden üblichen Bronzenominale; siehe etwa SC 1259, 1264 und 1268.

31 Le Rider 1994.

32 SC II, p. 68.

33 SC II, p. 44. Le Rider 1994, 19 vermutete, die Serie sei zwischen den beiden Feldzügen des Sechsten Syrischen Krieges entstanden.

34 SC II, p. 44 und 49.

35 Die Verehrung ägyptischer Gottheiten in seleukidischen Gebieten ist im Raphiadekret angedeutet: Ptolemaios IV. ließ Leichname von in Ägypten heiligen Tieren nach der Schlacht von Raphia in Ägypten bestatten. Kann daraus geschlossen werden, dass diese Tiere auch dort (von Ägyptern?) verehrt wurden? Siehe etwa Hoffmann 2000, 162 und Thissen 1966, 59–60. Zur Verehrung von Serapis im seleukidischen Herrschaftsgebiet siehe Bickerman 1938, 251 und Robert 1960. Tac. hist. 4.84.4, demzufolge Serapis aus Seleukeia am Tigris geholt worden war, deutet bei aller Skepsis auf eine Verbindung zwischen Seleukeia und Serapis hin. Zudem besaß im syrischen Raum Tyche zuweilen Attribute der Isis: Charbonneaux 1957, 139. Auch Zeus wurde nicht nur in Ägypten mit Serapis gleichgesetzt: Cook 1925, 188–191 und Charbonneaux 1957, 138. Aus Laodikeia am Meer sind für das Jahr 174 v. Chr. Priester des Serapis und der Isis belegt: Vidman 1969, 180 Nr. 356. In Seleukeia in Pieria wurde eine Isis-Aphrodite-Statuette gefunden: Stillwell 1941, 124 Nr. 365.

die beiden ägyptischen Götter durch das größte und das kleinste Nominal der Serie,
die Zeus und den König selbst auf den Aversen zeigen. Zeus ersetzte ab 173 v. Chr. in
vielen seleukidischen Prägestätten den bis dahin üblichen Apollon als Reversbild, und
Antiochos IV. scheint sich mit diesem Gott, der bereits auf den Münzen des Dynastiegründers zu finden war, besonders verbunden gefühlt zu haben.[36] Zwei der vier Averse
sind damit eher traditionell seleukidisch, zwei ptolemaiisch. Denkbar wäre, dass so
die doppelte Herrschaft des Königs im Seleukidenreich und in Ägypten symbolisiert
werden sollte. Das könnte auch den seitenverkehrten Adler erklären, der einerseits an
den ptolemaiischen Adler erinnert, aber eben doch bewusst verändert wurde. Auch
wenn sich diese Annahmen nicht belegen lassen, so ließen sich die für seleukidische
Verhältnisse ungewöhnlichen Aversdarstellungen von Serapis und Isis am ehesten im
Kontext des Sechsten Syrischen Krieges erklären. Vor dem Ausbruch des Kriegs im
Jahr 169 v. Chr. wären eher Apollon und Artemis oder andere griechische Gottheiten
erwartbar gewesen. Die Nutzer der Münzen wären wohl erstaunt gewesen, auf zwei
Nominalen vor 169 v. Chr. ägyptische Gottheiten vorzufinden, obwohl der von den
Ptolemaiern begonnene Krieg allenfalls zu erahnen und der für die Seleukiden äußerst
vorteilhafte Verlauf sicher nicht abzusehen waren. Auch wenn sich daher eine Datie-
rung ab 169 v. Chr. nicht beweisen lässt, deuten doch einige Indizien in diese Richtung.

Der Prägeort ergibt sich in erster Linie aus den Fundorten der Münzen und sti-
listischen Überlegungen.[37] Gerade die Fundortverteilung legt die Vermutung nahe,
dass die ungewöhnlichen Prägungen tatsächlich als Münzen in Syrien verwendet wurden und damit eine geldpolitische Bedeutung besaßen. Der wichtigste geldpolitische
Grund für diese Serie dürfte – wie Newell und Le Rider annahmen – die Erweiterung
der zuvor üblichen Palette an Nominalen gewesen sein. Schon während seiner Geiselhaft in Rom mag Antiochos IV. die Vorteile einer umfangreichen Bronzemünzprägung
kennengelernt haben. Dass die Serie aus Antiocheia sich dennoch eng an ptolemaiischen Münzen orientiert, könnte mit der großen geographischen Nähe erklärt werden. Interessanterweise wurde auch die Technik des Zentrierloches mitkopiert. Die
Fundorte der Münzen deuten darauf hin, dass es sich nicht um eine Kleingeldprägung
handelte, die lediglich in Antiocheia zirkulierte, sondern ähnlich wie in Ägypten eine
reichsweit einheitliche Kleingeldprägung geschaffen werden sollte.[38] Bis 173 v. Chr.

---

36   Zu den verschiedenen Indizien für eine besondere Beziehung zwischen Antiochos IV. und Zeus
      siehe Mittag 2006, 139–145. Siehe auch den Beitrag von Katharina Martin (S. 559–564) in diesem
      Band.
37   Newell 1918, 26–27 (vier Exemplare mit Fundort Syrien; ein Exemplar in Syrien gekauft; ein Exem-
      plar mit „syrischer" Patina; ein Exemplar [Svor. 1422] dessen Stil und Machart ägyptisch seien und
      das tatsächlich nach Ägypten gehört). Bei den Grabungen in Dura-Europos wurden zwei Münzen
      aus der Serie gefunden (Bellinger 1949, Nr. 67 und 68). Bei den amerikanischen Grabungen in
      Antiocheia des Jahres 1932 wurden keine Münzen Antiochos' IV. gefunden (Elderkin 1934). Auch
      die publizierten Münzschätze enthielten keine Münzen dieser Serie (vgl. IGCH und CH I–IX).
38   Siehe die Fundorte in Anm. 35.

waren die bereits von Seleukos IV. eingeführten Bronzenominale weiter geprägt worden;[39] die neuen Münzen sollten diese wohl ersetzen.

Der durch Serapis, Isis und den Adler gegebene enge Bezug auf die Doppelherrschaft im Seleukidenreich und in Ägypten war nach dem von den Römern erzwungenen Rückzug Antiochos' IV. problematisch; eine Einstellung der Serie lag daher nahe. Stattdessen wurde ab 169/168 v. Chr. in 26 Städten nach einem weitgehend einheitlichen Schema Kleingeld hergestellt.[40] Die neuen Bronzemünzen sind deutlich kleiner als die ‚ägyptische' Serie aus Antiocheia. Die deutlich kleineren Nominale könnten die Folge einer Verschiebung der Wertrelation zwischen Edelmetall und Kupfer gewesen sein. Möglicherweise führte die wohl vor allem aus Edelmetall bestehende Beute aus dem Sechsten Syrischen Krieg[41] zu einer Verschiebung dieser Wertrelation im seleukidischen Herrschaftsgebiet.[42] Wenn trotz der Kritik an Georges Le Riders Rekonstruktion dessen Wertrelationen zutreffend sein sollten, dann waren die ägyptisierenden Bronzemünzen nur leicht überbewertet, das heißt, ihr Materialwert lag nur wenig unterhalb des Nominalwertes.[43] Sollte es nach dem beutebeladenen Rückzug aus Ägypten zu einer Verschiebung der Wertrelationen der Münzmetalle gekommen sein, könnte der Materialwert den Nominalwert sogar überstiegen haben. Die Münzserie war damit wirtschaftlich nicht mehr sinnvoll und wurde durch lokal produzierte neue Bronzemünzen ersetzt. Auch wenn viele Details dieser besonderen Münzserie nach wie vor unklar sind, so stellt sie doch den ersten sicheren Fall von Ptolemaiischem auf seleukidischen Münzen dar.

2.5 Der ptolemaiische Adler auf seleukidischen Münzen aus Phoinikien

Ebenso wie diese ungewöhnliche Münzserie Antiochos' IV. einige Rätsel aufwirft, lassen sich die Hintergründe für eine münzpolitische Entscheidung seines Sohnes nur erahnen. Im südlichen Phoinikien war nach der Eroberung durch Antiochos III. das

---

39   SC II, p. 45.

40   Zur Datierung: SC II, p. 45, allgemein auch: Mørkholm 1966, 124–130; Mittag 2006, 182–191; Lichtenberger 2021.

41   Nach 1 Makk 1.20–24; 2 Makk 5.11–16; 4 Makk 4.21–22; Ios. ant. Iud. 12.246–247 entnahm Antiochos IV. auf dem Rückmarsch von Ägypten dem Jerusalemer Tempel darüber hinaus angeblich Gegenstände im Wert von 1.800 Talenten Silber.

42   Le Rider 1994, 27–28 hält es neben dieser Erklärung auch für möglich, dass der ‚Staat' die Münzen leichter machte, um einen höheren Gewinn aus der Münzprägung zu ziehen oder um dadurch mehr Münzen in Umlauf bringen zu können. Beide Erklärungen befriedigen nur dann, wenn sich bestätigen lässt, dass die Bronzemünzen aufgrund ihres Nominalwertes und nicht aufgrund ihres Materialwertes akzeptiert wurden.

43   Le Rider 1994, 20–21 und 27 rekonstruierte ein Nominalsystem aus silbernen Drachmen, Hemidrachmen, Diobolen und den vier bronzenen ‚ägyptischen' Nominalen, die seiner Meinung nach kaum überbewertet waren.

auf dem attischen Standard beruhende seleukidische Münzgewichtssystem eingeführt
worden. Während der ptolemaiischen Herrschaft lag der Münzprägung dagegen ein
reduzierter Standard zugrunde. Unter der kurzen Herrschaft von Antiochos V. (164–
162 v. Chr.) wurden in Ptolemaïs-Ake erstmals wieder Münzen nach diesem lokalen
phoinikischen Standard geprägt.[44] Zudem zeigen die Rückseiten der dort geprägten
Tetradrachmen nun den ‚ptolemaiischen‘ Adler auf einem Blitzbündel, die Legende ist
(wie auf ptolemaiischen Münzen üblich) dem Münzrund angepasst und der (seleukidische) Perlstabrand wurde durch einen (ptolemaiischen) Perlkreis ersetzt (Abb. 18).
Die Münzen sind somit weitgehend an den vorseleukidischen, also ptolemaiischen
Vorbildern ausgerichtet. Da in anderen phoinikischen Orten weiterhin nach seleukidischem Standard geprägt wurde, handelte es sich um eine lokal begrenzte und
vielleicht durch einen konkreten Anlass bedingte Maßnahme. Vor den nach phoinikischem Standard geprägten Tetradrachmen waren in Ptolemaïs-Ake für Antiochos V.
zwei unterschiedliche Serien von Tetradrachmen nach seleukidischem Standard hergestellt worden, die ‚phoinikischen‘ Tetradrachmen gehören also ans Ende der kurzen
Herrschaft dieses Seleukiden. In dieser Phase geriet seine anfänglich recht erfolgreiche Herrschaft ins Wanken, denn in Antiocheia probte Philippos einen Aufstand,[45] der
den seleukidischen König bzw. seinen Kanzler Lysias dazu zwang, trotz militärischer
Erfolge Frieden mit den aufständischen Juden zu schließen. Über diesen Friedensschluss waren die Einwohner von Ptolemaïs-Ake wenig erfreut und es bedurfte der
Überzeugungskraft des Lysias, um die Einwohner wieder zu beruhigen.[46] Vielleicht
war die Rückkehr zum vorseleukidischen Münzstandard und Design ein Zugeständnis
des Königs an die Bewohner dieser wichtigen Hafenstadt. Unklar bleibt jedoch, ob das
Zugeständnis darin bestand, zum alten, vorseleukidischen Standard zurückzukehren
oder zum vorseleukidischen Aussehen. Beides ging Hand in Hand, denn das Aussehen
orientierte sich an den vorseleukidischen Münzen, wohl in erster Linie, um zu signali-
sieren, dass diese Münzen nicht dem seleukidischen Standard folgten, sondern parallel
mit den älteren ptolemaiischen Münzen umlaufen sollten.

---

44 SC 1583. Ging man früher davon aus, dass diese Maßnahme erst unter Alexander Balas erfolgte und
    die Münzen im Namen Antiochos' V. posthum geprägt wurden, herrscht heute Konsens, dass sie
    bereits zu Lebzeiten Antiochos' V. entstanden (Mørkholm 1967, 78–79; Houghton – Le Rider 1985,
    76 und SC II, p. 136). Zu Beginn der Herrschaft Antiochos' V. wurden dort noch ‚seleukidische‘
    Tetradrachmen geprägt, gegen Ende der Herrschaft ‚ptolemaiische‘.
45 Ehling 2008, 119.
46 2 Makk 13.25–26.

Abb. 18 Antiochos V., Tetradrachme, Ptolemaïs-Ake, 164 v. Chr., SC 1583.

Abb. 19 Demetrios I., Gold-Oktadrachme, Antiocheia am Orontes, 151/150 v. Chr., SC 1628.

Abb. 20 Demetrios I., Gold-2,5-Stater, Antiocheia am Orontes, 151/150 v. Chr., SC 1630.

Abb. 21 Demetrios I., Gold-Distater, Antiocheia am Orontes, 151/150 v. Chr., SC 1631.

Abb. 22 Demetrios I, Goldstater, Antiocheia am Orontes, 151/150 v. Chr., SC 1632.

2.6 Ungewöhnliche Goldmünzen des Demetrios I.

Ähnlich wie die erwähnten Münzen Antiochos' IV. nur ein kurzes Zwischenspiel blieben und die Serie Antiochos' V. aus Ptolemaïs-Ake zunächst eine lokal und zeitlich begrenzte Maßnahme war, lehnte sich auch Demetrios I. nur in einer einzigen Serie möglicherweise eng an ptolemaiische Vorbilder an. Demetrios I. war 162 aus römischer Geiselhaft entflohen, hatte in Tripolis seleukidischen Boden betreten und die Ermordung von Antiochos V. und Lysias in die Wege geleitet. Er führte ein Reversmotiv ein, das weder Zeus noch Apollon zeigt, sondern eine thronende Tyche mit kurzem Zepter und Füllhorn (Abb. 19).[47] Unter dem Thron befindet sich eine kleine geflügelte weibliche Gestalt, die aufgrund ihres Fischleibes und der von der Ikonographie Nikes entlehnten Flügel auf die glückliche Seefahrt des Königs von Italien nach Syrien bezogen wurde.[48] Die thronende und ein Zepter haltende Tyche symbolisiert demnach das persönliche Schicksal des Königs.[49] Eine Serie von vier Goldnominalen, die 151/150 v. Chr. geprägt wurde (Jahr BΞP = 162 der seleukidischen Ära), zeigt diese Tyche – allerdings ohne die geflügelte Nike – als Aversmotiv (Abb. 20–22; keine Abb. des größten Nominals verfügbar); es handelt sich dabei um die einzige Edelmetallserie, deren Avers kein Bildnis des Herrschers trägt.[50] Ebenso ungewöhnlich ist der Revers, denn er zeigt ein Doppelfüllhorn und eine Legende, die dem Münzrund folgt, also zwei typisch ptolemaiische Gestaltungsmerkmale.[51]

Eine in vier verschiedenen Nominalen ausdifferenzierte Goldmünzserie hatten die Seleukiden bisher noch nie ausgebracht. Allem Anschein nach waren die Umstände für die Konzeption dieser Serie außergewöhnlich. Zuletzt wurde als Anlass das zehnjährige Thronjubiläum des Königs vermutet, allerdings sei es in Wirklichkeit darum gegangen, Unterstützung für den König zu sichern.[52] Obwohl die datierten Münzen durchaus zum zehnjährigen Thronjubiläum passen würden, ist doch auffällig, dass gerade diese Serie das Bildnis des Königs vermissen lässt, der Geehrte also sozusagen abwesend ist. Der Prägeanlass scheint sich vielmehr aus dem zweiten Aspekt zu ergeben, dem Versuch, mit Hilfe der Münzen Unterstützung zu gewinnen. Demetrios I. befand sich damals in einer wenig komfortablen Lage. 151/150 v. Chr. war der König

---

47   SC 1609–1617, 1620–1622, 1624–1626, 1628–1641, 1643, 1649–1653, 1659, 1678, 1681–1690, 1697, 1719, 1763; Bronzemünzen aus Seleukeia am Tigris zeigen auch abweichende Tyche-Darstellungen: 1695, 1699; in Uncertain Mint 81 wurden Drachmen und in einer Münzstätte im Osten des Reiches wurden Goldstatere geprägt, die eine thronende Tyche mit Pfeil und Füllhorn zeigen: 1722–1723, 1754; 1694 aus Seleukeia am Tigris: Agathos Daimon.
48   Fleischer 1986; Ehling 2004, 29; SC II, p. 154–155.
49   Smith 1994, 92.
50   SC 1629–1632.
51   Die Reverse weiterer Münzen, die auf dem Avers wie üblich das Herrscherbildnis tragen, zeigen ein einfaches Füllhorn, das von einer parallel angeordneten Legende flankiert wird: SC 1623, 1627, 1655–1657, 1698, 1716.
52   SC II, p. 166.

durch die Usurpation des Alexander Balas bereits in arge Bedrängnis geraten. Geradezu händeringend hatte er die Unterstützung der Juden gesucht[53] und sich sicher auch an
andere Untertanen gewandt. Im Jahr der Prägung kam Ptolemaios VI. nach Ptolemaïs-
Ake, um seine Tochter Kleopatra Thea mit Alexander Balas zu verheiraten.[54] Bereits
zuvor hatte der Ptolemaier Balas unterstützt, wodurch Demetrios I. in große Bedrängnis geraten war. In großer Hast wurden die Goldmünzen geprägt, wie die schlampige
Ausführung der Rückseitenlegenden und Monogramme[55] sowie die Verwendung von
Distater-Stempeln für die zweieinhalbfachen Statere zeigt.[56] Die Geschwindigkeit der
Prägung scheint einher gegangen zu sein mit einem enormen Geldbedarf, denn die
Goldmünzen repräsentierten einen viel höheren Geldbetrag als quantitativ vergleichbare Silbermünzen. Allem Anschein nach war die Eile so groß, dass man noch nicht
einmal genügend Zeit hatte, passende Aversstempel mit dem Herrscherbildnis anzu-
fertigen. Auch für die im Jahr zuvor geprägten Gold-Oktadrachmen hatte man bereits
abgenutzte Tetradrachmen-Aversstempel verwendet (Abb. 19) und Goldstatere mit
Hilfe von Drachmen-Aversstempeln geprägt.[57] Das zeigt deutlich, dass bereits damals
Eile geboten war. Offenbar hatte man zwar Stempelschneider zur Verfügung, die in
der Lage waren, Reversstempel anzufertigen, jedoch keine Aversstempelschneider. Da
Tyche vom Revers auf den Avers ,wanderte‘, lag es nahe, die Reverse mit dem Attribut
der Tyche zu schmücken. Aber die Reverse zeigen, dass auch die Graveure der Legende recht ungeübt waren. All das spricht für eine absolute Notprägung. Die Ähnlichkeit
der Münzrückseiten mit ptolemaiischen Vorbildern könnte daher eher zufällig und
keine bewusste Anlehnung an die Münzprägung des Kriegsgegners gewesen sein.[58]

2.7 Kleopatra Thea, die starke Ptolemaierin

Wohl anlässlich der Hochzeit von Alexander Balas mit Kleopatra Thea entstanden in
Ptolemaïs-Ake Tetradrachmen und Bronzemünzen (Abb. 23–24).[59] Auf den Tetradrachmen findet sich eine gestaffelte Doppelbüste von Kleopatra Thea mit Kalathos

---

53   1 Makk 10.1–45.
54   1 Makk 10.57–58.
55   SC 1629, siehe hierzu auch den Kommentar bei SC II, p. 167: „cat. no. 1629.2 (…) appears to be
      an emergency issue. The lettering was added somewhat carelessly to the reverse, so that the final
      Y of the king's name overlaps one end of the fillet. Both the right field monogram and the date are
      poorly written".
56   SC 1630; das Wertzeichen B unter dem Thron wurde schlampig eradiert und im linken Feld ein
      neues Wertzeichen angebracht.
57   SC 1627–1628 mit dem Kommentar bei SC II, p. 166.
58   Die Lage wurde sogar als so gefährlich eingeschätzt, dass Demetrios I. seine Söhne nach Knidos in
      Sicherheit bringen ließ: Iust. 35.2.1.
59   SC II, p. 210. Zur Hochzeit siehe 1 Makk 10.51–58 und Ios. ant. Iud. 13.80–82, der behauptet, Ptole-
      maios VI. habe seiner Tochter eine große Mitgift an Gold und Silber mit in die Ehe gegeben.

sowie Füllhorn und Alexander Balas.[60] Kleopatras Bedeutung wird dadurch unter-
strichen, dass sich ihr Bildnis vor dem ihres Gatten befindet; den Revers ziert jedoch
der seit Antiochos IV. übliche Zeus Nikephoros (allerdings steht Nike frontal und hält
ein Blitzbündel) und die parallel angeordnete Legende ΒΑΣΙΛΕΩΣ ΑΛΕΞΑΝΔΡΟΥ
ΘΕΟΠΑΤΟΡΟΣ ΕΥΕΡΓΕΤΟΥ.[61] Gewicht, Stil und Rückseitengestaltung sind somit
typisch seleukidisch, lediglich die Attribute, mit denen Kleopatras Bildnis ausgezeich-
net ist, könnten als ptolemaiische Entlehnungen gedeutet werden. Sie verweisen ähnlich wie die Füllhörner auf den älteren Prägungen für Ptolemaierinnen auf Frucht-
barkeit und Fülle. Die Kombination aus Kalathos und Füllhorn hat allerdings keine
exakten Vorbilder, so dass die konkrete Deutung unklar ist. Der Kalathos wurde mit
der Vergöttlichung Kleopatras in Verbindung gebracht,[62] allerdings scheint Kleopatra
Thea den Kultnamen Thea erst im Rahmen der Eheschließung mit Demetrios II. erhalten zu haben.[63] Das Füllhorn könnte auf Tyche verweisen,[64] allerdings trägt Tyche
üblicherweise keinen Kalathos.

Die Bronzemünzen zeigen wie die Tetradrachmen das Doppelporträt des Herrscherpaares,[65] wobei in zwei Fällen Reversbilder gewählt wurden, die mehr oder weniger deutliche Anspielungen auf ptolemaiische Traditonen aufweisen (SC 1845: Adler
mit Palmzweig; SC 1846: Isiskrone). Allerdings wurde bereits darauf hingewiesen,
dass der stehende Adler ein häufiges Reversmotiv ist, zudem wurde Isis in verschiedenen phoinikischen Küstenstädten bereits vor den Ptolemaiern verehrt,[66] so dass beide Reversmotive auch ohne die Ptolemaier erklärbar wären. Die Interpretation hängt
letztlich mit der Frage zusammen, wer die Adressaten der Münzen waren. Da sie in
seleukidischem Gewichtsstandard ausgebracht wurden, könnten primär nicht-ptole-
maiische Soldaten die Empfänger gewesen sein.

Scheint somit der ptolemaiische Einfluss auf die Münzprägung des seleukidisch-
ptolemaiischen Hochzeitspaares trotz der enormen Bedeutung Kleopatras Theas eher
gering gewesen zu sein, so präsentieren sich Goldmünzen im Namen Kleopatra Theas
weitgehend ‚ptolemaiisch' (Abb. 25). Sie zeigen auf dem Avers nur Kleopatra Thea
und auf dem Revers ein typisch ptolemaiisches Füllhorn und die dem Münzrund an-
gepasste Legende ΒΑΣΙΛΙΣΣΗΣ ΚΛΕΟΠΑΤΡΑΣ.[67] Lediglich der Gewichtsstandard
und der Stil entsprechen seleukidischen Konventionen, ansonsten folgt diese Prägung

60   Siehe Fleischer 1991, 76–77.
61   SC 1841; Houghton 1988; Ehling 2008, 155 Anm. 373 verweist zur Deutung des von Nike gehaltenen
     Blitzbündels auf die Gründungslegende von Seleukeia in Pieria bei App. Syr. 58.299.
62   Pinkwart 1965, 36–37.
63   Ehling 2008, 163.
64   So Fleischer 1991, 76 und Ehling 2008, 156, der völlig zurecht den von Brunelle 1976, 72 gezogenen
     Vergleich mit der kleinasiatischen Artemis ablehnt.
65   SC 1843–1846.
66   Siehe oben Anm. 33.
67   SC 1840.

ptolemaiischen Traditionen. Da das Bildnis eine junge Kleopatra Thea zeigt, liegt die Vermutung nahe, dass die Goldmünzen ebenfalls anlässlich der Hochzeit mit Alexander Balas in Ptolemaïs-Ake hergestellt wurden.[68] Sicher ist dies jedoch keineswegs, da Monogramme fehlen und Fundorte nicht bekannt sind.[69] Ähnliche Münzen waren bereits zwischen 244 und 221 – möglicherweise im ptolemaisch besetzten Seleukeia in Pierien – für Berenike II. geprägt worden (Abb. 26).[70] Der seleukidische Gewichtsstandard spricht dafür, dass diese Goldstatere für Personen hergestellt wurden, die sich nicht im ptolemaiischen, sondern im seleukidischen Wirtschaftsraum aufhielten. Um wen es sich dabei handelte, bleibt aber unklar. Bei Zahlungen an Soldaten würde man erwarten können, dass sie (auch) das Bildnis und den Namen des Königs tragen, der an ihrer Spitze ins Feld zog.

Abb. 23 Kleopatra Thea und Alexander Balas, Tetradrachme, Ptolemaïs-Ake, 150–149 v. Chr., SC 1841.

Abb. 24 Kleopatra Thea und Alexander Balas, Bronzemünze, Ptolemaïs-Ake, 150–149 v. Chr., SC 1846.

Abb. 25 Kleopatra Thea, Goldstater, Ptolemaïs-Ake (?), 150–149 v. Chr., SC 1840.

68   Auch die Verfasser des SC vermuten eine Prägung in Ptolemaïs-Ake.
69   Soweit ich sehe, existieren nur zwei Exemplare; eines befindet sich in einer Sammlung in Aleppo (SC 1840: „regional collection: Aleppo"), ein weiteres Exemplar tauchte 2016 im Münzhandel auf (Classical Numismatic Group, Triton XIX, 5.1.2016, Nr. 2072).
70   CPE 806.

Abb. 26 Berenike II., Gold-¼-Stater, Seleukeia in Pieria (?), CPE 806.

Abb. 27 Alexander Balas, Tetradrachme, Tyros, 146/5 v. Chr., SC 1835.6b.

Unter Alexander Balas wurde die von Demetrios I. unterbrochene Prägung von Tetradrachmen nach phoinikischem Standard wieder aufgenommen und sogar deutlich ausgeweitet (Abb. 27). Nicht nur in Ptolemaïs-Ake, sondern auch in Berytos, Sidon und Tyros wurden Tetradrachmen nach diesem Standard und ‚ptolemaiischem‘ Design geprägt, wobei der Adler nun einen Palmzweig unter seinem rechten Flügel trägt.[71] Auch unter den folgenden Königen wurden in den phoinikischen Küstenstädten Silbermünzen nach phoinikischem Standard geprägt – zum Teil parallel mit solchen nach seleukidischem Standard.[72] Die folgende Tabelle mag dies verdeutlichen.

---

71   Ptolemaïs-Ake: SC 1842, Berytos: SC 1824, siehe dazu auch Sawaya 2005, Sidon: SC 1830–1832, dort auch Tetradrachmen nach seleukidischem Standard: SC 1829, Tyros: SC 1835–1837.

72   Während der ersten Herrschaft von Demetrios II. entstanden in Berytos (SC 1952), Sidon (SC 1954–1956) und Tyros (SC 1959–1967) Silbermünzen nach phoinikischem Standard, in Sidon und Tyros wurden zudem auch Tetradrachmen nach seleukidischem Standard geprägt (SC 1953 bzw. 1958); unter Antiochos VI. wurde nur der phoinikische Standard verwendet: Byblos (SC 2020), Ptolemaïs-Ake (SC 2022) und Askalon (SC 2026); das gilt auch für Tryphon: Byblos (SC 2042–2043), Ptolemaïs-Ake (SC 2045–2046) und Askalon (SC 2047); unter Antiochos VII. wiederum sowohl nach seleukidischem (Sidon: SC 2101, Tyros: SC 2107–2108) als auch phoinikischem Standard (Sidon: SC 2102–2103, Tyros: SC 2109–2111, Ptolemaïs-Ake: SC 2116–2117, Askalon: SC 2124); während der zweiten Herrschaft Demetrios’ II. ebenfalls nach seleukidischem (Sidon: SC 2187, Tyros: SC 2193–2194, Ptolemaïs-Ake: SC 2201–2202) und phoinikischem Standard (Sidon: SC 2188, Tyros: SC 2195–2197, Ptolemaïs-Ake: SC 2203–2205, Askalon: SC 2206); unter Alexander Zabinas nach phoinikischem Standard in Askalon (SC 2253–2256); unter Kleopatra Thea in Ptolemaïs-Ake nach seleukidischem Standard (SC 2258); während der gemeinsamen Herrschaft von Kleopatra Thea und Antiochos VIII. nach seleukidischem Standard in Sidon (SC 2268) und Ptolemaïs-Ake (SC 2271), nach phoinikischem Standard in Sidon (SC 2269), Ptolemaïs-Ake (SC 2270, 2272–2273) und Askalon (SC 2276–2277); unter Antiochos VIII. nach seleukidischem Standard in Sidon (SC 2329–2330), Ptolemaïs-Ake (SC 2335–2336), nach phoinikischem Standard in Sidon (SC 2331–2332), Ptolemaïs-Ake (SC 2337–2338) und Askalon (SC 2339–2341); unter Antiochos IX. nach seleukidischem Standard in Tripolis (SC 2383), Sidon (SC 2384–2385) und Ptolemaïs-Ake

Tab. 2 Prägestandards in Phoinikien von Antiochos V. bis IX. (s. = seleukidischer, p. = phoinikischer Standard)

	Tripolis		Byblos		Berytos		Sidon		Tyros		Ptolemaïs-Ake		Askalon	
	s.	p.	s.	p.	s.	p.	s.	p.	s.	p.	s.	p.	s.	p.
Antiochos V.											x	x		
Demetrios I.											x			
Alexander I.						x	x	x			x			x
Demetrios II. (1)						x	x	x	x	x				
Antiochos VI.				x								x		x
Tryphon				x								x		x
Demetrios II. (2)							x	x	x	x	x	x		x
Alexander II.														x
Kleopatra Thea											x			
Kleopatra Thea und Antiochos VIII.							x	x			x	x		x
Antiochos VIII.							x	x			x	x		x
Antiochos IX.	x						x	x			x	x		x

Viele dieser Könige waren mit Kleopatra Thea verheiratet oder blutsverwandt. Interessanterweise prägte Kleopatra Thea während ihrer kurzen Alleinherrschaft in Ptolemaïs-Ake nur Tetradrachmen nach seleukidischem Standard und mit in parallelen Linien angeordneter Legende.[73] Zumindest in dieser Hinsicht sind sie völlig seleukidisch. Sie zeigen auf dem Revers ein ,ptolemaiisches' Doppelfüllhorn und auf dem Avers die Königin mit einer Korkenzieher-Frisur. Da diese seit dem frühen 2. Jh. v. Chr. auch bei Isisbüsten auf ptolemaiischen Münzen verwendet wird,[74] dürfte dieses Motiv eine Nähe Kleopatra Theas zu dieser Göttin zum Ausdruck gebracht haben (Abb. 28–29). Dieselbe Frisur trägt die Königin auch auf gemeinsamen Münzen mit ihrem Sohn Antiochos VIII. (Abb. 30).[75]

(SC 2390) und nach phoinikischem Standard in Sidon (SC 2386), Ptolemaïs-Ake (SC 2391–2392) und Askalon (SC 2395–2396).

73 SC 2258 (126/125 v. Chr.).
74 Pincock 2010.
75 SC 2259–2262, 2267–2273.

Abb. 28 Kleopatra Thea, Tetradrachme, Ptolemaïs-Ake, 126–125 v. Chr., SC 2258.

Abb. 29 Kleopatra I., Bronzemünze, Alexandreia, 180–176 v. Chr.

Abb. 30 Kleopatra Thea und Antiochos VIII., Tetradrachme, Antiocheia, 122–121 v. Chr., SC 2262.1d.

2.8 Die späten Seleukiden

Potentielle Anlehnungen an ptolemaiische Münzen finden sich bei den späteren Seleukiden nur noch selten. Im Jahr 129/128 v. Chr. entstanden in Antiocheia am Orontes
Bronzemünzen, die auf dem Avers einen nach rechts auf einem Blitzbündel stehenden
Adler zeigen, der unter seinem linken Flügel einen Thyrsos trägt (Abb. 31).[76] Der Thyrsos verweist auf Dionysos, der als einer der Stammväter der Ptolemaier galt (s. o.). In

---

76 SC 2171.

diesem Jahr verband sich Demetrios II. mit seiner Schwiegermutter Kleopatra II. gegen Ptolemaios VIII.[77] Vielleicht spielen die Bronzemünzen auf diese Verbindung an.

Abb. 31 Demetrios II., Bronzemünze, Antiocheia am Orontes, 129–128 v. Chr., SC 2171.

Als Reaktion auf die Übereinkunft zwischen Demetrios II. und Kleopatra II. baute Ptolemaios VIII. Alexander Zabinas als Gegenkandidaten zu Demetrios II. auf.[78] Möglicherweise war das der Grund, weshalb unter Alexander Zabinas das bei den Ptolemaiern beliebte Doppelfüllhorn das übliche Rückseitenmotiv der Drachmen aus Antiocheia am Orontes und Damaskos wurde (Abb. 32); auf Hemidrachmen findet sich ein einfaches Füllhorn, auch einige Bronzemünzen zeigen ein Doppelfüllhorn.[79] Ein Doppelfüllhorn findet sich auch auf Bronzemünzen aus Antiocheia am Orontes aus der Zeit Antiochos' VIII.[80]

Abb. 32 Alexander Zabinas, Drachme, Antiocheia am Orontes, 128–122 v. Chr., SC 2221.

3. Fazit

Sichere Anklänge an bzw. Anleihen aus dem Bereich der ptolemaiischen Münzprägung finden sich bei den Seleukiden vergleichsweise selten. In vielen Fällen handelt es sich um Ähnlichkeiten, ohne dass sich eine bewusste Übernahme ptolemaiischer Gestaltungselemente erkennen ließe. Das früheste sichere Beispiel bildet die Münzserie Antiochos' IV., die wahrscheinlich im Rahmen des Sechsten Syrischen Krieges in Antiocheia entstand. Möglicherweise handelte es sich um den Versuch, das seleuki-

---

77 Iust. 39.1.2; s. auch Euseb. Chron 1.257–258.
78 Iust. 39.1.4–5.
79 SC 2221, 2223, 2225, 2237 und 2249; Houghton, Lorber und Hoover, SC II, p. 443, bezeichnen es als „symbolic of Alexander's Egyptian patron". Unter Seleukos VI. war ein einfaches Füllhorn das Standardreversbild der Hemidrachmen aus Antiocheia am Orontes: SC 2419–2421.
80 SC 2312–2313.

dische Münzsystem in Kopie der ausgeklügelten ptolemaiischen Bronzemünzprägung zu reformieren, um Silber zu sparen. Der seitenverkehrte Adler auf dem Revers konnte sowohl als Anspielung auf den für die ptolemaiische Münzprägung typischen Adler angesehen werden als auch auf den unter Antiochos IV. üblicherweise auf den Reversen der Silbermünzen zu findenden Zeus. Die Averse der vier Nominale der Serie zeigen neben Zeus und Antiochos IV. die beiden ägyptischen Gottheiten Serapis und Isis und sind damit jeweils zur Hälfte ‚seleukidisch' und ‚ptolemaiisch'. Die Gestaltung der Münzaverse und -reverse konnte somit die doppelte Herrschaft des Königs über das Seleukiden- und das Ptolemaierreich symbolisieren. Sein Sohn Antiochos V. nahm gegen Ende seiner Herrschaft die Prägung von im Gewicht reduzierten Tetradrachmen in Ptolemaïs-Ake wieder auf, die in Gewicht und Aussehen an die hier in ptolemaiischer Zeit geprägten Tetradrachmen erinnerte. Wahrscheinlich handelt es sich dabei um ein Zugeständnis an die unzufriedenen Einwohner der wichtigen Hafenstadt. Viele Nachfolger ließen in verschiedenen phoinikischen Städten ebenfalls Münzen nach reduziertem Gewichtsstandard und ‚ptolemaiischem' Design prägen. Eine Goldnotprägung Demetrios' I., die auf dem Avers ausnahmsweise nicht das Herrscherporträt, sondern Tyche zeigt, trägt auf dem Avers eine dem Münzrund folgende Legende und das ‚ptolemaiische' Doppelfüllhorn. Ob es sich dabei eher um ein zufälliges Produkt nicht sehr geübter Stempelschneider oder um eine bewusste Anlehnung an die Münzprägung der Ptolemaier, mit denen sich Demetrios I. damals im Krieg befand, handelt, lässt sich nicht entscheiden.

Der vierte Fall sind seltene Goldstatere von Kleopatra Thea, die nach seleukidischem Gewichtsstandard und mit seleukidischem Stil, aber ptolemaiischem Design vielleicht im Rahmen der Eheschließung mit Alexander Balas entstanden. Die Hintergründe dieser Emission bleiben aber letztlich unklar. Die übrigen Münzen, die damals geprägt wurden, folgen eher seleukidischen Traditionen, wobei allein die Attribute Kleopatra Theas potentiell nach Ägypten verweisen. Interessanterweise wurden die Tetradrachmen, die Kleopatra Thea während ihrer Alleinherrschaft in Ptolemaïs-Ake herstellen ließ, nach seleukidischem Gewichtsstandard ausgebracht, obwohl davor und danach in der Region auch Tetradrachmen im reduzierten Gewicht und ‚ptolemaiischen' Design gefertigt wurden. Lediglich die Frisur der Königin und das Doppelfüllhorn des Reverses kopieren ptolemaiische Vorbilder. Möglicherweise erforderte der Anlass für diese Emission Tetradrachmen nach seleukidischem Gewichtsstandard, die bisher – abgesehen von der Goldnotprägung unter Demetrios I. – weitgehend auch dem seleukidischen Design entsprachen, um sie von den nach reduziertem Gewichtsstandard ausgeprägten Münzen leicht unterscheiden zu können. Die Wahl des Gewichtsstandards schränkte somit die Gestaltungsmöglichkeiten ein. Überhaupt sind metrologische Aspekte und die Übernahme ptolemaiischen Designs häufig sehr eng miteinander verbunden. Abgesehen von diesen Fällen gehen die anderen sicheren Übernahmen letztlich auf die Ehe zwischen der Ptolemaierin Kleopatra Thea und Alexander Balas und ihrem weiteren Wirken im Seleukidenreich zurück.

Literaturverzeichnis

Bellinger 1949: Bellinger, Alfred R., The Excavations of Dura-Europos VI: The Coins, New Haven et al. 1949

Bergmann 1998: Bergmann, Marianne, Die Strahlen der Herrscher. Theomorphes Herrscherbild und politische Symbolik im Hellenismus und in der römischen Kaiserzeit, Mainz 1998

Bickerman 1938: Bickerman, Elias, Institutions des Séleucides, Paris 1938

Brunelle 1976: Brunelle, Edelgard, Die Bildnisse der Ptolemäerinnen, Frankfurt am Main 1976

Bunge 1974: Bunge, Jochen G., „Theos Epiphanes". Zu den ersten fünf Regierungsjahren Antiochos' IV. Epiphanes, Historia 23, 1974, 57–85

Butcher 1988: Butcher, Kevin, Roman Provincial Coins. An Introduction to the ‚Greek Imperials', London 1988

Charbonneaux 1957: Charbonneaux, Jean, Serapis et Isis et la double corne d'abondance, Hommages à Waldemar Déonna, Brüssel 1957

Cohen 2011: Cohen, Edward, E., Dated Coins of Antiquity, Lancaster et al. 2011

Cook 1925: Cook, Arthur B., Zeus. A Study in Ancient Religion I: Zeus. God of the Bright Sky, Cambridge 1925

de Callataÿ 1993: de Callataÿ, François, Les tétradrachmes hellénistiques de Tripolis, Quaderni Ticinesi 22, 1993, 111–126

Dressel 1906: Dressel, Heinrich, Fünf Goldmedaillons aus dem Funde von Abukir, Berlin 1906, 1–86

Ehling 2004: Ehling, Kay, Geprägte Bilder. Münzen der Seleukiden aus Antiochia, Antike Welt 35.2, 2004, 27–31

Ehling 2008: Ehling, Kay, Untersuchungen zur Geschichte der späten Seleukiden (164–63 v. Chr.). Vom Tode des Antiochos IV. bis zur Einrichtung der Provinz Syria unter Pompeius, Stuttgart 2008

Elderkin 1934: Elderkin, Georges W., Antioch-on-the-Orontes. The Excavations of 1932, Princeton 1934

Fleischer 1986: Fleischer, Robert, Die Tyche des Demetrios I. von Syrien, Archäologischer Anzeiger 47.1, 1986, 699–706

Fleischer 1991: Fleischer, Robert, Studien zur seleukidischen Kunst I: Herrscherbildnisse, Mainz 1991

Guey – Picon 1968a: Guey, Julien – Picon, Maurice, Monnaies frappées sur les flans tournés ne présentant pa de cavités centrales, Bulletin de la Société française de numismatique 23.10, 1968, 336–337

Guey – Picon 1968b: Guey, Julien – Picon, Maurice, Quelques remarques sur la fabrication des grands bronzes lagides à cavités centrales, Bulletin de la Société française de numismatique 23.2, 1968, 240–241

Hall 1926: Hall, H. P., A Note on the Fabric of Ptolemaic Bronze, Numismatic Chronicle 6, 1926, 301–302

Hoffmann 2000: Hoffmann, Friedhelm, Ägypten. Kultur und Lebenswelt in griechisch-römischer Zeit. Eine Darstellung nach den demotischen Quellen, Berlin 2000

Hoover 2002: Hoover, Oliver, Laodice IV on the Bronze Coinage of Seleucus IV and Antiochus IV, American Journal of Numismatics 14, 2002, 81–87

Houghton 1988: Houghton, Arthur, The Double Portrait Coins of Alexander I Balas and Cleopatra Thea, Schweizerische Numismatische Rundschau 67, 1988, 85–93

Houghton – Le Rider 1985: Houghton, Arthur – Le Rider, Georges, Le deuxième fils d'Antiochos IV à Ptolémaïs, Schweizerische Numismatische Rundschau 64, 1985, 73–89

Icard 1979: Icard, Severin, Dictionary of Greek Coin Inscriptions, Chicago 1979

Kyrieleis 1973: Kyrieleis, Helmut, Die Porträtmünzen Ptolemaios' V. und seiner Eltern, Jahrbuch
des Deutschen Archäologischen Instituts 88, 1973, 213–246

Le Rider 1994: Le Rider, Georges, Antiochos IV (175–164) et le monnayage de bronze séleucide,
Bulletin des Correspondance Héllenique 118, 1994, 17–34

Lichtenberger 2021: Lichtenberger, Achim, Viele Mütter. Zu den quasi-municipalen seleukidischen
Lokalbronzen im hellenistischen Phönikien, in: J. Hoffmann-Salz (ed.), The Middle East as
Middle Ground? Cultural Interaction in the Ancient Middle East Revisited, Wien 2021, 65–86

Maresch 1996: Maresch, Klaus, Bronze und Silber, Opladen 1996

Mittag 2006: Mittag, Peter F., Antiochos IV. Epiphanes. Eine politische Biographie, Berlin 2006

Mørkholm 1963: Mørkholm, Otto, Studies in the Coinage of Antiochus IV of Syria, Kopenhagen
1963

Mørkholm 1966: Mørkholm, Otto, Antiochus IV of Syria, Kopenhagen 1966

Mørkholm 1967: Mørkholm, Otto, The Monetary System of the Seleucid Kings until 129 B. C., in:
A. Kindler (ed.), Phoenicia and Palestine in Antiquity, International Numismatic Convention,
Jerusalem 27.–31. December 1963, Tel Aviv 1967, 75–86

Mørkholm 1979: Mørkholm, Otto, The Portrait Coinage of Ptolemy V. The Main Series, in:
O. Mørkholm (ed.), Greek numismatics and archaeology. Essays in honor of Margaret Thompson, Wetteren 1979, 203–214

Mørkholm 1982: Mørkholm, Otto, Some Reflections on the Production and Use of Coinage in
Ancient Greece, Historia 31, 1982, 290–305

Muccioli 2013: Muccioli, Federicomaria, Gli epiteti ufficiali dei re ellenistici, Stuttgart 2013

Newell 1918: Newell, Edward T., The Seleucid Mint of Antioch, New York 1918, Nachdruck Chicago 1978

Noeske 2000: Noeske, Hans-Christoph, Die Münzen der Ptolemäer, Frankfurt a. M. 2000

Pincock 2010: Pincock, Richard, A Possible Unique Isis Head Bronze Coin of Cleopatra I (180–
176 BC), Numismatic Chronicle 170, 2010, 53–62

Pinkwart 1965: Pinkwart, Doris, Das Relief des Archelaos von Priene und die ,Musen des Philis-
kos', Kallmünz 1965

Robert 1960: Robert, Louis, Inscription hellénistique d'Iran, Hellenica 11/12, 1960, 85–91

Salzmann 2012: Salzmann, Dieter, Anmerkungen zur Typologie des hellenistischen Königsdiadems und zu anderen herrscherlichen Kopfbinden, in: A. Lichtenberger et al. (eds.), Das Diadem der hellenistischen Herrscher. Übernahme, Transformation oder Neuschöpfung eines
Herrschaftszeichens?, Bonn 2012, 337–383

Sawaya 2005: Sawaya, Ziad, Les Tétradrachmes Séleucides à l'Aigle de Bérytos, Numismatic
Chronicle 165, 2005, 99–124

Smith 1994: Smith, Amy C., Queens and Empresses as Goddesses. The Public Role of the Personal Tyche in the Graeco-Roman World, Yale University Art Gallery Bulletin, 1994, 86–105

Stillwell 1941: Stillwell, Richard (ed.), The Excavations 1937–1939, Antioch-on-the-Orontes 3,
Princeton 1941

Thissen 1966: Thissen, Heinz-Josef, Studien zum Raphiadekret, Meisenheim am Glan 1966

Vidman 1969: Vidman, Ladislaus, Sylloge inscriptionum religionis Isiacae et Sarapiacae, Berlin
1969

Wagner 1999: Wagner, Herfried E., Das zentrale Bohrloch auf antiken Bronzen, Helvetische
Münzzeitung 34.5, 1999, 269–273

Weiser 1995: Weiser, Wolfram, Katalog der ptolemäischen Bronzemünzen der Sammlung des Instituts für Altertumskunde der Universität zu Köln, Opladen 1995

Abbildungsverzeichnis

Peter F. Mittag studied ancient history, classical archaeology, and law at Freiburg. After his doctorate on the late antique contorniates, he first worked as a numismatist at the Römisch-Germanisches Museum in Cologne and returned to Freiburg for his habilitation on Antiochos IV. He is professor for ancient history at the University of Cologne since 2005. His research focuses on Hellenistic history and numismatics. Most recently he published a book on the history of the Hellenistic age and is currently working on two monographs on Roman medallions of the second and third century AD.

Victorious Kings
*Royal Victories over Galatians and a "Multidimensional" Hellenistic Kingship**

GIOVANNA PASQUARIELLO

Abstract: This chapter will discuss examples of royal victories over the so-called Galatians, "Celtic" tribes who migrated into Hellenistic Anatolia, plundered it, served as mercenaries for one king or another and eventually settled into a region later named after them: Galatia. With a focus on the 3rd and 2nd centuries BC, the chapter aims to highlight the role of the Galatian migration in monarchic self-presentation. The analysis will be both synchronic and diachronic. I will first look at aspects of comparison among dynasties with regard to the kings' depiction as victors over the Galatians, which will result in a generally consistent representation model, the one of "Galatersieger". I will then explore its origins and evolution up until the Galatian expedition of Manlius Vulso and conclude that this type of royal self-presentation is characterised by a certain Graeco-centrism, both in terms of tropes and imagery used and of addressees: the kings' victories over the Galatians are primarily exhibited as Greek victories for the Greeks. Practices such as royal philhellenism and euergetism certainly contribute to the model's characterization in this sense. I will then highlight that it is, ultimately, a "multidimensional" model, founded on the "vertical", diachronic depth of continuously vital Greek tropes, while "horizontally" looking at contemporary Greek attitudes towards the Galatian migration, as well as dynastic competition. In the end, its example offers a picture of Hellenistic monarchy that is also "multidimensional" – tautologically "vertical" in its autocratic structure, but also potentially "horizontal" in its active communication with Greek communities and in its use of models and imagery provided by Greek history itself.

* My thanks go to Prof. Andrew Erskine and Dr. Benedikt Eckhardt for their valuable comments and suggestions, to the editors of this volume and especially to Dr. Christoph Michels for reading and annotating this chapter. Any errors remain my own.

1. Introduction

Ever since the first defeat of an army of Galatians at Delphi in 279 BC, the Galatian migration into the Hellenistic world had been the object of a momentous ideological construction by Graeco-Macedonian powers, who – whenever they fought against Galatians – greatly celebrated their victories and often propagandistically exploited them.[1] It has long been noted, for instance, that among the strategies that the Aitolian *koinon* used to obtain hegemony over the Amphiktyony at Delphi in the mid-3rd century BC was an emphatic celebration of their contribution to the Galatian defeat of 279 BC, a contribution that – historically speaking – was not as prominent as the Aitolian celebrations may have us believe.[2] With regard to the Hellenistic kings, their propagandistic use of victories over Galatians is so significant for the geopolitics of the Greek world in the 3rd and 2nd centuries BC that Karl Strobel spoke about the Galatians as a 'politischer Mythos', the instrumentalisation of which was a fundamental legitimisation strategy of Hellenistic monarchy.[3] In this framework, the Attalid exploitation of the political myth of the Galatians is particularly prominent, so that it has been referred to by Clemens Koehn as the 'Galaterideologie', an instrument of Pergamene self-affirmation and justification of military interventions in Asia Minor.[4] In a way, both defi-

---

1　　Some premises are in order. This chapter being centred on a case-study analysis of monarchical representation, I will not emphasise the recently reiterated truth that the Galatians had their own agency as independent actors on the Hellenistic geopolitical scene, and were not just mere propagandistic instruments (Burghart 2022, Coşkun 2022a, Payen 2022). With regard to matters of ethnonymy, I will use terms such as "Celts" and "Celtic", and "Galatians" and "Galatian". However, the reader must be aware that the ethnonym "Celts", and its derived adjective "Celtic" (and so "Galatians" and "Galatian") are only conventional ethnographic categories used to address nomadic tribes of Europe, speaking an Indo-European language. They were politically disunited but culturally homogeneous – even though differentiation must be observed even in their linguistic and archaeological manifestations. Matters of "Celtic identity" are, thus, debated, hence the use of these ethnonyms must be cautious or, at least, aware of its own limits. Scholarship on the matter is vast and varied, and should be sought in the field of Celtic studies: in this instance, I will only mention Collis 2003 as a point of reference, but I am aware that I am oversimplifying the scholarly framework in the field. On the tribe of the Galatians who are generally included under the umbrella category of "Celts" and their migration into Hellenistic Anatolia, see – among scholars of ancient history – Mitchell 1993 and Strobel 2002. Many studies have been dedicated by Altay Coşkun to the Galatians; to mention just a few, the reader may want to look at Coşkun 2013 or Coşkun 2022b. On the image(s) of Celts and their re-functionalisation in the Greek Hellenistic world, see Kistler 2009. Savalli Lestrade 2020 focuses on the dynamics of exclusion and integration in the relationship between Attalids and Galatians. The latter is also treated by Gruen 2000 and Kaye 2022, 283–253.

2　　On the Aitolians at Delphi, see Sanchez 2001, 270–362. On Pausanias' account as a possible pre-Aitolian version of the battle of Delphi, see Bearzot 2020, 125–132. Nachtergael 1977 remains a point of reference for the study of the Galatian attack on Delphi and the documentation of the Soteria, instituted for the celebration of the Greek victory in 279 BC.

3　　Strobel 1994, 93.

4　　Koehn 2006, 110–127. In Koehn's view, Pergamon was a 'Mittelstaat', a middle state, meaning a regional force or a state "weaker" than leading powers on the geopolitical scene, and as such used ideological motifs to justify matters of foreign policy to its subjects.

nitions build on Gehrke's interpretation of the Hellenistic monarch as a "siegreicher König" modelled on Weber's "charismatische Herrschaft".[5]

Within a discourse on monarchical representation in the Hellenistic world, it is thus important to consider the numerous examples of royal victories over Galatians, as they certainly allow us to highlight aspects of comparison among dynasties with regard to celebrations, as well as the role of royal competition in the kings' self-presentation. With the ultimate aim of reconstructing the "anatomy" of an explanatory model of Hellenistic kingship, this chapter's analysis will be both synchronic and diachronic.[6] On the one hand, I will look at the ways different dynasties celebrated their own "Keltensiege": from the date of the first success of a king over Galatians in 277 BC, meaning the victory of Antigonos Gonatas at Lysimacheia, to Eumenes II's success in 166 BC.[7] I will then embrace a diachronic approach and retrace the origins and fortune of the celebrative motifs used in royal propaganda, from the parallel with the Persians to the expedition of Manlius Vulso against the Galatians in 189 BC. It will emerge that, on the one hand, the kings' self-presentation as victors over the Galatians is altogether consistent and a few similarities among dynasties can be observed. On the other, it will appear that the uniqueness of each victory, their contexts and the specific needs of each dynasty resulted in some differentiation, with kings focusing on one or another aspect of celebration. Overall, however, victorious kings presented themselves as benefactors and/or saviours of the Greeks and showed particular interest in communicating as such with the Greek cities of Asia Minor.[8] At the end of the chapter, I will conclude that the example provided by the Galatians favours an image of Hellenistic kingship that is at the same time "horizontal" and "vertical": it is evidently "vertical" in its claims of power and hegemony but also in its being diachronically anchored in Greek models; on the other hand, it is also "horizontal" because it communicates with the Greeks by drawing from a metaphorical "box" of Greek imagery and vocabulary.[9] In this way, Hellenistic kingship becomes a flexible, multi-dimensional structure.

---

5   Gehrke 1982. Koehn has been very critical of this (Koehn 2006, 77–88). Cf. Weber 1978. For a collection of essays on monarchy in ancient Greek history, see Luraghi (ed.) 2013.

6   'Die Galaterideologie: Erklärungsmodell' is the title of a sub-chapter in Koehn 2006 (114–127).

7   By using the term "Keltensiege", I quote the title of Strobel 1994, 'Keltensieg und Galatersieger'.

8   Despite the relevance of victoriousness in royal self-presentation, the latter is multifaceted and not limited to military potency. The chapter by Charalampos Chrysafis in this volume sheds light on the role of the king as a bringer of peace.

9   On the usability of cultural containers and on the idea of constructed "Greekness", see Lichtenberger 2021, who focuses on the example of Commagene. The reader should note that, while this chapter emphasises "philhellenic" elements in Hellenistic kingship, other contributions in this volume will show that these are certainly not the only aspect of royal self-presentation: while it plays a role in the context of victories over Galatians, "philhellenism" is not the one criterion defining Hellenistic monarchy in general.

2. Royal victories over Galatians: a synchronic analysis

Examples of victories of Hellenistic kings over Galatians are numerous and well-studied.[10] However, a fortunate preservation of sources and also of monumental archaeological remains, like the Great Altar of Pergamon, favours the prominence of the Attalid Galatian victories in tradition. Moreover, not negligible is the role of Rome in the amplification of Pergamene artistic motifs, with sculptures like the so-called Dying Gaul and the Ludovisi Gaul, which were originally located on the Akropolis of Pergamon and were subsequently transferred to Italy after the kingdom had become a province.[11] With regard to literary sources, Livy reports that, at a time when Asia Minor was so scared (*tantusque terror eorum nominis erat*) of the Galatian raids that even the Seleukids agreed to pay a tribute (*stipendium*) to them, Attalos I was the first who bravely broke the cycle and refused to pay, thus opening hostilities with the Galatians.[12] Against all expectations, he defeated the Galatian Tolistobogii at the river Kaikos.[13] On that occasion, he took the title of king and *Soter*, "Saviour", thus proclaiming the independence of Pergamon from the Seleukids, and dedicated altars in his own name.[14] Moreover, he enhanced the cults of Athena and Zeus in the city and made several dedications at Pergamon and all around the Greek world.[15] Sometime between 238 and 228 BC, he defeated the Galatians again: at the Aphrodision he prevailed over the

---

10   Aside from the already mentioned Strobel 1994, see also Hannestad 1996 and Strootman 2005.

11   Mitchell 1993, 21; Marszal 2000, 193–197. Cf. Kuttner 1995.

12   Liv. 38.16.14. Strobel 1994, 86 highlights the anti-Seleukid implications of the conflict. As for the tribute refused to pay by Attalos, it is difficult to establish what it was with certainty. Livy uses the Latin *stipendium*, which could be generally translated as a 'stipend', and therefore interpreted as pay for soldiers and mercenaries. This is how Mitchell understands it: as the promise of repartition of booty in the aftermath of the "brothers' war" between Antiochos and his Galatian mercenaries – or, rather, allies (Mitchell 1993, 20). Such an interpretation is possible, but leaves unaddressed any discussion of the *stipendium* paid by Pergamon and refused by Attalos. Allen 1983, 32, on the other side, considered the stipend a sort of "one-off" payment to bribe the Galatians whenever they threatened to plunder.

13   Liv. 38.16.13.

14   IvP I 43–45; Pol. 18.41.7; Liv. 33.21.3; Strab. 13.4.2. The date of the battle – and Attalos' proclamation as king – is unclear (cf. Mitchell 1993, 21–22; Strootman 2005, 122–123).

15   Marszal 2000, 204–212. Attalos implemented the cult of Athena Promachos, protector of Pergamon, by the dedication of a statue of the goddess and of a circular *bathron* in the peribolos of her temple on the Akropolis (cf. Hansen 1971, 31–32). The *bathron* served as a base for a group of sculptures celebrating the victory, like the so-called Dying Gaul and the Ludovisi Gaul. On the base, an inscription mentioned the battle (IvP I 20). Numerous dedications in the name of Attalos figure in cities of the Greek world. At Athens, he commissioned a stoa and four groups of bronze statues depicting Gigantomachies, Amazonomachies, the clash between Athenians and Persians and the one between Pergamon and the Galatians (Paus. 1.25.2). At Delos, statues of the king (IG XI, 4, 1110) and his general Epigenes (IG XI, 4, 1109) were erected. At Delphi, a stoa in the name of Attalos included the dedication of statues and panel paintings (Syll.³ 682). On Attalid cultural policy during the rulership of Philetairos and Attalos I, see Schalles 1985.

Tektosages, who were allied to Antiochos Hierax.[16] His successor Eumenes II defeated Galatians too: once in 184 BC, when they were led by Ortiagon and allies to Prusias I of Bithynia, and again in 166 BC.[17] On that occasion he reorganized the festival Nikephoria as Panhellenic.[18] Perhaps at that time, he commissioned the construction of the so-called Great Altar of Pergamon too, later brought to completion by his brother Attalos II (165–159/8 BC).[19] The abundance of evidence regarding the Attalid Galatian victories can thus overshadow examples from other dynasties, which are in comparison underrepresented in sources. In recent decades, however, scholarship on the Galatian migration has drawn attention to the complexity and variety of their settlement process and their relationships with Hellenistic dynasties.[20] This has consequently resulted in a re-assessment of the Attalid prominence mentioned above.

In fact, Antigonos Gonatas was, chronologically speaking, the first "Galatersieger" among the kings, and as such – according to Rolf Strootman – he marked the way for the others.[21] In 277 BC, he had met the Galatians, who were moving towards Byzantion to cross the Hellespont, and defeated them.[22] The king's role as victor did not, however, prevent him from hiring Galatian mercenaries when fighting to control Macedon.[23] Pyrrhos of Epeiros, who also had hegemonic claims on the region, could celebrate his

16   IvP I 23 = OGIS 275. Iust. 27.2–3 relates the battle to the so-called "brothers war", and the Attalid victory is recalled in Iust. prooem. 27, where – however – there is no mention of Antiochos. The battle finds reference in IvP I 247 too, a public calendar recording celebrations for events or people by popular decision.

17   Mitchell 1993, 24–26.

18   Syll.³ 629 and 630.

19   The dating and interpretation of the Great Altar are debated (cf. Michels 2004; Queyrel 2017). There exists a variety of possible opponents for allegorical representation at Pergamon, as Nelson points out when he mentions the Pergamene bronze plaque depicting Macedonians and Anatolians alongside the Galatians (Nelson 2022, 106–109). As Queyrel concludes, 'La grande frise de la gigantomachie ne transpose pas littéralement les épisodes d'une guerre particulière, mais propose une synthèse où les allusions historiques confèrent à l'image mythique une efficience mémorielle: l'image agit en célébrant une victoire de toute éternité qui parle à tous les Grecs' (Queyrel 2017, 215). In this volume, Noah Kaye also mentions the altar – and the related interpretative problems – for the representation of the Attalids as stabilizers of order.

20   An effort in highlighting the output of other dynasties is evident in Strootman 2005, but along these lines are also Coşkun's studies on Seleukid encounters with the Galatians (Coşkun 2012).

21   Strootman 2005, 113. Cf. also Waterfield 2021, 117–118 on the battle of Lysimacheia.

22   Diog. Laert. 2.141 quotes a decree from Eretria, moved by Menedemos, a friend of Antigonos, that honoured him for vanquishing the "barbarians" at Lysimacheia. Some coins, dated to the early 260s BC, bear the head of Pan and trophies, convincing scholars to explain the iconography of Pan with the *phobos panikos*, the panic brought on the Galatians by the god. Pausanias (10.23.7) mentions it at Delphi when the attackers were struck with inexplicable terrors, but no tradition of the phobos panikos is attested for the battle at Lysimacheia. In his chapter in this volume, Gregor Weber discusses the above-mentioned coins and the use of Pan as a tutelary god by Antigonos, likely unrelated to any epiphanic elements in the tradition of the battle of Lysimacheia.

23   We have notice of "Celtic" mercenaries among Greek armies. For instance, Dionysios I had sent Celts to fight alongside Sparta (Diod. 15.70.1). Tagliamonte 2020 is a recent overview of the studies on Celtic mercenaries.

own Galatian victory, as he had defeated Gonatas' mercenaries in around 274 BC.[24]
Galatian shields were dedicated at the temple of Itonian Athena in Thessaly, and
Macedonian spoils at the sanctuary of Zeus at Dodona.[25] In the mid-270s BC, Ptolemaios II had defeated Galatians too. These had originally been his mercenaries, who
had mutinied and were then beaten in the Nile Delta.[26] In the 3rd century BC, "Celtic"
shields (*thyreoi*) appear in Ptolemaic iconography.[27] However, this was perhaps not
Ptolemaios' only action against Galatians: the community of Limyra, in Lykia, dedicated a Ptolemaion to the king, who had presumably saved them from the assaults
of the Galatians.[28] Ptolemaios' intervention in Lykia must have happened sometime
in the 270s–260s BC when the Galatians were raiding various regions of Asia Minor.
Around the same time, Antiochos I had defeated some Galatians in an obscure "elephant battle", with which a statuette depicting an elephant trampling a Galatian warrior
is usually connected.[29] In the late 3rd century BC (ca. 214 BC), it was time for Prusias
I to claim his own Galatian victory, and it was Attalos who provided him with the
occasion: the king of Bithynia defeated the tribe of the Aigosages, called into Asia by
Pergamon to serve as mercenaries against Achaios, who had declared himself king of
the region around Laodikeia on the Lykos.[30]

In the course of the 3rd and 2nd centuries BC the Greek and Anatolian geopolitical
framework had become unstable, with young kingdoms and dynastic insecurity making the scenario particularly tense. It is somewhat tautological to point out that, under
those circumstances, victories over the "barbarian", nomadic Galatians were easily exploited for propaganda and legitimacy purposes. Antigonos' success at Lysimacheia
"did the trick" to support his claims over Macedon.[31] Similarly, Pyrrhos' victory over
Antigonos' Galatian mercenaries allowed him to present himself as victor over two
menaces, the raids of the Galatians and Antigonos' brutal treatment of Greece.[32] The

---

24   Pol. 5.77.2–78.
25   Paus. 1.13.3. The choice of making two separate dedications is notable and points to the active
     propagandistic policy of Pyrrhos in Northern Greece, directed to both Epeiros and Thessaly.
26   Paus. 1.7.2; Kall. h. 4.171–189. The reader shall note, however, that these Egyptian Galatians are not
     necessarily "ethnically" the same as the Galatians of Asia Minor. I have already mentioned the
     conventional character of "Celtic" ethnic categories in n.1.
27   For a discussion on oval shields in Ptolemaic iconography, see Kuzmin 2017, 521–523. IDélos 1417
     mentions a golden *thyreos* as a donation to the temple of Apollon at Delos by 'Ptolemaios son of
     Ptolemaios'. In Kallixeinos' description of the Great Procession at Alexandreia, some *thyreoi* ap-
     pear as trophies in the royal tent (BNJ 627 F2).
28   Mitchell 1990, 118. The metope depicts Kentauromachies. Cf. paragraph 3.1.
29   Coşkun 2012, however, argues for cautiousness in this regard. The sources on the battle are Luc.
     Zeux. 8–11 and App. Syr. 65. The details of the episode are obscure. Mitchell 1993, 18 sets a possible
     date to 269–268 BC.
30   The context of the battle remains unclear (Pol. 5.111.5–7; Michels 2009, 67–71). Cf. Pol. 5.77.2.
31   Waterfield 2021, 118.
32   Paus. 1.13.2–3: τῷ δὲ ἐν Δωδώνῃ Διὶ Μακεδόνων ἀνέθηκεν αὐτῶν τὰς ἀσπίδας. ἐπὶ γέγραπται δὲ καὶ
     ταύταις· Αἵδε ποτ' Ἀσίδα γαῖαν ἐπόρθησαν πολύχρυσον, αἵδε καὶ Ἕλλασι<ν> δουλοσύναν ἔπορον. νῦν

alleged intervention of Ptolemaios in support of Limyra might be seen in the context of anti-Antigonid manoeuvres in Anatolia.[33] In a similar way, Eumenes' exploitation of his success against Prusias' Galatian allies might have its roots in hegemonic conflicts with Bithynia.[34] Scholars have often pointed out that Attalos' Galatian victories were exploited as intrinsically anti-Seleukid, as they propagandistically supported the new king's claims of independence, but recent studies have suggested that at least until the end of the 3rd century BC the relationship between Attalids and Seleukids should not be seen as openly and unequivocally hostile.[35]

In any case, the celebration of Galatian victories often supported broader political aims, legitimating either a change in power or claims of hegemony. As a consequence, dynasts had to adapt their self-presentation as victorious kings to circumstances, with the result of modelling a specific image of "Galatersieger", a royal victor over Galatians.

3. "Galatersieger": (self-)presentation and celebrative patterns

Often kings presented themselves and their victories as bearers of salvation to the Greek communities who were threatened by marauding Galatians.[36] The motif of *soteria* could be expressed in the form of epithets.[37] It seems that Attalos took the title of king as well as of *Soter*, at the time of his first Galatian victory in 241 BC.[38] With regard to Antigonos, Craige Champion suggested that he instituted the festivals Paneia and Soteria at Delos to keep the memory of his Galatian victory alive.[39] Finally, Appian Syr. 65 attributes the epithet *Soter* to Antiochus I, and he is the only source directly connecting the title with the king's "elephant victory".[40]

δὲ Διὸς ναῷ ποτὶ κίονας ὀρφανὰ κεῖται τᾶς μεγαλαυχήτω σκῦλα Μακεδονίας. I suggest that αἵδε ... αἵδε refer, in order, to the Galatian shields and to the Macedonian ones, against translations such as Fraser's 'These shields once laid waste the golden Asian land, these shields brought slavery upon the Greek', closer to the Greek but more ambiguous in meaning as they hint to some unattested Macedonian raids in Asia Minor.

33 I.Kaunos 4 is dated to Antigonos' fifteenth regnal year (268 BC) and an unpublished inscription from Rhamnous honours an Athenian who had served for Antigonos in Asia. These texts suggest that at some point in the 260s Antigonos was in Asia Minor and had even taken Kaunos from Ptolemaios (cf. Waterfield 2021, 159).

34 Cf. Hopp 1977, 40–44.

35 Chrubasik 2013, who rather considers the first phases of Attalos' reign as a semi-autonomous kingdom. I am not thinking of Attalos' rule in these specific terms, but still embrace a more flexible approach to the Attalid/Seleukid antagonism at the time. For some comments on Chrubasik's interpretation, see Michels 2019, 334.

36 The Galatians plundered villages and sanctuaries, took captives and asked for ransoms in exchange for their liberation (Syll.³ 410, IK 49 Laodikea am Lykos 1, OGIS 765, TAM V 2, 881). Cf. Liv. 38.16.12–13.

37 On *Soter* as a royal epithet in general, see Muccioli 2013, 159–178.

38 Cf. note 14.

39 Champion 2004/2005.

40 Cf. Coşkun 2012, 62.

We can observe a metaphorical employment of the trope of salvation in the way royal Galatian victories are generally celebrated, by contrast with the motifs of peril and destruction that are associated with the Galatian migration. A Galatian victory corresponded to a foiled threat, to the civilizing power of "Greekness" overcoming "barbarism". This stereotyped representation is not a royal invention but has its model in the Amphiktyonic celebrations of the battle of Delphi instead. With the announcement of the Greek victory and the institution of the festival Soteria, the Amphiktyony established the official "soteric" narration of the Galatian defeat.[41] Not only the kings but also the communities who found themselves fighting against Galatians used the same vocabulary of salvation.[42] Royal celebrations re-used such stereotyped imagery, as well as iconographical motifs taken from mythical *exempla* of allegorical clashes between civilization and "barbarism".

3.1 Allegorical Galatomachies

Both the Attalids and the Ptolemies are known to have produced iconographical motifs of mythical clashes between Chthonian creatures and Olympic deities, with the Galatians being allegorically associated with Kentaurs or Giants/Titans.[43] Among the most prominent examples one should certainly enumerate the Great Altar of Pergamon, featuring a Gigantomachy – although of debated interpretation –, or Pausanias' description of Attalos' so-called Lesser (or Small) Dedication, composed of four scenes depicting respectively his victory over the Galatians, a Gigantomachy, an Amazonomachy and the Athenian triumph over the Persians.[44] While we cannot observe

41 Syll.³ 398, usually referred to as the Koan decree, is the response of Kos to the announcement of the Greek victory, presented as a triumph of Apollon and the Greeks and bearer of salvation. On the early Soteria and the Aitolian reorganisation of the festival as Panhellenic, see Nachtergael 1977, 299–373 and Lefèvre 1998. Of course, the use of *soteria* in religious and political contexts is much more ancient than the 3ʳᵈ century BC. Jim 2022 offers a thorough examination of the idea of salvation in the Greek world. Camassa 2020 individuates in the 5ᵗʰ century BC the moment when religious salvation took political connotations too.
42 Cf. OGIS 765, ll. 30–31: συνέχωντού[ς μετ]ὰ αὐτοῦ κινδυνεύοντα[ς ὑπὲρ τ]ῆς κοινῆς σωτηρίας τοῦ [δήμου] (from Priene); TAM V 2, 881, ll. 8–10: ὑπέρ τε τῆς αὐτοῦ καὶ τῆς γυναικὸς ὑγιείας καὶ τῆς τοῦ υἱοῦ Φανοκρίτου σωτηρίας (from Thyateira, in Lydia); IK Laodikeia am Lykos 1, ll. 24–26 θύειν δὲ καὶ Ἀχαιῶι κυρίωι τοῦ τοπου καὶ σωτῆρι κατ' ἐνιαυτὸν ἐμ μὲν τῶι τοῦ Διὸς ἱερῶι βοῦν (from Babakome and Kiddiokome, Phrygia). As for the latter example, it is especially interesting because it testifies to the attribution of the title *soter* to a non-royal recipient, Achaios, lord of the region before the refoundation of Diospolis/Rhoas as Laodikeia (cf. Bejor 2000, 16–19). It must be noted, however, that the decree does not say explicitly whether the title was given to Achaios on this occasion because of his help against the Galatians or had already been attributed to him for another reason. On this inscription, cf. Wörrle 1975 and D'Agostini 2013, 90–96.
43 Nelson 2022 provides a detailed overview of allegories and analogies in Hellenistic literature and art having the Galatians as protagonists.
44 Paus. 1.25.2. Cf. Stewart 2004.

Attalos' dedication on the Akropolis directly, Pausanias gives a description that closely mirrors the iconography of the Parthenon's metopes, decorated with scenes of Amazonomachies and episodes from the Trojan war and testifying to the process of allegorical memorialisation of the Persian wars started at the time of Perikles.[45] Two centuries later, the Attalids enhanced the cult of Athena Polias, made several dedications to the goddess and, thanks to a grandiose iconographical programme on Pergamon's Akropolis and a dedication at Athens, they implicitly associated the Galatians with the Persians and themselves with the Athenians, exploiting a centuries-old allegorical tradition.[46]

A Kentauromachy on the Ptolemaion at Limyra may also prove that the Chthonian imagery could be used allegorically, the association between Galatians and Kentaurs being made either by Ptolemaios himself or by the Greek community there.[47] A mythical parallel has a place in Kallimachos' *Hymn to Delos* too: in the context of a prophecy pronounced by Apollon himself from inside his mother's womb, Philadelphos is praised for having defeated the Celts, who are referred to as 'late-born Titans' (vv. 172–175): ὁππόταν οἱ μὲν ἐφ᾽ Ἑλλήνεσσι μάχαιραν | βαρβαρικὴν καὶ Κελτὸν ἀναστήσαντες Ἄρηα ὀψίγονοι Τιτῆνες ἀφ᾽ ἑσπέρου ἐσχατόωντος | ῥώσωνται ('when late-born Titans will storm from the furthest West, raising their barbarian dagger and Celtic Ares against the Greeks').[48] Moreover, the *Hymn* describes Ptolemaios' Galatian victory so that the king's deeds can be associated with those of Apollon at Delphi, and even allows for a possible intercultural dimension of the poem: with the Galatians being defeated by fire, just like Python or the Pharaoh's enemies, Ptolemaios' "Galatersieg" is the re-establishment of *kosmos*, or Egyptian *ma'at*.[49] The king established a "cosmological" royal image, associating his victory with the Olympic order and, specifically, with Apollon's "civilising" deeds. The Ptolemaic self-presentation would therefore fit into a mythical framework that would be familiar not only to the Greeks but, possibly, to the Egyptians too.

These allegories belong to a well-established mythico-historical tradition, stretching back to Herakles' labours and the Trojan wars and having its most recent anteced-

45   Hurwit 2004, 124–126.
46   Mitchell 1993, 21.
47   Cf. n. 28.
48   On the royal procession and Ptolemaios' victory over the Galatians, see Johstono 2019. On the representation of kingship in Kallimachos, see Barbantani 2011. On the Celts as late-born Titans, see Fantuzzi 2011, 440.
49   Kall. h. 4.185–187. Nelson 2022, 115–116. The author is, however, clear about the limits of an Egyptianising interpretation of the hymn. Similarly, Barbantani 2011, 186–189, who also mentions the hymn, questions a common interpretation of Kallimachos' *Hymn to Zeus* according to which the poem is fashioned to reflect a "bicultural monarchy".

ent in the Persian wars, making the royal Galatian victories a new founding moment of the shared history of the Greeks.[50]

3.2 Champions of Asia Minor

In the context of Asia Minor, the sources often describe the royal Galatian victories as acts of "liberation" of the Greeks. In the literary and epigraphic evidence, the kings pushed the Galatians away from Greek regions and/or cities and confined them somewhere further away, where their threat should not worry anymore. In this picture, a "Galatersieger" becomes primarily a liberator of the Greeks. The sources consistently depict the kings as such, and in some cases use similar vocabulary, too.

A good example in this regard is represented by IG XI,4 1105, a posthumous dedication to the founder of the Attalid dynasty, Philetairos, by a man named Sosikrates and possibly dated to around the late 3rd century BC.[51] The inscription is an epigram in elegiac couplets, which mentions a mysterious Galatian victory of the Pergamene ruler: ὥς ποτε δυσπολέμοις Γαλάταις θοὸν Ἄρεα μείξας | ἤλασας οἰκείων πολλὸν ὕπερθεν ὅρων (ll. 5–6, 'since you once engaged dextrous Ares with the unfortunate Galatians and pushed them far away from the homeland's borders'). Comparable information, and similar vocabulary, with the use of the verb ἐλαύνω, is found in Pausanias, where the rulers of Pergamon drove the Galatians away from coastal Asia Minor and confined them into that inner region later called Galatia: ἐς ταύτην Γαλάτας ἐλαύνουσιν ἀπὸ θαλάσσης ('they pushed them away from the sea into that area now called Galatia').[52] Lukianos describes in similar terms Antiochos' "elephant victory" that repulsed the Galatians into the mountains: Οἱ Γαλάται δὲ οἱ μὲν ἐτεθνήκεσαν, πολλοῦ τοῦ φόνου γενομένου, οἱ δὲ ζῶντες ἐλαμβάνοντο, πλὴν πάνυ ὀλίγοι ὁπόσοι ἔφθασαν εἰς τὰ ὄρη ἀναφυγόντες ('As for the Galatians, some of them had died, as a great massacre happened, and others were captured alive, except for the very few who escaped and reached the mountains').[53] Even Prusias' Galatian victory is narrated by Polybios as an act of liberation, this time of the cities on the Hellespont: πράξας δὲ ταῦτα μεγάλου μὲν ἀπέλυσε φόβου καὶ κινδύνου τὰς ἐφ' Ἑλλησπόντου πόλεις, καλὸν δὲ παράδειγμα τοῖς ἐπιγινομένοις ἀπέλιπε τοῦ μὴ ῥᾳδίαν ποιεῖσθαι τοὺς ἐκ τῆς Εὐρώπης βαρβάρους τὴν εἰς τὴν Ἀσίαν διάβασιν ('By this exploit he liberated the cities on the Hellespont from fear and danger, and provided a great example for the future: that the barbarians from Eu-

---

50   On a stele from Kyzikos, Herakles leaps onto a male figure whose *thyreos* and clothing tell us that he is a Galatian (Instanbul, Archaeological Museum 564). Cf. Strootman 2005, 131–134 on the Attalid Gigantomachies and the role of Herakles.

51   For the date of the inscription, see the discussion by Kosmetatou 2022, 176–177.

52   Paus. 1.4.5. The translation is based on Siebelis' restoration ἐς τὴν νῦν Γαλατίαν, in place of ἐς ταύτην Γαλάτας of the manuscript tradition.

53   Luk. Zeux. 8–11.

rope shall not easily cross to Asia').[54] Certainly, historically speaking, none of the kings' actions were actually decisive. The numerous tribes of so-called Galatians who were migrating into Asia kept raiding here and there for several decades; nonetheless, dynasties are depicted as "champions" of Asia Minor, with the sources thus reflecting a celebratory, if not self-celebratory intent.

A closer look at the evidence reveals that the Attalid and Seleukid Galatian victories are described in surprisingly similar terms, with an evident focus on how both liberated coastal Asia Minor and confined the plunderers in inner Anatolia. This juxtaposition of information is hardly coincidental and opens up a few – perhaps unanswerable – questions. The main interpretative issue is that there is no evidence of the victory of Philetairos aside from IG XI,4 1105.[55] Is his triumph an invention of the later Attalids, while he had never defeated the Galatians at all?

Some scholars have seen in the memorialisation of both the Attalids' and the Seleukids' Galatian victories a mutually competitive process. For instance, it has been suggested that Philetairos' victory was a Pergamene invention that projected back Attalos I's real successes against the Galatians. In this view, at the time of Attalos and Antiochos III, royal competition resulted in a revisitation of the Galatian discourse that aimed at affirming Attalos' dynastic legitimacy through the inheritance of the role of victor over the barbarians from Philetairos.[56] In this interpretation, the victory of the Attalid founding father in IG XI,4 1105 would only be a poetic and legitimating invention.

But is there any way to trust the information given by the Delian inscription? I want to highlight a neglected note in an old book on Pergamon by Pedroli that may offer a different solution. There, he suggested in passing that Philetairos took part in Antio-

---

54 Pol. 5.111.7. Assuming that the original information – and the relative vocabulary – comes from a source closer to the event, it seems that Polybios' – or rather his sources' – description of Prusias' Galatian victory reflects an already well-established way to describe Galatian defeats in Asia Minor. Moreover, the historian's phrasing is revealing not only of royal self-presentation but also of the way Greek communities described the Galatian attacks. Polybios says that thanks to the victory, the king could free the region from fear and danger (μεγάλου μὲν ἀπέλυσε φόβου καὶ κινδύνου τὰς ἐφ᾿ Ἑλλησπόντου πόλεις). This phrasing recalls the vocabulary of peril used by the Greek communities threatened by the Galatians and also the *terror* mentioned by Livy with regard to Attalos' first Galatian victory (Syll.³ 410, ll. 10–11; Livy 38.16.14).

55 The only cases when Philetairos is mentioned in relation to the Galatians are either indirect military support or financial interventions: OGIS 748 enlists his benefactions towards the Kyzikos, among which the fact that he sent money and troops for protection against some Galatian raids in 278/7 BC as well as wheat and barley to compensate for the depredations in 276/5 BC (note, however, that the first example is only connected to the Galatians by the editor's interpretation; cf. Hansen 1971, 18).

56 Kosmetatou 2022, 173–174. Coşkun 2013 also discusses the tradition of the battle from the perspective of the Attalid/Seleukid competition. I remind the reader, however, that the idea of open antagonism between the two dynasties at the time of Attalos I has been challenged by Chrubasik 2013, 83–119.

chos' "elephant victory", and that defeating the Galatians could only benefit his protectorate over the region.[57] Reasonably, Pedroli did not push speculation any further. On my end, I want to dare leave an open window for the possibility that Philetairos' Galatian victory in IG XI,4 1105 did happen and, perhaps, occurred in the framework of Antiochos' Galatian campaign. The Delian inscription – published at a time when the Attalids were rebranding their past for legitimacy purposes – might thus refer to a joint success, specifically one of Philetairos, in the same military context as Antiochos' "elephant victory". Perhaps, this could also explain why the narration of the battle of the elephants on one side and the Delian inscription on the other have similar phrasings: they reproduce the tradition of a (joint) victory that – at least temporarily – drove the Galatians away into inner Anatolia. Undoubtedly, the specificities of this campaign got lost soon, resulting in the nebulous tradition around the "elephant battle" and in Pausanias' even vaguer comment on the liberation of coastal Asia Minor by the Attalids. Of course, this interpretation shall remain in the domain of speculation unless further evidence is discovered that not only confirms that the elephant statuette found at Myrina can locate the battle, but also that the latter happened either on or close to Pergamene territory.[58] Leaving aside this question, there is little doubt that the motif of "liberation" became dominant in the royal celebrations of Galatian victories in Asia Minor, and especially in the self-presentation of the Attalid and Seleukid dynasties.

3.3 Euergetism and philhellenism

On some level, this is a "Graeco-centric" way to describe royal victories: despite the celebratory intent and the claims of legitimacy and hegemony behind many of the kings' activities in Asia Minor, Galatian victories stay – at their core – an act of service, which ultimately makes the victor a benefactor of the Greeks. In the case of Eumenes II's victory against Ortiagon and Prusias, a decree from Telmessos explicitly presents it as *euergesia*:

ἐπει|[δὴ βασι]λεὺς Εὐμένης ὁ σωτὴρ καὶ εὐεργέ|[της ἡμ]ῶν ἀναδεξάμενος τὸν πόλεμον οὐ μ[ό|νον ὑπ]ὲρ τῶν ὑφ' αὑτὸν τασσομένων ἀλλὰ καὶ| [τῶν ἄ]λλων τῶν κατοικούντωντ ἣν Ἀσίαν ὑ|[πέστ]η τὸν κίνδυνον (...)

---

57 Pedroli 1896, 6.
58 BCH 5, 283 records the borders of Pergamon between Myrina and Kyme. However, the paleography of the inscription only allows the editor to roughly date it to the 3rd century BC and does not give any information about whether the *horoi* were established before or after the independence of Pergamon.

Since King Eumenes, our benefactor and saviour, who has taken on the war not only on behalf of those under his command but also on behalf of the others dwelling in Asia and has endured the danger.[59]

As with many other elements discussed in this chapter, also the euergetic character of royal self-presentation has fundamentally Greek roots.[60] Euergetism is not only a very common practice of the Hellenistic world but also an exchange system of services and rewards that dates back to the Archaic and Classical ages.[61] When citizens were honoured for either having led the resistance against the Galatians or spent private money to face their raids, they were benefactors of the Greek community, in which they gained privileges.[62] The kings' euergetism and royal Galatian victories did not work much differently.

Since the 4th century BC, monarchic power was closely connected with euergetism. According to the tradition, Aristoteles wrote a letter on kingship to Alexander in which the idea of *euergesia* was so fundamental that his disciple affirmed that he had not been a king, because he had not made any benefaction to anyone.[63] Paul Veyne poignantly affirmed that 'donner est le geste royal par excellence' and Philippe Gauthier later brought examples from Aristoteles and Polybios to demonstrate that in Greek political thought 'l'essence royale doit se manifester et se prouver par l'*euergésia*'.[64] In the Hellenistic age, this was especially true for the recognition of royal power by Greek cities: in the inscriptions the title κοινὸς εὐεργέτης τῶν Ἑλλήνων is used for the kings and later associated with the Romans.[65] On the one hand, being *euergetai* brought honours and legitimisation to the "major" Hellenistic dynasties, like the Seleukids, and ultimately their euergetism was not much different from that operated by private Greek citizens. On the other hand, those monarchies usually considered "peripheral" or less "hellenised", such as Pontos, Kappadokia or Bithynia, could reinforce their own "Greekness" by benefactions.[66] In this way, euergetism and philhellenism are only distinguished by a faint line. Philhellenism – intended as the group of practices directed to the Greeks

---

59   Clara Rhodos 2, 1932, 172, 3, ll. 5–10; the translation above is Thonemann's, who emphasises that the Telmessians could not be directly involved in the war (Thonemann 2013, 35–36). This certainly makes the decree even more revealing of the extent of the Attalid propagandistic policy.

60   On royal *euergesia*, see Bringmann 1993 and 2000.

61   See Domingo Gygax 2016.

62   It is the case of Achaios at Laodikea on the Lykos (IK Laodikea am Lykos 1), Protogenes at Olbia Pontica (Syll.³ 495), Sotas at Priene (OGIS 765).

63   Aristot. fr. 646 Rose.

64   Veyne 1976, 232; Gauthier 1985, 40 who mentions Aristot. frg. 646 Rose (see note above), Pol. 10.3.1, 10.5.6, 34.2–35.2, 37.7–38.3.

65   Gauthier 1985, 42. Erskine 1994, however, points out that the epithet, despite having an antecedent in the association with Hellenistic kings, should not be oversimplified as a continuation of a Hellenistic practice.

66   Gauthier 1985, 42.

and not necessarily as a process of "Hellenization" – regards traditionally "non-Greek" monarchies but also dynasties whose Macedonian origin could make them "outsiders" from the perspective of a "properly" Greek, civic world.[67] In this framework, royal celebrations of Galatian victories are designed for an audience widely definable as "Greek" and reveal the kings' effort to meet their addressees in the "middle ground" of their own history.

4. Royal victories over Galatians: a diachronic analysis

The analysis above has shown that there is little originality in the presentation of royal Galatian victories after all. From the vocabulary of salvation to the exploitation of the memory of the Persian wars, the core elements at its roots were not an invention *ex novo* of Hellenistic monarchy but centuries-old tropes that were re-functionalised soon after the Galatian expedition into Greece and the battle at Delphi.

Immediately after that victory, the Aitolians had dedicated Galatian weapons to the Sanctuary of Apollon, on the opposite sides to where the Athenians had hung the shields of the Persians to commemorate the battle of Marathon.[68] When, in the 20th century, traces of a *thyreos* shape were found at the south-western corner of the temple, scholars connected the archaeological evidence with the testimony of Pausanias, who mentions golden Galatian weapons on the architraves as a trophy taken during the battle at Delphi.[69] It is difficult to deny that the early celebrations of the victory over the Galatians were designed to mirror the Persian wars. Whether this comparison was first promoted by the Amphiktyony or the Aitolian *koinon* is uncertain, but it surely became an immediate comparandum very soon and remained vital through the centuries.[70] If the sanctuary of Apollon marked the way of celebrations, the Aitolians not only appropriated but also enhanced them once they took control of the Amphiktyony in the mid-3rd century BC and reorganised the Soteria as Panhellenic.[71] It has to be noted that the Aitolian re-appropriation of the trope of a Greek victory over "barbarians" and in particular of the imagery of the Persian wars is significant for more than one reason: the Aitolians themselves have a history of hostile, semi-"barbaric" representation,

67   This is one of the arguments at the core of Michels 2009.
68   SEG 28.496. Cf. Amandry 1978.
69   Paus. 10.19.4. See also Syll.³ 398, 9–10. Cf. Flacelière 1937, 108; Amandry 1978, 578.
70   In the second half of the 2nd century BC, two poems – performed during a festival originally instituted to commemorate the battle of Plataiai – mentioned the Galatians (CID III 1, 25; CID III 2, 31–32). Bearzot 1989 compares passages from Pausanias, Diodoros and Iustinus on the Galatian attack on Delphi with Herodotos' account of the Persian invasion.
71   Epigraphic evidence is numerous; see Nachtergael 1977, Actes 21–27.

sometimes even on the same terms as the Galatians.[72] Drawing from the same stereotypes that discriminated against them is possibly one element that contributed to their
success in the 3rd century BC and their hegemony over the Amphiktyony.

Behind this practice of "enemy construction" for legitimacy purposes is a political
discourse that crossed the centuries from Classical Athens to Delphi in 279 BC. The
spectre of the Persian wars haunted the Greeks well after the battle of Plataiai.[73] It was
inherent in the foundation of the Delian League, and dominated the debate at Athens
on the rise of Macedon. A "Rachegedanke" war against the Persians and the dreams of
"Panhellenism" resonating in Isokrates' speeches kept the discourse vital until Philip
II could personify the ultimate Isokratean "Panhellenic" champion.[74] From the Greek
perspective, Philip's project of a Persian campaign was perfectly coherent with the
haunting hostility towards those eastern "barbarians". In this way, the "Rachegedanke"
war could take the form of a "crusade" and of a continuation of the 5th century's Persian
wars.[75] It does not matter that Philip's real objectives were political and economic, attracted as he was to the wealth of Asia.[76] When Alexander inherited his father's project,
that centuries-long tradition was fulfilled in the conquest of Persia. Eventually, when
the Galatians entered the Hellenistic world, the Graeco-Macedonian kingdoms that
had formed from the ashes of the Persian empire could programmatically use a vital
magma of well-established tropes.

It has been rightfully noted, however, that – in spite of the undeniable parallels
drawn by the sources – the Galatians were not exactly like the Persians in Hellenistic
political discourse, because they are not systematically associated with the imagery of
civic freedom and concord.[77] The Galatians migrated, plundered and occupied land,
they did not conquer to impose their system of government. There is no room for any

---

72 In the Ithyphallic Hymn to Demetrios Poliorketes, the Aitolian League is accused of raiding the
   wealth of Greece (Duris of Samos BNJ 76 F13 = Athen. 6.253 d–f). In the 2nd century BC, Polybios will describe the Aitolians as *asebeis*, impious, for plundering Dion (4.62). Inscriptions from
   Asia Minor highlight the impiety of the Galatians, see – for instance – OGIS 765 from Priene.
   Note, however, that Livy is the first author who explicitly uses the term *barbarus* for the Aitolians (34.24.3–4; 35.12.1). Because his source, Polybios, never calls them *barbaroi*, Antonetti 1990,
   139–141 suggested that the barbaric connotation of the Aitolians is an addition by Livy.

73 On the significance of Plataia in the early Hellenistic age and its relationship with Greek *eleutheria*,
   see Wallace 2011.

74 On the rhetoric of a war against the Persians as a "Rachegedanke" war in Isokrates' speeches, see
   Bloedow 2003, 261–265.

75 Diod. 16.89.2; Momigliano 1987, 165.

76 Ellis 1976, 234 who focuses on Philip's opportunistic motives. On the other hand, Bloedow 2003
   suggests a more flexible approach, seeing in the king's Persian campaign both a war of revenge and
   a war of conquest.

77 Wallace 2011, 212–215. On the cult of Homonoia of the Hellenes at Plataiai see Jung 2006, 328–329.
   On eleutheria in the Hellenistic age, see Wallace 2010 and 2011. In terms of the ides of a political
   menace to the Greek freedom, the Macedonians offer a more accurate parallel than the Galatians:
   anti-Macedonian imagery was also associated with the vocabulary the Persian wars. The Chremonidean decree offers a memorable example of this equation (IG II² 687, 7–13; cf. Nelson 2022, 103).

"Rachegedanke" war against them. Therefore, even though a parallel was established, and imagery was shared between Galatian victories and Persian wars, it is important to acknowledge the fundamental differences between them, thus the limits of such a comparison.

Nevertheless, when the kings did reuse imagery of the past, just like Philip and the Aitolians before them, they benefitted from being portrayed as victors over "barbarians": in this way, alongside the myth of the Galatians they were building their own, that of champions, of "saviours" of the Greeks, who should then recognise their power and "charisma". It is in the kings' relationship with their – in this case, "Greek" – subjects that we can see the peculiarity of the model of "Galatersieger", compared to the Aitolian self-presentation at Delphi. The king victor over the Galatians designs his image around his role of *phylax* and around the exchange system of benefaction that regulated his relations with the Greek cities. Seemingly, this relational model was to be appropriated by the Romans, too.

Soon after the battle of Magnesia, the Roman consul Manlius Vulso led a campaign into inner Anatolia against the Galatians, and eventually the Romans had their own Galatian victory. As our main source for the events, Livy describes the driving cause of the war as a sort of "punishment" of the Galatians, who had been allied to Antiochos, but the facts reported show that the Galatian campaign was aimed at securing control of the region and prevent a resurgence of Seleukid power, by annihilating the king's support network there.[78] The war allows Livy to include a digression on the Galatian migration; he then moves on to report Vulso's *exhortatio* to his army, a parainetic speech built on the emphasis of Roman valour against Galatian madness and Asiatic softness, together with a reminder of the first Gallic encounters of the Romans and of the fact that the *Gallograeci* they were going to meet were just a deteriorated version of those tumultuous Celts defeated by Rome in the past. However fictional Vulso's speech might be, his words – as reported by Livy – seem to evoke the stereotypical Celtic ethnography of Poseidonios rather than the "Galatersieger" motif employed by Hellenistic kings.[79] The passage has very little of the "soteric", Graeco-centric view of the Galatian victories that is so central in royal celebrations and that was to be reiterated only a few years later by Eumenes II.[80] Later in his work, however, the historian makes Vulso defend himself from the accusation of undertaking a "pirate" war. There, the consul says:

---

78 Liv. 38.12.1–38.28.9. Grainger provides a detailed study of Vulso's campaign, aimed at re-assessing a generalized negative sentiment towards the expedition and the consul, inherited from Livy's hostile description (Grainger 1995, 23–24).

79 Livian Vulso describes the Celts as fierce and dreadful, as they clash shields according to ancestral customs (cf. Poseidonios BNJ 87 F116). Emphasis on their tallness is stereotypical (cf. also Ptolemaios BNJ 138 F2).

80 Cf. Clara Rhodos 2, 1932, 172, 3, ll. 5–10, already mentioned above.

mittite, agedum, legatos circa omnes Asiae urbes, et quaerite utra graviore servitute, Antiocho ultra Tauri iuga emoto an Gallis subactis, liberati sint. quotiens agri eorum vastati sint quotiens praedae abactae referant, cum vix redimendi captivos copia esset, et mactatas humanas hostias immolatosque liberos suos audirent.

Come now, send delegations around all the cities of Asia and ask which was the heavier servitude from which they were delivered–was it from Antiochus when he was pushed back beyond the Taurus range or from the Gauls when they were brought to heel? Let them tell you how often their lands were devastated, how often their property pillaged–at a time when they barely had the wherewithal to ransom their prisoners and when they heard of human sacrifices and the immolation of their own children.[81]

Unlike the speech before, here Vulso's words reiterate the motif of liberation of Asia Minor. This passage recalls a similar comment of Polybios on the Roman victory over the Galatians:

διασαφήσομεν (…) τίνα τρόπον Ῥωμαῖοι καταλύσαντες τὴν Γαλατῶν ὕβριν ἀδήριτον μὲν σφίσι παρεσκεύασαν τὴν τῆς Ἀσίας ἀρχήν, ἀπέλυσαν δὲ τοὺς ἐπὶ τάδε τοῦ Ταύρου κατοικοῦντας βαρβαρικῶν φόβων καὶ τῆς Γαλατῶν παρανομίας.

I shall describe (…) how the Romans, suppressing the insolence of the Galatian Gauls, established their undisputed supremacy in Asia and freed its inhabitants on this side of the Taurus from the fear of barbarians and the lawless violence of these Gauls.[82]

Not only does Polybios use the same vocabulary of fear and lawlessness that was characteristic of some inscriptions, but he also portrays the victory in the same terms as Prusias' triumph over the Aigosages.[83] On the one hand, the Greek historian is clearly indebted to the imagery produced by royal self-presentation and perhaps uses it to explain how the Romans were able to obtain supremacy over Asia Minor. On the other, Livy – who perhaps uses Polybios as a source – is able to both design Vulso's exhortative speech for the fruition of a Roman audience and to mirror Polybios' portrayal of the Romans as typical "Galatersieger", liberators of the Greeks.

It seems that, even when new actors – the Romans – entered the scene, the model of "victor over the Galatians" remained specific to Graeco-centric discourses. The evident motif at its core is the kings' role as protectors of the Greeks of Asia Minor.

---

81   Liv. 38.47.11–12 (trans. Sage 1936).
82   Pol. 3.3.4–6 (trans. Paton 2010).
83   Cf. Pol. 5.111.7.

5. Conclusions

In spite of a relative disproportion in the sources – with dynasties such as the Attalids being more clearly represented than, for instance, Pyrrhos or the kings of Bithynia – examples of royal victories over the Galatians are numerous enough to allow for a
comparative analysis of the kings' self-presentation as victors over those "barbarians".
From a synchronic perspective, royal celebrations appear altogether consistent with
little differentiation, with dynasties focusing on one propagandistic aspect or another,
but without striking variations: they are both "the same, but different" and "different,
but the same". From a diachronic perspective, royal self-presentation was constructed
around centuries-long, well-affirmed Greek tropes, altogether crystallised in the Amphiktyonic celebrations of the battle of Delphi. These take inspiration from traditional
representations of victories over "barbarians" and the re-functionalisation of the Persian wars, but – as we have seen – some discontinuity with the past, especially with
regard to the imagery of the Persians, has to be noted.

The example provided by royal Galatian victories thus offers a coherent image of
"Galatersieger": a "saviour" king who liberated the Greeks from the menace of the
plundering Celts and/or whose triumph was allegorically compared to the re-estab-
lishment of cosmological order against the chaos represented by the "barbarians".
Attalid and Ptolemaic iconography hence offer scenes of Gigantomachies and Kentauromachies, as well as of Amazonomachies. Reference to stereotyped mythico-historical examples, allegorizing the Trojan myth and Persian wars, is evident and testifies
to the kings' programmatic self-inclusion in these traditions. They compared their own
Galatian victories with the Athenian triumph over the Persians, in the case of the Attalids, or with the civilizing deeds of Apollon, in the case of Philadelphos.

It is here where different experiences came into play in shaping unique, although
similar memories of the Galatian victories. The narration of Ptolemaios' Egyptian success, for instance, does not engage with aspects of territorial liberation, as the Seleukid
and Attalid victories do instead. This is because of diametrically different historical
contexts: Ptolemaios' victory against his mercenaries on the Nile was more exploita-
ble as an allegorical success – allowing for ideological parallels – than as a real, foiled
threat. On the contrary, royal victories against Galatians in Asia Minor are presented
in the sources as acts of "liberation" of Greek regions. Noticeable similarities have been
highlighted in the way they report the triumph of Pergamon, specifically a mysterious
Galatian victory of Philetairos and Antiochos' "elephant battle", raising questions regarding a possible joint "Galatian campaign" of the Pergamene ruler and the Seleukid
king. In general, royal attitudes towards the Greeks in the context of Galatian operations in Asia Minor follow a euergetic, philhellenic model. Royal *euergesia* has, in fact,
a long history, with deep roots in Greek civic euergetism but also in 4th century-discus-
sions on the euergetic nature of monarchy, finding in traditions around Alexander a
prominent antecedent for the practice of royal benefactions.

We have also seen that, despite the diachronic depth of the motifs behind the "Gala-tersieger" model, the latter seems specific to Graeco-centric discourses, focused on the relationships between the Greeks themselves and hegemonic powers. To profoundly understand the extent and complexity of this type of self-presentation, "multidimensionality" is the key: analysis must be both horizontal and vertical. As we have seen, elements of royal celebrations are illuminated by looking synchronically at examples from contemporary dynasties, but also diachronically at their earliest and most recent models. "Multidimensional" is also the Graeco-centrism of those Galatian victories: it is vertical insofar as it re-functionalizes continuously vital Greek tropes, but also horizontal insofar as it aligns with contemporary Greek attitudes towards the Galatian migration, namely the official Amphiktyonic celebrations of the battle of Delphi. Ultimately, the example of royal Galatian victories offers an image of Hellenistic kingship that is also "multidimensional": as an autocratic structure, it is intrinsically vertical, being founded on principles of authority and hegemony; however, this chapter has also highlighted how "horizontal" it can be: in its active communication with contemporary Greek communities and its effort to speak to them – metaphorically and literally – in their language, with their vocabulary, and their imagery. One may point out that the kings' aim ultimately is legitimacy and power over the Greeks they are talking to, but the "horizontality" of their means should not be dismissed as just a sneaky strategy. It actually demonstrates how deep royal self-presentation's debt to Greek history can be. And it serves to show, ultimately, that there is no simple way to approach Hellenistic kingship from one perspective, whereas a flexible, "multidimensional" approach is desirable instead.

Bibliography

Allen 1983: Allen, Robert E., The Attalid Kingdom. A Constitutional History, Oxford 1983

Amandry 1978: Amandry, Pierre, Consécration d'armes galates à Delphes, BCH 102, 1978, 571–586

Antonetti 1990: Antonetti, Claudia, Les Étoliens. Image et religion, Besançon-Paris 1990

Barbantani 2011: Barbantani, Silvia, Callimachus on Kings and Kingship, in: B. Acosta-Hughes – L. Lehnus – S. Stephens (eds.), Brill's Companion to Callimachus, Leiden et al. 2011, 178–200

Bearzot 1989: Bearzot, Cinzia, Fenomeni naturali e prodigi nell'attacco celtico a Delfi (279 a. C.), in: M. Sordi (ed.), Fenomeni naturali e avvenimenti storici dell'antichità, Milan 1989, 71–86

Bearzot 2020: Bearzot, Cinzia, I Galati a Delfi, in: C. Bearzot – F. Landucci – G. Zecchini (eds.), I Celti e il Mediterraneo. Impatto e trasformazioni, Milan 2020, 167–196

Bejor 2000: Bejor, Giorgio, Per una ricerca di Laodicea ellenistica, in: G. Traversari (ed.), Laodicea di Frigia. 1, Rome 2000, 15–23

Bloedow 2003: Bloedow, Edmund F., Why Did Philip and Alexander Launch a War Against the Persian Empire?, L'Antiquité Classique 72, 2003, 261–274

Bringmann 1993: Bringmann, Klaus, The King as Benefactor. Some Remarks on Ideal Kingship in the Age of Hellenism, in: A. W. Bulloch et al. (eds.), Images and Ideologies. Self-Definition in the Hellenistic World, Berkeley et al. 1993, 7–24

Bringmann 2000: Bringmann, Klaus, Geben und Nehmen. Monarchische Wohltätigkeit und Selbstdarstellung im Zeitalter des Hellenismus, Berlin 2000

Burghart 2022: Burghart, William D., When Galatians Attack: a Re-evaluation of the Impact of the Galatians on the International Affairs of 3rd-Century Hellenistic Asia Minor, in: Coşkun 2022a, 145–162

Camassa 2020: Camassa, Giorgio, Soter e soteria dal V secolo alle soglie dell'età ellenistica: qualche considerazione, Mythos 14, 1–17

Champion 2004/2005: Champion, Craige B., In Defense of Hellas. The Antigonid Soteria and Paneia at Delos and the Aetolian Soteria at Delphi, American Journal of Ancient History 3/4, 2004/2005, 72–88

Collis 2003: Collis, John, The Celts. Origins, Myths and Inventions, Stroud 2003

Coşkun 2012: Coşkun, Altay, Deconstructing a Myth of Seleucid History. The So-called "Elephant Victory" Revisited, Phoenix 66, 2012, 57–73

Coşkun 2013: Coşkun, Altay, Belonging and Isolation in Central Anatolia: The Galatians in the Graeco-Roman World, in: S. Ager – R. A. Faber (eds.), Belonging and Isolation in the Hellenistic World, Toronto 2013, 73–95

Coşkun 2022a: Coşkun, Altay (ed.), Galatian Victories and Other Studies into the Agency and Identity of the Galatians in the Hellenistic and Early Roman Periods, Leuven 2022

Coşkun 2022b: Coşkun, Altay, Pessinus, Kleonnaeion and Attalid Administration in Eastern Phrygia in Light of a Recently-found Royal Letter from Ballıhisar, in: Coşkun 2022a, 213–232

Chrubasik 2013: Chrubasik, Boris, The Attalids and the Seleukid Kings, 281–175 BC, in: P. Thonemann (ed.), Attalid Asia Minor. Money, International Relations, and the State, Oxford 2013, 83–119

D'Agostini 2013: D'Agostini, Monica, La strutturazione del potere seleucidico in Anatolia. Il caso di Acheo il Vecchio e Alessandro di Sardi, Erga-Logoi 1, 2013, 87–106

Domingo Gygax 2016: Domingo Gygax, Marc, Benefaction and Rewards in the Ancient Greek City. The Origins of Euergetism, Cambridge 2016

Ellis 1976: Ellis, John R., Philip II and Macedonian Imperialism, London 1976

Erskine 1994: Erskine, Andrew, The Romans as Common Benefactors, Historia 43, 1994, 70–87

Fantuzzi 2011: Fantuzzi, Marco, Speaking with Authority: Polyphony in Callimachus' Hymns, in: B. Acosta-Hughes – L. Lehnus – S. Stephens (eds.), Brill's Companion to Callimachus, Leiden et al. 2011, 429–453

Flacelière 1937: Flacelière, Robert, Les Aitoliens à Delphes. Contribution à l'histoire de la Grèce centrale au IIIe siècle av. J.-C., Paris 1937

Gauthier 1985: Gauthier, Philippe, Les cités grecques et leurs bienfaiteurs, Athens 1985

Gehrke 1982: Gehrke, Hans-Joachim, Der siegreiche König. Überlegungen zur hellenistischen Monarchie, Archiv für Kulturgeschichte 64, 1982, 247–277

Grainger 1995: Grainger, John D., The Campaign of Cn. Manlius Vulso in Asia Minor, Anatolian Studies 45, 1995, 23–42

Gruen 2000: Gruen, Erich S. 2000, Culture as Policy: The Attalids of Pergamon, in: N. T. de Grummond – B. S. Ridgway (eds.), From Pergamon to Sperlonga: Sculpture and Context, Berkeley 2000, 17–31

Hannestad 1996: Hannestad, Lise, Greeks and Celts: The Creation of a Myth, in: P. Bilde et al. (eds.), Centre and Periphery in the Hellenistic World, Aarhus 1996, 15–38

Hansen 1971: Hansen, Esther V., The Attalids of Pergamon, London 1971

Hopp 1977: Hopp, Joachim, Untersuchungen zur Geschichte der letzten Attaliden, Munich 1977

Hurwit 2004: Hurwit, Jeffrey M., The Acropolis in the Age of Pericles, Cambridge 2004

Jim 2022: Jim, Theodora S. F., Saviour Gods and Soteria in Ancient Greece, Oxford 2022

Johstono 2019: Johstono, Paul, The Grand Procession, Galatersieg, and Ptolemaic Kingship, in: T. Howe – F. Pownall (eds.), Ancient Macedonians in the Greek and Roman Sources. From History to Historiography, Swansea 2019, 181–200

Jung 2006: Jung, Michael, Marathon und Plataiai: Zwei Perserschlachten als "lieux de mémoire" im antiken Griechenland, Göttingen 2006

Kaye 2022: Kaye, Noah, The Attalids of Pergamon and Anatolia. Money, Culture and State Power, Cambridge 2022

Kistler 2009: Kistler, Erich, Funktionalisierte Keltenbilder. Die Indienstnahme der Kelten zur Vermittlung von Normen und Werten in der Hellenistischen Welt, Berlin 2009

Koehn 2007: Koehn, Clemens, Krieg – Diplomatie – Ideologie. Zur Außenpolitik hellenistischer Mittelstaaten, Stuttgart 2007

Kosmetatou 2022: Kosmetatou, Elizabeth, The Eunuch Philetairos: Pergamene Founding Father and Galatian-Slayer, in: Coşkun 2022, 163–192

Kuttner 1995: Kuttner, Anne, Republican Rome looks at Pergamon, Harvard Studies in Classical Philology 97, 1995, 157–178

Kuzmin 2017: Kuzmin, Yuri, New Perspectives on the Date of the New Festival of Ptolemy II, Klio 99, 2017, 513–527

Lefèvre 1998: Lefèvre, François, L'Amphictionie pyléo-delphique. Histoire et institutions, Paris 1998

Lichtenberger 2021: Lichtenberger, Achim, Hellenistic Commagene in Context. Is 'Global' the Answer and Do We Have to Overcome Cultural 'Containers'?, in: M. Blömer et al. (eds.) Common Dwelling Place of all the Gods. Commagene in its Local, Regional and Global Hellenistic Context, Stuttgart 2021, 579–587

Luraghi 2013: Luraghi, Nino (ed.), The Splendors and Miseries of Ruling Alone. Encounters with Monarchy from Archaic Greece to the Hellenistic Mediterranean, Stuttgart 2013

Marszal 2000: Marszal, John R., Ubiquitous Barbarians. Representation of the Gauls at Pergamon and Elsewhere, in: N. T. de Grummond – B. S. Ridgway (eds.), From Pergamon to Sperlonga. Sculpture and Context, Berkeley et al. 2000, 191–234

Merkel 1960: Merkel, Irwin L., The Silver Coinage of Antigonos Gonatas and Antigonos Doson, Museum Notes, American Numismatic Society 9, 1960, 39–52

Michels 2004: Michels, Christoph, Der Pergamonaltar als "Staatsmonument" der Attaliden. Zur Rolle des historischen Kontextes in den Diskussionen über Datierung und Interpretation der Bildfriese, Berlin 2004

Michels 2009: Michels, Christoph, Kulturtransfer und monarchischer 'Philhellenismus'. Bithynien, Pontos und Kappadokien in hellenistischer Zeit, Göttingen 2009

Michels 2019: Michels, Christoph, Unlike any Other? The Attalid Kingdom after Apameia, in: A. Coşkun – D. Engels (eds.), Rome and the Seleukid East, Brussels 2019, 333–352

Mitchell 1990: Mitchell, Stephen, Archaeology in Asia Minor 1985–1989, Archaeological Reports 36, 1990, 83–191

Mitchell 1993: Mitchell, Stephen, Anatolia. Land, Men, and Gods in Asia Minor I: The Celts in Anatolia and the Impact of Roman Rule, Oxford 1993

Momigliano 1987: Momigliano, Arnaldo, Filippo il Macedone. Saggio sulla storia greca del IV secolo a. C., Milan 1987

Muccioli 2013: Muccioli, Federicomaria, Gli epiteti ufficiali dei re ellenistici, Stuttgart 2013

Nachtergael 1977: Nachtergael, Georges, Les Galates en Grèce et les Sôtèria de Delphes. Recherches d'histoire et d'épigraphie hellénistiques, Paris 1977

Nelson 2022: Nelson, Thomas, Beating the Galatians: Ideologies, Analogies and Allegories in Hellenistic Literature and Art, in: Coşkun 2022, 97–144

Paton 2010: Paton, William R., tr. Polybius, The Histories. Books 3–4, Cambridge et al. 2010

Payen 2022: Payen, Germain, When Galatians unite? A geopolitical evaluation of the impact of the alleged Galatian unity in the 2nd century BC, in: Coşkun 2022, 193–212

Pedroli 1896: Pedroli, Uberto, Il Regno di Pergamo, Bologna 1896

Queyrel 2017: Queyrel, François, Les Galates comme nouveaux géants? De la métaphore au glissement interprétatif, in: F.-H. Massa-Pairault – C. Pouzadoux (eds.), Géants et Gigantomachies entre Orient et Occident, Naples 2017, 203–215

Sage 1936: Sage, Evan T., tr. Livy, History of Rome. Books XXXVIII–XXXIX, Cambridge et al. 1936

Sanchez 2001: Sanchez, Pierre, L'Amphictionie des Pyles et de Delphes: Recherches sur son rôle historique, des origines au IIe siècle de notre ère, Stuttgart 2001

Savalli Lestrade 2020: Savalli Lestrade, Ivana, I Galati e gli Attalidi. Tra esclusione e integrazione. The Galatians and the Attalids. Between exclusion and integration, in: C. Bearzot – F. Landucci – G. Zecchini (eds.), I Celti e il Mediterraneo. Impatto e trasformazioni, Milan 2020, 167–196

Schalles 1985: Schalles, Hans-Joachim, Untersuchungen zur Kulturpolitik der Pergamenischen Herrscher im dritten Jahrhundert vor Christus, Tübingen 1985

Scholten 1999: Scholten, Joseph, The Politics of Plunder. Aitolians and their Koinon in the Early Hellenisic Era, 279–217 BC, Berkeley et al. 1999

Stewart 2004: Stewart, Andrew, Attalos, Athens, and the Akropolis: the Pergamene "Little Barbarians" and their Roman and Renaissance Legacy, Cambridge et al. 2004

Strobel 1994: Strobel, Karl, Keltensieg und Galatersieger. Die Funktionalisierung eines historischen Phänomens als politischer Mythos der hellenistischen Welt, in: E. Schwerteim (ed.), Forschungen in Galatien, Bonn 1994, 67–96

Strobel 2002: Strobel, Karl, State formation by the Galatians of Asia Minor. Politico-Historical and Cultural Processes in Hellenistic Central Anatolia, Anatolica 28, 1–46

Strootman 2005: Strootman, Rolf, Kings against Celts. Deliverance from Barbarians as a Theme in Hellenistic Royal Propaganda, in: K. A. E. Enenkel – I. L. Pfeijffer (eds.), The Manipulative Mode: Political Propaganda in Antiquity. A Collection of Case Studies, Leiden 2005, 101–141

Tagliamonte 2020: Tagliamonte, Gianluca, I mercenari celtici, in: C. Bearzot – F. Landucci – G. Zecchini (eds.), I Celti e il Mediterraneo. Impatto e trasformazioni, Milan 2020, 63–92

Veyne 1976: Veyne, Paul, Le pain et le cirque: sociologie historique d'un pluralisme politique, Paris 1976

Wallace 2010: Wallace, Shane, The Significance of Plataia for Greek Eleutheria in the Early Hellenistic Period, in: A. Erskine – L. Llewellyn-Jones (eds.), Creating a Hellenistic World, Swansea 2010, 147–176

Wallace 2011: Wallace, Shane, Freedom of the Greeks in the early Hellenistic period (337–262 BC): a Study in Ruler-City Relations, Diss. Edinburgh 2011

Waterfield 2021: Waterfield, Robin, The Making of a King. Antigonus Gonatas of Macedon and the Greeks, Oxford 2021

Weber 1978: Weber, Max, Economy and Society. An Outline of Interpretive Sociology, 2 vols., ed. by G. Rothand – C. Wittich, Berkeley et al. 1978

Wörrle 1975: Wörrle, Michael, Antiochos I., Achaios der Ältere und die Galater. Eine Neue Inschrift in Denizli, Chiron 5, 1975, 59–88

Giovanna Pasquariello holds a doctorate from the University of Edinburgh. She studied the vocabulary used in Greek inscriptions of the 3rd and 2nd centuries BC to portray the Galatians. She explored the formation and circulation of stereotypical "Galatian imagery" in the Hellenistic world, with focus on the interface between epigraphy and literary accounts. She is also interested in educational outreach, cultural communication, and community engagement, as well as in the reception of Classics in contemporary political discourse.

Imitation and/or Innovation?
Royal Incest and the Mithradatids of Pontos

ALEX MCAULEY

Abstract: This chapter examines the context and ideology behind the two attested instances of brother-sister marriage among the Mithradatids of Pontos – namely the unions of Mithradates IV and his sister Laodike, and Mithradates VI's first marriage to his sister Laodike. These marriages have traditionally been viewed as an imitation of Ptolemaic or Achaimenid practice and therefore as an indication of the dynasty's broader cultural alignment in the Hellenistic milieu. Beginning with a detailed re-examination of the numismatic, epigraphic, and literary evidence, this chapter then situates these seemingly idiosyncratic marriages in the broader cultural and political context of the kingdom in order to determine how brother-sister marriage relates to the unique environment of Pontos. Throughout this chapter I argue that these incestuous marriages should not be exclusively taken as an imitation of either Ptolemaic or Achaimenid precedent but are also indicative of the kingdom's contemporary alignment with the emerging power of the Arsakids of Parthia and should be viewed as part of a wider effort to draw on a common Achaimenid heritage among eastern Anatolian dynasties. In this context I posit that these marriages could represent early instances of the Zoroastrian practice of xwēdōdah and relate to the more general combination of innovation and tradition in the self-representation of Hellenistic royalty.

1. Introduction

The theme of this volume – *the same, but different* – provides a fitting opportunity to reconsider some of the most basic aspects of monarchical representation in the Hellenistic world. Prominent among these considerations is the extent to which Hellenistic monarchies in various corners of the world, carved out by the campaigns of Alexander III, eagerly imitated existing models of dynastic practice and self-representation or created new royal practices of their own.[1] This balance between tradition and innovation, which lies at the core of Hellenistic monarchy, becomes all the more complicated when we turn our attention to the diverse dynastic landscape of the "High Hellenistic Period" of the second century BC. By this point in time we witness not only the ongoing dialogue of the "major" successor dynasties of the Seleukids, the Antigonids, and the Ptolemies with the dynastic traditions of their respective territories and subject populations, but also the emergence of "minor" Hellenistic dynasties in Asia Minor who in no small part modelled themselves on their more illustrious contemporaries.[2] All the while the *praxis* of Hellenistic monarchy had evolved over the course of the two centuries since the death of Alexander to the point of being accepted as the contemporary structure of power.

This in turn required another delicate negotiation: contemporary Hellenistic monarchs had to assimilate themselves to their predecessors in order to legitimize their rule while also differentiating themselves from them and their contemporaries in the creation of their own prestige. Against the backdrop of these broader considerations of continuity versus innovation and assimilation vs differentiation among the Hellenistic monarchies, in this chapter I will focus on the rather curious case study of royal incest among the Mithradatid dynasty of Pontos and what this practice reveals about the broader character of this Anatolian dynasty and its kingdom.

On a structural level the early generations of the Mithradatids behave very much like the other "minor" or "client" dynasties of Anatolia that developed in the shadow of the Seleukids.[3] This elite family of Iranian satrapal origin marries in to the Seleukid royal family with the union of Mithradates II and Laodike, daughter of the reigning king Antiochos II.[4] Thanks to this marriage Mithradates II was recognized both internally and externally as a *basileus* in his own right, and with their Hellenistic royal credentials well-established the royal couple then weave their own dynastic ties in Asia Minor. Their daughter Laodike – whose name both conforms with Seleukid tradition while

1   See, for instance, the recent edited volume of Anagnostou-Laoutides – Pfeiffer 2022, particularly the editor's introduction on how to re-approach questions of "Hellenisation" in this dynastic context, as well as the volume of Fischer-Bovet – von Reden 2021 comparing the Ptolemaic and Seleukid empires. The dynamic interplay between various cultural traditions and innovations has also been discussed in the context of Kleopatra III and Kleopatra Thea by Llewellyn-Jones and McAuley 2022. On broader courtly practices and cultural politics see also Strootman 2014.

2   On this occurrence in the Seleukid realm see McAuley 2021, and on the broader Philhellenism of Hellenistic royalty in Asia Minor see Michels 2009.

3   On these local dynasties in Hellenistic Asia Minor see the study of Kobes 1996. On Seleukid dynastic practice see also the contributions of Richter and Mittag in this volume.

4   See D'Agostini 2016 on the marriage practices of the Mithradatids and their evolving representation of their own history. This marriage is attested by Euseb. Chron. 1.40.6, Iust. 28.5.3, and discussed by Grainger 1997, 48. There is some debate as to whether it took place before or after the Battle of Ankyra, but the conflicting viewpoints are summarised by Erciyas 2006, 13–5. See also Bevan 1902, 1.22–28.

also advertising their pedigree – married another local dynast, Achaios "the Younger", who would later attempt to usurp the Seleukid throne.[5] Another daughter of the couple, also named Laodike, married back into her mother's family and would go on to become the highly-publicised wife of Antiochos III, who appears with remarkable prominence in the dynasty's public image.[6] Somewhat later Pharnakes I married another Seleukid princess, Nysa, in another union which treaded the line between exogamic and endogamic given the recurrent marriages between these two families. By this point the royal couple would have been cousins of one degree or another.[7]

Up to this point, the Mithradatids follow a fairly standard pattern among the Hellenistic dynasties: a local elite family marries into one of the major royal houses, adopts their naming traditions and court practices, is recognised as "royal" in its own right, and then proceeds to marry back into this family and other royal houses in subsequent generations.[8] Precisely the same sequence is found among the Attalids of Pergamon and the Ariarathids of Kappadokia, as well as in the Graeco-Baktrian kingdom in the Seleukid east.[9] But then suddenly in the third generation of the dynasty we find several attestations of Mithradates IV Philopator – or Mithradates III, following the sequence of Primo 2006 – marrying his full-blooded sister Laodike, and then somewhat later the famous Mithradates VI Eupator also married his sibling Laodike early in his reign.[10] These cases of royal sibling marriage in Pontos however have not garnered the same amount of scholarly attention as the more glamorously incestuous marriages of the Ptolemies or the enigmatic brother-sister union of the children of Antiochos III.[11] The prevailing tendency among contemporary scholars traditionally has been to view these incestuous marriages of the Mithradatids as an imitation of the Ptolemies intended as an ostentatious display of their *tryphē* as well as their Greekness. McGing describes one of the coin types broadcasting the marriage of Mithradates IV to his sister as 'a declaration of Hellenism.'[12] The message communicated by this manoeuvre, according to this line of reasoning, seems to be that if the Mithradatids practice the same martial strategies as the Ptolemies then they are royalty of equal standing to them, thus they should be counted among the great contemporary Hellenistic monarchies. Brian McGing does note, however, that there are some Persian elements lurking in the back-

---

5   On this marriage see D'Agostini 2018, and the discussion of Chrusbasik 2016, 65–115 in the Anatolian context.

6   Pol. 5.43.1–4 for this marriage; see Ma 2000's epigraphic dossier for the presence of the king and queen in Asia Minor.

7   App. Syr. 5, Pol. 32.30.8, Bevan 1902, 2.59–62.

8   See D'Agostini 2021 for a detailed discussion of Seleukid marriage alliances.

9   See again D'Agostini 2021, and Wenghofer – Houle 2016 for the Graeco-Baktrian context.

10   Primo 2006 makes a convincing case that Mithradates IV should be identified with Mithradates III, but this has not yet been broadly accepted in scholarship. In the interest of accessibility, I will identify Primo's Mithradates III as the conventionally-numbered Mithradates IV.

11   Ogden 1999, 135, Bielman-Sánchez 2003, 46.

12   McGing 1986, 35–36.

ground of this marriage and the iconography with which it was depicted.[13] François de Callataÿ argues essentially the same on the ground of numismatic iconography, which on the one hand seems to imitate the Ptolemies, but on the other to harken back to the dynasty's Persian roots.[14] Christoph Michels places the first of these incestuous marriages in its immediate dynastic context, emphasising that it was meant to ensure the continuity of the royal family and present an image of family cohesion at a time of dynastic uncertainty – all the while the iconography establishes a parallel between the royal couple and Zeus-Hera *à la lagide*.[15] Most recently, Luis Ballesteros Pastor views these marriages as an unsubtle reminder of the dynasty's Achaimenid roots, arguing that the Mithradatids were following a practice of consanguineous marriages well-attested among the Persians.[16]

The basic question thus seems to be "were the Mithradatids imitating the Ptolemies or the Achaimenids with these surprising brother-sister marriages?" In response to this, my argument in this chapter is that yes, these incestuous marriages do indeed appear to be an imitation of both Ptolemaic and the Achaimenids, but the dynamics of this *imitatio* are rather more complicated. In this case study we find an illustrative example of the polyvalence that lies at the core of Hellenistic royal representation here in Pontos and beyond. To develop these observations, we begin with what little primary evidence we have for Pontic royal incest before placing these marriages in the regional context of Pontos itself. We shall then consider how these marriages relate to western and eastern traditions among the courts of the Ptolemies in Alexandreia and the Parthians in Ktesiphon – especially the latter. In the end the adoption of royal brother-sister marriage among the Mithradatids is the product of imitation of perceived Egyptian and Persian traditions resurrected – and re-cast – in the Hellenistic present as a means of situating the Pontic kingdom among its contemporaries in the east and west.

2. Back to the evidence: representations of Pontic royal incest

It must be said at the outset that we have precious little evidence with which to work in reconstructing the history of the Mithradatids prior to the reign of Mithradates VI, and the chronology of the dynasty is sketchy at best. Attestations of these brother-sister marriages in the royal family are no exception to this general trend, though there is just

---

13   McGing 1986, 36–38.
14   De Callataÿ 2009, 79–83.
15   Michels 2009, 196–200. On Ptolemaic concepts of dynasty and representations thereof see Pfeiffer in this volume.
16   Ballesteros Pastor 2015, 428: 'Mitrídates Eupátor tuvo como primera esposa a su hermana Laódice, siguiendo una práctica de matrimonio consanguíneo que está bien atestiguada entre los persas' This, however, relies on accepting even difficult attestations of incestuous marriage among the Achaimenids.

enough evidence at our disposal to derive some observations. As mentioned above, the two attested instances of brother-sister marriage in the royal family of Pontos are the unions of Mithradates IV Philopator and Laodike, and Mithradates VI Eupator and Laodike. We shall discuss the immediate context and representations of each in turn.

At some point prior to ca. 155 BC Pharnakes I died after largely unsuccessful campaigns in Asia Minor during the 170s against Eumenes II of Pergamon and Ariarathes IV of Kappadokia. The peace settlement of these campaigns required the forfeiture of territory in Galatia and Paphlagonia, and from then onwards Pharnakes adopted a more pacific approach to kingship involving benefactions and displays of philhellenism in Delos and Athens. In conformity with the pattern set by previous generations of Anatolian royalty, Pharnakes married the Seleukid princess Nysa in another iteration of marital exchange confirming alliances among the Seleukids and minor dynasties of Asia Minor.[17] His son by Nysa, Mithradates V, was either too young to rule or was kept at bay by his uncle, as Pharnakes was succeeded on the throne by his younger brother Mithradates IV, who seems to have ruled as a regent of some sort for his nephew. Pharnakes and Mithradates had a sister named Laodike who was honoured with a statue at Delos erected at some point prior to her older brother's death – 160/159 according to Reinach – which identifies her as 'Laodike the sister of king Pharnakes and Mithradates'.[18] Note that she is not yet married at the date of this inscription, and only Pharnakes is identified as the reigning king given the genitive singular βασιλέως, so her marriage to her brother cannot yet have taken place at this point in the reign of Pharnakes.[19] The first attestation of Mithradates IV's reign, however, gives a clear indication of when this brother-sister marriage must have taken place. An inscription in both Greek and

17　The marriage is attested by OGIS 771, a decree of Athens at Delos in honour of Pharnakes and his wife Nysa. There is debate regarding both the identity of Nysa and the dating of the decree, which has been dated to either 196/5, 171/0, or 160. On this debate see Ghita 2011, 110–112 and Michels 2009: 89–95. The date of the inscription needs not detain us here; the relevant point to make is that Pharnakes was married to a distant relative of his in continuation of what by this point was a well-established pattern. In the same vein, Nysa has been identified as either a daughter of Antiochos III and Laodike III, or a daughter of Antiochos Neos and his sister Laodike. The latter seems far more plausible, and I agree with Michels 2009, 89–90 on the dating of the inscription to 196/5 and thus the beginning of his reign, and the identification of Nysa as the daughter of Antiochos III and Laodike III. The conclusion of Ghita that Antiochos IV was likely Nysa's father, and that the marriage came much later is problematic, as is the comment at 113 that this marriage was 'replenishing their [the Seleukids'] Iranian blood' given the longer marital history of these dynasties.

18　IDélos 1555: Λαοδίκην τὴν βασιλέως Φαρνάκου καὶ Μιθραδάτου ἀδελφήν.

19　If Laodike were married by this point, then we would expect this to be mentioned in this inscription but given that she is simply referred to as 'the sister' she must not yet have been married. While at first glance it would be curious that Laodike would be mentioned in this inscription at all, the same question could be asked of her brother Mithradates' presence as well given that he was not the ruling king. it seems that the precedent for the Pontic royal family's presence at Delos had been well-established by Pharnakes and Nysa in the document discussed above. The links between the Mithradatids and Delos were meant to transcend any one individual member of the royal family – hence the appearance of Pharnakes alongside his brother and sister in this inscription.

Latin on a rectangular stone base on the Capitoline hill in Rome records a dedication made by Mithradates IV to the people of Rome on account of his *amicitia* and *societas*. The king's titles are consistent in both languages of the dedication: the opening line in Latin reads *[rex Metradates Pilopator et Pil]adelpus* while the Greek a few lines later identifies him as [βασιλεὺς Μιθραδάτης Φιλ]οπάτωρ καὶ Φιλάδελφος.[20] Although the inscription had initially been dated to after the defeat of Mithradates VI in the first Mithradatic War, McGing noted that the combination of titles attested must refer to Mithradates IV rather than Eupator given that they are consistent with his numismatic titulary.[21] The title *philadelphos* can hardly have been an empty honorific, and Ptolemaic inspiration for this aspect in particular is certainly likely.[22] At some point shortly after taking the throne, then, Mithradates must have married his sister Laodike and taken the title *philadelphos*.

The marriage was also commemorated in a series of coin issues discussed by McGing, de Callataÿ, and Michels, dated to between ca. 152–150 BC, five of which survive today. Although Peter Green described the portrait of Mithradates IV as looking like a 'skid-row alcoholic' – marginally better than his 'neanderthal' older brother Pharnakes and 'escaped convict' ancestor – a more helpful analysis of this coin type makes the Ptolemaic connections clear.[23] The issue in question is a silver tetradrachm (fig. 1) bearing a jugate portrait of the royal couple Mithradates and Laodike on the obverse, and a reverse with the portrait of Zeus and Hera and the legend ΒΑΣΙΛΕΩΣ ΜΙΘΡΑΔΑΤΟΥ ΚΑΙ ΒΑΣΙΛΙΣΣΗΣ ΛΑΟΔΙΚΗΣ ΦΙΛΑΔΕΛΦΩΝ.[24]

20   OGIS 375 = IGUR I 9 and CIL I 730.
21   McGing 1986, 34–35.
22   On the ideology of family concord communicated by the Ptolemaic use of *philadelphos* and its attestation among other Hellenistic dynasties, see Muccioli 2013, 208–219, with discussion of Pontos at 212–213. The inspiration for his other title *philopator*, however, is more ambiguous: Ptolemaios IV bore the epithet during his reign from 221–204 BC, as did Seleukos IV from 185 to 175 BC. While the inclination may be to view the combination of these titles as a clear imitation of the Lagids, perhaps Mithradates was drawing on more than one dynasty for his inspiration. See again Pfeiffer in this volume on the title *philadelphos* in the Ptolemaic dynastic tradition.
23   Green 1990, 350. The full quotation: 'The early kings of Pontus resemble nothing so much as a family of escaped convicts: Pharnakes I (r. 185/183–170) has the profile of a Neanderthal, and Mithradates IV (r. 170–150) that of a skid-row alcoholic'.
24   De Callataÿ 2009, 77–78 for all surviving specimens of this coin type, which are largely consistent in their iconography. The only subtle difference seems to be whether the ends of Mithradates' diadem blend into his neckline or are shown as fluttering behind him. How this compared to the numismatic portraiture of the early Hellenistic kings more generally and the basic iconographic paradigms is also intriguing – on this see von den Hoff's contribution to this volume.

Fig. 1 Silver tetradrachm of Mithradates IV and Laodike, uncertain mint, Pontos.

The plural *philadelphōn* communicates an obvious message: this is a royal couple, king and queen, brother and sister, reigning just like Zeus and Hera who are both depicted standing with sceptres in their right hands. The layout of the coin is likewise unsubtle, given that the legend bearing the king's name is immediately to the right of the portrait of Zeus and the queen's name to the left of the portrait of Hera. As Michels has noted, the inspiration for this coin type must surely be Ptolemaic given literary depictions of the marriage of *theoi adelphoi* as another *hieros gamos* between Zeus and Hera in Theokritos 17, as well as the broader assimilation of the Ptolemaic royal family with the Olympians.[25] While all of these associations are meant to be brought to the numismatic portrait of this Pontic royal couple, Michels and Vlahogiannis however have pointed out that there are some idiosyncratic elements.[26] This depiction of Hera and Zeus as a royal-divine couple is common in Greek art but not in the numismatic context. The physical depiction of the king and queen likewise seem to leave a Pontic mark on this Ptolemaic paradigm. Rather than the older and more Rubenesque depiction of Ptolemaios II and Arsinoë II as the fleshy manifestation of Ptolemaic *tryphē*, Mithradates and Laodike appear much younger – though the former's fertility is highlighted by her double chin and round cheeks. This Pontic brother-sister pair clearly have the same facial structure, eye shape, and lips, all of which are quite distinct from the conventions of Ptolemaic numismatic portraiture. The dominant tone of this numismatic portraiture is not so much an outright imitation of Ptolemaic iconography related to marital practice, but rather an innovation on Ptolemaic precedents in the unique environment of Pontos. It is, to refer to the title of this volume again, the same, but different. The same can be said of the Hera-Zeus iconography of the reverse, which clearly borrows

25 Theokr. 17. On this and the multimedia representation of the *theoi adelphoi* Müller 2009 remains the best discussion, especially 262–300. On coin portraits in particular see Müller 2009, 335–347. See again Pfeiffer on the Ptolemies in this volume.
26 Michels 2009, 198–199 citing Vlahogiannis 1987, 271–279 (*non vidi*). On the representation of tutelary deities more generally among early Hellenistic royalty see also Weber's contribution to this volume.

from a Ptolemaic literary tradition establishing a parallel between the royal couple and Zeus and Hera but transplants it into a coin type.[27] The public image conveyed by this coin type goes beyond a simple facsimile of Ptolemaic incest by adapting this dynastic practice to the Pontic royal family.

Laodike's portraiture on this jugate series is consistent with her depiction in another silver tetradrachm issue possibly struck as a posthumous commemoration of the queen (fig. 2).[28] The single specimen of this type that survives is not in particularly good condition, though it is still possible to identify similarities between the jugate portrait of the queen and this solo depiction.

Fig. 2 Silver tetradrachm of Laodike, possibly posthumous, uncertain mint, Pontos.

While Laodike's cheeks are rather less fleshy and rounded than in the jugate portraiture, the queen still has the same slightly upturned nose and strong chin with which she and her brother were depicted alongside each other. In this solo issue, however, the queen is veiled and there is a hint of a diadem at her hairline, leading us to perhaps surmise that this was struck later in her married life than the jugate portrait, which appears at the beginning of the couple's reign. The depiction of Hera on the obverse is identical to the jugate issue: the goddess appears alone without her brother-husband, in a standing position with her right arm raised to hold a sceptre and her right resting on her hips, gathering the folds of a long dress that reaches to the ground. The legend on this coin is simply *basilissēs laodikēs*, without the titles on the previous jugate issue. Again, this issue seems to be an adaptation of Ptolemaic issues featuring solo portraits of queens but with a distinctly Mithradatic twist. A curiously idiosyncratic gold stater featuring a solo portrait of a queen in the obverse and the reverse legend *basilissēs*

27   Michels 2009, 199.
28   On the debate surrounding the identification of this Laodike see Michels 2009, 199–200, especially note 1030. Reinach originally identified her as otherwise unnamed queen of Mithradates V who could perhaps be equated with a Laodike, daughter of Antiochos IV, but the nearly identical similarity between the standing Hera on the reverse of this coin and the preceding jugate issue discussed above makes it far more likely this queen is still Laodike, sister-wife of Mithradates IV. See also de Callataÿ 2009, 78–79 for the purchase history of these coins.

laodikēs epiphanous kai philadelphou around a double cornucopia and six-rayed star was described by the cataloguer who sold it as depicting the wife and sister of Mithradates IV 'als junge Frau'. While the specimen sold for 220,000 CHF, it has convincingly been identified by de Callataÿ as a modern forgery.[29]

Contemporary counterfeits aside, the trend of Pontic adaptation (rather than outright replication) of Ptolemaic precedent can also be found in another coin issue of Mithradates IV. A silver tetradrachm (fig. 3) bears a solo portrait of the king consistent with his other numismatic depictions: diademed, bearded, gazing forward with the same identifiable eyes, nasal shape, and chin as in the jugate issue we have discussed earlier.[30] The reverse bears the legend inscription ΒΑΣΙΛΕΩΣ ΜΙΘΡΑΔΑΤΟΥ ΦΙΛΟΠΑΤΟΡΟΣ ΚΑΙ ΦΙΛΑΔΕΛΦΟΥ, his epithets are consistent with the dedication made on the Capitoline at the beginning of his reign.

Fig. 3 Silver tetradrachm of Mithradates IV, uncertain mint, Pontos.

The choice of *philopatōr* and *philadelphos* does certainly seem to draw on Ptolemaic titulary precedent, but the rest of the reverse's iconography is unique in the Hellenistic world. The top of the reverse features a seven-pointed star above a crescent moon in another iteration of the numismatic *pontisches Wappen* established during the reign of Pharnakes I. Below this 'coat of arms' is a standing portrait of Perseus wearing a chlamys, winged shoes, a Phrygian helmet and holding Medusa's head. As Michels has argued, the reverse of this coin represents the continued promotion of the cult of the moon god Men by the Pontic kings, and Perseus is here depicted in a way that borrows the associations of Men.[31] Perseus would later become a commonplace feature on the coin types of Mithradates VI and a means of advertising his dynasty's Persian roots through a commonplace hero that was resonant with a Greek audience, leading

---

29   See de Callataÿ 2009, 83–84 for a compelling argument as to why this odd gold stater of Laodike is likely a modern forgery.
30   Michels 2009, 196 and de Callataÿ 2009, 75–77.
31   Michels 2009, 195–197.

McGing to argue that this was a means of bridging eastern and western iconography.[32] While this certainly seems plausible and in keeping with the polyvalence of Hellenistic royal representations, there is no direct attestation of a cult of Perseus among the Pontic royal family. This leads Michels to conclude that the Perseus motif emphasizes the superhuman and heroic character of the king while also mimicking a recent emphasis on Perseus among the Antigonids of Macedon, therefore this was not primarily intended as a reference to the Iranian origins of the dynasty.[33] Nevertheless, these readings are by no means mutually exclusive, and in the end the iconography of Mithradates IV's coinage presents a unique twist on Greek, Pontic, and Iranian traditions while also drawing on the inspiration of contemporary Hellenistic monarchs.[34] These scant numismatic and epigraphic data represent the sum total of the ancient evidence for the brother-sister marriage of Mithradates IV and Laodike.

After the fairly standard marriage of Mithradates V to the Seleukid princess Laodike, consanguineous marriage returns in the next generation of the dynasty with the most (in)famous king of Pontos.[35] We have even less material to work with for the marriage of Mithradates VI Eupator to his younger sister Laodike, but still enough to assume that the marriage did in fact take place. After describing the early campaigns of Mithradates VI, Justin then recounts this typically scandalous tale: the conquering king returns home and learned that his sister-wife had given birth to a son, but when she assumed him dead, she had sordid affairs with his *philoi* who then tried to poison the king:

> After these campaigns he returned to his kingdom, and since he was believed to have died, he found an infant son whom his sister and wife Laodike had borne during his absence. In the midst of the celebration of his arrival after his long journey and on the birth of his son, Mithradates was in danger of being poisoned since his sister Laodike, believing him to be dead, had thrown herself into the bed of [his] *philoi*, and as if she could conceal the wicked deed by an even greater crime she prepared poison for him on his return. Mithradates, however, since he had learned of it from her female servants, took vengeance for the plot through punishing its authors.[36]

---

32   McGing 1986, 35, 94, and Michels 2009, 196–197.
33   Michels 2009, 197. For a comparison with how kingship among rivals is represented in Baktria see Hoo's contribution to this volume.
34   Michels 2009, 197.
35   Grainger 1997, 50. It is generally assumed that this Laodike is a daughter of Antiochos IV by his wife Laodike.
36   Iust. 37.3: *Post haec in regnum, cum iam perisse crederetur, reuersus est inuento paruulo filio, quem per absentiam eius soror uxorque Laodice enixa fuerat. Sed inter gratulationem post longam peregrinationem aduentus sui et filii geniti ueneno periclitatus est siquidem Laodice soror, cum perisse eum crederet, in concubitus amicorum proiecta, quasi admissum facinus maiori scelere tegere posset, uenenum aduenienti parauit. Quod cum ex ancillis Mithridates cognouisset, facinus in auctores uindicauit.*(my translation).

While the episode is clearly a prime example of Justin's eye for scandalous courtly intrigue and plotting, it is noteworthy here that the scandalous element of the tale is not so much Mithradates' marriage to his sister Laodike, but rather her dangerous liaisons with his *philoi* while he was away on campaign. If anything, the fact that Laodike was both his sister and his wife only seems to amplify the attempted betrayal rather than justify it – hence Justin labels her *soror* twice in just a few lines. While *topoi* like the infidelity of queens, female plots involving poison, and attempts to cover up transgressions with even more transgressions are all commonplace in Justin's epitome, here as elsewhere it is often the details in his account that are passed by without comment that seem the most reliable. From this literary testimonium there seems to be no reason to doubt that Mithradates was in fact married to his sister Laodike early in his reign. Valerius Maximus also attests that Mithradates was married to Laodike – who must be the same as his sister – and adds the interesting note that the pair gave birth a daughter, Drypetine, who had a double row of teeth on the top and bottom of her mouth. This same Drypetine, he adds, accompanied Mithradates when he fled from Pompeius after being defeated.[37] Beyond these two accounts, however, there are no further *testimonia* of the brother-sister marriage between Laodike and Mithradates VI. Unlike Mithradates IV, we do not find the epithet *philadelphos* in Eupator's numismatic *corpus* – his coin types are dominated either by Athena Nikephoros, a grazing Pegasos, or frequent assimilations of the king to Dionysos.[38] The famous monument of the Mithradatids at Delos likewise makes no explicit mention of Laodike, or any of the king's wives, for that matter, even though there is a remarkable retinue of Greek and Iranian elites featured on the monument's portrait medallions.[39] What, then, are we to make of these two episodes of royal incest among the Mithradatids, and what bearing does this have on our broader understanding of this kingdom in particular and Hellenistic royalty more generally? We shall first turn to the internal context of Pontos before considering how the kingdom fits into the broader dynastic landscape of the period.

3. The Mithradatids in their regional context

The practical rationale and royal ideology behind these brother-sister marriages among the Mithradatids gradually begins to come into focus when we consider them in the specific regional context of Pontos, and in the process we can begin to fill the gaps in our evidentiary record. There are three aspects of this regional context that merit further discussion as they relate to these two marriages: first, the royal family of the

---

37 Val. Max. 1.8e.13: *Mitridatis vero regis filia Drypetine, Laodice regina nata, duplici ordine dentium deformis admodum comes fugae patris a Pompeio devicti fuit.*
38 Michels 2009, 202–215.
39 On this monument see Michels 2009, 104–118 and Kreuz 2009.

Mithradatids; second, the immediate dynastic context of these marriages; and third, the religious and strategic geography of Pontos at the time of these rulers. We shall discuss each in turn. With regards to the dynastic environment, in a contribution to his 2009 edited volume Jakob Munk Højte made the following pertinent observation regarding our understanding of the dynasty's genealogy:

> The family tree of the Pontic kings, as we know it today from the sources, is very much a tree turned upside down with many branches at the bottom and thinning at the top. Of the families of the seven Pontic kings that preceded Mithridates VI, we only possess the names of four wives and three sisters. In comparison Mithridates is known to have had no less than 18 children and he had at least six siblings.[40]

In light of this disparity of attestation he then goes on to make the very reasonable conclusion that:

> We have no reason to believe that the structure of the Pontic royal family was any different before the time of Mithridates VI. It is a matter of scarcity of sources. We should therefore expect each generation of the house to have consisted of quite a large number of individuals.[41]

In practical terms Højte's conclusion permits us to assume that throughout the dynasty's history the royal family and court of the Mithradatids would have more closely resembled that of the Achaimenids or Philip II in scale than the Seleukids, for instance, and that here we are dealing with a large extended royal family comprised of multiple wives, relatives of the king, children, and therefore many potential rival claimants to the throne.

This drastically changes how we conceptualise the dynasty in general and these brother-sister marriages in particular. Prior generations of the Mithradatids would thus have been marked by the same existence of multiple royal wives, competing offspring of the king, and large extended family that so characterised the late Argeads and the Achaimenids.[42] Such large dynastic environments tend to breed instability given the large number of potential claimants to the throne, and competing family interests at court. The bitter rivalry between Adea-Eurydike and Olympias during the reign of Philip II is a particularly clear example of this, along with the amphimetric strife discussed by Daniel Ogden in his 1999 study.[43] Perhaps, then, these instances of brother-sister marriage were a means of clarifying and solidifying the couple's position within the family and thus at the head of the kingdom in the midst of a large dynastic environment. Whether this was done exclusively to the benefit of one partner or the

---

40   Højte 2009b, 126–127.
41   Højte 2009b, 126–127.
42   On the Argead context see Müller 2021 and Carney 2021.
43   Elaborated at Ogden 1999: *ix–xii*; see his discussion of the Argeads at 3–40.

other cannot be known, though the mechanism of marriage as a means of excluding possible rival claimants would certainly have been on the Pontic radar. Dareios I, for instance, cemented his claim to the Achaimenid throne by marrying all the former wives, sisters, and daughters of Cambyses and Bardiya, incorporated them into his household, and elevated their status at court. In the process, as Llewellyn-Jones has noted, Dareios himself was following in the footsteps of Rameses II, David of Israel, and his son Solomon after him.[44] In addition to clearly delineating courtly prestige and paths of succession, these marriages would have simplified the public image of the Pontic kings – especially to a Greek audience – by presenting a slimmed-down version of the royal family in the same manner as what I have described elsewhere as the Seleukid reigning triad.[45] Dynastic practicality and familial prestige are not mutually exclusive, and such a manoeuvre as brother-sister marriage would have been equally effective in the eyes of both domestic and foreign audiences.

This large dynastic environment is closely related to the second contextual observation to be made, namely that both of these incestuous marriages occurred in times of dynastic instability with other possible claimants to the throne. As discussed above, Mithradates IV came to the throne and married his sister after the death of his older brother Pharnakes, even though Pharnakes already had an heir in the form of his son Mithradates V – who would indeed go on to be king shortly after his aunt and uncle.[46] His accession took place at a precarious time for Pontos generally, following the largely unsuccessful campaigns of his older brother, and the kingdom itself was increasingly at risk of losing further territory in Asia Minor to its Anatolian rivals with the support of Rome. Mithradates VI likewise came to the throne in uncertain times: following the article of Ballesteros Pastor from 2013, he would only have been 11 or 12 at the sudden death of his father Mithradates V.[47] 'Everything', to quote Ballesteros Pastor, 'points to an inner quarrel within the court at Sinope'.[48] A rival faction trying to prevent his accession explains why the young king imprisoned the queen (his mother) and ordered the death of her and one of his brothers.[49] This also explains the alleged plot against his life in Justin, and why he ensured that two of his sisters remained unmarried into their 40s.[50] Both these kings, then, married their sisters as a means of stabilising their place on the throne and quieting internal dissent in the royal family. This incestuous marriage also becomes a sign of their legitimacy and prestige among a fairly crowded dynastic field and sets them out – at least temporarily – as the *primus inter pares* of the royal family, all the while closing off a possible dynastic rivalry by removing one of

---

44   Llewellyn-Jones 2013, 115–116.
45   McAuley 2022.
46   Michels 2009, 197–199.
47   Ballesteros Pastor 2013, 62.
48   Ballesteros Pastor 2013, 64.
49   Ballesteros Pastor 2013, 64.
50   Plut. Lucullus 18, discussed by Ballesteros Pastor 2013, 61–62.

their sisters from the picture. This transitional regnal context must be linked to this mechanism of incestuous marriage.

Our third and final observation relates to the kingdom of Pontos as a whole. As a consequence of the famous wars of Mithradates VI against the Romans along with his well-documented involvement in Western Anatolia and beyond, Pontos is often assumed to be a kingdom that looks to the west and that is primarily oriented towards the Greek and Roman world.[51] This is in no small part due to the nature of our source material for his reign and campaigns, which naturally sees them from a Graeco-Roman perspective. The religious geography of the kingdom, however, tells a very different story about its cultural and political orientation. As McGing discusses, aside from Greek cities on the Black Sea coast, in much of the kingdom's interior we are dealing with a non-Greek tribal culture previously ruled over by Achaimenid satraps rather than Greek-style civic communities. 'This geographical division of Pontus between coast and interior', he argues, 'reflects a sharp cultural division between Greek and Iranian / native Anatolian.'[52] While the kings of Pontos had managed to unify many of these tribal groups under their rule over the course of two centuries, according to Strabon even Eupator had to go on campaign in the east of the kingdom to subdue rebellious tribal groups.[53] In much of the interior of the kingdom the major land-holding institutions were temple estates rather than *poleis*.[54] In Kabeira there was a temple estate of the Anatolian god Men-Pharnakou, one of the chief deities of the royal family; Komana was home to a temple-estate of Ma, the priest of which was second in rank only to the king, while Zela had a temple estate of the Persian deities Anaitis, Omanos, and Anadatos.[55] Although much of the surviving material points to the worship of Zeus Ouranios and Zeus Stratios by the Mithradatid royal family, according to Sergej Saprykin's 2009 analysis there was a high degree of syncretism in the religious geography of the kingdom, which mutually recognised Hellenic, Phrygian/Anatolian, and Iranian deities.[56] Zeus Stratios was identified with Ahura Mazda, as well as Men-Pharnakou; Men was associated with Dionysos, Perseus with a variety of Iranian deities, especially Mithras, and the list of syncretic associations goes on.[57] The salient point is that while we tend to see only the Greek facet of this religious geography, the reality on the ground was

---

51   This is the implication that emerges from much of McGing 1986: even when discussing the early campaigns of Mithradates in Anatolia, the impression seems to be that Eupator is trying to make as many claims as possible without incurring the wrath of the Romans.

52   McGing 1986, 9.

53   McGing 1986, 9–11. Strab. 12.3.28, and see also 12.3.18 for his description of the eastern tribes. See also McGing 2014 on the cultural geography of the kingdom.

54   On these temple-estates and the institutional geography of Pontos see Olshausen 1990 and more recently Canepa 2018.

55   McGing 1986, 9.

56   Saprykin 2009, especially 258–262 on syncretism. The three tiers of Pontic religion are discussed at Saprykin 2009, 269.

57   See the preceding note, and Saprykin 2009, 255–258 on Ahura Mazda and Zeus Stratios.

much more diverse – and Iranian – than much of our literary source material would lead us to believe. As we shall discuss in further detail below, we must consider the diverse religious background and associated structures of regional power as part of the context in which these royal brother-sister marriages took place. In the Pontic context they could not, *de facto*, be addressed primarily to a Greek audience.

The contemporary strategic orientation of Pontos likewise casts these marriages in a different cultural light. Even though Mithradates VI was the alleged great enemy of the Republic, as Marek Jan Olbrycht noted in 2009 'if scholarly perspectives are limited to the interplay between Pontos and Rome, no coherent reconstruction of the period can be achieved.'[58] In order to round out our perspective on Pontos we must include its relationship with both its immediate western neighbours and the increasingly prominent presence of Arsakid Parthia. Eupator himself was certainly aware of this, given that for much of his early reign he – like his predecessors – was often looking to the east in order to cement his regional power and influence. He was not an exception in the longer trajectory of the Mithradatids: in the generations preceding Eupator we see a series of royal marriages of connecting the dynasty to the royal families of Kappadokia, Armenia, and Parthia. Olbrycht offers a convincing discussion of the evolving relationship between Mithradates VI and Iran as he rose to prominence: according to him, the early expansion of Mithradates would have put Pontos firmly on the Arsakid radar, and Parthia would be a crucial ally of any designs he had. Accordingly Olbrycht argues for a revival of old Iranian ties in the region that created an alliance among Parthia, Pontos, and Armenia predicated on common Achaimenid roots.[59] The Arsakids, for their part, were eager to step into the traditional role of the Achaimenid monarch: at the time of Mithradates II of Parthia, he had adopted the title 'king of kings', displayed himself with the royal tiara on coinage, and sent substantial sums of newly minted coinage to his allies in Eastern Anatolia.[60] The rather conspicuous inclusion of two envoys from the Parthian court in the heroon erected at Delos is perhaps indication that these ties were reciprocated publicly.[61] It follows logically that this pan-Iranian alliance would have had a cultural component to it beyond just *Realpolitik*. In sum, to understand royal incest

---

58   Olbrycht 2009, 163.
59   Olbrycht 2009, 169–177.
60   Olbrycht 2009, 165–167.
61   The heroon at Delos was dedicated by the Athenian citizen Helianax who stresses in the inscription that he built the structure out of his own resources (ἐκ τῶν ἰδίων ἀνέθηκεν) – on this see Sanders – Catling 1990, 330. On the dynamics of this dedicaton the relationship between Mithradates and Helianax see Morales 2021, 167–175, who agrees with the hypothesis of Roller 2020, 77 that Helianax and his family were of Rhodian origin and had been given Athenian citizenship at some point in the second century. The dedications on Delos thus 'added a new step in the Helianax family's established relations with the Pontic kingdom' (Morales 2021, 168). The inclusion of two Parthian envoys could therefore be the product of either Mithradates' encouragement, or of Helianax' own connections to the Parthian court. Either scenario, however, reveals how closely connected these royal courts were at this point.

specifically and the broader flavour of the kingdom of Pontos more generally, perhaps we need to look to the east, to Iran, and it is to this that we turn by means of conclusion.

4. Conclusions: from Alexandreia to Ktesiphon

As mentioned at the outset, besides borrowing elements of Ptolemaic royal practice and iconography, these incestuous marriages of the Mithradatids are often described as an imitation of an Achaimenid custom, but as we shall see this is not entirely the case. Instead, we need to look to the contemporary Parthian court to fully understand the eastern dynamics of brother-sister marriage at this point in Pontic history. In 1909 a clay jar was found in the northern Iraqi town of Avroman containing two parchments written in Greek which shed a great deal of light on the court of the Arsakids under Mithradates II. The first document relates to the sale of a vineyard in 88 BC, and the elaborate dating formula at the outset is as follows (my emphasis):

βασιλεύοντος βασιλέων Ἀρσάκου εὐεργέτου δικαίου ἐπιφα|νοῦς καὶ φιλέλληνος, καὶ βασιλισσῶν Σιάκης τε τῆς ὁμοπατρίας | αὐτοῦ ἀδελφῆς καὶ γυναικὸς καὶ Ἀρυαζάτης τῆς ἐπικαλουμένη[ς] | Ἀυτομὰ τῆς ἐγ βασιλέως μεγάλου Τιγράνου καὶ γυναικὸς αὐτ[οῦ] |⁵ καὶ Ἀζάτης τῆς ὁμοπατρίας αὐτοῦ ἀδελφῆς καὶ γυναικός.[62]

In the reign of the king of kings Arsakes (Mithradates) *euergetes dikaios epipha|nes* and *philhellenos*, and of the queens Siake, of the same father | his sister and his wife, and Aryazate surnamed | Automa, daughter of the great king Tigranes and his wife, |⁵ and of Azate, his sister of the same father and wife.

This fascinating document thus attests (in Greek) to three wives of the Arsakid king, two of whom are emphatically identified as his sisters of the same father. Given that the document itself is a record of a land transaction we can therefore assume that this dating formula would have been consistent throughout at least the Greek speaking areas of the kingdom. Although multiple wives of different rank are certainly an echo of Achaimenid courtly practice along with the identification of the king as 'king of kings', the prominence of two sisters as queens is *stricto sensu* a Persian tradition – at least not one which rests on any solid or consistent evidentiary ground.[63] In the same vein, the presence of two instances of brother-sister marriage in the royal family is cer-

---

62   My translation following the text of Minns 1915. See also Huber – Hartmann 2006, 486–488 on this document.
63   Llewellyn-Jones 2013, 116. Note that it was relatively common for Achaimenid kings to take half-sisters as their wives, but the only cases of fully incestuous marriage that we can be relatively certainly took place are between Artaxerxes II and his daughter Atossa and Amestris according to Plut. Artaxerxes 23.5.

tainly not something seen among the Ptolemies, so something else must lay behind this polygamous practice. Instead, Madreiter (Huber) and Hartmann argue that the document indicates that Mithradates like many Arsakid kings cultivated the particularly prestigious Zoroastrian practice of consanguineous marriage known in Middle Persian as *xwēdōdah*.[64]

By the Sasanian period this practice of *xwēdōdah* became routine to the point of obligation among Sasanian kings as a means of establishing and displaying their legitimacy, and even though much of our textual evidence for *xwēdōdah* is middle-Persian, it nevertheless sheds light on its early ideology among the Parthians – and their allies the Mithradatids, I argue. According to the Pahlavi sources, primordial acts of incest among deities provide the mythical prototypes of *xwēdōdah* among humans: incest among the gods produces the hero and mythical first king, Gayōmart, and his incest with his mother Spandārmad produced the first human couple Mašī and Mašyānī.[65] The incest between Mašī and Mašyānī then gives rise to humankind as a whole, thus all of humanity is a product of this divinely-inspired incest.[66] This imitation of divine incest among siblings is among the greatest religious duties to the point that the *Pahlavi Rivāyat* states 'And, of all those [things] he who practices *xwēdōdah* is greatest and best and foremost.'[67]

Beyond the imitation of the divine, *xwēdōdah* is a means of ensuring dynasty purity and the transmission of one's good character and power 'so that your lineage may go straighter'.[68] It is a means of repelling demons, slander, and witchcraft, and it is an atonement for sin and an assurance of devotion. Not only is the practice apotropaic, but also an atonement for sin: to quote the *Denkard*, 'Thus, it is certain that it is a good deed to cause the demons harm, pain, and fear and lead them astray, and, for those who practice good deeds in this manner, this is the road to making recompense and repayment.'[69] Little surprise, then, that the royal family of the Parthians and Sasanians

---

64 Huber – Hartmann 2006, 490–491.
65 Skjærvø 2013 provides a superbly detailed overview of *xwēdōdah* in the Zoroastrian tradition, along with its various attestations in mythological traditions and Zoroastrian texts. See this also for a detailed account of western scholarly interpretations of *xwēdōdah*. As with incestuous marriage in Egypt, the extent to which it was practiced outside royal and noble families is unclear, though it is well-attested among the Sasanians. I thank my colleague Eve MacDonald here at Cardiff for her fascinating discussions of this.
66 Following the account of Denkard 3.80: 'Mašī and Mašyānī, desiring offspring, had intercourse in the manner of males and females and produced children, which is called the *xwēdōdah* of brother and sister. A great family was born from them, who, having paired up, became husbands and wives. And, so, all humans who have been or are came from the original seed of *xwēdōdah*.'
67 Pahlavi *Rivāyat* 8c.1–2 (trans. Williams).
68 Denkard 3.80.
69 Denkard 3.81. The Pahlavi Rivāyat echoes this function as well: 'Just as today the most evil [comes] from anal intercourse, thus [also], when the Sōšāns comes, all men will practice *xwēdōdah*, and every demon will be destroyed through the miraculous power of *xwēdōdah*' Pahlavi *Rivāyat* 8c2 (trans. Williams).

would be so eager to broadcast their piety to their subjects through conspicuous incestuous marriage as a practice of *xwēdōdah*, which in turn serves the practical purpose of establishing a hierarchy among wives – and thus children – in a very crowded dynastic environment.[70] Given how the kingdom of Pontos under the Mithradatids pivoted towards Iran after the reign of Pharnakes, I would argue that we see a Greek echo of this distinctly Persian ideology of incestuous marriage in these attestations of the brother-sister marriages among these Pontic kings and queens.[71] Taken in the broader cultural and religious geography of the kingdom that we have just discussed, the contemporary Zoroastrian character of the kingdom and thus the marital practices of its ruling family become clear. This is thus not merely an expression of dynastic exclusivity and prestige, but also a religious practice deeply loaded with piety and devotion that would have resonated within Pontos itself and among the kingdom's eastern allies. This is not to say that more immediate context in which these royal marriages took place was irrelevant – far from it – but rather such pragmatism was only one motivation among many of this particular royal practice that would have been perceived differently by eastern and western eyes.

In this vein I would like to end with two closing thoughts that relate this particular case study of the Mithradatids to this volume as a whole. The first point is fairly straightforward. There has often been a tendency in scholarship to try to find the "true" or "unique" meaning of a given royal representation in the same manner as the "true" motivation behind a given strategy or manoeuvre has often been sought. In this particular case, it was to determine whether royal incest in Pontos is "Ptolemaic/Greek" or "Achaimenid". As mentioned at the outset, to me it is clearly both, and royal incest like many other aspects of royal representation in the period is polyvalent, and intended to be so. The same thing is perceived differently by the numerous audiences and their cultural traditions that comprise the diversity of the Hellenistic cultural landscape. The second is that royal incest in the period is usually understood as continuity with much older traditions: in Ptolemaic Egypt it was perceived as a continuation of pharaonic ideology and practice, and in the East as a continuation of Achaimenid royal ideology. But in Egypt this precedent never really existed outside the 17th dynasty, and attestations of brother-sister marriage among the Achaimenids rests on very uncertain evidentiary ground.[72] Instead, among the Ptolemies, the Parthians, the Mithradatids and beyond, we find not just the slavish imitation of tradition, but rather self-conscious

---

70   Madreiter – Hartmann 2021, 235–237.

71   The rock tombs of the Pontic kings in Amaseia are a particularly poignant example of this, as discussed by Fleischer 2009 especially 117–119. Fleischer notes that the rock-tombs in Amaseia follow a different trajectory from those elsewhere in Anatolia, which tend to exhibit some borrowed Greek forms initially and then become primarily "Greek" in appearance. 'In Amaseia', Fleischer notes, 'we are confronted with a development in the opposite directly' in which the Greek-inspired forms are replaced with non-Greek elements by the time of Pharnakes I.

72   See note 62 above. See also Ager 2021.

and selective innovation on traditional elements that are re-cast in new and unique ways. When it comes to practices such as royal incest or indeed Hellenistic monarchy more generally, tradition and innovation are indeed the same, but different.

Bibliography

Ager 2021: Ager, Sheila, Royal Brother-Sister Marriage, Ptolemaic and Otherwise, in: Carney – Müller 2021, 346–358

Anagnostou-Laoutides – Pfeiffer 2022: Anagnostou-Laoutides, Eva – Pfeiffer, Stefan (eds.), Culture and Ideology under the Seleukids. Unframing a Dynasty, Berlin 2022

Ballesteros Pastor 2013: Ballesteros Pastor, Luis, Eupator's Unmarried Sisters: an Approach to the Dynastic Struggle in Pontus after the Death of Mithridates V Euergetes, Anabasis 4, 2013, 61–72

Ballesteros Pastor 2015: Ballesteros Pastor, Luis, Los príncipes del ponto. La política onomástica de Mitridates Eupátor como factor de propaganda dinástica, REA 117, 2015, 425–445

Bevan 1902: Bevan, Edwyn, The House of Seleucus I–II, London 1902

Bielman-Sánchez 2003: Bielman-Sánchez, Anna, Régner au féminin. Réflexions sur les reines attalides et séleucides, in: F. Prost (ed.), L'Orient méditerranéen de la mort d'Alexandre aux campagnes de Pompée, Rennes 2003, 41–64

Canepa 2018: Canepa, Matthew P, The Iranian Expanse Transforming Royal Identity through Architecture, Landscape, and the Built Environment, 550 BCE – 642 CE, Oakland 2018

Carney 2021: Carney, Elizabeth, Women in Antigonid Monarchy, in: Carney – Müller 2021, 307–318

Carney – Müller 2021: Carney, Elizabeth – Müller, Sabine (eds.), The Routledge Companion to Women and Monarchy in the Ancient Mediterranean, London 2021

Chrubasik 2016: Chrubasik, Boris, The Men who would be King: Kings and Usurpers in the Seleukid Empire, Oxford 2016

de Callataÿ 2009: de Callataÿ, François, The First Royal Coinages of Pontos (from Mithridates III to Mithridates V), in: Højte 2009a, 63–94

D'Agostini 2016: D'Agostini, Monica, The Multicultural Ties of the Mithridatics: Sources, Tradition, and Promotional Image of the Dynasty of Pontus in 4th and 3rd centuries BC, Aevum 60, 2016, 83–96

D'Agostini 2018: D'Agostini, Monica, Asia Minor and the Many Shades of a Civil War. Observations on Achaios the Younger and his claim to the kingdom of Anatolia, in: K. Erickson (ed.), The Seleukid Empire 281–222 BC: War within the Family, Swansea 2018, 59–81

D'Agostini 2021: D'Agostini, Monica, Seleukid Marriage Alliances, in: Carney – Müller 2021, 198–209

Erciyas 2006: Erciyas, Deniz B., Wealth, Aristocracy and Royal Propaganda under the Hellenistic Kingdom of the Mithradatids in the Central Black Sea Region of Turkey, Leiden 2006

Fleischer 2009: Fleischer, Robert, The Rock-tombs of the Pontic Kings and Amaseia (Amasya), in: Højte 2009a, 109–120

Fischer-Bovet – von Reden 2021: Fischer-Bovet, Christelle – von Reden, Sitta (eds.), Comparing the Ptolemaic and Seleucid Empires. Integration, Communication, and Resistance, Cambridge 2022

Ghita 2011: Ghita, Cristian E., Nysa – A Seleucid Princess in an Anatolian Context, in: K. Erickson – G. Ramsey (eds.), Seleucid Dissolution: The Sinking of the Anchor, Wiesbaden 2011, 107–116

Grainger 1997: Grainger, John, A Seleukid Prosopography and Gazetteer, Leiden 1997

Green 1990: Green, Peter, Alexander to Actium: The Historical Evolution of the Hellenistic Age, Berkeley 1990

Højte 2009a: Højte, Jakob M. (ed.), Mithridates VI and the Pontic Kingdom, Aarhus 2009

Højte 2009b: Højte, Jakob M., The Death and Burial of Mithridates VI, in: Højte 2009a, 121–130

Huber – Hartmann 2003: Huber, Irene – Hartmann, Udo, 'Denn ihrem Diktat vermochte der König nicht zu widersprechen …' Die Position der Frauen am Hof der Arsakiden, in: A. Panaino – A. Piras (eds.), Proceedings of the 5th Conference of the Societas Iranologica Europaea I, Milan 2006, 485–518

Kobes 1996: Kobes, Jörn, "Kleine Könige". Untersuchungen zu den Lokaldynasten im hellenistischen Kleinasien (323–188 v. Chr.), St. Katharinen 1996

Kreuz 2009: Kreuz, Patric-Alexander, Monuments for the King: Royal Presence in the Late Hellenistic World of Mithridates VI, in: Højte 2009a, 131–144

Llewellyn-Jones – McAuley 2022: Llewellyn-Jones, Lloyd – McAuley, Alex, Sister-Queens in the High Hellenistic Period: Kleopatra III and Kleopatra Thea, London 2022

Llewellyn-Jones 2013: Llewellyn-Jones, Lloyd, King and Court in Ancient Persia, Edinburgh 2013

Ma 2000: Ma, John, Antiochos III and the Cities of Western Asia Minor, Oxford 2000

Madreiter – Hartmann 2021: Madreiter, Irene – Hartmann, Udo, Women at the Arsakid Court, in: Carney – Müller 2021, 234–245

McAuley 2021: McAuley, Alex, Daughters, Princesses, and Agents of Empire. Royal Women as Transcultural Agents in the Seleucid Empire, in: A. Stieldorf et al. (eds.), Geschlecht macht Herrschaft – Interdisziplinäre Studien zu vormoderner Macht und Herrschaft, Göttingen 2021, 221–242

McAuley 2022: McAuley, Alex, The Seleukid Royal Family as a Reigning Triad, in: Anagnostou-Laoutides – Pfeiffer 2022, 23–40

McGing 1986: McGing, Brian C., The Foreign Policy of Mithridates VI Eupator, King of Pontus, Leiden 1986

McGing 2014: McGing, Brian, Iranian Kings in Greek Dress? Cultural Identity in the Mithradatid Kingdom of Pontus, in: T. Bekker-Nielsen (ed.), Space, Place and Identity in Northern Anatolia, Stuttgart 2014, 21–37

Michels 2009: Michels, Christoph, Kulturtransfer und monarchischer "Philhellenismus": Bithynien, Pontos und Kappadokien in hellenistischer Zeit, Göttingen 2009

Minns 1915: Minns, Ellis H, Parchments of the Parthian Period from Avroman in Kurdistan, The Journal of Hellenic Studies 35, 1915, 22–65

Morales 2021: Morales, Fábio Augusto, Mithridates, Helianax and Late Hellenistic Delos as Global City: Urban Insularity and Integration Fields, Mare Nostrum 12.2, 2021, 165–197

Muccioli 2013: Muccioli, Federicomaria, Gli epiteti ufficiali dei re ellenistici, Stuttgart 2013

Müller 2009: Müller, Sabine, Das hellenistische Königspaar in der medialen Repräsentation: Ptolemaios II. und Arsinoe II., Berlin 2009

Müller 2021: Müller, Sabine, Argead Women, in: Carney – Müller 2021, 294–306

Ogden 1999: Ogden, Daniel, Polygamy, Prostitutes, and Death: The Hellenistic Dynasties, Swansea 1999

Olbrycht 2009: Olbrycht, Marek J., Mithridates VI Eupator and Iran, in: Højte 2009a, 163–190

Olshausen 1990: Olshausen, Eckart, Götter, Heroen und ihre Kulte in Pontos, ANRW II 18.3, 1990, 1865–1906

Primo 2006: Primo, Andrea, Mitridate III: Problemi di cronologia e identità nella dinastia pontica, Studi ellenistici 19, 2006, 307–331

Roller 2020: Roller, Duane W., Empire of the Black Sea: The rise and fall of the Mithridatic world, Oxford 2020

Sanders – Catling 1990: Sanders, Guy D. R. – Catling, Richard W. V., From Delos to Melos: A New Fragment of I. Delos 1562, ABSA 85, 1990, 327–332

Saprykin 2009: Saprykin, Sergey J., The Religion and Cults of the Pontic Kingdom: Political Aspects, in: Højte 2009a, 249–276

Skjærvø 2013: Skjærvø, Prods O., Marriage ii. Next of Kin Marriage in Zoroastrianism, Encyclopædia Iranica, online edition, 2013 (http://www.iranicaonline.org/articles/marriage-next-of-kin) last access: 24.07.2023

Strootman 2014: Strootman, Rolf, Courts and Elites in the Hellenistic Empires, Edinburgh 2014

Vlahogiannis 1987: Vlahogiannis, Nicholas, Diplomacy and War. Aspects of Mithridates Eupator's Foreign Policy, Diss.: Melbourne 1987

Wenghofer – Houle 2016: Wenghofer, Richard – Houle, Del John, Marriage Diplomacy and the Political Role of Royal Women in the Seleukid Far East, in A. Coşkun – A. McAuley (eds.), Seleukid Royal Women, Stuttgart 2016, 191–208

Figures

Fig. 1: Bibliothèque nationale de France, département Monnaies, médailles et antiques, B 829, ark:/12148/btv1b85602724

Fig. 2: Bibliothèque nationale de France, département Monnaies, médailles et antiques, Fonds général 12, ark:/12148/btv1b85602776

Fig. 3: Roma Numismatics Ltd, Auction XXV (22 September 2022), Lot number: 326.

Alex McAuley is Lecturer in Ancient Greek History and Language at Waipapa Taumata Rau University of Auckland in New Zealand, after previously teaching at Cardiff University, and the University of British Columbia. His main research interests are the royal ideology of the Successor dynasties of the Hellenistic World, and the dynamics of localism in the Hellenistic Greek Mainland. He has published widely on royal women, the dynastic practices and ideology of the successor dynasties, the genealogy of the Seleucid dynasty, and Greek local government in the Hellenistic Period. He has also written extensively on the reception of antiquity in film and television.

The King's Men
Loyalist Associations in the Hellenistic Kingdoms

BENEDIKT ECKHARDT

Abstract: Organised groups of loyalists are a well-known aspect of Hellenistic "associationalism", but their origin and function have not yet been subject to comparative analysis. This chapter gathers and compares relevant data from the four main Hellenistic kingdoms, taking due account of structural differences that may explain different manifestations of the phenomenon. In the Ptolemaic empire, the *basilistai* are quite literally "the king's men", but their purpose and sphere of activities remain debated. Like all associations, they were embedded into a network of social relations: there are notable connections with the military and the gymnasion. The chapter considers the role of founding figures and the way such groups interacted with their environment, both within and outside Egypt. The closest parallel at least on a terminological level are the *Attalistai* of Teos, but the context in which they operated was rather different, shaped by the activities and networks of Kraton the aulos player. They highlight the role agonistic networks and organisations could have in promoting loyalty to the kings and invite comparison with the Dionysiac *technitai*. There is no clear evidence for similar organisations from the Seleukid empire: instead, the gymnasion comes into view again, as well as the vexed question of how to understand groups like "the Antiochians in Ptolemais", or "the *politai* who are in Babylon" – should these be seen as associations of loyalists rather than cities? Finally, the Antigonid empire offers evidence for royal regulations of civic gymnasia: these can perhaps be understood as an attempt to curb associationalism and ensure loyalty through direct regulation. Precisely because of the different constellations that inspired and constrained them, loyalist associations can be seen as a window into the underlying values and institutional structures of Hellenistic kingdoms.

1. Introduction

One of the defining features of Hellenistic social history is the spread of membership-based organisations that united people of various backgrounds who shared common interests. The joint worship of a deity is usually the central activity of such groups that we can grasp in the epigraphic evidence, not least because the most common way of naming them was by reference to deities or rituals. However, other interests such as the forging of business networks, the pooling of resources or – for those who were not citizens – status elevation undoubtedly contributed to a development that has left its traces in almost every major Hellenistic city and many smaller ones as well.[1] Occasional discussions around categories notwithstanding, these groups have been understood since the 19th-century as a distinct phenomenon; Anglophone scholarship usually refers to them as private (or voluntary) associations.[2]

Among the hundreds of groups thus classified, a few are known that proclaimed loyalty to kings as their *raison d'être*. The aim of this chapter is to compare the evidence for such groups from the different Hellenistic kingdoms, with an inevitable focus on the Ptolemaic sphere because this is where they are most frequently attested, under the telling name of *basilistai*. The groups in question have traditionally been understood as merely one variant of the general Hellenistic trend towards the formation of cult associations: just as *Dionysiastai* can be assumed to have worshipped Dionysos, *basilistai* can be assumed to have worshipped the kings.[3] We will want to know if this tempting analogy does indeed hold: did these groups – which we can call "loyalist associations" – participate in the largely unregulated movement of people and ideas that enabled the surge of the associative phenomenon in the Hellenistic cities, or was their declared loyalism a response to royal oversight, perhaps even direct royal intervention? How did such groups interact with others in local contexts, and how do the histories of such interactions compare across kingdoms? In mapping this peculiar organisational field, many gaps will remain. However, by studying not only the composition and activities of individual groups but their position within a landscape of similar organisations, we can hope to reconstruct ways in which the same basic constellation (groups proclaiming loyalty to kings) could operate in different contexts and to different ends. This potentially allows for broader conclusions about organisation and societal cohesion in the respective kingdoms.

A few words on the selection of cases are in order. To make the comparison meaningful, the choice of material is restricted to corporate bodies with (potentially) a long-term perspective that explicitly present themselves as solely or mainly concerned with expressing their loyalty to kings. We are not interested here in irregular assemblies performing acts of loyalty, such as the priestly synods of Egypt. We are also not interested in organized groups that gave a show of loyalty on a specific occasion, which of course happened rather frequently. Military units in particular could act collectively to promote the worship of the king, like the *katoikoi hippeis* of the Hermopolites who built a temple and statues for Ptolemaios III and Berenike, or the much later case of the 'sol-

---

1   Early but still fundamental discussions: Ziebarth 1896; Poland 1909. On purposes (declared or suspected) see Gabrielsen 2009; Maillot 2021.
2   Justification of the term "private association": Gabrielsen – Thomsen 2015.
3   See their discussion as "Kultvereine" by Ziebarth 1896, 61–62; San Nicolò ²1972, 25–27.

diers stationed in Schedia' dedicating a *Kleopatreion*.[4] Apart from the question whether or not such dedications attest to the existence of permanent associations (rather than ad hoc collections of funds), the declared *raison d'être* of these groups is not loyalty but the organisation of the collective interests of fellow soldiers. Also not investigated here are associations of royal cultivators in Egypt, although these could be understood to be "king's men" (*basilikoi geōrgoi*): *basilikos* here designates not their attitude towards the kings but the status of the land they cultivated.[5] Finally, we are not interested in groups that were founded within the royal court itself, such as the "jesters" supposedly assembled by Ptolemaios IV as drinking companions, or the "inimitable livers" who were famously active in the final years of Kleopatra VII and Marcus Antonius.[6] It is obvious enough that groups of this type would have operated under rather different circumstances from those encountered by the average association of *Dionysiastai* or *Apolloniastai*: our question is precisely to what extent this was true for loyalist associations such as the Ptolemaic *basilistai*.

2. The Ptolemaic Kingdom

There are eight attestations in total of *basilistai*, *synbasilistai* or *philobasilistai*, four from Egypt and four from other places under Ptolemaic control. A ninth text that does not use the word but has been taken to refer to a group of this nature will be discussed below; a tenth could be added if the recent identification of a Demotic parallel were accepted, but the evidence appears inconclusive at this stage.[7] With one exception, the Egyptian texts cluster in the second half of the second century BC in Upper Egypt, whereas at least two of the four attestations from the Ptolemaic foreign possessions are significantly earlier. It may thus be possible to distinguish two phases and perhaps

---

4   I.Herm.Magn. 1; OGIS 738 (116–88 BC); cf. the discussion of similar cases by Launey 1949–1950, 1005–1018.

5   On these see Monson 2021. They could still be expected to demonstrate εὔνοια towards the royal πράγματα: UPZ I 110, l. 160.

6   Athen. 6.246c (citing Ptolemaios of Megalopolis) on the γελοιασταί assembled (συνάγεσθαι) by Ptolemaios IV; Plut. Antonius 28.2 on the σύνοδος ἀμιμητοβίων (dissolved and refounded as συναποθανούμενοι after Actium, 71.3); the latter also appears to be attested in an Alexandrian inscription of 34 BC (SEG 18.641). For a unifying but partly speculative reconstruction of the Ptolemaic "aulic *thiasos*" see Tondriau 1946.

7   P.Carlsberg 409 (Edfu, 132/131 BC) with the comments by Monson 2019, 48: 'Despite the editor's hesitation about the reading there is no doubt that it was a "royal association", the only attestation published so far of the Demotic equivalent for a Greek association of *basilistai* or *philobasilistai*. Moreover, the last word in that line before the fragment breaks off is sufficiently legible to recognize "horse" (*ḥtr*). The line should accordingly be translated: "the royal association of cavalrymen". The designation occurs as an entry in a list of accounts; we do not know enough about this group to establish its nature with certainty. It is of course not implausible as such that there should be a Demotic equivalent to βασιλισταί.

different contexts for the spread of βασιλισταί groups by looking at Ptolemaic garrisons outside Egypt first and then turning our attention to the situation within Egypt itself.

Perhaps the earliest text comes from Thera: an offertory box dedicated by Diokles and the *basilistai* to Serapis, Isis and Anubis. The date depends on the letter forms but is likely early, somewhere in the first half of the third century BC.[8] The *basilistai* of Thera were most likely soldiers from the local garrison. Later inscriptions reveal a bit more about their engagement with membership-based associations: the garrison commander and his wife were honoured (and registered as members) by an association of *Bakchistai* that may or may not have had a military background, and in (probably) 153/152 BC, the association of the *aleiphomenoi* honoured Baton, a member of the garrison, for having served as gymnasiarch for several years and supervising the *neoi*.[9] The second unambiguously early case is a recently published inscription from the acropolis of Limyra, dated to 199 BC. It records the gift of a vineyard by the local garrison commander to a group of *basilistai*, which not only gives some valuable details about some of their activities but also includes information about the topography of the Limyrean garrison. The membership list makes it all but certain that the 18 *basilistai* of Limyra were indeed Ptolemaic soldiers.[10] Here, too, a gymnasion seems to be implied as the place where the Herakleia were celebrated. Both Thera and Limyra are known to have had gymnasia, but in both cases it has been argued that the gymnasion used by the *basilistai* was a different institution connected to the garrison.[11] Two other groups of *basilistai* are known from Kypros (Lapethos and Paphos), but the texts are too fragmentary to draw significant conclusions. As Ptolemaic garrisons are known from both places, it is plausible to situate the groups in this context, and the fragment from La-

---

8   IG XII.3 443. Contrasting assessments are offered by Hiller von Gaertringen 1903, 90 ('Dem Schriftcharakter nach zu schliessen, vielleicht schon zu Lebzeiten des Soter') and S. Skaltsa in the *Database of the Copenhagen Associations Inventory* (CAPInv. 15: 'A date to the second half of the 3rd cent. BC on the basis of the letterforms (…) seems more likely'). To this author, the letters appear closer to late Classical examples than to inscriptions from the later third century. Skaltsa 2022, 132 now opts for 265–250 BC, with 272/271 (the introduction of the cult of the Theoi Adelphoi) as a terminus post quem because 'an association endorsing the cult of the sovereign could only properly be formed after that date'. Apart from the question of how central and local initiatives are related, it is not certain that the *basilistai* of Thera worshipped the king; cf. on the word n. 18 below.

9   Ἀλειφόμενοι: IG XII.3 331. Βακχισταί: IG XII.3 1296. Ladamos is first said (ll. 4–5) to have been [τεταγμέ]νος ὑπὸ τῶν βασιλέω[ν ἐπὶ Θήρας], which may suggest a non-military perspective, but on two occasions a distinction is made between 'the city and us' (l. 12) or 'us and the others' (l. 15), which Skaltsa 2022, 130–131 takes as evidence for the military nature of the *Bakchistai*.

10   For the full text and commentary see Wörrle 2021; the list of names was published earlier and discussed in detail by Wörrle 2015. The list has the typical form of mercenary lists; one member is from Limyra, the others are from places known to have been a reservoir of Ptolemaic manpower.

11   For Thera, IG XII.3 327 records the contributions of Ptolemaic soldiers to the restoration of a gymnasion. This could be the civic gymnasion (as assumed by Chaniotis 2002, 110), but the context of the inscription (a response by Ptolemaios VI to a petition παρὰ τῶν ἐν Θήραι τασσομένων στρατιωτῶν) perhaps suggests that the gymnasion was part of the garrison. This is also assumed (for both Thera and Limyra) by Wörrle 2021, 241.

pethos includes the word ἐλαιοχρίστιον, again pointing to a gymnasion as one of the places of activity.[12]

Given that all *basilistai* outside Egypt as well as the three later Egyptian attestations of *basilistai* appear to have a military background, the same has usually been assumed for the Egyptian outlier: a dedication of unknown provenance to king Ptolemaios, queen Berenike and the Dioskouroi by a priest and 'the *synbasilistai* and *Dioskouriastai* who are in the *nomē*', usually dated to 246–241 BC.[13] The reference to the *nomē* could be taken to imply a regional appointment or stationing, but apart from the fact that soldiers were not normally organised according to *nomai*, the vague ὑπάρχοντες is not as decisive as τεταγμένοι or τασσόμενοι. It is only here that we find *basilistai* with the *syn*- prefix, and it is also the only case where the designation is coupled with a typical theophoric association name. It is not obvious that this early Egyptian case comes from a military context; it may have assembled a wider group of loyalists in a *nomē*-wide organisation that was in possession of several buildings (οἰκήματα) and organized monthly sacrifices. It should perhaps be distinguished from the later Egyptian evidence, which strongly suggests a connection with the reinforcement of the Ptolemaic military presence in Upper Egypt after the Egyptian Revolt. The best-documented case comes from Setis island: in 143/142 BC, Herodes son of Demophon, *archisōmatophylax* and *stratēgos*, organized a dedication by 'the *basilistai* who come together on Setis' for the gods and *daimones* of the cataract.[14] The inscription includes a list of 30 names (mostly Greek, but a few are Egyptian); because of Herodes' own military background they are thought to belong to the members of the garrison on Setis. A military context is certain for the *philobasilistai* who are mentioned in a letter of 103 BC,

---

12   Peristianes, Gen. Hist. 945 no. 34 (Lapethos); Mitford 1961, 39 no. 105 (Paphos). Papantoniou 2013, 186 includes the βασιλισταί in his discussion of 'the manipulation of the ceremonial system' on Ptolemaic Kypros in the context of royal representation, but the texts themselves cannot contribute much to this interpretation. On gymnasia that served the army on Kypros see Stavrou 2020, 312–316. Βασιλισταί is in the dative in the text from Lapethos but in the genitive in the text from Paphos: this is presumably why Stavrou's table (321–324) classifies the former as 'recipients' and the latter as 'honouring body' (but given the state of the text, it could be e. g. [συνόδωι τῶν] βασιλιστῶν).

13   I.Varsovie 44: βασιλεῖ Πτολεμαίωι καὶ | βασιλίσσηι Βερενίκηι καὶ Διοσ|κούροις εἰς τὰς θυσίας τὰς κα|τὰ μῆνα γινομένας τὴν πρόσ|οδον τὴν ἀπὸ τῶν οἰκημάτων | Θέωρος ὁ ἱερεὺς καὶ οἱ συνβασι|λισταὶ καὶ Διοσκουριασταὶ | οἱ ὑπάρχοντες ἐν τῶι νομῶι. Cf. Pfeiffer ²2020, 75–77 no. 12 (246–243 BC). The date is based on the lack of the title *Euergetai*, and an assumption that Ptolemaios III and Berenike II are meant. An analysis of the letter forms alone would perhaps have suggested a later date: with a date in the 240s, this would be the first inscription from Egypt to feature both Alpha with broken crossbar and Theta with bisecting stroke (cf. the table in Crowther 2020, 265–266; photo of the inscription in Paganini 2020, 195). However, as both forms are attested individually in inscriptions of the later third century, there is no decisive reason to move the date down to the time of Ptolemaios IX and Berenike III.

14   OGIS 130 (= IThSy 303; Pfeiffer ²2020, 159–165 no. 27; Kloppenborg 2020, 374–380 no. 246).

written by soldiers on duty to the rest of their company stationed in Pathyris.[15] All addressees are labelled *philobasilistai*: as such, the term could be used as an unofficial label that does not presuppose an organisational reality (i. e., an association formally called *philobasilistai*). However, the only other attestation of the word does appear to suggest an official meaning within a military setting. The sentence in the trial of Hermias (119 BC), part of the archive of the Theban *choachytai*, is introduced with a list of four important people who were present: three of them are situated at different positions within the hierarchy of the *katoikoi hippeis*, whereas the fourth is 'Sesoosios, hekatontarchēs of the eager *philobasilistai*'.[16] The parallel with the *katoikoi hippeis* suggests that the *philobasilistai*, too, were an army unit, much like their namesakes in Pathyris. Again, we learn nothing about their organisation as an association, but if the term was merely an unofficial label used among fellow soldiers, it would perhaps be less likely to appear in a formal protocol.

While the evidence is very limited indeed, it appears to suggest that the organisation of military units as loyalist organisations – and the public expression of their readiness to support the king – became a relatively common occurrence in Upper Egypt in the second half of the second century BC, a challenging time shaped by the aftermath of the revolt and the ongoing throne wars. It has recently been observed that this period saw a transformation of Ptolemaic administration that directly integrated administrative, military and religious elites into the bureaucratic apparatus, creating an image of the state that transcended the person of the king and instead relied on a web of relations between privileged status groups.[17] The integration of different segments of society into a wider notion of the state would presumably be facilitated by their organisation as formal associations: the spread of loyalist military organisations fits this model. Their designation as *basilistai* very much appears to keep the king in the picture, but it should be noted that the term as such is not specific to a person. The root verb βασιλίζειν can be taken to refer to a general attitude that transcends the person of any one king: unlike *Dionysiastai* (to which a closer parallel would perhaps be the unattested **Ptolemaistai*), *basilistai* aims at the institution itself.[18] Of course individual acts

---

15 C.Jud.Syr.Eg. 1. That φιλοβασιλισταί does not describe only the two leaders Pates and Pachrates (as assumed in earlier studies) but the whole group was established by van't Dack in the commentary.

16 P.Tor.Choach. 11bis, l. 4: Σεσοώσιος (ἑκατοντάρχου) φιλοβασιλιστῶν προθύμων. That Sesoosios was ἑκατοντάρχης appears to be the accepted reading now, despite the doubts expressed by Wilcken 1935, 56.

17 Wackenier 2020.

18 A *nomen agentis* derived from an -ίζω or -άζω verb primarily indicates adherence or imitation, not necessarily cult. It is not the -ασταί ending per se that makes Διονυσιασταί a cultic designation, but the fact that Dionysos is a god (e. g. Διονυσιαστής from Διονυσιάζω, 'to celebrate the Dionysia' and hence worship Dionysos; given that the Ptolemaia were celebrated on an analogous cycle at least since Ptolemaios II, **Ptolemaistai* would hardly have been impossible). In contrast, the Σελευκίζοντες of Polyain. strat. 8.57 are clearly not worshippers of Seleukos I but his supporters against Lysimachos. There is clear evidence for ruler cult in the context of a few *basilistai* groups:

of loyalty would still be expected: the dedication on Setis is made 'on behalf of king Ptolemaios and queen Kleopatra', and the ninth text mentioned above as potentially relevant also keeps things personal: in Euergetis, the military settlement founded by Boethos in 132 BC, a newly formed association based in the gymnasion wrote to the city's chief magistrate to announce (and request approval for?) a meeting to honour Ptolemaios VIII and his queens.[19] Whether they would have referred to themselves as *basilistai* remains unknown (only the beginning of the letter has survived), but the emergence of an explicit loyalty association in a Ptolemaic military settlement in the Thebaid fits both the time and the region well.

Given that military organisations of *basilistai* are attested significantly earlier in the Ptolemaic foreign possessions, we would then have to assume an importation (or reimportation) of a known organisational model to Egypt in the mid-second century BC. The argument gains credibility if a parallel case is considered: there is now a broad consensus that ethnic *politeumata* were introduced to Egypt only in the time of Ptolemaios VI, and yet groups called *politeumata* and assembling soldiers from a specific place of origin are already known from Ptolemaic Sidon in the third century BC.[20] Like the emergence of *basilistai*, the introduction of *politeumata* in Egypt has plausibly been connected to the challenges the Ptolemaic empire faced in this period,

---

I.Varsovie 44 mentions Ptolemaios and Berenike on a par with the Dioskouroi as recipients of the dedication, and in Limyra, the garrison commander Menyllos obliged the *basilistai* 'to sacrifice to king Ptolemaios each year on the first of the month of Dystros, with a procession and a pig as sacrificial victim, carrying out the usual rites at the dedicated altar' (ll. 16–18). The mention of 'the dedicated altar' (ἐπὶ τοῦ ἀποδεδειγμένου βωμοῦ) could suggest – with Wörrle 2021, 238 – that this altar did not exist before the endowment. Perhaps it is possible to see in another dedication from Limyra by a group of Σαραπιασταί (SEG 55.1463bis, also discussed by Wörrle) the early history of the garrison's corporate organisation. On Setis, sacrifices 'on the eponymous days' (IThSy 303, l. 14) also appear to suggest ruler cult, although the recipients of the sacrifices are not specified. – An alternative would be to see the root word βασιλεύς as the more personal (rather than the more abstract) choice, expressing proximity to the man, not the divine figure of the Ptolemaia. One might point to the pleading βασιλεῦ in *enteuxeis* (but there as well, the point may be precisely to tie the individual ruler to a set of institutional obligations and expectations; truly personal designations could have been derived from epitheta, like the *Eupatoristai* on Delos, to be mentioned below). I thank Andrew Erskine for discussing this question with me.

19 P. UB Trier S 159–5 (unpublished; a – somewhat embellished – German translation is found in Kramer 2012, 38 no. 19). I thank Patrick Reinard for sharing a photo of the papyrus with me. For a comparable, non-military connection between the gymnasion and sacrifices 'on behalf of' the kings see I. Prose 40 (64 BC): an association of landowners in Psenamosis successfully petitioned Paris, a 'relative' of the king, to grant them land for a gymnasion and a house, ἐν αἷς συναγόμενοι θύομεν ὑπὲρ τῶν βασιλέων (ll. 11–12). Highlighting this particular activity was a strategic choice as emphasised by Paganini 2022, 240 – but in addition to the association's possible hope for 'royal benevolence' (*ibid.*), one should perhaps stress the interests of Paris himself, who became the priest of the association and could thus showcase his own loyalty to the royal house.

20 For this view on *politeumata* see, among others, Kayser 2013; Kruse 2015; Sänger 2019 (who also offers a discussion of the Sidonian cases on p. 229–239). Cf. also the paper by Patrick Sänger in this volume.

specifically the question of military recruitment; here as well, we may be dealing with a reimported and repurposed institution that could be integrated into an increasingly complex vision of delegated yet organized authority. However, while both *politeumata* and *basilistai* can thus be argued to reflect aspects of the same general transformation of the Ptolemaic state, there are also clear differences. While legal privileges could be granted to military status groups such as the *katoikoi hippeis*, the wide-ranging legal autonomy enjoyed by *politeumata* (which had their own jurisdiction in almost all matters) cannot be assumed for *basilistai*. The stakes were likely lower: while *politeumata* may have been a way to attract recruitment from certain regions, groups of *basilistai* were formed when soldiers were already recruited and stationed somewhere. Royal involvement must be assumed both for the creation of *politeumata* and for the stationing of soldiers who could eventually become *basilistai*, but in the latter case, the association as such appears to have been founded by individuals.[21] And while the evidence for membership in later Egyptian *basilistai* groups suggests a strong Egyptian presence, there is no reason to assume that ethnicity was a defining feature as in the case of *politeumata*, or the ethnic *koina* known from Kypros and Alexandreia.[22] This latter point is of particular relevance because it hints at wider questions regarding the impact of such groups on societal cohesion that are worth investigating a bit further.

It has recently been argued that associations, and particularly groups like the (*philo*)*basilistai*, fulfilled an integrative function in the Ptolemaic army and, by extension, wider Ptolemaic society.[23] Because Ptolemaic social hierarchies were not shaped by Greek citizenship and its strict legal distinctions (there being only three Greek cities in Egypt), there was more scope for other organisations to foster societal cohesion by uniting people of different backgrounds in groups with permeable status boundaries. In this view, the gymnasion in particular was not a separatist and carefully guarded institution with ethnic connotations, but a breeding ground for associations with overlapping memberships and regular interactions. An integrative associational culture based on military connections and loyalty to the kings thus provided Ptolemaic subjects with options for social mobility that their Seleukid rivals could not offer, because they relied on Greek cities as cornerstones of empire. These conceptual differences

---

21   Admittedly, we do not normally know this for certain, except perhaps in Setis where the role of Herodes son of Demophon is very prominent.

22   On the *koina* on Kypros see Kruse 2015, 292–295; cf. CPI I 55 and 56 for Alexandreia. For *basilistai* and *philobasilistai*, Launey 1949–1950, 1027–1030 assumed that they were Egyptians. If C. Jud. Syr. Eg. 3 is a list of the soldiers in Pathyris (the addressees of C. Jud. Syr. Eg. 1), then they do indeed have exclusively Egyptian names. In Thebes, we only know their leader, an Egyptian. The mix of Greek and Egyptian names in Setis does not prove much regarding ethnicity (but note Fischer-Bovet 2014, 289: 'a mixed community of Egyptians, Greco-Egyptians and Greeks'; Pfeiffer ²2020, 162 justly notes that the only person where we can be sure is the leader Herodes son of Demophon, who was from Pergamon).

23   For the argument summarized and discussed here, see Fischer-Bovet 2014, 280–299.

between Ptolemaic and Seleukid modes of societal integration are intriguing, and the model makes our modest groups of loyalists appear rather more important than we may so far have been led to believe. Indeed, apart from general assumptions about Ptolemaic gymnasia, the *basilistai* are the most important building block of this argument, which naturally has rather little use for ethnic *politeumata* and *koina*. However, beneath the laudable conceptual clarity lies a rather fragile evidence base: it is difficult to demonstrate the dynamic connections between different groups tied to the gymnasion, certainly for the *basilistai*. In the case from Pathyris, 'the young men of the company' (οἱ [ἐκ] τοῦ σημείου νεανίσκοι) wrote to the *philobasilistai* about the appointment of a president of the god Nechtpharaos. From this, three different associations have been deduced: the *neaniskoi*, the *philobasilistai* and a "guild of Nechtpharaos", with the gymnasion as an 'engine of integration' that brought together Greek, Greco-Egyptian and Egyptian strata of society.[24] But it is far from evident that there was indeed a separate association of the god Nechtpharaos, and if all addressees are *philobasilistai*, the writers (i. e. the *neaniskoi*) might be among them as well. Instead of three associations we would then have one. If we assume that the *neaniskoi* were Greeks trained in the gymnasion, there would still be a case for the *philobasilistai* as an inclusive umbrella group (given that at least some of the addressees bear Egyptian names) – but even that is far from certain.[25] For the *basilistai* of Setis, several entanglements with other groups and institutions have been proposed. They have been argued to have connections both with a local gymnasion and with another military association in Ptolemais, of which the Setis group would have been the "local chapter", but both assumptions are highly speculative.[26] More importantly, it is frequently argued that the *basilistai* are identical with the 'priests of the five tribes', who set up a very similar dedication a few years earlier, on the initiative of the same man, Herodes son of Demophon.[27] On this

---

24   Fischer-Bovet 2014, 288 (quotation 289); cf. already van't Dack – Clarysse – Cohen – Quaegebeur – Winicki 1989, 46–48 (leaving the relationship between the three postulated groups open).

25   That *neaniskoi* point to a gymnasion is assumed without argument by Fischer-Bovet 2014. But cf. Paganini 2021, 179: the word 'can be used neutrally to indicate a young person without any particular specification, or it may be applied to a young member of the gymnasion, or even to a young recruit or soldier in the army. (…) For the ambiguity of its meaning, it is clear that the presence of the term alone in a text does not necessarily involve a connection with the gymnasium'.

26   Local gymnasion: Fischer-Bovet 2014, 288, pointing to the fact that the current προστάτης, Papias son of Ammonius, seems to have originally been called something else, perhaps κοσμήτης. But perhaps the garrison had its own gymnasion? Local chapter: Fischer-Bovet 2020, 143–144. The argument is based on the observation that two names in the membership list from Setis, Asklepiades son of Ptolemaios and Ammonios son of Ammonios (not Ammonios son of Apollonios as in OGIS 130 and the editions of Pfeiffer and Kloppenborg), are also attested in an association in Ptolemais (CPI I 360, 138/137 BC). But an overlap of two common names (out of 30) is hardly decisive.

27   OGIS 111 = IThSy 302 (150–144 BC). Herodes is here acting together with οἱ ἄλλοι [ἱερεῖς τῆς πεν]-ταφυλίας … οἱ τὴ[ν] σύνοδον συνεσταμένο[ι εἰς τὸ ἐν Σήτει] ἱερό[ν]. The form of the monument is similar in both cases, and both inscriptions list the gods according to both their Greek and

reading, the *basilistai* of Setis could even be understood as a military priesthood, combining traditional Egyptian religion with Graeco-Macedonian military organisation: the model would fit well with the general image of this period as sketched above. But again, caution is advisable: Herodes may well have mobilized different groups for his dedications, which would then look similar for the simple reason that the same person was ultimately responsible for both of them. Thus, while the notion that *basilistai* were part of an emerging associational landscape that increased the integrative capacity of gymnasia offers an exciting perspective on the second century transformation of Ptolemaic Egypt, it cannot currently be demonstrated how such interactions would have worked in practice.

The case of Herodes son of Demophon throws the spotlight on the role of prominent individuals embedded into military hierarchies. Unlike the official *politeumata*, the emergence (or not) of *basilistai* depended on the initiative of Ptolemaic military elites – and what *they* wanted to achieve by this was perhaps not (or at least not primarily) the realization of an abstract ideal of societal cohesion. Individuals are singled out together with the *basilistai* on other occasions as well. Diokles in Thera and Menyllos in Limyra engaged in classic euergetism while at the same time demonstrating their loyalty to the royal house. In second-century Egypt, additional contexts can be envisaged: perhaps the organisation of one's subordinates as *basilistai* could translate into a claim to influence and recognition in a system that relied increasingly on the recruitment of an administrative elite drawn from various circles (temples, military cleruchs, indigenous army units). Herodes' involvement with (likely) two groups, the priests of Setis and the *basilistai*, can perhaps be understood as an attempt to pull the levers of a changing conception of the state: through the two monuments, he could show himself in control of priestly and military groups, both of which he oriented towards the overarching principal of loyalty to the royal house. One document may even allow us to observe the capacity of such groups to pave their leader's path to administrative relevance in action: the only reason we know anything at all about the *philobasilistai* of Thebes is that they serve in a protocol to locate their leader Sesoosios within an accepted hierarchical framework. Whether these groups could have a transformative effect on Ptolemaic society as a whole will depend on several factors that are beyond our reach (notably the number of such groups and their ethnic composition). But it is plausible to assume that they could do something for their founders, and that may well have been the most important factor contributing to their emergence.

Egyptian names. Launey 1949–1950, 1028 thought that Herodes founded a priestly association for the dynastic cult that was later enlarged – and renamed βασιλισταί – when the garrison members joined. More frequently, the inscriptions are simply treated as belonging to 'the same *synodos*' (Kloppenborg 2020, 377). Neither of these options is necessary if we accept that Herodes may have founded more than one group.

3. The Attalid Kingdom

No other Hellenistic kingdom provides evidence for the term *basilistai*. However, a close terminological and, perhaps, conceptual parallel has long been identified in an Attalid context: in the mid-second century BC, Kraton the aulos player, a well-known figure and member of the corporation of Dionysiac performers, founded an association of *Attalistai*. It is known to us from several documents: a posthumous honorific decree for Kraton found in Teos, the beginning of a letter by him to the group, and a joint dedication undertaken with other associations of Teos.[28] Kraton was no regular musician: he seems to have been on good terms with the kings themselves and promoted loyalty towards them in various capacities. Apart from the Dionysiac performers and his own *Attalistai*, he was involved with the *synagōnistai*, another group assembling performers.[29] An additional association with a very similar structure is attested in an inscription of unclear origin found in the Kaikos valley; the part that contained the name is missing, but the editors have rightly compared it to the *Attalistai*.[30]

Despite its fragmentary state and a number of textual problems, the posthumous honorific decree is the best source on the history and nature of the group.[31] Kraton bequeathed to his *Attalistai* a significant amount of money and a number of utensils, but he had already shown himself generous in his lifetime, most notably by donating to them an *Attaleion* and a house, both of which were likely located in Teos.[32] The name of the sanctuary suggests that the *Attalistai* engaged in some form of ruler cult, either for the deified Attalos I or for the dynasty as a whole.[33] We do not learn much about the association's activities, apart from the fact that members came together for 'sacrifices and meetings' and that they planned to celebrate 'days named after Kraton' in recognition of the latter's benefactions. But a hint may be found in the acknowledgment that Kraton's gifts were designed to free them from having to shoulder the maintenance

---

28   Posthumous decree: OGIS 326 (with a list of items given to the group by Kraton on the other side of the stone, CIG 3071). Beginning of a letter: OGIS 325. Joint dedication: BCH 4, 1880, 164 no. 21. Ἀτταλισταί have also been restored in a letter of Lucius Memmius (SEG 32.491).

29   On his career and networks, see Le Guen 2007.

30   SEG 52.1197, published with extensive commentary by Müller – Wörrle 2002.

31   The stone is lost; we rely on Chishull's transcript and Dittenberger's attempt (in OGIS) to make sense of it (cf. n. 38 below).

32   On the list of utensils, see Rigsby 1996. The location of the *Attaleion* is debated as some have argued for Pergamon; Radt 1999, 193–196 even knows the exact location. For Teos see Schwarzer 1999, 265–272 (but Le Guen 2007, 255–259 opts for Pergamon again). In my view, the note that Kraton 'ended his life in Pergamon' (OGIS 326, ll. 15–16) suggests that the *Attalistai* themselves (and hence their main building) were elsewhere, i. e. in Teos.

33   While Ἀτταλίζειν would suggest loyalty to (or worship of?) a person called Attalos, the Attalids are a better candidate than most for the emergence of an idea of *dynastic* loyalty (despite the reservations of Michels 2019, 344). Pertinent terminology is found relatively early: Strab. 6.4.2 does not call the "kings of Syria" Seleukids yet (a term much later invented by Appian), but refers to the rulers of Pergamon as βασιλεῖς Ἀτταλικοί.

costs of the sanctuary and 'the *chorēgia*'.[34] Earlier in the decree Kraton is said to have performed *chorēgia* himself, and other inscriptions show that he was honoured by the large synod of Dionysiac performers for having performed the same service (as well as many others) for them.[35] This may suggest that the *Attalistai*, too, were expected to organize theatrical performances, perhaps in honour of the king: it is a plausible assumption that Kraton had recruited the members of his loyalist association from his wider network of performers.[36] Kraton may even have promised the kings of Pergamon that such activities would be forthcoming: in a passage that looks back on the group's foundation, the *Attalistai* recall that 'he arranged many good things and gifts for the synod from the kings, who acknowledged both his loyalty towards them in every way and our disposition and gathering, which is worthy of their name'.[37] Kraton had thus convinced the kings of his own loyalty towards them and of his ability to guarantee proper conduct and worthy behaviour of his association. What appears to emerge from this is that Kraton had asked the kings (Eumenes II and Attalos II?) to officially recognize and support an association whose members he had picked himself;[38] we could even infer from it that naming an association *Attalistai* required such approval, at least in a place so close to the centre of Attalid power. In this context, he may have demonstrated how a group of Dionysiac performers worshipping the king would contribute to the public image the Attalids wanted to create for themselves.[39]

The context in which the *Attalistai* operated clearly differs from the situation of Ptolemaic *basilistai*. And yet the connection between theatrical groups and kings was not unique to the Attalids: we also find it in Egypt, where the Ptolemies had entertained good relations with "their" branch of Dionysiac performers much earlier. If the

---

34 OGIS 326, ll. 30–32: παραλῦσαι βουλόμενος καὶ τῆς εἰς ταῦτα δαπάνης καὶ χορηγίας τοὺς Ἀτταλιστάς.

35 IG XI.4 1061, l. 6; cf. CIG 3068.

36 Based on the Classical meaning of χορηγία, Strang 2007, 287 concludes that 'it seems likely that the Attalistai had a yearly festival for the Attalid monarch'. While this is plausible, it will be noted that the term can be used in less specific ways: the payment of χορηγία could be expected from many Teans around 300 BC (otherwise the temporary exemption for new citizens in SEG 2.79 is difficult to understand), and it can also mean more generally a liturgy or expense.

37 OGIS 326, ll. 8–13: ... καὶ πολλὰ μὲ{ι}ν [ἀγαθ]ὰ καὶ φιλάνθρωπα τῆι συνόδωι παρὰ τῶν βασιλέων ἐποίησεν, ἀποδεχομένων αὐτῶν τήν τε ἐκείνου ἅπαντα τρόπον πρὸς ἑαυτοὺς εὔνοιαν καὶ τὴν ἡμετέραν αἵρεσιν καὶ συναγωγὴν ἀξίαν οὖσαν τῆς ἑαυτῶν ἐπωνυμίας ... The text is understood very differently in the translation by Harland 2014, 326, but it cannot be Kraton who 'receives' (ἀποδεχομένων!) something, and it cannot be him who is worthy (οὖσαν!); ἑαυτούς and ἑαυτῶν must refer to the kings and not the σύνοδος. 'Our αἵρεσις' is probably not 'our group' (Harland), but 'our disposition'; cf. CPI I 55 (Alexandreia, 175–145 BC), ll. 8–9: ... τῆς τ[ε] ε[ἰς] τὸ κοινὸν αἱρέσεως καὶ φιλοτιμίας.

38 Stressed in OGIS 326, ll. 7–8: κατὰ κοινὸν τῶν ὑφ' ἑαυτοῦ συνηγμένων καὶ κε[κρι]μένων. The text transmitted by Chishull has κειμένων but does not seem to reliably indicate gaps; cf. Dittenberger ad loc.: 'οἱ κείμενοι de sodalibus omnino barbarum est'. Cf. the opening of Kraton's letter OGIS 325, ll. 3–5: Κράτω[ν Ζω][τίχο]υ τοῖς Ἀτταλισταῖς τοῖς ὑφ' ἑαυτοῦ συνηγμέ[νοις].

39 On the connections between Attalid ruler cult and the cult of Dionysos Kathegemon see Michels 2011.

technitai based in Teos did some unusual things for the Attalid kings in the 160s, like the introduction of an eponymous priest of Eumenes II,[40] this was a mere variation of what the Egyptian branch had done in the third century. In Ptolemais, the group had called itself τεχνῖται οἱ περὶ τὸν Διόνυσον καὶ θεοὺς Ἀδελφούς, adding the rulers to their name as would become common again much later, under the Roman emperors.[41] However, the similarities between Ptolemies and Attalids in this regard relate not to the world of small-scale private associations but to a different level of organisation, perhaps even to the world of peer polity interaction. The performers' associations of Ptolemais and particularly Teos could be seen as state-like actors: Eumenes famously tried to solve a dispute between the performers' association and the city of Teos by proposing a *synoikismos*, and the performers are the only association on record that issued its own coinage.[42] Gaining their support was important to Ptolemaic and Attalid kings alike, precisely because these corporations were not loyalist associations per se: they needed to be won over, and doing so could increase a king's international prestige. Kraton's offer to form an explicitly loyalist group within (or at least connected to) such an organisation must have been most welcome.

The *Attalistai* do not seem to be the only group of this kind. We have already mentioned briefly an inscription from the Kaikos valley dated to the 160s BC, set up by an apparently similar group. It organized contests of some sorts (one of its magistrates is the *agōnothetēs*), and the first regulation preserved in the inscription offers a remarkable image of loyalty: after the banquet, crowns are to be proclaimed 'for king Attalos and queen Apollonis, the gods; for the king, the queen, the king's brothers, the high priest, the priest of the synod, the *hemiolios*, the one in charge of the city, the *dioiketēs*, the *archeklogistēs*, the *oikonomos*, the *eklogistēs*, the *hieronomos*, the *agonothetēs*, the *grammateus* ...'.[43] While the last few offices are held within the association, the others represent Attalid administration all the way up to the royal house. Apart from the deified Attalos I and his wife, no names are given: the positions listed are worthy of honour no matter who holds them. The loyalty on display here is thus a general attitude towards an abstract conception of the Attalid government, not towards any particular (let alone "charismatic") king.[44] In this respect, there appears to be some conceptual

---

40 On this, see Aneziri 2003, 106–107, 130–131.
41 OGIS 50 and 51.
42 *Synoikismos*: RC 53; cf. Aneziri 2003, 100–104. Coinage: Lorber – Hoover 2003.
43 SEG 52.1197, ll. 8–13: [Σ]τέφανοι δὲ ἀνακηρυσσέσθωσαν μετὰ τὸ δεῖπνο[ν τῆι] [·· 6 ··] [ἡ]μέραι ὑπὸ τῶν ἀρχεπιμηνίων βασιλεῖ Ἀττάλωι κα[ὶ βασιλίσ]σηι Ἀπολλωνίδι θεοῖς · βασιλεῖ, βασιλίσσηι, βασιλέως ἀδ[ελ[φοῖς· ἀρ]χιερεῖ, ἱερεῖ τῆς συνόδου, ἡμιολίωι, τῶι ἐπὶ τῆς πόλεως, διοικη[τῆι], ἀρχεγλογιστῆι, οἰκονόμωι, ἐγλογιστῆι, ἱερονόμωι, ἀγωνοθέτηι, γραμματεῖ.
44 As Müller – Wörrle 2002, 231 note, the absence of names 'läßt die Kranzproklamation zur ritualisierten Loyalitätsbekundung nicht nur gegenüber dem Königshaus, sondern der monarchischen Herrschaft in ihrem konkret erfahrbaren institutionellen Aspekt werden'. Cf. on the offices mentioned Kaye 2022, 102.

overlap between the Ptolemaic *basilistai* and the loyalist associations of Teos and its environs.

The prominent position of Kraton son of Zotichos not just with the *Attalistai*, but within a network of agonistic associations again puts the spotlight on the founders and leaders of loyalist groups. If we accept that the two inscriptions from Setis organised by Herodes relate to two different groups, we have there another example of a declared "king's man" who instrumentalized both existing and recently founded groups to demonstrate his own allegiance to the royal house. For Teos, the potential benefits of leading a group of "king's men" are illuminated by a joined funerary dedication that connects 'the *Attalistai* who are with Kraton son of Zotichos' with several other groups led by presumably influential people.[45] While some of these groups appear to be private associations (such as a group of *orgeōnes* and another one of *mystai*), others assemble civic magistrates (the *synarchontes* and the *paraprytaneis*). A certain Athenodotos son of Metrodoros ostensibly trumped Kraton on this occasion by leading three groups involved in the dedication: much like the Attalid kings, he seems to have had a preference for mystery cults, while Kraton's recruitment focused on the world of agonistic performers.[46] What we can possibly grasp here is elite competition through an euergetism that involved not cities but a variety of smaller corporate organisations, some of which were presumably founded for this very purpose.[47] In this context, achieving recognition by the kings for the foundation of a group of *Attalistai*, and then tying that designation to one's own name ('those who are with Kraton'), could have been a major feat: Kraton's one group may well have equalled Metrodoros' three in terms of status and prestige. Once again, the question what a loyalist group could do for its founder comes to the fore; we may recall Sesoosios of Thebes, whose entrance ticket to the company of prominent "friends" of kings may have been his leadership of the *philobasilistai*. While the reservoirs of recruitment were patently different in Teos, the structural parallels thus identified appear to give some conceptual unity to the phenomenon of loyalist associations, at least in the second century BC.

4. The Seleukid Kingdom

Unlike the Attalids, the Seleukids do not seem to have entertained a particularly close relationship with agonistic associations. The Dionysiac artists are mentioned several times in the Teian decrees for Antiochos III and Laodike, but they are always paired

---

45   BCH 4, 1880, 164 no. 21. That the context is funerary emerges from similar dedications at Teos that also involve associations; cf. on the evidence Boulay 2013.

46   Athenodotos led the ὀργεῶνες, the μύσται and the Σαμοθρακιασταί.

47   We do not know the deceased: there is no reason to assume with Boulay 2013, 269–270 that he was a member in all the groups participating in the funerary dedication.

with the people of Teos, reflecting their prominent position in the city; they do not appear to have any independent relations with the king.[48] There is also no obvious term from anywhere in the Seleukid empire that would point to a loyalist association, like *basilistai* or *Attalistai* in our previous discussion. The only possible exception comes from Syrian Antiocheia: an inscription of AD 73/74 that lists the contributions of the city's "blocks" (*plintheia*) to the construction of the fullers' canal mentions, among many others, the *insulae* of the *Kerauniastai* and the *Euergesiastai*.[49] The first has been explained as an association of Zeus Keraunos and the second as a group celebrating Euergesia, but it is at least possible to think of a different context: both Keraunos and Euergetes were epitheta of Seleukid kings, and it is well-known that the Seleukid past was held in high regard in Antiocheia.[50] As the reference is likely to buildings on the respective *insulae*, we do not have to assume that the two groups were still active. Both designations could thus go back to the Hellenistic period and reflect loyalist associations using royal epithets to build a typical theophoric name; for a parallel, we can point to the "*Eupatoristai* of the gymnasium", who appear on a bronze bowl from (probably) Delos that was given to them by Mithradates VI.[51] However, even if this tentative suggestion were accepted,[52] not much would follow from it because we lack all information about the groups' activities and membership. For more relevant observations, we will have to turn elsewhere, and focus on a somewhat different organisational context.

We have already had occasion to briefly note a potentially important difference between the Ptolemaic and the Seleukid empire: the Ptolemies did not encourage the spread of cities with Greek citizen communities within their core territory, whereas the Seleukids relied heavily on the creation of such cities, either through foundation *ex nihilo* or (especially in the second century) through transformation of existing settlements.[53] The latter process in particular – now frequently and perhaps misleadingly called 'poliadisation'[54] – challenges the focus on small-scale groups adopted so far

---

48   SEG 41.1003 I and II (= Ma ²2005, 308–317 no. 17 and 18).

49   SEG 35.1483, with the commentary in Feissel 1985.

50   For Zeus Keraunos and Euergesia, see Feissel 1985, 101–102.

51   IDélos 1567 (= OGIS 367): βασιλεὺς Μιθραδάτης Εὐπάτωρ τοῖς ἀπὸ τοῦ γυμνασίου Εὐπατορισταῖς; cf. Michels 2009, 106–107. Nothing else is known about the group, which would otherwise be an important *comparandum*. We do not know if the members of the gymnasion would have referred to themselves as *Eupatoristai*, although this has usually been assumed. *Pace* Kreuz 2009, 132, we are not dealing with 'the dedication of an elaborate bronze vessel by the *eupatoristai*', but with a gift by the king to them; *pace* Mayor 2010, 249, it is therefore not certain that 'the members called themselves the *Eupatoristai* after their patron Eupator, who promised to liberate Greece'. All we know is that the king himself preferred to call them *Eupatoristai*.

52   For the second group, it may falter on the grounds that *Euergesiastai* should then be *Euergetistai*.

53   Possible reasons for this divergence are explored by Clancier and Gorre 2021.

54   For the terminology, see Couvenhes – Heller 2006, 17 n. 4. It is undoubtedly better than the alternative explored there ("politicization"), but it can still be misleading: "poliadisation" puts the emphasis on a term (*polis*) that plays no role in the process, and thereby suggests a constitutional focus whereas the participants appear to have concentrated on the creation of status groups.

in this enquiry on loyalist associations: should the people who created and sustained these new Greek citizen communities not also be understood as loyalist associations?[55] Some parallels can easily be noticed using our only literary source on poliadisation: the report given in the Second Book of Makkabees on the transformation of Jerusalem in 175/174 BC. Jason, brother of the high priest Onias III, had asked Antiochos IV to be allowed to create a gymnasion with an *ephēbeion*, and to register Jerusalemites "as Antiochenes".[56] Indeed, the new communities were frequently called *Antiocheis* or *Seleukeis*, leaving little doubt regarding their expected attitude towards the Seleukid kings. The transformation served Jason's interests because he became high priest in Onias' stead, but it also created a new status group hand-picked by him: he was acting not unlike Herodes in Setis or Kraton in Teos, although perhaps with wider ramifications. The gymnasion as a breeding ground for social organisation is familiar from our Ptolemaic section, and its important role in the creation of Greek citizen communities is corroborated by the pertinent evidence from Toriaion (under Eumenes II) and Babylon (under Antiochos III or IV).[57] For Babylon in particular, we know that 'the Greeks, as they are called, the citizens, who anoint themselves with oil just like the citizens who are in Seleukeia, the royal city',[58] could be regarded as a separate group by other Babylonians (like the one writing the chronicle just cited): they were, to some extent, a loyalist association tied to the gymnasion. That they also became the main addressees of royal letters and thus effectively took political control of the city makes it impossible to see them as a mere private organisation, but the experience of the *politai* of Babylon – and perhaps other groups such as the '*Antiocheis* in Ptolemais' or the '*Seleukeis* in Gaza' – would have had some similarity at least with that of small-scale associations such as the *basilistai*.[59]

Like other processes of institutional differentiation, poliadisation relied on the gymnasion as an engine of formal organisation around a symbolic centre, a point that we will return to at the end of this article. The phenomenon, mainly but not exclusively known in the Seleukid empire, can perhaps be regarded as the extreme end on a spectrum of loyalist organisation: it was the realisation of a potential that would, under different circumstances, have been inherent in all foundations of associations. Here as

55 A cognate suggestion (but the other way around) is made by Bernhardt 2017, 139: might the "Antiochians of Jerusalem" have constituted themselves as an association of the *basilistai/Attalistai*-type before Jerusalem "became a *polis*"? For the old idea that 'Antiochians in Jerusalem' etc. were *politeumata*, see Bickerman 1937, 61–62.

56 2 Makk. 4.8–9; cf. Ameling 2003.

57 Toriaion: SEG 47.1745 (= IK 62 Sultan Daği 393). Babylon: BCHP 14. The parallels especially between Jerusalem and Toriaion have often been noticed: apart from Ameling 2003, see Bringmann 2004, 327–328; Kennell 2005.

58 BCHP 14.

59 On the case of Babylon see Clancier 2017 (arguing for an altogether more integrative process than the one envisaged by the "apartheid" model of van der Spek 2009). For a comparative discussion, see Eckhardt 2021b.

well, loyalist groups in search of status recognition – and individual brokers who were partially out for themselves, like Jason – created exclusive corporate bodies that expressly declared their loyalty to the king, often in their very names. Elite competition undoubtedly played a role here: much like Kraton, Jason will have made sure to present his *Antiocheis* as "worthy of the king's name", giving him the edge over his brother and his presumably more traditional version of Jerusalemite society.[60] Apart from wider questions about the possibility to see the city as an association (a theoretical notion that goes back at least to Fustel de Coulanges and Max Weber), the role of Greek citizenship comes to the fore again, at least in a comparison between the Ptolemaic and the Seleukid kingdoms (where the existence of Greek citizen communities was not a given, as in the Attalid and Antigonid spheres of influence). We have already discussed a possible distinction between different approaches to societal cohesion in the two kingdoms: it is plausible to assume that different settlement policies opened different pathways towards ethnic coexistence, and the Ptolemaic tendency to settle cleruchs in the countryside rather than in civic 'îlôts de droit distinct' likely contributed to inclusive arrangements on an individual basis.[61] We have also seen that this model posits the spread of inclusive associations on the Ptolemaic side as a less conflictual, more integrative counterpart to divisive city foundation as practiced by the Seleukids. It may be possible to turn this argument on its head: Seleukid cities like Jerusalem or Babylon were divisive and exclusive in so far and because they, too, were associations. And as their integrative potential went well beyond the military, the number of people it could reach was potentially higher than in the case of the fragmented associational landscape of Egypt. In Ptolemaic Egypt, city foundation itself did not create citizenship communities or status groups, but this only meant that those with ambition created them through the foundation of associations: we may recall the foundation of a loyalist association in the gymnasion of newly founded Euergetis, which undoubtedly would have created a distinction between members and outsiders. In Jerusalem or Babylon, the city (as a citizen community) already was that kind of organisation. All associations exclude to some degree: societal fragmentation is the flipside of autonomous self-organisation. No solution was inherently better suited to foster cohesion and avoid ethnic conflict: even within the Seleukid sphere, what worked in Babylon failed in Jerusalem.

5. The Antigonid Kingdom

Once the Antigonid kingdom was basically confined to Macedonia and Greece, the conditions for the emergence of loyalist associations were perhaps not ideal. Unlike

---

60   On elite competition in the context of "poliadisation", see Savalli-Lestrade 2005.
61   Fischer-Bovet 2014, 280–299; see also Fischer-Bovet 2015, 42–44. The quotation is from Préaux 1955, 90.

the other three kingdoms we have discussed, the Antigonids did not promote a centrally organised ruler cult, and while individual cities outside the traditional core of the kingdom did occasionally engage in such worship on their own initiative, this general lack of an institutional foundation may have made the creation of an association of *basilistai* or *Antigonistai* a less obvious choice for declaring one's loyalty.[62] At the same time, city foundation played a less important role than in the Seleukid empire, with few foundations attributed with certainty to Antigonid kings after Demetrios Poliorketes. The gymnasion, so important in both the Ptolemaic and the Seleukid context, again merits investigation, but at least in the core of the Macedonian kingdom, we encounter a peculiarity: it is only here that we find kings regulating the affairs of this institution in detail, with possible implications for the emergence of associations of any kind.

There is evidence from all four major Hellenistic kingdoms for royal involvement with gymnasia: apart from the gymnasion's role in Seleukid poliadisation, we can point to the "joint venture" of the gymnasion at Pergamon, granted to the city by Eumenes II, or to an inscription of Ptolemaic Halikarnassos that records the rebuilding of a gymnasion (the *Philippeion*) after the king had granted permission (but no money).[63] The Antigonid case is different, because both the gymnasiarchic law of Beroia and the ephebarchic law of Amphipolis strongly suggest that at least the later Antigonid kings regulated the activities that took place in gymnasia throughout their kingdom.[64] Another document from Amphipolis shows that the king also interfered directly with the gymnasiarchic law in that city by having a new paragraph inserted.[65] The reason for this unusual degree of control has been argued to be the importance of Macedonian civic gymnasia in training soldiers for the Antigonid royal army, but it is unclear how helpful the kind of ephebic training described in these laws would actually be in that regard.[66] Perhaps a simpler solution is to take into account the nature of the gymnasion as a potential breeding ground for political activism: while there were constellations (such as Seleukid poliadisation, or the foundation of Euergetis in Egypt) where any groups

62   On the evidence for ruler cult in Macedonia, see Mari 2008. On the ruler cults of the Ptolemies and Seleukids cf. the chapters by Stefan Pfeiffer and Sonja Richter in this volume.

63   On the "joint venture" in Pergamon, see Wörrle 2007 (quotation 512); cf. now Kaye 2022, 234–282. Halikarnassos: Wilhelm 1908, 56–61 (McCabe, Halikarnassos 25).

64   Beroia: I. Beroia 1 (Gauthier – Hatzopoulos 1993). Amphipolis: SEG 65.420 (Lazaridou 2015). That both texts include some royal legislation is not in dispute, notably where they include two different options based on the conditions in a given city, which would be superfluous in a civic law. The nature of the law from Amphipolis is nevertheless debated because it was inscribed only in 24/23 BC, with a number of inconsistencies. Against the notion that it was a *verbatim* copy of a law by Philip V or Perseus (Lazaridou 2015; Hatzopoulos 2015/2016), others have argued that it is a patchwork of regulations from different periods (Rousset 2017), or at least an abridged version of a longer legislative text (Arnaoutoglou 2019). A fragmentary inscription with Hellenistic letter forms contains a few lines of text in what appears to be the same arrangement: Lazaridou 2015, 42.

65   Hatzopoulos 1996, no. 16.

66   See the doubts raised by Mann 2022, who privileges the civic context (but largely leaves open the question of royal regulations).

formed in the gymnasion were highly likely to be loyal to the king, the same was not necessarily true in cities like Amphipolis, where a lack of royal control over the composition of the citizen body presumably allowed for a diversity of views on Macedonian rule (or, indeed, occupation).[67] It is perhaps for this reason that the ephebarchic law of Amphipolis appears to discourage associationalism *tout court*: the ephebes are not allowed to eat together, nor is anyone else allowed to eat together with them.[68] While the second regulation is easily understood as one of the protective mechanisms that guard the ephebes against outside influence and potential abuse, the first is highly unusual. In the Aristotelian *Athēnaiōn Politeia*, common meals are explicitly mentioned as one of the ephebes' obligations,[69] but in Amphipolis they are banned, perhaps because of the well-known capacity of commensality to foster corporate organisation. Given the model character of the Athenian *ephēbeia* in other regards, this difference is telling: it foreshadows later Roman restrictions of associationalism, which could also focus on common meals,[70] and ultimately suggests that Antigonid kings could not be too sure about the outcome of young men banding together in their formative years.

There is no clear evidence for any loyalist associations in the Antigonid kingdom. Apart from a potentially restrictive environment, another reason may be the stronger presence of members of the royal court in the cities,[71] which could form their own organisations that may have made the foundation of independent loyalist associations less attractive. A case in point would be the 'royal hunters' (*basilikoi kynēgoi*), a category of courtiers mentioned by Polybios and epigraphically attested (as 'hunters of Herakles') in Macedonia and Thessaly. An inscription from Demetrias records a decree of Philip V that regulates the attire of the hunters not just there, but in all places where they could be found; it shows the same desire to regulate activities and appearance in detail that we know from the gymnasion-related legislation in Beroia and Amphipolis.[72] The royal hunters have been interpreted as royal ephebes, based on an extended analogy between the hierarchies of the civic gymnasion and the Antigonid court, but

---

67 On Amphipolis, see the remarks by Daubner 2018, 49–51. The case of Beroia is less clear because its early history is unknown. On Macedonian rule and stasis in Greek cities (a situation rather different from Ptolemaic or Seleucid rule in the East), see Börm 2021. An attempt to interfere with the composition of the citizen body is of course attested for Larisa in Thessaly (Syll.³ 543).

68 SEG 65.420, ll. 47–51: μὴ ἐξέστωι δὲ συσσειτεῖν μήτε αὐτοῖς μήτε ἄλλῳ μηθενὶ μετὰ τῶν ἐφήβων κατὰ μηδεμίαν πρόφασιν μηδὲ ἄλλοθι δειπνεῖν μηδὲ ἀριστᾶν ἀλλ' ἢ ἐν οἴκωι, εἰ δὲ μή, τὸν μὲν ἔφηβον κολαζέτω, τὸν δὲ ὑποδεξάμενον καὶ καλέσαντα ζημιούτωι …

69 [Aristot.] Ath. Pol. 42.3.

70 See the reference to σύνδειπνα in Ios. ant. Iud. 14.215. It may even be possible to see a Roman context behind this part of the law, as tentatively suggested by Eckhardt 2021a, 156–157. But given that the Hellenistic fragment (above, no. 64) appears to contain ll. 32–40 (i. e., it breaks off just seven lines before this passage), this is perhaps special pleading.

71 On the peculiarity of the Antigonid court and its role in 'constructing Antigonid space', see Ma 2011 (quotation 541).

72 SEG 56.625. Cf. Pol. 31.29.3–5.

there is no direct evidence for this equivalence.[73] They may well have formed associations that interacted with other groups (like the other Herakles associations known from Thessaly),[74] but if they were indeed created by royal *fiat* as a detachment of the royal court, they should be excluded from consideration here as outlined in the introduction to this chapter. The example nevertheless appears to support the notion that the Antigonid kings were invested in controlling the associational landscape of their realm, substituting royal agency for the potential creation of private associations akin to the Ptolemaic *basilistai* or their Attalid counterparts.

6. Conclusion

The same, but different? We have seen that very similar designations (*basilistai* and *Attalistai*) can hide rather different social realities: sameness gave way to difference on close analysis. Introducing a general analytical concept – elite competition – then reduced that notion of diversity and established some common ground, albeit on a more abstract level. On the next level of abstraction, even a very different process like the foundation of a new Antioch came into view. A common Greek institution like the gymnasion could link most of our cases, but closer inspection revealed fundamentally different constellations in the Ptolemaic, Seleukid and Antigonid spheres. Unsurprisingly, the choice between "same" and "different" depends on the granularity of our approach: both are true, always, in every area of comparative historical research.

The repeated appearance of the gymnasion in this study is no coincidence: as the place where new citizens were formed or – in Egypt and the Near East – where Greekness could be celebrated, it attracted the attention of kings and loyalists alike, from the *basilistai* to the hardly known *Eupatoristai* of Delos. The gymnasion and its age classes were also part of a common Greek concept of community formation, together with civic tribes and demes: associations have often been described as 'mirror-images of the city',[75] and the gymnasion was one place where models could be found. However, our comparison of four kingdoms has shown that beyond such generalities, everything depends on context. Loyalist associationalism centred on the gymnasion and supported by kings could create new citizen communities, as in Toriaion, Jerusalem or Babylon: on these occasions, the mirror-image of the city had itself become the city. On the other end of a scale of options, kings could curb associationalism in the gymnasia of their

---

73   For the argument, see Hatzopoulos 1994, 101–109; reprised with little variation by Intzesiloglou 2006.

74   Kravaritou 2018, 383–385 argues that a royal "hunter" might have led the civic ephebes of Demetrias. On other Herakles groups in the region, see Mili 2015, 124–125. That the "hunters" formed associations with Herakles as patron god was suggested already by Edson 1934, 228–229.

75   Arnaoutoglou 1998, 75.

realm, as was argued for the Antigonids. The reason for such variety of course is not (or at least not just) a mere difference in the respective interpretations of a king's relations to his subjects, but fundamentally different conditions created by the demographics and local traditions of Greece and Macedon on the one hand, rural Asia Minor and the Near East on the other. Within the parameters thus set, which also included the offers of participation made by royal systems of representation as highlighted for the Ptolemies and the Attalids, individuals could attempt to position groups of loyalists in a way that was advantageous to themselves, or they might not feel encouraged to do so (e. g. because groups of courtiers installed directly by the king left no "market" for private projects).

While many gaps remain in the evidence, loyalist associations can thus be seen as a window into the underlying values and institutional structures of Hellenistic kingdoms. Not everything we see through this window is new: that the primary contexts for loyalist organisation were the military in Egypt, the theatre in Pergamon and city foundation in the Seleukid empire would appear to reinforce traditional assumptions about these dynasties and their organisational priorities. But it has hopefully become clear how, apart from reasserting the familiar, a focus on associationalism helps to reveal how a widely shared set of basic institutions could support different dynamics of elite competition and even create different potentials for social cohesion, based on factors that went well beyond the individual decisions or character of any one king.

Bibliography

Ameling 2003: Ameling, Walter, Jerusalem als hellenistische Polis: 2 Makk 4,9–12 und eine neue Inschrift, Biblische Zeitschrift. N. F. 47, 2003, 105–111

Aneziri 2003: Aneziri, Sophia, Die Vereine der dionysischen Techniten im Kontext der hellenistischen Gesellschaft. Untersuchungen zur Geschichte, Organisation und Wirkung der hellenistischen Technitenvereine, Stuttgart 2003

Arnaoutoglou 1998: Arnaoutoglou, Ilias N., Between koinon and idion: Legal and Social Dimensions of Religious Associations in Ancient Athens, in: P. Cartledge – P. Millett – S. von Reden (eds.), Kosmos. Essays in Order, Conflict and Community in Classical Athens, Cambridge 1998, 68–83

Arnaoutoglou 2019: Arnaoutoglou, Ilias N., Between Minors and Adults: Ephebes in Amphipolis (AEph 2015, 1–40), in: L. Gagliardi – L. Pepe (eds.), Dike. Essays on Greek Law in Honor of Alberto Maffi, Mailand 2019, 1–28

Bernhardt 2017: Bernhardt, Johannes C., Die jüdische Revolution. Untersuchungen zu Ursachen, Verlauf und Folgen der hasmonäischen Erhebung, Berlin et al. 2017

Bickerman 1937: Bickerman, Elias, Der Gott der Makkabäer. Untersuchungen über Sinn und Ursprung der makkabäischen Erhebung, Berlin 1937

Börm 2021: Börm, Henning, Gespaltene Städte: Die Parteinahme für makedonische Könige in griechischen Poleis, in: S. Pfeiffer – G. Weber (eds.), Gesellschaftliche Spaltungen im Zeitalter des Hellenismus (4.–1. Jahrhundert v. Chr.), Stuttgart 2021, 21–55

Boulay 2013: Boulay, Thibaut, Les "groupes de référence" au sein du corps civique de Téos, in: P. Fröhlich – P. Hamon (eds.), Groupes et associations dans les cités grecques (IIIe siècle av. J.-C. – IIe siècle apr. J.-C.), Genf 2013, 251–275

Bringmann 2004: Bringmann, Klaus, Gymnasion und griechische Bildung im Nahen Osten, in: D. Kah – P. Scholz (eds.), Das hellenistische Gymnasion, Berlin 2004, 323–333

Chaniotis 2002: Chaniotis, Angelos, Foreign Soldiers – Native Girls? Constructing and Crossing Boundaries in Hellenistic Cities with Foreign Garrisons, in: A. Chaniotis – P. Ducrey (eds.), Army and Power in the Ancient World, Stuttgart 2002, 99–113

Clancier 2017: Clancier, Philippe, The Polis of Babylon. An Historiographical Approach, in: B. Chrubasik – D. King (eds.), Hellenism and the Local Communities of the Eastern Mediterranean. 400 BCE-250 CE, Oxford et al. 2017, 53–81

Clancier – Gorre 2021: Clancier, Philippe – Gorre, Gilles, The Integration of Indigenous Elites and the Development of Poleis in the Ptolemaic and Seleucid Empires, in: C. Fischer-Bovet – S. von Reden (eds.), Comparing the Ptolemaic and Seleucid Empires. Integration, Communication, and Resistance, Cambridge et al. 2021, 86–105

Couvenhes – Heller 2006: Couvenhes, Jean-Christophe – Heller, Anna, Les transferts culturels dans le monde institutionnel des cités et des royaumes à l'époque hellénistique, in: J.-C. Couvenhes – B. Legras (eds.), Transferts culturels et politique dans le monde hellénistique, Paris 2006, 15–52

Crowther 2020: Crowther, Charles, The Palaeography of Ptolemaic Inscriptions from Egypt, in: A. K. Bowman – C. Crowther (eds.), The Epigraphy of Ptolemaic Egypt, Oxford et al. 2020, 226–267

Daubner 2018: Daubner, Frank, Makedonien nach den Königen (168 v. Chr. – 14 n. Chr.), Stuttgart 2018

Eckhardt 2021a: Eckhardt, Benedikt, Romanisierung und Verbrüderung. Das Vereinswesen im römischen Reich, Berlin et al. 2021a

Eckhardt 2021b: Eckhardt, Benedikt, The Gymnasium of Jerusalem – a Middle Ground?, in: J. Hoffmann-Salz (ed.), The Middle East as Middle Ground? Cultural Interaction in the Ancient Middle East Revisited, Vienna 2021b, 179–197

Edson 1934: Edson, Charles F., The Antigonids, Heracles, and Beroea, Harvard Studies in Classical Philology 45, 1934, 213–246

Feissel 1985: Feissel, Denis, Deux listes de quartiers d'Antioche astreints au creusement d'un canal (73–74 après J.-C.), Syria 62, 1985, 77–103

Fischer-Bovet 2014: Fischer-Bovet, Christelle, Army and Society in Ptolemaic Egypt, Cambridge 2014

Fischer-Bovet 2015: Fischer-Bovet, Christelle, Social Unrest and Ethnic Coexistence in Ptolemaic Egypt and the Seleucid Empire, Past and Present 229, 2015, 3–45

Fischer-Bovet 2020: Fischer-Bovet, Christelle, Soldiers in the Epigraphy of Ptolemaic Egypt, in: A. K. Bowman – C. Crowther (eds.), The Epigraphy of Ptolemaic Egypt, Oxford Studies in Ancient Documents, Oxford et al. 2020, 127–158

Gabrielsen 2009: Gabrielsen, Vincent, Brotherhoods of Faith and Provident Planning: The Non-Public Associations of the Greek World, in: I. Malkin – C. Constantakopoulou – K. Panagopoulou (eds.), Greek and Roman Networks in the Mediterranean, London et al. 2009, 176–203

Gabrielsen – Thomsen 2015: Gabrielsen, Vincent – Thomsen, Christian A., Introduction: Private Groups, Public Functions?, in: V. Gabrielsen – C. A. Thomsen (eds.), Private Associations and the Public Sphere, Copenhagen 2015, 7–24

Gauthier – Hatzopoulos 1993: Gauthier, Philippe – Hatzopoulos, Miltiades B., La loi gymnasiarchique de Beroia, Athens et al. 1993

Harland 2014: Harland, Philip A., Greco-Roman Associations: Texts, Translations and Commentary II: North Coast of the Black Sea, Asia Minor, Berlin et al. 2014

Hatzopoulos 1994: Hatzopoulos, Miltiades B., Cultes et rites de passage en Macedoine, Athens et al. 1994

Hatzopoulos 1996: Hatzopoulos, Miltiades B., Macedonian Institutions under the Kings II: Epigraphic Appendix, Athens et al. 1996

Hatzopoulos 2015/2016: Hatzopoulos, Miltiades B., Comprendre la loi ephebarchique d'Amphipolis, Tekmeria 13, 2015/2016, 145–171

Hiller von Gaertringen 1903: Hiller von Gaertringen, Friedrich, Der Verein der Bakchisten und die Ptolemäerherrschaft in Thera, in: Festschrift zu Otto Hirschfelds sechzigstem Geburtstage, Berlin 1903, 87–99

Intzesiloglou 2006: Intzesiloglou, Babis G., The Inscription of the Kynegoi of Herakles from the Ancient Theatre of Demetrias, in: G. A. Pikoulas (ed.), Inscriptions and History of Thessaly. New Evidence. Proceedings of the International Symposium in Honor of Professor Christian Habicht, Volos 2006, 67–77

Kaye 2022: Kaye, Noah, The Attalids of Pergamon and Anatolia. Money, Culture, and State Power, Cambridge 2022

Kayser 2013: Kayser, François, Les communautés ethniques du type politeuma dans l'Égypte hellénistique, in: F. Delrieux – O. Mariaud (eds.), Communautés nouvelles dans l'Antiquité grecque. Mouvement, integrations et representations, Chambéry 2013, 121–153

Kennell 2005: Kennell, Nigel M., New Light on 2 Maccabees 4:7–15, Journal of Jewish Studies 56, 2005, 10–24

Kloppenborg 2020: Kloppenborg, John S., Greco-Roman Associations: Texts, Translations, and Commentary III: Ptolemaic and Early Roman Egypt, Berlin et al. 2020

Kramer 2012: Kramer, Bärbel, Fenster zur antiken Welt. 30 Jahre Trierer Papyrussammlung: Begleitheft zur Ausstellung, 14. Mai – 31. Juli 2012, Trier 2012

Kravaritou 2018: Kravaritou, Sofia, Cults and Rites of Passage in Ancient Thessaly, in: M. Kalaitzi et al. (eds.), Βορειοελλαδικά. Tales from the Lands of the ethne: Essays in Honour of Miltiades B. Hatzopoulos, Meletemata 78, Athens 2018, 377–396

Kreuz 2009: Kreuz, Patric-Alexander, Monuments for the King: Royal Presence in the Late Hellenistic World of Mithridates VI, in: J. Munk Højte (ed.), Mithridates VI and the Pontic Kingdom, Aarhus 2009, 131–144

Kruse 2015: Kruse, Thomas, Ethnic Koina and Politeumata in Ptolemaic Egypt, in: V. Gabrielsen – C. A. Thomsen (eds.), Private Associations and the Public Sphere, Copenhagen 2015, 270–300

Launey 1949–1950: Launey, Marcel, Recherches sur les armées hellénistiques, 2 vols., Paris 1949–1950

Lazaridou 2015: Lazaridou, Kalliopi, Ἐφηβαρχικὸς νόμος ἀπὸ τὴν Ἀμφίπολη, Archaiologike Ephemeris 154, 2015, 1–45

Le Guen 2007: Le Guen, Brigitte, Kraton, Son of Zotichos: Artists' Associations and Monarchic Power in the Hellenistic Period, in: P. Wilson (ed.), The Greek Theatre and Festivals, Oxford et al. 2007, 246–278

Lorber – Hoover 2003: Lorber, Catharine C. – Hoover, Oliver D., An Unpublished Tetradrachm Issued by the Artists of Dionysus, Numismatic Chronicle 163, 2003, 59–68

Ma ²2005: Ma, John, Antiochos III and the Cities of Western Asia Minor, Oxford et al. ²2005

Ma 2011: Ma, John, Court, King, and Power in Antigonid Macedonia, in: R.J. Lane Fox (ed.), Brill's Companion to Ancient Macedon. Studies in the Archaeology and History of Macedon, 650 BC – 300 AD, Leiden et al. 2011, 521–543

Maillot 2021: Maillot, Stéphanie, Associations dites d'étrangers, clientèles et groupes de travail à l'époque hellénistique, in: S. Maillot – J. Zurbach (eds.), Statuts personnels et main-d'œuvre en Méditerranée hellénistique, Clermont-Ferrand 2021, 285–313

Mann 2022: Mann, Christian, Sport und Erziehung im hellenistischen Makedonien. Überlegungen zum Ephebarchengesetz aus Amphipolis, Ancient Society 52, 2022, 125–169

Mari 2008: Mari, Manuela, The Ruler Cult in Macedonia, Studi Ellenistici 20, 2008, 219–268

Mayor 2010: Mayor, Adrienne, The Poison King. The Life and Legend of Mithradates, Rome's Deadliest Enemy, Princeton et al. 2010

Michels 2009: Michels, Christoph, Kulturtransfer und monarchischer "Philhellenismus": Bithynien, Pontos und Kappadokien in hellenistischer Zeit, Göttingen 2009

Michels 2011: Michels, Christoph, Dionysos Kathegemon und der attalidische Herrscherkult. Überlegungen zur Herrschaftsrepräsentation der Könige von Pergamon, in: L.-M. Günther – S. Plischke (eds.), Studien zum vorhellenistischen und hellenistischen Herrscherkult, Berlin 2011, 114–140

Michels 2019: Michels, Christoph, Unlike any Other? The Attalid Kingdom after Apameia, in: A. Coşkun – D. Engels (eds.), Rome and the Seleukid East, Leuven 2019, 333–352

Mili 2015: Mili, Maria, Religion and Society in Ancient Thessaly, Oxford et al. 2015

Mitford 1961: Mitford, Terence. B., The Hellenistic Inscriptions of Old Paphos, The Annual of the British School at Athens 56, 1961, 1–41

Monson 2019: Monson, Andrew, Political and Sacred Animals: Religious Associations in Greco-Roman Egypt, in: B. Eckhardt (ed.), Private Associations and Jewish Communities in the Hellenistic and Roman Cities, Leiden et al. 2019, 37–57

Monson 2021: Monson, Andrew, The Men of the Village: Royal Status and Agricultural Labor in Ptolemaic Egypt, in: S. Maillot – J. Zurbach (eds.), Statuts personnels et main-d'œuvre en Méditerranée hellénistique, Clermont-Ferrand 2021, 383–403

Müller – Wörrle 2002: Müller, Helmut – Wörrle, Michael, Ein Verein im Hinterland Pergamons zur Zeit Eumenes' II., Chiron 32, 2002, 191–235

Paganini 2020: Paganini, Mario C.D., Epigraphic Habits of Private Associations in the Ptolemaic Chora, in: A.K. Bowman – C. Crowther (eds.), The Epigraphy of Ptolemaic Egypt, Oxford et al. 2020, 179–207

Paganini 2021: Paganini, Mario C.D., Gymnasia and Greek Identity in Ptolemaic Egypt, Oxford et al. 2021

Paganini 2022: Paganini, Mario C.D., Religion and Leisure: A Gentry Association of Hellenistic Egypt, in: A. Cazemier – S. Skaltsa (eds.), Associations and Religion in Context. The Hellenistic and Roman Eastern Mediterranean, Liège 2022, 227–247

Papantoniou 2013: Papantoniou, Giorgos, Cypriot Autonomous Polities at the Crossroads of Empire: The Imprint of a Transformed Islandscape in the Classical and Hellenistic Periods, Bulletin of the American Schools of Oriental Research 370, 2013, 169–205

Pfeiffer ²2020: Pfeiffer, Stefan, Griechische und lateinische Inschriften zum Ptolemäerreich und zur römischen Provinz Aegyptus, Berlin ²2020

Poland 1909: Poland, Franz, Geschichte des griechischen Vereinswesens, Preisschriften, gekrönt und herausgegeben von der Fürstlich Jablonowski'schen Gesellschaft zu Leipzig 38, Leipzig 1909

Préaux 1955: Préaux, Claire, Institutions économiques et sociales des villes hellénistiques, principalement en Orient, in: Recueils de la Société Jean Bodin VII: La Ville. Deuxième Partie: Institutions économiques et sociales, Brussels 1955, 89–135

Radt 1999: Radt, Wolfgang, Pergamon. Geschichte und Bauten einer antiken Metropole, Darmstadt 1999

Rigsby 1996: Rigsby, Kent J., Craton's Legacy, Epigraphica Anatolica 26, 1996, 137–139

Rousset 2017: Rousset, Denis, Considérations sur la loi éphébarchique d'Amphipolis, Revue des études anciennes 119, 2017, 49–84

San Nicolò ²1972: San Nicolò, Marian, Ägyptisches Vereinswesen zur Zeit der Ptolemäer und Römer I: Die Vereinsarten, Munich ²1972

Sänger 2019: Sänger, Patrick, Die ptolemäische Organisationsform politeuma. Ein Herrschaftsinstrument zugunsten jüdischer und anderer hellenischer Gemeinschaften, Tübingen 2019

Savalli-Lestrade 2005: Savalli-Lestrade, Ivana, Devenir une cité: Poleis nouvelles et aspirations civiques en Asie Mineure à la basse époque hellénistique, in: P. Fröhlich – C. Müller (eds.), Citoyenneté et participation à la basse époque hellénistique, Genf 2005, 9–37

Schwarzer 1999: Schwarzer, Holger, Untersuchungen zum hellenistischen Herrscherkult in Pergamon, Mitteilungen des Deutschen Archäologischen Instituts. Istanbuler Abteilung 49, 1999, 249–300

Skaltsa 2022: Skaltsa, Stella, Associations in Ptolemaic Thera: Names, Identity, and Gatherings, in: A. Cazemier – S. Skaltsa (eds.), Associations and Religion in Context. The Hellenistic and Roman Eastern Mediterranean, Liège 2022, 125–147

Stavrou 2020: Stavrou, Dorothea, The Hellenistic *gymnasia* of Cyprus and Ptolemaic Propaganda, Journal of Greek Archaeology 5, 2020, 309–326

Strang 2007: Strang, Jonathan R., The City of Dionysos: A Social and Historical Study of the Ionian City of Teos, Diss. Buffalo 2007

Tondriau 1946: Tondriau, Jean, Les thiases dionysiaques royaux de la cour ptolémaïque, Chronique d'Égypte 21, 1946, 149–171

van der Spek 2009: van der Spek, Robartus J., Multi-Ethnicity and Ethnic Segregation in Hellenistic Babylon, in: T. Derks – N. Roymans (eds.), Ethnic Constructs in Antiquity. The Role of Power and Tradition, Amsterdam 2009, 101–115

van't Dack – Clarysse – Cohen – Quaegebeur – Winicki 1989: van't Dack, Edmond – Clarysse, Willy – Cohen, Getzel M. – Quaegebeur, Jan – Winicki, Jan K., The Judean-Syrian-Egyptian Conflict of 103–101 B. C. A Multilingual Dossier Concerning a "War of Sceptres", Brussels 1989

Wackenier 2020: Wackenier, Stéphanie, Splendeurs et misères des Lagides: le pouvoir personnel au service de la construction de l'état (milieu IIème-début Ier s.), in: G. Gorre – S. Wackenier (eds.), Quand la fortune du royaume ne dépend pas de la vertu du prince. Un renforcement de la monarchie lagide de Ptolemée VI à Ptolemée X (169–88 av. J.-C.)?, Louvain 2020, 95–111

Wilcken 1935: Wilcken, Ulrich, Urkunden der Ptolemäerzeit II: Papyri aus Oberägypten, Berlin et al. 1935

Wilhelm 1908: Wilhelm, Adolf, Inschriften aus Halikarnassos und Theangela, Jahreshefte des Österreichischen Archäologischen Institutes 11, 1908, 53–75

Wörrle 2007: Wörrle, Michael, Zu Rang und Bedeutung von Gymnasion und Gymnasiarchie im hellenistischen Pergamon, Chiron 37, 2007, 501–516

Wörrle 2015: Wörrle, Michael, Die ptolemäische Garnison auf der Burg von Limyra im Licht einer neuen Inschrift, in: B. Beck-Brandt – S. Ladstätter – B. Yener-Marksteiner (eds.), Turm und Tor. Siedlungsstrukturen in Lykien und benachbarten Kulturlandschaften. Akten des Gedenkkolloquiums für Thomas Marksteiner in Wien, November 2012, Vienna 2015, 291–304

Wörrle 2021: Wörrle, Michael, Epigraphische Forschungen zur Geschichte Lykiens XIII: Die
    Weinbergstiftung eines ptolemäischen Burgkommandanten von Limyra, Chiron 51, 2021,
    211–256
Ziebarth 1896: Ziebarth, Erich, Das griechische Vereinswesen, Leipzig 1896

Benedikt Eckhardt (*1983) gained his PhD in Ancient History from the University of Bochum
(2011) and obtained his Habilitation at the University of Bremen (2020). He has held positions at
the University of Münster (2008–2014) and the University of Bremen (2015–2018) before moving
to the University of Edinburgh in 2018, where he is currently Senior Lecturer in Ancient History. He
has published widely on Hellenistic and Roman history, and is the author of *Ethnos und Herrschaft*
(Berlin 2013), *Juden, Christen und Vereine im römischen Reich* (Berlin 2018, with C. Leonhard), *Herod
in History* (Oxford 2021, with K. Czajkowski), and *Romanisierung und Verbrüderung* (Berlin 2021).

The Image of the Ruler between Tradition and Innovation /
Das Herrscherbild zwischen Tradition und Innovation

The Twilight of Charisma
Hellenistic Kingship in Transition

NOAH KAYE

Abstract: This article contends that the dominance of Weberian charismatic kingship in studies of Hellenistic kingship fundamentally obscures an epochal change in the representation and practice of kingship from ca. 200 BC. This later Hellenistic kingship was defined by a shift toward precisely the legitimacy-seeking behavior that charismatic rulers by definition abjure. The sources show both a bottom-up withdrawal of the recognition of charisma, as evidenced in Hellenistic Jewish literature, but also a top-down abandonment of the same monarchic tropes, on full display in Ivana Savalli-Lestrade's new reconstruction of the correspondence of Eumenes II with Toriaion. As an adaptive response to Roman unipolarity in the Mediterranean interstate system, these later Hellenistic kings more actively cultivated traditional authorities such as cities, temples, and villages. Newfound symbolic and administrative entanglements thus characterize and distinguish these kings and their kingdoms from their predecessors of the age of Alexander and the Successors. Visually, such entanglement can be difficult to detect, since we find copious proxy coinages and a broad disappearance of the effigy of the monarch from coinage minted with royal bullion and oversight, such as the Attalid cistophoros and the so-called autonomous coinages of the Antigonids. However, in the epigraphic record, kings turn up more than ever in a particular genre: in a departure from the norm-breaking behavior of earlier charismatic kingship, rulers of this period begin to appear as parties to civic oaths. Instead of focusing their energies on rearranging the pantheon, these kings express care for the religious psychology of their subjects. The article points to the inadequacy of Weber's schema for describing a redefinition of Hellenistic kingship after ca. 200 BC around ideals of cosmic order and ethical discipline, calling for a new schema, one based on anthropologist Alan Strathern's recent comparative study of sacred kingship in world history.

1. Introduction

The invention and naming of periods is intrinsic to the craft of the historian, but we abandon our periods when they obscure more than they reveal about patterns in the past. In this regard, the Hellenistic period has proven remarkably durable, since

J. G. Droysen defined it in the first volume of his *Geschichte des Hellenismus* (1836) as the age from Alexander to Jesus, now secularized as "Alexander to Actium".[1] Yet what of its internal definition as a period? Evidently, Droysen chose the year 221 as his historiographical break, the hinge between the Kleomenic Wars and Polybios' jumping off point in the 140th Olympiad. Indeed, the Battle of Sellasia (222) still defines, in the textbook of Peter Green, the end of the Hellenistic zenith.[2] However, for a programmatic division of "early" from "late" Hellenistic history, one must look to epigraphers, to the French notion of the *basse époque hellénistique*: the rise of larger-than-life private benefactors in the Greek *polis* from ca. 150 BC, to whom other citizens were beholden at the expense of traditions of egalitarianism and democracy.[3] Yet, this is not totally satisfying as a caesura. First, it is left unmotivated. As Patrice Hamon has pointed out, the historical rupture that marks the transition eludes explanation on the present state of the evidence.[4] Second, kingship is left out of the story – it is simply described as in decline, and therefore, left unanalyzed. The omission is troubling since the Hellenistic period itself comes to be defined so often by a particular ideal type of monarchy, a type which cannot possibly retain its analytical utility across three centuries and an aristocratic takeover of Greek society.

Hellenistic kings, as Peter Thonemann explains in his primer on Hellenistic history, struck a familiar pose, from Alexander '(r)ight down to the end', neatly exemplified by the second-century ruler portrait, the "Terme Ruler," the heroic image of the superhuman warrior.[5] Meanwhile, however, from ca. 200 BC, as a resilient response to the pressures of Roman hegemony, Hellenistic rulers modulated their appearance in other contexts and visual media. Further, they even changed their behavior. These dynasts transformed the largely self-legitimating kingship bequeathed by the Successors into a style of rule that emphasized cosmic ordering and ethical discipline. Faced with annihilation, kings resuscitated traditional notions of kingship – and fell back on, more broadly, traditional authority – in order to survive. The evidence begins to stray dangerously far from the historian's ideal type, as has been recently noted by scholars such as Ulrich Gotter and Hans-Ulrich Wiemer.[6] Yet sounding out new ideal types in an age of academic hyper-specialization is daunting, especially given the ever-expanding body of evidence from every corner of the variegated Hellenistic world.[7] Can we – do

---

1   Momigliano 1970, 140. See now Chaniotis 2018 for a long Hellenistic age, stretching from Philip II to Hadrian.
2   Green 1990, 265: 'a watershed had been reached, as Polybios recognized, in the history of the Greek-speaking world.'
3   For a start date after ca. 150 BC, see Gauthier 1985, 57–58.
4   Hamon 2009, 377–379.
5   Thonemann 2018, 43.
6   Gotter 2013; Wiemer 2017.
7   Note the veritable troop of scholars assembled to compare the Ptolemaic and Seleukid empires – but also the two kingships – in Fischer-Bovet – von Reden 2021a.

we dare – generalize about Hellenistic kingship?[8] As John Ma wryly advises in a reference article on the subject, 'here, according to age of scholar and date of piece, quote homeopathic doses of Max Weber'.[9] Perhaps, then, the challenge is to approach the problem of generalization with a less reverent attitude toward Weber, who remains our starting point. In a 1982 article, reissued in 2013, Hans-Joachim Gehrke, proposed that of Weber's three types of legitimate domination – rational/legal, traditional, and charismatic – the third was the key to understanding Hellenistic kingship.[10] For Gehrke, Weber's charismatic king *is* the Hellenistic king: 'The concept has thus far proven to be perfectly in keeping with the historical reality'.[11] The ruler's spectacular and other-worldly performance of feats in war, including acts of liberation, inspired the confidence of the ruled in his ability to perpetually repeat those deeds, making the Hellenistic variety the quintessential personal, charismatic monarchy. As Weber had said, this rendered such a kingship highly unstable, and Hellenistic kings, writes Gehrke, since they were unable to transmit charisma to their heirs, unable to rely on the stabilizing process of the "routinization of charisma," the interleaving of charismatic with traditional and rational/legal authority, were thus left to wage a forever war.[12] They were trapped, and perhaps, so are we.

When we measure Hellenistic kings, especially later ones, with a purity standard of Weberian charisma, we tend to focus on what they did *not* do, rather than on what they *did* do. The creativity and agency of the kings is erased, and we lose sight of their ability to reformat their rule to meet the challenge of Roman hegemony. Gehrke was aware of the problem of change but tried to solve it with a tautology: 'Hellenistic monarchy was thus characterized by charisma until its decline'.[13] The historian's task is thereby reduced to marking the moment of decline. For Gotter, who takes the argument to its logical conclusion, late Hellenistic kings are non-kings, and all those who ruled after the Roman humiliation of Antiochos IV on the Day of Eleusis (168 BC) are characterized by their desperate, vain, and pathetic attempt to achieve charismatic kingship – they know no other way.[14] The approach of Wiemer is conservative in that it preserves Weberian orthodoxy by elaborating it, amplifying the role of euergetism in charismatic kingship

8   Or should we renounce the concept? A panel chaired by Sylvie Honigman at the 2021 annual of the European Association of Biblical Studies was entitled, 'The End of Hellenistic Kingship'.
9   Ma 2003, 179.
10   Gehrke 1982, reprinted in English as Gehrke 2013.
11   Gehrke 2013, 85.
12   Meanwhile, inside these kingdoms, a new civic ideology was cooling passions for interstate warfare. In the late Hellenistic polis of ca. 150 BC, as Benjamin Gray has argued (2017, 74–82), the new anti-democratic and paternalistic elites of this period, without fully renouncing the older militarism, began to pursue an idealistic type of world peace (*eirene*) that was conceptually akin to civic order.
13   Gehrke 2013, 88.
14   Gotter 2013, 207–208. While preserving Weberian orthodoxy, Brisson 2018, 438 still grants Antiochos IV charisma at Daphne in 166.

and arguing that German scholars in particular have just asked too much of the concept, underestimating the stabilizing role of royal institutions. Yet, as Wiemer admits, the question of why the Hellenistic public accepted these rulers remains an open one.[15] In fact, as Boris Chrubrasik has argued in a study of Seleukid usurpers, the approach of charisma is of limited help in answering that question.[16] Andrew Monson's recent contribution to the debate also charges charisma with a certain lack of explanatory power for Hellenistic history.[17] The performance of charisma, in Monson's provocative argument, does not confer legitimacy, pointing up the tension between norms-based legitimacy and Weberian charisma by reminding us of the central importance of the transgressive aspect of charisma.[18] Alexander was a Weberian charismatic insofar as he consciously transgressed against 'custom, law, morality, and truth'.[19] Legitimacy was not his concern. Later Hellenistic kings, by contrast, *were* much concerned with legitimacy since they lacked Alexander's resources and coercive power.[20] Therefore, charisma as a touchstone limits our ability to explain the historical evolution of Hellenistic kingship. For example, in his account of the 'highly innovative' form of a distinctively consensual late Attalid kingship, an adaptation to 'exceptionally fragile territorial legitimacy', Thonemann defaults to a description of the phenomenon as 'non-charismatic' kingship.[21]

Adaptation, indeed, is what we may be able to salvage from Weber's thought that is useful for the task of analyzing the transformation of Hellenistic kingship under the strain of Rome's advance. Pure charismatic authority, which is revolutionary and hostile to tradition, inevitably falters when the ruler fails to secure the subjects' recognition of his charisma. Faced with the withdrawal of recognition, a king turns to the process of the "routinization of charisma", the preservation of charisma via an unholy alliance with traditional-patrimonial and even rational-legal authority.[22] Implicitly, it

---

15   Wiemer 2017, 335.
16   Chrubrasik 2016, 8–9.
17   Monson 2020.
18   This transgressive aspect of Weber's charisma was actually the secular sociologist's novel twist on an idea he received from the Protestant legal historian Rudolph Sohm's "famous thesis" on *Kirchenrecht*, for which see Haley 1980, 195–197.
19   Monson 2020, 286.
20   Compare Alexander on this score to the late Attalids, who were famed in Antiquity for their money – a reputation still on display in the title of a 2013 volume edited by Peter Thonemann, *Attalid Asia Minor: Money, International Relations, and the State*. Yet the kings of Pergamon were actually not so rich, especially compared to late-fourth and third-century kings (see Kaye 2022, 37–38). Rather, it was the dynasty's qualitative relationship with money that earned them this reputation and legitimacy. Cf. Gotter 2013, 209–219, for whom the second-century Attalids use prodigious wealth to pose inauthentically as charismatic kings of the third-century, using art to effect a 'pathetic elevation of current politics to a cosmic level' (218).
21   Thonemann 2013, 5, 34, 46; cf. dissent of Wiemer 2017, 323, n. 64. On the waning utility of Weberian concepts in Hellenistic kingship studies, see now Djurslev 2021. See also Roisman 2020 on the inapplicability of the concept of charismatic kingship after the age of Alexander.
22   Weber 1978, 1122.

falls then to the king to withdraw from the public sphere, to renounce the flagrantly norm-defying performances that had previously characterized his rule. In essence, a crisis of authority compels the monarch to adopt a different mode of kingship, a scenario which fits the bill well for the period after the resounding Roman victories of the early second century BC, during which different royal behaviors and patterns of representations emerged. It is often pointed out that for decades, the victorious Romans eschewed direct rule. Yet even those earlier victories, from the conclusion of the First Macedonian War (205) until the Settlement of Apameia (188) – though they did not result in the destruction of kingdoms – seem to have changed the rules of interaction between Hellenistic rulers and their own subjects. Gehrke saw "routinization" in the history of Hellenistic kingship as an inevitable process of non-charismatic elements of legitimation acquiring some modest importance.[23] Yet these kings were marshalling an adaptative response. Now, they concealed themselves more and showed greater respect for norms when they did reenter the public sphere. They actively cultivated traditional authority by enmeshing themselves and their administrations in the inner workings of temples, cities, federations, and villages, even going so far as to rationally organize the finances of sub-royal institutions in order to render the impact of Hellenistic monarchy on local society more predictable and generate trust.

All this amounts to a dramatic shift away from the ideal of charismatic kingship typically held up in scholarship as still prescriptive (if no longer also descriptive) in the second century BC. The orthodox view is to take that ideal from a Byzantine encyclopedia, the *Suda*, s. v. "*basileia*" no. 147, which, we should note, has in fact only a dubious claim to be an 'emic theory of royal legitimation'.[24] In any case, this much-quoted first of two definitions of kingship in the *Suda* reads:

οὔτε φύσις οὔτε τὸ δίκαιον ἀποδιδοῦσι τοῖς ἀνθρώποις τὰς βασιλείας, ἀλλὰ τοῖς δυναμένοις ἡγεῖσθαι στρατοπέδου καὶ χειρίζειν πράγματα νουνεχῶς. οἷος ἦν Φίλιππος καὶ οἱ διάδοχοι Ἀλεξάνδρου.

It is neither descent nor legitimacy which gives monarchies to men, but the ability to command an army and to handle affairs competently. Such was the case with Philip and the Successors of Alexander.[25]

The lemma no. 147 is often taken to mean that a Hellenistic king was defined, accepted, and viewed as legitimate according to his personal ability to succeed in war and governance. However, scholars rarely examine the second definition, with its criteria for kingship based on stewardship of the commons, communal solidarity, and ethical behavior, s. v. '*basileia*' no. 148:

---

23 Gehrke 2013, 87 with n. 69.
24 For the phrase and critique, see Monson 2020, 268.
25 Trans. Austin ²2006, no. 45. See Eckstein 2009, 249, for a rare comment on *both* lemmata. Cf. Gehrke 2013, 76: 'According to one of the lemmata βασιλεία …' Similarly, Brisson 2018, 438 n. 68.

ὅτι ἡ βασιλεία κτῆμα τῶν κοινῶν, ἀλλ᾽ οὐ τὰ δημόσια τῆς βασιλείας κτήματα. διὸ τὰς ἐξ ἀνάγκης καὶ μεθ᾽ ὕβρεως εἰσπράξεις ὥσπερ τυραννικὰς ἀκολασίας μισεῖν δεῖ, τὰς δὲ σὺν λόγῳ καὶ φιλανθρωπίᾳ τῶν εἰσφορῶν ἀπαιτήσεις ὥσπερ κηδεμονίαν τιμᾶν.

Since kingship entails the possession of *ta koina* ["the commons" or common funds], but the public's property does not belong to the monarchy, it follows that one must detest, as the excesses of a tyrant, royal interventions made with force and arrogance; but one must honor like a solemn duty requests for contributions made persuasively and humanely.

The second definition recalls pre-Hellenistic views on kingship current among Greeks as much as it does the practice and representation of later Hellenistic kingship. At the very least, it exposes alternatives to charisma in ancient discourse. As Nino Luraghi has written, Greek thinkers were continually vexed by the problem of the good king and tended to imagine him in reductive fashion as a non-tyrant.[26] Yet the pressures of Roman hegemony on Hellenistic kings now beginning to hunger for legitimacy may have both churned up old ideals of good kingship and also finally stimulated the imagination of new ideals. In either case, to capture what transpired we need an update to the conceptual vocabulary of Weber.

2. From heroic to cosmic, to righteous kingship

The existence of various forms of sacred or "divinized" kingship is one of the great constants of premodern political and religious life.[27] Of course, kingship had a long history in the ancient Mediterranean before Alexander's reinvention of monarchy; and Octavian's equally radical reimagining of kingship marks for many a moment of eclipse. Kingship, in other words, is a seriated element in the historical record that allows us to track large-scale political and religious change and to compare societies. Ideal types such as Weber's charismatic kingship, or Alan Strathern's equally ambitious typology, with its heroic, cosmic, and righteous modes of kingship, are all etic concepts and by nature cannot account for all evidence. Ideal types, though, can help us to identify major shifts in the way power is exercised and represented.[28] Moreover, while historically, one ideal type never simply gave way to another, a schema of the succession of types provides a useful description of the historical process by which one mode of kingship outflanked another in response to a specific crisis of authority. Strathern's schema,

26 Luraghi 2013a, 18–20. Cf. Mitchell 2014, 1754 on a wider range of possibilities for sole rule in Greek thought.
27 Strathern 2019, 155–218; Moin – Strathern 2022, 1–30.
28 However, for the hazards of treating the transition from one Weberian type to another as an historical process, see Gotter 2008, 182–183.

from heroic to cosmic, and ultimately, to righteous kingship, is particularly useful for coming to grips with what comes after Weberian charisma fizzles out.[29]

Effectively, Strathern's heroic kingship draws its energy from the celerity of charisma-generating action. Heroic kingship, which resembles early Hellenistic kingship, depends on shocking, unprecedented, seemingly inhuman feats of achievement, especially in war. The heroic king has no interest in discourses of legitimacy, only status achieved through deeds. What matters is exposing the ruled to the 'revelation of the superlative individual', a king who in the manner of an amoral god transgresses the boundaries of social normativity and intervenes with arbitrary violence and wanton destruction in the lives of mortals.[30] In fact, early Hellenistic, ground-up ruler cult, may be seen as a "theologically sound" maneuver on the part of the ruled to tame, limit, or regularize the destructive interventions of god-kings into everyday life.[31] Yet heroic/charismatic kingship is fundamentally unstable and short-lived, falling into 'empirical jeopardy' just as soon as the ruler begins to lose battles.[32]

Whereas Weber emphasized the ruler's subsequent efforts to routinize charisma through ritual and bureaucracy – and therefore preserve it as the basis of authority – Strathern sees a successor to the heroic king in the rule of the "cosmic king", a much harder shift away from charisma and toward different, more durable sources of power. The cosmic king does not rule by dint of his unique personality, but by his ability to answer to the cognitive needs of the ruled. He is their bulwark against the supernatural forces of disorder, an intercessor, and a well-positioned cosmic pivot. The role garners him legitimacy, if performed correctly. However, correct performance requires abandoning many of the signature behaviors of the heroic king, trading in a disruptive focus on the display of deeds for the less visible, or at least less visually charged, more stylized work of symbolic ordering through ritual and the propitiation of unpredictable gods. In Hellenistic history, this would mean that at some point cosmic kingship was no longer isolated in Egypt, Babylon, or the overlooked former Hittite lands of Anatolia – where it also had deep roots – but spread throughout the eastern Mediterranean.[33]

---

29   On the usefulness of Strathern's work for historians of kingship and its relationship to the religious field, see Brack 2021.

30   Strathern 2019, 169.

31   Theologically sound, which means, not implying any insincerity of belief about the divinity of these kings. On the universal cognitive tendency to manipulate "metapersons", even in secular modernity, see Strathern 2019, 88. Here, I must disagree with Wiemer 2017, 337 on the less-than-sacred nature of Hellenistic ruler cult in the Greek city, on ruler cult as transactional in a specifically profane sense, politically contingent, and devoid of cosmic significance.

32   Strathern 2019, 69.

33   For Wiemer 2017, 337–338 cosmic kingship remained restricted to Egypt and Babylon. On the Hittite king as cosmic intercessor, see Beckman 1995, 530–531. As Strootman 2014 argues, *all* Hellenistic kingship was universal kingship, which placed kings at the center of the entire (civilized) world and indeed the cosmos. Yet Strootman 2014, 52 also notes: 'Expressions and images of the universalistic ideal varied'. To chart diachronic change in the representation of kingship, specifically, in

The cosmic king is an intimate of amoral gods and an advocate for the ruled in heaven. To discharge his duties of intercession, he can end up isolated from society, sometimes encased in ceremony. However, when he does interact with humanity, he treads lightly and respects norms. The second-century Attalids, for example, in their presentation of the Gigantomachy of the Great Altar of Pergamon, notably absented their own faces from the spectacle, while simultaneously fashioning themselves by means of this monument as the great stabilizers of the cycle of order and chaos.[34] If Andreas Scholl is right and the architectural ensemble of the Great Altar should be interpreted as the palatial hall of Zeus, these kings had even domesticated the Olympians by positioning the cosmic pivot within their own royal citadel.[35] Therefore, the concept of the cosmic king can help us understand the absence of Hellenistic royal images in certain media as potentially carrying meaning about the king's divinity, in addition to opening up space for local traditions and identities to express themselves.[36]

While the cosmic king can be strikingly absent, concealed from view, he also wants to be seen – especially when playing the role of coordinator between spheres. For example, such is the novel logic of Seleukos IV's otherwise oddly verbose and apologetic explanation of himself in a letter of 178 BC to an official named Heliodoros, which was first identified in a copy inscribed and displayed before a temple in the Idumean city of Maresha.[37] The first editors of the inscription, Hannah Cotton and Michael Wörrle, strongly emphasize the novelty of a royal rhetoric by which Seleukos IV forged 'a model to be followed by his successors', with his 'specific and remarkable formulation articulating the monarch's care for the welfare of his subjects, who at the same time distance themselves from his own rule and attend to their private affairs'.[38] Indeed, the letter parades before the public an image of the king performing acts of benevolent and providential coordination by way of placing a certain Olympiodoros in a supervisory role over sacred finance in the province of Koile Syria and Phoinike.[39] In other words, it is both a document of imperial administration, of Hellenistic kingdoms as 'bundles

terms of the relationship and responsibilities of the king to the rest of this world and the cosmos, is the goal of this paper.

34   Cf. Gotter 2013, 217–218, on the outer frieze of the Great Altar of Pergamon as a pretention to charismatic kingship. Such an interpretation is further weakened by studies such as Queyrel 2017 that call into question the Galatian allegory, endorsed, however, by Giovanna Pasquariello in this volume.

35   Scholl 2010.

36   Noteworthy too is the apparent absence of the Attalids from the Long Base from the sanctuary of Athena on the acropolis of Pergamon, for which see again Gotter 2013, 217–218, who nevertheless interprets the monument as advancing an unconvincing and historically revisionist claim to deeds-based charismatic kingship.

37   CIIP IV 2 no. 3511.

38   Cotton – Wörrle 2007, 196 with n. 28.

39   On Olympiodoros' title, either high priest (ἀρχιερεύς) or 'the one in charge of the sanctuaries' (ὁ ἐπὶ τῶν ἱερῶν), see Cotton-Paltiel – Ecker – Gera 2017, 2.

of institutions', and also a window on to the ideals of Hellenistic kingship.[40] The letter's lines 13–29 read:

Βασιλεὺς Σέλευκος Ἡλιοδώρωι τῶι ἀδελφῶι χαίρειν·| πλείστην πρόνοιαν ποιούμενοι περὶ τῆς τῶν ὑπο|[15] τεταγμένων ἀσφαλείας καὶ μέγιστον ἀγαθὸ[ν] | εἶναι νομίζοντες τοῖς πράγμασιν, ὅταν οἱ κατὰ | τὴν βασιλείαν ἀδεῶς τοὺς ἑαυτῶν βίους διοικῶ|σιν, καὶ συνθεωροῦντες, ὡς οὐθὲν δύναται μετα|λαμβάνειν τῆς καθηκούσης εὐδαιμονίας ἄνευ |[20] τῆς τῶν θεῶν εὐμ<ε>νείας, ἵνα μὲν τὰ καθιδρυ|μένα κατὰ τὰς ἄλλας σατραπείας ἱερὰ τὰς πατρίο[υς] | κομίζηται τιμὰς μετὰ τῆς ἁρμοζούσης θεραπ[είας], | [ἐ]ξ ἀρχῆς τυγχάνομεν τεταγμένοι, τῶν δὲ κ̣[ατὰ] [Κο]ἱ̣λ<η>ν Συρίαν καὶ Φοινίκην πραγμάτων οὐκ ἐχόντων |[25] [τὸν τα]σσόμενον πρὸς τῆι τούτων ἐπιμελείαι, κατε|[νοήσα]μεν ὅτι σωφρόνως προστήσεται τῆς εὐκοσ|μίας α[ὐ]τῶν Ὀλυμπιόδωρος, [τ]ὴν πίστιν ἡμῖν τῆς ὑπὲρ |αὐτοῦ διαλήψεως ἐκ τῶν προγεγονότων χρόνων | παρεισχημένος·

King Seleukos to Heliodoros his brother, greetings. We, taking the greatest care concerning the security of our subjects, and thinking it to be of the greatest good for our affairs when those who live throughout the kingdom lead their own lives without fear, and observing at the same time that nothing can partake of due good fortune without the favor of the gods, on the one hand we have prescribed from the beginning that the established sanctuaries throughout the other satrapies be provided with the ancestral honors with the proper service; and on the other hand, as the affairs in Koile Syria and Phoinike lack someone in charge for the care of such, we believed that Olympiodoros would prudently see to their proper conduct, for he has won our confidence in his judgement from times gone by.[41]

Seleukos IV casts the province of Koile Syria and Phoinike as out of sync with the other satrapies of the kingdom in terms of the management of human relations with the divine. This administrative reform at regional scale thus aims to correct a cosmic imbalance. It is important to note that the publication clause (Fragment E, lines 12–15) of the dossier provides for an identical letter to be inscribed in a conspicuous location in other sanctuaries. Recently, a second copy was discovered at Byblos, while a third, also now provenanced from Maresha – from a different temple than the first? – points to intensive canvassing of the message, with more than one shrine in a single settlement receiving a copy.[42] Naturally, the king shows off his own piety – an old trope; but he also displays a stunning new interest in the religious psychology of his subjects, who should live their lives without fear and under providence. Cotton and Wörrle heralded this document as a more authentic account of part of the backstory to the Makkabean Revolt than the tale of temple robbers and angels found in 2 Makkabees; but the king

---

40   The phrase is from Ma 2013, 335, discussed by Wiemer 2017, 318 in terms of divergent scholarly traditions, one focused on the kings, another on the kingdoms.

41   Trans. Cotton – Wörrle 2007.

42   Yon 2015; Cotton-Paltiel – Ecker – Gera 2017.

also offers his own 'partisan and dramatized perspective' by framing his interventions into the finances of many a local temple as a single project aiming to bring the province – and ultimately his entire realm – into cosmic equilibrium.[43] Michael J. Taylor has written of the episode as an act of 'administrative spoliation' and predatory revenue seeking, dressed up in soothing Seleukid 'administrative prose', and though to indigenous eyes, it surely counted as spoliation, we can also see it as a more banal withdrawal of costly concessions awarded to temple communities in the southern Levant by a victorious Antiochos III just two decades prior.[44] In any case, rhetorically, in order to sell the local priests and populace on higher taxes, Seleukos IV was actually heightening the emotional stakes by adding a cosmic dimension to a genre of interaction in which it was previously unknown.

A hypothesis of a shift from heroic to cosmic kingship that begins ca. 200 BC and reveals itself as an historical process in a variety of later Hellenistic documents and artifacts takes account for the way the two modes overlap in Strathern's model. That is to say, the emergence of cosmic kingship does not permanently eradicate heroic elements, which continually resurface, like the earlier portrait styles that make a comeback in both Ptolemaic and Seleukid portraiture of the second century BC.[45] However, we can offer a synthetic explanation for the new phenomena identified by epigraphers, such as the rhetoric of Seleukos IV, by numismatists, such as the visual strangeness of cistophoric coinage, and by legal historians, such as Hellenistic kings' sudden rush to begin swearing oaths with polis partners. Meanwhile, flashes of the heroic streak across the second-century evidence, the pose of the Terme Ruler, the royal portrait on the so-called pseudo-municipal coinages of Antiochos IV, or the transgressions, if they were that, of the vilified Attalos III with his unprecedented honors at Pergamon.[46] Yet none

43   Cotton – Wörrle 2007, 203.
44   Taylor 2014, 231; cf. Cotton-Paltiel – Ecker – Gera 2017, 12–14. On the fiscal reform of Seleukos IV, see now Girardin 2022, 162–168, underscoring that the king was *not* bankrupt, and thereby, removing what these other scholars imply was a motivation for norm-breaking behavior.
45   See both Ralf von den Hoff and Martin Kovacs in this volume.
46   For pseudo-municipal (also known as pseudo-autonomous) coinage of Antiochos IV, see SC 1441–1496 with Meyer 2020 and Katharina Martin in this volume. The behavior and self-presentation of Antiochos IV at the procession of Daphne in 166 is also an important datum, for which see Pol. 30.25–27. Brisson 2018, 426, 436–442 understands the event as the king's play for a Weberian recognition of his charisma, a 'politique de grandeur' that is at once both an agile reaction to the new Roman unipolarity, reinforced at Pydna, and also just 'tradition hellénistique'. However, as has been pointed out by Von Hesberg 1999 (esp. 69, 74), the king was quite simply not on stage in the case of Antiochos IV at Daphne in the way he was in the procession of Ptolemaios Philadelphos (Athen. 5.201d). Like the statue of Philip II placed among the Olympians at Aigai, royal portrait statues, including Ptolemaios II's, appeared alongside images of gods and personifications at Alexandreia. Meanwhile, at Daphne, where the immense quantity of images was too great to relate (τὸ δὲ τῶν ἀγαλμάτων πλῆθος οὐ δυνατὸν ἐξηγήσασθαι), royal portraits evidently did not appear in the pageant, which Polybios describes as an encyclopedic presentation of gods and heroes (30.25.13–15). Admittedly, Brisson 2018, 439 can point to an extraordinary gold coinage associated with the festival that bears the royal portrait with the inscription ΒΑΣΙΛΕΩΣ ΑΝΤΙΟΧΟΥ ΘΕΟΥ

of this invalidates the hypothesis of a shift away from heroic/charismatic kingship as a response to a crisis of authority, rather than as a crisis of kingship *per se*.

As an ideal type, the cosmic king disciplines the amoral gods, but no one disciplines him, for he is the embodiment of morality, law incarnate. In world history, it took the profoundest of changes, what is known as the Axial Age transformation of the first millennium BC, the passage from immanence to transcendence as the dominant form of religion, to create kingship with ethical discipline, i. e., the "righteous king."[47] The transcendentalism of the Axial Age disenchants kingship by opening up an "ontological breach" between this world and the beyond, relativizing the political arrangements of the present, and thereby stripping kingly power of its "just so" status. Now, kings no longer make divine law but conform to it; public opinion measures their morality according to an ethical canon of revealed truths. While the ideal type of the righteous king only arrives historically when Buddhism and monotheisms such as Christianity and Islam become imperial religions, the Greeks gave voice to the transcendentalist critique of kingship, as Lynette Mitchell has argued, from the very beginning of their literature.[48] For Mitchell, though, a pre-Hellenistic Greek king always saw his own *aretê* as justification enough for his rule, and Greek theorists were pessimistic about the possibility of a real-life monarch ever being constrained by transcendent law. Thus, despite all the philosophizing critique and the potency of the charge of tyranny, for the archaic and classical Greeks, both in practice and theory, kingship remained largely heroic/charismatic. Then, in Mitchell's view, Alexander and the Successors, with their iconoclastic claims to divinity, pushed the pendulum farther than ever before in the direction of the heroic mode; 'the question of how to rule in relation to law was repositioned, and the lines were redrawn'.[49] Indeed, we can see in the epiphanic figure of Demetrios Poliorketes at Athens a quintessential divinized king, one unconstrained by law or any transcendent canon of ethics.[50]

Yet the old critique never went away. In fact, during the Age of the Successors, it seems to have cast its shadow from a perch on the Panathenaic Way at the heart of the Agora: the 3 m-high, four-part monument of the Tyrannicides, both those of Kritios

ΕΠΙΦΑΝΟΥΣ ΝΙΚΗΦΟΡΟΥ. Note, though, that the epithet Nikephoros had been introduced at Antioch in 168 on silver tetradrachms that *removed* the royal portrait and replaced it with the image of Zeus (SC 1394, 1398). Further on Daphne, see now Strootman 2019, 192–195, casting the event as a Hellenistic New Year's Festival, which makes of the understated Antiochos patrolling the sidelines on his thin horse a veritable cosmic king. Finally, for Attalos III's unprecedented honors, see OGIS 332 with Chin 2018; and for a deconstruction of his infamy, see Daubner 2006, 13–17.

47 For the "righteous king," see Strathern 2019, 195–203; for immanence and transcendence, see conveniently Moin – Strathern 2022, 5–14.

48 Mitchell 2022; Strathern 2019, 83 emphasizes the intriguing 'proto-transcendentalism' of ancient Greek culture.

49 Mitchell 2022, 130.

50 Demetrios at Athens: Plut. Demetrios 2.4.3–4; Athen. 6.253b-f, an example cited by Gehrke 2013, 82, as well as Mitchell 2022, 130, as evidence of heroic/charismatic kingship. See also Michels 2017.

and Nesiotes and their antecedents, those of Antenor which were returned from Susa by either Alexander or Seleukos I and jointly reinstalled, thereby doubling a statue group that was (literally) an affront to heroic kingship.[51] Still, early Hellenistic kingship firmly resisted ethical discipline. Tellingly, the courtly genre of *peri basileias* ("On Kingship") treatises, which, at least as preserved, is a third-century phenomenon, had only discursive effects, shaping the communication between kings and cities and burnishing the image of rulers. As Matthias Haake has argued, these writings had no direct consequences for the practice of politics through the exercise of kingship.[52] By contrast, in the second century, the vision of the good king in Polybios seems to reflect the stronger ethical claims of broader public opinion – intimations, again, of righteous kingship in Greek history – and a demand for accountability, which kings began to answer to once they no longer had a choice.

3. Kingship under pressure

At the turn from the third to the second century, the Hellenistic kingdoms witnessed warfare on a scale unseen in a century. Yet the outburst of fighting did not result in a retrenchment of the old claims to kingship, since the old interstate system, as Arthur Eckstein has shown, had perished by 188 BC, taking with it key aspects of the diplomatic culture. In humbling the Macedonians in two wars, battling down Antiochos III in a third, and dividing up Seleukid cis-Tauric Asia among allies in the Settlement of Apameia, the Roman Republic had destroyed the old anarchic system and erected in its place a new unipolar system.[53] This unipolarity – under a non-royal power, note – was unstable in its own way. Ultimately, it was a transitional stage on the road to Roman hegemony, but in the short term, it dictated a modification of ideals of kingship and new patterns of interaction between kings and their subjects. In the 180s, this is evident in the correspondence of a small community in Phrygia Paroreios called Toriaion with the Attalid king Eumenes II, which discusses the town's upgrade to the status of polis. The remarkably strange lines 19 to 24 of Eumenes' first letter read:

ἐγὼ δὲ ἐθεώρουμ μὲν οὐκ εἰς μικρὰ | διαφέρον ἐμοὶ τὸ συνχωρῆσαι τὰ ἀξιούμενα, πρὸ[ς] με[ί]|ζονα δὲ καὶ πολλὰ πράγματα ἀνῆκον· καὶ γὰρ νῦν ὑμ[ῖν] |²⁰ γένοιτ᾿ ἂν βεβαία παρ᾿ ἐμοῦ δο[θ]εῖσα, ἐκτημένου κυρ[ί]|ως διὰ τὸ παρὰ τῶν κρατησάντων καὶ πολέμωι καὶ σ[υν]|θήκαις εἰληφέναι Ῥωμαίων, ἀλλ | οὐκ ἡ γραφεῖσα ὑπὸ | τῶν μὴ κυριευόντων· κενὴ γὰρ ἡ χάρις αὕτη καὶ δωρ[ε]|ὰ κρίνοιτ᾿ ἂν ὑπὸ πάντων ἀληθῶς· κτλ.

51   Stewart – Frischer – Abdelaziz 2022, esp. 339 for juxtaposition with the monument of the Eponymoi and its Antigonid portraits.
52   Haake 2013, esp. 185–87.
53   Eckstein 2012, 25–27.

For my part, I have observed that it is no small thing for me to consent to your demands, since it is directly related to many matters of great consequence. Indeed, now an unrequited gift would be yours securely if it is granted by me because I am the possessor (of the territory) with full authority since I have received it from the Romans who have prevailed both in war and in treaty; while that (*sc.* unrequited gift) granted by those who do not have full authority would not be; such an unrequited gift would truly be considered by all devoid of value, etc.[54]

As if the windy explanation were not strange enough, Eumenes invokes Roman authority – of his own accord. This now brings in a third party as the decisive partner in the interaction. The move has been viewed as a sign of insecurity and weakness, an incongruous bit of royal rhetoric addressed to a tiny, semi-Hellenized community in southeastern Phrygia.[55] However, in light of current research in the plain of Ilgın, the settlement profile of Toriaion remains to be determined. Therefore, we are in fact not in a position to evaluate the community's bargaining power, to define the limits of its leverage. Intensive archaeological study of the site of Kale Tepesi has now identified it as a fortified city of the early Hittite Empire, a Bronze Age monument and not a Hellenistic one. Its inclusion in the settlement profile of Toriaion is therefore hazardous.[56]

Irrespective of the actual balance of power between king and subject community, the expression that Eumenes used to justify the grant of territory to Toriaion was new and unparalleled as a strategy of legitimation in Hellenistic royal speech. The king claims to have received the territory with full, as it were, legal title, from the Romans, who themselves had in the first place had the authority to grant it to him because they had 'prevailed both in war and in treaty (τῶν κρατησάντων καὶ πολέμωι καὶ σ[υν]|θήκαις)'. This legal or quasi-legal framework was just as novel as the emphasis on a source of authority other than the king or his ancestors. As scholars such as Laurent Capdetrey and Lauro Boffo, followed recently by Ivana Savalli-Lestrade have argued, the Treaty of Apameia opened up cis-Tauric Asia as a "legal space", albeit a contentious one, especially for the losers of the new order, most notably, for Prusias I of Bithynia.[57] Thus alongside the time-honored appeal to the prerogative of the conqueror, a new way of justifying territorial rights in the Hellenistic world appears, one based on rational/legal authority, in Weber's terms, rather than the charismatic authority of the concept of "spear-won land" (χώρα δορίκτητος).[58] And the new concept proved to be no aberration. By the end of the century, it had achieved such currency that it appears in

54 Trans. based on both Jonnes – Ricl 1997 (ed. pr.) and also Savalli-Lestrade 2018, 172–173, using her new text, which includes readings of Georg Petzl.
55 Thonemann 2013, 6.
56 E. g., Paganini 2021, 35–36. See Johnson – Harmanşah 2015 on Kale Tepesi.
57 Savalli-Lestrade 2018, esp. 170–175; Capdetrey 2012; Boffo 2001. For Payen 2020, Anatolia gains coherence as a geopolitical space after Apameia.
58 Charismatic nature of concept of spear-won land: Gehrke 2013, 87 n. 16.

an inter-polis agreement without a royal partner, the arbitration of Magnesia on the Maiander for Hierapytna and Itanos on Krete of 112/111 BC. There, we find a four-fold typology of legitimate land ownership: 'People possess authoritative claims to terri-tory either because they inherited them, or they purchased them with money, or they won them by the spear, or they received them from those who won them so,' ([... ἄν] θρωποι τὰς κατὰ τῶν τόπων ἔχουσι κυριείας ἢ παρὰ προγόνων π[αραλαβόν]τες αὐτοὶ [ἢ πριάμενοι] [κατ'] ἀργυρίου δόσιν ἢ δόρατι κρατήσαντες ἢ παρά τινος τῶν κρεισσόν[ων σχόντες).[59] Remarkably, there is no hierarchy here, and conquest by the spear appears to be just one option among many for the legitimation of a claim. Perhaps, this four-fold typology of legitimate land ownership had long governed inter-polis arbitrations. Or, after nearly a century of diplomacy, an idea that was new to royal discourse at To-riaion in the 180s had trickled down and become normalized.

Eumenes was both reacting to and shaping the public's view of legitimate authority. From the beginning, he had acted as if authority that was not spear-won was neverthe-less perfectly legitimate. This is confirmed by his characterization of *charis* in a speech delivered to the Roman senate in 189 BC. The king contended that if the Romans were to liberate the cities of Asia Minor in response to the Rhodians' plea, the Greeks would not in fact be freed, but a debt of *charis* would actually place them under the dominion of Rhodos. 'For such is the nature of things (τὰ γὰρ πράγματα φύσιν ἔχει τοιαύτην)', he argued.[60] Almost immediately, we see the same king employing this new-fangled conception of *charis* at Toriaion – with the same normative force. According to the text of Savalli-Lestrade and Georg Petzl, what was conveyed to this polis by the king was *charis* itself, not land as such. The word at the end of line 23 and the beginning of line 24 is now read as δωρ[ε]||ά – a gift, paired with the adjacent χάρις in a hendi-adys – a "concession gracieuse," which I have translated as "unrequited gift" in order to skirt the Christian overtones of "grace gift," while still signaling the non-reciprocal quality of the transaction. Both of these terms ring of the old Hellenistic kingship, of gift estates for courtiers (*doreai*) and of a specifically royal version of *charis* as a con-cession of incommensurate value, granted by an unencumbered authority rooted in one's own victory in war or that of one's ancestors. This is what Antiochos III had told the Romans at Lysimacheia after explaining that the kingdom of Lysimachos belonged to him because it had been spear-won by Seleukos I: 'It was proper that the cities of Asia be autonomous by virtue of his *charis*, not by an order (*epitagê*) of the Romans' (τὰς δ' αὐτονόμους τῶν κατὰ τὴν Ἀσίαν πόλεων οὐ διὰ τῆς Ῥωμαίων ἐπιταγῆς δέον εἶναι τυγχάνειν τῆς ἐλευθερίας, ἀλλὰ διὰ τῆς αὐτοῦ χάριτος).[61] What could be a greater sign of a shift in the ideology of kingship than the Attalid gift of *charis* proffered to a city in cis-Tauric Asia under precisely the rational/legal authority rejected a few years earlier

59   I.Cret. III iv *9, ll. 133–134; for this interpretation, see Savalli-Lestrade 2018, 171.
60   Pol. 21.19.10.
61   Pol. 18.51.9.

by the Seleukid king at the conference of Lysimacheia in 196?[62] What we see at Toriaion is a redefinition of royal *charis* that was a swift and agile response to the collapse of the old interstate system. In our terms, this also marks indelibly a turn away from charismatic kingship.

A redefinition of kingship around ideals of cosmic order and ethical discipline reflects pressure from below as well as above. For many contemporary observers, kingship in the heroic/charismatic mode must have seemed anachronistic. Two examples from Hellenistic Jewish literature point in this direction. In the *Letter of Aristeas*, we seem to possess a second-century witness to Alexandrian Jewish perspectives on monarchy. The final sections of the *Letter* are the so-called Symposia, which narrate seven consecutive nights of banqueting (187–300). This is a highly literary account of a supposed meeting between 72 Jewish elders and king Ptolemaios II – early in the Hellenistic period, on narrative chronology – in the context of the pivotal translation of the Hebrew Bible into Greek. The character "Aristeas", as presented in the text, poses as a Gentile member of the court of Ptolemaios II. In truth, the author of the narrative was a Jewish Alexandrian, who seems to have lived in the second half of the second century BC.[63] In other words, the author lived after the momentous transformation of Ptolemaic state and society relations that took place ca. 220–160 BC, a response to a crisis of foreign invasion, civil war, and increasing Roman pressure.[64] Naturally, the historical context of the author will have colored his vision of the world of the early Ptolemies. He himself was living in a world in which Ptolemaic kings had turned their attention away from the Aegean and toward the social and economic integration of multi-ethnic Egypt. It was a world in which Hellenistic kingship had evolved – had been forced to adapt to new circumstances. He was not living in the world of Ptolemaios Philadelphos, of whom Theokritos had sung in his famous encomium: 'All the sea, every land, and each of the sounding rivers acknowledges his dominion' (θάλασσα δὲ πᾶσα καὶ αἶα καὶ ποταμοὶ κελάδοντες ἀνάσσονται Πτολεμαίῳ).[65] He was living in a world in which rulers could no longer count on their own subjects' recognition of charismatic authority, let alone credibly claim such acknowledgment from rivers and islands.

Indeed, a lack of recognition of that hoary claim to universal dominion is implicit in one of the questions posed in the imagined symposion. The possibility of interminable conquest is broached when the fictional Ptolemaios II asks his Jewish interlocutor, 'How he [the king] could be invincible (ἀήττητος) in military affairs?' (Πῶς ὢν ἐν ταῖς πολεμικαῖς χρείαις ἀήττητος εἴη;).[66] The answer is, as Jonathan More notes in an analysis

---

62   See Boffo 2001, 234–236, cited by Savalli-Lestrade 2015, 170 n. 47.
63   For this date, see Wright 2015, 21–30 with endorsement of Honigman 2019, 223. For slightly earlier date, ca. 160 BC, see Fraser 1972, v. 1, 696.
64   Fischer-Bovet 2014, esp. 7.
65   Theokr. 17.92.3. Cf. Kall. epigr. 4.166–170.
66   [Ps.-]Aristeas 193.

of kingship ideology in the *Letter* – from an early Hellenistic standpoint – quite counter-cultural: the king can achieve invincibility by *not* trusting in his own military might, but rather by trusting in God. On the one hand, this is essentially a Jewish answer, which echoes much earlier biblical texts like Psalm 20:8 (Ps. 19 [70].8), but also the *Temple Scroll* of the Dead Sea Scrolls.[67] However, that attribute of invincibility (*aêttêsia*) does not appear in the Septuagint, while it does appear in Greek philosophical texts from Platon to the Stoics.[68] Further, the logic of genre and literary strategy dictate that this particular question, namely, "How could the king be invincible," derives from the *realia* of life at the court of a second-century Hellenistic king. It may be that, as Gunther Zuntz writes: 'Never was an answer like this given by a Greek adviser to a Greek king.'[69] However, the question was evidently a standard one – at that time – and perhaps part of the broader discussion and debate on the utopian *politeia* that best fit ideals of Greek *paideia* in multi-ethnic Alexandreia. Sylvie Honigman has argued that the author explicitly rejected the generic style of 'brachyology', a quick give-and-take language which reeked of archaic Greek popular wisdom, in favor of an ultra-modern philosophical style.[70] Is it possible that in the process of updating the Symposium to his present, the author of the *Letter* introduced an anachronism? Would a question about the mere possibility of invincibility – let alone an answer, by a genuine or would-be literary courtier, which suggested a royal comportment of non-aggression and negotiation – have ever appeared in, for example, a treatise on kingship of the early Hellenistic Age?

Another hint of a transition away from the charisma of perpetual military victory is contained within the apocalyptic prophecies of the late Biblical book of Daniel. It presents the testimony of a subject of a Hellenistic kingdom (usually thought to be Seleukid), ca. 165 BC. From one angle, the author of Daniel defines kingship as a zero-sum proposition. The tale is set in the Neo-Babylonian period, and when Nebuchadnezzar finally accepts the fact that the god of Daniel is the only true king, he is then deemed fit to receive absolute power on earth. On the other hand, the author seems to describe different types of kings, each associated with different stages in world history. Significantly, the kings of the actual time of the text's composition are described as distinctly weak. The author presents four successive kingdoms: the Babylonian (gold), the Median (silver), the Persian (bronze), and the Greek (iron). This fourth, "Greek" kingdom is first defined as iron – the iron of Alexander the Great, which 'crushes and smashes everything' that preceded it.[71] However, Alexander's iron kingdom degenerates into a mixture of mere clay and iron, an alloy which is structurally unsound and

---

67   More 2009, 313–315.
68   Plat. Mx. 243d; rep. 375b; Zen. fr. 157 (Pearson). The attribute also turns up in the works of two
       second-century Greek historians: Pol. 15.5.3; Agatharchides De Mari Erythraeo 1.17.
69   Zuntz 1959, 23.
70   Honigman 2019, 14.
71   Dan 2.40–44.

'will not hold together', despite the dynastic marriages of the Ptolemies and Seleukids, which are alluded to in the text. This contrast between Alexander and his successors is repeated in the more detailed vision of Hellenistic history prophesied at the end of the book.[72] There, Alexander is a "warrior king", who possesses sovereignty (משל; κυριεία in 11.3) – who can 'take action as he pleases', according to his will (כרצונו). That particular form of sovereignty and that unrestrained, in Biblical terms, God-like freedom of action, the prophet seems to argue, did not outlive the Macedonian conqueror. Not only was Alexander's kingdom broken into pieces because he had no heir, but sovereignty (משל/κυριεία) itself was not bequeathed. The eschatology of the vision does not allow for the contemporary kings of the author's actual historical context to ever return to the unqualified state of power that earlier generations of monarchs had enjoyed.[73]

For the evil, so-called "little horn" of the prophecy, Antiochos IV, a more serious humbling is said to be in store. This is the famous verse 11.30: 'For ships of/from (?) Kittim shall come against him.' The verb *wnk'h* is frequently translated 'discouraged' or 'checked' – but the author and the Ptolemaic (?) subjects who translated the verse into the Septuagint seem to have understood the event in even starker terms. The event from the Sixth Syrian War is usually taken to be the Day of Eleusis, the confrontation of Antiochos with the Roman legate Popilius Laenas.[74] In a revisionist account of the historical context, Benjamin Scolnic and Thomas Davis have pointed out the much stronger force of the verb *nkh* in other Biblical texts such as Psalms 109:16 and Hiob 30:6–8. Its meaning is closer to 'chased to death and stricken from the earth' than merely 'checked'.[75] Thus, the Septuagint resorts here to an exegetical translation: 'chased out and rebuked him', (ἐξώσουσιν αὐτὸν καὶ ἐμβριμήσονται αὐτῷ). In other words, the text documents a severe humbling of the king with which the contemporary readership was keenly familiar. This was not a prophetic fantasy of resistance to empire, but rather an interpretation of contemporary events as an unraveling of kingship.

4. Kingship ethicized

One may object that the evidence gathered from Toriaion and these Jewish sources is poor testimony of a general downshift from heroic to non-heroic kingship, of a global Hellenistic withdrawal of the recognition of charisma, particularly when such evidence is weighed against the persistence of charismatic representations of kingship. Assuming we understand it correctly, how far can we extrapolate from the case of Toriaion? Many scholars have adduced the case of Toriaion to explicate the birth of Anti-

72   Dan 11.2–4.
73   On the bygone charisma of Alexander in the vision of Daniel, see Köhler 2020, 159–161.
74   For the numerous sources for the event, see Gera 1998, 172 n. 171.
75   Scolnic – Davis 2015, 316–317.

ocheia-in-Jerusalem, while Robert Parker, on the other hand, has pointed out that the
epigraphical dossier from southeastern Phrygia in fact shows no sign of the adoption
of Greek religion by the Toriaitoi, who may well have also taken a pass on Hellenic
sacred kingship.[76] For their part, the alterity of the Jewish authors is generally evident
in their ideological commitment to the demonstration of the singular and absolute
sovereignty of a heavenly royal power in the physical world. Thus, to guard against the
danger of extrapolating too widely from peripheral or sectarian views, we can juxta-
pose these texts with monarchic discourse in Polybios. We know that Polybios was not
dogmatically anti-monarchy, despite his relationship to the Roman Republic and the
Achaian Koinon. This was the conclusion of the foundational study of Karl-Wilhelm
Welwei, which Arthur Eckstein and Boris Dreyer have since elaborated.[77] In addition,
Polybios turns out to be, as Dreyer has cogently argued, a reliable source for popular
views about monarchy in the second century, some of which coincide nicely with ob-
servable shifts in the representation and exercise of kingship.[78]

Indeed, the perspective of a wider Hellenistic public shines through when we compare Polybios with a second-century Jewish source on the same events. A trenchant
example is public awareness of the kings' payment of war reparations to Rome, conceived of as tribute (*phoros*), which is central to the Polybian theodicy of the downfalls
of Antiochos III and Philip V. Both kings, the historian gloats, were justly rewarded
for a specifically lawless (*paranomos*) way of lusting after the Ptolemaic kingdom with
the loss of their own sovereignty and payment of tribute to Rome.[79] Did a broader
(literate) public, including local elites and sub-elites, have knowledge of such war reparations and interpret them as a degradation of royal sovereignty? A strong indication
in favor of this view is the mention of the penalty at 1 Makk 1.8. The rebel leader Judas
hears of the Seleukid indemnity (ca. 160s), then weighs it as a factor in favor of a Roman alliance. The author of 1 Makkabees, writing in Hebrew for a local Judean audience, publicized the information, perhaps ca. 110 BC or during the preceding two decades. Daniel Schwartz has noted the anonymous author's 'evident lack of familiarity
with the Hellenistic world', but such a detail of international diplomacy was apparently
well-known.[80] By then, the indemnity had ceased. Still, the damage to the image of the
dynasty could not be undone.

The testimony of Polybios is critical because the historian shines a bright light on
the behavior and comportment of many a king, particularly when writing their obitu-
aries.[81] Only then, Polybios thought, was it possible to carefully distill the truth about

76   On Toriaion and Jerusalem, see Berthelot 2021, 370 n. 128 with references. Religious life of the
     settlement unaffected by its new status: Parker 2017, 213.
77   Welwei 1963; Eckstein 1985.
78   Dreyer 2013.
79   Pol. 15.20.6–7.
80   Schwartz 2022, 8, also on date of composition.
81   On these "death notices", see Pomeroy 1986.

their character by reconciling all the facts.[82] For example, Hieron II only *appeared* dissolute, but his longevity indicates a stoic restraint of his passions. In the act of dying, the interpretation of a king's life becomes clear: the impious Antiochos IV dies in an attempted temple-robbing, while the virtuous Massinissa savors his last meal of a filthy crust of bread on the battlefield.[83] Polybios is also rigorously comparative in his evaluation of kings: Eumenes II was his generation's greatest benefactor of Greek cities, while Pharnakes I was the most lawless king ever.[84] Fascinatingly, the standard of judgement for Polybios and his cast of characters is often set by previous generations of rulers, as when, for instance, the Argeads become a foil for the Antigonids. An explicit comparison between earlier and later Hellenistic kingship would have made good sense to an observer who summed up the heroic achievements of the generation of the Successors, writing: 'It is unnecessary to mention anyone by name. And after the death of Alexander, when they disputed the empire of the greater part of the world, they left a record so glorious in numerous histories (…)'.[85]

Polybios also studied and thought deeply about concepts of kingship, most famously in his account of the cycle of constitutional forms (*anakyklosis*) in Book 6, with its eclectic mix of earlier Platonic thought and contemporary Stoic ideas.[86] For him, the political community as such is born into primitive monarchy, just as soon as the biological *anakyklosis* begins. Further, in a passage of prehistory, Polybios claims that basic notions of human morality – the very consciousness of goodness (*to kalon*) and fairness (*to dikaion*) – first come into existence alongside the institution of "true", i. e., consensual kingship, in which subjects are ruled voluntarily. The preservation of this form of kingship (*basileia*) comes to depend on the emergence in the archaic political community of a specific moral sensibility, which is the ability to ethicize the ruler and his descendants.[87] Therefore, Polybios, who spent much of his career managing royal relationships, believed wholeheartedly in both the necessity and efficacy of frank talk with kings.[88] Good counsel can arrest or delay the cycle of decay, prevent Hellenic kingship from turning into barbaric tyranny – an idea at least as old as Greek literature.[89] Accordingly, if a king were only rational enough to accept feedback, cognizant of the axiomatic fact that the self-interested choice for a king *is* to act ethically – as Aratos

---

82 Cf. Polybios' criticism of Theopompos on this score (8.11–13).
83 Pol. 31.9; 36.16.12.
84 Pol. 32.8.6; 27.17.
85 Pol. 8.10.11–12: οὐδὲν ἂν δέοι μνημονεύειν ἐπ' ὀνόματος. μετὰ δὲ τὸν Ἀλεξάνδρου θάνατον οὕτω περὶ τῶν πλείστων μερῶν τῆς οἰκουμένης ἀμφισβητήσαντες παραδόσιμον ἐποίησαν τὴν ἑαυτῶν δόξαν ἐν πλείστοις ὑπομνήμασιν …
86 On the philosophical influences on the *anakyklosis*, see Walbank 1957, 643–648.
87 Pol. 6.7.1–2.
88 Such is the implication of the historian's editorial comment about the fitting, albeit inopportune candor (*parrhêsia*) of the young Roman ambassador who confronted Queen Teuta (Pol. 2.8.10).
89 Mitchell 2022, 119–125. On Hellenic kingship in Polybios, see further Nicholson 2020.

counsels the young Philip V in an episode veiled with tragic irony – then perhaps he could cheat Tyche and avoid the destruction of his monarchy, a teleological eventuality which Polybios had of course witnessed in the case of Antigonid Macedonia and set down as the terminus of his work according to its original plan.[90] Polybios, in other words, seems to see ethical discipline as a survival strategy for any king or dynasty in the new Mediterranean of Roman hegemony.

Two key planks of the Polybian ideal of ethical discipline, laid out for the monarch who would survive Rome, exist in tension. One the one hand, the king is asked to carefully withdraw from or conceal himself in contexts open to earlier Hellenistic monarchs to enter and exit as they pleased. On the other hand, he is asked to coordinate among smaller polities and cultic communities, and therefore interact with civic actors and local institutions to a far greater extent than ever before. Paradoxically, with his very gentleness (*praotês*), the king nurtures and becomes further enmeshed with traditional authority. Hellenistic royal pageantry need not cease entirely, but the good king treads lightly even if he refuses to renounce the limelight altogether, like Antiochos IV tracking (*paratrexô*) the procession at Daphne on what Polybios deems a cheap pony.[91] Certainly, this king avoids the arbitrary violence and transgression of norms associated with heroic/charismatic kingship.[92] Ptolemaios VI, for example, is gentle (*praos*) and good (*chrêstos*), more so, Polybios believes, than any of the earlier Ptolemies, the greatest proof being the fact that the king never executed an Alexandrian citizen, neither courtier nor commoner.[93] In short, his inaction and lack of notoriety are now his glory.

In 200 BC, Attalos I modeled this do-nothing behavior in paradigmatic fashion at Athens.[94] According to Polybios, the war-panicked Athenians were almost embarrassingly busy, throwing open their temple doors and organizing processions. He describes the reception and escort of the king from Peiraieus to town as a singular and spectacular event. However, it appears that Polybios misunderstood the norms of the Athenian protocol of *apantêsis*, mischaracterized certain honors as unprecedented, and simply retailed stereotypes of royal pageantry.[95] Yet in Polybios' telling, these ex-

---

90   Aratos counsels Philip that what is royal and what is self-interested are one in the same: καὶ γὰρ βασιλικὸν εἶναι τὸ τοιοῦτο καὶ πρὸς πᾶν συμφέρον (Pol. 4.85.6). The destruction of the Macedonian kingdom is placed as the final event in original plan of the work at Pol. 3.3.8. The work is haunted by the specter of kingship destroyed by *katalusis*, the most momentous form of constitutional collapse in Polybios' world. Cf. Philip's melancholy meditation on the dissolution of the Spartan diarchy in his speech to his sons (Pol. 23.11.5); or the historian's characterization of the Day of Eleusis as a narrowly averted Ptolemaic disappearance (Pol. 29.27.13).

91   Pol. 30.26.4.

92   Pol. 26.1.7: '... some looking upon him as a plain simple man and others as a madman ...' (... οἱ μὲν γὰρ ἀφελῆ τινα αὐτὸν εἶναι ὑπελάμβανον, οἱ δὲ μαινόμενον ...); Loeb trans.

93   Pol. 39.7.4.

94   Pol. 16.25–26.

95   Perrin-Saminadayar 2004. Regarding precedent for the honors, see comment by Christian Habicht in Loeb ed. v. 5, p. 66 n. 60.

aggerations of Athenian servility before royal power only serve to accentuate the merit of Attalos. Upon arrival, the Athenians request the king's presence at the assembly. The latter, however, 'begged to be excused, saying that it would be bad taste (*phortikon*) on his part to appear in person'.[96] The subtle gesture reveals his virtue and is not at all ironic. Attalos successfully avoids the burdensome intrusion of *to phortikon* among the Athenians. For Polybios, Attalos is the exemplar of the king who reads the room, comprehends and respects civic norms even when they are being flouted by others, and conceals himself, thereby winning renown by staying pat at just the right time.

Both the performance and ultimately the inversion of the ideal are on full display in Polybios' presentation of Philip V, who possesses outsized traits, both good and bad.[97] Indeed, the peak of the arc of Philip's career – and reputation – are explicitly linked to an act of non-violent coordination. At this moment, the Greek public is "in love" with Philip on account of his euergetic disposition.[98] Royal euergetism, in this case, is not gift-giving. Polybios employs a single vignette to explain how it affectively attaches the public to the king, 'a most conspicuous and striking example of the value of honorable principles and good faith' (*pistis*).[99] This was Philip's greatest moment: a bloodless co-ordination between Kretan cities that resulted in an unprecedented alliance on the restive island.[100] Conceptually, it seems that we have returned to an ideal of pre-Alexander fourth-century kings, the monarch as coordinator, perhaps not capable of producing a Common Peace, but no longer operating under the heroic/charismatic mandate of endless warfare. However, what actually happens, as Polybios resumes his narrative, is that Philip descends directly from this acme toward the ethical nadir of the siege of Messene, where he destroys his own *pistis* with norm-breaking and violent, impious behavior. In the end, Philip was his own foil.

---

96 Pol. 16.26.2: παραιτουμένου δὲ καὶ φάσκοντος εἶναι φορτικὸν τὸ κατὰ πρόσωπον εἰσελθόντα (…).

97 Pol. 10.26.7: Philip is said to have surpassed all of his predecessors in both good and bad qualities.

98 Pol. 7.11.8: 'In fact, as a whole, if one may use a somewhat extravagant phrase, one might say most aptly of Philip that he was the darling of the whole of Greece owing to his beneficent policy.' (καθόλου γε μήν, εἰ δεῖ μικρὸν ὑπερβολικώτερον εἰπεῖν, οἰκειότατ᾽ ἂν οἶμαι περὶ Φιλίππου τοῦτο ῥηθῆναι, διότι κοινός τις οἷον ἐρώμενος ἐγένετο τῶν Ἑλλήνων διὰ τὸ τῆς αἱρέσεως εὐεργετικόν); Loeb trans.

99 Pol. 7.11.8–9: 'A most conspicuous and striking proof of the value of honorable principles and good faith is that all the Cretans united and entering into one confederacy elected Philip president of the whole island, this being accomplished without any appeal to arms or violence, a thing of which it would be difficult to find a previous instance.' (καθόλου γε μήν, εἰ δεῖ μικρὸν ὑπερβολικώτερον εἰπεῖν, οἰκειότατ᾽ ἂν οἶμαι περὶ Φιλίππου τοῦτο ῥηθῆναι, διότι κοινός τις οἷον ἐρώμενος ἐγένετο τῶν Ἑλλήνων διὰ τὸ τῆς αἱρέσεως εὐεργετικόν. ἐκφανέστατον δὲ καὶ μέγιστον δεῖγμα περὶ τοῦ τί δύναται προαίρεσις καλοκἀγαθικὴ καὶ πίστις, τὸ πάντας Κρηταιεῖς συμφρονήσαντας καὶ τῆς αὐτῆς μετασχόντας συμμαχίας ἕνα προστάτην ἑλέσθαι τῆς νήσου Φίλιππον, καὶ ταῦτα συντελεσθῆναι χωρὶς ὅπλων καὶ κινδύνων, ὃ πρότερον οὐ ῥᾳδίως ἂν εὕροι τις γεγονός); Loeb trans.

100 What is significant here is the ideal. The fact that the historian may have exaggerated the peace on Krete is thus of no consequence. As the new Loeb eds. point out, doubts have been expressed about Polybios' characterization of the military situation by Chaniotis 1996, 441 n. 76.

Polybios later shows us the same king's inversion of the ideal of concealment during Philip's sojourn in Argos.[101] The Macedonian's behavior contrasts markedly with that of Attalos I at Athens. Like Attalos, Philip aims to conceal himself – but fails utterly. Here, a disapproving Polybios lays the irony on thickly. For all his efforts, Philip does not achieve his goal of appearing the unobtrusive political equal of the Argives, even though he manages to get elected as agonothete of the Nemean Games.[102] He even changes his clothes to appear democratic, but his monarchic character shines through all the more. What is particularly striking is the way that an otherwise banal negative character trait of lust is cast as a violation of civic norms and an impious invasion of both public and private space. When one of the Argive women refuses Philip's advances, she – or, worse, her husband – receives a summons from the king that is likened to a royal edict (*prostagma*). And if that fails to convince, the king shows up at their private residence, clogging up the streets and polluting the soundscape with a merry if also menacing band of revelers, a fake version of the rite of *kômos*. In a similarly botched attempt at concealment, Philip reveals his moral bankruptcy and fickleness (*athesia*) when he partners with his kinsman Prusias I to destroy the Propontic city of Kios.[103] The event was a trauma that seems to have become a watchword for the monarchic enslavement of a Greek city.[104] According to Polybios, Philip himself was blind to the obvious (*prophanon*) fact of his own disgrace and found himself exposed when the ugly news reached the Rhodian prytaneion just as his envoys were declaiming about the king's magnanimity. In Polybios' account of Philip's villainy, the king is exposed precisely where he aims to be concealed.

Thus, even by castigating a monarch for an ironical breach of norms, Polybios presents an ethical ideal. In practical politics, such a standard must have provided succor to kings who lived in a world in which monarchy was under renewed ideological assault. This is brought out in the historian's description of the debate in the council of the Achaian League in 185 BC. First, Apollonidas of Sikyon asserts that monarchy and democracy are two 'warring forces of nature' (*enantiai physeis*), and that 'most of our debates and the most important deal with our differences with the kings'.[105] Then, Polybios implicitly undermines that argument by narrating the very next order of League business: the entry of Achaian representatives who announce the swearing of an oath

---

101   Pol. 10.26.
102   Liv. 27.30.9; 17.
103   Pol. 15.22.
104   According to Pol. 15.22.3, Philip earned at Kios, 'a legacy of infamy throughout the whole of Greece as a violator of all that was sacred' (κληρονομήσειν παρὰ πᾶσι τοῖς Ἕλλησι τὴν ἐπ᾽ ἀσεβείᾳ δόξαν). Further on the Panhellenic significance of this event, see Nicholson 2020, 58.
105   Pol. 22.8.6: τῶν δὲ πραγμάτων ἐναντίαν φύσιν ἐχόντων τοῖς βασιλεῦσι καὶ ταῖς δημοκρατίαις, καὶ τῶν πλείστων καὶ μεγίστων διαβουλίων ἀεὶ γινομένων <περὶ τῶν> πρὸς τοὺς βασιλεῖς ἡμῖν διαφερόντων (...).

of alliance by Ptolemaios V.[106] In an increasingly hostile climate, a Hellenistic king now needed to signal that he was accountable, and the customary oath was a key tool in this regard. Public opinion mattered and was up for grabs. The stakes were perhaps highest during the hammering out of the Apameian settlement in the Senate in 189. There, the Rhodian delegation presented arguments, which also appear in Livy and seem to derive from official Roman documents, that Greek freedom and monarchy in cis-Tauric Asia were fundamentally incompatible – arguments, which were apparently well received.[107] Obviously, the Attalids and their partisans disagreed, and somehow, won the day.

In a certain sense, kings in Polybios are just normal people, virtuous or not. They may conform to an ethical standard, or flout it. The historian must have believed in the possibility of ethical discipline, as he warned against the courtier who would negatively influence royal behavior.[108] Kings, though, were accountable like anyone else for amoral behavior. For example, Antiochos III and Philip V invited Tyche to punish them for their attempt on the kingdom of Ptolemaios V, then a minor.[109] On the other hand, for Polybios, the true king has a specific nature, which is only perceptible through his actions. Certainly, these might be heroic, shock-and-awe deeds of the spear, such as those of the *anabasis* of Antiochos III, which, Polybios famously writes, made him appear worthy of kingship to the inhabitants of Asia and Europe.[110] However, the revelation of a kingly nature was now more likely to be a subtle and moderate expression – a sense of *sophrosyne* – a greatness of spirit (*megalopsychia*) and benevolent action (*euergesia*) taken on behalf of subjects and humankind (*philanthropia*).[111] Theoretically, such was the restraint of the ideal monarch that Polybios views the "natural king" as nearly indistinguishable from his subjects.[112] Yet in practice, the good king cuts a figure like Hieron II already in Book 1, who rules placidly under the Roman umbrella.[113] Such a king gains the title by his own effort – of which military victory plays a part, but he must also – in Weber's terms – routinize and institutionalize charisma with socially responsible

---

106 Pol. 22.9.9.

107 Pol. 21.22; cf. Livy 37.54. See Dreyer 2013, 239 n. 31 and Dreyer 2007, 332–333 on underlying sources.

108 E. g., Pol. 9.23: The influence of the courtier is seen as a powerful camouflage that obscures the king's true nature. Cf. 28.21: Ptolemaios VI is able to overcome the influence of a bad courtier in the context of the 6th Syrian War.

109 Pol. 15.20. On divine punishment of these kings for their amoral behavior, see Dreyer 2013, 236–237.

110 Pol. 11.34.16: διὰ γὰρ ταύτης τῆς στρατείας ἄξιος ἐφάνη τῆς βασιλείας οὐ μόνον τοῖς κατὰ τὴν Ἀσίαν, ἀλλὰ καὶ τοῖς κατὰ τὴν Εὐρώπην. See also the account of the same king's campaign in Baktria (10.49), with comments of Wiemer 2017, 312–313.

111 Eckstein 1985, 267. See Pol. 5.90.5–8 for grumbling about the small-scale giving (*mikrodosia*) of contemporary kings, as compared to earlier kings. However, the Attalid case suggests that the *frequency* of giving over time had increased by Polybios' day, for which see Kaye 2022, 37.

112 Pol. 6.7.

113 Pol.1.16.10: ἀδεῶς ἐβασίλευε. As Eckstein 1985, 269 notes, this seems to be Polybios' perspective on Hieron II, not that of Fabius Pictor.

gifting, busying himself with the physical security of his people and their borders, and securing a peaceful succession.

Yet because Polybios trained his eye to look for the moral failing that catalyzed the destruction of a man's kingship, and *post eventum*, saw each man's life as a totalizing expression of his character, the historian perhaps underestimated the extent to which kings were in fact striving to conform to an ethical standard – now chastised by voices like his. This is suggested by the randomized documentary record of epigraphy, which represents a useful check on the literary distortions of Polybios. Apparently, the idea of Hellenic kingship as righteous kingship was back in vogue. This is one way to explain the sharp increase in kings' use of the so-called customary oath (*nomimos horkos*) in interstate agreements.[114] As noted, Polybios mentions the oath of Ptolemaios V sworn with the Achaians, but he omits a raft of other instances, including those sworn by those kings he depicts as characteristically lawless. There is almost no epigraphic evidence for an early Hellenistic king personally swearing such an oath. The sole exception is a fragmentary text from Ilion that may relate to an agreement between Antiochos II and Lysimacheia.[115] Dynasts such as Eumenes I or satraps like Eupolemos may swear in first-person, but those who don the diadem, like Ptolemaios II in the Chremonides Decree, seem to avoid it.[116] Then, precisely when Polybios would have us believe that Philip V had become incapable of renouncing arbitrary violence, building consensus, and acquiring the public's trust again, the Antigonid swore an oath at Lysimacheia in 202 BC – publicly displayed in Dion and maybe even epitomized on a gold tablet held in a royal treasury.[117] Also, Pharnakes I, who for Polybios was the most lawless king ever, swore one with Tauric Chersonessos in 180/79.[118] So too did Attalos I at Lato and Mallos, ca. 200 BC; and Antiochos III at Perinthos (ca. 196) and Lysimacheia (190s). R. M. Errington has even suggested that this Seleukid is the third-party lurking in the fragmentary agreement of alliance between Arykanda and Tragalassos, struck ca. 200–189 BC.[119] We know that this tool was available to early Hellenistic kings, as it had been employed in the late Classical period, not by the larger-than-life Achaimenid kings, but by the Argeads. Yet Alexander and the Successors, like the Homeric lords they emulated, simply had no use for the institution.[120] It only reemerged ca. 200 BC with

---

114   On this term, see references of Cook 2022, 213 n. 23.

115   IK 3 Ilion 45b. See commentary of StV 721 for suggestion of Antiochos II in the fragment.

116   Eumenes I: OGIS 266. Eupolemos swears with Theangela in StV 429. In Chremonides' decree (StV 476), note, the idiosyncratic Spartan kings *do* swear, but Ptolemaios II does not.

117   StV 549; for tablet, see Cook 2022.

118   For context, see Errington 2014.

119   StV 608, 609, 615, 620, 649, and 721. See further the literary sources, StV 637 and 671; and the mid-second century case of the Anatolian tyrant Moagetes, 668a.

120   On kings as partners to interstate oaths, see Sommerstein and Bayliss 2013, 175–179, with p. 148 on the origin of the institution in the Archaic period and the absence of such oaths in the Homeric world.

the turn away from heroic/charismatic kingship, when public commitment to norms and accountability resurfaced as an aspect of royal style.

5. Traditional authority renewed

To return to Strathern's schema: in the end, a pre-Christian, proto-transcendentalist Greek political philosophy could only chasten kings. Late Hellenistic kings may have been ethicized, but they were still not righteous. Instead, monarchs adapted to the loss of face before Roman hegemony by strengthening coordination with traditional authorities, especially those at the helm of cities and other civic organisms, as well as temple communities. For Boris Dreyer and François Gerardin, this was the peak in deal-making with local elites that characterized both the Ptolemaic and Seleukid kingdoms in the decades after ca. 200 BC, plainly explicable as a response to Roman pressure.[121] The king now acquired greater control over the lives and symbols of his subjects, while also removing himself from view in ways that a modern historian is bound to find perplexing.[122] Inevitably, from a Weberian perspective, the devolution of agency if not also real power on to traditional authorities meant that charisma now ceded way to its old antagonist: tradition.

The Seleukid southern Levant after the conquest of Antiochos III in 198 BC provides us with a clear-cut case of the elevation of traditional authorities. In a decades-long process, spanning the reigns of Antiochos III, Seleukos IV, and Antiochos IV, the new regime traded out the centralized administrative apparatus of the Ptolemies for one that relied heavily on cities, temples, local elites, and priests. A multidisciplinary team of scholars has illuminated this process in a 2017 study, which charts both immediate changes, such as those evidenced in the Charter of Jerusalem, as well as delayed ones, such as the decoupling of the roles of governor and provincial high priest after the death of the holdover figure Ptolemaios son of Thraseas.[123] Already under Antiochos III, we see the first-ever attempt to integrate the Jerusalem temple and *gerousia* into a royal apparatus. For the second-century Seleukids, entrenched local power holders such as the Jerusalemite priesthood collected taxes; for the third-century Ptolemies, it had been tax farmers who answered directly to the regime. Further, excavation in Samaria suggests that the priestly administration on Mount Gerizim found itself in a similar position. There, the Ptolemies had thoroughly neglected the Persian-period precinct, while the Seleukids transformed it: 700 coins of Antiochos III have been recovered in exca-

---

121 Dreyer – Gerardin 2021.
122 Fischer-Bovet – von Reden 2021b, 5 define "Period B," ca. 220–160 BC, as marked by important reforms that led to tighter royal control of territory in both the Ptolemaic and Seleukid kingdoms.
123 Charter of Jerusalem: Ios. ant. Iud. 13.138–144. For what follows, see Ecker – Finkielsztejn – Gorre – Honigman – Syon 2017, esp. 173–175, 181–182.

vation, along with 400 Aramaic votive inscriptions said to date to the first half of the second century. Under Seleukos IV, the local temples seem to have taken on an even larger administrative role, such is the main message of the aforementioned Heliodoros decree and the associated episode in 2 Makk 4.1–6. Perhaps, only the form rather than the measure of domination had changed since Ptolemaic relations with temples in Egypt of the third century suggest a conscious decision to circumvent the Judean and Samarian ones. Yet in addition to administrative efficiency, if not also greater revenues, this new way of running an empire produced ideological gains: it allowed the king to assume the posture of the guardian of cosmic order, who coordinated between the priestly sphere, the heavenly, and the profane. That the Hasmoneans later depicted him as the disruptor of cosmic order in their memorialization of the Makkabean Revolt does not change the fact that the king had been aiming for just the opposite.[124]

In the wider Levant, with its native city-state culture, the nesting of royal administrative structures within civic ones was also very much a means of leveraging traditional authority – even when this resulted in a jarring linguistic switch into documentary Greek, as in the ostraka from Maresha.[125] Under Antiochos IV, in particular, cities of the region, some now re-founded, were afforded enhanced administrative roles in the form of a collaborative regulation and sanctioning of economic life. Besides the introduction of pseudo-municipal coinages, Antiochos was responsible for a penetrating reorganization of weights and measures, while his overhaul of market surveillance (*agoranomia*) carried forward the reform of Seleukos IV, who had introduced the office.[126] For the first time, we now find official weights from Koile Syria and Phoinikia bearing both a Seleukid regnal year and the name of the local *agoranomos*. On these sacred objects, the two authorities were shown as co-guarantors of justice and order in the transactional sphere of everyday commerce.

For its part, the Greek polis, exhibits aspects of Weberian traditional authority, since 'rules which in fact are innovations can be legitimized only by the claim that they have been 'valid of yore'', or consistent with the "constitution of our fathers (*patrion politeia*)", etc.'[127] Consequently, as a storehouse of traditional authority, the polis was an administrative and ideological resource for a Hellenistic king scrambling to find his footing. For instance, in the years after Apameia, an Attalid general named Korragos was honored by a Hellespontine city for the following services of mediation with Eumenes II:

---

124 For this ancient Near Eastern trope in the definition of power, shared by both the Seleukids and the Judean rebels, see Honigman – Veïsse 2021, 316–318.
125 Ecker – Finkielsztejn – Gorre – Honigman – Syon 2017, 188–191.
126 Finkielsztejn 2020, 298–299; 2 Makk 3.4, for *agoranomos* under Seleukos IV.
127 Weber 1978, 227.

ὑπό τε τὴν παράληψιν τῆς πόλεως | ἠξίωσεν τὸν βασιλέα ἀποδοθῆναι τούς τε ν[ό]|¹⁰μους καὶ
τὴν πάτριον πολιτείαν καὶ τὰ ἱερὰ τεμέ|νη καὶ τὸ εἰς τὰ ἱερὰ καὶ πόλεως διοίκησιν ἀργύριον
καὶ | τὸ τοῖς νέοις ἔλαιον καὶ τὰ ἄλλα ἅπερ ἐξ ἀρχῆς ὑπῆ[ρ]|χεν τῶι δήμῳ

... when he took over the city he requested from the king the restoration of our laws, the
ancestral constitution, the sacred precincts, the funds for cult expenses and the administration of the city, the oil for the young men (*neoi*) and everything else which originally
belonged to the People ...[128]

Could the citizenry of the Korragos Decree have come to imagine monarchy as a cosmic institution and not just a political fact?[129] Indeed, the case of the Attalids and the
cities of cis-Tauric Asia suggests that the concept of cosmic kingship holds heuristic
value beyond those parts of the Hellenistic world that belonged to the ancient Near
East. On the one hand, the late kings of Pergamon seem to have retreated, devolving
power on to local civic institutions, both those of the Greek poleis, but also, and to a
greater extent than has been recognized, those belonging to non-polis civic organisms
in the Anatolian countryside. While certain Seleukid administrative structures were
retained, over time, a radical decentralization occurred marked by three practices.
The first was budgetary earmarking, the habit of leaving important portions of taxes
in the hands of civic officials, designating them for basic functions of civic life. The
second was an unprecedented royal investment in the gymnasion, an institution which
the Attalids succeeded in transforming into what Louis Robert named the "second
agora".[130] The third was the creation of a decentralized monetary system based around
the *cistophoros*, an "iconoclastic" coin, which neither mentions the king nor shows his
face.[131] On the other hand, however, the king now held a lien against the deployment of
communal symbols, the production of collective memory, and even communication
with ancestral gods. When a king such as Eumenes II, in the Korragos decree, assumed
perennial responsibility for 'the funds for cult expenses and the administration of the
city, the oil for the young men' (*neoi*), was he not also taking guardianship of the most
essential elements of social order, not to mention, the means of bringing them into
cosmic alignment with the divine?

---

128 I.Prusa 1001, ll. 8–13.
129 Wiemer 2017, 337: 'Für die Bürger griechischer Städte war die Monarchie keine kosmische Institu-
     tion, sondern ein politisches Faktum.'
130 Robert, OMS II, 812–814, esp. 814 n. 3; VI, 422–423.
131 For new evidence telling in favor the low date of ca. 166 BC for the introduction of the *cistophoros*,
     as well as discussion of the high date of shortly before 190, see Meadows 2020. However, Eumenes
     II did issue silver tetradrachms bearing his portrait, for which see Marcellesi 2012, 123. Yet with only
     two examples extant – one, in Paris, with a probable findspot outside of the Attalid kingdom – the
     visual impact of Eumenes' portrait coinage upon his subjects will not have been comparable to that
     of the cistophori.

6. The great disappearance

A final adaptation to consider is a change in coin design of which the *cistophoros* is only the most well-known exemplar. In scholarship, the debate over that coin's categorization as "royal" or "civic" has run its course.[132] The point to underscore is that the king had now removed his face from the visual field and disguised the imperialism. In the background, the monarchy was stepping up its coordination of an entire monetary system, but in the foreground, the king had now ceded the visual field to local, traditional authorities, whose symbols and collective identities began to appear on ever greater volumes of coinage. For example, a cistophoric tetradrachm of Tralles (fig. 1) carries on its reverse the civic emblem of the zebu, known from coins that the city minted under its dynastic name Seleukeia, as well as its post-Attalid coinage.[133] The legend on the obverse can be resolved as an ethnic Τρα[λλιανῶν] "of the Tralleans." Yet noticeably lacking is a portrait of the king or one of his ancestors. This marks a clear turn away from the royal pageantry that Andrew Stewart identifies as a key feature of Hellenistic art, and it is a development that flies in the face of claims that kings garnered legitimacy by remaining omnipresent before their subjects via the mass medium of coinage.[134] Quite the opposite – in the course of the second century, rulers responded to a crisis of legitimacy by adapting the medium of coinage to register their absence.

It is important to notice that this change in coin design occurred in kingdoms with different political economies and therefore testifies to a broader shift in the representation of monarchy. In other words, it allows coinage – usually deployed as documentary evidence for the 'Soziologie der Imperien' – to offer a comment on the 'Soziologie der Herrschaft'.[135]

---

132   For history of scholarship, see Kleiner – Noe 1977, 10. Two attempts to create new terminology: Thonemann 2015, 77–80 employs the term 'pseudo-federal coinage'; Kaye 2022, 173–177 prefers 'coordinated coinage', placing the accent on the interleaving of royal and civic administrative structures.

133   For the zebu on the coinage of Tralles, see Ashton – Kinns – Meadows 2014, 18.

134   Stewart 2014, 7; Wiemer 2017, 335–336: 'Omnipräsent war allein das Bild des Königs auf seinen Münzen'.

135   On this distinction, see Wiemer 2017, 332.

Fig. 1 Cistophoros of Tralles (12.67g), serpent with cista mystica/serpents with gorytos type. Legend: Τρα[λλιανῶν]; the zebu is a civic symbol of the polis of Tralles, Attalid period, post-167 BC.

Fig. 2 Silver tetradrachm of the "autonomous" Amphaxians (16.93g), Macedonian shield/club within an oak wreath type, ca. 187–167 BC.

Fig. 3 Silver hemidrachm of the "autonomous" Macedonians (1.91g), nymph/prow type (Kremydi Series I), ca. 220–197 BC.

Fig. 4 Reduced Aiginetan silver hemidrachm of Histiaia (1.94g), maenad/nymph with stylis
seated on ship's stern, 3rd and 2nd centuries BC.

Fig. 5 Silver tetradrachm of the First Macedonian Meris (16.86 g), Artemis Tauropolos/club
within an oak wreath type, Roman Macedonia, post-168 BC.

Fig. 6 Silver didrachm of the First Macedonian Meris (7.83g), Macedonian shield/club
within an oak wreath type, ca. 187–179 BC.

Fig. 7 Silver tetradrachm of King Amyntas of Galatia (15.85g), Athena/Nike, ca. 37–36 BC.

Recently, Sophia Kremydi has invoked the cistophori as a key point of comparison for the so-called autonomous coinages of the late Antigonids (fig. 2). These are silver coins, overwhelmingly fractional denominations, which were minted on regional standards. Thus, the late Antigonids also issued coins for internal use that bore neither the effigy nor the name of the king under whose authority they were minted. Kremydi has identified a strong visual parallel between the contemporary Antigonid and Attalid coinages, but it is only when she seeks to reconstruct the administrative relationships underlying the minting of these coins – the elusive power dynamics between royal and civic or regional authorities – that the comparison seems to break down.[136] Yet in the Attalid case, we simply have no independent document for the administrative relationship between the cities or citizenries evoked on the cistophori and the royal apparatus. That relationship seems to have been *sui generis*. Was the Antigonid case any less unique? It bears recalling that the *Makedones*, i. e., the *ethnos* that deliberated in a national assembly and is represented on the majority of these coins, was just as much as the king, a constituent part of the state.[137] Further, as a monarchical and loosely integrated ethnic-federal state, the Antigonid kingdom preserved earlier ethnic structures such as those that show up on two smaller issues of these coins. These are the Botteatai, the people in the plain around Pella, and the Amphaxians, the people between the Axios and the Strymon river. Already under royal rule, their territories became administra-

---

136 For Kremydi 2018, 42, the cistophori are 'anonymous, but royal'. See, further, 250: 'Antigonid autonomous coinages relate both to the unique character of the Antigonid Macedonian monarchy, but also to federal coinages of mainland Greece, with which they were meant to be exchangeable according to common weight standard.' Katharina Martin, in her contribution to this volume, confronts the same problem in differentiating the "quasi-munizipale" coinage mintued under Antiochos IV from the "pseudo-städtische" coinage minted under Mithradates VI.

137 Hatzopoulos 1996, v. 1, 491. On Argead and Antigonid representations of the relationship of the king to the *Makedones*, see Mari 2020, 202–210, emphasizing the enduring visibility of this political community. Note also that τὸ ἔθνος τὸ Μακεδόνων has now appeared twice in civic decrees from the growing *asylia* dossier from Kos (243/242), for which see Bosnakis – Hallof 2020, 297.

tive districts (*merides*) and minting authorities.[138] In addition, Antigonid Macedonia contained cities with strong civic identities and institutions such as Thessalonike, Amphipolis, and Pella. Ultimately, these diverse administrative structures were essential components of a new monetary system, while these regional and civic identities were expressed on the coins themselves. However, no more here than in the Pergamene case did the singular political economy of a kingdom dictate the absence of the king from the visual field.

Nevertheless, in both cases, royal coordination is discernible.[139] For example, the Antigonid coins share mintmarks with silver coins of royal type that seem to proliferate from at least the earlier part of the reign of Philp V, if not the reign of Antigonos Doson, ca. 224 BC. It has also been suggested that the naval Series I (fig. 3) and II could be linked to payments for the construction and maintenance of Philip V's fleet. Crucially, the mintmarks seem to show that Antigonid control over this coinage only increased through the reign of Philip's successor, Perseus.[140] Coincident with a change in coin design that was decreasing the king's imprint on the visual field was another process: the administrative role of royal bureaucracy in minting and the interleaving of royal and civic structures were increasing.

To meet his monetary needs, whether the subsides of Doson's symmachy or Philip's navy, an Antigonid was forced to choose in the late third century between minting fractional silver that bore his own name and likeness – or some other type. Admittedly, the larger denomination silver coinage of the late Antigonids does evince classic charisma, returning to the practice of Demetrios Poliorketes. Earlier, Antigonos Gonatas, with his Pan and Poseidon-type tetradrachms, had generally placed his name, but not his face on the coin; though once the god put on a diadem, we can consider the image to be a pseudo-portrait.[141] Since the Pan and Poseidon tetradrachms in the name of Gonatas were quite small issues, the need for at least fractional silver earlier in the third century may have been met by lingering drachms minted in the name of Alexander the Great.[142] The final Antigonids, then, might have resuscitated those familiar types

---

138   Kremydi-Sicilianou 2007 demonstrated that the *merides* predated Roman rule; now endorsed by Panagopoulou 2020, 334.
139   For the Attalids, see Kaye 2022, 138–140, 149–152.
140   Kremydi 2018, 188 (table 2b), 211–214, 383. This revises Hugo Gaebler's view that the so-called autonomous coinages represent the weakening of the central state under the last Antigonids.
141   For chronology, see Panagopoulou 2020, 286–303. The legend 'of King Antigonos' appears early on in the reign of Gonatas on his silver coinage with types of Alexander III; on the Pan/Athena types from the 260s, and on the Poseidon types from the late 240s, both continuing to the end of Doson's reign. For pseudo-portrait of Gonatas as Pan, see 107–109, 147 with n. 26; on early Antigonid portraits, see Ralf von den Hoff in this volume.
142   On the mismatch between the small amount of silver minted in the king's name and the Antigonid budget, see Panagopoulou 2020, 328–329.

and burnished the Argead connection.[143] Instead, local markets were flooded with these "autonomous" types – especially, it seems, after the Battle of Kynoskephalai – coins that bear generic Macedonian icons, the shield and the helmet, the nymph and the ship's prow. And unlike proper royal silver, these coins were issued on a reduced weight standard. Their circulation was therefore confined to Macedonia itself and neighboring territories. The audience for these images was comprised of royal subjects. Yet they saw – and read – themselves on these coins, not the kings. While the Antigonids may not have been ceding autonomy, as was once thought, they were ceding the visual field and a very powerful medium for the dissemination of images across ancient society.

To get a sense of the scale of the shift, it is also worth considering as a form of Antigonid money a fractional silver coinage minted in the name of the polis of Histiaia on the island of Euboia (fig. 4). In fact, François de Callataÿ has argued adamantly that these understudied silver fractions were used to meet the enormous military expenses of combatants in the Third Macedonian War.[144] The coinage is far too large and its circulation far too wide for any medium-sized polis of the late third and second centuries BC. In addition, numerous references to the coinage are made in the Delian inventories of the sanctuary of Apollon.[145] Curiously, the city of Histiaia, though subjected to the Antigonids down to 196, appears to have provided royal moneyers with the inspiration for the autonomous Series 1 with nymph/stern types.[146] As the weight of these reduced Aiginetan hemidrachms was quite close to those of the Macedonian fractional silver, a user could easily have mistaken them for each other. In fact, the large size of the Histiaian coinage has led to suspicion that it was minted by or for Perseus, or for the Romans, to make payments in the Third Macedonian War. Considering that Perseus has also been suspected of minting pseudo-Rhodian coins, the turn away from monarchical self-representation at the end of the dynasty appears even more pronounced.[147]

Late Hellenistic Greece and Asia Minor were awash in proxy coinage. The pseudo-civic bronze issues of Mithradates VI appear to have been massive.[148] The Romans waged campaigns, built provinces, and even after Pompey's reorganization, until the late first century BC, continued to pay their expenses in local coinage. The Romans minted by proxy, but the size of the issues and other clues have allowed numismatists,

---

143 Cf. the Alexander III types of the large, long-running bronze issues in the name of "King Antigonos" that circulated throughout southern Greece in the third century, described by Panagopoulou 2020, 356–358.
144 De Callataÿ 2016, 325 n. 58.
145 E. g., IDélos 442 and 443.
146 Kremydi, 2018, 215.
147 On weight standard and more generally on Histiaian silver: Kremydi 2018, 225–230. Perseus and pseudo-Rhodian drachms: Ashton 1998, 226.
148 However, just how massive they were remains to be determined. See Tekin 1999, 106 for the suggestion of an original die count in the tens of thousands, which is considered improbable by De Callataÿ 2011a, 463. As Katharina Martin notes in this volume, these coins lack both the image and the name of the king.

especially de Callataÿ, to track Roman military expenditure in Greece and the northern Balkans through die counts.[149] Moreover, Lucia Carbone, has recently written of what she calls the "hidden power" of Rome, exercised from the start in the province of Asia through tight control of the production of post-Attalid cistophori.[150] In minting proxy coinage, Roman administrators had borrowed the role and not just the coin type from the Pergamene kings: they were now the coordinating force of the monetary system, and the allusion of the visual absence pointed toward them. Similarly, the First Macedonian *Meris* coinage minted in gobs for the Romans had a royal precedent, which can be dated to the reign of Philip V (figs. 5 and 6).[151] Among the Antigonids, the practice seems to pick up significantly after 187 with the launching of Philip's reforms. Among the Attalids, it is also important to realize that the cistophori are just one half of the story. Die counts compel us to see the Attalid treasury as the source for the silver bullion of the prolific Wreathed Coinages, minted in the names of cities.[152] In sum, in the eastern Mediterranean from ca. 150 BC, the corpus of royal images and the king's share in the finite number of anthropomorphic images that a person saw in a lifetime were rapidly diminishing.[153] This was a reversal of the trend in the third century, when a monarch such as Ptolemaios III managed his Achaian and Spartan alliances by flooding the Peloponnese with his own image in the form of a desperately needed large-module bronze coinage.[154] The change happened by design, and not because of a Roman suppression of those images, such that by ca. 37/36 BC, a new king like Amyntas of Galatia, though he owed his power to Antonius, seems to follow his royal peers by absenting his face and even employing an imitative civic type of Side (fig. 7).[155] If kings willingly ceded part of the visual field of the coin, one of the only mass media of Antiquity, an explanation is in order. Numismatists of late have tended

---

149   De Callataÿ 2011b.

150   Carbone 2020.

151   Kremydi-Sicilianou 2007; Kremydi-Sicilianou 2009, 197, for post-168 date of *Meris* tetradrachms with monogram HP (illustrated here as fig. 5); Kremydi 2011, 175–176; endorsed by Panagopoulou 2020, 334; cf. Juhel 2011.

152   Martin, this volume fig. 24–25.

153   For this interpretation of the Wreathed Coinages, see de Callataÿ 2013, 229–236. Consider also the wider perspective of the same study's table 6.13 (p. 241). There, de Callataÿ quantifies a large, but not exhaustive selection of the major silver coinages in this period. In ca. 150 BC, the wreathed coinages and the cistophori together made up 37 % of what entered circulation each year, a significant and deliberate reduction of the proportion of royal images in the public domain, which the Attalids themselves were carrying out.

154   See Cavagna 2017, 275–288. This coinage (Svor. 1000; CPE B408) appears to have met an acute need for bronze at this weight in the later third-century Peloponnese. It is almost unique at this denomination for a period of time and was an important part of the money supply of the entire peninsula. Importantly, it was a coinage that Ptolemaic authorities minted exclusively for the Peloponnese, purposively parading the king's image before a large swathe of the Greek public.

155   Roman suppression: Crawford 1985, 132; tentatively endorsed by de Callataÿ 2016, 331. Amyntas: BMC Galatia, Amyntas 1–16.

to see this as a pragmatic choice, a sign of insouciance about the relationship between political autonomy and the authority to mint. Yet it corresponds to a broader shift in Hellenistic kingship, the transition from charismatic/heroic kingship to a style of rule that showcased partnerships with traditional authorities while purposively absenting the ruler from the picture.

7. Conclusion

This account of the evolution of Hellenistic kingship has aimed to spring these monarchs from the methodological trap of charisma. Scholarship of the charisma school has shown us "same, but *not* different." It has shown us kings who are locked into endless war, trapped by an ideal, and barreling toward self-destruction like Weber's beloved berserkers.[156] The concept is supposed to have been a dead end for them. Has it not also become one for us, too? Nevertheless, it was suggested that Weber offers a way to describe a set of changes in both imperial governance and the representation of Hellenistic kingship: the ascendance of traditional authorities in the wake of the collapse of charisma. One way to slip loose of Weber's ghost is to borrow from the comparativist project of Strathern and a team of scholars investigating sacred kingship in premodern world history. Usefully, historical anthropology offers us ideal types such as heroic kingship, which respond to Weber's legacy, while also providing a schema for historical change. Indeed, the goal here was to recover both the agency of the kings and to delineate the contours of a specifically *late* Hellenistic kingship. In the cosmic mode, kings become 'meeting points … conduits, pivots, cruxes.'[157] The transgressions of the heroic/charismatic mode are replaced by acts of coordination between different spheres, human and divine. These functions require a certain distance from society and an absence from the field of vision. Later, transcendentalist religion provides the righteous king with a sense of ethical discipline that is equally foreign to the charismatic hero. While cosmic models were available in the Near East and ethical models in proto-transcendentalist Greece, Hellenistic kings of the third century could afford to deploy or reject this inheritance at will. The toolkit was always available. For example, Laure Marest has shown with Hellenistic sealings that kings could absent their faces entirely from their own seals, but also construct power and agency at second hand with a distribution of portrait-bearing seals within a social network.[158]

The critical period of change seems to have begun ca. 200 BC when the victorious Romans began to transform the geopolitical system of the Hellenistic world. The top-

---

156 Haley 1980, 196: 'Distinct motifs of unrestraint, frenzy, and disregard for inherited commands are added in the Weberian conception.'
157 Strathern 2019, 174.
158 Marest 2021.

down perspective of Toriaion and the bottom-up view of second-century Jewish literature indicate that charismatic kingship was untenable and indeed undesirable once unipolarity had arrived by way of the Settlement of Apameia. By mid-century, something had changed such that Polybios could describe the unmartial death of Attalos I in 197 in Thebes as glorious – a crippling stroke that arrived while the king was speaking at length in the assembly.[159] Such a death could only have been deemed glorious once Hellenistic kingship had come to rely so heavily on the traditional authority of temples, cities, leagues, and other civic organisms, not only as a partner in governance, but also as a source of legitimacy. Thus, the interleaving of what we call "royal" and "civic" institutions increased, but we also find more mixing of symbolic repertoires and a broader visual field for the expression of sub-royal collective identities. The Roman victories of 197, 189, and 167 fundamentally altered the relationship of kings to their own subjects. Hellenistic monarchy adapted by transitioning on the fly toward non-charismatic forms of legitimate domination that stand in need of study. This can only sharpen our understanding of the paradigmatic changes in the history of monarchy that bookend the Hellenistic period. As Weber mused, 'To have established the principate as an office was the achievement of Augustus, whose reform appeared to contemporaries as the preservation and restoration of Roman tradition and liberty, in contrast to the notion of a Hellenistic monarchy that was probably on Caesar's mind'.[160] Indeed, only by defining this late-breaking iteration of our subject can we properly approach the problem of Roman contact.

Bibliography

Ashton 1998: Ashton, Richard, The Pseudo-Rhodian Drachms of Kos, The Numismatic Chronicle 158, 1998, 223–228

Ashton – Kinns – Meadows 2014: Ashton, Richard – Kinns, Philip – Meadows, Andrew, Opuscula Anatolica IV, The Numismatic Chronicle 174, 2014, 1–27

Beckman 1995: Beckman, Gary, Royal Ideology and State Administration in Hittite Anatolia, in: J. M. Sasson (ed.), Civilizations of the Ancient Near East, New York 1995, 529–543

Boffo 2001: Boffo, Laura, Lo statuto di terre, insediamenti e persone nell'Anatolia ellenistica. Documenti recenti e problemi antichi, Dike 4, 2001, 233–255

Bosnakis – Hallof 2020: Bosnakis, Dimitris – Hallof, Klaus, Alte und neue Inschriften aus Kos VI, Chiron 50, 2020, 287–326

Brack 2021: Brack, David, Rev. of: Strathern 2019, Journal of Early Modern History 25, 2021, 573–583

Brisson 2018: Brisson, Pierre-Luc, Antiochos IV et les festivités de Daphnè: Aspects de la politique séleucide sous l'unipolarité romaine, Revue des Études Grecques 131, 2018, 415–449

159 Pol. 18.17.6, 18.41.9; Liv. 33.2, 33.21.1, based on Polybios, for which see Pomeroy 1988, 175.
160 Weber 1978, 1125.

Capdetrey 2012: Capdetrey, Laurent, Droit de la force ou force du droit ? Paradigme juridique et sujétion des cités en Asie Mineure à la haute époque hellénistique, in: C. Feyel (ed.), Communautés locales et pouvoir central dans l'Orient hellénistique et romain, Nancy 2012, 31–64

Carbone 2020: Carbone, Lucia F., Hidden Power: Late Cistophoric Production and the Organization of the *Provincia Asia* (128–89 BC), New York 2020

Cavagna 2017: Cavagna, Alessandro, Le monete di Tolemeo III nel Peloponneso: circolazione monetaria, tipologia e strutture ponderali, Annuario della Scuola Archeologica Italiana di Atene 95, 2017, 273–287

Chaniotis 1996: Chaniotis, Angelos, Die Verträge zwischen kretischen Poleis in der hellenistischen Zeit, Stuttgart 1996

Chaniotis 2018: Chaniotis, Angelos, Age of Conquests: The Greek World from Alexander to Hadrian, Cambridge, MA 2018

Chin 2018: Chin, Marcus Jia Hao, *OGIS* 332 and Civic Authority at Pergamon in the Reign of Attalos III, Zeitschrift für Papyrologie und Epigraphik 208, 2018, 121–137

Chrubasik 2016: Chrubasik, Boris, Kings and Usurpers in the Seleukid Empire: The Men who would be King, Oxford 2016

Cojocaru – Schuler 2014: Cojocaru, Victor – Schuler, Christof (eds.), Die Außenbeziehungen pontischer und kleinasiatischer Städte in hellenistischer und römischer Zeit: Akten einer deutsch-rumänischen Tagung in Constanța, 20.–24. September 2010, Stuttgart 2014

Cook 2022: Cook, Brad L., Philip V and Lysimacheia: An Oath in Gold, Greek, Roman, and Byzantine Studies 62, 2022, 203–238

Cotton – Wörrle 2007: Cotton, Hannah M. – Wörrle, Michael, Seleukos IV to Heliodoros: A New Dossier of Royal Correspondence from Israel, Zeitschrift für Papyrologie und Epigraphik 159, 2007, 191–205

Cotton-Paltiel – Ecker – Gera 2017: Cotton-Paltiel, Hannah M. – Ecker, Avner – Gera, Dov, Juxtaposing Literary and Documentary Evidence: A New Copy of the So-Called Heliodoros Stele and the Corpus Inscriptionum Iudaeae/Palaestinae (CIIP), Bulletin of the Institute of Classical Studies 60.1, 2017, 1–15

Crawford 1985: Crawford, Michael H., Coinage and Money under the Roman Republic: Italy and the Mediterranean Economy, Berkeley 1985

Daubner 2006: Daubner, Frank, Bellum Asiaticum: Der Krieg der Römer gegen Aristonikos von Pergamon und die Einrichtung der Provinz Asia, Munich 2006

de Callataÿ 2011a: de Callataÿ, François, Productions et circulations monétaires dans le Pont, la Paphlagonie et la Bithynie: deux horizons différents (Ve–Ier s. av. J.-C.), in: T. Faucher – M.-C. Marcellesi – O. Picard (eds.), Nomisma: la circulation monétaire dans le monde grec antique, Athens 2011, 455–482

de Callataÿ 2011b: de Callataÿ, François, More Than it Would Seem: The Use of Coinage by the Romans in Late Hellenistic Asia Minor (133–63 BC), American Journal of Numismatics 23, 2011, 55–86

de Callataÿ 2013: de Callataÿ, François, The Coinages of the Attalids and their Neighbours: A Quantified Overview, in: P. Thonemann (ed.), Attalid Asia Minor: Money, International Relations, and the State, Oxford 2013, 207–244

de Callataÿ 2016: de Callataÿ, François, The Coinages Struck for the Romans in Hellenistic Greece: A Quantified Overview (mid 2nd-mid 1st c. BCE), Nomismata 9, 2016, 315–338

Djurslev 2021: Djurslev, Christian T., Rev. of: Trampedach – Meeus 2020, Bryn Mawr Classical Review 10.11.2021 (https://bmcr.brynmawr.edu/2021/2021.11.10/) last access 20.5.2024

Dreyer 2007: Dreyer, Boris, Die römische Nobilitätsherrschaft und Antiochos III. (205 bis 188 v. Chr.), Hennef 2007

Dreyer 2013: Dreyer, Boris, Polybios und die hellenistischen Monarchien, in: V. Grieb – C. Koehn (eds.), Polybios und seine Historien, Stuttgart 2013, 233–249

Dreyer – Gerardin 2021: Dreyer, Boris – Gerardin, François, Antiochus III, Ptolemy IV and Local Elites: Deal-Making Politics at its Peak, in: Fischer-Bovet – von Reden 2021a, 262–300

Ecker – Finkielsztejn – Gorre – Honigman – Syon 2017: Ecker, Avner – Finkielsztejn, Gérald – Gorre, Gilles – Honigman, Sylvie – Syon, Danny, The Southern Levant in Antiochos III's Time: Between Continuity and Immediate or Delayed Changes, in: C. Feyel – L. Graslin-Thomé (eds.), Antiochos III et l'Orient: Journées d'études franco-allemandes, Nancy 6–8 juin 2016, Paris 2017, 161–207

Eckstein 2009: Eckstein, Arthur M., Hellenistic Monarchy in Theory and Practice, in: R. K. Balot (ed.), A Companion to Greek and Roman Political Thought, Malden 2009, 247–265

Eckstein 2012: Eckstein, Arthur M., Rome Enters the Greek East: From Anarchy to Hierarchy in the Hellenistic Mediterranean, Malden 2012

Errington 2014: Errington, Robert M., Rom und das Schwarze Meer im 2. Jh. v. Chr., in: Cojocaru – Schuler 2014, 37–44

Finkielsztejn 2020: Finkielsztejn, Gérald, The City Organization in the Seleucid Southern Levant: Some Archeological Evidence and Prospects, in: Oetjen 2020, 296–311

Fischer-Bovet 2014: Fischer-Bovet, Christelle, Army and Society in Ptolemaic Egypt, Cambridge 2014

Fischer-Bovet – von Reden 2021a: Fischer-Bovet, Christelle – von Reden, Sitta (eds.), Comparing the Ptolemaic and Seleucid Empires. Integration, Communication, and Resistance, Cambridge 2021a

Fischer-Bovet – von Reden 2021b: Fischer-Bovet, Christelle – von Reden, Sitta, Introduction, in: Fischer-Bovet – von Reden 2021a, 1–14

Fraser 1972: Fraser, Peter M., Ptolemaic Alexandria, 3 vols., Oxford 1972

Gauthier 1985: Gauthier, Philippe, Les cités grecques et leurs bienfaiteurs, Paris 1985

Gehrke 2013: Gehrke, Hans-Joachim, The Victorious King: Reflections on the Hellenistic Monarchy, in: Luraghi 2013b, 207–230

Gera 1998: Gera, Dov, Judaea and Mediterranean Politics, 219 to 161 B. C. E., Leiden 1998

Girardin 2022: Girardin, Michaël, L'offrande et le tribut: Histoire politique de la fiscalité en Judée hellénistique et romaine (200 a. C.-135 p. C.), Bordeaux 2022

Gotter 2008: Gotter, Ulrich, Die Nemesis des Allgemeingültigen: Max Webers Charisma-Konzept und die antiken Monarchien, in: P. Rychterova et al. (eds.), Das Charisma. Funktionen und symbolische Repräsentationen, Berlin 2008, 173–186

Gotter 2013: Gotter, Ulrich, The Castrated King, or: The Everyday Monstrosity of Late Hellenistic Kingship, in: Luraghi 2013b, 207–230

Gray 2017: Gray, Benjamin, Reconciliation in later Classical and post-Classical Greek Cities, in: E. P. Moloney – M. S. Williams (eds.), Peace and Reconciliation in the Classical World, London 2017, 66–85

Green 1990: Green, Peter, Alexander to Actium: The Historical Evolution of the Hellenistic Age, Berkeley 1990

Haake 2013: Haake, Matthias, Writing Down the King: The Communicative Function of Treatises on Kingship in the Hellenistic Period, in: Luraghi 2013b, 165–206

Haley 1980: Haley, Peter, Rudolph Sohm on Charisma, The Journal of Religion 60, 1980, 185–197

Hamon 2009: Hamon, Patrice, Démocraties grecques après Alexandre. À propos de trois ouvrages récents, Topoi 16, 2009, 347–382

Hatzopoulos 1996: Hatzopoulos, Miltiades B, Macedonian Institutions under the Kings, 2 vols., Paris 1996

Honigman 2019: Honigman, Sylvie, Literary Genres and Identity in the *Letter of Aristeas*, in: D. R. Katz et al. (eds.), A Question of Identity: Social, Political, and Historical Aspects of Identity Dynamics in Jewish and Other Contexts, Berlin 2019

Honigman – Veïsse 2021: Honigman, Sylvie – Veïsse, Anne-Emmanuelle (eds.), Regional Revolts in the Seleucid and Ptolemaic Empires, in: Fischer-Bovet – von Reden 2021a, 301–328

Johnson – Harmanşah 2015: Johnson, Peri – Harmanşah, Ömür, Landscape, Politics, and Water in the Hittite Borderlands: Yalburt Yaylası Archaeological Landscape Research Project 2010–2014, in: S. R. Steadman – G. McMahon (eds.), The Archaeology of Anatolia: Recent Discoveries (2011–2014) I, Newcastle upon Tyne 2015, 255–277

Jonnes – Ricl 1997: Jonnes, Lloyd – Ricl, Marijana, A New Royal Inscription from Phrygia Paroreios: Eumenes II grants Tyriaion the Status of a Polis, Epigraphica Anatolica 28, 1997, 1–30

Juhel 2011: Juhel, Pierre O., Un fantôme de l'histoire hellénistique: le 'district' macédonien, Greek, Roman, and Byzantine Studies 51, 2011, 579–612

Kaye 2022: Kaye, Noah, The Attalids of Pergamon and Anatolia: Money, Culture, and State Power, Cambridge 2022

Kleiner – Noe 1977: Kleiner, Fred S. – Noe, Sydney P., The Early Cistophoric Coinage, New York 1977

Köhler 2020: Köhler, Wilhelm, Legitimation – Unwitting and Unrequested: Alexander of Macedon's Portrayal as Divine Tool in Zechariah 9, in: Trampedach – Meeus 2020, 145–164

Kremydi 2011: Kremydi, Sophia, Coinage and Finance, in: R. J. L. Fox (ed.), Brill's Companion to Ancient Macedon: Studies in the Archaeology and History of Macedon, 650 BC-300 AD, Leiden 2011, 159–178

Kremydi 2018: Kremydi, Sophia, "Autonomous" Coinages under the Late Antigonids, Athens 2018

Kremydi-Sicilianou 2007: Kremydi-Sicilianou, Sophia, ΜΑΚΕΔΟΝΩΝ ΠΡΟΩΤΗΣ ΜΕΡΙΔΟΣ: Evidence for a Coinage under the Antigonids, Revue Numismatique 163, 2007, 91–100

Kremydi-Sicilianou 2009: Kremydi-Sicilianou, Sophia, The Tauropolos Tetradrachms of the First Macedonian *Meris*: Provenance, Iconography and Dating, in: S. Drougou et al. (eds.), Κερμάτια φιλίας: τιμητικός τόμος για τον Ιωάννη Τουράτσογλου I, Athens 2009, 191–201

Luraghi 2013a: Luraghi, Nino, Ruling Alone: Monarchy in Greek Politics and Thought, in: Luraghi 2013b, 11–24

Luraghi 2013b: Luraghi, Nino (ed.), The Splendors and Miseries of Ruling Alone: Encounters with Monarchy from Archaic Greece to the Hellenistic Mediterranean, Stuttgart 2013b

Ma 2003: Ma, John, Kings, in: A. Erskine (ed.), A Companion to the Hellenistic World, Malden 2003, 175–195

Ma 2013: Ma, John, Hellenistic Empires, in: P. F. Bang – W. Scheidel (eds.), The Oxford Handbook of the State in the Ancient Near East and Mediterranean, Oxford 2013, 324–360

Marcellesi 2008: Marcellesi, Marie-Christine, Une cité devenue capitale royale: L'histoire monétaire de Pergame dans son contexte micrasiatique, in: M. Kohl (ed.), Pergame: Histoire et archéologie d'un centre urbain depuis ses origines jusqu'à la fin de l'antiquité, Villeneuve d'Ascq 2008, 245–256

Marcellesi 2012: Marcellesi, Marie-Christine, Pergame de la fin du Ve au début du Ier siècle avant J. C.: pratiques monétaires et histoire, Pisa 2012

Marest 2021: Marest, Laure, Patterns of Use of Royal Portraits in Hellenistic Archives, in: B. van Oppen de Ruiter – R. Wallenfels (eds.), Hellenistic Sealings & Archives: Proceedings of the Edfu Connection, an international Conference, 23–24 January 2018, Allard Pierson Museum, Amsterdam, Turnhout 2021, 163–178

Mari 2020: Mari, Manuela, Alexander, The King of the Macedonians, in: Trampedach – Meeus 2020, 197–217

Michels 2017: Michels, Christoph, Überlegungen zum 'kosmischen' Herrscherornat des Demetrios I. Poliorketes, in: H. Beck et al. (eds.), Von Magna Graecia nach Asia Minor. Festschrift für L.-M. Günther, Wiesbaden 2017, 211–224

Meadows 2020: Meadows, Andrew, An Attalid Overstrike and its Implications, Revue Numismatique 177, 2020, 117–127

Meyer 2020: Meyer, Marion, King Antiochus IV and the Cities in the Levant, in: Oetjen 2020, 525–539

Mitchell 2014: Mitchell, Lynette G., Rev. of: Luraghi 2013b, American Historical Review 119, 2014, 1753–1755

Mitchell 2022: Mitchell, Lynette G., King, Divinity, and Law in Ancient Greece, in: Moin – Strathern 2022, 111–136

Moin – Strathern 2022: Moin, A. Azfar – Strathern, Alana (eds.), Sacred Kingship in World History: Between Immanence and Transcendence, New York 2022

Momigliano 1970: Momigliano, Arnaldo, J. G. Droysen Between Greeks and Jews, History and Theory 9, 1970, 139–153

Monson 2020: Monson, Andrew, Alexander's Tributary Empire, in: Trampedach – Meeus 2020, 263–290

More 2009: More, Jonathan, Kingship Ideology: A Neglected Element in Aristeas' Charter Myth for Alexandrian Judaism, in: J. Cook (ed.), Septuagint and Reception: Essays Prepared for the Association for the Study of the Septuagint in South Africa, Leiden et al. 2009, 299–319

Nicholson 2020: Nicholson, Emma, Hellenic Romans and Barbaric Macedonians: Polybius on Hellenism and Changing Hegemonic Powers, Ancient History Bulletin 34, 2020, 38–73

Oetjen 2020: Oetjen, Roland (ed.), New Perspectives in Seleucid History, Archaeology and Numismatics: Studies in Honor of Getzel M. Cohen, Berlin 2020

Paganini 2021: Paganini, Mario C. D., Gymnasia and Greek Identity in Ptolemaic Egypt, Oxford 2021

Panagopoulou 2020: Panagopoulou, Katerina, The Early Antigonids: Coinage, Money, and the Economy, New York 2020

Payen 2020: Payen, Germain, Dans l'ombre des empires: les suites géopolitiques du traité d'Apamée en Anatolie, Québec 2020

Parker 2017: Parker, Robert, Greek Gods Abroad: Names, Natures, and Transformations, Berkeley 2017

Perrin-Saminadayar 2004: Perrin-Saminadayar, Éric, L'accueil officiel des souverains et des princes à Athènes à l'époque hellénistique, Bulletin de Correspondance Hellénique 128, 2004, 351–375

Pomeroy 1986: Pomeroy, Arthur J., Polybius' Death Notices, Phoenix 40, 1986, 407–423

Pomeroy 1988: Pomeroy, Arthur J., Livy's Death Notices, Greece & Rome 35, 1988, 172–183

Queyrel 2017: Queyrel, François, Les Galates comme nouveaux géants? De la métaphore au glissement interprétatif, in: F.-H. Massa-Pairault – C. Pouzadoux (eds.), Géants et Gigantomachies entre Orient et Occident, Naples 2017, 203–215

Roisman 2020: Roisman, Joseph, Charismatic Leaders in Ancient Greece, in: J. P. Zúquete (ed.), Routledge International Handbook of Charisma, Abingdon et al. 2020, 53–64

Savalli-Lestrade 2018: Savalli-Lestrade, Ivana, Nouvelles considérations sur le dossier épigraphique de Toriaion (*SEG* 47. 1745; *I. Sultan Dağı* I, 393), Zeitschrift für Papyrologie und Epigraphik 205, 2018, 165–177

Scholl 2009: Scholl, Andreas, Ὀλυμπίου ἔνδοθεν αὐλή – Zur Deutung des Pergamonaltars als Palast des Zeus, Jahrbuch des Deutschen Archäologischen Instituts 129, 2009, 251–278

Schwartz 2022: Schwartz, Daniel R., 1 Maccabees: A New Translation with Introduction and Commentary, New Haven 2022

Scolnic – Davis 2015: Scolnic, Benjamin – Davis, Thomas, How Kittim became 'Rome': Dan 11,30 and the Importance of Cyprus in the Sixth Syrian War, Zeitschrift für die alttestamentliche Wissenschaft 127, 2015, 304–319

Sommerstein 2013: Sommerstein, Alan H. – Bayliss, Andrew J., Oath and State in Ancient Greece, Berlin 2013

Stewart 2014: Stewart, Andrew, Art in the Hellenistic World: An Introduction, Cambridge 2014

Stewart – Frischer – Abdelaziz 2022: Stewart, Andrew – Frischer, Bernard – Abdelaziz, Mohamed, Fear and Loathing in the Hellenistic Agora: Antenor's Tyrannicides Return, Hesperia 91, 2022, 311–350

Strathern 2019: Strathern, Alan, Unearthly Powers: Religious and Political Change in World History, Cambridge 2019

Strootman 2014: Strootman, Rolf, Hellenistic Imperialism and the Idea of World Unity, in: C. Rapp – H. A. Drake (eds.), The City in the Classical and Post-Classical World: Changing Contexts of Power and Identity, Cambridge 2014, 38–61

Strootman 2019: Strootman, Rolf, Antiochos IV and Rome: The Festival at Daphne (Syria), the Treaty of Apameia and the Revival of Seleukid Expansionism in the West, in: A. Coşkun – D. Engels (eds.), Rome and the Seleukid East, Brussels 2019, 173–216

Taylor 2014: Taylor, Michael J., Sacred Plunder and the Seleucid Near East, Greece & Rome 61, 2014, 222–241

Tekin 1999: Tekin, Oğuz, Sivas definesi: VI. Mithradates dönemi Pontos ve Paphlagonia kentlerinin bronz sikkeleri, Istanbul 1999

Thonemann 2013: Thonemann, Peter, The Attalid State: 188–133 BC, in: id. (ed.), Attalid Asia Minor: Money, International Relations, and the State, Oxford 2013, 1–48

Thonemann 2015: Thonemann, Peter, The Hellenistic World: Using Coins as Sources, Cambridge 2015

Thonemann 2018: Thonemann, Peter, The Hellenistic Age: A Very Short Introduction, Oxford 2018

Trampedach – Meeus 2020: Trampedach, Kai – Meeus, Alexander (eds.), The Legitimation of Conquest: Monarchical Representation and the Art of Government in the Empire of Alexander the Great, Stuttgart 2020

von Hesberg 1999: von Hesberg, Henner, The King on Stage, Studies in the History of Art 56, 1999, 64–75

Walbank 1957–1979: Walbank, Frank W., A Historical Commentary on Polybius, 3 vols., Oxford 1957–1979

Weber 1978: Weber, Max, Economy and Society: An Outline of Interpretive Sociology, Berkeley 1978

Welwei 1963: Welwei, Karl-Wilhelm, Könige und Königtum im Urteil des Polybios, Diss. Cologne 1963

Wiemer 2017: Wiemer, Hans-Ulrich, Siegen oder untergehen? Die hellenistische Monarchie in der neueren Forschung, in: S. Rebenich (ed.), Monarchische Herrschaft im Altertum, Berlin 2017, 305–340

Wright 2015: Wright, Benjamin G., The Letter of Aristeas: "Aristeas to Philocrates" or "On the translation of the Law of the Jews", Berlin et al. 2015

Yon 2015: Yon, Jean-Baptiste, De Marisa à Byblos avec le courrier de Séleucos IV. Quelques données sur Byblos hellénistique, Topoi Supplément 13, 2015, 89–105

Figures

Fig. 1: Bibliothèque nationale de France, département Monnaies, médailles et antiques, 1965.986.

Fig. 2: Bibliothèque nationale de France, département Monnaies, médailles et antiques, Fonds général 343.

Fig. 3: Bibliothèque nationale de France, département Monnaies, médailles et antiques, AA.GR.16911.

Fig. 4: Bibliothèque nationale de France, département Monnaies, médailles et antiques, Fonds général 204.

Fig. 5: Bibliothèque nationale de France, département Monnaies, médailles et antiques, 1966.453.1072.

Fig. 6: Bibliothèque nationale de France, département Monnaies, médailles et antiques, 1973.1.80.

Fig. 7: Bibliothèque nationale de France, département Monnaies, médailles et antiques, Fonds général 12.

Noah Kaye is Assistant Professor in the Department of History at Michigan State University. The key concern of his work is the historical anthropology of economic life, the way that culture, religion, identity, and language mediate economic behavior for groups and individuals. Much of his research investigates the political economy of the Hellenistic kingdoms of the eastern Mediterranean using epigraphy and numismatics. He is also an ancient historian with significant experience in field archaeology, which he gained as a resident fellow at Koç University (Istanbul), the American School of Classical Studies at Athens, and the University of Haifa (Israel). He received his PhD from the Graduate Group in Ancient History and Mediterranean Archaeology at the University of California-Berkeley in 2012. In 2022, he published his first book *The Attalids of Pergamon and Anatolia: Money, Culture, and State Power* (Cambridge). He is now investigating Toriaion in Phrygia with the Kale Tepesi Excavations.

König & Stadt
Kommunikationsstrategien in der hellenistischen Münzprägung

KATHARINA MARTIN

Abstract: Starting point for questions of monarchical representation with regard to interaction with the cities and their elites treated in this chapter is the Seleukid Empire and the diverse spectrum of coins circulating there. For a concrete inter-dynastic comparison ("same, but different"), the so-called quasi-municipal coinage in the Seleukid Empire since Antiochos IV and the so-called pseudo-autonomous coins of Mithradates VI in Pontos and Paphlagonia – both bronze coinages, which have similar intentions but different structures – are suitable. The silver coinage of the late Seleukids from Mallos, Tarsos and Damaskos, with its reference to indigenous cults, brings civic traditions into monarchical representation. Finally, the Attic-weight wreathed coinages from Asia Minor, also circulating in the Seleukid Empire, illustrate the growing opportunities of presenting civic structures within the framework of monarchical systems.

1. Vorbemerkung

Die Münzprägung im Hellenismus ist vielfältig und in gewissem Maße unübersichtlich.[1] Um überregionalen Handel zu erleichtern und zu vereinfachen, hat Alexander der Große in seinem großen Weltreich eine einheitliche trimetallische (Gold-, Silber- und Bronze-)Währung nach attischem Münzfuß eingeführt:[2] So werden überall in seinem Reich von zahlreichen alten und neuen Münzstätten dieselben festgelegten Nominale mit denselben Motiven ausgegeben. Doch bleibt die Geldwirtschaft in seiner Nachfolge divers und in der Verantwortung verschiedener Münzherren. Neben dem postum umlaufenden und kontinuierlich weiter ausgemünzten Alexandergeld entste-

---

1   Thonemann 2015.
2   Das Material ist von Price 1991 vorgelegt.

hen in den verschiedenen Diadochenreichen eigene königliche Währungen, daneben stehen städtische Prägungen.[3]

Dieses auf mehreren Säulen stehende System funktioniert über die Jahrhunderte. Spätestens ab dem 2. Jh. v. Chr. zeichnen sich äußerliche Veränderungen ab, die sich besonders im Verhältnis König und Stadt zeigen.[4] Im folgenden Beitrag soll anhand einiger Fallbeispiele untersucht werden, wie die verschiedenen monetären Systeme miteinander interagieren und wie der König und seine Untergebenen (in Gestalt der Städte) miteinander mittels Bildern und Texten auf den Münzen kommunizieren.[5] Immer geht es dabei auch um das Profil des jeweiligen Königs, der sich u. a. im Verhältnis zu den Städten in seinem Reich positioniert.

2. Münzen als Zahlungs- und Kommunikationsmittel

Alle hellenistischen Dynastien nutzen Münzen nicht nur in ihrer primären Geldfunktion, sondern auch als Kommunikationsmittel. Der Umgang mit dem Medium ist dabei in den hellenistischen Reichen dynastiespezifisch. Für die Vorderseiten insbesondere der Edelmetallprägungen wird in der Regel sehr bald das Porträt des Königs als verantwortlicher Münzherr (und damit Wertgarant) und allgegenwärtiger Herrscher gewählt.[6] Auf den programmatischen Rückseiten stehen Gottheiten und ihre Attribute für das Selbstverständnis der Dynastie; später werden die Bilder individualisiert oder ,personalisiert' und charakterisieren den jeweiligen Herrscher und sein Herrschaftsprogramm. Die Ikonographie der Münzen bleibt lange ,griechisch' – das gilt für Bilder und Texte. Zumindest von den nicht-monetären Aspekten scheinen also vornehmlich die griechisch geprägten Eliten im Reich angesprochen worden zu sein. Mit dem 2. Jh. ändert sich einiges: Das Motivspektrum wird insgesamt vielfältiger, auch tauchen aus griechischem Blickwinkel mitunter ,fremdartig' scheinende Gottheiten oder wenig königliche Motive auf. Lokale oder regionale Einflüsse machen sich bemerkbar. Meist

---

3   Hortzusammensetzungen belegen das Nebeneinander verschiedener Währungen, wobei königliche und städtische Münzen nicht immer gemeinsam deponiert sind, dazu auch Biedermann 2014, 44–45 et passim, der die im IGCH gelisteten Hortfunde ausgewertet hat und dabei u. a. nach verschiedenen Prägeautoritäten (königlich vs. nicht-königlich) differenziert hat, z. B. mit Tab. 14 (Kleinasien und Zypern: 15,7 % gemischte Horte) oder Tab. 17 (Levante: 26,8 % gemischte Horte); zum Hortungsverhalten s. auch Kaye 2022, 168.

4   Houghton 2005, 54.

5   Zur Interaktion zwischen Königen und Städten siehe hier auch den Beitrag von Noah Kaye in diesem Band, bes. S. 520–522, 537–547.

6   Auch der Umgang mit dem Herrscherporträt ist dynastiespezifisch; so finden sich bei den Seleukiden alle Könige und Usurpatoren mit Münzporträt, die Ptolemaier hingegen setzten den Fokus auf die Familie und zeigten, bis auf wenige Ausnahmen, den Dynastiegründer Ptolemaios I. Einen Vergleich der Münzpolitik der beiden großen Dynastien liefern zuletzt Iossif – Lorber 2021. Vgl. dazu auch den Beitrag von Ralf von den Hoff in diesem Band.

liegt die Verantwortung für solche Veränderungen – direkt oder indirekt, wie sich zeigen wird – beim Hof. Es stellt sich daher die Frage nach der Intention: Präsentieren die hellenistischen Könige mit den anderen/neuen/fremden Gottheiten ein neues Herrschaftsverständnis, agieren sie also im eigenen Interesse oder reagieren sie auf (geänderte) politisch-soziale Gegebenheiten?

Bei der Frage nach monarchischer Repräsentation in den numismatischen Quellen bietet es sich besonders an, auf die Münzprägung der Seleukiden zu blicken, insofern uns hier a) alle Könige und Usurpatoren im Porträt überliefert sind, wir also ein Gesicht des herrschenden Königs vor Augen haben und b) die vielfältigen kulturellen Traditionen gerade dieses großen Reiches verschiedene Reaktionen und Strategien auf die königliche Präsenz erwarten lassen.[7]

Während meist die Silberprägung im Fokus der Betrachtung steht (Tetradrachmen und Drachmen sind in der Regel sorgfältiger produziert, besser erhalten, über Hortfunde besser überliefert und besser aufgearbeitet), lohnt immer auch ein Blick auf das bronzene ‚Kleingeld'. Denn die Münzen aus Buntmetall sind oft vielfältiger, weniger standardisiert und weniger streng konzipiert. Und: Sie verengen den Blick nicht auf eine elitäre, dem Hof nahestehende oder militärische Nutzergruppe,[8] sondern erschließen breitere Felder.

Nicht immer ist auf diesen kleinen Nominalen der königlichen Münzen der König abgebildet, oft finden sich auf den Vorderseiten in bewährter Tradition alte und neue Gottheiten – insgesamt sind hellenistische Bronzemünzen ‚religiöser' strukturiert als Edelmetallprägungen.[9] Der Name des königlichen Münzherrn bleibt jedoch. Die Produktion erfolgt in seinem Auftrag (und in seinem Sinne). Auch zeigen die Rückseitenbilder nicht immer ‚klassisch griechische' Motive, sie ergänzen vielmehr das Image des Königs um indigene Traditionen und andere lokale Komponenten. Dazu kommen im 2. Jh. v. Chr. Münzen, die von städtischen Instanzen ausgegeben werden, dafür aber den König abbilden (s. u.). Lokale oder regionale Bezüge in der königlichen Münzprägung lassen ebenso wie monarchische Reflexe auf städtischen Münzen auf Interaktion zwischen König und Bevölkerung, zwischen Herrscher und Beherrschten schließen.[10]

---

7   Zu dieser Konstellation siehe auch den Beitrag von Sonja Richter in diesem Band.
8   Zu verschiedenen Ziel- und Nutzergruppen s. de Callataÿ 2014, 59–77 oder Eckhardt – Martin 2016, 37–40.
9   Panagiotis Iossif hat dieses Phänomen mehrfach untersucht und publiziert, s. besonders Iossif 2011 oder Iossif 2018, 282–283 oder 288–289 mit Tabellen und Graphiken.
10   Explizit Ehling 2008, 82 (konkret zu den sog. quasi-munizipalen Prägungen in Palästina und Phoinikien).

3. Königlich – städtisch – quasi-munizipal:
seleukidische Praxis unter Antiochos IV.

Beim Nebeneinander von Münzen verschiedener Prägeautoritäten scheint sich im 2. Jh. v. Chr. insgesamt das Verhältnis zugunsten der Städte zu bewegen. Unter Antiochos IV. beginnen seit 169/168 v. Chr. insgesamt 19 Städte[11] in verschiedenen Regionen des Seleukidenreichs Bronzemünzen auszugeben, die auf der Rückseite städtische Motive und eine städtische Legende, auf der Vorderseite aber den Kopf des Königs zeigen. Diese neue Bronzegeld-Gruppe wird insbesondere unter Alexander I. und Demetrios II. weitergeführt. Unter den ausgebenden Städten sind zahlreiche Orte, die mit einem (meist ephemeren) seleukidischen Namen einen neuen hellenisierten Charakter erhalten haben (z. B. Tarsos als „Antiocheia-Kydnos", Adana als „Antiocheia am Saros", Edessa als „Antiocheia-Kallirrhoe" oder Nisibis als „Antiocheia in Mygdonia") – hier schafft schon die Verwendung des dynastischen Namens eine äußerliche Bindung an den König.[12]

Neben dem Alexandergeld und der königlichen Reichsprägung sowie einer zu diesem Zeitpunkt überschaubaren echten städtischen Prägung, die alle auch die kleinen Nominale bedienen, etabliert sich damit eine weitere Kategorie von Münzen, die städtische und königliche Interessen zu verbinden scheint. Es geht hier konkret um ‚Kleingeld', das für alltägliche (lokal oder regional definierte) Transaktionen geeignet ist und für einen wachsenden Grad an Monetarisierung im seleukidischen Reich spricht. Um die verschiedenen Charakteristika zu unterscheiden und diese neuen Münzen als eine besondere, zumindest formal abgrenzbare, Gruppe zu benennen, hat sich in der Literatur der Begriff ‚quasi-munizipal' etabliert.[13] Er evoziert städtische Prägehoheit unter einer externen Aufsicht. Die Frage ‚wieviel König' und ‚wieviel Stadt' hinter diesen Münzen steckt, wird nach wie vor diskutiert, wenngleich die Nennung des Ethnikons

---

11   Es sind dies Adana, Mopsos, Hierapolis Kastabala, Aigeai und Alexandreia ad Issum in Kilikien,
      Antiocheia am Orontes, Seleukeia Pieria, Apameia, Laodikeia am Meer, Hierapolis Bambyke,
      Edessa, Nisibis im seleukidischen Kernland, Ake-Ptolemais und Askalon in Koile Syria sowie die
      Städte in Phoinikien, die zuvor zum ptolemaiischen Reich gehörten: Berytos, Byblos, Sidon, Tri-
      polis und Tyros. Siehe dazu zuletzt Hoover 2005, 488–491, 497–498; SC II S. xxiii–xxiv, 45–46
      („the degree to which the quasi-municipal coinages of Antiochus IV and Alexander I were inspired
      by royal design or local civic interests remains in question", ebd. S. xxiv); Iossif 2014; Lorber 2015,
      68–71; Meyer 2020; Iossif – Lorber 2021, 199–200.
12   So Meyer 2020, 531 zu den Stadtumbenennungen und den damit im Zusammenhang stehenden
      „Selbsthellenisierungstendenzen der lokalen Eliten" (so Mittag 2006, 202–204), die sich großen-
      teils schon in die Zeit vor Antiochos IV. datieren lassen.
13   So z. B. bei SC II,2 S. 44–45 et passim; Houghton 2005, 64–65; Hoover 2009, 126; Meyer 2020, 525;
      Lichtenberger 2021a; Kaye in diesem Band S. 522–523, 538 („pseudo-municipal"). Im Folgenden
      werden hier die Hilfsbegriffe ohne Anführungszeichen benutzt.

die Stadt als offiziellen Prägeherrn identifiziert[14] und von einem auf Stadt und Chora beschränkten Umlauf auszugehen ist.[15]

Die quasi-munizipale Münzprägung ist je nach Münzstätte unterschiedlich stark differenziert; es werden wie in der regulären Bronzewährung unterschiedliche Nominalwerte ausgegeben, die sich den antiken Nutzern durch bestimmte festgelegte Rückseitenbilder erschließen und die wir heute nach bestimmten Durchmessergrößen kategorisieren.[16] Drei Nominalwerte („Nominale B-D", also Doppelstücke, Bronzeeinheiten und -halbstücke) werden für die quasi-munizipalen Münzen vermehrt genutzt. Auf diesen verteilt sich ein jeweils ortsspezifisches Bildprogramm. In der Regel werden, wie auch in der königlichen Bronzeprägung, griechische Gottheiten und ihre Symbole abgebildet. Vielfach findet sich Zeus auf den neuen Münzen; einige Städte wie Adana, Seleukeia in Pierien oder Nisibis übernehmen den thronenden Zeus Nikephoros,[17] den Antiochos zuvor in der Reichsprägung für seine neuen Tetradrachmen in Antiocheia am Orontes eingeführt hat. Die Stadt Antiocheia selbst wählt – wie Apameia, Hierapolis, Ake oder Kallirhoë – einen stehenden Zeus,[18] wie ihn Antiochos zuvor auf seinen königlichen Bronzen präsentiert hat.[19]

Lokal individuelle Motive entwickeln besonders die phoinikischen Küstenstädte, die durch ihre vorherige Zugehörigkeit zum ptolemaiischen Reich traditionell (kulturell wie numismatisch) anders geprägt sind und die Ägypten auch weiter verbunden bleiben.

---

14   Wie Hoover 2005, 488 oder Meyer 2020, 525 formulieren, ist die offizielle Autorität durch die Legende definiert; Meadows 2001, 59–60; Iossif 2014, 79 und Iossif – Lorber 2021, 200 sehen die Initiative beim König (‚top-down'-Praktiken), Lorber 2015, 69 differenziert: „This is strong evidence that the cities themselves designed these coin issues and valued the opportunity for civic self-promotion, even if the political and fiscal realities behind the quasi-municipal coinage remain obscure and debatable". Lichtenberger 2021a fokussiert auf die phoinikischen Prägungen, bei denen regelmäßig der Königsname auf der Vorderseite zum Stadtnamen bzw. Ethnikon auf der Rückseite hinzutritt, was den Charakter dieser Gruppe als „Zwitter" (ebd. S. 65) noch hervorhebt.

15   SC II,1 S. xxiv; Lichtenberger 2021a, 80. Anders als für Edelmetall liegen Fund- und Hortdaten für Bronzemünzen nicht in vergleichbarer Dichte vor, sodass Umlaufräume nicht mit derselben Bestimmtheit definiert werden können, dennoch: „Find evidence suggests that the quasi-municipal bronzes were generally very restricted in their circulation even by comparison with the regular royal issues, which themselves did not normally travel very far outside of the region they were struck" (so Oliver Hoover in SC II,2 S. 44).

16   Unterschieden werden verschiedene Wertstufen; für die quasi-munizipalen Münzen relevant sind in der Regel: Nominal A (‚Vierfachstück', ca. 22–29 mm), B (‚Doppelstück', ca. 17–22 mm), C (‚Einheit', ca. 15–21 mm), D (‚Halbstück', ca. 12–14 mm) und selten E (‚Viertelstück', ca. 8–11 mm), vgl. SC II,1 S. 9–42 (Appendix 2A) und S. 45–52 (Appendix 2B). Nur selten sind, wie in Nisibis, konkrete Wertangaben auf den Münzen zu finden, die hier die Münze als Tetrachalkon, Dichalkon und Chalkous auszeichnen (SC II, Nr. 1502–1504).

17   SC II, Nr. 1379–1380 (Adana); Nr. 1427 (Seleukeia in Pierien) oder Nr. 1502 (Nisibis).

18   SC II, Nr. 1416–1418 (Antiocheia am Orontes); Nr. 1428 (Apameia); Nr. 1432–1433 (Hierapolis); Nr. 1480 (Ake) oder Nr. 1499–1500 (Kallirhoë).

19   SC II, Nr. 1408–1409.

– So zeigen Sidon mit der Galeere (Abb. 1) und Tyros mit Schiffsbug oder -heck auf ihren großen Nominalen nautische Motive, die damit zum einen auf ihre maritime Lage und damit einhergehend auf ihre wichtige wirtschaftliche und strategische Bedeutung verweisen, zum anderen – im Fall von Sidon – aber auch altbekannte identitätsstiftende Bilder ihrer vorhellenistischen Münzprägung aufnehmen.[20] Hier kommt mit Astarte auf dem Schiffsbug (Abb. 2) ab Antiochos VII. ein weiteres Motiv in der quasi-munizipalen Münzprägung hinzu.[21] Dabei wird das altbekannte Parasemon reduziert und mit der Stadtgottheit kombiniert; die griechische Rückseitenlege ΣΙΔΩΝΟΣ ΘΕΑΣ verdeutlicht die Funktion der Göttin. Diese Kombination wird später in der städtischen Münzprägung übernommen (Abb. 3).

– Beide Städte thematisieren zudem auf kleineren Bronzen mit Europa auf dem Stier (Abb. 4)[22] ein Motiv aus dem (griechischen) Mythos, den beide für sich reklamieren. Die phoinikische Königstochter Europa gilt als Tochter von Agenor oder Phoinix – nach einigen Quellen König von Sidon, nach anderen König von Tyros; sicher ist nur das geschwisterliche Verhältnis zum Bruder Kadmos.[23] Beide Städte verwenden dasselbe Bild, Sidon prägt es erneut unter Demetrios I. aus; in Tyros bleibt es auf die eine quasi-munizipale Emission beschränkt. Über die städtische Münzprägung führen beide Städte ihre Konkurrenz um Europa aber bis in die Kaiserzeit weiter.[24] Der Konkurrenzkampf der beiden Städte spiegelt sich auch in den z. T. ausführlichen bilinguen Legenden der Münzen, die die Städte gegeneinander ausspielen: So nennt sich Tyros in den phoinikischen Legende „Mutter der Sidonier", während Sidon sich im Gegenzug als „Mutter von Kambe, Hippos, Kition und Tyros" bezeichnet.[25]

20   Sidon: SC II, Nr. 1453; Tyros: SC II, Nr. 1463–1468. Zu den vorhellenistischen Münzen von Sidon: Elayi 2004.
21   SC II, Nr. 2105 (Antiochos VII.); Nr. 2189 (Demetrios II.); Nr. 2333 (Antiochos VIII.).
22   SC II, Nr. 1455–1456 und 1668 (Sidon) und SC II, Nr. 1469 (Tyros); Lichtenberger 2021a, 70–73 (Sidon) und 74–75 (Tyros). Die Darstellung auf den Münzen mit der einen Hand am Horn des Stieres und dem gebauschten Gewand entspricht exakt der Schilderung des Mythos bei Moschos II (ΕΥΡΩΠΗ), Z. 125–130.
23   Die meisten antiken Autoren nennen nur die Vaterschaft, nicht die konkrete Heimatstadt. Sidon findet sich z. B. bei Hyg. fab. 178 oder Ov. met. 2.840; ältere Autoren wie Palaiphatos 15 (περὶ Εὐρώπης) oder Hdt. 2,49,2 erwähnen Tyros. Bei Eur. Phoen. 5 wird Kadmos im Zusammenhang mit Sidon genannt, in 639 bezeichnet er ihn als Tyrer.
24   Dazu Lichtenberger 2009, 152, 160–161.
25   Mittag 2006, 189 mit ausführlicher Anm. 45. Zu Anspruch und Reaktion in Bild und Text s. Meyer 2020, 534–535, die vermutet, dass zunächst Sidon das Bild der Europa einführt und so – numismatisch – den Anspruch auf sie erhebt und Tyros mit demselben Bild reagiert, während Sidon mit der ausführlicheren Legende auf Tyros' Anspruch, älter zu sein, antwortet. Eine detaillierte Auflistung der quasi-munizipalen Münzen in Phoinikien bei Lichtenberger 2021a; zum Konkurrenzverhältnis der beiden Städte ebd. bes. S. 66, 73–76, das auf der Ebene der vermeintlichen Mutterschaft in hellenistischer Zeit jedoch bald wieder einschläft.

Abb. 1 Sidon (Phoinikien), quasi-munizipale AE des Antiochos IV. mit Galeere, ca. 168–164 v. Chr. (SC 1453).

Abb. 2 Sidon (Phoinikien), quasi-munizipale AE des Demetrios II. mit Astarte auf Schiff, 127/126 v. Chr. (SC 2189).

Abb. 3 Sidon (Phoinikien), städtische AE mit Astarte auf Schiff, 97/96 v. Chr.

Abb. 4 Sidon (Phoinikien), quasi-munizipale AE des Antiochos IV. mit Europa auf dem Stier, ca. 168–164 v. Chr. (SC 1456).

Abb. 5 Berytos (Phoiniken), quasi-munizipale AE des Alexander Balas mit Baal-Berit, ca. 168–164 v. Chr. (SC 1825).

Abb. 6 Berytos (Phoinikien), quasi-munizipale AE des Alexander Balas mit Astarte
und Schiffsbug, ca. 151–149 v. Chr. (SC 1826).

Abb. 7 Byblos (Phoinikien), quasi-munizipale AE des Antiochos IV. mit Kronos-El,
ca. 168–164 v. Chr. (SC 1443).

Abb. 8 Byblos (Phoinikien), städtische AE mit Kronos-El, 50–49 v. Chr.

– Ebenfalls maritim gibt sich Berytos, das Baal-Berit, den lokalen Hauptgott, als
  Erscheinungsform des griechischen Poseidon, (Nominal B, Abb. 5) abbildet
  sowie Astarte mit Steuerruder auf einem Schiffsbug (Nominal C, Abb. 6) und
  das kleine Nominal mit Gerätschaften und Tieren wie Ruder, Dreizack, Delfin
  schmückt. Hier wird die quasi-munizipale Münzprägung – zumindest mit Baal-
  Berit und dem bronzenen Hauptnominal – unter weiteren Königen bis ins frühe
  1. Jh. v. Chr. weitergeführt.[26] Die Wiedergabe der Gottheiten entspricht, vielleicht
  bis auf den durchgängig frontalen Blick Baals, bekannter griechischer Götteriko-
  nographie.
– Byblos zeigt mit dem vielfach geflügelten Kronos-El (Abb. 7) einen der phoinikischen Urgötter, der sich in seiner Ikonographie von den sonst üblichen ‚grie-

26 Unter Antiochos IV.: SC II, Nr. 1448–1449 (Baal-Berit), 1450 (Astarte), 1451–1452 (Ruder, Drei-
    zack); unter Antiochos V.: 1579 (Baal-Berit); unter Alexander Balas: SC II, Nr. 1825 (Baal-Berit),
    1826 (Astarte), 1827 (Delfin); unter Demetrios II.: SC II, Nr. 2185–2186 (Baal-Berit); unter Alexan-
    der Zabinas: SC II, Nr. 2250–2252 (Baal-Berit); unter Antiochos VIII.: SC II, Nr. 2326–2327 (Baal-
    Berit).

chischen' Göttern abgrenzt.[27] Die Art der ‚Mehrfachflügel' erinnert an die nicht identifizierte geflügelte männliche Figur auf Stateren und kleineren Nominalen im kilikischen Mallos,[28] das Standmotiv mit seiner Kombination aus Profil und Frontalität ist ägyptisch, ebenso die Hörnerkrone. Dazu kommen die ägyptischen Gottheiten Isis (Nominal C) und Harpokrates (Nominal D) und die Isiskrone auf dem selten ausgeprägten kleinsten Nominal.[29] Kronos-El wird später unter Tryphon (142–138 v. Chr.) auf königlichen Didrachmen und auf städtischen Prägungen übernommen (Abb. 8).[30]

Charakteristisch für die quasi-munizipalen Prägungen bleibt überall die Präsenz des Königsporträts auf der Vorderseite. Bei aller aufkommenden städtischen Individualität, die sich vornehmlich in Phoinikien zeigt, sonst aber durch griechische Götterwelt und Ikonographie geprägt ist, scheint die Initiative für diese (vermeintlich?) städtischen Prägungen vom König ausgegangen zu sein. Die meisten Orte mit quasi-munizipaler Münzprägung liegen an wichtigen Häfen oder zentralen Handelsrouten, sodass mit der Ausgabe zusätzlichen Kleingeldes eine Stärkung der lokalen/regionalen Wirtschaft anzunehmen ist.[31] Dies liegt im Interesse des Königs – aber letztlich auch in demjenigen der Städte. Ist darin also ein Recht oder eine Pflicht zu sehen? Ein Recht auf eine eigene Münzprägung? Oder die Verpflichtung, das königliche Währungssystem zu unterstützen? Offizielle Prägerechtsverleihungen sind in der Antike äußerst selten;[32] ein konkretes königliches Dekret lässt sich hier ebenso wenig nachweisen. Zumindest der Auftrag wird vom Hof gekommen sein;[33] das legt schon die gleichzeitige Einführung der Münzen nahe. Die konkrete Umsetzung, die Organisation (und Finanzierung) der Prägungen wird dann den Städten überlassen; dafür spricht die lokal jeweils unterschiedliche Ausführung.

27   SC II, Nr. 1443–1444 (Antiochos IV.), 1578 (Antiochos V.), 1822 (Alexander Balas), 2099 (Antiochos VII.); Wright 2009/2010, 194.
28   Casabonne 2004, Typ 2; die Unterteilung der Flügel grenzt sie klar von Ahura Mazda ab, wenngleich die Sonnenscheibe ein verbindendes Element ist.
29   Unter Antiochos IV.: SC II, Nr. 1442 (Isis Pelagia); Nr. 1445 (Isis mit Zepter); Nr. 1446 (Harpokrates); unter Alexander Balas: SC II, Nr. 1823 (Harpokrates); unter Antiochos VI.: SC II, Nr. 2021 (Isis Pelagia).
30   SC II, Nr. 2044 und BMC Phoenicia Nr. 12.
31   Mittag 2006, 187, 190 und 207.
32   Speziell der Hinweis auf 1 Makk 15.6–7, wonach Antiochos VII. den Juden unter Simon Münzrecht gewährt, ist problematisch zu bewerten, da von diesem Recht offenbar kein Gebrauch gemacht worden ist, d. h. keine entsprechenden Münzen nachgewiesen sind, s. Mittag 2006, 184.
33   Iossif 2014, 73 spricht von der „predominance of Greek culture and language, those of the royal administration and of the local elites. Once again, the decision is a top-to-bottom one, with the city simply following royal policy".

Der Beginn der quasi-munizipalen Münzen geht oftmals einher mit dem Start einer
‚echten' städtischen Münzprägung.[34] Die Grenzen sind fließend;[35] möglicherweise
nehmen die quasi-munizipalen Münzen die später gängige römische Praxis der sogenannten Roman Provincials vorweg, die letztlich städtische Prägungen, aber eingebunden in das römische Währungssystem sind und in der Regel den Kaiserkopf auf
der Vorderseite zeigen.[36] Wenngleich mit Kronos-El, Astarte, Isis, Europa u. a. fraglos
lokale Gottheiten oder allgegenwärtig vertraute Mythen abgebildet werden,[37] die Identität reflektieren oder den Städten ein Alleinstellungsmerkmal geben, so sind diese
Motive in der Münzprägung neu; erst in der Folge werden sie ins reguläre städtische
Typenrepertoire übernommen.[38]

4. Pseudo-städtische Bronzen: Pontos unter Mithradates VI.

Später, aber in ihrer Intention vergleichbar sind die sogenannten pseudo-städtischen
oder pseudo-autonomen Bronzemünzen, die Mithradates VI. Eupator in seinem
Machtbereich in verschiedenen Städten in Pontos und Paphlagonien ausgeben lässt.
Auch hier hat die Forschung einen Hilfsbegriff eingeführt, der die formalen Besonderheiten der Prägungen umschreibt, die den Anschein erwecken, von Städten ausgegeben worden zu sein.[39]
    Auf seinen zentral produzierten Gold- und Silbermünzen nennt sich Mithradates
als Prägeherr (ΒΑΣΙΛΕΩΣ ΜΙΘΡΑΔΑΤΟΥ) und setzt sein idealisiertes Porträt in
der Tradition des Alexanderbildes auf die Vorderseite.[40] Als erster pontischer König
lässt er auch Kleingeld aus Buntmetall produzieren; dies erfolgt dezentral in vielen
verschiedenen Städten und Festungen in Pontos, Paphlagonien, Bosporus und Kolchis.[41] Vorder- und Rückseiten sind inhaltlich aufeinander abgestimmt, sie zeigen

---

34   Lorber 2015, 70–71.
35   Syon 2008, 299–302 kann dies für Tyros sauber abgrenzen.
36   So möchte Hoover 2020, 770–771, 773 sie verstehen; ähnlich bereits Lorber 2015, 69. Auch inner-
      halb der Provincials gibt es wieder eine Gruppe sogenannter pseudo-autonomer Münzen, die
      nämlich *nicht* den Kaiser auf der Vorderseite zeigen. Diese Gruppe unterscheidet sich aber ledig-
      lich formal von den restlichen und wird in der Forschung nicht anders bewertet.
37   Lorber 2015, 69 („it is probably significant that they refer to glories of the distant past"); Meyer
      2020, 533–536.
38   Iossif 2014, 78; Lichtenberger 2021a, 65.
39   Olshausen 2009; Michels 2009, 203–205; Bendschus 2017, 114–116, 123–128; Kaye in diesem Band,
      S. 545–546.
40   De Callataÿ 1997, 4–51; Michels 2009, 202–215; Bendschus 2017, 112–114, 127–122. Zur *imitatio
      Alexandri* bei Mithradates s. Kovacs 2022, 424–434.
41   In Amaseia, Amisos, Chabakta, Gaziura, Dia, Kabeira, Komana, Pharnakeia, Sarbanissa, Taulara
      (Pontos), in Abonuteichos, Amastris, Pimolisa, Sinope (Paphlagonien), in Gorgippia, Phanago-
      reia und Pantikapaion (kimmerischer Bosporos), Dioskurias in Kolchis. Dazu de Callataÿ 1997,
      296–297; id. 2005, 122–136; Erciyas 2006, 115–120; Michels 2009, 203–205; Bendschus 2017, 114–117,

aber weder sein Porträt noch nennen sie den Namen des Königs. Die Rückseitenlegenden bezeichnen die jeweiligen Städte – auffallend sind hier vielfach die Städ-
tenamen im Genitiv Singular (ΑΒΟΝΟΥΤΕΙΧΟΥ, ΑΜΑΣΕΙΑΣ, ΑΜΙΣΟΥ, ΔΙΑΣ,
ΔΙΟΣΚΟΥΡΙΑΔΟΣ, ΛΑΟΔΙΚΕΙΑΣ, ΦΑΡΝΑΚΕΙΑΣ, ΣΙΝΩΠΗΣ) und nicht, wie
sonst meist üblich, die Ethnika im Genitiv Plural (ΑΜΑΣΤΡΙΕΩΝ, ΓΑΖΙΟΥΡΩΝ,
ΓΟΡΓΙΠΠΕΩΝ, ΚΑΒΗΡΩΝ, ΚΟΜΑΝΩΝ, ΠΑΝΤΙΚΑΠΑΙΤΩΝ, ΠΙΜΩΛΙΣΩΝ,
ΣΑΡΒΑΝΙΣΕΩΝ, ΤΑΥΛΑΡΩΝ, ΦΑΝΑΓΟΡΙΤΩΝ, ΧΑΒΑΚΤΩΝ).[42] Dieses Phänomen
mischt sich in den verschiedenen Landschaften und tritt in bedeutenden Orten ebenso
wie in kleinen auf, die sonst keine Münzen ausgeben. Die Angabe der Stadt und nicht
der Bürgerschaft mag darauf hindeuten, dass es sich um einen Münzort und weniger
um eine Prägeautorität handelt.[43] Vielleicht ist diese grammatikalische Besonderheit
vielerorts (und gerade in den beiden bedeutendsten und prägestärksten Städten Amisos und Sinope) dahingehend zu verstehen, dass nicht die Bürgerschaft eigenständig
die Typen bestimmt, sondern dass sich die Stadt in ein übergeordnetes System einfügt
und sich so eng an den König bindet.

Denn anders als im Seleukidenreich zeigt sich hier ein fest vorgegebenes Bildprogramm, es gibt eine Nominalbindung und klar festgelegte Typen, die (nicht alle in
allen, aber) in verschiedenen Orten auf dieselbe Weise produziert werden.[44]

– In Amisos und Sinope werden die meisten der pseudo-städtischen Münzen produziert. Zwei der häufigsten Typen, die zudem in einer Vielzahl von Prägestätten
   ausgegeben werden, sind klar militärisch konnotiert: Sie zeigen a) auf der Vorderseite die Ägis mit einem zentralen Gorgoneion und auf der Rückseite Nike

---

123–128, 453–474. Die umfangreichsten Emissionen geben Amaseia, Amisos, Amastris und Sinope
aus. Für ‚Dia‘ (Typ: Zeuskopf/Adler) und ‚Dioskurias‘ (Typ: Dioskurenköpfe / Thyrsos) sind nur
Einzeltypen bekannt, die Legenden ΔΙΑΣ und ΔΙΟΣΚΟΥΡΙΑΔΟΣ stehen zudem in engem in-
haltlichen Bezug zu den dargestellten Göttern, sodass eine Deutung als Ortsnamen/Münzstätten-
bezeichnung fraglich ist. Im Falle von Sarbanissa ist nur ein einziges Exemplar nachgewiesen, bei
dem ein Stempel aus Amisos offenbar umgeschnitten worden ist (dazu Ireland – Cook 2008); auch
aus Abonuteichos ist nur eine Münze bekannt (SNG Ashmolean Nr. 202 = Hoover 2012, Nr. 351).

42 Für Pharnakeia lässt sich ein konkreter Wechsel vom städtischen Ethnikon im Genitiv Plural zum
    Stadtnamen im Genitiv Singular nachweisen: Hoover 2012, 90.

43 Vgl. Hoover 2012, 65, der eine Produktion „in the fortress rather than by the authority of the in-
    habitants of the city below" (für Amaseia) vermutet oder ebd. 53, dass die „authority for the coin-
    age came from the king, rather than from the citizen body" (für Dioskurias). Eine bewusst unter-
    schiedliche Verwendung von Ethnikon und Stadtnamen betont auch Lichtenberger 2021a, 71 im
    Fall der quasi-munizipalen Münzen in Phoinikien.

44 Olshausen 2009 und Ireland 2000 haben knapp 6.000 Münzen im Museum von Samsun, dem an-
    tiken Amisos, und gut 1.000 Münzen in Amasya, dem antiken Amaseia, aufgenommen. Es handelt
    sich großenteils um Fundmünzen aus der Region. Es verwundert nicht, dass jeweils die Anzahl
    der vor Ort geprägten Münzen besonders hoch ist. De Callataÿ 2010 weist in seiner Rezension
    S. 264–265 darauf hin, dass trotz der großen Gesamtzahl in Samsun dort nur etwa die Hälfte aller
    bekannten Kombinationen vorhanden ist. Mehr liefern seine Tabellen 2–4; ausführlicher de Cal-
    lataÿ 2005, 123–135.

mit einem Palmzweig (Abb. 9–11)[45] bzw. b), den Kopf des Ares und ein Schwert in Schwertscheide.[46] Den Kriegsgott mit Waffe abzubilden und zugleich mit der Ägis göttlichen Schutz und das Siegeszeichen *par excellence* für sich zu reklamieren, sind ideale Motive für eine Prägung in Kriegszeiten. Dazu kommt der Zeus-Adler-Typ,[47] ein universell einsetzbares Münzbild, das von Unteritalien über Makedonien, Epeiros und Kleinasien bis zu den ptolemaiischen Bronzemünzen in der Mittelmeerwelt geläufig ist.

– Insgesamt wird ein breites Spektrum aus der griechischen Götterwelt thematisiert; auffallend sind zudem mehrere Perseus-Typen (Abb. 12–15).[48] Der Heros ist bereits von Mithradates IV. in die pontische Münzikonographie eingeführt;[49] möglicherweise weist er auf iranische Ursprünge der Mithradatiden, auch wenn eigentlich eher seine griechische Rezeption thematisiert wird.

Abb. 9 Amastris (Paphlagonien), pseudo-städtische AE des Mithradates VI. mit Ägis/Nike-Typus, ca. 105–85 v. Chr.

Abb. 10 Amisos (Pontos), pseudo-städtische AE des Mithradates VI. mit Ägis/Nike-Typus, ca. 105–85 v. Chr.

45 Bendschus 2017, Typ PON46, Tetrachalkos, geprägt in Amastris, Amisos, Chabakta, Kabeira, Komana Pontika, Laodikeia und Sinope.
46 Bendschus 2017, Typ PON44, Tetrachalkos, geprägt in Amaseia, Amastris, Amisos, Chabakta, Gaziura, Kabeira, Laodikeia, Pimolisa, Sinope und Taulara.
47 Bendschus 2017, Typ PON43, Diobol, geprägt in Amaseia, Amisos, Gaziura, Kabeira, Komana, Laodikeia, Pimolisa, Sinope und Taulara und als Tetrachalkos in Abonouteichos, Amaseia, Amastris, Amisos, Dia, Pharnakeia und Sinope.
48 Michels 2009, 204.
49 Michels 2009, 196–197; Bendschus 2017, PON 6.

Abb. 11 Sinope (Paphlagonien), pseudo-städtische AE des Mithradates VI.
mit Ägis/Nike-Typus, ca. 105–85 v. Chr.

Abb. 12 Komana (Pontos), pseudo-städtische AE des Mithradates VI. mit Athena/Perseus
mit Medusa, ca. 85–65 v. Chr.

Abb. 13 Chabakta (Pontos), pseudo-städtische AE des Mithradates VI. mit Perseus/Pegasos,
ca. 100–85 v. Chr.

Abb. 14 Amisos (Pontos), pseudo-städtische AE des Mithradates VI. mit Perseus/Füllhorn
und Piloi, ca. 120–111 oder 110–100 v. Chr.

Abb. 15 Amisos (Pontos), pseudo-städtische AE des Mithradates VI. mit Perseus/Harpa,
ca. 85–65 v. Chr.

Anders als die seleukidischen quasi-munizipalen Münzen zeigen die pontischen pseudo-städtischen Prägungen nicht den Kopf des Königs auf der Vorderseite, der ihre
Produktion initiiert hat; sie sind in ihrer Gestaltung also auf den ersten Blick weniger
‚monarchisch' konzipiert. Durch die Verwendung derselben Typen in vielen Münzstätten, die keine lokale Individualität erlaubt, sondern ein zentral verordnetes königliches Programm darstellt, ist einerseits eine reichsweite Gültigkeit gewährleistet. Andererseits sind diese pseudo-städtischen Münzen tatsächlich deutlich monarchischer
in ihrer Ausprägung als die seleukidischen quasi-munizipalen Bronzen. In Pontos
zeigt sich, dass allerorten die verschiedensten Städte die Politik von Mithradates mit-
tragen (müssen); im Seleukidenreich organisieren sich die Städte individuell. Haben
wir in beiden Fällen eine gleiche Ausgangslage, nämlich den königlichen Auftrag an
die Städte, mit der Ausgabe von Bronzemünzen die (Klein-)Geldversorgung im Reich
zu unterstützen, um auf lokaler und regionaler Ebene die Wirtschaft anzukurbeln, die
Monetarisierung auszuweiten und damit (militärische) Alltagsgeschäfte zu gewährleisten,[50] so entwickelt sich die Realisierung dieses Auftrags in den beiden Dynastien
völlig unterschiedlich.

5. Indigene Gottheiten in Kilikien und Damaskos: Königliche Initiativen in Silber

Blicken wir zurück zu den Seleukiden. Wechselwirkungen zwischen königlichen und
städtischen Interessen rund um die Instrumentalisierung indigener Kulte und alter
oder altertümlicher Kultbilder finden sich auch in der Silberprägung. Umlaufraum
und Zielgruppen sind damit anders intendiert.

–   Frühester Reflex eines indigenen Kultes in der königlich-seleukidischen Münz-
     prägung ist das Bild der Magarsia im kilikischen Mallos: Ihr Kultbild (Abb. 16)
     findet sich von Demetrios I. (162–150 v. Chr.) bis Antiochos IX. (116–96 v. Chr.)
     auf hier ausgegebenen königlichen Tetradrachmen,[51] außerdem unter Deme-
     trios II. (in seiner ersten und zweiten Regierungszeit 145–139 und 129–125 v. Chr.)
     und Antiochos VII. (138–129 v. Chr.) gelegentlich auch auf Drachmen.[52] Die Göt-
     tin trägt Helm, Speer und Ägis und weist so auf ihren griechischen Charakter
     als Athena hin; die formale Gestaltung mit ihrer geschlossenen Körperkontur
     spricht jedoch für einen indigenen anatolisch-hethitischen Kult.[53] Die Stadt ist

---

50   Zur Verwendung von Bronzegeld: Houghton 2005, 51, 64–67; de Callataÿ 2014, 73–75.
51   SC II, Nr. 1618–1619 (Demetrios I.); Nr. 1779 (Alexander Balas); Nr. 1896 (Demetrios II.); Nr. 1998
      und 2059 (Antiochos VI.); Nr. 2059 (Antiochos VII.); Nr. 2162 (Demetrios II.); Nr. 2290 (Antio-
      chos VIII.); Nr. 2357 (Antiochos IX.). Stempelstudien bei Houghton 1984, 94–97.
52   SC II, Nr. 1897 und 2163 (Demetrios II.); Nr. 2060 (Antiochos VII.).
53   Fleischer 1973, 260–263; Houghton 1984, 102–110; Pohl – Sayar 2004, 98–107; Wright 2009/2010,
      195–196.

alt, auch eine reiche Münzprägung reicht in die Perserzeit zurück.[54] Ein Hinweis auf Magarsia findet sich jedoch erst spät, in einer Inschrift von ca. 160–140 v. Chr.[55] und in den etwa zeitgleichen Münzen. Nach eingehender Analyse der einzelnen auf den Münzen überlieferten Bilddetails kommen Daniela Pohl und Mustafa H. Sayar zu dem Schluss, dass es sich zwar um einen alten Kult handelt, dass das auf den Münzen überlieferte Kultbild jedoch erst zwischen dem 4. Jh. und dem Erscheinen der ersten Münzen in der Mitte des 2. Jhs. v. Chr. Form angenommen hat. Dafür spricht der Eklektizismus der einzelnen Bildbestandteile und der Archaismus einiger Details. Es handelt sich also nicht um ein archaisches, sondern um ein archaistisches Kultbild, das durch ‚künstliche Alterung' Altehrwürdigkeit vermitteln soll.[56]

„Die Wiedergabe des Bildes einer lokalen Göttin auf Münzen der Reichsprägung muß im besonderen Interesse des Königs gelegen haben", vermuten Pohl und Sayar.[57] Der Monarch bringt damit zum Ausdruck, dass er Herr über die Region mit ihren alten Traditionen ist und zugleich in einem besonders engen Nahverhältnis zu den Bürgern steht, die ihm in kritischer Situation zur Seite stehen. Interessant ist allerdings erneut – wie bei Kronos-El in Byblos –, dass diese Magarsia auf den *städtischen* Prägungen im Hellenismus kaum eine Rolle spielt.

– Auch in Tarsos beruft man sich auf einen alten Kult: Seit Alexander I. Balas (152/150–145 v. Chr.) thematisieren verschiedene seleukidische Könige den lokalen Sandankult. Das geschieht mit zwei unterschiedlichen Motiven, dem sogenannten Schrein des Sandan[58] (Abb. 18) und dem Bild des Gottes, der auf einem gehörnten, löwenähnlichen Fabelwesen steht und Pfeil- und Bogenköcher sowie einen Hammer hält (Abb. 19).[59] Auf königlichen Tetradrachmen wird der ‚Schrein' des Sandan, auf Drachmen der Gott selbst abgebildet. Anders als in Mallos korrespondieren in Tarsos die Typen der *königlichen* und der *städtischen* Münzen miteinander, da sie dieselben Bilder verwendeten und damit dieselbe Intention einer Betonung lokaler Kulttraditionen verbreiteten: Der auf dem Tier stehende Gott wird auf städtischen (Silber-)Drachmen und auf Bronzen geprägt (Abb. 20), und der ‚Schrein' ist ein gängiges Motiv in der Bronzeprägung (Abb. 21).

54 Babelon 1910, 867–884 Nr. 1385–1415; SNG von Aulock Nr. 5705–5721, 8698–8699.
55 Ehling u. a. 2004, 221 Inschrift Nr. 1 (Appendix).
56 Pohl – Sayar 2004, 102, 105 und öfter. Möglicherweise handelt es sich um „invented traditions"; zum Phänomen s. Lichtenberger 2021b, 580–581.
57 So Pohl – Sayar 2004, 97.
58 SC II, Nr. 1996 (Antiochos VI.); Nr. 2057 (Antiochos VII.); Nr. 2160 (Demetrios II.); Nr. 2260 (Kleopatra Thea und Antiochos VII.); Nr. 2284–2286 und 2288 (Antiochos VIII.); Nr. 2348–2350 und 2355 (Antiochos IX.); Nr. 2407 (Seleukos VI.).
59 SC II, Nr. 1778 (unter Alexander Balas); Nr. 1895, 2159, 2161 und 2212 (Demetrios II.); Nr. 1997 (Antiochos VI.); Nr. 2058 (Antiochos VII.); Nr. 2287 und 2289 (Antiochos VIII.); Nr. 2351 und 2356 (Antiochos IX.).

Die königlichen Münzen nehmen ein in der städtischen Münzprägung bereits kurz zuvor (als Tarsos kurzzeitig mit ‚Antiocheia am Kydnos' einen dynastischen Namen trägt[60]) eingeführtes Motiv auf. Pohl hat auch seine Münzbilder ausgewertet und einzelne (vorderasiatische und griechische) Bildtraditionen herausgearbeitet, die in der Figur des Sandan zusammenfließen und so gleichzeitig auf kultische Persistenz und Akkulturation verweisen. Sandan ist ein alter, hethitisch-luwischer Gott, der hier in einem Götterbild verewigt wird, das klar in lokalen bzw. regionalen (nicht in griechischen) Bildtraditionen steht.[61]

Beide kilikischen Gottheiten, Magarsia und Sandan, werden später bis weit in die römische Kaiserzeit zu gängigen städtischen Münzmotiven und dienen als Erkennungszeichen und charakteristische Stadtgottheiten/Repräsentanten auf den Roman Provincials.[62]

– Ähnliche lokale Besonderheiten lassen sich am Ende der seleukidischen Herrschaft unter Demetrios III. (95–88 v. Chr.) und Antiochos XII. (87–83/82 v. Chr.) in dem inzwischen zusammengeschrumpften Restreich fassen. In Damaskos, das als „Demetrias" kurzzeitig einen dynastischen Namen trägt, lässt Demetrios ein altertümlich orientalisches oder orientalisierendes weibliches Kultbild auf seine Tetradrachmen prägen (Abb. 14),[63] später sein Bruder und Nachfolger ein vergleichbares männliches Kultbild (Abb. 15).[64] Die Figuren lassen sich als Atargatis (auch Züge der Derketo mögen verwoben sein) und Hadad deuten. Wie in Mallos und Tarsos erinnern die amorphen Gestalten mit menschlichen Gesichtern und aus- bzw. vorgestreckten Armen an altanatolische Figuren. Attribute weisen auf den fruchtbaren Charakter beider Gottheiten. Auch diese beiden Typen werden über mehrere Jahre und aus jeweils mehreren Stempeln geprägt. Es handelt sich also nicht um kleine, unbedeutende Ausnahmeprägungen, sondern in dieser Spätzeit um regelmäßige Ausgaben der großen Edelmetallnominale.[65]

Kay Ehling bemerkt, dass die königlichen Prägungen die außergewöhnlichen ‚nicht-griechischen' Gottheiten zeigten, während die städtischen Prägungen rein griechische Motive (Stadttyche mit Flussgott, stehende Tyche, Zeus, Nike) auf-

---

60   Darauf weisen Pohl 2004, 74 und Tekin 2021, 98 (Gruppe A) hin.
61   Pohl 2004, 76, 82, 87–88, 91–93; Wright 2009/2010, 195–196; Eckhardt – Martin 2016, 42–43; Tekin 2021, 105. Zur Relevanz solcher Kategorien („cultural containers") Lichtenberger 2021b, 583–586.
62   Zu Sandan in Tarsos z. B. RPC III Nr. 3266–3268 (hadrianische Tetradrachmen) sowie auf Bronzemünzen: RPC III Nr. 3307–3310; RPC IV Temp. Nr. 8506; RPC VI Temp. Nr. 7111; RPC VII Nr. 3098–3099, 3150; RPC IX Nr. 1361, 1382, 1385, 1387 und öfter. Bis ins 2. Jh. n. Chr. bleibt die Ikonographie eng den hellenistischen Vorbildern verhaftet. Dazu Ehling 2004b, 140–144 und Tekin 2021, 102–105. Zu Magarsia in Mallos z. B. RPC I Nr. 4016, 4023–4024A; RPC II Nr. 1739; RPC IV Temp. Nr. 4981, 5816, 10297, 10733. Dazu Ehling 2004a, 126–128.
63   SC II, Nr. 2450–2451; Stempelstudie bei Hoover et al. 2008, 225–233.
64   SC II, Nr. 2471–2472A; Stempelstudie bei Hoover et al. 2008, 233–234.
65   Siehe die Zusammenstellungen bei Eckhardt – Martin 2016, 32–34; s. auch Fleischer 1973, 263–369 (Atargatis) und 379–380 (Hadad); Wright 2009/2010, 198–199.

weisen.[66] Bedeutet das, dass sich der seleukidische König mit indigenen Kulten beschäftigt, während die Bürgerschaft der Stadt selbst so sehr hellenisiert ist, dass sie keinen Wert auf ihre eigenen Traditionen legt? Tatsächlich sind die Unterschiede in den Nominalen zu sehen, denn nur das ‚große' Geld, die Tetradrachmen, zeigen die altertümlichen Gottheiten; alle kleineren Nominale in Silber und Bronze sind jeweils (bei Demetrios und Antiochos) griechisch geprägt. Das gilt für die städtische und die königliche Prägung, denn auch die kleinen Werte der königlichen Emissionen zeigen gängige Götterbilder wie Nike (Drachmen), ein Diadem (Hemidrachmen) und Tyche/Zeus/Nike, Apollon/Hermes/Nike oder Dreifuß/Hermes in Bronze. Es sind daher offenbar nicht die jeweiligen Münzherren – König oder Stadt –, die unterschiedliche kulturelle Welten thematisieren oder ansprechen, sondern dies geschieht über die Geldwerte, d. h. es handelt sich um eine nominalspezifische Differenzierung der Bildmotive.[67]

Es lässt sich vermuten, dass die Absicht speziell dieser neu eingeführten Bilder darin besteht, auf überregionaler Ebene mittels der Silbermünzen eine *Außen*-Repräsentation zu schaffen, die ein Vertrauen des Herrschers auf lokale Kräfte vermittelt und im Gegenzug – in unsicheren Zeiten – deren Verlässlichkeit und ein harmonisches Miteinander von König und Stadt suggeriert. Anders als bei den kilikischen Gottheiten, die bis in die römische Kaiserzeit als städtische Identifikationsfiguren verwendet werden, bleiben die damaszenischen eine numismatische Ausnahmeerscheinung; beide Gottheiten finden nach Antiochos XII. keine Verwendung mehr. Möglicherweise haben Demetrios III. und Antiochos XII. mit ihren Tetradrachmen in Damaskos traditionellen lokalen Gottheiten eine in griechischen Augen orientalische bzw. indigen erscheinende Gestalt gegeben, also ein neues, aber alt anmutendes Erscheinungsbild geschaffen, das so jedoch im Kultgeschehen von Damaskos nicht wirklich verwurzelt war.

Abb. 16 Mallos (Kilikien), Tetradrachme des Antiochos VII. mit Magarsia, ca. 138–129 v. Chr. (SC 2059).

---

66 Ehling 2008, 109.
67 Martin – Eckhardt 2016, 36–37.

Abb. 17 Mallos (Kilikien), städtische AE mit Magarsia, ca. 1. Jh. v. Chr.

Abb. 18 Tarsos (Kilikien), Tetradrachme des Antiochos VIII. mit dem Schrein des Sandan,
ca. 121–113 v. Chr.

Abb. 19 Tarsos (Kilikien), Drachme des Antiochos IX. mit Sandan auf einem löwenähnlichen
Tier, 96/95 v. Chr.

Abb. 20 Tarsos (Kilikien), städtische AE mit Sandan auf einem löwenähnlichen Tier stehend,
ca. 2./1. Jh. v. Chr.

Abb. 21 Tarsos (Kilikien), städtische AE mit dem sog. Schrein des Sandan,
ca. 2./1. Jh. v. Chr.

Abb. 22 Damaskos (Koile Syria), Tetradrachme des Demetrios III. mit Atargatis,
92/91 v. Chr. (SC 2451).

Abb. 23 Damaskos (Koile Syria), Tetradrachme des Antiochos XII. mit Hadad,
87/86 v. Chr. (SC 2471).

6. Ausblick

Es stellt sich bei all diesen lokalspezifischen Emissionen die Frage der Bedeutung. Und es stellt sich neben der Frage nach den Empfängern respektive Nutzern dieser Münzen (für wen sind sie konzipiert und wer nutzt diese Münzen? Wen sollen und wen können sie erreichen?) auch diejenige nach den Initiatoren und Auftraggebern. Wenngleich am Anfang immer der König steht (bzw. der Hof / die königliche Entourage, die für den König oder mit ihm geldwirtschaftliche und repräsentative Entscheidungen trifft), sind in den genannten Beispielen mit den unterschiedlich aufgestellten Städten andere Akteure hinzugetreten.

Interessanterweise gelangen etwa ab der Mitte des 2. Jh. v. Chr. auch aus dem Attalidenreich Tetradrachmen mit städtischem Charakter in den seleukidischen Münzumlauf.[68] Wie das ptolemaiische Ägypten, so ist ab Eumenes II. (197–158 v. Chr.) auch das attalidische Kleinasien ein abgegrenzter Währungsraum, da dieser den deutlich

---

68   Eine Zusammenstellung von Horten bzw. das Vorkommen von „Attic weight tetradrachms of cities of Western Asia minor in hoards buried in Seleukid Syria" findet sich bei Psoma 2013, 269–272, 297–299.

reduzierten Kistophor als Leitnominal einführt.[69] Für Wirtschaftskontakte mit anderen Dynastien werden daher in zahlreichen Städten Tetradrachmen nach attischem Standard produziert – Münzen, deren Rückseitenmotiv in der Regel von einem Kranz (στεφανός, daher ihr Rufname als Stephanophoren) gerahmt ist und die das Alexandergeld ablösen.[70] Ihre Münzbilder sind, ganz anders als die einheitlichen Kistophoren, stadtspezifisch individuell und basieren oft auf vorhellenistischen Traditionen.[71] Gelegentlich werden die Motive mit königlichen Details kombiniert und nehmen so bei aller städtischen Individualität monarchische Repräsentationsformen mit auf. Dies zeigt sich beispielsweise in Lebedos, das mit einem Diadem-umwundenen Doppelfüllhorn Bezug auf seine ehemalige Zugehörigkeit zum Ptolemaierreich zeigt (Abb. 24),

Abb. 24 Lebedos (Ionien), sog. stephanophore Tetradrachme, ca. 160–140 v. Chr.

Abb. 25 Myrina (Aiolis), sog. stephanophore Tetradrachme, ca. 160–140 v. Chr.

---

69 Zuletzt Kaye 2022, 129–187, der eine strenge Kategorisierung als ‚königlich' oder ‚städtisch' in Bezug auf die Kistophoren für nicht zielführend hält (ebd. 186–187), stattdessen von dezentralisierter Produktion bei zentralisierter Kontrolle spricht (ebd. 153) und von einer Kooperation der Städte mit dem Herrscher (ebd. 130, 174–175), so dass er auch hier wachsende Eigenständigkeit der Städte sieht. Siehe auch seinen Beitrag in diesem Band (bes. S. 538–544), in dem er die Kistophoren als ein Zugehen der Monarchen auf die Städte sieht. Speziell im Vergleich zu den Stephanophoren (s. u.) ist eine Stärkung der städtischen Position anhand der Kistophoren m. E. jedoch wenig greifbar. Zum abgegrenzten Währungsraum der Attaliden Kaye 2022, 169–173, der jedoch anders als der ptolemaiische (ebd. 163–169) funktioniert.
70 Houghton 2005, 57–58; Psoma 2013, 279; Meadows 2018, 308; Kaye 2022, 144–145, 183–185.
71 Thonemann 2015, 56–61 spricht vom „revival of civic types"; Meadows 2018, 298 et passim von der „great transformation" der griechischen Münzikonographie im 2. Jh. v. Chr.

oder in Myrina, dessen Apollon auf der Vorderseite einen Kranz mit Diademenden trägt (Abb. 25) – in beiden Fällen klar königliche Elemente, bei Lebedos wird zudem das ptolemaiische Doppelfüllhorn modifiziert.

Im Fokus der hier dargelegten Überlegungen standen jedoch bewusst nicht nur Edelmetallprägungen, sondern besonders auch das bronzene Kleingeld. Hier finden sich Entsprechungen, aber auch abweichende Muster. Jeweils unterschiedliche Zielgruppen und Umlaufgebiete werden hierdurch angesprochen. Und auch der Vergleich zum Motivspektrum der oftmals parallel betriebenen städtischen Prägestätten ist aufschlussreich. So geht es um Austauschprozesse und Wechselwirkungen zwischen königlichen und städtischen Ideen, um lokale Einflüsse und die Auseinandersetzung mit indigenen Traditionen und lokalen Kräften, was für Aspekte der königlichen Repräsentation in Bezug auf die Erwartungshaltung der Bevölkerung bedeutsam ist. Interessant ist, dass es oftmals die Könige sind, die zuerst regionale Themen in der Münzprägung aufnehmen (wie Magarsia in Mallos oder indirekt Europa/Stier und Astarte/Schiffsbug auf den quasi-munizipalen Prägungen), erst später werden sie dann auch von der städtischen Münze übernommen.[72]

Was bringt das für die „monarchische Repräsentation"? Ganz offenbar ist es den späten Seleukiden ein Anliegen, die Städte auf numismatischer Ebene in die monarchische Repräsentation einzubinden (Silbermünzen in Mallos, Tarsos oder Damaskos) oder ihnen im Rahmen monarchischer Repräsentation eigene Gestaltungsspielräume zu geben (mit den quasi-munizipalen Prägungen), die sie aber wohl selbst finanzieren müssen. Mithradates VI. in Pontos hingegen gibt sein Programm vor und lässt seinen Münzstätten in numismatischer Hinsicht keine Optionen. Währungspolitisch ist dies sinnvoll, weil so ein reichsweit einheitliches Geldsystem zur Verfügung steht. In vielen Fällen sind die königlichen Münzen Wegbereiter für später produziertes städtisches Geld. Prägetechnische Infrastruktur ist in den Städten der Levante vielerorts vorhanden; in Pontos muss sie an den meisten Orten erst geschaffen werden, ist aber oft nur ephemer, im Attalidenreich wird mit den Stephanophoren dieselbe Währung wie zuvor nun in neuer Gestalt geprägt: auch gleich, nur anders.

Literaturverzeichnis

Babelon 1910: Babelon, Ernest, Le grand roi ou le dieu? Remarques sur quelques types monétaires de Cilicie et de Transeuphratène à l'époque achéménide et romaines I–III, Paris 1910

Bendschus 2017: Bendschus, Torsten, Münzen als Medium der Herrschaftskommunikation von Kleinkönigen im hellenistischen Osten. Die Königreiche von Kappadokien, Pontos, dem Reg-

---

72 So z. B. für Tyros: Syon 2008, 296–297 und Iossif 2014, 78: „*later*, these types became *unambiguously* Tyrian and civic but they were not at the time of the Seleucid conquest" (Hervorhebungen P. Iossif).

num Bosporanum, Armenien und Kommagene im Hellenismus und in der frühen Kaiserzeit, Diss. Rostock 2015/2016, Open Access unter https://doi.org/10.18453/rosdok_id00001850 (last access: 20.5.2024)

Biedermann 2014: Biedermann, David, Hortfundanalysen. Spiegelt sich in getrennten Edelmetall- und Bronzehorten eine nominalspezifische Wahrnehmung?, in: Lichtenberger et al. 2014, 7–58

Casabone 2004: Casabonne, Olivier, La Cilicie à l'époque achéménide, Paris 2004

Chankowski – Duryat 2005: Chankowski, Véronique – Duyrat, Frédérique (eds.), Le Roi et l'économie. Autonomies locales et structures royales dans l'économie de l'empire séleucide, actes des rencontres de Lille (23 juin 2003) et d'Orléans (29–30 janvier 2004), Paris 2004 (2005)

de Callataÿ 1997: de Callataÿ, François, L'histoire des guerres Mithridatiques vue par les monnaies, Louvain-La-Neuve 1997

de Callataÿ 2005: de Callataÿ, François, Coins and Archaeology: The (Mis)Use of Mithridatic Coins for Chronological Purposes in the Bosporan Area, in: V. F. Stolba – L. Hannestadt (eds.), Chronologies of the Black Sea Area in the Period c. 400–100 BC, Aarhus 2005, 119–136

de Callataÿ 2010: de Callataÿ, François, Rez. zu Olshausen 2009, in: Revue suisse de Numismatique 89, 2010, 263–272

de Callataÿ 2014: de Callataÿ, François, For Whom Were Royal Hellenistic Coins Struck? The Choice of Metals and Denominations, in: Lichtenberger et al. 2014, 59–77

Eckhardt – Martin 2016: Eckhardt, Benedikt – Martin, Katharina, De-Hellenisierung/Re-Hellenisierung? Zu ,indigenen Motiven' auf damaszenischen Münzen der späten Seleukidenzeit, in: B. Eckhardt – K. Martin (eds.), Eine neue Prägung. Innovationspotentiale von Münzen in der griechisch-römischen Antike, Wiesbaden 2016, 31–56

Ehling 2004a: Ehling, Kay, Athena Magarsia und Amphilochos auf den kaiserzeitlichen Münzen von Mallos, in: Ehling – Pohl – Sayyar 2004, 126–130

Ehling 2004b: Ehling, Kay, Die Götterwelt von Tarsos, in: Ehling – Pohl – Sayyar 2004, 130–153

Ehling 2008: Ehling, Kay, Untersuchungen zur Geschichte der späten Seleukiden (164–63 v. Chr.). Vom Tode des Antiochos IV. bis zur Einrichtung der Provinz Syria unter Pompeius, Stuttgart 2008

Ehling – Pohl – Sayyar 2004: Ehling, Kay – Pohl, Daniela – Sayyar, Mustafa H., Kulturbegegnung in einem Brückenland. Gottheiten und Kulte als Indikatoren von Akkulturationsprozessen im Ebenen Kilikien, ed. von Marion Meyer und Ruprecht Ziegler, Bonn 2004

Elayi 2004: Elayi, Josette, Le monnayage de la cité phénicienne de Sidon à l'époque Perse (Ve– IVe s. av. J.-C.), Paris 2004

Erciyas 2006: Erciyas, Deniz B., Wealth, Aristocracy, and Royal Propaganda under the Hellenistic Kingdom of Mithradatids in Central Black Sea Region in Turkey, Leiden 2006

Fleischer 1973: Fleischer, Robert, Artemis von Ephesos und verwandte Kultstatuen aus Anatolien und Syrien, Leiden 1973

Hoover 2005: Hoover, Oliver D., Ceci n'est pas l'autonomie. The Coinage of Seleucid Phoenicia as Royal and Civic Power Discourse, in: Chankowski – Duyrat 2005, 485–507

Hoover 2009: Hoover, Oliver D., Handbook of Syrian Coins. Royal and Civic Issues, Fourth to First Centuries BC, Lancaster 2009

Hoover 2012: Hoover, Oliver D., Handbook of Coins of Northern and Central Anatolia, Pontos, Paphlagonia, Bithynia, Phrygia, Galatia, Lykaonia, and Kappadokia (with Kolchis and the Kimmerian Bosporos), Fifth to First Centuries BC, Lancaster 2012

Hoover 2020: Hoover, Oliver D., The Beginning of the End or the End of the Beginning? Seleucid Coinage and the Roman Provincial Paradigm, in: Oetjen 2020, 765–775

Hoover et al. 2008: Hoover, Oliver D. – Houghton, Arthur – Veselý, Petr, The Silver Mint of Damascus under Demetrius III and Antiochus XII (97/6 BC–83/2 BC), American Journal of Numismatics 20, 2008, 203–234

Houghton 1984: Houghton, Arthur, The Seleucid Mint of Mallus and the Cult Figure of Athena Magarsia, in: A. Houghton et al. (eds.), Festschrift für Leo Mildenberg, Wetteren 1984, 91–110

Houghton 2005: Houghton, Arthur, Seleucid Coinage and Monetary Policy of the 2nd c. B. C. Reflections on the Monetization of the Seleucid Economy, in: Chankowski – Duyrat 2005, 49–79

Iossif 2011: Iossif, Panagiotis, Seleucid Religion through Coins: Is it Possible to Quantify ‚Iconography‘ and ‚Religion‘?, in: F. de Callataÿ (ed.), Quantifying Monetary Supplies in Graeco-Roman Times, Bari 2011, 213–249

Iossif 2014: Iossif, Panagiotis P., The Last Seleucids in Phoenicia: Juggling Civic and Royal Identity, American Journal of Numismatics 26, 2014, 61–87

Iossif 2018: Iossif, Panagiotis, Divine Attributes on Hellenistic Coinages: From Noble to Humble and Back, in: Iossif – de Callataÿ – Veymiers 2018, 269–295

Iossif – de Callataÿ – Veymiers 2018: Iossif, Panagiotis – de Callataÿ, François – Veymiers, Richard (eds.), TYPOI. Greek and Roman Coins Seen Through Their Images. Noble Issuers, Humble Users?, Liège 2018

Iossif – Lorber 2021: Iossif, Panagiotis – Lorber, Catharine C., Monetary Policies, Coin Production, and Currency Supply in the Seleucid and Ptolemaic Empires II. Communication and Exchange, in: C. Fischer-Bovet – S. von Reden (eds.), Comparing the Ptolemaic and Seleucid Empires. Integration, Communication, and Resistance, Cambridge 2021, 191–230

Ireland – Cook 2008: Ireland, Stanley – Cook, Peter, A New Mint for Mithradates VI of Pontus?, Numismatic Chronicle 168, 2008, 135–139

Kaye 2022: Kaye, Noah, The Attalids of Pergamon and Anatolia. Money, Culture, and State Power, Cambridge 2022

Kovacs 2022: Kovacs, Martin, Vom Herrscher zum Heros. Die Bildnisse Alexanders des Großen und die Imitatio Alexandri, Rahden 2022

Lichtenberger 2009: Lichtenberger, Achim, Tyros und Berytos. Zwei Fallbeispiele städtischer Identitäten in Phönikien, in: M. Blömer – M. Facella – E. Winter (eds.), Lokale Identität im Römischen Nahen Osten. Kontexte und Perspektiven, Stuttgart 2009, 151–175

Lichtenberger 2021a: Lichtenberger, Achim, Viele Mütter. Zu den quasi-municipalen seleukidischen Lokalbronzen im hellenistischen Phönikien, in: J. Hoffmann-Salz (ed.), The Middle East as Middle Ground?. Cultural Interaction in the Ancient Middle East Revisited, Wien 2021, 65–86

Lichtenberger 2021b: Lichtenberger, Achim, Hellenistic Commagene in Context. Is ‚Global‘ the Answer and Do We Have to Overcome Cultural ‚Containers‘?, in: M. Blömer et al. (eds.), Common Dwelling Place of all the Gods. Commagene in its Local, Regional and Global Hellenistic Context, Stuttgart 2021, 579–587

Lichtenberger et al. 2014: Lichtenberger, Achim et al. (eds.), BildWert. Nominalspezifische Kommunikationsstrategien in der Münzprägung hellenistischer Herrscher, Bonn 2014

Lorber 2015: Lorber, Catharine C., Royal Coinage in Hellenistic Phoenicia: Expressions of Continuity, Agents of Change, in: J. Aliquot – C. Bonnet (eds.), La Phénicie hellénistique. Actes du colloque international de Toulouse (18–20 février 2013), Paris 2015, 55–88

Meadows 2001: Meadows, Andrew, Money, Freedom, and Empire in the Hellenistic World, in: A. Meadows – K. Shipton (eds.), Money and its Uses in the Ancient World, Oxford 2001, 53–63

Meadows 2018: Meadows, Andrew, The Grand Transformation. Civic Coins Design in the Second Century BC, in: Iossif – de Callataÿ – Veymiers 2018, 297–318

Meyer 2020: Meyer, Marion, King Antiochus IV and the Cities in the Levant, in: Oetjen 2020, 525–539

Michels 2009: Michels, Christoph, Kulturtransfer und monarchischer „Philhellenismus": Bithynien, Pontos und Kappadokien in hellenistischer Zeit, Göttingen 2009

Mittag 2006: Mittag, Peter F., Antiochos IV. Epiphanes. Eine politische Biographie, Stuttgart 2006

Oetjen 2020: Oetjen, Roland (ed.), New Perspectives in Seleucid History, Archaeology and Numismatics. Studies in Honour of Getzel M. Cohen, Berlin u. a. 2020

Olshausen 2009: Olshausen, Eckart, Bronzemünzen aus der Zeit des Mithradates' VI. im Museum von Samsun, Stuttgart 2009

Pohl 2004: Pohl, Daniela, Sandan in Tarsos, in: Ehling – Pohl – Sayyar 2004, 73–93

Pohl – Sayar 2004: Pohl, Daniela – Sayar, Mustafa H., Athena Magarsia in Mallos, in: Ehling – Pohl – Sayyar 2004, 93–107

Price 1991: Price, Martin J., The Coinage in the Name of Alexander the Great and Philip Arrhidaeus, London 1991

Psoma 2013: Psoma, Selene, War or Trade? Attic-Weight Tetradrachms from Second-Century BC Attalid Asia Minor in Seleukid Syria after the Peace of Apameia and their Historical Context, in: P. Thonemann (ed.), Attalid Asia Minor. Money, International Relations, and the State, Oxford 2013, 265–300

Syon 2008: Syon, Danny, The Bronze Coinage of Tyre: The First Years of Autonomy, American Journal of Numismatics 20, 2008, 295–304

Thonemann 2015: Thonemann, Peter, The Hellenistic World. Using Coins as Sources, Cambridge 2015

Tekin 2021: Tekin, Oğuz, Sandan on the Coins of Tarsus in Cilica, in: S. Kerschbaum – H. Vidin (eds.), Traditions through Empires. Cities of Asia Minor and their Coin Images, Bonn 2021, 97–107

Wright 2009/2010: Wright, Nicholas L., Non-Greek Religious Imagery on the Coinage of Seleucid Syria, Mediterranean Archaeology 22/23, 2009/2010, 193–206

Abbildungsverzeichnis

Abb. 1:   ANS, Inv. 1992.54.1566, © American Numismatic Society, New York.

Abb. 2:   Münzsammlung der Universität Münster, M 1504, Foto Robert Dylka.

Abb. 3:   Münzkabinett der Staatlichen Museen zu Berlin, Objektnummer 18209961, Foto Reinhard Saczewski.

Abb. 4:   Münzsammlung der Universität Münster, M 1507, Foto Robert Dylka.

Abb. 5:   ANS, Inv. 1992.54.1733, © American Numismatic Society, New York.

Abb. 6:   BNF, Inv. FRBNF44996731, © Bibliothèque nationale de France, Paris.

Abb. 7:   ANS, Inv. 1944.100.77142, © American Numismatic Society, New York.

Abb. 8:   CNG, E-Auction 344 (2015-02-15) Nr. 149, © Classical Numismatic Group Inc., Lancaster.

Abb. 9:   Münzsammlung der Universität Münster, Inv. M 952, Foto Robert Dylka.

Abb. 10: Münzsammlung der Universität Münster, Inv. M 939, Foto Robert Dylka.

Abb. 11: Münzsammlung der Universität Münster, Inv. M 956, Foto Robert Dylka.

Abb. 12: Münzkabinett der Staatlichen Museen zu Berlin, Objektnummer 18276535, Foto Bernhard Weisser.

Abb. 13: Münzkabinett der Staatlichen Museen zu Berlin, Objektnummer 18276523, Foto Bernhard Weisser.

Abb. 14: Münzsammlung der Universität Stuttgart, Inv.-Nr. AGS 6.2, Foto Leah Frey.

Abb. 15: Münzkabinett der Staatlichen Museen zu Berlin, Objektnummer 18275978, Foto Bernhard Weisser.

Abb. 16: Leu, Auktion 8 (2021-10-23) Nr. 150, © Leu Numismatik AG, Winterthur.

Abb. 17: Universität Düsseldorf, Inv. Ls4252.32.67, Foto Sebastian Lindermann.

Abb. 18: Münzkabinett der Staatlichen Museen zu Berlin, Objektnummer 18200452, Foto Lutz-Jürgen Lübke.

Abb. 19: ANS, Inv. 1944.100.78090, © American Numismatic Society, New York.

Abb. 20: Münzsammlung der Universität Münster, Inv. M 1322, Foto Robert Dylka.

Abb. 21: Münzsammlung der Universität Münster, Inv. M 2913, Foto Robert Dylka.

Abb. 22: ANS, Inv. 1944.100.78015, © American Numismatic Society, New York.

Abb. 23: CNG, Auction 121 (2022-10-06) Nr. 533, © Classical Numismatic Group Inc., Lancaster.

Abb. 24: Münzsammlung der Katholischen Universität Eichstätt, Inv. 288, Foto Kristina Hamacher.

Abb. 25: Münzsammlung des Martin von Wagner Museums der Universität Würzburg, Inv. Ka 1723 = H 6298, Foto Lukas Jansen.

Katharina Martin is curator of the coin collection at the Archaeological Museum of Münster University. She studied Classical Archaeology, Ancient History and Arabic/Islamic Studies in Münster and Cairo. Both her master thesis and her PhD dissertation focus on topics from the field of numismatics. First specialising in Roman provincial coinage, she later also did research in the field of Hellenistic coins. Another focus of her work is digitisation; within this context, she has coordinated the "Network of University Coin Collections in Germany" (NUMiD) since 2017 and is co-editor of the "Online Zeitschrift zur Antiken Numismatik" (OZeAN).

Being "Greek" in Egypt
The Ptolemies of the Second and First Century and Ethno-cultural Concepts[*]

PATRICK SÄNGER

Abstract: This paper deals with the later Ptolemaic period, when the Ptolemaic empire had already passed its zenith but had far from given up its claim to be a leading political player on the international stage. The question of Ptolemaic legitimation and self-representation will be examined in this temporal context, with a focus on how ethnic groups and concepts were dealt with. The aim is to show strategies that the Ptolemies pursued on an administrative and social level in order to assert their former role as a maritime power in the eastern Mediterranean on an ideological level. The institution of the politeuma, whose introduction can probably be linked to Ptolemaios VI, will serve as the pivotal point for the considerations. This institution seems to have created a specific form of association that was apparently intended for organised groups of people who lived within an urban area and were named after an ethnic designation. In establishing the politeumata, the Ptolemies used ethnicity for ideological reasons that were probably related to domestic and foreign policy developments and strategic considerations. The Ptolemies' intention was probably to set an example for their settlement policy and to keep Egypt attractive for immigrants from foreign cities or regions. The politeumata could be understood as a compensatory strategy aimed at continuing in the second and first centuries patterns that were characteristic of Ptolemaic politics in the third century and obviously formative for the dynasty's self-image.

Could a Hellenistic king legitimize himself through establishing institutions as an expression of his benevolent and successful administrative or social policies? Did reforms or innovations in these areas serve self-representation and who were the addressees?

In principle, these questions tie in with the major patterns of interpretation of the Hellenistic monarchies: on the one hand, with the approach of Hans-Joachim Gehrke, who associated the Hellenistic monarchy with charismatic rule in the sense of Max

---

[*] The present text contains single passages of my articles 2021 and 2022; on the topic see also Sänger 2019, 191–196.

Weber;[1] on the other hand, with those in Anglo-American and Francophone scholarship, who understand the Hellenistic monarchies as empires in which the king at
the top exercised power over institutions or institutional structures – this research approach of a patrimonial-bureaucratic rule (again corresponding to Weber) is inextricably linked with the name of Elias Bickerman.[2] Basically, then, a "sociology of rule" is
opposed here to a "sociology of empires".[3] Both approaches have their strengths and
weaknesses, point to specific possibilities and emphases in interpretation as well as respective analytical limits, and it is not my intention to continue or deepen this discussion here. Incidentally, it was recently addressed in detail by Ulrich Wiemer, who did
not confine himself to a mere summary of the state of research. Rather, in a synopsis,
he has undertaken a programmatic harmonization of the "sociology of rule" and the
"sociology of empires", thus arguing – in my understanding – for the inclusion of both
approaches in the discussion of Hellenistic monarchies. Wiemer reminds us that, on
the one hand, there is the character that the rule of Hellenistic kings possessed, and
this can undoubtedly be described by the term "personal monarchy" – this brings the
personality of the king into focus and implies the need for the king to be able to fulfill
the expectations that the relevant social groups have of his qualities; victory in war is
an important aspect of this, but by no means the only one, because the king also had
to prove himself a benefactor, a *euergetes*. On the other hand, Wiemer comes to the
conclusion that Hellenistic monarchies were resilient, which cannot be explained by
the features of a "personal monarchy" alone, but must also take into account the patrimonial-bureaucratic organization of rule, thus the ability to exercise power through
institutions. Accordingly, when Wiemer finally highlights the stability of Hellenistic
monarchies such as those of the Ptolemies, Seleukids, and Antigonids, he attributes
this characteristic in large parts to institutional structures.[4]

In this paper, I would like to develop the idea that the Ptolemies knew how to actively play the institutional card to meet their goals in terms of dynastic legitimation and
self-representation. In doing so, I would like to draw attention to the fact that Hellenistic kingship, which is to be understood as a "personal monarchy", was not only able
to articulate its power and sociopolitical claim through potential or asserted victoriousness and euergetism and their sometimes abstract translation into rituals, images,
and texts. Rather, the example of the Ptolemies will illustrate that a regime could also
resort to institutional or administrative instruments to do justice to its ideology and
self-image and perhaps to the expectations of certain population groups. In this con-

1   Gehrke 1982; for a critical evaluation and further development of the approach, see e. g., Gotter
     2013 and Wiemer 2017. On the use of Max Weber's typology (Weber 1976) cf. also the paper by
     Noah Kaye in this volume.
2   Bickerman 1938 and 1966; cf. Wiemer 2017, 319–323.
3   On these currents within recent research see Wiemer 2017, 332–338.
4   As in the preceding note.

text, the concept of "being 'Greek' in Egypt" will come into focus touching on the self-understanding of the Ptolemies as a Graeco-Macedonian ruling dynasty – an area where it was meaningless what realities lay behind "being 'Greek' in Egypt" over the centuries in terms of ethnicity, culture, and identity.[5]

The paper will explore these issues by looking at the later Ptolemaic period, when the Ptolemaic kingdom had passed its zenith but had by no means given up its claim to be a leading political player on the international stage. Our starting point is the first half of the second century, when the Ptolemaic kingdom was seriously tested, both in terms of foreign policy and domestic policies: Ptolemaios V had lost all Ptolemaic outer possessions in Asia Minor and Koile-Syria in the 190s. Although a few years later his reign saw the end of the great twenty-year-long revolt of the Thebaid or Upper Egypt in 186, Egypt continued to be affected by several domestic political crises under his successor Ptolemaios VI. In 169 and 168 the Seleukids invaded Lower Egypt and soon after (*ca.* 165) the revolt of Dionysios Petosarapis started near Alexandreia and obviously spread through the Herakleopolite nome in Middle Egypt.[6] At roughly the same time another uprising broke out in the Thebaid.[7] Finally, Egypt was burdened by the dispute between Ptolemaios VI and Ptolemaios VIII because the latter, although his authority had been limited to the Kyrenaika in 164/163, continued to pose a significant threat to his older brother's rule over Egypt in the 150s.

The weak political position of the Ptolemaic kingdom from the second century onward brought changes in recruitment patterns, which manifested themselves in the army's increased use of Graeco-Egyptian or Egyptian recruits in the composition of its troops. Indeed, in the second and first centuries, mercenaries or professional soldiers were increasingly recruited from Graeco-Egyptian or Egyptian milieus, that is, from within Egypt.[8] From the second century onward, changes also occurred with regard to the recruitment of cleruchs in that recruits from Egyptian families were now increas-

---

5   Overviews of the vast literature on ethnicity and ethnic identity in Ptolemaic Egypt – an issue entangled with the question of the fusion or separation of the Graeco-Macedonian and indigenous populations, and with scholarly contributions often inspired by colonial or post-colonial experiences and European imperialism – are provided by Moyer 2011, 11–36 and (focusing the Ptolemaic army and its social role) Fischer-Bovet 2014, 4–6; recently, Coussement 2016 took up this topic in connection with the phenomenon of double names. Of relevance in this context, of course, are also the approaches to the facets and degrees of Jewish assimilation or separation in the Greek and Egyptian cultures of Ptolemaic Egypt; the tendencies of research are reflected, for example, in: Tcherikover 1959, 298–305, Smallwood 1976, 225–226, Applebaum 1974a, 430, 452, id. 1974b, 465, and Kasher 1985, with a summary on pp. 356–357; Mélèze Modrzejewski 1997, 80–83; 2014, 153–157; Ritter 2015; Sänger 2019; Kugler 2022.

6   See McGing, 1997, 293.

7   See Hölbl 1994, 157–158. On revolts in Ptolemaic Egypt see, in general, McGing 1997; Veïsse 2004; Pfeiffer 2021.

8   On this change in mercenary recruitment practices, see also Fischer-Bovet 2014, 119, 262, 269, 273–279 and 293 as well as Scheuble 2009, 220.

ingly accepted into the higher ranks of the cleruchy system, which had previously been reserved for soldiers of Graeco-Macedonian descent.[9]

What did not change, however, was the categorization of Egypt's population, which largely adhered to third century principles: Persons who were assigned to the population categories of the *Hellenes* and *Makedones* retained their fiscally privileged and prestigious positions of the third century in the second and first centuries.[10] In administrative and sociopolitical terms, a certain ideological significance must be attributed to this adherence to old patterns, in the sense of a harking back to "the good old days" when the Ptolemaic kingdom was at the height of its political power, and a continuation of the associated image of success. This continuity in the ethno-cultural categorization of population groups provided a certain degree of domestic political stability,[11] but it did not provide any innovative strength in a time of obvious loss of power.

It is precisely at this point that an institution called *politeuma* comes into play, whose earliest secured attestation falls into the reign of Ptolemaios VI (180–145).[12] With the *politeumata*, the Ptolemies seem to have created a specific form of association which is only attested in their realm and was apparently destined for organized groups of persons living within an urban area and named after an ethnic designation.[13] In Hellenistic Egypt, *politeumata* of Kilikians and Kretans, which are both perhaps to be located in the Arsinoite nome, a *politeuma* of Boiotians in Xois in the Delta, one of Idumaeans in Memphis, and one of Jews in Herakleopolis are attested.[14] In Roman times we encounter – probably as a relic of the Ptolemaic period – one other Jewish *politeuma* which was located in Berenike in the Kyrenaika, a *politeuma* of Phrygians, whose location in Egypt is unknown, and a *politeuma* of Lykians which existed in Alexandreia.[15]

---

9   See Fischer-Bovet 2014, 216–221; Scheuble-Reiter 2012, 138–139.

10   On the continuing use of the categories "Greeks" or *Hellenes* and "Egyptians" in administrative language, see P.Tebt. I 5 = C.Ord.Ptol. 53, 207–210 (118) with Mélèze Modrzejewski 1983, 255; Thompson 2001, 302–303. On the tax-*Hellenes*, see specifically Huß 2011, 247–248 with reference to BGU 14, 2429, 13 (Herakl., after 94 or 61 [?]). On the category of *Makedones* see Thompson 2001, 306; Vandorpe 2008; Fischer-Bovet 2014, 177–191.

11   On the preservation of the Greek Macedonian image of the Ptolemies, see Buraselis 2011, 159; La'Da 2003, 166–167; Spawforth 2006, 5–7.

12   This has led to the widespread assumption that the form of organization in question was introduced by this king: see Launey 1949/1950, 1077; Honigman 2003, 67; Thompson 2011b, 21–22 with further bibliographical references at n. 47; cf. also Fischer-Bovet 2014, 293–294.

13   On the evidence for the *politeumata* see most recently Sänger 2019, 29–91.

14   Boiotians: SEG 2.871 = SB III 6664. Kretans: P.Tebt. I 32 = W.Chr. 448. Idumaeans: OGIS 737 = Milne 1905, 18–19 no. 33027 = SB V 8929 = I.Prose 25; on the identification of the Idumaean politeuma see Thompson 1984 and 2012, 93–96. Cilicians: SB IV 7270 = SEG 8.573 = I.Fay. I 15 = I.gr. Eg.Nub. Louvre 22. Jews: P.Polit.Iud.

15   Jews: CIG III 5362 = SEG 16.931 = Lüderitz 1983, no. 70 (Augustan period?) and CIG III 5361 = Lüderitz 1983, no. 71 (AD 24/25). Phrygians: IG XIV 701 = OGIS 658 = SB V 7875 = IGR I 458 = Kayser 1994, no. 74; on the provenance of the inscription see also Huß 2011, 299 with further bibliographical references in n. 232. Lycians: SB III 6025 = V 8757 = IGR I 1078 = SEG 2.848 = I.Prose 61 = Kayser 1994, no. 24.

The peculiarity of this specific form of association is that it is likely to be interpreted as an administrative unit that was based on a (semi-autonomous) community and its territorial base.[16] Furthermore, the location of the *politeumata* and their connection with military groups suggest that these communities resulted from mercenary groups. This approach is based on the fact that the Ptolemies recruited full-time mercenary soldiers to use in war, but who also functioned in peacetime to garrison strategically important points.[17] A significant proportion of such military bases were in larger or urban settlements.[18] Furthermore, the ethnic designations the *politeumata* bore might support their mercenary background: Statistical analyses show that, at least in the third century, mercenaries or professional soldiers were recruited by preference in regions where the Ptolemies had possessions or influence, as in Asia Minor, Krete, and the Levant.[19] Therefore, it is fair to assume that the *politeumata* were rooted in ethnically defined mercenaries whose units had been stationed – as far as can be precisely determined – in nome capitals (Xois, Memphis, Herakleopolis) or *poleis* closely intertwined with the Ptolemaic claim to power (Alexandreia, Berenike). In both cases most of these professional soldiers will have lived in the same neighborhood and probably in the vicinity of their garrison.[20] However, the connection with third-century recruitment patterns does not mean that our ethnically defined mercenary groups must have migrated to Egypt in the third century, which will be discussed below.

The fact that the ethnically categorized *politeumata* show a connection with the reign of Ptolemaios VI is probably no coincidence. After decades of domestic and foreign political challenges, they seem to represent an attempt to consolidate the acceptance of the Ptolemaic government through a newly created institution and in this way to articulate claims to power. And in this context, it is precisely the link to ethno-cultural concepts that may have had a certain ideological significance. In this regard, it should first be pointed out that all ethnic groups encountered in the *politeumata* – Boiotians, Kilikians, Kretans, Idumeans, Jews, Lykians, Phrygians – were subsumed by the Ptolemaic fiscal administration since the third century under the previously mentioned collective category of *Hellenes* which were exempt from the obol tax: a very modest fiscal privilege.[21]

---

16   See Kruse 2010, 95, 97, 99–100; Sänger 2019, 130–135, 147–150, 180–184.

17   See Scheuble 2009, 214–215; Fischer-Bovet 2014, 261–263, 269–279.

18   The roots of this system lay in late Pharaonic times and can be traced back to the seventh century; see Fischer-Bovet 2014, 18–37.

19   See Bagnall 1984, 16; Stefanou 2013, 127–131.

20   The *politeumata* are without doubt the best example for a process described by Thompson 2011a, 112–113: 'Local ethnic communities in the Ptolemaic period often derived in origin from military groups; [but] in their developed form they were total communities, consisting of far more than just the military.'

21   On the category of *Hellenes* see, in general, Mélèze Modrzejewski 1983; Thompson 2001; Clarysse – Thompson 2006, 138–147, 154–157. Although Egyptians could become members of this group, too, as a result of their occupation, see Thompson 2001, 310–312 and Clarysse – Thompson 2006, 142–

Moreover, it is striking that the ethnic designations mentioned above, which serve to specify the *politeumata*, refer to regions that once represented outlying possessions, or, at least, to areas which did not belong to the remaining parts of the Ptolemaic kingdom (such as Kypros and the Kyrenaika); from the perspective of the second and first centuries, these ethnic designations thus, alluded to times when the Ptolemies ruled the eastern Mediterranean: in this respect, then, the ethnically categorized *politeumata* likewise embodied continuity and allowed for linkage to a glorious past. Furthermore, it is noticeable that the *politeumata* were set up as conspicuously "Greek" focal points at strategic locations especially in Lower and Middle Egypt and, therefore, close to the Mediterranean and the connecting route to Palestine, the only land bridge to the Levant and the Greek core areas.[22] Behind this geographical scattering, another political message could be hidden, as whose addressee the Seleukid kingdom could be identified and to which a concrete double signaling effect could easily be attributed: on the one hand, that the Ptolemies kept a sharp eye on Judea – which until the middle of the second century was an apple of discord between the Ptolemaic and Seleukid kingdoms – and, on the other hand, that Ptolemaic Egypt had much to offer to Jewish immigrants and their communities in terms of structural anchoring – as the establishment of a Jewish *politeuma* in Herakleopolis and the Jewish military colony at Leontopolis in the eastern delta, associated with the person of Onias (see further below), were able to prove.[23]

With the *politeumata*, then, the Ptolemies may have emphasized, in a mixture of diplomatic and military strategies, a turning toward regions of the eastern Mediterranean and their inhabitants – possibly to express an affinity that resulted from ancient claims to power and/or to invite immigrants to Ptolemaic Egypt. This latter aspect, which opens a socio-political perspective on the issue under consideration, would also touch on a continuum with the policies pursued by the Ptolemies in the third century. For

---

145, the term *Hellen* (Ἕλλην), in practice, mostly denoted an "immigrant" or a "foreign settler" who was to be distinguished from "native Egyptians" (*Aigyptioi*); see Bagnall 1997, 7; Clarysse – Thompson 2006, 142–143, 155.

22   For an overview of the locations of the *politeumata*, see the map in Sänger 2019, XV.

23   Political confusion in Judaea, a consequence of the revolt of the Makkabees, drove Onias – accompanied by fellow Jews – to Egypt, and he was allowed by Ptolemaios VI to found a Jewish temple and form a military colony in Leontopolis (south-east of the Nile Delta); see Ios. bell. Iud. 1.33; 7.427; ant. Iud. 13.65–66. The Oniads were the descendants of Zadok, high priest under Solomon, whose ancestors had held the office of high priest at Jerusalem since Onias I (ca. 320–280). It is still not possible to determine with certainty whether Onias should be identified with Onias III or his son, though the second possibility is slightly preferred in the literature: see Kasher 1985, 132–135, for the controversy, but who leaves open whether Onias III or IV is meant. Parente 1994 argued for Onias III, as did (with more or less conviction), Taylor 1998, 298–310 and Ameling 2008, 118–119. Mélèze Modrzejewski 1997, 124–125 identifies Onias with Onias IV, an identification also preferred by Gruen 1997, 47–57 (n. 26 cites older literature for this position); Capponi 2007, 42–53; Nadig 2011, 188–194. As to whether the military colony of Onias was organized as a *politeuma*, which seems likely, see Sänger 2015.

they had, from the beginning of their rule, created structures to make Egypt a promising and attractive country for immigration: one need only think, first, of the categorical highlighting of the *Hellenes* and the practice of using ethnic designations in everyday legal life as important identification markers, thus marking certain groups of people as "immigrants";[24] second, of the establishment of the *dikasterion*, a "Hellenic" court or court of *Hellenes*;[25] and third and finally, of the Ptolemaic legal system, into which the *politikoi nomoi*, the "civil rights," of the *Hellenes* were integrated.[26] Here, then, the efforts of the Ptolemies to preserve and promote the Graeco-Macedonian element in the population of Egypt had entailed domestic measures at the categorical level on the one hand and at the institutional level on the other, which were intended to attract further immigrants from the Greek world and the Levant and to promise them a privileged position in society.

Even if models of historical migration research based on developments in modern history cannot be applied to pre-modern conditions without reservation, one could in some respects recognize features of a migration regime in Ptolemaic immigration policy or in the socio-political course-setting to be observed in this context.[27] One particular type of this model – for instance, in addition to the coercive, educational and wealth migration regimes – is the labor migration regime, which was aimed at recruiting laborers. This intention can also be attributed to a large extent to the Ptolemaic migration regime under consideration, and it emerges particularly clearly in military contexts.

Indeed, a look at Ptolemaic military policy reveals two broad patterns that seem to have been directed at making the military purpose of recruits dependent on their origin: In the third century, military settlers or cleruchs were recruited with preference from Macedonia, mainland Greece, and Thrace, that is, from outside the Ptole-

---

24 See above n. 21.
25 See Wolff 1962, 37–48; Grotkamp 2018, 24–41.
26 See Wolff 1953, 39–44 and id. 2002, 55–58; Mélèze Modrzejewski 1988, 177; cf. for instance id. 1966; 1983, 258–260; 1997, 107–112; 2014, 142–169.
27 On the model, see basically Jochen Oltmer, http://ome-lexikon.uni-oldenburg.de/begriffe/migration/#c110143 (last access: 20.5.2024): 'Jenseits der Zwangsmigrationen und jenseits der geschilderten individuell oder gruppenspezifisch wirksamen Faktoren beeinflussten Migrationsregime die Umsetzung und Gestaltung von Migrationsoptionen, kontrollierten, förderten, steuerten oder begrenzten das Handeln von Akteuren im Prozess der Migration. Elemente von Migrationsregimen sind für die Rahmung und Gestaltung von Migrationsprozessen relevante weltanschauliche und politische Prinzipien, obrigkeitlich bzw. staatlich gesetzte Regeln, institutionelle Gefüge und administrative Entscheidungsprozeduren. Migrationsregime verweisen damit auf das weit ausgreifende Wechselverhältnis von Staat und Migration. Obrigkeiten bzw. Staaten konnten räumliche Bevölkerungsbewegungen und deren Begleit- und Folgeerscheinungen als wirtschaftliche, soziale, rechtliche, kulturelle oder innen- bzw. außenpolitische Herausforderung wahrnehmen. Art und Grad dieser Problemperzeption orientierten sich dabei an der staatlichen Selbstzuschreibung von Verantwortungsbereichen und Aufgabenstellungen sowie an den damit verbundenen Zielvorstellungen. Der Wandel von Staatlichkeit und Staatsverständnis, von Staatsform und Staatstätigkeit, von staatlicher Legitimation und staatlicher Repräsentation bedingte die Veränderung staatlicher Perzeptionen von Migration.'

maic kingdom,[28] while mercenaries or professional soldiers, as has already been stated, tended to be recruited in the Ptolemaic outer possessions.[29] In this context, the ethnic designations used to name the *politeumata* probably show that the Ptolemies attempted to follow third-century patterns in dealing with mercenary troops even in the second and first centuries, when said foreign possessions or claims to power in the eastern Mediterranean were no longer existent and professional soldiers were primarily recruited from within Egypt.[30] There is indeed some evidence suggesting that even after the territory of the Ptolemaic kingdom had been reduced to Egypt, Kypros, and the Kyrenaika, the Ptolemies were still eager and able to recruit soldiers from other regions.[31] From lands once Ptolemaic but now under hostile control, powerful political refugees and their existing forces or retainers were natural recruits, a fact illustrated by the Ptolemaic reception of the Judaean Onias, member of the Oniad family.[32] Some years later, Idumaens possibly took refuge in Egypt after Idumea had been captured and annexed by the Jewish leader John Hyrcanus in ca. 125 BC.[33] In short, even in a period of declining Ptolemaic power, there is no reason to think the influx of outside soldiers into Egypt ever came to an abrupt end. It rather continued to a lesser degree even in an altered geo-political context.[34]

The division of foreign soldiers into two different occupational groups is also reflected in the divergent strategies used to bind these immigrants to Egypt. On the one hand, cleruchs, who were intended for long-term employment in their capacity as military reservists, were assigned a plot of land (*kleros*) to supply them. On the other hand, there were the *politeumata*, which integrated certain communities of mercenaries of the same origin into the administrative structure of the Ptolemaic kingdom. Since *politeumata* have so far only been attested in urban settlements, they can be seen as an urban counterweight to the settlement of cleruchs, which was largely concentrated in

---

28 See Bagnall 1984; Scheuble-Reiter 2012, 18–23, 114–118; Stefanou 2013.
29 See above n. 19.
30 See above n. 8.
31 Until the reign of Ptolemaios VI Philometor (180–145) active Ptolemaic policy in the Aegean is attested, and until his reign Ptolemaic garrisons were kept in Itanos (north-eastern Krete), Methana (Eastern Peloponnese on the Saronic Gulf), and on the Aegean island of Thera; see Buraselis 2011; Winter 2011; Scheuble-Reiter 2012, 117–118; Fischer-Bovet 2014, 168–169. All these outposts could have assisted recruitment in the surrounding areas. The Ptolemies also employed trusted recruitment officers (xenologoi) to hire soldiers outside Egypt (Pol. 5.63.8–9; 15.25.16–18). Stefanou 2013, 118–120 concluded (p. 120): 'that individual Macedonians might render their services to the Ptolemies, regardless of Ptolemaic relations with the Antigonids', and see pp. 120–121 for Ptolemaic recruitment of prisoners of war and renegades.
32 See above n. 23.
33 See Rapaport 1969, 78–79, 81–82; Thompson 1984, 1071–1072; (2012) 79–80; Honigman 2003, 66 n. 22, 83–84.
34 See Fischer-Bovet 2014, 293: "Indeed, the reorganization of the army during the period of crisis (Period B) [c. 220 and c. 160] favored the use of professional soldiers in garrisons. Even if recruitment was mainly internal to Egypt, foreigners were also hired at times."

rural areas.[35] In any case, both measures attest to the Ptolemies' efforts to create incentives for service in the royal army and to strengthen relations between military personnel and the regime.

Systematically, the essential features of the Ptolemaic labor migration regime expressed through the cleruchy and *politeumata* can be paralleled as follows: if the granting of a plot of land in the third century provided an incentive for recruits from certain regions to join the Ptolemaic cleruchic army and remain in Egypt, in the second and first centuries, it may have been the institution of the *politeuma* that should specifically attract mercenary groups coming from abroad and bind them to their place of service or foster communities that had been present in Egypt for some time. These groups were ethnically defined and provided professional soldiers.[36] If the Ptolemaic cleruchy provided the framework for extensive immigration in the third century, the Ptolemies seem to have set a rather targeted but at the same time distinctive mark in their settlement policy by establishing *politeumata*; and this measure was additionally flanked by likewise attested city foundations, which generally lent a special and dynamic character to the Ptolemaic settlement policy that can be traced in the second century.[37] If Ptolemaic foreign policy after the end of the third century could not match its former glory and consequently the number of immigrants decreased massively, it at least (i. a. by means of the *politeumata*) sought to maintain its reputation for willingly welcoming recruits from the Greek and Levantine regions and offering them further prospects for a life in Egypt[38] – a strategy that may be explained by an increased need for security and

35 On the settlement of cleruchs, see Scheuble-Reiter 2012, 27–32; on villages as places of residence of cleruchs ibid., 33–38; Fischer-Bovet 2014, 239–242.

36 One can certainly agree with Thompson 1984, 1074–1075; ead. 2011a, 109–113; 2011b, 21–22 that the institution of the *politeuma* might have been an alternative to the allocation of *kleroi*. At the same time, however, there is no evidence to suggest that *politeumata* were intended as a substitute for the settlement cleruchs. This is because cleruch settlements are also attested (to a limited extent) for the second and first centuries; see Scheuble-Reiter 2012, 23–24; Fischer-Bovet 2014, 204–206.

37 This concerns the initiatives of Ptolemaios VI and Ptolemaios VIII who both entrusted Boethos, a high-ranking official with the epithet κτίστης or "founder," with city foundations in the Nile valley, first Philometoris and Kleopatra in the Triakontaschoinus (Lower Nubia) and then Euergetis, which unpublished papyri locate in the Herakleopolite. The foundation of Philometoris, Kleopatra and Euergetis was probably, as the *politeumata*, a security-motivated response to the great revolt of the Thebaid and/or to other domestic and foreign political crises that threatened the Ptolemaic kingdom in the first half of the second century: the geographic position of Philometoris and Kleopatra, though not precisely identified, suggests that these cities were intended to be military outposts, and in Euergetis a large part of the population demonstrably seems to have been employed as soldiers. For Philometoris and Kleopatra see the inscription OGIS 111 (IThSy 302 = I.gr.Eg.Nub. Louvre 14) which comes from the southern border zone of Egypt and is dated to the reign of Ptolemaios VI, for Euergetis SB XXIV 15973 (prov. unknown, 132) and 15974 (prov. unknown, 129); see also Thompson 2011a, 103 with n. 8. On Boethos and his city foundations see Kramer 1997; Heinen 1997 and Fischer-Bovet 2021, 75–78.

38 On the good image that the Ptolemies had in the third century with regard to the remuneration of soldiers, see Theokr. 14.58, 65–68; Scheuble-Reiter 2012, 19.

a reduced influx of foreign mercenaries into Egypt. Thus, in addition to establishing continuity, which manifested itself in the recourse to and promotion of ethnic concepts and groups, the *politeumata* were also concerned with creating stability in terms of the goodwill of and access to mercenary troops.

Continuity and stability are indeed the keywords that can be employed to describe the institutional principles and course set in Ptolemaic administrative and social policy in the second and first centuries. An essential pivot of this continuity and stability was the concept "of being 'Greek' in Egypt", and in terms of their political function and external impact, the highlighted ethno-cultural concepts based on group definition and categorization – regardless of the question of their actual authenticity – can be broken down to mere ideology-laden labels. We are dealing with ideologemes that emphasized the Graeco-Macedonian image of the Ptolemies as a manifestation of their successful presence in the eastern Mediterranean. At this level, "being 'Greek' in Egypt" was an important representational feature in the "political game" of the Ptolemies. In the second and first centuries, the framework conditions for this "political game" had changed significantly, because foreign policy successes and political influence – as guarantors of open channels for immigration to Egypt – could no longer easily serve as its backdrop. A determining factor in this development was that the Ptolemies, as well as other Hellenistic kings, had to resign themselves in the course of the second century to Roman supremacy in the eastern Mediterranean, which manifested itself bluntly in the events surrounding the Day of Eleusis in 168. The Hellenistic kings had thus entered a phase of their rule in which they were deprived of an essential basis of their legitimacy and acceptance: they could no longer credibly present themselves as victors without any "ifs and buts" and in this respect became – to use Ulrich Gotter's pithy diction – "castrated kings" in diplomatic dependence on Rome.[39]

In this context, the aim of the present study was to draw attention to the remarkable fact that the compensation for an irretrievable past could also reach into the institutional sphere, and even lead to innovations here, namely, in the case of the Ptolemies, to the establishment of an institution such as we encounter in the *politeuma*. However strong its effect on foreign policy might have been, domestically, this institution was capable of reflecting to some extent – at least in Lower and Middle Egypt – the political claim of the Ptolemies, inherited from the third century and also expressed in ethno-cultural concepts, to establish Egypt as a center of attraction and a home for Graeco-Macedonian and Semitic population groups. And it was capable of continuing a consistent military policy alongside the Ptolemaic cleruchy that especially sought to anchor soldiers socially, thus setting this branch of Ptolemaic policy apart from the other Hellenistic kingdoms, which had not developed such a clearly militaristically de-

---

39   Gotter 2013. See on the consequences of this also the chapter by Noah Kaye in this volume.

fined cleruchy and even lacked an institution such as the *politeuma*.[40] The view opened
here thus demonstrates how administrative and social policies were instrumentalized
for self-representation and a form of expression of a political agenda; and it reveals
a neuralgic point in Ptolemaic history where the "personal monarchy" made use of
the possibilities of patrimonial-bureaucratic organization to compensate for lost sine-
cures. The "sociology of rule" merges with the "sociology of empires" – a connection
that should be given increased attention in the future.

Bibliography

Ameling 2008: Ameling, Walter, Die jüdischen Gemeinden im antiken Kleinasien, in: R. Jütte –
A. P. Kustermann (eds.), Jüdische Gemeinden und Organisationsformen von der Antike bis
zur Gegenwart, Vienna et al. 1996, 29–55

Applebaum 1974a: Applebaum, Shimon, The Legal Status of the Jewish Communities in the Diaspora, in: S. Safrai – M. Stern (eds.), The Jewish People in the First Century. Historical Geography, Political History, Social, Cultural and Religious Life and Institutions I, Assen 1974,
420–463

Applebaum 1974b: Applebaum, Shimon, The Organization of the Jewish Communities in the
Diaspora, in: S. Safrai – M. Stern (eds.), The Jewish People in the First Century. Historical
Geography, Political History, Social, Cultural and Religious Life and Institutions I, Assen 1974,
464–503

Bagnall 1984: Bagnall, Roger S., The Origins of Ptolemaic Cleruchs, Bulletin of the American
Society of Papyrologists 21, 1984, 7–20

Bagnall 1997: Bagnall, Roger S., The People of the Roman Fayum, in: M. L. Bierbrier, (ed.), Portraits and Masks: Burial Customs in Roman Egypt, London 1997, 7–15 (also published in:
R. S. Bagnall (ed.), Hellenistic and Roman Egypt. Sources and Approaches, Aldershot et al.
2006, 1–19)

Bickerman 1938: Bickerman, Elias J., Institutions des Séleucides, Paris 1938

Bickerman 1966: Bickerman, Elias J., The Seleucids and the Achaemenids, in: A. Monteverdi
(ed.), La Persia e il mondo greco-romano, Accademia Nazionale dei Lincei 76, Rome 1966,
87–117; also published in: E. J. Bickerman, Religion and Politics in the Hellenistic and Roman
Periods, Como 1985, 491–521

Buraselis 2011: Buraselis, Kostas, A Lively "Indian Summer": Remarks on the Ptolemaic Role in
the Aegean under Philometor, in: Jördens – Quack 2011, 151–160

Capponi 2007: Capponi, Livia, Il tempio di Leontopoli in Egitto: Identità politica e religiosa dei
Giudei di Onia (c. 150 a. C. – 73 d. C.), Pisa 2007

Clarysse – Thompson 2006: Clarysse, Willy – Thompson, Dorothy J., Counting the People in
Hellenistic Egypt II: Historical Studies, Cambridge Classical Studies, Cambridge 2006

Coussement 2016: Coussement, Sandra, 'Because I am Greek'. Polyonymy as an Expression of
Ethnicity in Ptolemaic Egypt, Leuven 2016

---

40   On the cleruchy and the *politeumata* in the context of the ruling practices of the Antigonid, Attalid
and Seleukid kingdoms, see Sänger 2019, 198–206 and id. 2021, 118–125.

Fischer-Bovet 2014: Fischer-Bovet, Christelle, Army and Society in Ptolemaic Egypt, Cambridge 2014

Fischer-Bovet 2021: Fischer-Bovet, Christelle, Reassessing Ptolemaic Settlement Policies: Another Look at the poleis, in: Fischer-Bovet – von Reden 2021, 64–84

Fischer-Bovet – von Reden 2021: Fischer-Bovet, Christelle – von Reden, Sitta (eds.), Comparing the Ptolemaic and Seleucid Empires. Integration, Communication, and Resistance, Cambridge 2021

Gehrke 1982: Gehrke, Hans-Joachim, Der siegreiche König. Überlegungen zur hellenistischen Monarchie, Archiv für Kulturgeschichte 64, 1982, 247–277

Gotter 2013: Gotter, Ulrich, The Castrated King, or: The Everyday Monstrosity of Late Hellenistic Kingship, in: N. Luraghi (ed.), The Splendors and Miseries of Ruling Alone. Encounters with Monarchy from Archaic Greece to the Hellenistic Mediterranean, Stuttgart 2013, 207–230

Grotkamp 2018: Grotkamp, Nadine, Rechtsschutz im hellenistischen Ägypten, Munich 2018

Gruen 1997: Gruen, Erich S., The Origins and Objectives of Onias' Temple, Scripta Classica Israelica 16, 1997, 47–70

Heinen 1997: Heinen, Heinz, Der κτίστης Boethos und die Einrichtung einer neuen Stadt. Teil II, Archiv für Papyrusforschung 43, 1997, 340–363

Hölbl 1994: Hölbl, Günther, Geschichte des Ptolemäerreiches. Politik, Ideologie und religiöse Kultur von Alexander dem Großen bis zur römischen Eroberung, Darmstadt 1994

Honigman 2003: Honigman, Sylvie, Politeumata and Ethnicity in Ptolemaic Egypt, Ancient Society 33, 2003, 61–102

Huß 2011: Huß, Werner, Die Verwaltung des ptolemaiischen Reiches, Munich 2011

Jördens – Quack 2011: Jördens, Andrea – Quack, Joachim F. (eds.), Ägypten zwischen innerem Zwist und äußerem Druck. Die Zeit Ptolemaios' VI. bis VIII. Internationales Symposion Heidelberg 16.–19.9.2007, Philippika. Marburger altertumskundliche Abhandlungen 45, Wiesbaden 2011

Kasher 1985: Kasher, Aryeh, The Jews in Hellenistic and Roman Egypt. The Struggle for Equal Rights, Tübingen 1985

Kayser 1994: Kayser, François, Recueil des inscriptions grecques et latines (non funéraires) d'Alexandrie impériale (Ier–IIIe s. apr. J.-C.), Le Caire 1994

Kramer 1997: Kramer, Bärbel, Der κτίστης Boethos und die Einrichtung einer neuen Stadt. Teil I, Archiv für Papyrusforschung 43, 1997, 315–339

Kruse 2010: Kruse, Thomas, Das jüdische politeuma von Herakleopolis und die Integration fremder Ethnien im Ptolemäerreich, in: V. V. Dement'eva – T. Schmitt (eds.), Volk und Demokratie im Altertum, Göttingen 2010, 93–105

Kugler 2022: Kugler, Robert A., Resolving Disputes in Second Century BCE Herakleopolis: A Study in Jewish Legal Reasoning in Hellenistic Egypt, Leiden 2022

La'Da 2003: La'Da, Csaba, Encounters with Ancient Egypt: The Hellenistic Greek Experience, in: R. Matthews – C. Roemer (eds.), Ancient Perspectives on Egypt, London 2003, 157–169

Launey 1949/1950: Launey, Marcel, Recherches sur les armées hellénistiques, Paris 1949/1950

Lüderitz 1983: Lüderitz, Gert, Corpus jüdischer Zeugnisse aus der Cyrenaika mit einem Anhang von Joyce M. Reynolds, Wiesbaden 1983

McGing 1997: McGing, Brian, Revolt Egyptian Style. Internal Opposition to Ptolemaic Rule, Archiv für Papyrusforschung 43, 1997, 273–314

Mélèze Modrzejewski 1966: Mélèze Modrzejewski, Joseph, La règle de droit dans l'Égypte ptolémaïque, in: A. E. Samuel (ed.), Essays in Honor of Bradford Welles, New Haven 1966, 125–173

Mélèze Modrzejewski 1983: Mélèze Modrzejewski, Joseph, Le statut des Hellènes dans l'Égypte lagide: Bilan et perspectives des recherches, Revue des Études Grecques 96, 1983, 241–268

Mélèze Modrzejewski 1988: Mélèze Modrzejewski, Joseph, Nochmals zum Justizwesen der Ptolemäer, Zeitschrift der Savigny-Stiftung für Rechtsgeschichte 105, 1988, 165–179

Mélèze Modrzejewski 1997: Mélèze Modrzejewski, Joseph, The Jews of Egypt. From Ramses II to Emperor Hadrian, trans. by R. Cornman; with a foreword by S. J. D. Cohen repr. with corrections, Princeton 1997

Mélèze Modrzejewski 2014: Mélèze Modrzejewski, Joseph, Loi et coutume dans l'Égypte grecque et romaine, Warsaw 2014

Milne 1905: Milne, Joseph G., Greek Inscriptions, Service des Antiquités de l'Égypte: Catalogue géneral des antiquités égyptiennes du Musée du Caire, Oxford 1905

Moyer 2011: Moyer, Ian S., Egypt and the Limits of Hellenism, Cambridge 2011

Nadig 2011: Nadig, Peter, Zur Rolle der Juden unter Ptolemaios VI. und Ptolemaios VIII., in: Jördens – Quack 2011, 186–200

Parente 1994: Parente, Fausto, Onias III' Death and the Founding of the Temple of Leontopolis, in: F. Parente – J. Sievers (eds.), Josephus and the History of the Greco-Roman Period. Essays in Memory of Morton Smith, Leiden et al. 1994, 69–98

Pfeiffer 2021: Pfeiffer, Stefan, Innere Konflikte und herrschaftliche Versöhnungsstrategien im ptolemäischen Ägypten, in: St. Pfeiffer – G. Weber (eds.), Gesellschaftliche Spaltungen im Zeitalter des Hellenismus (4.–1. Jahrhundert v. Chr.), Stuttgart 2021, 107–128

Rapaport 1969: Rapaport, Uriel, Des Iduméens en Égypte, Revue de Philologie, de Littérature et d'Histoire Anciennes 43, 1969, 73–82

Ritter 2015: Ritter, Bradley, Judaeans in the Greek Cities of the Roman Empire. Rights, Citizenship and Civil Discord, Leiden 2015

Sänger 2015: Sänger, Patrick, Considerations on the Administrative Organisation of the Jewish Military Colony in Leontopolis: A Case of Generosity and Calculation, in: J. Tolan (ed.), Expulsion and Diaspora Formation: Religious and Ethnic Identities in Flux from Antiquity to the Seventeenth Century, Turnhout 2015, 171–194

Sänger 2019: Sänger, Patrick, Die ptolemäische Organisationsform politeuma. Ein Herrschaftsinstrument zugunsten jüdischer und anderer hellenischer Gemeinschaften, Tübingen 2019

Sänger 2021: Sänger, Patrick, Contextualizing a Ptolemaic Solution: The Institution of the Ethnic politeuma, in: Fischer-Bovet – von Reden 2021, 106–126

Sänger 2022: Sänger, Patrick, Immigrant Soldiers and Ptolemaic Policy in Hellenistic Egypt (Late Fourth Century–30 BCE), in: G. Christ – P. Sänger – M. Carr (eds.), Military Diasporas: Building of Empire in the Middle East and Europe (550 BCE–1500 CE), London 2022, 51–81

Scheuble 2009: Scheuble, Sandra, Bemerkungen zu den μισθοφόροι und τακτόμισθοι im ptolemäischen Ägypten, in: R. Eberhard et al. (eds.), "… vor dem Papyrus sind alle gleich!" Papyrologische Beiträge zu Ehren von Bärbel Kramer (P. Kramer), Berlin et al. 2009, 213–222

Scheuble-Reiter 2012: Scheuble-Reiter, Sandra, Die Katökenreiter im ptolemäischen Ägypten, Munich 2012

Smallwood 1976: Smallwood, Mary, The Jews under Roman Rule from Pompey to Diocletian, Leiden 1976

Spawforth 2006: Spawforth, Tony, 'Macedonian Times': Hellenistic Memories in the Provinces of the Roman Near East, in: D. Konstan – S. Saïd (eds.), Greeks on Greekness. Viewing the Past under the Roman Empire, Cambridge 2006, 1–26

Stefanou 2013: Stefanou, Mary, Waterborne Recruits: The Military Settlers of Ptolemaic Egypt, in: K. Buraselis – M. Stefanou – D.J. Thompson (eds.), The Ptolemies, the Sea and the Nile. Studies in Waterborne Power, Cambridge 2013, 108–131

Taylor 1998: Taylor, Joan E., A Second Temple in Egypt: The Evidence for the Zadokite Temple of Onias, Journal for the Study of Judaism 29, 1998, 297–321

Tcherikover 1959: Tcherikover, Victor A., Hellenistic Civilisation and the Jews, Philadelphia et al. 1959

Thompson 1984: Thompson, Dorothy J., The Idumaeans of Memphis and the Ptolemaic Politeuma, in: Atti del XVII Congresso Internazionale di Papirologia (Napoli, 19–26 maggio 1983), Centro Internazionale per lo Studio dei Papiri Ercolanesi, Naples 1984, 1069–1075

Thompson 2001: Thompson, Dorothy J., Hellenistic Hellenes: The Case of Ptolemaic Egypt, in: I. Malkin (ed.), Ancient Perceptions of Greek Ethnicity, Center for Hellenic Studies Colloquia 5, Cambridge et al. 2001, 301–322

Thompson 2011a: Thompson, Dorothy J., Ethnic Minorities in Hellenistic Egypt, in: O.M. van Nijf – R. Alston (eds.), Political Culture in the Greek City After the Classical Age, Groningen-Royal Holloway Studies on the Greek City after the Classical Age 2, Leuven 2011a, 101–117

Thompson 2011b: Thompson, Dorothy J., The Sons of Ptolemy V in a post-secession World, in: Jördens – Quack 2011, 10–23

Thompson 2012: Thompson, Dorothy J., Memphis under the Ptolemies, Princeton et al. 2012

Vandorpe 2008: Vandorpe, Katelijn, Persian Soldiers and Persians of the Epigone. Social Mobility of Soldiers-Herdsmen in Upper Egypt, Archiv für Papyrusforschung 54, 2008, 87–108

Veïsse 2004: Veïsse, Anne-Emmanuelle, Les "révoltes égyptiennes". Recherches sur les troubles intérieurs en Égypte du règne de Ptolémée III à la conquête romaine, Leuven 2004

Weber 1976: Weber, Max, Wirtschaft und Gesellschaft. Studienausgabe, 5. Aufl., Tübingen 1976

Wiemer 2017: Wiemer, Hans-Ulrich, Siegen oder untergehen? Die hellenistische Monarchie in der neueren Forschung, in: S. Rebenich (ed.), Monarchische Herrschaft im Altertum, Berlin et al. 2017, 305–339

Winter 2011: Winter, Eva, Formen ptolemäischer Präsenz in der Ägäis zwischen schriftlicher Überlieferung und archäologischem Befund, in: F. Daubner (ed.), Militärsiedlungen und Territorialherrschaft in der Antike, Berlin et al. 2011, 65–77

Wolff 1953: Wolff, Hans J., Faktoren der Rechtsbildung im hellenistisch-römischen Ägypten, Zeitschrift der Savigny-Stiftung für Rechtsgeschichte 70, 1953, 20–57

Wolff 1962: Wolff, Hans J., Das Justizwesen der Ptolemäer, Munich 1962, 37–48

Wolff 2002: Wolff, Hans J., Das Recht der griechischen Papyri Ägyptens in der Zeit der Ptolemäer und des Prinzipats I: Bedingungen und Triebkräfte der Rechtsentwicklung, ed. H.-A. Rupprecht, Handbuch der Altertumswissenschaft 10.5.1, Munich 2002

Patrick Sänger is Professor of Ancient History at the Universität Münster. His main interests are the administrative, legal and social history of the eastern Mediterranean, especially of Egypt from the Hellenistic to the Late Antique period. He has also worked on the editing of documentary papyri and of Ephesian inscriptions. His most recent book examines a particular Ptolemaic form of association called politeuma (2019). He is currently searching for new ways to narrate the history of Greco-Roman Egypt and its intertwining with papyrology.

Dynastic Image and the Visual Imitation of Alexander the Great
Seleukid Kings between Tradition and Innovation in the Second Century BC

MARTIN KOVACS

In memory of Andrew F. Stewart

Abstract: Analysing portraits of the Seleukids of the late 3rd and 2nd centuries BC, different, semantically significant lines of tradition and trends appear discernible. On the one hand, different strategies of dynastically influenced modes of representation can be detected, in which representatives of the supposedly legitimate dynasty formulate dynastic prestige with the help of direct visual references to their forefathers. On the other hand, various transgressive moments can be identified in the representational culture of the Seleukids. Antiochos IV renounced the established, rather more mature forms of stylization with a short, stringy hairstyle and sought a more charismatic staging of his reign through a youthful portrait with curly hair and Anastolé, which comes remarkably close to the visual image of Alexander the Great. This can be linked to specific political ambitions, at times in demarcation from the Ptolemaic empire. In contrast, the usurper Diodotos Tryphon takes the game with the image of Alexander to a new extreme. Like no other Hellenistic ruler before him, he adapts an Alexander-like, long-haired coiffure with raised strands on the forehead and has new coin images designed, of which the depiction of a Boiotian equestrian helmet with diadem, divine attributes and a horn of a unicorn is particularly striking. These, but also other pictorial creations, seek to establish the ruler's own legitimacy; a ruler who also programmatically places himself outside the dynasty. The *imitatio Alexandri* functions here as a promise in which Alexander's achievements as conqueror of the eastern satrapies of the Persian Empire are characterized as repeatable. The remarkable innovations in the stylizations of the 2nd century BC as well as the handling of Alexander the Great's image, but also the competing, stabilizing, and tradition-building tendencies in contrast, illustrate an increasingly differentiated spectrum of ideas of Greek kingship during Hellenism, each of which responded to different political, cultural, and social challenges.

1. Preface: Alexander the Great – Alexander the (almost) Unreachable

With the successive establishment of the empires of the Diadochi, from the death of Alexander the Great until the final episode of the wars of the Diadochi, the battle at Kouroupedion in 281 BC, all prevailing kings were trying to define their own representations and strategies to legitimize their rule in images – combining divine references and specific stylizations in their portraiture – and in articulating their relationship with and dependence of Alexander the Great.[1] Regarding the last aspect, this seemed, at first hand, to be rather problematic. Alexander embodied the idea of a vast, unified empire from Macedonia to India. In contrast to this, the officers who were turning on each other were trying to set up their own kingdoms.[2] All of these battle-hardened officers aspired for a distinctive monarchic position. In this way, the Diadochi had to lose the ties to Alexander's idea of a unified empire, covering the known world. Nevertheless, Alexander continued to function as an important figure of reference,[3] that was, to varying degrees, incorporated into the respective representation strategies of the Diadochi. In this way, Alexander either became a distant divine figure, as in the case of Ptolemaios I, a soldier-king embodying the essence of heroic leadership as a role model, as in the example of Lysimachos, or he was simply neglected, as it was done by Seleukos Nikator.[4] After a short period of emitting gold denominations in the latest 4th century, showing the head of Alexander the Great on the obverse, which were partially copied from the early Ptolemaic coinage,[5] Seleukos rapidly established his own representational strategy incorporating divine attributes and programmatically signalizing his ties to the Persian satrapies.[6] Additionally, Demetrios Poliorketes, adopting iconographies both from the Ptolemaic coinage and those of Lysimachos, also tried to formulate a distinctive representation and established a strategy, through which the

---

1   On the portraiture of Alexander the Great see in particular Hölscher 1971; Stewart 1993; von den Hoff 2020; Kovacs 2022. Cf. the chapter by Ralf von den Hoff on the portraiture of the 3rd century in this volume.
2   For the famous peace treaty from 311 BC, in conclusion of the 3rd Diachochi War, which defined spheres of influence for the Diadochi see Simpson 1954; Errington 1977; Anson 2006. In contrast, Gruen 1985 points out that, except for Kassander, none of the Diadochi have a territorial limit in their titulature; all are equally "king", like Alexander. To what extent, however, there is an actual claim behind this that announces a (renewed) unity of the empire under one ruler seems questionable to me. The proclaimed universality, in contrast to the established, traditional, and well-known Macedonian kingship, seems to refer in particular and primarily to the status and rank in principle, and not to the body of the empire itself.
3   Cf. the literary evidence Meuus 2009.
4   See the discussions in Kovacs 2022, 136–150 (Ptolemaios I); 187–197 (Lysimachos); 226–236 (Seleukos I).
5   Stewart 1993, 313–318 fig. 115; Dahmen 2007, 49; 117–118 pl. 7; Kovacs 2022, 226–227 fig. 47.
6   Compare the famous, very rare coins with a depiction of a horned rider on the reverse from Ekbatana (early 3rd century BC). The identification is, however, disputed. Houghton – Stewart 2008 pleaded for Alexander. See in contrast to this Erickson 2013; Kovacs 2022, 231–233 fig. 53 (Seleukos I).

son of Antigonos Monophthalmos could even be seen as a different, or even a "better" Alexander, and simply as a ruler, who incorporates military competence and divine charisma in his own way.[7] Nevertheless, both Diadochi, Seleukos and Demetrios, were operating within a visual system which was defined by the presence of Alexander and his relation to divine and heroic power.

Loosening the historic ties to Alexander and abandoning the idea of a unified empire, which became but distant prospect for any Hellenistic ruler in the 3rd century BC, highlighted the almost mythic, enormous accomplishment of Alexander as conqueror of the world, or as *theos aniketos*, as the Athenians put it.[8] With this, Alexander was paralleled with Herakles, Dionysos and Zeus, and with the deeds of the mythical heroes of the Greek world. This distant, unrepeatable achievement helped to construct a specific role for Alexander, which could only be fulfilled by Alexander himself. It was out of the question that any of the Diadochi could repeat the military campaign conducted by Alexander against the Persian empire or the Indian realm of Maurya.[9] Due to this, the role of *aniketos theos* with all its connotations interwoven with Alexander became unreachable for any Hellenistic monarch, which prevented other early Hellenistic kings to establish themselves as *new Alexanders*: It proved to be simply implausible to the audiences to appear in this way. In connection with the well-known spear-won-land (*doriktetos chora*) ideology,[10] in which the individual capability of a general to conquer and to rule his realm constituted the central criterion for legitimate kingship, it is becoming clear that while the Diadochi had to establish their legitimacy on their own, it seemed impossible to gain the full amount of prestige and victoriousness of Alexander.

Therefore, Alexander's figurations were altered and heavily transformed, in order to make at least some aspects of his kingship linkable to Hellenistic kingship in general. The first aspect is defined by royal insignia, like the diadem, which were partially invented by the Diadochi themselves but subsequently reconnected to Alexander to enhance their prestige.[11] In consequence, the Diadochi appeared as experienced and matured generals, pointing to their military capabilities. In other cases, they re-established a connection with Alexander, as they were shown together with the great

---

7   Therefore, in the case of Demetrios Poliorketes, it is misleading to talk about a coherent *imitatio Alexandri*. Cf. Kovacs 2022, 196–197; 360–363.

8   For Hyp. 5 frg. 7 see Stewart 1993, 100–101; 381–382. For Alexander's invincibility see Pfister 1964, 39–47. See further Muccioli 2013, 37–62; 347–352.

9   It was only at the time when the Seleukids had largely lost control of the eastern satrapies that Antiochos III attempted in his *anabasis* (212–204 BC), in the form of long-lasting military campaigns agains the Parthians and the Graeco-Bactrian empire, to re-establish suzerainty in these areas, cf. Grainger 2015a, 55–79.

10 Diod. 17.17.2. See also Pol. 4.77.2 for a clear statement on the essential capabilities of a Hellenistic ruler: πρᾶξις καὶ τόλμα πολεμική. Compare Instinsky 1949; Gehrke 1982, 273; Zahrnt 1996; von den Hoff 2020, 17–18.

11 Compare the important discussions in Lichtenberger et al. 2012. See recently, pleading for an invention of the diadem by the Diadochi, Kovacs 2022, 195–197.

king fulfilling heroic deeds, like in the Krateros *anathema* in Delphi or on the famous so-called Alexander sarcophagus from the royal necropolis in Sidon.[12] However, these selective appropriations of the Alexander figure and its varying constructions[13] by the Diadochi proved to be exceptional phenomena that only rarely established a tradition. Furthermore, it has to be pointed out that a direct visual imitation of the likeness of Alexander and a programmatic approach to present oneself as a *new Alexander* was consequently completely absent.

2. Signs of age, signs of experience or divine appearances. Seleukid ruler portraiture in the late 3rd century BC

Looking at the Seleukid kingdom delivers some eye-catching archaeological and numismatic evidence for the question when, how, and in with what purpose Alexander-like iconographies were used for monarchic representation. Following the conventions established by the Diadochi, the portraits of the Seleukids usually show clear signs of age.[14] The features of Antiochos III appear haggard and even slightly emaciated, both in coinage and also on the well-known head in the Louvre in Paris (fig. 1a, b).[15] The hairstyle appears relatively simple, with short strands. This portrait stylization proves to be neither particularly youthful nor does it evoke ostentatious dynamism. This seems even more remarkable because Antiochos III, in his extensive campaigns in the far east of the Seleukid empire, seemed to come closer to Alexander's deeds or his entitlement than any Hellenistic ruler before him if one disregards Seleukos I's peace treaty with Chandragupta in 303 BC.[16] The king's actions therefore had no consequences for the portrait representation and did not promote a visual *imitatio Alexandri*.

---

12   Votive of Krateros at Delphi (322/321 BC): Hölscher 1973, 181–185; Saatsoglou-Palliadeli 1989; Stewart 1993, 270–277; 390–392; Völcker-Janssen 1993, 117–132; Bringmann – von Steuben 1995, 141–142 no. 90; Schmidt-Dounas 2000, 183–185; Seyer 2007, 143–164; Kovacs 2022, 197–205. Istanbul, Archaeological Museum inv. no. 370 ("Alexander sarcophagus"): von Graeve 1970; Hölscher 1973, 189–196; Messerschmidt 1989; Stewart 1993, 294–306; von den Hoff 2020, 33–36; Kovacs 2022, 236–244.

13   For the idea of *figuration* see Elias 1997, 46–73. On the appropriation of this concept for Alexander the Great see in general Kovacs 2022, 21–23.

14   For the iconography of Hellenistic rulers of the 3rd century BC and the term of 'Porträtkonzept', established in this context, see the paper by Ralf von den Hoff in this volume.

15   Paris, Louvre inv. no. MA 1204. See Fleischer 1991, 99–102, pl. 56 a-d; von den Hoff 1994, 107 fig. 198; Smith 1988, 161 no. 30 pl. 24, 1–3; L. Laugier, in: Picón – Hemingway 2016, 215–216 no. 143.

16   See also Strootman 2020, 146, referring to the title of *megas* of Antiochos III (App. Syr. 11.3.15): 'There is no reason to assume that Antiochos' use of the title megas was a reference to Alexander or, for that matter, that Antiochos' eastern anabasis was an attempt to imitate Alexander. The assumption that Alexander was an example for Macedonian rulers in the third century is a modern overestimation of his postmortem influence based on the retrospective projection of an image of Alexander that developed only in the second century BCE.'

Significant for this question, however, appears to be a posthumous coinage used by Antiochos Hierax from 241 BC in connection with the succession wars with Seleukos II and issued in western Asia Minor mints such as Alexandreia Troas (fig. 2).[17] It very likely shows a rejuvenated portrait of Antiochos I, recognizable by the peculiar, steeply rising curve of the brow, although the deep folds and the hanging neck have disappeared.[18] However, above the ear a wing of Hermes has been added, which grows out of the head below the diadem and above the ear. Additionally, the head also shows a clearly recognizable Anastolé, which falls onto the forehead in a short sweep. The hair remains short, but it is a different hairstyle from the one otherwise attested for Antiochos I. He usually wears a simple strand of hair.

Fig. 1 Portrait of Antiochos III. Paris, Musée de Louvre inv. MA 1204.

17   Newell ²1977, 336–341 no. 1567–1579 pl. 72,12; 73, 1–12; 74, 1–6; Smith 1988, 42. 45; Fleischer 1991, 22–23 pl. 12 d (Alexandreia Troas, 230s BC).
18   Against an identification with Hierax himself speaks the decisively different, considerably even younger, and slender physiognomy on tetradrachms showing a diademed head, most certainly portraying Hierax, cf. in particular SC 836. 842. 897–900.

Fig. 2 The rejuvenated Antiochos I with wings. Tetradrachm of Antiochos Hierax, Alexandreia Troas, 230s BC.

Fig. 3 Alexander the Great. Tetradrachm of Lysimachos, Ainos, 297–281 BC.

Fig. 4 Seleukos I with bull's horns. Tetradrachm of Antiochos I, Sardeis, 276–274 BC.

The theomorphic attribute of Hermes does not appear understandable here at first glance, although their supra-regional distribution does not suggest a local cult or corresponding peculiarity, but rather a specific image conception which is intended to present the deceased king as Hermes-like and youthfully idealized. In this context, it would also be conceivable to regard the wings of Hermes as the iconographic equivalent of Alexander's ram's horns on the Lysimachos coinage (fig. 3) or the bull's horns of Seleukos I Nikator on the posthumous coinage under Antiochos I (fig. 4).[19] In this way, the image reflects the attempt to place the deceased Antiochos I on the same level as the founder of the dynasty using his own iconographic means. What seems important here is the frame of reference in which the respective predecessors are placed. The deceased predecessors are clearly above the incumbent rulers in rank, but this can enhance the legitimacy of the current monarch.

However, the question also arises whether the wings of Hermes, the Anastolé and the rejuvenation should rather be understood as a reference to an image of the god Hermes. The Anastolé is known to have been used for the depiction of Herakles in Macedonian coinage already during Alexander's lifetime.[20] The slightly later coinage of Tenos with the depiction of Apollon Karneios from the 3rd century BC even precisely adopts the Alexander image of the Lysimachos coinage.[21] It therefore seems conceivable that in the course of a general availability of features of Alexander's iconography for representations of gods there is no direct semantic referencing of Alexander's image here, but rather an indirect one that evokes the image of a god or divine qualities in general. It is, however, important to note that Alexander-like iconographies do not necessarily point directly to a specific, programmatic reference to Alexander.[22] The posthumous coin image thereby sought to glorify the predecessor or the father and, in the case of Antiochos Hierax, the grandfather Antiochos I, and thus strove to establish legitimacy through the divine charisma of the grandfather, ignoring and overwriting the legitimate claim of Antiochos' Hierax brother, Seleukos II.

19   Fleischer 1991, 5–8 pl. 1 a-d; SC 322. 363. 364. This is also the case for the representation of Demetrios Poliorketes with bull's horns: Ehling 2000; Kovacs 2022, 361–363. See further Günther 2011, 102–103, who points out the resemblance of the images of the coin emission of Demetrios to the known Macedonian coinage under Alexander the Great.

20   Price 1991, 27–29; de Callataÿ 2012, 178; Mittag 2016, 164–165. Decisively Dorka Moreno 2019, 119–136.

21   Kovacs 2022, 192–193 fig. 37.

22   Schörner 1992; Lichtenberger 2013; Dorka Moreno 2019, 32–41; Kovacs 2022, 56 ('Entsemantisierung'); 369–395.

3. Antiochos IV and the charismatization[23] of royal representation

Antiochos IV is probably one of the most enigmatic figures of the Hellenistic period and has been the subject of extensive scholarly debate right up to the present day.[24] The fact that the portrait head on coins from the mint of Antiocheia, which at the beginning of his reign in 175 BC showed clear signs of old age, was massively rejuvenated in a second, later phase from 173/172 BC onward, has already been recognized.[25] The receding hairline, the wrinkles and the protruding cheekbone disappear in favour of an ageless, youthful portrait with full hair and a pronounced Anastolé (fig. 5). Some stamps even show both curls of the Anastolé. At the same time, the conventional coin legend "Basileus Antiochos" is provided with an epithet celebrating the ruler as *theos epiphanes*. In addition, a star sometimes decorates the obverse, which is placed above the diadem.[26] The images on the reverse first show Apollon, the dynastic god of the Seleukids, and later the enthroned Zeus, to whom Nike – standing on the hand of the father of the gods – hands a victory wreath.[27]

Fig. 5 The rejuvenated Antiochos IV. Tetradrachm, Antiocheia on the Orontes, 173–168 BC.

---

23   Fundamentally Gehrke 1982. See for a profound and recent discussion of the concept, based on Max Weber's *Herrschaftssoziologie*, Trampedach – Meuus 2020, 9–13, in particular p. 11: 'Yet, for Weber the demonstration and performance of charisma constitute a very effective strategy of legitimation – albeit depending on the audience – serving to highlight the superhuman achievements of the leader. While the various peoples in Alexander's empire had different conceptions of kingship, for all of them the ideal ruler was expected to possess a series of virtues: in the Greek and Macedonian context, for instance, the king had to display ἀρετή, victoriousness, personal bravery, beauty, generosity, μεγαλοψυχία. These qualities which proved the charisma of the heroic king did not necessarily imply moral greatness.' Regarding 'superhuman' qualities, I therefore regard the deliberate use of divine attributes, epithets, as well as with heroic aspects, including Alexander-like elements, as opposed to other, more traditional forms of legitimation, such as dynastic argumentation structures, as decidedly and intentionally charismatic features of Hellenistic ruler representation, cf. Gehrke 1982, 252–253.

24   See in general Mørkholm 1966; Mittag 2006.

25   Mørkholm 1963. In summary Fleischer 1991, 44–52, and in particular Bergmann 1998, 61–66.

26   Fleischer 1991, 46 pl. 21 f; 22d; SC 1424. 1463. 1512. 1517. 1518. On the solar iconography in the images of Antiochos IV see also Bunge 1975.

27   See SC 1397 (Antiocheia on the Orontes).

The political implications of these multifaceted and allusive changes in Antiochos IV's representation have been extensively discussed, which is why they will only be briefly summarized here.[28] These changes are at least partially due to an immediate political rivalry with the Ptolemaic Empire, which culminated in the context of the Sixth Syrian War. Antiochos occupied the Nile delta but was prevented by Rome from annexing the Ptolemaic Empire.[29] The solar pictorial elements that emerged earlier, such as the star above the diadem or the sporadically appearing radiant aureole, both in coinage and on official seals (fig. 6),[30] react directly to already established Ptolemaic pictorial creations. This also applies to the epithet *epiphanes*, which Antiochos IV had adopted from his brother-in-law Ptolemaios V to increase his authority in order to assert sovereignty over Koile-Syria, which was supposedly handed over to the Ptolemaic Empire as a dowry when Kleopatra I, Antiochos III's daughter, married Ptolemaios V in the course of the succession dispute.

Fig. 6 Antiochos IV with radiate aureole. Clay seal from Uruk.

The epithet *epiphanes*, however, contains a further component, which is connected with the solar attributes of the radiant aureole and the star.[31] The head of Apollon is

---

28   Bunge 1974; Mittag 2006, 128–139.
29   On the 6th Syrian War 168/167 BC see Hölbl 1994, 129–134; Huß 2001, 544–563; Mittag 2006, 159–181.
30   See also the extensive study by Bunge 1975. Further Svenson 1995, 19–23; Mittag 2006, 130–136; Iossif – Lorber 2012, 207–208.
31   The radiant aureole is predominantly present on bronze nominals, although there are some silver hemidrachms from Antioch on the Orontes: SC 1405. Cf. the epithet *epiphanes* Muccioli 2013, 281–308.

crowned with the solar attribute, while some coins from Seleukia on the Tigris even show a bust of Helios next to the image of Apollon.[32] While the former patron god of Seleukos is supplemented with a solar component, the reigning ruler Antiochos IV visibly places himself under his protection or appropriates and condenses both Apollonian and solar qualities. This politically competitive situation thus led to the development of a number of iconographic peculiarities, of which the youthful, Alexander-like portrait is an essential feature, although it must be seen in conjunction with other elements, such as addition of divine attributes and various attributions. The radical, even revolutionary re-stylization of the 40-year-old ruler, which initially corresponded to a more realistic portrait in accordance with the Seleukid tradition,[33] appears even more clearly when one considers his earlier portrait type in the form of an under-life-size head in Berlin (fig. 7a. b).[34] Here, the features are repeated: A high forehead, where individual curls can still just be pulled out from under the diadem, sunken cheeks and pointedly protruding cheekbones. Once again, however, it seems remarkable that although there is a general, unspecific visual reference to the image of Alexander in the form of the conspicuous Anastolé and the emphasized agelessness of the coinage since 173/172 BC, Alexander's long hair does not appear, although it can be considered as an essential feature. If one associates the visual change more with the image of a god[35] such as Helios, then this peculiarity is all the more surprising, especially since Helios also had long hair, and usually even longer hair than Alexander's.[36] Although this is a far-reaching visual assimilation, as individualising features were still "left standing", an essential, constitutive element of the iconography of Alexander is not incorporated.

Another artifact which may be significant for understanding the iconography of Antiochos IV but has not yet been sufficiently considered is an under life-size statue from Pompeii, now in the Museo Nazionale in Naples. It wears a cloak over its left, bent forearm (fig. 8a. b).[37] The statue is shown in contrapposto pose, but combined with a rather softly modelled upper body, the not quite strictly balanced stance and a striking frontality. It characteristically combines stylistic elements of the 5th and 4th

---

32   Le Rider 1965, 138 pl. 25 g. h; Bergmann 1998, 65 pl. 11, 9; SC 1517.

33   From Seleukos I to Antiochos IV, clear signs of age and individualizing formulas can be observed almost universally, such as sunken cheeks, receding hairline, wrinkles on the forehead, slight corpulence or pointed noses, compare Fleischer 1991, 120–123.

34   Berlin, Antikensammlung inv. no. 1975.5: Kyrieleis 1980; Himmelmann 1989, 133; 138 fig. 55; Fleischer 1991, 52–53 pl. 23 c. 24–27; R. von den Hoff, 104179: Bildniskopf des Antiochos IV. von Syrien (http://arachne.uni-koeln.de/item/objekt/104179) last access: 20.5.2024.

35   See for this interpretation La Rocca 1994, 17–25.

36   Letta 1988; Matern 2002; Dorka Moreno 2019, 156–168.

37   Naples, Museo Nazionale inv. no. 126249, H 70 cm. See with the older literature Fröhlich 1998, 195–200; 281–283 no. 22; Queyrel 2003, 252–254 no. F5 pl. 46–48. The proposed identification with Attalos III seems to me to be non-binding. Against Fröhlich's interpretation that it portrays Ptolemaios VI can be used the fact that the portrait has an Anastolé which does not occur at all in the otherwise well-documented iconography of the Ptolemies, compare Kyrieleis 1975, 58–62.

century BC and the Hellenistic era.[38] The statue apparently depicts a military commander, since the support to the left shows a cuirass of decisively Hellenistic type. The head appears ageless, with short hair in crescent-shaped curls and a separate, almost isolated Anastolé, which has no organic connection with the rest of the hair. Previous identifications, for example with Ptolemaios VI or Attalos III, can hardly be verified. Regarding the prominent Anastolé as well as the short curls arranged in rows as well as the youthful physiognomy in comparison with the coin portraits since 173/172 BC, it seems plausible that this may be a statue of Antiochos IV, which represents a later type of portrait than the famous marble head in Berlin. The hair on the calotte of the statuette's head appears similar in single motifs. Particularly close seem to be the short, crescent-shaped curls. However, there are no clear typological relations to coinages of the mint of Antiocheia.[39] Strikingly similar prove to be both the straight, steeply sloping bridge of the nose as well as the slightly protruding, blunt chin, which has been on the coins since the earliest images of Antiochos IV.[40] The absence of the diadem cannot be seen as a sufficient criterion to exclude the statue from the stock of Hellenistic ruler portraits.[41]

38   Kreikenbom 1990, 172 considers the statue to be a Hellenistic reshaping after the Doryphoros of Polykleitos. Cf. the discussion in Fröhlich 1998, 197–198. Furthermore, the conspicuous shift of the upper body to the side of the playing leg in combination with the bent right arm appears as if the support typical for Praxitelean sculptures is missing.

39   Cf. Fleischer 1991, 49.

40   The specific shape of the chin also contradicts other possible identifications. The chin of the image of Alexander Balas, which is comparable in terms of hairstyle typology, is clearly more massive, protrudes further and determines the physiognomy to a great extent, cf. Fleischer 1991, 60–63 pl. 31 c–h. A Hellenistic head from Limyra, found in the vicinity of the Ptolemaion, could also represent Antiochos IV: Borchhardt 2001, 423–424 fig. 6. 7; Stanzl 2015, 188–189 fig. 21; Stanzl 2016, 739 fig. 12. The identification with Ptolemaios III by Stanzl seems to contradict the known iconography of the Ptolemaic king, cf. Kyrieleis 1975, 25–42. The feisty stylization, typical of the portraits of Ptolemaios III, is completely absent in the head from Limyra. In addition, the almond shape of the eyes, the stronger emphasis on the skull, and the differentiated drilling technique of the hair seem to indicate a date within the 2nd century B. C. Also, the rather tight-fitting cap of hair in the portraits of Ptolemaios III seems to be rather different from the voluminous, loosened and freely unfolding curl formations of the head from Limyra.

41   Compare for example the famous herm portraying Demetrios Poliorketes from the Villa dei Papiri (Naples, Museo Archeologico Nazionale inv. no. 6149), wearing a narrow hair band, not a diadem: Smith 1988, 64–65; 156 no. 4 pl. 4–5, or the small-scale portrait (H 7 cm) of Ptolemaios VIII (?) without headdress in Washington, Dumbarton Oaks inv. no. 48.10, which has a replica with a rolled diadem (?) in Athens, Benaki Museum inv. no. 22586: Stanwick 2002, 113 no. C6–C7 fig. 86–89. One may also add the famous statue of the 'Terme Ruler' in Rome, Museo Nazionale Romano inv. no. 1049; however, it is still disputed, whether it portrays a Hellenistic ruler or a Roman general: Smith 1988, 164 no. 44 pl. 31–32; Himmelmann 1989, 126–150; Queyrel 2003, 200–234 no. E1 pl. 32–34; Hallett 2003, 57–59 pl. 30.

Fig. 7 Antiochos IV, first portrait type.

Fig. 8 Statue of Antiochos IV (?). Naples, Museo Archeologico Nazionale di Napoli
inv. no. 126249.

The clear military connotation of the armor speaks against an interpretation as an athlete or an ephebe, but rather as a Hellenistic monarch.[42] What is striking about the
head of the statue in Naples is a peculiarly individual, yet ageless physiognomy. The
modelling of the face reveals a subtle surface treatment. The individual forms seem to
flow into one another and even seem to blur virtually.[43] The wide mouth with its thick-

42   Bergmann 1991, 240 n. 37 ('hellenistischer Prinz').
43   These are stylistic features characteristic of the second quarter of the 2nd century BC, compare for
      example some of the heads of the Telephos frieze from the Great Altar from Pergamon in Berlin:

er lips is framed by small folds at the corners, the cheekbones stand out high above, without, however, showing the angular accentuation of the portrait in Berlin. The youthfulness appears together with the Anastolé, which is applied here in a formulaic manner, within the context of military representation. The nudity bears a heroizing, almost old-fashioned reference to classical statuary motifs that refer to agonal practices, which makes the representation appear even more nobilitised.[44]

Together with a number of seal impressions showing Antiochos IV with an elephant *exuvia*,[45] this also alludes to his victoriousness, which is expressed by the coinage since 169/168 BC in the form of the added legend Nikephoros.[46] The proclaimed victory over Egypt, which was decisively sabotaged by the Romans,[47] as well as the earlier victory over the Galatians in Asia Minor obviously enabled the exaggerated staging, which visually and linguistically not only evoked divine qualities, but – through the youthful stylisation with the Anastolé – sought comparison with Alexander the Great and his achievements. A novelty in the representation of Antiochos IV thus lies in the fact that a wide variety of pictorial motifs were used which strikingly exaggerated the ruler and related him to various gods, as well as using Alexander the Great to a previously unknown extent as a subtly present, almost merely connoted reference figure.[48] The youthfulness and the Anastolé evoked a king who, like Alexander, had divine abilities, indeed was a present, "appeared" god, and could therefore act as a victorious general (*nikephoros*).

4. Adopting the Alexander image – in a moderate way: Demetrios I

The eldest son of Seleukos IV, Demetrios I did not assume power until 160 BC, after he had initially been passed over by the Roman Senate as a hostage in Rome during the

---

Winnefeld 1910, 173–174 pl. 36, 5.

44 See the discussion by Hallett 2003, 57–60.

45 Fleischer 1991, 53–54 pl. 28 a; Svenson 1995, 111–112 pl. 53; SC 1533.

46 Summarized pointedly by Chaniotis 2003, 433: 'If kings had a claim to divine honours it was because of their achievements and benefactions. This is what the epithets attributed to monarchs indicate: "the Saviour" (Soter, attested, e. g., for Antigonos Monophthalmos and Demetrios Poliorketes, Ptolemaios I, Antiochos I, Antigonos Gonatas, Attalos I, Achaios, Philip V, Eumenes II, Seleukos III, Ptolemaios IX and Kleopatra), "the one with the manifest power" (Epiphanes, attested for Antiochos IV); or "the winner of fair victories" (Kallinikos, attested for Seleukos II and Mithradates I).' See further in detail de Callataÿ – Lorber 2011. For *nikephoros* in particular cf. Muccioli 2013, 345–347.

47 See in particular Gotter 2013.

48 Compare pointedly Mittag 2006, 139: 'Er konnte mit den Epitheta versuchen, seine eigene Stellung zu legitimieren und weiter zu festigen ohne konkrete Taten vollbringen zu müssen. Charisma, das sich aus seiner Abstammung und seiner Nähe zur göttlichen Sphäre speiste, sollte leistungsabhängiges Charisma ersetzen.'

succession rulings in 175 BC and 164 BC.[49] In 162 BC, after escaping from Roman custody, he had the minor Antiochos V, the son of Antiochos IV, poisoned and was then able to consolidate his rule in Syria against the usurper Timarchos. This was initially marked by the successful attempt to regain Judea, which had previously broken away under Judas Maccabeus, who was, however, defeated by the Seleukid in 160 BC. The latter's portraits are also subject to changes which, although not as radical as those of Antiochos IV, prove to be programmatically significant because of the addition of the Anastolé.[50] At the beginning of his reign, the latter appears with a massive skull sitting on a broad neck. The nose is hooked, the cheekbones are prominent, and forehead wrinkles are partly visible. The hair is of medium length and parted in widely curved crescents, while at the forehead a single strand is combed to the side (fig. 9). In contrast to the emphatically youthful stylisations of Antiochos IV as well as his successor Antiochos V, a more realistic portrait is pursued here, which follows on from older models. The massive skull with the accentuated cheekbones, for example, can be seen in Antiochos III, who also shows a peculiarly individualised, long nose.[51]

In the portrait of Demetrios I, it is noticeable that the hair on the forehead is completely redesigned from 155 BC onwards (fig. 10). A straggly Anastolé now dominates the appearance, in which the individual upward curls are led to the side in waves across the forehead. The hair at the nape becomes somewhat longer, the individual features are slightly retracted, although they do not disappear completely.

Fig. 9 Demetrios I Soter, first portrait type.
Tetradrachm, Antiocheia on the Orontes, 162–154 BC

49   Willrich 1901.
50   For the chronology of the series see Newell 1917, 34–46; Fleischer 1991, 56–57.
51   Fleischer 1991, 56–57 pl. 29 a-c. Compare in particular SC 985. 986. 1005–1009 (uncertain mints).
      The development becomes clearly visible when looking at the early Antiochian emissions: Newell
      1917, 34–37 no. 79–95 pl. 5. 6.

Fig. 10 Demetrios I Soter, second portrait type.
Tetradrachm, Antiocheia on the Orontes, 153–152 BC

The change in hairstyle as well as the youthfulness of the portrait are again programmatically significant. Ernst Pfuhl and Hans Peter L'Orange had already argued that this iconographic detail is a reference to Alexander the Great.[52] In fact, the Anastolé no longer appears here as a single almost isolated element, but determines the hairstyle decisively. The raised strands are similarly dominant as in the famous Azara type.[53] There is, however, no typologically compelling reference to a specific image of Alexander. Furthermore, in analogy to Antiochos IV, there are numerous examples of bronze coins showing the ruler with an elephant *exuvia*.[54] Caroline Bohm has interpreted this series of visual imitations of Alexander in the mid-2nd century BC as a sign of political crisis of the Seleukid kingship, which was constantly exposed to new usurpations and dynastic disputes, and faced increasing military threats from the Parthians in the east and the Romans and Pergamon in the west.[55] At the very least, the situation of a constant threat from other powers, including the Ptolemaic Empire or Ptolemaios VI, who was allied with Rome and ultimately helped to overthrow Demetrios I under Alexander Balas, could have led to this special representation in the sense of an ostentatious self-assertion against foreign threats.

The parallel emergence of images depicting the ruler with an elephant's scalp also seems significant. The king of the Seleukid empire was militarily active in the same areas as Alexander and defended them against insurgents. The scalp was a symbol of the heroic elements of his kingship as well as his powerful armies, of which elephants were an active part. More than any other monarch, the ruler of the Seleukid Empire, despite various crises during the 2nd century BC, was the only legitimate successor to

---

52   Pfuhl 1930, 29; L'Orange 1947, 39–40.
53   Kovacs 2022, 118–129 pl. 24–29.
54   Le Rider 1977, 145. 348 pl. 28 m. n; Fleischer 1991, 57 pl. 29 f.; SC 1696.
55   Bohm 1989, 101: 'Die verloren gegangene Stabilität der seleukidischen Monarchie und die Schwäche des königlichen Regiments geben den historischen Hintergrund ab, vor dem die *imitatio Alexandri* der Seleukiden zu sehen ist.'

Alexander and the preserver of the empire he had created, if one considers Alexander's successful war against the barbarians east of the Persian heartland as far as India as an essential link. The endeavour to restore the past greatness of the Seleukid empire, is articulated, among others, in the king's attempt to wrest Kypros from the Ptolemies. Since this was an open breach of the peace treaty of Apameia, Demetrios was forced to assume that Rome, too, would consider this an agression.[56]

In documenting the legitimate claim to power, the Seleukid coinage also contains a further novelty which, in analogy to the images under Antiochos IV, once again refers back to Ptolemaic schemes. Under Demetrios I, a double portrait is used in Seleukid coinage, showing Demetrios I and his wife Laodike.[57] The latter was a daughter of Seleukos IV, formerly the wife of the Antigonid king Perseus and the sister of Demetrios. This image proclaims the legitimacy of the ruling dynasty, which in the case of the Seleukids, however, was constantly exposed to internal disputes, in continuation of the double portraits that had been introduced by the Ptolemies in the 3rd century BC.[58] The adoption of this well-known image scheme, which had functioned as the visual epitome of dynastic continuity and was present in various media, underpinned Demetrios I's claim to represent an equally successful dynasty himself.

In this context of intensified competition between the respective Hellenistic ruling dynasties for supremacy in the eastern Mediterranean region during the later 3rd and 2nd centuries BC, the purposeful adaptation of elements of Alexander's iconography may have been an additional factor that tied in with Alexander's immediate succession as king of the eastern satrapies and as conqueror of the Parthians and Indians. In contrast to Antiochos IV and his son Antiochos V, the fundamentally more individualising conception of the portrait refers to the tradition of the more realistic Seleukid portraits of the 3rd century BC.[59] In this way, partially innovative image designs – like the visual imitation of Alexander and its integration into a traditional image discourse – are mixed, and in this way they reflect the different legitimation strategies of Demetrios I.

5. Proclaiming dynastic continuity – Alexander Balas, a "true" Alexander

Alexander Balas, supported by Rome, Pergamon and Ptolemaios VI, overthrew Demetrios I in 150 BC, whose attempt to establish his own dynasty and to restore the empire had thus failed.[60] Balas, who was educated in Pergamon and presented there as the sup-

---

56   Cf. the foreign policy of Demetrios I Ehling 2008, 139–153.
57   Fleischer 1991, 58 pl. 30 d–g; SC 1687. 1688. Cf. the chapter by Peter Mittag in this volume on this phenomenon.
58   Kyrieleis 1975, 17 pl. 8, 1–3.
59   See von den Hoff 2021, 170–171; 175–178.
60   Bohm 1989, 105–116; Volkmann 1923.

posed son of Antiochos IV, married Kleopatra Thea after coming to power, and was a more comfortable ruler for Rome and the Attalid kingdom than Demetrios I had been. As with Demetrios I, double portraits were struck on coins presenting the new ruling couple. In taking up the double portrait coinage of Demetrios, the dynastic succession of Antiochos IV's line and the new alliance with the Ptolemaic Empire were demonstratively affirmed.[61] In this way, the images that had previously been placed in clear competition virtually formulated the opposite. Significant for a habitual *imitatio Alexandri*[62] was the choice of Alexander's name, which was, according to Claudia Bohm, deliberately made at the Pergamene royal court in order to increase the legitimacy of the pretender.[63] Another facet of the name, however, is the visual *Imitatio Alexandri* of Demetrios I, who openly and recognisably operated with essential features of Alexander's iconography and in this way justified his rule by charismatic means.

In the dispute over the throne, it could therefore be insinuated that this was a "true" Alexander, who rightfully took over the inheritance of the Seleukid empire. The portraits of Alexander Balas, on the other hand, are less directly linked to the image of Alexander than to the youthful portrait of Antiochos IV, his supposed father, for whom he had coins issued posthumously in Antiocheia (fig. 11).[64] Virtually identical is the full, richly moving hairstyle, which is divided into short curls. In addition, age features are omitted, although the massive and characteristic chin, as well as a slight nose hump on some coinages,[65] stand out as individualising features. It follows from this that in the present case a supposed visual *imitatio Alexandri* cannot be assumed without taking into account the similar stylisation of his predecessor Antiochos IV, his presumed father.[66] The divine as well as the heroic pictorial formulas must initially be understood as a deliberate link to the appearance of Antiochos. The reference in ancient literature to the fact that Balas was said to resemble his alleged brother Antiochos V Eupator,[67] whose coinage was also

---

61   SC 1798. 1841. The origin of Balas seems to be completely unclear according to the ancient historiographers, above all Pol. 33.18.9, cf. the compilation of sources by Will ²1982, 373–376; Bohm 1989, 109 n. 43.

62   See for the heuristic distinction between *habitual* and *visual* imitation Kovacs 2015, *passim*.

63   Cf. Bohm 1989, 111–113, with reference to Iust. 35.1.6–7: *Itaque adiuuantibus et Ptolemeo, rege Aegypti, et Attalo, rege Asiae, et Ariarathe Cappadociae, bello a Demetrio lacessiti subornant propolam quendam, sortis extremae iuuenem, qui Syriae regnum uelut paternum armis repeteret, et ne quid contumeliae deesset, nomen ei Alexandri inditur genitusque ab Antiocho rege dicitur.*

64   Mørkholm 1960; Fleischer 1991, 63–64 pl. 32 e. Issues with the portrait of Antiochos IV on the obverse: SC 1883. 1884.

65   While the massive chin is almost omnipresent in the portraiture of Alexander Balas, especially some high-quality coins show also a characteristic nose with a pronounced hump: SC 1782.2 (Antiocheia on the Orontes); 1867.7 (Susa). Cf. Gorny & Mosch, Auction 236, Munich, 7 March 2016, no. 284.

66   Compare in contrast to this Chrubasik 2016, 198, who argues that both Balas and Zabinas referred to Alexander the Great directly, ignoring the 'conventional' Seleukid portraiture. However, that seems inaccurate to me. For Alexander Zabinas see below.

67   Fleischer 1991, 54–55 pl. 28 c-f. See further in particular SC 1573–1575.

assimilated to that of Antiochos IV, may be directly attributed to the visual representation and political communication of Alexander Balas.[68] Consequently, the portrait of the
son of Balas and Kleopatra Thea, the barely two-year-old Antiochos VI, also seems to
resemble his predecessors in his short, curly hair and his physiognomy.[69]

Since the Anastolé does not appear regularly on the coin portraits of Alexander Balas, a deliberate visual assimilation to Alexander the Great is not sufficiently evident
at this level. The Anastolé can be seen particularly clearly on some tetradrachms from
the years 149/148 BC, which were minted in Seleukia on the Tigris as well as in Antiocheia.[70] The Anastolé appears rather small-scale and is almost unrecognisable in the
moving mop of curls. Nevertheless, the visual evidence for an *imitatio Alexandri* in
Alexander Balas remains remarkably sparse; his image is instead oriented towards his
proclaimed father Antiochos IV, which becomes especially clear when considering the
combination with some reverses typical for the coinage of Antiochos IV, like those
showing the seated Zeus, who is accompanied by a crowning Nike (fig. 11).[71]

Fig. 11 Alexander Balas. Tetradrachm, Antiocheia on the Orontes, 150–149 BC.

Fig. 12 Diodotos Tryphon. Tetradrachm, Antiocheia on the Orontes, 141–138 BC.

68   Diod. 31.31 a. Compare Bohm 1989, 109. The kinship of Balas with Antiochos IV was apparently put
      forward in Rome by the allied kings, cf. Iust. 35.1.6.
69   Fleischer 1991, 67–68 pl. 37 a. b; SC 1885–1887.
70   The reverse shows Athena, the ruler is also provided with the epithets *theopatros* and *euergetes*:
      Newell 1917, 48 no. 150; SC 1783.
71   Newell 1917, 47–48 no. 142–148; SC 1780–1782. 1784.

6. Adopting the Alexander image – in a hard way: Diodotos Tryphon, a charismatic usurper

The turmoil over the succession to the Seleukid throne was not to end.[72] Although Alexander Balas had initially prevailed, he was soon threatened again when Demetrios I's son, Demetrios II, led a rebellion (since 147 BC) which finally overthrew Alexander Balas in 145 BC, who was also betrayed by his ally, Ptolemaios VI.[73] Kleopatra Thea was consequently married to the new ruler Demetrios II. The general Diodotos Tryphon, on the other hand, proclaimed himself as counter-king in the same year. In contrast to Balas, Diodotos did not strive for a fictitious lineage or incorporation into the Seleukid ruling family, but rather placed his abilities as a general at the centre of his representation from the very beginning. The epithet *autokrator*, which was without precedent in Seleukid history, as well as the counting of the years after a new era founded by Diodotos,[74] clarified the claim of the king.

On the reverses of the tetradrachms now appears, almost omnipresent, a Boiotian equestrian helmet framed by a laurel wreath; the cheek-flap is decorated with a lightning bolt (fig. 12). At the back, the ends of the king's diadem fall out, and stars can be seen.[75] Furthermore, a large horn, curling like a volute at the upper end, is attached to the helmet, which comes from a unicorn, a mythical creature of Indian origin.[76] This image thus refers to his abilities as commander-in-chief of a Macedonian Hetaireian cavalry, the proclaimed world domination, and his kingship. The portrait of Diodotos also proves to be revealing. For he is the first Seleukid king to wear long, flowing hair that ruffles wildly as if moving in the wind. Furthermore, the hair at the nape falls far down to the shoulders. In contrast to the Seleukid tradition, there are hardly any

---

72   See in general Chrubasik 2016, 123–200.

73   On this episode Bohm 1989, 116–120. On Diodotos in detail Baldus 1970; Fischer 1972; Grainger 1997, 69–70.

74   Baldus 1970, 224–225.

75   SC 2029–2040. For the ancient naming see the evidence in Xen. equ. rat. 12.3: κράνος γε μὴν κράτιστον εἶναι νομίζομεν τὸ βοιωτιουργές, and Ail. nat. 3.24: κράνος Βοιωτιουργές. This helmet was used also within the ranks of Alexander's cavalry. See for the archaeological evidence Dintsis 1986, 3; 13–16. The innovative aspect of the iconography is also noted by Chrubasik 2016, 158–160.

76   The idea advocated by Ehling 1997 that the horn may be a reference to Kretan mercenaries, who helped Diodotos to gain the throne from Demetrios I, seems to me unfounded. Firstly, this is clearly the helmet of the king himself, with the diadem. Secondly, the helmet only shows a single horn mounted on the forehead, which seems confusing, as usually two horns are attached to the sides, corresponding to the animal referenced. Needless to say, the Cretan mountain goat to which Ehling refers also has two horns. The famous ram's horns on the Lysimachos tetradrachms which can be found on the portrait of Alexander, do illustrate the issue (fig. 3). The horn is mounted at the side of the head, not on the forehead! The third issue is revealed by the question of why Hellenistic Kretan mercenaries should represent themselves with one (!) horn of a goat on their helmets. Material from the Bronze Age should be excluded from the discussion. See also Hoover 2007, 100; Chrubasik 2016, 160 n. 134.

individualising features to be found here. The ruler is ageless and conforms to a stand-ardised image of youth, but with one significant deviating detail: the small chin, which merges almost vertically into the neck, signals a considerable corpulence, which is also indicated in the epithet, Tryphon. The dynamic stylisation of the ruler's long hair and the emphatically military staging of his person thus adapt and integrate an essential virtue of Ptolemaic rulers.[77]

Fig. 13 Diodotos Tryphon. Collection of the late George Ortiz, Geneva.

Fig. 14 Alexander the Great, Boston/Capitol type, right profile view.

77   App. Syr. 68.358; Diod. 33.4 a; Strab. 14.5.2; Ios. ant. Iud. 13.132. See further Bohm 1989, 126, who argues for a link between Diodotos and Dionysos, in accordance with Heinen 1983, 119.

The obesity, the youthful, sparsely individualised physiognomy as well as the diadem in the long hair are also found in a marble portrait of the 2nd century BC from the area of Apameia on the Orontes, interpreted convincingly by Robert Fleischer as a portrait of Diodotos (fig. 13a. b).[78] The dedicatory inscription on the surface of the fragment, which can be dated to the Hellenistic period and was documented in detail by Seyrig,[79] names a certain Panderos who, having been commanded to do so in a dream, conse-crated the portrait as a votive offering in a sanctuary of Artemis. However, it remains important to note that the long hair, the intensified dynamic formulas, and the youth-ful physiognomy did not appear before in this iconographic condensation. Therefore, the portrait of Diodotos appears as an amalgamation of different features which – al-though not exclusively attested for images of Alexander – in their combination in a king's portrait make Diodotos appear closer to Alexander's image than any Hellenistic ruler before him. In the visual *imitatio Alexandri* of Diodotos, there is no direct refer-ence to a specific image of Alexander, but a portrait of Alexander at the time might well have looked like this,[80] if one leaves out the corpulence of the ruler: the Boston/ Capitol type (fig. 14) or the so-called Inopos from Delos in the Louvre in Paris, both of which show, however, an Anastolé, can be cited here.[81] The waving hair is typical of the coin depictions of Alexander on the Macedonian Aesillas coinage as well as for the Alexander-like stylised coin portraits of Mithradates VI from 88 BC.[82] Seemingly com-peting semantic aspects obviously overlap in one concept, but they were apparently perceived as coherent and complementary.

The reverse of the tetradrachms with the Boiotian equestrian helmet can be seen as an innovative image creation that rhetorically and aspirationally ties in with the rep-resentation of Alexander the Great. The horn as a trophy from a battle with a mythical creature native to India represents a semantic equivalent to Alexander's elephant *exu-via*, and to the obverse of the Poros decadrachms, depicting a war elephant, perceived

---

78   Collection of the late George Ortiz, Geneva. See Fischer 1971, 56 pl. 24, 1–5. First Seyrig 1965, 28–30 (portrait of Alexander the Great). For the dating in the 2nd century BC, based on stylistic evidence, see especially Niemeier 1985, 45. Furthermore Jucker – Willers 1982, 24–25 no. 5; Smith 1988, 181 no. 17; Fleischer 1991, 69–70 pl. 37 e-41. Recently Tonghini 2012, 51.

79   Seyrig 1965, 29–30 fig. 2; Fleischer 1991, 70 pl. 37 e: Πάνδερος δὶς [σω] θεὶς ἐγ μεγάλων κινδύνων κατ᾽ ὄ[ναρ] τῆ(ι) Ἀρτέμιδι.

80   See also Fleischer 2002, 68–69: 'He did not choose for himself the name Alexander, but his long hair and his face on the coins clearly resemble him.'

81   Boston/Capitol type: H. von Steuben, in: Helbig II⁴ (1966) 229–230 no. 1423; Smith 1988, 62; Stew-art 1993, 44; 333–334; Kovacs 2022, 290–295 pl. 100. 101. "Inopos" from Delos (Paris, Louvre inv. no. MA 855): Smith 1988, 172 no. 89 pl. 54, 6; Kreikenbom 1992, 118–119 no. 17; Kovacs 2022, 214–217 pl. 72.

82   Aesillas coins: Stewart 1993, 328–330; de Callataÿ 1996; Bauslaugh 2002; Dahmen 2007, 18–20; Tzvetkova 2016; Kovacs 2022, 220–226. Alexander-like portraits of Mithradates VI: Smith 1988, 113; Bohm 1989, 168–171; Højte 2009; Michels 2009, 202–215; Kovacs 2015, 48–57; Kovacs 2022, 424–434. For the chronology of the Mithradatic coinage see de Callataÿ 1997.

as an exotic and overpowering beast, which is put to flight by Alexander.[83] The Boiotian equestrian helmet magnificently adorned with the diadem also refers to the leadership of a Macedonian cavalry unit and thereby also connects to Alexander. The lightning bolt as an attribute of Zeus, in turn, corresponds to world domination that was won as a result of military victories, a message that the image of Alexander crowned by Nike on the obverse of the Poros dekadrachms can also convey.[84]

However, the coin image of Diodotos was meant prospectively, and not as a proclamation of victory as with Alexander. Between 141 and 139 BC, the Parthians had occupied Mesopotamia and thus directly threatened the existence of the empire.[85] Diodotos, who propagated his own legitimation based on his abilities and charisma – the epithet *autokrator*, the ruler from within himself,[86] is to be given a programmatic meaning – promised the restoration of the empire to its former greatness. This promise, combined with the visual appearance, was reminiscent of Alexander's achievements, suggesting Diodotos would achieve something similar to Alexander.[87]

7. Back to the roots. Antiochos VII and the reestablishment of dynastic ruler portraiture

The urgency of the restoration of Seleukid rule over the Mesopotamian and Persian satrapies is demonstrated by the immense efforts of Diodotos' successor, Antiochos VII Sidetes, who marched east with a large army and, after initial successes, ultimately failed.[88] In his portrait (fig. 15),[89] however, the latter stylised himself as a representative of the legitimate Seleukid dynasty with his simple hairstyle in a rather traditional manner in the sense of dynastic iconography by imitating the coiffure of Antiochos I (fig. 16).[90] And this claim can be enforced with literary evidence. In the first book of the Makkabees, Sidetes tells the Jewish high priest Simon in Jerusalem, while still lingering

---

83   See Bohm 1989, 124–126. One could argue that the horn is not the headdress of a unicorn because it is rolled up at the tip. However, it is said that the horn in question was used as a drinking vessel, which in turn, in connection with the Graeco-Persian rhyta widespread in Hellenism, cf. in particular Bernard 1985; Bernard 1991; Pappalardo 2008, suggests that the horn of the unicorn may have been imagined as curved in antiquity. Compare Wellmann 1903. For the relevance of elephants within the Seleukid context already under Seleukos I see Iossif – Lorber 2010.

84   Cf. the Poros dekadrachm, issued ca. 326/323 BC in Babylon (?) Price 1982; Bernard 1985; Holt 2003; Le Rider 2007, Dahmen 2007, 7–8; 109–110; Kovacs 2022, 107–110.

85   Vgl. Dąbrowa 1992; van Wickevoort Crommelin 1998, 267.

86   Cf. in detail Gehrke 1982, 266.

87   In her contribution to this volume, Katharina Martin points out the communicative relevance of the respective coinages, which were used on high-value nominals.

88   Fischer 1970; Ehling 1998; Ehling 2008, 200–216; Grainger 2015b.

89   Cf. in particular SC 2061 (Antiocheia on the Orontes).

90   Compare for example SC 379. He also adopted the title *megas* after the reconquest of Babylonia (cf. Iust. 38.10.6), probably referring directly to the *anabasis* of his famous forefather Antiochos III,

on Rhodos, that the king is determined to regain the empire of his fathers, with which he refers to the dynastically legitimized claim for the throne.[91]

> A few criminals have usurped the rule over the empire of our fathers. I now want to take over the empire again and restore the old order in it. I have recruited numerous forces and equipped warships and want to land with them to bring to justice all those who have ruined our country and depopulated so many cities in my empire.

The hope for a future victory of the Greeks against the Parthians, based on the achievements and abilities of Alexander the Great, also intensified once more under the usurper Alexander Zabinas. Since the latter was positioned by Ptolemaios VIII as a fictitious son of Antiochos VII against Demetrios II, his portrait was modelled on his great predecessor (fig. 17).[92] Even individual curls on the calotte and the forehead partially correspond. Nevertheless, bronze coins were once again issued in this period showing the ruler with the elephant *exuvia* or attributing to him Herakles-like abilities via a lion scalp.[93] Both attributes can be interpreted – in the context of the greatest foreign policy crisis as well as in the struggle for legitimacy of rule against Demetrios II – as expressions of Alexander-like abilities of Zabinas.[94]

Fig. 15 Antiochos VII Sidetes. Tetradrachm, Antiocheia on the Orontes, 138–129 BC.

---

see Strootman 2020, 147–148. On the the *megas* title see also the paper by Shane Wallace in this volume.

91 1 Makk 15.3–4: ἐπεί τινες λοιμοὶ κατεκράτησαν τῆς βασιλείας τῶν πατέρων ἡμῶν, βούλομαι δὲ ἀντιποιήσασθαι τῆς βασιλείας, ὅπως ἀποκαταστήσω αὐτὴν ὡς ἦν τὸ πρότερον, ἐξενολόγησα δὲ πλῆθος δυνάμεων καὶ κατεσκεύασα πλοῖα πολεμικά, (4) βούλομαι δὲ ἐκβῆναι κατὰ τὴν χώραν, ὅπως μετέλθω τοὺς κατεφθαρκότας τὴν χώραν ἡμῶν καὶ τοὺς ἠρημωκότας πόλεις πολλὰς ἐν τῇ βασιλείᾳ μου, (…).

92 SC 2219.

93 Fleischer 1991, 75 pl. 43 c. d; SC 2231. Furthermore, Zwierlein-Diehl 2007, 65; 372 fig. 227 identifies a glass cameo on the Shrine of the Three Kings in the Cologne Cathedral, showing a Hellenistic ruler with a lion's skin over his head, with Alexander Zabinas.

94 For the episode of the usurpation of Alexander Zabinas cf. Bohm 1989, 127–129; Ehling 1998, 144–147; Chrubasik 2016, 142–145.

Fig. 16 Antiochos I. Tetradrachm of Antiochos II, Seleukia on the Tigris, 261–246 BC.

Fig. 17 Alexander Zabinas. Tetradrachm, Antiocheia on the Orontes, 128–122 BC.

At this point, a decisive turn in the semantic quality and visual possibilities of the *imitatio Alexandri* in the Hellenistic age becomes apparent. Whereas the greatness of the unconquered (ἀνίκητος)[95] Alexander had previously been perceived as unattainable and his deeds unrepeatable, making Alexander as referenced by Hellenistic monarchs a more or less distanced, mythically and divinely transfigured character, the crisis of the mid-2nd century BC allowed a new semantic quality to arise. A paradigm shift in the treatment of the figure of Alexander seems to have taken place, which was first marked by the experiment of Diodotos. The latter claimed to carry out the conquest of Persia and India again, as Alexander himself and his predecessor, Antiochos III, successfully had once done[96], whereby the visual representation in the sense of a "new Alexander" could be considered a tangible and, in the historical-cultural situation, also credible option, which had not been possible before. In the example of Diodotos Tryphon, the Alexander-model became available in an unprecedented, far-reaching form for the visual representation of Hellenistic rulers who did not want to or could not inscribe themselves in dynastic traditions, but intended to formulate a corresponding charisma

95   See note 8.
96   In the case of Antiochos III, there is also a direct connection between his epithet *megas* and his military sucesses in the east, cf. Spranger 1958, 30–31; Ma 2000, 271–276; Engels 2017, 50; Strootman 2020, 145–148.

that would place them in the vicinity of the great conqueror. This paved the way for the ultimate Alexander imitator, Mithradates VI.[97]

The pronounced Alexander-like representation of Diodotos Tryphon remained but an episode in the face of his failure and the reassertion of the old Seleukid dynasty. From the 120s BC, the empire entered an accelerating process of political marginalisation and became more than ever a plaything for other competing powers, above all Rome and the Parthian Empire. The visual representation of the last Seleukid rulers, however, is oriented towards their great predecessors again, especially Antiochos IV.

The hairstyle of Antiochos VII Sidetes roughly echoes that of Antiochos I, as discussed above, whereas Antiochos VIII quotes the feisty stylisation of Sidetes, and on some coinage portraits the moving curly hairstyle of the later portrait of the rejuvenated portrait of Antiochos IV, slightly altered with a pronounced hooked nose[98]. Sidetes also resembled Alexander Zabinas in a striking way.[99] These elements define the essential components of Seleukid portrait representation until the end of the dynasty. Antiochos IX introduced a luxurious beard, shaved out above the upper lip and on the chin, as a further iconographic detail, which was adopted by several other rulers.[100] The only one that stands out is the portrait of Demetrios II after his release by the Parthians (128 to 125 BC). He stylises himself in a peculiar way with a long, smoothly streaked beard and wreath of hair, and seems to be reminiscent of images of gods of the Severe Style.[101]

Fig. 18 Antiochos XIII. Tetradrachm, Antiocheia on the Orontes, 65–64 BC.

97   See note 82.
98   Fleischer 1991, 80–82 pl. 45 c–f; SC 2309.
99   Fleischer 1991, 75 pl. 43 a. b.
100 Houghton 1984; Fleischer 1991, 82–85 pl. 46 b–g. SC 2263. 2366–2368.
101 Fleischer 1991, 71–74 pl. 42 d–f. Compare numerous issues from different mints: SC 2155–2168 (Antiocheia on the Orontes); 2177–2183 (Damaskos); 2187–2188 (Berytos); 2193–2194 (Tyre); 2201–2206 (Ake). See in contrast the resemblance to images of Zeus on coins of Antiochos IV: Fleischer 1991, pl. 22 g; 23 a. Ehling 1998, 143–144, however, argues, that the beard of Demetrios II represented a Parthian identity of the king.

While the physiognomy of Antiochos XIII (fig. 18)[102] is reminiscent of Seleukos VI (nose, mouth and chin),[103] the curly hairstyle with the Anastolé is reminiscent of the second portrait type of Antiochos IV as well as of Alexander Balas. The overall ageless stylisation seems to invoke once again the heritage as well as the heroizing and theomorphic representation of the famous king, who was the last Seleukid ruler to lead successful campaigns against Egypt and in Judea. The fact that the reverse sides are decorated with Zeus enthroned and crowned by a Nike also fits in with this. This image design seems to have been deliberately introduced at the same time as the change in the portrait model of Antiochos IV to the ageless, heroic portrait. A concrete programmatic reference to Alexander the Great is evident here once again only in an indirect refraction, in which the connection to an older Seleukid ruler image played a greater role. In this way, the originally transgressive, charismatic redesign[104] of the ruler portrait under Antiochos IV became a more conventional and traditional form of representation in which precisely the supposed stability and continuity of the dynasty could be emphasised. The exaggerated, heroic and divine connotations, which may once have been decidedly dominant in the conception, now seem to have played a rather subordinate role.

8. Conclusion: dynastic image versus visual imitation of Alexander the Great, and the dynamics of change in visual representation as a cultural-historical phenomenon

In the overall view of the portrait stylisations of the Seleukid rulers, several trends and conjunctures can be identified. First of all, it is striking that the rulers who legitimised themselves directly through the dynastic line inscribed themselves in specific traditions. While in the late 3rd and early 2nd century BC references to Antiochos I can be detected, and thus a preference for features of age and a simpler coiffure, it is only with the representation of Antiochos IV, and especially with his second portrait type, that a remarkable innovation emerges, which initially removes the ruler from the narrow dynastic tradition and claims instead a charismatic legitimation. The new, intensified references to gods, the adoption of attributes of the gods as well as the youthful stylization, which is complemented by the heroically impregnated Anastolé, prove to be successful in the portrait of Antiochos IV. Therefore, numerous successors who place themselves in a direct dynastic line with the king, such as Alexander Balas, followed this model. In this way, it is possible to grasp a tradition of dynastic portrait representa-

---

102   Houghton at al. 2008, no. 2487.
103   Compare in particular SC 2414. 2415.
104   For transgressivity as one criterion for a charismatic shaping of monarchic representation cf. Trampedach – Meuus 2020, 11.

tion that was consolidated and remained stable. Although it originally represented an open break with established conventions, it still represented a point of reference for the last Seleukid kings in the early 1st century BC.

On the other hand, operating with iconographic features of the Alexander portrait proves to be a specific feature of those rulers who ostentatiously evaded dynastic legitimation; either because as usurpers they turned against the representative of the established succession anyway, like Demetrios I or Diodotos Tryphon, or, as in the case of Antiochos IV, because they relied heavily on charismatic elements in their representation. The visual proximity to Alexander the Great thereby gained increased momentum when the Seleukid Empire was confronted with crisis-like events both externally and internally. It became particularly plausible in a political climate in which the emerging kings, especially ostentatiously Diodotos Tryphon, appeared as saviours and restorers of the empire as well as protectors of the Greek cities in the eastern satrapies. The performance necessary for this, which was to lead prospectively to a restoration of the ancient greatness and integrity of the Seleukid Empire, resembled the achievements of Alexander the Great in his military campaign against the Persian Empire. This potential repeatability of Alexander's heroic deeds represents the decisive difference here to early Hellenism, in which the Diadochi strove to develop their own strategies of ruler representation allowing the considerable internal variance in the visual staging of Greek kingship to develop between Macedonia, Asia and Egypt. The replicability of Alexander's achievements, as well as the extensive visual assimilation to the great Macedonian, opened the way for Mithradates VI, who, although he did not turn east against the Parthian Empire, did intend to regain the freedom of the Greek cities with vast military campaigns against the omnipresent Roman Empire.

The clear emphasis on the military qualities of the kings, but also the charismatic references to decidedly heroic and divine aspects, are to be understood in this sense. The peculiar Boiotian equestrian helmet of Diodotos Tryphon, novel and singular in its iconographic conception, as well as the reference to the Dioskuroi, who were known as helpers in battle, repeatedly invoked by the later Seleukid kings, embody this claim in a special way.

Noah Kaye, in his programmatic contribution to this volume, seeks to dismiss the concept of charismatic rulership for the 2nd century BC in general. However, in the light of his observations and considering the tendencies addressed here, it is precisely the diversity and the only *seemingly* contradictory aspects of Hellenistic kingship that become clear. Furthermore, different communication media appear to be of high importance in this context. While the ruler could assume a charismatic/heroic role on coin images, or, one might add, in the panegyric imagery of the highly precious

Hellenistic cameos deriving from Ptolemaic court art,[105] he could present himself in a progressively different role in interaction with the poleis or various sanctuaries, making him appear more accessible and more politically tangible. These emerging roles are not contradictory, but should be understood as complementary aspects of Hellenistic ruler representation, which could be activated (or not) in different forms and conjunctures, as well as depending on the conventions of different visual media and their praxeological contexts.[106]

One could therefore describe the period studied here as an age of alternating experiments in the visual culture of the Seleukid kings, in view of the crisis-like events resulting from rapid changes of rulers and external threats. If one wants to draw a historical parallel, then the observed phenomena of the chequered history of different concepts of rulership and competing models of portraiture seem not dissimilar to the situation of the Roman Empire in the 3rd century AD. Due to the rapid change of rulers as a result of contingent events, the stylisation of the emperors' portraits shows sometimes radical transformations as well as subtle links to specific iconographic traditions,[107] as well as in the imagery of the coin images on the reverses. For example, the charismatic portrayal of Emperor Gallienus was also a response to a situation perceived as particularly crisis-ridden showing that he too used this representation to present himself as the potential saviour of the empire.[108]

In connection with the developments in the representation of the Seleukid image in the 2nd century BC, overarching conjunctures and transformations become apparent. Particularly in the later 2nd and then in the early 1st century, an increasing range in the stylisation of portraits can be observed. These include, for example, the decidedly old portraits of (client) rulers, to whom a pro-Roman attitude was attributed in this way in an alleged imitation of republican portraits.[109] However, it seems essential to note that it was the transformations and changes in the visual representation of previous rulers, sometimes induced by crises, that noticeably expanded the field of possibilities for the following period. The image of the middle-aged, mature, usually beardless gen-

---

105   See for the 'visual language' of Hellenistic court art, referring to the example of cameos, Bergmann 2008.
106   See also the papers by Katharina Martin and Achim Lichtenberger in this volume. In this regard, the tradition of ruler representation in its varying medial and praxeological contexts in the Roman imperial period appears to be comparable, exemplified by the portraits of Caligula: von den Hoff 2009, 255–258.
107   Cf. Bergmann 2015 with further references.
108   Cf. Kovacs 2015, 70–78.
109   See for example the elderly portrait of the Kappadokian ruler Ariobarzanes (95–63 BC): Smith 1988, 130–132 pl. 78, 9–10; 79, 1. The idea, however, is disputed by Salzmann 2007. See further Michels 2009, 235–237. Older, individualizing physiognomies are also basically apparent in civic late Hellenistic portraiture in Athens and on Delos, cf. Stewart 1979, and recently Kovacs 2018, 43–44.

eral with stringy hair,[110] which prevailed in the Seleukid Empire in the 3rd century BC and to whom charismatic or divine traits could be cumulatively inscribed,[111] gradually lost its binding force in the advancing 2nd century BC. In a discourse in which, on the one hand, traits of Alexander iconography were increasingly adopted, and on the other hand, and also directly as a result, heroic and charismatic contents gained in importance, a differentiation and both selective and dynamic redefinition of Graeco-Macedonian, i. e., Hellenistic kingship is expressed.

Bibliography

R.-Alföldi 1984: R.-Alföldi, Maria, Der Stater des T. Quinctius Flamininus, Numismatische Zeitschrift 98, 1984, 19–26

Amela Valverde 2012: Amela Valverde, Luis, La emisión de T. Qvincti (RRC 548), OMNI. Revista Numismática 5, 2012, 38–42

Anson 2006: Anson, Edward M., The Chronology of the Third Diadoch War, Phoenix 60, 2006, 226–235

Baldus 1970: Baldus, Hans R., Der Helm des Tryphon und die seleukidische Chronologie 146–138 v. Chr., Jahrbuch für Numismatik und Geldgeschichte 20, 1970, 217–239

Bergmann 1991: Bergmann, Marianne, Ein Fragment klassizistischer Kritik am hellenistischen Figurenstil, Jahrbuch des Deutschen Archäologischen Instituts 106, 1991, 231–241

Bergmann 1998: Bergmann, Marianne, Die Strahlen der Herrscher. Theomorphes Herrscherbild und politische Symbolik im Hellenismus und in der römischen Kaiserzeit, Mainz 1998

Bergmann 2008: Bergmann, Marianne, Zur Bildsprache römischer Kaiserkameen, in: G. Platz-Horster (ed.), Mythos und Macht. Erhabene Bilder in Edelstein, Berlin 2008, 13–21

Bergmann 2015: Bergmann, Marianne, Gli imperatori e le stilizzazioni delle loro immagini, in: E. La Rocca – C. Parisi Presicce – QA. Lo Monaco (eds.), L'età dell'Angoscia. Da Commodo a Diocleziano. 180–305 d. C., Rome 2015, 74–83

Bernard 1985: Bernard, Paul, Le monnayage d'Eudamos, satrape grec du Pandjab et "maître des éléphants", in: G. Gnoli – L. Lanciotti (eds.), Orientalia Josephi Tucci memoriae dicata, Rome 1985, 65–94

Bernard 1991: Bernard, Paul, Les rhytons de Nisa. A quoi, à qui ont-ils servi?, in: P. Bernard – F. Grenet (eds.), Histoire et cultes de l'Asie Centrale préislamique. Sources écrites et documents archéologiques. Actes du Colloque international du CNRS, Paris 22–28 novembre 1988, Paris 1991, 31–38

110 This model was also used, albeit in a bearded version, and hardly by chance, for the portrait of Quinctius Flamininus on the famous gold staters, issued 196 BC in Greece: Boyce 1962; Smith 1981, 26–27 pl. 2 2; R.-Alföldi 1984, Amela Valverde 2012; Campana 2016.

111 Although, in contrast to this, in the Ptolemaic Empire in the 3rd century the ideal of *tryphe*, which deviated from this, was predominant, and thus exceptionally corpulent stylizations of portraits, a greater range of possible stylizations is also apparent there in the 2nd century, cf. Kyrieleis 1975, 52–64. For a recent comparison of the portraiture of both empires see von den Hoff 2021. For retrospective tendencies in the portraiture of the Antigonid rulers in the 2nd century see Kovacs 2022, 365–366.

Bohm 1989: Bohm, Caroline, Imitatio Alexandri im Hellenismus. Untersuchungen zum politischen Nachwirken Alexanders des Großen in den hoch- und späthellenistischen Monarchien,
Munich 1989

Borchhardt 2001: Borchhardt, Jürgen, Bericht der Grabungskampagne in Limyra 2000, Kazı
Sonuçları Toplantısı 23.1, 2001, 419–426

Boyce 1962: Boyce, A. Abaecherli, The Gold Staters of T. Quinctius Flamininus, in: M. Renard
(ed.), Hommages à Albert Grenier I, Brussels 1962, 342–350

Bringmann – von Steuben 1995: Bringmann, Klaus – von Steuben, Hans, Schenkungen hellenistischer Herrscher an griechische Städte und Heiligtümer I: Zeugnisse und Kommentare, Berlin 1995

Bunge 1974: Bunge, Jochen G., "Theos Epiphanes". Zu den ersten fünf Regierungsjahren Antiochos' IV. Epiphanes, Historia 24, 1974, 57–85

Bunge 1975: Bunge, Jochen G., "Antiochos-Helios": Methoden und Ergebnisse der Reichspolitik
Antiochos' IV. Epiphanes von Syrien im Spiegel seiner Münzen, Historia 25, 1975, 164–188

Campana 2016: Campana, Alberto, La Monetazione di T. Quinctius Flamininus. Un aureo elle-
nistico (RRC 548/1), Cassino 2016

Chaniotis 2003: Chaniotis, Angelos, The Divinity of Hellenistic Rulers, in: A. Erskine (ed.), A
Companion to the Hellenistic World, Oxford 2003, 431–445

Chrubasik 2016: Chrubasik, Boris, Kings and Usurpers in the Seleukid Empire: The Men Who
Would Be King, Oxford 2016

Dąbrowa 1992: Dąbrowa, Edward, Könige Syriens in der Gefangenschaft der Parther. Zwei Epi-
soden aus der Geschichte der Beziehungen der Seleukiden zu den Arsakiden, Tyche 7, 1992,
45–54

Dahmen 2007: Dahmen, Karsten, The Legend of Alexander the Great on Greek and Roman
Coins, New York 2007

de Callataÿ – Lorber 2011: de Callataÿ, François – Lorber, Catharine C., The Pattern of Royal Epithets on Hellenistic Coinages, in: P. P. Iossif – A. S. Chankowski – C. C. Lorber (eds.), More
than Men, Less than Gods. Studies on Royal Cult and Imperial Worship, Leuven 2011, 417–456

de Callataÿ 1996: de Callataÿ, François, Les monnaies au nom d'Aesillas, in: T. Hackens – G. Mou-
charte (eds.), Italian fato profugi. Hesperinaque venerunt litora. Numismatic Studies Dedicated to Vladimir and Elvira Eliza Clain-Stefanelli, Leuven 1996, 113–151

de Callataÿ 1997: de Callataÿ, François, L'histoire des guerres mithridatiques vue par les monnaies, Leuven 1997

de Callataÿ 2012: de Callataÿ, François, Royal Hellenistic Coinages: From Alexander to Mithradates, in: W. Metcalf (ed.), The Oxford Handbook of Greek and Roman Coinage, New York
2012, 175–190

Dintsis 1986: Dintsis, Petros, Hellenistische Helme, Rome 1986

Dorka Moreno 2019: Dorka Moreno, Martin, Imitatio Alexandri? Ähnlichkeitsrelationen zwischen Götter- und Heroenbildern und Porträts Alexanders des Großen in der griechisch-
römischen Antike, Rahden 2019

Ehling 1997: Ehling, Kay, Überlegungen zur Herkunft und Bedeutung des Helms auf den Münzen
Antiochos' VI. und Tryphons, Jahrbuch für Numismatik und Geldgeschichte 47, 1997, 21–27

Ehling 1998: Ehling, Kay, Seleukidische Geschichte zwischen 130 und 121 v. Chr., Historia 47, 1998,
141–151

Ehling 2000: Ehling, Kay, Stierdionysos oder Sohn des Poseidon: Zu den Hörnern des Demetrios
Poliorketes, Göttinger Forum für Altertumswissenschaft 3, 2000, 153–160

Ehling 2008: Ehling, Kay, Untersuchungen zur Geschichte der späten Seleukiden (164–63 v. Chr.). Vom Tode des Antiochos IV. bis zur Einrichtung der Provinz Syria unter Pompeius, Stuttgart 2008

Elias 1997: Elias, Norbert, Über den Prozeß der Zivilisation I. Soziogenetische und psychogenetische Untersuchungen, Amsterdam 1997

Engels 2017: Engels, David, Benefactors, Kings, Rulers. Studies on the Seleukid Empire between East and West, Leuven 2017

Erickson 2013: Erickson, Kyle, Seleucus I, Zeus and Alexander, in: L. Mitchell – A. Melville (eds.), Every Inch a King. Comparative Studies on King and Kingship in the Ancient and Medieval Worlds, Leiden 2013, 120–124

Errington 1977: Errington, Robert M., Diodorus Siculus and the Chronology of the Early Diadochoi, 320–311 B. C., Hermes 105, 1977, 478–504

Fischer 1970: Fischer, Thomas, Untersuchungen zum Partherkrieg Antiochos' VII. im Rahmen der Seleukidengeschichte, Diss. Munich 1970

Fischer 1971: Fischer, Thomas, Ein Bildnis des Tryphon in Basel?, Antike Kunst 14, 1971, 56

Fischer 1972: Fischer, Thomas, Zu Tryphon, Chiron 2, 1972, 201–213

Fleischer 1991: Fleischer, Robert, Studien zur seleukidischen Kunst I: Herrscherbildnisse, Mainz 1991

Fleischer 2002: Fleischer, Robert, True Ancestors and False Ancestors in Hellenistic Rulers' Portrait, in: J. M. Højte (ed.), Images of Ancestors, Aarhus 2002, 59–74

Fröhlich 1998: Fröhlich, Brigitte, Die statuarischen Darstellungen der hellenistischen Herrscher, Hamburg 1998

Gehrke 1982: Gehrke, Hans-Joachim, Der siegreiche König. Überlegungen zur hellenistischen Monarchie, Archiv für Kulturgeschichte 64, 1982, 247–277

Gotter 2013: Gotter, Ulrich, The Castrated King, or: The Everyday Monstrosity of Late Hellenistic Kingship, in: N. Luraghi (ed.), The Splendors and Miseries of Ruling Alone. Encounters with Monarchy from Archaic Greece to the Hellenistic Mediterranean, Stuttgart 2013, 207–230

Grainger 1997: Grainger, John D., A Seleukid Prosopography and Gazetteer, Leiden 1997

Grainger 2015a: Grainger, John D., The Seleukid Empire of Antiochus III (223–187 BC), Barnsley 2015a

Grainger 2015b: Grainger, John D., The Fall of the Seleukid Empire, 187–75 B. C., Barnsley 2015b

Gruen 1985: Gruen, Erich S., The Coronation of the Diadochi, in: J. Eadie – J. Ober (eds.), The Craft of the Ancient Historian, London 1985, 253–271 (repr. in. Karanos 1, 2018, 109–119)

Günther 2011: Günther, Linda-Marie, Herrscher als Götter – Götter als Herrscher? Zur Ambivalenz hellenistischer Münzbilder, in: L.-M. Günther – S. Plischke (eds.), Studien zum vorhellenistischen und hellenistischen Herrscherkult, Berlin 2011, 98–113

Hallett 2003: Hallett, Christopher H., The Roman Nude. Heroic Portrait Statuary 200 B. C.–A. D. 300, Oxford 2005

Heinen 1983: Heinen, Heinz, Die Tryphé des Ptolemaios VIII. Euergetes II. Beobachtungen zum ptolemäischen Herrscherideal und zu einer römischen Gesandtschaft in Ägypten (140/139 v. Chr.), in: H. Heinen (ed.), Althistorische Studien. Festschrift Hermann Bengtson, Wiesbaden 1983, 116–128

Himmelmann 1989: Himmelmann, Nikolaus, Herrscher und Athlet. Die Bronzen vom Quirinal, Milan 1989

Højte 2009: Højte, Jakob M., Portraits and Statues of Mithridates VI, in: id. (ed.), Mithridates VI and the Pontic Kingdom, Aarhus 2009, 145–162

Hölbl 1994: Hölbl, Günther, Geschichte des Ptolemäerreiches. Von Alexander dem Großen bis
    zur römischen Eroberung, Darmstadt 1994

Hölscher 1971: Hölscher, Tonio, Ideal und Wirklichkeit in den Bildnissen Alexanders des Großen,
    Heidelberg 1971

Hölscher 1973: Hölscher, Tonio, Griechische Historienbilder des 5. und 4. Jahrhunderts v. Chr.,
    Würzburg 1973

Hölscher 2009: Hölscher, Tonio, Herrschaft und Lebensalter. Alexander der Große: Politisches
    Image und anthropologisches Modell, Basel 2009

Holt 2003: Holt, Frank L., Alexander the Great and the Mystery of the Elephant Medallions,
    Berkeley 2003

Hoover 2007: Hoover, Oliver D., Coins of the Seleucid Empire from the Collection of Arthur
    Houghton II, New York 2007

Houghton 1984: Houghton, Arthur, The Portrait of Antiochus IX., Antike Kunst 27, 1984, 123–128

Houghton – Stewart 2008: Houghton, Arthur – Stewart, Andrew F., The Equestrian Portrait of
    Alexander the Great on a New Tetradrachm of Seleucus I, Schweizerische Numismatische
    Rundschau 78, 1999, 27–33

Huß 2001: Huß, Werner, Ägypten in hellenistischer Zeit 332–30 v. Chr., Munich 2001

Instinsky 1949: Instinsky, Hans U., Alexander der Große am Hellespont, Godesberg 1949

Iossif – Lorber 2010: Iossif, Panagiotis P. – Lorber, Catharine C., The Elephantarches Bronze of
    Seleucos I Nikator, Syria 87, 2010, 147–164

Iossif – Lorber 2012: Iossif, Panagiotis P. – Lorber, Catharine C., The Rays of the Ptolemies, Revue
    Numismatique 169, 2012, 197–224

Jucker – Willers 1982: Jucker, Hans – Willers, Dietrich (eds.), Gesichter. Griechische und Römi-
    sche Bildnisse aus Schweizer Besitz, Bern 1982

Kovacs 2015: Kovacs, Martin, Imitatio Alexandri – Zu Aneignungs- und Angleichungsphänome-
    nen im römischen Porträt, in: R. von den Hoff et al. (eds.), Imitatio heroica. Heldenanglei-
    chung im Bildnis, Würzburg 2015, 47–84

Kovacs 2018: Kovacs, Martin, Charakter und Präsenz im griechischen Porträt. Realistische Bild-
    nisentwürfe zwischen Klassik und Hellenismus, in: C. Nowak – L. Winkler-Horacek (eds.),
    Auf der Suche nach Wirklichkeit. Realismen in der griechischen Plastik, Rahden 2018, 27–49

Kovacs 2022: Kovacs, Martin, Vom Herrscher zum Heros. Die Bildnisse Alexanders des Großen
    und die Imitatio Alexandri, Rahden 2022

Kreikenbom 1990: Kreikenbom, Detlev, Bildwerke nach Polyklet. Kopienkritische Untersuchun-
    gen zu den männlichen statuarischen Typen nach Werken Polyklets. Diskophoros, Hermes,
    Doryphoros, Herakles, Diadumenos, Berlin 1990

Kreikenbom 1992: Kreikenbom, Detlev, Griechische und römische Kolossalporträts bis zum spä-
    ten 1. Jahrhundert n. Chr., Berlin 1992

Kyrieleis 1975: Kyrieleis, Helmut, Bildnisse der Ptolemäer, Berlin 1975

Kyrieleis 1980: Kyrieleis, Helmut, Ein Bildnis des Königs Antiochos IV. von Syrien, Berlin 1980

La Rocca 1994: La Rocca, Eugenio, Theoi epiphaneis. Linguaggio figurativo e culto dinastico da
    Antioco IV ad Augusto, in: K. Rosen (ed.), Macht und Kultur im Rom der Kaiserzeit, Bonn
    1994, 9–63

L'Orange 1947: L'Orange, Hans P., Apotheosis in Ancient Portraiture, Oslo 1947

Le Rider 1965: Le Rider, Georges, Suse sous les Séleucides et les Parthes. Trouvailles monétaires
    et l'histoire de la ville, Paris 1965

Le Rider 1977: Le Rider, Georges, Le monnayage d'argent et d'or de Philippe II frappé en Macé-
    doine de 359 à 294, Paris 1977

Le Rider 2007: Le Rider, Georges, Coinage, Finances, and Policy, Philadelphia 2007

Letta 1988: Letta, Cesare, s. v. Helios/Sol, LIMC IV.1, 1988, 592–625

Lichtenberger 2013: Lichtenberger, Achim, Der Zeus Nemeios des Lysipp und Alexander der Große, in: G. Kalaitzoglu – G. Lüdorf (eds.), Petasos. Festschrift für Hans Lohmann, Paderborn 2013, 179–192

Lichtenberger et al. 2012: Lichtenberger, Achim et al. (eds.), Das Diadem der hellenistischen Herrscher. Übernahme, Transformation oder Neuschöpfung eines Herrschaftszeichens, Bonn 2012

Ma 2000: Ma, John, Antiochos III and the Cities of Western Asia Minor, Oxford 2000

Matern 2002: Matern, Petra, Helios und Sol. Kulte und Ikonographie des griechischen und römischen Sonnengottes, Istanbul 2002

Messerschmidt 1989: Messerschmidt, Wolfgang, Historische und ikonographische Untersuchungen zum Alexandersarkophag, Boreas 12, 1989, 64–92

Meeus 2009: Meeus, Alexander, Alexander's Image in the Age of the Successors, in: W. Heckel – L. A. Tritle (eds.), Alexander the Great: A New History, Malden 2009, 235–250

Michels 2009: Michels, Christoph, Kulturtransfer und monarchischer "Philhellenismus": Bithynien, Pontos und Kappadokien in hellenistischer Zeit, Göttingen 2009

Mittag 2006: Mittag, Peter F., Antiochos IV. Epiphanes. Eine politische Biographie, Berlin 2006

Mittag 2016: Mittag, Peter F., Griechische Numismatik. Eine Einführung, Berlin 2016

Mørkholm 1960: Mørkholm, Otto, A Posthumous Issue of Antiochus IV of Syria, Numismatic Chronicle 20, 1960, 25–30

Mørkholm 1963: Mørkholm, Otto, Studies in the Coinage of Antiochos IV of Syria, Copenhagen 1963

Mørkholm 1966: Mørkholm, Otto, Antiochus IV of Syria, Copenhagen 1966

Muccioli 2013: Muccioli, Federicomaria, Gli epiteti ufficiali dei re ellenistici, Stuttgart 2013

Newell 1917: Newell, Edward T., The Seleucid Mint of Antioch, American Journal of Numismatics 51, 1917, 1–151

Newell ²1977: Newell, Edward T., The Coinage of the Western Seleucid Mints from Seleucus I to Antiochus III, New York ²1977

Niemeier 1985: Niemeier, Jörg-Peter, Kopien und Nachahmungen im Hellenismus. Ein Beitrag zum Klassizismus des 2. und frühen 1. Jhs. v. Chr., Bonn 1985

Pappalardo 2008: Pappalardo, Eleonora, The Rhyton no. 52 from Old Nisa. An Interpretative Proposal, Parthica 10, 2008, 63–80

Pfister 1964: Pfister, Friedrich, Alexander der Große. Die Geschichte seines Ruhms im Lichte seiner Beinamen, Historia 13, 1964, 37–79

Pfuhl 1930: Pfuhl, Ernst, Ikonographische Beiträge zur Stilgeschichte der hellenistischen Kunst, Jahrbuch des Deutschen Archäologischen Instituts 45, 1930, 1–61

Picón – Hemingway 2016: Picón, Carlos A. – Hemingway, Seán (eds.), Pergamon and the Hellenistic Kingdoms of the Ancient World, New York 2016

Price 1982: Price, Martin J., The 'Porus' Coinage of Alexander the Great: A Symbol of Concord and Community, in: S. Scheers (ed.), Studia Paulo Naster Oblata I: Numismatica Antiqua, Leuven 1982, 75–88

Price 1991: Price, Martin J., The Coinage in the Name of Alexander the Great and Philip Arrhidaeus. A British Museum Catalogue, London 1991

Queyrel 2003: Queyrel, François, Les portraits des Attalides. Fonction et representation, Paris 2003

Saatsoglou-Palliadeli 1989: Saatsoglou-Palliadeli, Chrysoula, Το ανάθημα του Κρατερού στους Δελφούς. Μεθοδολογικά προβλήματα, Egnatia 1, 1989, 81–99

Salzmann 2007: Salzmann, Dieter, Zur Selbstdarstellung von Klientelherrschern im griechischen Osten, in: M. Meyer (ed.), Neue Zeiten – Neue Sitten. Zu Rezeption und Integration römischen und italischen Kulturguts in Kleinasien, Vienna 2007, 37–43

Schmidt-Dounas 2000: Schmidt-Dounas, Barbara, Geschenke erhalten die Freundschaft. Politik und Selbstdarstellung im Spiegel der Monumente, Schenkungen hellenistischer Herrscher an griechische Städte und Heiligtümer 2.2: Archäologische Auswertung, Berlin 2000

Schörner 1993: Schörner, Günther, Helios und Alexander. Zum Einfluß der Herrscherikonographie auf das Götterbild, Archäologischer Anzeiger 2001, 59–68

Seyer 2007: Seyer, Martin, Der Herrscher als Jäger: Untersuchungen zur königlichen Jagd im persischen und makedonischen Reich vom 6.–4. Jh. v. Chr. sowie unter den Diadochen Alexanders des Großen, Vienna 2007

Seyrig 1965: Seyrig, Henri, Antiquités syriennes 88: Deux pièces énigmatiques. 1: Tête de marbre avec inscription, Syria 42, 1965, 28–30

Simpson 1954: Simpson, Richard H., The Historical Circumstances of the Peace of 311, The Journal of Hellenic Studies 74, 1954, 25–31

Smith 1981: Smith, Roland R. R., Greeks, Foreigners, and Roman Republican Portraits, Journal of Roman Studies 71, 1981, 24–38

Smith 1988: Smith, Roland R. R., Hellenistic Royal Portraits, Oxford 1988

Spranger 1978: Spranger, Peter, Der Große. Untersuchungen zur Entstehung des historischen Beinamens der Antike, Saeculum 9, 1958, 22–58

Stanwick 2002: Stanwick, Paul E., Portraits of the Ptolemies. Greek Kings as Egyptian Pharaohs, Austin 2002

Stanzl 2015: Stanzl, Günther, Das Ptolemaion von Limyra, in: J. des Courtils (ed.), L'Architecture monumentale grecque au IIIe siècle a. C., Bordeaux 2015, 175–196

Stanzl 2016: Stanzl, Günther, Neue Forschungen zum Ptolemaion von Limyra, in: K. Dörtlük et al. (eds.), The IIIrd Symposium on Lycia. Symposium Proceedings, 7–10 November 2005, Antalya, II, Antalya 2016, 735–745

Stewart 1979: Stewart, Andrew F., Attika. Studies in Athenian Sculpture of the Hellenistic Age, London 1979

Stewart 1993: Stewart, Andrew F., Faces of Power. Alexander's Image and Hellenistic Politics, Berkeley 1993

Strootman 2020: Strootman, Rolf, The Great Kings of Asia: Imperial Titulature in the Seleukid and Post-Seleukid Middle East, in: R. Oetjen (ed.), New Perspektives in Seleucid History, Archaeology and Numismatics. Studies in Honor of Getzel M. Cohen, Berlin et al. 2020, 123–157

Svenson 1995: Svenson, Dominique, Darstellungen hellenistischer Könige mit Götterattributen, Frankfurt a. M. 1995

Tonghini 2012: Tonghini, Cristina, Shayzar I: The Fortification of the Citadel, Leiden 2012

Trampedach – Meeus 2020: Trampedach, Kai – Meuus, Alexander, Introduction: Understanding Alexander's Relations with his Subjects, in: id. (eds.), The Legitimation of Conquest. Monarchical Representation and the Art of Government in the Empire of Alexander the Great, Stuttgart 2020, 9–18

Tzetkova 2016: Tzvetkova, Julia, Die Aesillas-Münzen in Thrakien im Lichte einiger neuer Funde, in: H. Schwarzer – H.-H. Nieswandt (eds.), "Man kann es sich nicht prächtig genug vorstellen!", Festschrift für Dieter Salzmann, Marsberg 2016, 199–210 van Wickevoort Crommelin 1998: van Wickevoort Crommelin, Bernard R., Die Parther und die parthische Geschichte bei Pompeius Trogus-Iustin, in: J. Wiesehöfer (ed.), Das Partherreich und seine Zeugnisse, Stuttgart 1998, 259–277

Völcker-Janssen 1993: Völcker-Janssen, Wilhelm, Kunst und Gesellschaft an den Höfen Alexanders des Großen und seiner Nachfolger, Munich 1993

Volkmann 1923: Volkmann, Hans, Zur Münzprägung des Demetrios I. und Alexander I. von Syrien, Zeitschrift für Numismatik 34, 1923, 51–66

von den Hoff 1994: von den Hoff, Ralf, Philosophenporträts des Früh- und Hochhellenismus, Munich 1994

von den Hoff 2009: von den Hoff, Ralf, Caligula. Zur visuellen Repräsentation eines römischen Kaisers, Archäologischer Anzeiger 2009, 237–263

von den Hoff 2020: von den Hoff, Ralf, Handlungsbild und Herrscherbild. Die Heroisierung der Tat in Bildnissen Alexanders des Großen, Göttingen 2020

von den Hoff 2021: von den Hoff, Ralf, The Visual Representation of Ptolemaic and Seleucid Kings, in: C. Fischer-Bovet – S. von Reden (eds.), Comparing the Ptolemaic and Seleucid Empires. Integration, Communication, and Resistance, Cambridge 2021, 164–190

von Graeve 1970: von Graeve, Volkmar, Der Alexandersarkophag und seine Werkstatt, Berlin 1970

Wellmann 1903: Wellmann, Max, s. v. Einhorn, RE V.2, 1905, 2114–2115

Will ²1982: Will, Ernest, Histoire politique du monde hellénistique (323–30 av. J.-C.) II: Des avènements d'Antiochos III et de Philippe V à la fin des Lagides, Nancy ²1982

Willrich 1901: Willrich, Hugo, s. v. Demetrios [40], RE IV.2, 1901, 2795–2798

Winnefeld 1910: Winnefeld, Hermann, Die Friese des großen Altars, Altertümer von Pergamon 3.2, Berlin 1910

Zahrnt 1996: Zahrnt, Michael, Alexanders Übergang über den Hellespont, Chiron 26, 1996, 129–147

Zwierlein-Diehl 2007: Zwierlein-Diehl, Erika, Antike Gemmen und ihr Nachleben, Berlin 2007

Figures

Fig. 1:   Paris, Musée de Louvre inv. MA 1204. © Musée du Louvre / Maurice et Pierre Chuzeville.

Fig. 2:   Berlin, Staatliche Museen/SMPK – Münzkabinett. Photograph: Dirk Sonnenwald.

Fig. 3:   Berlin, Staatliche Museen/SMPK – Münzkabinett. Photograph: Reinhard Saczewski.

Fig. 4:   Berlin, Staatliche Museen/SMPK – Münzkabinett. Photograph: Reinhard Saczewski.

Fig. 5:   American Numismatic Society 1908.115.38. Public Domain.

Fig. 6:   Berlin, Staatliche Museen/SMPK. Vorderasiatisches Museum. Photograph: Olaf M. Teßner.

Fig. 7:   Berlin, Staatliche Museen/SMPK – Antikensammlung (plaster cast Göttingen). Photographs: Stephan Eckardt.

Fig. 8:   Naples, Museo Archeologico Nazionale di Napoli inv. no. 126249. Photo: DAI Rom, D-DAI-ROM-38.576 (8a), DAI Rom, D-DAI-ROM-59.374R (8b).

Fig. 9:   American Numismatic Society 1944.100.75330. Public Domain.

Fig. 10: American Numismatic Society 1957.172.2008. Public Domain.

Fig. 11: American Numismatic Society 1944.100.76405. Public Domain.

Fig. 12: Berlin, Staatliche Museen/SMPK – Münzkabinett. Photographs: Lutz-Jürgen Lübke (Lübke und Wiedemann).

Fig. 13:   © J. Zbinden, Institut für Archäologische Wissenschaften, Universität Bern.
Fig. 14:   Rome, Museo Capitolino. Sala del Gallo Morente inv. no. 732. Forschungsarchiv für Antike Plastik, Universität zu Köln (Barbara Malter).
Fig. 15:   Berlin, Staatliche Museen/SMPK – Münzkabinett. Photograph: Dirk Sonnenwald.
Fig. 16:   Berlin, Staatliche Museen/SMPK – Münzkabinett. Photograph: Dirk Sonnenwald.
Fig. 17:   Berlin, Staatliche Museen/SMPK – Münzkabinett. Photograph: Reinhard Saczewski.
Fig. 18:   American Numismatic Society 1952.81.9. Public Domain.

Martin Kovacs is a university lecturer in Classical Archaeology at the University of Freiburg. Following the completion of his dissertation in Göttingen in 2011 (published: *Kaiser, Senatoren und Gelehrte – Untersuchungen zum spätantiken männlichen Privatporträt* (Wiesbaden 2014)), he received the travel grant from the German Archaeological Institute for 2011/2012, and was subsequently employed as a research assistant at the Institute for Classical Archaeology in Freiburg up to 2016, where he earned his habilitation with a thesis on the portraits of Alexander the Great in 2018 (published: *Vom Herrscher zum Heros. Die Bildnisse Alexanders des Großen und die Imitatio Alexandri* (Rahden 2022)). Since then, he has held substitute professorships in Saarbrücken, Freiburg and Würzburg. He has been working at the Institute of Archaeology at the University of Tübingen since 2017 and is currently part of the CRC 1391 ('Different Aesthetics'). His research focuses on the cultural history of ancient sculpture and portraiture, the representation of rulers and elites, and the archaeology of late antiquity.

City Foundations in Late Hellenistic Kingdoms

ACHIM LICHTENBERGER

Abstract: A characteristic of the Hellenistic period was the royal foundation of cities which were typically named after the king or members of the local dynasty. In the late Hellenistic period kings continued this practice but now, cities are named not only after king's own family but also after the Roman imperial family. The paper argues that such a dynastic naming relating to other than the ruler's own family occurred only in this period, and even in structurally comparable situations of kingdoms dependent on Parthia, such naming did not happen. This observation suggests that Rome expected the imperial name to be given to cities to underline the loyalty of the client kings towards Rome and the emperor.

1. Introduction

The foundation of cities belonged very much to the public image cultivated by Hellenistic kings.[1] Starting with Philipp II of Macedon and continued on a large scale by Alexander the Great, the Diadochi maintained the practice of founding cities.[2] The foundations, some of them genuine new foundations, others mere re-foundations of existing settlements served different purposes. On the one hand they promoted urbanization and opened up economic possibilities for kings and settlers and safeguarded territories. On the other hand, they served an ideological purpose, glorifying the king and the dynasty by often carrying dynastic names.

In the following, I will look at how the royal practice of founding and naming cities was continued in the late Hellenistic kingdoms, especially in the minor kingdoms often dependent on or dominated by Rome or Parthia. These kings are today called client kings, although recent research has shown that they cannot be taken as a homog-

---

[1]   On Hellenistic city foundations see still Tscherikower 1927; Leschhorn 1984 and more recently and systematically Cohen 1995; 2006; 2013.
[2]   On Philipp of Macedon cf. Lichtenberger 2001.

enous group but need to be differentiated geographically and chronologically.[3] It is the late 1st century BC to the early 1st century AD which will be the focus of the discussion. How did the still strong Hellenistic idea of royal city foundations continue to be a model for the Late Hellenistic kingdoms, and how did the smaller kingdoms cope with the challenge of acting as strong and independent kings while in fact being restricted by their limited political autonomy? The paper will focus on the naming of the royal foundations.

2. Naming cities in the shadow of world empires

The Jewish client king Herodes the Great (40/37–4 BC) is the starting point, because his building program and city foundations are well attested in the literary sources and by archaeological evidence (fig. 1).[4]

King Herodes is the founder of several cities most of which seem to be modelled on the Greek *polis*.[5] In general, he followed the ideal of Hellenistic kings, acted as *ktistes* founding cities, displaying his *euergesia, tryphe, megalopsychia, arete*, being successful and courageous in war and claiming a strong *physis*. It is apparent that he emulated Hellenistic kings and followed a Hellenistic canon of virtue.[6] However, Herodes, who became king only with the support of Rome, was also a "client king" and he ruled over Judaea, a country whose population did not fully endorse pagan Hellenistic culture. Therefore, city foundations and the naming of cities occurred in a challenging political context:

Tab. 1 Herodian city foundations and their names

Name	Naming	Character
Kypros	Dynastic, mother	Foundation
Sebaste	Rome, emperor	Re-foundation
Herodeion (possibly two)	Dynastic, king	Foundation
Kaisareia	Rome, emperor	Foundation
Antipatris	Dynastic, father	Foundation
Phasaelis	Dynastic, brother	Foundation
Agrippias	Rome, Marcus Agrippa	Re-foundation
Drusias	Rome, Drusus	Foundation

3 On client kingship cf. Braund 1984; Paltiel 1991; Coşkun 2005; Kaizer – Facella 2010; Baltrusch – Wilker 2015.
4 On the building activities of Herodes cf. Roller 1998; Lichtenberger 1999; Japp 2000; Netzer 2006.
5 Cf. however, the critical remarks on the idea of Greek *poleis* being special van der Spek 1987, 58–59.
6 Jacobson 1988; Lichtenberger 1999, 179–185.

Obviously, Herodes honored himself and his father, mother and brother with foundations. These dynastic names stand in the tradition of Hellenistic royal city foundations. What is remarkable in this respect, however, is that the Herodian city foundations all are named after people. This is different from the earlier Hellenistic foundations which were given a wide spectrum of toponyms, not only dynastic names but often also relating to toponyms from Macedon and Greece or toponyms pertaining to natural fea-

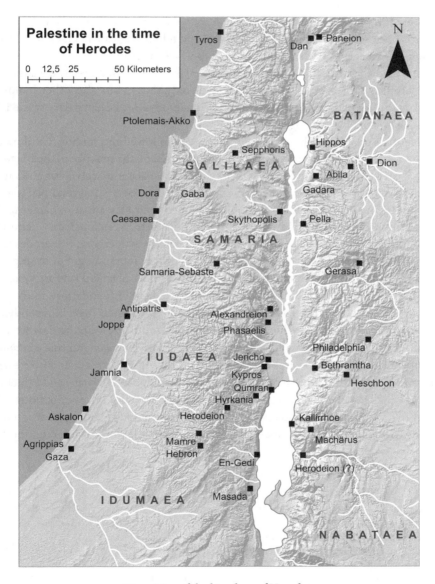

Fig. 1 Map of the kingdom of Herodes.

tures and divinities. Some were even given fantasy names.[7] In the case of Herodes, the new city foundations are named predominantly after members of his own family or of the Roman imperial family.

The city foundations were also accompanied, in the case of Herodes, by the naming of important buildings, such as towers, after members of his family, namely after his wife Mariamme and his brother Phasael. The dynastic naming of towers seems to have been a local or regional peculiarity which is not necessarily in a broader Hellenistic tradition.[8] It is interesting that Herodes also named towers after Romans such as, e. g., the Drusion tower in the harbor of Kaisareia and a building called Tiberieion/Tiberieum in the same place, which too had probably been a tower in the harbor.[9] Also, the Antonia temple fortress in Jerusalem, possibly evoked a tower fortress, and was named after Herodes' patron Marcus Antonius.[10] Not only towers but also other buildings were named after people: for instance, rooms in Herodes' Jerusalem palace carried the names *Kaisareios oikos* and *Agrippeios oikos*.[11]

In Herodes' kingdom, the city foundations also followed the tradition of the high priest-kings of the Hasmoneans, which in turn recurred on the practice of the Macedonian dynasties. Herodes had fought against the Hasmonaeans in a civil war and finally prevailed with the help of Rome and became king. Interestingly, several places such as Alexandreion, Hyrkania and Aristobulias retained their Hasmonaean names under Herodes and were not renamed (nor was the Antonia fortress renamed after Actium).[12] Indeed, not a single case of a Hasmonaean place being renamed under Herodes is attested. Previously, there is some evidence of this kind of rebranding. For example, in Southern Syria Ptolemaic Scythopolis was renamed under Seleukid rule as Nysa, and Pella lost its royal Ptolemaic name Berenike.[13] Also, Seleukid foundations in the East lost their Seleukid dynastic names after the regions had gained their independence, and there were also cases in which former Antigonid foundations in the East were renamed after regime change.[14] However, there is nothing like a general rule of *damnatio memoriae* of city names after changes of dynastic supremacy, as can also be seen with prominent former Ptolemaic cities such as Philadelphia (Amman) and Ptolemais (Akko), which retained their names under Seleukid rule and beyond, although the case of Akko is particularly interesting, since under Seleukid rule the citizens minted coins as "Antiochenes in Ptolemais", suggesting that some kind of intervention had

---

7   Cf. Cohen 2013, 349–359.
8   On the local tradition of the naming of towers cf. Lichtenberger 1999, 95.
9   Alföldy 1999; 2002.
10   Lichtenberger 1999, 35–39.
11   Ios. bell. Iud. 1.402. Cf. Lichtenberger 1999, 96–98.
12   Lichtenberger 1999, 17–20. 51–54. 159.
13   Lichtenberger 2003, 128–130. 171.
14   Cf. Leschhorn 1984, 257–258. On the rarity of numismatic *damnatio memoriae* cf. now de Callataÿ 2020.

taken place (fig. 2).[15] In the case of Herodes, the retention of Hasmonaean city names probably also relates to an intended and conscious programmatic connection to the Hasmoneans who were still highly esteemed by parts of the local population. Herodes' wife Mariamme was of the Hasmonean family, and Herodes, who was not of priestly descent, had in some measure to refer to the prestige and the legitimacy of the Hasmoneans.

It is also worth mentioning that the naming of places with Herodian dynastic names relates to foundations in the heartland of Judaea and Jewish settlements: Herodion, Kypros and Phasaelis were in Judaea, Antipatris in the coastal plain. This observation probably impacts on the target group of the Herodian naming of cities, i. e. the local Jewish population to which the new dynasty is presented.

Fig. 2 Bronze coin of Antiocheia in Ptolemais under Antiochos IV.

Different is the case with the naming of cities after Romans: Kaisareia was a new foundation on the Mediterranean coast, Sebaste was the re-foundation of a Hellenistic city in Samaria, Agrippias was a re-foundation of the Hellenistic town Anthedon, the harbor of Gaza, and Drusias has not yet been identified. These foundations were located in mostly non-Jewish or at least not traditionally Jewish parts of Herodes' kingdom and apparently had a different audience than the naming after members of the Herodian family.

With this geographical observation we move to the naming of cities after Romans. This of course has often been noted as a characteristic of the late Hellenistic Roman client kings who founded cities and named them after the emperor of the time. Herodes is not alone in this and especially several Caesareas/Kaisareias and Sebastes along the Mediterranean coast attest to this. Suetonius in his vita of Augustus reports: 'The kings, his friends and allies, built cities in their respective kingdoms, to which they gave the

15   Cohen 2006, 213–214 (on Akko) and 268–269 (on Philadelphia). On the Akko coins cf. Kadman 1961, 92–105 nos. 1–63.

name of Caesarea'[16]. David Braund explained this as follows: 'the kings announced that the kingdom had two rulers, the royal and the imperial families'[17] And: 'Implicit also is the suggestion that the two were on a par, in so far as they stood as alternatives.'[18] Fergus Millar termed the entire situation a 'two-level sovereignty'[19], describing the same phenomenon but implying that the relationship was less being on a par.

What is remarkable here is the Herodian naming of cities after Marcus Agrippa and Drusus, which is quite rare in the overall context. To the best of my knowledge, there is no other Drusias and the only other Agrippias is in the Bosporan kingdom, to which we will return. Usually, the city foundations with Roman focus refer only to the emperor himself as is appropriate in an autocratic principate. Herodes' successors also named cities after other members of the imperial family, such as Livias and Iulias, but this seems to be an idiosyncrasy of the Herodian kings. In general, such an extension of naming to family members other than the emperor very rarely happened elsewhere in client kingdoms. One of the few examples of such a naming is king Archelaos of Kappadokia (36 BC–17 AD) who founded not only an Archelais, but also a Sebaste and a Kaisareia.[20] Here we see the same pattern as with his contemporary Herodes. In Kommagene a comparable foundation is also attested, with king Antiochos IV (38–72 AD) founding a city Germanikeia in honor of the emperor Caligula and/or emperor Claudius, both of whom carried the name Germanicus[21]; in this case, however, the naming is again related directly to the emperor comparable as in the case of Sebaste and Kaisareia.

It has always been noted that the naming of client kings' cities after the emperor relates to the *Realpolitik* situation, namely that these kingdoms were dependent on Rome and the client kings not only honored the emperor but could also show the population that they were a friend of the Roman emperor. This of course is true, but two questions remain:

1. In a diachronic perspective: Are there antecedents in the Hellenistic world of giving names to cities that relate to dynasties other than the one ruling the kingdom?
2. In a synchronic perspective: Are there other contemporary, or at least late Hellenistic, examples for such naming other than related to Rome?

---

16   Suet. Aug. 60: *Reges amici atque socii et singuli in suo quisque regno Caesareas urbes condiderunt* (…). Cf. also Eutr. 7.10.
17   Braund 1984, 111.
18   Braund 1984, 112.
19   Millar 1996.
20   On Archelaos as founder of cities cf. Michels 2009, 325–334. It remains unsure, whether the city of Liviopolis (Plin. nat. 6.11) also belongs to his foundations as Sänger-Böhm 2016, 62 n. 12 assumes.
21   French 1991, 18; Facella 2006, 61 n. 46.

To the best of my knowledge, there are no previous cases of a city being named after a member of a dynasty other than the own.[22] There is no instance, e. g., of a kingdom that had gained independence or semi-independence from the Seleukid kingdom naming a city after Seleukid rulers such as could be expected, e. g., from the early Hasmonaeans. This also did not happen in kingdoms such as, e. g., Kommagene, which traced their ancestry back to the Seleukids.[23] Also, no other cases are known in Asia Minor or in the kingdoms and ethnarchies of the Near East. This means that the cross-dynastic naming of cities seems to be unique to the late Hellenistic kingdoms confronted with the superpower Rome. Naming a city after a non-local "dynasty" (= imperial house in Rome) is something new, although the basic idea of dynastic names of city foundations stems from an earlier Hellenistic tradition; it is a nice example of: "same but different".

This leads to the synchronic perspective and the question if in similar political situations the same naming practice can be observed. A comparable entity to the Roman empire is the Parthian empire, and there, too, we can observe the phenomenon of petty kings and a "two-level sovereignty".[24] The kingdom of Armenia can be taken as a test case. In Orontid and Artaxiad Armenia several cities were founded that carried dynastic names, among them Jerewandashat, Artaxata and several Tigranokertas. These were all cities named after Armenian kings, although the syntax of the names is somewhat different from that of the Greek foundations, because they often include specific aspects, like the "joy of", suggesting a local tradition of such names that not necessarily is a direct copy of the Greek dynastic names.

What is remarkable is that in Armenia, which during several periods was dominated either by Rome or Parthia, we have evidence that Artaxata at one point was renamed Neronias after the emperor Nero.[25] The name was given by the Armenian king Tigranes, who was installed by Nero. The Roman name fits the pattern known from Herodes and other client kings of Rome, and it should be mentioned that the Armenian king Tigranes was the great grandson of king Herodes of Judaea.

However, we have no clear evidence that any city in Armenia took its name from Parthian kings, especially in the 2nd/1st centuries BC when Parthian influence in Armenia was very strong. Only one possible case is known to me, though this possibly dates to an earlier time. On the 5th century AD map Tabula Peutingeriana, a Philadelphia is

22   The only remotely comparable example is Cities called Alexandreia and founded by later Diadochi such as Lysimachos who renamed Antigoneia Alexandreia Troas. Cf. Leschhorn 1984, 254–255. This naming however has to do mainly with the overarching significance of Alexander for the Diadochi and did not relate to a contemporary person.

23   On the Seleukid dynastic lineage cf. Lichtenberger 2015, 118.

24   Fowler 2010, esp. 70–71; but see also p. 75–77 where Fowler stresses that Roman relations to client kings were more "vertically" than in the Parthian empire.

25   Paltiel 1991, 247.

mentioned on the road from Artaxata to Ekbatana (fig. 3).[26] Usually this Philadelphia is considered to be related to a Seleukid foundation by the Seleukid king Demetrios II Theos Philadelphos (145–139/138 and 129–125 BC), but it has also been suggested that it was founded by the Arsakid king Arsakes II Philadelphos (approx. 211–185 BC) or by Artabanos I Philadelphos (approx. 126–122 BC).[27] The site of Philadelphia has not yet been identified but it must be situated somewhere north of Lake Urmia, meaning that it is not sure whether it belonged to Armenia or Media Atropatene, a kingdom heavily dependent on Parthia.

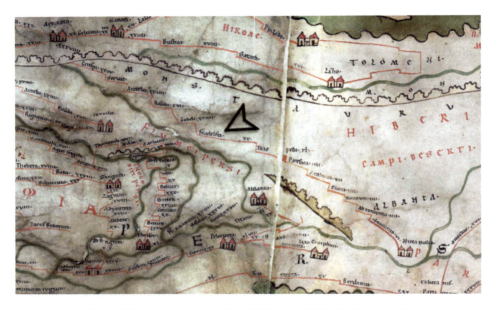

Fig. 3 Tabula Peutingeriana XI.4–XII.1, with Philadelphia marked.

The discussion about the identity of the eponym must also consider who possibly initiated the foundation and assigned the name: Was it the person whose name it took or was it someone from another dynasty, who was dependent on the overlord, be it Parthia or the Seleukids? The origin of this Philadelphia thus remains unknown, and until further evidence is available, it is unclear whether it was founded by a king dependent on Parthia or on the Seleukids. This is the only case known to me where possibly a comparable naming of a dependent Hellenistic kingdom took place. If so, it would be an antecedent to the naming of city foundations after Romans in the client kingdoms.

26   Tabula Peutingeriana XI.5. For the following cf. Chaumont 1993, 440; Cohen 2013, 49–50.
27   Tscherikower 1927, 83.

However, this proposition remains doubtful because in Parthia there was no attested tradition of naming cities after members of the dynasty[28] so that if Philadelphia really related to a Parthian king, this would be a very rare exception, and it might even be explained by a local (Armenian?) tradition of founding and naming cities. The Parthians in general seem to have been less interested in naming cities after rulers. Several cities in Parthia even retained their Seleukid names after Parthian conquest, although there is also one example of a Seleukid city name being changed under Parthian rule, namely Seleukid Europos Rhagai which was renamed Arsakia.[29] In this case, a dynastic name replaced a non-dynastic name.

It seems that the naming of cities after dynastic members other than from the ruler's own family mainly happened in deference to Rome. The reason for this is not only the superpower status of Rome, as we have seen with Armenian client kings of the Parthian empire, where in a structurally comparable situation this was not or hardly practiced. In this context it should not be ruled out that there was some expectation on the part of Rome for cities of local dynasties to be named after the emperor. Although this expectation has been downplayed by authors such as Andreas Kropp, who suggests more a local than a Roman audience for these kinds of naming[30], the Armenian example where we have a Neronias but no Parthian equivalent suggests that Rome played a more active role in these processes. This active role of Rome and the emperor again could explain why – with the exception of the Roman examples – it is rather rare for a city to be named after members of a dynasty other than one's own.[31]

However, we should not understand this as a practice prescribed by Rome, since local agency should not be underestimated as could be seen in the case of Herodes, who used Roman names other than that of the emperor.

Fig. 4 Bronze coin of Agrippias (Phanagoreia), early Roman.

28 See, however, the title *ktistes* on Parthian coins Leschhorn 1984, 288–293 underlining the importance of founding (empires?).
29 Cohen 2016, 209–210.
30 Kropp 2013, 346–348.
31 See also Michels 2009, 330–331.

Another remarkable example is the renaming of Phanagoreia as Agrippias (fig. 4). This
is the only other known example of a city named after Marcus Agrippa. In the Bosporan kingdom there is again a strong tradition of naming cities after rulers. The city
of Gorgippia in fact is contemporary with the first known example in the Greek world,
namely Philippoi (named after Philipp II of Macedon).[32] When Phanagoreia was renamed Agrippias, Pantikapaion was assigned the name Kaisareia by king Polemon I
(16 or 13/12–8 BC).[33] Whereas in the case of Herodes and Agrippa we have a lot of
information about their good relationship and even of a visit by Agrippa to Herodes'
kingdom,[34] such information is rare in the case of Polemon of Pontos. Polemon was
also strongly supported by Agrippa in gaining the throne and this could be the main
reason for the renaming. Agrippa's support also included the supply of ships, some of
which were commanded by Herodes himself.[35] Therefore, it is likely that Polemon and
Herodes in fact actually met. Whoever had the idea to name a city after Agrippa, he
probably shared it with the other. This story is therefore important, because it provides
a stage for how these ideas were actually exchanged.[36] Such an exchange also happened
of course through intermarriage which connected many of the client kingdoms, including the previously discussed Judaea, Kappadokia, Kommagene, Armenia and the
Bosporan Kingdom.[37]

3. Conclusion

To conclude: The foundation of cities and the naming of the new cities by late Hellenistic kings followed the tradition of the late Classical and earlier Hellenistic royal
foundations. These in turn link into a Greek tradition of founding cities.[38]

1.   As in earlier periods, the late Hellenistic kings founded and renamed cities, and
     these foundations were either genuine new foundations or re-foundations of pre-
     vious cities.

2.   Many cities were named after members of the local dynasty and this is very much
     in line with earlier foundations.

3.   What is different in the late Hellenistic period compared to earlier foundations
     is that there seems to be a dominance of dynastic names; hardly any cities with

32   Lichtenberger 2001.
33   See most recently Millar 1996, 172; Heinen 2011.
34   Ios. ant. Iud. 16.12–20.
35   Ios. ant. Iud. 16.21–23.
36   On this kind of client king networking cf. Jacobson 2001, 27–30. See also the possible connection
     of Herodes stimulating the naming of Elaiussa in Kappadocia as Sebaste: Michels 2009, 329.
37   On Herodian prosopography attesting to these royal family relations cf. Kokkinos 1998. See also
     Jacobson 2001, 23–24.
38   See for this the still excellent study by Leschhorn 1984.

non-dynastic names were established. This underlines the dynastic importance and focus of the late Hellenistic foundations.

4. The dynastic names relate not only to the local dynasty but also to Rome. This extension of dynastic naming appears to be an innovation of the time when the client kings were confronted with the Roman superpower. Although earlier asymmetric power relations between Hellenistic kingdoms can be observed, no other examples of cities being named after a foreign dynasty are known, with one possible exception in Armenia/Media Atropatene, where a city named Philadelphia might relate to an Arsakid Parthian or to a Seleukid king.

5. It is worth considering why especially when confronted with Rome the non-local dynastic naming emerges. Is this something Roman? I have the impression that it also has to do with Roman expectations, expectations which other Hellenistic dynasties did not face. And, these expectations were not only self-perceived expectations but they relate to a different concept: In the Parthian world, the relationship between the king of kings and the client kings was less hierarchical than the relationship between the Roman emperor and his client kings.[39] The naming of cities in client kingdoms after Romans therefore seems to have been a response to Roman expectations and expressed loyalty towards Rome and the emperor.[40]

Bibliography

Alföldy 1999: Alföldy, Géza, Pontius Pilatus und das Tiberieum von Caesarea Maritima, Scripta Classica Israelica 18, 1999, 85–108

Alföldy 2002: Alföldy, Géza, Nochmals: Pontius Pilatus und das Tiberieum von Caesarea Maritima, Scripta Classica Israelica 21, 133–148

Baltrusch – Wilker 2015: Baltrusch, Ernst – Wilker, Julia (eds.), Amici – socii – clientes? Abhängige Herrschaft im Imperium Romanum, Berlin 2015

Braund 1984: Braund, David, Rome and the Friendly King, New York 1984

Chaumont 1993: Chaumont, Marie-Louise, Fondations séleucides en Arménie méridionale, Syria 70, 1993, 431–441

Cohen 1995: Cohen, Getzel M., The Hellenistic Settlements in Europe, the Islands, and Asia Minor, Berkeley et al. 1995

Cohen 2006: Cohen, Getzel M., The Hellenistic Settlements in Syria, the Red Sea Basin, and North Africa, Berkeley et al. 2006

Cohen 2013: Cohen, Getzel M., The Hellenistic Settlements in the East from Armenia and Mesopotamia to Bactria and India, Berkeley et al. 2013

---

39 See above n. 22.
40 Eastern client kings were also confronted with cities named after Romans but founded by Romans such as Pompeiopolis in Paphlagonia, founded in 64 BC (Strab. 12.3.1; Cass. Dio. 37.20.2) and later several other such cities, cf. Mitchell 1993, 78.

Coşkun 2005: Coşkun, Altay (ed.), Roms auswärtige Freunde in der späten Republik und im frühen Prinzipat, Göttingen 2005

de Callataÿ 2020: de Callataÿ, François, Remelted or Overstruck: Cases of Monetary Damnatio Memoriae in Hellenistic Times?, in: R.A. Faber (ed.), Celebrity, Fame, and Infamy in the Hellenistic World, Toronto et al. 2020, 90–110

Facella 2006: Facella, Margherita, La dinastia degli Orontidi nella Commagene ellenistico-romana, Pisa 2006

Fowler 2010: Fowler, Richard, King, Bigger King, King of Kings: Structuring Power in the Parthian World, in: Kaizer – Facella 2010, 57–77

French 1991: French, David H., Commagene: Territorial Definitions, Studien zum antiken Kleinasien, Bonn, 1991, 11–19

Heinen 2011: Heinen, Heinz, Kaisareia und Agrippeia: das Tor zur Maiotis als augusteisches Monument, in: N. Povalahev – V. Kuznetsov (eds.), Phanagoreia und seine historische Umwelt. Von den Anfängen der griechischen Kolonisation (8. Jh. v. Chr.) bis zum Chasarenreich (10. Jh. n. Chr.), Göttingen 2011, 225–240

Jacobson 1988: Jacobson, David M., King Herod's Public "Heroic" Image, Revue Biblique 95, 1988, 386–403

Jacobson 2001: Jacobson, David M., Three Roman Client Kings: Herod of Judaea, Archelaos of Cappadocia and Juba of Mauretania, Palestine Exploration Quarterly 133, 2001, 22–38

Japp 2000: Japp, Sarah, Die Baupolitik Herodes' des Großen. Die Bedeutung der Architektur für die Herrschaftslegitimation eines römischen Klientelkönigs, Rahden 2000

Kadman 1961: Kadman, Leo, The Coins of Akko Ptolemais, Tel Aviv et al 1961

Kaizer – Facella 2010: Kaizer, Ted – Facella, Margherita (eds.), Kingdoms and Principalities in the Roman Near East, Stuttgart 2010

Kokkinos 1998: Kokkinos, Nikos, The Herodian Dynasty. Origins, Role in Society and Eclipse, Sheffield 1998

Kropp 2013: Kropp, Andreas J.M., Images and Monuments of Near Eastern Dynasts, 100 BC–AD 100, Oxford 2013

Leschhorn 1984: Leschhorn, Wolfgang, "Gründer der Stadt". Studien zu einem politisch-religiösen Phänomen der griechischen Geschichte, Stuttgart 1984

Lichtenberger 1999: Lichtenberger, Achim, Die Baupolitik Herodes des Großen, Wiesbaden 1999

Lichtenberger 2001: Lichtenberger, Achim, Philippoi oder Gorgippia – Zum Beginn der Benennung von Städten nach Herrschern in der griechischen Welt, in: H. Klinkott (ed.), Anatolien im Lichte kultureller Wechselwirkungen. Akkulturationsphänomene in Kleinasien und seinen Nachbarregionen während des 2. und 1. Jahrtausends v. Chr., Tübingen 2001, 167–180

Lichtenberger 2003: Lichtenberger, Achim, Kulte und Kultur der Dekapolis. Untersuchungen zu numismatischen, archäologischen und epigraphischen Zeugnissen, Wiesbaden 2003

Lichtenberger 2015: Lichtenberger, Achim, Herod, Zoilos, Philopappos. Multiple Identities in the Graeco-Roman World, Eretz-Israel 31 (Ehud Netzer Volume), 2015, 110*–122*

Michels 2009: Michels, Christoph, Kulturtransfer und monarchischer "Philhellenismus". Bithynien, Pontos und Kappadokien in hellenistischer Zeit, Göttingen 2009

Millar 1996: Millar, Fergus, Emperors, Kings and Subjects: The Politics of Two-Level Sovereignty, Scripta Classica Israelica 15, 1996, 159–173

Mitchell 1993: Mitchell, Stephen, Anatolia. Land, Men, and Gods in Asia Minor I: The Celts in Anatolia and the Impact of Roman Rule, Oxford 1993

Netzer 2006: Netzer, Ehud, The Architecture of Herod, the Great Builder, Tübingen 2006

Paltiel 1991: Paltiel, Eliezer, Vassals and Rebels in the Roman Empire. Julio-Claudian Policies in Judaea and the Kingdoms of the East, Brussels 1991

Roller 1998: Roller, Duane W., The Building Program of Herod the Great, Berkeley et al. 1998

Sänger-Böhm 2016: Sänger-Böhm, Kerstin, Weibliche Diplomatie zwischen Gesandtschaften und Erziehung: Zum Verhältnis von Juden und römischen Kaiserinnen, in: P. Sänger (ed.), Minderheiten und Migration in der griechisch-römischen Welt. Politische, rechtliche, religiöse und kulturelle Aspekte, Paderborn 2016, 59–72

Tscherikower 1927: Tscherikower, Victor, Die hellenistischen Städtegründungen von Alexander dem Grossen bis auf die Römerzeit, Leipzig 1927

van der Spek 1987: van der Spek, Robartus J., The Babylonian City, in: A, Kuhrt – S. Sherwin-White (eds.), Hellenism in the East. The interaction of Greek and non-Greek civilizations from Syria to Central Asia after Alexander, London 1987, 57–74

Figures

Fig. 1: © Marian Helm.

Fig. 2: © Numismatica Ars Classica, Auction 64, 17 May 2012, lot 1471.

Fig. 3: © Alexandra Kaiser, Kartographie und Mediendesign, Katholische Universität Eichstätt-Ingolstadt (https://tiles.arcgis.com/tiles/ng2xfLT71MDOMwFn/arcgis/rest/services/ TP_1to11_WTL1/MapServer) last access 20.5.2024.

Fig. 4: © Archäologisches Museum der Universität Münster M 927.

Achim Lichtenberger, Professor of Classical Archaeology at Münster University and Director of the Archaeological Museum. His research focusses on the archaeology of the eastern Mediterranean, ancient religious history and numismatics and he is active in excavations in Armenia, Israel and Jordan. Lichtenbergers monographs include *Der Olymp. Sitz der Götter zwischen Himmel und Erde* (Urban Taschenbücher; Stuttgart 2021), *Terrakotten aus Beit Nattif. Eine Untersuchung zur religiösen Alltagspraxis im spätantiken Judäa* (Contextualizing the Sacred 7; Turnhout 2016), *Severus Pius Augustus. Studien zur sakralen Repräsentation und Rezeption der Herrschaft des Septimius Severus und seiner Familie (193–211 n. Chr.)* (Impact of Empire 14; Leiden 2011), *Kulte und Kultur der Dekapolis. Untersuchungen zu numismatischen, archäologischen und epigraphischen Zeugnissen* (ADPV 29; Wiesbaden 2003) and *Die Baupolitik Herodes des Großen* (ADPV 26; Wiesbaden 1999). In the framework of Münsters Cluster of Excellence "Religion and Politics", he conducts a research project on the Imperial coinage of Tyre.

Concluding Remarks / Schlussbetrachtungen

The Tapestry of Hellenistic Rule
Reflections on the Fabric of Monarchy in a World of Transition

JOHANNES WIENAND

Premises and Pursuits. Between the conquests of Alexander the Great and the rise of the Roman and Parthian empires, vast stretches of the Mediterranean world and the Near and Middle East, including parts of South and Central Asia, formed a multipolar landscape of kingdoms that we are accustomed to calling "Hellenistic." We typically classify these monarchies by particular royal dynasties, each centering around a series of more or less well-known kings – and a number of queens, for that matter: the Ptolemies of Egypt, the Seleucids of Asia, the Antigonids of Macedonia and Greece, the Attalids of Pergamon, the Euthydemids of Bactria, as well as Sicilian, Pontic, and Armenian kingdoms, among others. The term "Hellenistic" sets these monarchies apart from other ancient autocratic regimes, implying they share specific traits that distinguish them in terms of governance and administrative practices, cultural and ideological dissemination, and their unique approach to hegemony and diplomacy. When the German scholar Johann Gustav Droysen first used the concept in this way, he specifically aimed to capture the idea of a particular blend of Greek culture with local elements in these regions, resulting in a distinct cultural and historical period with its characteristic social and political configurations. This opened the way to investigating the period beyond simply writing biographies of rulers along the different family lines: Droysen's approach helped to overcome the idea that history was forged primarily by the will of great men on the royal throne, facilitating comparative investigations and pointing beyond the political sphere towards the social, cultural, and economic developments of the period.

Still, the concept has been widely challenged, and rightly so: The term "Hellenistic" centers on Graeco-Macedonian influence, potentially underplaying the rich, pre-existing cultures and traditions of the regions in question and inadvertently tending to overshadow the role of local contexts in shaping the "Hellenistic" world. The concept, then, oversimplifies the complex network of developments and interactions that characterized the period, placing more emphasis on the dynamics of Greek influence while implying that local and regional identities were more static. Using a single term to encompass such a vast geographical area with diverse populations and traditions potentially obscures the varied and distinct effects in different regions and communities. Also, Droysen failed to offer persuasive explanations for how legitimate kingship was forged in the "Hellenistic" era, how power was successfully centralized over wider regions of a world with strong traditions of local pride and civic autonomy, how "Hellenistic" monarchies differed systemically from other ancient monarchical political systems, and how these systems transformed under the rising impact of Rome and Parthia. While stemming from the same Graeco-Macedonian roots, legitimate kingship depended not only on support from the ruling elites and administrators but also on the acceptance of local elites, soldiers, and the wider populace. Indeed, monarchical authority was contingent on successful interaction and communication within the different cultural milieus surrounding the various centers of power, which put the monarchies in question on distinct trajectories even when navigating comparable sets of external pressures and internal exigencies.

Thus, the question arises: Does this label, "Hellenistic," have any heuristic value, beyond defining the chronological boundaries, for understanding the inner workings of a particular subset of ancient monarchies? How does it help us to grasp the social, political, and cultural settings of these monarchies that held sway over vast territories for roughly three centuries? Is there anything that, in Austrian philosopher Ludwig Wittgenstein's sense, could be referred to as a "family resemblance" between the various "Hellenistic" monarchies? And where exactly do these resemblances end? The present volume establishes a triadic research matrix to tackle these essential questions along the following three principal axes of investigation:

1.   The volume provides a comprehensive assessment of Hellenistic rule across the various monarchical systems in question. It achieves this by integrating the two most successful scholarly approaches to monarchical power structures: one derived from empire studies, emphasizing institutions and administration, and the other from a sociological understanding of political authority, focusing on strategies of legitimation. This dual approach of joining complementary perspectives on monarchical rule offers a more comprehensive understanding of the inner mechanics of the historical regimes under investigation.

2.   The volume also develops a comparative approach to examining the configuration of power and authority across different monarchies within the given chronological and geographical frame. The investigations complement synchronic analyses of various monarchies with diachronic perspectives that trace their historical evolutions, thereby providing a more fine-grained understanding of the diverse regimes, their interdependencies, and their distinctiveness over time.

3.   Finally, the volume addresses the complex relations and interdependencies of global and local factors to shed light on the intricacies of monarchical rule during the period under investigation. Sensitivity towards the interplay – and the trade-

offs – between the global and the local is vital for a thorough understanding of power dynamics and communication strategies in the ancient world. The mutual impacts and frictions between cross-cutting norms and ideologies on the one hand and local practices and values on the other imposed significant constraints on the configuration and expression of these monarchies, influencing how kings, ruling elites, and administrators navigated the complexities of their empires when engaging with local elites, soldiers, and the wider populace.

With this triadic approach, the volume seeks to better understand the multifaceted natures of the monarchies in question, the intricacies of royal governance, and the strategies of legitimation. It explores the alignment and disparities between the general idea of "Hellenistic" kingship and the actual mechanics of the different systems of governance in various territories, time spans, and contexts. The in-depth analyses reveal the varied ways these kingdoms molded and were influenced by socio-political predispositions on the local level and their collective role in defining what we understand as "Hellenistic" in a historical and cultural sense. In this way, the volume sheds light on the polyvalent character of these regimes, providing insights into their distinct adjustments and the broader effects of monarchical rule on the era's social, political, and cultural fabric. This concluding chapter reflects on the methodological and conceptual premises of these investigations, synthesizes the essential elements of the resulting picture of Hellenistic rule, and discusses the explanatory potential and interpretive challenges arising from the historical sources.

Empires and Monarchies. More recent research has underscored the analytical value of combining the two main approaches typically adopted when investigating the inner workings of ancient monarchies: Traditionally, scholars tend to focus either on the institutions and administrative processes that constituted an empire as an organizational structure in its entirety, or on the communicative processes that created the integrative forces of its political authority. The first approach focuses on questions of institutional resilience, and the second on questions of personalized rule. Both approaches have their strengths and weaknesses. It is high time to overcome the binary divide and merge the explanatory power of these perspectives. Hellenistic monarchies are both: complex institutional structures *and* administrative practices, and fields of political authority and socio-cultural integration. Political authority is not solely a question of state institutions and administration, nor is an empire held together by communicative strategies of legitimation alone. To understand how monarchies work, we need to account for the interplay between structural assets (demographics and resources, infrastructure and technologies, production and consumption, etc.) and the practices and discourses aimed at mitigating the risks of societal fragmentation and instability inherent in human societies (rituals of power, ideologies of kingship, dynastic policies, ruler cult, etc.).

This volume proceeds from the presumption that a close analysis of the structural features of Hellenistic kingdoms in combination with a proper conceptualization of political authority – if adequately refined and applied to the changing historical landscapes between Alexander's conquests and the rise of the Roman and Parthian empires – can yield a powerful theory of Hellenistic governance. Such an understanding helps us transcend the limitations of a Weberian "Idealtypus" (ideal type) of rule, embracing the multifaceted and intricate nature of social interactions across a broad spectrum of time, space, and culture. Pursuing this path is highly demanding, as it requires tailoring the analytical matrix to the diverse political cultures in question as closely as possible. At the same time, it involves the creation of comparative analytical models (including, in this volume, a juxtaposition with the early Chinese monarchy of the Qin dynasty), facilitating a broader understanding of the overarching characteristics of monarchical rule in the period under investigation. Effective exercise of monarchical power depended on socially embedded structural assets and the interaction between ruler and ruled. In both regards, Hellenistic kingdoms were simultaneously shaped by cultural preconditions and historical dynamics that transcended individual empires and by constraints and opportunities resulting from their specific local and regional contexts.

Starting from these methodological and conceptual axioms, this volume shows how a more nuanced understanding of Hellenistic rule can be gained by comparative historical investigations of monarchical rule that account for subtle calibrations between commonalities and variabilities in the everyday exercise of power, yielding a more differentiated anatomy of governance and authority, both chronologically and geographically. Four aspects of Hellenistic rule are of particular interest to the investigations assembled here, and they are addressed from multiple angles throughout the different thematic sections of this volume: the relationship between kings and cities, the roles of courts and dynasties, the ideology of military leadership, and the impact of Roman supremacy. The structures, functions, and dynamics associated with these factors open viable pathways towards a richer interpretation of how institutional structures and political authority engaged in the exercise of Hellenistic rule.

Kings and Cities. The interaction between kings and cities constitutes the core of what we might call the political dimension of Hellenistic rule. In its classical understanding, however, the Greek concept "political" means "pertaining to the affairs of a polis." In this sense, Hellenistic monarchies were not political entities proper but suprapolitical structures. Nonetheless, Hellenistic monarchies did not operate in a political void; they were linked in manifold ways to urban settlements as highly complex and dynamic socio-political entities that both empowered the monarchies and presented them with significant governance challenges – even in regions beyond the world of the Greek polis. For one, population hubs were important nodes of public and private services, production, and trade. As venues of societal integration, stratification, and differentiation, urban centers (with associated villages and rural territories) also played a pivotal role in consolidating monarchical power by mobilizing human resources and serving as recruitment grounds for the military and the royal administration.

Urban populations were often heterogeneous in their social, cultural, and ethnic composition. The total population of a city usually comprised both urbanized and rural segments covering a broad spectrum of strata characterized by vastly differing preconditions and opportunities, including a highly competitive and socially privileged civic elite, a citizen body organized into demes and civic tribes, a wide range of corporate organizations and associations, and other more or less structured groups (such as military or ethnic), as well as distinct categories like mercenaries, settlers, commercial travelers, resident foreigners, and enslaved people. Reducing potential friction within such a complex social emulsion required investing significant resources to foster cohesion and counteract disintegrative forces and, from time to time, even to suppress open societal conflict or stasis (civil war).

Royal investments in social cohesion first and foremost aimed to preserve peace, maintain security, and ensure civic eunomia (i. e., a proper constitution based on good legislation). Hellenistic kings appointed administrative officials and judicial officers to maintain public order within the cities of their kingdom, and soldiers were deployed to protect and control cities and their territories. They also invested in constructing and preserving basic infrastructure (roads, bridges, water conduits), public spaces (agorai, theaters, gymnasia, temples), and military installations (camps, defense works, port infrastructure). Hellenistic kings also created incentives (granting of privileges, tax concessions, endowments, recognition of asylia) to deepen the social commitment of civic elites and loyalist subgroups at the king's service. Patronage and euergetic practice evolved into important axes of interaction between kings and cities: Through the role of the king as a benefactor, royal power was linked to local prosperity, and the swift and authoritative administration of justice counted among his most essential tasks. In a fruitful relationship with the city, the Hellenistic ruler could forge his image as an ideal basileus, the antithesis of a tyrant.

These activities – which unfolded through a constant flow of interaction via emissaries and delegations, through royal letters and honorific responses – tied the exercise of royal power directly to local sociospheres with their particular values, needs, and opportunities. As this volume shows, this direct and inherently power-related bond with local communities and their specific predispositions and inclinations was perhaps the most substantial incentive for Hellenistic monarchies to diversify their repertoire of communicative options, tailoring their strategies of engagement with subject groups to ensure the responses were finely attuned to particular cultural expectations. Thus, when superregional monarchies began to overlay and overarch a world of cities and other hubs of local pride and self-administration (such as priesthoods) with established networks of social obligations and loyalties, the new realities had to be reconciled with deeply rooted norms and values that could even include anti-monarchical sentiments, as in the case of traditionally autonomous Greek city-states. Hellenistic rule had a particularly high chance of succeeding when both sides were willing to meet halfway. The superior power of Hellenistic monarchies challenged political ideals prevalent throughout the ancient world and enforced realignments of loyalties and administrative processes on the local level. Vice versa, kings adapted to the cultural logic of cities as the essential social, administrative, and economic building blocks of their superior power, with locally coded models of communication and local traditions putting constraints on how they could effectively interact with civic communities.

The emergence of federal leagues (koina) was a highly versatile institutional answer to this challenge that served the needs of both kings and cities. Leagues, which were often regarded as instruments of resilience forged by cities to counter monarchical dominance, were in fact tools jointly forged by kings and cities in an intermediary sphere, responding to both global and local interests: Leagues provided different cities with a joint platform for their interactions with the royal court, while Hellenistic monarchs could utilize federalism strategically to manage their political arena more efficiently. In the interplay between cities and the court, leagues gave cities a tool to coordinate their local interests and balance them vis-à-vis the center of power. As suprapolitical but sub-monarchical entities, federal leagues bridged the gap between the two spheres and helped to anchor the Hellenistic monarchies politically.

Courts and Dynasties. The royal court was the Hellenistic monarchy's administrative and military powerhouse and its political, religious, economic, and cultural kernel. In terms of a distinct physical space, the court was the residence for the king and the ruling dynasty, and it provided the essential bureaucratic infrastructure for the operation of government and diplomacy. As a realm of representation and functionality, a Hellenistic palace complex could accommodate the royal chancellery, the royal treasury, the library, archives, and offices as well as audience halls and conference chambers, dining rooms, and service facilities. As far as archaeological evidence indicates, monumental courtyards, bathing structures, hunting areas, and stables were regular components, and palatial structures could integrate (preexisting or newly built) sanctuaries or even gymnasia and spaces for athletic and theatrical games. As such, the Hellenistic court embodied the power and prestige of the monarchy, and it exerted a kind of cultural magnetism through royal patronage of the arts and sciences, festivals and celebrations of all sorts, and cultic performances.

In terms of its agents and networks, the court was the primary platform for fostering loyalties, integrating elites, and negotiating social status and prestige, and it played a pivotal role in recruiting personnel for vital governmental positions, effectively attracting both Graeco-Macedonian and local elites. The Hellenistic court thus provided the ruler and royal officials with a versatile platform for developing and shaping personal networks around the ruling dynasty, which, in turn, was significantly more than just a group of people with family ties to the king. The royal dynasty was an instrument of authority, influence, and control, embodying the ruling monarchy's past, present, and future. Specifically, royal dynasties could bridge the critical power transition when a monarch died – a situation that called for a profound realignment of command hierarchies and support networks. In such volatile moments, the stabilizing potential of an established royal clan could effectively reduce the degree of contingency in Hellenistic kingship which was otherwise an inherently precarious system of rule.

However, establishing and maintaining a well-integrated dynasty was a demanding task, which, if not mastered, could allow internal frictions, rivalries between family branches, or competing claims to the throne to escalate into open conflict, as in the Ptolemaic civil wars of the second century. Even in less turbulent times, the unique status and privileged role of dynasty members had to be justified to the subjects. Transforming a group of relatives and inlaws into a ruling dynasty necessitated the skillful crafting of narratives and practices that portrayed the family as divinely chosen for a blessed destiny. As this volume shows, these representational strategies, ultimately directed at securing and maintaining monarchical rule, followed general premises, established precedents, and entrenched customs and required, on the other hand, contextual adaptability, cultural sensitivity, and situational awareness.

The stories, symbols, and rituals that emerged from this process revolved around the display of internal unity, which itself could go as far as public expressions of sibling love. The narratives and images of dynastic glory and power extended into wider communicative fields (genealogical founding myths and divine lineage; ancestral achievements and divinized predecessors; exceptional physical dispositions and divine incarnations; legitimate offspring and inter-dynastic bonds; patron deities and ruler cults). Within these broader contexts, female members of the royal clan could assume prominent public roles far beyond mere marriage politics. Just as the relationship between kings and cities, these fields of monarchical practice and discourse were likewise characterized by an interplay between overarching ideologies and local influences.

Wars and Victories. Hellenistic monarchies were steeped in an agonistic culture of war and victory – at least until the rise of Roman supremacy. Set against the backdrop of Alexander's conquests and his model of oikoumenic rule, military achievements seemingly exceeding human capabilities were the benchmark of charismatic authority in the Hellenistic world. The ideology of military success structured the relationship between kings on the one hand and their divine patrons and progenitors on the other; charismatic military leadership could even compensate for a lack of dynastic legitimacy. Rulers' military engagements targeted foreign empires, "barbarian" groups, and adversaries in domestic conflicts such as rebellions or civil wars. For Hellenistic kings, heroic leadership thus combined the gain and defense of their "spear-won land" in wars against external foes with the building and preservation of social and political stability, which served to legitimize the ruler's authority and maintain control within. Triumphal rulership was thus conditioned by an understanding of monarchy that transcended the interaction between the king and his soldiers, reaching far into the civ-il sphere and linking the requirement of security from external threats to demands for inner stability and harmony. These complex interdependencies, so the volume shows, formed fields of tensions between transversal ideologies and situational constraints.

Seen as an inevitable prerequisite for attaining a persistent state of both outward strength and domestic cohesion, military triumph was a decisive source of royal legiti-macy, and the charismatic war leader was an effective and adaptable focal point within monarchical discourse and practice. Consequentially, triumphal ideology was ubiqui-tous, and the king's role as a warrior in the narrower sense typically featured various interrelations with associated fields of monarchical representation. Hellenistic rulers, the elite, and other loyalist groups and individuals employed a wide array of media, communicative strategies, and practices to convey and perpetuate a triumphal ruler image. These included ceremonial events such as victory parades and commemorative festivals; donations and endowments from captured riches and dedications of spoils; other symbolic actions, including adoption of victory titles and triumphal epithets; the erection of inscribed monuments and works of art, or the distribution of specific coin designs; and the oral and written dissemination of ruler biographies and historio-graphic accounts, panegyrics, hymns, and epinician literature.

The idea of a victorious military leader who fights for peace and security and lavish-es captured riches on his people resonated deeply within the diverse body of subjects, and the idea was especially pertinent in reinforcing the bonds of loyalty forged with elite groups and the military. However, even if these comparably homogeneous social groups were willing in principle to serve the monarchy, they still formed a conglom-erate of individual organisms driven by partially incompatible interests. These groups had the potential to effectively challenge the ruler, and Hellenistic history provides numerous examples of fatal cracks in the supposedly solidified elite and military or-ganization. Tailoring triumphal ideology to its intended audiences was thus challeng-ing, even with regard to groups that were closely interleaved with the power apparatus: What we broadly refer to as the military, in fact, represented a broad spectrum of or-ganizational units that were individually embedded in their own social, cultural, and economic environments (elite guards and professional soldiers at court; soldiers and mercenaries in border outposts, field camps, or city garrisons; auxiliary units, cleruchs, and other military reservists of various backgrounds; ephebic groups and distinct elit-ist units with specific competences, responsibilities, and obligations). Finely tuned tri-umphal ideology played a crucial role in the relationship between the kings and these various military groups, and this relationship conspicuously changed when Roman power came into play.

Greeks and Romans. The integration of triumphal ideology into the broader ideological and social contexts enabled Hellenistic monarchs to steer ruler discourse and govern-ance practice more towards civic matters when Rome's expanding supremacy (with

Parthia capitalizing on its effects) limited their scope for military accomplishments. Rome's gradual rise from city-state to world power, the process that triggered these systemic changes in Hellenistic governance, effectively spanned the entire Hellenistic period and increasingly affected the fortunes of the monarchies in question. When the Wars of the Diadochi were still raging, the spheres of interest of Carthage and Rome already began to collide in the Western Mediterranean, with Sicily becoming a hotspot of the protracted conflict, eventually falling under direct Roman control in the course of the First Punic War. The formation and expansion of a Roman-Republican imperium then exerted increasing pressure on Hellenistic kingdoms throughout the Eastern Mediterranean and beyond, which was only increased by the Parthians, who at the end of the Hellenistic period were the only remaining power in the East that could effectively force the Romans to the negotiating table.

The emerging Roman hegemony became more and more evident not only in spectacular military achievements, strategic support of select dynasties, and dictates of bilateral and interstate treaties, but also in conversions of Hellenistic monarchies into client-kingdoms, in the dissolution of ruling dynasties, and the creation of Roman provinces. Hellenistic kingdoms, increasingly caught in the stress field created by Rome and Parthia, had to respond to the large-scale changes in a period marked by heightened military conflict and civil unrest. As long as they did not vanish in the process, Hellenistic monarchies, inherently flexible organisms from their inception, eventually adapted their governance frameworks to the new rules of a power game they were compelled to play with forceful new foreign competitors. However, due to the decisively non-monarchical logic of Roman hegemony, they could not simply adjust established strategies of interstate interaction. As this volume shows, the rise of Rome demanded an outright reinvention of Hellenistic rulership.

We can grasp these innovative adaptive strategies and their broader implications for late Hellenistic kingship more clearly when focusing on the subtle ways in which the mechanics of Hellenistic rule were realigned in this process – and, conversely, on how the Roman political system was influenced in its dealings with the political, economic, and cultural achievements of Hellenistic kingdoms. The development markedly differed from the process in the late fourth and third centuries BC, when Eastern Mediterranean, Near Eastern, and Middle Eastern cultures integrated with the newly emerging Hellenistic monarchies. Despite all superpower competition, Hellenistic kings generally recognized each other as basileis, while Rome enforced a subordination of royal power under the overarching umbrella of Roman-Republican supremacy. The ramifications of this were evident on the "Day of Eleusis" when a Hellenistic king had to submit to the dictates of a Roman legate.

As military resistance against Rome was not successful in the long run, Hellenistic kings eventually responded by profoundly redefining royal authority, developing non-charismatic strategies of legitimation. Royal interactions with subjects were increasingly modeled on ideals of reliable governance and accountability – on norm-based partnerships with local traditional institutions such as leagues, cities, civic organisms, and temples. Conversely, the encounter with the Hellenistic world also had a profound impact on Rome. As the imperium evolved into a political system tailored to the leading role of towering individuals – and eventually a single princeps – Roman official authority was increasingly imagined as a personal quality of the office-holder while competing families drew inspiration from Hellenistic court culture, Greek paideia, and royal dynastic representation. Hellenistic kings and elites did their part to develop a common language with Rome, further bridging the divide. The prominent role of emperor worship in the East and related phenomena, such as city dedications by client-kings to members of the ruling dynasty of Rome, indicated the significant impact of Hellenistic rule on the Roman political system. Augustus ultimately established a monarchy that was conspicuously distinct from Hellenistic models. But the Roman principate, in a way, precipitated the sublation of Hellenistic kingship in Hegel's threefold sense of "Aufhebung," i. e., negation, preservation, and elevation.

Sources and Traditions. The virtually unrivaled financial resources of the royal dynasties afforded vast opportunities for ideological expression, which, in turn, influenced contemporary perceptions and informed subsequent traditions. The present volume explores the dynamics of Hellenistic rule through various literary and material sources, such as historiography and biographical literature, monuments and buildings, encomia and epinikia, royal portraiture and reliefs, inscriptions, and coins. For one, we need these sources to establish the historical facts, but often the sources themselves were once embedded in the historical processes they reflect, so they may carry direct traces of Hellenistic ideological dissemination. Sometimes, our sources even served as media of interaction and communication for the various historical actors and agents who brought about, shaped, and transformed the political cultures of the Hellenistic world. As communication was never a straightforward top-down process, such media played the role of interactive reference points in complex forms of social, cultural, economic, and political exchange structured and influenced by all those who interacted with the monarchy in one way or another. Hence, beyond their value for reconstructing the course of events or the logic of tradition and reception, investigations into our sources also raise questions about discourse and practice, representation strategies, target groups, and impact.

In these regards, coins are of particular interest and accordingly play a prominent role in this volume. The unique source value of coins is due to their comparatively extensive survival, their technical characteristics, and their role as serially produced tokens carrying both text and image: Scholars can often date the production of specific coin series with considerable precision, identify their geographical origins, and at least partially evaluate scales of production and the dynamics and reach of circulation. Such preserved artifacts thus provide a dense chronological and geographical matrix, helping to analyze the development, dissemination, and impact of certain aspects of monarchical representation. On this basis, the varying coin designs indicate how communicative strategies were constantly adapted to the changing circumstances of interaction between the monarchical center on the one hand, where royal portraiture and dynastic iconography were entrusted to specialized artists with close ties to court culture, and the urban and rural dwellers, soldiers, settlers, merchants, and manufacturers on the other, as key societal groups that dealt with coins in everyday transactions. While the design of royal coinages was used to assert monarchical authority, local coinage could provide cities with a means for civic self-representation, albeit within the constraints of the overarching ideological system, establishing a certain dialogue between civic traditions and monarchical representation.

However, coins were not primarily minted and brought into circulation as portable mini-monuments; their production, distribution, and exchange patterns depended on their monetary function. How various monetary systems interacted was determined by the nature of their economic and trade environments, by royal investments (in infrastructure, the military, or maritime assets, for instance), subsidies and interstate payments, and more. This is particularly interesting in three respects: First, in terms of how (on a global level) the monetary systems and coin designs of the Hellenistic kingdoms shared certain traits, differed from each other in particular aspects, and also responded to and influenced one another at specific points. Second, on a regional and local level, civic coinage could overlap and interfere with royal coinage in various ways, revealing mechanisms of mutual influence and differentiation and creating localized resonance spaces for representation, which also served as platforms for relating ruler ideology to local traditions. And thirdly, the introduction of the so-called quasi-municipal coinage (as in the case of the Seleucids), pseudo-civic coinage (kingdom of Pontus), and the cistophoric standard (Attalids) reveals an increasingly intricate intertwining of royal and civic administrative practices in the contexts of expanding monetization, strengthening local markets, rising military expenditures, and the growing influence of Roman hegemony.

Hellenistic coinage was thus by no means a homogeneous phenomenon, even if we can observe overarching trends such as the roughly synchronous introduction of ruler portraits by several (though not all) dynasties in the late classical and early Hellenistic era. This was nothing less than a revolution that put the portrayed human on a par with gods and heroes. Also, the production of coins was more consistently subject to royal administrative oversight than the creation of other physical media of representation. Sculptures, reliefs, wall paintings, cameos, or inscribed monuments also experienced a lower chance of survival simply due to less favorable generic properties. Comparing coins with other media also highlights a distinction between monarchical self-representation and ideological expressions of the subjects, with the former reflecting a higher degree of central influence and the latter emerging from more decentralized, self-regulatory processes, which could trigger successful innovations but may also have produced highly idiosyncratic forms with limited impact.

The difference was gradual rather than binary, which can be seen again in the case of the ruler portrait: At first glance, it was a highly standardized element of Hellenistic coinage, but the portrait design in fact varied across different workshops, even under the same dynasty, due to the absence of a strictly coordinated distribution of royal portrait models, providing the workshops with enough leeway to blend strategies of monarchical self-display with local iconographic traditions. Nonetheless, common artistic developments and time-specific iconographic trends could simultaneously influence the visual languages of Hellenistic monarchies across vast geographical distances. Decreasing similarity may consequentially indicate increasingly competitive legitimation. Even when different dynasties came up with broadly comparable strategies, they were never uniform, and even the slightest dissimilarities may yield valuable historical information.

Ultimately, our record of historical sources is inhomogeneous far beyond Hellenistic coinage, relief sculpture, and portraiture in the round. Different genera vary not only in their survival rate but also in their chronological and geographical coverage, which means that they reflect the discourses and practices of Hellenistic monarchies in different ways. We need to take into account a varying degree of consistency in scope and transmission when approaching epigraphic and literary sources as well: Greek historiographers such as Polybios, Diodoros, Appian, or Plutarch only draw on Iranian or indigenous accounts to a very limited extent, if at all, while the ancient Near and Middle East feature significantly less pronounced traditions of historical writing than what we know from the Greek polis. The epigraphic habit also varies geographically: A plethora of inscriptions from Greek cities offers insights into local administrative processes, while we have a much more limited understanding of the civic decision-making mechanisms in the Eastern Hellenistic world. Perceived inconsistencies, differences, or contradictions within the historical record, which also affect the investigations presented here, may thus be due to discrepancies in the available source material. We also need to consider that our understanding of Hellenistic monarchies partially depends on the perspectives provided by Roman receptions: notably, one of the most frequently cited characterizations of the nature of Hellenistic kingship stems from a Byzantine lexicon.

Retrospects and Prospects. To conclude, this volume explores the nature of Hellenistic rule, specifically aiming to bridge the gap between the common ideological fabric of Hellenistic monarchies and the nuanced realities of individual governance frameworks. In doing so, it seeks to enhance our understanding of how Hellenistic monarchies derived from deep roots while also adapting to local contexts and traditions. Despite these efforts, it is evident that much work remains to be done.

First and foremost, scholars might want to continue reconciling the different approaches to Hellenistic monarchy to gain a more integrated understanding. This particularly involves exploring more comprehensively the ways in which personalized rule and political authority were predicated on structural assets and institutional resilience. Furthermore, refining comparative perspectives is crucial to understanding how the general concept of "Hellenistic" kingship aligns with or diverges from the actual practices and experiences of monarchical rule across the diverse political systems in question. This entails further investigations into how and why governance practices varied across time and space. Additionally, scholarship must delve deeper into the interplay between global preconditions and local dynamics that influenced how dynasties forged recognition, prestige, and legitimacy. To further substantiate the notion of a distinct "Hellenistic" form of kingship within the intricate tapestry of ancient governance and political authority, we must ultimately advance our efforts toward a comprehensive and ambitious comparative investigation between the ancient monarchies traditionally termed "Hellenistic" and those that fall outside this intriguing category. The present volume informs and inspires such future investigations.

Johannes Wienand is Professor of Ancient History at University of Braunschweig, Germany. His research interests range across politics, civil war and religion in the Graeco-Roman world, and he has published widely on Greek democracy, the Roman empire, and late antiquity. He is the author of a recent monograph on the Athenian public funeral (*Der politische Tod*, 2023), and he has co-edited books about Constantinople and Jerusalem in late antiquity (2022), the Roman triumph (2017), and civil war in ancient Greece and Rome (2016). Johannes Wienand has founded the international academic network "Internal War: Society, Social Order and Political Conflict in Antiquity" and an international numismatic digitization consortium (numid.online). He is editor-in-chief of the book series "Studies in Ancient Civil War" (De Gruyter) and full member of the German Archaeological Institute.

Indices

Index of Persons

Index of Deities and Mythological Figures

Geographical Index

Index Locorum

I. Literary Sources

II. Inscriptions

III. Papyri

IV. Coins

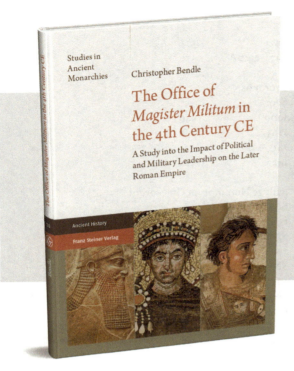

Studies in
Ancient
Monarchies

Christopher Bendle

The Office of
Magister Militum in
the 4th Century CE

A Study into the Impact of Political
and Military Leadership on the Later
Roman Empire

Ancient History

Franz Steiner Verlag

Christopher Bendle

**The Office of *Magister Militum* in
the 4th Century CE**

A Study into the Impact of Political and Military
Leadership on the Later Roman Empire

STUDIES IN ANCIENT MONARCHIES – VOLUME 10
2024. 236 pages with 5 col. figs. and 4 tables

978-3-515-13614-3 HARDCOVER
978-3-515-13621-1 E-BOOK

This monograph presents a novel investigation of the *magistri militum*, the highest-ranking officers within the late Roman army. It posits that between 340 and 395 CE, specific *magistri* seized opportune moments, notably during the political voids following emperors' deaths, to reshape the character of their office and expand its pivotal role in the military-political sphere. This transformation played a decisive role in the eventual dissolution of the Western Roman Empire. Furthermore, the study employs the prosopographical method to reevaluate previous scholarship regarding the proportion of barbarian and Roman generals. Notably, the research posits that the balance between Roman and non-Roman officers was far more equitably distributed than hitherto conjectured. Additionally, prosopography is used to reconstruct the fourth-century *cursus honorum*.

Finally, this work utilizes the analytical framework of social network analysis, predicated upon the application of mathematical equations and formulae to elucidate the intricate dynamics of positive and negative relationships. The findings of this study furnish valuable insights and prospects for further research.

THE AUTHOR

Christopher Bendle currently teaches Latin in Philadelphia, where he moved in 2020. He also studies Classics at the University of Pennsylvania. His research interests center on the Later Roman Empire and 'big picture' history, especially the military and political reasons for the dissolution of the western empire, as well as Roman vs. non-Roman identities, leadership, and the successor kingdoms.

Franz Steiner
Verlag

Order online at:
service@steiner-verlag.de

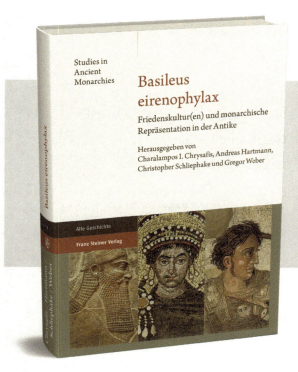

Studies in Ancient Monarchies

Basileus eirenophylax

Friedenskultur(en) und monarchische Repräsentation in der Antike

Herausgegeben von
Charalampos I. Chrysafis, Andreas Hartmann,
Christopher Schliephake und Gregor Weber

Alte Geschichte

Franz Steiner Verlag

Charalampos I. Chrysafis / Andreas Hartmann /
Christopher Schliephake / Gregor Weber (Hg.)

Basileus eirenophylax

Friedenskultur(en) und monarchische Repräsentation in der Antike

STUDIES IN ANCIENT MONARCHIES – BAND 9
2023. 550 Seiten mit 55 s/w-Abbildungen und einer Tabelle

978-3-515-13477-4 GEBUNDEN
978-3-515-13481-1 E-BOOK

Die militärische Sieghaftigkeit gilt in der gegenwärtigen Forschung als wichtiges Legitimationsmittel der antiken Monarchien. Zwar wird dabei oft eine notwendig bellizistische Ausrichtung monarchischen Handelns a priori gesetzt, doch ist der Aspekt der Sieghaftigkeit im Kontext monarchischer Selbstdarstellung entsprechend zu gewichten. Der Band geht der zentralen Frage nach, ob Krieg vorrangig als Mittel zur Herstellung von Frieden oder als Weg zur Aneignung materieller Ressourcen konzeptualisiert wird. Führende internationale ExpertInnen zur antiken Monarchie betrachten dafür nicht die politische Praxis selbst, sondern deren Repräsentation und Reflexion in verschiedenen Medien und Texten. In den Blick genommen werden die monarchischen Traditionen des Vorderen Orients, das hellenistische Königtum, das römische Kaisertum sowie die Transformation der Spätantike zum Mittelalter. Neben einem darstellenden sowie analytischen Teil enthalten die Beiträge eine Sammlung von zentralen Quellen, die für die zukünftige Beschäftigung mit dem Thema des Friedens in der Antike eine unerlässliche Grundlage bereitstellen wird.

MIT BEITRÄGEN VON

Josef Wiesehöfer / Anke Ilona Blöbaum / Andreas Hartmann / Charalampos I. Chrysafis / Hans Joachim Gehrke / Kostas Buraselis / Peter Franz Mittag / Gregor Weber / Rolf Strootman / Estelle Galbois / Ulrich Gotter / Werner Eck / Carlos Noreña / Damien Nelis / Stephan Faust / Stefan Rebenich / Felix K. Maier / Fernando Lopez Sanchez / Mischa Meier / Wolfram Drews

Franz Steiner
Verlag

Hier bestellen:
service@steiner-verlag.de

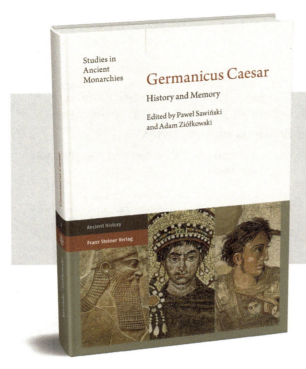

Paweł Sawinski / Adam Ziółkowski (Ed.)

Germanicus Caesar

History and Memory

STUDIES IN ANCIENT MONARCHIES – VOL. 8
2023. 170 pages with 4 b/w- and 16 col. figs. + 4 graphics

978-3-515-13440-8 HARDCOVER
978-3-515-13446-0 E-BOOK

The historical memory of the principate is for obvious reasons dominated by the emperors, with one exception: Germanicus Caesar, who, though not a ruler, appears in the sources as if he had been one. Chosen by Augustus as his ultimate heir, the embodiment of the dynastic principle, yet never the emperor; put at the head of one third of the Roman army to reconquer Germania, but recalled before the task's completion; the last to hold an imperium which made him almost a co-regent of the emperor, cut short by his sudden death – he reflects like no one the transition of the principate from the Augustan phase to its mature form. Equally significant is the longevity of the memory of his person and the variety of ways in which it was expressed: the only non-emperor commemorated in the *Feriale Duranum*, he figures on coins struck long after the end of the Julio-Claudians and an edict of his, quoted in a legal text of the 3rd century, appears in the Digesta. To give justice to his memorability, our contributions approach him in the perspective of not only history, classical philology, art history/archaeology and numismatics, but also Egyptology and Roman law.

THE EDITORS

Paweł Sawinski studied history at the Adam Mickiewicz University in Poznań. 2002 PhD in history and 2016 Habilitation with the „Succession of Imperial Power under the Julio-Claudian Dynasty (30 BCE – 68 CE)". Appointment as professor of Adam Mickiewicz University in 2017.

Adam Ziółkowski studied at the University of Warsaw. M.A. in 1973, Ph.D. in 1981 and Habilitation in 1989. First lectureship at the Catholic University of Lublin and since 1988 at the Institute of History (now Faculty of History) of the University of Warsaw. Still teaching as a professor emeritus on a part-time basis, Roman history and historiography, and Rome's topography.

Franz Steiner
Verlag

Hier bestellen:
service@steiner-verlag.de